10
European Cups

Claude Girault and Guy Mislin
Mike Hammond

Editor
Bruce Smith

Published by Burlington Publishing Co. Ltd.

ISBN: 1-873-05710-5

Front cover photos:
1991 European Cups action from Allsport

Book Design by Carolyn Knight

Packaged by
Bruce Smith Books Ltd.,
Smug Oak Green Business Centre, Lye Lane,
Bricket Wood, Herts, AL2 3UG

Printed by Richard Clay Ltd., Bungay, Suffolk.

Foreword by Michel Platini

The European Celebration

The European Cups are a reflection on life itself. They bring immense joy, but also, occasionally, sadness and tears.

Thanks to the European Cups, I was able, during my time at Saint-Etienne and, especially Juventus, to enjoy many moments of intense happiness. But once, because of them, on an evening when the folly of man took over, I cried.

My lasting memory though, will be of the unique flavour and atmosphere of the great European occasions – those nights when it really felt that there was a touch of magic in the air...

With this book – *100 European Cups* – and its extraordinary and unprecedented collection of figures and tables, my friends Claude Girault, an ardent statistician, and Guy Mislin, a journalist with *France Football,* allow you to enter into this fascinating and passionate world.

Finally, to all those for whom this book will become a reference, I offer this message.

Football is a game, the European Cups are a celebration, and the stadium a theatre where the actors and audience must first and foremost, regardless of the result, enjoy the experience together.

Contents

Claude Girault was born in Nice, France, where he went to school. He joined the French Navy as a paymaster before moving to California to teach French.

He is a delegate elected by French citizens residing in the western United States to represent them in Paris at the prestigious Superior Council of the French from Overseas.

For more than 15 years he has worked on football statistics making researches in nearly all the countries whose clubs qualified for the UEFA Cups. He is the author of three poetry books and a broad range of essays and articles published in France and the U.S.

Guy Mislin, Editor of the magazine *France Football*, was born on April 10th, 1942 at Orléansville, Algeria. After studying at the Sorbonne in Paris, he started working in 1965 on the daily newspaper *Le Parisien Libéré* before contributing to the football monthly *Onze*, for which he made several reports from abroad.

In 1978 he entered the sports department after the 1982 World Cup in Spain, remaining in this post until 1987 when he joined the editorial team at *France Football*.

Guy Mislin is also co-author, with television presenter Therry Roland, of a two-volume work entitled *La Fabuleuse Histoire de la Coupe d'Europe* (The Fabulous History of the European Cups).

Mike Hammond is a freelance writer and researcher specialising in European football. He shares both his birthdate (30/1/60) and his home town (Leicester) with England captain Gary Lineker and is an ardent, if occasionally disillusioned, supporter of Leicester City.

A graduate in Modern Languages from the University of Bradford, he has written many articles on the subject of European football in magazines such as *90 Minutes, Football Today* and the American monthly, *Soccer International*, but is probably best known in his capacity as General Editor of his self-confessed labour of love, *The European Football Yearbook*.

Editor **Bruce Smith** is an award winning journalist with over 40 books to his credit, in addition to being the editor of several major works. A freelance writer and author for over 10 years he has written on a wide range of subjects from football and hockey to his second pet love home computers.

A dual Arsenal and Barnet supporter he was for a time Editor of the highly acclaimed *Non-League Football Magazine*. A regular broadcaster, he has appeared on several TV programmes and reports regularly on football and hockey for BBC Radio Bedfordshire.

Editor's Acknowledgments

One of the major headaches in producing this book has been in deciding which material to include and which to leave out. The material hereonin represents around 75% of that which was originally supplied; indeed had it all been included the book would have burst at the seams at well over 1,000 pages. While Guy and Claude have spent years of painstaking research in compiling the data, they would wish to thank **Bernard Marcault** for his sterling efforts in computerising the information.

It is a sobering fact that both authors have already produced several larger folders of new information that will hopefully find its way into a second volume at some time in the future.

I am grateful to **Mike Hammond** for authoring the highly readable reviews which adorn each seasons statistics. Working to a tight spec. and word count is not the easiest of tasks even for the most seasoned of writers.

In-house thanks go to **Mark Webb** and **Martin Ritchie** who had the mammoth responsibility for typesetting and proof-reading the pages through many many revisions.

Another major headache has been to standardise on the spelling of club names. This has become more of a problem in recent years as the advent of satellite TV has allowed more foreign league games to be shown in English homes. Thus, Fiorentina is now an accepted Italian club name whereas five years ago, Florence might have been more common. We have tried to be consistent throughout, following as closely as possible Mike's *The European Football Yearbook*, but there will no doubt be points of contention.

On May 29th, 1991, in the San Nicola stadium in Bari, Italy, Red Star Belgrade beat Olympique Marseille in a penalty shoot-out and entered their name in the record books as the winners of the 36th European Champions' Cup.

Bari represented an important milestone in the history of the European club competitions. For the 60,000 fans packed into the futuristic World Cup stadium were witnessing the *100th* European Final – all three Cups included.

During the course of this book, particularly in the statistical headings, we shall refer to the three European Cups under the abbreviations C1, C2 and C3.

C1, the *Champions' Cup*, and the first of the three competitions to be introduced, in 1955-56, is the most prestigious, as it brings together all the national champion clubs of Europe. C2, the *Cup-winners' Cup*, followed five years later, in 1960-61. C3, on the other hand, did not become the UEFA Cup until 1972, having been reserved since 1958 for towns possessing an international trade fair, hence the original title *Fairs' Cup*. From an undistinguished beginning (the clubs involved in those days were not necessarily amongst the best in their own country), C3 took on a completely different dimension in 1972 when, as the re-named *UEFA Cup*, it brought together those clubs who had finished in the places just below the national champions. Nowadays, there are many who believe that the UEFA Cup has become the most difficult of the three Cups to win – both because of the quality of the participating teams and because of the length of the competition. With 64 teams lining up at the start (as opposed to 32 in both the Champions' Cup and the Cup-winners' Cup), an extra round has to be negotiated before a team reaches the quarter-finals.

A Brief History of the European Cups

Before entering into the complex and mysterious world of European Cup statistics, it is worthwhile to look briefly at the history of the competitions. It was in 1955, under the initiative of French journalist Gabriel Hanot, that the first European Cup was born. The idea of a competition involving clubs from different European countries found instant favour with the Danish president of UEFA, Ebbe Schwartz, although it was not until its second year that this new European Cup was reserved exclusively for the national champions. The inaugural participants were selected on the basis of their prestige.

The English football authorities, ever faithful to their traditional *wait and see* policy, neglected to allow Chelsea to compete, preferring to delay judgement until after the first year's competition had been completed. So Chelsea's place was taken instead by Polish club Gwardia Warsaw, who joined up with such respected opponents as PSV Eindhoven (the Netherlands), AC Milan (Italy), Real Madrid (Spain), Partizan Belgrade (Yugoslavia), Rapid Vienna (Austria), Rot-Weiss Essen (West Germany), Hibernian (Scotland), Anderlecht (Belgium), Sporting Lisbon (Portugal) and Stade Reims (France). Nobody at the time could have imagined just how prodigiously successful this new European Champions' Cup would become.

An Exceptional Real Madrid

One club, and one club alone, was to dominate the early years of the competition – Real Madrid. The famous Spanish club carved its name indelibly into European Cup legend by winning the trophy five times on the trot, from the inaugural 1955-56 season to 1959-60, and then once again in 1965-66, thereby establishing a record of six victories which still remains unmatched 25 years later.

It was the discovery of this formidable Spanish armada, dressed all in white and practising a brand of football that was as spectacular as it was successful, that did much to capture the European football public's imagination for this new competition. The team included such memorable figures as the *blond arrow* from Argentina, Alfredo Di Stéfano, the *galloping major* from Hungary, Ferenc Puskás, the Frenchman Raymond Kopa and several gifted Spaniards such as Rial, Muñoz, Santamaria and the one man to play a part in all six Champions' Cup triumphs, Gento.

And this interest spread even further after a decade or so of competition when the Northern Europeans from Britain, the Netherlands and Germany woke up at last to challenge the hegemony of the Latin clubs. From 1956 to 1966, in addition to Real Madrid's six victories, there were two wins each for Benfica, of Lisbon, and Inter, of Milan, and one for Inter's city rivals, AC Milan. It was not until 1967 that the splendid silver trophy was to find its way to the northern reaches of the old continent. And it was the Scottish club, Celtic, forerunners of the celebrated new playing style known as *total football* which would bring such glory to Johan Cruijff and his Ajax Amsterdam side a few years later, who made the first breach of the Latin fortress.

Following in their footsteps, a year later, were Manchester United, resurgent at last after the air tragedy which had decimated the club a decade earlier. In 1958, on the way back from a European Cup match in Belgrade, the plane carrying the Manchester United team crashed shortly after take-off in Munich, where it had stopped to refuel. Seven members of the famous *Busby Babes* side were to die in the wreckage, an eighth, the great Duncan Edwards, finally succumbing to his injuries a fortnight later.

Amongst those who survived were manager Matt Busby and future England World Cup hero Bobby Charlton. And both these men were to play important roles in the Champions' Cup final victory at Wembley in 1968 when United overcame Benfica and their *Black Pearl*, Eusébio, to win the trophy 4-1 after extra-time.

The Northern Europeans Make Their Mark

But if Celtic were the first Northern European club to break the supremacy of the Latins in the Champions' Cup, it should also be mentioned that back in 1963, Tottenham Hotspur had won the third European Cup-winners' Cup by beating the holders, Atlético Madrid, 5-1 in the final! That said, it was not until the start of the '70s that the North Europeans, and notably the Anglo Saxons, really established a stranglehold of their own over the Latins and began to reign supreme in all three UEFA competitions.

The roll-of-honour in the Champions' Cup from 1970, when Dutch club Feyenoord took the trophy, illustrates the domination of clubs from the North: three triumphs for the Ajax of Cruijff, Neeskens, Keizer, Haan, Hulshoff and Blankenburg, in 1971, 1972 and 1973; three in a row also for Bayern Munich, led by the impeccable Franz Beckenbauer and ably supported by his lieutenants, all of them World Cup winners with West Germany in 1974, Gerd Müller, Sepp Maier, Georg Schwarzenbeck and Uli Hoeness, in 1974, 1975 and 1976.

From 1977 right up to 1984, it was the turn of English clubs to display their superiority. Four victories for Liverpool (1977, 1978, 1981, 1984), with their stars Kevin Keegan, Ray Clemence, Steve Heighway and Phil Neal, and later Kenny Dalglish, Bruce Grobbelaar, Graeme Souness and Ian Rush; two wins for Nottingham Forest and their enigmatic Brian Clough, who took them from the English Second Division to Champions' Cup success (1979, 1980) within the space of two years; and one triumph also for Aston Villa, who disposed of former champions, and red-hot favourites, Bayern Munich in the 1982 final in Rotterdam.

The Heysel Tragedy

The English domination, continued in 1985 by a victory for Liverpool's Merseyside rivals Everton in the final of the Cup Winners' Cup (3-1 v Rapid Vienna), was to come to a brutal and tragic halt a fortnight later. On May 29th, 1985, at the Heysel stadium in Brussels, a terrible tragedy was to occur prior to the Champions' Cup final between Liverpool and Juventus.

Several charges by the English supporters towards the Italian fans massed in the infamous "Z" section of the old stadium were to end in disaster as a wall collapsed, leading to the death by suffocation of 39 innocent people and serious injuries to hundreds of others.

The tragedy was to send European football into mourning and bring about tough new measures in the war against hooliganism. As far as English football was concerned, the punishment was alarming in its severity: an indefinite ban from European club competitions on all its clubs and an additional suspension for Liverpool. The exile lasted five long years, with Liverpool finally being allowed back a year later, when the UEFA Executive Committee convened in London in April 1991.

Remarkably, in the first year back for English clubs after the ban, Manchester United proved what the competitions had been missing by winning the Cup-winners' Cup at the expense of Barcelona in the Rotterdam final, this after eliminating, in the quarter-finals, French club Montpellier (earlier conquerors of both PSV Eindhoven and Steaua Bucharest) and, in the semi-finals, Legia Warsaw, the Polish club who had previously accounted for holders Sampdoria. It was an extraordinary achievement for Manchester United, and of particular significance was the exemplary behaviour of their supporters, who had been a credit to the club all through the competition.

By September 1991, English clubs were back in force in European competition, with Arsenal in the Champions' Cup, Tottenham Hotspur and holders Manchester United in the Cup-winners' Cup and Liverpool in the UEFA Cup. And the general feeling throughout the continent was that the European Cups were back once again to their true status.

An Electric AC Milan

Even if it is difficult to prove in real terms, the absence of English clubs certainly went a long way towards helping Latin football to re-establish itself at the top of the European tree. And amidst this renaissance of the Southern powers emerged one formidable team, that of AC Milan, led by their celebrated Dutch trio of Ruud Gullit, Marco van Basten and Frank Rijkaard, all European Championship winners with the Netherlands in 1988, and boosted by the home-grown Italian contributions of, amongst others, Franco Baresi, Roberto Donadoni and Paolo Maldini. Champions' Cup winners in 1989 (4-0 against Steaua Bucharest in Barcelona's Nou Camp stadium, where they were cheered on by 90,000 passionate *tifosi*!), they retained the trophy in 1990 by disposing of Benfica 1-0 in the Vienna final. The team, pieced together by club president and media magnate Silvio Berlusconi, were aiming to follow in the footsteps of Ajax and Bayern Munich and win a third successive trophy in 1990-91, but they met their match in the quarter-finals against Olympique Marseille.

The French club, themselves run by an ambitious multi-millionaire businessman, Bernard Tapie, were attempting to become a new giant in European football by capturing the trophy for the first time, but in the final they fell into the trap set by Red Star Belgrade, going down in a penalty shoot-out. Prosinecki, Savicevic, Pancev, Belodedic and the rest gave Yugoslavia its first Champions' Cup, whereas France, the country which originated the competition and whose football is considered as one of the best in the continent, still awaits its first European triumph.

A New Champions' Cup

The Champions' Cup meeting between Red Star and Marseille in Bari was not just the 100th European final. It also marked the closing of a particular chapter in European Cup history. For since the beginning of the 1991-92 season a new Champions' Cup has seen the light, the old formula having undergone fundamental changes, 36 years after its creation in 1955.

Dundee United striker Ian Redford (left) heads the ball in from of IFK Gothenburg defender Peter Larsson during the 1986-87 UEFA Cup Final at Tannadice Stadium.

UEFA, whose intention is to try out the reforms only in the Champions' Cup for the time being, are nevertheless prepared to introduce them into the other two competitions if the experiment proves a success.

In its desire to satisfy the wishes of the big European clubs – several of whom had even threatened to form their own breakaway European League – but also with the objective of adding a breath of fresh air to the Champions' Cup, UEFA decided that from the 1991-92 season the eight clubs left in the competition after the first two rounds would be distributed into two groups of four teams, with matches to be played on a league basis (2 points for a win, 1 for a draw, 0 for a defeat) and the two winners of each group going into the final.

In these groups each team plays six matches (three at home, three away) before the final instead of two under the old system if a club was eliminated in the quarter-finals and four if a club went out in the semi-finals.

Up until now, the Champions' Cup, like the Cup-winners' and UEFA Cups, was played from start to finish under traditional Cup rules, i.e. a complete draw from the first round to the semi-finals and elimination in each round after home and away matches. Since the 1990-91 season, UEFA has tried to pacify those big clubs who complained of being drawn against each other early on in the competition by introducing a *league table* of those clubs taking part in the three competitions. This table is drawn up on the basis of the clubs' performance index (number of points plus bonus points divided by number of games played). These teams are classified from 1 to 32 in the Champions' and Cup-winners' Cups and from 1 to 64 in the UEFA Cup.

The first 16 ranked teams in each of the three competitions are given seeded status and, as a result, can not meet in the first two rounds.

For the Champions' Cup and the Cup-winners' Cup there are simply two *hats*, one containing the seeded clubs and one containing the rest of the clubs, those classified 17 to 32.

For the UEFA Cup, however, it is somewhat more complicated because of the greater number of clubs at the start – 64. In this case, UEFA decided to *manipulate* the draw by composing eight groups of eight clubs and placing two seeded teams (1 to 16) and six other teams (17 to 64) in each group.

The same system is carried through up until the quarter-final stages, when a conventional draw is made to determine both the distribution of the two four-team groups in the Champions' Cup and the four quarter-final pairings in the Cup-winners' and UEFA Cups.

The Power of Figures

One hundred European Cups have passed (36 Champions' Cups, 31 Cup-winners' Cups, 33 Fairs' and UEFA Cups) and a new Champions' Cup has been created, so there has never been a more appropriate time to look back on the history of the three competitions and study them in fine statistical detail.

This collection of facts and figures, some of which have never previously been published, is the most complete and detailed summary of its kind and will become the ultimate reference work for all those who are interested in the history of the three UEFA competitions and who display a particular passion for those confrontations between clubs from different countries.

Arrangement

For ease of reference we have divided our statistics broadly into five sections each of which is clearly headed and is preceded with a comprehensive description using a worked example. These sections, and their contents are:

Year by Year:

A year by year account of the first 35 years of European competition. This is the largest of the sections and paints a marvellous picture that depicts the fall and rise of clubs and countries. Every result is given along with the UEFA coefficients (outlined below) for each country at the completion of the season.

Champions' Cup, Cup Winners' Cup, UEFA Cup:

This gives a summary of the individual cup components over the entire history of the competitions. Areas detailed include national performances by index and club performances by points over 35, 10 and 5 year periods, a country by country record of points gained against clubs from other countries to name but a few.

All Three Cups:

These final section provides cumulative facts about all three cups over the entire history of the competitions, an alphabetical list of countries and the clubs which have represented them year by year in each competition, plus much more.

Official Formula

We should reveal here that all of our statistics have been compiled using the same official formula adopted by UEFA in establishing classifications of clubs and countries at the end of each season. All countries participating in the European Cups (with the exception of Wales, who have only ever been represented in the Cup-winners' Cup during the first 100 European Cups due to the absence of a national Welsh League) are attributed a performance index, calculated on the basis of the number of points obtained by their clubs, the bonus points earned from the quarter-final stage and the number of clubs entered by each country.

Simply by looking at the list of trophy winners, it can be gauged, for example, that:

- Spain and England are the two countries which have reached the most European Finals, (all three Cups included): 36 and 34 respectively.
- Italy is the country which has reached most Champions' Cup finals (14).
- Juventus is the only team to have been victorious in all three competitions: Champions' Cup in 1985, Cup-winners' Cup in 1984, and UEFA Cup in 1977 and 1990.
- Leeds United, Hamburg and Fiorentina have been finalists in all three competitions.
- Real Madrid have won the most trophies, with six Champions' Cups and two UEFA Cups (but no Cup-winners' Cups).

But these facts are just scratching the surface. For this study we have delved much deeper into the European Cup archives. Of particular interest is the publication of complete results for each season and for each of the three competitions, followed by the classifications by points and by performance index, by club and by country, cup by cup and all three competitions together, season after season, from the first year to the last, over ten years and five years.

But before we go into the salient points of these statistics, we should establish what the *rules of the game* are in the European Cups.

What You Need to Know

Since 1955-56, when the first European Cup was created, the three UEFA competitions have been run on a two-leg basis, with the conventional *cup* formula, whereby the team scoring more goals over the two matches – the aggregate score – qualifies for the next round. If the number of goals scored is the same for both sides, then those goals scored away from home are deemed to count double.

Example:

1st leg:	A v B:	2-0
2nd leg:	B v A:	3-1

The aggregate score is 3-3 but team A qualifies because it scored one away goal in the second leg and team B did not score in the first leg.

If the two results are identical, 30 minutes' extra-time is played to separate the teams. If no further goals are scored, the tie is decided on penalty kicks.

UEFA Co-efficients

Since the creation in 1972 of the UEFA Cup, a competition, as we have explained, which brings together those clubs who have finished just behind their respective national champions, UEFA has classified the 32 competing countries by according them a performance index at the end of each season, using a co-efficient calculated on the basis of the performances of their clubs and the number of clubs entered. Added together over five seasons, these co-efficients enable UEFA to allocate the 64 UEFA Cup places according to the classification of the 32 countries, as follows:

Countries in positions 1 to 3:	4 clubs
Countries in positions 4 to 8:	3 clubs
Countries in positions 9 to 21:	2 clubs
Countries in positions 22 to 32:	1 club

To calculate the co-efficients, UEFA uses the following formula:

1. The total number of points accumulated by a country during the course of the season (2 points for a victory, 1 point for a draw, 0 for a defeat) are added to any bonus points gained. One bonus point is obtained for each team qualifying for the quarter-finals, the semi-finals and the final.
2. This total is then divided by the number of clubs who entered the three competitions, shown as No./T in the table.

Example:

At the start of the season Italy enters five clubs, one in the Champions' Cup, one in the Cup-winners' Cup and three in the UEFA Cup. These five clubs earn a total of 56 points, plus 8 bonus points, giving a grand total of 64 points.

Italy's performance index for this season is therefore the following:

64 (number of points) /5 (number of teams) = 12.800

This index is then added to those of the previous four seasons and it is this *cumulative index* over five seasons which enables UEFA to classify the countries before allocating the UEFA Cup places.

As the European Cups are run parallel to national championships (USSR and the Scandinavian countries excepted), the UEFA Cup place allocation is made a year ahead of the actual competition. Thus, to make the allocation for the 1991-92 season, the five seasons from 1985-86 to 1989-90 are the ones taken into account.

Finally, it should also be pointed out that in the event of a penalty shoot-out, the points are shared as if the match were drawn, with one point each for the winner and the loser. So, for example, when the 1991 Champions' Cup final between Red Star Belgrade and Marseille ended 0-0 after extra-time, both teams earned one point each.

Barcelona's Gary Lineker holds the European Cup Winners' Cup aloft after Barca's 2-0 1988-89 win over Sampdoria in Berne.

One Season Under the Spotlight

The first part of our statistical work looks at the complete results, season by season, of all three Cups, since the beginning (1955-56) to the 100th European Cup in 1991. The running head across the top of the page gives the competition and year to which the page's statistics apply. To help you understand what information the figures convey and how to read them, let us look at the 1976-77 season by way of example (pages 229 to 239) and the Champions' Cup won that year by Liverpool.

Round by round information is provided and each round lists seven columns of information across the page, typically thus:

First Round

Team 1	Cnty	Team 2	Cnty	1st leg	2nd leg	Agg
Liverpool	Eng	Crusaders	Nir	2-0	5-0	7-0
Austria Vienna	Aut	Bor. Mönchengladbach	FRG	1-0	0-3	1-3
Club Bruges	Bel	Steaua Bucharest	Rom	2-1	1-1	3-2

Each line of results includes the following information:

Team 1 the name of the club playing the first leg at home
Cnty the club's three-letter (Olympic) country code
Team 2 the name of the away club in the first leg
Cnty the away club's three letter country code
1st leg the first leg score
2nd leg the second leg score (with the first team given first)
Agg the total aggregate score

Thus in Liverpool's first round tie they were drawn at home to Crusaders of Northern Ireland in the first leg. Liverpool won the first leg 2-0 and then won the second leg (away) 5-0, giving the Reds a 7-0 aggregate victory.

Each European Cup round is punctuated with a running record of the points obtained, the total number of matches played, the number of goals scored and the average number of goals per match for each round. The first round details are summarised thus:

	Pts	P	W	D	L	F	A	Diff	B	Goals/P
Total	64	32	25	14	25	88	88	0	0	2.750

So, in the first round a total of 64 points were obtainable. Thirty two games were played (16 ties of two legs) resulting in 25 wins, 14 draws and 25 defeats. Eighty eight goals were scored (for and against). The goal difference will always be 0 and, by virtue of being the first round, no bonus points were available. The 2.750 figure is the average number of goals scored per game. These figures are repeated for each round. Thus we can see that the average goals per game drops to two goals per match in the second round (32 goals in 16 games) before increasing in both the quarter-finals and semi-finals to give a total for the season of 2.541 goals per match (155 goals in 61 games).

Kiev Better Than Mönchengladbach?

At the end of each season, for each of the three competitions, a general league table of clubs (by points won) and of countries (by UEFA performance index) has been established, so that it is possible to compare the overall performances of the countries with those of the clubs which have represented them. The top of the table looks like this:

Pos'n	Club	Cnty	Pts	P	W	D	L	F	A	Diff	B	Pts/P	F/P
1	Liverpool	Eng	17	9	7	0	2	22	5	17	3	1.889	2.444
2	Dinamo Kiev	URS	14	8	6	0	2	14	3	11	2	1.750	1.750
3	Bor. Mönchengladbach	FRG	13	9	4	2	3	11	8	3	3	1.444	1.222

In 1976-77 Liverpool defeated Borussia Mönchengladbach in the Champions' Cup Final 3-1. Not surprisingly, they finish at the top of the table with a total of 17 points. The 17 points have been obtained as follows:

7 wins	2 points per win	Total 14	points
0 draws	1 point per draw	Total 0	points
2 defeats	0 points per defeat	Total 0	points
Bonus points	1 for each round from quarter finals	Total 3	points
		Total 17	points

Much of the table should be self explanatory. The column under B lists bonus points which are calculated as described earlier. The next column Pts/P is the average number of points won by the club in relation to the number of matches played (including bonus points). Let us take Liverpool as an example:

17 (number of points) / 9 (number of matches) = 1.889 points

The second column indicates the average number of goals scored by the club. Liverpool again:

22 (number of goals scored) / 9 (number of matches) = 2.444

But this 1976-77 Champions' Cup table also shows us that the club which finishes up at the end of the season in second place behind Liverpool is not runners-up Borussia Mönchengladbach, but Dinamo Kiev! The explanation is simple: Kiev gained one point more than the German club despite playing one game less (they were knocked out by Mönchengladbach in the semi-finals). The Ukrainians have a grand total of 14 points (8 matches, 6 victories, 2 defeats, 2 bonus points) against Mönchengladbach's 13 (9 matches, 4 victories, 2 draws, 3 defeats, 3 bonus points).

There are other peculiarities to be found in the table. For example, Ferencváros, in ninth position, have the most efficient attack with an average of three goals per match (12 goals in four games). Saint-Etienne, in sixth place, eliminated in the quarter-finals by eventual winners Liverpool, only scored four goals in six matches and conceded only three. Three too many in fact, as they conceded them all in one match, away to Liverpool at Anfield!

Go for Goal!

The changes in the average number of goals scored per match over the years give an interesting indication of how the game has evolved from the beginning of the European Cups to the present day.

It can be seen that after reaching figures of around four goals per match (sometimes even going as high as 4.5!) between 1956 and 1963, the average number of goals fell sharply in 1964 with the advent of the infamous *catenaccio* tactics practised by Helenio Herrera's Inter Milan. This figure even dropped to around 2.8 goals per match in the '70s and '80s, with a record low for the 87-88 season of 2.3 goals per match, all three competitions included.

This dramatic fall in the goals per game average is not exclusive to the European Cups. It has also been evident in certain national championships and, notably, in recent World Cups. There are two explanations for this:

1. With the exception of a few countries, such as Luxembourg and Malta, whose clubs continue to get beaten heavily in European competition, most teams, including those from other small countries (e.g. Iceland, Cyprus etc) are now much better prepared both mentally and tactically and are consequently much less likely to cave in to superior opposition quite so readily as they once did in the past.

   There are, of course, exceptions such as the 5-0 drubbing which AC Milan handed out to Real Madrid in 1989, but, generally speaking, high-scoring victories are much rarer these days. Certainly, there is virtually no chance whatsoever of seeing a Champions' Cup final ending up with a 7-3 scoreline, such as Real Madrid and Eintracht Frankfurt managed back in 1960!

2. The massive injection of money into the game, through advertising, television and sponsorship, has not just made the rich clubs even richer but has also, to a certain extent, had a damaging effect on the spirit of the game. So popular and important have the three European club competitions become that the difference between winning and losing has never been greater. In effect the stakes have become so high that the first priority for teams going into European Cup matches, even finals, is not to go out and defeat the opposition, but to make sure that they don't lose. Hence the over-cautious tactics one sees these days, where the result takes all precedence over the spectacle, the most poignant recent example of course being the last Champions' Cup final in Bari. The brilliant

performance of Red Star Belgrade in the semi-final against Bayern Munich led most experts to believe that the final would be a classic of enterprising, attacking football, but in Bari the Yugoslavs put all their resources into defence, in effect *shutting up shop* and attempting to hold out for the penalty shoot-out. In the end, they could claim that the result proved them right, that the risk was worth taking, but tactics such as those are hardly likely to bring in the crowds.

This negative trend, amply illustrated in the last World Cup in Italy, has prompted football's governing body, FIFA, to set up a commission of footballing experts (including French national team coach Michel Platini, German striker Rudi Völler and the Danish referee Peter Mikkelsen) under the direction of the Swedish president of UEFA, Lennart Johansson. This commission, which meets at regular intervals in Zürich, has been given the task of seeking out remedies to make football more attractive.

This large-scale operation, which began with a study of certain possible rule changes proposed by the International Board, was baptised *Football 2000* and launched by FIFA general secretary Joseph Blatter under the slogan *Go For Goal!* The objective of it all is to restore the *beautiful game* and that means getting players and coaches to change their negative habits and to rediscover their taste for attacking football, technical excellence and, above all, scoring goals.

The *magic* of the European Cups exists because a number of great teams down the years have gone out onto the field of play with the dual intention of winning matches and entertaining the crowds. Real Madrid in the '50s and '60s, Ajax in 1972, Bayern Munich in 1974, Liverpool in 1977 and 1978, Milan in 1989, not forgetting the Juventus of Platini, Tardelli and Rossi, the Benfica of Eusébio or the Barcelona of Rexach and Cruijff. These are all clubs with marvellous records in European competition and which – it is no coincidence – sit proudly at the head of our various statistical tables.

Annual and Accumulative Tables

Each year is rounded off by two pages of tables which provide details of national performances by points and by index. There are two tables for each – the first being the season's record and the second being the on-going total from the first season of European competition, namely 1955-56. Again, these tables should be largely self-explanatory but for the sake of completeness a brief description follows, using the 1976-77 season as an example (page 237).

The first two tables are headed National Performance by Points. The uppermost lists by country the total points accumulated by its participating clubs in all three competitions. The layout provides a standard PWDLFA summary along with bonus points and averages for points per game and goals per game.

Pos'n	Cnty	Pts	P	W	D	L	F	A	Diff	B	Pts/P	F/P
1	FRG	65	44	25	8	11	93	47	46	7	1.477	2.114
2	Esp	50	38	18	8	12	62	44	18	6	1.316	1.632
3	Eng	48	33	21	1	11	86	37	49	5	1.455	2.606
4	Bel	47	31	16	9	6	50	27	23	6	1.516	1.613
5	Ita	47	34	18	6	10	47	30	17	5	1.382	1.382

It is interesting that, despite the fact that Juventus won the Fairs' Cup in the season in question, Italy are listed in only fifth position in the season's point totals. In the accumulator (below) it is England who ride high in the charts – a position they would retain at the end of the first 100 European Cups.

1	Eng	946	637	349	133	155	1273	666	607	115	1.485	1.998
2	Esp	840	604	310	113	181	1181	754	427	107	1.391	1.955
3	FRG	795	574	302	106	166	1182	765	417	85	1.385	2.059
4	Ita	780	560	285	119	156	905	574	331	91	1.393	1.616
5	Sco	507	405	197	65	143	735	553	182	48	1.252	1.815

The second set of tables lists National Performances by Index (page 238) – as an average of the country's co-efficient, first by year and then as an average calculated over all three competitions since their inception.

Pos'n	Cnty	Ave	Pts	P	W	D	L	F	A	Diff	B	No./T
1	Spain	10.000	50	38	18	8	12	62	44	18	6	5
2	Belgium	9.400	47	31	16	9	6	50	27	23	6	5
3	W. Germany	9.285	65	44	25	8	11	93	47	46	7	7
4	England	8.000	48	33	21	1	11	86	37	49	5	6
5	Italy	7.833	47	34	18	6	10	47	30	17	5	6

The first of these shows that it is Spain who had the best co-efficient for 1976-77, despite finishing second to West Germany in the season's points table. England were ranked fourth. However, as the second listing shows, England had a far superior accumulative co-efficient to second-placed Spain – 9.274 compared to 8.000.

1	England	9.274	946	637	349	133	155	1273	666	607	115	102
2	Spain	8.000	840	604	310	113	181	1181	754	427	107	105
3	Italy	7.572	780	560	285	119	156	905	574	331	91	103
4	W. Germany	7.361	795	574	302	106	166	1182	765	417	85	108
5	USSR	6.333	209	153	84	27	42	240	149	91	14	33

Below: Nottingham Forest striker Trevor Francis dives to head past Malmo 'keeper Jan Moeller to score the only goal of the 1978-78 Champions' Cup Final.

Country Codes

The following is a list of country codes used throughout this book, arranged alphabetically by country code.

Alb	Albania	Lux	Luxembourg
Aut	Austria	Mlt	Malta
Bel	Belgium	Ned	The Netherlands
Bul	Bulgaria	Nir	Northern Ireland
Cyp	Cyprus	Nor	Norway
Den	Denmark	Pol	Poland
Eng	England	Por	Portugal
Esp	Spain	Rom	Romania
Fin	Finland	Sco	Scotland
Fra	France	Sui	Switzerland
FRG	West Germany	Swe	Sweden
GDR	East Germany	Tch	Czechoslovakia
Gre	Greece	Tur	Turkey
Hun	Hungary	URS	USSR
Irl	Republic of Ireland	Wal	Wales
Isl	Iceland	Yug	Yugoslavia
Ita	Italy		

Below: Alan Sealey (right) jumps for joy as his close range shot beats Munich 'keeper Peter Radenovic. Martin Peters joins in as West Ham United win the the 1964-65 Cup Winners' Cup Final at Wembley.

Real Madrid

1955 – 1956

First Round

Team 1	Cnty	Team 2	Cnty	1st leg	2nd leg	Agg
Rapid Vienna	Aut	PSV Eindhoven	Ned	6-1	0-1	6-2
AGF Aarhus	Den	Stade Reims	Fra	0-2	2-2	2-4
MTK-VM	Hun	Anderlecht	Bel	6-3	4-1	10-4
AC Milan	Ita	Saarbrücken	FRG	3-4	4-1	7-5
Sporting Lisbon	Por	Partizan Belgrade	Yug	3-3	2-5	5-8
Rot-Weiss Essen	FRG	Hibernian	Sco	0-4	1-1	1-5
Djurgården SIF	Swe	Gwardia Warsaw	Pol	0-0	4-1	4-1
Servette	Sui	Real Madrid	Esp	0-2	0-5	0-7

	Pts	P	W	D	L	F	A	Diff	Goals/P
Total	32	16	12	8	12	71	71	0	4.438

Quarter Finals

Rapid Vienna	Aut	AC Milan	Ita	1-1	2-7	3-8
Hibernian	Sco	Djurgården SIF	Swe	3-1	1-0	4-1
Real Madrid	Esp	Partizan Belgrade	Yug	4-0	0-3	4-3
Stade Reims	Fra	MTK-VM	Hun	4-2	4-4	8-6

	Pts	P	W	D	L	F	A	Diff	Goals/P
Total	16	8	6	4	6	37	37	0	4.625

Semi Finals

Real Madrid	Esp	AC Milan	Ita	4-2	1-2	5-4
Stade Reims	Fra	Hibernian	Sco	2-0	1-0	3-0

	Pts	P	W	D	L	F	A	Diff	Goals/P
Total	8	4	4	0	4	12	12	0	3.000

Final

Real Madrid	Esp	Stade Reims	Fra	4-3		4-3

	Pts	P	W	D	L	F	A	Diff	Goals/P
Total	2	1	1	0	1	7	7	0	7.000

	Pts	P	W	D	L	F	A	Diff	Goals/P
Total	58	29	23	12	23	127	127	0	4.379

European Cup 1955-56

Pos'n	Club	Cnty	Pts	P	W	D	L	F	A	Diff	B	Pts/P	F/P
1	Real Madrid	Esp	13	7	5	0	2	20	10	10	3	1.857	2.857
2	Stade Reims	Fra	13	7	4	2	1	18	12	6	3	1.857	2.571
3	AC Milan	Ita	9	6	3	1	2	19	13	6	2	1.500	3.167
4	Hibernian	Sco	9	6	3	1	2	9	5	4	2	1.500	1.500
5	MTK-VM	Hun	6	4	2	1	1	16	12	4	1	1.500	4.000
6	Partizan Belgrade	Yug	6	4	2	1	1	11	9	2	1	1.500	2.750
7	Djurgården SIF	Swe	4	4	1	1	2	5	5	0	1	1.000	1.250
8	Rapid Vienna	Aut	4	4	1	1	2	9	10	-1	1	1.000	2.250
9	Saarbrücken	FRG	2	2	1	0	1	5	7	-2	0	1.000	2.500
10	PSV Eindhoven	Ned	2	2	1	0	1	2	6	-4	0	1.000	1.000
11	AGF Aarhus	Den	1	2	0	1	1	2	4	-2	0	0.500	1.000
12	Sporting Lisbon	Por	1	2	0	1	1	5	8	-3	0	0.500	2.500
13	Gwardia Warsaw	Pol	1	2	0	1	1	1	4	-3	0	0.500	0.500
14	Rot-Weiss Essen	FRG	1	2	0	1	1	1	5	-4	0	0.500	0.500
15	Anderlecht	Bel	0	2	0	0	2	4	10	-6	0	0.000	2.000
16	Servette	Sui	0	2	0	0	2	0	7	-7	0	0.000	0.000
	Total		**72**	**58**	**23**	**12**	**23**	**127**	**127**	**0**	**14**	**1.241**	**4.379**

National Performances by Points

1955-56

Pos'n	Cnty	Pts	P	W	D	L	F	A	Diff	B	Pts/P	F/P
1	Esp	13	7	5	0	2	20	10	10	3	1.857	2.857
2	Fra	13	7	4	2	1	18	12	6	3	1.857	2.571
3	Ita	9	6	3	1	2	19	13	6	2	1.500	3.167
4	Sco	9	6	3	1	2	9	5	4	2	1.500	1.500
5	Hun	6	4	2	1	1	16	12	4	1	1.500	4.000
6	Yug	6	4	2	1	1	11	9	2	1	1.500	2.750
7	Swe	4	4	1	1	2	5	5	0	1	1.000	1.250
8	Aut	4	4	1	1	2	9	10	-1	1	1.000	2.250
9	FRG	3	4	1	1	2	6	12	-6	0	0.750	1.500
10	Ned	2	2	1	0	1	2	6	-4	0	1.000	1.000
11	Den	1	2	0	1	1	2	4	-2	0	0.500	1.000
12	Por	1	2	0	1	1	5	8	-3	0	0.500	2.500
13	Pol	1	2	0	1	1	1	4	-3	0	0.500	0.500
14	Bel	0	2	0	0	2	4	10	-6	0	0.000	2.000
15	Sui	0	2	0	0	2	0	7	-7	0	0.000	0.000
	Total	**72**	**58**	**23**	**12**	**23**	**127**	**127**	**0**	**14**	**1.241**	**4.379**

National Performances by Index

1955-56

Pos'n	Cnty	Ave	Pts	P	W	D	L	F	A	Diff	B	No./T
1	Spain	13.000	13	7	5	0	2	20	10	10	3	1
–	France	13.000	13	7	4	2	1	18	12	6	3	1
3	Scotland	9.000	9	6	3	1	2	9	5	4	2	1
–	Italy	9.000	9	6	3	1	2	19	13	6	2	1
5	Hungary	6.000	6	4	2	1	1	16	12	4	1	1
–	Yugoslavia	6.000	6	4	2	1	1	11	9	2	1	1
7	Austria	4.000	4	4	1	1	2	9	10	-1	1	1
–	Sweden	4.000	4	4	1	1	2	5	5	0	1	1
9	Netherlands	2.000	2	2	1	0	1	2	6	-4	0	1
10	W. Germany	1.500	3	4	1	1	2	6	12	-6	0	2
11	Denmark	1.000	1	2	0	1	1	2	4	-2	0	1
–	Poland	1.000	1	2	0	1	1	1	4	-3	0	1
–	Portugal	1.000	1	2	0	1	1	5	8	-3	0	1
14	Belgium	0.000	0	2	0	0	2	4	10	-6	0	1
–	Switzerland	0.000	0	2	0	0	2	0	7	-7	0	1
	Total		**72**	**58**	**23**	**12**	**23**	**127**	**127**	**0**	**14**	**4.379**

By Invitation Only

The inaugural European Cup was more of an invitational tournament than a bringing-together of the national champions of Europe. Of the 16 teams which took part in the first *Champions' Cup,* less than half were entering as the holders of their own domestic league title. Only Rot-Weiss Essen (West Germany), Anderlecht (Belgium), Djurgården (Sweden), AGF (Denmark), Reims (France), Milan (Italy) and Real Madrid (Spain) came into that category. The remaining nine teams were simply selected by their own federations as being their country's most worthy representatives.

Of the many European nations not taking part, England's absence was the most notable. Chelsea, the English champions at the time, were invited to compete, but, after heeding the dissuasive advice of the Football League, eventually elected not to enter.

Despite these initial teething problems, Gabriel Hanot's brainchild was to enjoy a relatively healthy first year of life. The tournament kicked off with an exciting 3-3 draw between Portugal's Sporting Lisbon and Yugoslavia's Partizan Belgrade and that abundance of goals was to be replicated through the entire competition. The return match saw Partizan progress through to the next round with a thumping 5-2 victory, their prize being a quarter-final encounter with Spanish champions, Real Madrid.

Real, one of the pre-tournament favourites, had waltzed through their first-round tie, defeating the Swiss side, Servette of Geneva, 7-0 on aggregate, and they were to treat the Madrid public to a festive feast of attacking football with a 4-0 victory over Partizan on Christmas Day. The return leg, played in snowbound Belgrade, was a different matter entirely, with the Yugoslavs winning the game 3-0 and almost staging a miraculous comeback.

Real's semi-final opponents were Italian champions, AC Milan, who had begun the tournament inauspiciously with a 3-4 home defeat against Saarbrücken but had later proved their worth with a 7-2 destruction of Rapid Vienna in the quarter-finals. The first leg of the semi-finals, held in Madrid's Chamartin stadium (later to be named after their pioneering president of the day, Santiago Bernabéu), went the way of the Spaniards, with star player Alfredo Di Stéfano scoring the last goal in a 4-2 victory. It was a victory margin which proved too great for Milan in the return leg, and a single Real goal from Joseito was enough to take the Spaniards through to the first European Cup final in Paris.

There to meet them were the French representatives, Stade Reims. Inspired by international centre-forward Raymond Kopa, Reims had won both of their semi-final matches against Scotland's Hibernian and, with the advantage of playing on home territory, they looked forward to the June 13th final with plenty of confidence.

The French champions made the perfect start in front of a partisan, sell-out crowd. With 12 minutes gone they were already two goals up through Leblond and Templin. But Real, masterminded by Di Stéfano, soon came back into the match and by half-time the scores were level at 2-2. Michel Hidalgo, later to become a successful coach to the French national side, taking them to the European Championship crown in 1984, then put Reims ahead again with a header from a Kopa free-kick, but the lead did not last long. A deflected shot from defender Marquitos restored parity before, with just ten minutes left on the clock, left-winger Paco Gento sped away up the wing to provide the winning goal for Real's Argentinian inside-forward, Hector Rial.

Reims tried desperately to respond, and Templin hit the bar in the dying seconds. But it was not to be and Albert Batteux's side could only gain consolation from being gallant losers in an enthralling contest. Which Frenchman in the crowd could have possibly thought then that 99 European Cups later, his country would still be awaiting their first ever European trophy?

The first European Cup, then, had gone to Real Madrid, 4-3, after a truly exhilarating final. There could have been no finer advert for the competition than that match in Paris. And, sure enough, it was to spark off a fresh bout of interest for the first Champions' Cup proper the following season.

Real Madrid

1956 – 1957

First Round

Team 1	Cnty	Team 2	Cnty	1st leg	2nd leg	Agg
Anderlecht	Bel	Manchester United	Eng	0-2	0-10	0-12
AGF Åarhus	Den	Nice	Fra	1-1	1-5	2-6
FC Porto	Por	Athletic Bilbao	Esp	1-2	2-3	3-5
Borussia Dortmund	FRG	Spora Luxembourg	Lux	4-3	1-2	12-5
		Dortmund won the replay 7-0				
Dinamo Bucharest	Rom	Galatasaray	Tur	3-1	1-2	4-3
Slovan Bratislava	Tch	Legia Warsaw	Pol	4-0	0-2	4-2

	Pts	P	W	D	L	F	A	Diff	Goals/P
Total	26	13	12	2	12	58	58	0	4.462

Second Round

Team 1	Cnty	Team 2	Cnty	1st leg	2nd leg	Agg
Manchester United	Eng	Borussia Dortmund	FRG	3-2	0-0	3-2
CSKA Sofia	Bul	Dinamo Bucharest	Rom	8-1	2-3	10-4
Rangers	Sco	Nice	Fra	2-1	1-2	4-6
		Nice won the replay 1-3				
Athletic Bilbao	Esp	Honvéd	Hun	3-2	3-3	6-5
Real Madrid	Esp	Rapid Vienna	Aut	4-2	1-3	7-5
		Madrid won the replay 2-0				
Fiorentina	Ita	IFK Norrköping	Swe	1-1	1-0	2-1
Roda JC	Ned	Red Star Belgrade	Yug	3-4	0-2	3-6
Slovan Bratislava	Tch	Grasshoppers Zürich	Sui	1-0	0-2	1-2

	Pts	P	W	D	L	F	A	Diff	Goals/P
Total	36	18	15	6	15	67	67	0	3.722

Quarter Finals

Team 1	Cnty	Team 2	Cnty	1st leg	2nd leg	Agg
Athletic Bilbao	Esp	Manchester United	Eng	5-3	0-3	5-6
Real Madrid	Esp	Nice	Fra	3-0	3-2	6-2
Fiorentina	Ita	Grasshoppers Zürich	Sui	3-1	2-2	5-3
Red Star Belgrade	Yug	CSKA Sofia	Bul	3-1	1-2	4-3

	Pts	P	W	D	L	F	A	Diff	Goals/P
Total	16	8	7	2	7	34	34	0	4.250

Semi Finals

Team 1	Cnty	Team 2	Cnty	1st leg	2nd leg	Agg
Real Madrid	Esp	Manchester United	Eng	3-1	2-2	5-3
Red Star Belgrade	Yug	Fiorentina	Ita	0-1	0-0	0-1

	Pts	P	W	D	L	F	A	Diff	Goals/P
Total	8	4	2	4	2	9	9	0	2.250

Final

Team 1	Cnty	Team 2	Cnty	1st leg	2nd leg	Agg
Real Madrid	Esp	Fiorentina	Ita	2-0		2-0

	Pts	P	W	D	L	F	A	Diff	Goals/P
Total	2	1	1	0	1	2	2	0	2.000

European Cup 1956-57

	Pts	P	W	D	L	F	A	Diff	Goals/P
Total	88	44	37	14	37	170	170	0	3.864

Pos'n	Club	Cnty	Pts	P	W	D	L	F	A	Diff	B	Pts/P	F/P
1	Real Madrid	Esp	16	8	6	1	1	20	10	10	3	2.000	2.500
2	Manchester United	Eng	12	8	4	2	2	24	12	12	2	1.500	3.000
3	Fiorentina	Ita	12	7	3	3	1	8	6	2	3	1.714	1.143
–	Athletic Bilbao	Esp	10	6	4	1	1	16	14	2	1	1.667	2.667
5	Red Star Belgrade	Yug	9	6	3	1	2	10	7	3	2	1.500	1.667
6	Nice	Fra	8	7	3	1	3	14	12	2	1	1.143	2.000
7	Borussia Dortmund	FRG	5	5	2	1	2	14	8	6	0	1.000	2.800
8	CSKA Sofia	Bul	5	4	2	0	2	13	8	5	1	1.250	3.250
9	Slovan Bratislava	Tch	4	4	2	0	2	5	4	1	0	1.000	1.250
10	Grasshoppers Zürich	Sui	4	4	1	1	2	5	6	-1	1	1.000	1.250
11	Dinamon Bucharest	Rom	4	4	2	0	2	8	13	-5	0	1.000	2.000
12	Galatasaray	Tur	2	2	1	0	1	3	4	-1	0	1.000	1.500
13	Rapid Vienna	Aut	2	3	1	0	2	5	7	-2	0	0.667	1.667
14	Rangers	Sco	2	3	1	0	2	4	6	-2	0	0.667	1.333
15	Legia Warsaw	Pol	2	2	1	0	1	2	4	-2	0	1.000	1.000
16	Spora Luxembourg	Lux	2	3	1	0	2	5	12	-7	0	0.667	1.667
17	Honvéd	Hun	1	2	0	1	1	5	6	-1	0	0.500	2.500
18	IFK Norrköping	Swe	1	2	0	1	1	1	2	-1	0	0.500	0.500
19	AGF Åarhus	Den	1	2	0	1	1	2	6	-4	0	0.500	1.000
20	FC Porto	Por	0	2	0	0	2	3	5	-2	0	0.000	1.500
21	Roda JC	Ned	0	2	0	0	2	3	6	-3	0	0 000	1.500
22	Anderlecht	Bel	0	2	0	0	2	0	12	-12	0	0.000	0.000
	Total		**102**	**88**	**37**	**14**	**37**	**170**	**170**	**0**	**14**	**1.159**	**3.864**

1956-57

Pos'n	Cnty	Pts	P	W	D	L	F	A	Diff	B	Pts/P	F/P
1	Esp	26	14	10	2	2	36	24	12	4	1.857	2.571
2	Eng	12	8	4	2	2	24	12	12	2	1.500	3.000
3	Ita	12	7	3	3	1	8	6	2	3	1.714	1.143
4	Yug	9	6	3	1	2	10	7	3	2	1.500	1.667
5	Fra	8	7	3	1	3	14	12	2	1	1.143	2.000
6	FRG	5	5	2	1	2	14	8	6	0	1.000	2.800
7	Bul	5	4	2	0	2	13	8	5	1	1.250	3.250
8	Tch	4	4	2	0	2	5	4	1	0	1.000	1.250
9	Sui	4	4	1	1	2	5	6	-1	1	1.000	1.250
10	Rom	4	4	2	0	2	8	13	-5	0	1.000	2.000
11	Tur	2	2	1	0	1	3	4	-1	0	1.000	1.500
12	Aut	2	3	1	0	2	5	7	-2	0	0.667	1.667
13	Sco	2	3	1	0	2	4	6	-2	0	0.667	1.333
14	Pol	2	2	1	0	1	2	4	-2	0	1.000	1.000
15	Lux	2	3	1	0	2	5	12	-7	0	0.667	1.667
16	Hun	1	2	0	1	1	5	6	-1	0	0.500	2.500
17	Swe	1	2	0	1	1	1	2	-1	0	0.500	0.500
18	Den	1	2	0	1	1	2	6	-4	0	0.500	1.000
19	Por	0	2	0	0	2	3	5	-2	0	0.000	1.500
20	Ned	0	2	0	0	2	3	6	-3	0	0.000	1.500
21	Bel	0	2	0	0	2	0	12	-12	0	0.000	0.000
	Total	**102**	**88**	**37**	**14**	**37**	**170**	**170**	**0**	**14**	**1.159**	**3.864**

1955-56 to 1956-57

1	Esp	39	21	15	2	4	56	34	22	7	1.857	2.667
2	Fra	21	14	7	3	4	32	24	8	4	1.500	2.286
3	Ita	21	13	6	4	3	27	19	8	5	1.615	2.077
4	Yug	15	10	5	2	3	21	16	5	3	1.500	2.100
5	Eng	12	8	4	2	2	24	12	12	2	1.500	3.000
6	Sco	11	9	4	1	4	13	11	2	2	1.222	1.444
7	FRG	8	9	3	2	4	20	20	0	0	0.889	2.222
8	Hun	7	6	2	2	2	21	18	3	1	1.167	3.500
9	Aut	6	7	2	1	4	14	17	-3	1	0.857	2.000
10	Bul	5	4	2	0	2	13	8	5	1	1.250	3.250
11	Swe	5	6	1	2	3	6	7	-1	1	0.833	1.000
12	Tch	4	4	2	0	2	5	4	1	0	1.000	1.250
13	Rom	4	4	2	0	2	8	13	-5	0	1.000	2.000
14	Sui	4	6	1	1	4	5	13	-8	1	0.667	0.833
15	Pol	3	4	1	1	2	3	8	-5	0	0.750	0.750
16	Tur	2	2	1	0	1	3	4	-1	0	1.000	1.500
17	Den	2	4	0	2	2	4	10	-6	0	0.500	1.000
18	Lux	2	3	1	0	2	5	12	-7	0	0.667	1.667
–	Ned	2	4	1	0	3	5	12	-7	0	0.500	1.250
20	Por	1	4	0	1	3	8	13	-5	0	0.250	2.000
21	Bel	0	4	0	0	4	4	22	-18	0	0.000	1.000
	Total	**174**	**146**	**60**	**26**	**60**	**297**	**297**	**0**	**28**	**1.192**	**4.068**

National Performance by Index

1956-57

Pos'n	Cnty	Ave	Pts	P	W	D	L	F	A	Diff	B	No./T
1	Spain	13.000	26	14	10	2	2	36	24	12	4	2
2	England	12.000	12	8	4	2	2	24	12	12	2	1
–	Italy	12.000	12	7	3	3	1	8	6	2	3	1
4	Yugoslavia	9.000	9	6	3	1	2	10	7	3	2	1
5	France	8.000	8	7	3	1	3	14	12	2	1	1
6	Bulgaria	5.000	5	4	2	0	2	13	8	5	1	1
–	W. Germany	5.000	5	5	2	1	2	14	8	6	0	1
8	Romania	4.000	4	4	2	0	2	8	13	-5	0	1
–	Switzerland	4.000	4	4	1	1	2	5	6	-1	1	1
–	Czechoslovakia	4.000	4	4	2	0	2	5	4	1	0	1
11	Austria	2.000	2	3	1	0	2	5	7	-2	0	1
–	Scotland	2.000	2	3	1	0	2	4	6	-2	0	1
–	Luxembourg	2.000	2	3	1	0	2	5	12	-7	0	1
–	Poland	2.000	2	2	1	0	1	2	4	-2	0	1
–	Turkey	2.000	2	2	1	0	1	3	4	-1	0	1
16	Denmark	1.000	1	2	0	1	1	2	6	-4	0	1
–	Hungary	1.000	1	2	0	1	1	5	6	-1	0	1
–	Sweden	1.000	1	2	0	1	1	1	2	-1	0	1
19	Belgium	0.000	0	2	0	0	2	0	12	-12	0	1
–	Netherlands	0.000	0	2	0	0	2	3	6	-3	0	1
–	Portugal	0.000	0	2	0	0	2	3	5	-2	0	1
	Total		**102**	**88**	**37**	**14**	**37**	**170**	**170**	**0**	**14**	**3.864**

1955-56 to 1956-57

Pos'n	Cnty	Ave	Pts	P	W	D	L	F	A	Diff	B	No./T
1	Spain	13.000	39	21	15	2	4	56	34	22	7	3
2	England	12.000	12	8	4	2	2	24	12	12	2	1
3	France	10.500	21	14	7	3	4	32	24	8	4	2
–	Italy	10.500	21	13	6	4	3	27	19	8	5	2
5	Yugoslavia	7.500	15	10	5	2	3	21	16	5	3	2
6	Scotland	5.500	11	9	4	1	4	13	11	2	2	2
7	Bulgaria	5.000	5	4	2	0	2	13	8	5	1	1
8	Romania	4.000	4	4	2	0	2	8	13	-5	0	1
–	Czechoslovakia	4.000	4	4	2	0	2	5	4	1	0	1
10	Hungary	3.500	7	6	2	2	2	21	18	3	1	2
11	Austria	3.000	6	7	2	1	4	14	17	-3	1	2
12	W. Germany	2.667	8	9	3	2	4	20	20	0	0	3
13	Sweden	2.500	5	6	1	2	3	6	7	-1	1	2
14	Luxembourg	2.000	2	3	1	0	2	5	12	-7	0	1
–	Switzerland	2.000	4	6	1	1	4	5	13	-8	1	2
–	Turkey	2.000	2	2	1	0	1	3	4	-1	0	1
17	Poland	1.500	3	4	1	1	2	3	8	-5	0	2
18	Denmark	1.000	2	4	0	2	2	4	10	-6	0	2
–	Netherlands	1.000	2	4	1	0	3	5	12	-7	0	2
20	Portugal	0.500	1	4	0	1	3	8	13	-5	0	2
21	Belgium	0.000	0	4	0	0	4	4	22	-18	0	2
	Total		**174**	**146**	**60**	**26**	**60**	**297**	**297**	**0**	**28**	**4. 068**

Manchester Takes On Madrid

Twenty one national champions, plus holders Real Madrid, made up the field for the second edition of the European Champions' Cup. This entry figure of 22 teams meant that a preliminary round was necessary in order to come to a more manageable 16-team complement for the first round proper. So while Real and nine other clubs were afforded byes, the remaining 12 went into early battle in the preliminaries.

One of these clubs was Manchester United. Defying the Football League's veto, they duly took their rightful place in the tournament as English champions and promptly announced their arrival in stunning fashion with a 12-0 aggregate defeat of Belgian side, Anderlecht. Their 10-0 win at Maine Road (there were no floodlights at Old Trafford) in the return leg was to remain the biggest victory in the competition until Benfica equalled it in 1965-66 against Stade Dudelange of Luxembourg and Feyenoord surpassed it with a 12-2 win against Icelandic side KR four years later.

The preliminary round of the 1956-57 tournament was also notable for bringing about the first play-off in the competition, when Borussia Dortmund, of West Germany, defeated Spora Luxembourg 7-0 after the tie had finished 5-5 on aggregate. In those days, when sides were equal after the two legs, there was no resorting to away goals or penalty shoot-outs. Instead, a third match, a play-off, was required to decide the winner. In Dortmund's case, they were fortunate enough to stage the play-off in their home stadium, but in later years these deciding matches were taken to neutral venues.

Manchester United and Borussia Dortmund were drawn together in the first round proper and it was the English champions who progressed, holding Dortmund to a goalless draw in the Ruhr after beating them 3-2 in Manchester. United's next opponents were Spanish champions Atlético Bilbao (known at the time under their Spanish title, before Franco's death enabled them to restore their original English name of Athletic) and they got through that tie as well, winning 3-0 at home after going down 5-3 away.

By this stage, United's centre-forward Dennis Viollet had scored nine goals in six games to become the competition's leading scorer, but in the semi-final against Real Madrid he could only fire blanks and the Spanish Cup holders, led as ever by the brilliant Di Stéfano, surged through to their second successive final.

Had the away goals rule been in force back in these early days of the competition, Real's defence of their trophy would not have lasted long. In the first round they lost 3-1 away to Rapid Vienna (all three Austrian goals scored by a future Champions' Cup-winning coach, Ernst Happel) after a 4-2 home win. Like Dortmund, they too enjoyed home advantage in the play-off and eventually sneaked through to the quarter-finals with a 2-0 win in Madrid.

Real were equally fortunate to be able to play the final in their home stadium. Originally selected as the final venue as a kind of *reward* for Real's victory in the inaugural tournament, the Chamartin stadium was not replaced even though its inhabitants were one of the two teams taking part. So, with a 100% record in their seven European home games so far, and with a guaranteed capacity crowd of 125,000 partisan fans to cheer them on, the Spaniards were clear favourites to retain their trophy when they faced Italian champions Fiorentina in the Chamartin at the end of May.

Fiorentina had conceded only four goals in their six games leading up to the final and their reputation as a formidable defensive unit was to be enhanced in Madrid. They kept Real's glittering attack at bay for 70 minutes until a controversial penalty was awarded by the Dutch referee and converted by Di Stéfano. Gento made it 2-0 shortly afterwards and the Italians' brave resistance was over. Captain Miguel Muñoz (later to coach the side to European glory in 1960) celebrated his last game for the club by collecting the Cup from one of Real Madrid's best-known supporters, General Franco.

Real Madrid

Barcelona

1957 – 1958

First Round

Team 1	Cnty	Team 2	Cnty	1st leg	2nd leg	Agg
CSKA Sofia	Bul	Vasas SC	Hun	2-1	1-6	3-7
AGF Aarhus	Den	Glenavon	Nir	0-0	3-0	3-0
Rangers	Sco	Saint-Etienne	Fra	3-1	1-2	4-3
Shamrock Rovers	Irl	Manchester United	Eng	0-6	2-3	2-9
Seville	Esp	Benfica	Por	3-1	0-0	3-1
AC Milan	Ita	Rapid Vienna	Aut	4-1	2-5	10-8
		Milan won the replay 4-2				
Stade Dudelange	Lux	Red Star Belgrade	Yug	0-5	1-9	1-14
Gwardia Warsaw	Pol	Karl-Marx-Stadt	GDR	3-1	1-3	5-5
		The replay resulted in a 1-1 draw				

	Pts	P	W	D	L	F	A	Diff	Goals/P
Total	36	18	15	6	15	78	78	0	4.333

Second Round

Manchester United	Eng	Dukla Prague	Tch	3-0	0-1	3-1
Antwerp	Bel	Real Madrid	Esp	1-2	0-6	1-8
Rangers	Sco	AC Milan	Ita	1-4	0-2	1-6
Seville	Esp	AGF Aarhus	Den	4-0	0-2	4-2
Borussia Dortmund	FRG	Steaua Bucharest	Rom	4-2	1-3	8-6
		Dortmund won the replay 3-1				
IFK Norrköping	Swe	Red Star Belgrade	Yug	2-2	1-2	3-4
Young Boys Berne	Sui	Vasas SC	Hun	1-1	1-2	2-3
Karl-Marx-Stadt	GDR	Ajax	Ned	1-3	0-1	1-4

	Pts	P	W	D	L	F	A	Diff	Goals/P
Total	34	17	15	4	15	57	57	0	3.353

Quarter Finals

Manchester United	Eng	Red Star Belgrade	Yug	2-1	3-3	5-4
Real Madrid	Esp	Seville	Esp	8-0	2-2	10-2
Ajax	Ned	Vasas SC	Hun	2-2	0-4	2-6
Borussia Dortmund	FRG	AC Milan	Ita	1-1	1-4	2-5

	Pts	P	W	D	L	F	A	Diff	Goals/P
Total	16	8	4	8	4	36	36	0	4.500

Semi Finals

Manchester United	Eng	AC Milan	Ita	2-1	0-4	2-5
Real Madrid	Esp	Vasas SC	Hun	4-0	0-2	4-2

	Pts	P	W	D	L	F	A	Diff	Goals/P
Total	8	4	4	0	4	13	13	0	3.250

Final

Real Madrid	Esp	AC Milan	Ita	3-2		3-2

	Pts	P	W	D	L	F	A	Diff	Goals/P
Total	2	1	1	0	1	5	5	0	5.000

	Pts	P	W	D	L	F	A	Diff	Goals/P
Total	96	48	39	18	39	189	189	0	3.938

Pos'n	Club	Cnty	Pts	P	W	D	L	F	A	Diff	B	Pts/P	F/P
1	AC Milan	Ita	16	10	6	1	3	28	16	12	3	1.600	2.800
2	Real Madrid	Esp	14	7	5	1	1	25	7	18	3	2.000	3.571
3	Manchester United	Eng	13	8	5	1	2	19	12	7	2	1.625	2.375
4	Vasas SC	Hun	12	8	4	2	2	18	11	7	2	1.500	2.250
5	Red Star Belgrade	Yug	9	6	3	2	1	22	9	13	1	1.500	3.667
6	Seville	Esp	7	6	2	2	2	9	13	-4	1	1.167	1.500
7	Borussia Dortmund	FRG	6	5	2	1	2	10	11	-1	1	1.200	2.000
8	Ajax	Ned	6	4	2	1	1	6	7	-1	1	1.500	1.500
9	AGF Aarhus	Den	5	4	2	1	1	5	4	1	0	1.250	1.250
10	Gwardia Warsaw	Pol	3	3	1	1	1	5	5	0	0	1.000	1.667
11	Karl-Marx-Stadt	GDR	3	5	1	1	3	6	9	-3	0	0.600	1.200
12	Saint-Etienne	Fra	2	2	1	0	1	3	4	-1	0	1.000	1.500
13	Rapid Vienna	Aut	2	3	1	0	2	8	10	-2	0	0.667	2.667
14	Steaua Bucharest	Rom	2	3	1	0	2	6	8	-2	0	0.667	2.000
15	Dukla Prague	Tch	2	2	1	0	1	1	3	-2	0	1.000	0.500
16	Rangers	Sco	2	4	1	0	3	5	9	-4	0	0.500	1.250
17	CSKA Sofia	Bul	2	2	1	0	1	3	7	-4	0	1.000	1.500
18	IFK Norrköping	Swe	1	2	0	1	1	3	4	-1	0	0.500	1.500
19	Young Boys Berne	Sui	1	2	0	1	1	2	3	-1	0	0.500	1.000
20	Benfica	Por	1	2	0	1	1	1	3	-2	0	0.500	0.500
21	Glenavon	Nir	1	2	0	1	1	0	3	-3	0	0.500	0.000
22	Shamrock Rovers	Irl	0	2	0	0	2	2	9	-7	0	0.000	1.000
23	Antwerp	Bel	0	2	0	0	2	1	8	-7	0	0.000	0.500
24	Stade Dudelange	Lux	0	2	0	0	2	1	14	-13	0	0.000	0.500
	Total		**110**	**96**	**39**	**18**	**39**	**189**	**189**	**0**	**14**	**1.146**	**3.938**

First Round

Team 1	Cnty	Team 2	Cnty	1st leg	2nd leg	Agg
Chelsea	Eng	Eintracht Frankfurt	FRG	3-2	0-1	3-3
Inter Milan	Ita	Birmingham City	Eng	0-0	1-2	1-2
Eintracht Frankfurt	FRG	FC Basle	Sui	5-1	2-6	7-7
FC Basle	Sui	Chelsea	Eng	0-5	0-1	0-6
Dinamo Zagreb	Yug	Birmingham City	Eng	0-1	0-3	0-4
Dinamo Zagreb	Yug	Inter Milan	Ita	0-1	0-4	0-5

	Pts	P	W	D	L	F	A	Diff	Goals/P
Total	24	12	11	2	11	38	38	0	3.167

Quarter Finals

Barcelona	Esp	BK Frem	Den	6-2	1-1	7-3
Lausanne-Sports	Sui	Lokomotive Leipzig	GDR	7-3	3-6	10-9

	Pts	P	W	D	L	F	A	Diff	Goals/P
Total	8	4	3	2	3	29	29	0	7.250

Semi Finals

Birmingham City	Eng	Barcelona	Esp	4-3	0-1	5-6
		Barcelona won the replay 1-2				
Lausanne-Sports	Sui	Chelsea	Eng	2-1	0-2	2-3

	Pts	P	W	D	L	F	A	Diff	Goals/P
Total	10	5	5	0	5	16	16	0	3.200

Final

Chelsea	Eng	Barcelona	Esp	2-2	0-6	2-8

	Pts	P	W	D	L	F	A	Diff	Goals/P
Total	4	2	1	2	1	10	10	0	5.000

	Pts	P	W	D	L	F	A	Diff	Goals/P
Total	46	23	20	6	20	93	93	0	4.043

Pos'n	Club	Cnty	Pts	P	W	D	L	F	A	Diff	B	Pts/P	F/P
1	Barcelona	Esp	12	7	4	2	1	21	10	11	2	1.714	3.000
2	Chelsea	Eng	11	8	4	1	3	14	13	1	2	1.375	1.750
3	Birmingham City	Eng	10	7	4	1	2	11	7	4	1	1.429	1.571
4	Inter Milan	Ita	5	4	2	1	1	6	2	4	0	1.250	1.500
5	Lausanne-Sports	Sui	5	4	2	0	2	12	12	0	1	1.250	3.000
6	Eintracht Frankfurt	FRG	4	4	2	0	2	10	10	0	0	1.000	2.500
–	Lokomotive Leipzig	GDR	2	2	1	0	1	9	10	-1	0	1.000	4.500
8	FC Basle	Sui	2	4	1	0	3	7	13	-6	0	0.500	1.750
9	BK Frem	Den	1	2	0	1	1	3	7	-4	0	0.500	1.500
10	Dinamo Zagreb	Yug	0	4	0	0	4	0	9	-9	0	0.000	0.000
	Total		**52**	**46**	**20**	**6**	**20**	**93**	**93**	**0**	**6**	**1.130**	**4.043**

1957-58

Pos'n	Cnty	Pts	P	W	D	L	F	A	Diff	B	Pts/P	F/P
1	Eng	34	23	13	3	7	44	32	12	5	1.478	1.913
2	Esp	33	20	11	5	4	55	30	25	6	1.650	2.750
3	Ita	21	14	8	2	4	34	18	16	3	1.500	2.429
4	Hun	12	8	4	2	2	18	11	7	2	1.500	2.250
5	FRG	10	9	4	1	4	20	21	-1	1	1.111	2.222
6	Yug	9	10	3	2	5	22	18	4	1	0.900	2.200
7	Sui	8	10	3	1	6	21	28	-7	1	0.800	2.100
8	Ned	6	4	2	1	1	6	7	-1	1	1.500	1.500
9	Den	6	6	2	2	2	8	11	-3	0	1.000	1.333
10	GDR	5	7	2	1	4	15	19	-4	0	0.714	2.143
11	Pol	3	3	1	1	1	5	5	0	0	1.000	1.667
12	Fra	2	2	1	0	1	3	4	-1	0	1.000	1.500
13	Aut	2	3	1	0	2	8	10	-2	0	0.667	2.667
14	Rom	2	3	1	0	2	6	8	-2	0	0.667	2.000
15	Tch	2	2	1	0	1	1	3	-2	0	1.000	0.500
16	Sco	2	4	1	0	3	5	9	-4	0	0.500	1.250
17	Bul	2	2	1	0	1	3	7	-4	0	1.000	1.500
18	Swe	1	2	0	1	1	3	4	-1	0	0.500	1.500
19	Por	1	2	0	1	1	1	3	-2	0	0.500	0.500
20	Nir	1	2	0	1	1	0	3	-3	0	0.500	0.000
21	Irl	0	2	0	0	2	2	9	-7	0	0.000	1.000
22	Bel	0	2	0	0	2	1	8	-7	0	0.000	0.500
23	Lux	0	2	0	0	2	1	14	-13	0	0.000	0.500
	Total	**162**	**142**	**59**	**24**	**59**	**282**	**282**	**0**	**20**	**1.141**	**3.972**

1955-56 to 1957-58

1	Esp	72	41	26	7	8	111	64	47	13	1.756	2.707
2	Eng	46	31	17	5	9	68	44	24	7	1.484	2.194
3	Ita	42	27	14	6	7	61	37	24	8	1.556	2.259
4	Yug	24	20	8	4	8	43	34	9	4	1.200	2.150
5	Fra	23	16	8	3	5	35	28	7	4	1.438	2.188
6	Hun	19	14	6	4	4	39	29	10	3	1.357	2.786
7	FRG	18	18	7	3	8	40	41	-1	1	1.000	2.222
8	Sco	13	13	5	1	7	18	20	-2	2	1.000	1.385
9	Sui	12	16	4	2	10	26	41	-15	2	0.750	1.625
10	Aut	8	10	3	1	6	22	27	-5	1	0.800	2.200
11	Ned	8	8	3	1	4	11	19	-8	1	1.000	1.375
12	Den	8	10	2	4	4	12	21	-9	0	0.800	1.200
13	Bul	7	6	3	0	3	16	15	1	1	1.167	2.667
14	Tch	6	6	3	0	3	6	7	-1	0	1.000	1.000
15	Swe	6	8	1	3	4	9	11	-2	1	0.750	1.125
16	Pol	6	7	2	2	3	8	13	-5	0	0.857	1.143
17	Rom	6	7	3	0	4	14	21	-7	0	0.857	2.000
18	GDR	5	7	2	1	4	15	19	-4	0	0.714	2.143
19	Tur	2	2	1	0	1	3	4	-1	0	1.000	1.500
20	Por	2	6	0	2	4	9	16	-7	0	0.333	1.500
21	Lux	2	5	1	0	4	6	26	-20	0	0.400	1.200
22	Nir	1	2	0	1	1	0	3	-3	0	0.500	0.000
23	Irl	0	2	0	0	2	2	9	-7	0	0.000	1.000
24	Bel	0	6	0	0	6	5	30	-25	0	0.000	0.833
	Total	**336**	**288**	**119**	**50**	**119**	**579**	**579**	**0**	**48**	**1.167**	**4.021**

1957-58

Pos'n	Cnty	Ave	Pts	P	W	D	L	F	A	Diff	B	No./T
1	Hungary	12.000	12	8	4	2	2	18	11	7	2	1
2	England	11.333	34	23	13	3	7	44	32	12	5	3
3	Spain	11.000	33	20	11	5	4	55	30	25	6	3
4	Italy	10.500	21	14	8	2	4	34	18	16	3	2
5	Netherlands	6.000	6	4	2	1	1	6	7	-1	1	1
6	W. Germany	5.000	10	9	4	1	4	20	21	-1	1	2
7	Yugoslavia	4.500	9	10	3	2	5	22	18	4	1	2
8	Denmark	3.000	6	6	2	2	2	8	11	-3	0	2
–	Poland	3.000	3	3	1	1	1	5	5	0	0	1
10	Switzerland	2.666	8	10	3	1	6	21	28	-7	1	3
11	E. Germany	2.500	5	7	2	1	4	15	19	-4	0	2
12	Austria	2.000	2	3	1	0	2	8	10	-2	0	1
–	Bulgaria	2.000	2	2	1	0	1	3	7	-4	0	1
–	Scotland	2.000	2	4	1	0	3	5	9	-4	0	1
–	France	2.000	2	2	1	0	1	3	4	-1	0	1
–	Romania	2.000	2	3	1	0	2	6	8	-2	0	1
–	Czechoslovakia	2.000	2	2	1	0	1	1	3	-2	0	1
18	N. Ireland	1.000	1	2	0	1	1	0	3	-3	0	1
–	Portugal	1.000	1	2	0	1	1	1	3	-2	0	1
–	Sweden	1.000	1	2	0	1	1	3	4	-1	0	1
21	Belgium	0.000	0	2	0	0	2	1	8	-7	0	1
–	Rep. of Ireland	0.000	0	2	0	0	2	2	9	-7	0	1
–	Luxembourg	0.000	0	2	0	0	2	1	14	-13	0	1
	Total		**162**	**142**	**59**	**24**	**59**	**282**	**282**	**0**	**20**	**3.972**

1955-56 to 1957-58

1	Spain	12.000	72	41	26	7	8	111	64	47	13	6
2	England	11.500	46	31	17	5	9	68	44	24	7	4
3	Italy	10.500	42	27	14	6	7	61	37	24	8	4
4	France	7.666	23	16	8	3	5	35	28	7	4	3
5	Hungary	6.333	19	14	6	4	4	39	29	10	3	3
6	Yugoslavia	6.000	24	20	8	4	8	43	34	9	4	4
7	Scotland	4.333	13	13	5	1	7	18	20	-2	2	3
8	W. Germany	3.600	18	18	7	3	8	40	41	-1	1	5
9	Bulgaria	3.500	7	6	3	0	3	16	15	1	1	2
10	Romania	3.000	6	7	3	0	4	14	21	-7	0	2
–	Czechoslovakia	3.000	6	6	3	0	3	6	7	-1	0	2
12	Austria	2.666	8	10	3	1	6	22	27	-5	1	3
–	Netherlands	2.666	8	8	3	1	4	11	19	-8	1	3
14	E. Germany	2.500	5	7	2	1	4	15	19	-4	0	2
15	Switzerland	2.400	12	16	4	2	10	26	41	-15	2	5
16	Denmark	2.000	8	10	2	4	4	12	21	-9	0	4
–	Poland	2.000	6	7	2	2	3	8	13	-5	0	3
–	Sweden	2.000	6	8	1	3	4	9	11	-2	1	3
–	Turkey	2.000	2	2	1	0	1	3	4	-1	0	1
20	N. Ireland	1.000	1	2	0	1	1	0	3	-3	0	1
–	Luxembourg	1.000	2	5	1	0	4	6	26	-20	0	2
22	Portugal	0.666	2	6	0	2	4	9	16	-7	0	3
23	Belgium	0.000	0	6	0	0	6	5	30	-25	0	3
–	Rep. of Ireland	0.000	0	2	0	0	2	2	9	-7	0	1
	Total		**336**	**288**	**119**	**50**	**119**	**579**	**579**	**0**	**48**	**4.021**

Three in a Row

Real Madrid won the Champions' Cup for the third year in a row, but the 1957-58 competition was clouded by the terrible air tragedy that befell Manchester United's famous *Busby Babes* team. A side of immense promise horrifically cut down in its prime, eight players killed, manager Matt Busby himself critically injured, as the plane that carried the team back from their quarter-final in Belgrade failed to take off after refuelling in Munich and crashed into a house at the end of the runway.

Who knows whether that United team could have wrested the Cup from Real's grip had it survived? The question will forever remain unanswered. In the event, the fragments of the team that remained put on an astonishingly courageous performance in the first leg of the semi-final against AC Milan, but in the return the Italians were too strong and they, not United, went on to face Real Madrid in the Brussels final.

Real, under new coach Luis Carniglia who had replaced José Villalonga at the start of the season, made comfortable progress to their third consecutive final. Their home form, in particular, was formidable. Given another bye into the last 16, they hammered Antwerp 6-0 before dishing out even rougher treatment to fellow Spaniards Seville in the quarter-finals. Seville, who had qualified as runners-up to Real in the previous season's Spanish League (such means of qualification are no longer valid in the Champions' Cup), felt the full force of the holders in Madrid, going down 8-0, with Di Stéfano scoring four goals and Raymond Kopa, the former Reims player, hitting two more.

Di Stéfano bagged another hat-trick in the first leg of the semi-final, against surprise qualifiers Vasas of Hungary, to give Real another convincing home win, but, just to prove that they were not invincible, the Spaniards lost the second leg 2-0 in Budapest – their first defeat of the competition.

Milan, like Real the previous season, had enormous difficulty getting past Austrian champions Rapid Vienna in their first outing of the tournament. Winners 4-1 at home, they were beaten 5-2 in Vienna and thus required a 4-2 victory in the play-off (played this time in neutral Zürich) to see themselves safely through. A play-off was also required to resolve the first-round tie between Gwardia Warsaw and Karl-Marx-Stadt. But with the scores still level (1-1) after extra-time, the rules of the day stated that the teams had to be separated by the drawing of lots. The luck, on this occasion, was with Karl-Marx-Stadt.

Luck also played a part in the Real Madrid-AC Milan final in Brussels. Milan, with talented individuals such as the Uruguayan Juan Schiaffino and the Swede Nils Liedholm, gave Real as good as they got throughout the 90 minutes and into extra-time, but fate decreed that the Spaniards would achieve their hat-trick of Cup successes, and it was a goal by Paco Gento at the start of the second extra period that eventually settled an extremely closely-fought match in the Spanish side's favour – this after they had twice come from behind in normal time.

Some four weeks before Real Madrid renewed their acquaintance with the Champions' Cup trophy, their domestic rivals Barcelona had also given evidence of Spanish strength by winning the inaugural Fairs' Cup. This competition, played over a duration of two years and restricted to representative teams from European cities with international trade fairs, was not greeted with anything like the fervour which accompanied the introduction of the Champions' Cup. There were only ten participants in the first tournament, with England and Switzerland both providing two teams and Denmark, Spain, Italy, Yugoslavia, East Germany and West Germany each entering one.

Birmingham, Barcelona, Lausanne and a London selection including such famous names as Greaves (Chelsea), Haynes (Fulham) and Blanchflower (Tottenham) made it through the initial group phase to the two-legged semi-finals. Having disposed of Birmingham after a semi-final play-off in their own Nou Camp stadium, Barcelona captured the trophy by drawing away to the London selection and then beating them 6-0 in Spain.

1958 – 1959

Real Madrid

European Cup 1958-59

First Round

Team 1	Cnty	Team 2	Cnty	1st leg	2nd leg	Agg
Standard Liège	Bel	Heart of Midlothian	Sco	5-1	1-2	6- 3
KB Copenhagen	Den	Schalke 04	FRG	3-0	2-5	6-8
		Schalke 04 won the replay 1-3				
Atlético Madrid	Esp	Drumcondra	Irl	8-0	5-1	13-1
Ards	Irl	Stade Reims	Fra	1-4	2-6	3-10
Juventus	Ita	Wiener Sport-Club	Aut	3-1	0-7	3-8
Jeunesse Esch	Lux	IFK Gothenburg	Swe	1-2	1-0	3-7
		Gothenburg won the replay 1-5				
Utrecht	Ned	Sporting Lisbon	Por	3-4	1-2	4-6
Polonia Bytom	Pol	MTK-VM	Hun	0-3	0-3	0-6
Dinamo Zagreb	Yug	Dukla Prague	Tch	2-2	1-2	3-4
Karl-Marx-Stadt	GDR	Petrolul Ploiesti	Rom	4-2	0-2	8-4
		Karl-Marx-Stadt won the replay 4-0				

	Pts	P	W	D	L	F	A	Diff	Goals/P
Total	46	23	22	2	22	106	106	0	4.609

Second Round

Wolverhampton Wanderers	Eng	Schalke 04	FRG	2-2	1-2	3-4
Wiener Sport-Club	Aut	Dukla Prague	Tch	3-1	0-1	3-2
Atlético Madrid	Esp	CSKA Sofia	Bul	2-1	0-1	5-3
		Atlético Madrid won the replay 3-1				
Real Madrid	Esp	Besiktas	Tur	2-0	1-1	3-1
Stade Reims	Fra	HPS Helsinki	Fin	4-0	3-0	7-0
MTK-VM	Hun	Young Boys Berne	Sui	1-2	1-4	2-6
Sporting Lisbon	Por	Standard Liège	Bel	2-3	0-3	2-6
IFK Gothenburg	Swe	Karl-Marx-Stadt	GDR	2-2	0-4	2-6

	Pts	P	W	D	L	F	A	Diff	Goals/P
Total	34	17	14	6	14	55	55	0	3.235

Quarter Finals

Wiener Sport-Club	Aut	Real Madrid	Esp	0-0	1-7	1-7
Standard Liège	Bel	Stade Reims	Fra	2-0	0-3	2-3
Atlético Madrid	Esp	Schalke 04	FRG	3-0	1-1	4-1
Young Boys Berne	Sui	Karl-Marx-Stadt	GDR	2-2	0-0	4-3
		Berne won the replay 2-1				

	Pts	P	W	D	L	F	A	Diff	Goals/P
Total	18	9	5	8	5	25	25	0	2.778

Semi Finals

Real Madrid	Esp	Atlético Madrid	Esp	2-1	0-1	4-3
		Real Madrid won the replay 2-1				
Young Boys Berne	Sui	Stade Reims	Fra	1-0	0-3	1-3

	Pts	P	W	D	L	F	A	Diff	Goals/P
Total	10	5	5	0	5	11	11	0	2.200

Final

Real Madrid	Esp	Stade Reims	Fra	2-0	2-0

	Pts	P	W	D	L	F	A	Diff	Goals/P
Total	2	1	1	0	1	2	2	0	2.000

	Pts	P	W	D	L	F	A	Diff	Goals/P
Total	110	55	47	16	47	199	199	0	3.618

Pos'n	Club	Cnty	Pts	P	W	D	L	F	A	Diff	B	Pts/P	F/P
1	Atlético Madrid	Esp	15	10	6	1	3	25	9	16	2	1.500	2.500
2	Stade Reims	Fra	15	9	6	0	3	23	8	15	3	1.667	2.556
3	Real Madrid	Esp	15	8	5	2	1	16	5	11	3	1 875	2.000
4	Young Boys Berne	Sui	12	7	4	2	1	11	8	3	2	1.714	1.571
5	Karl-Marx-Stadt	GDR	10	8	3	3	2	17	10	7	1	1.250	2.125
6	Standard Liège	Bel	9	6	4	0	2	14	8	6	1	1.500	2.333
7	Schalke 04	FRG	9	7	3	2	2	13	13	0	1	1.286	1.857
8	Wiener Sport-Club	Aut	6	6	2	1	3	12	12	0	1	1.000	2.000
9	IFK Gothenburg	Swe	5	5	2	1	2	9	9	0	0	1.000	1.800
10	Dukla Prague	Tch	5	4	2	1	1	6	6	0	0	1.250	1.500
11	MKT-VM	Hun	4	4	2	0	2	8	6	2	0	1.000	2.000
12	Sporting Lisbon	Por	4	4	2	0	2	8	10	-2	0	1.000	2.000
13	KB Copenhagen	Den	2	3	1	0	2	6	8	-2	0	0.667	2.000
14	CSKA Sofia	Bul	2	3	1	0	2	3	5	-2	0	0.667	1.000
15	Heart of Midlothian	Sco	2	2	1	0	1	3	6	-3	0	1.000	1.500
16	Petrolul Ploiesti	Rom	2	3	1	0	2	4	8	-4	0	0.667	1.333
17	Jeunesse Esch	Lux	2	3	1	0	2	3	7	-4	0	0.667	1.000
18	Juventus	Ita	2	2	1	0	1	3	8	-5	0	1.000	1.500
19	Wolverhampton Wanderers	Eng	1	2	0	1	1	3	4	-1	0	0.500	1.500
–	Dinamo Zagreb	Yug	1	2	0	1	1	3	4	-1	0	0.500	1.500
21	Besiktas	Tur	1	2	0	1	1	1	3	-2	0	0.500	0.500
22	Utrecht	Ned	0	2	0	0	2	4	6	-2	0	0.000	2.000
23	Polonia Bytom	Pol	0	2	0	0	2	0	6	-6	0	0.000	0.000
24	Ards	Nir	0	2	0	0	2	3	10	-7	0	0.000	1.500
25	HPS (Helsinki)	Fin	0	2	0	0	2	0	7	-7	0	0.000	0.000
26	Drumcondra	Irl	0	2	0	0	2	1	13	-12	0	0.000	0.500
	Total		**124**	**110**	**47**	**16**	**47**	**199**	**199**	**0**	**14**	**1.127**	**3.618**

1958-59

Pos'n	Cnty	Pts	P	W	D	L	F	A	Diff	B	Pts/P	F/P
1	Esp	30	18	11	3	4	41	14	27	5	1.667	2.278
2	Fra	15	9	6	0	3	23	8	15	3	1.667	2.556
3	Sui	12	7	4	2	1	11	8	3	2	1.714	1.571
4	GDR	10	8	3	3	2	17	10	7	1	1.250	2.125
5	Bel	9	6	4	0	2	14	8	6	1	1.500	2.333
6	FRG	9	7	3	2	2	13	13	0	1	1.286	1.857
7	Aut	6	6	2	1	3	12	12	0	1	1.000	2.000
8	Swe	5	5	2	1	2	9	9	0	0	1.000	1.800
9	Tch	5	4	2	1	1	6	6	0	0	1.250	1.500
10	Hun	4	4	2	0	2	8	6	2	0	1.000	2.000
11	Por	4	4	2	0	2	8	10	-2	0	1.000	2.000
12	Den	2	3	1	0	2	6	8	-2	0	0.667	2.000
13	Bul	2	3	1	0	2	3	5	-2	0	0.667	1.000
14	Sco	2	2	1	0	1	3	6	-3	0	1.000	1.500
15	Rom	2	3	1	0	2	4	8	-4	0	0.667	1.333
16	Lux	2	3	1	0	2	3	7	-4	0	0.667	1.000
17	Ita	2	2	1	0	1	3	8	-5	0	1.000	1.500
18	Eng	1	2	0	1	1	3	4	-1	0	0.500	1.500
–	Yug	1	2	0	1	1	3	4	-1	0	0.500	1.500
20	Tur	1	2	0	1	1	1	3	-2	0	0.500	0.500
21	Ned	0	2	0	0	2	4	6	-2	0	0.000	2.000
22	Pol	0	2	0	0	2	0	6	-6	0	0.000	0.000
23	Nir	0	2	0	0	2	3	10	-7	0	0.000	1.500
24	Fin	0	2	0	0	2	0	7	-7	0	0.000	0.000
25	Irl	0	2	0	0	2	1	13	-12	0	0.000	0.500
	Total	**124**	**110**	**47**	**16**	**47**	**199**	**199**	**0**	**14**	**1.127**	**3. 618**

1955-56 to 1958-59

1	Esp	102	59	37	10	12	152	78	74	18	1.729	2.576
2	Eng	47	33	17	6	10	71	48	23	7	1.424	2.152
3	Ita	44	29	15	6	8	64	45	19	8	1.517	2.207
4	Fra	38	25	14	3	8	58	36	22	7	1.520	2.320
5	FRG	27	25	10	5	10	53	54	-1	2	1.080	2.120
6	Yug	25	22	8	5	9	46	38	8	4	1.136	2.091
7	Sui	24	23	8	4	11	37	49	-12	4	1.043	1.609
8	Hun	23	18	8	4	6	47	35	12	3	1.278	2.611
9	GDR	15	15	5	4	6	32	29	3	1	1.000	2.133
10	Sco	15	15	6	1	8	21	26	-5	2	1.000	1.400
11	Aut	14	16	5	2	9	34	39	-5	2	0.875	2.125
12	Tch	11	10	5	1	4	12	13	-1	0	1.100	1.200
13	Swe	11	13	3	4	6	18	20	-2	1	0.846	1.385
14	Den	10	13	3	4	6	18	29	-11	0	0.769	1.385
15	Bul	9	9	4	0	5	19	20	-1	1	1.000	2.111
16	Bel	9	12	4	0	8	19	38	-19	1	0.750	1.583
17	Ned	8	10	3	1	6	15	25	-10	1	0.800	1.500
18	Rom	8	10	4	0	6	18	29	-11	0	0.800	1.800
19	Por	6	10	2	2	6	17	26	-9	0	0.600	1.700
20	Pol	6	9	2	2	5	8	19	-11	0	0.667	0.889
21	Lux	4	8	2	0	6	9	33	-24	0	0.500	1.125
22	Tur	3	4	1	1	2	4	7	-3	0	0.750	1.000
23	Nir	1	4	0	1	3	3	13	-10	0	0.250	0.750
24	Fin	0	2	0	0	2	0	7	-7	0	0.000	0.000
25	Irl	0	4	0	0	4	3	22	-19	0	0.000	0.750
	Total	**460**	**398**	**166**	**66**	**166**	**778**	**778**	**0**	**62**	**1.156**	**3.910**

1958-59

Pos'n	Cnty	Ave	Pts	P	W	D	L	F	A	Diff	B	No./T
1	Spain	15.000	30	18	11	3	4	41	14	27	5	2
-	France	15.000	15	9	6	0	3	23	8	15	3	1
3	Switzerland	12.000	12	7	4	2	1	11	8	3	2	1
4	E. Germany	10.000	10	8	3	3	2	17	10	7	1	1
5	Belgium	9.000	9	6	4	0	2	14	8	6	1	1
-	W. Germany	9.000	9	7	3	2	2	13	13	0	1	1
7	Austria	6.000	6	6	2	1	3	12	12	0	1	1
8	Sweden	5.000	5	5	2	1	2	9	9	0	0	1
-	Czechoslovakia	5.000	5	4	2	1	1	6	6	0	0	1
10	Hungary	4.000	4	4	2	0	2	8	6	2	0	1
-	Portugal	4.000	4	4	2	0	2	8	10	-2	0	1
12	Bulgaria	2.000	2	3	1	0	2	3	5	-2	0	1
-	Denmark	2.000	2	3	1	0	2	6	8	-2	0	1
-	Scotland	2.000	2	2	1	0	1	3	6	-3	0	1
-	Italy	2.000	2	2	1	0	1	3	8	-5	0	1
-	Luxembourg	2.000	2	3	1	0	2	3	7	-4	0	1
-	Romania	2.000	2	3	1	0	2	4	8	-4	0	1
18	England	1.000	1	2	0	1	1	3	4	-1	0	1
-	Turkey	1.000	1	2	0	1	1	1	3	-2	0	1
-	Yugoslavia	1.000	1	2	0	1	1	3	4	-1	0	1
21	Rep. of Ireland	0.000	0	2	0	0	2	1	13	-12	0	1
-	Finland	0.000	0	2	0	0	2	0	7	-7	0	1
-	N. Ireland	0.000	0	2	0	0	2	3	10	-7	0	1
-	Netherlands	0.000	0	2	0	0	2	4	6	-2	0	1
-	Poland	0.000	0	2	0	0	2	0	6	-6	0	1
	Total		**124**	**110**	**47**	**16**	**47**	**199**	**199**	**0**	**14**	**3.618**

1955-56 to 1958-59

1	Spain	12.750	102	59	37	10	12	152	78	74	18	8
2	France	9.500	38	25	14	3	8	58	36	22	7	4
3	England	9.400	47	33	17	6	10	71	48	23	7	5
4	Italy	8.800	44	29	15	6	8	64	45	19	8	5
5	Hungary	5.750	23	18	8	4	6	47	35	12	3	4
6	Yugoslavia	5.000	25	22	8	5	9	46	38	8	4	5
-	E. Germany	5.000	15	15	5	4	6	32	29	3	1	3
8	W. Germany	4.500	27	25	10	5	10	53	54	-1	2	6
9	Switzerland	4.000	24	23	8	4	11	37	49	-12	4	6
10	Scotland	3.750	15	15	6	1	8	21	26	-5	2	4
11	Czechoslovakia	3.666	11	10	5	1	4	12	13	-1	0	3
12	Austria	3.500	14	16	5	2	9	34	39	-5	2	4
13	Bulgaria	3.000	9	9	4	0	5	19	20	-1	1	3
14	Sweden	2.750	11	13	3	4	6	18	20	-2	1	4
15	Romania	2.666	8	10	4	0	6	18	29	-11	0	3
16	Belgium	2.250	9	12	4	0	8	19	38	-19	1	4
17	Denmark	2.000	10	13	3	4	6	18	29	-11	0	5
-	Netherlands	2.000	8	10	3	1	6	15	25	-10	1	4
19	Poland	1.500	6	9	2	2	5	8	19	-11	0	4
-	Portugal	1.500	6	10	2	2	6	17	26	-9	0	4
-	Turkey	1.500	3	4	1	1	2	4	7	-3	0	2
22	Luxembourg	1.333	4	8	2	0	6	9	33	-24	0	3
23	N. Ireland	0.500	1	4	0	1	3	3	13	-10	0	2
24	Rep. of Ireland	0.000	0	4	0	0	4	3	22	-19	0	2
-	Finland	0.000	0	2	0	0	2	0	7	-7	0	1
	Total		**460**	**398**	**166**	**66**	**166**	**778**	**778**	**0**	**62**	**3. 910**

Di Stefano and Puskas Duo

Real Madrid welcomed one more superstar into their side for their Champions' Cup defence in 1958-59. Ferenc Puskás, the Hungarian who had captained his country to a legendary 6-3 victory against England at Wembley in 1953 and who had been a star of the 1954 World Cup, arrived in Madrid to form, with Di Stéfano, one of the greatest attacking partnerships in European Cup history.

Injury, sadly, prevented Puskás from appearing in the final, which Real reached yet again, but he was a principal figure in the club's epic semi-final confrontation with city rivals, Atlético Madrid, scoring the winning goal in the play-off which enabled Real to go through and renew their acquaintance with French champions Stade Reims in the Stuttgart final.

The 1958-59 competition had its largest entry yet – 26 teams, as opposed to 24 the previous season. Manchester United were handed an honorary place in the competition by UEFA as a show of understanding and sympathy for their terrible tragedy of the previous year, but under insensitive pressure from the English authorities, they were obliged to decline the offer. The first Republic of Ireland representative, Drumcondra of Dublin, suffered a painful baptism, thrashed 13-1 over two legs by Atlético Madrid, who, like Seville the year before, were in the tournament only as runners-up to Real Madrid in the Spanish championship.

Real, given their customary bye into the second round, preserved their perfect home record with victories over Besiktas of Turkey and Wiener Sport-Club of Austria, although they were held to draws in both away legs. Atlético, meanwhile, reached the semi-final after a play-off victory over CDNA Sofia (later to become CSKA Sofia) and a trouble-free quarter-final triumph over the German representatives, Schalke 04.

The all-Madrid semi-final was the highlight of the competition. Real won the first leg in the Chamartin 2-1, but only after they had recovered from going a goal down and their goalkeeper, Rogelio Domínguez, had saved a late penalty. The return leg was won by Atlético, 1-0, with a goal by Spanish international Enrique Collar. As in the Rapid Vienna tie two years earlier, application of the away goals rule would have seen Real eliminated by this result, but instead they went to Zaragoza for the decider. Collar again found the target for Atlético, but goals from the dynamic duo of Di Stéfano and Puskás ultimately carried Real into their fourth successive final.

Their opponents in Stuttgart were the team they had defeated in their first Champions' Cup final three years earlier, Stade Reims, still led by their legendary coach Albert Batteux and boasting several members of the French national squad which had finished third in the 1958 World Cup.

Just Fontaine, whose 13 goals in the '58 World Cup still stand as the highest total scored by any player in one single Finals tournament, played a major part in getting Reims to the final. Beaten 2-0 in the first leg of the quarter-finals by Standard Liège, the French club were indebted to two goals from their international forward in the return fixture to give them the 3-0 victory they required to progress. In the semi-finals, Reims survived a similar scenario against Swiss side Young Boys Berne, losing the first leg 1-0 before finding their form again at home with another 3-0 victory. Young Boys, incidentally, were only in the competition as a result of Manchester United's withdrawal, and in 100 European Cups no Swiss side has ever come closer to reaching a final than they did in 1959.

Reims were no match for Real in the final – despite the absence of Puskás and despite the early foul inflicted by Reims winger Jean Vincent on his fellow countryman Raymond Kopa, virtually putting him out of the game. Real scored after only two minutes through Mateos and the remarkable Di Stéfano maintained his record of scoring in every one of Real's Champions' Cup finals by hitting the decisive second goal early in the second half.

1959 - 1960

Real Madrid

Barcelona

European Cup 1959-60

First Round

Team 1	Cnty	Team 2	Cnty	1st leg	2nd leg	Agg
Wiener Sport-Club	Aut	Petrolul Ploiesti	Rom	0-0	2-1	2-1
CSKA Sofia	Bul	Barcelona	Esp	2-2	2-6	4-8
Rangers	Sco	Anderlecht	Bel	5-2	2-0	7-2
Nice	Fra	Shamrock Rovers	Irl	3-2	1-1	4-3
Olympiakos Pireus	Gre	AC Milan	Ita	2-2	1-3	3-5
Linfield	Nir	IFK Gothenburg	Swe	2-1	1-6	3-7
Jeunesse Esch	Lux	LKS Lódź	Pol	5-0	1-2	6-2
Inter Bratislava	Tch	FC Porto	Por	2-1	2-0	4-1
Fenerbahçe	Tur	Csepel	Hun	1-1	3-2	4-3
Vorwärts Frankfurt/Oder	GDR	Wolverhampton Wanderers	Eng	2-1	0-2	2-3

	Pts	P	W	D	L	F	A	Diff	Goals/P
Total	40	20	15	10	15	74	74	0	3.700

Second Round

B 1909 Odense	Den	Wiener Sport-Club	Aut	0-3	2-2	2-5
Rangers	Sco	Inter Bratislava	Tch	4-3	1-1	5-4
Real Madrid	Esp	Jeunesse Esch	Lux	7-0	5-2	12-2
AC Milan	Ita	Barcelona	Esp	0-2	1-5	1-7
Sparta Rotterdam	Ned	IFK Gothenburg	Swe	3-1	1-3	7-5
		Sparta won the replay 3-1				
Young Boys Berne	Sui	Eintracht Frankfurt	FRG	1-4	1-1	2-5
Fenerbahçe	Tur	Nice	Fra	2-1	1-2	4-8
		Nice won the replay 1-5				
Red Star Belgrade	Yug	Wolverhampton Wanderers	Eng	1-1	0-3	1-4

	Pts	P	W	D	L	F	A	Diff	Goals/P
Total	36	18	14	8	14	74	74	0	4.111

Quarter Finals

Barcelona	Esp	Wolverhampton Wanderers	Eng	4-0	5-2	9-2
Nice	Fra	Real Madrid	Esp	3-2	0-4	3-6
Sparta Rotterdam	Ned	Rangers	Sco	2-3	1-0	5-6
		Rangers won the replay 2-3				
Eintracht Frankfurt	FRG	Wiener Sport-Club	Aut	2-1	1-1	3-2

	Pts	P	W	D	L	F	A	Diff	Goals/P
Total	18	9	8	2	8	36	36	0	4.000

Semi Finals

Real Madrid	Esp	Barcelona	Esp	3-2	3-1	6-3
Eintracht Frankfurt	FRG	Rangers	Sco	6-1	6-3	12-4

	Pts	P	W	D	L	F	A	Diff	Goals/P
Total	8	4	4	0	4	25	25	0	6.250

Final

Real Madrid	Esp	Eintracht Frankfurt	FRG	7-3	7-3

	Pts	P	W	D	L	F	A	Diff	Goals/P
Total	2	1	1	0	1	10	10	0	10.000

	Pts	P	W	D	L	F	A	Diff	Goals/P
Total	104	52	42	20	42	219	219	0	4.212

Pos'n	Club	Cnty	Pts	P	W	D	L	F	A	Diff	B	Pts/P	F/P
1	Real Madrid	Esp	15	7	6	0	1	31	11	20	3	2.143	4.429
2	Barcelona	Esp	13	8	5	1	2	27	13	14	2	1.625	3.375
3	Eintracht Frankfurt	FRG	13	7	4	2	1	23	15	8	3	1.857	3.286
4	Rangers	Sco	13	9	5	1	3	22	23	-1	2	1.444	2.444
5	Nice	Fra	10	7	4	1	2	15	13	2	1	1.429	2.143
6	Wiener Sport-Club	Aut	8	6	2	3	1	9	6	3	1	1.333	1.500
7	Sparta Rotterdam	Ned	7	6	3	0	3	12	11	1	1	1.167	2.000
8	Wolverhampton Wanderers	Eng	6	6	2	1	3	9	12	-3	1	1.000	1.500
9	Inter Bratislava	Tch	5	4	2	1	1	8	6	2	0	1.250	2.000
10	Fenerbahçe	Tur	5	5	2	1	2	8	11	-3	0	1.000	1.600
11	IFK Gothenburg	Swe	4	5	2	0	3	12	10	2	0	0.800	2.400
12	AC Milan	Ita	3	4	1	1	2	6	10	-4	0	0.750	1.500
13	Vorwärts Frankfurt/Oder	GDR	2	2	1	0	1	2	3	-1	0	1.000	1.000
14	Linfield	Nir	2	2	1	0	1	3	7	-4	0	1.000	1.500
15	LKS Lódź	Pol	2	2	1	0	1	2	6	-4	0	1.000	1.000
16	Jeunesse Esch	Lux	2	4	1	0	3	8	14	-6	0	0.500	2.000
17	Shamrock Rovers	Irl	1	2	0	1	1	3	4	-1	0	0.500	1.500
–	Csepel	Hun	1	2	0	1	1	3	4	-1	0	0.500	1.500
19	Petrolul Ploiesti	Rom	1	2	0	1	1	1	2	-1	0	0.500	0.500
20	Olympiakos Pireus	Gre	1	2	0	1	1	3	5	-2	0	0.500	1.500
21	B 1909 Odense	Den	1	2	0	1	1	2	5	-3	0	0.500	1.000
–	Young Boys Berne	Sui	1	2	0	1	1	2	5	-3	0	0.500	1.000
23	Red Star Belgrade	Yug	1	2	0	1	1	1	4	-3	0	0.500	0.500
24	CSKA Sofia	Bul	1	2	0	1	1	4	8	-4	0	0.500	2.000
25	FC Porto	Por	0	2	0	0	2	1	4	-3	0	0.000	0.500
26	Anderlecht	Bel	0	2	0	0	2	2	7	-5	0	0.000	1.000
	Total		**118**	**104**	**42**	**20**	**42**	**219**	**219**	**0**	**14**	**1.135**	**4.212**

UEFA Cup 1958-60

First Round

Team 1	Cnty	Team 2	Cnty	1st leg	2nd leg	Agg
Birmingham City	Eng	Cologne	FRG	2-0	2-2	4-2
Chelsea	Eng	BK Frem	Den	4-1	3-1	7-2
Union St-Gilloise	Bel	Lokomotive Leipzig	GDR	6-1	0-1	6-2
Barcelona	Esp	FC Basle	Sui	5-2	2-1	7-3
Inter Milan	Ita	Olympique Lyon	Fra	7-0	1-1	8-1
Roma	Ita	Hannover 96	FRG	1-1	3-1	4-2
OFK Belgrade	Yug	Lausanne-Sports	Sui	6-1	5-3	11-4
Dinamo Zagreb	Yug	Vasas SC	Hun	4-2	0-1	4-3

	Pts	P	W	D	L	F	A	Diff	Goals/P
Total	32	16	13	6	13	70	70	0	4.375

Quarter Finals

Chelsea	Eng	OFK Belgrade	Yug	1-0	1-4	2-4
Union St-Gilloise	Bel	Roma	Ita	2-0	1-1	3-1
Barcelona	Esp	Inter Milan	Ita	4-0	4-2	8-2
Dinamo Zagreb	Yug	Birmingham City	Eng	3-3	0-1	3-4

	Pts	P	W	D	L	F	A	Diff	Goals/P
Total	16	8	6	4	6	27	27	0	3.375

Semi Finals

Birmingham City	Eng	Union St-Gilloise	Bel	4-2	4-2	8-4
OFK Belgrade	Yug	Barcelona	Esp	1-1	1-3	2-4

	Pts	P	W	D	L	F	A	Diff	Goals/P
Total	8	4	3	2	3	18	18	0	4.500

Final

Barcelona	Esp	Birmingham City	Eng	1-1	4-1	5-2

	Pts	P	W	D	L	F	A	Diff	Goals/P
Total	4	2	1	2	1	7	7	0	3.500

	Pts	P	W	D	L	F	A	Diff	Goals/P
Total	60	30	23	14	23	122	122	0	4.067

Pos'n	Club	Cnty	Pts	P	W	D	L	F	A	Diff	B	Pts/P	F/P
1	Barcelona	Esp	17	8	6	2	0	24	9	15	3	2.125	3.000
2	Birmingham City	Eng	14	8	4	3	1	18	14	4	3	1.750	2.250
3	OFK Belgrade	Yug	9	6	3	1	2	17	10	7	2	1.500	2.833
4	Chelsea	Eng	7	4	3	0	1	9	6	3	1	1.750	2.250
5	St-Gilloise Union	Bel	7	6	2	1	3	13	11	2	2	1.167	2.167
6	Roma	Ita	5	4	1	2	1	5	5	0	1	1.250	1.250
7	Inter Milan	Ita	4	4	1	1	2	10	9	1	1	1.000	2.500
8	Dinamo Zagreb	Yug	4	4	1	1	2	7	7	0	1	1.000	1.750
9	Vasas SC	Hun	2	2	1	0	1	3	4	-1	0	1.000	1.500
10	Lokomotiv Leipzig	GDR	2	2	1	0	1	2	6	-4	0	1.000	1.000
11	Cologne	FRG	1	2	0	1	1	2	4	-2	0	0.500	1.000
–	Hannover 96	FRG	1	2	0	1	1	2	4	-2	0	0.500	1.000
13	Olympique Lyon	Fra	1	2	0	1	1	1	8	-7	0	0.500	0.500
14	FC Basle	Sui	0	2	0	0	2	3	7	-4	0	0.000	1.500
15	BK Frem	Den	0	2	0	0	2	2	7	-5	0	0.000	1.000
16	Lausanne Sports	Sui	0	2	0	0	2	4	11	-7	0	0.000	2.000
	Total		**74**	**60**	**23**	**14**	**23**	**122**	**122**	**0**	**14**	**1.233**	**4.067**

National Performance by Points

1959-60

Pos'n	Cnty	Pts	P	W	D	L	F	A	Diff	B	Pts/P	F/P
1	Esp	45	23	17	3	3	82	33	49	8	1.957	3.565
2	Eng	27	18	9	4	5	36	32	4	5	1.500	2.000
3	FRG	15	11	4	4	3	27	23	4	3	1.364	2.455
4	Yug	14	12	4	3	5	25	21	4	3	1.167	2.083
5	Sco	13	9	5	1	3	22	23	-1	2	1.444	2.444
6	Ita	12	12	3	4	5	21	24	-3	2	1.000	1.750
7	Fra	11	9	4	2	3	16	21	-5	1	1.222	1.778
8	Aut	8	6	2	3	1	9	6	3	1	1.333	1.500
9	Ned	7	6	3	0	3	12	11	1	1	1.167	2.000
10	Bel	7	8	2	1	5	15	18	-3	2	0.875	1.875
11	Tch	5	4	2	1	1	8	6	2	0	1.250	2.000
12	Tur	5	5	2	1	2	8	11	-3	0	1.000	1.600
13	Swe	4	5	2	0	3	12	10	2	0	0.800	2.400
14	GDR	4	4	2	0	2	4	9	-5	0	1.000	1.000
15	Hun	3	4	1	1	2	6	8	-2	0	0.750	1.500
16	Nir	2	2	1	0	1	3	7	-4	0	1.000	1.500
17	Pol	2	2	1	0	1	2	6	-4	0	1.000	1.000
18	Lux	2	4	1	0	3	8	14	-6	0	0.500	2.000
19	Irl	1	2	0	1	1	3	4	-1	0	0.500	1.500
20	Rom	1	2	0	1	1	1	2	-1	0	0.500	0.500
21	Gre	1	2	0	1	1	3	5	-2	0	0.500	1.500
22	Bul	1	2	0	1	1	4	8	-4	0	0.500	2.000
23	Den	1	4	0	1	3	4	12	-8	0	0.250	1.000
24	Sui	1	6	0	1	5	9	23	-14	0	0.167	1.500
25	Por	0	2	0	0	2	1	4	-3	0	0.000	0.500
	Total	**192**	**164**	**65**	**34**	**65**	**341**	**341**	**0**	**28**	**1.171**	**4.159**

1955-56 to 1959-60

1	Esp	147	82	54	13	15	234	111	123	26	1.793	2.854
2	Eng	74	51	26	10	15	107	80	27	12	1.451	2.098
3	Ita	56	41	18	10	13	85	69	16	10	1.366	2.073
4	Fra	49	34	18	5	11	74	57	17	8	1.441	2.176
5	FRG	42	36	14	9	13	80	77	3	5	1.167	2.222
6	Yug	39	34	12	8	14	71	59	12	7	1.147	2.088
7	Sco	28	24	11	2	11	43	49	-6	4	1.167	1.792
8	Hun	26	22	9	5	8	53	43	10	3	1.182	2.409
9	Sui	25	29	8	5	16	46	72	-26	4	0.862	1.586
10	Aut	22	22	7	5	10	43	45	-2	3	1.000	1.955
11	GDR	19	19	7	4	8	36	38	-2	1	1.000	1.895
12	Tch	16	14	7	2	5	20	19	1	0	1.143	1.429
13	Bel	16	20	6	1	13	34	56	-22	3	0.800	1.700
14	Swe	15	18	5	4	9	30	30	0	1	0.833	1.667
15	Ned	15	16	6	1	9	27	36	-9	2	0.938	1.688
16	Den	11	17	3	5	9	22	41	-19	0	0.647	1.294
17	Bul	10	11	4	1	6	23	28	-5	1	0.909	2.091
18	Rom	9	12	4	1	7	19	31	-12	0	0.750	1.583
19	Tur	8	9	3	2	4	12	18	-6	0	0.889	1.333
20	Pol	8	11	3	2	6	10	25	-15	0	0.727	0.909
21	Por	6	12	2	2	8	18	30	-12	0	0.500	1.500
22	Lux	6	12	3	0	9	17	47	-30	0	0.500	1.417
23	Nir	3	6	1	1	4	6	20	-14	0	0.500	1.000
24	Gre	1	2	0	1	1	3	5	-2	0	0.500	1.500
25	Irl	1	6	0	1	5	6	26	-20	0	0.167	1.000
26	Fin	0	2	0	0	2	0	7	-7	0	0.000	0.000
	Total	**652**	**562**	**231**	**100**	**231**	**1119**	**1119**	**0**	**90**	**1.160**	**3.982**

1959-60

Pos'n	Cnty	Ave	Pts	P	W	D	L	F	A	Diff	B	No./T
1	Spain	15.000	45	23	17	3	3	82	33	49	8	3
2	Scotland	13.000	13	9	5	1	3	22	23	-1	2	1
3	England	9.000	27	18	9	4	5	36	32	4	5	3
4	Austria	8.000	8	6	2	3	1	9	6	3	1	1
5	Netherlands	7.000	7	6	3	0	3	12	11	1	1	1
6	France	5.500	11	9	4	2	3	16	21	-5	1	2
7	W. Germany	5.000	15	11	4	4	3	27	23	4	3	3
–	Czechoslovakia	5.000	5	4	2	1	1	8	6	2	0	1
–	Turkey	5.000	5	5	2	1	2	8	11	-3	0	1
10	Yugoslavia	4.667	14	12	4	3	5	25	21	4	3	3
11	Italy	4.000	12	12	3	4	5	21	24	-3	2	3
–	Sweden	4.000	4	5	2	0	3	12	10	2	0	1
13	Belgium	3.500	7	8	2	1	5	15	18	-3	2	2
14	N. Ireland	2.000	2	2	1	0	1	3	7	-4	0	1
–	Luxembourg	2.000	2	4	1	0	3	8	14	-6	0	1
–	Poland	2.000	2	2	1	0	1	2	6	-4	0	1
–	E. Germany	2.000	4	4	2	0	2	4	9	-5	0	2
18	Hungary	1.500	3	4	1	1	2	6	8	-2	0	2
19	Bulgaria	1.000	1	2	0	1	1	4	8	-4	0	1
–	Rep. of Ireland	1.000	1	2	0	1	1	3	4	-1	0	1
–	Greece	1.000	1	2	0	1	1	3	5	-2	0	1
–	Romania	1.000	1	2	0	1	1	1	2	-1	0	1
23	Denmark	0.500	1	4	0	1	3	4	12	-8	0	2
24	Switzerland	0.333	1	6	0	1	5	9	23	-14	0	3
25	Portugal	0.000	0	2	0	0	2	1	4	-3	0	1
	Total		**192**	**164**	**65**	**34**	**65**	**341**	**341**	**0**	**28**	**4.159**

1955-56 to 1959-60

Pos'n	Cnty	Ave	Pts	P	W	D	L	F	A	Diff	B	No./T
1	Spain	13.363	147	82	54	13	15	234	111	123	26	11
2	England	9.250	74	51	26	10	15	107	80	27	12	8
3	France	8.166	49	34	18	5	11	74	57	17	8	6
4	Italy	7.000	56	41	18	10	13	85	69	16	10	8
5	Scotland	5.600	28	24	11	2	11	43	49	-6	4	5
6	Yugoslavia	4.875	39	34	12	8	14	71	59	12	7	8
7	W. Germany	4.666	42	36	14	9	13	80	77	3	5	9
8	Austria	4.400	22	22	7	5	10	43	45	-2	3	5
9	Hungary	4.333	26	22	9	5	8	53	43	10	3	6
10	Czechoslovakia	4.000	16	14	7	2	5	20	19	1	0	4
11	E. Germany	3.800	19	19	7	4	8	36	38	-2	1	5
12	Netherlands	3.000	15	16	6	1	9	27	36	-9	2	5
–	Sweden	3.000	15	18	5	4	9	30	30	0	1	5
14	Switzerland	2.777	25	29	8	5	16	46	72	-26	4	9
15	Belgium	2.666	16	20	6	1	13	34	56	-22	3	6
–	Turkey	2.666	8	9	3	2	4	12	18	-6	0	3
17	Bulgaria	2.500	10	11	4	1	6	23	28	-5	1	4
18	Romania	2.250	9	12	4	1	7	19	31	-12	0	4
19	Poland	1.600	8	11	3	2	6	10	25	-15	0	5
20	Denmark	1.571	11	17	3	5	9	22	41	-19	0	7
21	Luxembourg	1.500	6	12	3	0	9	17	47	-30	0	4
22	Portugal	1.200	6	12	2	2	8	18	30	-12	0	5
23	Greece	1.000	1	2	0	1	1	3	5	-2	0	1
–	N. Ireland	1.000	3	6	1	1	4	6	20	-14	0	3
25	Rep. of Ireland	0.333	1	6	0	1	5	6	26	-20	0	3
26	Finland	0.000	0	2	0	0	2	0	7	-7	0	1
	Total		**652**	**562**	**231**	**100**	**231**	**1119**	**1119**	**0**	**90**	**3.982**

Real's Record Achievement

This will always be remembered as the season when Real Madrid captured their record fifth Champions' Cup (no team has ever matched that achievement in the 31 years since) with victory in one of the most memorable matches ever played. The 7-3 victory over Eintracht Frankfurt at Hampden Park on 18 May, 1960 is still talked about today and, quite clearly, in these times of functional, pragmatic football, such a match is unlikely ever to be seen again.

But if 1960 was the year of Real's crowning glory, their arch-rivals Barcelona did everything they could to try and steal it from them. Barcelona, coached by the Argentinian Helenio Herrera, later to gain infamy with his highly defensive, but extremely successful, *catenaccio* tactics for Inter Milan, nearly brought off a unique European Cup *double* in 1960 – one which, under current regulations, would be impossible to achieve.

For a start, they retained their Fairs' Cup, winning six of their eight games (including a four-goal double against Inter) and drawing the other two to become the first winner of a European trophy to go through the tournament undefeated. Their victims in the final were once again an English side, Birmingham, beaten 4-1 in Barcelona after a first-leg goalless draw.

Thanks to their 1959 Spanish championship victory – they finished four points clear of runners-up Real Madrid – Barcelona were also entitled to compete, simultaneously, in the Champions' Cup. And what an impression they made on their first appearance! They began with an 8-4 aggregate win over CDNA Sofia, followed that with a 7-1 destruction of AC Milan and then, in the quarter-finals, annihilated English champions Wolverhampton Wanderers with two magnificent performances, winning 4-0 at home in the first leg before crushing the West Midlanders 5-2 in the return.

The Barcelona side included such luminaries as Hungarian attackers Zoltán Czibor and Sándor Kocsis, Spanish international Luis Suárez and the greatly gifted Ladislao Kubala, later to coach both Barcelona and the Spanish national team.

But another future Spanish national coach, Miguel Muñoz, stood in Barcelona's way to their first Champions' Cup final. Real's former captain had only just taken over the coaching reins at the club, replacing the unpopular Paraguayan Fleitas Soltich, who had steered Real through the two earlier rounds against Jeunesse Esch and Nice.

Muñoz's first major task as Real's coach was to plot a course past Barcelona into the Champions' Cup final, and in the first leg, in Madrid, his players did not let him down. Di Stéfano, majestic as ever, scored twice and Puskás once to give Real a deserved 3-1 lead. Real had comfortably preserved their 100% European home record, but could they do the business in the furnace of the Nou Camp? The answer was an emphatic yes. Two more goals from Puskás and a third from Gento repeated the 3-1 victory of the first leg. Real were in their fifth final and Barcelona, despite a valiant effort, had to be content with the Fairs' Cup and another Spanish championship.

Eintracht Frankfurt were Real's opponents in the final. Up until the semi-finals they had made unspectacular progress, but against Rangers they suddenly came alive, thrashing the Scottish champions 6-1 at home and then 6-3 in Glasgow.

It was to Glasgow that Eintracht returned for the final, and within ten minutes they had taken the lead through inside-right Richard Kress. But that was to prove a false dawn for the Germans. Real came roaring back and by half-time they were well in control, 3-1 up after two goals from Di Stéfano and one, from an almost impossible angle, from Puskás. The second half turned into a procession of electrifying football from the men in white. Puskás struck three more times before Di Stéfano, too, collected his hat-trick. Frankfurt pulled back two consolation goals, but their's was a hopeless cause. They had been destroyed by a truly great performance from a truly great team. And the 127,000 Hampden crowd knew it. As the Real players collected the Cup for an amazing fifth time, the Scottish spectators stayed behind, almost to a man, to acknowledge the club's achievement with a raucous standing ovation.

1960 – 1961

Benfica

Fiorentina

Roma

European Cup 1960-61

First Round

Team 1	Cnty	Team 2	Cnty	1st leg	2nd leg	Agg
Rapid Vienna	Aut	Besiktas	Tur	4-0	0-1	3-1
AGF Aarhus	Den	Legia Warsaw	Pol	3-0	0-1	3-1
Heart of Midlothian	Sco	Benfica	Por	1-2	0-3	1-5
Limerick	Irl	Young Boys Berne	Sui	0-6	2-4	2-10
Barcelona	Esp	Lierse	Bel	2-0	3-0	5-0
HIFK Helsinki	Fin	Malmö FF	Swe	1-3	1-2	2-5
Stade Reims	Fra	Jeunesse Esch	Lux	6-1	5-0	11-1
Juventus	Ita	CSKA Sofia	Bul	2-0	1-4	3-4
Fredrikstad FK	Nor	Ajax	Ned	4-3	0-0	4-3
Red Star Belgrade	Yug	Ujpesti Dózsa	Hun	1-2	0-3	1-5

	Pts	P	W	D	L	F	A	Diff	Goals/P
Total	40	20	19	2	19	71	71	0	3.550

Second Round

Burnley	Eng	Stade Reims	Fra	2-0	2-3	4-3
Rapid Vienna	Aut	Karl-Marx-Stadt	GDR	3-1	0-2	4-3
		Rapid Vienna won the replay 1-0				
AGF Aarhus	Den	Fredrikstad FK	Nor	3-0	1-0	4-0
Real Madrid	Esp	Barcelona	Esp	2-2	1-2	3-4
Benfica	Por	Ujpesti Dózsa	Hun	6-2	1-2	7-4
Malmö FF	Swe	CSKA Sofia	Bul	1-0	1-1	2-1
Young Boys Berne	Sui	Hamburg	FRG	0-5	3-3	3-8
Spartak Hradec Králové	Tch	Panathinaikos	Gre	1-0	0-0	1- 0

	Pts	P	W	D	L	F	A	Diff	Goals/P
Total	34	17	13	8	13	51	51	0	3.000

Quarter Finals

Burnley	Eng	Hamburg	FRG	3-1	1-4	4-5
Rapid Vienna	Aut	Malmö FF	Swe	2-0	2-0	4-0
Barcelona	Esp	Spartak Hradec Králové	Tch	4-0	1-1	5- 1
Benfica	Por	AGF Aarhus	Den	3-1	4-2	7-3

	Pts	P	W	D	L	F	A	Diff	Goals/P
Total	16	8	7	2	7	29	29	0	3.625

Semi Finals

Barcelona	Esp	Hamburg	FRG	1-0	1-2	3-2
		Barcelona won the replay 1-0				
Benfica	Por	Rapid Vienna	Aut	3-0	1-1	4-1

	Pts	P	W	D	L	F	A	Diff	Goals/P
Total	10	5	4	2	4	10	10	0	2.000

Final

Benfica	Por	Barcelona	Esp	3-2	3-2

	Pts	P	W	D	L	F	A	Diff	Goals/P
Total	2	1	1	0	1	5	5	0	5.000

	Pts	P	W	D	L	F	A	Diff	Goals/P
Total	102	51	44	14	44	166	166	0	3.255

Pos'n	Club	Cnty	Pts	P	W	D	L	F	A	Diff	B	Pts/P	F/P
1	Benfica	Por	18	9	7	1	1	26	11	15	3	2.000	2.889
2	Barcelona	Esp	17	10	6	2	2	19	9	10	3	1.700	1.900
3	Rapid Vienna	Aut	13	9	5	1	3	13	8	5	2	1.444	1.444
4	Hamburg	FRG	9	7	3	1	3	15	10	5	2	1.286	2.143
5	Malmö FF	Swe	8	6	3	1	2	7	7	0	1	1.333	1.167
6	AGF Aarhus	Den	7	6	3	0	3	10	8	2	1	1.167	1.667
7	Stade Reims	Fra	6	4	3	0	1	14	5	9	0	1.500	3.500
8	Ujpesti Dózsa	Hun	6	4	3	0	1	9	8	1	0	1.500	2.250
9	Young Boys Berne	Sui	5	4	2	1	1	13	10	3	0	1.250	3.250
10	Burnley	Eng	5	4	2	0	2	8	8	0	1	1.250	2.000
11	Spartak Hradec Králové	Tch	5	4	1	2	1	2	5	-3	1	1.250	0.500
12	CSKA Sofia	Bul	3	4	1	1	2	5	5	0	0	0.750	1.250
13	Fredrikstad FK	Nor	3	4	1	1	2	4	7	-3	0	0.150	1.000
14	Juventus	Ita	2	2	1	0	1	3	4	-1	0	1.000	1.500
–	Karl-Marx-Stadt	GDR	2	3	1	0	2	3	4	-1	0	0.667	1.000
16	Legia Warsaw	Pol	2	2	1	0	1	1	3	-2	0	1.000	0.500
17	Besiktas	Tur	2	2	1	0	1	1	4	-3	0	1.000	0.500
18	Real Madrid	Esp	1	2	0	1	1	3	4	-1	0	0.500	1.500
–	Ajax	Ned	1	2	0	1	1	3	4	-1	0	0 500	1 500
20	Panathinaikos	Gre	1	2	0	1	1	0	1	-1	0	0 500	0 000
21	HIFK Helsinki	Fin	0	2	0	0	2	2	5	-3	0	0.000	1.000
22	Heart of Midlothian	Sco	0	2	0	0	2	1	5	-4	0	0.000	0.500
–	Red Star Belgrade	Yug	0	2	0	0	2	1	5	-4	0	0.000	0.500
24	Lierse	Bel	0	2	0	0	2	0	5	-5	0	0.000	0.000
25	Limerick	Irl	0	2	0	0	2	2	10	-8	0	0.000	1.000
26	Jeunesse Esch	Lux	0	2	0	0	2	1	11	-10	0	0 000	0 500
	Total		**116**	**102**	**44**	**14**	**44**	**166**	**166**	**0**	**14**	**1.137**	**3.255**

European Cup Winners' Cup 1960-61

First Round

Team 1	Cnty	Team 2	Cnty	1st leg	2nd leg	Agg
Rangers	Sco	Ferencváros	Hun	4-2	1-2	5-4
Vorwärts Frankfurt/Oder	GDR	Zbrojovka Brno	Tch	2-1	0-2	2-3

	Pts	P	W	D	L	F	A	Diff	Goals/P
Total	8	4	4	0	4	14	14	0	3.500

Quarter Finals

Austria Vienna	Aut	Wolverhampton Wanderers	Eng	2-0	0-5	2-5
Bor. Mönchengladbach	FRG	Rangers	Sco	0-3	0-8	0-11
Lucerne	Sui	Fiorentina	Ita	0-3	2-6	2-9
Zbrojovka Brno	Tch	Dinamo Zagreb	Yug	0-0	0-2	0-2

	Pts	P	W	D	L	F	A	Diff	Goals/P
Total	16	8	7	2	7	31	31	0	3.875

Semi Finals

Rangers	Sco	Wolverhampton Wanderers	Eng	2-0	1-1	3-1
Fiorentina	Ita	Dinamo Zagreb	Yug	3-0	1-2	4-2

	Pts	P	W	D	L	F	A	Diff	Goals/P
Total	8	4	3	2	4	10	10	0	2.500

Final

Rangers	Sco	Fiorentina	Ita	0-2	1-2	1-4

	Pts	P	W	D	L	F	A	Diff	Goals/P
Total	4	2	2	0	2	5	5	0	2.500

	Pts	P	W	D	L	F	A	Diff	Goals/P
Total	36	18	16	4	16	60	60	0	3.333

Pos'n	Club	Cnty	Pts	P	W	D	L	F	A	Diff	B	Pts/P	F/P
1	Fiorentina	Ita	12	6	5	0	1	17	5	12	2	2.000	2.833
2	Rangers	Sco	12	8	4	1	3	20	9	11	3	1.500	2.500
3	Dinamo Zagreb	Yug	6	4	2	1	1	4	4	0	1	1.500	1.000
4	Wolverhampton Wanderers	Eng	4	4	1	1	2	6	5	1	1	1.000	1.500
5	Zbrojovka Brno	Tch	4	4	1	1	2	3	4	-1	1	1.000	0.750
6	Ferencváros	Hun	2	2	1	0	1	4	5	-1	0	1.000	2.000
7	Vorwärts Frankfurt/Oder	GDR	2	2	1	0	1	2	3	-1	0	1.000	1.000
8	Austria Vienna	Aut	2	2	1	0	1	2	5	-3	0	1.000	1.000
9	Lucerne	Sui	0	2	0	0	2	2	9	-7	0	0.000	1.000
10	Bor. Mönchengladbach	FRG	0	2	0	0	2	0	11	-11	0	0.000	0.000
	Total		**44**	**36**	**16**	**4**	**16**	**60**	**60**	**0**	**8**	**1.222**	**3.333**

First Round

Birmingham City	Eng	Vasas SC	Hun	3-2	2-1	5-3
Union St-Gilloise	Bel	Roma	Ita	0-0	1-4	1-4
KB Copenhagen	Den	FC Basle	Sui	8-1	3-3	11-4
Olympique Lyon	Fra	Cologne	FRG	1-3	1-2	2-5
Inter Milan	Ita	Hannover 96	FRG	8-2	6-1	14-3
NK Zagreb	Yug	Barcelona	Esp	1-1	3-4	4-5
Lokomotive Leipzig	GDR	OFK Belgrade	Yug	5-2	1-4	6-8
		OFK Belgrade won the replay 0-2				

	Pts	P	W	D	L	F	A	Diff	Goals/P
Total	30	15	12	6	12	75	75	0	5.000

Quarter Finals

Birmingham City	Eng	KB Copenhagen	Den	5-0	4-4	9-4
Barcelona	Esp	Hibernian	Sco	4-4	2-3	6-7
Inter Milan	Ita	OFK Belgrade	Yug	5-0	0-1	5-1
Cologne	FRG	Roma	Ita	2-0	0-2	3-6
		Roma won the replay 1-4				

	Pts	P	W	D	L	F	A	Diff	Goals/P
Total	18	9	7	4	7	41	41	0	4.556

Semi Finals

Inter Milan	Ita	Birmingham City	Eng	1-2	1-2	2-4
Roma	Ita	Hibernian	Sco	3-3	2-2	11-5
		Roma won the replay 6-0				

	Pts	P	W	D	L	F	A	Diff	Goals/P
Total	10	5	3	4	3	22	22	0	4.000

Final

Roma	Ita	Birmingham City	Eng	2-0	2-2	4-2

	Pts	P	W	D	L	F	A	Diff	Goals/P
Total	4	2	1	2	1	6	6	0	3.000

	Pts	P	W	D	L	F	A	Diff	Goals/P
Total	62	31	23	16	23	144	144	0	4.645

UEFA Cup 1960-61

Pos'n	Club	Cnty	Pts	P	W	D	L	F	A	Diff	B	Pts/P	F/P
1	Roma	Ita	17	10	5	4	1	25	11	14	3	1.700	2.500
2	Birmingham City	Eng	15	8	5	2	1	20	13	7	3	1.875	2.500
3	Inter Milan	Ita	8	6	3	0	3	21	8	13	2	1.333	3.500
4	Cologne	FRG	7	5	3	0	2	8	8	0	1	1.400	1.600
5	OFK Belgrade	Yug	7	5	3	0	2	9	11	-2	1	1.400	1.800
6	Hibernian	Sco	6	5	1	3	1	12	17	-5	1	1.200	2.400
7	KB Copenhagen	Den	5	4	1	2	1	15	13	2	1	1.250	3.750
8	Barcelona	Esp	5	4	1	2	1	11	11	0	1	1.250	2.750
9	Lokomotive Leipzig	GDR	2	3	1	0	2	6	8	-2	0	0.667	2.000
10	NK Zagreb	Yug	1	2	0	1	1	4	5	-1	0	0.500	2.000
11	St-Gilloise Union	Bel	1	2	0	1	1	1	4	-3	0	0.500	0.500
12	FC Basle	Sui	1	2	0	1	1	4	11	-7	0	0.500	2.000
13	Vasas SC	Hun	0	2	0	0	2	3	5	-2	0	0.000	1.500
14	Olympique Lyon	Fra	0	2	0	0	2	2	5	-3	0	0.000	1.000
15	Hanover 96	FRG	0	2	0	0	2	3	14	-11	0	0.000	1.500
	Total		**75**	**62**	**23**	**16**	**23**	**144**	**144**	**0**	**13**	**1.210**	**4.645**

1960-61

Pos'n	Cnty	Pts	P	W	D	L	F	A	Diff	B	Pts/P	F/P
1	Ita	39	24	14	4	6	66	28	38	7	1.625	2.750
2	Eng	24	16	8	3	5	34	26	8	5	1.500	2.125
3	Esp	23	16	7	5	4	33	24	9	4	1.438	2.063
4	Por	18	9	7	1	1	26	11	15	3	2.000	2.889
5	Sco	18	15	5	4	6	33	31	2	4	1.200	2.200
6	FRG	16	16	6	1	9	26	43	-17	3	1.000	1.625
7	Aut	15	11	6	1	4	15	13	2	2	1.364	1.364
8	Yug	14	13	5	2	6	18	25	-7	2	1.077	1.385
9	Den	12	10	4	2	4	25	21	4	2	1.200	2.500
10	Tch	9	8	2	3	3	5	9	-4	2	1.125	0.625
11	Swe	8	6	3	1	2	7	7	0	1	1.333	1.167
12	Hun	8	8	4	0	4	16	18	-2	0	1.000	2.000
13	Fra	6	6	3	0	3	16	10	6	0	1.000	2.667
14	GDR	6	8	3	0	5	11	15	-4	0	0.750	1.375
15	Sui	6	8	2	2	4	19	30	-11	0	0.750	2.375
16	Bul	3	4	1	1	2	5	5	0	0	0.750	1.250
17	Nor	3	4	1	1	2	4	7	-3	0	0.750	1.000
18	Pol	2	2	1	0	1	1	3	-2	0	1.000	0.500
19	Tur	2	2	1	0	1	1	4	-3	0	1.000	0.500
20	Ned	1	2	0	1	1	3	4	-1	0	0.500	1.500
21	Gre	1	2	0	1	1	0	1	-1	0	0.500	0.000
22	Bel	1	4	0	1	3	1	9	-8	0	0.250	0.250
23	Fin	0	2	0	0	2	2	5	-3	0	0.000	1.000
24	Irl	0	2	0	0	2	2	10	-8	0	0.000	1.000
25	Lux	0	2	0	0	2	1	11	-10	0	0.000	0.500
	Total	**235**	**200**	**83**	**34**	**83**	**370**	**370**	**0**	**35**	**1.175**	**3.700**

1955-56 to 1960-61

1	Esp	170	98	61	18	19	267	135	132	30	1.735	2.724
2	Eng	98	67	34	13	20	141	106	35	17	1.463	2.104
3	Ita	95	65	32	14	19	151	97	54	17	1.462	2.323
4	FRG	58	52	20	10	22	106	120	-14	8	1.115	2.038
5	Fra	55	40	21	5	14	90	67	23	8	1.375	2.250
6	Yug	53	47	17	10	20	89	84	5	9	1.128	1.894
7	Sco	46	39	16	6	17	76	80	-4	8	1.179	1.949
8	Aut	37	33	13	6	14	58	58	0	5	1.121	1.758
9	Hun	34	30	13	5	12	69	61	8	3	1.133	2.300
10	Sui	31	37	10	7	20	65	102	-37	4	0.838	1.757
11	Tch	25	22	9	5	8	25	28	-3	2	1.136	1.136
12	GDR	25	27	10	4	13	47	53	-6	1	0.926	1.741
13	Por	24	21	9	3	9	44	41	3	3	1.143	2.095
14	Swe	23	24	8	5	11	37	37	0	2	0.958	1.542
15	Den	23	27	7	7	13	47	62	-15	2	0.852	1.741
16	Bel	17	24	6	2	16	35	65	-30	3	0.708	1.458
17	Ned	16	18	6	2	10	30	40	-10	2	0.889	1.667
18	Bul	13	15	5	2	8	28	33	-5	1	0.867	1.867
19	Tur	10	11	4	2	5	13	22	-9	0	0.909	1.182
20	Pol	10	13	4	2	7	11	28	-17	0	0.769	0.846
21	Rom	9	12	4	1	7	19	31	-12	0	0.750	1.583
22	Lux	6	14	3	0	11	18	58	-40	0	0.429	1.286
23	Nor	3	4	1	1	2	4	7	-3	0	0.750	1.000
24	Nir	3	6	1	1	4	6	20	-14	0	0.500	1.000
25	Gre	2	4	0	2	2	3	6	-3	0	0.500	0.750
26	Irl	1	8	0	1	7	8	36	-28	0	0.125	1.000
27	Fin	0	4	0	0	4	2	12	-10	0	0.000	0.500
	Total	**887**	**762**	**314**	**134**	**314**	**1489**	**1489**	**0**	**125**	**1.164**	**3.908**

National Performance by Index

1960-61

Pos'n	Cnty	Ave	Pts	P	W	D	L	F	A	Diff	B	No./T
1	Portugal	18.000	18	9	7	1	1	26	11	15	3	1
2	Italy	9.750	39	24	14	4	6	66	28	38	7	4
3	England	8.000	24	16	8	3	5	34	26	8	5	3
–	Sweden	8.000	8	6	3	1	2	7	7	0	1	1
5	Spain	7.666	23	16	7	5	4	33	24	9	4	3
6	Austria	7.500	15	11	6	1	4	15	13	2	2	2
7	Denmark	6.000	12	10	4	2	4	25	21	4	2	2
–	Scotland	6.000	18	15	5	4	6	33	31	2	4	3
9	Czechoslovakia	4.500	9	8	2	3	3	5	9	-4	2	2
10	W. Germany	4.000	16	16	6	1	9	26	43	-17	3	4
11	Yugoslavia	3.500	14	13	5	2	6	18	25	-7	2	4
12	Bulgaria	3.000	3	4	1	1	2	5	5	0	0	1
–	France	3.000	6	6	3	0	3	16	10	6	0	2
–	Norway	3.000	3	4	1	1	2	4	7	-3	0	1
15	Hungary	2.666	8	8	4	0	4	16	18	-2	0	3
16	Poland	2.000	2	2	1	0	1	1	3	-2	0	1
–	Switzerland	2.000	6	8	2	2	4	19	30	-11	0	3
–	Turkey	2.000	2	2	1	0	1	1	4	-3	0	1
–	E. Germany	2.000	6	8	3	0	5	11	15	-4	0	3
20	Greece	1. 000	1	2	0	1	1	0	1	-1	0	1
–	Netherlands	1.000	1	2	0	1	1	3	4	-1	0	1
22	Belgium	0.500	1	4	0	1	3	1	9	-8	0	2
23	Rep. of Ireland	0.000	0	2	0	0	2	2	10	-8	0	1
–	Finland	0.000	0	2	0	0	2	2	5	-3	0	1
–	Luxembourg	0.000	0	2	0	0	2	1	11	-10	0	1
	Total		**235**	**200**	**83**	**34**	**83**	**370**	**370**	**0**	**35**	**3.700**

1955-56 to 1960-61

Pos'n	Cnty	Ave	Pts	P	W	D	L	F	A	Diff	B	No./T
1	Spain	12.142	170	98	61	18	19	267	135	132	30	14
2	England	8.909	98	67	34	13	20	141	106	35	17	11
3	Italy	7.916	95	65	32	14	19	151	97	54	17	12
4	France	6.875	55	40	21	5	14	90	67	23	8	8
5	Scotland	5.750	46	39	16	6	17	76	80	-4	8	8
6	Austria	5.285	37	33	13	6	14	58	58	0	5	7
7	W. Germany	4.461	58	52	20	10	22	106	120	-14	8	13
8	Yugoslavia	4.416	53	47	17	10	20	89	84	5	9	12
9	Czechoslovakia	4.166	25	22	9	5	8	25	28	-3	2	6
10	Portugal	4.000	24	21	9	3	9	44	41	3	3	6
11	Sweden	3.833	23	24	8	5	11	37	37	0	2	6
12	Hungary	3.777	34	30	13	5	12	69	61	8	3	9
13	E. Germany	3.125	25	27	10	4	13	47	53	-6	1	8
14	Norway	3.000	3	4	1	1	2	4	7	-3	0	1
15	Netherlands	2.666	16	18	6	2	10	30	40	-10	2	6
16	Bulgaria	2.600	13	15	5	2	8	28	33	-5	1	5
17	Switzerland	2.583	31	37	10	7	20	65	102	-37	4	12
18	Denmark	2.555	23	27	7	7	13	47	62	-15	2	9
19	Turkey	2.500	10	11	4	2	5	13	22	-9	0	4
20	Romania	2.250	9	12	4	1	7	19	31	-12	0	4
21	Belgium	2.125	17	24	6	2	16	35	65	-30	3	8
22	Poland	1.666	10	13	4	2	7	11	28	-17	0	6
23	Luxembourg	1.200	6	14	3	0	11	18	58	-40	0	5
24	Greece	1.000	2	4	0	2	2	3	6	-3	0	2
–	N. Ireland	1.000	3	6	1	1	4	6	20	-14	0	3
26	Rep. of Ireland	0.250	1	8	0	1	7	8	36	-28	0	4
27	Finland	0.000	0	4	0	0	4	2	12	-10	0	2
	Total		**887**	**762**	**314**	**134**	**314**	**1489**	**1489**	**0**	**125**	**3.908**

And Then There Were Three

The 1960-61 season saw the introduction of a third European competition – the Cup-winners' Cup. Like the Champions' Cup, the new competition received only lukewarm support in its inaugural year. A mere ten clubs chose to enter, and not all of those were actually the reigning Cup holders in their own country.

One of that group was Fiorentina, the eventual winners of the competition. They had qualified for the Cup-winners' Cup as runners-up in the Italian Cup because the team that had defeated them in the final, Juventus, also won the Italian championship and, consequently, had entered the Champions' Cup. Wary of the precedent set by Barcelona's double appearances in Fairs' and Champions' Cups, UEFA made it clear from the outset that no team could enter both the Champions' and the Cup-winners' Cups.

Fiorentina, the 1957 Champions' Cup runners-up, made light work of becoming the first Italian side to win a European trophy. They comfortably beat Lucerne and Dinamo Zagreb before winning both matches of the two-legged final against Rangers.

There was also an Italian winner in the final of the Fairs' Cup. Again, as in the previous year, Birmingham City were the beaten finalists, and once more they drew the first leg at home before losing the return. This had been the pattern of all three Fairs' Cup finals to date, with the English team beaten into second place on each occasion. At least Birmingham had prevented an all-Italian final by defeating Inter Milan home and away in the semis. A Roma-Inter final would have to wait another 30 years, when the competition would be called the UEFA Cup.

Barcelona were deprived of a third successive Fairs' Cup triumph when they lost their quarter-final tie against Scotland's Hibernian, 7-6 on aggregate. But by then they had already made their mark in the Champions' Cup.

Having defeated Lierse of Belgium in the preliminary round, Barcelona were drawn to face holders Real Madrid – a repeat of their semi-final confrontation of the previous season. This time, though, it was the Catalans who were to come out on top, inflicting on Real their first elimination from the competition after 21 ties. Both games were tarnished with suspect refereeing decisions, but two goals from Luis Suárez gave Barcelona a 2-2 draw in Madrid (the first time Real had failed to win at home in a European match) and a 2-1 win for Barcelona in the Nou Camp finally brought Real's long reign to an end.

Having eliminated Real, Barcelona were now red-hot favourites to go on and take the Cup. They did need a play-off victory in Brussels to get past Hamburg in the semi-finals, but most people regarded the team, with its thrilling front line of Kubala, Kocsis, Evaristo, Suárez and Czibor, as a worthy potential successor to Real.

Barcelona's opponents in the Berne final were Benfica, the champions of Portugal. Coached by the ageing Hungarian, Bela Guttmann, they had sailed through every one of their four ties. Their only defeat was away to Ujpesti Dózsa, but as they had already won the home leg 6-2, that gave no cause for alarm. Their hairiest moment came in Vienna, in the semi-final second leg against Rapid, when the Austrian players and spectators ran riot after they had been denied a late penalty. With the tie over as a contest at that stage anyway, it was an extraordinary way for the Austrians to react. The game was duly abandoned, with Benfica declared the winners.

The final itself was packed wth excitement. Barcelona, as expected, opened the scoring, through Kocsis, and seemed to have everything well in control until two Benfica goals within a minute suddenly transformed the match. Coluna, the Benfica captain, added a third goal early in the second half, but Barcelona came back, made it 3-2 through Czibor and came excruciatingly close to scoring the equaliser that would have sent the game into extra time. But Benfica, desperately, held out, ensuring that their name, and not Barcelona's, would be the first to accompany Real Madrid's on the giant silver trophy.

Benfica

Atlético Madrid

Valencia

1961 – 1962

First Round

Team 1	Cnty	Team 2	Cnty	1st leg	2nd leg	Agg
Standard Liège	Bel	Fredrikstad FK	Nor	2-1	2-0	4-1
CSKA Sofia	Bul	Dukla Prague	Tch	4-4	1-2	5-6
Monaco	Fra	Rangers	Sco	2-3	2-3	4-6
Panathinaikos	Gre	Juventus	Ita	1-1	1-2	2-3
Vasas SC	Hun	Real Madrid	Esp	0-2	1-3	1-5
Spora Luxembourg	Lux	B 1913 Odense	Den	0-6	2-9	2-15
Górnik Zabrze	Pol	Tottenham Hotspur	Eng	4-2	1-8	5-10
Sporting Lisbon	Por	Partizan Belgrade	Yug	1-1	0-2	1-3
Nuremberg	FRG	Drumcondra	Irl	5-0	4-1	9-1
Steaua Bucharest	Rom	Austria Vienna	Aut	0-0	0-2	0-2
IFK Gothenburg	Swe	Feyenoord	Ned	0-3	2-8	2-11
Servette	Sui	Hibernians	Mlt	5-0	2-1	7-1
Vorwärts Frankfurt/Oder	GDR	Linfield	Nir	3-0		3-0

	Pts	P	W	D	L	F	A	Diff	Goals/P
Total	50	25	21	8	21	109	109	0	4.360

Second Round

Team 1	Cnty	Team 2	Cnty	1st leg	2nd leg	Agg
Austria Vienna	Aut	Benfica	Por	1-1	1-5	2-6
Standard Liège	Bel	Haka Valkeakoski	Fin	5-1	2-0	7-1
B 1913 Odense	Den	Real Madrid	Esp	0-3	0-9	0-12
Feyenoord	Ned	Tottenham Hotspur	Eng	1-3	1-1	2-4
Geneva Servette	Sui	Dukla Prague	Tch	4-3	0-2	4-5
Fenerbahçe	Tur	Nuremberg	FRG	1-2	0-1	1-3
Partizan Belgrade	Yug	Juventus	Ita	1-2	0-5	1-7
Vorwärts Frankfurt/Oder	GDR	Rangers	Sco	1-2	1-4	2-6

	Pts	P	W	D	L	F	A	Diff	Goals/P
Total	32	16	14	4	14	63	63	0	3.938

Quarter Finals

Team 1	Cnty	Team 2	Cnty	1st leg	2nd leg	Agg
Standard Liège	Bel	Rangers	Sco	4-1	0-2	4-3
Juventus	Ita	Real Madrid	Esp	0-1	1-0	2-4
		Real Madrid won the replay 1-3				
Nuremberg	FRG	Benfica	Por	3-1	0-6	3-7
Dukla Prague	Tch	Tottenham Hotspur	Eng	1-0	1-4	2-4

	Pts	P	W	D	L	F	A	Diff	Goals/P
Total	18	9	9	0	9	29	29	0	3.222

Semi Finals

Team 1	Cnty	Team 2	Cnty	1st leg	2nd leg	Agg
Real Madrid	Esp	Standard Liège	Bel	4-0	2-0	6-0
Benfica	Por	Tottenham Hotspur	Eng	3-1	1-2	4-3

	Pts	P	W	D	L	F	A	Diff	Goals/P
Total	8	4	4	0	4	13	13	0	3.250

Final

Benfica	Por	Real Madrid	Esp	5-3	5-3

	Pts	P	W	D	L	F	A	Diff	Goals/P
Total	2	1	1	0	1	8	8	0	8.000

	Pts	P	W	D	L	F	A	Diff	Goals/P
Total	110	55	49	12	49	222	222	0	4.036

Pos'n	Club	Cnty	Pts	P	W	D	L	F	A	Diff	B	Pts/P	F/P
1	Real Madrid	Esp	19	10	8	0	2	30	8	22	3	1.900	3.000
2	Benfica	Por	12	7	4	1	2	22	11	11	3	1.714	3.143
3	Standard Liège	Bel	12	8	5	0	3	15	11	4	2	1.500	1.875
4	Tottenham Hotspur	Eng	11	8	4	1	3	21	13	8	2	1.375	2.625
5	Nuremberg	FRG	11	6	5	0	1	15	9	6	1	1.833	2.500
6	Rangers	Sco	11	6	5	0	1	15	10	5	1	1.833	2.500
7	Juventus	Ita	10	7	4	1	2	12	7	5	1	1.429	1.714
8	Dukla Prague	Tch	8	6	3	1	2	13	13	0	1	1.333	2.167
9	Servette	Sui	6	4	3	0	1	11	6	5	0	1.500	2.750
10	Feyenoord	Ned	5	4	2	1	1	13	6	7	0	1.250	3.250
11	B 1913 Odense	Den	4	4	2	0	2	15	14	1	0	1.000	3.750
12	Austria Vienna	Aut	4	4	1	2	1	4	6	-2	0	1.000	1.000
13	Partizan Belgrade	Yug	3	4	1	1	2	4	8	-4	0	0.750	1.000
14	Vorwärts Frankfurt/Oder	GDR	2	3	1	0	2	5	6	-1	0	0.667	1.667
15	Górnik Zabrze	Pol	2	2	1	0	1	5	10	-5	0	1.000	2.500
16	CSKA Sofia	Bul	1	2	0	1	1	5	6	-1	0	0.500	2.500
17	Panathinaikos	Gre	1	2	0	1	1	2	3	-1	0	0.500	1.000
18	Sporting Lisbon	Por	1	2	0	1	1	1	3	-2	0	0.500	0.500
19	Steaua Bucharest	Rom	1	2	0	1	1	0	2	-2	0	0.500	0.000
20	Monaco	Fra	0	2	0	0	2	4	6	-2	0	0.000	2.000
21	Fenerbahçe	Tur	0	2	0	0	2	1	3	-2	0	0.000	0.500
22	Fredrikstad FK	Nor	0	2	0	0	2	1	4	-3	0	0.000	0.500
23	Linfield	Nir	0	1	0	0	1	0	3	-3	0	0.000	0.000
24	Vasas SC	Hun	0	2	0	0	2	1	5	-4	0	0.000	0.500
25	Haka Valkeakoski	Fin	0	2	0	0	2	1	7	-6	0	0.000	0.500
–	Hibernians	Mlt	0	2	0	0	2	1	7	-6	0	0.000	0.500
27	Drumcondra	Irl	0	2	0	0	2	1	9	-8	0	0.000	0.500
28	IFK Gothenburg	Swe	0	2	0	0	2	2	11	-9	0	0.000	1.000
29	Spora Luxembourg	Lux	0	2	0	0	2	2	15	-13	0	0.000	1.000
	Total		**124**	**110**	**49**	**12**	**49**	**222**	**222**	**0**	**14**	**1.127**	**4.036**

First Round

Team 1	Cnty	Team 2	Cnty	1st leg	2nd leg	Agg
Rapid Vienna	Aut	Spartak Varna	Bul	0-0	5-2	5-2
Dunfermline Athletic	Sco	St. Patrick's Athletic	Irl	4-1	4-0	8-1
Sedan	Fra	Atlético Madrid	Esp	2-3	1-4	3-7
Swansea City	Wal	Carl Zeiss Jena	GDR	2-2	1-5	3-7
Glenavon	Nir	Leicester City	Eng	1-4	1-3	2-7
Floriana	Mlt	Ujpesti Dózsa	Hun	2-5	2-10	4-15
La Chaux-de-Fonds	Sui	Leixões	Por	6-2	0-5	6-7

	Pts	P	W	D	L	F	A	Diff	Goals/P
Total	28	14	12	4	12	77	77	0	5.500

Second Round

Leicester City	Eng	Atlético Madrid	Esp	1-1	0-2	1-3
Dunfermline Athletic	Sco	Vardar Skoplje	Yug	5-0	0-2	5-2
Olympiakos Pireus	Gre	Dynamo Zilina	Tch	2-3	0-1	2-4
Fiorentina	Ita	Rapid Vienna	Aut	3-1	6-2	9-3
Ajax	Ned	Ujpesti Dózsa	Hun	2-1	1-3	3-4
Leixões	Por	Progresul Bucharest	Rom	1-1	1-0	2-1
Werder Bremen	FRG	AGF Aarhus	Den	2-0	3-2	5-2
Carl Zeiss Jena	GDR	Alliance Dudelange	Lux	7-0	2-2	9-2

	Pts	P	W	D	L	F	A	Diff	Goals/P
Total	32	16	13	6	13	57	57	0	3.563

Quarter Finals

Ujpesti Dózsa	Hun	Dunfermline Athletic	Sco	4-3	1-0	5-3
Werder Bremen	FRG	Atlético Madrid	Esp	1-1	1-3	2-4
Dynamo Zilina	Tch	Fiorentina	Ita	3-2	0-2	3-4
Carl Zeiss Jena	GDR	Leixões	Por	1-1	3-1	4-2

	Pts	P	W	D	L	F	A	Diff	Goals/P
Total	16	8	6	4	6	27	27	0	3.375

Semi Finals

Fiorentina	Ita	Ujpesti Dózsa	Hun	2-0	1-0	3-0
Carl Zeiss Jena	GDR	Atlético Madrid	Esp	1-1	0-4	1- 5

	Pts	P	W	D	L	F	A	Diff	Goals/P
Total	8	4	3	2	3	9	9	0	2.250

Final

Atlético Madrid	Esp	Fiorentina	Ita	1-1	3-0	4-1

	Pts	P	W	D	L	F	A	Diff	Goals/P
Total	4	2	1	2	1	5	5	0	2.500

European Cup Winners Cup 1961-62

	Pts	P	W	D	L	F	A	Diff	Goals/P
Total	88	44	35	18	35	175	175	0	3.977

Pos'n	Club	Cnty	Pts	P	W	D	L	F	A	Diff	B	Pts/P	F/P
1	Atlético Madrid	Esp	19	10	6	4	0	23	8	15	3	1.900	2.300
2	Fiorentina	Ita	14	8	5	1	2	17	10	7	3	1.750	2.125
3	Ujpesti Dózsa	Hun	12	8	5	0	3	24	13	11	2	1.500	3.000
4	Carl Zeiss Jena	GDR	12	8	3	4	1	21	12	9	2	1.500	2.625
5	Dunfermline Athletic	Sco	7	6	3	0	3	16	8	8	1	1.167	2.667
6	Dynamo Zilina	Tch	7	4	3	0	1	7	6	1	1	1.750	1.750
7	Leixões	Por	7	6	2	2	2	11	11	0	1	1.167	1.833
8	Werder Bremen	FRG	6	4	2	1	1	7	6	1	1	1.500	1.750
9	Leicester City	Eng	5	4	2	1	1	8	5	3	0	1.250	2.000
10	Rapid Vienna	Aut	3	4	1	1	2	8	11	-3	0	0.750	2.000
11	La Chaux-de-Fonds	Sui	2	2	1	0	1	6	7	-1	0	1.000	3.000
12	Ajax	Ned	2	2	1	0	1	3	4	-1	0	1.000	1.500
13	Vardar Skoplje	Yug	2	2	1	0	1	2	5	-3	0	1.000	1.000
14	Progresul Bucharest	Rom	1	2	0	1	1	1	2	-1	0	0.500	0.500
15	Spartak Varna	Bul	1	2	0	1	1	2	5	-3	0	0.500	1.000
16	Swansea City	Wal	1	2	0	1	1	3	7	-4	0	0.500	1.500
17	Alliance Dudelange	Lux	1	2	0	1	1	2	9	-7	0	0.500	1.000
18	Olympiakos Pireus	Gre	0	2	0	0	2	2	1	-2	0	0.000	1.000
19	AGF Aarhus	Den	0	2	0	0	2	2	5	-3	0	0.000	1.000
20	Sedan	Fra	0	2	0	0	2	3	7	-4	0	0.000	1.500
21	Glenavon	Nir	0	2	0	0	2	2	7	-5	0	0.000	1.000
22	St. Patrick's Athletic	Irl	0	2	0	0	2	1	8	-7	0	0.000	0.500
23	Floriana	Mal	0	2	0	0	2	4	15	-11	0	0.000	2.000
	Total		**102**	**88**	**35**	**18**	**35**	**175**	**175**	**0**	**14**	**1.159**	**3.977**

First Round

Team 1	Cnty	Team 2	Cnty	1st leg	2nd leg	Agg
Heart of Midlothian	Sco	Union St-Gilloise	Bel	2-0	3-1	5-1
Valencia	Esp	Nottingham Forest	Eng	2-0	5-1	7-1
Olympique Lyon	Fra	Sheffield Wednesday	Eng	4-2	2-5	6-7
Strasbourg	Fra	MTK-VM	Hun	1-3	2 -10	3-13
AC Milan	Ita	Vojvodina Novi Sad	Yug	0-0	0-2	0- 2
Belenenses	Por	Hibernian	Sco	1-3	3-3	4-6
Hertha Berlin	FRG	Barcelona	Esp	1-0	0-3	1-3
Cologne	FRG	Inter Milan	Ita	4-2	0-2	7-9
		Inter Milan won the replay 3-5				
Hannover 96	FRG	Español	Esp	0-1	0-2	0-3
FC Basle	Sui	Red Star Belgrade	Yug	1-1	1-4	2-5
Zbrojovka Brno	Tch	Lokomotive Leipzig	GDR	2-2	1-4	3-6
Dinamo Zagreb	Yug	KB Copenhagen	Den	2-2	7-2	9-4

	Pts	P	W	D	L	F	A	Diff	Goals/P
Total	50	25	20	10	20	107	107	0	4.280

Second Round

Sheffield Wednesday	Eng	Roma	Ita	4-0	0-1	4-1
Heart of Midlothian	Eco	Inter Milan	Ita	0-1	0-4	0- 5
Español	Esp	Birmingham City	Eng	5-2	0-1	5-3
Barcelona	Esp	Dinamo Zagreb	Yug	5-1	2-2	7-3
Valencia	Esp	Lausanne-Sports	Sui	4-3		4-3
Iraklis	Gre	Vojvodina Novi Sad	Yug	2-1	1-9	3-10
MTK-VM	Hun	Lokomotive Leipzig	GDR	3-0	0-3	5-3
		MTK-VM won the replay 2-0				
Red Star Belgrade	Yug	Hibernian	Sco	4-0	1-0	5-0

	Pts	P	W	D	L	F	A	Diff	Goals/P
Total	32	16	15	2	15	61	61	0	3.813

Quarter Finals

Sheffield Wednesday	Eng	Barcelona	Esp	3-2	0-2	3-4
Valencia	Esp	Inter Milan	Ita	2-0	3-3	5-3
Red Star Belgrade	Yug	Español	Esp	5-0	1-2	6-2
Vojvodina Novi Sad	Yug	MTK-VM	Hun	1-4	1-2	2-6

	Pts	P	W	D	L	F	A	Diff	Goals/P
Total	16	8	7	2	7	31	31	0	3.875

Semi Finals

Barcelona	Esp	Red Star Belgrade	Yug	4-1	0-2	4-3
MTK-VM	Hun	Valencia	Esp	3-7	0-3	3-10

	Pts	P	W	D	L	F	A	Diff	Goals/P
Total	8	4	4	0	4	20	20	0	5.000

Final

Valencia	Esp	Barcelona	Esp	6-2	1-1	7-3

	Pts	P	W	D	L	F	A	Diff	Goals/P
Total	4	2	1	2	1	10	10	0	5.000

	Pts	P	W	D	L	F	A	Diff	Goals/P
Total	110	55	47	16	47	229	229	0	4.164

Pos'n	Club	Cnty	Pts	P	W	D	L	F	A	Diff	B	Pts/P	F/P
1	Valencia	Esp	19	9	7	2	0	33	13	20	3	2.111	3.661
2	MTK-VM	Hun	14	9	6	0	3	27	18	9	2	1.556	3.000
3	Red Star Belgrade	Yug	13	8	5	1	2	19	8	11	2	1.625	2.375
4	Barcelona	Esp	13	10	4	2	4	21	17	4	3	1.300	2.000
5	Inter Milan	Ita	10	7	4	1	2	17	12	5	1	1.429	2.429
6	Español	Esp	9	6	4	0	2	10	9	1	1	1.500	1.667
7	Sheffield Wednesday	Eng	7	6	3	0	3	14	11	3	1	1.167	2.333
8	Vojvodina Novi Sad	Yug	6	6	2	1	3	14	9	5	1	1.000	2.333
9	Lokomotive Leipzig	GDR	5	5	2	1	2	9	8	1	0	1.000	1.800
10	Dinamo Zagreb	Yug	4	4	1	2	1	12	11	1	0	1.000	3.000
11	Hearts of Midlothian	Sco	4	4	2	0	2	5	6	-1	0	1.000	1.250
12	Hibernian	Sco	3	4	1	1	2	6	9	-3	0	0.750	1.500
13	Olympique Lyon	Fra	2	2	1	0	1	6	7	-1	0	1.000	3.000
14	Cologne	FRG	2	3	1	0	2	7	9	-2	0	0.667	2.333
15	Birmingham City	Eng	2	2	1	0	1	3	5	-2	0	1.000	1.500
16	Hertha Berlin	FRG	2	2	1	0	1	1	3	-2	0	1.000	0.500
17	Roma	Ita	2	2	1	0	1	1	4	-3	0	1.000	0.500
18	Iraklis	Gre	2	2	1	0	1	3	10	-7	0	1.000	1.500
19	Belenenses	Por	1	2	0	1	1	4	6	-2	0	0.500	2.000
20	AC Milan	Ita	1	2	0	1	1	0	2	-2	0	0.500	0.000
21	Zbrojovka Brno	Tch	1	2	0	1	1	3	6	-3	0	0.500	1.500
22	FC Basle	Sui	1	2	0	1	1	2	5	-3	0	0.500	1.000
23	KB Copenhagen	Den	1	2	0	1	1	4	9	-5	0	0.500	2.000
24	Lausanne-Sports	Sui	0	1	0	0	1	3	4	-1	0	0.000	3.000
25	Hannover 96	FRG	0	2	0	0	2	0	3	-3	0	0.000	0.000
26	St-Gilloise Union	Bel	0	2	0	0	2	1	5	-4	0	0.000	0.500
27	Nottingham Forest	Eng	0	2	0	0	2	1	7	-6	0	0.000	0.500
28	Strasbourg	Fra	0	2	0	0	2	3	13	-10	0	0.000	1.500
	Total		**124**	**110**	**47**	**16**	**47**	**229**	**229**	**0**	**14**	**1.127**	**4.164**

1961-62

Pos'n	Cnty	Pts	P	W	D	L	F	A	Diff	B	Pts/P	F/P
1	Esp	79	45	29	8	8	117	55	62	13	1.756	2.600
2	Ita	37	26	14	4	8	47	35	12	5	1.423	1.808
3	Yug	28	24	10	5	9	51	41	10	3	1.167	2.125
4	Hun	26	19	11	0	8	52	36	16	4	1.368	2.737
5	Sco	25	20	11	1	8	42	33	9	2	1.250	2.100
6	Eng	25	22	10	2	10	47	41	6	3	1.136	2.136
7	Por	21	17	6	5	6	38	31	7	4	1.235	2.235
8	FRG	21	17	9	1	7	30	30	0	2	1.235	1.765
9	GDR	19	16	6	5	5	35	26	9	2	1.188	2.188
10	Tch	16	12	6	2	4	23	25	-2	2	1.333	1.917
11	Bel	12	10	5	0	5	16	16	0	2	1.200	1.600
12	Sui	9	9	4	1	4	22	22	0	0	1.000	2.444
13	Ned	7	6	3	1	2	16	10	6	0	1.167	2.667
14	Aut	7	8	2	3	3	12	17	-5	0	0.875	1.500
15	Den	5	8	2	1	5	21	28	-7	0	0.625	2.625
16	Gre	3	6	1	1	4	7	17	-10	0	0.500	1.167
17	Rom	2	4	0	2	2	1	4	-3	0	0.500	0.250
18	Bul	2	4	0	2	2	7	11	-4	0	0.500	1.750
19	Pol	2	2	1	0	1	5	10	-5	0	1.000	2.500
20	Fra	2	8	1	0	7	16	33	-17	0	0.250	2.000
21	Wal	1	2	0	1	1	3	7	-4	0	0.500	1.500
22	Lux	1	4	0	1	3	4	24	-20	0	0.250	1.000
23	Tur	0	2	0	0	2	1	3	-2	0	0.000	0.500
24	Nor	0	2	0	0	2	1	4	-3	0	0.000	0.500
25	Fin	0	2	0	0	2	1	7	-6	0	0.000	0.500
26	Nir	0	3	0	0	3	2	10	-8	0	0.000	0.667
27	Swe	0	2	0	0	2	2	11	-9	0	0.000	1.000
28	Irl	0	4	0	0	4	2	17	-15	0	0.000	0.500
29	Mlt	0	4	0	0	4	5	22	-17	0	0.000	1.250
	Total	**350**	**308**	**131**	**46**	**131**	**626**	**626**	**0**	**42**	**1.136**	**4.065**

1955-56 to 1961-62

1	Esp	249	143	90	26	27	384	190	194	43	1.741	2.685
2	Ita	132	91	46	18	27	198	132	66	22	1.451	2.176
3	Eng	123	89	44	15	30	188	147	41	20	1.382	2.112
4	Yug	81	71	27	15	29	140	125	15	12	1.141	1.972
5	FRG	79	69	29	11	29	136	150	-14	10	1.145	1.971
6	Sco	71	59	27	7	25	118	113	5	10	1.203	2.000
7	Hun	60	49	24	5	20	121	97	24	7	1.224	2.469
8	Fra	57	48	22	5	21	106	100	6	8	1.188	2.208
9	Por	45	38	15	8	15	82	72	10	7	1.184	2.158
10	GDR	44	43	16	9	18	82	79	3	3	1.023	1.907
11	Aut	44	41	15	9	17	70	75	-5	5	1.073	1.707
12	Tch	41	34	15	7	12	48	53	-5	4	1.206	1.412
13	Sui	40	46	14	8	24	87	124	-37	4	0.870	1.891
14	Bel	29	34	11	2	21	51	81	-30	5	0.853	1.500
15	Den	28	35	9	8	18	68	90	-22	2	0.800	1.943
16	Ned	23	24	9	3	12	46	50	-4	2	0.958	1.917
17	Swe	23	26	8	5	13	39	48	-9	2	0.885	1.500
18	Bul	15	19	5	4	10	35	44	-9	1	0.789	1.842
19	Pol	12	15	5	2	8	16	38	-22	0	0.800	1.067
20	Rom	11	16	4	3	9	20	35	-15	0	0.688	1.250
21	Tur	10	13	4	2	7	14	25	-11	0	0.769	1.077
22	Lux	7	18	3	1	14	22	82	-60	0	0.389	1.222
23	Gre	5	10	1	3	6	10	23	-13	0	0.500	1.000
24	Nor	3	6	1	1	4	5	11	-6	0	0.500	0.833
25	Nir	3	9	1	1	7	8	30	-22	0	0.333	0.889
26	Wal	1	2	0	1	1	3	7	-4	0	0.500	1.500
27	Irl	1	12	0	1	11	10	53	-43	0	0.083	0.833
28	Fin	0	6	0	0	6	3	19	-16	0	0.000	0.500
29	Mlt	0	4	0	0	4	5	22	-17	0	0.000	1.250
	Total	**1237**	**1070**	**445**	**180**	**445**	**2115**	**2115**	**0**	**167**	**1.156**	**3.953**

1961-62

Pos'n	Cnty	Ave	Pts	P	W	D	L	F	A	Diff	B	No./T
1	Spain	15.800	79	45	29	8	8	117	55	62	13	5
2	Hungary	8.667	26	19	11	0	8	52	36	16	4	3
3	Italy	7.400	37	26	14	4	8	47	35	12	5	5
4	E. Germany	6.333	19	16	6	5	5	35	26	9	2	3
5	Scotland	6.250	25	20	11	1	8	42	33	9	2	4
6	Belgium	6.000	12	10	5	0	5	16	16	0	2	2
7	Yugoslavia	5.600	28	24	10	5	9	51	41	10	3	5
8	Czechoslovakia	5.333	16	12	6	2	4	23	25	-2	2	3
9	Portugal	5.250	21	17	6	5	6	38	31	7	4	4
10	England	5.000	25	22	10	2	10	47	41	6	3	5
11	W. Germany	4.200	21	17	9	1	7	30	30	0	2	5
12	Austria	3.500	7	8	2	3	3	12	17	-5	0	2
–	Netherlands	3.500	7	6	3	1	2	16	10	6	0	2
14	Switzerland	2.250	9	9	4	1	4	22	22	0	0	4
15	Poland	2.000	2	2	1	0	1	5	10	-5	0	1
16	Denmark	1.667	5	8	2	1	5	21	28	-7	0	3
17	Bulgaria	1.000	2	4	0	2	2	7	11	-4	0	2
–	Wales	1.000	1	2	0	1	1	3	7	-4	0	1
–	Greece	1.000	3	6	1	1	4	7	17	-10	0	3
–	Romania	1.000	2	4	0	2	2	1	4	-3	0	2
21	France	0.500	2	8	1	0	7	16	33	-17	0	4
–	Luxembourg	0.500	1	4	0	1	3	4	24	-20	0	2
23	Rep. of Ireland	0.000	0	4	0	0	4	2	17	-15	0	2
–	Finland	0.000	0	2	0	0	2	1	7	-6	0	1
–	N. Ireland	0.000	0	3	0	0	3	2	10	-8	0	2
–	Malta	0.000	0	4	0	0	4	5	22	-17	0	2
–	Norway	0.000	0	2	0	0	2	1	4	-3	0	1
–	Sweden	0.000	0	2	0	0	2	2	11	-9	0	1
–	Turkey	0.000	0	2	0	0	2	1	3	-2	0	1
	Total		**350**	**308**	**131**	**46**	**131**	**626**	**626**	**0**	**42**	**4.065**

1955-56 to 1961-62

Pos'n	Cnty	Ave	Pts	P	W	D	L	F	A	Diff	B	No./T
1	Spain	13.105	249	143	90	26	27	384	190	194	43	19
2	Italy	7.764	132	91	46	18	27	198	132	66	22	17
3	England	7.687	123	89	44	15	30	188	147	41	20	16
4	Scotland	5.916	71	59	27	7	25	118	113	5	10	12
5	Hungary	5.000	60	49	24	5	20	121	97	24	7	12
6	Austria	4.888	44	41	15	9	17	70	75	-5	5	9
7	Yugoslavia	4.764	81	71	27	15	29	140	125	15	12	17
8	France	4.750	57	48	22	5	21	106	100	6	8	12
9	Czechoslovakia	4.555	41	34	15	7	12	48	53	-5	4	9
10	Portugal	4.500	45	38	15	8	15	82	72	10	7	10
11	W. Germany	4.388	79	69	29	11	29	136	150	-14	10	18
12	E. Germany	4.000	44	43	16	9	18	82	79	3	3	11
13	Sweden	3.285	23	26	8	5	13	39	48	-9	2	7
14	Belgium	2.900	29	34	11	2	21	51	81	-30	5	10
15	Netherlands	2.875	23	24	9	3	12	46	50	-4	2	8
16	Switzerland	2.500	40	46	14	8	24	87	124	-37	4	16
17	Denmark	2.333	28	35	9	8	18	68	90	-22	2	12
18	Bulgaria	2.142	15	19	5	4	10	35	44	-9	1	7
19	Turkey	2.000	10	13	4	2	7	14	25	-11	0	5
20	Romania	1.833	11	16	4	3	9	20	35	-15	0	6
21	Poland	1.714	12	15	5	2	8	16	38	-22	0	7
22	Norway	1.500	3	6	1	1	4	5	11	-6	0	2
23	Wales	1.000	1	2	0	1	1	3	7	-4	0	1
–	Greece	1.000	5	10	1	3	6	10	23	-13	0	5
–	Luxembourg	1.000	7	18	3	1	14	22	82	-60	0	7
26	N. Ireland	0.600	3	9	1	1	7	8	30	-22	0	5
27	Rep. of Ireland	0.166	1	12	0	1	11	10	53	-43	0	6
28	Finland	0.000	0	6	0	0	6	3	19	-16	0	3
–	Malta	0.000	0	4	0	0	4	5	22	-17	0	2
	Total		**1237**	**1070**	**445**	**180**	**445**	**2115**	**2115**	**0**	**167**	**3.953**

Best Final Ever

Benfica had an exciting new talent to add to their squad for the Champions' Cup defence – Eusébio, the prodigious teenager from Mozambique, later to become a star of the 1966 World Cup, where he finished as the tournament's leading goalscorer. He it was who made the difference in the final against Real Madrid in Amsterdam, scoring two second-half goals to give Benfica a memorable 5-3 victory.

There were 29 teams competing in the Champions' Cup now. And with the arrival of some of the smaller nations came some ridiculous scorelines, such as Odense's 15-2 aggregate victory (6-0, 9-2) over Spora Luxembourg, particularly remarkable considering that in the next round the Danish club were hammered 12-0 over two legs by Real Madrid! Tottenham Hotspur, too, hit the headlines in the preliminary round by thrashing Górnik Zabrze of Poland 8-1 at White Hart Lane – this after losing the away leg 4-2.

Tottenham came into the tournament as the first winners of the English Cup and League double this century and, as such, were expected to go far in the tournament. They did in fact make it into the semi-finals, after further wins over Feyenoord and Dukla Prague, but that was where their run came to a halt. Benfica narrowly beat them, 4-3 over two legs, to deprive England of a first ever representative in the Champions' Cup final. Real Madrid were obliged to play in the preliminary round for the first time since the inaugural tournament in 1955-56, but, with Di Stéfano, Puskás and Gento, amongst others, still going strong in their side, they were still a force to be reckoned with – as Odense discovered to their cost in the first round proper! Juventus proved a decidedly tougher obstacle in the quarter-finals. Real actually won the first leg in Turin with a single Di Stéfano goal, but lost the return by the same 0-1 scoreline in the Chamartin – their first home defeat in Europe. A play-off in Paris saw Real emerge 3-1 winners and they cantered through their next tie against Standard Liège to reach their sixth final in seven seasons.

Amsterdam's Olympic stadium was the setting for what many experts still describe as the best Champions' Cup final ever played. The 1960 final had offered breathtaking football and plenty of goals, but it had been one-sided. This final offered two great teams at the peak of their game – Germano, Coluna, Aguas and Eusébio on the one side, Di Stéfano, Puskás, Santamaria and Del Sol on the other – and the outcome was always unpredictable.

Puskás it was who grabbed the initiative early on, putting Real 2-0 up and then completing his hat-trick after Benfica had equalised through Aguas and Cavem. But as Real's ageing limbs creaked in the second half, Coluna brought the scores level to 3-3 and the sprightly youngster Eusébio took centre stage to hit Benfica's fourth and fifth goals and seal the victory. The final score was 5-3 and Benfica had retained their trophy and Real, for the first time, had ended a Champions' Cup final on the losing side.

The other two European trophies did, however, end up in Spanish hands. Real's city rivals, Atlético Madrid, won the Cup-winners' Cup, whilst Valencia, in their first season of European competition, took the Fairs' Cup.

Interestingly, both teams went through their respective competitions undefeated. Atlético accounted for Sedan, Leicester City, Werder Bremen and Carl Zeiss Jena before overcoming Cup holders Fiorentina in the final. Unlike the previous year, the Cup-winners' Cup final was played as a single one-off match at a neutral venue. But as that game, in Glasgow, ended up 1-1 after extra time, a second match was needed anyway. In Stuttgart, Atlético easily defeated their Italian opponents 3-0 with goals from Jones, Mendonca and Peiro.

As for Valencia, they established a new European record by going through their first nine games unbeaten. It should have been ten, but Lausanne, their second-round opponents, withdrew after losing their home leg 3-4. Valencia's finest hour came in the final against fellow Spaniards Barcelona, themselves chasing a third Fairs' Cup win in four attempts. They destroyed the Catalans 6-2 in the home leg and held out comfortably for a 1-1 draw in the return.

1962 – 1963

AC Milan

Tottenham Hotspur

Valencia

First Round

Team 1	Cnty	Team 2	Cnty	1st leg	2nd leg	Agg
Austria Vienna	Aut	HIFK Helsinki	Fin	5-3	2-0	7-3
CSKA Sofia	Bul	Partizan Belgrade	Yug	2-1	4-1	6-2
Dundee	Sco	Cologne	FRG	8-1	0-4	8-5
Shelbourne	Irl	Sporting Lisbon	Por	0-2	1-5	1-7
Real Madrid	Esp	Anderlecht	Bel	3-3	0-1	3-4
Linfield	Nir	Esbjerg FB	Den	1-2	0-0	1-2
AC Milan	Ita	Union Luxembourg	Lux	8-0	6-0	14-0
Floriana	Mlt	Ipswich Town	Eng	1-4	0-10	1-14
Fredrikstad FK	Nor	Vasas SC	Hun	1-4	0-7	1-11
Polonia Bytom	Pol	Panathinaikos	Gre	2-1	4-1	6-2
Dinamo Bucharest	Rom	Galatasaray	Tur	1-1	0-3	1-4
IFK Norrköping	Swe	Partizani Tirana	Alb	2-0	1-1	3-1
Servette	Sui	Feyenoord	Ned	1-3	3-1	5-7
		Feyenoord won the replay 1-3				
Vorwärts Frankfurt/Oder	GDR	Dukla Prague	Tch	0-3	0-1	0-4

	Pts	P	W	D	L	F	A	Diff	Goals/P
Total	58	29	25	8	25	123	123	0	4.241

Second Round

Team 1	Cnty	Team 2	Cnty	1st leg	2nd leg	Agg
Austria Vienna	Aut	Stade Reims	Fra	3-2	0-5	3-7
CSKA Sofia	Bul	Anderlecht	Bel	2-2	0-2	2-4
Esbjerg FB	Den	Dukla Prague	Tch	0-0	0-5	0-5
AC Milan	Ita	Ipswich Town	Eng	3-0	1-2	4-2
Feyenoord	Ned	Vasas SC	Hun	1-1	2-2	4-3
		Feyenoord won the replay 1-0				
Sporting Lisbon	Por	Dundee	Sco	1-0	1-4	2-4
IFK Norrköping	Swe	Benfica	Por	1-1	1-5	2-6
Galatasaray	Tur	Polonia Bytom	Pol	4-1	1-0	5-1

	Pts	P	W	D	L	F	A	Diff	Goals/P
Total	34	17	12	10	12	54	54	0	3.176

Quarter Finals

Team 1	Cnty	Team 2	Cnty	1st leg	2nd leg	Agg
Anderlecht	Bel	Dundee	Sco	1-4	1-2	2-6
Stade Reims	Fra	Feyenoord	Ned	0-1	1-1	1-2
Benfica	Por	Dukla Prague	Tch	2-1	0-0	2-1
Galatasaray	Tur	AC Milan	Ita	1-3	0-5	1-8

	Pts	P	W	D	L	F	A	Diff	Goals/P
Total	16	8	6	4	6	23	23	0	2.875

Semi Finals

Team 1	Cnty	Team 2	Cnty	1st leg	2nd leg	Agg
AC Milan	Ita	Dundee	Sco	5-1	0-1	5-2
Feyenoord	Ned	Benfica	Por	0-0	1-3	1-3

	Pts	P	W	D	L	F	A	Diff	Goals/P
Total	8	4	3	2	3	11	11	0	2.750

European Cup 1962-63

Final

AC Milan	Ita	Benfica	Por	2-1	2-1

	Pts	P	W	D	L	F	A	Diff	Goals/P
Total	2	1	1	0	1	3	3	0	3.000

	Pts	P	W	D	L	F	A	Diff	Goals/P
Total	118	59	47	24	47	214	214	0	3.627

Pos'n	Club	Cnty	Pts	P	W	D	L	F	A	Diff	B	Pts/P	F/P
1	AC Milan	Ita	17	9	7	0	2	33	6	27	3	1.889	3.667
2	Feyenoord	Ned	14	10	4	4	2	14	12	2	2	1.400	1.400
3	Dundee	Sco	12	8	5	0	3	20	14	6	2	1 500	2.500
4	Benfica	Por	12	7	3	3	1	12	6	6	3	1.714	1.714
5	Dukla Prague	Tch	9	6	3	2	1	10	2	8	1	1.500	1.667
6	Galatasaray	Tur	8	6	3	1	2	10	10	0	1	1.333	1.667
7	Anderlecht	Bel	7	6	2	2	2	10	11	-1	1	1.167	1.667
8	Ipswich Town	Eng	6	4	3	0	1	16	5	11	0	1.500	4.000
9	Vasas SC	Hun	6	5	2	2	1	14	5	9	0	1.200	2.800
10	Sporting Lisbon	Por	6	4	3	0	1	9	5	4	0	1.500	2.250
11	Austria Vienna	Aut	6	4	3	0	1	10	10	0	0	1.500	2.500
12	CSKA Sofia	Bul	5	4	2	1	1	8	6	2	0	1.250	2.000
13	Stade Reims	Fra	4	4	1	1	2	8	5	3	1	1.000	2.000
14	Polonia Bytom	Pol	4	4	2	0	2	7	7	0	0	1.000	1.750
15	IFK Norrköping	Swe	4	4	1	2	1	5	7	-2	0	1.000	1.250
16	Esbjerg FB	Den	4	4	1	2	1	2	6	-4	0	1.000	0.500
17	Servette	Sui	2	3	1	0	2	5	7	-2	0	0.667	1.667
18	Cologne	FRG	2	2	1	0	1	5	8	-3	0	1.000	2.500
19	Real Madrid	Esp	1	2	0	1	1	3	4	-1	0	0.500	1.500
20	Linfield	Nir	1	2	0	1	1	1	2	-1	0	0.500	0.500
21	Tirana Partizan	Alb	1	2	0	1	1	1	3	-2	0	0.500	0.500
22	Bucarest Dinano	Rom	1	2	0	1	1	1	4	-3	0	0.500	0.500
23	HIFK Helsinki	Fin	0	2	0	0	2	3	7	-4	0	0.000	1.500
24	Panathinaikos	Gre	0	2	0	0	2	2	6	-4	0	0.000	1.000
–	Partizan Belgrade	Yug	0	2	0	0	2	2	6	-4	0	0.000	1.000
26	Vorwärts Frankfurt/Oder	GDR	0	2	0	0	2	0	4	-4	0	0.000	0.000
27	Shelbourne	Irl	0	2	0	0	2	1	7	-6	0	0.000	0.500
28	Fredrikstad FK	Nor	0	2	0	0	2	1	11	-10	0	0.000	0.500
29	Floriana	Mlt	0	2	0	0	2	1	14	-13	0	0.000	0.500
30	Union Luxembourg	Lux	0	2	0	0	2	0	14	-14	0	0.000	0.000
	Total		**132**	**118**	**47**	**24**	**47**	**214**	**214**	**0**	**14**	**1.119**	**3.627**

First Round

Team 1	Cnty	Team 2	Cnty	1st leg	2nd leg	Agg
Rangers	Sco	Seville	Esp	4-0	0-2	4-2
Saint-Etienne	Fra	Vitória Setúbal	Por	1-1	3-0	4-1
Bangor City	Wal	Napoli	Ita	2-0	1-3	4-5
		Napoli won the replay 1-2				
Ujpesti Dózsa	Hun	Zaglebie Sosnowiec	Pol	5-0	0-0	5-0
Alliance Dudelange	Lux	B 1909 Odense	Den	1-1	1-8	2-9
Steaua Bucharest	Rom	Trakia Plovdiv	Bul	3-2	1-5	4-7
Lausanne-Sports	Sui	Sparta Rotterdam	Ned	3-0	2-4	5-4
OFK Belgrade	Yug	Chemie Halle	GDR	2-0	3-3	5-3

	Pts	P	W	D	L	F	A	Diff	Goals/P
Total	34	17	13	8	13	64	64	0	3.765

Second Round

Team 1	Cnty	Team 2	Cnty	1st leg	2nd leg	Agg
Tottenham Hotspur	Eng	Rangers	Sco	5-2	3-2	8-4
Grazer AK	Aut	B 1909 Odense	Den	1-1	3-5	4-6
Shamrock Rovers	Irl	Trakia Plovdiv	Bul	0-4	0-1	0- 5
Atlético Madrid	Esp	Hibernians	Mlt	4-0	1-0	5-0
Saint-Etienne	Fra	Nuremberg	FRG	0-0	0-3	0-3
Ujpesti Dózsa	Hun	Napoli	Ita	1-1	1-1	3-5
		Napoli won the replay 1-3				
Lausanne-Sports	Sui	Slovan Bratislava	Tch	1-1	0-1	1-2
OFK Belgrade	Yug	Portadown	Nir	5-1	2-3	7-4

	Pts	P	W	D	L	F	A	Diff	Goals/P
Total	34	17	12	10	12	57	57	0	3.353

Quarter Finals

Team 1	Cnty	Team 2	Cnty	1st leg	2nd leg	Agg
Trakia Plovdiv	Bul	Atlético Madrid	Esp	1-1	0-4	1-5
B 1909 Odense	Den	Nuremberg	FRG	0-1	0-6	0- 7
Slovan Bratislava	Tch	Tottenham Hotspur	Eng	2-0	0-6	2-6
OFK Belgrade	Yug	Napoli	Ita	2-0	1-3	6-4
		OFK Belgrade won the replay 3-1				

	Pts	P	W	D	L	F	A	Diff	Goals/P
Total	18	9	8	2	8	31	31	0	3.444

Semi Finals

Team 1	Cnty	Team 2	Cnty	1st leg	2nd leg	Agg
Nuremberg	FRG	Atlético Madrid	Esp	2-1	0-2	2-3
OFK Belgrade	Yug	Tottenham Hotspur	Eng	1-2	1-3	2-5

	Pts	P	W	D	L	F	A	Diff	Goals/P
Total	8	4	4	0	4	12	12	0	3.000

Final

Tottenham Hotspur	Eng	Atlético Madrid	Esp	5-1	5-1

	Pts	P	W	D	L	F	A	Diff	Goals/P
Total	2	1	1	0	1	6	6	0	6.000

	Pts	P	W	D	L	F	A	Diff	Goals/P
Total	96	48	38	20	38	170	170	0	3.542

Pos'n	Club	Cnty	Pts	P	W	D	L	F	A	Diff	B	Pts/P	F/P
1	Tottenham Hotspur	Eng	15	7	6	0	1	24	9	15	3	2.143	3.429
2	Atlético Madrid	Esp	12	7	4	1	2	14	8	6	3	1.714	2.000
3	Nuremberg	FRG	11	6	4	1	1	12	3	9	2	1.833	2.000
4	Belgrade OFK	Yug	11	9	4	1	4	20	16	4	2	1.222	2.222
5	Napoli	Ita	11	9	4	2	3	14	13	1	1	1.222	1.556
6	Trakia Plovdiv	Bul	8	6	3	1	2	13	9	4	1	1.333	2.167
7	B 1909 Odense	Den	7	6	2	2	2	15	13	2	1	1.167	2.500
8	Slovan Bratislava	Tch	6	4	2	1	1	4	7	-3	1	1.500	1.000
9	Ujpesti Dózsa	Hun	5	5	1	3	1	8	5	3	0	1.000	1.600
10	Saint-Etienne	Fra	4	4	1	2	1	4	4	0	0	1.000	1.000
11	Lausanne-Sports	Sui	3	4	1	1	2	6	6	0	0	0.750	1.500
12	Bangor City	Wal	2	3	1	0	2	4	5	-1	0	0.667	1.333
-	Sparta Rotterdam	Ned	2	2	1	0	1	4	5	-1	0	1.000	2.000
14	Rangers	Sco	2	4	1	0	3	8	10	-2	0	0.500	2.000
15	Seville	Esp	2	2	1	0	1	2	4	-2	0	1.000	1.000
16	Portadown	Nir	2	2	1	0	1	4	7	-3	0	1.000	2.000
-	Steaua Bucharest	Rom	2	2	1	0	1	4	7	-3	0	1.000	2.000
18	Grazer AK	Aut	1	2	0	1	1	4	6	-2	0	0.500	2.000
19	Chemie Halle	GDR	1	2	0	1	1	3	5	-2	0	0.500	1.500
20	Vitória Setúbal	Por	1	2	0	1	1	1	4	-3	0	0.500	0.500
21	Zaglebie Sosnowiec	Pol	1	2	0	1	1	0	5	-5	0	0.500	0.000
22	Alliance Dudelange	Lux	1	2	0	1	1	2	9	-7	0	0.500	1.000
23	Shamrock Rovers	Irl	0	2	0	0	2	0	5	-5	0	0.000	0.000
	Hibernians	Mlt	0	2	0	0	2	0	5	-5	0	0.000	0.000
	Total		**110**	**96**	**38**	**20**	**38**	**170**	**170**	**0**	**14**	**1.146**	**3.542**

First Round

Team 1	Cnty	Team 2	Cnty	1st leg	2nd leg	Agg
Everton	Eng	Dunfermline Athletic	Sco	1-0	0-2	1-2
Rapid Vienna	Aut	Red Star Belgrade	Yug	1-1	0-1	1-2
Hibernian	Sco	KB Copenhagen	Den	4-0	3-2	7-2
Drumcondra	Irl	B 1913 Odense	Den	4-1	2-4	6-5
Barcelona	Esp	Belenenses	Por	1-1	1-1	5-4
		Barcelona won the replay 3-2				
Valencia	Esp	Celtic	Sco	4-2	2-2	6-4
Olympique Marseille	Fra	Union St-Gilloise	Bel	1-0	2-4	3-4
Glentoran	Nir	Real Zaragoza	Esp	0-2	2-6	2-8
Sampdoria	Ita	Aris Bonnevoie	Lux	1-0	2-0	3-0
Utrecht	Ned	Tasmania Berlin	FRG	3-2	2-1	5-3
FC Porto	Por	Dinamo Zagreb	Yug	1-2	0-0	1-2
Viktoria Cologne	FRG	Ferencváros	Hun	4-3	1-4	5-7
Bayern Munich	FRG	FC Basle	Sui	3-0		3-0
Petrolul Ploiesti	Rom	Zbrojovka Brno	Tch	4-0	1-0	5-0
Altay	Tur	Roma	Ita	2-3	1-10	3-13
Vojvodina Novi Sad	Yug	Lokomotive Leipzig	GDR	1-0	0-2	1-2

	Pts	P	W	D	L	F	A	Diff	Goals/P
Total	64	32	27	10	27	115	115	0	3.594

Second Round

Real Zaragoza	Esp	Roma	Ita	2-4	1-2	3-6
Valencia	Esp	Dunfermline Athletic	Sco	4-0	2-6	7-6
		Valencia won the replay 1-0				
Sampdoria	Ita	Ferencváros	Hun	1-0	0-6	1-6
Utrecht	Ned	Hibernian	Sco	0-1	1-2	1-3
Bayern Munich	FRG	Drumcondra	Irl	6-0	0-1	6-1
Petrolul Ploiesti	Rom	Lokomotive Leipzig	GDR	1-0	0-1	2-1
		Petrolul Ploiesti won the replay 1-0				
Red Star Belgrade	Yug	Barcelona	Esp	3-2	0-1	4-3
		Red Star Belgrade won the replay 1-0				
Dinamo Zagreb	Yug	Union St-Gilloise	Bel	2-1	0-1	5-4
		Dinamo Zagreb won the replay 3-2				

	Pts	P	W	D	L	F	A	Diff	Goals/P
Total	40	20	20	0	20	59	59	0	2.950

Quarter Finals

Valencia	Esp	Hibernian	Sco	5-0	1-2	6-2
Ferencváros	Hun	Petrolul Ploiesti	Rom	2-0	0-1	2-1
Roma	Ita	Red Star Belgrade	Yug	3-0	0-2	3-2
Dinamo Zagreb	Yug	Bayern Munich	FRG	4-1	0-0	4-1

	Pts	P	W	D	L	F	A	Diff	Goals/P
Total	16	8	7	2	7	21	21	0	2.625

UEFA Cup 1962-63

Semi Finals

Valencia	Esp	Roma	Ita	3-0	0-1	3-1
Dinamo Zagreb	Yug	Ferencváros	Hun	2-1	1-0	3-1

	Pts	P	W	D	L	F	A	Diff	Goals/P
Total	8	4	4	0	4	8	8	0	2.000

Final

Valencia	Esp	Dinamo Zagreb	Yug	2-0	2-1	4-1

	Pts	P	W	D	L	F	A	Diff	Goals/P
Total	4	2	2	0	2	5	5	0	2.500

	Pts	P	W	D	L	F	A	Diff	Goals/P
Total	132	66	60	12	60	208	208	0	3.152

Pos'n	**Club**	**Cnty**	**Pts**	**P**	**W**	**D**	**L**	**F**	**A**	**Diff**	**B**	**Pts/P**	**F/P**
1	Valencia	Esp	18	11	7	1	3	26	14	12	3	1.636	2.364
2	Dinamo Zagreb	Yug	17	11	6	2	3	15	11	4	3	1.545	1.364
3	Roma	Ita	14	8	6	0	2	23	11	12	2	1.750	2.875
4	Petrolul Ploiesti	Rom	11	7	5	0	2	8	3	5	1	1.571	1.143
5	Hibernian	Sco	11	6	5	0	1	12	9	3	1	1.833	2.000
6	Red Star Belgrade	Yug	10	7	4	1	2	8	7	1	1	1.429	1.143
7	Ferencváros	Hun	8	8	3	0	5	16	10	6	2	1.000	2.000
8	Bayern Munich	FRG	6	5	2	1	2	10	5	5	1	1.200	2.000
9	Barcelona	Esp	6	6	2	2	2	8	8	0	0	1.000	1.333
10	Sampdoria	Ita	6	4	3	0	1	4	6	-2	0	1.500	1.000
11	Real Zaragoza	Esp	4	4	2	0	2	11	8	3	0	1.000	2.750
12	St-Gilloise Union	Bel	4	5	2	0	3	8	8	0	0	0.800	1.600
–	Dunfermline Athletic	Sco	4	5	2	0	3	8	8	0	0	0.800	1.600
14	Utrecht	Ned	4	4	2	0	2	6	6	0	0	1.000	1.500
15	Lokomotive Leipzig	GDR	4	5	2	0	3	3	3	0	0	0.800	0.600
16	Drumcondra	Irl	4	4	2	0	2	7	11	-4	0	1.000	1.750
17	B 1913 Odense	Den	2	2	1	0	1	5	6	-1	0	1.000	2.500
18	Belenenses	Por	2	3	0	2	1	4	5	-1	0	0.667	1.333
19	Olympique Marseille	Fra	2	2	1	0	1	3	4	-1	0	1.000	1.500
20	Everton	Eng	2	2	1	0	1	1	2	-1	0	1.000	0.500
–	Vojvodina Novi Sad	Yug	2	2	1	0	1	1	2	-1	0	1.000	0.500
22	Viktoria Cologne	FRG	2	2	1	0	1	5	7	-2	0	1.000	2.500
23	Rapid Vienna	Aut	1	2	0	1	1	1	2	-1	0	0.500	0.500
–	FC Porto	Por	1	2	0	1	1	1	2	-1	0	0.500	0.500
25	Celtic	Sco	1	2	0	1	1	4	6	-2	0	0.500	2.000
26	Tasmania Berlin	FRG	0	2	0	0	2	3	5	-2	0	0.000	1.500
27	Aris Bonnevoie	Lux	0	2	0	0	2	0	3	-3	0	0.000	0.000
–	FC Basle	Sui	0	1	0	0	1	0	3	-3	0	0.000	0.000
29	KB Copenhagen	Den	0	2	0	0	2	2	7	-5	0	0.000	1.000
30	Zbrojovka Brno	Tch	0	2	0	0	2	0	5	-5	0	0.000	0.000
31	Glentoran	Nir	0	2	0	0	2	2	8	-6	0	0.000	1.000
32	Altay	Tur	0	2	0	0	2	3	13	-10	0	0.000	1.500
	Total		**146**	**132**	**60**	**12**	**60**	**208**	**208**	**0**	**14**	**1.106**	**3.152**

1962-63

Pos'n	Cnty	Pts	P	W	D	L	F	A	Diff	B	Pts/P	F/P
1	Ita	48	30	20	2	8	74	36	38	6	1.600	2.467
2	Esp	43	32	16	5	11	64	46	18	6	1.344	2.000
3	Yug	40	31	15	4	12	46	42	4	6	1.290	1.484
4	Sco	30	25	13	1	11	52	47	5	3	1.200	2.080
5	Eng	23	13	10	0	3	41	16	25	3	1.769	3.154
6	Por	22	18	6	7	5	27	22	5	3	1.222	1.500
7	FRG	21	17	8	2	7	35	28	7	3	1.235	2.059
8	Ned	20	16	7	4	5	24	23	1	2	1.250	1.500
9	Hun	19	18	6	5	7	38	20	18	2	1.056	2.111
10	Tch	15	12	5	3	4	14	14	0	2	1.250	1.167
11	Rom	14	11	6	1	4	13	14	-1	1	1.273	1.182
12	Bul	13	10	5	2	3	21	15	6	1	1.300	2.100
13	Den	13	14	4	4	6	24	32	-8	1	0.929	1.714
14	Bel	11	11	4	2	5	18	19	-1	1	1.000	1.636
15	Fra	10	10	3	3	4	15	13	2	1	1.000	1.500
16	Aut	8	8	3	2	3	15	18	-3	0	1.000	1.875
17	Tur	8	8	3	1	4	13	23	-10	1	1.000	1.625
18	Sui	5	8	2	1	5	11	16	-5	0	0.625	1.375
19	Pol	5	6	2	1	3	7	12	-5	0	0.833	1.167
20	GDR	5	9	2	1	6	6	12	-6	0	0.556	0.667
21	Swe	4	4	1	2	1	5	7	-2	0	1.000	1.250
22	Irl	4	8	2	0	6	8	23	-15	0	0.500	1.000
23	Nir	3	6	1	1	4	7	17	-10	0	0.500	1.167
24	Wal	2	3	1	0	2	4	5	-1	0	0.667	1.333
25	Alb	1	2	0	1	1	1	3	-2	0	0.500	0.500
26	Lux	1	6	0	1	5	2	26	-24	0	0.167	0.333
27	Fin	0	2	0	0	2	3	7	-4	0	0.000	1.500
28	Gre	0	2	0	0	2	2	6	-4	0	0.000	1.000
29	Nor	0	2	0	0	2	1	11	-10	0	0.000	0 500
30	Mal	0	4	0	0	4	1	19	-18	0	0.000	0.250
	Total	**388**	**346**	**145**	**56**	**145**	**592**	**592**	**0**	**42**	**1.121**	**3.422**

1955-56 to 1962-63

1	Esp	292	175	106	31	38	448	236	212	49	1.669	2.560
2	Ita	180	121	66	20	35	272	168	104	28	1.488	2.248
3	Eng	146	102	54	15	33	229	163	66	23	1.431	2.245
4	Yug	121	102	42	19	41	186	167	19	18	1.186	1.824
5	Sco	101	84	40	8	36	170	160	10	13	1.202	2.024
6	FRG	100	86	37	13	36	171	178	-7	13	1.163	1.988
7	Hun	79	67	30	10	27	159	117	42	9	1.179	2.373
8	Por	67	56	21	15	20	109	94	15	10	1.196	1.946
9	Fra	67	58	25	8	25	121	113	8	9	1.155	2.086
10	Tch	56	46	20	10	16	62	67	-5	6	1.217	1.348
11	Aut	52	49	18	11	20	85	93	-8	5	1.061	1.735
12	GDR	49	52	18	10	24	88	91	-3	3	0.942	1.692
13	Sui	45	54	16	9	29	98	140	-42	4	0.833	1.815
14	Ned	43	40	16	7	17	70	73	-3	4	1.075	1.750
15	Den	41	49	13	12	24	92	122	-30	3	0.837	1.878
16	Bel	40	45	15	4	26	69	100	-31	6	0.889	1.533
17	Bul	28	29	10	6	13	56	59	-3	2	0.966	1.931
18	Swe	27	30	9	7	14	44	55	-11	2	0.900	1.467
19	Rom	25	27	10	4	13	33	49	-16	1	0.926	1.222
20	Tur	18	21	7	3	11	27	48	-21	1	0.857	1.286
21	Pol	17	21	7	3	11	23	50	-27	0	0.810	1.095
22	Lux	8	24	3	2	19	24	108	-84	0	0.333	1.000
23	Nir	6	15	2	2	11	15	47	-32	0	0.400	1.000
24	Gre	5	12	1	3	8	12	29	-17	0	0.417	1.000
25	Irl	5	20	2	1	17	18	76	-58	0	0.250	0.900
26	Wal	3	5	1	1	3	7	12	-5	0	0.600	1.400
27	Nor	3	8	1	1	6	6	22	-16	0	0.375	0.750
28	Alb	1	2	0	1	1	1	3	-2	0	0.500	0.500
29	Fin	0	8	0	0	8	6	26	-20	0	0.000	0.750
30	Mlt	0	8	0	0	8	6	41	-35	0	0.000	0.750
	Total	**1625**	**1416**	**590**	**236**	**590**	**2707**	**2707**	**0**	**209**	**1.148**	**3.823**

National Performances by Index

1962-63

Pos'n	Cnty	Ave	Pts	P	W	D	L	F	A	Diff	B	No./T
1	Italie	12.000	48	30	20	2	8	74	36	38	6	4
2	Yugoslavia	8.000	40	31	15	4	12	46	42	4	6	5
3	England	7.667	23	13	10	0	3	41	16	25	3	3
4	Spain	7.167	43	32	16	5	11	64	46	18	6	6
5	Netherlands	6.667	20	16	7	4	5	24	23	1	2	3
6	Bulgaria	6.500	13	10	5	2	3	21	15	6	1	2
7	Hungary	6.333	19	18	6	5	7	38	20	18	2	3
8	Scotland	6.000	30	25	13	1	11	52	47	5	3	5
9	Belgium	5.500	11	11	4	2	5	18	19	-1	1	2
10	Czechoslovakia	5.000	15	12	5	3	4	14	14	0	2	3
11	Romania	4.667	14	11	6	1	4	13	14	-1	1	3
12	Portugal	4.400	22	18	6	7	5	27	22	5	3	5
13	W. Germany	4.200	21	17	8	2	7	35	28	7	3	5
14	Sweden	4.000	4	4	1	2	1	5	7	-2	0	1
–	Turkey	4.000	8	8	3	1	4	13	23	-10	1	2
16	France	3.333	10	10	3	3	4	15	13	2	1	3
17	Denmark	3.250	13	14	4	4	6	24	32	-8	1	4
18	Austria	2.667	8	8	3	2	3	15	18	-3	0	3
19	Poland	2.500	5	6	2	1	3	7	12	-5	0	2
20	Wales	2.000	2	3	1	0	2	4	5	1	0	1
21	Switzerland	1.667	5	8	2	1	5	11	16	-5	0	3
–	E. Germany	1.667	5	9	2	1	6	6	12	6	0	3
23	Rep. of Ireland	1.333	4	8	2	0	6	8	23	-15	0	3
24	Albania	1.000	1	2	0	1	1	1	3	-2	0	1
–	N. Ireland	1.000	3	6	1	1	4	7	17	-10	0	3
26	Luxembourg	0.333	1	6	0	1	5	2	26	-24	0	3
27	Finland	0.000	0	2	0	0	2	3	7	-4	0	1
–	Greece	0.000	0	2	0	0	2	2	6	-4	0	1
–	Malta	0.000	0	4	0	0	4	1	19	-18	0	2
–	Norway	0.000	0	2	0	0	2	1	11	-10	0	1
	Total		**388**	**346**	**145**	**56**	**145**	**592**	**592**	**0**	**42**	**3.422**

1955-56 to 1962-63

Pos'n	Cnty	Ave	Pts	P	W	D	L	F	A	Diff	B	No./T
1	Spain	11.680	292	175	106	31	38	448	236	212	49	25
2	Italy	8.571	180	121	66	20	35	272	168	104	28	21
3	England	7.684	146	102	54	15	33	229	163	66	23	19
4	Scotland	8.941	101	84	40	8	36	170	160	10	13	17
5	Yugoslavia	5.500	121	102	42	19	41	186	167	19	18	22
6	Hungary	5.266	79	67	30	10	27	159	117	42	9	15
7	Czechoslovakia	4.666	56	46	20	10	16	62	67	-5	6	12
8	France	4.466	67	58	25	8	25	121	113	8	9	15
–	Portugal	4.466	67	56	21	15	20	109	94	15	10	15
10	W. Germany	4.347	100	86	37	13	36	171	178	-7	13	23
11	Austria	4.333	52	49	18	11	20	85	93	-8	5	12
12	Netherlands	3.909	43	40	16	7	17	70	73	-3	4	11
13	E. Germany	3.500	49	52	18	10	24	88	91	-3	3	14
14	Sweden	3.375	27	30	9	7	14	44	55	-11	2	8
15	Belgium	3.333	40	45	15	4	26	69	100	-31	6	12
16	Bulgaria	3.111	28	29	10	6	13	56	59	-3	2	9
17	Romania	2.777	25	27	10	4	13	33	49	-16	1	9
18	Turkey	2.571	18	21	7	3	11	27	48	-21	1	7
19	Denmark	2.562	41	49	13	12	24	92	122	-30	3	16
20	Switzerland	2.368	45	54	16	9	29	98	140	-42	4	19
21	Poland	1.888	17	21	7	3	11	23	50	-27	0	9
22	Wales	1.500	3	5	1	1	3	7	12	-5	0	2
23	Albania	1.000	1	2	0	1	1	1	3	-2	0	1
–	Norway	1.000	3	8	1	1	6	6	22	-16	0	3
25	Greece	0.833	5	12	1	3	8	12	29	-17	0	6
26	Luxembourg	0.800	8	24	3	2	19	24	108	-84	0	10
27	N. Ireland	0.750	6	15	2	2	11	15	47	-32	0	8
28	Rep. of Ireland	0.555	5	20	2	1	17	18	76	-58	0	9
29	Finland	0.000	0	8	0	0	8	6	26	-20	0	4
–	Malta	0.000	0	8	0	0	8	6	41	-35	0	4
	Total		**1625**	**1416**	**590**	**236**	**590**	**2707**	**2707**	**0**	**209**	**3.823**

First British Success

All three of the previous season's European Cup winners reached the final of their respective competition again in 1962-63, but only Valencia, in the Fairs' Cup, succeeded in retaining their trophy.

Benfica, aiming to emulate Real Madrid with a hat-trick of Champions' Cup victories, were denied in the Wembley final by AC Milan, who thus became the first Italian winners of the Cup.

The star of the final, and of the whole tournament for that matter, was Milan's Brazilian centre-forward José Altafini. He scored twice in the second half at Wembley, feeding on two excellent passes from Milan's playmaker, Gianni Rivera, to wipe out the lead given to Benfica by Eusébio in the 18th minute and take his total for the competition to a record 14 goals.

Over half of that total came in Milan's opening tie against Union Luxembourg. Altafini scored five times in the 8-0 home leg win and hit a hat-trick in the 6-0 second-leg victory. His eight-goal total for a single tie set a new record for the competition and went one better than Ipswich Town's Ray Crawford who also broke the old record with seven goals in his club's 14-1 aggregate demolition of Maltese side, Floriana.

Curiously enough, Crawford and Altafini came face to face in the following round and although the Englishman scored another goal in that tie to join Altafini on eight goals, it was the Brazilian's team which qualified for the quarter-finals, winning 4-2 on aggregate after a first-leg 3-0 victory in the San Siro.

The biggest surprise of the opening round was Real Madrid's elimination by Anderlecht. Held 3-3 in Madrid, they lost to a single Jef Jurion goal in Brussels, enabling the Belgians to win their first ever Champions' Cup tie at the fourth attempt. Anderlecht progressed to the quarter-finals, but were easily beaten there by Scotland's Dundee, 2-6 on aggregate after losing 1-4 at home!

Like Hibernian, Manchester United, Rangers and Tottenham before them, Dundee were unable to break new ground for a British club and actually reach the final. A 5-1 defeat away to Milan in the first leg of the semi-final left them with too much to do in the return and they went out, along with Dutch club Feyenoord, beaten 3-1 by Benfica over the two legs.

There was, however, a first British success in the Cup-winners' Cup. Tottenham Hotspur, containing such famous names as Greaves, Blanchflower, White, Smith and Dyson, destroyed holders Atlético Madrid 5-1 in the final to become the first English club to capture any of the three European trophies. In doing so, they set two interesting precedents.

Firstly, the venue of their triumph in the final, Rotterdam, was to become an equally happy hunting ground for other English clubs in years to come. Aston Villa won the Champions' Cup there in 1982, and Everton (1985) and Manchester United (1991) followed suit in the Cup-winners' Cup. As yet, no English club has ever lost a one-off final in Rotterdam, although Tottenham did lose there to Feyenoord in the first leg of the UEFA Cup final in 1974.

Secondly, Atlético's failure to hold on to their trophy continued the trend set by Fiorentina the year before – and one which as yet has never been broken. Several clubs have since emulated Atlético and Fiorentina by reaching the Cup-winners' Cup final in defence of their trophy (AC Milan in 1974, Anderlecht in 1977, Ajax in 1988), but none has ever won the Cup back-to-back. This is of course in stark contrast to the Champions' Cup, which has been successfully defended no fewer than 13 times!

Valencia, though, emulated their compatriots of Barcelona and retained the Fairs' Cup, defeating Dinamo Zagreb 4-1 on aggregate in the two-legged final, which, for the first time, had been brought forward to June from its usual autumn scheduling. Valencia eliminated three Scottish clubs on the way to the final, but they did need a play-off victory in the second round against Dunfermline. They had brought the Spanish club's record unbeaten run to an abrupt halt, winning 6-2 at home to cancel out Valencia's 4-0 first leg win.

1963 – 1964

Inter Milan

Sporting Lisbon

Valencia

First Round

Team 1	Cnty	Team 2	Cnty	1st leg	2nd leg	Agg
Partizani Tirana	Alb	Trakia Plovdiv	Bul	1-0	1-3	2-3
Everton	Eng	Inter Milan	Ita	0-0	0-1	0-1
Standard Liège	Bel	IFK Norrköping	Swe	1-0	0-2	1-2
Esbjerg FB	Den	PSV Eindhoven	Ned	3-4	1-7	4-11
Rangers	Sco	Real Madrid	Esp	0-1	0-6	0-7
Dundalk	Irl	FC Zürich	Sui	0-3	2-1	2-4
Haka Valkeakoski	Fin	Jeunesse Esch	Lux	4-1	0-4	4-5
Monaco	Fra	AEK Athens	Gre	7-2	1-1	8-3
Distillery	Nir	Benfica	Por	3-3	0-5	3-8
SFK Lyn	Nor	Borussia Dortmund	FRG	2-4	0-2	2-6
Górnik Zabrze	Pol	Austria Vienna	Aut	1-0	0-1	3-2
		Górnik Zabrze won the replay 2-1				
Dinamo Bucharest	Rom	Carl Zeiss Jena	GDR	2-0	1-0	3-0
Dukla Prague	Tch	Valletta	Mlt	6-0	2-0	8-0
Galatasaray	Tur	Ferencváros	Hun	6-0	0-2	6-2
Partizan Belgrade	Yug	Anorthosis Famagusta	Cyp	3-0	3-1	6-1

	Pts	P	W	D	L	F	A	Diff	Goals/P
Total	62	31	28	6	28	107	107	0	3.452

Second Round

Trakia Plovdiv	Bul	PSV Eindhoven	Ned	0-1	0-0	0-1
Inter Milan	Ita	Monaco	Fra	1-0	3-1	4-1
Jeunesse Esch	Lux	Partizan Belgrade	Yug	2-1	2-6	4-7
Górnik Zabrze	Pol	Dukla Prague	Tch	2-0	1-4	3-4
Benfica	Por	Borussia Dortmund	FRG	2-1	0-6	2-7
Dinamo Bucharest	Rom	Real Madrid	Esp	1-3	3-5	4-8
IFK Norrköping	Swe	AC Milan	Ita	1-1	2-5	3-6
FC Zürich	Sui	Galatasaray	Tur	2-0	0-2	4-4
		The replay resulted in a 2-2 draw				

	Pts	P	W	D	L	F	A	Diff	Goals/P
Total	34	17	14	6	14	62	62	0	3.647

Quarter Finals

Real Madrid	Esp	AC Milan	Ita	4-1	0-2	4-3
PSV Eindhoven	Ned	FC Zürich	Sui	1-0	1-3	2-3
Dukla Prague	Tch	Borussia Dortmund	FRG	0-4	3-1	3-5
Partizan Belgrade	Yug	Inter Milan	Ita	0-2	1-2	1-4

	Pts	P	W	D	L	F	A	Diff	Goals/P
Total	16	8	8	0	8	25	25	0	3.125

Semi Finals

Borussia Dortmund	FRG	Inter Milan	Ita	2-2	0-2	2-4
FC Zürich	Sui	Real Madrid	Esp	1-2	0-6	1-8

	Pts	P	W	D	L	F	A	Diff	Goals/P
Total	8	4	3	2	3	15	15	0	3.750

Final

Inter Milan	Ita	Real Madrid	Esp	3-1	3-1

	Pts	P	W	D	L	F	A	Diff	Goals/P
Total	2	1	1	0	1	4	4	0	4.000

	Pts	P	W	D	L	F	A	Diff	Goals/P
Total	122	61	54	14	54	213	213	0	3.492

Pos'n	Club	Cnty	Pts	P	W	D	L	F	A	Diff	B	Pts/P	F/P
1	Inter Milan	Ita	19	9	7	2	0	16	5	11	3	2.111	1.778
2	Real Madrid	Esp	17	9	7	0	2	28	11	17	3	1.889	3.111
3	Borussia Dortmund	FRG	11	8	4	1	3	20	11	9	2	1.375	2.500
4	PSV Eindhoven	Ned	10	6	4	1	1	14	7	7	1	1.667	2.333
5	Dukla Prague	Tch	9	6	4	0	2	15	8	7	1	1.500	2.500
6	FC Zürich	Sui	9	9	3	1	5	12	16	-4	2	1.000	1.333
7	Partizan Belgrade	Yug	7	6	3	0	3	14	9	5	1	1.167	2.333
8	AC Milan	Ita	6	4	2	1	1	9	7	2	1	1.500	2.250
9	Górnik Zabrze	Pol	6	5	3	0	2	6	6	0	0	1.200	1.200
10	Galatasaray	Tur	5	5	2	1	2	10	6	4	0	1.000	2.000
11	Benfica	Por	5	4	2	1	1	10	10	0	0	1.250	2.500
12	Bucarest Dinamo	Rom	4	4	2	0	2	7	8	-1	0	1.000	1.750
13	Jeunesse Esch	Lux	4	4	2	0	2	9	11	-2	0	1.000	2.250
14	Monaco	Fra	3	4	1	1	2	9	7	2	0	0.750	2.250
15	Trakia Plovdiv	Bul	3	4	1	1	2	3	3	0	0	0.750	0.750
16	IFK Norrköping	Swe	3	4	1	1	2	5	7	-2	0	0.750	1.250
17	Haka Valkeakoski	Fin	2	2	1	0	1	4	5	-1	0	1.000	2.000
18	Tirana Partizan	Alb	2	2	1	0	1	2	3	-1	0	1.000	1.000
–	Austria Vienna	Aut	2	3	1	0	2	2	3	-1	0	0.667	0.667
20	Standard Liège	Bel	2	2	1	0	1	1	2	-1	0	1.000	0.500
21	Dundalk	Irl	2	2	1	0	1	2	4	-2	0	1.000	1.000
22	Ferencváros	Hun	2	2	1	0	1	2	6	-4	0	1.000	1.000
23	Everton	Eng	1	2	0	1	1	0	1	-1	0	0.500	0.000
24	AEK Athens	Gre	1	2	0	1	1	3	8	-5	0	0.500	1.500
–	Distillery	Nir	1	2	0	1	1	3	8	-5	0	0.500	1.500
26	Carl Zeiss Jena	GDR	0	2	0	0	2	0	3	-3	0	0.000	0.000
27	SFK Lyn	Nor	0	2	0	0	2	2	6	-4	0	0.000	1.000
28	Anorthosis Famagusta	Cyp	0	2	0	0	2	1	6	-5	0	0.000	0.500
29	Esbjerg FB	Den	0	2	0	0	2	4	11	-7	0	0.000	2.000
30	Rangers	Sco	0	2	0	0	2	0	7	-7	0	0.000	0.000
31	Valletta	Mlt	0	2	0	0	2	0	8	-8	0	0.000	0.000
	Total		**136**	**122**	**54**	**14**	**54**	**213**	**213**	**0**	**14**	**1.115**	**3.492**

First Round

Team 1	Cnty	Team 2	Cnty	1st leg	2nd leg	Agg
Linzer ASK	Aut	Dinamo Zagreb	Yug	1-0	0-1	2-2
		The replay resulted in a 1-1 draw				
Apoel Nicosia	Cyp	Gjøvik/Lyn	Nor	6-0	0-1	6-1
Shelbourne	Irl	Barcelona	Esp	0-2	1-3	1-5
HPS Helsinki	Fin	Slovan Bratislava	Tch	1-4	1-8	2-12
Olympique Lyon	Fra	B 1913 Odense	Den	3-1	3-1	6-2
Olympiakos Pireus	Gre	Zaglebie Sosnowiec	Pol	2-1	0-1	4-2
		Olympiakos Pireus won the replay 2-0				
MTK-VM	Hun	Slavia Sofia	Bul	1-0	1-1	2-1
Atalanta	Ita	Sporting Lisbon	Por	2-0	1-3	4-6
		Sporting Lisbon won the replay 1-3				
Sliema Wanderers	Mlt	Borough United	Wal	0-0	0-2	0-2
Willem II	Ned	Manchester United	Eng	1-1	1-6	2-7
Hamburg	FRG	Union Luxembourg	Lux	4-0	3-2	7-2
FC Basle	Sui	Celtic	Sco	1-5	0-5	1-10
Fenerbahçe	Tur	Petrolul Ploiesti	Rom	4-1	0-1	4-2

	Pts	P	W	D	L	F	A	Diff	Goals/P
Total	58	29	25	8	25	95	95	0	3.276

Second Round

Tottenham Hotspur	Eng	Manchester United	Eng	2-0	1-4	3-4
Celtic	Sco	Dinamo Zagreb	Yug	3-0	1-2	4-2
Barcelona	Esp	Hamburg	FRG	4-4	0-0	6-7
		Hamburg won the replay 2-3				
Olympique Lyon	Fra	Olympiakos Pireus	Gre	4-1	1-2	5-3
Borough United	Wal	Slovan Bratislava	Tch	0-1	0-3	0-4
Sporting Lisbon	Por	Apoel Nicosia	Cyp	16-1	2-0	18-1
Fenerbahçe	Tur	Linfield	Nir	4-1	0-2	4-3
Sachsenning Zwickau	GDR	MTK-VM	Hun	1-0	0-2	1-2

	Pts	P	W	D	L	F	A	Diff	Goals/P
Total	34	17	15	4	15	67	67	0	3.941

Quarter Finals

Manchester United	Eng	Sporting Lisbon	Por	4-1	0-5	4-6
Celtic	Sco	Slovan Bratislava	Tch	1-0	1-0	2-0
MTK-VM	Hun	Fenerbahçe	Tur	2-0	1-3	4-3
		MTK-VM won the replay 1-0				
Hamburg	FRG	Olympique Lyon	Fra	1-1	0-2	1-3

	Pts	P	W	D	L	F	A	Diff	Goals/P
Total	18	9	8	2	8	23	23	0	2.556

Semi Finals

Celtic	Sco	MTK-VM	Hun	3-0	0-4	3-4
Olympique Lyon	Fra	Sporting Lisbon	Por	0-0	1-1	1-2
		Sporting Lisbon won the replay 0-1				

European Cup Winners Cup 1963-64

	Pts	P	W	D	L	F	A	Diff	Goals/P
Total	10	5	3	4	3	10	10	0	2.000

Final

Sporting Lisbon	Por	MTK-VM	Hun	3-3	1-0	4-3

	Pts	P	W	D	L	F	A	Diff	Goals/P
Total	4	2	1	2	1	7	7	0	3.500

	Pts	P	W	D	L	F	A	Diff	Goals/P
Total	124	62	52	20	52	202	202	0	3.258

Pos'n	Club	Cnty	Pts	P	W	D	L	F	A	Diff	B	Pts/P	F/P
1	Sporting Lisbon	Por	20	12	7	3	2	36	13	23	3	1.667	3.000
2	MTK-VM	Hun	15	11	5	2	4	15	12	3	3	1.364	1.364
3	Celtic	Sco	14	8	6	0	2	19	7	12	2	1.750	2.375
4	Olympique Lyon	Fra	13	9	4	3	2	15	8	7	2	1.444	1.667
5	Hamburg	FRG	10	7	3	3	1	15	11	4	1	1.429	2.143
6	Slovan Bratislava	Tch	9	6	4	0	2	16	4	12	1	1.500	2.667
7	Manchester United	Eng	8	6	3	1	2	15	11	4	1	1.333	2.500
8	Fenerbahçe	Sur	7	7	3	0	4	11	9	2	1	1.000	1.571
9	Barcelona	Esp	6	5	2	2	1	11	8	3	0	1.200	2.200
10	Olympiakos Pireus	Gre	6	5	3	0	2	7	7	0	0	1.200	1.400
11	Dinamo Zagreb	Rom	5	5	2	1	2	4	6	-2	0	1.000	0 800
12	Linzer ASK	Aut	3	3	1	1	1	2	2	0	0	1.000	0.667
13	Borough United	Wal	3	4	1	1	2	2	4	-2	0	0.750	0.500
14	Tottenham Hotspur	Eng	2	2	1	0	1	3	4	-1	0	1.000	1.500
–	Linfield	Nir	2	2	1	0	1	3	4	-1	0	1.000	1.500
16	Sachsenning Zwickau	GDR	2	2	1	0	1	1	2	-1	0	1.000	0.500
17	Atalanta	Ita	2	3	1	0	2	4	6	-2	0	0.667	1.333
18	Zaglebie Sosnowiec	Pol	2	3	1	0	2	2	4	-2	0	0.667	0.667
–	Petrolul Ploiesti	Rom	2	2	1	0	1	2	4	-2	0	1.000	1.000
20	Gjøvik/Lyn	Nor	2	2	1	0	1	1	6	-5	0	1.000	0.500
21	Apoel Nicosia	Cyp	2	4	1	0	3	7	19	-12	0	0.500	1.750
22	Slavia Sofia	Bul	1	2	0	1	1	1	2	-1	0	0.500	0.500
23	Sliema Wanderers	Mlt	1	2	0	1	1	0	2	-2	0	0.500	0.000
24	Willen II	Ned	1	2	0	1	1	2	7	-5	0	0.500	1.000
25	B 1913 Odense	Den	0	2	0	0	2	2	6	-4	0	0.000	1.000
26	Shelbourne	Irl	0	2	0	0	2	1	5	-4	0	0.000	0.500
27	Union Luxembourg	Lux	0	2	0	0	2	2	7	-5	0	0.000	1.000
28	FC Basle	Sui	0	2	0	0	2	1	10	-9	0	0.000	0.500
29	HPS Helsinki	Fin	0	2	0	0	2	2	12	-10	0	0.000	1.000
	Total		**138**	**121**	**52**	**20**	**52**	**202**	**202**	**0**	**14**	**1.113**	**3.258**

First Round

Team 1	Cnty	Team 2	Cnty	1st leg	2nd leg	Agg
Arsenal	Eng	KB Copenhagen	Den	3-2	7-1	10-3
Rapid Vienna	Aut	Racing Club Paris	Fra	1-0	3-2	4-2
FC Liège	Bel	Aris Bonnevoie	Lux	0-0	2-0	2-0
Lokomotiv Plovdiv	Bul	Red Flag Brasov	Rom	2-1	3-1	5-2
Shamrock Rovers	Irl	Valencia	Esp	0-1	2-2	2- 3
Atlético Madrid	Esp	FC Porto	Por	2-1	0-0	2-1
Real Zaragoza	Esp	Iraklis	Gre	6-1	3-0	9-1
Ujpesti Dózsa	Hun	Lokomotive Leipzig	GDR	3-2	0-0	3-2
Glentoran	Nir	Partick Thistle	Sco	1-4	0-3	1-7
Juventus	Ita	OFK Belgrade	Yug	2-1	1-2	4-3
		Juventus won the replay 1-0				
Utrecht	Ned	Sheffield Wednesday	Eng	1-4	1-4	2-8
Hertha Berlin	FRG	Roma	Ita	1-3	0-1	1-5
Cologne	FRG	Gent	Bel	3-1	1-1	4-2
Lausanne-Sports	Sui	Heart of Midlothian	Sco	2-2	4-4	9-8
		Lausanne-Sports won the replay 3-2				
Zbrojovka Brno	Tch	Servette	Sui	5-0	2-1	7-1
Tresnjevka Zagreb	Yug	Belenenses	Por	0-2	1-2	1-4

	Pts	P	W	D	L	F	A	Diff	Goals/P
Total	68	34	27	14	27	118	118	0	3.471

Second Round

Arsenal	Eng	FC Liège	Bel	1-1	1-3	2-4
Rapid Vienna	Aut	Valencia	Esp	0-0	2-3	2-3
Partick Thistle	Sco	Zbrojovka Brno	Tch	3-2	0-4	3-6
Ujpesti Dózsa	Hun	Lokomotiv Plovdiv	Bul	0-0	3-1	3-1
Roma	Ita	Belenenses	Por	2-1	1-0	3-1
Juventus	Ita	Atlético Madrid	Esp	1-0	2-1	3-1
Cologne	FRG	Sheffield Wednesday	Eng	3-2	2-1	5-3
Lausanne-Sports	Sui	Real Zaragoza	Esp	1-2	0-3	1-5

	Pts	P	W	D	L	F	A	Diff	Goals/P
Total	32	16	13	6	13	46	46	0	2.875

Quarter Finals

FC Liège	Bel	Zbrojovka Brno	Tch	2-0	0-2	3-2
		FC Liège won the replay 1-0				
Valencia	Esp	Ujpesti Dózsa	Hun	5-2	1-3	6-5
Roma	Ita	Cologne	FRG	3-1	0-4	3-5
Juventus	Ita	Real Zaragoza	Esp	0-0	2-3	2-3

	Pts	P	W	D	L	F	A	Diff	Goals/P
Total	18	9	8	2	8	29	29	0	3.222

Semi Finals

FC Liège	Bel	Real Zaragoza	Esp	1-0	1-2	2-4
		Real Zaragoza won the replay 0-2				
Valencia	Esp	Cologne	FRG	4-1	0-2	4-3

	Pts	P	W	D	L	F	A	Diff	Goals/P
Total	10	5	5	0	5	13	13	0	2.600

Final

Real Zaragoza	Esp	Valencia	Esp	2-1	2-1

	Pts	P	W	D	L	F	A	Diff	Goals/P
Total	2	1	1	0	1	3	3	0	3.000

	Pts	P	W	D	L	F	A	Diff	Goals/P
Total	130	65	54	22	54	209	209	0	3.215

Pos'n	Club	Cnty	Pts	P	W	D	L	F	A	Diff	B	Pts/P	F/P
1	Real Zaragoza	Esp	20	10	8	1	1	23	7	16	3	2.000	2.300
2	FC Liège	Bel	14	10	5	2	3	11	8	3	2	1.400	1.100
3	Cologne	FRG	13	8	5	1	2	17	12	5	2	1.625	2.125
4	Valencia	Esp	13	9	4	2	3	17	14	3	3	1.444	1.889
5	Roma	Ita	11	6	5	0	1	11	7	4	1	1.833	1.833
6	Juventus	Ita	10	7	4	1	2	9	7	2	1	1.429	1.286
7	Zbrojovka Brno	Tch	9	7	4	0	3	15	7	8	1	1.286	2.143
8	Ujpesti Dózsa	Hun	9	6	3	2	1	11	9	2	1	1.500	1.833
9	Partick Thistle	Sco	6	4	3	0	1	10	7	3	0	1 500	2 500
10	Arsenal	Eng	5	4	2	1	1	12	7	5	0	1.250	3.000
11	Rapid Vienna	Aut	5	4	2	1	1	6	5	1	0	1.250	1.500
–	Lokomotiv Plovdiv	Bul	5	4	2	1	1	6	5	1	0	1.250	1.500
13	Sheffield Wednesday	Eng	4	4	2	0	2	11	7	4	0	1.000	2.750
14	Belenenses	Por	4	4	2	0	2	5	4	1	0	1.000	1.250
15	Lausanne-Sports	Sui	4	5	1	2	2	10	13	-3	0	0.800	2.000
16	Atlético Madrid	Esp	3	4	1	1	2	3	4	-1	0	0.750	0.750
17	Heart of Midlothian	Sco	2	3	0	2	1	8	9	-1	0	0.667	2.667
18	OFK Belgrade	Yug	2	3	1	0	2	3	4	-1	0	0.667	1.000
19	Shamrock Rovers	Irl	1	2	0	1	1	2	3	-1	0	0.500	1.000
–	Lokomotive Leipzig	GDR	1	2	0	1	1	2	3	-1	0	0.500	1.000
21	FC Porto	Por	1	2	0	1	1	1	2	-1	0	0.500	0.500
22	Gent	Bel	1	2	0	1	1	2	4	-2	0	0.500	1.000
23	Aris Bonnevoie	Lux	1	2	0	1	1	0	2	-2	0	0.500	0.000
24	Racing Club Paris	Fra	0	2	0	0	2	2	4	-2	0	0.000	1.000
25	Red Flag Brasov	Rom	0	2	0	0	2	2	5	-3	0	0.000	1.000
26	Tresnjevka Zagreb	Yug	0	2	0	0	2	1	4	-3	0	0.000	0.500
27	Hertha Berlin	FRG	0	2	0	0	2	1	5	-4	0	0.000	0.500
28	Utrecht	Ned	0	2	0	0	2	2	8	-6	0	0.000	1.000
29	Glentoran	Nir	0	2	0	0	2	1	7	-6	0	0.000	0.500
–	Servette	Sui	0	2	0	0	2	1	7	-6	0	0.000	0.500
31	KB Copenhagen	Den	0	2	0	0	2	3	10	-7	0	0.000	1.500
32	Iraklis	Gre	0	2	0	0	2	1	9	-8	0	0.000	0.500
	Total		**144**	**130**	**54**	**22**	**54**	**209**	**209**	**0**	**14**	**1.108**	**3.215**

1963-64

Pos'n	Cnty	Pts	P	W	D	L	F	A	Diff	B	Pts/P	F/P
1	Esp	59	37	22	6	9	82	44	38	9	1.595	2.216
2	Ita	48	29	19	4	6	49	32	17	6	1.655	1.690
3	FRG	34	25	12	5	8	53	39	14	5	1.360	2.120
4	Por	30	22	11	5	6	52	29	23	3	1.364	2.364
5	Tch	27	19	12	0	7	46	19	27	3	1.421	2.421
6	Hun	26	19	9	4	6	28	27	1	4	1.368	1.474
7	Sco	22	17	9	2	6	37	30	7	2	1.294	2.176
8	Eng	20	18	8	3	7	41	30	11	1	1.111	2.278
9	Bel	17	14	6	3	5	14	14	0	2	1.214	1.000
10	Fra	16	15	5	4	6	26	19	7	2	1.067	1.733
11	Yug	14	16	6	1	9	22	23	-1	1	0.875	1.375
12	Sui	13	18	4	3	11	24	46	-22	2	0.722	1.333
13	Tur	12	12	5	1	6	21	15	6	1	1.000	1.750
14	Ned	11	10	4	2	4	18	22	-4	1	1.100	1.800
15	Aut	10	10	4	2	4	10	10	0	0	1.000	1.000
16	Bul	9	10	3	3	4	10	10	0	0	0.900	1.000
17	Pol	8	8	4	0	4	8	10	-2	0	1.000	1.000
18	Gre	7	9	3	1	5	11	24	-13	0	0.778	1.222
19	Rom	6	8	3	0	5	11	17	-6	0	0.750	1.375
20	Lux	5	8	2	1	5	11	20	-9	0	0.625	1.375
21	Swe	3	4	1	1	2	5	7	-2	0	0.750	1.250
22	Wal	3	4	1	1	2	2	4	-2	0	0.750	0.500
23	GDR	3	6	1	1	4	3	8	-5	0	0.500	0.500
24	Irl	3	6	1	1	4	5	12	-7	0	0.500	0.833
25	Nir	3	6	1	1	4	7	19	-12	0	0.500	1.167
26	Alb	2	2	1	0	1	2	3	-1	0	1.000	1.000
27	Nor	2	4	1	0	3	3	12	-9	0	0.500	0.750
28	Fin	2	4	1	0	3	6	17	-11	0	0.500	1.500
29	Cyp	2	6	1	0	5	8	25	-17	0	0.333	1.333
30	Mlt	1	4	0	1	3	0	10	-10	0	0.250	0.000
31	Den	0	6	0	0	6	9	27	-18	0	0.000	1.500
	Total	**418**	**376**	**160**	**56**	**160**	**624**	**624**	**0**	**42**	**1.112**	**3.319**

1955-56 to 1963-64

1	Esp	351	212	128	37	47	530	280	250	58	1.656	2.500
2	Ita	228	150	85	24	41	321	200	121	34	1.520	2.140
3	Eng	166	120	62	18	40	270	193	77	24	1.383	2.250
4	Yug	135	118	48	20	50	208	190	18	19	1.144	1.763
5	FRG	134	111	49	18	44	224	217	7	18	1.207	2.018
6	Sco	123	101	49	10	42	207	190	17	15	1.218	2.050
7	Hun	105	86	39	14	33	187	144	43	13	1.221	2.174
8	Por	97	78	32	20	26	161	123	38	13	1.244	2.064
9	Tch	83	65	32	10	23	108	86	22	9	1.277	1.662
10	Fra	83	73	30	12	31	147	132	15	11	1.137	2.014
11	Aut	62	59	22	13	24	95	103	-8	5	1.051	1.610
12	Sui	58	72	20	12	40	122	186	-64	6	0.806	1.694
13	Bel	57	59	21	7	31	83	114	-31	8	0.966	1.407
14	Ned	54	50	20	9	21	88	95	-7	5	1.080	1.760
15	GDR	52	58	19	11	28	91	99	-8	3	0.897	1.569
16	Den	41	55	13	12	30	101	149	-48	3	0.745	1.836
17	Bul	37	39	13	9	17	66	69	-3	2	0.949	1.692
18	Rom	31	35	13	4	18	44	66	-22	1	0.886	1.257
19	Swe	30	34	10	8	16	49	62	-13	2	0.882	1.441
20	Tur	30	33	12	4	17	48	63	-15	2	0.909	1.455
21	Pol	25	29	11	3	15	31	60	-29	0	0.862	1.069
22	Lux	13	32	5	3	24	35	128	-93	0	0.406	1.094
23	Gre	12	21	4	4	13	23	53	-30	0	0.571	1.095
24	Nir	9	21	3	3	15	22	66	-44	0	0.429	1.048
25	Irl	8	26	3	2	21	23	88	-65	0	0.308	0.885
26	Wal	6	9	2	2	5	9	16	-7	0	0.667	1.000
27	Nor	5	12	2	1	9	9	34	-25	0	0.417	0.750
28	Alb	3	4	1	1	2	3	6	-3	0	0.750	0.750
29	Cyp	2	6	1	0	5	8	25	-17	0	0.333	1.333
30	Fin	2	12	1	0	11	12	43	-31	0	0.167	1.000
31	Mlt	1	12	0	1	11	6	51	-45	0	0.083	0.500
	Total	**2043**	**1792**	**750**	**292**	**750**	**3331**	**3331**	**0**	**251**	**1.140**	**3.718**

1963-64

Pos'n	Cnty	Ave	Pts	P	W	D	L	F	A	Diff	B	Eng
1	Spain	11.800	59	37	22	6	9	82	44	38	9	5
2	Italy	9.600	48	29	19	4	6	49	32	17	6	5
3	Czechoslovakia	9.000	27	19	12	0	7	46	19	27	3	3
4	Hungary	8.666	26	19	9	4	6	28	27	1	4	3
5	W. Germany	8.500	34	25	12	5	8	53	39	14	5	4
6	Portugal	7.500	30	22	11	5	6	52	29	23	3	4
7	Turkey	6.000	12	12	5	1	6	21	15	6	1	2
8	Belgium	5.666	17	14	6	3	5	14	14	0	2	3
9	Scotland	5.500	22	17	9	2	6	37	30	7	2	4
10	France	5.333	16	15	5	4	6	26	19	7	2	3
11	England	4.000	20	18	8	3	7	41	30	11	1	5
–	Poland	4.000	8	8	4	0	4	8	10	-2	0	2
13	Netherlands	3.666	11	10	4	2	4	18	22	-4	1	3
14	Yugoslavia	3.500	14	16	6	1	9	22	23	-1	1	4
15	Austria	3.333	10	10	4	2	4	10	10	0	0	3
16	Switzerland	3.250	13	18	4	3	11	24	46	-22	2	4
17	Bulgaria	3.000	9	10	3	3	4	10	10	0	0	3
–	Wales	3.000	3	4	1	1	2	2	4	-2	0	1
–	Sweden	3.000	3	4	1	1	2	5	7	-2	0	1
20	Greece	2.333	7	9	3	1	5	11	24	-13	0	3
21	Albania	2.000	2	2	1	0	1	2	3	-1	0	1
–	Romania	2.000	6	8	3	0	5	11	17	-6	0	3
23	Luxembourg	1.666	5	8	2	1	5	11	20	-9	0	3
24	Cyprus	1.000	2	6	1	0	5	8	25	-17	0	2
–	Rep. of Ireland	1.000	3	6	1	1	4	5	12	-7	0	3
–	Finland	1.000	2	4	1	0	3	6	17	-11	0	2
–	N. Ireland	1.000	3	6	1	1	4	7	19	-12	0	3
–	Norway	1.000	2	4	1	0	3	3	12	-9	0	2
–	E. Germany	1.000	3	6	1	1	4	3	8	-5	0	3
30	Malta	0.500	1	4	0	1	3	0	10	-10	0	2
31	Denmark	0.000	0	6	0	0	6	9	27	-18	0	3
	Total		**418**	**376**	**160**	**56**	**160**	**624**	**624**	**0**	**42**	**3.319**

1955-56 to 1963-64

Pos'n	Cnty	Ave	Pts	P	W	D	L	F	A	Diff	B	Eng
1	Spain	11.700	351	212	128	37	47	530	280	250	58	30
2	Italy	8.769	228	150	85	24	41	321	200	121	34	26
3	England	6.916	166	120	62	18	40	270	193	77	24	24
4	Scotland	5.857	123	101	49	10	42	207	190	17	15	21
5	Hungary	5.833	105	86	39	14	33	187	144	43	13	18
6	Czechoslovakia	5.533	83	65	32	10	23	108	86	22	9	15
7	Yugoslavia	5.192	135	118	48	20	50	208	190	18	19	26
8	Portugal	5.105	97	78	32	20	26	161	123	38	13	19
9	W. Germany	4.962	134	111	49	18	44	224	217	7	18	27
10	France	4.611	83	73	30	12	31	147	132	15	11	18
11	Austria	4.133	62	59	22	13	24	95	103	-8	5	15
12	Netherlands	3.857	54	50	20	9	21	88	95	-7	5	14
13	Belgium	3.800	57	59	21	7	31	83	114	-31	8	15
14	Sweden	3.333	30	34	10	8	16	49	62	-13	2	9
–	Turkey	3.333	30	33	12	4	17	48	63	-15	2	9
16	Bulgaria	3.083	37	39	13	9	17	66	69	-3	2	12
17	E. Germany	3.058	52	58	19	11	28	91	99	-8	3	17
18	Romania	2.583	31	35	13	4	18	44	66	-22	1	12
19	Switzerland	2.521	58	72	20	12	40	122	186	-64	6	23
20	Poland	2.272	25	29	11	3	15	31	60	-29	0	11
21	Denmark	2.157	41	55	13	12	30	101	149	-48	3	19
22	Wales	2.000	6	9	2	2	5	9	16	-7	0	3
23	Albania	1.500	3	4	1	1	2	3	6	-3	0	2
24	Greece	1.333	12	21	4	4	13	23	53	-30	0	9
25	Cyprus	1.000	2	6	1	0	5	8	25	-17	0	2
–	Luxembourg	1.000	13	32	5	3	24	35	128	-93	0	13
–	Norway	1.000	5	12	2	1	9	9	34	-25	0	5
28	N. Ireland	0.818	9	21	3	3	15	22	66	-44	0	11
29	Rep. of Ireland	0.666	8	26	3	2	21	23	88	-65	0	12
30	Finland	0.333	2	12	1	0	11	12	43	-31	0	6
31	Malta	0.166	1	12	0	1	11	6	51	-45	0	6
	Total		**2043**	**1792**	**750**	**292**	**750**	**3331**	**3331**	**0**	**251**	**3.718**

A Clash of Soccer Styles

The family of nations competing in the European Cups rose to 31 with the introduction of Cyprus for the 1963-64 competitions. At this stage, only Iceland and the Soviet Union had not entered the fray. Iceland would join the following season; the Soviet Union the season after that.

Of the two Cypriot clubs which entered, Anorthosis came and went without much ado in the Champions' Cup, losing 6-1 on aggregate to Partizan Belgrade in the opening round, but Apoel were to go through the full gamut of emotions in their Cup-winners' Cup baptism.

They began with a 6-0 victory over the Norwegians Gjøvik/Lyn in the first round, then won the return 1-0 to qualify with ease. But awaiting them in the next round was the biggest defeat ever suffered by any team in European competition. The record scoreline was 16-1 as Apoel went down to eventual winners Sporting Lisbon. After that, the 0-2 defeat at home in the second leg must have come as some relief to the Cypriot novices!

Sporting's performance against Apoel was particularly remarkable considering that they had almost failed to reach that stage of the competition, requiring a play-off in Barcelona to see off Italian side Atalanta in the first round. But Sporting's blistering home form was in evidence once again in the quarter-finals when they came back from a 4-1 away defeat to win 5-0 in Lisbon against Manchester United – the team that had eliminated holders Tottenham in the all-English tie of the previous round.

With the two English representatives and pre-tournament favourites Barcelona eliminated early on, the semi-finals had an unusual look about them. Both ties, as expected, were very close, with the Hungarians of MTK-VM staging a remarkable comeback against Celtic and Sporting again requiring a third match before overcoming French side Lyon. The final, too, required a replay, with Sporting and MTK-VM sharing a 3-3 draw in Brussels before the Portuguese club took their first European trophy with a 1-0 win in Antwerp two days later.

The Champions' Cup remained in Italy, and in the city of Milan, but it was not the holders AC Milan who won the trophy – they were knocked out in the quarter-finals by Real Madrid – but their city rivals, Inter.

Inter, coached by former Barcelona boss Helenio Herrera and featuring star inside-forwards Luis Suárez and Sandro Mazzola, made solid progress on their first ever appearance in the competition, eliminating English champions Everton by a single goal in the opening round and then preserving their unbeaten run in subsequent ties against Monaco, Partizan Belgrade and, second-round conquerors of Benfica, Borussia Dortmund.

Real Madrid, with several survivors from their vintage 1960 team, including Di Stéfano, Puskás, Gento and coach Muñoz, were troubled only once on the way to their seventh final. But the 0-2 quarter-final defeat by AC Milan in the San Siro was good enough to see them through to an easy semi-final tie with FC Zürich after their 4-1 victory in the first leg.

The final, in Vienna's Prater stadium, was notable for the clash of styles of the two coaches. Herrera, high priest of *catenaccio*, against Muñoz, the man responsible for Real's flowing open style, so brilliantly epitomised in the 1960 final. This, however, was to be Herrera's, and Inter's, day as Real's defence went to pieces, conceding three goals, two of them to man-of-the-match Mazzola. Inter won 3-1 and thus became the first Champions' Cup winners to go through the entire competition without losing a match.

If Spanish fortunes were beginning to fade in the Champions' Cup, they were still riding high in the Fairs' Cup where, for the second time in three seasons, the final was an all-Spanish affair, between Valencia and Real Zaragoza. Valencia, bidding for an unprecedented Fairs' Cup hat-trick, were the favourites to retain the Cup, but for the final they agreed to forego the usual home-and-away formula – a surprise given that they had won all 14 of their previous home games in the Fairs' Cup – and in the one-off match in neutral Barcelona, Zaragoza came out 2-1 winners.

1964 – 1965

Inter Milan

West Ham United

Ferencváros

First Round

Team 1	Cnty	Team 2	Cnty	1st leg	2nd leg	Agg
Partizani Tirana	Alb	Cologne	FRG	0-0	0-2	0-2
Rapid Vienna	Aut	Shamrock Rovers	Irl	3-0	2-0	5-0
Anderlecht	Bel	Bologna	Ita	1-0	1-2	2-2
		The replay resulted in a 0-0 draw				
Lokomotiv Sofia	Bul	Malmö FF	Swe	8-3	0-2	8-5
B1909 Odense	Den	Real Madrid	Esp	2-5	0-4	2-9
Rangers	Sco	Red Star Belgrade	Yug	3-1	2-4	8-6
		Rangers won the replay 3-1				
Reipas Lahti	Fin	SFK Lyn	Nor	2-1	0-3	2-4
Saint-Etienne	Fra	La Chaux-de-Fonds	Sui	2-2	1-2	3-4
Glentoran	Nir	Panathinaikos	Gre	2-2	2-3	4-5
KR Reykjavik	Isl	Liverpool	Eng	0-5	1-6	1-11
Aris Bonnevoie	Lux	Benfica	Por	1-5	1-5	2-10
Sliema Wanderers	Mlt	Dinamo Bucharest	Rom	0-2	0-5	0-7
FC Amsterdam	Ned	Fenerbahçe	Tur	3-1	1-0	4-1
Dukla Prague	Tch	Górnik Zabrze	Pol	4-1	0-3	4-4
		The replay resulted in a 0-0 draw				
Chemie Leipzig	GDR	Rába ETO	Hun	0-2	2-4	2-6

	Pts	P	W	D	L	F	A	Diff	Goals/P
Total	66	33	28	10	28	123	123	0	3.727

Second Round

Liverpool	Eng	Anderlecht	Bel	3-0	1-0	4-0
Rangers	Sco	Rapid Vienna	Aut	1-0	2-0	3-0
Real Madrid	Esp	Dukla Prague	Tch	4-0	2-2	6-2
Panathinaikos	Gre	Cologne	FRG	1-1	1-2	2-3
Rába ETO	Hun	Lokomotiv Sofia	Bul	5-3	3-4	8-7
Inter Milan	Ita	Dinamo Bucharest	Rom	6-0	1-0	7-0
FC Amsterdam	Ned	SFK Lyn	Nor	5-0	3-1	8-1
La Chaux-de-Fonds	Sui	Benfica	Por	1-1	0-5	1-6

	Pts	P	W	D	L	F	A	Diff	Goals/P
Total	32	16	13	6	13	58	58	0	3.625

Quarter Finals

Inter Milan	Ita	Rangers	Sco	3-1	0-1	3-2
FC Amsterdam	Ned	Rába ETO	Hun	1-1	0-1	1-2
Benfica	Por	Real Madrid	Esp	5-1	1-2	6-3
Cologne	FRG	Liverpool	Eng	0-0	0-0	2-2
		The replay resulted in a 2-2 draw				

	Pts	P	W	D	L	F	A	Diff	Goals/P
Total	18	9	5	8	5	21	21	0	2.333

Semi Finals

Liverpool	Eng	Inter Milan	Ita	3-1	0-3	3-4
Rába ETO	Hun	Benfica	Por	0-1	0-4	0-5

European Cup 1964-65

	Pts	P	W	D	L	F	A	Diff	Goals/P
Total	8	4	4	0	4	12	12	0	3.000

Final

Inter Milan	Ita	Benfica	Por	1-0	1-0

	Pts	P	W	D	L	F	A	Diff	Goals/P
Total	2	1	1	0	1	1	1	0	1.000

	Pts	P	W	D	L	F	A	Diff	Goals/P
Total	126	63	51	24	51	215	215	0	3.413

Pos'n	Club	Cnty	Pts	P	W	D	L	F	A	Diff	B	Pts/P	F/P
1	Benfica	Por	16	9	6	1	2	27	7	20	3	1.778	3.000
2	Liverpool	Eng	15	9	5	3	1	20	7	13	2	1.667	2.222
3	Inter Milan	Ita	13	7	5	0	2	15	5	10	3	1.857	2.143
4	Rangers	Sco	11	7	5	0	2	13	9	4	1	1.571	1.857
5	Rába ETO	Hun	11	8	4	1	3	16	15	1	2	1.375	2.000
6	FC Amsterdam	Ned	10	6	4	1	1	13	4	9	1	1.667	2.167
7	Real Madrid	Esp	10	6	4	1	1	18	10	8	1	1.667	3.000
8	Cologne	FRG	10	7	2	5	0	7	4	3	1	1.429	1.000
9	Lokomotiv Sofia	Bul	4	4	2	0	2	15	13	2	0	1.000	3.750
10	Rapid Vienna	Aut	4	4	2	0	2	5	3	2	0	1.000	1.250
11	Panathinaikos	Gre	4	4	1	2	1	7	7	0	0	1.000	1.750
–	Dinamo Bucarest	Rom	4	4	2	0	2	7	7	0	0	1.000	1.750
13	Dukla Prague	Tch	4	5	1	2	2	6	10	-4	0	0.800	1.200
14	La Chaux-de-Fonds	Sui	4	4	1	2	1	5	9	-4	0	1.000	1.250
15	Górnik Zabrze	Pol	3	3	1	1	1	4	4	0	0	1.000	1.333
16	Bologna	Ita	3	3	1	1	1	2	2	0	0	1.000	0.667
17	Anderlecht	Bel	3	5	1	1	3	2	6	-4	0	0. 600	0.400
18	Red Star Belgrade	Yug	2	3	1	0	2	6	8	-2	0	0.667	2.000
19	Reipas Lahti	Fin	2	2	1	0	1	2	4	-2	0	1.000	1.000
20	Malmö FF	Swe	2	2	1	0	1	5	8	-3	0	1.000	2.500
21	SFK Lyn	Nor	2	4	1	0	3	5	10	-5	0	0.500	1.250
22	Glentoran	Nir	1	2	0	1	1	4	5	-1	0	0.500	2.000
23	Saint-Etienne	Fra	1	2	0	1	1	3	4	-1	0	0.500	1.500
24	Tirana Partizan	Alb	1	2	0	1	1	0	2	-2	0	0.500	0.000
25	Fenerbahçe	Tur	0	2	0	0	2	1	4	-3	0	0.000	0.500
26	Chemie Leipzig	GDR	0	2	0	0	2	2	6	-4	0	0.000	1.000
27	Shamrock Rovers	Irl	0	2	0	0	2	0	5	-5	0	0.000	0.000
28	B 1909 Odense	Den	0	2	0	0	2	2	9	-7	0	0.000	1.000
29	Sliema Wanderers	Mlt	0	2	0	0	2	0	7	-7	0	0.000	0.000
30	Aris Bonnevoie	Lux	0	2	0	0	2	2	10	-8	0	0.000	1.000
31	KR Reykjavik	Isl	0	2	0	0	2	1	11	-10	0	0.000	0.500
	Total		**140**	**126**	**51**	**24**	**51**	**215**	**215**	**0**	**14**	**1.111**	**3. 413**

First Round

Team 1	Cnty	Team 2	Cnty	1st leg	2nd leg	Agg
Admira Wacker	Aut	Legia Warsaw	Pol	1-3	0-1	1-4
Gent	Bel	West Ham United	Eng	0-1	1-1	1-2
Esbjerg FB	Den	Cardiff City	Wal	0-0	0-1	0-1
Cork Celtic	Irl	Slavia Sofia	Bul	0-2	1-1	1-3
AEK Athens	Gre	Dinamo Zagreb	Yug	2-0	0-3	2-3
Torino	Ita	Fortuna Sittard	Ned	3-1	2-2	5-3
Union Luxembourg	Lux	1860 Munich	FRG	0-4	0-6	0-10
Valletta	Mlt	Real Zaragoza	Esp	0-3	1-5	1-8
FK Skeid	Nor	Haka Valkeakoski	Fin	1-0	0-2	1-2
FC Porto	Por	Olympique Lyon	Fra	3-0	1-0	4-0
Steaua Bucharest	Rom	Derry City	Nir	3-0	2-0	5-0
Lausanne-Sports	Sui	Honvéd	Hun	2-0	0-1	2-1
Sparta Prague	Tch	Anorthosis Nicosia	Cyp	10-0	6-0	16-0
Magdeburg	GDR	Galatasaray	Tur	1-1	1-1	3-3
		The replay resulted in a 1-1 draw				

	Pts	P	W	D	L	F	A	Diff	Goals/P
Total	58	29	22	14	22	82	82	0	2.828

Second Round

West Ham United	Eng	Sparta Prague	Tch	2-0	1-2	3- 2
Slavia Sofia	Bul	Lausanne-Sports	Sui	1-0	1-2	4-5
		Lausanne-Sports won the replay 2-3				
Dundee	Sco	Real Zaragoza	Esp	2-2	1-2	3-4
Haka Valkeakoski	Fin	Torino	Ita	0-1	0-5	0-6
Legia Warsaw	Pol	Galatasaray	Tur	2-1	0-1	3-2
		Legia Warsaw won the replay 1-0				
Sporting Lisbon	Por	Cardiff City	Wal	1-2	0-0	1-2
FC Porto	Por	1860 Munich	FRG	0-1	1-1	1-2
Steaua Bucharest	Rom	Dinamo Zagreb	Yug	1-3	0-2	1-5

	Pts	P	W	D	L	F	A	Diff	Goals/P
Total	36	18	15	6	15	44	44	0	2.444

Quarter Finals

Cardiff City	Wal	Real Zaragoza	Esp	0-1	2-2	2-3
Torino	Ita	Dinamo Zagreb	Yug	1-1	2-1	3-2
Legia Warsaw	Pol	1860 Munich	FRG	0-4	0-0	0-4
Lausanne-Sports	Sui	West Ham United	Eng	1-2	3-4	4-6

	Pts	P	W	D	L	F	A	Diff	Goals/P
Total	16	8	5	6	5	24	24	0	3.000

Semi Finals

West Ham United	Eng	Real Zaragoza	Esp	2-1	1-1	3-2
Torino	Ita	1860 Munich	FRG	2-0	1-3	3-5
		1860 Munich won the replay 0-2				

	Pts	P	W	D	L	F	A	Diff	Goals/P
Total	10	5	4	2	4	13	13	0	2.600

Final

West Ham United	Eng	1860 Munich	FRG	2-0	2-0

	Pts	P	W	D	L	F	A	Diff	Goals/P
Total	2	1	1	0	1	2	2	0	2.000

	Pts	P	W	D	L	F	A	Diff	Goals/P
Total	122	61	47	28	47	165	165	0	2.705

Pos'n	Club	Cnty	Pts	P	W	D	L	F	A	Diff	B	Pts/P	F/P
1	1860 Munich	FRG	17	10	6	2	2	21	6	15	3	1.700	2.100
2	West Ham United	Eng	17	9	6	2	1	16	9	7	3	1.889	1.778
3	Torino	Ita	14	9	5	2	2	17	10	7	2	1.556	1.889
4	Real Zaragoza	Esp	13	8	4	3	1	17	9	8	2	1.625	2.125
5	Legia Warsaw	Pol	10	7	4	1	2	7	7	0	1	1.429	1.000
6	Dinamo Zagreb	Yug	8	6	3	1	2	10	6	4	1	1.333	1.667
7	Cardiff City	Wal	8	6	2	3	1	5	4	1	1	1.333	0.833
8	Lausanne-Sports	Sui	7	7	3	0	4	11	11	0	1	1.000	1.571
9	Sparta Prague	Tch	6	4	3	0	1	18	3	15	0	1.500	4.500
10	FC Porto	Por	5	4	2	1	1	5	2	3	0	1.250	1.250
11	Slavia Sofia	Bul	5	5	2	1	2	7	6	1	0	1.000	1.400
12	Galatasaray	Tur	5	6	1	3	2	5	6	-1	0	0.833	0.833
13	Steaua Bucharest	Rom	4	4	2	0	2	6	5	1	0	1.000	1.500
14	Magdeburg	GDR	3	3	0	3	0	3	3	0	0	1.000	1.000
15	AEK Athens	Gre	2	2	1	0	1	2	3	-1	0	1.000	1.000
16	Honvéd	Hun	2	2	1	0	1	1	2	-1	0	1.000	0.500
-	FK Skeid	Nor	2	2	1	0	1	1	2	-1	0	1.000	0.500
18	Haka Valkeakoski	Fin	2	4	1	0	3	2	7	-5	0	0.500	0.500
19	Dundee	Sco	1	2	0	1	1	3	4	-1	0	0.500	1.500
20	Gent	Bel	1	2	0	1	1	1	2	-1	0	0.500	0.500
-	Sporting Lisbon	Por	1	2	0	1	1	1	2	-1	0	0.500	0.500
22	Esbjerg FB	Den	1	2	0	1	1	0	1	-1	0	0.500	0.000
23	Fortuna Sittard	Ned	1	2	0	1	1	3	5	-2	0	0.500	1.500
24	Cork Celtic	Irl	1	2	0	1	1	1	3	-2	0	0.500	0.500
25	Admira Wacker	Aut	0	2	0	0	2	1	4	-3	0	0.000	0.500
26	Olympique Lyon	Fra	0	2	0	0	2	0	4	-4	0	0.000	0.000
27	Derry City	Nir	0	2	0	0	2	0	5	-5	0	0.000	0.000
28	Valletta	Mlt	0	2	0	0	2	1	8	-7	0	0.000	0.500
29	Union Luxembourg	Lux	0	2	0	0	2	0	10	-10	0	0.000	0.000
30	Anorthosis Nicosia	Cyp	0	2	0	0	2	0	16	-16	0	0.000	0.000
	Total		**136**	**122**	**47**	**28**	**47**	**165**	**165**	**0**	**14**	**1.115**	**2.705**

First Round

Team 1	Cnty	Team 2	Cnty	1st leg	2nd leg	Agg
Everton	Eng	Vålerengen SIF	Nor	4-2	5-2	9-4
Manchester United	Eng	Djurgården SIF	Swe	6-1	1-1	7-2
Wiener Sport-Club	Aut	Lokomotive Leipzig	GDR	2-1	1-0	3-1
Antwerp	Bel	Hertha Berlin	FRG	2-0	1-2	3-2
FC Liège	Bel	Valencia	Esp	3-1	1-1	4-2
Lokomotiv Plovdiv	Bul	Vojvodina NoviSad	Yug	1-1	1-1	4-2
		Lokomotiv Plovdiv won the replay 2-0				
Dunfermline Athletic	Sco	Örgryte IS	Swe	4-2	0-0	4-2
Celtic	Sco	Leixões	Por	3-0	1-1	4-1
Shelbourne	Irl	Belenenses	Por	0-0	1-1	3-2
		Shelbourne won the replay 2-1				
Athletic Bilbao	Esp	OFK Belgrade	Yug	2-2	2-0	4-2
Atlético Madrid	Esp	Servette	Sui	6-1	2-2	8-3
Stade Français	Fra	Real Betis	Esp	2-0	1-1	3-1
Strasbourg	Fra	AC Milan	Ita	2-0	0-1	2-1
Ferencváros	Hun	Zbrojovka Brno	Tch	2-0	0-1	2-1
Fiorentina	Ita	Barcelona	Esp	0-2	1-0	1-2
Roma	Ita	Aris Salonika	Gre	3-0	0-0	3-0
Juventus	Ita	Union St-Gilloise	Bel	1-0	1-0	2-0
Utrecht	Ned	KB Copenhagen	Den	2-1	4-3	6-4
Borussia Dortmund	FRG	Girondins Bordeaux	Fra	4-1	0-2	4-3
Eintracht Frankfurt	FRG	Kilmarnock	Sco	3-0	1-5	4-5
VFB Stuttgart	FRG	B 1913 Odense	Den	3-1	1-0	4-1
Petrolul Ploiesti	Rom	Göztepe	Tur	2-1	1-0	3-1
FC Basle	Sui	Spora Luxembourg	Lux	2-0	0-1	2-1
NK Zagreb	Yug	Grazer AK	Aut	3-2	6-0	9-2

	Pts	P	W	D	L	F	A	Diff	Goals/P
Total	100	50	38	24	38	143	143	0	2.860

Second Round

Everton	Eng	Kilmarnock	Sco	4-1	2-0	6-1
Manchester United	Eng	Borussia Dortmund	FRG	4-0	6-1	10-1
FC Liège	Bel	Utrecht	Ned	2-0	2-0	4-0
Lokomotiv Plovdiv	Bul	Petrolul Ploiesti	Rom	2-0	0-1	2-1
Dunfermline Athletic	Sco	VFB Stuttgart	FRG	1-0	0-0	1-0
Barcelona	Esp	Celtic	Sco	3-1	0-0	3-1
Athletic Bilbao	Esp	Antwerp	Bel	2-0	1-0	3-0
Atlético Madrid	Esp	Shelbourne	Irl	1-0	1-0	2-0
Strasbourg	Fra	FC Basle	Sui	5-2	1-0	6-2
Ferencváros	Hun	Wiener Sport-Club	Aut	2-1	0-1	4-2
		Ferencváros won the replay 2-0				
Roma	Ita	NK Zagreb	Yug	1-0	1-1	2-1
Juventus	Ita	Stade Français	Fra	1-0	0-0	1-0

	Pts	P	W	D	L	F	A	Diff	Goals/P
Total	50	25	21	8	21	53	53	0	2.120

Third Round

Manchester United	Eng	Everton	Eng	1-1	2-1	3-2
FC Liège	Bel	Atlético Madrid	Esp	1-0	0-2	1-2
Athletic Bilbao	Esp	Dunfermline Athletic	Sco	1-0	0-1	3-2
		Athletic Bilbao won the replay 2-1				
Strasbourg	Fra	Barcelona	Esp	0-0	2-2	2-2
		The replay resulted in a 0-0 draw				
Roma	Ita	Ferencváros	Hun	1-2	0-1	1-3
Juventus	Ita	Lokomotiv Plovdiv	Bul	1-1	1-1	4-3
		Juventus won the replay 2-1				

	Pts	P	W	D	L	F	A	Diff	Goals/P
Total	30	15	9	12	9	28	28	0	1.867

Quarter Finals

Strasbourg	Fra	Manchester United	Eng	0-5	0-0	0-5
Ferencváros	Hun	Athletic Bilbao	Esp	1-0	1-2	5-2
		Ferencváros won the replay 3-0				

	Pts	P	W	D	L	F	A	Diff	Goals/P
Total	10	5	4	2	4	12	12	0	2.400

Semi Finals

Manchester United	Eng	Ferencváros	Hun	3-2	0-1	4-5
		Ferencváros won the replay 1-2				
Atlético Madrid	Esp	Juventus	Ita	3-1	1-3	5-7
		Juventus won the replay 1-3				

	Pts	P	W	D	L	F	A	Diff	Goals/P
Total	12	6	6	0	6	21	21	0	3.500

Final

Juventus	Ita	Ferencváros	Hun	0-1		0-1

	Pts	P	W	D	L	F	A	Diff	Goals/P
Total	2	1	1	0	1	1	1	0	1.000

	Pts	P	W	D	L	F	A	Diff	Goals/P
Total	204	102	79	46	79	258	258	0	2.529

Pos'n	Club	Cnty	Pts	P	W	D	L	F	A	Diff	B	Pts/P	F/P
1	Ferencváros	Hun	23	14	10	0	4	20	10	10	3	1.643	1.429
2	Manchester United	Eng	17	11	6	3	2	29	10	19	2	1.545	2.636
3	Juventus	Ita	17	11	6	3	2	14	9	5	2	1.545	1.273
4	Athletic Bilbao	Esp	14	10	6	1	3	12	9	3	1	1.400	1.200
5	Atlético Madrid	Esp	12	9	5	1	3	17	11	6	1	1.333	1.889
6	Strasbourg	Fra	11	9	3	4	2	10	10	0	1	1.222	1.111
7	Everton	Eng	9	6	4	1	1	17	8	9	0	1.500	2.833
8	FC Liège	Bel	9	6	4	1	1	9	4	5	0	1.500	1.500
9	Barcelona	Esp	8	7	2	4	1	7	4	3	0	1.143	1.000
10	Lokomotiv Plovdiv	Bul	8	8	2	4	2	9	7	2	0	1.000	1.125
11	Dunfermline Athletic	Sco	8	7	3	2	2	7	5	2	0	1.143	1.000
12	Roma	Ita	6	6	2	2	2	6	4	2	0	1.000	1.000
13	Petrolul Ploiesti	Rom	6	4	3	0	1	4	3	1	0	1.500	1.000
14	Wiener Sport-Club	Aut	6	5	3	0	2	5	5	0	0	1.200	1.000
15	NK Zagreb	Yug	5	4	2	1	1	10	4	6	0	1.250	2.500
16	VFB Stuttgart	FRG	5	4	2	1	1	4	2	2	0	1.250	1.000
17	Celtic	Sco	4	4	1	2	1	5	4	1	0	1.000	1.250
18	Stade Français	Fra	4	4	1	2	1	3	2	1	0	1.000	0.750
19	Shelbourne	Irl	4	5	1	2	2	3	4	-1	0	0.800	0.600
20	Utrecht	Ned	4	4	2	0	2	6	8	-2	0	1.000	1.500
21	Eintracht Frankfurt	FRG	2	2	1	0	1	4	5	-1	0	1.000	2.000
22	Girondins Bordeaux	Fra	2	2	1	0	1	3	4	-1	0	1.000	1.500
23	Belenenses	Por	2	3	0	2	1	2	3	-1	0	0.667	0.667
–	Hertha Berlin	FRG	2	2	1	0	1	2	3	-1	0	1.000	1.000
25	Fiorentina	Ita	2	2	1	0	1	1	2	-1	0	1.000	0.500
–	AC Milan	Ita	2	2	1	0	1	1	2	-1	0	1.000	0.500
–	Spora Luxembourg	Lux	2	2	1	0	1	1	2	-1	0	1.000	0.500
–	Zbrojovka Brno	Tch	2	2	1	0	1	1	2	-1	0	1.000	0.500
29	Antwerp	Bel	2	4	1	0	3	3	5	-2	0	0.500	0.750
30	Vojvodina Novi Sad	Yug	2	3	0	2	1	2	4	-2	0	0.667	0.667
31	FC Basle	Sui	2	4	1	0	3	4	7	-3	0	0.500	1.000
32	Kilmarnock	Sco	2	4	1	0	3	6	10	-4	0	0.500	1.500
33	Borussia Dortmund	FRG	2	4	1	0	3	5	13	-8	0	0.500	1.250
34	Valencia	Esp	1	2	0	1	1	2	4	-2	0	0.500	1.000
–	Örgryte IS	Swe	1	2	0	1	1	2	4	-2	0	0.500	1.000
–	OFK Belgrade	Yug	1	2	0	1	1	2	4	-2	0	0.500	1.000
37	Real Betis	Esp	1	2	0	1	1	1	3	-2	0	0.500	0.500
38	Leixões	Por	1	2	0	1	1	1	4	-3	0	0.500	0.500
39	Aris Salonika	Gre	1	2	0	1	1	0	3	-3	0	0.500	0.000
40	Servette	Sui	1	2	0	1	1	3	8	-5	0	0.500	1.500
41	Djurgården SIF	Swe	1	2	0	1	1	2	7	-5	0	0.500	1.000
42	KB Copenhagen	Den	0	2	0	0	2	4	6	-2	0	0.000	2.000
43	Göztepe	Tur	0	2	0	0	2	1	3	-2	0	0.000	0.500
–	Lokomotive Leipzig	GDR	0	2	0	0	2	1	3	-2	0	0.000	0.500
45	St-Gilloise Union	Bel	0	2	0	0	2	0	2	-2	0	0.000	0.000
46	B 1913 Odense	Den	0	2	0	0	2	1	4	-3	0	0.000	0.500
47	Vålerengen SIF	Nor	0	2	0	0	2	4	9	-5	0	0.000	2.000
48	Grazer AK	Aut	0	2	0	0	2	2	9	-7	0	0.000	1.000
	Total		**214**	**204**	**79**	**46**	**79**	**258**	**258**	**0**	**10**	**1.049**	**2.529**

1964-65

Pos'n	Cnty	Pts	P	W	D	L	F	A	Diff	B	Pts/P	F/P
1	Esp	59	44	21	12	11	74	50	24	5	1.341	1.682
2	Eng	58	35	21	9	5	82	34	48	7	1.657	2.343
3	Ita	57	40	21	8	11	56	34	22	7	1.425	1.400
4	FRG	38	29	13	8	8	43	33	10	4	1.310	1.483
5	Hun	36	24	15	1	8	37	27	10	5	1.500	1.542
6	Sco	26	24	10	5	9	34	32	2	1	1.083	1.417
7	Por	25	20	8	6	6	36	18	18	3	1.250	1.800
8	Yug	18	18	6	5	7	30	26	4	1	1.000	1.667
9	Fra	18	19	5	7	7	19	24	-5	1	0.947	1.000
10	Bul	17	17	6	5	6	31	26	5	0	1.000	1.824
11	Ned	15	12	6	2	4	22	17	5	1	1.250	1.833
12	Bel	15	19	6	3	10	15	19	-4	0	0.789	0.789
13	Rom	14	12	7	0	5	17	15	2	0	1.167	1.417
14	Sui	14	17	5	3	9	23	35	-12	1	0.824	1.353
15	Pol	13	10	5	2	3	11	11	0	1	1.300	1.100
16	Tch	12	11	5	2	4	25	15	10	0	1.091	2.273
17	Aut	10	13	5	0	8	13	21	-8	0	0.769	1.000
18	Wal	8	6	2	3	1	5	4	1	1	1.333	0.833
19	Gre	7	8	2	3	3	9	13	-4	0	0.875	1.125
20	Tur	5	10	1	3	6	7	13	-6	0	0.500	0.700
21	Irl	5	9	1	3	5	4	12	-8	0	0.556	0.444
22	Fin	4	6	2	0	4	4	11	-7	0	0.667	0.667
23	Swe	4	6	1	2	3	9	19	-10	0	0.667	1.500
24	Nor	4	8	2	0	6	10	21	-11	0	0.500	1.250
25	GDR	3	7	0	3	4	6	12	-6	0	0.429	0.857
26	Lux	2	6	1	0	5	3	22	-19	O	0.333	0.500
27	Alb	1	2	0	1	1	0	2	-2	0	0.500	0.000
28	Nir	1	4	0	1	3	4	10	-6	0	0.250	1.000
29	Den	1	8	0	1	7	7	20	-13	0	0.125	0.875
30	Isl	0	2	0	0	2	1	11	-10	0	0.000	0.500
31	Mlt	0	4	0	0	4	1	15	-14	0	0.000	0.250
32	Cyp	0	2	0	0	2	0	16	-16	0	0.000	0.000
	Total	**490**	**452**	**177**	**98**	**177**	**638**	**638**	**0**	**38**	**1.084**	**2.823**

1955-56 to 1964-65

1	Esp	410	256	149	49	58	604	330	274	63	1.602	2.359
2	Ita	285	190	106	32	52	377	234	143	41	1.500	1.984
3	Eng	224	155	83	27	45	352	227	125	31	1.445	2.271
4	FRG	172	140	62	26	52	267	250	17	22	1.229	1.907
5	Yug	153	136	54	25	57	238	216	22	20	1.125	1.750
6	Sco	149	125	59	15	51	241	222	19	16	1.192	1.928
7	Hun	141	110	54	15	41	224	171	53	18	1.282	2.036
8	Por	122	98	40	26	32	197	141	56	16	1.245	2.010
9	Fra	101	92	35	19	38	166	156	10	12	1.098	1.804
10	Tch	95	76	37	12	27	133	101	32	9	1.250	1.750
11	Aut	72	72	27	13	32	108	124	-16	5	1.000	1.500
12	Bel	72	78	27	10	41	98	133	-35	8	0.923	1.256
13	Sui	72	89	25	15	49	145	221	-76	7	0.809	1.629
14	Ned	69	62	26	11	25	110	112	-2	6	1.113	1.774
15	GDR	55	65	19	14	32	97	111	-14	3	0.846	1.492
16	Bul	54	56	19	14	23	97	95	2	2	0.964	1.732
17	Rom	45	47	20	4	23	61	81	-20	1	0.957	1.298
18	Den	42	63	13	13	37	108	169	-61	3	0.667	1.714
19	Pol	38	39	16	5	18	42	71	-29	1	0.974	1.077
20	Tur	35	43	13	7	23	55	76	-21	2	0.814	1.279
21	Sua	34	40	11	10	19	58	81	-23	2	0.850	1.450
22	Gra	19	29	6	7	16	32	66	-34	0	0.655	1.103
23	Lux	15	38	6	3	29	38	150	-112	0	0.395	1.000
24	Wal	14	15	4	5	6	14	20	-6	1	0.933	0.933
25	Irl	13	35	4	5	26	27	100	-73	0	0.371	0.771
26	Nir	10	25	3	4	18	26	76	-50	0	0.400	1.040
27	Nor	9	20	4	1	15	19	55	-36	0	0.450	0.950
28	Fin	6	18	3	0	15	16	54	-38	0	0.333	0.889
29	Alb	4	6	1	2	3	3	8	-5	0	0.667	0.500
30	Cyp	2	8	1	0	7	8	41	-33	0	0.250	1.000
31	Mlt	1	16	0	1	15	7	66	-59	0	0.063	0.438
32	Isl	0	2	0	0	2	1	11	-10	0	0.000	0.500
	Total	**2533**	**2244**	**927**	**390**	**927**	**3969**	**3969**	**0**	**289**	**1.129**	**3.537**

1964-65

Pos'n	Cnty	Ave	Pts	P	W	D	L	F	A	Diff	B	No./T
1	England	14.500	58	35	21	9	5	82	34	48	7	4
2	Hungary	12.000	36	24	15	1	8	37	27	10	5	3
3	Spain	8.428	59	44	21	12	11	74	50	24	5	7
4	Italy	8.142	57	40	21	8	11	56	34	22	7	7
5	Wales	8.000	8	6	2	3	1	5	4	1	1	1
6	Poland	6.500	13	10	5	2	3	11	11	0	1	2
7	W. Germany	6.333	38	29	13	8	8	43	33	10	4	6
8	Bulgaria	5.666	17	17	6	5	6	31	26	5	0	3
9	Scotland	5.200	26	24	10	5	9	34	32	2	1	5
10	Netherlands	5.000	15	12	6	2	4	22	17	5	1	3
–	Portugal	5.000	25	20	8	6	6	36	18	18	3	5
12	Romania	4.666	14	12	7	0	5	17	15	2	0	3
13	Czechoslovakia	4.000	12	11	5	2	4	25	15	10	0	3
14	France	3.600	18	19	5	7	7	19	24	-5	1	5
–	Yugoslavia	3.600	18	18	6	5	7	30	26	4	1	5
16	Switzerland	3.500	14	17	5	3	9	23	35	-12	1	4
17	Belgium	3.000	15	19	6	3	10	15	19	-4	0	5
18	Austria	2.500	10	13	5	0	8	13	21	-8	0	4
19	Greece	2.333	7	8	2	3	3	9	13	-4	0	3
20	Finland	2.000	4	6	2	0	4	4	11	-7	0	2
21	Rep. of Ireland	1.666	5	9	1	3	5	4	12	-8	0	3
–	Turkey	1.666	5	10	1	3	6	7	13	-6	0	3
23	Norway	1.333	4	8	2	0	6	10	21	-11	0	3
–	Sweden	1.333	4	6	1	2	3	9	19	-10	0	3
25	Albania	1.000	1	2	0	1	1	0	2	-2	0	1
–	E. Germany	1.000	3	7	0	3	4	6	12	-6	0	3
27	Luxembourg	0.666	2	6	1	0	5	3	22	-19	0	3
28	N. Ireland	0.500	1	4	0	1	3	4	10	-6	0	2
29	Denmark	0.250	1	8	0	1	7	7	20	-13	0	4
30	Cyprus	0.000	0	2	0	0	2	0	16	-16	0	1
–	Iceland	0.000	0	2	0	0	2	1	11	-10	0	1
–	Malta	0.000	0	4	0	0	4	1	15	-14	0	2
	Total		**490**	**452**	**177**	**98**	**177**	**638**	**638**	**0**	**38**	**2.823**

1955-56 to 1964-65

Pos'n	Cnty	Ave	Pts	P	W	D	L	F	A	Diff	B	No./T
1	Spain	11.081	410	256	149	49	58	604	330	274	63	37
2	Italy	8.636	285	190	106	32	52	377	234	143	41	33
3	England	8.000	224	155	83	27	45	352	227	125	31	28
4	Hungary	6.714	141	110	54	15	41	224	171	53	18	21
5	Scotland	5.730	149	125	59	15	51	241	222	19	16	26
6	Czechoslovakia	5.277	95	76	37	12	27	133	101	32	9	18
7	W. Germany	5.212	172	140	62	26	52	267	250	17	22	33
8	Portugal	5.083	122	98	40	26	32	197	141	56	16	24
9	Yugoslavia	4.935	153	136	54	25	57	238	216	22	20	31
10	France	4.391	101	92	35	19	38	166	156	10	12	23
11	Netherlands	4.058	69	62	26	11	25	110	112	-2	6	17
12	Austria	3.789	72	72	27	13	32	108	124	-16	5	19
13	Belgium	3.600	72	78	27	10	41	98	133	-35	8	20
–	Bulgaria	3.600	54	56	19	14	23	97	95	2	2	15
15	Wales	3.500	14	15	4	5	6	14	20	-6	1	4
16	Romania	3.000	45	47	20	4	23	61	81	-20	1	15
17	Poland	2.923	38	39	16	5	18	42	71	-29	1	13
18	Turkey	2.916	35	43	13	7	23	55	76	-21	2	12
19	Sweden	2.833	34	40	11	10	19	58	81	-23	2	12
20	E. Germany	2.750	55	65	19	14	32	97	111	-14	3	20
21	Switzerland	2.666	72	89	25	15	49	145	221	-76	7	27
22	Denmark	1.826	42	63	13	13	37	108	169	-61	3	23
23	Greece	1.583	19	29	6	7	16	32	66	-34	0	12
24	Albania	1.333	4	6	1	2	3	3	8	-5	0	3
25	Norway	1.125	9	20	4	1	15	19	55	-36	0	8
26	Luxembourg	0.937	15	38	6	3	29	38	150	-112	0	16
27	Rep. of Ireland	0.866	13	35	4	5	26	27	100	-73	0	15
28	N. Ireland	0.769	10	25	3	4	18	26	76	-50	0	13
29	Finland	0.750	6	18	3	0	15	16	54	-38	0	8
30	Cyprus	0.666	2	8	1	0	7	8	41	-33	0	3
31	Malta	0.125	1	16	0	1	15	7	66	-59	0	8
32	Iceland	0.000	0	2	0	0	2	1	11	-10	0	1
	Total		**2533**	**2244**	**927**	**390**	**927**	**3969**	**3969**	**0**	**289**	**3.537**

Home Advantage – in the Final!

Inter Milan did what their rivals AC Milan could not do the previous season and succeeded in emulating Real Madrid and Benfica by retaining the Champions' Cup the year after their first triumph.

Things were certainly made easy for Helenio Herrera and his team when the venue for the final against Benfica was confirmed as their own San Siro stadium. The precedent for such an eventuality had been set, back in 1956-57, when Real Madrid had been permitted to play the final on their own ground against Fiorentina, so despite Benfica's vehement protests, UEFA felt obliged to go along with their original choice. It would take another 20 years and more before UEFA finally decided to prohibit the possibility of a team playing the final on its own ground – but not until Roma, too, had benefited from it, or rather, failed to benefit from it, in the 1984 final against Liverpool.

Inter, however, did take advantage of their good fortune, sending Benfica to their second final defeat in three seasons with a 1-0 victory on a muddy, waterlogged San Siro pitch. It was the lowest score ever recorded in a Champions' Cup final and was in keeping with Inter's functional, risk-free approach to the game.

Inter had only just made it into the final in the first place. They scraped past Rangers, 3-2 on aggregate, in the quarter-finals and then profited from some highly dubious refereeing decisions to put out English champions, and European debutantes, Liverpool in the semis. Benfica, on the other hand, had played quite splendidly throughout the tournament, their best display coming in the quarter-final when they pulverised Real Madrid 5-1 in front of a packed crowd in the Stadium of Light. It was Real's heaviest ever defeat in the Champions' Cup and remained as such until their 5-0 hammering by AC Milan in the 1988-89 semi-final.

Like Inter in the Champions' Cup, West Ham United also had the advantage of playing the final of the Cup-winners' Cup in their home city, even if Wembley stadium was not actually their home ground. Their opponents in the final were a German side, 1860 Munich, and in retrospect, with Moore, Hurst and Peters in the West Ham side, the match proved to be something of a dress rehearsal for the World Cup final between England and West Germany the following year. The outcome was certainly similar, with West Ham clinching the trophy, and thus following another London club, Tottenham Hotspur, onto the Cup-winners' Cup roll-of-honour, thanks to two goals in three minutes midway through the second half from right-winger Sealey.

The fact that West Ham and 1860 Munich, two clubs which had never won their own domestic championship (although the Germans did so the next year), should be in the Cup-winners' final was evidence of the fairly poor quality of the 1964-65 tournament. There were no true European giants in the competition and even holders Sporting Lisbon could not make it past the second round, beaten at home and subsequently eliminated by Welsh Cup winners Cardiff City, then of the English Second Division.

The Fairs' Cup, gradually moving away from its original conception, welcomed an enlarged cast of 48 for its 1964-65 edition. This was all very well in respect of the competitions prestige, but in terms of organisation, with no teams being allowed exemption from the first round, it eventually ended up in a mixture of farce and chaos, with Atlético Madrid and Juventus both being given byes at the quarter-final stage.

Following the example of the previous season, the Fairs' Cup final was played as a single match, but unlike the Zaragoza-Valencia clash, there was to be no neutral venue for the Ferencváros-Juventus final. The preferential treatment afforded to Inter in the Champions' Cup was extended also to Juventus, with the match taking place in Juve's own Stadio Comunale in Turin. On this occasion, though, the hand that feeds was bitten and Ferencváros, to enormous surprise, won the match 1-0, becoming the first club from Eastern Europe to win one of the three European trophies.

1965 – 1966

Inter Milan

Borussia Dortmund

Barcelona

European Cup 1965-66

First Round

Team 1	Cnty	Team 2	Cnty	1st leg	2nd leg	Agg
17 Nëntori Tirana	Alb	Kilmarnock	Sco	0-0	0-1	0-1
Linzer ASK	Aut	Górnik Zabrze	Pol	1-3	1-2	2-5
Apoel Nicosia	Cyp	Werder Bremen	FRG	0-5	0-5	0-10
Drumcondra	Irl	Vorwärts Frankfurt/Oder	GDR	1-0	1-2	2-5
		Vorwärts won the replay 0-3				
HJK Helsinki	Fin	Manchester United	Eng	2-3	0-6	2-9
Panathinaikos	Gre	Sliema Wanderers	Mlt	4-1	0-1	4-2
IBK Keflavik	Isl	Ferencváros	Hun	1-4	1-9	2-13
Stade Dudelange	Lux	Benfica	Por	0-8	0-10	0-18
SFK Lyn	Nor	Derry City	Nir	5-3	1-5	6- 8
Feyenoord	Ned	Real Madrid	Esp	2-1	0-5	2-6
Dinamo Bucharest	Rom	B 1909 Odense	Den	4-0	3-2	7-2
Djurgården SIF	Swe	Levski Sofia	Bul	2-1	0-6	2-7
Lausanne-Sports	Sui	Sparta Prague	Tch	0-0	0-4	0-4
Fenerbahçe	Tur	Anderlecht	Bel	0-0	1-5	1-5
Partizan Belgrade	Yug	Nantes	Fra	2-0	2-2	4-2

	Pts	P	W	D	L	F	A	Diff	Goals/P
Total	62	31	27	8	27	131	131	0	4.226

Second Round

Anderlecht	Bel	Derry City	Nir	9-0		9-0
Levski Sofia	Bul	Benfica	Por	2-2	2-3	4-5
Kilmarnock	Sco	Real Madrid	Esp	2-2	1-5	3-7
Ferencváros	Hun	Panathinaikos	Gre	0-0	3-1	3-1
Dinamo Bucharest	Rom	Inter Milan	Ita	2-1	0-2	2-3
Sparta Prague	Tch	Górnik Zabrze	Pol	3-0	1-2	4-2
Partizan Belgrade	Yug	Werder Bremen	FRG	3-0	0-1	3-1
Vorwärts Frankfurt/Oder	GDR	Manchester United	Eng	0-2	1-3	1-5

	Pts	P	W	D	L	F	A	Diff	Goals/P
Total	30	15	12	6	12	53	53	0	3.533

Quarter Finals

Manchester United	Eng	Benfica	Por	3-2	5-1	8-3
Anderlecht	Bel	Real Madrid	Esp	1-0	2-4	3-4
Inter Milan	Ita	Ferencváros	Hun	4-0	1-1	5-1
Sparta Prague	Tch	Partizan Belgrade	Yug	4-1	0-5	4-6

	Pts	P	W	D	L	F	A	Diff	Goals/P
Total	16	8	7	2	7	34	34	0	4.250

Semi Finals

Real Madrid	Esp	Inter Milan	Ita	1-0	1-1	2-1
Partizan Belgrade	Yug	Manchester United	Eng	2-0	0-1	2-1

	Pts	P	W	D	L	F	A	Diff	Goals/P
Total	8	4	3	2	3	6	6	0	1.500

Final

Real Madrid	Esp	Partizan Belgrade	Yug	2-1	2-1

	Pts	P	W	D	L	F	A	Diff	Goals/P
Total	2	1	1	0	1	3	3	0	3.000

	Pts	P	W	D	L	F	A	Diff	Goals/P
Total	118	59	50	18	50	227	227	0	3.847

Pos'n	Club	Cnty	Pts	P	W	D	L	F	A	Diff	B	Pts/P	F/P
1	Manchester United	Eng	16	8	7	0	1	23	8	15	2	2.000	2.875
2	Real Madrid	Esp	15	9	5	2	2	21	10	11	3	1.667	2.333
3	Partizan Belgrade	Yug	12	9	4	1	4	16	10	6	3	1.333	1.778
4	Ferencváros	Hun	9	6	3	2	1	17	8	9	1	1.500	2.833
5	Benfica	Por	8	6	3	1	2	26	12	14	1	1.333	4.333
6	Anderlecht	Bel	8	5	3	1	1	17	5	12	1	1.600	3.400
7	Sparta Prague	Tch	8	6	3	1	2	12	8	4	1	1.333	2.000
8	Inter Milan	Ita	8	6	2	2	2	9	5	4	2	1.333	1.500
9	Werder Bremen	FRG	6	4	3	0	1	11	3	8	0	1.500	2.750
10	Bucarest Dinamo	Rom	6	4	3	0	1	9	5	4	0	1.500	2.250
11	Górnik Zabrze	Pol	6	4	3	0	1	7	6	1	0	1.500	1.750
12	Vorwärts Frankfurt/Oder	GDR	4	5	2	0	3	6	7	-1	0	0.800	1.200
13	Kilmarnock	Sco	4	4	1	2	1	4	7	-3	0	1.000	1.000
14	Levski Sofia	Bul	3	4	1	1	2	11	7	4	0	0.750	2.750
15	Panathinaikos	Gre	3	4	1	1	2	5	5	0	0	0.750	1.250
16	SFK Lyn	Nor	2	2	1	0	1	6	8	-2	0	1 000	3.000
17	Sliema Wanderers	Mlt	2	2	1	0	1	2	4	-2	0	1.000	1.000
18	Drumcondra	Irl	2	3	1	0	2	2	5	-3	0	0.667	0.667
19	Feyenoord	Ned	2	2	1	0	1	2	6	-4	0	1.000	1.000
20	Djurgården SIF	Swe	2	2	1	0	1	2	7	-5	0	1.000	1.000
21	Derry City	Nir	2	3	1	0	2	8	15	-7	0	0.667	2.667
22	17 Nëntori Tirana	Alb	1	2	0	1	1	0	1	-1	0	0 500	0.000
23	Nantes	Fra	1	2	0	1	1	2	4	-2	0	0.500	1.000
24	Fenerbahçe	Tur	1	2	0	1	1	1	5	-4	0	0.500	0.500
25	Lausanne-Sports	Sui	1	2	0	1	1	0	4	-4	0	0.500	0.000
26	Linzer ASK	Aut	0	2	0	0	2	2	5	-3	0	0.000	1.000
27	B 1909 Odense	Den	0	2	0	0	2	2	7	-5	0	0.000	1.000
28	HJK Helsinki	Fin	0	2	0	0	2	2	9	-7	0	0.000	1.000
29	Apoel Nicosia	Cyp	0	2	0	0	2	0	10	-10	0	0.000	0.000
30	IBK Keflavik	Isl	0	2	0	0	2	2	13	-11	0	0.000	1.000
31	Stade Dudelange	Lux	0	2	0	0	2	0	18	-18	0	0.000	0.000
	Total		**132**	**118**	**50**	**18**	**50**	**227**	**227**	**0**	**14**	**1.119**	**3.847**

European Cup Winners Cup 1965-66

First Round

Team 1	Cnty	Team 2	Cnty	1st leg	2nd leg	Agg
Wiener Neustadt	Aut	Universitatea Cluj	Rom	0-1	0-2	0-3
Omonia Nicosia	Cyp	Olympiakos Pireus	Gre	0-1	1-1	1-2
AGF Aarhus	Den	Vitória Setúbal	Por	2-1	2-1	4-2
Limerick	Irl	CSKA Sofia	Bul	1-2	0-2	1-4
Atlético Madrid	Esp	Dinamo Zagreb	Yug	4-0	1-0	5-0
Reipas Lahti	Fin	Honvéd	Hun	2-10	0-6	2-16
Cardiff City	Wal	Standard Liège	Bel	1-2	0-1	1-3
Coleraine	Nir	Dinamo Kiev	URS	1-6	0-4	1-10
KR Reykjavik	Isl	Rosenborg BK	Nor	1-3	1-3	2-6
Juventus	Ita	Liverpool	Eng	1-0	0-2	1-2
Floriana	Mlt	Borussia Dortmund	FRG	1-5	0-8	1-13
Go Ahead Eagles	Ned	Celtic	Sco	0-6	0-1	0-7
Sion	Sui	Galatasaray	Tur	5-1	1-2	6-3
Dukla Prague	Tch	Stade Rennes	Fra	2-0	0-0	2-0
Magdeburg	GDR	Spora Luxembourg	Lux	1-0	2-0	3-0

	Pts	P	W	D	L	F	A	Diff	Goals/P
Total	**60**	**30**	**28**	**4**	**28**	**101**	**101**	**0**	**3.367**

Second Round

Liverpool	Eng	Standard Liège	Bel	3-1	2-1	5-2
West Ham United	Eng	Olympiakos Pireus	Gre	4-0	2-2	6-2
AGF Aarhus	Den	Celtic	Sco	0-1	0-2	0-3
Rosenborg BK	Nor	Dinamo Kiev	URS	1-4	0-2	1-6
Borussia Dortmund	FRG	CSKA Sofia	Bul	3-0	2-4	5-4
Universitatea Cluj	Rom	Atlético Madrid	Esp	0-2	0-4	0-6
Dukla Prague	Tch	Honvéd	Hun	2-3	2-1	4-4
Magdeburg	GDR	Sion	Sui	8-1	2-2	10-3

	Pts	P	W	D	L	F	A	Diff	Goals/P
Total	**32**	**16**	**14**	**4**	**14**	**61**	**61**	**0**	**3.813**

Quarter Finals

West Ham United	Eng	Magdeburg	GDR	1-0	1-1	2-1
Celtic	Sco	Dinamo Kiev	URS	3-0	1-1	4-1
Atlético Madrid	Esp	Borussia Dortmund	FRG	1-1	0-1	1-2
Honvéd	Hun	Liverpool	Eng	0-0	0-2	0-2

	Pts	P	W	D	L	F	A	Diff	Goals/P
Total	**16**	**8**	**4**	**8**	**4**	**13**	**13**	**0**	**1.625**

Semi Finals

West Ham United	Eng	Borussia Dortmund	FRG	1-2	1-3	2-5
Celtic	Sco	Liverpool	Eng	1-0	0-2	1-2

	Pts	P	W	D	L	F	A	Diff	Goals/P
Total	**8**	**4**	**4**	**0**	**4**	**10**	**10**	**0**	**2.500**

Final

Borussia Dortmund	FRG	Liverpool	Eng	2-1	2-1

	Pts	P	W	D	L	F	A	Diff	Goals/P
Total	2	1	1	0	1	3	3	0	3.000

	Pts	P	W	D	L	F	A	Diff	Goals/P
Total	118	59	51	16	51	188	188	0	3.186

Pos'n	Club	Cnty	Pts	P	W	D	L	F	A	Diff	B	Pts/P	F/P
1	Borussia Dortmund	FRG	18	9	7	1	1	27	9	18	3	2.000	3.000
2	Celtic	Sco	15	8	6	1	1	15	3	12	2	1.875	1.875
3	Liverpool	Eng	14	9	5	1	3	12	6	6	3	1.556	1.333
4	Dinamo Kiev	URS	10	6	4	1	1	17	6	11	1	1.667	2.833
5	Atlético Madrid	Esp	10	6	4	1	1	12	2	10	1	1.667	2.000
6	Magdeburg	GDR	9	6	3	2	1	14	5	9	1	1.500	2.333
7	Honvéd	Hun	8	6	3	1	2	20	8	12	1	1.333	3.333
8	West Ham United	Eng	8	6	2	2	2	10	8	2	2	1.333	1.667
9	CSKA Sofia	Bul	6	4	3	0	1	8	6	2	0	1.500	2.000
10	Dukla Prague	Tch	5	4	2	1	1	6	4	2	0	1.250	1.500
11	Rosenborg BK	Nor	4	4	2	0	2	7	8	-1	0	1.000	1.750
12	Standard Liège	Bel	4	4	2	0	2	5	6	-1	0	1.000	1.250
13	AGF Aarhus	Den	4	4	2	0	2	4	5	-1	0	1.000	1.000
14	Olympiakos Pireus	Gre	4	4	1	2	1	4	7	-3	0	1.000	1.000
15	Universitatea Cluj	Rom	4	4	2	0	2	3	6	-3	0	1.000	0.750
16	Sion	Sui	3	4	1	1	2	9	13	-4	0	0.750	2.250
17	Juventus	Ita	2	2	1	0	1	1	2	-1	0	1.000	0.500
18	Galatasaray	Tur	2	2	1	0	1	3	6	-3	0	1.000	1.500
19	Omonia Nicosia	Cyp	1	2	0	1	1	1	2	-1	0	0.500	0.500
20	Stade Rennes	Fra	1	2	0	1	1	0	2	-2	0	0.500	0.000
21	Vitória Setúbal	Por	0	2	0	0	2	2	4	-2	0	0.000	1.000
22	Cardiff City	Wal	0	2	0	0	2	1	3	-2	0	0.000	0.500
23	Limerick	Irl	0	2	0	0	2	1	4	-3	0	0.000	0.500
24	Wiener Neustadt	Aut	0	2	0	0	2	0	3	-3	0	0.000	0.000
–	Spora Luxemburg	Lux	0	2	0	0	2	0	3	-3	0	0.000	0.000
26	KR Reykjavik	Isl	0	2	0	0	2	2	6	-4	0	0.000	1.000
27	Dinamo Zagreb	Rom	0	2	0	0	2	0	5	-5	0	0.000	0.000
28	Go Ahead Eagles	Ned	0	2	0	0	2	0	7	-7	0	0.000	0.000
29	Coleraine	Nir	0	2	0	0	2	1	10	-9	0	0.000	0.500
30	Floriana	Mlt	0	2	0	0	2	1	13	-12	0	0.000	0.500
31	Reipas Lahti	Fin	0	2	0	0	2	2	16	-14	0	0.000	1.000
	Total		**132**	**118**	**51**	**16**	**51**	**188**	**188**	**0**	**14**	**1.119**	**3.186**

First Round

Team 1	Cnty	Team 2	Cnty	1st leg	2nd leg	Agg
Leeds United	Eng	Torino	Ita	2-1	0-0	2-1
Chelsea	Eng	Roma	Ita	4-1	0-0	4-1
Antwerp	Bel	Glentoran	Nir	1-0	3-3	4-3
FC Liège	Bel	NK Zagreb	Yug	1-0	0-2	1-2
Hibernian	Sco	Valencia	Esp	2-0	0-2	2-5
		Valencia won the replay 0-3				
Girondins Bordeaux	Fra	Sporting Lisbon	Por	0-4	1-6	1-10
Stade Français	Fra	FC Porto	Por	0-0	0-1	0-1
PAOK Salonika	Gre	Wiener Sport-Club	Aut	2-1	0-6	2-7
AC Milan	Ita	Strasbourg	Fra	1-0	1-2	3-3
		The replay resulted in a 1-1 draw				
Utrecht	Ned	Barcelona	Esp	0-0	1-7	1-7
Cologne	FRG	Union Luxembourg	Lux	13-0	4-0	17-0
Nuremberg	FRG	Everton	Eng	1-1	0-1	1-2
Malmö FF	Swe	1860 Munich	FRG	0-3	0-4	0-7
AIK	Swe	RWD Molenbeek	Bel	3-1	0-0	3-1
Zbrojovka Brno	Tch	Lokomotiv Plovdiv	Bul	2-0	0-1	2-1
Red Star Belgrade	Yug	Fiorentina	Ita	0-4	1-3	1-7

	Pts	P	W	D	L	F	A	Diff	Goals/P
Total	68	34	26	16	26	102	102	0	3.000

Second Round

Chelsea	Eng	Wiener Sport-Club	Aut	2-0	0-1	2-1
Dunfermline Athletic	Sco	B1903 Copenhagen	Den	5-0	4-2	9-2
Heart of Midlothian	Sco	Vålerengen SIF	Nor	1-0	3-1	4-1
Shamrock Rovers	Irl	Real Zaragoza	Esp	1-1	1-2	2-3
Barcelona	Esp	Antwerp	Bel	2-0	1-2	3-2
Valencia	Esp	FC Basle	Sui	5-1	3-1	8-2
Aris Salonika	Gre	Cologne	FRG	2-1	0-2	2-3
Ujpesti Dózsa	Hun	Everton	Eng	3-0	1-2	4-2
Fiorentina	Ita	Zbrojovka Brno	Tch	2-0	0-4	2-4
AC Milan	Ita	Barreirense	Por	2-0	0-2	3-2
		AC Milan won the replay 1-0				
Sporting Lisbon	Por	Español	Esp	2-1	3-4	6-7
		Español won the replay 1-2				
Hannover 96	FRG	FC Porto	Por	5-0	1-2	6-2
AIK	Swe	Servette	Sui	2-1	1-4	3-5
Göztepe	Tur	1860 Munich	FRG	2-1	1-9	3-10
NK Zagreb	Yug	Red Flag Brasov	Rom	2-2	0-1	2-3
Lokomotive Leipzig	GDR	Leeds United	Eng	1-2	0-0	1-2

	Pts	P	W	D	L	F	A	Diff	Goals/P
Total	68	34	31	6	31	111	111	0	3.265

Third Round

Leeds United	Eng	Valencia	Esp	1-1	1-0	2-1
Heart of Midlothian	Sco	Real Zaragoza	Esp	3-3	2-2	5-6
		Real Zaragoza won the replay 0-1				
Español	Esp	Red Flag Brasov	Rom	3-1	2-4	6-5
		Español won the replay 1-0				
AC Milan	Ita	Chelsea	Eng	2-1	1-2	4-4
		The replay resulted in a 1-1 draw				
Cologne	FRG	Ujpesti Dózsa	Hun	3-2	0-4	3-6
Hannover 96	FRG	Barcelona	Esp	2-1	0-1	3-3
		The replay resulted in a 1-1 draw				
Servette	Sui	1860 Munich	FRG	1-1	1-4	2-5
Zbrojovka Brno	Tch	Dunfermline Athletic	Sco	0-0	0-2	0-2

	Pts	P	W	D	L	F	A	Diff	Goals/P
Total	40	20	13	14	13	57	57	0	2.850

Quarter Finals

Leeds United	Eng	Ujpesti Dózsa	Hun	4-1	1-1	5-2
Barcelona	Esp	Español	Esp	1-0	1-0	2-0
Real Zaragoza	Esp	Dunfermline Athletic	Sco	4-2	0-1	4-3
1860 Munich	FRG	Chelsea	Eng	2-2	0-1	2-3

	Pts	P	W	D	L	F	A	Diff	Goals/P
Total	16	8	6	4	6	21	21	0	2.625

Semi Finals

Barcelona	FRG	Chelsea	Eng	2-0	0-2	7-2
		Barcelona won the replay 5-0				
Real Zaragoza	Esp	Leeds United	Eng	1-0	1-2	5-3
		Real Zaragoza won the replay 3-1				

	Pts	P	W	D	L	F	A	Diff	Goals/P
Total	12	6	6	0	6	17	17	0	2.833

Final

Barcelona	Esp	Real Zaragoza	Esp	0-1	4-2	4-3

	Pts	P	W	D	L	F	A	Diff	Goals/P
Total	4	2	2	0	2	7	7	0	3.500

	Pts	P	W	D	L	F	A	Diff	Goals/P
Total	208	104	84	40	84	315	315	0	3.029

UEFA Cup 1965-66

Pos'n	Club	Cnty	Pts	P	W	D	L	F	A	Diff	B	Pts/P	F/P
1	Barcelona	Esp	21	14	8	2	4	26	11	15	3	1.500	1.857
2	Real Zaragoza	Esp	18	21	6	3	3	21	17	4	3	1.500	1.750
3	Leeds United	Eng	16	11	5	4	2	14	10	4	2	1.455	1.273
4	Chelsea	Eng	15	12	5	3	4	15	15	0	2	1.250	1.250
5	1860 Munich	FRG	11	8	4	2	2	24	8	16	1	1.375	3.000
6	Dunfermline Athletic	Sco	10	6	4	1	1	14	6	8	1	1.667	2.333
7	AC Milan	Ita	10	9	4	2	3	10	9	1	0	1.111	1.111
8	Valencia	Esp	9	7	4	1	2	14	6	8	0	1.286	2.000
9	Español	Esp	9	8	4	0	4	13	13	0	1	1.125	1.625
10	Cologne	FRG	8	6	4	0	2	23	8	15	0	1.333	3.833
11	Sporting Lisbon	Por	6	5	3	0	2	16	8	8	0	1.200	3.200
12	Fiorentina	Ita	6	4	3	0	1	9	5	4	0	1.500	2.250
13	Ujpesti Dósza	Hun	6	6	2	1	3	12	10	2	1	1.000	2.000
14	Heart of Midlothian	Sco	6	5	2	2	1	9	7	2	0	1.200	1.800
15	Hannover 96	FRG	5	5	2	1	2	9	5	4	0	1.000	1.800
16	Zbrojovka Brno	Tch	5	6	2	1	3	6	5	1	0	0.833	1.000
17	Red Flag Brasov	Rom	5	5	2	1	2	8	8	0	0	1.000	1.600
18	Antwerp	Bel	5	4	2	1	1	6	6	0	0	1.250	1.500
–	AIK	Swe	5	4	2	1	1	6	6	0	0	1.250	1.500
20	Everton	Eng	5	4	2	1	1	4	5	-1	0	1.250	1.000
21	FC Porto	Por	5	4	2	1	1	3	6	-3	0	1.250	0.750
22	Wiener Sport-Club	Aut	4	4	2	0	2	8	4	4	0	1.000	2.000
23	NK Zagreb	Yug	3	4	1	1	2	4	4	0	0	0.750	1.000
24	Strasbourg	Fra	3	3	1	1	1	3	3	0	0	1.000	1.000
25	Servette	Sui	3	4	1	1	2	7	8	-1	0	0.750	1.750
26	Aris Salonika	Gre	2	2	1	0	1	2	3	-1	0	1.000	1.000
–	Barreirense	Por	2	3	1	0	2	2	3	-1	0	0.667	0.667
28	FC Liège	Bel	2	2	1	0	1	1	2	-1	0	1.000	0.500
–	Lokomotiv Plovdiv	Bul	2	2	1	0	1	1	2	-1	0	1.000	0.500
30	Hibernian	Sco	2	3	1	0	2	2	5	-3	0	0.667	0.667
31	PAOK Salonika	Gre	2	2	1	0	1	2	7	-5	0	1.000	1.000
32	Göztepe	Tur	2	2	1	0	1	3	10	-7	0	1.000	1.500
33	Glentoran	Nir	1	2	0	1	1	3	4	-1	0	0.500	1.500
34	Shamrock Rovers	Irl	1	2	0	1	1	2	3	-1	0	0.500	1.000
35	Torino	Ita	1	2	0	1	1	1	2	-1	0	0.500	0.500
–	Nuremberg	FRG	1	2	0	1	1	1	2	-1	0	0.500	0.500
–	Lokomotive Leipzig	GDR	1	2	0	1	1	1	2	-1	0	0.500	0.500
38	Stade Français	Fra	1	2	0	1	1	0	1	-1	0	0.500	0.000
39	RWD Molenbeek	Bel	1	2	0	1	1	1	3	-2	0	0.500	0.500
40	Roma	Ita	1	2	0	1	1	1	4	-3	0	0.500	0.500
41	Utrecht	Ned	1	2	0	1	1	1	7	-6	0	0.500	0.500
42	Vålerengen SIF	Nor	0	2	0	0	2	1	4	-3	0	0.000	0.500
43	FC Basle	Sui	0	2	0	0	2	2	8	-6	0	0.000	1.000
44	Red Star Belgrade	Yug	0	2	0	0	2	1	7	-6	0	0.000	0.500
45	B 1903 Copenhagen	Den	0	2	0	0	2	2	9	-7	0	0.000	1.000
46	Malmö FF	Swe	0	2	0	0	2	0	7	-7	0	0.000	0.000
47	Girondins Bordeaux	Fra	0	2	0	0	2	1	10	-9	0	0.000	0.500
48	Union Luxembourg	Lux	0	2	0	0	2	0	17	-17	0	0.000	0.000
	Total		**222**	**208**	**84**	**40**	**84**	**315**	**315**	**0**	**14**	**1.067**	**3.029**

1965-66

Pos'n	Cnty	Pts	P	W	D	L	F	A	Diff	B	Pts/P	F/P
1	Esp	82	56	31	9	16	107	59	48	11	1.464	1.911
2	Eng	74	50	26	11	13	78	52	26	11	1.480	1.560
3	FRG	49	34	20	5	9	95	35	60	4	1.441	2.794
4	Sco	37	26	14	6	6	44	28	16	3	1.423	1.692
5	Ita	28	25	10	6	9	31	27	4	2	1.120	1.240
6	Hun	23	18	8	4	6	49	26	23	3	1.278	2.722
7	Por	21	20	9	2	9	49	33	16	1	1.050	2.450
8	Bel	20	17	8	3	6	30	22	8	1	1.176	1.765
9	Tch	18	16	7	3	6	24	17	7	1	1.125	1.500
10	Rom	15	13	7	1	5	20	19	1	0	1.154	1.538
11	Yug	15	17	5	2	10	21	26	-5	3	0.882	1.235
12	GDR	14	13	5	3	5	21	14	7	1	1.077	1.615
13	Bul	11	10	5	1	4	20	15	5	0	1.100	2.000
14	Gre	11	12	4	3	5	13	22	-9	0	0.917	1.083
15	URS	10	6	4	1	1	17	6	11	1	1.667	2.833
16	Swe	7	8	3	1	4	8	20	-12	0	0.875	1.000
17	Sui	7	12	2	3	7	18	33	-15	0	0.583	1.500
18	Pol	6	4	3	0	1	7	6	1	0	1.500	1.750
19	Nor	6	8	3	0	5	14	20	-6	0	0.750	1.750
20	Fra	6	11	1	4	6	6	20	-14	0	0.545	0.545
21	Tur	5	6	2	1	3	7	21	-14	0	0.833	1.167
22	Aut	4	8	2	0	6	10	12	-2	0	0.500	1.250
23	Den	4	8	2	0	6	8	21	-13	0	0.500	1.000
24	Irl	3	7	1	1	5	5	12	-7	0	0.429	0.714
25	Nir	3	7	1	1	5	12	29	-17	0	0.429	1.714
26	Ned	3	6	1	1	4	3	20	-17	0	0.500	0.500
27	Mlt	2	4	1	0	3	3	17	-14	0	0.500	0.750
28	Alb	1	2	0	1	1	0	1	-1	0	0.500	0.000
29	Cyp	1	4	0	1	3	1	12	-11	0	0.250	0.250
30	Wal	0	2	0	0	2	1	3	-2	0	0.000	0.500
31	Isl	0	4	0	0	4	4	19	-15	0	0.000	1.000
32	Fin	0	4	0	0	4	4	25	-21	0	0.000	1.000
33	Lux	0	6	0	0	6	0	38	-38	0	0.000	0.000
	Total	**486**	**444**	**185**	**74**	**185**	**730**	**730**	**0**	**42**	**1.095**	**3.288**

1955-56 to 1965-66

Pos'n	Cnty	Pts	P	W	D	L	F	A	Diff	B	Pts/P	F/P
1	Esp	492	312	180	58	74	711	389	322	74	1.577	2.279
2	Ita	313	215	116	38	61	408	261	147	43	1.456	1.898
3	Eng	298	205	109	38	58	430	279	151	42	1.454	2.098
4	FRG	221	174	82	31	61	362	285	77	26	1.270	2.080
5	Sco	186	151	73	21	57	285	250	35	19	1.232	1.887
6	Yug	168	153	59	27	67	259	242	17	23	1.098	1.693
7	Hun	164	128	62	19	47	273	197	76	21	1.281	2.133
8	Por	143	118	49	28	41	246	174	72	17	1.212	2.085
9	Tch	113	92	44	15	33	157	118	39	10	1.228	1.707
10	Fra	107	103	36	23	44	172	176	-4	12	1.039	1.670
11	Bel	92	95	35	13	47	128	155	-27	9	0.968	1.347
12	Sui	79	101	27	18	56	163	254	-91	7	0.782	1.614
13	Aut	76	80	29	13	38	118	136	-18	5	0.950	1.475
14	Ned	72	68	27	12	29	113	132	-19	6	1.059	1.662
15	GDR	69	78	24	17	37	118	125	-7	4	0.885	1.513
16	Bul	65	66	24	15	27	117	110	7	2	0.985	1.773
17	Rom	60	60	27	5	28	81	100	-19	1	1.000	1.350
18	Den	46	71	15	13	43	116	190	-74	3	0.648	1.634
19	Pol	44	43	19	5	19	49	77	-28	1	1.023	1.140
20	Swe	41	48	14	11	23	66	101	-35	2	0.854	1.375
21	Tur	40	49	15	8	26	62	97	-35	2	0.816	1.265
22	Gre	30	41	10	10	21	45	88	-43	0	0.732	1.098
23	Irl	16	42	5	6	31	32	112	-80	0	0.381	0.762
24	Nor	15	28	7	1	20	33	75	-42	0	0.536	1.179
25	Lux	15	44	6	3	35	38	188	-150	0	0.341	0.864
26	Wal	14	17	4	5	8	15	23	-8	1	0.824	0.882
27	Nir	13	32	4	5	23	38	105	-67	0	0.406	1.188
28	URS	10	6	4	1	1	17	6	11	1	1.667	2.833
29	Fin	6	22	3	0	19	20	79	-59	0	0.273	0.909
30	Alb	5	8	1	3	4	3	9	-6	0	0.625	0.375
31	Cyp	3	12	1	1	10	9	53	-44	0	0.250	0.750
32	Mlt	3	20	1	1	18	10	83	-73	0	0.150	0.500
33	Isl	0	6	0	0	6	5	30	-25	0	0.000	0.833
	Total	**3019**	**2688**	**1112**	**464**	**1112**	**4699**	**4699**	**0**	**331**	**1.123**	**3.496**

National Performance by Index

1965-66

Pos'n	Cnty	Ave	Pts	P	W	D	L	F	A	Diff	B	No./T
1	Spain	13.666	82	56	31	9	16	107	59	48	11	6
2	England	12.333	74	50	26	11	13	78	52	26	11	6
3	USSR	10.000	10	6	4	1	1	17	6	11	1	1
4	W. Germany	8.166	49	34	20	5	9	95	35	60	4	6
5	Hungary	7.666	23	18	8	4	6	49	26	23	3	3
6	Scotland	7.400	37	26	14	6	6	44	28	16	3	5
7	Poland	6.000	6	4	3	0	1	7	6	1	0	1
–	Czechoslovakia	6.000	18	16	7	3	6	24	17	7	1	3
9	Romania	5.000	15	13	7	1	5	20	19	1	0	3
10	Italy	4.666	28	25	10	6	9	31	27	4	2	6
–	E. Germany	4.666	14	13	5	3	5	21	14	7	1	3
12	Portugal	4.200	21	20	9	2	9	49	33	16	1	5
13	Belgium	4.000	20	17	8	3	6	30	22	8	1	5
14	Yugoslavia	3.750	15	17	5	2	10	21	26	-5	3	4
15	Bulgaria	3.666	11	10	5	1	4	20	15	5	0	3
16	Greece	2.750	11	12	4	3	5	13	22	-9	0	4
17	Sweden	2.333	7	8	3	1	4	8	20	-12	0	3
18	Norway	2.000	6	8	3	0	5	14	20	-6	0	3
19	Switzerland	1.750	7	12	2	3	7	18	33	-15	0	4
20	Turkey	1.666	5	6	2	1	3	7	21	-14	0	3
21	Austria	1.333	4	8	2	0	6	10	12	-2	0	3
–	Denmark	1.333	4	8	2	0	6	8	21	-13	0	3
23	France	1.200	6	11	1	4	6	6	20	-14	0	5
24	Albania	1.000	1	2	0	1	1	0	1	-1	0	1
–	Rep. of Ireland	1.000	3	7	1	1	5	5	12	-7	0	3
–	N. Ireland	1.000	3	7	1	1	5	12	29	-17	0	3
–	Malta	1.000	2	4	1	0	3	3	17	-14	0	2
–	Netherlands	1.000	3	6	1	1	4	3	20	-17	0	3
29	Cyprus	0.500	1	4	0	1	3	1	12	-11	0	2
30	Finland	0.000	0	4	0	0	4	4	25	-21	0	2
–	Wales	0.000	0	2	0	0	2	1	3	-2	0	1
–	Iceland	0.000	0	4	0	0	4	4	19	-15	0	2
–	Luxembourg	0.000	0	6	0	0	6	0	38	-38	0	3
	Total		**486**	**444**	**185**	**74**	**185**	**730**	**730**	**0**	**42**	**3.288**

1955-56 to 1965-66

1	Spain	11.441	492	312	180	58	74	711	389	322	74	43
2	USSR	10.000	10	6	4	1	1	17	6	11	1	1
3	England	8.764	298	205	109	38	58	430	279	151	42	34
4	Italy	8.025	313	215	116	38	61	408	261	147	43	39
5	Hungary	6.833	164	128	62	19	47	273	197	76	21	24
6	Scotland	6.000	186	151	73	21	57	285	250	35	19	31
7	W. Germany	5.666	221	174	82	31	61	362	285	77	26	39
8	Czechoslovakia	5.380	113	92	44	15	33	157	118	39	10	21
9	Portugal	4.931	143	118	49	28	41	246	174	72	17	29
10	Yugoslavia	4.800	168	153	59	27	67	259	242	17	23	35
11	France	3.821	107	103	36	23	44	172	176	-4	12	28
12	Belgium	3.680	92	95	35	13	47	128	155	-27	9	25
13	Bulgaria	3.611	65	66	24	15	27	117	110	7	2	18
14	Netherlands	3.600	72	68	27	12	29	113	132	-19	6	20
15	Austria	3.454	76	80	29	13	38	118	136	-18	5	22
16	Romania	3.333	60	60	27	5	28	81	100	-19	1	18
17	Poland	3.142	44	43	19	5	19	49	77	-28	1	14
18	E. Germany	3.000	69	78	24	17	37	118	125	-7	4	23
19	Wales	2.800	14	17	4	5	8	15	23	-8	1	5
20	Sweden	2.733	41	48	14	11	23	66	101	-35	2	15
21	Turkey	2.666	40	49	15	8	26	62	97	-35	2	15
22	Switzerland	2.548	79	101	27	18	56	163	254	-91	7	31
23	Greece	1.875	30	41	10	10	21	45	88	-43	0	16
24	Denmark	1.769	46	71	15	13	43	116	190	-74	3	26
25	Norway	1.363	15	28	7	1	20	33	75	-42	0	11
26	Albania	1.250	5	8	1	3	4	3	9	-6	0	4
27	Rep. of Ireland	0.888	16	42	5	6	31	32	112	-80	0	18
28	N. Ireland	0.812	13	32	4	5	23	38	105	-67	0	16
29	Luxembourg	0.789	15	44	6	3	35	38	188	-150	0	19
30	Cyprus	0.600	3	12	1	1	10	9	53	-44	0	5
–	Finland	0.600	6	22	3	0	19	20	79	-59	0	10
32	Malta	0.300	3	20	1	1	18	10	83	-73	0	10
33	Iceland	0.000	0	6	0	0	6	5	30	-25	0	3
	Total		**3019**	**2688**	**1112**	**464**	**1112**	**4699**	**4699**	**0**	**331**	**3.496**

Puskás Swansong Season

The 1965-66 season marked a fleeting return to the old established order as Real Madrid won their first Champions' Cup in six years, and a record sixth in all, and their great Spanish rivals Barcelona captured their third Fairs' Cup. There was to be no Spanish treble, however, as Atlético Madrid went out in the quarter-finals of the Cup-winners' Cup to the eventual winners, Borussia Dortmund.

Real didn't get off to the best of starts in their 11th successive Champions' Cup campaign, losing 2-1 in Rotterdam to Dutch champions Feyenoord (or Feijenoord as they were then known before their name was internationalised). But that defeat was swiftly nullified in the second leg in Madrid, where Puskás, in his swansong season at the club, fired four goals, his last in European competition, to give the team a 5-0 victory. Kilmarnock were given similar treatment in the next round and then it was time for Real to reap their revenge on their 1962-63 conquerors Anderlecht with a 4-3 aggregate victory.

Real's major achievement was to deny Inter Milan in the semi-finals. Inter, going for a hat-trick of victories, lost the first leg in Madrid, but only by a single goal scored by right-half Pirri. They might have fancied their chances in the return, but with Real's courage matched by that of the Hungarian referee who refused to be bribed into giving the Italians the match, the game ended 1-1, allowing Real, not Inter, to progress into the final.

The other finalists, surprisingly, were Partizan Belgrade. They had caused a major shock by knocking out Manchester United in the semi-final. United had given one of the great European performances in the previous round, when, inspired by two-goal George Best, they destroyed Benfica 5-1 in the Stadium of Light – a ground on which the Portuguese club had won every single one of their previous 18 European Cup matches!

The final was played in Brussels, the first venue to be selected twice for the Champions' Cup final and a favourite venue of Real, victors there in 1958. But it looked to be heading for an upset when Partizan, through a goal by Vasovic, led with just 20 minutes to go. But Amaro Amancio, as he had done the round before in Milan, popped up to score the crucial equaliser before right-winger Serena gave Real the trophy with a late winner. Interestingly, Real's line-up for the final was made up entirely of Spanish players, with one of them, Paco Gento, winning his sixth Champions' Cup winner's medal – an achievement which is unlikely ever to be equalled.

Barcelona, quite literally, needed the luck of the draw on the way to winning the Fairs' Cup. In the third round, after a play-off against Hannover 96 had ended 1-1, they won the draw by lots to progress into the quarter-finals. After eliminating city rivals Español, they were then forced into another play-off by Chelsea in the semi-finals, but this time they won 5-0 and made it through to the final against 1963-64 winners Zaragoza. Zaragoza had also accounted for English opposition in a semi-final play-off, defeating Leeds United 3-1 to make the Fairs' Cup final an all-Spanish affair for the third time in five seasons.

Zaragoza caused a sensation when they won the first leg of the final (now restored to two matches) 1-0 in Barcelona – only the second time in 25 Fairs' Cup matches that Barcelona had lost at home. But it was not enough. Barcelona restored parity in the second leg and won the match in extra-time with a hat-trick from their left-winger Pujol.

Borussia Dortmund's success in the Cup-winners' Cup marked the first victory for a West German side in any of the three European Cups. For the second year running the final brought together German and English opposition, but this time the outcome was different, with Dortmund defeating Liverpool 2-1 after extra time in Glasgow. Dortmund had also knocked out the holders West Ham in the semi-finals thanks to four goals from their star striker Lothar Emmerich, which took his total for the competition to 14. Surprisingly, he did not get his name on the scoresheet in the final. That honour went to his West German international team-mates Held and Libuda, with Roger Hunt replying for Liverpool.

Celtic

Bayern Munich

Real Madrid

1966 – 1967

Preliminary Round

Team 1	Cnty	Team 2	Cnty	1st leg	2nd leg	Agg
Waterford United	Irl	Vorwärts Frankfurt/Oder	GDR	1-6	0-6	1-12
Sliema Wanderers	Mlt	CSKA Sofia	Bul	1-2	0-4	1-6

	Pts	P	W	D	L	F	A	Diff	Goals/P
Total	8	4	4	0	4	20	20	0	5.000

First Round

Liverpool	Eng	Petrolul Ploiesti	Rom	2-0	1-3	5-3
		Liverpool won the replay 2-0				
Admira Wacker	Aut	Vojvodina Novi Sad	Yug	0-1	0-0	0-1
CSKA Sofia	Bul	Olympiakos Pireus	Gre	3-1	0-1	3-2
Esbjerg FB	Den	Dukla Prague	Tch	0-2	0-4	0-6
Celtic	Sco	FC Zürich	Sui	2-0	3-0	5-0
Haka Valkeakoski	Fin	Anderlecht	Bel	1-10	0-2	1-12
Vasas SC	Hun	Sporting Lisbon	Por	5-0	2-0	7-0
KR Reykjavik	Isl	Nantes	Fra	2-3	2-5	4-8
Inter Milan	Ita	Torpedo Moscow	URS	1-0	0-0	1-0
Aris Bonnevoie	Lux	Linfield	Nir	3-3	1-6	4-9
Ajax	Ned	Besiktas	Tur	2-0	2-1	4-1
Górnik Zabrze	Pol	Vorwärts Frankfurt/Oder	GDR	2-1	3-1	6-4
		Górnik Zabrze won the replay 3-1				
1860 Munich	FRG	Omonia Nicosia	Cyp	8-0	2-1	10-1
Malmö FF	Swe	Atlético Madrid	Esp	0-2	1-3	1-5

	Pts	P	W	D	L	F	A	Diff	Goals/P
Total	60	30	27	6	27	103	103	0	3.433

Second Round

CSKA Sofia	Bul	Górnik Zabrze	Pol	4-0	0-3	4-3
Nantes	Fra	Celtic	Sco	1-3	1-3	2-6
Inter Milan	Ita	Vasas SC	Hun	2-1	2-0	4-1
Vålerengen SIF	Nor	Linfield	Nir	1-4	1-1	2-5
Ajax	Ned	Liverpool	Eng	5-1	2-2	7-3
1860 Munich	FRG	Real Madrid	Esp	1-0	1-3	2-3
Dukla Prague	Tch	Anderlecht	Bel	4-1	2-1	6-2
Vojvodina Novi Sad	Yug	Atlético Madrid	Esp	3-1	0-2	6-5
		Vojvodina Novi Sad won the replay 3-2				

	Pts	P	W	D	L	F	A	Diff	Goals/P
Total	34	17	15	4	15	61	61	0	3.588

Quarter Finals

Linfield	Nir	CSKA Sofia	Bul	2-2	0-1	2-3
Inter Milan	Ita	Real Madrid	Esp	1-0	2-0	3-0
Ajax	Ned	Dukla Prague	Tch	1-1	1-2	2-3
Vojvodina Novi Sad	Yug	Celtic	Sco	1-0	0-2	1-2

	Pts	P	W	D	L	F	A	Diff	Goals/P
Total	16	8	6	4	6	16	16	0	2.000

Semi Finals

Celtic	Sco	Dukla Prague	Tch	3-1	0-0		3-1
Inter Milan	Ita	CSKA Sofia	Bul	1-1	1-1		3-2
		Inter Milan won the replay 1-0					

	Pts	P	W	D	L	F	A	Diff	Goals/P
Total	10	5	2	6	2	9	9	0	1.800

Final

Celtic	Sco	Inter Milan	Ita	2-1	2-1

	Pts	P	W	D	L	F	A	Diff	Goals/P
Total	2	1	1	0	1	3	3	0	3.000

	Pts	P	W	D	L	F	A	Diff	Goals/P
Total	130	65	55	20	55	212	212	0	3.262

Pos'n	Club	Cnty	Pts	P	W	D	L	F	A	Diff	B	Pts/P	F/P
1	Celtic	Sco	18	9	7	1	1	18	5	13	3	2.000	2.000
2	Inter Milan	Ita	18	10	6	3	1	12	5	7	3	1.800	1.200
3	CSKA Sofia	Bul	15	11	5	3	3	18	11	7	2	1.364	1.636
4	Dulka Prague	Tch	14	8	5	2	1	16	7	9	2	1.750	2.000
5	Vojvodina Novi Sad	You	10	7	4	1	2	8	7	1	1	1.429	1.143
6	Ajax	Ned	9	6	3	2	1	13	7	6	1	1.500	2.167
7	Linfield	Nir	8	6	2	3	1	16	9	7	1	1.333	2.667
8	Vorwärts Frankfurt/Oder	GDR	6	5	3	0	2	16	7	9	0	1.200	3.200
9	1860 Munich	FRG	6	4	3	0	1	12	4	8	0	1.500	3.000
10	Atlético Madrid	Esp	6	5	3	0	2	10	7	3	0	1.200	2.000
11	Górnik Zabrze	Pol	6	5	3	0	2	9	8	1	0	1.200	1.800
12	Liverpool	Eng	5	5	2	1	2	8	10	-2	0	1.000	1.600
13	Anderlecht	Bel	4	4	2	0	2	14	7	7	0	1.000	3.500
14	Vasas SC	Hun	4	4	2	0	2	8	4	4	0	1.000	2.000
15	Nantes	Fra	4	4	2	0	2	10	10	0	0	1.000	2.500
16	Real Madrid	Esp	3	4	1	0	3	3	5	-2	1	0.750	0.750
17	Olympiakos Pireus	Gre	2	2	1	0	1	2	3	-1	0	1.000	1.000
18	Petrolul Ploeisti	Rom	2	3	1	0	2	3	5	-2	0	0.667	1.000
19	Admira Wacker	Aut	1	2	0	1	1	0	1	-1	0	0.500	0.000
–	Torpedo Moscow	URS	1	2	0	1	1	0	1	-1	0	0.500	0.000
21	Vålerengen SIF	Nor	1	2	0	1	1	2	5	-3	0	0.500	1.000
22	Aris Bonnevoie	Lux	1	2	0	1	1	4	9	-5	0	0.500	2.000
23	Besiktas	Tur	0	2	0	0	2	1	4	-3	0	0.000	0.500
24	KR Reykjavik	Isl	0	2	0	0	2	4	8	-4	0	0.000	2.000
25	Malmö FF	Swe	0	2	0	0	2	1	5	-4	0	0.000	0.500
26	Sliema Wanderers	Mlt	0	2	0	0	2	1	6	-5	0	0.000	0.500
27	FC Zürich	Sui	0	2	0	0	2	0	5	-5	0	0.000	0.000
28	Esbjerg FB	Den	0	2	0	0	2	0	6	-6	0	0.000	0.000
29	Sporting Lisbon	Por	0	2	0	0	2	0	7	-7	0	0.000	0.000
30	Omonia Nicosia	Cyp	0	2	0	0	2	1	10	-9	0	0.000	0.500
31	Waterford	Irl	0	2	0	0	2	1	12	-11	0	0.000	0.500
–	Haka Valkeakoski	Fin	0	2	0	0	2	1	12	-11	0	0.000	0.500
	Total		**144**	**130**	**55**	**20**	**55**	**212**	**212**	**0**	**14**	**1.108**	**3.262**

Preliminary Round

Team 1	Cnty	Team 2	Cnty	1st leg	2nd leg	Agg
Valur Reykjavik	Isl	Standard Liège	Bel	1-1	1-8	2-9

	Pts	P	W	D	L	F	A	Diff	Goals/P
Total	4	2	1	2	1	11	11	0	5.500

First Round

Rapid Vienna	Aut	Galatasaray	Tur	4-0	5-3	9-3
Standard Liège	Bel	Apollon Limassol	Cyp	5-1	1-0	6-1
AaB Aalborg	Den	Everton	Eng	0-0	1-2	1-2
Shamrock Rovers	Irl	Spora Luxembourg	Lux	4-1	4-1	8-2
Strasbourg	Fra	Steaua Bucharest	Rom	1-0	1-1	2-1
Swansea City	Wal	Slavia Sofia	Bul	1-1	0-4	1-5
AEK Athens	Gre	Sporting Braga	Por	0-1	2-3	2-4
Glentoran	Nir	Rangers	Sco	1-1	0-4	1-5
Fiorentina	Ita	Rába ETO	Hun	1-0	2-4	3-4
Floriana	Mlt	Sparta Rotterdam	Ned	1-1	0-6	1-7
FK Skeid	Nor	Real Zaragoza	Esp	3-2	1-3	4-5
Servette	Sui	TPS Turku	Fin	1-1	2-1	3-2
Tatran Presov	Tch	Bayern Munich	FRG	1-1	2-3	3-4
OFK Belgrade	Yug	Spartak Moscow	URS	1-3	0-3	1-6
Chemie Leipzig	GDR	Legia Warsaw	Pol	3-0	2-2	5-2

	Pts	P	W	D	L	F	A	Diff	Goals/P
Total	60	30	22	16	22	103	103	0	3.433

Second Round

Rangers	Sco	Borussia Dortmund	FRG	2-1	0-0	2-1
Shamrock Rovers	Irl	Bayern Munich	FRG	1-1	2-3	3-4
Real Zaragoza	Esp	Everton	Eng	2-0	0-1	2-1
Strasbourg	Fra	Slavia Sofia	Bul	1-0	0-2	1-2
Rába ETO	Hun	Sporting Braga	Por	3-0	0-2	3-2
Servette	Sui	Sparta Rotterdam	Ned	2-0	0-1	2-1
Spartak Moscow	URS	Rapid Vienna	Aut	1-1	0-1	1-2
Chemie Leipzig	GDR	Standard Liège	Bel	2-1	0-1	2-2

	Pts	P	W	D	L	F	A	Diff	Goals/P
Total	32	16	13	6	13	31	31	0	1.938

Quarter Finals

Rapid Vienna	Aut	Bayern Munich	FRG	1-0	0-2	1-2
Rangers	Sco	Real Zaragoza	Esp	2-0	0-2	2-2
Rába ETO	Hun	Standard Liège	Bel	2-1	0-2	2-3
Servette	Sui	Slavia Sofia	Bul	1-0	0-3	1-3

	Pts	P	W	D	L	F	A	Diff	Goals/P
Total	16	8	8	0	8	16	16	0	2.000

European Cup Winners Cup 1966-67

Semi Finals

Slavia Sofia	Bul	Rangers	Sco	0-1	0-1	0-2
Bayern Munich	FRG	Standard Liège	Bel	2-0	3-1	5-1

	Pts	P	W	D	L	F	A	Diff	Goals/P
Total	8	4	4	0	4	8	8	0	2.000

Final

Bayern Munich	FRG	Rangers	Sco	1-0	1-0

	Pts	P	W	D	L	F	A	Diff	Goals/P
Total	2	1	1	0	1	1	1	0	1.000

	Pts	P	W	D	L	F	A	Diff	Goals/P
Total	122	61	49	24	49	170	170	0	2.787

Pos'n	Club	Cnty	Pts	P	W	D	L	F	A	Diff	B	Pts/P	F/P
1	Bayern Munich	FRG	17	9	6	2	1	16	8	8	3	1.889	1.778
2	Rangers	Sco	15	9	5	2	2	11	5	6	3	1.667	1.222
3	Standard Liège	Bel	13	10	5	1	4	21	12	9	2	1.300	2.100
4	Rapid Vienna	Aut	10	6	4	1	1	12	6	6	1	1.667	2.000
5	Slavia Sofia	Bul	9	8	3	1	4	10	5	5	2	1.125	1.250
6	Servette	Sui	8	6	3	1	2	6	6	0	1	1.333	1.000
7	Real Zaragoza	Esp	7	6	3	0	3	9	7	2	1	1.167	1.500
8	Rába ETO	Hun	7	6	3	0	3	9	8	1	1	1.167	1.500
9	Sporting Braga	Por	6	4	3	0	1	6	5	1	0	1.500	1.500
10	Shamrock Rovers	Irl	5	4	2	1	1	11	6	5	0	1.250	2.750
11	Sparta Rotterdam	Ned	5	4	2	1	1	8	3	5	0	1.250	2.000
12	Spartak Moscow	URS	5	4	2	1	1	7	3	4	0	1.250	1.750
13	Chemie Leipzig	GDR	5	4	2	1	1	7	4	3	0	1.250	1.750
14	Everton	Eng	5	4	2	1	1	3	3	0	0	1.250	0.750
15	Strasbourg	Fra	5	4	2	1	1	3	3	0	0	1.250	0.750
16	FK Skeid	Nor	2	2	1	0	1	4	5	-1	0	1.000	2.000
17	Fiorentina	Ita	2	2	1	0	1	3	4	-1	0	1.000	1.500
18	Tatran Presov	Tch	1	2	0	1	1	3	4	-1	0	0.500	1.500
19	TPS Turku	Fin	1	2	0	1	1	2	3	-1	0	0.500	1.000
20	AaB Aalborg	Den	1	2	0	1	1	1	2	-1	0	0.500	0.500
21	Borrusia Dortmund	FRG	1	2	0	1	1	1	2	-1	0	0.500	0.500
22	Steaua Bucharest	Rom	1	2	0	1	1	1	2	-1	0	0.500	0.500
23	Legia Warsaw	Pol	1	2	0	1	1	2	5	-3	0	0.500	1.000
24	Swansea City	Wal	1	2	0	1	1	1	5	-4	0	0.500	0.500
25	Glentoran	Nir	1	2	0	1	1	1	5	-4	0	0.500	0.500
26	Floriana	Mlt	1	2	0	1	1	1	7	-6	0	0.500	0.500
27	Valur Reykjavik	Isl	1	2	0	1	1	2	9	-7	0	0.500	1.000
28	AEK Athens	Gre	0	2	0	0	2	2	4	-2	0	0.000	1.000
29	Apollon Limassol	Cyp	0	2	0	0	2	1	6	-5	0	0.000	0.500
30	OFK Belgrade	Yug	0	2	0	0	2	1	6	-5	0	0.000	0.500
31	Galatasaray	Tur	0	2	0	0	2	3	9	-6	0	0.000	1.500
32	Spora Luxembourg	Lux	0	2	0	0	2	2	8	-6	0	0.000	1.000
	Total		**136**	**122**	**49**	**24**	**49**	**170**	**170**	**0**	**14**	**1.115**	**2.787**

First Round

Team 1	Cnty	Team 2	Cnty	1st leg	2nd leg	Agg
Wiener Sport-Club	Aut	Napoli	Ita	1-2	1-3	2-5
Drumcondra	Irl	Eintracht Frankfurt	FRG	0-2	1-6	1-8
Nice	Fra	Örgryte IS	Swe	2-2	1-2	3-4
Aris Salonika	Gre	Juventus	Ita	0-2	0-5	0-7
Union Luxembourg	Lux	Antwerp	Bel	0-1	0-1	0-2
SK Frigg	Nor	Dunfermline Athletic	Sco	1-3	1-3	2-6
Utrecht	Ned	FC Basle	Sui	2-1	2-2	4-3
FC Porto	Por	Girondins Bordeaux	Fra	2-1	1-2	3-3
Nuremberg	FRG	Valencia	Esp	1-2	0-2	1-4
VFB Stuttgart	FRG	Burnley	Eng	1-1	0-2	1-3
Dinamo Bucharest	Rom	Seville	Esp	2-0	2-2	4-2
Djurgården SIF	Swe	Lokomotive Leipzig	GDR	1-3	1-2	2-5
Zbrojovka Brno	Tch	Dinamo Zagreb	Yug	2-0	0-2	2-2
Göztepe	Tur	Bologna	Ita	1-2	1-3	2-5
Red Star Belgrade	Yug	Athletic Bilbao	Esp	5-0	0-2	5-2
Olimpija Ljubljana	Yug	Ferencváros	Hun	3-3	0-3	3-6

	Pts	P	W	D	L	F	A	Diff	Goals/P
Total	64	32	27	10	27	102	102	0	3.188

Second Round

Antwerp	Bel	Kilmarnock	Sco	0-1	2-7	2-8
Gent	Bel	Girondins Bordeaux	Fra	1-0	0-0	1-0
Trakia Plovdiv	Bul	Benfica	Por	1-1	0-3	1-4
B 1909 Odense	Den	Napoli	Ita	1-4	1-2	2-6
Dunfermline Athletic	Sco	Dinamo Zagreb	Yug	4-2	0-2	4-4
Barcelona	Esp	Dundee United	Sco	1-2	0-2	1-4
Valencia	Esp	Red Star Belgrade	Yug	1-0	2-1	3-1
Toulouse	Fra	Dinamo Bucharest	Rom	3-0	1-5	4-5
Juventus	Ita	Vitória Setúbal	Por	3-1	2-0	5-1
FC Amsterdam	Ned	Leeds United	Eng	1-3	1-5	2-8
Utrecht	Ned	West Bromwich Albion	Eng	1-1	2-5	3-6
Eintracht Frankfurt	FRG	Hvidovre IF	Den	5-1	2-2	7-3
Örgryte IS	Swe	Ferencváros	Hun	0-0	1-7	1-7
Lausanne-Sports	Sui	Burnley	Eng	1-3	0-5	1-8
Sparta Prague	Tch	Bologna	Ita	2-2	1-2	3-4
Lokomotive Leipzig	GDR	FC Liège	Bel	0-0	1-0	1-0

	Pts	P	W	D	L	F	A	Diff	Goals/P
Total	64	32	25	14	25	110	110	0	3.438

Third Round

Burnley	Eng	Napoli	Ita	3-0	0-0	3-0
Leeds United	Eng	Valencia	Esp	1-1	2-0	3-1
Kilmarnock	Sco	Gent	Bel	1-0	2-1	3-1
Bologna	Ita	West Bromwich Albion	Eng	3-0	3-1	6-1
Juventus	Ita	Dundee United	Sco	3-0	0-1	3-1
Eintracht Frankfurt	FRG	Ferencváros	Hun	4-1	1-2	5-3
Dinamo Bucharest	Rom	Dinamo Zagreb	Yug	0-1	0-0	0-1
Lokomotive Leipzig	GDR	Benfica	Por	3-1	1-2	4-3

UEFA Cup 1966-67

	Pts	P	W	D	L	F	A	Diff	Goals/P
Total	32	16	13	6	13	38	38	0	2.375

Quarter Finals

Bologna	Ita	Leeds United	Eng	1-0	0-1	1-1
Juventus	Ita	Dinamo Zagreb	Yug	2-2	0-3	2-5
Eintracht Frankfurt	FRG	Burnley	Eng	1-1	2-1	3-2
Lokomotive Leipzig	GDR	Kilmarnock	Sco	1-0	0-2	1-2

	Pts	P	W	D	L	F	A	Diff	Goals/P
Total	16	8	6	4	6	17	17	0	2.125

Semi Finals

Leeds United	Eng	Kilmarnock	Sco	4-2	0-0	4-2
Eintracht Frankfurt	FRG	Dinamo Zagreb	Yug	3-0	0-4	3-4

	Pts	P	W	D	L	F	A	Diff	Goals/P
Total	8	4	3	2	3	13	13	0	3.250

Final

Dinamo Zagreb	Yug	Leeds United	Eng	2-0	0-0	2-0

	Pts	P	W	D	L	F	A	Diff	Goals/P
Total	4	2	1	2	1	2	2	0	3.000

	Pts	P	W	D	L	F	A	Diff	Goals/P
Total	188	94	75	38	75	282	282	0	3.000

Pos'n	Club	Cnty	Pts	P	W	D	L	F	A	Diff	B	Pts/P	F/P
1	Dinamo Zagreb	Yug	18	12	6	3	3	18	11	7	3	1.500	1.500
2	Eintracht Frankfurt	FRG	16	10	6	2	2	26	13	13	2	1.600	2.600
3	Leeds United	Eng	16	10	5	3	2	16	8	8	3	1.600	1.600
4	Bologna	Ita	14	8	6	1	1	16	7	9	1	1.750	2.000
5	Kilmarnock	Sco	13	8	5	1	2	15	8	7	2	1.625	1.875
6	Burnley	Eng	12	8	4	3	1	16	5	11	1	1.500	2.000
7	Juventus	Ita	12	8	5	1	2	17	7	10	1	1.500	2.125
8	Locomotive Leipzig	GDR	12	8	5	1	2	11	7	4	1	1.500	1.375
9	Napoli	Ita	9	6	4	1	1	11	7	4	0	1.500	1.833
10	Valencia	Esp	9	6	4	1	1	8	5	3	0	1.500	1.333
11	Ferencváros	Hun	8	6	3	2	1	16	9	7	0	1.333	2.667
12	Dunfermline Athletic	Sco	6	4	3	0	1	10	6	4	0	1.500	2.500
13	Dinamo Bucharest	Rom	6	6	2	2	2	9	7	2	0	1.000	1.500
14	Dundee United	Sco	6	4	3	0	1	5	4	1	0	1.500	1.250
15	Benfica	Por	5	4	2	1	1	7	5	2	0	1.250	1.750
16	Utrecht	Ned	4	4	1	2	1	7	9	-2	0	1.000	1.750
17	Antwerp	Bel	4	4	2	0	2	4	8	-4	0	1.000	1.000
18	Örgryte IS	Swe	4	4	1	2	1	5	10	-5	0	1.000	1.250
19	Girondins Bordeaux	Fra	3	4	1	1	2	3	4	-1	0	0.750	0.750
20	Gent	Bel	3	4	1	1	2	2	3	-1	0	0.750	0.500
21	West Bromwich Albion	Eng	3	4	1	1	2	7	9	-2	0	0.750	1.750
22	Red Star Belgrade	Yug	2	4	1	0	3	6	5	1	0	0.500	1.500
23	FC Porto	Por	2	2	1	0	1	3	3	0	0	1.000	1.500
24	Zbrojovka Brno	Tch	2	2	1	0	1	2	2	0	0	1.000	1.000
25	Toulouse	Irl	2	2	1	0	1	4	5	-1	0	1.000	2.000
26	Athletic Bilbao	Esp	2	2	1	0	1	2	5	-3	0	1.000	1.000
27	Nice	Fra	1	2	0	1	1	3	4	-1	0	0.500	1.500
–	FC Basle	Sui	1	2	0	1	1	3	4	-1	0	0.500	1.500
–	Sparta Prague	Tch	1	2	0	1	1	3	4	-1	0	0.500	1.500
30	FC Lèige	Bel	1	2	0	1	1	0	1	-1	0	0.500	0.000
31	Seville	Esp	1	2	0	1	1	2	4	-2	0	0.500	1.000
32	VFB Stuttgart	FRG	1	2	0	1	1	1	3	-2	0	0.500	0.500
33	Olimpija Ljubljana	Yug	1	2	0	1	1	3	6	-3	0	0.500	1.500
34	Trakia Plovdiv	Bul	1	2	0	1	1	1	4	-3	0	0.500	0.500
35	Hvidovre IF	Den	1	2	0	1	1	3	7	-4	0	0.500	1.500
36	Union Luxembourg	Lux	0	2	0	0	2	0	2	-2	0	0.000	0.000
37	Wiener Sport-Club	Aut	0	2	0	0	2	2	5	-3	0	0.000	1.000
–	Djurgården SIF	Swe	0	2	0	0	2	2	5	-3	0	0.000	1.000
–	Gøztepe	Tur	0	2	0	0	2	2	5	-3	0	0.000	1.000
40	Barcelona	Esp	0	2	0	0	2	1	4	-3	0	0.000	0.500
–	Nuremberg	FRG	0	2	0	0	2	1	4	-3	0	0.000	0.500
42	B 1909 Odense	Den	0	2	0	0	2	2	6	-4	0	0.000	1.000
–	SK Frigg	Nor	0	2	0	0	2	2	6	-4	0	0.000	1.000
44	Vitória Setúbal	Por	0	2	0	0	2	1	5	-4	0	0.000	0.500
45	FC Amsterdam	Ned	0	2	0	0	2	2	8	-6	0	0.000	1.000
46	Drumcondra	Irl	0	2	0	0	2	1	8	-7	0	0.000	0.500
–	Lausanne-Sports	Sui	0	2	0	0	2	1	8	-7	0	0.000	0.500
48	Aris Salonika	Gre	0	2	0	0	2	0	7	-7	0	0.000	0.000
	Total		**202**	**188**	**75**	**38**	**75**	**282**	**282**	**0**	**14**	**1.074**	**3.000**

1966-67

Pos'n	Cnty	Pts	P	W	D	L	F	A	Diff	B	Pts/P	F/P
1	Sco	58	34	23	4	7	59	28	31	8	1.706	1.735
2	Ita	55	34	22	6	6	59	30	29	5	1.618	1.735
3	FRG	41	29	15	6	8	57	34	23	5	1.414	1.966
4	Eng	41	31	14	9	8	50	35	15	4	1.323	1.613
5	Yug	31	27	11	5	11	36	35	1	4	1.148	1.333
6	Esp	28	27	12	2	13	35	37	-2	2	1.037	1.296
7	Bel	25	24	10	3	11	41	31	10	2	1.042	1.708
8	Bul	25	21	8	5	8	29	20	9	4	1.190	1.381
9	GDR	23	17	10	2	5	34	18	16	1	1.353	2.000
10	Hun	19	16	8	2	6	33	21	12	1	1.188	2.063
11	Tch	18	14	6	4	4	24	17	7	2	1.286	1.714
12	Ned	18	16	6	5	5	30	27	3	1	1.125	1.875
13	Fra	15	16	6	3	7	23	26	-3	0	0.938	1.438
14	Por	13	14	6	1	7	17	25	-8	0	0.929	1.214
15	Aut	11	10	4	2	4	14	12	2	1	1.100	1.400
16	Nir	9	8	2	4	2	17	14	3	1	1.125	2.125
17	Rom	9	11	3	3	5	13	14	-1	0	0.818	1.182
18	Sui	9	12	3	2	7	10	23	-13	1	0.750	0.833
19	Pol	7	7	3	1	3	11	13	-2	0	1.000	1.571
20	URS	6	6	2	2	2	7	4	3	0	1.000	1.167
21	Irl	5	8	2	1	5	13	26	-13	0	0.625	1.625
22	Swe	4	8	1	2	5	8	20	-12	0	0.500	1.000
23	Nor	3	6	1	1	4	8	16	-8	0	0.500	1.333
24	Gre	2	6	1	0	5	4	14	-10	0	0.333	0.667
25	Den	2	8	0	2	6	6	21	-15	0	0.250	0.750
26	Wal	1	2	0	1	1	1	5	-4	0	0.500	0.500
27	Isl	1	4	0	1	3	6	17	-11	0	0.250	1.500
28	Mlt	1	4	0	1	3	2	13	-11	0	0.250	0.500
29	Fin	1	4	0	1	3	3	15	-12	0	0.250	0.750
30	Lux	1	6	0	1	5	6	19	-13	0	0.167	1.000
31	Tur	0	6	0	0	6	6	18	-12	0	0.000	1.000
32	Cyp	0	4	0	0	4	2	16	-14	0	0.000	0.500
	Total	**482**	**440**	**179**	**82**	**179**	**664**	**664**	**0**	**42**	**1.095**	**3.018**

1955-56 to 1966-67

Pos'n	Cnty	Pts	P	W	D	L	F	A	Diff	B	Pts/P	F/P
1	Esp	520	339	192	60	87	746	426	320	76	1.534	2.201
2	Ita	368	249	138	44	67	467	291	176	48	1.478	1.876
3	Eng	339	236	123	47	66	480	314	166	46	1.436	2.034
4	FRG	262	203	97	37	69	419	319	100	31	1.291	2.064
5	Sco	244	185	96	25	64	344	278	66	27	1.319	1.859
6	Yug	199	180	70	32	78	295	277	18	27	1.106	1.639
7	Hun	183	144	70	21	53	306	218	88	22	1.271	2.125
8	Por	156	132	55	29	48	263	199	64	17	1.182	1.992
9	Tch	131	106	50	19	37	181	135	46	12	1.236	1.708
10	Fra	122	119	42	26	51	195	202	-7	12	1.025	1.639
11	Bel	117	119	45	16	58	169	186	-17	11	0.983	1.420
12	GDR	92	95	34	19	42	152	143	9	5	0.968	1.600
13	Bul	90	87	32	20	35	146	130	16	6	1.034	1.678
14	Ned	90	84	33	17	34	143	159	-16	7	1.071	1.702
15	Sui	88	113	30	20	63	173	277	-104	8	0.779	1.531
16	Aut	87	90	33	15	42	132	148	-16	6	0.967	1.467
17	Rom	69	71	30	8	33	94	114	-20	1	0.972	1.324
18	Pol	51	50	22	6	22	60	90	-30	1	1.020	1.200
19	Den	48	79	15	15	49	122	211	-89	3	0.608	1.544
20	Swe	45	56	15	13	28	74	121	-47	2	0.804	1.321
21	Tur	40	55	15	8	32	68	115	-47	2	0.727	1.236
22	Gre	32	47	11	10	26	49	102	-53	0	0.681	1.043
23	Nir	22	40	6	9	25	55	119	-64	1	0.550	1.375
24	Irl	21	50	7	7	36	45	138	-93	0	0.420	0.900
25	Nor	18	34	8	2	24	41	91	-50	0	0.529	1.206
26	URS	16	12	6	3	3	24	10	14	1	1.333	2.000
27	Lux	16	50	6	4	40	44	207	-163	0	0.320	0.880
28	Wal	15	19	4	6	9	16	28	-12	1	0.789	0.842
29	Fin	7	26	3	1	22	23	94	-71	0	0.269	0.885
30	Alb	5	8	1	3	4	3	9	-6	0	0.625	0.375
31	Mlt	4	24	1	2	21	12	96	-84	0	0.167	0.500
32	Cyp	3	16	1	1	14	11	69	-58	0	0.188	0.688
33	Isl	1	10	0	1	9	11	47	-36	0	0.100	1.100
	Total	**3501**	**3128**	**1291**	**546**	**1291**	**5363**	**5363**	**0**	**373**	**1.119**	**3.429**

1966-67

Pos'n	Cnty	Ave	Pts	P	W	D	L	F	A	Diff	B	No./T
1	Scotland	11.600	58	34	23	4	7	59	28	31	8	5
2	Italy	11.000	55	34	22	6	6	59	30	29	5	5
3	Bulgaria	8.333	25	21	8	5	8	29	20	9	4	3
4	England	8.200	41	31	14	9	8	50	35	15	4	5
5	E. Germany	7.666	23	17	10	2	5	34	18	16	1	3
6	W. Germany	6.833	41	29	15	6	8	57	34	23	5	6
7	Hungary	6.333	19	16	8	2	6	33	21	12	1	3
8	Yugoslavia	6.200	31	27	11	5	11	36	35	1	4	5
9	Belgium	5.000	25	24	10	3	11	41	31	10	2	5
10	N. Ireland	4.500	9	8	2	4	2	17	14	3	1	2
–	Netherlands	4.500	18	16	6	5	5	30	27	3	1	4
–	Czechoslovakia	4.500	18	14	6	4	4	24	17	7	2	4
13	Spain	4.000	28	27	12	2	13	35	37	-2	2	7
14	Austria	3.666	11	10	4	2	4	14	12	2	1	3
15	Poland	3.500	7	7	3	1	3	11	13	-2	0	2
16	France	3.000	15	16	6	3	7	23	26	-3	0	5
–	Romania	3.000	9	11	3	3	5	13	14	-1	0	3
–	USSR	3.000	6	6	2	2	2	7	4	3	0	2
19	Portugal	2.600	13	14	6	1	7	17	25	-8	0	5
20	Switzerland	2.250	9	12	3	2	7	10	23	-13	1	4
21	Rep. of Ireland	1.666	5	8	2	1	5	13	26	-13	0	3
22	Sweden	1.333	4	8	1	2	5	8	20	-12	0	3
23	Wales	1.000	1	2	0	1	1	1	5	-4	0	1
–	Norway	1.000	3	6	1	1	4	8	16	-8	0	3
25	Greece	0.666	2	6	1	0	5	4	14	-10	0	3
26	Denmark	0.500	2	8	0	2	6	6	21	-15	0	4
–	Finland	0.500	1	4	0	1	3	3	15	-12	0	2
–	Iceland	0.500	1	4	0	1	3	6	17	-11	0	2
–	Malta	0.500	1	4	0	1	3	2	13	-11	0	2
30	Luxembourg	0.333	1	6	0	1	5	6	19	-13	0	3
31	Cyprus	0.000	0	4	0	0	4	2	16	-14	0	2
–	Turkey	0.000	0	6	0	0	6	6	18	-12	0	3
	Total		**482**	**440**	**179**	**82**	**179**	**664**	**664**	**0**	**42**	**3.018**

1955-56 to 1966-67

Pos'n	Cnty	Ave	Pts	P	W	D	L	F	A	Diff	B	No./T
1	Spain	10.400	520	339	192	60	87	746	426	320	76	50
2	England	8.692	339	236	123	47	66	480	314	166	46	39
3	Italy	8.363	368	249	138	44	67	467	291	176	48	44
4	Scotland	6.777	244	185	96	25	64	344	278	66	27	36
–	Hungary	6.777	183	144	70	21	53	306	218	88	22	27
6	W. Germany	5.822	262	203	97	37	69	419	319	100	31	45
7	USSR	5.333	16	12	6	3	3	24	10	14	1	3
8	Czechoslovakia	5.240	131	106	50	19	37	181	135	46	12	25
9	Yugoslavia	4.975	199	180	70	32	78	295	277	18	27	40
10	Portugal	4.588	156	132	55	29	48	263	199	64	17	34
11	Bulgaria	4.285	90	87	32	20	35	146	130	16	6	21
12	Belgium	3.900	117	119	45	16	58	169	186	-17	11	30
13	Netherlands	3.750	90	84	33	17	34	143	159	-16	7	24
14	France	3.696	122	119	42	26	51	195	202	-7	12	33
15	E. Germany	3.538	92	95	34	19	42	152	143	9	5	26
16	Austria	3.480	87	90	33	15	42	132	148	-16	6	25
17	Romania	3.285	69	71	30	8	33	94	114	-20	1	21
18	Poland	3.187	51	50	22	6	22	60	90	-30	1	16
19	Switzerland	2.514	88	113	30	20	63	173	277	-104	8	35
20	Wales	2.500	15	19	4	6	9	16	28	-12	1	6
–	Sweden	2.500	45	56	15	13	28	74	121	-47	2	18
22	Turkey	2.222	40	55	15	8	32	68	115	-47	2	18
23	Greece	1.684	32	47	11	10	26	49	102	-53	0	19
24	Denmark	1.600	48	79	15	15	49	122	211	-89	3	30
25	Norway	1.285	18	34	8	2	24	41	91	-50	0	14
26	Albania	1.250	5	8	1	3	4	3	9	-6	0	4
27	N. Ireland	1.222	22	40	6	9	25	55	119	-64	1	18
28	Rep. of Ireland	1.000	21	50	7	7	36	45	138	-93	0	21
29	Luxembourg	0.727	16	50	6	4	40	44	207	-163	0	22
30	Finland	0.583	7	26	3	1	22	23	94	-71	0	12
31	Cyprus	0.428	3	16	1	1	14	11	69	-58	0	7
32	Malta	0.333	4	24	1	2	21	12	96	-84	0	12
33	Iceland	0.200	1	10	0	1	9	11	47	-36	0	5
	Total		**3501**	**3128**	**1291**	**546**	**1291**	**5363**	**5363**	**0**	**373**	**3.429**

Scots Fly High

The 1966-67 season was a highly successful one for Scottish football. Pride of place belonged indisputably to Celtic, who became the first non-Latin club to capture the Champions' Cup, but their Glasgow rivals Rangers also reached the final of the Cup-winners' Cup, and in the Fairs' Cup both Kilmarnock and Dundee United excelled themselves, the former reaching the semi-finals and the latter winning both of their second-round matches against holders Barcelona.

Celtic's Champions' Cup triumph was seen by many as a watershed in the competition's history. Managed by the legendary Jock Stein, the team played a brand of football that was fast, skilful and, above all, exciting for the spectators. The antithesis of Celtic's exuberant open play were Helenio Herrera's Inter Milan, and it was they whom Celtic faced, and overcame, in the Lisbon final.

Inter, seeking to win the trophy for the third time in four years, were overwhelming favourites to win the final. They had gone through the first four rounds of the competition undefeated, their infamous *catenaccio* defence, led by Burgnich and Facchetti, conceding the miserly total of three goals in nine matches. They had surprisingly required a third match to put out CSKA Sofia in the semi-finals after two 1-1 draws, but in the previous round they had given a masterful performance against holders Real Madrid, winning 2-0 in the Bernabéu after a 1-0 success in Milan.

Real's city rivals, Atlético Madrid, had also lost at home in the Spanish capital in their second-round play-off decider against Vojvodina Novi Sad. Vojvodina, bidding to emulate Partizan Belgrade and become the second successive Yugoslav club to reach the final, then gave Celtic a major fright, winning the quarter-final first leg 1-0 and holding the Scots to the same scoreline in Glasgow until a minute from time when Celtic skipper Billy McNeill headed the winning goal.

Celtic defeated Dukla Prague 3-1 on aggregate in a gruelling semi-final to become the first British side to reach a Champions' Cup final. But in Lisbon, against Inter, it looked for a long time as if Stein's men would return to Scotland empty-handed. Sandro Mazzola put the Italians into an early lead from the penalty spot after six minutes and, true to their reputation, Inter opted to hold on to what they had and spent the next hour camped in defence. This time, however, the spoiling tactics failed to pay off. Celtic attacked incessantly and were at last rewarded with an equaliser from their left-back Tommy Gemmell. The Italian wall had collapsed and with just seven minutes left centre-forward Steve Chalmers popped up to score the goal that deservedly gave Celtic the Cup.

The Cup-winners' Cup final, which took place six days later, welcomed back Glasgow Rangers, who had reached the first of the competition's finals six years earlier. They had lost on that occasion to Fiorentina, and they were to lose again, this time to Bayern Munich, who, with the final staged in the Bavarian city of Nuremberg, were virtually playing at home. The Scots did all they could to emulate their Glaswegian rivals and return home with the silverware, but a single goal, scored in extra-time by left-half Franz Roth, kept the trophy in German hands for the second year in a row.

Extra-time had also been introduced in the earlier rounds of all three European Cups for the first time, and both finalists were involved in the first Cup-winners' Cup ties to be decided in this way. Bayern owed their quarter-final success over Rapid Vienna to an extra-time winner from Gerd Müller – one of eight goals he scored in the competition – and Rangers also prevailed, albeit after a toss of the coin, in their extended quarter-final tie against Zaragoza.

The Fairs' Cup winners, Dinamo Zagreb, also required a lucky toss of the coin against Spartak Brno in the first round on their way to becoming Yugoslavia's first European trophy winners. The highlight of their campaign was a 5-1 aggregate victory over Juventus in the quarter-finals and they repeated that form in the final to defeat Leeds United 2-0 over the two legs. Leeds thus became the fourth English finalist out of four to lose the Fairs' Cup final.

1967 – 1968

Manchester United

AC Milan

Leeds United

European Cup 1967-68

First Round

Team 1	Cnty	Team 2	Cnty	1st leg	2nd leg	Agg
Manchester United	Eng	Hibernians	Mlt	4-0	0-0	4-0
Trakia Plovdiv	Bul	Rapid Bucarest	Rom	2-0	0-3	2-3
Olympiakos Nicosia	Cyp	Sarajevo	Yug	2-2	1-3	3-5
Celtic	Sco	Dinamo Kiev	URS	1-2	1-1	2-3
Dundalk	Irl	Vasas SC	Hun	0-1	1-8	1-9
Saint-Etienne	Fra	KuPS Kuopio	Fin	2-0	3-0	5-0
Olympiakos Pireus	Gre	Juventus	Ita	0-0	0-2	0-2
Glentoran	Nir	Benfica	Por	1-1	0-0	1-1
Valur Reykjavik	Isl	Jeunesse Esch	Lux	1-1	3-3	4-4
FK Skeid	Nor	Sparta Prague	Tch	0-1	1-1	1-2
Ajax	Ned	Real Madrid	Esp	1-1	1-2	2-3
Górnik Zabrze	Pol	Djurgården SIF	Swe	3-0	1-0	4-0
FC Basle	Sui	Hvidovre IF	Den	1-2	3-3	4-5
Besiktas	Tur	Rapid Vienna	Aut	0-1	0-3	0-4
Karl-Marx-Stadt	GDR	Anderlecht	Bel	1-3	1-2	2-5

	Pts	P	W	D	L	F	A	Diff	Goals/P
Total	60	30	19	22	19	81	81	0	2.700

Second Round

Rapid Vienna	Aut	Eintracht Braunschweig	FRG	1-0	0-2	1-2
Hvidovre IF	Den	Real Madrid	Esp	2-2	1-4	3-6
Vasas SC	Hun	Valur Reykjavik	Isl	6-0	5-1	11-1
Juventus	Ita	Rapid Bucarest	Rom	1-0	0-0	1-0
Benfica	Por	Saint-Etienne	Fra	2-0	0-1	2-1
Sparta Prague	Tch	Anderlecht	Bel	3-2	3-3	6-5
Dinamo Kiev	URS	Górnik Zabrze	Pol	1-2	1-1	2-3
Sarajevo	Yug	Manchester United	Eng	0-0	1-2	1-2

	Pts	P	W	D	L	F	A	Diff	Goals/P
Total	32	16	11	10	11	47	47	0	2.938

Quarter Finals

Manchester United	Eng	Górnik Zabrze	Pol	2-0	0-1	2-1
Real Madrid	Esp	Sparta Prague	Tch	3-0	1-2	4-2
Vasas SC	Hun	Benfica	Por	0-0	0-3	0-3
Eintracht Braunschweig	FRG	Juventus	Ita	3-2	0-1	3-4
		Juventus won the replay 0-1				

	Pts	P	W	D	L	F	A	Diff	Goals/P
Total	18	9	8	2	8	19	19	0	42.111

Semi Finals

Manchester United	Eng	Real Madrid	Esp	1-0	3-3	4-3
Benfica	Por	Juventus	Ita	2-0	1-0	3-0

	Pts	P	W	D	L	F	A	Diff	Goals/P
Total	8	4	3	2	3	10	10	0	2.500

Final

Manchester United	Eng	Benfica	Por	4-1	4-1

	Pts	P	W	D	L	F	A	Diff	Goals/P
Total	2	1	1	0	1	5	5	0	5.000

	Pts	P	W	D	L	F	A	Diff	Goals/P
Total	120	60	42	36	42	162	162	0	2.700

Pos'n	Club	Cnty	Pts	P	W	D	L	F	A	Diff	B	Pts/P	F/P
1	Manchester United	Eng	16	9	5	3	1	16	6	10	3	1.778	1.778
2	Benfica	Por	14	9	4	3	2	10	6	4	3	1.556	1.111
3	Juventus	Ita	12	9	4	2	3	7	6	1	2	1.333	0.778
4	Real Madrid	Esp	11	8	3	3	2	16	11	5	2	1.375	2.000
5	Vasas SC	Hun	10	6	4	1	1	20	5	15	1	1.667	3.333
6	Górnik Zabrze	Pol	10	6	4	1	1	8	4	4	1	1.667	1.333
7	Sparta Prague	Tch	9	6	3	2	1	10	10	0	1	1.500	1.667
8	Saint-Etienne	Fra	6	4	3	0	1	6	2	4	0	1.500	1.500
9	Rapid Vienna	Aut	6	4	3	0	1	5	2	3	0	1.500	1.250
10	Anderlecht	Bel	5	4	2	1	1	10	8	2	0	1.250	2.500
11	Eintracht Braunschweig	FRG	5	5	2	0	3	5	5	0	1	1.000	1.000
12	Sarajevo	Yug	4	4	1	2	1	6	5	1	0	1.000	1.500
13	Dinamo Kiev	URS	4	4	1	2	1	5	5	0	0	1.000	1.250
14	Hvidovre IF	Den	4	4	1	2	1	8	10	-2	0	1.000	2.000
15	Rapid Bucharest	Rom	3	4	1	1	2	3	3	0	0	0.750	0.750
16	Jeunesse Esch	Lux	2	2	0	2	0	4	4	0	0	1.000	2.000
17	Glentoran	Nir	2	2	0	2	0	1	1	0	0	1.000	0.500
18	Trakia Plovdiv	Bul	2	2	1	0	1	2	3	-1	0	1.000	1.000
19	Valur Reykjavik	Isl	2	4	0	2	2	5	15	-10	0	0.500	1.250
20	FC Basle	Sui	1	2	0	1	1	4	5	-1	0	0.500	2.000
21	Celtic	Sco	1	2	0	1	1	2	3	-1	0	0.500	1.000
–	Ajax	Ned	1	2	0	1	1	2	3	-1	0	0.500	1.000
23	FK Skeid	Nor	1	2	0	1	1	1	2	-1	0	0.500	0.500
24	Olympiakos Nicosia	Cyp	1	2	0	1	1	3	5	-2	0	0.500	1.500
25	Olympiakos Pireus	Gre	1	2	0	1	1	0	2	-2	0	0.500	0.000
26	Hibernians	Mlt	1	2	0	1	1	0	4	-4	0	0.500	0.000
27	Karl-Marx-Stadt	GDR	0	2	0	0	2	2	5	-3	0	0.000	1.000
28	Djurgården SIF	Swe	0	2	0	0	2	0	4	-4	0	0.000	0.000
–	Besiktas	Tur	0	2	0	0	2	0	4	-4	0	0.000	0.000
30	KuPS Kuopio	Fin	0	2	0	0	2	0	5	-5	0	0.000	0.000
31	Dundalk	Irl	0	2	0	0	2	1	9	-8	0	0.000	0.500
	Total		**134**	**120**	**42**	**36**	**42**	**162**	**162**	**0**	**14**	**1.117**	**2.700**

European Cup Winners Cup 1967-68

First Round

Team 1	Cnty	Team 2	Cnty	1st leg	2nd leg	Agg
Austria Vienna	Aut	Steaua Bucarest	Rom	0-2	1-2	1-4
Aberdeen	Sco	KR Reykjavik	Isl	10-0	4-1	14-1
Shamrock Rovers	Irl	Cardiff City	Wal	1-1	0-2	1-3
Valencia	Esp	Crusaders	Nir	4-0	4-2	8-2
HJK Helsinki	Fin	Wisla Kraków	Pol	1-4	0-4	1-8
Rába ETO	Hun	Apollon Limassol	Cyp	5-0	4-0	9-0
AC Milan	Ita	Levski Sofia	Bul	5-1	1-1	6-2
Aris Bonnevoie	Lux	Olympique Lyon	Fra	0-3	1-2	1-5
Floriana	Mal	NAC Breda	Ned	1-2	0-1	1-3
Fredrikstad FK	Nor	Vitória Setúbal	Por	1-5	1-2	2-7
Hamburg	FRG	Randers Freja FC	Den	5-3	2-0	7-3
Bayern Munich	FRG	Panathinaikos	Gre	5-0	2-1	7-1
Lausanne-Sports	Sui	Spartak Trnava	Tch	3-2	0-2	3-4
Altay	Tur	Standard Liège	Bel	2-3	0-0	2-3
Torpedo Moscow	URS	Sachsenning Zwickau	GDR	0-0	1-0	1-0
Hajduk Split	Yug	Tottenham Hotspur	Eng	0-2	3-4	3-6

	Pts	P	W	D	L	F	A	Diff	Goals/P
Total	64	32	28	8	28	119	119	0	3.719

Second Round

Standard Liège	Bel	Aberdeen	Sco	3-0	0-2	3-2
Valencia	Esp	Steaua Bucarest	Rom	3-0	0-1	3-1
Olympique Lyon	Fra	Tottenham Hotspur	Eng	1-0	3-4	4-4
Rába ETO	Hun	AC Milan	Ita	2-2	1-1	3-3
NAC Breda	Ned	Cardiff City	Wal	1-1	1-4	2-5
Wisla Kraków	Pol	Hamburg	FRG	0-1	0-4	0-5
Bayern Munich	FRG	Vitória Setúbal	Por	6-2	1-1	7-3
Torpedo Moscow	URS	Spartak Trnava	Tch	3-0	3-1	6-1

	Pts	P	W	D	L	F	A	Diff	Goals/P
Total	32	16	12	8	12	52	52	0	3.250

Quarter Finals

Valencia	Esp	Bayern Munich	FRG	1-1	0-1	1-2
Cardiff City	Wal	Torpedo Moscow	URS	1-0	0-1	2-1
		Cardiff won the replay 1-0				
AC Milan	Ita	Standard Liège	Bel	1-1	1-1	4-2
		AC Milan won the replay 2-0				
Hamburg	FRG	Olympique Lyon	Fra	2-0	0-2	4-2
		Hamburg won the replay 2-0				

	Pts	P	W	D	L	F	A	Diff	Goals/P
Total	22	11	8	6	8	18	18	0	1.636

Semi Finals

AC Milan	Ita	Bayern Munich	FRG	2-0	0-0	2-0
Hamburg	FRG	Cardiff City	Wal	1-1	3-2	4-3

	Pts	P	W	D	L	F	A	Diff	Goals/P
Total	8	4	2	4	2	9	9	0	2.250

Final

AC Milan	Ita	Hamburg	FRG	2-0	2-0

	Pts	P	W	D	L	F	A	Diff	Goals/P
Total	2	1	1	0	1	2	2	0	2.000

	Pts	P	W	D	L	F	A	Diff	Goals/P
Total	128	64	51	26	51	200	200	0	3.125

Pos'n	Club	Cnty	Pts	P	W	D	L	F	A	Diff	B	Pts/P	F/P
1	Hamburg	FRG	18	10	7	1	2	20	10	10	3	1.800	2.000
2	AC Milan	Ita	17	10	4	6	0	17	7	10	3	1.700	1.700
3	Bayern Munich	FRG	13	8	4	3	1	16	7	9	2	1.625	2.000
4	Cardiff City	Wal	13	9	4	3	2	13	8	5	2	1.444	1.444
5	Torpedo Moscow	URS	10	7	4	1	2	8	3	5	1	1.429	1.143
6	Olympique Lyon	Fra	9	7	4	0	3	11	9	2	1	1.286	1.571
7	Valencia	Esp	8	6	3	1	2	12	5	7	1	1.333	2.000
8	Standard Liège	Bel	8	7	2	3	2	8	8	0	1	1.143	1.143
9	Aberdeen	Sco	6	4	3	0	1	16	4	12	0	1.500	4.000
10	Rába ETO	Hun	6	4	2	2	0	12	3	9	0	1.500	3.000
11	Tottenham Hotspur	Eng	6	4	3	0	1	10	7	3	0	1.500	2.500
12	Steaua Bucharest	Rom	6	4	3	0	1	5	4	1	0	1.500	1.250
13	Vitória Setúbal	Por	5	4	2	1	1	10	9	1	0	1.250	2.500
14	NAC Breda	Ned	5	4	2	1	1	5	6	-1	0	1.250	1.250
15	Wisla Kraków	Pol	4	4	2	0	2	8	6	2	0	1.000	2.000
16	Lausanne-Sports	Sui	2	2	1	0	1	3	4	-1	0	1.000	1.500
17	Spartak Trnava	Tch	2	4	1	0	3	5	9	-4	0	0.500	1.250
18	Altay	Tur	1	2	0	1	1	2	3	-1	0	0.500	1.000
19	Sachsenning Zwickau	GDR	1	2	0	1	1	0	1	-1	0	0.500	0.000
20	Shamrock Rovers	Irl	1	2	0	1	1	1	3	-2	0	0.500	0.500
21	Levski Sofia	Bul	1	2	0	1	1	2	6	-4	0	0.500	1.000
22	Floriana	Mlt	0	2	0	0	2	1	3	-2	0	0.000	0.500
23	Hajduk Split	Yug	0	2	0	0	2	3	6	-3	0	0.000	1.500
24	Austria Vienna	Aut	0	2	0	0	2	1	4	-3	0	0.000	0.500
25	Randers Freja FC	Den	0	2	0	0	2	3	7	-4	0	0.000	1.500
26	Aris Bonnevoie	Lux	0	2	0	0	2	1	5	-4	0	0.000	0.500
27	Fredrikstad FK	Nor	0	2	0	0	2	2	7	-5	0	0.000	1.000
28	Crusaders	Nir	0	2	0	0	2	2	8	-6	0	0.000	1.000
29	Panathinaikos	Gre	0	2	0	0	2	1	7	-6	0	0.000	0.500
30	HJK Helsinki	Fin	0	2	0	0	2	1	8	-7	0	0.000	0.500
31	Apollon Limassol	Cyp	0	2	0	0	2	0	9	-9	0	0.000	0.000
32	KR Reykjavik	Isl	0	2	0	0	2	1	14	-13	0	0.000	0.500
	Total		**142**	**128**	**51**	**26**	**51**	**200**	**200**	**0**	**14**	**1.109**	**3.125**

First Round

Team 1	Cnty	Team 2	Cnty	1st leg	2nd leg	Agg
Wiener Sport-Club	Aut	Atlético Madrid	Esp	2-5	1-2	3-7
Antwerp	Bel	Göztepe	Tur	1-2	0-0	1-2
Club Bruges	Bel	Sporting Lisbon	Por	0-0	1-2	1-2
FC Liège	Bel	PAOK Salonika	Gre	3-2	2-0	5-2
Hibernian	Sco	FC Porto	Por	3-0	1-3	4-3
Rangers	Sco	Dynamo Dresden	GDR	2-1	1-1	3-2
St. Patrick's Athletic	Irl	Girondins Bordeaux	Fra	1-3	3-6	4-9
Athletic Bilbao	Esp	BK Frem	Den	3-2	1-0	4-2
Nice	Fra	Fiorentina	Ita	0-1	0-4	0-5
Bologna	Ita	SFK Lyn	Nor	2-0	0-0	2-0
Napoli	Ita	Hannover 96	FRG	4-0	1-1	5-1
Spora Luxembourg	Lux	Leeds United	Eng	0-9	0-7	0-16
FC Amsterdam	Ned	Dundee United	Sco	2-1	0-3	2-4
Utrecht	Ned	Real Zaragoza	Esp	3-2	1-3	4-5
Cologne	FRG	Slavia Prague	Tch	2-0	2-2	4-2
Eintracht Frankfurt	FRG	Nottingham Forest	Eng	0-1	0-4	0-5
Arges Pitesti	Rom	Ferencváros	Hun	3-1	0-4	3-5
Malmö FF	Swe	Liverpool	Eng	0-2	1-2	1-4
Servette	Sui	1860 Munich	FRG	2-2	0-4	2-6
FC Zürich	Sui	Barcelona	Esp	3-1	0-1	3-2
Partizan Belgrade	Yug	Lokomotiv Plovdiv	Bul	5-1	1-1	6-2
Vojvodina Novi Sad	Yug	Barreirense	Por	1-0	3-1	4-1
Dinamo Zagreb	Yug	Petrolul Ploiesti	Rom	5-0	0-2	5-2
Lokomotive Leipzig	GDR	Linfield	Nir	5-1	0-1	5-2

	Pts	P	W	D	L	F	A	Diff	Goals/P
Total	96	48	40	16	40	162	162	0	3.375

Second Round

Liverpool	Eng	1860 Munich	FRG	8-0	1-2	9-2
Nottingham Forest	Eng	FC Zürich	Sui	2-1	0-1	2-2
Dundee United	Sco	FC Liège	Bel	3-1	4-1	7-2
Rangers	Sco	Cologne	FRG	3-0	1-3	4-3
Atlético Madrid	Esp	Göztepe	Tur	2-0	0-3	2-3
Real Zaragoza	Esp	Ferencváros	Hun	2-1	0-3	2-4
Girondins Bordeaux	Fra	Athletic Bilbao	Esp	1-3	0-1	1-4
Bologna	Ita	Dinamo Zagreb	Yug	0-0	2-1	2-1
Napoli	Ita	Hibernian	Sco	4-1	0-5	4-6
Sporting Lisbon	Por	Fiorentina	Ita	2-1	1-1	3-2
Partizan Belgrade	Yug	Leeds United	Eng	1-2	1-1	2-3
Vojvodina Novi Sad	Yug	Lokomotive Leipzig	GDR	0-0	2-0	2-0

	Pts	P	W	D	L	F	A	Diff	Goals/P
Total	48	24	20	8	20	72	72	0	3.000

Third Round

Leeds United	Eng	Hibernian	Sco	1-0	1-1	2-1
Ferencváros	Hun	Liverpool	Eng	1-0	1-0	2-0
FC Zürich	Sui	Sporting Lisbon	Por	3-0	0-1	3-1
Vojvodina Novi Sad	Yug	Göztepe	Tur	1-0	1-0	2-0

	Pts	P	W	D	L	F	A	Diff	Goals/P
Total	16	8	7	2	7	11	11	0	1.375

Quarter Finals

Dundee United	Sco	FC Zürich	Sui	1-0	1-0	2-0
Rangers	Sco	Leeds United	Eng	0-0	0-2	0-2
Ferencváros	Hun	Athletic Bilbao	Esp	2-1	2-1	4-2
Bologna	Ita	Vojvodina Novi Sad	Yug	0-0	2-0	2-0

	Pts	P	W	D	L	F	A	Diff	Goals/P
Total	16	8	6	4	6	12	12	0	1.500

Semi Finals

Leeds United	Eng	Dundee United	Sco	1-0	1-1	2-1
Ferencváros	Hun	Bologna	Ita	3-2	2-2	5-4

	Pts	P	W	D	L	F	A	Diff	Goals/P
Total	8	4	2	4	2	12	12	0	3.000

Final

Leeds United	Eng	Ferencváros	Hun	1-0	0-0	1-0

	Pts	P	W	D	L	F	A	Diff	Goals/P
Total	4	2	1	2	1	1	1	0	0.500

	Pts	P	W	D	L	F	A	Diff	Goals/P
Total	188	94	76	36	76	270	270	0	2.872

UEFA Cup 1967-68

Pos'n	Club	Cnty	Pts	P	W	D	L	F	A	Diff	B	Pts/P	F/P
1	Leeds United	Eng	22	12	7	5	0	26	4	22	3	1.833	2.167
2	Ferencváros	Hun	19	12	7	2	3	20	12	8	3	1.583	1.667
3	Dundee United	Sco	13	8	5	1	2	14	6	8	2	1.625	1.750
4	Vojvodina Novi Sad	Yug	13	8	5	2	1	8	3	5	1	1.625	1.000
5	Bologna	Ita	12	8	3	4	1	10	6	4	2	1.500	1.250
6	Athletic Bilbao	Esp	9	6	4	0	2	10	7	3	1	1.500	1.667
7	Sporting Lisbon	Por	8	6	3	2	1	6	6	0	0	1.333	1.000
8	FC Zürich	Sui	7	8	3	0	5	8	7	1	1	0.875	1.000
9	Rangers	Sco	7	6	2	2	2	7	7	0	1	1.167	1.167
10	Liverpool	Eng	6	6	3	0	3	13	5	8	0	1.000	2.167
11	Nottingham Forest	Eng	6	4	3	0	1	7	2	5	0	1.500	1.750
12	Atlético Madrid	Esp	6	4	3	0	1	9	6	3	0	1.500	2.250
13	Fiorentina	Ita	5	4	2	1	1	7	3	4	0	1.250	1.750
14	Hibernian	Sco	5	6	2	1	3	11	9	2	0	0.833	1.833
15	Napoli	Ita	5	4	2	1	1	9	7	2	0	1.250	2.250
16	Cologne	FRG	5	4	2	1	1	7	6	1	0	1.250	1.750
17	Göztepe	Tur	5	6	2	1	3	5	5	0	0	0.833	0.833
18	1860 Munich	FRG	5	4	2	1	1	8	11	-3	0	1.250	2.000
19	Partizan Belgrade	Yug	4	4	1	2	1	8	5	3	0	1.000	2.000
20	Girondins Bordeaux	Fra	4	4	2	0	2	10	8	2	0	1.000	2.500
21	Real Zaragoza	Esp	4	4	2	0	2	7	8	-1	0	1.000	1.750
22	FC Liège	Bel	4	4	2	0	2	7	9	-2	0	1.000	1.750
23	Dinamo Zagreb	Yug	3	4	1	1	2	6	4	2	0	0.750	1.500
24	Lokomotive Leipzig	GDR	3	4	1	1	2	5	4	1	0	0.750	1.250
25	Utrecht	Ned	2	2	1	0	1	4	5	-1	0	1.000	2.000
26	FC Porto	Por	2	2	1	0	1	3	4	-1	0	1.000	1.500
27	Barcelona	Esp	2	2	1	0	1	2	3	-1	0	1.000	1.000
28	Arges Pitesti	Rom	2	2	1	0	1	3	5	-2	0	1.000	1.500
29	FC Amsterdam	Ned	2	2	1	0	1	2	4	-2	0	1.000	1.000
30	Linfield	Nir	2	2	1	0	1	2	5	-3	0	1.000	1.000
-	Petrolul Ploiesti	Rom	2	2	1	0	1	2	5	-3	0	1.000	1.000
32	Dynamo Dresden	GDR	1	2	0	1	1	2	3	-1	0	0.500	1.000
33	Antwerp	Bel	1	2	0	1	1	1	2	-1	0	0.500	0.500
-	Club Bruges	Bel	1	2	0	1	1	1	2	-1	0	0.500	0.500
35	Slavia Prague	Tch	1	2	0	1	1	2	4	-2	0	0.500	1.000
36	SFK Lyn	Nor	1	2	0	1	1	0	2	-2	0	0.500	0.000
37	Lokomotiv Plovdiv	Bul	1	2	0	1	1	2	6	-4	0	0.500	1.000
-	Servette	Sui	1	2	0	1	1	2	6	-4	0	0.500	1.000
39	Hannover 96	FRG	1	2	0	1	1	1	5	-4	0	0.500	0.500
40	BK Frem	Den	0	2	0	0	2	2	4	-2	0	0.000	1.000
41	PAOK Salonika	Gre	0	2	0	0	2	2	5	-3	0	0.000	1.000
42	Barreirense	Por	0	2	0	0	2	1	4	-3	0	0.000	0.500
-	Malmö FF	Swe	0	2	0	0	2	1	4	-3	0	0.000	0.500
44	Wiener Sport-Club	Aut	0	2	0	0	2	3	7	-4	0	0.000	1.500
45	St. Patrick's Athletic	Irl	0	2	0	0	2	4	9	-5	0	0.000	2.000
46	Nice	Fra	0	2	0	0	2	0	5	-5	0	0.000	0.000
-	Eintracht Frankfurt	FRG	0	2	0	0	2	0	5	-5	0	0.000	0.000
48	Spora Luxembourg	Lux	0	2	0	0	2	0	16	-16	0	0.000	0.000
	Total		**202**	**188**	**76**	**36**	**76**	**270**	**270**	**0**	**14**	**1.074**	**2.872**

1967-68

Pos'n	Cnty	Pts	P	W	D	L	F	A	Diff	B	Pts/P	F/P
1	Eng	56	35	21	8	6	72	24	48	6	1.600	2.057
2	Ita	51	35	15	14	6	50	29	21	7	1.457	1.429
3	FRG	47	35	17	7	11	57	49	8	6	1.343	1.629
4	Esp	40	30	16	4	10	56	40	16	4	1.333	1.867
5	Hun	35	22	13	5	4	52	20	32	4	1.591	2.364
6	Sco	32	26	12	5	9	50	29	21	3	1.231	1.923
7	Por	29	23	10	6	7	30	29	1	3	1.261	1.304
8	Yug	24	22	8	7	7	31	23	8	1	1.091	1.409
9	Fra	19	17	9	0	8	27	24	3	1	1.118	1.588
10	Bel	19	19	6	6	7	27	29	-2	1	1.000	1.421
11	Pol	14	10	6	1	3	16	10	6	1	1.400	1.600
12	URS	14	11	5	3	3	13	8	5	1	1.273	1.182
13	Wal	13	9	4	3	2	13	8	5	2	1.444	1.444
14	Rom	13	12	6	1	5	13	17	-4	0	1.083	1.083
15	Tch	12	12	4	3	5	17	23	-6	1	1.000	1.417
16	Sui	11	14	4	2	8	17	22	-5	1	0.786	1.214
17	Ned	10	10	4	2	4	13	18	-5	0	1.000	1.300
18	Aut	6	8	3	0	5	9	13	-4	0	0.750	1.125
19	Tur	6	10	2	2	6	7	12	-5	0	0.600	0.700
20	GDR	5	10	1	3	6	9	13	-4	0	0.500	0.900
21	Den	4	8	1	2	5	13	21	-8	0	0.500	1.625
22	Bul	4	6	1	2	3	6	15	-9	0	0.667	1.000
23	Nir	4	6	1	2	3	5	14	-9	0	0.667	0.833
24	Nor	2	6	0	2	4	3	11	-8	0	0.333	0.500
25	Lux	2	6	0	2	4	5	25	-20	0	0.333	0.833
26	Isl	2	6	0	2	4	6	29	-23	0	0.333	1.000
27	Mlt	1	4	0	1	3	1	7	-6	0	0.250	0.250
28	Cyp	1	4	0	1	3	3	14	-11	0	0.250	0.750
–	Gre	1	6	0	1	5	3	14	-11	0	0.167	0.500
30	Irl	1	6	0	1	5	6	21	-15	0	0.167	1.000
31	Swe	0	4	0	0	4	1	8	-7	0	0.000	0.250
32	Fin	0	4	0	0	4	1	13	-12	0	0.000	0.250
	Total	**478**	**436**	**169**	**98**	**169**	**632**	**632**	**0**	**42**	**1.096**	**2.899**

1955-56 to 1967-68

1	Esp	560	369	208	64	97	802	466	336	80	1.518	2.173
2	Ita	419	284	153	58	73	517	320	197	55	1.475	1.820
3	Eng	395	271	144	55	72	552	338	214	52	1.458	2.037
4	FRG	309	238	114	44	80	476	368	108	37	1.298	2.000
5	Sco	276	211	108	30	73	394	307	87	30	1.308	1.867
6	Yug	223	202	78	39	85	326	300	26	28	1.104	1.614
7	Hun	218	166	83	26	57	358	238	120	26	1.313	2.157
8	Por	185	155	65	35	55	293	228	65	20	1.194	1.890
9	Tch	143	118	54	22	42	198	158	40	13	1.212	1.678
10	Fra	141	136	51	26	59	222	226	-4	13	1.037	1.632
11	Bel	136	138	51	22	65	196	215	-19	12	0.986	1.420
12	Ned	100	94	37	19	38	156	177	-21	7	1.064	1.660
13	Sui	99	127	34	22	71	190	299	-109	9	0.780	1.496
14	GDR	97	105	35	22	48	161	156	5	5	0.924	1.533
15	Bul	94	93	33	22	38	152	145	7	6	1.011	1.634
16	Aut	93	98	36	15	47	141	161	-20	6	0.949	1.439
17	Rom	82	83	36	9	38	107	131	-24	1	0.988	1.289
18	Pol	65	60	28	7	25	76	100	-24	2	1.083	1.267
19	Den	52	87	16	17	54	135	232	-97	3	0.598	1.552
20	Tur	46	65	17	10	38	75	127	-52	2	0.708	1.154
21	Swe	45	60	15	13	32	75	129	-54	2	0.750	1.250
22	Gre	33	53	11	11	31	52	116	-64	0	0.623	0.981
23	URS	30	23	11	6	6	37	18	19	2	1.304	1.609
24	Wal	28	28	8	9	11	29	36	-7	3	1.000	1.036
25	Nir	26	46	7	11	28	60	133	-73	1	0.565	1.304
26	Irl	22	56	7	8	41	51	159	-108	0	0.393	0.911
27	Nor	20	40	8	4	28	44	102	-58	0	0.500	1.100
28	Lux	18	56	6	6	44	49	232	-183	0	0.321	0.875
29	Fin	7	30	3	1	26	24	107	-83	0	0.233	0.800
30	Alb	5	8	1	3	4	3	9	-6	0	0.625	0.375
31	Mlt	5	28	1	3	24	13	103	-90	0	0.179	0.464
32	Cyp	4	20	1	2	17	14	83	-69	0	0.200	0.700
33	Isl	3	16	0	3	13	17	76	-59	0	0.188	1.063
	Total	**3979**	**3564**	**1460**	**644**	**1460**	**5995**	**5995**	**0**	**415**	**1.116**	**3.364**

National Performance by Index

1967-68

Pos'n	Cnty	Ave	Pts	P	W	D	L	F	A	Diff	B	No./T
1	Wales	13.000	13	9	4	3	2	13	8	5	2	1
2	Hungary	11.666	35	22	13	5	4	52	20	32	4	3
3	England	11.200	56	35	21	8	6	72	24	48	6	5
4	Italy	10.200	51	35	15	14	6	50	29	21	7	5
5	Poland	7.000	14	10	6	1	3	16	10	6	1	2
–	USSR	7.000	14	11	5	3	3	13	8	5	1	2
7	W. Germany	6.714	47	35	17	7	11	57	49	8	6	7
8	Spain	6.666	40	30	16	4	10	56	40	16	4	6
9	Scotland	6.400	32	26	12	5	9	50	29	21	3	5
10	Portugal	5.800	29	23	10	6	7	30	29	1	3	5
11	Yugoslavia	4.800	24	22	8	7	7	31	23	8	1	5
12	France	4.750	19	17	9	0	8	27	24	3	1	4
13	Czechoslovakia	4.000	12	12	4	3	5	17	23	-6	1	3
14	Belgium	3.800	19	19	6	6	7	27	29	-2	1	5
15	Romania	3.250	13	12	6	1	5	13	17	-4	0	4
16	Switzerland	2.750	11	14	4	2	8	17	22	-5	1	4
17	Netherlands	2.500	10	10	4	2	4	13	18	-5	0	4
18	Austria	2.000	6	8	3	0	5	9	13	-4	0	3
–	Turkey	2.000	6	10	2	2	6	7	12	-5	0	3
20	Bulgaria	1.333	4	6	1	2	3	6	15	-9	0	3
–	Denmark	1.333	4	8	1	2	5	13	21	-8	0	3
–	N. Ireland	1.333	4	6	1	2	3	5	14	-9	0	3
23	E. Germany	1.250	5	10	1	3	6	9	13	-4	0	4
24	Iceland	1.000	2	6	0	2	4	6	29	-23	0	2
25	Luxembourg	0.666	2	6	0	2	4	5	25	-20	0	3
–	Norway	0.666	2	6	0	2	4	3	11	-8	0	3
27	Cyprus	0.500	1	4	0	1	3	3	14	-11	0	2
–	Malta	0.500	1	4	0	1	3	1	7	-6	0	2
29	Rep.of Ireland	0.333	1	6	0	1	5	6	21	-15	0	3
–	Greece	0.333	1	6	0	1	5	3	14	-11	0	3
31	Finland	0.000	0	4	0	0	4	1	13	-12	0	2
–	Sweden	0.000	0	4	0	0	4	1	8	-7	0	2
	Total		**478**	**436**	**169**	**98**	**169**	**632**	**632**	**0**	**42**	**2.899**

1955-56 to 1967-68

Pos'n	Cnty	Ave	Pts	P	W	D	L	F	A	Diff	B	No./T
1	Spain	10.000	560	369	208	64	97	802	466	336	80	56
2	England	8.977	395	271	144	55	72	552	338	214	52	44
3	Italy	8.551	419	284	153	58	73	517	320	197	55	49
4	Hungary	7.266	218	166	83	26	57	358	238	120	26	30
5	Scotland	6.731	276	211	108	30	73	394	307	87	30	41
6	USSR	6.000	30	23	11	6	6	37	18	19	2	5
7	W. Germany	5.942	309	238	114	44	80	476	368	108	37	52
8	Czechoslovakia	5.107	143	118	54	22	42	198	158	40	13	28
9	Yugoslavia	4.955	223	202	78	39	85	326	300	26	28	45
10	Portugal	4.743	185	155	65	35	55	293	228	65	20	39
11	Wales	4.000	28	28	8	9	11	29	36	-7	3	7
12	Bulgaria	3.916	94	93	33	22	38	152	145	7	6	24
13	Belgium	3.885	136	138	51	22	65	196	215	-19	12	35
14	France	3.810	141	136	51	26	59	222	226	-4	13	37
15	Poland	3.611	65	60	28	7	25	76	100	-24	2	18
16	Netherlands	3.571	100	94	37	19	38	156	177	-21	7	28
17	Austria	3.321	93	98	36	15	47	141	161	-20	6	28
18	Romania	3.280	82	83	36	9	38	107	131	-24	1	25
19	E. Germany	3.233	97	105	35	22	48	161	156	5	5	30
20	Switzerland	2.538	99	127	34	22	71	190	299	-109	9	39
21	Sweden	2.250	45	60	15	13	32	75	129	-54	2	20
22	Turkey	2.190	46	65	17	10	38	75	127	-52	2	21
23	Denmark	1.575	52	87	16	17	54	135	232	-97	3	33
24	Greece	1.500	33	53	11	11	31	52	116	-64	0	22
25	Albania	1.250	5	8	1	3	4	3	9	-6	0	4
26	N. Ireland	1.238	26	46	7	11	28	60	133	-73	1	21
27	Norway	1.176	20	40	8	4	28	44	102	-58	0	17
28	Rep. of Ireland	0.916	22	56	7	8	41	51	159	-108	0	24
29	Luxembourg	0.720	18	56	6	6	44	49	232	-183	0	25
30	Finland	0.500	7	30	3	1	26	24	107	-83	0	14
31	Cyprus	0.444	4	20	1	2	17	14	83	-69	0	9
32	Iceland	0.428	3	16	0	3	13	17	76	-59	0	7
33	Malta	0.357	5	28	1	3	24	13	103	-90	0	14
	Total		**3979**	**3564**	**1460**	**644**	**1460**	**5995**	**5995**	**0**	**415**	**3.364**

Leeds Progress to the Fair's Cup

The 1967-68 season saw the introduction of the away goals rule, although this was only applicable to the earlier rounds of the three competitions. From the quarter-finals onwards, play-offs were still required to determine the outcome of stalemate ties.

There were two first-round beneficiaries of the new rule in the Champions' Cup. Surprisingly, one of them was Benfica, who were held to a goalless draw at home by Glentoran after a 1-1 draw in Belfast. But the former Cup winners subsequently took full advantage of their good fortune and, with victories over Saint-Etienne, Vasas Budapest and Juventus, succeeded in reaching their fifth Champions' Cup final.

But this was to be the year of the English and, most poignantly and most significantly, of Manchester United. Ten full years after the club had been torn apart by the Munich air disaster, United reached their first Champions' Cup final, to be staged, as luck would have it, in the temple of English football, Wembley stadium.

United's road to Wembley was not, however, without its pitfalls. They failed to win a single one of their four away matches and were close to elimination in each of their ties against Sarajevo, Górnik Zabrze and Real Madrid. Real, in the semi-final, inevitably proved to be the toughest nut to crack – not simply because of the strength of the opposition but because United had failed at the semi-final stage of all three of their previous Champions' Cup campaigns. This time, however, the semi-final jinx was at last laid to rest. Two late goals from David Sadler and the veteran Bill Foulkes gave United an unexpected 3-3 draw in the Bernabeu, which, added to the 1-0 win at Old Trafford, took them into the final at the expense of the team that had eliminated them at the same stage of the competition 11 years earlier.

Dressed unusually in all-blue, United bestrode the Wembley turf as marginal favourites to defeat Benfica and keep the Champions' Cup trophy on British soil. This was the most important match played at Wembley since the World Cup final less than two years earlier, and it was one of the heroes of '66, Bobby Charlton, who gave United the lead with a looping header early in the second half. But as in the England-West Germany match, the visiting team were to score a late equaliser, through Graça, and take the match into extra-time. Matt Busby, like Charlton a survivor from the Munich crash, urged on his troops and they responded immediately and decisively with three goals in the first extra period – the first a magnificent solo effort from George Best, followed by a header from 19-year-old birthday boy Brian Kidd and a second from the irrepressible Charlton. Europe's premier club trophy was in English hands at last.

The Cup-winners' Cup, featuring a full cast of 32 for the first time, went to AC Milan, making them the first club to win two different European trophies – they had already captured the Champions' Cup in 1963.

Milan went through the entire tournament undefeated, but they won just four matches out of ten played. They had to resort to the new away goals rule to see off the Hungarians Rába Eto of Györ in the second round, and were then taken to a play-off by Standard Liège in the quarter-finals. But they recovered their best form to eliminate holders Bayern Munich, 2-0 on aggregate, in the semis before repeating the dose against another West German club, Hamburg, in the Rotterdam final. Two early goals from Swedish striker Kurt Hamrin gave Milan the Cup and thus prevented a German side from taking the trophy for the third year in a row.

The Fairs' Cup, at long last, came to England, and it was to remain there for the next six years. The first English winners, fittingly enough, were Leeds United, who thus continued their progression in three years of Fairs' Cup participation from semi-finalists in 1965-66 to beaten finalists in 1966-67 to winners in 1967-68! The 1-0 aggregate scoreline in the final against 1964-65 winners Ferencváros was hardly surprising, given that, their first-round 16-0 annihilation of Spora Luxembourg apart, Leeds had failed to score more than two goals in any of their other eight matches. But Mick Jones' solitary goal was sufficient to give Leeds their first European trophy and, together with Manchester United's Champions' Cup victory, enable England to become the third nation, after Spain and Italy, to provide winners in all three European competitions.

AC Milan

Slovan Bratislava

Newcastle United

1968 – 1969

First Round

Team 1	Cnty	Team 2	Cnty	1st leg	2nd leg	Agg
Manchester City	Eng	Fenerbahçe	Tur	0-0	1-2	1-2
Anderlecht	Bel	Glentoran	Nir	3-0	2-2	5-2
Waterford United	Irl	Manchester United	Eng	1-3	1-7	2-10
Real Madrid	Esp	AEL Limassol	Cyp	6-0	6-0	12-0
Reipas Lahti	Fin	Floriana	Mlt	2-0	1-1	3-1
Saint-Etienne	Fra	Celtic	Sco	2-0	0-4	2-4
AEK Athens	Gre	Jeunesse Esch	Lux	3-0	2-3	5-3
Valur Reykjavik	Isl	Benfica	Por	0-0	1-8	1-8
Rosenborg BK	Nor	Rapid Vienna	Aut	1-3	3-3	4-6
Nuremberg	FRG	Ajax	Ned	1-1	0-4	1-5
Steaua Bucharest	Rom	Spartak Trnava	Tch	3-1	0-4	3-5
Malmö FF	Swe	AC Milan	Ita	2-1	1-4	3-5
FC Zürich	Sui	AB Copenhagen	Den	1-3	2-1	3-4

	Pts	P	W	D	L	F	A	Diff	Goals/P
Total	52	26	20	12	20	100	100	0	3.846

Second Round

Manchester United	Eng	Anderlecht	Bel	3-0	1-3	4-3
Rapid Vienna	Aut	Real Madrid	Esp	1-0	1-2	2-2
Celtic	Sco	Red Star Belgrade	Yug	5-1	1-1	6-2
Reipas Lahti	Fin	Spartak Trnava	Tch	1-9	1-7	2 -16
AEK Athens	Gre	AB Copenhagen	Den	0-0	2-0	2-0
Ajax	Ned	Fenerbahçe	Tur	2-0	2-0	4-0

	Pts	P	W	D	L	F	A	Diff	Goals/P
Total	24	12	10	4	10	43	43	0	3.583

Quarter Finals

Manchester United	Eng	Rapid Vienna	Aut	3-0	0-0	3-0
AC Milan	Ita	Celtic	Sco	0-0	1-0	1-0
Ajax	Ned	Benfica	Por	1-3	3-1	7-4
		Ajax won the replay 3-0				
Spartak Trnava	Tch	AEK Athens	Gre	2-1	1-1	3-2

	Pts	P	W	D	L	F	A	Diff	Goals/P
Total	18	9	6	6	6	20	20	0	2.222

Semi Finals

AC Milan	Ita	Manchester United	Eng	2-0	0-1	2-1
Ajax	Ned	Spartak Trnava	Tch	3-0	0-2	3-2

	Pts	P	W	D	L	F	A	Diff	Goals/P
Total	8	4	4	0	4	8	8	0	2.000

Final

AC Milan	Ita	Ajax	Ned	4-1	4-1

	Pts	P	W	D	L	F	A	Diff	Goals/P
Total	2	1	1	0	1	5	5	0	5.000

	Pts	P	W	D	L	F	A	Diff	Goals/P
Total	104	52	41	22	41	176	176	0	3.385

Pos'n	Club	Cnty	Pts	P	W	D	L	F	A	Diff	B	Pts/P	F/P
1	Ajax	Ned	16	10	6	1	3	20	11	9	3	1.600	2.000
2	Spartak Trnava	Tch	13	8	5	1	2	26	10	16	2	1.625	3.250
3	Manchester United	Eng	13	8	5	1	2	18	7	11	2	1.625	2.250
4	AC Milan	Ita	12	7	4	1	2	12	5	7	3	1.714	1.714
5	Celtic	Sco	7	6	2	2	2	10	5	5	1	1.167	1.667
6	AEK Athens	Gre	7	6	2	2	2	9	6	3	1	1.167	1.500
7	Rapid Vienna	Aut	7	6	2	2	2	8	9	-1	1	1.167	1.333
8	Real Madrid	Esp	6	4	3	0	1	14	2	12	0	1.500	3.500
9	Benfica	Por	6	5	2	1	2	12	8	4	1	1.200	2.400
10	Anderlecht	Bel	5	4	2	1	1	8	6	2	0	1.250	2.000
11	AB Copenhagen	Den	3	4	1	1	2	4	5	-1	0	0.750	1.000
12	Fenerbahçe	Tur	3	4	1	1	2	2	5	-3	0	0.750	0.500
13	Reipas Lahti	Fin	3	4	1	1	2	5	17	-12	0	0.750	1.250
14	FC Zürich	Sui	2	2	1	0	1	3	4	-1	0	1.000	1.500
15	Jeunesse Esch	Lux	2	2	1	0	1	3	5	-2	0	1.000	1.500
–	Steaua Bucharest	Rom	2	2	1	0	1	3	5	-2	0	1.000	1.500
–	Malmö FF	Swe	2	2	1	0	1	3	5	-2	0	1.000	1.500
18	Saint-Etienne	Fra	2	2	1	0	1	2	4	-2	0	1.000	1.000
19	Manchester City	Eng	1	2	0	1	1	1	2	-1	0	0.500	0.500
20	Rosenborg BK	Nor	1	2	0	1	1	4	6	-2	0	0.500	2.000
21	Floriana	Mlt	1	2	0	1	1	1	3	-2	0	0.500	0.500
22	Glentoran	Nir	1	2	0	1	1	2	5	-3	0	0.500	1.000
23	Red Star Belgrade	Yug	1	2	0	1	1	2	6	-4	0	0.500	1.000
24	Nuremberg	FRG	1	2	0	1	1	1	5	-4	0	0.500	0.500
25	Valur Reykjavik	Isl	1	2	0	1	1	1	8	-7	0	0.500	0.500
26	Waterford United	Irl	0	2	0	0	2	2	10	-8	0	0.000	1.000
27	AEL Limassol	Cyp	0	2	0	0	2	0	12	-12	0	0.000	0.000
	Total		**118**	**104**	**41**	**22**	**41**	**176**	**176**	**0**	**14**	**1.135**	**3385**

First Round

Team 1	Cnty	Team 2	Cnty	1st leg	2nd leg	Agg
Partizani Tirana	Alb	Torino	Ita	1-0	1-3	2-3
Club Bruges	Bel	West Bromwich Albion	Eng	3-1	0-2	3-3
Dunfermline Athletic	Sco	Apoel Nicosia	Cyp	10-1	2-0	12-1
Shamrock Rovers	Irl	Randers Freja FC	Den	1-2	0-1	1-3
Girondins Bordeaux	Fra	Cologne	FRG	2-1	0-3	2-4
Cardiff City	Wal	FC Porto	Por	2-2	1-2	3-4
Olympiakos Pireus	Gre	KR Reykjavik	Isl	2-0	2-0	4-0
Crusaders	Nir	IFK Norrköping	Swe	2-2	1-4	3-6
US Rumelange	Lux	Sliema Wanderers	Mlt	2-1	0-1	2-2
FC Den Haag	Ned	Grazer AK	Aut	4-1	2-0	6-1
Lugano	Sui	Barcelona	Esp	0-1	0-3	0-4
Slovan Bratislava	Tch	Borovo	Yug	3-0	0-2	3-2
Altay	Tur	SFK Lyn	Nor	3-1	1-4	4-5

	Pts	P	W	D	L	F	A	Diff	Goals/P
Total	52	26	24	4	24	83	83	0	3.192

Second Round

Randers Freja FC	Den	Sliema Wanderers	Mlt	6-0	2-0	8-0
Dunfermline Athletic	Sco	Olympiakos Pireus	Gre	4-0	0-3	4-3
SFK Lyn	Nor	IFK Norrköping	Swe	2-0	2-3	4-3
FC Den Haag	Ned	Cologne	FRG	0-1	0-3	0-4
FC Porto	Por	Slovan Bratislava	Tch	1-0	0-4	1-4
Dinamo Bucharest	Rom	West Bromwich Albion	Eng	1-1	0-4	1-5

	Pts	P	W	D	L	F	A	Diff	Goals/P
Total	24	12	11	2	11	37	37	0	3.083

Quarter Finals

Dunfermline Athletic	Sco	West Bromwich Albion	Eng	0-0	1-0	1-0
Barcelona	Esp	SFK Lyn	Nor	3-2	2-2	5-4
Torino	Ita	Slovan Bratislava	Tch	0-1	1-2	1-3
Cologne	FRG	Randers Freja FC	Den	2-1	3-0	5-1

	Pts	P	W	D	L	F	A	Diff	Goals/P
Total	16	8	6	4	6	20	20	0	2.500

Semi Finals

Dunfermline Athletic	Sco	Slovan Bratislava	Tch	1-1	0-1	1-2
Cologne	FRG	Barcelona	Esp	2-2	1-4	3-6

	Pts	P	W	D	L	F	A	Diff	Goals/P
Total	8	4	2	4	2	12	12	0	3.000

Final

Slovan Bratislava	Tch	Barcelona	Esp	3-2	3-2

	Pts	P	W	D	L	F	A	Diff	Goals/P
Total	2	1	1	0	1	5	5	0	5.000

	Pts	P	W	D	L	F	A	Diff	Goals/P
Total	102	51	44	14	44	157	157	0	3.078

Pos'n	Club	Cnty	Pts	P	W	D	L	F	A	Diff	B	Pts/P	F/P
1	Slovan Bratislava	Tch	16	9	6	1	2	15	7	8	3	1.778	1.667
2	Barcelona	Esp	13	7	4	2	1	17	10	7	3	1.857	2.429
3	Cologne	FRG	13	8	5	1	2	16	9	7	2	1.625	2.000
4	Dunfermline Athletic	Sco	12	8	4	2	2	18	6	12	2	1.500	2.250
5	Randers Freja FC	Den	9	6	4	0	2	12	6	6	1	1.500	2.000
6	West Bromwich Albion	Eng	7	6	2	2	2	8	5	3	1	1.167	1.333
7	Olympiakos Pireus	Gre	6	4	3	0	1	7	4	3	0	1.500	1.750
8	SFK Lyn	Nor	6	6	2	1	3	13	12	1	1	1.000	2.167
9	IFK Norrköping	Swe	5	4	2	1	1	9	7	2	0	1.250	2.250
10	FC Porto	Por	5	4	2	1	1	5	7	-2	0	1.250	1.250
11	FC Den Haag	Ned	4	4	2	0	2	6	5	1	0	1.000	1.500
12	Torino	Ita	3	4	1	0	3	4	5	-1	1	0. 750	1.000
13	Club Bruges	Bel	2	2	1	0	1	3	3	0	0	1.000	1.500
14	US Rumelange	Lux	2	2	1	0	1	2	2	0	0	1.000	1.000
15	Altay	Tur	2	2	1	0	1	4	5	-1	0	1.000	2.000
16	Partizani Tirana	Alb	2	2	1	0	1	2	3	-1	0	1.000	1.000
–	Borovo	Yug	2	2	1	0	1	2	3	-1	0	1.000	1.000
18	Girondins Bordeaux	Fra	2	2	1	0	1	2	4	-2	0	1.000	1.000
19	Sliema Wanderers	Mlt	2	4	1	0	3	2	10	-8	0	0.500	0.500
20	Cardiff City	Wal	1	2	0	1	1	3	4	-1	0	0.500	1.500
21	Crusaders	Nir	1	2	0	1	1	3	6	-3	0	0.500	1.500
22	Dinamo Bucharest	Rom	1	2	0	1	1	1	5	-4	0	0.500	0.500
23	Shamrock Rovers	Irl	0	2	0	0	2	1	3	-2	0	0.000	0.500
24	KR Reykjavik	Isl	0	2	0	0	2	0	4	-4	0	0.000	0.000
–	Lugano	Sui	0	2	0	0	2	0	4	-4	0	0.000	0.000
26	Grazer AK	Aut	0	2	0	0	2	1	6	-5	0	0.000	0.500
27	Apoel Nicosia	Cyp	0	2	0	0	2	1	12	-11	0	0.000	0.500
	Total		**116**	**102**	**44**	**14**	**44**	**157**	**157**	**0**	**14**	**1.137**	**3.078**

First Round

Team 1	Cnty	Team 2	Cnty	1st leg	2nd leg	Agg
Chelsea	Eng	Morton	Sco	5-0	4-3	9-3
Newcastle United	Eng	Feyenoord	Ned	4-0	0-2	4-2
FC Tirol	Aut	Eintracht Frankfurt	FRG	2-2	0-3	2-5
Wiener Sport-Club	Aut	Slavia Prague	Tch	1-0	0-5	1-5
Beerschot	Bel	FC Amsterdam	Ned	1-1	1-2	2-3
Standard Liège	Bel	Leeds United	Eng	0-0	2-3	2-3
RWD Molenbeek	Bel	Panathinaikos	Gre	2-1	0-2	2-3
Trakia Plovdiv	Bul	Real Zaragoza	Esp	3-1	0-2	3-3
Slavia Sofia	Bul	Aberdeen	Sco	0-0	0-2	0-2
Rangers	Sco	Vojvodina Novi Sad	Yug	2-0	0-1	2-1
Athletic Bilbao	Esp	Liverpool	Eng	2-1	1-2	3-3
Atlético Madrid	Esp	Waregem	Bel	2-1	0-1	2-2
Olympique Lyon	Fra	Academica Coimbra	Por	1-0	0-1	1-1
Metz	Fra	Hamburg	FRG	1-4	2-3	3-7
Aris Salonika	Gre	Hibernians	Mlt	1-0	6-0	7-0
Bologna	Ita	FC Basle	Sui	4-1	2-1	6-2
Napoli	Ita	Grasshoppers Zürich	Sui	3-1	0-1	3-2
FK Skeid	Nor	AIK	Swe	1-1	1-2	2-3
Utrecht	Ned	Dundalk	Irl	1-1	1-2	2-3
Legia Warsaw	Pol	1860 Munich	FRG	6-0	3-2	9-2
Sporting Lisbon	Por	Valencia	Esp	4-0	1-4	5-4
Leixões	Por	Arges Pitesti	Rom	1-1	0-0	1-1
Vitória Setúbal	Por	Linfield	Nir	3-0	3-1	6-1
Hannover 96	FRG	OB Odense	Den	3-2	1-0	4-2
Rapid Bucharest	Rom	OFK Belgrade	Yug	3-1	1-6	4-7
Lausanne-Sports	Sui	Juventus	Ita	0-2	0-2	0-4
Göztepe	Tur	Olympique Marseille	Fra	2-0	0-2	2-2
Olimpija Ljubljana	Yug	Hibernian	Sco	0-3	1-2	1-5
Dinamo Zagreb	Yug	Fiorentina	Ita	1-1	1-2	2-3
Hansa Rostock	GDR	Nice	Fra	3-0	1-2	4-2

	Pts	P	W	D	L	F	A	Diff	Goals/P
Total	120	60	51	18	51	180	180	0	3.000

Second Round

Leeds United	Eng	Napoli	Ita	2-0	0-2	2-2
Chelsea	Eng	FC Amsterdam	Ned	0-0	0-0	0-0
Waregem	Bel	Legia Warsaw	Pol	1-0	0-2	1-2
Aberdeen	Sco	Real Zaragoza	Esp	2-1	0-3	2-4
Hibernian	Sco	Lokomotive Leipzig	GDR	3-1	1-0	4-1
Rangers	Sco	Dundalk	Irl	6-1	3-0	9-1
Panathinaikos	Gre	Athletic Bilbao	Esp	0-0	0-1	0-1
Aris Salonika	Gre	Ujpesti Dózsa	Hun	1-2	1-9	2-11
Juventus	Ita	Eintracht Frankfurt	FRG	0-0	0-1	0-1
Sporting Lisbon	Por	Newcastle United	Eng	1-1	0-1	1-2
Vitória Setúbal	Por	Olympique Lyon	Fra	5-0	2-1	7-1
Hamburg	FRG	Slavia Prague	Tch	4-1	1-3	5-4
AIK	Swe	Hannover 96	FRG	4-2	2-5	6-7
Göztepe	Tur	Arges Pitesti	Rom	3-0	2-3	5-3
OFK Belgrade	Yug	Bologna	Ita	1-0	1-1	2-1
Hansa Rostock	GDR	Fiorentina	Ita	3-2	1-2	4-4

UEFA Cup 1968-69

	Pts	P	W	D	L	F	A	Diff	Goals/P
Total	64	32	26	12	26	95	95	0	2.969

Third Round

Leeds United	Eng	Hannover 96	FRG	5-1	2-1	7-2
Athletic Bilbao	Esp	Eintracht Frankfurt	FRG	1-0	1-1	2-1
Real Zaragoza	Esp	Newcastle United	Eng	3-2	1-2	4-4
FC Amsterdam	Ned	Rangers	Sco	0-2	1-2	1-4
Legia Warsaw	Pol	Ujpesti Dózsa	Hun	0-1	2-2	2-3
Vitória Setúbal	Por	Fiorentina	Ita	3-0	1-2	4-2
Hamburg	FRG	Hibernian	Sco	1-0	1-2	2-2
OFK Belgrade	Yug	Göztepe	Tur	3-1	0-2	3-3

	Pts	P	W	D	L	F	A	Diff	Goals/P
Total	32	16	14	4	14	46	46	0	2.875

Quarter Finals

Leeds United	Eng	Ujpesti Dózsa	Hun	0-1	0-2	0-3
Newcastle United	Eng	Vitória Setúbal	Por	5-1	1-3	6-4
Rangers	Sco	Athletic Bilbao	Esp	4-1	0-2	4-3

	Pts	P	W	D	L	F	A	Diff	Goals/P
Total	12	6	6	0	6	20	20	0	3.333

Semi Finals

Newcastle United	Eng	Rangers	Sco	2-0	0-0	2-0
Göztepe	Tur	Ujpesti Dózsa	Hun	1-4	0-4	1-8

	Pts	P	W	D	L	F	A	Diff	Goals/P
Total	8	4	3	2	3	11	11	0	2.750

Final

Newcastle United	Eng	Ujpesti Dózsa	Hun	3-0	3-2	6-2

	Pts	P	W	D	L	F	A	Diff	Goals/P
Total	4	2	2	0	2	8	8	0	4.000

	Pts	P	W	D	L	F	A	Diff	Goals/P
Total	240	120	102	36	102	360	360	0	3.000

Pos'n	Club	Cnty	Pts	P	W	D	L	F	A	Diff	B	Pts/P	F/P
1	Newcastle United	Eng	19	12	7	2	3	24	13	11	3	1.583	2.000
2	Ujpesti Dózsa	Hun	18	10	7	1	2	27	11	16	3	1.800	2.700
3	Rangers	Sco	15	10	6	1	3	19	8	11	2	1.500	1.900
4	Vitória Setúbal	Por	13	8	6	0	2	21	10	11	1	1.625	2.625
5	Athletic Bilbao	Esp	11	8	4	2	2	9	8	1	1	1.375	1.125
6	Hibernian	Sco	10	6	5	0	1	11	4	7	0	1.667	1.833
7	Leeds United	Eng	10	8	4	1	3	12	9	3	1	1.250	1.500
8	Hamburg	FRG	8	6	4	0	2	14	9	5	0	1.333	2.333
9	Legia Warsaw	Pol	7	6	3	1	2	13	6	7	0	1.167	2.167
10	OFK Belgrade	Yug	7	6	3	1	2	12	8	4	0	1.167	2.000
11	Eintracht Frankfurt	FRG	7	6	2	3	1	7	4	3	0	1.167	1.167
12	Fiorentina	Ita	7	6	3	1	2	9	10	-1	0	1.167	1.500
13	Göztepe	Tur	7	8	3	0	5	11	16	-5	1	0.875	1.375
14	Chelsea	Eng	6	4	2	2	0	9	3	6	0	1.500	2.250
15	Real Zaragoza	Esp	6	6	3	0	3	11	9	2	0	1.000	1.833
16	Hannover 96	FRG	6	6	3	0	3	13	15	-2	0	1.000	2.167
17	Bologna	Ita	5	4	2	1	1	7	4	3	0	1.250	1.750
18	Juventus	Ita	5	4	2	1	1	4	1	3	0	1.250	1.000
19	AIK	Swe	5	4	2	1	1	9	9	0	0	1.250	2.250
20	Aberdeen	Sco	5	4	2	1	1	4	4	0	0	1.250	1.000
21	FC Amsterdam	Ned	5	6	1	3	2	4	6	-2	0	0.833	0.667
22	Slavia Prague	Tch	4	4	2	0	2	9	6	3	0	1.000	2.250
23	Hansa Rostock	GDR	4	4	2	0	2	8	6	2	0	1.000	2.000
24	Napoli	Ita	4	4	2	0	2	5	4	1	0	1.000	1.250
25	Waregem	Bel	4	4	2	0	2	3	4	-1	0	1.000	0.750
26	Aris Salonika	Gre	4	4	2	0	2	9	11	-2	0	1.000	2.250
27	Arges Pitesti	Rom	4	4	1	2	1	4	6	-2	0	1.000	1.000
28	Sporting Lisbon	Por	3	4	1	1	2	6	6	0	0	0.750	1.500
29	Panathinaikos	Gre	3	4	1	1	2	3	3	0	0	0.750	0.750
30	Dundalk	Irl	3	4	1	1	2	4	11	-7	0	0.750	1.000
31	Liverpool	Eng	2	2	1	0	1	3	3	0	0	1.000	1.500
–	Trakia Plovdiv	Bul	2	2	1	0	1	3	3	0	0	1.000	1.500
33	Atlético Madrid	Esp	2	2	1	0	1	2	2	0	0	1.000	1.000
–	Olympique Marseille	Fra	2	2	1	0	1	2	2	0	0	1.000	1.000
35	Academica Coimbra	Por	2	2	1	0	1	1	1	0	0	1.000	0.500
–	Leixões	Por	2	2	0	2	0	1	1	0	0	1.000	0.500
37	Valencia	Esp	2	2	1	0	1	4	5	-1	0	1.000	2.000
38	RWD Molenbeek	Bel	2	2	1	0	1	2	3	-1	0	1.000	1.000
–	Grasshoppers Zürich	Sui	2	2	1	0	1	2	3	-1	0	1.000	1.000
40	Vojvodina Novi Sad	Yug	2	2	1	0	1	1	2	-1	0	1.000	0.500
41	Nice	Fra	2	2	1	0	1	2	4	-2	0	1.000	1.000
–	Feyenoord	Ned	2	2	1	0	1	2	4	-2	0	1.000	1.000
43	Rapid Bucharest	Rom	2	2	1	0	1	4	7	-3	0	1.000	2.000
44	Wiener Sport-Club	Aut	2	2	1	0	1	1	5	-4	0	1.000	0.500
45	Olympique Lyon	Fra	2	4	1	0	3	2	8	-6	0	0.500	0.500
46	Beerschot	Bel	1	2	0	1	1	2	3	-1	0	0.500	1.000
–	Standard Liège	Bel	1	2	0	1	1	2	3	-1	0	0.500	1.000
–	FK Skeid	Nor	1	2	0	1	1	2	3	-1	0	0.500	1.000
–	Utrecht	Ned	1	2	0	1	1	2	3	-1	0	0.500	1.000
–	Dinamo Zagreb	Yug	1	2	0	1	1	2	3	-1	0	0.500	1.000
51	Slavia Sofia	Bul	1	2	0	1	1	0	2	-2	0	0.500	0.000
52	FC Tirol	Aut	1	2	0	1	1	2	5	-3	0	0.500	1.000
53	OB Odense	Den	0	2	0	0	2	2	4	-2	0	0.000	1.000
54	Lokomotive Leipzig	GDR	0	2	0	0	2	1	4	-3	0	0.000	0.500
55	Metz	Fra	0	2	0	0	2	3	7	-4	0	0.000	1.500
56	FC Basle	Sui	0	2	0	0	2	2	6	-4	0	0.000	1.000
57	Olimpija Ljubljana	Yug	0	2	0	0	2	1	5	-4	0	0.000	0.500
58	Lausanne-Sports	Sui	0	2	0	0	2	0	4	-4	0	0.000	0.000
59	Linfield	Nir	0	2	0	0	2	1	6	-5	0	0.000	0.500
60	Morton	Sco	0	2	0	0	2	3	9	-6	0	0.000	1.500
61	1860 Munich	FRG	0	2	0	0	2	2	9	-7	0	0.000	1.000
62	Hibernians	Mlt	0	2	0	0	2	0	7	-7	0	0.000	0.000
	Total		**252**	**240**	**102**	**36**	**102**	**360**	**360**	**0**	**12**	**1.050**	**3.000**

1968-69

Pos'n	Cnty	Pts	P	W	D	L	F	A	Diff	B	Pts/P	F/P
1	Eng	58	42	21	9	12	75	42	33	7	1.381	1.786
2	Sco	49	36	19	6	11	65	36	29	5	1.361	1.806
3	Esp	40	29	16	4	9	57	36	21	4	1.379	1.966
4	Ita	36	29	14	4	11	41	29	12	4	1.241	1.414
5	FRG	35	30	14	5	11	53	51	2	2	1.167	1.767
6	Tch	33	21	13	2	6	50	23	27	5	1.571	2.381
7	Por	31	25	12	5	8	46	33	13	2	1.240	1.840
8	Ned	28	24	10	5	9	34	29	5	3	1.167	1.417
9	Gre	20	18	8	3	7	28	24	4	1	1.111	1.556
10	Hun	18	10	7	1	2	27	11	16	3	1.800	2.700
11	Bel	15	16	6	3	7	20	22	-2	0	0.938	1.250
12	Yug	13	16	5	3	8	20	27	-7	0	0.813	1.250
13	Den	12	12	5	1	6	18	15	3	1	1.000	1.500
14	Swe	12	10	5	2	3	21	21	0	0	1.200	2.100
15	Tur	12	14	5	1	8	17	26	-9	1	0.857	1.214
16	Aut	10	12	3	3	6	12	25	-13	1	0.833	1.000
17	Fra	10	14	5	0	9	13	29	-16	0	0.714	0.929
18	Rom	9	10	3	3	4	12	23	-11	0	0.900	1.200
19	Nor	8	10	2	3	5	19	21	-2	1	0.800	1.900
20	Pol	7	6	3	1	2	13	6	7	0	1.167	2.167
21	GDR	4	6	2	0	4	9	10	-1	0	0.667	1.500
22	Lux	4	4	2	0	2	5	7	-2	0	1.000	1.250
23	Sui	4	10	2	0	8	7	21	-14	0	0.400	0.700
24	Bul	3	4	1	1	2	3	5	-2	0	0.750	0.750
25	Fin	3	4	1	1	2	5	17	-12	0	0.750	1.250
26	Irl	3	8	1	1	6	7	24	-17	0	0.375	0.875
27	Mlt	3	8	1	1	6	3	20	-17	0	0.375	0.375
28	Alb	2	2	1	0	1	2	3	-1	0	1.000	1.000
29	Nir	2	6	0	2	4	6	17	-11	0	0.333	1.000
30	Wal	1	2	0	1	1	3	4	-1	0	0.500	1.500
31	Isl	1	4	0	1	3	1	12	-11	0	0.250	0.250
32	Cyp	0	4	0	0	4	1	24	-23	0	0.000	0.250
	Total	**486**	**446**	**187**	**72**	**187**	**693**	**693**	**0**	**40**	**1.090**	**3.108**

1955-56 to 1968-69

Pos'n	Cnty	Pts	P	W	D	L	F	A	Diff	B	Pts/P	F/P
1	Esp	600	398	224	68	106	859	502	357	84	1.508	2.158
2	Ita	455	313	167	62	84	558	349	209	59	1.454	1.783
3	Eng	453	313	165	64	84	627	380	247	59	1.447	2.003
4	FRG	344	268	128	49	91	529	419	110	39	1.284	1.974
5	Sco	325	247	127	36	84	459	343	116	35	1.316	1.858
6	Hun	236	176	90	27	59	385	249	136	29	1.341	2.188
7	Yug	236	218	83	42	93	346	327	19	28	1.083	1.587
8	Por	216	180	77	40	63	339	261	78	22	1.200	1.883
9	Tch	176	139	67	24	48	248	181	67	18	1.266	1.784
10	Fra	151	150	56	26	68	235	255	-20	13	1.007	1.567
11	Bel	151	154	57	25	72	216	237	-21	12	0.981	1.403
12	Ned	128	118	47	24	47	190	206	-16	10	1.085	1.610
13	Aut	103	110	39	18	53	153	186	-33	7	0.936	1.391
14	Sui	103	137	36	22	79	197	320	-123	9	0.752	1.438
15	GDR	101	111	37	22	52	170	166	4	5	0.910	1.532
16	Bul	97	97	34	23	40	155	150	5	6	1.000	1.598
17	Rom	91	93	39	12	42	119	154	-35	1	0.978	1.280
18	Pol	72	66	31	8	27	89	106	-17	2	1.091	1.348
19	Den	64	99	21	18	60	153	247	-94	4	0.646	1.545
20	Tur	58	79	22	11	46	92	153	-61	3	0.734	1.165
21	Swe	57	70	20	15	35	96	150	-54	2	0.814	1.371
22	Gre	53	71	19	14	38	80	140	-60	1	0.746	1.127
23	URS	30	23	11	6	6	37	18	19	2	1.304	1.609
24	Wal	29	30	8	10	12	32	40	-8	3	0.967	1.067
25	Nor	28	50	10	7	33	63	123	-60	1	0.560	1.260
26	Nir	28	52	7	13	32	66	150	-84	1	0.538	1.269
27	Irl	25	64	8	9	47	58	183	-125	0	0.391	0.906
28	Lux	22	60	8	6	46	54	239	-185	0	0.367	0.900
29	Fin	10	34	4	2	28	29	124	-95	0	0.294	0.853
30	Mlt	8	36	2	4	30	16	123	-107	0	0.222	0.444
31	Alb	7	10	2	3	5	5	12	-7	0	0.700	0.500
32	Isl	4	20	0	4	16	18	88	-70	0	0.200	0.900
33	Cyp	4	24	1	2	21	15	107	-92	0	0.167	0.625
	Total	**4465**	**4010**	**1647**	**716**	**1647**	**6688**	**6688**	**0**	**455**	**1.113**	**3.336**

1968-69

Pos'n	Cnty	Ave	Pts	P	W	D	L	F	A	Diff	B	No./T
1	Hungary	18.000	18	10	7	1	2	27	11	16	3	1
2	Czechoslovakia	11.000	33	21	13	2	6	50	23	27	5	3
3	England	8.285	58	42	21	9	12	75	42	33	7	7
4	Scotland	8.166	49	36	19	6	11	65	36	29	5	6
5	Poland	7.000	7	6	3	1	2	13	6	7	0	1
6	Spain	6.666	40	29	16	4	9	57	36	21	4	6
7	Italy	6.000	36	29	14	4	11	41	29	12	4	6
8	W. Germany	5.833	35	30	14	5	11	53	51	2	2	6
9	Netherlands	5.600	28	24	10	5	9	34	29	5	3	5
10	Portugal	5.166	31	25	12	5	8	46	33	13	2	6
11	Greece	5.000	20	18	8	3	7	28	24	4	1	4
12	Denmark	4.000	12	12	5	1	6	18	15	3	1	3
–	Sweden	4.000	12	10	5	2	3	21	21	0	0	3
–	Turkey	4.000	12	14	5	1	8	17	26	-9	1	3
15	Finland	3.000	3	4	1	1	2	5	17	-12	0	1
16	Norway	2.666	8	10	2	3	5	19	21	-2	1	3
17	Austria	2.500	10	12	3	3	6	12	25	-13	1	4
–	Belgium	2.500	15	16	6	3	7	20	22	-2	0	6
19	Romania	2.250	9	10	3	3	4	12	23	-11	0	4
20	Yugoslavia	2.166	13	16	5	3	8	20	27	-7	0	6
21	Albania	2.000	2	2	1	0	1	2	3	-1	0	1
–	Luxembourg	2.000	4	4	2	0	2	5	7	-2	0	2
–	E. Germany	2.000	4	6	2	0	4	9	10	-1	0	2
24	France	1.666	10	14	5	0	9	13	29	-16	0	6
25	Bulgaria	1.500	3	4	1	1	2	3	5	-2	0	2
26	Rep. of Ireland	1.000	3	8	1	1	6	7	24	-17	0	3
–	Wales	1.000	1	2	0	1	1	3	4	-1	0	1
–	Malta	1.000	3	8	1	1	6	3	20	-17	0	3
29	Switzerland	0.800	4	10	2	0	8	7	21	-14	0	5
30	N. Ireland	0.666	2	6	0	2	4	6	17	-11	0	3
31	Iceland	0.500	1	4	0	1	3	1	12	-11	0	2
32	Cyprus	0.000	0	4	0	0	4	1	24	-23	0	2
	Total		**486**	**446**	**187**	**72**	**187**	**693**	**693**	**0**	**40**	**3.108**

1955-56 to 1968-69

Pos'n	Cnty	Ave	Pts	P	W	D	L	F	A	Diff	B	No./T
1	Spain	9.677	600	398	224	68	106	859	502	357	84	62
2	England	8.882	453	313	165	64	84	627	380	247	59	51
3	Italy	8.272	455	313	167	62	84	558	349	209	59	55
4	Hungary	7.612	236	176	90	27	59	385	249	136	29	31
5	Scotland	6.914	325	247	127	36	84	459	343	116	35	47
6	USSR	6.000	30	23	11	6	6	37	18	19	2	5
7	W. Germany	5.931	344	268	128	49	91	529	419	110	39	58
8	Czechoslovakia	5.677	176	139	67	24	48	248	181	67	18	31
9	Portugal	4.800	216	180	77	40	63	339	261	78	22	45
10	Yugoslavia	4.627	236	218	83	42	93	346	327	19	28	51
11	Netherlands	3.878	128	118	47	24	47	190	206	-16	10	33
12	Poland	3.789	72	66	31	8	27	89	106	-17	2	19
13	Bulgaria	3.730	97	97	34	23	40	155	150	5	6	26
14	Belgium	3.682	151	154	57	25	72	216	237	-21	12	41
15	Wales	3.625	29	30	8	10	12	32	40	-8	3	8
16	France	3.511	151	150	56	26	68	235	255	-20	13	43
17	Austria	3.218	103	110	39	18	53	153	186	-33	7	32
18	E. Germany	3.156	101	111	37	22	52	170	166	4	5	32
19	Romania	3.137	91	93	39	12	42	119	154	-35	1	29
20	Sweden	2.478	57	70	20	15	35	96	150	-54	2	23
21	Turkey	2.416	58	79	22	11	46	92	153	-61	3	24
22	Switzerland	2.340	103	137	36	22	79	197	320	-123	9	44
23	Greece	2.038	53	71	19	14	38	80	140	-60	1	26
24	Denmark	1.777	64	99	21	18	60	153	247	-94	4	36
25	Albania	1.400	7	10	2	3	5	5	12	-7	0	5
–	Norway	1.400	28	50	10	7	33	63	123	-60	1	20
27	N. Ireland	1.166	28	52	7	13	32	66	150	-84	1	24
28	Rep. of Ireland	0.925	25	64	8	9	47	58	183	-125	0	27
29	Luxembourg	0.814	22	60	8	6	46	54	239	-185	0	27
30	Finland	0.666	10	34	4	2	28	29	124	-95	0	15
31	Malta	0.470	8	36	2	4	30	16	123	-107	0	17
32	Iceland	0.444	4	20	0	4	16	18	88	-70	0	9
33	Cyprus	0.363	4	24	1	2	21	15	107	-92	0	11
	Total		**4465**	**4010**	**1647**	**716**	**1647**	**6688**	**6688**	**0**	**455**	**3.336**

Eastern European Boycott en Bloc

Champions' Cup holders Manchester United were joined in the 1968-69 competition by their local rivals Manchester City, but the recently crowned English champions did not last long on their European debut. Unable to manage more than a goalless draw at home to Turkish side Fenerbahçe, they lost the return 2-1 in Istanbul and went crashing out of the competition in the first round.

City could certainly have done with the goalscoring instincts of their old boy Denis Law, who, having missed the 1968 final through injury, now became United's star, scoring seven goals in their 10-2 aggregate demolition of Irish part-timers Waterford United in the first round and another two in the second-round tie against Anderlecht, which United won 4-3 on aggregate.

United had little trouble disposing of Rapid Vienna in the next round to preserve their remarkable record of reaching the semi-finals on each of their five Champions' Cup appearances. But this time, unlike the previous year, their semi-final jinx returned to haunt them and they went out of the competition to Cup-winners' Cup holders, AC Milan.

With the competition thrown into chaos after the politically-enforced withdrawals of several Eastern bloc participants, Milan had earned a bye into the quarter-finals after their first round victory over Malmö of Sweden. They eventually emerged victorious from two tough encounters with 1967 winners Celtic, winning 1-0 in Glasgow after being held scoreless at the San Siro. Another team afforded a direct route into the quarter-finals were Benfica and they looked certain to progress when they won their first leg 3-1 away to Dutch champions Ajax. But in a remarkable turnaround, Ajax came back to register a 3-1 victory of their own in Lisbon, with two of the goals going to a young Johan Cruijff. In the Paris play-off Cruijff was again the star, scoring twice more to help the Amsterdammers to a handsome 3-0 victory.

As Milan put out holders Manchester United, Ajax went through to their first ever Champions' Cup final with a 3-2 aggregate win over Czechoslovakia's Spartak Trnava. But the final, staged in Madrid, proved to be something of a bridge too far for the young Dutchmen, and the Italians capitalised on their inexperience with a comprehensive 4-1 victory – the same score as in the previous year's final, but this time achieved in the regulation 90 minutes with Pierino Prati proving to be Milan's hero by scoring the Champions' Cup final's first hat-trick since Puskás in 1962 and goalkeeper Fabio Cudicini becoming the first player to earn a winner's medal in all three European competitions – he was with Roma when they won the Fairs' Cup in 1961.

Milan's participation in the Champions' Cup meant that for the first time ever the Cup-winners' Cup holders were not there to defend their trophy. This left a relatively weak field (made weaker still by the mass Eastern European boycott), in which Barcelona were the only team of international repute, the only team to have previously won a European trophy.

The Spaniards duly confirmed all the predictions by reaching the final undefeated after eliminating Lugano, SFK Lyn and Cologne. But in Basle, against surprise package Slovan Bratislava, they were to go down to one of their most humiliating defeats ever in European competition. The Slovaks, who had accounted for FC Porto and Torino, amongst others, in earlier rounds, scored in the opening minute through right-winger Cvetler and left Barcelona in the unaccustomed role of having to chase the game. They did equalise, through Zaldua, in the 15th minute, but further strikes from Hrivnak and Jan Capkovic before half-time proved decisive and Carlos Rexach's second-half goal served merely as a consolation.

Slovan's victory gave Czechoslovakia its first, and as yet only, European trophy, whereas Newcastle United, with a 6-2 aggregate triumph over Hungary's Ujpesti Dózsa in the Fairs' Cup final, became the fifth different English club (after Tottenham, West Ham, Manchester United and Leeds) to add their name to the European roll-of-honour. It was the second Anglo-Hungarian Fairs' Cup final in a row, and although an English club had also come out on top the year before, there was an element of revenge in Newcastle's final victory, because Ujpesti had knocked out holders Leeds in the quarter-finals. Three goals from Newcastle captain Bobby Moncur saw to it, however, that the Cup remained in the North of England, albeit in a different location, for another twelve months.

1969 - 1970

Feyenoord

Manchester City

Arsenal

European Cup 1969-70

Preliminary Round

Team 1	Cnty	Team 2	Cnty	1st leg	2nd leg	Agg
TPS Turku	Fin	KB Copenhagen	Den	0-1	0-4	0-5

	Pts	P	W	D	L	F	A	Diff	Goals/P
Total	4	2	2	0	2	5	5	0	2.500

First Round

Leeds United	Eng	SFK Lyn	Nor	10-0	6-0	16-0
Austria Vienna	Aut	Dinamo Kiev	URS	1-2	1-3	2-5
Standard Liège	Bel	17 Nëntori Tirana	Alb	3-0	1-1	4-1
CSKA Sofia	Bul	Ferencváros	Hun	2-1	1-4	3-5
Real Madrid	Esp	Olympiakos Nicosia	Cyp	8-0	6-1	14-1
Fiorentina	Ita	Öster SIF	Swe	1-0	2-1	3-1
AC Milan	Ita	Avenir Beggen	Lux	5-0	3-0	8-0
Hibernians	Mlt	Spartak Trnava	Tch	2-2	0-4	2-6
Feyenoord	Ned	KR Reykjavik	Isl	12-2	4-0	16-2
Benfica	Por	KB Copenhagen	Den	2-0	3-2	5-2
Bayern Munich	FRG	Saint-Etienne	Fra	2-0	0-3	2-3
UT Arad	Rom	Legia Warsaw	Pol	1-2	0-8	1-10
FC Basle	Sui	Celtic	Sco	0-0	0-2	0-2
Galatasaray	Tur	Waterford United	Irl	2-0	3-2	5-2
Red Star Belgrade	Yug	Linfield	Nir	8-0	4-2	12-2
Vorwärts Frankfurt/Oder	GDR	Panathinaikos	Gre	2-0	1-1	3-1

	Pts	P	W	D	L	F	A	Diff	Goals/P
Total	64	32	28	8	28	139	139	0	4.344

Second Round

Leeds United	Eng	Ferencváros	Hun	3-0	3-0	6-0
Standard Liège	Bel	Real Madrid	Esp	1-0	3-2	4-2
Celtic	Sco	Benfica	Por	3-0	0-3	3-3
AC Milan	Ita	Feyenoord	Ned	1-0	0-2	1-2
Legia Warsaw	Pol	Saint-Etienne	Fra	2-1	1-0	3-1
Spartak Trnava	Tch	Galatasaray	Tur	1-0	0-1	1-1
Dinamo Kiev	URS	Fiorentina	Ita	1-2	0-0	1-2
Vorwärts Frankfurt/Oder	GDR	Red Star Belgrade	Yug	2-1	2-3	4-4

	Pts	P	W	D	L	F	A	Diff	Goals/P
Total	32	16	15	2	15	38	38	0	2.375

Quarter Finals

Standard Liège	Bel	Leeds United	Eng	0-1	0-1	0-2
Celtic	Sco	Fiorentina	Ita	3-0	0-1	3-1
Galatasaray	Tur	Legia Warsaw	Pol	1-1	0-2	1-3
Vorwärts Frankfurt/Oder	GDR	Feyenoord	Ned	1-0	0-2	1-2

	Pts	P	W	D	L	F	A	Diff	Goals/P
Total	16	8	7	2	7	13	13	0	1.625

Semi Finals

Leeds United	Eng	Celtic	Sco	0-1	1-2	1-3
Legia Warsaw	Pol	Feyenoord	Ned	0-0	0-2	0-2

	Pts	P	W	D	L	F	A	Diff	Goals/P
Total	8	4	3	2	3	6	6	0	1.500

Final

Feyenoord	Ned	Celtic	Sco	2-1		2-1

	Pts	P	W	D	L	F	A	Diff	Goals/P
Total	2	1	1	0	1	3	3	0	3.000

	Pts	P	W	D	L	F	A	Diff	Goals/P
Total	126	63	56	14	56	204	204	0	3.238

Pos'n	Club	Cnty	Pts	P	W	D	L	F	A	Diff	B	Pts/P	F/P
1	Feyenoord	Ned	16	9	6	1	2	24	5	19	3	1.778	2.667
2	Leeds United	Eng	14	8	6	0	2	25	3	22	2	1.750	3.125
3	Legia Warsaw	Pol	14	8	5	2	1	16	5	11	2	1.750	2.000
4	Celtic	Sco	14	9	5	1	3	12	7	5	3	1.556	1.333
5	Fiorentina	Ita	10	6	4	1	1	6	5	1	1	1.667	1.000
6	Standard Liège	Bel	8	6	3	1	2	8	5	3	1	1.333	1.333
7	Vorwärts Frankfurt/Oder	GDR	8	6	3	1	2	8	7	1	1	1.333	1.333
8	Galatasaray	Tur	8	6	3	1	2	7	6	1	1	1.333	1.167
9	Red Star Belgrade	Yug	6	4	3	0	1	16	6	10	0	1.500	4.000
10	AC Milan	Ita	6	4	3	0	1	9	2	7	0	1.500	2.250
11	Benfica	Por	6	4	3	0	1	8	5	3	0	1.500	2.000
12	Spartak Trnava	Tch	5	4	2	1	1	7	3	4	0	1.250	1.750
13	Dinamo Kiev	URS	5	4	2	1	1	6	4	2	0	1.250	1.500
14	Real Madrid	Esp	4	4	2	0	2	16	5	11	0	1.000	4.000
15	KB Copenhagen	Den	4	4	2	0	2	7	5	2	0	1.000	1.750
16	Saint-Etienne	Fra	2	4	1	0	3	4	5	-1	0	0.500	1.000
17	Bayern Munich	FRG	2	2	1	0	1	2	3	-1	0	1.000	1.000
18	CSKA Sofia	Bul	2	2	1	0	1	3	5	-2	0	1.000	1.500
19	Ferencváros	Hun	2	4	1	0	3	5	9	-4	0	0.500	1.250
20	Panathinaikos	Gre	1	2	0	1	1	1	3	-2	0	0.500	0.500
21	FC Basle	Sui	1	2	0	1	1	0	2	-2	0	0.500	0.000
22	17 Nëntori Tirana	Alb	1	2	0	1	1	1	4	-3	0	0.500	0.500
23	Hibernians	Mlt	1	2	0	1	1	2	6	-4	0	0.500	1.000
24	Öster SIF	Swe	0	2	0	0	2	1	3	-2	0	0.000	0.500
25	Austria Vienna	Aut	0	2	0	0	2	2	5	-3	0	0.000	1.000
–	Waterford United	Irl	0	2	0	0	2	2	5	-3	0	0.000	1.000
27	TPS Turku	Fin	0	2	0	0	2	0	5	-5	0	0.000	0.000
28	Avenir Beggen	Lux	0	2	0	0	2	0	8	-8	0	0.000	0.000
29	UT Arad	Rom	0	2	0	0	2	1	10	-9	0	0.000	0.500
30	Linfield	Nir	0	2	0	0	2	2	12	-10	0	0.000	1.000
31	Olympiakos Nicosie	Cyp	0	2	0	0	2	1	14	-13	0	0.000	0.500
32	KR Reykjavik	Isl	0	2	0	0	2	2	16	-14	0	0.000	1.000
33	SFK Lyn	Nor	0	2	0	0	2	0	16	-16	0	0.000	0.000
	Total		**140**	**126**	**56**	**14**	**56**	**204**	**204**	**0**	**14**	**1.111**	**3.238**

European Cup Winners Cup 1969-70

Preliminary Round

Team 1	Cnty	Team 2	Cnty	1st leg	2nd leg	Agg
Rapid Vienna	Aut	Torpedo Moscow	URS	0-0	1-1	1-1

	Pts	P	W	D	L	F	A	Diff	Goals/P
Total	4	2	0	4	0	2	2	0	1.000

First Round

Rapid Vienna	Aut	PSV Eindhoven	Ned	1-2	2-4	3-6
Lierse	Bel	Apoel Nicosia	Cyp	10-1	1-0	11-1
BK Frem	Den	St-Gallen	Sui	2-1	0-1	2-2
Rangers	Sco	Steaua Bucharest	Rom	2-0	0-0	2-0
Shamrock Rovers	Irl	Schalke 04	FRG	2-1	0-3	2- 4
Athletic Bilbao	Esp	Manchester City	Eng	3-3	0-3	3-6
Olympiakos Pireus	Gre	Górnik Zabrze	Pol	2-2	0-5	2-7
Ards	Nir	Roma	Ita	0-0	1-3	1-3
IBV Vestmannaeyjar	Isl	Levski Sofia	Bul	0-4	0-4	0-8
Mjøndalen IF	Nor	Cardiff City	Wal	1-7	1-5	2-12
Academica Coimbra	Por	KuPS Kuopio	Fin	0-0	1-0	1-0
IFK Norrköping	Swe	Sliema Wanderers	Mlt	5-1	0-1	5-2
Dukla Prague	Tch	Olympique Marseille	Fra	1-0	0-2	1-2
Göztepe	Tur	Union Luxembourg	Lux	3-0	3-2	6-2
Dinamo Zagreb	Yug	Slovan Bratislava	Tch	3-0	0-0	3-0
Magdeburg	GDR	MTK-VM	Hun	1-0	1-1	2-1

	Pts	P	W	D	L	F	A	Diff	Goals/P
Total	64	32	25	14	25	102	102	0	3.188

Second Round

Lierse	Bel	Manchester City	Eng	0-3	0-5	0-8
Levski Sofia	Bul	St-Gallen	Sui	4-0	0-0	4-0
Olympique Marseille	Fra	Dinamo Zagreb	Yug	1-1	0-2	1-3
Roma	Ita	PSV Eindhoven	Ned	1-0	0-1	1-1
Górnik Zabrze	Pol	Rangers	Sco	3-1	3-1	6-2
IFK Norrköping	Swe	Schalke 04	FRG	0-0	0-1	0-1
Göztepe	Tur	Cardiff City	Wal	3-0	0-1	3-1
Magdeburg	GDR	Academica Coimbra	Por	1-0	0-2	1-2

	Pts	P	W	D	L	F	A	Diff	Goals/P
Total	32	16	13	6	13	34	34	0	2.125

Quarter Finals

Levski Sofia	Bul	Górnik Zabrze	Pol	3-2	1-2	4-4
Roma	Ita	Göztepe	Tur	2-0	0-0	2-0
Academica Coimbra	Por	Manchester City	Eng	0-0	0-1	0-1
Dinamo Zagreb	Yug	Schalke 04	FRG	1-3	0-1	1-4

	Pts	P	W	D	L	F	A	Diff	Goals/P
Total	16	8	6	4	6	16	16	0	2.000

Semi Finals

Roma	Ita	Górnik Zabrze	Pol	1-1	2-2	4-4
		The replay resulted in a 1-1 draw				
Schalke 04	FRG	Manchester City	Eng	1-0	1-5	2-5

	Pts	P	W	D	L	F	A	Diff	Goals/P
Total	10	5	2	6	2	15	15	0	3.000

Final

Manchester City	Eng	Górnik Zabrze	Pol	2-1		2-1

	Pts	P	W	D	L	F	A	Diff	Goals/P
Total	2	1	1	0	1	3	3	0	3.000

	Pts	P	W	D	L	F	A	Diff	Goals/P
Total	128	64	47	34	47	172	172	0	2.688

Pos'n	Club	Cnty	Pts	P	W	D	L	F	A	Diff	B	Pts/P	F/P
1	Manchester City	Eng	17	9	6	2	1	22	6	16	3	1.889	2.444
2	Górnik Zabrze	Pol	15	10	4	4	2	22	14	8	3	1.500	2.200
3	Roma	Ita	13	9	3	5	1	10	6	4	2	1.444	1.111
4	Schalke 04	FRG	13	8	5	1	2	11	8	3	2	1.625	1.375
5	Levski Sofia	Bul	10	6	4	1	1	16	4	12	1	1.667	2.667
6	Göztepe	Tur	8	6	3	1	2	9	5	4	1	1.333	1.500
7	Dinamo Zagreb	Yug	7	6	2	2	2	7	5	2	1	1.167	1.167
8	Academica Coimbra	Por	7	6	2	2	2	3	2	1	1	1.167	0.500
9	Cardiff City	Wal	6	4	3	0	1	13	5	8	0	1.500	3.250
10	PSV Eindhoven	Ned	6	4	3	0	1	7	4	3	0	1.500	1.750
11	Magdeburg	GDR	5	4	2	1	1	3	3	0	0	1.250	2.750
12	Lierse	Bel	4	4	2	0	2	11	9	2	0	1.000	2.750
13	IFK Norrköping	Swe	3	4	1	1	2	5	3	2	0	0.750	1.250
14	Olympique Marseille	Fra	3	4	1	1	2	3	4	-1	0	0.750	0.750
15	Rangers	Sco	3	4	1	1	2	4	6	-2	0	0.750	1.000
16	St-Gallen	Sui	3	4	1	1	2	2	6	-4	0	0.750	0.500
17	BK Frem	Den	2	2	1	0	1	2	2	0	0	1.000	1.000
18	Torpedo Moscow	URS	2	2	0	2	0	1	1	0	0	1.000	0.500
19	Dukla Prague	Tch	2	2	1	0	1	1	2	-1	0	1.000	0.500
20	Shamrock Rovers	Irl	2	2	1	0	1	2	4	-2	0	1.000	1.000
21	Rapid Vienna	Aut	2	4	0	2	2	4	7	-3	0	0.500	1.000
22	Sliema Wanderers	Mlt	2	2	1	0	1	2	5	-3	0	1.000	1.000
23	MTK-VM	Hun	1	2	0	1	1	1	2	-1	0	0.500	0.500
24	KuPS Kuopio	Fin	1	2	0	1	1	0	1	-1	0	0.500	0.000
25	Ards	Nir	1	2	0	1	1	1	3	-2	0	0.500	0.500
26	Steaua Bucharest	Rom	1	2	0	1	1	0	2	-2	0	0.500	0.000
27	Athletic Bilbao	Esp	1	2	0	1	1	3	6	-3	0	0.500	1.500
28	Slovan Bratislava	Tch	1	2	0	1	1	0	3	-3	0	0.500	0.000
29	Olympiakos Pireus	Gre	1	2	0	1	1	2	7	-5	0	0.500	1.000
30	Union Luxembourg	Lux	0	2	0	0	2	2	6	-4	0	0.000	1.000
31	IBV Vestmannaeyjar	Isl	0	2	0	0	2	0	8	-8	0	0.000	0.000
32	Mjøndalen IF	Nor	0	2	0	0	2	2	12	-10	0	0.000	1.000
33	Apoel Nicosia	Cyp	0	2	0	0	2	1	11	-10	0	0.000	0.500
	Total		**142**	**128**	**47**	**34**	**47**	**172**	**172**	**0**	**14**	**1.109**	**2.688**

First Round

Team 1	Cnty	Team 2	Cnty	1st leg	2nd leg	Agg
Liverpool	Eng	Dundalk	Irl	10-0	4-0	14-0
Arsenal	Eng	Glentoran	Nir	3-0	0-1	3-1
Wiener Sport-Club	Aut	Ruch Chorzów	Pol	4-2	1-4	5-6
Anderlecht	Bel	Valur Reykjavik	Isl	6-0	2-0	8-0
Charleroi	Bel	NK Zagreb	Yug	2-1	3-1	5-2
Slavia Sofia	Bul	Valencia	Esp	2-0	1-1	3-1
Hvidovre IF	Den	FC Porto	Por	1-2	0-2	1-4
Dundee United	Sco	Newcastle United	Eng	1-2	0-1	1-3
Dunfermline Athletic	Sco	Girondins Bordeaux	Fra	4-0	0-2	4-2
Barcelona	Esp	B 1913 Odense	Den	4-0	2-0	6-0
Las Palmas	Esp	Hertha Berlin	FRG	0-0	0-1	0-1
Sabadell	Esp	Club Bruges	Bel	2-0	1-5	3-5
Metz	Fra	Napoli	Ita	1-1	1-2	2-3
Rouen	Fra	Twente Enschede	Ned	2-0	0-1	2-1
Aris Salonika	Gre	Cagliari	Ita	1-1	0-3	1-4
Inter Milan	Ita	Sparta Prague	Tch	3-0	1-0	4-0
Juventus	Ita	Lokomotiv Plovdiv	Bul	3-1	2-1	5-2
Jeunesse Esch	Lux	Coleraine	Nir	3-2	0-4	3-6
Rosenborg BK	Nor	Southampton	Eng	1-0	0-2	1-2
Vitória Guimarães	Por	Banik Ostrava	Tch	1-0	1-1	2-1
Sporting Lisbon	Por	Linzer ASK	Aut	4-0	2-2	6-2
Vitória Setúbal	Por	Rapid Bucharest	Rom	3-1	4-1	7-2
Hannover 96	FRG	Ajax	Ned	2-1	0-3	2-4
1860 Munich	FRG	FK Skeid	Nor	2-2	1-2	3-4
VFB Stuttgart	FRG	Malmö FF	Swe	3-0	1-1	4-1
Bacau	Rom	Floriana	Mlt	6-0	0-1	6-1
Lausanne-Sports	Sui	Rába ETO	Hun	1-2	1-2	2-4
FC Zürich	Sui	Kilmarnock	Sco	3-2	1-3	4-5
Partizan Belgrade	Yug	Ujpesti Dózsa	Hun	2-1	0-2	2-3
Vojvodina Novi Sad	Yug	Gwardia Warsaw	Pol	1-1	0-1	1-2
Carl Zeiss Jena	GDR	Altay	Tur	1-0	0-0	1-0
Hansa Rostock	GDR	Panionios	Gre	3-0	0-2	3-2

	Pts	P	W	D	L	F	A	Diff	Goals/P
Total	128	64	54	20	54	188	188	0	2.938

Second Round

Anderlecht	Bel	Coleraine	Nir	6-1	7-3	13-4
Club Bruges	Bel	Ujpesti Dózsa	Hun	5-2	0-3	5-5
Charleroi	Bel	Rouen	Fra	3-1	0-2	3-3
Dunfermline Athletic	Sco	Gwardia Warsaw	Pol	2-1	1-0	3-1
Kilmarnock	Sco	Slavia Sofia	Bul	4-1	0-2	4-3
Rába ETO	Hun	Barcelona	Esp	2-3	0-2	2-5
FK Skeid	Nor	Bacau	Rom	0-0	0-2	0-2
Ajax	Ned	Ruch Chorzów	Pol	7-0	2-1	9-1
Vitória Guimarães	Por	Southampton	Eng	3-3	1-5	4-8
Sporting Lisbon	Por	Arsenal	Eng	0-0	0-3	0-3
FC Porto	Por	Newcastle United	Eng	0-0	0-1	0-1
Vitória Setúbal	Por	Liverpool	Eng	1-0	2-3	3-3
Hertha Berlin	FRG	Juventus	Ita	3-1	0-0	3-1
VFB Stuttgart	FRG	Napoli	Ita	0-0	0-1	0-1
Carl Zeiss Jena	GDR	Cagliari	Ita	2-0	1-0	3-0
Hansa Rostock	GDR	Inter Milan	Ita	2-1	0-3	2-4

	Pts	P	W	D	L	F	A	Diff	Goals/P
Total	64	32	26	12	26	99	99	0	3.094

Third Round

Newcastle United	Eng	Southampton	Eng	0-0	1-1	1-1
Anderlecht	Bel	Dunfermline Athletic	Sco	1-0	2-3	3-3
Kilmarnock	Sco	Bacau	Rom	1-1	0-2	1-3
Barcelona	Esp	Inter Milan	Ita	1-2	1-1	2-3
Rouen	Fra	Arsenal	Eng	0-0	0-1	0-1
Napoli	Ita	Ajax	Ned	1-0	0-4	1-4
Vitória Setúbal	Por	Hertha Berlin	FRG	1-1	0-1	1-2
Carl Zeiss Jena	GDR	Ujpesti Dózsa	Hun	1-0	3-0	4-0

	Pts	P	W	D	L	F	A	Diff	Goals/P
Total	32	16	10	12	10	30	30	0	1.875

Quarter Finals

Anderlecht	Bel	Newcastle United	Eng	2-0	1-3	3-3
Hertha Berlin	FRG	Inter Milan	Ita	1-0	0-2	1-2
Bacau	Rom	Arsenal	Eng	0-2	1-7	1-9
Carl Zeiss Jena	GDR	Ajax	Ned	3-1	1-5	4-6

	Pts	P	W	D	L	F	A	Diff	Goals/P
Total	16	8	8	0	8	29	29	0	3.625

Semi Finals

Arsenal	Eng	Ajax	Ned	3-0	0-1	3-1
Anderlecht	Bel	Inter Milan	Ita	0-1	2-0	2-1

	Pts	P	W	D	L	F	A	Diff	Goals/P
Total	8	4	4	0	4	7	7	0	1.750

Final

Anderlecht	Bel	Arsenal	Eng	3-1	0-3	3-4

	Pts	P	W	D	L	F	A	Diff	Goals/P
Total	4	2	2	0	2	7	7	0	3.500

	Pts	P	W	D	L	F	A	Diff	Goals/P
Total	252	126	104	44	104	360	360	0	2.857

UEFA Cup 1969-70

Pos'n	Club	Cnty	Pts	P	W	D	L	F	A	Diff	B	Pts/P	F/P
1	Anderlecht	Bel	19	12	8	0	4	32	15	17	3	1.583	2.667
2	Arsenal	Eng	19	12	7	2	3	23	6	17	3	1.583	1.917
3	Inter Milan	Ita	15	10	6	1	3	14	7	7	2	1.500	1.400
4	Ajax	Ned	14	10	6	0	4	24	11	13	2	1.400	2.400
5	Carl Zeiss Jena	GDR	14	8	6	1	1	12	6	6	1	1.750	1.500
6	Newcastle United	Eng	12	8	4	3	1	8	5	3	1	1.500	1.000
7	Hertha Berlin	FRG	12	8	4	3	1	7	4	3	1	1.500	0.875
8	Barcelona	Esp	9	6	4	1	1	13	5	8	0	1.500	2.167
9	Bacau	Rom	9	8	3	2	3	12	11	1	1	1.125	1.500
10	Dunfermline Athletic	Sco	8	6	4	0	2	10	6	4	0	1.333	1.667
11	Napoli	Ita	8	6	3	2	1	5	6	-1	0	1.333	0.833
12	Southampton	Eng	7	6	2	3	1	11	6	5	0	1.167	1.833
13	Vitória Setúbal	Por	7	6	3	1	2	11	7	4	0	1.167	1.833
14	Liverpool	Eng	6	4	3	0	1	17	3	14	0	1.500	4.250
15	Charleroi	Bel	6	4	3	0	1	8	5	3	0	1.500	2.000
16	FC Porto	Por	5	4	2	1	1	4	2	2	0	1.250	1.000
17	Slavia Sofia	Bul	5	4	2	1	1	6	5	1	0	1.250	1.500
–	Juventus	Ita	5	4	2	1	1	6	5	1	0	1.250	1.500
19	Kilmarnock	Sco	5	6	2	1	3	10	10	0	0	0.833	1.667
20	Rouen	Fra	5	6	2	1	3	5	5	0	0	0.833	0.833
21	Club Bruges	Bel	4	4	2	0	2	10	8	2	0	1.000	2.500
22	VFB Stuttgart	FRG	4	4	1	2	1	4	2	2	0	1.000	1.000
23	Sporting Lisbon	Por	4	4	1	2	1	6	5	1	0	1.000	1.500
24	Rába ETO	Hun	4	4	2	0	2	6	7	-1	0	1.000	1.500
25	Hansa Rostock	GDR	4	4	2	0	2	5	6	-1	0	1.000	1.250
26	FK Skeid	Nor	4	4	1	2	1	4	5	-1	0	1.000	1.000
27	Ujpesti Dózsa	Hun	4	6	2	0	4	8	11	-3	0	0.667	1.333
28	Vitória Guimarães	Por	4	4	1	2	1	6	9	-3	0	1.000	1.500
29	Cagliari	Ita	3	4	1	1	2	4	4	0	0	0.750	1.000
30	Gwardia Warsaw	Pol	3	4	1	1	2	3	4	-1	0	0.750	0.750
31	Wiener Sport-Club	Aut	2	2	1	0	1	5	6	-1	0	1.000	2.500
32	FC Zürich	Sui	2	2	1	0	1	4	5	-1	0	1.000	2.000
33	Panionios	Gre	2	2	1	0	1	2	3	-1	0	1.000	1.000
–	Partizan Belgrade	Yug	2	2	1	0	1	2	3	-1	0	1.000	1.000
35	Rosenborg BK	Nor	2	2	1	0	1	1	2	-1	0	1.000	0.500
–	Twente Enschede	Ned	2	2	1	0	1	1	2	-1	0	1.000	0.500
37	Sabadell	Esp	2	2	1	0	1	3	5	-2	0	1.000	1.500
38	Girondins Bordeaux	Fra	2	2	1	0	1	2	4	-2	0	1.000	1.000
–	Hannover 96	FRG	2	2	1	0	1	2	4	-2	0	1.000	1.000
40	Glentoran	Nir	2	2	1	0	1	1	3	-2	0	1.000	0.500
41	Jeunesse Esch	Lux	2	2	1	0	1	3	6	-3	0	1.000	1.500
42	Floriana	Mlt	2	2	1	0	1	1	6	-5	0	1.000	0.500
43	Coleraine	Nir	2	4	1	0	3	10	16	-6	0	0.500	2.500
44	Ruch Chorzów	Pol	2	4	1	0	3	7	14	-7	0	0.500	1.750
45	1860 Munich	FRG	1	2	0	1	1	3	4	-1	0	0.500	1.500
46	Metz	Fra	1	2	0	1	1	2	3	-1	0	0.500	1.000
47	Banik Ostrava	Tch	1	2	0	1	1	1	2	-1	0	0.500	0.500
–	Vojvodina Novi Sad	Yug	1	2	0	1	1	1	2	-1	0	0.500	0.500
49	Las Palmas	Esp	1	2	0	1	1	0	1	-1	0	0.500	0.000
–	Altay	Tur	1	2	0	1	1	0	1	-1	0	0.500	0.000
51	Valencia	Esp	1	2	0	1	1	1	3	-2	0	0.500	0.500
52	Aris Salonika	Gre	1	2	0	1	1	1	4	-3	0	0.500	0.500
–	Malmö FF	Swe	1	2	0	1	1	1	4	-3	0	0.500	0.500
54	Linzer ASK	Aut	1	2	0	1	1	2	6	-4	0	0.500	1.000
55	Lausanne-Sports	Sui	0	2	0	0	2	2	4	-2	0	0.000	1.000
56	Dundee United	Sco	0	2	0	0	2	1	3	-2	0	0.000	0.500
57	Lokomotiv Plovdiv	Bul	0	2	0	0	2	2	5	-3	0	0.000	1.000
–	NK Zagreb	Yug	0	2	0	0	2	2	5	-3	0	0.000	1.000
59	Hvidovre IF	Den	0	2	0	0	2	1	4	-3	0	0.000	0.500
60	Sparta Prague	Tch	0	2	0	0	2	0	4	-4	0	0.000	0.000
61	Rapid Bucharest	Rom	0	2	0	0	2	2	7	-5	0	0.000	1.000
62	B 1913 Odense	Den	0	2	0	0	2	0	6	-6	0	0.000	0.000
63	Valur Reykjavik	Isl	0	2	0	0	2	0	8	-8	0	0.000	0.000
64	Dundalk	Irl	0	2	0	0	2	0	14	-14	0	0.000	0.000
	Total		**266**	**252**	**104**	**44**	**104**	**360**	**360**	**0**	**14**	**1.056**	**2.857**

1969-70

Pos'n	Cnty	Pts	P	W	D	L	F	A	Diff	B	Pts/P	F/P
1	Eng	75	47	28	10	9	106	29	77	9	1.596	2.255
2	Ita	60	43	22	11	10	54	35	19	5	1.395	1.256
3	Bel	41	30	18	1	11	69	42	27	4	1.367	2.300
4	Ned	38	25	16	1	8	56	22	34	5	1.520	2.240
5	Pol	34	26	11	7	8	48	37	11	5	1.308	1.846
6	FRG	34	26	12	7	7	29	25	4	3	1.308	1.115
7	Por	33	28	12	8	8	38	30	8	1	1.179	1.357
8	GDR	31	22	13	3	6	28	22	6	2	1.409	1.273
9	Sco	30	27	12	3	12	37	32	5	3	1.111	1.370
10	Esp	18	18	7	4	7	36	25	11	0	1.000	2.000
11	Bul	17	14	7	2	5	27	19	8	1	1.214	1.929
12	Tur	17	14	6	3	5	16	12	4	2	1.214	1.143
13	Yug	16	16	6	3	7	28	21	7	1	1.000	1.750
14	Fra	13	18	5	3	10	16	21	-5	0	0.722	0.889
15	Hun	11	16	5	1	10	20	29	-9	0	0.688	1.250
16	Rom	10	14	3	3	8	15	30	-15	1	0.714	1.071
17	Tch	9	12	3	3	6	9	14	-5	0	0.750	0.750
18	URS	7	6	2	3	1	7	5	2	0	1.167	1.167
19	Wal	6	4	3	0	1	13	5	8	0	1.500	3.250
20	Den	6	10	3	0	7	10	17	-7	0	0.600	1.000
21	Sui	6	10	2	2	6	8	17	-9	0	0.600	0.800
22	Nor	6	10	2	2	6	7	35	-28	0	0.600	0.700
23	Aut	5	10	1	3	6	13	24	-11	0	0.500	1.300
24	Gre	5	8	1	3	4	6	17	-11	0	0.625	0.750
25	Mlt	5	6	2	1	3	5	17	-12	0	0.833	0.833
26	Nir	5	10	2	1	7	14	34	-20	0	0.500	1.400
27	Swe	4	8	1	2	5	7	10	-3	0	0.500	0.875
28	Lux	2	6	1	0	5	5	20	-15	0	0.333	0.833
29	Irl	2	6	1	0	5	4	23	-19	0	0.333	0.667
30	Alb	1	2	0	1	1	1	4	-3	0	0.500	0.500
31	Fin	1	4	0	1	3	0	6	-6	0	0.250	0.000
32	Cyp	0	4	0	0	4	2	25	-23	0	0.000	0.500
33	Isl	0	6	0	0	6	2	32	-30	0	0.000	0.333
	Total	**548**	**506**	**207**	**92**	**207**	**736**	**736**	**0**	**42**	**1.083**	**2.909**

1955-56 to 1969-70

Pos'n	Cnty	Pts	P	W	D	L	F	A	Diff	B	Pts/P	F/P
1	Esp	618	416	231	72	113	895	527	368	84	1.486	2.151
2	Eng	528	360	193	74	93	733	409	324	68	1.467	2.036
3	Ita	515	356	189	73	94	612	384	228	64	1.447	1.719
4	FRG	378	294	140	56	98	558	444	114	42	1.286	1.898
5	Sco	355	274	139	39	96	496	375	121	38	1.296	1.810
6	Yug	252	234	89	45	100	374	348	26	29	1.077	1.598
7	Por	249	208	89	48	71	377	291	86	23	1.197	1.813
8	Hun	247	192	95	28	69	405	278	127	29	1.286	2.109
9	Bel	192	184	75	26	83	285	279	6	16	1.043	1.549
10	Tch	185	151	70	27	54	257	195	62	18	1.225	1.702
11	Ned	166	143	63	25	55	246	228	18	15	1.161	1.720
12	Fra	164	168	61	29	78	251	276	-25	13	0.976	1.494
13	GDR	132	133	50	25	58	198	188	10	7	0.992	1.489
14	Bul	114	111	41	25	45	182	169	13	7	1.027	1.640
15	Sui	109	147	38	24	85	205	337	-132	9	0.741	1.395
16	Aut	108	120	40	21	59	166	210	-44	7	0.900	1.383
17	Pol	106	92	42	15	35	137	143	-6	7	1.152	1.489
18	Rom	101	107	42	15	50	134	184	-50	2	0.944	1.252
19	Tur	75	93	28	14	51	108	165	-57	5	0.806	1.161
20	Den	70	109	24	18	67	163	264	-101	4	0.642	1.495
21	Swe	61	78	21	17	40	103	160	-57	2	0.782	1.321
22	Gre	58	79	20	17	42	86	157	-71	1	0.734	1.089
23	URS	37	29	13	9	7	44	23	21	2	1.276	1.517
24	Wal	35	34	11	10	13	45	45	0	3	1.029	1.324
25	Nor	34	60	12	9	39	70	158	-88	1	0.567	1.167
26	Nir	33	62	9	14	39	80	184	-104	1	0.532	1.290
27	Irl	27	70	9	9	52	62	206	-144	0	0.386	0.886
28	Lux	24	66	9	6	51	59	259	-200	0	0.364	0.894
29	Mlt	13	42	4	5	33	21	140	-119	0	0.310	0.500
30	Fin	11	38	4	3	31	29	130	-101	0	0.289	0.763
31	Alb	8	12	2	4	6	6	16	-10	0	0.667	0.500
32	Isl	4	26	0	4	22	20	120	-100	0	0.154	0.769
33	Cyp	4	28	1	2	25	17	132	-115	0	0.143	0.607
	Total	**5013**	**4516**	**1854**	**808**	**1854**	**7424**	**7424**	**0**	**497**	**1.110**	**3.288**

National Performance by Index

1969-70

Pos'n	Cnty	Ave	Pts	P	W	D	L	F	A	Diff	B	No./T
1	England	12.500	75	47	28	10	9	106	29	77	9	6
2	Netherlands	9.500	38	25	16	1	8	56	22	34	5	4
3	Italy	8.571	60	43	22	11	10	54	35	19	5	7
4	Poland	8.500	34	26	11	7	8	48	37	11	5	4
5	Belgium	8.200	41	30	18	1	11	69	42	27	4	5
6	E. Germany	7.750	31	22	13	3	6	28	22	6	2	4
7	Scotland	6.000	30	27	12	3	12	37	32	5	3	5
–	Wales	6.000	6	4	3	0	1	13	5	8	0	1
9	W. Germany	5.666	34	26	12	7	7	29	25	4	3	6
–	Turkey	5.666	17	14	6	3	5	16	12	4	2	3
11	Portugal	5.500	33	28	12	8	8	38	30	8	1	6
12	Bulgaria	4.250	17	14	7	2	5	27	19	8	1	4
13	USSR	3.500	7	6	2	3	1	7	5	2	0	2
14	Yugoslavia	3.200	16	16	6	3	7	28	21	7	1	5
15	Spain	3.000	18	18	7	4	7	36	25	11	0	6
16	Hungary	2.750	11	16	5	1	10	20	29	-9	0	4
17	France	2.600	13	18	5	3	10	16	21	-5	0	5
18	Romania	2.500	10	14	3	3	8	15	30	-15	1	4
19	Czechoslovakia	1.800	9	12	3	3	6	9	14	-5	0	5
20	Malta	1.666	5	6	2	1	3	5	17	-12	0	3
21	Denmark	1.500	6	10	3	0	7	10	17	-7	0	4
–	Norway	1.500	6	10	2	2	6	7	35	-28	0	4
–	Switzerland	1.500	6	10	2	2	6	8	17	-9	0	4
24	Sweden	1.333	4	8	1	2	5	7	10	-3	0	3
25	Austria	1.250	5	10	1	3	6	13	24	-11	0	4
–	Greece	1.250	5	8	1	3	4	6	17	-11	0	4
–	N. Ireland	1.250	5	10	2	1	7	14	34	-20	0	4
28	Albania	1.000	1	2	0	1	1	1	4	-3	0	1
29	Rep. of Ireland	0.666	2	6	1	0	5	4	23	-19	0	3
–	Luxembourg	0.666	2	6	1	0	5	5	20	-15	0	3
31	Finland	0.500	1	4	0	1	3	0	6	-6	0	2
32	Cyprus	0.000	0	4	0	0	4	2	25	-23	0	2
–	Iceland	0.000	0	6	0	0	6	2	32	-30	0	3
	Total		**548**	**506**	**207**	**92**	**207**	**736**	**736**	**0**	**42**	**2.909**

1955-56 to 1969-70

Pos'n	Cnty	Ave	Pts	P	W	D	L	F	A	Diff	B	No./T
1	England	9.263	528	360	193	74	93	733	409	324	68	57
2	Spain	9.088	618	416	231	72	113	895	527	368	84	68
3	Italy	8.306	515	356	189	73	94	612	384	228	64	62
4	Hungary	7.057	247	192	95	28	69	405	278	127	29	35
5	Scotland	6.826	355	274	139	39	96	496	375	121	38	52
6	W. Germany	5.906	378	294	140	56	98	558	444	114	42	64
7	USSR	5.285	37	29	13	9	7	44	23	21	2	7
8	Czechoslovakia	5.138	185	151	70	27	54	257	195	62	18	36
9	Portugal	4.882	249	208	89	48	71	377	291	86	23	51
10	Poland	4.608	106	92	42	15	35	137	143	-6	7	23
11	Yugoslavia	4.500	252	234	89	45	100	374	348	26	29	56
12	Netherlands	4.486	166	143	63	25	55	246	228	18	15	37
13	Belgium	4.173	192	184	75	26	83	285	279	6	16	46
14	Wales	3.888	35	34	11	10	13	45	45	0	3	9
15	Bulgaria	3.800	114	111	41	25	45	182	169	13	7	30
16	E. Germany	3.666	132	133	50	25	58	198	188	10	7	36
17	France	3.416	164	168	61	29	78	251	276	-25	13	48
18	Romania	3.060	101	107	42	15	50	134	184	-50	2	33
19	Austria	3.000	108	120	40	21	59	166	210	-44	7	36
20	Turkey	2.777	75	93	28	14	51	108	165	-57	5	27
21	Sweden	2.346	61	78	21	17	40	103	160	-57	2	26
22	Switzerland	2.270	109	147	38	24	85	205	337	-132	9	48
23	Greece	1.933	58	79	20	17	42	86	157	-71	1	30
24	Denmark	1.750	70	109	24	18	67	163	264	-101	4	40
25	Norway	1.416	34	60	12	9	39	70	158	-88	1	24
26	Albania	1.333	8	12	2	4	6	6	16	-10	0	6
27	N. Ireland	1.178	33	62	9	14	39	80	184	-104	1	28
28	Rep. of Ireland	0.900	27	70	9	9	52	62	206	-144	0	30
29	Luxembourg	0.800	24	66	9	6	51	59	259	-200	0	30
30	Malta	0.650	13	42	4	5	33	21	140	-119	0	20
31	Finland	0.647	11	38	4	3	31	29	130	-101	0	17
32	Iceland	0.333	4	26	0	4	22	20	120	-100	0	12
33	Cyprus	0.307	4	28	1	2	25	17	132	-115	0	13
	Total		**5013**	**4516**	**1854**	**808**	**1854**	**7424**	**7424**	**0**	**497**	**3.288**

Northern Leading Lights

A new decade of European Cup football began with a confirmation of the shift in power from south to north. For the first time in 15 years there were no Latins on the winner's podium at the end of the season. Furthermore, all six clubs appearing in the three European finals of 1969-70 came from Northern European countries.

This Latin fall from grace was particularly bruising in the Champions' Cup where previous winners Benfica and Real Madrid and two Italian clubs, Fiorentina and holders AC Milan, represented a formidable quartet. But all four were knocked out by clubs from colder northern climes, with not one reaching even the semi-finals. Benfica were the most unfortunate, losing to Celtic on a toss of a coin after both matches had finished 3-0 in the second round, and they were accompanied out of the competition at this stage by both Real, who went down home and away against Standard Liège, and Milan, narrowly beaten by Feyenoord.

Fiorentina's run ended in the quarter-finals after a heavy defeat in Glasgow, and this heralded an epic semi-final encounter between their victors, Celtic, and England's Champions' Cup debutants Leeds United. It was the first time that English and Scottish opposition had met in the Champions' Cup, and Celtic's greater experience told as they won both games, 1-0 in Leeds and 2-1 in Glasgow, where an amazing 136,000 people crammed into Hampden Park to cheer the team into their second Champions' Cup final.

Meanwhile, Feyenoord, having seen off Milan in the second round, earned a return ticket to the San Siro for the final by comfortably disposing of modest Eastern Europeans Vorwärts Frankfurt/Oder and Legia Warsaw in the next two rounds.

There was no doubt that Celtic were favourites to win in Milan. Still coached by Jock Stein, the team retained several names from the victorious 1966-67 side – Gemmell, Murdoch, McNeill, Johnstone, Wallace, Auld and Lennox – and, after their comprehensive success against Leeds and a runaway victory in the Scottish domestic championship, they looked invincible. There was certainly no sign of an upset when Gemmell, a scorer three years earlier in Lisbon, did it again after half an hour to put Celtic into the lead. But less than two minutes later Feyenoord, coached by the Austrian Ernst Happel, were back in the game through their commanding sweeper Rinus Israel. The match eventually went into extra-time with the Dutch looking the stronger and, just four minutes from time, with a replay looking likely, Feyenoord's Swedish striker Ove Kindvall took advantage of a mistake by Celtic captain McNeill and fired home the winning goal. Feyenoord had succeded where their great domestic rivals, Ajax, had failed a year earlier and given Netherlands its first Champions' Cup.

The other two European trophies were to go to English clubs. Manchester City and Arsenal took the number of different English teams to have won a European trophy to a record seven.

Manchester City emerged victorious from yet another poor-quality field in the Cup-winners' Cup. Holders Slovan Bratislava were instantly despatched by Dinamo Zagreb and, those two teams apart, only one other previous European winner – Roma – was included on the 33-team starting grid. The Italians, who eliminated PSV Eindhoven on a toss of a coin in the second round, were denied a second European final place in the same manner after three draws (play-off included) against Górnik Zabrze. Górnik thus became the only team ever to win a semi-final on the toss of a coin and the only Polish team ever to reach a European final. But they could not take the trophy, despite the excellence of their inside-forward Lubanski, who had contributed so greatly to the downfall of Roma, and Glasgow Rangers before them. Manchester City were too good for them in Vienna and goals from Neil Young (their FA Cup final hero a year earlier) and Francis Lee, from a penalty, gave them a deserved 2-1 win.

Arsenal's triumph came after a highly exciting Fairs' Cup final with Anderlecht, who had dumped holders Newcastle out of the competition on the away goals rule (now used in all rounds of the Fairs' Cup) in the quarter-finals. Arsenal came back from a 3-1 defeat in Brussels to repeat the 3-0 home victory of their semi-final against Ajax with goals from Eddie Kelly, John Radford and, decisively, Jon Sammels. Ray Kennedy – who would make is make in Europe with Liverpool in years to come scored the vital goal in Brussels.

Ajax

Chelsea

Leeds United

1970 – 1971

Preliminary Round

Team 1	Cnty	Team 2	Cnty	1st leg	2nd leg	Agg
Levski Sofia	Bul	Austria Vienna	Aut	3-1	0-3	3-4

	Pts	P	W	D	L	F	A	Diff	Goals/P
Total	4	2	2	0	2	7	7	0	3.500

First Round

Team 1	Cnty	Team 2	Cnty	1st leg	2nd leg	Agg
17 Nëntori Tirana	Alb	Ajax	Ned	2-2	0-2	2-4
Everton	Eng	IBK Keflavik	Isl	6-2	3-0	9-2
EPA Larnaca	Cyp	Bor. Mönchengladbach	FRG	0-6	0-10	0-16
Celtic	Sco	KPV Kokkola	Fin	9-0	5-0	14-0
Atlético Madrid	Esp	Austria Vienna	Aut	2-0	2-1	4-1
Ujpesti Dózsa	Hun	Red Star Belgrade	Yug	2-0	0-4	2-4
Glentoran	Nir	Waterford United	Irl	1-3	0-1	1-4
Cagliari	Ita	Saint-Etienne	Fra	3-0	0-1	3-1
Jeunesse Esch	Lux	Panathinaikos	Gre	1-2	0-5	1-7
Rosenborg BK	Nor	Standard Liège	Bel	0-2	0-5	0-7
Feyenoord	Ned	UT Arad	Rom	1-1	0-0	1-1
Sporting Lisbon	Por	Floriana	Mlt	5-0	4-0	9-0
IFK Gothenburg	Swe	Legia Warsaw	Pol	0-4	1-2	1-6
Slovan Bratislava	Tch	B 1903 Copenhagen	Den	2-1	2-2	4-3
Fenerbahçe	Tur	Carl Zeiss Jena	GDR	0-4	0-1	0-5
Spartak Moscow	URS	FC Basle	Sui	3-2	1-2	4-4

	Pts	P	W	D	L	F	A	Diff	Goals/P
Total	64	32	28	8	28	120	120	0	3.750

Second Round

Team 1	Cnty	Team 2	Cnty	1st leg	2nd leg	Agg
Standard Liège	Bel	Legia Warsaw	Pol	1-0	0-2	1-2
Waterford United	Irl	Celtic	Sco	0-7	2-3	2-10
Panathinaikos	Gre	Slovan Bratislava	Tch	3-0	1-2	4-2
Cagliari	Ita	Atlético Madrid	Esp	2-1	0-3	2-4
Ajax	Ned	FC Basle	Sui	3-0	2-1	5-1
Bor. Mönchengladbach	FRG	Everton	Eng	1-1	1-1	2-2
Red Star Belgrade	Yug	UT Arad	Rom	3-0	3-1	6-1
Carl Zeiss Jena	GDR	Sporting Lisbon	Por	2-1	2-1	4-2

	Pts	P	W	D	L	F	A	Diff	Goals/P
Total	32	16	14	4	14	50	50	0	3.125

Quarter Finals

Team 1	Cnty	Team 2	Cnty	1st leg	2nd leg	Agg
Everton	Eng	Panathinaikos	Gre	1-1	0-0	1-1
Atlético Madrid	Esp	Legia Warsaw	Pol	1-0	1-2	2-2
Ajax	Ned	Celtic	Sco	3-0	0-1	3-1
Carl Zeiss Jena	GDR	Red Star Belgrade	Yug	3-2	0-4	3-6

	Pts	P	W	D	L	F	A	Diff	Goals/P
Total	16	8	6	4	6	19	19	0	2.375

Semi Finals

Athlético Madrid	Esp	Ajax	Ned	1-0	0-3		1-3
Red Star Belgrade	Yug	Panathinaikos	Gre	4-1	0-3		4-4

	Pts	P	W	D	L	F	A	Diff	Goals/P
Total	8	4	4	0	4	12	12	0	3.000

Final

Ajax	Ned	Panathinaikos	Gre	2-0	2-0

	Pts	P	W	D	L	F	A	Diff	Goals/P
Total	2	1	1	0	1	2	2	0	2.000

	Pts	P	W	D	L	F	A	Diff	Goals/P
Total	126	63	55	16	55	210	210	0	3.333

Pos'n	Club	Cnty	Pts	P	W	D	L	F	A	Diff	B	Pts/P	F/P
1	Ajax	Ned	16	9	6	1	2	17	5	12	3	1.778	1.889
2	Panathinaikos	Gre	13	9	4	2	3	16	10	6	3	1.444	1.778
3	Red Star Belgrade	Yug	12	8	5	0	3	20	10	10	2	1.500	2.500
4	Atlético Madrid	Esp	12	8	5	0	3	11	8	3	2	1.500	1.375
5	Celtic	Sco	11	6	5	0	1	25	5	20	1	1.833	4.167
6	Carl Zeiss Jena	GDR	11	6	5	0	1	12	8	4	1	1.833	2.000
7	Everton	Eng	9	6	2	4	0	12	5	7	1	1.500	2.000
8	Legia Warsaw	Pol	9	6	4	0	2	10	4	6	1	1.500	1.667
9	Bor. Monchengladbach	FRG	6	4	2	2	0	18	2	16	0	1.500	4.500
10	Standard Liège	Bel	6	4	3	0	1	8	2	6	0	1.500	2.000
11	Slovan Bratislava	Tch	5	4	2	1	1	6	7	-1	0	1.250	1.500
12	Sporting Lisbon	Por	4	4	2	0	2	11	4	7	0	1.000	2.750
13	Cagliari	Ita	4	4	2	0	2	5	5	0	0	1.000	1.250
14	Waterford United	Irl	4	4	2	0	2	6	11	-5	0	1.000	1.500
15	Spartak Moscow	URS	2	2	1	0	1	4	4	0	0	1.000	2.000
16	Feyenoord	Ned	2	2	0	2	0	1	1	0	0	1.000	0.500
17	Levski Sofia	Bul	2	2	1	0	1	3	4	-1	0	1.000	1.500
18	Austria Vienna	Aut	2	4	1	0	3	5	7	-2	0	0.500	1.250
19	Ujpesti Dózsa	Hun	2	2	1	0	1	2	4	-2	0	1.000	1.000
20	Saint-Etienne	Fra	2	2	1	0	1	1	3	-2	0	1.000	0.500
21	FC Basle	Sui	2	4	1	0	3	5	9	-4	0	0.500	1.250
22	UT Arad	Rom	2	4	0	2	2	2	7	-5	0	0.500	0.500
23	B 1903 Copenhagen	Den	1	2	0	1	1	3	4	-1	0	0.500	1.500
24	17 Nëntori Tirana	Alb	1	2	0	1	1	2	4	-2	0	0.500	1.000
25	Glentoran	Nir	0	2	0	0	2	1	4	-3	0	0.000	0.500
26	IFK Gothenburg	Swe	0	2	0	0	2	1	6	-5	0	0.000	0.500
27	Fenerbahçe	Tur	0	2	0	0	2	0	5	-5	0	0.000	0.000
28	Jeunesse Esch	Lux	0	2	0	0	2	1	7	-6	0	0.000	0.500
29	IBK Keflavik	Isl	0	2	0	0	2	2	9	-7	0	0.000	1.000
30	Rosenborg BK	Nor	0	2	0	0	2	0	7	-7	0	0.000	0.000
31	Floriana	Mlt	0	2	0	0	2	0	9	-9	0	0.000	0.000
32	KPV Kokkola	Fin	0	2	0	0	2	0	14	-14	0	0.000	0.000
33	EPA Larnaca	Cyp	0	2	0	0	2	0	16	-16	0	0.000	0.000
	Total		**140**	**126**	**55**	**16**	**55**	**210**	**210**	**0**	**14**	**1.111**	**3.333**

Preliminary Round

Team 1	Cnty	Team 2	Cnty	1st leg	2nd leg	Agg
Bohemians	Irl	TJ Gottwaldov	Tch	1-2	2-2	3-4
Åtvideberg SFF	Swe	Partizani Tirana	Alb	1-1	0-2	1-3

	Pts	P	W	D	L	F	A	Diff	Goals/P
Total	8	4	2	4	2	11	11	0	2.750

First Round

Manchester City	Eng	Linfield	Nir	1-0	1-2	2-2
FC Tirol	Aut	Partizani Tirana	Alb	3-2	2-1	5-3
CSKA Sofia	Bul	Haka Valkeakoski	Fin	9-0	2-1	11-1
AaB Aalborg	Den	Górnik Zabrze	Pol	0-1	1-8	1-9
Aberdeen	Sco	Honvéd	Hun	3-1	1-3	4-4
Cardiff City	Wal	Pezoporikos Larnaca	Cyp	8-0	0-0	8-0
Aris Salonika	Gre	Chelsea	Eng	1-1	1-5	2-6
Hibernians	Mlt	Real Madrid	Esp	0-0	0-5	0-5
Strømgodset IF	Nor	Nantes	Fra	0-5	3-2	3-7
Kickers Offenbach	FRG	Club Bruges	Bel	2-1	0-2	2-3
FC Zürich	Sui	IBA Akureyri	Isl	7-1	7-0	14-1
TJ Gottwaldov	Tch	PSV Eindhoven	Ned	2-1	0-1	2-2
Göztepe	Tur	Union Luxembourg	Lux	5-0	0-1	5-1
Karpaty Lvov	URS	Steaua Bucharest	Rom	0-1	3-3	3-4
Olimpija Ljubljana	Yug	Benfica	Por	1-1	1-8	2-9
Vorwärts Frankfurt/Oder	GDR	Bologna	Ita	0-0	1-1	1-1

	Pts	P	W	D	L	F	A	Diff	Goals/P
Total	64	32	25	14	25	123	123	0	3.844

Second Round

Club Bruges	Bel	FC Zürich	Sui	2-0	2-3	4-3
CSKA Sofia	Bul	Chelsea	Eng	0-1	0-1	0-2
Real Madrid	Esp	FC Tirol	Aut	0-1	2-0	2- 1
Cardiff City	Wal	Nantes	Fra	5-1	2-1	7-2
Honvéd	Hun	Manchester City	Eng	0-1	0-2	0-3
PSV Eindhoven	Ned	Steaua Bucharest	Rom	4-0	3-0	7-0
Benfica	Por	Vorwärts Frankfurt/Oder	GDR	2-0	0-2	2-2
Göztepe	Tur	Górnik Zabrze	Pol	0-1	0-3	0-4

	Pts	P	W	D	L	F	A	Diff	Goals/P
Total	32	16	16	0	16	39	39	0	2.438

Quarter Finals

Club Bruges	Bel	Chelsea	Eng	2-0	0-4	2-4
Cardiff City	Wal	Real Madrid	Esp	1-0	0-2	1-2
PSV Eindhoven	Ned	Vorwärts Frankfurt/Oder	GDR	2-0	0-1	2-1
Górnik Zabrze	Pol	Manchester City	Eng	2-0	0-2	3-5
		Manchester City won the replay 1-3				

	Pts	P	W	D	L	F	A	Diff	Goals/P
Total	18	9	9	0	9	20	20	0	2.222

Semi Finals

Chelsea	Eng	Manchester City	Eng	1-0	1-0	2-0
PSV Eindhoven	Ned	Real Madrid	Esp	0-0	1-2	1-2

	Pts	P	W	D	L	F	A	Diff	Goals/P
Total	8	4	3	2	3	5	5	0	1.250

Final

Chelsea	Eng	Real Madrid	Esp	1-1	2-1	3-2

	Pts	P	W	D	L	F	A	Diff	Goals/P
Total	4	2	1	2	1	5	5	0	2.500

	Pts	P	W	D	L	F	A	Diff	Goals/P
Total	134	67	56	22	56	203	203	0	3.030

Pos'n	Club	Cnty	Pts	P	W	D	L	F	A	Diff	B	Pts/P	F/P
1	Chelsea	Eng	19	10	7	2	1	17	6	11	3	1.900	1.700
2	Real Madrid	Esp	14	10	4	3	3	13	6	7	3	1.400	1.300
3	Manchester City	Eng	12	9	5	0	4	10	7	3	2	1.333	1.111
4	Górnik Zabrze	Pol	11	7	5	0	2	16	6	10	1	1.571	2.286
5	PSV Eindhoven	Ned	11	8	4	1	3	12	5	7	2	1.375	1.500
6	Cardiff City	Wal	10	6	4	1	1	16	4	12	1	1.667	2.667
7	Club Bruges	Bel	7	6	3	0	3	9	9	0	1	1.167	1.500
8	Vorwärts Frankfurt/Oder	GDR	7	6	2	2	2	4	5	-1	1	1.167	0.667
9	FC Zürich	Sui	6	4	3	0	1	17	5	12	0	1.500	4.250
10	FC Tirol	Aut	6	4	3	0	1	6	5	1	0	1.500	1.500
11	Benfica	Por	5	4	2	1	1	11	4	7	0	1.250	2.750
12	TJ Gottwaldov	Tch	5	4	2	1	1	6	5	1	0	1.250	1.500
13	CSKA Sofia	Bul	4	4	2	0	2	11	3	8	0	1.000	2.750
14	Partizani Tirana	Alb	3	4	1	1	2	6	6	0	0	0.750	1.500
15	Steaua Bucharest	Rom	3	4	1	1	2	4	10	-6	0	0.750	1.000
16	Göztepe	Tur	2	4	1	0	3	5	5	0	0	0.500	1.250
17	Aberdeen	Sco	2	2	1	0	1	4	4	0	0	1.000	2.000
18	Linfield	Nir	2	2	1	0	1	2	2	0	0	1.000	1.000
19	Bologna	Ita	2	2	0	2	0	1	1	0	0	1.000	0.500
20	Nantes	Fra	2	4	1	0	3	9	10	-1	0	0.500	2.250
21	Kickers Offenbach	FRG	2	2	1	0	1	2	3	-1	0	1.000	1.000
22	Honvéd	Hun	2	4	1	0	3	4	7	-3	0	0.500	1.000
23	Strømgodset IF	Nor	2	2	1	0	1	3	7	-4	0	1.000	1.500
24	Union Luxembourg	Lux	2	2	1	0	1	1	5	-4	0	1.000	0.500
25	Bohemians	Irl	1	2	0	1	1	3	4	-1	0	0.500	1.500
–	Karpaty Lvov	URS	1	2	0	1	1	3	4	-1	0	0.500	1.500
27	Åtvidaberg SFF	Swe	1	2	0	1	1	1	3	-2	0	0.500	0.500
28	Aris Salonika	Gre	1	2	0	1	1	2	6	-4	0	0.500	1.000
29	Hibernians	Mlt	1	2	0	1	1	0	5	-5	0	0.500	0.000
30	Olimpija Ljubljana	Yug	1	2	0	1	1	2	9	-7	0	0.500	1.000
31	Pezoporikos Larnaca	Cyp	1	2	0	1	1	0	8	-8	0	0.500	0.000
32	AaB Aalborg	Den	0	2	0	0	2	1	9	-8	0	0.000	0.500
33	Haka Valkeakoski	Fin	0	2	0	0	2	1	11	-10	0	0.000	0.500
34	IBA Akureyri	Isl	0	2	0	0	2	1	14	-13	0	0.000	0.500
	Total		**148**	**134**	**56**	**22**	**56**	**203**	**203**	**0**	**14**	**1.104**	**3.030**

First Round

Team 1	Cnty	Team 2	Cnty	1st leg	2nd leg	Agg
Liverpool	Eng	Ferencváros	Hun	1-0	1-1	2-1
Wiener Sport-Club	Aut	Beveren	Bel	0-2	0-3	0-5
Gent	Bel	Hamburg	FRG	0-1	1-7	1-8
Trakia Plovdiv	Bul	Coventry City	Eng	1-4	0-2	1-6
AB Copenhagen	Den	Sliema Wanderers	Mlt	7-0	3-2	10-2
B 1901 Nykobing	Den	Hertha Berlin	FRG	2-4	1-4	3-8
Dundee United	Sco	Grasshoppers Zürich	Sui	3-2	0-0	3-2
Hibernian	Sco	Malmö FF	Swe	6-0	3-2	9-2
Cork Hibernians	Irl	Valencia	Esp	0-3	1-3	1-6
Seville	Esp	Eskisehirspor	Tur	1-0	1-3	2-3
Ilves Tampere	Fin	Sturm Graz	Aut	4-2	0-3	4-5
AEK Athens	Gre	Twente Enschede	Ned	0-1	0-3	0-4
Coleraine	Nir	Kilmarnock	Sco	1-1	3-2	4-3
Inter Milan	Ita	Newcastle United	Eng	1-1	0-2	1-3
Lazio	Ita	Arsenal	Eng	2-2	0-2	2-4
Juventus	Ita	US Rumelange	Lux	7-0	4-0	11-0
IF Sarpsborg	Nor	Leeds United	Eng	0-1	0-5	0-6
Sparta Rotterdam	Ned	IA Akranes	Isl	6-0	9-0	15-0
Ruch Chorzów	Pol	Fiorentina	Ita	1-1	0-2	1-3
GKS Katowice	Pol	Barcelona	Esp	0-1	2-3	2-4
Barreirense	Por	Dinamo Zagreb	Yug	2-0	1-6	3-6
Vitória Guimarães	Por	Angoulême	Fra	3-0	1-3	4-3
Cologne	FRG	Sedan	Fra	5-1	0-1	5-2
Bayern Munich	FRG	Rangers	Sco	1-0	1-1	2-1
Dinamo Bucharest	Rom	PAOK Salonika	Gre	5-0	0-1	5-1
Universitatea Craiova	Rom	Pécs Dózsa	Hun	2-1	0-3	2-4
Lausanne-Sports	Sui	Vitória Setúbal	Por	0-2	1-2	1-4
Sparta Prague	Tch	Athletic Bilbao	Esp	2-0	1-1	3-1
Spartak Trnava	Tch	Olympique Marseille	Fra	2-0	0-2	2-2
Partizan Belgrade	Yug	Dynamo Dresden	GDR	0-0	0-6	0-6
Zeljeznicar Sarajevo	Yug	Anderlecht	Bel	3-4	4-5	7-9
Hajduk Split	Yug	Slavia Sofia	Bul	3-0	0-1	3-1

	Pts	P	W	D	L	F	A	Diff	Goals/P
Total	128	64	55	18	55	224	224	0	3.500

Second Round

Leeds United	Eng	Dynamo Dresden	GDR	1-0	1-2	2-2
Liverpool	Eng	Dinamo Bucharest	Rom	3-0	1-1	4-1
Newcastle United	Eng	Pécs Dózsa	Hun	2-0	0-2	2-2
Sturm Graz	Aut	Arsenal	Eng	1-0	0-2	1-2
AB Copenhagen	Den	Anderlecht	Bel	1-3	0-4	1-7
Hibernian	Sco	Vitória Guimarães	Por	2-0	1-2	3-2
Barcelona	Esp	Juventus	Ita	1-2	1-2	2-4
Valencia	Esp	Beveren	Bel	0-1	1-1	1-2
Fiorentina	Ita	Cologne	FRG	1-2	0-1	1-3
Sparta Rotterdam	Ned	Coleraine	Nir	2-0	2-1	4-1
Vitória Setúbal	Por	Hajduk Split	Yug	2-0	1-2	3-2
Hertha Berlin	FRG	Spartak Trnava	Tch	1-0	1-3	2-3
Bayern Munich	FRG	Coventry City	Eng	6-1	1-2	7-3
Sparta Prague	Tch	Dundee United	Sco	3-1	0-1	3-2
Eskisehirspor	Tur	Twente Enschede	Ned	3-2	1-6	4-8
Dinamo Zagreb	Yug	Hamburg	FRG	4-0	0-1	4-1

	Pts	P	W	D	L	F	A	Diff	Goals/P
Total	64	32	30	4	30	89	89	0	2.781

Third Round

Leeds United	Eng	Sparta Prague	Tch	6-0	3-2	9-2
Arsenal	Eng	Beveren	Bel	4-0	0-0	4-0
Anderlecht	Bel	Vitória Setúbal	Por	2-1	1-3	3-4
Hibernian	Sco	Liverpool	Eng	0-1	0-2	0-3
Pécs Dózsa	Hun	Juventus	Ita	0-1	0-2	0-3
Bayern Munich	FRG	Sparta Rotterdam	Ned	2-1	3-1	5-2
Spartak Trnava	Tch	Cologne	FRG	0-1	0-3	0-4
Dinamo Zagreb	Yug	Twente Enschede	Ned	2-2	0-1	2-3

	Pts	P	W	D	L	F	A	Diff	Goals/P
Total	32	16	14	4	14	44	44	0	2.750

Quarter Finals

Leeds United	Eng	Vitória Setúbal	Por	2-1	1-1	3-2
Liverpool	Eng	Bayern Munich	FRG	3-0	1-1	4-1
Arsenal	Eng	Cologne	FRG	2-1	0-1	2-2
Juventus	Ita	Twente Enschede	Ned	2-0	2-2	4-2

	Pts	P	W	D	L	F	A	Diff	Goals/P
Total	16	8	5	6	5	20	20	0	2.500

Semi Finals

Liverpool	Eng	Leeds United	Eng	0-1	0-0	0-1
Cologne	FRG	Juventus	Ita	1-1	0-2	1-3

	Pts	P	W	D	L	F	A	Diff	Goals/P
Total	8	4	2	4	2	5	5	0	1.250

Final

Juventus	Ita	Leeds United	Eng	2-2	1-1	3-3

	Pts	P	W	D	L	F	A	Diff	Goals/P
Total	4	2	0	4	0	6	6	0	3.000

	Pts	P	W	D	L	F	A	Diff	Goals/P
Total	252	126	106	40	106	388	388	0	3.079

Pos'n	Club	Cnty	Pts	P	W	D	L	F	A	Diff	B	Pts/P	F/P
1	Juventus	Ita	23	12	8	4	0	28	8	20	3	1.917	2.333
2	Leeds United	Eng	21	12	7	4	1	24	9	15	3	1.750	2.000
3	Liverpool	Eng	16	10	5	4	1	13	4	9	2	1.600	1.300
4	Cologne	FRG	15	10	6	1	3	15	8	7	2	1.500	1.500
5	Twente Enschede	Ned	11	8	4	2	2	17	10	7	1	1.375	2.125
6	Arsenal	Eng	11	8	4	2	2	12	5	7	1	1.375	1.500
7	Bayern Munich	FRG	11	8	4	2	2	15	10	5	1	1.375	1.875
8	Anderlecht	Bel	10	6	5	0	1	19	12	7	0	1.667	3.167
9	Vitória Setúbal	Por	10	8	4	1	3	13	9	4	1	1.250	1.625
10	Sparta Rotterdam	Ned	8	6	4	0	2	21	6	15	0	1.333	3.500
11	Beveren	Bel	8	6	3	2	1	7	5	2	0	1.333	1.167
12	Hibernian	Sco	6	6	3	0	3	12	7	5	0	1.000	2.000
13	Hertha Berlin	FRG	6	4	3	0	1	10	6	4	0	1.500	2.500
14	Hamburg	FRG	6	4	3	0	1	9	5	4	0	1.500	2.250
15	Coventry City	Eng	6	4	3	0	1	9	8	1	0	1.500	2.250
16	Dynamo Dresden	GDR	5	4	2	1	1	8	2	6	0	1.250	2.000
17	Dinamo Zagreb	Yug	5	6	2	1	3	12	7	5	0	0.833	2.000
18	Valencia	Esp	5	4	2	1	1	7	3	4	0	1.250	1.750
19	Newcastle United	Eng	5	4	2	1	1	5	3	2	0	1.250	1.250
20	Dundee United	Sco	5	4	2	1	1	5	5	0	0	1.250	1.250
21	Sparta Prague	Tch	5	6	2	1	3	8	12	-4	0	0.833	1.333
22	AB Copenhagen	Den	4	4	2	0	2	11	9	2	0	1.000	2.750
23	Hajduk Split	Yug	4	4	2	0	2	5	4	1	0	1.000	1.250
24	Sturm Graz	Aut	4	4	2	0	2	6	6	0	0	1.000	1.500
–	Barcelona	Esp	4	4	2	0	2	6	6	0	0	1.000	1.500
–	Vitória Guimarães	Por	4	4	2	0	2	6	6	0	0	1.000	1.500
27	Pécs Dózsa	Hun	4	6	2	0	4	6	7	-1	0	0.667	1.000
28	Eskisehirspor	Tur	4	4	2	0	2	7	10	-3	0	1.000	1.750
29	Spartak Trnava	Tch	4	6	2	0	4	5	8	-3	0	0.667	0.833
30	Dinamo Bucharest	Rom	3	4	1	1	2	6	5	1	0	0.750	1.500
31	Fiorentina	Ita	3	4	1	1	2	4	4	0	0	0.750	1.000
32	Coleraine	Nir	3	4	1	1	2	5	7	-2	0	0.750	1.250
33	Olympique Marseille	Fra	2	2	1	0	1	2	2	0	0	1.000	1.000
34	Ilves Tampere	Fin	2	2	1	0	1	4	5	-1	0	1.000	2.000
35	Angoulême	Fra	2	2	1	0	1	3	4	-1	0	1.000	1.500
36	Seville	Esp	2	2	1	0	1	2	3	-1	0	1.000	1.000
37	Universitatea Craiova	Rom	2	2	1	0	1	2	4	-2	0	1.000	1.000
38	Slavia Sofia	Bul	2	2	1	0	1	1	3	-2	0	1.000	0.500
39	Barreirense	Por	2	2	1	0	1	3	6	-3	0	1.000	1.500
40	Sedan	Fra	2	2	1	0	1	2	5	-3	0	1.000	1.000
41	PAOK Salonika	Gre	2	2	1	0	1	1	5	-4	0	1.000	0.500
42	Kilmarnock	Sco	1	2	0	1	1	3	4	-1	0	0.500	1.500
43	Grasshoppers Zürich	Sui	1	2	0	1	1	2	3	-1	0	0.500	1.000
44	Rangers	Sco	1	2	0	1	1	1	2	-1	0	0.500	0.500
–	Ferencváros	Hun	1	2	0	1	1	1	2	-1	0	0.500	0.500
46	Lazio	Ita	1	2	0	1	1	2	4	-2	0	0.500	1.000
47	Athletic Bilbao	Esp	1	2	0	1	1	1	3	-2	0	0.500	0.500
–	Inter Milan	Ita	1	2	0	1	1	1	3	-2	0	0.500	0.500
–	Ruch Chorzów	Pol	1	2	0	1	1	1	3	-2	0	0.500	0.500
50	Partizan Belgrade	Yug	1	2	0	1	1	0	6	-6	0	0.500	0.000
51	Zeljeznicar Sarajevo	Yug	0	2	0	0	2	7	9	-2	0	0.000	3.500
52	GKS Katowice	Pol	0	2	0	0	2	2	4	-2	0	0.000	1.000
53	Lausanne-Sports	Sui	0	2	0	0	2	1	4	-3	0	0.000	0.500
54	AEK Athens	Gre	0	2	0	0	2	0	4	-4	0	0.000	0.000
55	B 1901 Nykobing	Den	0	2	0	0	2	3	8	-5	0	0.000	1.500
56	Trakia Plovdiv	Bul	0	2	0	0	2	1	6	-5	0	0.000	0.500
–	Cork Hibernians	Irl	0	2	0	0	2	1	6	-5	0	0.000	0.500
58	Wiener Sport-Club	Aut	0	2	0	0	2	0	5	-5	0	0.000	0.000
59	IF Sarpsborg	Nor	0	2	0	0	2	0	6	-6	0	0.000	0.000
60	Malmö FF	Swe	0	2	0	0	2	2	9	-7	0	0.000	1.000
61	Gent	Bel	0	2	0	0	2	1	8	-7	0	0.000	0.500
62	Sliema Wanderers	Mlt	0	2	0	0	2	2	10	-8	0	0.000	1.000
63	US Rumelange	Lux	0	2	0	0	2	0	11	-11	0	0.000	0.000
64	IA Akranes	Isl	0	2	0	0	2	0	15	-15	0	0.000	0.000
	Total		**266**	**252**	**106**	**40**	**106**	**388**	**388**	**0**	**14**	**1.056**	**3.079**

National Performances by Points

1970-71

Pos'n	Cnty	Pts	P	W	D	L	F	A	Diff	B	Pts/P	F/P
1	Eng	99	63	35	17	11	102	47	55	12	1.571	1.619
2	Ned	48	33	18	6	9	68	27	41	6	1.455	2.061
3	FRG	46	32	19	5	8	69	34	35	3	1.438	2.156
4	Esp	38	30	14	5	11	40	29	11	5	1.267	1.333
5	Ita	34	26	11	9	6	41	25	16	3	1.308	1.577
6	Bel	31	24	14	2	8	44	36	8	1	1.292	1.833
7	Sco	26	22	11	3	8	50	27	23	1	1.182	2.273
8	Por	25	22	11	2	9	44	29	15	1	1.136	2.000
9	GDR	23	16	9	3	4	24	15	9	2	1.438	1.500
10	Yug	23	24	9	3	12	46	45	1	2	0.958	1.917
11	Pol	21	17	9	1	7	29	17	12	2	1.235	1.706
12	Tch	19	20	8	3	9	25	32	-7	0	0.950	1.250
13	Gre	16	15	5	3	7	19	25	-6	3	1.067	1.267
14	Aut	12	14	6	0	8	17	23	-6	0	0.857	1.214
15	Wal	10	6	4	1	1	16	4	12	1	1.667	2.667
16	Fra	10	12	5	0	7	17	24	-7	0	0.833	1.417
17	Rom	10	14	3	4	7	14	26	-12	0	0.714	1.000
18	Sui	9	12	4	1	7	25	21	4	0	0.750	2.083
19	Hun	9	14	4	1	9	13	20	-7	0	0.643	0.929
20	Bul	8	10	4	0	6	16	16	0	0	0.800	1.600
21	Tur	6	10	3	0	7	12	20	-8	0	0.600	1.200
22	Nir	5	8	2	1	5	8	13	-5	0	0.625	1.000
23	Irl	5	8	2	1	5	10	21	-11	0	0.625	1.250
24	Den	5	10	2	1	7	18	30	-12	0	0.500	1.800
25	Alb	4	6	1	2	3	8	10	-2	0	0.667	1.333
26	URS	3	4	1	1	2	7	8	-1	0	0.750	1.750
27	Nor	2	6	1	0	5	3	20	-17	0	0.333	0.500
28	Lux	2	6	1	0	5	2	23	-21	0	0.333	0.333
29	Fin	2	6	1	0	5	5	30	-25	0	0.333	0.833
30	Swe	1	6	0	1	5	4	18	-14	0	0.167	0.667
31	Mlt	1	6	0	1	5	2	24	-22	0	0.167	0.333
32	Cyp	1	4	0	1	3	0	24	-24	0	0.250	0.000
33	Isl	0	6	0	0	6	3	38	-35	0	0.000	0.500
	Total	**554**	**512**	**217**	**78**	**217**	**801**	**801**	**0**	**42**	**1.082**	**3.129**

1955-56 to 1970-71

1	Esp	656	446	245	77	124	935	556	379	89	1.471	2.096
2	Eng	627	423	228	91	104	835	456	379	80	1.482	1.974
3	Ita	549	382	200	82	100	653	409	244	67	1.437	1.709
4	FRG	424	326	159	61	106	627	478	149	45	1.301	1.923
5	Sco	381	296	150	42	104	546	402	144	39	1.287	1.845
6	Yug	275	258	98	48	112	420	393	27	31	1.066	1.628
7	Por	274	230	100	50	80	421	320	101	24	1.191	1.830
8	Hun	256	206	99	29	78	418	298	120	29	1.243	2.029
9	Bel	223	208	89	28	91	329	315	14	17	1.072	1.582
10	Ned	214	176	81	31	64	314	255	59	21	1.216	1.784
11	Tch	204	171	78	30	63	282	227	55	18	1.193	1.649
12	Fra	174	180	66	29	85	268	300	-32	13	0.967	1.489
13	GDR	155	149	59	28	62	222	203	19	9	1.040	1.490
14	Pol	127	109	51	16	42	166	160	6	9	1.165	1.523
15	Bul	122	121	45	25	51	198	185	13	7	1.008	1.636
16	Aut	120	134	46	21	67	183	233	-50	7	0.896	1.366
17	Sui	118	159	42	25	92	230	358	-128	9	0.742	1.447
18	Rom	111	121	45	19	57	148	210	-62	2	0.917	1.223
19	Tur	81	103	31	14	58	120	185	-65	5	0.786	1.165
20	Den	75	119	26	19	74	181	294	-113	4	0.630	1.521
21	Gre	74	94	25	20	49	105	182	-77	4	0.787	1.117
22	Swe	62	84	21	18	45	107	178	-71	2	0.738	1.274
23	Wal	45	40	15	11	14	61	49	12	4	1.125	1.525
24	URS	40	33	14	10	9	51	31	20	2	1.212	1.545
25	Nir	38	70	11	15	44	88	197	-109	1	0.543	1.257
26	Nor	36	66	13	9	44	73	178	-105	1	0.545	1.106
27	Irl	32	78	11	10	57	72	227	-155	0	0.410	0.923
28	Lux	26	72	10	6	56	61	282	-221	0	0.361	0.847
29	Mlt	14	48	4	6	38	23	164	-141	0	0.292	0.479
30	Fin	13	44	5	3	36	34	160	-126	0	0.295	0.773
31	Alb	12	18	3	6	9	14	26	-12	0	0.667	0.778
32	Cyp	5	32	1	3	28	17	156	-139	0	0.156	0.531
33	Isl	4	32	0	4	28	23	158	-135	0	0.125	0.719
	Total	**5567**	**5028**	**2071**	**886**	**2071**	**8225**	**8225**	**0**	**539**	**1.107**	**3.272**

1970-71

Pos'n	Cnty	Ave	Pts	P	W	D	L	F	A	Diff	B	No./T
1	England	12.375	99	63	35	17	11	102	47	55	12	8
2	Wales	10.000	10	6	4	1	1	16	4	12	1	1
3	Netherlands	9.600	48	33	18	6	9	68	27	41	6	5
4	W. Germany	7.666	46	32	19	5	8	69	34	35	3	6
–	E. Germany	7.666	23	16	9	3	4	24	15	9	2	3
6	Spain	6.333	38	30	14	5	11	40	29	11	5	6
7	Belgium	6.200	31	24	14	2	8	44	36	8	1	5
8	Italy	5.666	34	26	11	9	6	41	25	16	3	6
9	Poland	5.250	21	17	9	1	7	29	17	12	2	4
10	Portugal	5.000	25	22	11	2	9	44	29	15	1	5
11	Czechoslovakia	4.750	19	20	8	3	9	25	32	-7	0	4
12	Scotland	4.333	26	22	11	3	8	50	27	23	1	6
13	Greece	4.000	16	15	5	3	7	19	25	-6	3	4
14	Yugoslavia	3.833	23	24	9	3	12	46	45	1	2	6
15	Austria	3.000	12	14	6	0	8	17	23	-6	0	4
16	Romania	2.500	10	14	3	4	7	14	26	-12	0	4
17	Switzerland	2.250	9	12	4	1	7	25	21	4	0	4
18	Albania	2.000	4	6	1	2	3	8	10	-2	0	2
–	Bulgaria	2.000	8	10	4	0	6	16	16	0	0	4
–	France	2.000	10	12	5	0	7	17	24	-7	0	5
–	Turkey	2.000	6	10	3	0	7	12	20	-8	0	3
22	Hungary	1.800	9	14	4	1	9	13	20	-7	0	5
23	Rep. of Ireland	1.666	5	8	2	1	5	10	21	-11	0	3
–	N. Ireland	1.666	5	8	2	1	5	8	13	-5	0	3
25	USSR	1.500	3	4	1	1	2	7	8	-1	0	2
26	Denmark	1.250	5	10	2	1	7	18	30	-12	0	4
27	Finland	0.666	2	6	1	0	5	5	30	-25	0	3
–	Luxembourg	0.666	2	6	1	0	5	2	23	-21	0	3
–	Norway	0.666	2	6	1	0	5	3	20	-17	0	3
30	Cyprus	0.500	1	4	0	1	3	0	24	-24	0	2
31	Malta	0.333	1	6	0	1	5	2	24	-22	0	3
–	Sweden	0.333	1	6	0	1	5	4	18	-14	0	3
33	Iceland	0.000	0	6	0	0	6	3	38	-35	0	3
	Total		**554**	**512**	**217**	**78**	**217**	**801**	**801**	**0**	**42**	**3.129**

1955-56 to 1970-71

Pos'n	Cnty	Ave	Pts	P	W	D	L	F	A	Diff	B	No./T
1	England	9.646	627	423	228	91	104	835	456	379	80	65
2	Spain	8.864	656	446	245	77	124	935	556	379	89	74
3	Italy	8.073	549	382	200	82	100	653	409	244	67	68
4	Scotland	6.568	381	296	150	42	104	546	402	144	39	58
5	Hungary	6.564	256	206	99	29	78	418	298	120	29	39
6	W. Germany	6.057	424	326	159	61	106	627	478	149	45	70
7	Czechoslovakia	5.100	204	171	78	30	63	282	227	55	18	40
8	Netherlands	5.095	214	176	81	31	64	314	255	59	21	42
9	Portugal	4.892	274	230	100	50	80	421	320	101	24	56
10	Poland	4.703	127	109	51	16	42	166	160	6	9	27
11	Wales	4.500	45	40	15	11	14	61	49	12	4	10
12	USSR	4.444	40	33	14	10	9	51	31	20	2	9
13	Yugoslavia	4.435	275	258	98	48	112	420	393	27	31	62
14	Belgium	4.372	223	208	89	28	91	329	315	14	17	51
15	E. Germany	3.974	155	149	59	28	62	222	203	19	9	39
16	Bulgaria	3.588	122	121	45	25	51	198	185	13	7	34
17	France	3.283	174	180	66	29	85	268	300	-32	13	53
18	Austria	3.000	120	134	46	21	67	183	233	-50	7	40
–	Romania	3.000	111	121	45	19	57	148	210	-62	2	37
20	Turkey	2.700	81	103	31	14	58	120	185	-65	5	30
21	Switzerland	2.269	118	159	42	25	92	230	358	-128	9	52
22	Greece	2.176	74	94	25	20	49	105	182	-77	4	34
23	Sweden	2.137	62	84	21	18	45	107	178	-71	2	29
24	Denmark	1.704	75	119	26	19	74	181	294	-113	4	44
25	Albania	1.500	12	18	3	6	9	14	26	-12	0	8
26	Norway	1.333	36	66	13	9	44	73	178	-105	1	27
27	N. Ireland	1.225	38	70	11	15	44	88	197	-109	1	31
28	Rep. of Ireland	0.969	32	78	11	10	57	72	227	-155	0	33
29	Luxembourg	0.787	26	72	10	6	56	61	282	-221	0	33
30	Finland	0.650	13	44	5	3	36	34	160	-126	0	20
31	Malta	0.608	14	48	4	6	38	23	164	-141	0	23
32	Cyprus	0.333	5	32	1	3	28	17	156	-139	0	15
33	Iceland	0.266	4	32	0	4	28	23	158	-135	0	15
	Total		**5567**	**5028**	**2071**	**886**	**2071**	**8225**	**8225**	**0**	**539**	**3.272**

Cruijff's Ajax Win with Ease

This was the season when UEFA finally did away with the highly unsatisfactory tossing of a coin after drawn ties and replaced it with the penalty shoot-out.

The first tie to be settled in this way was the Fairs' Cup first round encounter between Spartak Trnava and Marseille. Twenty years on the French club would have to endure the torment of losing the Champions' Cup final after a shoot-out, and on this occasion too they were the unfortunate victims.

The first team to suffer the fate of a penalty shoot-out defeat in the Champions' Cup were Borussia Mönchengladbach, knocked out by English champions Everton in the second round after two 1-1 draws. Everton, having prevailed from the penalty spot, then became victims themselves of another UEFA regulation in the next round when they lost on away goals to Panathinaikos. This rule was now in force for every round of the competition, not just the first two rounds as before.

Panathinaikos, coached by the legendary Ferenc Puskás, broke new ground for Greek football with their accession to the semi-finals, and in coming back from a 4-1 defeat in the first leg of those semi-finals against Red Star Belgrade to win 3-0 in Athens, they not only succeeded in making further use of the away goals rule, but became the only Greek club ever to reach a European final.

Panathinaikos's success was a major surprise, but if the underdog was to have its day, then the 1970-71 season was the time to have it because of the 33 clubs which took part, only two were former winners of the competition – the previous season's finalists, Feyenoord and Celtic. For the first time ever, the Champions' Cup had set off without Real Madrid on board. There was no Benfica either, and no team from Milan.

Feyenoord's hold on the Cup did not last long. Held 1-1 at home by UT Arad, they could do no better than a 0-0 draw in Romania and thus went out on away goals in the first round. Fortunately, however, Netherlands was also represented by Ajax, and they succeeded in eliminating 17 Nëntori Tirana, Basle, Celtic and Atlético Madrid to reach their second final in three seasons, conceding not a single goal in their four home ties along the way.

The final against Panathinaikos went pretty much to plan for Rinus Michels' team. With Johan Cruijff orchestrating things in midfield, Ajax were rarely troubled after Dick van Dijk had given them an early lead. The match was far from exciting for the 90,000 spectators packed into Wembley stadium, but Ajax were always in control and a late second goal from substitute Arie Haan confirmed both their superiority and their victory.

Real Madrid, lost to the Champions' Cup, were the Spanish representatives in the Cup-winners' Cup and, not surprisingly, they reached the final, albeit with some bumpy moments along the way such as losing at home to Wacker Innsbruck (later to become FC Tirol) and away to Cardiff City. Holders Manchester City were denied in their quest to retain the trophy by fellow Football League representatives Chelsea, who won 1-0 both home and away in the semi-final. The final, in Athens, had to go to a replay when Real's left-half Zoco equalised Peter Osgood's earlier goal in the very last minute of the game. Two days later, at the same venue, Chelsea scored twice in the first half, through Dempster and Osgood, and Real could only pull one goal back, through Fleitas, with 15 minutes to go. So the Cup remained in England, with an eighth different English club now adding its name to the list of European winners.

The first English team to win a second trophy were Leeds United. They regained the Fairs' Cup three years after their first victory and, in so doing, defeated two famous clubs still seeking their first European title – Liverpool in the semi-finals and Juventus in the final. The first leg of the final, in Turin, was abandoned after 51 minutes with the score 0-0 when the pitch became unplayable. Two days later they tried again and this time Leeds clocked up two valuable away goals, from Madeley and Bates, in another evenly contested draw. They proved essential, for in the return at Elland Road Leeds could only draw 1-1, which meant that they took the Cup on the away goals rule.

1971 – 1972

Ajax

Rangers

Tottenham Hotspur

European Cup 1971-72

Preliminary Round

Team 1	Cnty	Team 2	Cnty	1st leg	2nd leg	Agg
Valencia	Esp	Union Luxembourg	Lux	3-1	1-0	4-1

	Pts	P	W	D	L	F	A	Diff	Goals/P
Total	4	2	2	0	2	5	5	0	2.500

First Round

FC Tirol	Aut	Benfica	Por	0-4	1-3	1-7
Standard Liège	Bel	Linfield	Nir	2-0	3-2	5-2
CSKA Sofia	Bul	Partizani Tirana	Alb	3-0	1-0	4-0
B 1903 Copenhagen	Den	Celtic	Sco	2-1	0-3	2-4
Cork Hibernians	Irl	Bor. Mönchengladbach	FRG	0-5	1-2	1-7
Valencia	Esp	Hajduk Split	Yug	0-0	1-1	1-1
Reipas Lahti	Fin	Grasshoppers Zürich	Sui	1-1	0-8	1-9
Olympique Marseille	Fra	Górnik Zabrze	Pol	2-1	1-1	3-2
Ujpesti Dózsa	Hun	Malmö FF	Swe	4-0	0-1	4-1
Inter Milan	Ita	AEK Athens	Gre	4-1	2-3	6-4
Sliema Wanderers	Mlt	IA Akranes	Isl	4-0	0-0	4-0
Strømgodset IF	Nor	Arsenal	Eng	1-3	0-4	1-7
Ajax	Ned	Dynamo Dresden	GDR	2-0	0-0	2-0
Feyenoord	Ned	Olympiakos Nicosia	Cyp	8-0	9-0	17-0
Dinamo Bucharest	Rom	Spartak Trnava	Tch	0-0	2-2	2-2
Galatasaray	Tur	CSKA Moscow	URS	1-1	0-3	1-4

	Pts	P	W	D	L	F	A	Diff	Goals/P
Total	64	32	23	18	23	105	105	0	3.281

Second Round

Celtic	Sco	Sliema Wanderers	Mlt	5-0	2-1	7-1
Valencia	Esp	Ujpesti Dózsa	Hun	0-1	1-2	1-3
Olympique Marseille	Fra	Ajax	Ned	1-2	1-4	2-6
Inter Milan	Ita	Bor. Mönchengladbach	FRG	4-2	0-0	4-2
Benfica	Por	CSKA Sofia	Bul	2-1	0-0	2-1
Dinamo Bucharest	Rom	Feyenoord	Ned	0-3	0-2	0-5
Grasshoppers Zürich	Sui	Arsenal	Eng	0-2	0-3	0-5
CSKA Moscow	URS	Standard Liège	Bel	1-0	0-2	1-2

	Pts	P	W	D	L	F	A	Diff	Goals/P
Total	32	16	14	4	14	42	42	0	2.625

Quarter Finals

Ujpesti Dózsa	Hun	Celtic	Sco	1-2	1-1	2-3
Inter Milan	Ita	Standard Liège	Bel	1-0	1-2	2-2
Ajax	Ned	Arsenal	Eng	2-1	1-0	3-1
Feyenoord	Ned	Benfica	Por	1-0	1-5	2-5

	Pts	P	W	D	L	F	A	Diff	Goals/P
Total	16	8	7	2	7	20	20	0	2.500

Semi Finals

Inter Milan	Ita	Celtic	Sco	0-0	0-0	0-0
Ajax	Ned	Benfica	Por	1-0	0-0	1-0

	Pts	P	W	D	L	F	A	Diff	Goals/P
Total	8	4	1	6	1	1	1	0	0.250

Final

Ajax	Ned	Inter Milan	Ita	2-0	2-0

	Pts	P	W	D	L	F	A	Diff	Goals/P
Total	2	1	1	0	1	2	2	0	2.000

	Pts	P	W	D	L	F	A	Diff	Goals/P
Total	126	63	48	30	48	175	175	0	2.778

Pos'n	Club	Cnty	Pts	P	W	D	L	F	A	Diff	B	Pts/P	F/P
1	Ajax	Ned	19	9	7	2	0	14	3	11	3	2.111	1.556
2	Celtic	Sco	13	8	4	3	1	14	5	9	2	1.625	1.750
3	Benfica	Por	12	8	4	2	2	14	5	9	2	1.500	1.750
4	Inter Milan	Ita	12	9	3	3	3	12	10	2	3	1.333	1.333
5	Feyenoord	Ned	11	6	5	0	1	24	5	19	1	1.833	4.000
6	Arsenal	Eng	9	6	4	0	2	13	4	9	1	1.500	2.167
7	Standard Liège	Bel	9	6	4	0	2	9	5	4	1	1.500	1.500
8	Ujpesti Dózsa	Hun	8	6	3	1	2	9	5	4	1	1.333	1.500
9	Valencia	Esp	6	6	2	2	2	6	5	1	0	1.000	1.000
10	Bor. Mönchengladbach	FRG	5	4	2	1	1	9	5	4	0	1.250	2.250
11	CSKA Sofia	Bul	5	4	2	1	1	5	2	3	0	1.250	1.250
12	CSKA Moscow	URS	5	4	2	1	1	5	3	2	0	1.250	1.250
13	Grasshoppers Zürich	Sui	3	4	1	1	2	9	6	3	0	0.750	2.250
14	Sliema Wanderers	Mlt	3	4	1	1	2	5	7	-2	0	0.750	1.250
15	Olympique Marseille	Fra	3	4	1	1	2	5	8	-3	0	0.750	1.250
16	Spartak Trnava	Tch	2	2	0	2	0	2	2	0	0	1.000	1.000
17	Hajduk Split	Yug	2	2	0	2	0	1	1	0	0	1.000	0.500
18	AEK Athens	Gre	2	2	1	0	1	4	6	-2	0	1.000	2.000
19	B 1903 Copenhagen	Den	2	2	1	0	1	2	4	-2	0	1.000	1.000
20	Malmö FF	Swe	2	2	1	0	1	1	4	-3	0	1.000	0.500
21	Dinamo Bucharest	Rom	2	4	0	2	2	2	7	-5	0	0.500	0.500
22	Górnik Zabrze	Pol	1	2	0	1	1	2	3	-1	0	0.500	1.000
23	Dynamo Dresden	GDR	1	2	0	1	1	0	2	-2	0	0.500	0.000
24	Galatasaray	Tur	1	2	0	1	1	1	4	-3	0	0.500	0.500
25	IA Akranes	Isl	1	2	0	1	1	0	4	-4	0	0.500	0.000
26	Reipas Lahti	Fin	1	2	0	1	1	1	9	-8	0	0.500	0.500
27	Linfield	Nir	0	2	0	0	2	2	5	-3	0	0.000	1.000
28	Union Luxembourg	Lux	0	2	0	0	2	1	4	-3	0	0.000	0.500
29	Partizani Tirana	Alb	0	2	0	0	2	0	4	-4	0	0.000	0.000
30	FC Tirol	Aut	0	2	0	0	2	1	7	-6	0	0.000	0.500
–	Cork Hibernians	Irl	0	2	0	0	2	1	7	-6	0	0.000	0.500
–	Strømgodset IF	Nor	0	2	0	0	2	1	7	-6	0	0.000	0.500
33	Olympiakos Nicosia	Cyp	0	2	0	0	2	0	17	-17	0	0.000	0.000
	Total		**140**	**126**	**18**	**30**	**48**	**175**	**175**	**0**	**14**	**1.111**	**2.778**

European Cup Winners Cup 1971-72

Preliminary Round

Team 1	Cnty	Team 2	Cnty	1st leg	2nd leg	Agg
B 1909 Odense	Den	Austria Vienna	Aut	4-2	0-2	4-4
Hibernians	Mlt	Fram Reykjavik	Isl	3-0	0-2	3-2

	Pts	P	W	D	L	F	A	Diff	Goals/P
Total	8	4	4	0	4	13	13	0	3.250

First Round

Dinamo Tirana	Alb	Austria Vienna	Aut	1-1	0-1	1-2
Beerschot	Bel	Anorthosis Famagusta	Cyp	7-0	1-0	8-0
Levski Sofia	Bul	Sparta Rotterdam	Ned	1-1	0-2	1-3
Limerick	Irl	Torino	Ita	0-1	0-4	0-5
MP Mikkeli	Fin	Eskisehirspor	Tur	0-0	0-4	0-4
Stade Rennes	Fra	Rangers	Sco	1-1	0-1	1-2
Olympiakos Pireus	Gre	Dinamo Moscow	URS	0-2	2-1	2-3
Komló	Hun	Red Star Belgrade	Yug	2-7	2-1	4-8
Distillery	Nir	Barcelona	Esp	1-3	0-4	1-7
Jeunesse Hautcharage	Lux	Chelsea	Eng	0-8	0-13	0-21
Hibernians	Mlt	Steaua Bucharest	Rom	0-0	0-1	0-1
Zaglebie Sosnowiec	Pol	Åtvidaberg SFF	Swe	3-4	1-1	4-5
Sporting Lisbon	Por	SFK Lyn	Nor	4-0	3-0	7-0
Servette	Sui	Liverpool	Eng	2-1	0-2	2-3
Skoda Plzen	Tch	Bayern Munich	FRG	0-1	1-6	1-7
Dynamo Berlin	GDR	Cardiff City	Wal	1-1	1-1	2-2

	Pts	P	W	D	L	F	A	Diff	Goals/P
Total	64	32	24	16	24	107	107	0	3.344

Second Round

Liverpool	Eng	Bayern Munich	FRG	0-0	1-3	1-3
Beerschot	Bel	Dynamo Berlin	GDR	1-3	1-3	2-6
Rangers	Sco	Sporting Lisbon	Por	3-2	3-4	6-6
Barcelona	Esp	Steaua Bucharest	Rom	0-1	1-2	1-3
Torino	Ita	Austria Vienna	Aut	1-0	0-0	1-0
Sparta Rotterdam	Ned	Red Star Belgrade	Yug	1-1	1-2	2-3
Åtvidaberg SFF	Swe	Chelsea	Eng	0-0	1-1	1-1
Eskisehirspor	Tur	Dinamo Moscow	URS	0-1	0-1	0-2

	Pts	P	W	D	L	F	A	Diff	Goals/P
Total	32	16	11	10	11	38	38	0	2.375

Quarter Finals

Torino	Ita	Rangers	Sco	1-1	0-1	1-2
Steaua Bucharest	Rom	Bayern Munich	FRG	1-1	0-0	1-1
Åtvidaberg SFF	Swe	Dynamo Berlin	GDR	0-2	2-2	2-4
Red Star Belgrade	Yug	Dinamo Moscow	URS	1-2	1-1	2-3

	Pts	P	W	D	L	F	A	Diff	Goals/P
Total	16	8	3	10	3	16	16	0	2.000

Semi Finals

Bayern Munich	FRG	Rangers	Sco	1-1	0-2	1-3
Dynamo Berlin	GDR	Dinamo Moscow	URS	1-1	1-1	2-2

	Pts	P	W	D	L	F	A	Diff	Goals/P
Total	8	4	1	6	1	8	8	0	2.000

Final

Rangers	Sco	Dinamo Moscow	URS	3-2		3-2

	Pts	P	W	D	L	F	A	Diff	Goals/P
Total	2	1	1	0	1	5	5	0	5.000

	Pts	P	W	D	L	F	A	Diff	Goals/P
Total	130	65	44	42	44	187	187	0	2.877

Pos'n	Club	Cnty	Pts	P	W	D	L	F	A	Diff	B	Pts/P	F/P
1	Rangers	Sco	16	9	5	3	1	16	11	5	3	1.778	1.778
2	Dinamo Moscow	URS	14	9	4	3	2	12	9	3	3	1.556	1.333
3	Dynamo Berlin	GDR	13	8	3	5	0	14	8	6	2	1.625	1.750
4	Bayern Munich	FRG	12	8	3	4	1	12	6	6	2	1.500	1.500
5	Steaua Bucharest	Rom	10	6	3	3	0	5	2	3	1	1.667	0.833
6	Torino	Ita	9	6	3	2	1	7	2	5	1	1.500	1.167
7	Red Star Belgrade	Yug	7	6	2	2	2	13	9	4	1	1.167	2.167
8	Åtvidaberg SFF	Swe	7	6	1	4	1	8	9	-1	1	1.167	1.333
9	Chelsea	Eng	6	4	2	2	0	22	1	21	0	1.500	5.500
10	Sporting Lisbon	Por	6	4	3	0	1	13	6	7	0	1.500	3.250
11	Austria Vienna	Aut	6	6	2	2	2	6	6	0	0	1.000	1.000
12	Beerschot	Bel	4	4	2	0	2	10	6	4	0	1.000	2.500
13	Barcelona	Esp	4	4	2	0	2	8	4	4	0	1.000	2.000
14	Sparta Rotterdam	Ned	4	4	1	2	1	5	4	1	0	1.000	1.250
15	Eskisehirspor	Tur	3	4	1	1	2	4	2	2	0	0.750	1.000
16	Hibernians	Mlt	3	4	1	1	2	3	3	0	0	0.750	0.750
17	Liverpool	Eng	3	4	1	1	2	4	5	-1	0	0.750	1.000
18	B 1909 Odense	Den	2	2	1	0	1	4	4	0	0	1.000	2.000
19	Cardiff City	Wal	2	2	0	2	0	2	2	0	0	1.000	1.000
20	Olympiakos Pireus	Gre	2	2	1	0	1	2	3	-1	0	1.000	1.000
–	Fram Reykjavik	Isl	2	2	1	0	1	2	3	-1	0	1.000	1.000
–	Servette	Sui	2	2	1	0	1	2	3	-1	0	1.000	1.000
23	Komló	Hun	2	2	1	0	1	4	8	-4	0	1.000	2.000
24	Zaglebie Sosnowiec	Pol	1	2	0	1	1	4	5	-1	0	0.500	2.000
25	Dinamo Tirana	Alb	1	2	0	1	1	1	2	-1	0	0.500	0.500
–	Stade Rennes	Fra	1	2	0	1	1	1	2	-1	0	0.500	0.500
27	Levski Sofia	Bul	1	2	0	1	1	1	3	-2	0	0.500	0.500
28	MP Mikkeli	Fin	1	2	0	1	1	0	4	-4	0	0.500	0.000
29	Limerick	Irl	0	2	0	0	2	0	5	-5	0	0.000	0.000
30	Distillery	Nir	0	2	0	0	2	1	7	-6	0	0.000	0.500
–	Skoda Plzen	Tch	0	2	0	0	2	1	7	-6	0	0.000	0.500
32	SFK Lyn	Nor	0	2	0	0	2	0	7	-7	0	0.000	0.000
33	Anorthosis Famagusta	Cyp	0	2	0	0	2	0	8	-8	0	0.000	0.000
34	Jeunesse Hautcharage	Lux	0	2	0	0	2	0	21	-21	0	0.000	0.000
	Total		**144**	**130**	**44**	**42**	**44**	**187**	**187**	**0**	**14**	**1.108**	**2.877**

First Round

Team 1	Cnty	Team 2	Cnty	1st leg	2nd leg	Agg
Southampton	Eng	Athletic Bilbao	Esp	2-1	0-2	2-3
Wolverhampton Wanderers	Eng	Academica Coimbra	Por	3-0	4-1	7-1
Lierse	Bel	Leeds United	Eng	0-2	4-0	4-2
Dundee	Sco	AB Copenhagen	Den	4-2	1-0	5-2
Atlético Madrid	Esp	Panionios	Gre	2-1	0-1	2-2
Celta Vigo	Esp	Aberdeen	Sco	0-2	0-1	0-3
Saint-Etienne	Fra	Cologne	FRG	1-1	1-2	2-3
Vasas SC	Hun	Shelbourne	Irl	1-0	1-1	2-1
Glentoran	Nir	Eintracht Braunschweig	FRG	0-1	1-6	1-7
IBK Keflavik	Isl	Tottenham Hotspur	Eng	1-6	0-9	1-15
Bologna	Ita	Anderlecht	Bel	1-1	2-0	3-1
AC Milan	Ita	Akritas Morphou	Cyp	4-0	3-0	7-0
Napoli	Ita	Rapid Bucharest	Rom	1-0	0-2	1-2
Marsa	Mlt	Juventus	Ita	0-6	0-5	0-11
Rosenborg BK	Nor	HIFK Helsinki	Fin	3-0	1-0	4-0
FC Den Haag	Ned	Aris Bonnevoie	Lux	5-0	2-2	7-2
Zaglebie Walbrzych	Pol	Union Teplice	Tch	1-0	3-2	4-2
FC Porto	Por	Nantes	Fra	0-2	1-1	1-3
Vitória Setúbal	Por	Nîmes Olympique	Fra	1-0	1-2	2-2
Hertha Berlin	FRG	IF Elfsborg	Swe	3-1	4-1	7-2
Hamburg	FRG	St. Johnstone	Sco	2-1	0-3	2-4
UT Arad	Rom	SV Salzburg	Aut	4-1	1-3	5-4
FC Basle	Sui	Real Madrid	Esp	1-2	1-2	2-4
Lugano	Sui	Legia Warsaw	Pol	1-3	0-0	1-3
Fenerbahçe	Tur	Ferencváros	Hun	1-1	1-3	2-4
Spartak Moscow	URS	VSS Kosice	Tch	2-0	1-2	3-2
OFK Belgrade	Yug	Djurgården SIF	Swe	4-1	2-2	6-3
Zeljeznicar Sarajevo	Yug	Club Bruges	Bel	3-0	1-3	4-3
Dinamo Zagreb	Yug	Botev Vratsa	Bul	6-1	2-1	8-2
Carl Zeiss Jena	GDR	Lokomotiv Plovdiv	Bul	3-0	1-3	4-3

	Pts	P	W	D	L	F	A	Diff	Goals/P
Total	120	60	52	16	52	195	195	0	3.250

Second Round

St. Johnstone	Sco	Vasas SC	Hun	2-0	0-1	2-1
Real Madrid	Esp	PSV Eindhoven	Ned	3-1	0-2	3-3
Nantes	Fra	Tottenham Hotspur	Eng	0-0	0-1	0-1
Ferencváros	Hun	Panionios	Gre	6-0	6-0	6-0
AC Milan	Ita	Hertha Berlin	FRG	4-2	1-2	5-4
Juventus	Ita	Aberdeen	Sco	2-0	1-1	3-1
Rosenborg BK	Nor	Lierse	Bel	4-1	0-3	4-4
FC Den Haag	Ned	Wolverhampton Wanderers	Eng	1-3	0-4	1-7
Zaglebie Walbrzych	Pol	UT Arad	Rom	1-1	1-2	2-3
Eintracht Braunschweig	FRG	Athletic Bilbao	Esp	2-1	2-2	4-3
Cologne	FRG	Dundee	Sco	2-1	2-4	4-5
Rapid Bucharest	Rom	Legia Warsaw	Pol	4-0	0-2	4-2
Spartak Moscow	URS	Vitória Setúbal	Por	0-0	0-4	0-4
OFK Belgrade	Yug	Carl Zeiss Jena	GDR	1-1	0-4	1-5
Zeljeznicar Sarajevo	Yug	Bologna	Ita	1-1	2-2	3-3
Dinamo Zagreb	Yug	Rapid Vienna	Aut	2-2	0-0	2-2

	Pts	P	W	D	L	F	A	Diff	Goals/P
Total	62	31	21	20	21	92	92	0	2.968

Third Round

Tottenham Hotspur	Eng	Rapid Bucharest	Rom	3-0	2-0	5-0
Rapid Vienna	Aut	Juventus	Ita	0-1	1-4	1-5
St. Johnstone	Sco	Zeljeznicar Sarajevo	Yug	1-0	1-5	2-5
AC Milan	Ita	Dundee	Sco	3-0	0-2	3-2
PSV Eindhoven	Ned	Lierse	Bel	1-0	0-4	1-4
Eintracht Braunschweig	FRG	Ferencváros	Hun	1-1	2-5	3-6
UT Arad	Rom	Vitória Setúbal	Por	3-0	0-1	3-1
Carl Zeiss Jena	GDR	Wolverhampton Wanderers	Eng	0-1	0-3	0-4

	Pts	P	W	D	L	F	A	Diff	Goals/P
Total	32	16	15	2	15	45	45	0	2.813

Quarter Finals

Ferencváros	Hun	Zeljeznicar Sarajevo	Yug	1-2	2-1	3-3
AC Milan	Ita	Lierse	Bel	2-0	1-1	3-1
Juventus	Ita	Wolverhampton Wanderers	Eng	1-1	1-2	2-3
UT Arad	Rom	Tottenham Hotspur	Eng	0-2	1-1	1-3

	Pts	P	W	D	L	F	A	Diff	Goals/P
Total	16	8	5	6	5	19	19	0	2.375

Semi Finals

Tottenham Hotspur	Eng	AC Milan	Ita	2-1	1-1	3-2
Ferencváros	Hun	Wolverhampton Wanderers	Eng	2-2	1-2	3-4

	Pts	P	W	D	L	F	A	Diff	Goals/P
Total	8	4	2	4	2	12	12	0	3.000

Final

Wolverhampton Wanderers	Eng	Tottenham Hotspur	Eng	1-2	1-1	2-3

	Pts	P	W	D	L	F	A	Diff	Goals/P
Total	4	2	1	2	1	5	5	0	2.500

	Pts	P	W	D	L	F	A	Diff	Goals/P
Total	242	121	96	50	96	368	368	0	3.041

UEFA Cup 1971-72

Pos'n	Club	Cnty	Pts	P	W	D	L	F	A	Diff	B	Pts/P	F/P
1	Tottenham Hotspur	Eng	23	12	8	4	0	30	6	24	3	1.917	2.500
2	Wolverhampton Wanderers	Eng	22	12	8	3	1	27	10	17	3	1.833	2.250
3	AC Milan	Ita	14	10	5	2	3	20	10	10	2	1.400	2.000
4	Juventus	Ita	13	8	5	2	1	21	5	16	1	1.625	2.625
5	Ferencváros	Hun	13	9	4	3	2	22	12	10	2	1.444	2.444
6	Zeljeznicar Sarajevo	Yug	9	8	3	2	3	15	11	4	1	1.125	1.875
7	UT Arad	Rom	9	8	3	2	3	12	10	2	1	1.125	1.500
8	Eintracht Braunschweig	FRG	8	6	3	2	1	14	10	4	0	1.333	2.333
9	Lierse	Bel	8	8	3	1	4	13	10	3	1	1.000	1.625
10	Dundee	Sco	8	6	4	0	2	12	9	3	0	1.333	2.000
11	Vitória Setúbal	Por	7	6	3	1	2	7	5	2	0	1.167	1.167
12	Dinamo Zagreb	Yug	6	4	2	2	0	10	4	6	0	1.500	2.500
13	Hertha Berlin	FRG	6	4	3	0	1	11	7	4	0	1.500	2.750
14	Rosenborg BK	Nor	6	4	3	0	1	8	4	4	0	1.500	2.000
15	Real Madrid	Esp	6	4	3	0	1	7	5	2	0	1.500	1.750
16	St. Johnstone	Sco	6	6	3	0	3	8	8	0	0	1.000	1.333
17	Bologna	Ita	5	4	1	3	0	6	4	2	0	1.250	1.500
18	Carl Zeiss Jena	GDR	5	6	2	1	3	9	8	1	0	0.833	1.500
19	Zaglebie Watbrzych	Pol	5	4	2	1	1	6	5	1	0	1.250	1.500
20	Aberdeen	Sco	5	4	2	1	1	4	3	1	0	1.250	1.000
21	Cologne	FRG	5	4	2	1	1	7	7	0	0	1.250	1.750
22	Legia Warsaw	Pol	5	4	2	1	1	5	5	0	0	1.250	1.250
23	Vasas SC	Hun	5	4	2	1	1	3	3	0	0	1.250	0.750
24	Nantes	Fra	4	4	1	2	1	3	2	1	0	1.000	0.750
25	OFK Belgrade	Yug	4	4	1	2	1	7	8	-1	0	1.000	1.750
26	Rapid Bucharest	Rom	4	6	2	0	4	6	8	-2	0	0.667	1.000
27	PSV Eindhoven	Ned	4	4	2	0	2	4	7	-3	0	1.000	1.000
28	Athletic Bilbao	Esp	3	4	1	1	2	6	6	0	0	0.750	1.500
29	FC Den Haag	Ned	3	4	1	1	2	8	9	-1	0	0.750	2.000
30	Spartak Moscow	URS	3	4	1	1	2	3	6	-3	0	0.750	0.750
31	Atlético Madrid	Esp	2	2	1	0	1	2	2	0	0	1.000	1.000
–	Nîmes Olympique	Fra	2	2	1	0	1	2	2	0	0	1.000	1.000
33	SV Salzburg	Aut	2	2	1	0	1	4	5	-1	0	1.000	2.000
34	Club Bruges	Bel	2	2	1	0	1	3	4	-1	0	1.000	1.500
–	Lokomotiv Plovdiv	Bul	2	2	1	0	1	3	4	-1	0	1.000	1.500
36	Southampton	Eng	2	2	1	0	1	2	3	-1	0	1.000	1.000
-	VSS Kosice	Tch	2	2	1	0	1	2	3	-1	0	1.000	1.000
38	Napoli	Ita	2	2	1	0	1	1	2	-1	0	1.000	0.500
39	Leeds United	Eng	2	2	1	0	1	2	4	-2	0	1.000	1.000
–	Hamburg	FRG	2	2	1	0	1	2	4	-2	0	1.000	1.000
41	Rapid Vienna	Aut	2	4	0	2	2	3	7	-4	0	0.500	0.750
42	Panionios	Gre	2	3	1	0	2	2	8	-6	0	0.667	0.667
43	Saint-Etienne	Fra	1	2	0	1	1	2	3	-1	0	0.500	1.000
44	Shelbourne	Irl	1	2	0	1	1	1	2	-1	0	0.500	0.500
45	Fenerbahçe	Tur	1	2	0	1	1	2	4	-2	0	0.500	1.000
46	Anderlecht	Bel	1	2	0	1	1	1	3	-2	0	0.500	0.500
–	FC Porto	Por	1	2	0	1	1	1	3	-2	0	0.500	0.500
–	Lugano	Sui	1	2	0	1	1	1	3	-2	0	0.500	0.500
49	Djurgården SIF	Swe	1	2	0	1	1	3	6	-3	0	0.500	1.500
50	Aris Bonnevoie	Lux	1	2	0	1	1	2	7	-5	0	0.500	1.000
51	FC Basle	Sui	0	2	0	0	2	2	4	-2	0	0.000	1.000
–	Union Teplice	Tch	0	2	0	0	2	2	4	-2	0	0.000	1.000
53	AB Copenhagen	Den	0	2	0	0	2	2	5	-3	0	0.000	1.000
54	Celta Vigo	Esp	0	2	0	0	2	0	3	-3	0	0.000	0.000
55	HIFK Helsinki	Fin	0	2	0	0	2	0	4	-4	0	0.000	0.000
56	IF Elfsborg	Swe	0	2	0	0	2	2	7	-5	0	0.000	1.000
57	Botev Vratsa	Bul	0	2	0	0	2	2	8	-6	0	0.000	1.000
58	Glentoran	Nir	0	2	0	0	2	1	7	-6	0	0.000	0.500
–	Academica Coimbra	Por	0	2	0	0	2	1	7	-6	0	0.000	0.500
60	Akritas Morphou	Cyp	0	2	0	0	2	0	7	-7	0	0.000	0.000
61	Marsa	Mlt	0	2	0	0	2	0	11	-11	0	0.000	0.000
62	IBK Keflavik	Isl	0	2	0	0	2	1	15	-14	0	0.000	0.500
	Total		**256**	**242**	**96**	**50**	**96**	**368**	**368**	**0**	**14**	**1.058**	**3.041**

1971-72

Pos'n	Cnty	Pts	P	W	D	L	F	A	Diff	B	Pts/P	F/P
1	Eng	67	42	25	10	7	100	33	67	7	1.595	2.381
2	Ita	55	39	18	12	9	67	33	34	7	1.410	1.718
3	Sco	48	33	18	7	8	54	36	18	5	1.455	1.636
4	Ned	41	27	16	5	6	55	28	27	4	1.519	2.037
5	FRG	38	28	14	8	6	55	39	16	2	1.357	1.964
6	Yug	28	24	8	10	6	46	33	13	2	1.167	1.917
7	Hun	28	21	10	5	6	38	28	10	3	1.333	1.810
8	Por	26	22	10	4	8	36	26	10	2	1.182	1.636
9	Rom	25	24	8	7	9	25	27	-2	2	1.042	1.042
10	Bel	24	22	10	2	10	36	28	8	2	1.091	1.636
11	URS	22	17	7	5	5	20	18	2	3	1.294	1.176
12	Esp	21	22	9	3	10	29	25	4	0	0.955	1.318
13	GDR	19	16	5	7	4	23	18	5	2	1.188	1.438
14	Pol	12	12	4	4	4	17	18	-1	0	1.000	1.417
15	Fra	11	14	3	5	6	13	17	-4	0	0.786	0.929
16	Aut	10	14	3	4	7	14	25	-11	0	0.714	1.000
17	Swe	10	12	2	5	5	14	26	-12	1	0.833	1.167
18	Bul	8	10	3	2	5	11	17	-6	0	0.800	1.100
19	Sui	6	10	2	2	6	14	16	-2	0	0.600	1.400
20	Nor	6	8	3	0	5	9	18	-9	0	0.750	1.125
21	Gre	6	7	3	0	4	8	17	-9	0	0.857	1.143
22	Mlt	6	10	2	2	6	8	21	-13	0	0.600	0.800
23	Tur	5	8	1	3	4	7	10	-3	0	0.625	0.875
24	Den	4	6	2	0	4	8	13	-5	0	0.667	1.333
25	Tch	4	8	1	2	5	7	16	-9	0	0.500	0.875
26	Isl	3	6	1	1	4	3	22	-19	0	0.500	0.500
27	Wal	2	2	0	2	0	2	2	0	0	1.000	1.000
28	Fin	2	6	0	2	4	1	17	-16	0	0.333	0.167
29	Alb	1	4	0	1	3	1	6	-5	0	0.250	0.250
30	Irl	1	6	0	1	5	2	14	-12	0	0.167	0.333
31	Lux	1	6	0	1	5	3	32	-29	0	0.167	0.500
32	Nir	0	6	0	0	6	4	19	-15	0	0.000	0.667
33	Cyp	0	6	0	0	6	0	32	-32	0	0.000	0.000
	Total	**540**	**498**	**188**	**122**	**188**	**730**	**730**	**0**	**42**	**1.084**	**2.932**

1955-56 to 1971-72

1	Eng	694	465	253	101	111	935	489	446	87	1.492	2.011
2	Esp	677	468	254	80	134	964	581	383	89	1.447	2.060
3	Ita	604	421	218	94	109	720	442	278	74	1.435	1.710
4	FRG	462	354	173	69	112	682	517	165	47	1.305	1.927
5	Sco	429	329	168	49	112	600	438	162	44	1.304	1.824
6	Yug	303	282	106	58	118	466	426	40	33	1.074	1.652
7	Por	300	252	110	54	88	457	346	111	26	1.190	1.813
8	Hun	284	227	109	34	84	456	326	130	32	1.251	2.009
9	Ned	255	203	97	36	70	369	283	86	25	1.256	1.818
10	Bel	247	230	99	30	101	365	343	22	19	1.074	1.587
11	Tch	208	179	79	32	68	289	243	46	18	1.162	1.615
12	Fra	185	194	69	34	91	281	317	-36	13	0.954	1.448
13	GDR	174	165	64	35	66	245	221	24	11	1.055	1.485
14	Pol	139	121	55	20	46	183	178	5	9	1.149	1.512
15	Rom	136	145	53	26	66	173	237	-64	4	0.938	1.193
16	Bul	130	131	48	27	56	209	202	7	7	0.992	1.595
17	Aut	130	148	49	25	74	197	258	-61	7	0.878	1.331
18	Sui	124	169	44	27	98	244	374	-130	9	0.734	1.444
19	Tur	86	111	32	17	62	127	195	-68	5	0.775	1.144
20	Gre	80	101	28	20	53	113	199	-86	4	0.792	1.119
21	Den	79	125	28	19	78	189	307	-118	4	0.632	1.512
22	Swe	72	96	23	23	50	121	204	-83	3	0.750	1.260
23	URS	62	50	21	15	14	71	49	22	5	1.240	1.420
24	Wal	47	42	15	13	14	63	51	12	4	1.119	1.500
25	Nor	42	74	16	9	49	82	196	-114	1	0.568	1.108
26	Nir	38	76	11	15	50	92	216	-124	1	0.500	1.211
27	Irl	33	84	11	11	62	74	241	-167	0	0.393	0.881
28	Lux	27	78	10	7	61	64	314	-250	0	0.346	0.821
29	Mlt	20	58	6	8	44	31	185	-154	0	0.345	0.534
30	Fin	15	50	5	5	40	35	177	-142	0	0.300	0.700
31	Alb	13	22	3	7	12	15	32	-17	0	0.591	0.682
32	Isl	7	38	1	5	32	26	180	-154	0	0.184	0.684
33	Cyp	5	38	1	3	34	17	188	-171	0	0.132	0.447
	Total	**6107**	**5526**	**2259**	**1008**	**2259**	**8955**	**8955**	**0**	**581**	**1.105**	**3.241**

1971-72

Pos'n	Cnty	Ave	Pts	P	W	D	L	F	A	Diff	B	No./T
1	Scotland	9.600	48	33	18	7	8	54	36	18	5	5
2	England	9.571	67	42	25	10	7	100	33	67	7	7
3	Italy	9.166	55	39	18	12	9	67	33	34	7	6
4	Netherlands	8.200	41	27	16	5	6	55	28	27	4	5
5	USSR	7.333	22	17	7	5	5	20	18	2	3	3
6	Hungary	7.000	28	21	10	5	6	38	28	10	3	4
7	W. Germany	6.333	38	28	14	8	6	55	39	16	2	6
–	E. Germany	6.333	19	16	5	7	4	23	18	5	2	3
9	Romania	6.250	25	24	8	7	9	25	27	-2	2	4
10	Yugoslavia	5.600	28	24	8	10	6	46	33	13	2	5
11	Portugal	5.200	26	22	10	4	8	36	26	10	2	5
12	Belgium	4.800	24	22	10	2	10	36	28	8	2	5
13	Spain	3.500	21	22	9	3	10	29	25	4	0	6
14	Poland	3.000	12	12	4	4	4	17	18	-1	0	4
15	Austria	2.500	10	14	3	4	7	14	25	-11	0	4
–	Sweden	2.500	10	12	2	5	5	14	26	-12	1	4
17	France	2.200	11	14	3	5	6	13	17	-4	0	5
18	Bulgaria	2.000	8	10	3	2	5	11	17	-6	0	4
–	Wales	2.000	2	2	0	2	0	2	2	0	0	1
–	Greece	2.000	6	7	3	0	4	8	17	-9	0	3
–	Malta	2.000	6	10	2	2	6	8	21	-13	0	3
–	Norway	2.000	6	8	3	0	5	9	18	-9	0	3
23	Turkey	1.666	5	8	1	3	4	7	10	-3	0	3
24	Switzerland	1.500	6	10	2	2	6	14	16	-2	0	4
25	Denmark	1.333	4	6	2	0	4	8	13	-5	0	3
26	Iceland	1.000	3	6	1	1	4	3	22	-19	0	3
–	Czechoslovakia	1.000	4	8	1	2	5	7	16	-9	0	4
28	Finland	0.666	2	6	0	2	4	1	17	-16	0	3
29	Albania	0.500	1	4	0	1	3	1	6	-5	0	2
30	Rep. of Ireland	0.333	1	6	0	1	5	2	14	-12	0	3
–	Luxembourg	0.333	1	6	0	1	5	3	32	-29	0	3
32	Cyprus	0.000	0	6	0	0	6	0	32	-32	0	3
–	N. Ireland	0.000	0	6	0	0	6	4	19	-15	0	3
	Total		**540**	**498**	**188**	**122**	**188**	**730**	**730**	**0**	**42**	**2.932**

1955-56 to 1971-72

Pos'n	Cnty	Ave	Pts	P	W	D	L	F	A	Diff	B	No./T
1	England	9.638	694	465	253	101	111	935	489	446	87	72
2	Spain	8.462	677	468	254	80	134	964	581	383	89	80
3	Italy	8.162	604	421	218	94	109	720	442	278	74	74
4	Scotland	6.809	429	329	168	49	112	600	438	162	44	63
5	Hungary	6.604	284	227	109	34	84	456	326	130	32	43
6	W. Germany	6.078	462	354	173	69	112	682	517	165	47	76
7	Netherlands	5.425	255	203	97	36	70	369	283	86	25	47
8	USSR	5.166	62	50	21	15	14	71	49	22	5	12
9	Portugal	4.918	300	252	110	54	88	457	346	111	26	61
10	Czechoslovakia	4.727	208	179	79	32	68	289	243	46	18	44
11	Yugoslavia	4.522	303	282	106	58	118	466	426	40	33	67
12	Poland	4.483	139	121	55	20	46	183	178	5	9	31
13	Belgium	4.410	247	230	99	30	101	365	343	22	19	56
14	Wales	4.272	47	42	15	13	14	63	51	12	4	11
15	E. Germany	4.142	174	165	64	35	66	245	221	24	11	42
16	Bulgaria	3.421	130	131	48	27	56	209	202	7	7	38
17	Romania	3.317	136	145	53	26	66	173	237	-64	4	41
18	France	3.189	185	194	69	34	91	281	317	-36	13	58
19	Austria	2.954	130	148	49	25	74	197	258	-61	7	44
20	Turkey	2.606	86	111	32	17	62	127	195	-68	5	33
21	Switzerland	2.214	124	169	44	27	98	244	374	-130	9	56
22	Sweden	2.181	72	96	23	23	50	121	204	-83	3	33
23	Greece	2.162	80	101	28	20	53	113	199	-86	4	37
24	Denmark	1.680	79	125	28	19	78	189	307	-118	4	47
25	Norway	1.400	42	74	16	9	49	82	196	-114	1	30
26	Albania	1.300	13	22	3	7	12	15	32	-17	0	10
27	N. Ireland	1.117	38	76	11	15	50	92	216	-124	1	34
28	Rep. of Ireland	0.916	33	84	11	11	62	74	241	-167	0	36
29	Malta	0.769	20	58	6	8	44	31	185	-154	0	26
30	Luxembourg	0.750	27	78	10	7	61	64	314	-250	0	36
31	Finland	0.652	15	50	5	5	40	35	177	-142	0	23
32	Iceland	0.388	7	38	1	5	32	26	180	-154	0	18
33	Cyprus	0.277	5	38	1	3	34	17	188	-171	0	18
	Total		**6107**	**5526**	**2259**	**1008**	**2259**	**8955**	**8955**	**0**	**581**	**3.241**

All British UEFA Final

This season saw the birth of a new competition – the UEFA Cup. In essence, there was nothing new about it. It was simply a renamed version of the Fairs' Cup, whose title now seemed irrelevant as the clubs participating in it were not those from trade fair towns, as had been the original concept, rather those who had finished just behind the champion clubs in their own domestic leagues.

If the title of the competition had changed, there was nothing to indicate that the outcome would be any different. English clubs had won the last four Fairs' Cups and once again they were to the fore in the inaugural UEFA Cup, with Tottenham Hotspur and Wolverhampton Wanderers qualifying for the first, and as yet only, all-English European final.

Tottenham reached the final unbeaten, their best performance being the semi-final victory over AC Milan, who were seeking to become the first club to win all three European trophies. Wolves, meanwhile, also reached the final at the expense of Italian opposition, becoming the third English club to knock Juventus out of Europe in as many meetings. The final looked to be all over after the first leg when Martin Chivers scored twice to give Tottenham a 2-1 victory in Wolverhampton. But Wolves staged a spirited fightback in the return and were unfortunate to earn nothing more than a 1-1 draw, which, of course, gave Tottenham the Cup and enabled the North Londoners to become the first English club to win two different European trophies.

There was British success too in the Cup-winners' Cup, with Glasgow Rangers taking the trophy after a 3-2 victory over Dinamo Moscow in the Barcelona final. Cup holders Chelsea made a remarkable start to their defence by thrashing Luxembourg's Jeunesse Hautcharage by a record 21-0 margin in the first round, but, to enormous surprise, they were knocked out in the next round on away goals by little-known Swedish team Åtvidaberg. Liverpool, taking part in the competition as runners-up in the FA Cup to the Arsenal double-winning team of the season before, were also knocked out in the second round, 3-1 on aggregate by Bayern Munich.

But Rangers kept British interest alive with an away goals win over Sporting Lisbon before knocking out both Torino and Bayern on their way to the final. Their opponents in the Nou Camp were Dinamo Moscow, who had become the first Soviet team to reach a European final thanks to a penalty shoot-out victory over Dynamo Berlin. Rangers were favourites to win and they justified that billing by roaring into a 3-0 lead thanks to an opening goal from Colin Stein and two from Willie Johnstone. But the Russians came back strongly in the second half and almost pulled back the deficit. In the end, though, Rangers held on to the 3-2 scoreline and took the Cup back to Glasgow.

The Champions' Cup was won, for the second year in succession, by Ajax. Now coached by the Romanian, Stefan Kovacs, they reached the final with an impressive unbeaten run, knocking out Dynamo Dresden, Marseille, Arsenal and Benfica along the way. The semi-final victory over Benfica tasted particularly sweet as the Portuguese champions had put out Feyenoord in the previous round.

The semi-finals were made up of four previous winners – Ajax and Benfica, Celtic and Inter – but the four matches yielded just a solitary goal, scored by Johan Cruijff in Amsterdam. The Celtic-Inter tie was decided on penalties in favour of the Italians, who were obviously on a lucky run, having come back from the dead in the second round when a 7-1 defeat away to Borussia Mönchengladbach was annulled by UEFA after the Inter forward Boninsegna had been struck on the head by a drinks can thrown from the terraces.

The final was held in Rotterdam, which clearly favoured Ajax. Of six previous one-off European finals staged in the country of one of the participating teams, only one had been won by the visitors – Real Madrid in the inaugural final against Stade Reims in Paris. And, sure enough, it was Ajax, inspired by two-goal Johan Cruijff, who won the match and retained their trophy with a comprehensive 2-0 victory. *Catenaccio* had been destroyed by the new reality of Total Football.

Ajax

AC Milan

Liverpool

1972 – 1973

First Round

Team 1	Cnty	Team 2	Cnty	1st leg	2nd leg	Agg
Derby County	Eng	Zeljeznicar Sarajevo	Yug	2-0	2-1	4-1
FC Tirol	Aut	Dinamo Kiev	URS	0-1	0-2	0-3
Anderlecht	Bel	Vejle BK	Den	4-2	3-0	7-2
CSKA Sofia	Bul	Panathinaikos	Gre	2-1	2-0	4-1
Celtic	Sco	Rosenborg BK	Nor	2-1	3-1	5-2
Waterford United	Irl	Omonia Nicosia	Cyp	2-1	0-2	2-3
Real Madrid	Esp	IBK Keflavik	Isl	3-0	1-0	4-0
Olympique Marseille	Fra	Juventus	Ita	1-0	0-3	1-3
Ujpesti Dózsa	Hun	FC Basle	Sui	2-0	2-3	4-3
Aris Bonnevoie	Lux	Arges Pitesti	Rom	0-2	0-4	0-6
Sliema Wanderers	Mlt	Górnik Zabrze	Pol	0-5	0-5	0-10
Malmö FF	Swe	Benfica	Por	1-0	1-4	2-4
Galatasaray	Tur	Bayern Munich	FRG	1-1	0-6	1-7
Magdeburg	GDR	TPS Turku	Fin	6-0	3-1	9-1

	Pts	P	W	D	L	F	A	Diff	Goals/P
Total	56	28	27	2	27	89	89	0	3.179

Second Round

Derby County	Eng	Benfica	Por	3-0	0-0	3-0
CSKA Sofia	Bul	Ajax	Ned	1-3	0-3	1-6
Celtic	Sco	Ujpesti Dózsa	Hun	2-1	0-3	2-4
Juventus	Ita	Magdeburg	GDR	1-0	1-0	2-0
Bayern Munich	FRG	Omonia Nicosia	Cyp	9-0	4-0	13-0
Arges Pitesti	Rom	Real Madrid	Esp	2-1	1-3	3-4
Spartak Trnava	Tch	Anderlecht	Bel	1-0	1-0	2-0
Dinamo Kiev	URS	Górnik Zabrze	Pol	2-0	1-2	3-2

	Pts	P	W	D	L	F	A	Diff	Goals/P
Total	32	16	15	2	15	45	45	0	2.813

Quarter Finals

Juventus	Ita	Ujpesti Dózsa	Hun	0-0	2-2	2-2
Ajax	Ned	Bayern Munich	FRG	4-0	1-2	5-2
Spartak Trnava	Tch	Derby County	Eng	1-0	0-2	1-2
Dinamo Kiev	URS	Real Madrid	Esp	0-0	0-3	0-3

	Pts	P	W	D	L	F	A	Diff	Goals/P
Total	16	8	5	6	5	17	17	0	2.125

Semi Finals

Juventus	Ita	Derby County	Eng	3-1	0-0	3-1
Ajax	Ned	Real Madrid	Esp	2-1	1-0	3-1

	Pts	P	W	D	L	F	A	Diff	Goals/P
Total	8	4	3	2	3	8	8	0	2.000

Final

Ajax	Ned	Juventus	Ita	1-0	1-0

	Pts	P	W	D	L	F	A	Diff	Goals/P
Total	2	1	1	0	1	1	1	0	1.000

	Pts	P	W	D	L	F	A	Diff	Goals/P
Total	114	57	51	12	51	160	160	0	2.807

Pos'n	Club	Cnty	Pts	P	W	D	L	F	A	Diff	B	Pts/P	F/P
1	Ajax	Ned	15	7	6	0	1	15	4	11	3	2.143	2.143
2	Juventus	Ita	14	9	4	3	2	10	5	5	3	1.556	1.111
3	Derby County	Eng	12	8	4	2	2	10	5	5	2	1.500	1.250
4	Real Madrid	Esp	11	8	4	1	3	12	6	6	2	1.375	1.500
5	Bayern Munich	FRG	10	6	4	1	1	22	6	16	1	1.667	3.667
6	Dinamo Kiev	URS	8	6	3	1	2	6	5	1	1	1.333	1.000
7	Ujpesti Dózsa	Hun	7	6	2	2	2	10	7	3	1	1.167	1.667
8	Spartak Trnava	Tch	7	4	3	0	1	3	2	1	1	1.750	0.750
9	Górnik Zabrze	Pol	6	4	3	0	1	12	3	9	0	1.500	3.000
10	Arges Pitesti	Rom	6	4	3	0	1	9	4	5	0	1.500	2.250
11	Celtic	Sco	6	4	3	0	1	7	6	1	0	1.500	1.750
12	Magdeburg	GDR	4	4	2	0	2	9	3	6	0	1.000	2.250
13	Anderlecht	Bel	4	4	2	0	2	7	4	3	0	1.000	1.750
14	CSKA Sofia	Bul	4	4	2	0	2	5	7	-2	0	1.000	1.250
15	Benfica	Por	3	4	1	1	2	4	5	-1	0	0.750	1.000
16	FC Basle	Sui	2	2	1	0	1	3	4	-1	0	1.000	1.500
17	Waterford United	Irl	2	2	1	0	1	2	3	-1	0	1.000	1.000
18	Malmö FF	Swe	2	2	1	0	1	2	4	-2	0	1.000	1.000
19	Olympique Marseille	Fra	2	2	1	0	1	1	3	-2	0	1.000	0.500
20	Omonia Nicosia	Cyp	2	4	1	0	3	3	15	-12	0	0.500	0.750
21	Galatasaray	Tur	1	2	0	1	1	1	7	-6	0	0.500	0.500
22	Rosenborg BK	Nor	0	2	0	0	2	2	5	-3	0	0.000	1.000
23	Panathinaikos	Gre	0	2	0	0	2	1	4	-3	0	0.000	0.500
–	Zeljeznicar Sarajevo	Yug	0	2	0	0	2	1	4	-3	0	0.000	0.500
25	FC Tirol	Aut	0	2	0	0	2	0	3	-3	0	0.000	0.000
26	IBK Keflavik	Isl	0	2	0	0	2	0	4	-4	0	0.000	0.000
27	Vejle BK	Den	0	2	0	0	2	2	7	-5	0	0.000	1.000
28	Aris Bonnevoie	Lux	0	2	0	0	2	0	6	-6	0	0.000	0.000
29	TPS Turku	Fin	0	2	0	0	2	1	9	-8	0	0.000	0.500
30	Sliema Wanderers	Mlt	0	2	0	0	2	0	10	-10	0	0.000	0.000
	Total		**128**	**114**	**51**	**12**	**51**	**160**	**160**	**0**	**14**	**1.123**	**2.807**

First Round

Team 1	Cnty	Team 2	Cnty	1st leg	2nd leg	Agg
Rapid Vienna	Aut	PAOK Salonika	Gre	0-0	2-2	2-2
Standard Liège	Bel	Sparta Prague	Tch	1-0	2-4	3-4
BK Fremad Amager	Den	Besa Kavajë	Alb	1-1	0-0	1-1
Cork Hibernians	Irl	Pezoporikos Larnaca	Cyp	2-1	4-1	6-2
Bastia	Fra	Atlético Madrid	Esp	0-0	1-2	1-2
Vikingur Reykjavik	Isl	Legia Warsaw	Pol	0-2	0-9	0-11
Red Boys Differdange	Lux	AC Milan	Ita	1-4	0-3	1-7
Floriana	Mlt	Ferencváros	Hun	1-0	0-6	1-6
Sporting Lisbon	Por	Hibernian	Sco	2-1	1-6	3-7
Schalke 04	FRG	Slavia Sofia	Bul	2-1	3-1	5-2
Rapid Bucharest	Rom	Landskrona BOIS	Swe	3-0	0-1	3-1
FC Zürich	Sui	Wrexham	Wal	1-1	1-2	2-3
Ankaragücü	Tur	Leeds United	Eng	1-1	0-1	1-2
Spartak Moscow	URS	FC Den Haag	Ned	1-0	0-0	1-0
Hajduk Split	Yug	Fredrikstad FK	Nor	1-0	1-0	2-0
Carl Zeiss Jena	GDR	MP Mikkeli	Fin	6-1	2-3	8-4

	Pts	P	W	D	L	F	A	Diff	Goals/P
Total	64	32	24	16	24	94	94	0	2.938

Second Round

Rapid Vienna	Aut	Rapid Bucharest	Rom	1-1	1-3	2-4
Hibernian	Sco	Besa Kavajë	Alb	7-1	1-1	8-2
Cork Hibernians	Irl	Schalke 04	FRG	0-0	0-3	0-3
Atlético Madrid	Esp	Spartak Moscow	URS	3-4	2-1	5-5
Wrexham	Wal	Hajduk Split	Yug	3-1	0-2	3-3
Ferencváros	Hun	Sparta Prague	Tch	2-0	1-4	3-4
Legia Warsaw	Pol	AC Milan	Ita	1-1	1-2	2-3
Carl Zeiss Jena	GDR	Leeds United	Eng	0-0	0-2	0-2

	Pts	P	W	D	L	F	A	Diff	Goals/P
Total	32	16	11	10	11	49	49	0	3.063

Quarter Finals

Leeds United	Eng	Rapid Bucharest	Rom	5-0	3-1	8-1
Hibernian	Sco	Hajduk Split	Yug	4-2	0-3	4-5
Schalke 04	FRG	Sparta Prague	Tch	2-1	0-3	2-4
Spartak Moscow	URS	AC Milan	Ita	0-1	1-1	1-2

	Pts	P	W	D	L	F	A	Diff	Goals/P
Total	16	8	7	2	7	27	27	0	3.375

Semi Finals

Leeds United	Eng	Hajduk Split	Yug	1-0	0-0	1-0
AC Milan	Ita	Sparta Prague	Tch	1-0	1-0	2-0

	Pts	P	W	D	L	F	A	Diff	Goals/P
Total	8	4	3	2	3	3	3	0	0.750

Final

AC Milan	Ita	Leeds United	Eng	1-0	1-0

	Pts	P	W	D	L	F	A	Diff	Goals/P
Total	2	1	1	0	1	1	1	0	1.000

	Pts	P	W	D	L	F	A	Diff	Goals/P
Total	122	61	46	30	46	174	174	0	2.852

Pos'n	Club	Cnty	Pts	P	W	D	L	F	A	Diff	B	Pts/P	F/P
1	AC Milan	Ita	19	9	7	2	0	15	4	11	3	2.111	1.667
2	Leeds United	Eng	16	9	5	3	1	13	3	10	3	1.778	1.444
3	Hajduk Split	Yug	11	8	4	1	3	10	8	2	2	1.375	1.250
4	Schalke 04	FRG	10	6	4	1	1	10	6	4	1	1.667	1.667
5	Hibernian	Sco	8	6	3	1	2	19	10	9	1	1.333	3.167
6	Sparta Prague	Tch	8	8	3	0	5	12	10	2	2	1.000	1.500
7	Spartak Moscow	URS	7	6	2	2	2	7	7	0	1	1.167	1.167
8	Rapid Bucharest	Rom	6	6	2	1	3	8	11	-3	1	1.000	1.333
9	Legia Warsaw	Pol	5	4	2	1	1	13	3	10	0	1.250	3.250
10	Atlético Madrid	Esp	5	4	2	1	1	7	6	1	0	1.250	1.750
11	Cork Hibernians	Irl	5	4	2	1	1	6	5	1	0	1.250	1.500
–	Wrexham	Wal	5	4	2	1	1	6	5	1	0	1.250	1.500
13	Ferencváros	Hun	4	4	2	0	2	9	5	4	0	1.000	2.250
14	Carl Zeiss Jena	GDR	3	4	1	1	2	8	6	2	0	0.750	2.000
15	Rapid Vienna	Aut	3	4	0	3	1	4	6	-2	0	0.750	1.000
16	Besa Kavajë	Alb	3	4	0	3	1	3	9	-6	0	0.750	0.750
17	PAOK Salonika	Gre	2	2	0	2	0	2	2	0	0	1.000	1.000
18	BK Fremad Amager	Den	2	2	0	2	0	1	1	0	0	1.000	0.500
19	Standard Liège	Bel	2	2	1	0	1	3	4	-1	0	1.000	1.500
20	Landskrona BOIS	Swe	2	2	1	0	1	1	3	-2	0	1.000	0.500
21	MP Mikkeli	Fin	2	2	1	0	1	4	8	-4	0	1.000	2.000
22	Sporting Lisbon	Por	2	2	1	0	1	3	7	-4	0	1.000	1.500
23	Floriana	Mlt	2	2	1	0	1	1	6	-5	0	1.000	0.500
24	FC Zürich	Sui	1	2	0	1	1	2	3	-1	0	0.500	1.000
25	Bastia	Fra	1	2	0	1	1	1	2	-1	0	0.500	0.500
–	Ankaragücü	Tur	1	2	0	1	1	1	2	-1	0	0.500	0.500
27	FC Den Haag	Ned	1	2	0	1	1	0	1	-1	0	0.500	0.000
28	Fredrikstad FK	Nor	0	2	0	0	2	0	2	-2	0	0.000	0.000
29	Slavia Sofia	Bul	0	2	0	0	2	2	5	-3	0	0.000	1.000
30	Pezoporikos Larnaca	Cyp	0	2	0	0	2	2	6	-4	0	0.000	1.000
31	Red Boys Differdange	Lux	0	2	0	0	2	1	7	-6	0	0.000	0.500
32	Vikingur Reykjavik	Isl	0	2	0	0	2	0	11	-11	0	0.000	0.000
	Total		**136**	**122**	**46**	**30**	**16**	**174**	**174**	**0**	**14**	**1.115**	**2.852**

First Round

Team 1	Cnty	Team 2	Cnty	1st leg	2nd leg	Agg
Liverpool	Eng	Eintracht Frankfurt	FRG	2-0	0-0	2-0
Manchester City	Eng	Valencia	Esp	2-2	1-2	3-4
Stoke City	Eng	Kaiserslautern	FRG	3-1	0-4	3-5
RWD Molenbeek	Bel	Barreirense	Por	0-1	0-2	0-3
Beroe Stara Zagora	Bul	Austria Vienna	Aut	7-0	3-1	10-1
EPA Larnaca	Cyp	Ararat Erevan	URS	0-1	0-1	0-2
Aberdeen	Sco	Bor. Mönchengladbach	FRG	2-3	3-6	5-9
Angers	Fra	Dynamo Berlin	GDR	1-1	1-2	2-3
Nîmes Olympique	Fra	Grasshoppers Zürich	Sui	1-2	1-2	2-4
Sochaux	Fra	BK Frem	Den	1-3	1-2	2-5
AEK Athens	Gre	Salgótarján	Hun	3-1	1-1	4-2
Olympiakos Pireus	Gre	Cagliari	Ita	2-1	1-0	3-1
Honvéd	Hun	Partick Thistle	Sco	1-0	3-0	4-0
Inter Milan	Ita	Valletta	Mlt	6-1	1-0	7-1
Torino	Ita	Las Palmas	Esp	2-0	0-4	2-4
SFK Lyn	Nor	Tottenham Hotspur	Eng	3-6	0-6	3-12
IL Viking	Nor	IBV Vestmannaeyjar	Isl	1-0	0-0	1-0
Feyenoord	Ned	US Rumelange	Lux	9-0	12-0	21-0
Ruch Chorzów	Pol	Fenerbahçe	Tur	3-0	0-1	3-1
FC Porto	Por	Barcelona	Esp	3-1	1-0	4-1
Vitória Setúbal	Por	Zaglebie Sosnowiec	Pol	6-1	0-1	6-2
Cologne	FRG	Bohemians	Irl	2-1	3-0	5-1
UT Arad	Rom	IFK Norrköping	Swe	1-2	0-2	1-4
Universitatea Cluj	Rom	Levski Sofia	Bul	4-1	1-5	5-6
Åtvidaberg SFF	Swe	Club Bruges	Bel	3-5	2-1	5-6
Slovan Bratislava	Tch	Vojvodina Novi Sad	Yug	6-0	2-1	8-1
Dukla Prague	Tch	OFK Belgrade	Yug	2-2	1-3	3-5
Eskisehirspor	Tur	Fiorentina	Ita	1-2	0-3	1-5
Dinamo Tbilisi	URS	Twente Enschede	Ned	3-2	0-2	3-4
Red Star Belgrade	Yug	Lausanne-Sports	Sui	5-1	2-3	7-4
Dynamo Dresden	GDR	Vöest Linz	Aut	2-0	2-2	4-2

	Pts	P	W	D	L	F	A	Diff	Goals/P
Total	124	62	55	14	55	227	227	0	3.661

Second Round

Liverpool	Eng	AEK Athens	Gre	3-0	3-1	6-1
Tottenham Hotspur	Eng	Olympiakos Pireus	Gre	4-0	0-1	4-1
Beroe Stara Zagora	Bul	Honvéd	Hun	3-0	0-1	3-1
BK Frem	Den	Twente Enschede	Ned	0-5	0-4	0-9
Las Palmas	Esp	Slovan Bratislava	Tch	2-2	1-0	3-2
Inter Milan	Ita	IFK Norrköping	Swe	2-2	2-0	4-2
IL Viking	Nor	Cologne	FRG	1-0	1-9	2-9
Feyenoord	Ned	OFK Belgrade	Yug	4-3	1-2	5-5
Ruch Chorzów	Pol	Dynamo Dresden	GDR	0-1	0-3	0-4
Barreirense	Por	Kaiserslautern	FRG	1-3	1-0	2-3
FC Porto	Por	Club Bruges	Bel	3-0	2-3	5-3
Vitória Setúbal	Por	Fiorentina	Ita	1-0	1-2	2-2
Bor. Mönchengladbach	FRG	Hvidovre IF	Den	3-0	3-1	6-1
Grasshoppers Zürich	Sui	Ararat Erevan	URS	1-3	2-4	3-7
Red Star Belgrade	Yug	Valencia	Esp	3-1	1-0	4-1
Dynamo Berlin	GDR	Levski Sofia	Bul	3-0	0-2	3-2

	Pts	P	W	D	L	F	A	Diff	Goals/P
Total	64	32	30	4	30	105	105	0	3.281

Third Round

Tottenham Hotspur	Eng	Red Star Belgrade	Yug	2-0	0-1	2-1
Twente Enschede	Ned	Las Palmas	Esp	3-0	1-2	4-2
FC Porto	Por	Dynamo Dresden	GDR	1-2	0-1	1-3
Vitória Setúbal	Por	Inter Milan	Ita	2-0	0-1	2-1
Cologne	FRG	Bor. Mönchengladbach	FRG	0-0	0-5	0-5
Ararat Erevan	URS	Kaiserslautern	FRG	2-0	0-2	2-2
OFK Belgrade	Yug	Beroe Stara Zagora	Bul	0-0	3-1	3-1
Dynamo Berlin	GDR	Liverpool	Eng	0-0	1-3	1-3

	Pts	P	W	D	L	F	A	Diff	Goals/P
Total	32	16	13	6	13	33	33	0	2.063

Quarter Finals

Liverpool	Eng	Dynamo Dresden	GDR	2-0	1-0	3-0
Tottenham Hotspur	Eng	Vitória Setúbal	Por	1-0	1-2	2-2
Kaiserslautern	FRG	Bor. Mönchengladbach	FRG	1-2	1-7	2-9
OFK Belgrade	Yug	Twente Enschede	Ned	3-2	0-2	3-4

	Pts	P	W	D	L	F	A	Diff	Goals/P
Total	16	8	8	0	8	25	25	0	3.125

Semi Finals

Liverpool	Eng	Tottenham Hotspur	Eng	1-0	1-2	2-2
Bor. Mönchengladbach	FRG	Twente Enschede	Ned	3-0	2-1	5-1

	Pts	P	W	D	L	F	A	Diff	Goals/P
Total	8	4	4	0	4	10	10	0	2.500

Final

Liverpool	Eng	Bor. Mönchengladbach	FRG	3-0	0-2	3-2

	Pts	P	W	D	L	F	A	Diff	Goals/P
Total	4	2	2	0	2	5	5	0	2.500

	Pts	P	W	D	L	F	A	Diff	Goals/P
Total	248	124	112	24	112	405	405	0	3.266

Pos'n	Club	Cnty	Pts	P	W	D	L	F	A	Diff	B	Pts/P	F/P
1	Bor. Mönchengladbach	FRG	24	12	10	1	1	36	12	24	3	2.000	3.000
2	Liverpool	Eng	21	12	8	2	2	19	6	13	3	1.750	1.583
3	Tottenham Hotspur	Eng	14	10	6	0	4	22	9	13	2	1.400	2.200
4	Twente Enschede	Ned	12	10	5	0	5	22	13	9	2	1.200	2.200
5	Dynamo Dresden	GDR	12	8	5	1	2	11	6	5	1	1.500	1.375
6	OFK Belgrade	Yug	11	8	4	2	2	16	13	3	1	1.375	2.000
7	Ararat Erevan	URS	10	6	5	0	1	11	5	6	0	1.667	1.833
8	Inter Milan	Ita	9	6	4	1	1	12	5	7	0	1.500	2.000
9	Vitória Setúbal	Por	9	8	4	0	4	12	7	5	1	1.125	1.500
10	Red Star Belgrade	Yug	8	6	4	0	2	12	7	5	0	1.333	2.000
11	Beroe Stara Zagora	Bul	7	6	3	1	2	14	5	9	0	1.167	2.333
12	Cologne	FRG	7	6	3	1	2	14	8	6	0	1.167	2.333
13	Las Palmas	Esp	7	6	3	1	2	9	8	1	0	1.167	1.500
14	Kaiserslautern	FRG	7	8	3	0	5	12	16	-4	1	0.875	1.500
15	Feyenoord	Ned	6	4	3	0	1	26	5	21	0	1.500	6.500
16	Fiorentina	Ita	6	4	3	0	1	7	3	4	0	1.500	1.750
17	FC Porto	Por	6	6	3	0	3	10	7	3	0	1.000	1.667
18	Honvéd	Hun	6	4	3	0	1	5	3	2	0	1.500	1.250
–	Barreirense	Por	6	4	3	0	1	5	3	2	0	1.500	1.250
20	Dynamo Berlin	GDR	6	6	2	2	2	7	7	0	0	1.000	1.167
21	Olympiakos Pireus	Gre	6	4	3	0	1	4	5	-1	0	1.500	1.000
22	Slovan Bratislava	Tch	5	4	2	1	1	10	4	6	0	1.250	2.500
23	IFK Norrköping	Swe	5	4	2	1	1	6	5	1	0	1.250	1.500
24	IL Viking	Nor	5	4	2	1	1	3	9	-6	0	1.250	0.750
25	Levski Sofia	Bul	4	4	2	0	2	8	8	0	0	1.000	2.000
26	Club Bruges	Bel	4	4	2	0	2	9	10	-1	0	1.000	2.250
27	Grasshoppers Zürich	Sui	4	4	2	0	2	7	9	-2	0	1.000	1.750
28	BK Frem	Den	4	4	2	0	2	5	11	-6	0	1.000	1.250
29	Valencia	Esp	3	4	1	1	2	5	7	-2	0	0.750	1.250
30	AEK Athens	Gre	3	4	1	1	2	5	8	-3	0	0.750	1.250
31	Universitatea Cluj	Rom	2	2	1	0	1	5	6	-1	0	1.000	2.500
–	Åtvidaberg SFF	Swe	2	2	1	0	1	5	6	-1	0	1.000	2.500
33	Dynamo Tbilisi	URS	2	2	1	0	1	3	4	-1	0	1.000	1.500
34	Stoke City	Eng	2	2	1	0	1	3	5	-2	0	1.000	1.500
–	Ruch Chorzów	Pol	2	4	1	0	3	3	5	-2	0	0.500	0.750
36	Torino	Ita	2	2	1	0	1	2	4	-2	0	1.000	1.000
37	Fenerbahçe	Tur	2	2	1	0	1	1	3	-2	0	1.000	0.500
38	Lausanne-Sports	Sui	2	2	1	0	1	4	7	-3	0	1.000	2.000
39	Zaglebie Sosnowiec	Pol	2	2	1	0	1	2	6	-4	0	1.000	1.000
40	Manchester City	Eng	1	2	0	1	1	3	4	-1	0	0.500	1.500
41	Angers	Fra	1	2	0	1	1	2	3	-1	0	0.500	1.000
42	IBV Vestmannaeyjar	Isl	1	2	0	1	1	0	1	-1	0	0.500	0.000
43	Dukla Prague	Tch	1	2	0	1	1	3	5	-2	0	0.500	1.500
44	Vöest Linz	Aut	1	2	0	1	1	2	4	-2	0	0.500	1.000
–	Salgótarján	Hun	1	2	0	1	1	2	4	-2	0	0.500	1.000
46	Eintracht Frankfurt	FRG	1	2	0	1	1	0	2	-2	0	0.500	0.000
47	Nîmes Olympique	Fra	0	2	0	0	2	2	4	-2	0	0.000	1.000
48	Cagliari	Ita	0	2	0	0	2	1	3	-2	0	0.000	0.500
49	EPA Larnaca	Cyp	0	2	0	0	2	0	2	-2	0	0.000	0.000
50	Sochaux	Fra	0	2	0	0	2	2	5	-3	0	0.000	1.000
51	Barcelona	Esp	0	2	0	0	2	1	4	-3	0	0.000	0.500
–	UT Arad	Rom	0	2	0	0	2	1	4	-3	0	0.000	0.500
53	RWD Molenbeek	Bel	0	2	0	0	2	0	3	-3	0	0.000	0.000
54	Aberdeen	Sco	0	2	0	0	2	5	9	-4	0	0.000	2.500
55	Bohemians	Irl	0	2	0	0	2	1	5	-4	0	0.000	0.500
–	Eskisehirspor	Tur	0	2	0	0	2	1	5	-4	0	0.000	0.500
57	Partick Thistle	Sco	0	2	0	0	2	0	4	-4	0	0.000	0.000
58	Hvidovre IF	Den	0	2	0	0	2	1	6	-5	0	0.000	0.500
59	Valletta	Mlt	0	2	0	0	2	1	7	-6	0	0.000	0.500
60	Vojvodina Novi Sad	Yug	0	2	0	0	2	1	8	-7	0	0.000	0.500
61	SFK Lyn	Nor	0	2	0	0	2	3	12	-9	0	0.000	1.500
62	Austria Vienna	Aut	0	2	0	0	2	1	10	-9	0	0.000	0.500
63	US Rumelange	Lux	0	2	0	0	2	0	21	-21	0	0.000	0.000
	Total		**262**	**248**	**112**	**24**	**112**	**405**	**405**	**0**	**14**	**1.056**	**3.266**

National Performances by Points

1972-73

Pos'n	Cnty	Pts	P	W	D	L	F	A	Diff	B	Pts/P	F/P
1	Eng	66	43	24	8	11	70	32	38	10	1.535	1.628
2	FRG	59	40	24	5	11	94	50	44	6	1.475	2.350
3	Ita	50	32	19	6	7	47	24	23	6	1.563	1.469
4	Ned	34	23	14	1	8	63	23	40	5	1.478	2.739
5	Yug	30	26	12	3	11	40	40	0	3	1.154	1.538
6	URS	27	20	11	3	6	27	21	6	2	1.350	1.350
7	Por	26	24	12	1	11	34	29	5	1	1.083	1.417
8	Esp	26	24	10	4	10	34	31	3	2	1.083	1.417
9	GDR	25	22	10	4	8	35	22	13	1	1.136	1.591
10	Tch	21	18	8	2	8	28	21	7	3	1.167	1.556
11	Hun	18	16	7	3	6	26	19	7	1	1.125	1.625
12	Pol	15	14	7	1	6	30	17	13	0	1.071	2.143
13	Bul	15	16	7	1	8	29	25	4	0	0.938	1.813
14	Sco	14	14	6	1	7	31	29	2	1	1.000	2.214
15	Rom	14	14	6	1	7	23	25	-2	1	1.000	1.643
16	Swe	11	10	5	1	4	14	18	-4	0	1.100	1.400
17	Gre	11	12	4	3	5	12	19	-7	0	0.917	1.000
18	Bel	10	12	5	0	7	19	21	-2	0	0.833	1.583
19	Sui	9	10	4	1	5	16	23	-7	0	0.900	1.600
20	Irl	7	8	3	1	4	9	13	-4	0	0.875	1.125
21	Den	6	10	2	2	6	9	25	-16	0	0.600	0.900
22	Wal	5	4	2	1	1	6	5	1	0	1.250	1.500
23	Nor	5	10	2	1	7	8	28	-20	0	0.500	0.800
24	Fra	4	10	1	2	7	8	17	-9	0	0.400	0.800
25	Tur	4	8	1	2	5	4	17	-13	0	0.500	0.500
26	Aut	4	10	0	4	6	7	23	-16	0	0.400	0.700
27	Alb	3	4	0	3	1	3	9	-6	0	0.750	0.750
28	Fin	2	4	1	0	3	5	17	-12	0	0.500	1.250
29	Cyp	2	8	1	0	7	5	23	-18	0	0.250	0.625
30	Mlt	2	6	1	0	5	2	23	-21	0	0.333	0.333
31	Isl	1	6	0	1	5	0	16	-16	0	0.167	0.000
32	Lux	0	6	0	0	6	1	34	-33	0	0.000	0.167
	Total	**526**	**484**	**209**	**66**	**209**	**739**	**739**	**0**	**42**	**1.087**	**3.054**

1955-56 to 1972-73

Pos'n	Cnty	Pts	P	W	D	L	F	A	Diff	B	Pts/P	F/P
1	Eng	760	508	277	109	122	1005	521	484	97	1.496	1.978
2	Esp	703	492	264	84	144	998	612	386	91	1.429	2.028
3	Ita	654	453	237	100	116	767	466	301	80	1.444	1.693
4	FRG	521	394	197	74	123	776	567	209	53	1.322	1.970
5	Sco	443	343	174	50	119	631	467	164	45	1.292	1.840
6	Yug	333	308	118	61	129	506	466	40	36	1.081	1.643
7	Por	326	276	122	55	99	491	375	116	27	1.181	1.779
8	Hun	302	243	116	37	90	482	345	137	33	1.243	1.984
9	Ned	289	226	111	37	78	432	306	126	30	1.279	1.912
10	Bel	257	242	104	30	108	384	364	20	19	1.062	1.587
11	Tch	229	197	87	34	76	317	264	53	21	1.162	1.609
12	GDR	199	187	74	39	74	280	243	37	12	1.064	1.497
13	Fra	189	204	70	36	98	289	334	-45	13	0.926	1.417
14	Pol	154	135	62	21	52	213	195	18	9	1.141	1.578
15	Rom	150	159	59	27	73	196	262	-66	5	0.943	1.233
16	Bul	145	147	55	28	64	238	227	11	7	0.986	1.619
17	Aut	134	158	49	29	80	204	281	-77	7	0.848	1.291
18	Sui	133	179	48	28	103	260	397	-137	9	0.743	1.453
19	Gre	91	113	32	23	58	125	218	-93	4	0.805	1.106
20	Tur	90	119	33	19	67	131	212	-81	5	0.756	1.101
21	URS	89	70	32	18	20	98	70	28	7	1.271	1.400
22	Den	85	135	30	21	84	198	332	-134	4	0.630	1.467
23	Swe	83	106	28	24	54	135	222	-87	3	0.783	1.274
24	Wal	52	46	17	14	15	69	56	13	4	1.130	1.500
25	Nor	47	84	18	10	56	90	224	-134	1	0.560	1.071
26	Irl	40	92	14	12	66	83	254	-171	0	0.435	0.902
27	Nir	38	76	11	15	50	92	216	-124	1	0.500	1.211
28	Lux	27	84	10	7	67	65	348	-283	0	0.321	0.774
29	Mlt	22	64	7	8	49	33	208	-175	0	0.344	0.516
30	Fin	17	54	6	5	43	40	194	-154	0	0.315	0.741
31	Alb	16	26	3	10	13	18	41	-23	0	0.615	0.692
32	Isl	8	44	1	6	37	26	196	-170	0	0.182	0.591
33	Cyp	7	46	2	3	41	22	211	-189	0	0.152	0.478
	Total	**6633**	**6010**	**2468**	**1074**	**2468**	**9694**	**9694**	**0**	**623**	**1.104**	**3.226**

1972-73

Pos'n	Cnty	Ave	Pts	P	W	D	L	F	A	Diff	B	No./T
1	England	11.000	66	43	24	8	11	70	32	38	10	6
2	W. Germany	9.833	59	40	24	5	11	94	50	44	6	6
3	Netherlands	8.500	34	23	14	1	8	63	23	40	5	4
4	Italy	8.333	50	32	19	6	7	47	24	23	6	6
5	USSR	6.750	27	20	11	3	6	27	21	6	2	4
6	E. Germany	6.250	25	22	10	4	8	35	22	13	1	4
7	Yugoslavia	6.000	30	26	12	3	11	40	40	0	3	5
8	Czechoslovakia	5.250	21	18	8	2	8	28	21	7	3	4
9	Spain	5.200	26	24	10	4	10	34	31	3	2	5
–	Portugal	5.200	26	24	12	1	11	34	29	5	1	5
11	Wales	5.000	5	4	2	1	1	6	5	1	0	1
12	Hungary	4.500	18	16	7	3	6	26	19	7	1	4
13	Bulgaria	3.750	15	16	7	1	8	29	25	4	0	4
–	Poland	3.750	15	14	7	1	6	30	17	13	0	4
15	Scotland	3.500	14	14	6	1	7	31	29	2	1	4
–	Romania	3.500	14	14	6	1	7	23	25	-2	1	4
17	Albania	3.000	3	4	0	3	1	3	9	-6	0	1
18	Greece	2.750	11	12	4	3	5	12	19	-7	0	4
–	Sweden	2.750	11	10	5	1	4	14	18	-4	0	4
20	Belgium	2.500	10	12	5	0	7	19	21	-2	0	4
21	Rep. of Ireland	2.333	7	8	3	1	4	9	13	-4	0	3
22	Switzerland	2.250	9	10	4	1	5	16	23	-7	0	4
23	Denmark	1.500	6	10	2	2	6	9	25	-16	0	4
24	Norway	1.250	5	10	2	1	7	8	28	-20	0	4
25	Austria	1.000	4	10	0	4	6	7	23	-16	0	4
–	Finland	1.000	2	4	1	0	3	5	17	-12	0	2
–	Turkey	1.000	4	8	1	2	5	4	17	-13	0	4
28	France	0.800	4	10	1	2	7	8	17	-9	0	5
29	Cyprus	0.666	2	8	1	0	7	5	23	-18	0	3
–	Malta	0.666	2	6	1	0	5	2	23	-21	0	3
31	Iceland	0.333	1	6	0	1	5	0	16	-16	0	3
32	Luxembourg	0.000	0	6	0	0	6	1	34	-33	0	3
	Total		**526**	**484**	**209**	**66**	**209**	**739**	**739**	**0**	**42**	**3.054**

1955-56 to 1972-73

1	England	9.743	760	508	277	109	122	1005	521	484	97	78
2	Spain	8.270	703	492	264	84	144	998	612	386	91	85
3	Italy	8.175	654	453	237	100	116	767	466	301	80	80
4	Scotland	6.611	443	343	174	50	119	631	467	164	45	67
5	Hungary	6.425	302	243	116	37	90	482	345	137	33	47
6	W. Germany	6.353	521	394	197	74	123	776	567	209	53	82
7	Netherlands	5.666	289	226	111	37	78	432	306	126	30	51
8	USSR	5.562	89	70	32	18	20	98	70	28	7	16
9	Portugal	4.939	326	276	122	55	99	491	375	116	27	66
10	Czechoslovakia	4.770	229	197	87	34	76	317	264	53	21	48
11	Yugoslavia	4.625	333	308	118	61	129	506	466	40	36	72
12	Poland	4.400	154	135	62	21	52	213	195	18	9	35
13	Wales	4.333	52	46	17	14	15	69	56	13	4	12
14	E. Germany	4.326	199	187	74	39	74	280	243	37	12	46
15	Belgium	4.283	257	242	104	30	108	384	364	20	19	60
16	Bulgaria	3.452	145	147	55	28	64	238	227	11	7	42
17	Romania	3.333	150	159	59	27	73	196	262	-66	5	45
18	France	3.000	189	204	70	36	98	289	334	-45	13	63
19	Austria	2.791	134	158	49	29	80	204	281	-77	7	48
20	Turkey	2.432	90	119	33	19	67	131	212	-81	5	37
21	Sweden	2.243	83	106	28	24	54	135	222	-87	3	37
22	Greece	2.219	91	113	32	23	58	125	218	-93	4	41
23	Switzerland	2.216	133	179	48	28	103	260	397	-137	9	60
24	Denmark	1.666	85	135	30	21	84	198	332	-134	4	51
25	Albania	1.454	16	26	3	10	13	18	41	-23	0	11
26	Norway	1.382	47	84	18	10	56	90	224	-134	1	34
27	N. Ireland	1.117	38	76	11	15	50	92	216	-124	1	34
28	Rep. of Ireland	1.025	40	92	14	12	66	83	254	-171	0	39
29	Malta	0.758	22	64	7	8	49	33	208	-175	0	29
30	Luxembourg	0.692	27	84	10	7	67	65	348	-283	0	39
31	Finland	0.680	17	54	6	5	43	40	194	-154	0	25
32	Iceland	0.380	8	44	1	6	37	26	196	-170	0	21
33	Cyprus	0.333	7	46	2	3	41	22	211	-189	0	21
	Total		**6633**	**6010**	**2468**	**1074**	**2468**	**9694**	**9694**	**0**	**623**	**3.226**

Ajax Take Third Title

Ajax became the first team since Real Madrid to register a hat-trick of Champions' Cup victories when they defeated Juventus 1-0 in the 1972-73 final in Belgrade. The final itself was a drab, unexciting affair, with Johnny Rep heading the only goal of the game after four minutes, but Ajax's claim to be the top side in Europe was beyond argument. No fewer than nine of the team which defeated Juventus in Belgrade had also appeared in the previous two final victories – Stuy, Suurbier, Neeskens, Blankenburg, Hulshoff, Haan, Mühren, Keizer and the incomparable Johan Cruijff – and many of those players also featured in the Dutch national team that was to gain universal praise the following year for its brilliant performances in the 1974 World Cup.

Whereas Juventus's path to their first Champions' Cup final had been strewn with controversy, especially in the semi-final win over Derby County, Ajax had proved their worth in the quarter and semi-finals with magnificent victories over Bayern Munich and Real Madrid. The first leg against Bayern saw Ajax at their brilliant best. Goals from Haan (2), Mühren and Cruijff gave them a decisive 4-0 victory and the right to proclaim themselves as the champions of Total Football. Bayern won the second leg 2-1 but they were never really in the hunt. Next up for Ajax came Real, back in the competition after a two-year absence. The Dutchmen could only manage a slender 2-1 lead from the home leg, but a goal from Gerrie Mühren gave them a second victory in the Bernabéu and they were into the final for the fourth time in five seasons.

AC Milan had entered the Cup-winners' Cup once before, in 1967-68, and they had won the trophy then, beating Hamburg 2-0 in the final. Now, in their second participation, they won the Cup again, beating Leeds United 1-0 in the final and thus preventing a British team from landing the trophy for the fourth season on the trot – an achievement made easier by the absence of holders Rangers, banned for a year for the misbehaviour of a section of their supporters at the previous year's final in Barcelona.

Milan reached the 1973 final, in Salonika, undefeated, as they had done on the occasion of their last triumph six years earlier. But so, too, did Leeds, who conceded just two goals in their eight matches. The final was the first single-match European encounter between English and Italian opposition and it was difficult to predict the outcome. In the end, it was Milan who emerged victorious from a brutal, hard-fought game, decided, like the Champions' Cup final, by a goal in the first few minutes, from Milan's left-winger Chiarugi, who had also scored both of his team's goals in the semi-final defeat of Sparta Prague.

The second UEFA Cup tournament brought yet another success for England and provided another new club to add to the list of English winners. Liverpool, with a 3-2 aggregate victory over Borussia Mönchengladbach in the final, kept the trophy in English hands for the sixth year in a row and became the ninth different Football league club to win a European Cup.

To achieve that, Liverpool had to overcome holders Tottenham Hotspur in the semi-final, which they managed, only just, by virtue of the away goals rule. Their four previous opponents – Eintracht Frankfurt, AEK Athens, Dynamo Berlin and Dynamo Dresden – had presented considerably fewer problems. Awaiting Liverpool in the final were yet another German side – and the first from that country to reach a UEFA/Fairs' Cup final – Borussia Mönchengladbach. They had enjoyed a remarkable run, winning nine of their ten matches and drawing the other, with fellow Bundesliga teams Cologne and Kaiserslautern among their victims.

But at Anfield, Mönchengladbach's unbeaten run was brought to a conclusive end. Two goals from Kevin Keegan and one from Larry Lloyd gave Liverpool a 3-0 victory and what appeared to be an unassailable lead. The Germans made a valiant effort to claw their way back in the return, but two goals from striker Jupp Heynckes were all they could muster and Liverpool held onto their aggregate lead to lift the Cup.

1973 – 1974

Bayern Munich

Magdeburg

Feyenoord

First Round

Team 1	Cnty	Team 2	Cnty	1st leg	2nd leg	Agg
Club Bruges	Bel	Floriana	Mlt	8-0	2-0	10-0
CSKA Sofia	Bul	FC Tirol	Aut	3-0	1-0	4-0
Vejle BK	Den	Nantes	Fra	2-2	1-0	3-2
Waterford United	Irl	Ujpesti Dózsa	Hun	2-3	0-3	2-6
Atlético Madrid	Esp	Galatasaray	Tur	0-0	1-0	1-0
TPS Turku	Fin	Celtic	Sco	1-6	0-3	1-9
Crusaders	Nir	Dinamo Bucharest	Rom	0-1	0-11	0-12
Jeunesse Esch	Lux	Liverpool	Eng	1-1	0-2	1-3
IL Viking	Nor	Spartak Trnava	Tch	1-2	0-1	1-3
Benfica	Por	Olympiakos Pireus	Gre	1-0	1-0	2-0
Bayern Munich	FRG	Åtvidaberg SFF	Swe	3-1	1-3	4-4
FC Basle	Sui	Fram Reykjavik	Isl	5-0	6-2	11-2
Zaria Voroshilovgrad	URS	Apoel Nicosia	Cyp	2-0	1-0	3-0
Red Star Belgrade	Yug	Stal Mielec	Pol	2-1	1-0	3-1
Dynamo Dresden	GDR	Juventus	Ita	2-0	2-3	4-3

	Pts	P	W	D	L	F	A	Diff	Goals/P
Total	60	30	27	6	27	95	95	0	3.167

Second Round

Team 1	Cnty	Team 2	Cnty	1st leg	2nd leg	Agg
Club Bruges	Bel	FC Basle	Sui	2-1	4-6	6-7
Celtic	Sco	Vejle BK	Den	0-0	1-0	1-0
Ajax	Ned	CSKA Sofia	Bul	1-0	0-2	1-2
Benfica	Por	Ujpesti Dózsa	Hun	1-1	0-2	1-3
Bayern Munich	FRG	Dynamo Dresden	GDR	4-3	3-3	7-6
Dinamo Bucharest	Rom	Atlético Madrid	Esp	0-2	2-2	2-4
Spartak Trnava	Tch	Zaria Voroshilovgrad	URS	0-0	1-0	1-0
Red Star Belgrade	Yug	Liverpool	Eng	2-1	2-1	4-2

	Pts	P	W	D	L	F	A	Diff	Goals/P
Total	32	16	11	10	11	47	47	0	2.938

Quarter Finals

Team 1	Cnty	Team 2	Cnty	1st leg	2nd leg	Agg
Bayern Munich	FRG	CSKA Sofia	Bul	4-1	1-2	5-3
FC Basle	Sui	Celtic	Sco	3-2	2-4	5-6
Spartak Trnava	Tch	Ujpesti Dózsa	Hun	1-1	1-1	2-2
Red Star Belgrade	Yug	Atlético Madrid	Esp	0-2	0-0	0-2

	Pts	P	W	D	L	F	A	Diff	Goals/P
Total	16	8	5	6	5	25	25	0	3.125

Semi Finals

Team 1	Cnty	Team 2	Cnty	1st leg	2nd leg	Agg
Celtic	Sco	Atlético Madrid	Esp	0-0	0-2	0-2
Ujpesti Dózsa	Hun	Bayern Munich	FRG	1-1	0-3	1-4

	Pts	P	W	D	L	F	A	Diff	Goals/P
Total	8	4	2	4	2	7	7	0	1.750

Final

Bayern Munich	FRG	Atlético Madrid	Esp	1-1	4-0	5-1

	Pts	P	W	D	L	F	A	Diff	Goals/P
Total	4	2	1	2	1	6	6	0	3.000

	Pts	P	W	D	L	F	A	Diff	Goals/P
Total	120	60	46	28	46	180	180	0	3.000

Pos'n	Club	Cnty	Pts	P	W	D	L	F	A	Diff	B	Pts/P	F/P
1	Bayern Munich	FRG	16	10	5	3	2	25	15	10	3	1.600	2.500
2	Atlético Madrid	Esp	16	10	4	5	1	10	7	3	3	1.600	1.000
3	Celtic	Sco	12	8	4	2	2	16	8	8	2	1.500	2.000
4	Ujpesti Dózsa	Hun	12	8	3	4	1	12	9	3	2	1.500	1.500
5	Spartak Trnava	Tch	10	6	3	3	0	6	3	3	1	1.667	1.000
6	Red Star Belgrade	Yug	10	6	4	1	1	7	5	2	1	1.667	1.167
7	FC Basle	Sui	9	6	4	0	2	23	14	9	1	1.500	3.833
8	CSKA Sofia	Bul	9	6	4	0	2	9	6	3	1	1.500	1.500
9	Club Bruges	Bel	6	4	3	0	1	16	7	9	0	1.500	4.000
10	Dinamo Bucharest	Rom	5	4	2	1	1	14	4	10	0	1.250	3.500
11	Zana Voroshilovgrad	URS	5	4	2	1	1	3	1	2	0	1.250	0.750
12	Benfica	Por	5	4	2	1	1	3	3	0	0	1.250	0.750
13	Vejle BK	Den	4	4	1	2	1	3	3	0	0	1.000	0.750
14	Dynamo Dresden	GDR	3	4	1	1	2	10	10	0	0	0.750	2.500
15	Liverpool	Eng	3	4	1	1	2	5	5	0	0	0.750	1.250
16	Åtvidaberg SFF	Swe	2	2	1	0	1	4	4	0	0	1.000	2.000
17	Juventus	Ita	2	2	1	0	1	3	4	-1	0	1.000	1.500
18	Ajax	Ned	2	2	1	0	1	1	2	-1	0	1.000	0.500
19	Nantes	Fra	1	2	0	1	1	2	3	-1	0	0.500	1.000
20	Galatasaray	Tur	1	2	0	1	1	0	1	-1	0	0.500	0.000
21	Jeunesse Esch	Lux	1	2	0	1	1	1	3	-2	0	0.500	0.500
22	IL Viking	Nor	0	2	0	0	2	1	3	-2	0	0.000	0.500
–	Stal Mielec	Pol	0	2	0	0	2	1	3	-2	0	0.000	0.500
24	Olympiakos Pireus	Gre	0	2	0	0	2	0	2	-2	0	0.000	0.000
25	Apoel Nicosia	Cyp	0	2	0	0	2	0	3	-3	0	0.000	0.000
26	Waterford United	Irl	0	2	0	0	2	2	6	-4	0	0.000	1.000
27	FC Tirol	Aut	0	2	0	0	2	0	4	-4	0	0.000	0.000
28	TPS Turku	Fin	0	2	0	0	2	1	9	-8	0	0.000	0.500
29	Fram Reykjavik	Isl	0	2	0	0	2	2	11	-9	0	0.000	1.000
30	Floriana	Mlt	0	2	0	0	2	0	10	-10	0	0.000	0.000
31	Crusaders	Nir	0	2	0	0	2	0	12	-12	0	0.000	0.000
	Total		**134**	**120**	**46**	**28**	**46**	**180**	**180**	**0**	**14**	**1.117**	**3.000**

European Cup Winners Cup 1973-74

First Round

Team 1	Cnty	Team 2	Cnty	1st leg	2nd leg	Agg
Anderlecht	Bel	FC Zürich	Sui	3-2	0-1	3-3
Beroe Stara Zagora	Bul	Fola Esch	Lux	7-0	4-1	11-1
Pezoporikos Larnaca	Cyp	Malmö FF	Swe	0-0	0-11	0-11
Randers Freja FC	Den	Rapid Vienna	Aut	0-0	1-2	1-2
Reipas Lahti	Fin	Olympique Lyon	Fra	0-0	0-2	0-2
Cardiff City	Wal	Sporting Lisbon	Por	0-0	0-2	0-2
Vasas SC	Hun	Sunderland	Eng	0-2	0-1	0-3
IBV Vestmannaeyjar	Isl	Bor. Mönchengladbach	FRG	0-7	1-9	1-16
AC Milan	Ita	Dinamo Zagreb	Yug	3-1	1-0	4-1
Gzira United	Mlt	SK Brann	Nor	0-2	0-7	0-9
NAC Breda	Ned	Magdeburg	GDR	0-0	0-2	0-2
Legia Warsaw	Pol	PAOK Salonika	Gre	1-1	0-1	1-2
Chimia Râmnicu Vâlcea	Rom	Glentoran	Nir	2-2	0-2	2-4
Banik Ostrava	Tch	Cork Hibernians	Irl	1-0	2-1	3-1
Ankaragücü	Tur	Rangers	Sco	0-2	0-4	0-6
Torpedo Moscow	URS	Athletic Bilbao	Esp	0-0	0-2	0-2

	Pts	P	W	D	L	F	A	Diff	Goals/P
Total	64	32	24	16	24	93	93	0	2.906

Second Round

Sunderland	Eng	Sporting Lisbon	Por	2-1	0-2	2-3
Beroe Stara Zagora	Bul	Athletic Bilbao	Esp	3-0	0-1	3-1
Olympique Lyon	Fra	PAOK Salonika	Gre	3-3	0-4	3-7
AC Milan	Ita	Rapid Vienna	Aut	0-0	2-0	2-0
SK Brann	Nor	Glentoran	Nir	1-1	1-3	2-4
Bor. Mönchengladbach	FRG	Rangers	Sco	3-0	2-3	5-3
FC Zürich	Sui	Malmö FF	Swe	0-0	1-1	1-1
Banik Ostrava	Tch	Magdeburg	GDR	2-0	0-3	2-3

	Pts	P	W	D	L	F	A	Diff	Goals/P
Total	32	16	11	10	11	42	42	0	2.625

Quarter Finals

Glentoran	Nir	Bor. Mönchengladbach	FRG	0-2	0-5	0-7
AC Milan	Ita	PAOK Salonika	Gre	3-0	2-2	5-2
Sporting Lisbon	Por	FC Zürich	Sui	3-0	1-1	4-1
Magdeburg	GDR	Beroe Stara Zagora	Bul	2-0	1-1	3-1

	Pts	P	W	D	L	F	A	Diff	Goals/P
Total	16	8	5	6	5	23	23	0	2.875

Semi Finals

AC Milan	Ita	Bor. Mönchengladbach	FRG	2-0	0-1	2-1
Sporting Lisbon	Por	Magdeburg	GDR	1-1	1-2	2-3

	Pts	P	W	D	L	F	A	Diff	Goals/P
Total	8	4	3	2	3	8	8	0	2.000

Final

Magdeburg	GDR	AC Milan	Ita	2-0	2-0

	Pts	P	W	D	L	F	A	Diff	Goals/P
Total	2	1	1	0	1	2	2	0	2.000

	Pts	P	W	D	L	F	A	Diff	Goals/P
Total	122	61	44	34	44	168	168	0	2.754

Pos'n	Club	Cnty	Pts	P	W	D	L	F	A	Diff	B	Pts/P	F/P
1	Magdeburg	GDR	16	9	5	3	1	13	5	8	3	1.778	1.444
2	AC Milan	Ita	15	9	5	2	2	13	6	7	3	1.667	1.444
3	Bor. Mönchengladbach	FRG	14	8	6	0	2	29	6	23	2	1.750	3.625
4	Sporting Lisbon	Por	11	8	3	3	2	11	6	5	2	1.375	1.375
5	Beroe Stara Zagora	Bul	8	6	3	1	2	15	5	10	1	1.333	2.500
6	PAOK Salonika	Gre	8	6	2	3	1	11	9	2	1	1.333	1.833
7	Glentoran	Nir	7	6	2	2	2	8	11	-3	1	1.167	1.333
8	Rangers	Sco	6	4	3	0	1	9	5	4	0	1.500	2.250
9	Sunderland	Eng	6	4	3	0	1	5	3	2	0	1.500	1.250
10	Banik Ostrava	Tch	6	4	3	0	1	5	4	1	0	1.500	1.250
11	FC Zürich	Sui	6	6	1	3	2	5	8	-3	1	1.000	0.833
12	Malmö FF	Swe	5	4	1	3	0	12	1	11	0	1.250	3.000
13	SK Brann	Nor	5	4	2	1	1	11	4	7	0	1.250	2.750
14	Athletic Bilbao	Esp	5	4	2	1	1	3	3	0	0	1.250	0.750
15	Rapid Vienna	Aut	4	4	1	2	1	2	3	-1	0	1.000	0.500
16	Olympique Lyon	Fra	4	4	1	2	1	5	7	-2	0	1.000	1.250
17	Anderlecht	Bel	2	2	1	0	1	3	3	0	0	1.000	1.500
18	Randers Freja FC	Den	1	2	0	1	1	1	2	-1	0	0.500	0.500
–	Legia Warsaw	Pol	1	2	0	1	1	1	2	-1	0	0.500	0.500
20	Chimia Râmnicu Vâlcea	Rom	1	2	0	1	1	2	4	-2	0	0.500	1.000
21	Reipas Lahti	Fin	1	2	0	1	1	0	2	-2	0	0.500	0.000
–	Cardiff City	Wal	1	2	0	1	1	0	2	-2	0	0.500	0.000
–	NAC Breda	Ned	1	2	0	1	1	0	2	-2	0	0.500	0.000
–	Torpedo Moscow	URS	1	2	0	1	1	0	2	-2	0	0.500	0.000
25	Pezoporikos Larnaca	Cyp	1	2	0	1	1	0	11	-11	0	0.500	0.000
26	Cork Hibernians	Irl	0	2	0	0	2	1	3	-2	0	0.000	0.500
27	Dinamo Zagreb	Yug	0	2	0	0	2	1	4	-3	0	0.000	0.500
28	Vasas SC	Hun	0	2	0	0	2	0	3	-3	0	0.000	0.000
29	Ankaragücü	Tur	0	2	0	0	2	0	6	-6	0	0.000	0.000
30	Gzira United	Mlt	0	2	0	0	2	0	9	-9	0	0.000	0.000
31	Fola Esch	Lux	0	2	0	0	2	1	11	-10	0	0.000	0.500
32	IBV Vestmannaeyjar	Isl	0	2	0	0	2	1	16	-15	0	0.000	0.500
	Total		**136**	**122**	**44**	**34**	**44**	**168**	**168**	**0**	**14**	**1.115**	**2.754**

First Round

Team 1	Cnty	Team 2	Cnty	1st leg	2nd leg	Agg
Ipswich Town	Eng	Real Madrid	Esp	1-0	0-0	1-0
Admira Wacker	Aut	Inter Milan	Ita	1-0	1-2	2-2
B 1903 Copenhagen	Den	AIK	Swe	2-1	1-1	3-2
Aberdeen	Sco	Finn Harps	Irl	4-1	3-1	7-2
Dundee	Sco	Twente Enschede	Ned	1-3	2-4	3-7
Hibernian	Sco	IBK Keflavik	Isl	2-0	1-1	3-1
Español	Esp	RWD Molenbeek	Bel	0-3	2-1	2-4
Nice	Fra	Barcelona	Esp	3-0	0-2	3-2
Panathinaikos	Gre	OFK Belgrade	Yug	1-2	1-0	2-2
Panahaiki	Gre	Grazer AK	Aut	2-1	1-0	3-1
Ferencváros	Hun	Gwardia Warsaw	Pol	0-1	1-2	1-3
Ards	Nir	Standard Liège	Bel	3-2	1-6	4-8
Fiorentina	Ita	Universitatea Craiova	Rom	0-0	0-1	0-1
Lazio	Ita	Sion	Sui	3-0	1-3	4-3
Torino	Ita	Lokomotive Leipzig	GDR	1-2	1-2	2-4
Union Luxembourg	Lux	Olympique Marseille	Fra	0-5	1-7	1-12
Sliema Wanderers	Mlt	Lokomotiv Plovdiv	Bul	0-2	0-1	0-3
Strømgodset IF	Nor	Leeds United	Eng	1-1	1-6	2-7
Fredrikstad FK	Nor	Dinamo Kiev	URS	0-1	0-4	0-5
Ruch Chorzów	Pol	Wuppertal	FRG	4-1	4-5	8-6
Belenenses	Por	Wolverhampton Wanderers	Eng	0-2	1-2	1-4
Vitória Setúbal	Por	Beerschot	Bel	2-0	2-0	4-0
Fortuna Düsseldorf	FRG	Naestved IF	Den	1-0	2-2	3-2
VFB Stuttgart	FRG	Olympiakos Nicosia	Cyp	9-0	4-0	13-0
Öster SIF	Swe	Feyenoord	Ned	1-3	1-2	2-5
Grasshoppers Zürich	Sui	Tottenham Hotspur	Eng	1-5	1-4	2-9
VSS Kosice	Tch	Honvéd	Hun	1-0	2-5	3-5
Tatran Presov	Tch	Velez Mostar	Yug	4-2	1-1	5-3
Eskisehirspor	Tur	Cologne	FRG	0-0	0-2	0-2
Fenerbahçe	Tur	Arges Pitesti	Rom	5-1	1-1	6-2
Dinamo Tbilisi	URS	Slavia Sofia	Bul	4-1	0-2	4-3
Carl Zeiss Jena	GDR	MP Mikkeli	Fin	3-0	3-0	6-0

	Pts	P	W	D	L	F	A	Diff	Goals/P
Total	128	64	55	18	55	210	210	0	3.281

Second Round

Ipswich Town	Eng	Lazio	Ita	4-0	2-4	6-4
Leeds United	Eng	Hibernian	Sco	0-0	0-0	0-0
Admira Wacker	Aut	Fortuna Düsseldorf	FRG	2-1	0-3	2-4
Standard Liège	Bel	Universitatea Craiova	Rom	2-0	1-1	3-1
Lokomotiv Plovdiv	Bul	Honvéd	Hun	3-4	2-3	5-7
Aberdeen	Sco	Tottenham Hotspur	Eng	1-1	1-4	2-5
Olympique Marseille	Fra	Cologne	FRG	2-0	0-6	2-6
Nice	Fra	Fenerbahçe	Tur	4-0	0-2	4-2
Panahaiki	Gre	Twente Enschede	Ned	1-1	0-7	1-8
Feyenoord	Ned	Gwardia Warsaw	Pol	3-1	0-1	3-2
Ruch Chorzów	Pol	Carl Zeiss Jena	GDR	3-0	0-1	3-1
Vitória Setúbal	Por	RWD Molenbeek	Bel	1-0	1-2	2-2
VFB Stuttgart	FRG	Tatran Presov	Tch	3-1	5-3	8-4
Dinamo Kiev	URS	B 1903 Copenhagen	Den	1-0	2-1	3-1
Dinamo Tbilisi	URS	OFK Belgrade	Yug	3-0	5-1	8-1
Lokomotive Leipzig	GDR	Wolverhampton Wanderers	Eng	3-0	1-4	4-4

	Pts	P	W	D	L	F	A	Diff	Goals/P
Total	64	32	27	10	27	108	108	0	3.375

Third Round

Ipswich Town	Eng	Twente Enschede	Ned	1-0	2-1	3-1
Leeds United	Eng	Vitória Setúbal	Por	1-0	1-3	2-3
Standard Liège	Bel	Feyenoord	Ned	3-1	0-2	3-3
Nice	Fra	Cologne	FRG	1-0	0-4	1-4
Honvéd	Hun	Ruch Chorzów	Pol	2-0	0-5	2-5
Fortuna Düsseldorf	FRG	Lokomotive Leipzig	GDR	2-1	0-3	2-4
Dinamo Kiev	URS	VFB Stuttgart	FRG	2-0	0-3	2-3
Dinamo Tbilisi	URS	Tottenham Hotspur	Eng	1-1	1-5	2-6

	Pts	P	W	D	L	F	A	Diff	Goals/P
Total	32	16	15	2	15	46	46	0	2.875

Quarter Finals

Ipswich Town	Eng	Lokomotive Leipzig	GDR	1-0	0-1	1-1
Ruch Chorzów	Pol	Feyenoord	Ned	1-1	1-3	2-4
Cologne	FRG	Tottenham Hotspur	Eng	1-2	0-3	1-5
VFB Stuttgart	FRG	Vitória Setúbal	Por	1-0	2-2	3-2

	Pts	P	W	D	L	F	A	Diff	Goals/P
Total	16	8	6	4	6	19	19	0	2.375

Semi Finals

Feyenoord	Ned	VFB Stuttgart	FRG	2-1	2-2	4-3
Lokomotive Leipzig	GDR	Tottenham Hotspur	Eng	1-2	0-2	1-4

	Pts	P	W	D	L	F	A	Diff	Goals/P
Total	8	4	3	2	3	12	12	0	3.000

Final

Tottenham Hotspur	Eng	Feyenoord	Ned	2-2	0-2	2-4

	Pts	P	W	D	L	F	A	Diff	Goals/P
Total	4	2	1	2	1	6	6	0	3.000

	Pts	P	W	D	L	F	A	Diff	Goals/P
Total	252	126	107	38	107	401	401	0	3.183

UEFA Cup 1973-74

Pos'n	Club	Cnty	Pts	P	W	D	L	F	A	Diff	B	Pts/P	F/P
1	Tottenham Hotspur	Eng	22	12	8	3	1	31	12	19	3	1.833	2.583
2	Feyenoord	Ned	20	12	7	3	2	23	14	9	3	1.667	1.917
3	VFB Stuttgart	FRG	16	10	6	2	2	30	12	18	2	1.600	3.000
4	Ipswich Town	Eng	12	8	5	1	2	11	6	5	1	1.500	1.375
5	Lokomotive Leipzig	GDR	12	10	5	0	5	14	13	1	2	1.200	1.400
6	Dinamo Kiev	URS	10	6	5	0	1	10	4	6	0	1.667	1.667
7	Vitória Setúbal	Por	10	8	4	1	3	11	7	4	1	1.250	1.375
8	Ruch Chorzów	Pol	8	8	3	1	4	18	13	5	1	1.000	2.250
9	Cologne	FRG	8	8	3	1	4	13	8	5	1	1.000	1.625
10	Honvéd	Hun	8	6	4	0	2	14	13	1	0	1.333	2.333
11	Twente Enschede	Ned	7	6	3	1	2	16	7	9	0	1.167	2.667
12	Standard Liège	Bel	7	6	3	1	2	14	8	6	0	1.167	2.333
13	Dinamo Tbilisi	URS	7	6	3	1	2	14	10	4	0	1.167	2.333
14	Leeds United	Eng	7	6	2	3	1	9	5	4	0	1.167	1.500
15	Fortuna Düsseldorf	FRG	7	6	3	1	2	9	8	1	0	1.167	1.500
16	Olympique Marseille	Fra	6	4	3	0	1	14	7	7	0	1.500	3.500
17	Carl Zeiss Jena	GDR	6	4	3	0	1	7	3	4	0	1.500	1.750
18	Wolverhampton Wanderers	Eng	6	4	3	0	1	8	5	3	0	1.500	2.000
19	Gwardia Warsaw	Pol	6	4	3	0	1	5	4	1	0	1.500	1.250
20	Nice	Fra	6	6	3	0	3	8	8	0	0	1.000	1.333
21	Aberdeen	Sco	5	4	2	1	1	9	7	2	0	1.250	2.250
22	Fenerbahçe	Tur	5	4	2	1	1	8	6	2	0	1.250	2.000
23	Hibernian	Sco	5	4	1	3	0	3	1	2	0	1.250	0.750
24	Panahaiki	Gre	5	4	2	1	1	4	9	-5	0	1.250	1.000
25	RWD Molenbeek	Bel	4	4	2	0	2	6	4	2	0	1.000	1.500
26	Lokomotiv Plovdiv	Bul	4	4	2	0	2	8	7	1	0	1.000	2.000
27	Lazio	Ita	4	4	2	0	2	8	9	-1	0	1.000	2.000
28	Universitatea Craiova	Rom	4	4	1	2	1	2	3	-1	0	1.000	0.500
29	Admira Wacker	Aut	4	4	2	0	2	4	6	-2	0	1.000	1.000
30	B 1903 Copenhagen	Den	3	4	1	1	2	4	5	-1	0	0.750	1.000
31	Tatran Presov	Tch	3	4	1	1	2	9	11	-2	0	0.750	2.250
32	Panathinaikos	Gre	2	2	1	0	1	2	2	0	0	1.000	1.000
33	Inter Milan	Ita	2	2	1	0	1	2	2	0	0	1.000	1.000
34	Slavia Sofia	Bul	2	2	1	0	1	3	4	-1	0	1.000	1.500
–	Sion	Sui	2	2	1	0	1	3	4	-1	0	1.000	1.500
36	Barcelona	Esp	2	2	1	0	1	2	3	-1	0	1.000	1.000
37	Wuppertal	FRG	2	2	1	0	1	6	8	-2	0	1.000	3.000
38	VSS Kosice	Tch	2	2	1	0	1	3	5	-2	0	1.000	1.500
39	Español	Esp	2	2	1	0	1	2	4	-2	0	1.000	1.000
40	Ards	Nir	2	2	1	0	1	4	8	-4	0	1.000	2.000
41	OFK Belgrade	Yug	2	4	1	0	3	3	10	-7	0	0.500	0.750
42	Naestved IF	Den	1	2	0	1	1	2	3	-1	0	0.500	1.000
–	AIK	Swe	1	2	0	1	1	2	3	-1	0	0.500	1.000
44	Real Madrid	Esp	1	2	0	1	1	0	1	-1	0	0.500	0.000
–	Fiorentina	Ita	1	2	0	1	1	0	1	-1	0	0.500	0.000
46	Velez Mostar	Yug	1	2	0	1	1	3	5	-2	0	0.500	1.500
47	IBK Keflavik	Isl	1	2	0	1	1	1	3	-2	0	0.500	0.500
48	Eskisehirspor	Tur	1	2	0	1	1	0	2	-2	0	0.500	0.000
49	Arges Pitesti	Rom	1	2	0	1	1	2	6	-4	0	0.500	1.000
50	Strømgodset IF	Nor	1	2	0	1	1	2	7	-5	0	0.500	1.000
51	Torino	Ita	0	2	0	0	2	2	4	-2	0	0.000	1.000
52	Grazer AK	Aut	0	2	0	0	2	1	3	-2	0	0.000	0.500
–	Ferencváros	Hun	0	2	0	0	2	1	3	-2	0	0.000	0.500
54	Öster SIF	Swe	0	2	0	0	2	2	5	-3	0	0.000	1.000
55	Belenenses	Por	0	2	0	0	2	1	4	-3	0	0.000	0.500
56	Sliema Wanderers	Mlt	0	2	0	0	2	0	3	-3	0	0.000	0.000
57	Dundee	Sco	0	2	0	0	2	3	7	-4	0	0.000	1.500
58	Beerschot	Bel	0	2	0	0	2	0	4	-4	0	0.000	0.000
59	Finn Harps	Irl	0	2	0	0	2	2	7	-5	0	0.000	1.000
60	Fredrikstad FK	Nor	0	2	0	0	2	0	5	-5	0	0.000	0.000
61	MP Mikkeli	Fin	0	2	0	0	2	0	6	-6	0	0.000	0.000
62	Grasshoppers Zürich	Sui	0	2	0	0	2	2	9	-7	0	0.000	1.000
63	Union Luxembourg	Lux	0	2	0	0	2	1	12	-11	0	0.000	0.500
64	Olympiakos Nicosia	Cyp	0	2	0	0	2	0	13	-13	0	0.000	0.000
	Total		**266**	**252**	**107**	**38**	**107**	**401**	**401**	**0**	**14**	**1.056**	**3.183**

1973-74

Pos'n	Cnty	Pts	P	W	D	L	F	A	Diff	B	Pts/P	F/P
1	FRG	63	44	24	7	13	112	57	55	8	1.432	2.545
2	Eng	56	38	22	8	8	69	36	33	4	1.474	1.816
3	GDR	37	27	14	4	9	44	31	13	5	1.370	1.630
4	Ned	30	22	11	5	6	40	25	15	3	1.364	1.818
5	Sco	28	22	10	6	6	40	28	12	2	1.273	1.818
6	Por	26	22	9	5	8	26	20	6	3	1.182	1.182
7	Esp	26	20	8	7	5	17	18	-1	3	1.300	0.850
8	Ita	24	21	9	3	9	28	26	2	3	1.143	1.333
9	Bul	23	18	10	1	7	35	22	13	2	1.278	1.944
10	URS	23	18	10	3	5	27	17	10	0	1.278	1.500
11	Tch	21	16	8	4	4	23	23	0	1	1.313	1.438
12	Hun	20	18	7	4	7	27	28	-1	2	1.111	1.500
13	Bel	19	18	9	1	8	39	26	13	0	1.056	2.167
14	Fra	17	16	7	3	6	29	25	4	0	1.063	1.813
15	Sui	17	16	6	3	7	33	35	-2	2	1.063	2.063
16	Pol	15	16	6	2	8	25	22	3	1	0.938	1.563
17	Gre	15	14	5	4	5	17	22	-5	1	1.071	1.214
18	Yug	13	14	5	2	7	14	24	-10	1	0.929	1.000
19	Rom	11	12	3	5	4	20	17	3	0	0.917	1.667
20	Den	9	12	2	5	5	10	13	-3	0	0.750	0.833
21	Nir	9	10	3	2	5	12	31	-19	1	0.900	1.200
22	Swe	8	10	2	4	4	20	13	7	0	0.800	2.000
23	Aut	8	12	3	2	7	7	16	-9	0	0.667	0.583
24	Tur	7	10	2	3	5	8	15	-7	0	0.700	0.800
25	Nor	6	10	2	2	6	14	19	-5	0	0.600	1.400
26	Wal	1	2	0	1	1	0	2	-2	0	0.500	0.000
27	Fin	1	6	0	1	5	1	17	-16	0	0.167	0.167
28	Lux	1	6	0	1	5	3	26	-23	0	0.167	0.500
29	Isl	1	6	0	1	5	4	30	-26	0	0.167	0.667
30	Cyp	1	6	0	1	5	0	27	-27	0	0.167	0.000
31	Irl	0	6	0	0	6	5	16	-11	0	0.000	0.833
32	Mlt	0	6	0	0	6	0	22	-22	0	0.000	0.000
	Total	**536**	**494**	**197**	**100**	**197**	**749**	**749**	**0**	**42**	**1.085**	**3.032**

1955-56 to 1973-74

1	Eng	816	546	299	117	130	1074	557	517	101	1.495	1.967
2	Esp	729	512	272	91	149	1015	630	385	94	1.424	1.982
3	Ita	678	474	246	103	125	795	492	303	83	1.430	1.677
4	FRG	584	438	221	81	136	888	624	264	61	1.333	2.027
5	Sco	471	365	184	56	125	671	495	176	47	1.290	1.838
6	Por	352	298	131	60	107	517	395	122	30	1.181	1.735
7	Yug	346	322	123	63	136	520	490	30	37	1.075	1.615
8	Hun	322	261	123	41	97	509	373	136	35	1.234	1.950
9	Ned	319	248	122	42	84	472	331	141	33	1.286	1.903
10	Bel	276	260	113	31	116	423	390	33	19	1.062	1.627
11	Tch	250	213	95	38	80	340	287	53	22	1.174	1.596
12	GDR	236	214	88	43	83	324	274	50	17	1.103	1.514
13	Fra	206	220	77	39	104	318	359	-41	13	0.936	1.445
14	Pol	169	151	68	23	60	238	217	21	10	1.119	1.576
15	Bul	168	165	65	29	71	273	249	24	9	1.018	1.655
16	Rom	161	171	62	32	77	216	279	-63	5	0.942	1.263
17	Sui	150	195	54	31	110	293	432	-139	11	0.769	1.503
18	Aut	142	170	52	31	87	211	297	-86	7	0.835	1.241
19	URS	112	88	42	21	25	125	87	38	7	1.273	1.420
20	Gre	106	127	37	27	63	142	240	-98	5	0.835	1.118
21	Tur	97	129	35	22	72	139	227	-88	5	0.752	1.078
22	Den	94	147	32	26	89	208	345	-137	4	0.639	1.415
23	Swe	91	116	30	28	58	155	235	-80	3	0.784	1.336
24	Wal	53	48	17	15	16	69	58	11	4	1.104	1.438
25	Nor	53	94	20	12	62	104	243	-139	1	0.564	1.106
26	Nir	47	86	14	17	55	104	247	-143	2	0.547	1.209
27	Irl	40	98	14	12	72	88	270	-182	0	0.408	0.898
28	Lux	28	90	10	8	72	68	374	-306	0	0.311	0.756
29	Mlt	22	70	7	8	55	33	230	-197	0	0.314	0.471
30	Fin	18	60	6	6	48	41	211	-170	0	0.300	0.683
31	Alb	16	26	3	10	13	18	41	-23	0	0.615	0.692
32	Isl	9	50	1	7	42	30	226	-196	0	0.180	0.600
33	Cyp	8	52	2	4	46	22	238	-216	0	0.154	0.423
	Total	**7169**	**6504**	**2665**	**1174**	**2665**	**10443**	**10443**	**0**	**665**	**1.102**	**3.211**

National Performance by Index

1973-74

Pos'n	Cnty	Ave	Pts	P	W	D	L	F	A	Diff	B	No./T
1	W. Germany	10.500	63	44	24	7	13	112	57	55	8	6
2	England	9.333	56	38	22	8	8	69	36	33	4	6
3	E. Germany	9.250	37	27	14	4	9	44	31	13	5	4
4	Netherlands	7.500	30	22	11	5	6	40	25	15	3	4
5	Portugal	6.500	26	22	9	5	8	26	20	6	3	4
6	Bulgaria	5.750	23	18	10	1	7	35	22	13	2	4
–	USSR	5.750	23	18	10	3	5	27	17	10	0	4
8	Scotland	5.600	28	22	10	6	6	40	28	12	2	5
9	Czechoslovakia	5.250	21	16	8	4	4	23	23	0	1	4
10	Spain	5.200	26	20	8	7	5	17	18	-1	3	5
11	Hungary	5.000	20	18	7	4	7	27	28	-1	2	4
12	France	4.250	17	16	7	3	6	29	25	4	0	4
–	Switzerland	4.250	17	16	6	3	7	33	35	-2	2	4
14	Italy	4.000	24	21	9	3	9	28	26	2	3	6
15	Belgium	3.800	19	18	9	1	8	39	26	13	0	5
16	Greece	3.750	15	14	5	4	5	17	22	-5	1	4
–	Poland	3.750	15	16	6	2	8	25	22	3	1	4
18	Yugoslavia	3.250	13	14	5	2	7	14	24	-10	1	4
19	N. Ireland	3.000	9	10	3	2	5	12	31	-19	1	3
20	Romania	2.750	11	12	3	5	4	20	17	3	0	4
21	Denmark	2.250	9	12	2	5	5	10	13	-3	0	4
22	Austria	2.000	8	12	3	2	7	7	16	-9	0	4
–	Sweden	2.000	8	10	2	4	4	20	13	7	0	4
24	Turkey	1.750	7	10	2	3	5	8	15	-7	0	4
25	Norway	1.500	6	10	2	2	6	14	19	-5	0	4
26	Wales	1.000	1	2	0	1	1	0	2	-2	0	1
27	Cyprus	0.333	1	6	0	1	5	0	27	-27	0	3
–	Finland	0.333	1	6	0	1	5	1	17	-16	0	3
–	Iceland	0.333	1	6	0	1	5	4	30	-26	0	3
–	Luxembourg	0.333	1	6	0	1	5	3	26	-23	0	3
31	Rep. of Ireland	0.000	0	6	0	0	6	5	16	-11	0	3
–	Malta	0.000	0	6	0	0	6	0	22	-22	0	3
	Total		**536**	**494**	**197**	**100**	**197**	**749**	**749**	**0**	**42**	**3.032**

1955-56 to 1973-74

Pos'n	Cnty	Ave	Pts	P	W	D	L	F	A	Diff	B	No./T
1	England	9.714	816	546	299	117	130	1074	557	517	101	84
2	Spain	8.100	729	512	272	91	149	1015	630	385	94	90
3	Italy	7.883	678	474	246	103	125	795	492	303	83	86
4	W. Germany	6.636	584	438	221	81	136	888	624	264	61	88
5	Scotland	6.541	471	365	184	56	125	671	495	176	47	72
6	Hungary	6.313	322	261	123	41	97	509	373	136	35	51
7	Netherlands	5.800	319	248	122	42	84	472	331	141	33	55
8	USSR	5.600	112	88	42	21	25	125	87	38	7	20
9	Portugal	5.028	352	298	131	60	107	517	395	122	30	70
10	Czechoslovakia	4.807	250	213	95	38	80	340	287	53	22	52
11	E. Germany	4.720	236	214	88	43	83	324	274	50	17	50
12	Yugoslavia	4.552	346	322	123	63	136	520	490	30	37	76
13	Poland	4.333	169	151	68	23	60	238	217	21	10	39
14	Belgium	4.246	276	260	113	31	116	423	390	33	19	65
15	Wales	4.076	53	48	17	15	16	69	58	11	4	13
16	Bulgaria	3.652	168	165	65	29	71	273	249	24	9	46
17	Romania	3.285	161	171	62	32	77	216	279	-63	5	49
18	France	3.074	206	220	77	39	104	318	359	-41	13	67
19	Austria	2.730	142	170	52	31	87	211	297	-86	7	52
20	Turkey	2.365	97	129	35	22	72	139	227	-88	5	41
21	Greece	2.355	106	127	37	27	63	142	240	-98	5	45
22	Switzerland	2.343	150	195	54	31	110	293	432	-139	11	64
23	Sweden	2.219	91	116	30	28	58	155	235	-80	3	41
24	Denmark	1.709	94	147	32	26	89	208	345	-137	4	55
25	Albania	1.454	16	26	3	10	13	18	41	-23	0	11
26	Norway	1.394	53	94	20	12	62	104	243	-139	1	38
27	N. Ireland	1.270	47	86	14	17	55	104	247	-143	2	37
28	Rep. of Ireland	0.952	40	98	14	12	72	88	270	-182	0	42
29	Malta	0.687	22	70	7	8	55	33	230	-197	0	32
30	Luxembourg	0.666	28	90	10	8	72	68	374	-306	0	42
31	Finland	0.642	18	60	6	6	48	41	211	-170	0	28
32	Iceland	0.375	9	50	1	7	42	30	226	-196	0	24
33	Cyprus	0.333	8	52	2	4	46	22	238	-216	0	24
	Total		**7169**	**6504**	**2665**	**1174**	**2665**	**10443**	**10443**	**0**	**665**	**3.211**

German Success, Both East and West

The baton of Total Football was relinquished by Ajax after a three-year tenure and passed on, via the Bulgarian army club CSKA Sofia, to Bayern Munich.

Bayern, containing over half of the team that would go on to win the World Cup for West Germany – Maier, Breitner, Schwarzenbeck, Beckenbauer, Hoeness and Müller – were spared a repeat of their previous season's quarter-final meeting with Ajax when the Amsterdam club, now lacking Barcelona-bound Johan Cruijff, were surprisingly beaten in the second round by CSKA Sofia, 2-1 on aggregate after extra-time. In the following round Bayern beat the Bulgarians 4-1 at home and sealed the tie with a 2-1 defeat in Sofia.

Ajax were not the only surprise losers in the second round. Liverpool, playing in the Champions' Cup for the first time in seven years, also went out after losing 2-1 to Red Star Belgrade in both matches. The defeat at Anfield remains their one and only in 12 years of Champions' Cup participation, and was significant in changing the way in which the club approached future European fixtures.

Red Star, like CSKA Sofia, succumbed in the next round, beaten 2-0 on aggregate by Atlético Madrid. Both Atlético goals were scored away from home in what was their third away victory of the competition after previous successes in Turkey and Romania. In the semi-final they were pitted against Champions' Cup diehards Celtic. They didn't extend their sequence of away victories in Glasgow, but they did obtain a goalless draw, despite having three players sent off in a thoroughly ugly and brutal performance. The hardest part over, Atlético finished Celtic off in Madrid with a 2-0 victory to reach their first Champions' Cup final.

Bayern, meanwhile, having required penalties in the first round to get past the troublesome Swedes of Åtvidaberg, improved as the competition went on, with their dual strike force of Müller and Torstensson sharing the team's four goals against Ujpesti Dózsa in the semi-final which enabled Bayern to become the first West German Champions' Cup finalists since Eintracht Frankfurt in 1960.

With Bayern and Atlético Madrid in the final, there was sure to be a new name on the trophy. Remarkably, it was the first time since 1961 that the final had brought together two teams which had never reached this stage of the competition before!

Brussels' Heysel stadium staged the final, equalling Wembley as the most frequently used venue for the Champions' Cup final and then surpassing it when Bayern and Atlético drew 1-1, thus taking the tie to a replay, also at Heysel, two days later. Bayern had been perilously close to defeat in that first match, equalising in the last seconds of injury-time through Georg Schwarzenbeck, but in the second match they completely annihilated the Spaniards. Uli Hoeness and Gerd Müller scored twice each to give Bayern a 4-0 victory, the biggest margin of victory seen in a Champions' Cup final since 1960.

If Bayern's victory was more or less to be expected, the success of Magdeburg, from East Germany, in the Cup-winners' Cup was a massive surprise, especially as their victims in the final were none other than holders AC Milan, who had extended their long unbeaten run in the competition to a remarkable 26 matches before their 1-0 defeat away to Borussia Mönchengladbach in the semi-final. But, led by striker Jürgen Sparwasser, whose name was to become famous when he scored East Germany's winning goal against West Germany in the 1974 World Cup, Magdeburg upset all the odds and beat the Italians 2-0 in the Rotterdam final to register the first, and last, East German success in European competition.

Another East German club, Lokomotive Leipzig, did well in the UEFA Cup, reaching the semi-finals before succumbing to the tournament's specialists, Tottenham Hotspur. The Londoners, having won the first UEFA Cup in 1972 and reached the semi-finals the following year, now rode into the final once again on the back of ten games without a defeat, eight of them victories. That record made them favourites to keep the UEFA Cup in England for yet another year but Feyenoord, who had suffered a much rougher passage to the final, came good when it mattered and took the Cup with a 2-0 win in Rotterdam after holding Spurs to a 2-2 draw at White Hart Lane.

1974–1975

Bayern Munich

Dinamo Kiev

Borussia Mönchengladbach

First Round

Team 1	Cnty	Team 2	Cnty	1st leg	2nd leg	Agg
Leeds United	Eng	FC Zürich	Sui	4-1	1-2	5-3
Vöest Linz	Aut	Barcelona	Esp	0-0	0-5	0-5
Levski Sofia	Bul	Ujpesti Dózsa	Hun	0-3	1-4	1-7
Hvidovre IF	Den	Ruch Chorzów	Pol	0-0	1-2	1-2
Celtic	Sco	Olympiakos Pireus	Gre	1-1	0-2	1-3
Saint-Etienne	Fra	Sporting Lisbon	Por	2-0	1-1	3-1
Jeunesse Esch	Lux	Fenerbahçe	Tur	2-3	0-2	2-5
Valletta	Mlt	HJK Helsinki	Fin	1-0	1-4	2-4
IL Viking	Nor	Ararat Erevan	URS	0-2	2-4	2-6
Feyenoord	Ned	Coleraine	Nir	7-0	4-1	11-1
Universitatea Craiova	Rom	Åtvidaberg SFF	Swe	2-1	1-3	3-4
Slovan Bratislava	Tch	Anderlecht	Bel	4-2	1-3	5-5
Hajduk Split	Yug	IBK Keflavik	Isl	7-1	2-0	9-1

	Pts	P	W	D	L	F	A	Diff	Goals/P
Total	52	26	22	8	22	92	92	0	3.538

Second Round

Anderlecht	Bel	Olympiakos Pireus	Gre	5-1	0-3	5-4
Cork Celtic	Irl	Ararat Erevan	URS	1-2	0-5	1-7
HJK Helsinki	Fin	Åtvidaberg SFF	Swe	0-3	0-1	0-4
Ujpesti Dózsa	Hun	Leeds United	Eng	1-2	0-3	1-5
Feyenoord	Ned	Barcelona	Esp	0-0	0-3	0-3
Ruch Chorzów	Pol	Fenerbahçe	Tur	2-1	2-0	4-1
Bayern Munich	FRG	Magdeburg	GDR	3-2	2-1	5-3
Hajduk Split	Yug	Saint-Etienne	Fra	4-1	1-5	5-6

	Pts	P	W	D	L	F	A	Diff	Goals/P
Total	32	16	15	2	15	54	54	0	3.375

Quarter Finals

Leeds United	Eng	Anderlecht	Bel	3-0	1-0	4-0
Barcelona	Esp	Åtvidaberg SFF	Swe	2-0	3-0	5-0
Ruch Chorzów	Pol	Saint-Etienne	Fra	3-2	0-2	3-4
Bayern Munich	FRG	Ararat Erevan	URS	2-0	0-1	2-1

	Pts	P	W	D	L	F	A	Diff	Goals/P
Total	16	8	8	0	8	19	19	0	2.375

Semi Finals

Leeds United	Eng	Barcelona	Esp	2-1	1-1	3-2
Saint-Etienne	Fra	Bayern Munich	FRG	0-0	0-2	0-2

	Pts	P	W	D	L	F	A	Diff	Goals/P
Total	8	4	2	4	2	7	7	0	1.750

Final

Bayern Munich	FRG	Leeds United	Eng	2-0	2-0

	Pts	P	W	D	L	F	A	Diff	Goals/P
Total	2	1	1	0	1	2	2	0	2.000

	Pts	P	W	D	L	F	A	Diff	Goals/P
Total	110	55	48	14	48	174	174	0	3.164

Pos'n	Club	Cnty	Pts	P	W	D	L	F	A	Diff	B	Pts/P	F/P
1	Leeds United	Eng	16	9	6	1	2	17	8	9	3	1.778	1.889
2	Bayern Munich	FRG	14	7	5	1	1	11	4	7	3	2.000	1.571
3	Barcelona	Esp	13	8	4	3	1	15	3	12	2	1.625	1.875
4	Ararat Erevan	URS	11	6	5	0	1	14	5	9	1	1.833	2.333
5	Ruch Chorzów	Pol	10	6	4	1	1	9	6	3	1	1.667	1.500
6	Saint-Etienne	Fra	10	8	3	2	3	13	11	2	2	1.250	1.625
7	Åtvidaberg SFF	Swe	7	6	3	0	3	8	8	0	1	1.167	1.333
8	Hajduk Split	Yug	6	4	3	0	1	14	7	7	0	1.500	3.500
9	Feyenoord	Ned	5	4	2	1	1	11	4	7	0	1.250	2.750
10	Olympiakos Pireus	Gre	5	4	2	1	1	7	6	1	0	1.250	1.750
11	Anderlecht	Bel	5	6	2	0	4	10	13	-3	1	0.833	1.667
12	Ujpesti Dózsa	Hun	4	4	2	0	2	8	6	2	0	1.000	2.000
13	Fenerbahçe	Tur	4	4	2	0	2	6	6	0	0	1.000	1.500
14	Slovan Bratislava	Tch	2	2	1	0	1	5	5	0	0	1.000	2.500
15	Universitatea Craiova	Rom	2	2	1	0	1	3	4	-1	0	1.000	1.500
16	HJK Helsinki	Fin	2	4	1	0	3	4	6	-2	0	0.500	1.000
17	FC Zürich	Sui	2	2	1	0	1	3	5	-2	0	1.000	1.500
18	Valletta	Mlt	2	2	1	0	1	2	4	-2	0	1.000	1.000
19	Hvidovre IF	Den	1	2	0	1	1	1	2	-1	0	0.500	0.500
20	Celtic	Sco	1	2	0	1	1	1	3	-2	0	0.500	0.500
–	Sporting Lisbon	Por	1	2	0	1	1	1	3	-2	0	0.500	0.500
22	Vöest Linz	Aut	1	2	0	1	1	0	5	-5	0	0.500	0.000
23	Magdeburg	GDR	0	2	0	0	2	3	5	-2	0	0.000	1.500
24	Jeunesse Esch	Lux	0	2	0	0	2	2	5	-3	0	0.000	1.000
25	IL Viking	Nor	0	2	0	0	2	2	6	-4	0	0.000	1.000
26	Levski Sofia	Bul	0	2	0	0	2	1	7	-6	0	0.000	0.500
–	Cork Celtic	Irl	0	2	0	0	2	1	7	-6	0	0.000	0.500
28	IBKKeflavik	Isl	0	2	0	0	2	1	9	-8	0	0.000	0.500
29	Coleraine	Nir	0	2	0	0	2	1	11	-10	0	0.000	0.500
	Total		**124**	**110**	**48**	**14**	**48**	**174**	**174**	**0**	**14**	**1.127**	**3.164**

First Round

Team 1	Cnty	Team 2	Cnty	1st leg	2nd leg	Agg
Liverpool	Eng	Strømgodset IF	Nor	11-0	1-0	12-0
Waregem	Bel	Austria Vienna	Aut	2-1	1-4	3-5
Dundee United	Sco	Jiul Petrosani	Rom	3-0	0-2	3-2
PAOK Salonika	Gre	Red Star Belgrade	Yug	1-0	0-2	1-2
Ferencváros	Hun	Cardiff City	Wal	2-0	4-1	6-1
Fram Reykjavik	Isl	Real Madrid	Esp	0-2	0-6	0-8
Sliema Wanderers	Mlt	Reipas Lahti	Fin	2-0	1-4	3-4
PSV Eindhoven	Ned	Ards	Nir	10-0	4-1	14-1
Gwardia Warsaw	Pol	Bologna	Ita	2-1	1-2	3-3
Benfica	Por	Vanløse IF	Den	4-0	4-1	8-1
Eintracht Frankfurt	FRG	Monaco	Fra	3-0	2-2	5-2
Malmö FF	Swe	Sion	Sui	1-0	0-1	1-1
Slavia Prague	Tch	Carl Zeiss Jena	GDR	1-0	0-1	1-1
Bursaspor	Tur	Finn Harps	Irl	4-2	0-0	4-2
Dinamo Kiev	URS	CSKA Sofia	Bul	1-0	1-0	2-0

	Pts	P	W	D	L	F	A	Diff	Goals/P
Total	60	30	28	4	28	99	99	0	3.300

Second Round

Liverpool	Eng	Ferencváros	Hun	1-1	0-0	1-1
Dundee United	Sco	Bursaspor	Tur	0-0	0-1	0-1
Real Madrid	Esp	Austria Vienna	Aut	3-0	2-2	5-2
Avenir Beggen	Lux	Red Star Belgrade	Yug	1-6	1-5	2-11
Gwardia Warsaw	Pol	PSV Eindhoven	Ned	1-5	0-3	1-8
Eintracht Frankfurt	FRG	Dinamo Kiev	URS	2-3	1-2	3-5
Malmö FF	Swe	Reipas Lahti	Fin	3-1	0-0	3-1
Carl Zeiss Jena	GDR	Benfica	Por	1-1	0-0	1-1

	Pts	P	W	D	L	F	A	Diff	Goals/P
Total	32	16	9	14	9	46	46	0	2.875

Quarter Finals

Real Madrid	Esp	Red Star Belgrade	Yug	2-0	0-2	2-2
PSV Eindhoven	Ned	Benfica	Por	0-0	2-1	2-1
Malmö FF	Swe	Ferencváros	Hun	1-3	1-1	2-4
Bursaspor	Tur	Dinamo Kiev	URS	0-1	0-2	0-3

	Pts	P	W	D	L	F	A	Diff	Goals/P
Total	16	8	6	4	6	16	16	0	2.000

Semi Finals

Ferencváros	Hun	Red Star Belgrade	Yug	2-1	2-2	4-3
Dinamo Kiev	URS	PSV Eindhoven	Ned	3-0	1-2	4-2

	Pts	P	W	D	L	F	A	Diff	Goals/P
Total	8	4	3	2	3	13	13	0	3.250

European Cup Winners Cup 1974-75

Final

Dinamo Kiev	URS	Ferencváros	Hun	3-0	3-0

	Pts	P	W	D	L	F	A	Diff	Goals/P
Total	2	1	1	0	1	3	3	0	3.000

	Pts	P	W	D	L	F	A	Diff	Goals/P
Total	118	59	47	24	47	177	177	0	3.000

Pos'n	Club	Cnty	Pts	P	W	D	L	F	A	Diff	B	Pts/P	F/P
1	Dinamo Kiev	URS	19	9	8	0	1	17	5	12	3	2.111	1.889
2	PSV Eindhoven	Ned	15	8	6	1	1	26	7	19	2	1.875	3.250
3	Ferencváros	Hun	15	9	4	4	1	15	10	5	3	1.667	1.667
4	Red Star Belgrade	Yug	11	8	4	1	3	18	9	9	2	1.375	2.250
5	Real Madrid	Esp	10	6	4	1	1	15	4	11	1	1.667	2.500
6	Benfica	Por	8	6	2	3	1	10	4	6	1	1.333	1.667
7	Malmö FF	Swe	7	6	2	2	2	6	6	0	1	1.167	1.000
8	Bursaspor	Tur	7	6	2	2	2	5	5	0	1	1.167	0.833
9	Liverpool	Eng	6	4	2	2	0	13	1	12	0	1.500	3.250
10	Carl Zeiss Jena	GDR	4	4	1	2	1	2	2	0	0	1.000	0.500
11	Eintracht Frankfurt	FRG	3	4	1	1	2	8	7	1	0	0.750	2.000
12	Dundee United	Sco	3	4	1	1	2	3	3	0	0	0.750	0.750
13	Austria Vienna	Aut	3	4	1	1	2	7	8	-1	0	0.750	1.750
14	Reipas Lahti	Fin	3	4	1	1	2	5	6	-1	0	0.750	1.250
15	Bologna	Ita	2	2	1	0	1	3	3	0	0	1.000	1.500
16	Sion	Sui	2	2	1	0	1	1	1	0	0	1.000	0.500
–	Slavia Prague	Tch	2	2	1	0	1	1	1	0	0	1.000	0.500
18	Sliema Wanderers	Mlt	2	2	1	0	1	3	4	-1	0	1.000	1.500
19	Jiul Petrosani	Rom	2	2	1	0	1	2	3	-1	0	1.000	1.000
20	PAOK Salonika	Gre	2	2	1	0	1	1	2	-1	0	1.000	0.500
21	Waregem	Bel	2	2	1	0	1	3	5	-2	0	1.000	1.500
22	Gwardia Warsaw	Pol	2	4	1	0	3	4	11	-7	0	0.500	1.000
23	Finn Harps	Irl	1	2	0	1	1	2	4	-2	0	0.500	1.000
24	Monaco	Fra	1	2	0	1	1	2	5	-3	0	0.500	1.000
25	CSKA Sofia	Bul	0	2	0	0	2	0	2	-2	0	0.000	0.000
26	Cardiff City	Wal	0	2	0	0	2	1	6	-5	0	0.000	0.500
27	Vanløse IF	Den	0	2	0	0	2	1	8	-7	0	0.000	0.500
28	Fram Reykjavik	Isl	0	2	0	0	2	0	8	-8	0	0.000	0.000
29	Avenir Beggen	Lux	0	2	0	0	2	2	11	-9	0	0.000	1.000
30	Strømgodset IF	Nor	0	2	0	0	2	0	12	-12	0	0.000	0.000
31	Ards	Nir	0	2	0	0	2	1	14	-13	0	0.000	0.500
	Total		**132**	**118**	**47**	**24**	**47**	**177**	**177**	**0**	**14**	**1.119**	**3.000**

First Round

Team 1	Cnty	Team 2	Cnty	1st leg	2nd leg	Agg
Derby County	Eng	Servette	Sui	4-1	2-1	6-2
Ipswich Town	Eng	Twente Enschede	Ned	2-2	1-1	3-3
Stoke City	Eng	Ajax	Ned	1-1	0-0	1-1
Sturm Graz	Aut	Antwerp	Bel	2-1	0-1	2-2
FC Tirol	Aut	Bor. Mönchengladbach	FRG	2-1	0-3	2-4
Rapid Vienna	Aut	Aris Salonika	Gre	3-1	0-1	3-2
RWD Molenbeek	Bel	Dundee	Sco	1-0	4-2	5-2
Lokomotiv Plovdiv	Bul	Rába ETO	Hun	3-1	1-3	4-4
Etar Veliko Tarnovo	Bul	Inter Milan	Ita	0-0	0-3	0-3
KB Copenhagen	Den	Atlético Madrid	Esp	3-2	0-4	3-6
Randers Freja FC	Den	Dynamo Dresden	GDR	1-1	0-0	1-1
Real Sociedad	Esp	Banik Ostrava	Tch	0-1	0-4	0-5
Olympique Lyon	Fra	Red Boys Differdange	Lux	7-0	4-1	11-1
Nantes	Fra	Legia Warsaw	Pol	2-2	1-0	3-2
Valur Reykjavik	Isl	Portadown	Nir	0-0	1-2	1-2
Napoli	Ita	Videoton	Hun	2-0	1-1	3-1
Torino	Ita	Fortuna Düsseldorf	FRG	1-1	1-3	2-4
IK Start	Nor	Djurgården SIF	Swe	1-2	0-5	1-7
Rosenborg BK	Nor	Hibernian	Sco	2-3	1-9	3 -12
FC Amsterdam	Ned	Hibernians	Mlt	5-0	7-0	12-0
Górnik Zabrze	Pol	Partizan Belgrade	Yug	2-2	0-3	2-5
FC Porto	Por	Wolverhampton Wanderers	Eng	4-1	1-3	5-4
Vitória Setúbal	Por	Real Zaragoza	Esp	1-1	0-4	1-5
Cologne	FRG	KPV Kokkola	Fin	5-1	4-1	9-2
Hamburg	FRG	Bohemians	Irl	3-0	1-0	4-0
Öster SIF	Swe	Dinamo Moscow	URS	3-2	1-2	4-4
Grasshoppers Zürich	Sui	Panathinaikos	Gre	2-0	1-2	3-2
Boluspor	Tur	Dinamo Bucharest	Rom	0-1	0-3	0-4
Besiktas	Tur	Red Flag Brasov	Rom	2-0	0-3	2-3
Spartak Moscow	URS	Velez Mostar	Yug	3-1	0-2	3-3
Vorwärts Frankfurt/Oder	GDR	Juventus	Ita	2-1	0-3	2-4

	Pts	P	W	D	L	F	A	Diff	Goals/P
Total	124	62	49	26	49	201	201	0	3.242

Second Round

Derby County	Eng	Atlético Madrid	Esp	2-2	2-2	4-4
Rapid Vienna	Aut	Mostar Velez	Yug	1-1	0-1	1-2
Hibernian	Sco	Juventus	Ita	2-4	0-4	2-8
Nantes	Fra	Banik Ostrava	Tch	1-0	0-2	1-2
Rába ETO	Hun	Fortuna Düsseldorf	FRG	2-0	0-3	2-3
Inter Milan	Ita	FC Amsterdam	Ned	1-2	0-0	1-2
Napoli	Ita	FC Porto	Por	1-0	1-0	2-0
Ajax	Ned	Antwerp	Bel	1-0	1-2	2-2
Twente Enschede	Ned	RWD Molenbeek	Bel	2-1	1-0	3-1
Hamburg	FRG	Red Flag Brasov	Rom	8-0	2-1	10-1
Bor. Mönchengladbach	FRG	Olympique Lyon	Fra	1-0	5-2	6-2
Dinamo Bucharest	Rom	Cologne	FRG	1-1	2-3	3-4
Djurgården SIF	Swe	Dukla Prague	Tch	0-2	1-3	1-5
Grasshoppers Zürich	Sui	Real Zaragoza	Esp	2-1	0-5	2-6
Partizan Belgrade	Yug	Portadown	Nir	5-0	1-1	6-1
Dynamo Dresden	GDR	Dinamo Moscow	URS	1-0	0-1	1-1

	Pts	P	W	D	L	F	A	Diff	Goals/P
Total	64	32	26	12	26	91	91	0	2.844

Third Round

Derby County	Eng	Mostar Velez	Yug	3-1	1-4	4-5
Napoli	Ita	Banik Ostrava	Tch	0-2	1-1	1-3
Juventus	Ita	Ajax	Ned	1-0	1-2	2-2
FC Amsterdam	Ned	Fortuna Düsseldorf	FRG	3-0	2-1	5-1
Hamburg	FRG	Dynamo Dresden	GDR	4-1	2-2	6-3
Bor. Mönchengladbach	FRG	Real Zaragoza	Esp	5-0	4-2	9-2
Dukla Prague	Tch	Twente Enschede	Ned	3-1	0-5	3-6
Partizan Belgrade	Yug	Cologne	FRG	1-0	1-5	2-5

	Pts	P	W	D	L	F	A	Diff	Goals/P
Total	32	16	14	4	14	59	59	0	3.688

Quarter Finals

Juventus	Ita	Hamburg	FRG	2-0	0-0	2-0
Cologne	FRG	FC Amsterdam	Ned	5-1	3-2	8-3
Banik Ostrava	Tch	Bor. Mönchengladbach	FRG	0-1	1-3	1-4
Mostar Velez	Yug	Twente Enschede	Ned	1-0	0-2	1-2

	Pts	P	W	D	L	F	A	Diff	Goals/P
Total	16	8	7	2	7	21	21	0	2.625

Semi Finals

Twente Enschede	Ned	Juventus	Ita	3-1	1-0	4-1
Cologne	FRG	Bor. Mönchengladbach	FRG	1-3	0-1	1-4

	Pts	P	W	D	L	F	A	Diff	Goals/P
Total	8	4	4	0	4	10	10	0	2.500

Final

Bor. Mönchengladbach	FRG	Twente Enschede	Ned	0-0	5-1	5-1

	Pts	P	W	D	L	F	A	Diff	Goals/P
Total	4	2	1	2	1	6	6	0	3.000

	Pts	P	W	D	L	F	A	Diff	Goals/P
Total	248	124	101	46	101	388	388	0	3.129

Pos'n	Club	Cnty	Pts	P	W	D	L	F	A	Diff	B	Pts/P	F/P
1	Bor. Mönchengladbach	FRG	24	12	10	1	1	32	9	23	3	2.000	2.667
2	Twente Enschede	Ned	18	12	6	3	3	19	14	5	3	1.500	1.583
3	Cologne	FRG	15	10	6	1	3	27	14	13	2	1.500	2.700
4	Hamburg	FRG	13	8	5	2	1	20	6	14	1	1.625	2.500
5	Juventus	Ita	13	10	5	1	4	17	10	7	2	1.300	1.700
6	FC Amsterdam	Ned	12	8	5	1	2	22	10	12	1	1.500	2.750
7	Banik Ostrava	Tch	10	8	4	1	3	11	6	5	1	1.250	1.375
8	Velez Mostar	Yug	10	8	4	1	3	11	10	1	1	1.250	1.375
9	Partizan Belgrade	Yug	8	6	3	2	1	13	8	5	0	1.333	2.167
10	Derby County	Eng	8	6	3	2	1	14	11	3	0	1.333	2.333
11	Napoli	Ita	8	6	3	2	1	6	4	2	0	1.333	1.000
12	Dukla Prague	Tch	6	4	3	0	1	8	7	1	0	1.500	2.000
13	Ajax	Ned	6	6	2	2	2	5	5	0	0	1.000	0.833
14	Dinamo Bucharest	Rom	5	4	2	1	1	7	4	3	0	1.250	1.750
15	Real Zaragoza	Esp	5	6	2	1	3	13	12	1	0	0.833	2.167
16	Nantes	Fra	5	4	2	1	1	4	4	0	0	1.250	1.000
17	Fortuna Düsseldorf	FRG	5	6	2	1	3	8	9	-1	0	0.833	1.333
18	Dynamo Dresden	GDR	5	6	1	3	2	5	8	-3	0	0.833	0.833
19	Olympique Lyon	Fra	4	4	2	0	2	13	7	6	0	1.000	3.250
20	Hibernian	Sco	4	4	2	0	2	14	11	3	0	1.000	3.500
21	Atlético Madrid	Esp	4	4	1	2	1	10	7	3	0	1.000	2.500
22	Djurgården SIF	Swe	4	4	2	0	2	8	6	2	0	1.000	2.000
23	Inter Milan	Ita	4	4	1	2	1	4	2	2	0	1.000	1.000
24	RWD Molenbeek	Bel	4	4	2	0	2	6	5	1	0	1.000	1.500
25	Dinamo Moscow	URS	4	4	2	0	2	5	5	0	0	1.000	1.250
26	Antwerp	Bel	4	4	2	0	2	4	4	0	0	1.000	1.000
27	Rába ETO	Hun	4	4	2	0	2	6	7	-1	0	1.000	1.500
28	Grasshoppers Zürich	Sui	4	4	2	0	2	5	8	-3	0	1.000	1.250
29	Portadown	Nir	4	4	1	2	1	3	7	-4	0	1.000	0.750
30	Rapid Vienna	Aut	3	4	1	1	2	4	4	0	0	0.750	1.000
31	Lokomotiv Plovdiv	Bul	2	2	1	0	1	4	4	0	0	1.000	2.000
–	Öster SIF	Swe	2	2	1	0	1	4	4	0	0	1.000	2.000
33	Ipswich Town	Eng	2	2	0	2	0	3	3	0	0	1.000	1.500
–	Spartak Moscow	URS	2	2	1	0	1	3	3	0	0	1.000	1.500
35	Sturm Graz	Aut	2	2	1	0	1	2	2	0	0	1.000	1.000
36	Stoke City	Eng	2	2	0	2	0	1	1	0	0	1.000	0.500
–	Randers Freja FC	Den	2	2	0	2	0	1	1	0	0	1.000	0.500
38	FC Porto	Por	2	4	1	0	3	5	6	-1	0	0.500	1.250
39	Wolverhampton Wanderers	Eng	2	2	1	0	1	4	5	-1	0	1.000	2.000
40	Panathinaikos	Gre	2	2	1	0	1	2	3	-1	0	1.000	1.000
–	Aris Salonika	Gre	2	2	1	0	1	2	3	-1	0	1.000	1.000
–	Besiktas	Tur	2	2	1	0	1	2	3	-1	0	1.000	1.000
43	FC Tirol	Aut	2	2	1	0	1	2	4	-2	0	1.000	1.000
–	Vorwärts Frankfurt/Oder	GDR	2	2	1	0	1	2	4	-2	0	1.000	1.000
45	KB Copenhagen	Den	2	2	1	0	1	3	6	-3	0	1.000	1.500
46	Red Flag Brasov	Rom	2	4	1	0	3	4	12	-8	0	0.500	1.000
47	Legia Warsaw	Pol	1	2	0	1	1	2	3	-1	0	0.500	1.000
48	Valur Reykjavik	Isl	1	2	0	1	1	1	2	-1	0	0.500	0.500
49	Torino	Ita	1	2	0	1	1	2	4	-2	0	0.500	1.000
50	Videoton	Hun	1	2	0	1	1	1	3	-2	0	0.500	0.500
51	Górnik Zabrze	Pol	1	2	0	1	1	2	5	-3	0	0.500	1.000
52	Etar Veliko Tarnovo	Bul	1	2	0	1	1	0	3	-3	0	0.500	0.000
53	Vitória Setúbal	Por	1	2	0	1	1	1	5	-4	0	0.500	0.500
54	Dundee	Sco	0	2	0	0	2	2	5	-3	0	0.000	1.000
55	Servette	Sui	0	2	0	0	2	2	6	-4	0	0.000	1.000
56	Bohemians	Irl	0	2	0	0	2	0	4	-4	0	0.000	0.000
–	Boluspor	Tur	0	2	0	0	2	0	4	-4	0	0.000	0.000
58	Real Sociedad	Esp	0	2	0	0	2	0	5	-5	0	0.000	0.000
59	IK Start	Nor	0	2	0	0	2	1	7	-6	0	0.000	0.500
60	KPV Kokkola	Fin	0	2	0	0	2	2	9	-7	0	0.000	1.000
61	Rosenborg BK	Nor	0	2	0	0	2	3	12	-9	0	0.000	1.500
62	Red Boys Differdange	Lux	0	2	0	0	2	1	11	-10	0	0.000	0.500
63	Hibernians	Mlt	0	2	0	0	2	0	12	-12	0	0.000	0.000
	Total		**262**	**248**	**101**	**46**	**101**	**388**	**388**	**0**	**14**	**1.056**	**3.129**

1974-75

Pos'n	Cnty	Pts	P	W	D	L	F	A	Diff	B	Pts/P	F/P
1	FRG	74	47	29	7	11	106	49	57	9	1.574	2.255
2	Ned	56	38	21	8	9	83	40	43	6	1.474	2.184
3	Eng	36	25	12	9	4	52	29	23	3	1.440	2.080
4	URS	36	21	16	0	5	39	18	21	4	1.714	1.857
5	Yug	35	26	14	4	8	56	34	22	3	1.346	2.154
6	Esp	32	26	11	7	8	53	31	22	3	1.231	2.038
7	Ita	28	24	10	6	8	32	23	9	2	1.167	1.333
8	Hun	24	19	8	5	6	30	26	4	3	1.263	1.579
9	Tch	20	16	9	1	6	25	19	6	1	1.250	1.563
10	Fra	20	18	7	4	7	32	27	5	2	1.111	1.778
11	Swe	20	18	8	2	8	26	24	2	2	1.111	1.444
12	Bel	15	16	7	0	9	23	27	-4	1	0.938	1.438
13	Pol	14	14	5	3	6	17	25	-8	1	1.000	1.214
14	Tur	13	14	5	2	7	13	18	-5	1	0.929	0.929
15	Por	12	14	3	5	6	17	18	-1	1	0.857	1.214
16	Gre	11	10	5	1	4	12	14	-2	0	1.100	1.200
17	Rom	11	12	5	1	6	16	23	-7	0	0.917	1.333
18	GDR	11	14	3	5	6	12	19	-7	0	0.786	0.857
19	Aut	11	14	4	3	7	15	23	-8	0	0.786	1.071
20	Sco	8	12	3	2	7	20	22	-2	0	0.667	1.667
21	Sui	8	10	4	0	6	11	20	-9	0	0.800	1.100
22	Fin	5	10	2	1	7	11	21	-10	0	0.500	1.100
23	Den	5	8	1	3	4	6	17	-11	0	0.625	0.750
24	Mlt	4	6	2	0	4	5	20	-15	0	0.667	0.833
25	Nir	4	8	1	2	5	5	32	-27	0	0.500	0.625
26	Bul	3	8	1	1	6	5	16	-11	0	0.375	0.625
27	Irl	1	6	0	1	5	3	15	-12	0	0.167	0.500
28	Isl	1	6	0	1	5	2	19	-17	0	0.167	0.333
29	Wal	0	2	0	0	2	1	6	-5	0	0.000	0.500
30	Lux	0	6	0	0	6	5	27	-22	0	0.000	0.833
31	Nor	0	8	0	0	8	6	37	-31	0	0.000	0.750
	Total	**518**	**476**	**196**	**84**	**196**	**739**	**739**	**0**	**42**	**1.088**	**3.105**

1955-56 to 1974-75

Pos'n	Cnty	Pts	P	W	D	L	F	A	Diff	B	Pts/P	F/P
1	Eng	852	571	311	126	134	1126	586	540	104	1.492	1.972
2	Esp	761	538	283	98	157	1068	661	407	97	1.414	1.985
3	Ita	706	498	256	109	133	827	515	312	85	1.418	1.661
4	FRG	658	485	250	88	147	994	673	321	70	1.357	2.049
5	Sco	479	377	187	58	132	691	517	174	47	1.271	1.833
6	Yug	381	348	137	67	144	576	524	52	40	1.095	1.655
7	Ned	375	286	143	50	93	555	371	184	39	1.311	1.941
8	Por	364	312	134	65	113	534	413	121	31	1.167	1.712
9	Hun	346	280	131	46	103	539	399	140	38	1.236	1.925
10	Bel	291	276	120	31	125	446	417	29	20	1.054	1.616
11	Tch	270	229	104	39	86	365	306	59	23	1.179	1.594
12	GDR	247	228	91	48	89	336	293	43	17	1.083	1.474
13	Fra	226	238	84	43	111	350	386	-36	15	0.950	1.471
14	Pol	183	165	73	26	66	255	242	13	11	1.109	1.545
15	Rom	172	183	67	33	83	232	302	-70	5	0.940	1.268
16	Bul	171	173	66	30	77	278	265	13	9	0.988	1.607
17	Sui	158	205	58	31	116	304	452	-148	11	0.771	1.483
18	Aut	153	184	56	34	94	226	320	-94	7	0.832	1.228
19	URS	148	109	58	21	30	164	105	59	11	1.358	1.505
20	Gre	117	137	42	28	67	154	254	-100	5	0.854	1.124
21	Swe	111	134	38	30	66	181	259	-78	5	0.828	1.351
22	Tur	110	143	40	24	79	152	245	-93	6	0.769	1.063
23	Den	99	155	33	29	93	214	362	-148	4	0.639	1.381
24	Wal	53	50	17	15	18	70	64	6	4	1.060	1.400
25	Nor	53	102	20	12	70	110	280	-170	1	0.520	1.078
26	Nir	51	94	15	19	60	109	279	-170	2	0.543	1.160
27	Irl	41	104	14	13	77	91	285	-194	0	0.394	0.875
28	Lux	28	96	10	8	78	73	401	-328	0	0.292	0.760
29	Mlt	26	76	9	8	59	38	250	-212	0	0.342	0.500
30	Fin	23	70	8	7	55	52	232	-180	0	0.329	0.743
31	Alb	16	26	3	10	13	18	41	-23	0	0.615	0.692
32	Isl	10	56	1	8	47	32	245	-213	0	0.179	0.571
33	Cyp	8	52	2	4	46	22	238	-216	0	0.154	0.423
	Total	**7687**	**6980**	**2861**	**1258**	**2861**	**11182**	**11182**	**0**	**707**	**1.101**	**3.204**

1974-75

Pos'n	Cnty	Ave	Pts	P	W	D	L	F	A	Diff	B	No./T
1	W. Germany	12.333	74	47	29	7	11	106	49	57	9	6
2	Netherlands	11.200	56	38	21	8	9	83	40	43	6	5
3	USSR	9.000	36	21	16	0	5	39	18	21	4	4
4	Yugoslavia	8.750	35	26	14	4	8	56	34	22	3	4
5	Spain	6.400	32	26	11	7	8	53	31	22	3	5
6	England	6.000	36	25	12	9	4	52	29	23	3	6
–	Hungary	6.000	24	19	8	5	6	30	26	4	3	4
8	Italy	5.600	28	24	10	6	8	32	23	9	2	5
9	France	5.000	20	18	7	4	7	32	27	5	2	4
–	Sweden	5.000	20	18	8	2	8	26	24	2	2	4
–	Czechoslovakia	5.000	20	16	9	1	6	25	19	6	1	4
12	Belgium	3.750	15	16	7	0	9	23	27	-4	1	4
13	Poland	3.500	14	14	5	3	6	17	25	-8	1	4
14	Turkey	3.250	13	14	5	2	7	13	18	-5	1	4
15	Portugal	3.000	12	14	3	5	6	17	18	-1	1	4
16	Greece	2.750	11	10	5	1	4	12	14	-2	0	4
–	Romania	2.750	11	12	5	1	6	16	23	-7	0	4
–	E. Germany	2.750	11	14	3	5	6	12	19	-7	0	4
19	Austria	2.200	11	14	4	3	7	15	23	-8	0	5
20	Scotland	2.000	8	12	3	2	7	20	22	-2	0	4
–	Switzerland	2.000	8	10	4	0	6	11	20	-9	0	4
22	Finland	1.666	5	10	2	1	7	11	21	-10	0	3
23	N. Ireland	1.333	4	8	1	2	5	5	32	-27	0	3
–	Malta	1.333	4	6	2	0	4	5	20	-15	0	3
25	Denmark	1.250	5	8	1	3	4	6	17	-11	0	4
26	Bulgaria	0.750	3	8	1	1	6	5	16	-11	0	4
27	Rep. of Ireland	0.333	1	6	0	1	5	3	15	-12	0	3
–	Iceland	0.333	1	6	0	1	5	2	19	-17	0	3
29	Wales	0.000	0	2	0	0	2	1	6	-5	0	1
–	Luxembourg	0.000	0	6	0	0	6	5	27	-22	0	3
–	Norway	0.000	0	8	0	0	8	6	37	-31	0	4
	Total		**518**	**476**	**196**	**84**	**196**	**739**	**739**	**0**	**42**	**3.105**

1955-56 to 1974-75

1	England	9.466	852	571	311	126	134	1126	586	540	104	90
2	Spain	8.010	761	538	283	98	157	1068	661	407	97	95
3	Italy	7.758	706	498	256	109	133	827	515	312	85	91
4	W. Germany	7.000	658	485	250	88	147	994	673	321	70	94
5	Scotland	6.302	479	377	187	58	132	691	517	174	47	76
6	Hungary	6.290	346	280	131	46	103	539	399	140	38	55
7	Netherlands	6.250	375	286	143	50	93	555	371	184	39	60
8	USSR	6.166	148	109	58	21	30	164	105	59	11	24
9	Portugal	4.918	364	312	134	65	113	534	413	121	31	74
10	Czechoslovakia	4.821	270	229	104	39	86	365	306	59	23	56
11	Yugoslavia	4.762	381	348	137	67	144	576	524	52	40	80
12	E. Germany	4.574	247	228	91	48	89	336	293	43	17	54
13	Poland	4.255	183	165	73	26	66	255	242	13	11	43
14	Belgium	4.217	291	276	120	31	125	446	417	29	20	69
15	Wales	3.785	53	50	17	15	18	70	64	6	4	14
16	Bulgaria	3.420	171	173	66	30	77	278	265	13	9	50
17	Romania	3.245	172	183	67	33	83	232	302	-70	5	53
18	France	3.183	226	238	84	43	111	350	386	-36	15	71
19	Austria	2.684	153	184	56	34	94	226	320	-94	7	57
20	Sweden	2.466	111	134	38	30	66	181	259	-78	5	45
21	Turkey	2.444	110	143	40	24	79	152	245	-93	6	45
22	Greece	2.387	117	137	42	28	67	154	254	-100	5	49
23	Switzerland	2.323	158	205	58	31	116	304	452	-148	11	68
24	Denmark	1.677	99	155	33	29	93	214	362	-148	4	59
25	Albania	1.454	16	26	3	10	13	18	41	-23	0	11
26	N. Ireland	1.275	51	94	15	19	60	109	279	-170	2	40
27	Norway	1.261	53	102	20	12	70	110	280	-170	1	42
28	Rep. of Ireland	0.911	41	104	14	13	77	91	285	-194	0	45
29	Malta	0.742	26	76	9	8	59	38	250	-212	0	35
30	Finland	0.741	23	70	8	7	55	52	232	-180	0	31
31	Luxembourg	0.622	28	96	10	8	78	73	401	-328	0	45
32	Iceland	0.370	10	56	1	8	47	32	245	-213	0	27
33	Cyprus	0.333	8	52	2	4	46	22	238	-216	0	24
	Total		**7687**	**6980**	**2861**	**1258**	**2861**	**11182**	**11182**	**0**	**707**	**3.204**

Leeds Bow Out to Bayern

Bayern Munich became the fifth club to make a successful defence of the Champions' Cup when they defeated Leeds United 2-0 in Paris. Their victory, however, was an extremely contentious one. Leeds, the first English team to reach the Champions' Cup final since Manchester United in 1968, were denied two clear-cut penalties and also had a goal harshly ruled out by the French referee when the score stood at 0-0.

Bayern did score two fine goals in the last 20 minutes, through Franz Roth and Gerd Müller, to win the game, but what had gone before left a distinctly bitter taste in the mouth. Certainly, the thousands of Leeds United fans massed behind one of the goals could not contain their sense of injustice. They tore up seats and hurled them on to the pitch, injuring several innocent bystanders. But their behaviour simply added to the pain of defeat. UEFA, having gathered together all the evidence, banned Leeds from competing in Europe for the next three years.

The Yorkshire club subsequently made just one further appearance in European competition, in the 1979-80 UEFA Cup, but, to all intents, the sad drama of Paris had brought about the end of an era. There were grounds for considering Leeds as the foremost English club in the early years of the European competitions. They had been competing in Europe for ten years without a break and had reached five finals in that time, becoming the first English club to reach the finals of all three competitions.

The only other club to have achieved that feat before Leeds were Barcelona, and it was they whom Leeds overcame to reach the final in Paris. Goals from Billy Bremner and Allan Clarke gave them a 2-1 win in the first leg and they survived the attacking threat of a team containing former Ajax stars Cruijff and Neeskens to earn a 1-1 draw in the Nou Camp.

Bayern made fairly light work of Saint-Etienne in their semi-final, but, the majestic Beckenbauer and free-scoring Müller apart, they had not been particularly impressive in their previous confrontations against Magdeburg and Ararat Erevan. The replacement of former coach Udo Lattek with the less adventurous Dettmar Cramer had not been a popular move, but in a season when Bayern finished a miserable tenth in the Bundesliga (their worst ever placing), the Champions' Cup proved to be the club's, and the coach's, salvation.

Borussia Mönchengladbach were the new domestic kings in West Germany, winning the 1974-75 championship by six clear points, and they secured a unique double by adding the UEFA Cup, a trophy they had come close to winning two years earlier when they narrowly lost the final to Liverpool.

This time, however, after powering their way to the final with nine straight wins, they became West Germany's first winners of the competition by crushing Dutch club Twente Enschede 5-1 on aggregate. All the goals, surprisingly, were scored in the second leg in Netherlands, where Borussia simply overran the team that had dared to hold them to a goalless draw in Mönchengladbach. A hat-trick for Jupp Heynckes, plus two goals for Danish international Allan Simonsen, wrapped the tie up comprehensively for the Germans.

There was to be no West German hat-trick, though. Eintracht Frankfurt only lasted until the second round of the Cup-winners' Cup. But at least they had the consolation of being eliminated by the eventual winners, Dinamo Kiev.

Kiev won both games against Frankfurt and held a 100% record in the competition until they lost the second leg of their semi-final 2-1 against PSV Eindhoven. But that was irrelevant as they had already won the first leg 3-0 to become the second Soviet team, after Dinamo Moscow four years earlier, to make it into a European final. Their opponents, Ferencváros, were in their third European final (a record for a club from the Eastern bloc) but they were helpless bystanders in Basle as the powerful Ukrainians tore them apart, led by dynamic strikers Onishenko and Blokhin. The latter, who made the final score 3-0 after Onishenko had hit two goals in the first half, was later voted European Footballer of the Year for 1975, beating no lesser names than Beckenbauer and Cruijff into second and third place.

1975 - 1976

Bayern Munich

Anderlecht

Liverpool

European Cup 1975-76

First Round

Team 1	Cnty	Team 2	Cnty	1st leg	2nd leg	Agg
RWD Molenbeek	Bel	IL Viking	Nor	3-2	1-0	4-2
CSKA Sofia	Bul	Juventus	Ita	2-1	0-2	2-3
Omonia Nicosia	Cyp	IA Akranes	Isl	2-1	0-4	2-5
KB Copenhagen	Den	Saint-Etienne	Fra	0-2	1-3	1-5
Rangers	Sco	Bohemians	Irl	4-1	1-1	5-2
Real Madrid	Esp	Dinamo Bucharest	Rom	4-1	0-1	4-2
Olympiakos Pireus	Gre	Dinamo Kiev	URS	2-2	0-1	2-3
Ujpesti Dózsa	Hun	FC Zürich	Sui	4-0	1-5	5-5
Linfield	Nir	PSV Eindhoven	Ned	1-2	0-8	1-10
Jeunesse Esch	Lux	Bayern Munich	FRG	0-5	1-3	1-8
Floriana	Mlt	Hajduk Split	Yug	0-5	0-3	0-8
Ruch Chorzów	Pol	KuPS Kuopio	Fin	5-0	2-2	7-2
Benfica	Por	Fenerbahçe	Tur	7-0	0-1	7-1
Bor. Mönchengladbach	FRG	FC Tirol	Aut	1-1	6-1	7- 2
Malmö FF	Swe	Magdeburg	GDR	2-1	1-2	3-3
Slovan Bratislava	Tch	Derby County	Eng	1-0	0-3	1-3

	Pts	P	W	D	L	F	A	Diff	Goals/P
Total	64	32	28	8	28	116	116	0	3.625

Second Round

Derby County	Eng	Real Madrid	Esp	4-1	1-5	5-6
Saint-Etienne	Fra	Rangers	Sco	2-0	2-1	4-1
Ruch Chorzów	Pol	PSV Eindhoven	Ned	1-3	0-4	1-7
Benfica	Por	Ujpesti Dózsa	Hun	5-2	1-3	6-5
Bor. Mönchengladbach	FRG	Juventus	Ita	2-0	2-2	4-2
Malmö FF	Swe	Bayern Munich	FRG	1-0	0-2	1-2
Dinamo Kiev	URS	IA Akranes	Isl	3-0	2-0	5-0
Hajduk Split	Yug	RWD Molenbeek	Bel	4-0	3-2	7-2

	Pts	P	W	D	L	F	A	Diff	Goals/P
Total	32	16	15	2	15	58	58	0	3.625

Quarter Finals

Benfica	Por	Bayern Munich	FRG	0-0	1-5	1-5
Bor. Mönchengladbach	FRG	Real Madrid	Esp	2-2	1-1	3-3
Dinamo Kiev	URS	Saint-Etienne	Fra	2-0	0-3	2-3
Hajduk Split	Yug	PSV Eindhoven	Ned	2-0	0-3	2-3

	Pts	P	W	D	L	F	A	Diff	Goals/P
Total	16	8	5	6	5	22	22	0	2.750

Semi Finals

Real Madrid	Esp	Bayern Munich	FRG	1-1	0-2	1-3
Saint-Etienne	Fra	PSV Eindhoven	Ned	1-0	0-0	1-0

	Pts	P	W	D	L	F	A	Diff	Goals/P
Total	8	4	2	4	2	5	5	0	1.250

Final

Bayern Munich	FRG	Saint-Etienne	Fra	1-0	1-0

	Pts	P	W	D	L	F	A	Diff	Goals/P
Total	2	1	1	0	1	1	1	0	1.000

	Pts	P	W	D	L	F	A	Diff	Goals/P
Total	122	61	51	20	51	202	202	0	3.311

Pos'n	Club	Cnty	Pts	P	W	D	L	F	A	Diff	B	Pts/P	F/P
1	Bayern Munich	FRG	17	9	6	2	1	19	4	15	3	1.889	2.111
2	Saint-Etienne	Fra	16	9	6	1	2	13	5	8	3	1.778	1.444
3	PSV Eindhoven	Ned	13	8	5	1	2	20	5	15	2	1.625	2.500
4	Hajduk Split	Yug	11	6	5	0	1	17	5	12	1	1.833	2.833
5	Dinamo Kiev	URS	10	6	4	1	1	10	5	5	1	1.667	1.667
6	Bor. Mönchengladbach	FRG	9	6	2	4	0	14	7	7	1	1.500	2.333
7	Real Madrid	Esp	9	8	2	3	3	14	13	1	2	1.125	1.750
8	Benfica	Por	6	6	2	1	3	14	11	3	1	1.000	2.333
9	Derby County	Eng	4	4	2	0	2	8	7	1	0	1.000	2.000
10	Ujpesti Dózsa	Hun	4	4	2	0	2	10	11	-1	0	1.000	2.500
11	Malmö FF	Swe	4	4	2	0	2	4	5	-1	0	1.000	1.000
12	RWD Molenbeek	Bel	4	4	2	0	2	6	9	-3	0	1.000	1.500
13	Rangers	Sco	3	4	1	1	2	6	6	0	0	0.750	1.500
14	Ruch Chorzów	Pol	3	4	1	1	2	8	9	-1	0	0.750	2.000
15	Juventus	Ita	3	4	1	1	2	5	6	-1	0	0.750	1.250
16	FC Zürich	Sui	2	2	1	0	1	5	5	0	0	1.000	2.500
17	Magdeburg	GDR	2	2	1	0	1	3	3	0	0	1.000	1.500
18	CSKA Sofia	Bul	2	2	1	0	1	2	3	-1	0	1.000	1.000
19	IA Akranes	Isl	2	4	1	0	3	5	7	-2	0	0.500	1.250
20	Dinamo Bucharest	Rom	2	2	1	0	1	2	4	-2	0	1.000	1.000
21	Slovan Bratislava	Tch	2	2	1	0	1	1	3	-2	0	1.000	0.500
22	Omonia Nicosia	Cyp	2	2	1	0	1	2	5	-3	0	1.000	1.000
23	Fenerbahçe	Tur	2	2	1	0	1	1	7	-6	0	1.000	0.500
24	Olympiakos Pireus	Gre	1	2	0	1	1	2	3	-1	0	0.500	1.000
25	Bohemians	Irl	1	2	0	1	1	2	5	-3	0	0.500	1.000
26	FC Tirol	Aut	1	2	0	1	1	2	7	-5	0	0.500	1.000
–	KuPS Kuopio	Fin	1	2	0	1	1	2	7	-5	0	0.500	1.000
28	IL Viking	Nor	0	2	0	0	2	2	4	-2	0	0.000	1.000
29	KB Copenhagen	Den	0	2	0	0	2	1	5	-4	0	0.000	0.500
30	Jeunesse Esch	Lux	0	2	0	0	2	1	8	-7	0	0.000	0.500
31	Floriana	Mlt	0	2	0	0	2	0	8	-8	0	0.000	0.000
32	Linfield	Nir	0	2	0	0	2	1	10	-9	0	0.000	0.500
	Total		**136**	**122**	**51**	**20**	**51**	**202**	**202**	**0**	**14**	**1.115**	**3.311**

European Cup Winners Cup 1975-76

First Round

Team 1	Cnty	Team 2	Cnty	1st leg	2nd leg	Agg
Sturm Graz	Aut	Slavia Sofia	Bul	3-1	0-1	3-2
Vejle BK	Den	FC Den Haag	Ned	0-2	0-2	0-4
Home Farm	Irl	Lens	Fra	1-1	0-6	1-7
Reipas Lahti	Fin	West Ham United	Eng	2-2	0-3	2- 5
Wrexham	Wal	Djurgården SIF	Swe	2-1	1-1	3-2
Panathinaikos	Gre	Sachsenning Zwickau	GDR	0-0	0-2	0-2
Haladás	Hun	Valletta	Mlt	7-0	1-1	8-1
Valur Reykjavik	Isl	Celtic	Sco	0-2	0-7	0-9
FK Skeid	Nor	Stal Rzeszów	Pol	1-4	0-4	1-8
Eintracht Frankfurt	FRG	Coleraine	Nir	5-1	6-2	11-3
Rapid Bucharest	Rom	Anderlecht	Bel	1-0	0-2	1-2
FC Basle	Sui	Atlético Madrid	Esp	1-2	1-1	2-3
Spartak Trnava	Tch	Boavista	Por	0-0	0-3	0-3
Besiktas	Tur	Fiorentina	Ita	0-3	0-3	0-6
Ararat Erevan	URS	Anorthosis Famagusta	Cyp	9-0	1-1	10-1
Borac Banja Luka	Yug	US Rumelange	Lux	9-0	5-1	14-1

	Pts	P	W	D	L	F	A	Diff	Goals/P
Total	64	32	24	16	24	115	115	0	3.594

Second Round

Sturm Graz	Aut	Haladás	Hun	2-0	1-1	3-1
Anderlecht	Bel	Borac Banja Luka	Yug	3-0	0-1	3-1
Atlético Madrid	Esp	Eintracht Frankfurt	FRG	1-2	0-1	1-3
Wrexham	Wal	Stal Rzeszów	Pol	2-0	1-1	3-1
Fiorentina	Ita	Sachsenning Zwickau	GDR	1-0	0-1	1-1
FC Den Haag	Ned	Lens	Fra	3-2	3-1	6-3
Boavista	Por	Celtic	Sco	0-0	1-3	1-3
Ararat Erevan	URS	West Ham United	Eng	1-1	1-3	2-4

	Pts	P	W	D	L	F	A	Diff	Goals/P
Total	32	16	12	8	12	37	37	0	2.313

Quarter Finals

Sturm Graz	Aut	Eintracht Frankfurt	FRG	0-2	0-1	0-3
Anderlecht	Bel	Wrexham	Wal	1-0	1-1	2-1
Celtic	Sco	Sachsenning Zwickau	GDR	1-1	0-1	1-2
FC Den Haag	Ned	West Ham United	Eng	4-2	1-3	5-5

	Pts	P	W	D	L	F	A	Diff	Goals/P
Total	16	8	6	4	6	19	19	0	2.375

Semi Finals

Eintracht Frankfurt	FRG	West Ham United	Eng	2-1	1-3	3-4
Sachsenning Zwickau	GDR	Anderlecht	Bel	0-3	0-2	0-5

	Pts	P	W	D	L	F	A	Diff	Goals/P
Total	8	4	4	0	4	12	12	0	3.000

Final

Anderlecht	Bel	West Ham United	Eng	4-2	4-2

	Pts	P	W	D	L	F	A	Diff	Goals/P
Total	2	1	1	0	1	6	6	0	6.000

	Pts	P	W	D	L	F	A	Diff	Goals/P
Total	122	61	47	28	47	189	189	0	3.098

Pos'n	Club	Cnty	Pts	P	W	D	L	F	A	Diff	B	Pts/P	F/P
1	Eintracht Frankfurt	FRG	16	8	7	0	1	20	8	12	2	2.000	2.500
2	Anderlecht	Bel	16	9	6	1	2	16	5	11	3	1.778	1.778
3	West Ham United	Eng	13	9	4	2	3	20	16	4	3	1.444	2.222
4	FC Den Haag	Ned	11	6	5	0	1	15	8	7	1	1.833	2.500
5	Sachsenning Zwickau	GDR	10	8	3	2	3	5	7	-2	2	1.250	0.625
6	Celtic	Sco	9	6	3	2	1	13	3	10	1	1.500	2.167
7	Wrexham	Wal	8	6	2	3	1	7	5	2	1	1.333	1.167
8	Borac Banja Luka	Yug	6	4	3	0	1	15	4	11	0	1.500	3.750
9	Fiorentina	Ita	6	4	3	0	1	7	1	6	0	1.500	1.750
10	Sturm Graz	Aut	6	6	2	1	3	6	6	0	1	1.000	1.000
11	Stal Rzeszów	Pol	5	4	2	1	1	9	4	5	0	1.250	2.250
12	Ararat Erevan	URS	4	4	1	2	1	12	5	7	0	1.000	3.000
13	Haladás	Hun	4	4	1	2	1	9	4	5	0	1.000	2.250
14	Boavista	Por	4	4	1	2	1	4	3	1	0	1.000	1.000
15	Lens	Fra	3	4	1	1	2	10	7	3	0	0.750	2.500
16	Atlético Madrid	Esp	3	4	1	1	2	4	5	-1	0	0.750	1.000
17	Slavia Sofia	Bul	2	2	1	0	1	2	3	-1	0	1.000	1.000
18	Rapid Bucharest	Rom	2	2	1	0	1	1	2	-1	0	1.000	0.500
19	Djurgården SIF	Swe	1	2	0	1	1	2	3	-1	0	0.500	1.000
–	FC Basle	Sui	1	2	0	1	1	2	3	-1	0	0.500	1.000
21	Panathinaikos	Gre	1	2	0	1	1	0	2	-2	0	0.500	0.000
22	Reipas Lahti	Fin	1	2	0	1	1	2	5	-3	0	0.500	1.000
23	Spartak Trnava	Tch	1	2	0	1	1	0	3	-3	0	0.500	0.000
24	Home Farm	Irl	1	2	0	1	1	1	7	-6	0	0.500	0.500
25	Valletta	Mlt	1	2	0	1	1	1	8	-7	0	0.500	0.500
26	Anorthosis Famagusta	Cyp	1	2	0	1	1	1	10	-9	0	0.500	0.500
27	Vejle BK	Den	0	2	0	0	2	0	4	-4	0	0.000	0.000
28	Besiktas	Tur	0	2	0	0	2	0	6	-6	0	0.000	0.000
29	FK Skeid	Nor	0	2	0	0	2	1	8	-7	0	0.000	0.500
30	Coleraine	Nir	0	2	0	0	2	3	11	-8	0	0.000	1.500
31	Valur Reykjavik	Isl	0	2	0	0	2	0	9	-9	0	0.000	0.000
32	US Rumelange	Lux	0	2	0	0	2	1	14	-13	0	0.000	0.500
	Total		**136**	**122**	**47**	**28**	**47**	**189**	**189**	**0**	**14**	**1.115**	**3.098**

First Round

Team 1	Cnty	Team 2	Cnty	1st leg	2nd leg	Agg
Everton	Eng	AC Milan	Ita	0-0	0-1	0-1
Vöest Linz	Aut	Vasas SC	Hun	2-0	0-4	2-4
Rapid Vienna	Aut	Galatasaray	Tur	1-0	1-3	2-3
Antwerp	Bel	Aston Villa	Eng	4-1	1-0	5-1
Levski Sofia	Bul	Eskisehirspor	Tur	3-0	4-1	7-1
Holbaek BIF	Den	Stal Mielec	Pol	0-1	1-2	1-3
Hibernian	Sco	Liverpool	Eng	1-0	1-3	2-3
Athlone Town	Irl	Vålerengen SIF	Nor	3-1	1-1	4-2
Olympique Lyon	Fra	Club Bruges	Bel	4-3	0-3	4-6
PAOK Salonika	Gre	Barcelona	Esp	1-0	1-6	2-6
Glentoran	Nir	Ajax	Ned	1-6	0-8	1-14
IBK Keflavik	Isl	Dundee United	Sco	0-2	0-4	0-6
Roma	Ita	Dunav Ruse	Bul	2-0	0-1	2-1
Sliema Wanderers	Mlt	Sporting Lisbon	Por	1-2	1-3	2-5
Molde FK	Nor	Öster SIF	Swe	1-0	0-6	1-6
Feyenoord	Ned	Ipswich Town	Eng	1-2	0-2	1-4
FC Porto	Por	Avenir Beggen	Lux	7-0	3-0	10-0
Hertha Berlin	FRG	HJK Helsinki	Fin	4-1	2-1	6-2
Cologne	FRG	B 1903 Copenhagen	Den	2-0	3-2	5-2
MSV Duisburg	FRG	Paralimni	Cyp	7-1	3-2	10-3
Universitatea Craiova	Rom	Red Star Belgrade	Yug	1-3	1-1	2-4
ASA Tîrgu Mures	Rom	Dynamo Dresden	GDR	2-2	1-4	3-6
GAIS	Swe	Slask Wroclaw	Pol	2-1	2-4	4-5
AIK	Swe	Spartak Moscow	URS	1-1	0-1	1-2
Young Boys Berne	Sui	Hamburg	FRG	0-0	2-4	2-4
Grasshoppers Zürich	Sui	Real Sociedad	Esp	3-3	1-1	4-4
Inter Bratislava	Tch	Real Zaragoza	Esp	5-0	3-2	8-2
Bohemians Prague	Tch	Honvéd	Hun	1-2	1-1	2-3
Torpedo Moscow	URS	Napoli	Ita	4-1	1-1	5-2
Chernomorets Odessa	URS	Lazio	Ita	1-0	0-3	1-3
Vojvodina Novi Sad	Yug	AEK Athens	Gre	0-0	1-3	1-3
Carl Zeiss Jena	GDR	Olympique Marseille	Fra	3-0	1-0	4-0

	Pts	P	W	D	L	F	A	Diff	Goals/P
Total	128	64	53	22	53	215	215	0	3.359

Second Round

Ipswich Town	Eng	Club Bruges	Bel	3-0	0-4	3-4
Dundee United	Sco	FC Porto	Por	1-2	1-1	2-3
Athlone Town	Irl	AC Milan	Ita	0-0	0-3	0-3
Real Sociedad	Esp	Liverpool	Eng	1-3	0-6	1-9
Honvéd	Hun	Dynamo Dresden	GDR	2-2	0-1	2-3
Vasas SC	Hun	Sporting Lisbon	Por	3-1	1-2	4-3
Lazio	Ita	Barcelona	Esp	0-3	0-4	0-7
Slask Wroclaw	Pol	Antwerp	Bel	1-1	2-1	3-2
Hertha Berlin	FRG	Ajax	Ned	1-0	1-4	2-4
MSV Duisburg	FRG	Levski Sofia	Bul	3-2	1-2	4-4
Öster SIF	Sue	Roma	Ita	1-0	0-2	1-2
Inter Bratislava	Tch	AEK Athens	Gre	2-0	1-3	3-3
Galatasaray	Tur	Torpedo Moscow	URS	2-4	0-3	2-7
Spartak Moscow	URS	Cologne	FRG	2-0	1-0	3-0
Red Star Belgrade	Yug	Hamburg	FRG	1-1	0-4	1-5
Carl Zeiss Jena	GDR	Stal Mielec	Pol	1-0	0-1	1-1

	Pts	P	W	D	L	F	A	Diff	Goals/P
Total	64	32	27	10	27	92	92	0	2.875

Third Round

Club Bruges	Bel	Roma	Ita	1-0	1-0	2-0
Barcelona	Esp	Vasas SC	Hun	3-1	1-0	4-1
AC Milan	Ita	Spartak Moscow	URS	4-0	0-2	4-2
Ajax	Ned	Levski Sofia	Bul	2-1	1-2	3-3
Slask Wroclaw	Pol	Liverpool	Eng	1-2	0-3	1-5
Hamburg	FRG	FC Porto	Por	2-0	1-2	3-2
Inter Bratislava	Tch	Stal Mielec	Pol	1-0	0-2	1-2
Dynamo Dresden	GDR	Torpedo Moscow	URS	3-0	1-3	4-3

	Pts	P	W	D	L	F	A	Diff	Goals/P
Total	32	16	16	0	16	40	40	0	2.500

Quarter Finals

Club Bruges	Bel	AC Milan	Ita	2-0	1-2	3-2
Barcelona	Esp	Levski Sofia	Bul	4-0	4-5	8-5
Hamburg	FRG	Stal Mielec	Pol	1-1	1-0	2-1
Dynamo Dresden	GDR	Liverpool	Eng	0-0	1-2	1-2

	Pts	P	W	D	L	F	A	Diff	Goals/P
Total	16	8	6	4	6	24	24	0	3.000

Semi Finals

Barcelona	Esp	Liverpool	Eng	0-1	1-1	1-2
Hamburg	FRG	Club Bruges	Bel	1-1	0-1	1-2

	Pts	P	W	D	L	F	A	Diff	Goals/P
Total	8	4	2	4	2	6	6	0	1.500

Final

Liverpool	Eng	Club Bruges	Bel	3-2	1-1	4-3

	Pts	P	W	D	L	F	A	Diff	Goals/P
Total	4	2	1	2	1	7	7	0	3.500

	Pts	P	W	D	L	F	A	Diff	Goals/P
Total	252	126	105	42	105	384	384	0	3.048

UEFA Cup 1975-76

Pos'n	Club	Cnty	Pts	P	W	D	L	F	A	Diff	B	Pts/P	F/P
1	Liverpool	Eng	22	12	8	3	1	25	9	16	3	1.833	2.083
2	Club Bruges	Bel	17	12	6	2	4	20	14	6	3	1.417	1.667
3	Barcelona	Esp	15	10	6	1	3	26	10	16	2	1.500	2.600
4	Hamburg	FRG	14	10	4	4	2	15	8	7	2	1.400	1.500
5	AC Milan	Ita	11	8	4	2	2	10	5	5	1	1.375	1.250
6	Levski Sofia	Bul	11	8	5	0	3	19	16	3	1	1.375	2.375
7	Dynamo Dresden	GDR	10	8	3	3	2	14	10	4	1	1.250	1.750
8	Stal Mielec	Pol	10	8	4	1	3	7	5	2	1	1.250	0.875
9	FC Porto	Por	9	6	4	1	1	15	5	10	0	1.500	2.500
10	Torpedo Moscow	URS	9	6	4	1	1	15	8	7	0	1.500	2.500
11	Spartak Moscow	URs	9	6	4	1	1	7	5	2	0	1.500	1.167
12	Ajax	Ned	8	6	4	0	2	21	6	15	0	1.333	3.500
13	Inter Bratislava	Tch	8	6	4	0	2	12	7	5	0	1.333	2.000
14	MSV Duisburg	FRG	6	4	3	0	1	14	7	7	0	1.500	3.500
15	Carl Zeiss Jena	GDR	6	4	3	0	1	5	1	4	0	1.500	1.250
16	Sporting Lisbon	Por	6	4	3	0	1	8	6	2	0	1.500	2.000
–	Hertha Berlin	FRG	6	4	3	0	1	8	6	2	0	1.500	2.000
18	Ipswich Town	Eng	6	4	3	0	1	7	5	2	0	1.500	1.750
19	Dundee United	Sco	5	4	2	1	1	8	3	5	0	1.250	2.000
20	Antwerp	Bel	5	4	2	1	1	7	4	3	0	1.250	1.750
21	AEK Athens	Gre	5	4	2	1	1	6	4	2	0	1.250	1.500
22	Slask Wroclaw	Pol	5	6	2	1	3	9	11	-2	0	0.833	1.500
23	Öster SIF	Swe	4	4	2	0	2	7	3	4	0	1.000	1.750
24	Vasas SC	Hun	4	6	2	0	4	9	9	0	0	0.667	1.500
25	Honvéd	Hun	4	4	1	2	1	5	5	0	0	1.000	1.250
–	Cologne	FRG	4	4	2	0	2	5	5	0	0	1.000	1.250
27	Roma	Ita	4	6	2	0	4	4	4	0	0	0.667	0.667
28	Athlone Town	Irl	4	4	1	2	1	4	5	-1	0	1.000	1.000
29	Red Star Belgrade	Yug	4	4	1	2	1	5	7	-2	0	1.000	1.250
30	Grasshoppers Zürich	Sui	2	2	0	2	0	4	4	0	0	1.000	2.000
31	GAIS	Swe	2	2	1	0	1	4	5	-1	0	1.000	2.000
32	Rapid Vienna	Aut	2	2	1	0	1	2	3	-1	0	1.000	1.000
–	Hibernian	Sco	2	2	1	0	1	2	3	-1	0	1.000	1.000
34	Dunav Ruse	Bul	2	2	1	0	1	1	2	-1	0	1.000	0.500
35	Olympique Lyon	Fra	2	2	1	0	1	4	6	-2	0	1.000	2.000
36	Vöest Linz	Aut	2	2	1	0	1	2	4	-2	0	1.000	1.000
37	Chernomorets Odessa	URS	2	2	1	0	1	1	3	-2	0	1.000	0.500
38	Galatasaray	Tur	2	4	1	0	3	5	9	-4	0	0.500	1.250
39	PAOK Salonika	Gre	2	2	1	0	1	2	6	-4	0	1.000	1.000
40	Lazio	Ita	2	4	1	0	3	3	8	-5	0	0.500	0.750
41	Molde FK	Nor	2	2	1	0	1	1	6	-5	0	1.000	0.500
42	Real Sociedad	Esp	2	4	0	2	2	5	13	-8	0	0.500	1.250
43	Bohemians Prague	Tch	1	2	0	1	1	2	3	-1	0	0.500	1.000
44	AIK	Swe	1	2	0	1	1	1	2	-1	0	0.500	0.500
45	Everton	Eng	1	2	0	1	1	0	1	-1	0	0.500	0.000
46	Vålerengen SIF	Nor	1	2	0	1	1	2	4	-2	0	0.500	1.000
–	Universitatea Craiova	Rom	1	2	0	1	1	2	4	-2	0	0.500	1.000
–	Young Boys Berne	Sui	1	2	0	1	1	2	4	-2	0	0.500	1.000
49	Vojvodina Novi Sad	Yug	1	2	0	1	1	1	3	-2	0	0.500	0.500
50	ASA Tîrgu Mures	Rom	1	2	0	1	1	3	6	-3	0	0.500	1.500
51	Napoli	Ita	1	2	0	1	1	2	5	-3	0	0.500	1.000
52	Holbaek BIF	Den	0	2	0	0	2	1	3	-2	0	0.000	0.500
53	B 1903 Copenhagen	Den	0	2	0	0	2	2	5	-3	0	0.000	1.000
–	Sliema Wanderers	Mlt	0	2	0	0	2	2	5	-3	0	0.000	1.000
55	Feyenoord	Ned	0	2	0	0	2	1	4	-3	0	0.000	0.500
56	HJK Helsinki	Fin	0	2	0	0	2	2	6	-4	0	0.000	1.000
57	Aston Villa	Eng	0	2	0	0	2	1	5	-4	0	0.000	0.500
58	Olympique Marseille	Fra	0	2	0	0	2	0	4	-4	0	0.000	0.000
59	Real Zaragoza	Esp	0	2	0	0	2	2	8	-6	0	0.000	1.000
60	Eskisehirspor	Tur	0	2	0	0	2	1	7	-6	0	0.000	0.500
61	IBK Keflavik	Isl	0	2	0	0	2	0	6	-6	0	0.000	0.000
62	Paralimni	Cyp	0	2	0	0	2	3	10	-7	0	0.000	1.500
63	Avenir Beggen	Lux	0	2	0	0	2	0	10	-10	0	0.000	0.000
64	Glentoran	Nir	0	2	0	0	2	1	14	-13	0	0.000	0.500
	Total		**266**	**252**	**105**	**42**	**105**	**384**	**384**	**0**	**14**	**1.056**	**3.048**

1975-76

Pos'n	Cnty	Pts	P	W	D	L	F	A	Diff	B	Pts/P	F/P
1	FRG	72	45	27	10	8	95	45	50	8	1.600	2.111
2	Eng	46	33	17	6	10	61	43	18	6	1.394	1.848
3	Bel	42	29	16	4	9	49	32	17	6	1.448	1.690
4	URS	34	24	14	5	5	45	26	19	1	1.417	1.875
5	Ned	32	22	14	1	7	57	23	34	3	1.455	2.591
6	Esp	29	28	9	7	12	51	49	2	4	1.036	1.821
7	GDR	28	22	10	5	7	27	21	6	3	1.273	1.227
8	Ita	27	28	11	4	13	31	29	2	1	0.964	1.107
9	Por	25	20	10	4	6	41	25	16	1	1.250	2.050
10	Pol	23	22	9	4	9	33	29	4	1	1.045	1.500
11	Yug	22	16	9	3	4	38	19	19	1	1.375	2.375
12	Fra	21	17	8	2	7	27	22	5	3	1.235	1.588
13	Sco	19	16	7	4	5	29	15	14	1	1.188	1.813
14	Bul	17	14	8	0	6	24	24	0	1	1.214	1.714
15	Hun	16	18	6	4	8	33	29	4	0	0.889	1.833
16	Swe	12	14	5	2	7	18	18	0	0	0.857	1.286
17	Tch	12	12	5	2	5	15	16	-1	0	1.000	1.250
18	Aut	11	12	4	2	6	12	20	-8	1	0.917	1.000
19	Gre	9	10	3	3	4	10	15	-5	0	0.900	1.000
20	Wal	8	6	2	3	1	7	5	2	1	1.333	1.167
21	Sui	6	8	1	4	3	13	16	-3	0	0.750	1.625
22	Rom	6	8	2	2	4	8	16	-8	0	0.750	1.000
23	Irl	6	8	1	4	3	7	17	-10	0	0.750	0.875
24	Tur	4	10	2	0	8	7	29	-22	0	0.400	0.700
25	Nor	3	8	1	1	6	6	22	-16	0	0.375	0.750
26	Cyp	3	6	1	1	4	6	25	-19	0	0.500	1.000
27	Fin	2	6	0	2	4	6	18	-12	0	0.333	1.000
28	Isl	2	8	1	0	7	5	22	-17	0	0.250	0.625
29	Mlt	1	6	0	1	5	3	21	-18	0	0.167	0.500
30	Den	0	8	0	0	8	4	17	-13	0	0.000	0.500
31	Nir	0	6	0	0	6	5	35	-30	0	0.000	0.833
32	Lux	0	6	0	0	6	2	32	-30	0	0.000	0.333
	Total	**538**	**496**	**203**	**90**	**203**	**775**	**775**	**0**	**42**	**1.085**	**3.125**

1955-56 to 1975-76

1	Eng	898	604	328	132	144	1187	629	558	110	1.487	1.965
2	Esp	790	566	292	105	169	1119	710	409	101	1.396	1.977
3	Ita	733	526	267	113	146	858	544	314	86	1.394	1.631
4	FRG	730	530	277	98	155	1089	718	371	78	1.377	2.055
5	Sco	498	393	194	62	137	720	532	188	48	1.267	1.832
6	Ned	407	308	157	51	100	612	394	218	42	1.321	1.987
7	Yug	403	364	146	70	148	614	543	71	41	1.107	1.687
8	Por	389	332	144	69	119	575	438	137	32	1.172	1.732
9	Hun	362	298	137	50	111	572	428	144	38	1.215	1.919
10	Bel	333	305	136	35	134	495	449	46	26	1.092	1.623
11	Tch	282	241	109	41	91	380	322	58	23	1.170	1.577
12	GDR	275	250	101	53	96	363	314	49	20	1.100	1.452
13	Fra	247	255	92	45	118	377	408	-31	18	0.969	1.478
14	Pol	206	187	82	30	75	288	271	17	12	1.102	1.540
15	Bul	188	187	74	30	83	302	289	13	10	1.005	1.615
16	URS	182	133	72	26	35	209	131	78	12	1.368	1.571
17	Rom	178	191	69	35	87	240	318	-78	5	0.932	1.257
18	Aut	164	196	60	36	100	238	340	-102	8	0.837	1.214
19	Sui	164	213	59	35	119	317	468	-151	11	0.770	1.488
20	Gre	126	147	45	31	71	164	269	-105	5	0.857	1.116
21	Swe	123	148	43	32	73	199	277	-78	5	0.831	1.345
22	Tur	114	153	42	24	87	159	274	-115	6	0.745	1.039
23	Den	99	163	33	29	101	218	379	-161	4	0.607	1.337
24	Wal	61	56	19	18	19	77	69	8	5	1.089	1.375
25	Nor	56	110	21	13	76	116	302	-186	1	0.509	1.055
26	Nir	51	100	15	19	66	114	314	-200	2	0.510	1.140
27	Irl	47	112	15	17	80	98	302	-204	0	0.420	0.875
28	Lux	28	102	10	8	84	75	433	-358	0	0.275	0.735
29	Mlt	27	82	9	9	64	41	271	-230	0	0.329	0.500
30	Fin	25	76	8	9	59	58	250	-192	0	0.329	0.763
31	Alb	16	26	3	10	13	18	41	-23	0	0.615	0.692
32	Isl	12	64	2	8	54	37	267	-230	0	0.188	0.578
33	Cyp	11	58	3	5	50	28	263	-235	0	0.190	0.483
	Total	**8225**	**7476**	**3064**	**1348**	**3064**	**11957**	**11957**	**0**	**749**	**1.100**	**3.199**

1975-76

Pos'n	Cnty	Ave	Pts	P	W	D	L	F	A	Diff	B	No./T
1	Belgium	10.500	42	29	16	4	9	49	32	17	6	4
2	W. Germany	10.285	72	45	27	10	8	95	45	50	8	7
3	Wales	8.000	8	6	2	3	1	7	5	2	1	1
–	Netherlands	8.000	32	22	14	1	7	57	23	34	3	4
5	England	7.666	46	33	17	6	10	61	43	18	6	6
6	E. Germany	7.000	28	22	10	5	7	27	21	6	3	4
7	USSR	6.800	34	24	14	5	5	45	26	19	1	5
8	Portugal	6.250	25	20	10	4	6	41	25	16	1	4
9	Spain	5.800	29	28	9	7	12	51	49	2	4	5
10	Poland	5.750	23	22	9	4	9	33	29	4	1	4
11	Yugoslavia	5.500	22	16	9	3	4	38	19	19	1	4
12	France	5.250	21	17	8	2	7	27	22	5	3	4
13	Scotland	4.750	19	16	7	4	5	29	15	14	1	4
14	Italy	4.500	27	28	11	4	13	31	29	2	1	6
15	Bulgaria	4.250	17	14	8	0	6	24	24	0	1	4
16	Hungary	4.000	16	18	6	4	8	33	29	4	0	4
17	Czechoslovakia	3.000	12	12	5	2	5	15	16	-1	0	4
18	Austria	2.750	11	12	4	2	6	12	20	-8	1	4
19	Sweden	2.400	12	14	5	2	7	18	18	0	0	5
20	Greece	2.250	9	10	3	3	4	10	15	-5	0	4
21	Rep. of Ireland	2.000	6	8	1	4	3	7	17	-10	0	3
22	Romania	1.500	6	8	2	2	4	8	16	-8	0	4
–	Switzerland	1.500	6	8	1	4	3	13	16	-3	0	4
24	Cyprus	1.000	3	6	1	1	4	6	25	-19	0	3
–	Turkey	1.000	4	10	2	0	8	7	29	-22	0	4
26	Norway	0.750	3	8	1	1	6	6	22	-16	0	4
27	Finland	0.666	2	6	0	2	4	6	18	-12	0	3
–	Iceland	0.666	2	8	1	0	7	5	22	-17	0	3
29	Malta	0.333	1	6	0	1	5	3	21	-18	0	3
30	Denmark	0.000	0	8	0	0	8	4	17	-13	0	4
–	N. Ireland	0.000	0	6	0	0	6	5	35	-30	0	3
–	Luxembourg	0.000	0	6	0	0	6	2	32	-30	0	3
	Total		**538**	**496**	**203**	**90**	**203**	**775**	**775**	**0**	**42**	**3.125**

1955-56 to 1975-76

Pos'n	Cnty	Ave	Pts	P	W	D	L	F	A	Diff	B	No./T
1	England	9.354	898	604	328	132	144	1187	629	558	110	96
2	Spain	7.900	790	566	292	105	169	1119	710	409	101	100
3	Italy	7.556	733	526	267	113	146	858	544	314	86	97
4	W. Germany	7.227	730	530	277	98	155	1089	718	371	78	101
5	Netherlands	6.359	407	308	157	51	100	612	394	218	42	64
6	USSR	6.275	182	133	72	26	35	209	131	78	12	29
7	Scotland	6.225	498	393	194	62	137	720	532	188	48	80
8	Hungary	6.135	362	298	137	50	111	572	428	144	38	59
9	Portugal	4.987	389	332	144	69	119	575	438	137	32	78
10	Yugoslavia	4.797	403	364	146	70	148	614	543	71	41	84
11	E. Germany	4.741	275	250	101	53	96	363	314	49	20	58
12	Czechoslovakia	4.700	282	241	109	41	91	380	322	58	23	60
13	Belgium	4.561	333	305	136	35	134	495	449	46	26	73
14	Poland	4.382	206	187	82	30	75	288	271	17	12	47
15	Wales	4.066	61	56	19	18	19	77	69	8	5	15
16	Bulgaria	3.481	188	187	74	30	83	302	289	13	10	54
17	France	3.293	247	255	92	45	118	377	408	-31	18	75
18	Romania	3.122	178	191	69	35	87	240	318	-78	5	57
19	Austria	2.688	164	196	60	36	100	238	340	-102	8	61
20	Sweden	2.460	123	148	43	32	73	199	277	-78	5	50
21	Greece	2.377	126	147	45	31	71	164	269	-105	5	53
22	Turkey	2.326	114	153	42	24	87	159	274	-115	6	49
23	Switzerland	2.277	164	213	59	35	119	317	468	-151	11	72
24	Denmark	1.571	99	163	33	29	101	218	379	-161	4	63
25	Albania	1.454	16	26	3	10	13	18	41	-23	0	11
26	Norway	1.217	56	110	21	13	76	116	302	-186	1	46
27	N. Ireland	1.186	51	100	15	19	66	114	314	-200	2	43
28	Rep. of Ireland	0.979	47	112	15	17	80	98	302	-204	0	48
29	Finland	0.735	25	76	8	9	59	58	250	-192	0	34
30	Malta	0.710	27	82	9	9	64	41	271	-230	0	38
31	Luxembourg	0.583	28	102	10	8	84	75	433	-358	0	48
32	Cyprus	0.407	11	58	3	5	50	28	263	-235	0	27
33	Iceland	0.400	12	64	2	8	54	37	267	-230	0	30
	Total		**8225**	**7476**	**3064**	**1348**	**3064**	**11957**	**11957**	**0**	**749**	**3.199**

Bayern Make It Three in a Row

Bayern Munich secured their place in European Cup history by doing what only Real Madrid and Ajax had done before them and winning the Champions' Cup for the third year in a row.

Unlike the season before, Bayern faced a perilous route to the final. Jeunesse Esch of Luxembourg posed no problem in the first round, but Malmö FF, of Sweden, put the Germans through a rigorous ordeal in the second round and it was only with two questionable goals from Dürnberger and Torstensson that Bayern progressed. In the quarter-finals came Benfica. Bayern managed a goalless draw in Lisbon and then treated their fans in the Olympiastadion to arguably the best performance of their three successful Champions' Cup campaigns. Two goals each from Dürnberger and Müller, plus one from newcomer Karl-Heinz Rummenigge, gave Bayern a superb 5-1 victory, taking them into a semi-final Clash of the Titans with Real Madrid.

Real were not the most popular team in West Germany at the time. Their talented team contained the highly gifted West German international Günter Netzer, but in the previous round they had knocked out Netzer's former club, UEFA Cup holders Borussia Mönchengladbach, in highly controversial fashion on the away goals rule. Revenge was in the air, and it was in this tie that Gerd Müller, now 30, proved his everlasting quality in front of goal, scoring once in the Bernabéu to earn his side a 1-1 draw and then striking twice more in Munich to take his team through to the final in Glasgow.

French football had been through a long barren spell in the late '60s and early '70s, so it came as some relief when Saint-Etienne, semi-finalists the year before, became the first French team since Reims in 1959 to reach the Champions' Cup final. This they achieved by eliminating KB of Denmark, Glasgow Rangers, Cup-winners' Cup holders Dinamo Kiev and PSV Eindhoven along the way. At Hampden Park, though, fortune was to smile once again on Bayern in a match of high drama and considerable entertainment, even if just one goal decided the contest. That goal came once again from the right boot of free-kick specialist Franz Roth, his second winning strike in successive finals, after 57 minutes. A thrilling climax was ensured by the late introduction of injured French winger Dominique Rocheteau, who turned the Bayern defence inside out in the last ten minutes, but the Germans' luck held and captain Franz Beckenbauer was able to step forward and collect the Champions' Cup for the third year in a row.

Belgian football received an enormous boost to its prestige in the 1975-76 season with the presence of two of its clubs in European finals – Anderlecht, their only previous European finalists (1970 Fairs' Cup), in the Cup-winners' Cup, and Club Bruges in the UEFA Cup.

Anderlecht were fortunate enough to play the Cup-winners' Cup final in their home city of Brussels. West Ham United, their opponents, had enjoyed a similar advantage when they took the trophy 11 years earlier at Wembley, but now the Londoners had to travel, and on their route to the final, via Helsinki, Erevan, The Hague and Frankfurt, they had not won a single match away from home. Anderlecht, on the other hand, had triumphed in all their matches on home soil. And in the final they made it five wins out of five, triumphing 4-2 in an exhilarating match which saw Anderlecht's Dutch international Robbie Rensenbrink extend his record of scoring in every round with two further goals to add to another brace from his striking colleague François Van der Elst.

Anderlecht's win gave Belgium a first ever European trophy, but Club Bruges, coached by former Feyenoord boss Ernst Happel, could not make it two despite a marvellous run in the UEFA Cup which saw them reach the final at the expense of such highly-ranked clubs as Roma, Milan and Hamburg. Their chances of taking the trophy remained after a narrow 3-2 defeat in the first leg of the final at Anfield. But in the return, Liverpool, whose away form had been exceptional, culminating in a 1-0 semi-final victory in Barcelona, achieved the draw they needed courtesy of a goal from their nippy forward Kevin Keegan, who had also scored in the first leg. Liverpool thus took the trophy for the second time in four years, bringing it back to England for a record seventh time.

Liverpool

Hamburg

Juventus

1976 – 1977

First Round

Team 1	Cnty	Team 2	Cnty	1st leg	2nd leg	Agg
Liverpool	Eng	Crusaders	Nir	2-0	5-0	7-0
Austria Vienna	Aut	Bor. Mönchengladbach	FRG	1-0	0-3	1-3
Club Bruges	Bel	Steaua Bucharest	Rom	2-1	1-1	3-2
CSKA Sofia	Bul	Saint-Etienne	Fra	0-0	0-1	0-1
Omonia Nicosia	Cyp	PAOK Salonika	Gre	0-2	1-1	1-3
Køge BK	Den	Bayern Munich	FRG	0-5	1-2	1-7
Rangers	Sco	FC Zürich	Sui	1-1	0-1	1-2
Dundalk	Irl	PSV Eindhoven	Ned	1-1	0-6	1-7
Ferencváros	Hun	Jeunesse Esch	Lux	5-1	6-2	11-3
IA Akranes	Isl	Trabzonspor	Tur	1-3	2-3	3-6
Torino	Ita	Malmö FF	Swe	2-1	1-1	3-2
Sliema Wanderers	Mlt	TPS Turku	Fin	2-1	0-1	2-2
IL Viking	Nor	Banik Ostrava	Tch	2-1	0-2	2-3
Stal Mielec	Pol	Real Madrid	Esp	1-2	0-1	1-3
Dinamo Kiev	URS	Partizan Belgrade	Yug	3-0	2-0	5-0
Dynamo Dresden	GDR	Benfica	Por	2-0	0-0	2-0

	Pts	P	W	D	L	F	A	Diff	Goals/P
Total	64	32	25	14	25	88	88	0	2.750

Second Round

Real Madrid	Esp	Club Bruges	Bel	0-0	0-2	0-2
Saint-Etienne	Fra	PSV Eindhoven	Ned	1-0	0-0	1-0
Ferencváros	Hun	Dynamo Dresden	GDR	1-0	0-4	1-4
Torino	Ita	Bor. Mönchengladbach	FRG	1-2	0-0	1-2
FC Zürich	Sui	TPS Turku	Fin	2-0	1-0	3-0
Banik Ostrava	Tch	Bayern Munich	FRG	2-1	0-5	2-6
Trabzonspor	Tur	Liverpool	Eng	1-0	0-3	1-3
Dinamo Kiev	URS	PAOK Salonika	Gre	4-0	2-0	6-0

	Pts	P	W	D	L	F	A	Diff	Goals/P
Total	32	16	13	6	13	32	32	0	2.000

Quarter Finals

Saint-Etienne	Fra	Liverpool	Eng	1-0	1-3	2-3
Bayern Munich	FRG	Dinamo Kiev	URS	1-0	0-2	1-2
Bor. Mönchengladbach	FRG	Club Bruges	Bel	2-2	1-0	3-2
FC Zürich	Sui	Dynamo Dresden	GDR	2-1	2-3	4-4

	Pts	P	W	D	L	F	A	Diff	Goals/P
Total	16	8	7	2	7	21	21	0	2.625

Semi Finals

FC Zürich	Sui	Liverpool	Eng	1-3	0-3	1-6
Dinamo Kiev	URS	Bor. Mönchengladbach	FRG	1-0	0-2	1-2

	Pts	P	W	D	L	F	A	Diff	Goals/P
Total	8	4	4	0	4	10	10	0	2.500

Final

Liverpool	Eng	Bor. Mönchengladbach	FRG	3-1	3-1

	Pts	P	W	D	L	F	A	Diff	Goals/P
Total	2	1	1	0	1	4	4	0	4.000

	Pts	P	W	D	L	F	A	Diff	Goals/P
Total	122	61	50	22	50	155	155	0	2.541

Pos'n	Club	Cnty	Pts	P	W	D	L	F	A	Diff	B	Pts/P	F/P
1	Liverpool	Eng	17	9	7	0	2	22	5	17	3	1.889	2.444
2	Dinamo Kiev	URS	14	8	6	0	2	14	3	11	2	1.750	1.750
3	Bor. Mönchengladbach	FRG	13	9	4	2	3	11	8	3	3	1.444	1.222
4	FC Zürich	Sui	11	8	4	1	3	10	11	-1	2	1.375	1.250
5	Bayern Munich	FRG	9	6	4	0	2	14	5	9	1	1.500	2.333
6	Saint-Etienne	Fra	9	6	3	2	1	4	3	1	1	1.500	0.667
7	Dynamo Dresden	GDR	8	6	3	1	2	10	5	5	1	1.333	1.667
8	Club Bruges	Bel	8	6	2	3	1	7	5	2	1	1.333	1.167
9	Ferencváros	Hun	6	4	3	0	1	12	7	5	0	1.500	3.000
10	Trabzonspor	Tur	6	4	3	0	1	7	6	1	0	1.500	1.750
11	Real Madrid	Esp	5	4	2	1	1	3	3	0	0	1.250	0.750
12	PSV Eindhoven	Ned	4	4	1	2	1	7	2	5	0	1.000	1.750
13	Torino	Ita	4	4	1	2	1	4	4	0	0	1.000	1.000
14	Banik Ostrava	Tch	4	4	2	0	2	5	8	-3	0	1.000	1.250
15	PAOK Salonika	Gre	3	4	1	1	2	3	7	-4	0	0.750	0.750
16	Sliema Wanderers	Mlt	2	2	1	0	1	2	2	0	0	1.000	1.000
17	IL Viking	Nor	2	2	1	0	1	2	3	-1	0	1.000	1.000
18	Austria Vienna	Aut	2	2	1	0	1	1	3	-2	0	1.000	0.500
19	TPS Turku	Fin	2	4	1	0	3	2	5	-3	0	0.500	0.500
20	Steaua Bucharest	Rom	1	2	0	1	1	2	3	-1	0	0.500	1.000
–	Malmö FF	Swe	1	2	0	1	1	2	3	-1	0	0.500	1.000
22	Rangers	Sco	1	2	0	1	1	1	2	-1	0	0.500	0.500
23	CSKA Sofia	Bul	1	2	0	1	1	0	1	-1	0	0.500	0.000
24	Omonia Nicosia	Cyp	1	2	0	1	1	1	3	-2	0	0.500	0.500
25	Benfica	Por	1	2	0	1	1	0	2	-2	0	0.500	0.000
26	Dundalk	Irl	1	2	0	1	1	1	7	-6	0	0.500	0.500
27	Stal Mielec	Pol	0	2	0	0	2	1	3	-2	0	0.000	0.500
28	IA Akranes	Isl	0	2	0	0	2	3	6	-3	0	0.000	1.500
29	Partizan Belgrade	Yug	0	2	0	0	2	0	5	-5	0	0.000	0.000
30	Køge BK	Den	0	2	0	0	2	1	7	-6	0	0.000	0.500
31	Crusaders	Nir	0	2	0	0	2	0	7	-7	0	0.000	0.000
32	Jeunesse Esch	Lux	0	2	0	0	2	3	11	-8	0	0.000	1.500
	Total		**136**	**122**	**50**	**22**	**50**	**155**	**155**	**0**	**14**	**1.115**	**2.541**

Preliminary Round

Team 1	Cnty	Team 2	Cnty	1st leg	2nd leg	Agg
Cardiff City	Wal	Servette	Sui	1-0	1-2	2-2

	Pts	P	W	D	L	F	A	Diff	Goals/P
Total	4	2	2	0	2	4	4	0	2.000

First Round

Southampton	Eng	Olympique Marseille	Fra	4-0	1-2	5-2
Rapid Vienna	Aut	Atlético Madrid	Esp	1-2	1-1	2-3
Anderlecht	Bel	Roda JC	Ned	2-1	3-2	5-3
Lierse	Bel	Hajduk Split	Yug	1-0	0-3	1-3
Levski Sofia	Bul	Reipas Lahti	Fin	12-2	7-1	19-3
Bohemians	Irl	Esbjerg FB	Den	2-1	1-0	3-1
Cardiff City	Wal	Dinamo Tbilisi	URS	1-0	0-3	1-3
Iraklis	Gre	Apoel Nicosia	Cyp	0-0	0-2	0-2
MTK-VM	Hun	Sparta Prague	Tch	3-1	1-1	4-2
Carrick Rangers	Nir	Aris Bonnevoie	Lux	3-1	1-2	4-3
Floriana	Mlt	Slask Wraclaw	Pol	1-4	0-2	1-6
SFK Bodø/Glimt	Nor	Napoli	Ita	0-2	0-1	0-3
Hamburg	FRG	IBK Keflavik	Isl	3-0	1-1	4-1
CSU Galati	Rom	Boavista	Por	2-3	0-2	2-5
AIK	Swe	Galatasaray	Tur	1-2	1-1	2-3
Lokomotive Leipzig	GDR	Heart of Midlothian	Sco	2-0	1-5	3- 5

	Pts	P	W	D	L	F	A	Diff	Goals/P
Total	64	32	27	10	27	104	104	0	3.250

Second Round

Anderlecht	Bel	Galatasaray	Tur	5-1	5-1	10-2
Apoel Nicosia	Cyp	Napoli	Ita	1-1	0-2	1-3
Atlético Madrid	Esp	Hajduk Split	Yug	1-0	2-1	3-1
Carrick Rangers	Nir	Southampton	Eng	2-5	1-4	3-9
Slask Wraclaw	Pol	Bohemians	Irl	3-0	1-0	4-0
Boavista	Por	Levski Sofia	Bul	3-1	0-2	3-3
Hamburg	FRG	Heart of Midlothian	Sco	4-2	4-1	8- 3
Dinamo Tbilisi	URS	MTK-VM	Hun	1-4	0-1	1-5

	Pts	P	W	D	L	F	A	Diff	Goals/P
Total	32	16	15	2	15	59	59	0	3.688

Quarter Finals

Anderlecht	Bel	Southampton	Eng	2-0	1-2	3-2
Levski Sofia	Bul	Atlético Madrid	Esp	2-1	0-2	2-3
MTK-VM	Hun	Hamburg	FRG	1-1	1-4	2-5
Slask Wraclaw	Pol	Napoli	Ita	0-0	0-2	0-2

	Pts	P	W	D	L	F	A	Diff	Goals/P
Total	16	8	6	4	6	19	19	0	2.375

European Cup Winners Cup 1976-77

Semi Finals

Atlético Madrid	Esp	Hamburg	FRG	3-1	0-3	3-4
Napoli	Ita	Anderlecht	Bel	1-0	0-2	1-2

	Pts	P	W	D	L	F	A	Diff	Goals/P
Total	8	4	4	0	4	10	10	0	2.500

Final

Hamburg	FRG	Anderlecht	Bel	2-0	2-0

	Pts	P	W	D	L	F	A	Diff	Goals/P
Total	2	1	1	0	1	2	2	0	2.000

	Pts	P	W	D	L	F	A	Diff	Goals/P
Total	126	63	55	16	55	198	198	0	3.143

Pos'n	Club	Cnty	Pts	P	W	D	L	F	A	Diff	B	Pts/P	F/P
1	Hamburg	FRG	17	9	6	2	1	23	9	14	3	1.889	2.556
2	Anderlecht	Bel	15	9	6	0	3	20	10	10	3	1.667	2.222
3	Napoli	Ita	14	8	5	2	1	9	3	6	2	1.750	1.125
4	Atlético Madrid	Esp	13	8	5	1	2	12	9	3	2	1.625	1.500
5	Slask Wroclaw	Pol	10	6	4	1	1	10	3	7	1	1.667	1.667
6	Levski Sofia	Bul	9	6	4	0	2	24	9	15	1	1.500	4.000
7	Southampton	Eng	9	6	4	0	2	16	8	8	1	1.500	2.667
8	MTK-VM	Hun	9	6	3	2	1	11	8	3	1	1.500	1.833
9	Boavista	Por	6	4	3	0	1	8	5	3	0	1.500	2.000
10	Apoel Nicosia	Cyp	4	4	1	2	1	3	3	0	0	1.000	0.750
11	Bohemians	Irl	4	4	2	0	2	3	5	-2	0	1.000	0.750
–	Cardiff City	Wal	4	4	2	0	2	3	5	-2	0	1.000	0.750
13	Galatasaray	Tur	3	4	1	1	2	5	12	-7	0	0.750	1.250
14	Hajduk Split	Yug	2	4	1	0	3	4	4	0	0	0.500	1.000
15	Servette	Sui	2	2	1	0	1	2	2	0	0	1.000	1.000
16	Aris Bonnevoie	Lux	2	2	1	0	1	3	4	-1	0	1.000	1.500
17	Dinamo Tbilisi	URS	2	4	1	0	3	4	6	-2	0	0.500	1.000
18	Lokomotive Leipzig	GDR	2	2	1	0	1	3	5	-2	0	1.000	1.500
19	Lierse	Bel	2	2	1	0	1	1	3	-2	0	1.000	0.500
20	Heart of Midlothian	Sco	2	4	1	0	3	8	11	-3	0	0.500	2.000
21	Olympique Marseille	Fra	2	2	1	0	1	2	5	-3	0	1.000	1.000
22	Carrick Rangers	Nir	2	4	1	0	3	7	12	-5	0	0.500	1.750
23	Rapid Vienna	Aut	1	2	0	1	1	2	3	-1	0	0.500	1.000
–	AIK	Swe	1	2	0	1	1	2	3	-1	0	0.500	1.000
25	Sparta Prague	Tch	1	2	0	1	1	2	4	-2	0	0.500	1.000
26	Iraklis	Gre	1	2	0	1	1	0	2	-2	0	0.500	0.000
27	IBK Keflavik	Isl	1	2	0	1	1	1	4	-3	0	0.500	0.500
28	Roda JC	Ned	0	2	0	0	2	3	5	-2	0	0.000	1.500
29	Esbjerg FB	Den	0	2	0	0	2	1	3	-2	0	0.000	0.500
30	CSU Galati	Rom	0	2	0	0	2	2	5	-3	0	0.000	1.000
31	SFK Bodø/Glimt	Nor	0	2	0	0	2	0	3	-3	0	0.000	0.000
32	Floriana	Mlt	0	2	0	0	2	1	6	-5	0	0.000	0.500
33	Reipas Lahti	Fin	0	2	0	0	2	3	19	-16	0	0.000	1.500
	Total		**140**	**126**	**55**	**16**	**55**	**198**	**198**	**0**	**14**	**1.111**	**3.143**

First Round

Team 1	Cnty	Team 2	Cnty	1st leg	2nd leg	Agg
Derby County	Eng	Finn Harps	Irl	12-0	4-1	16-1
Queen's Park Rangers	Eng	SK Brann	Nor	4-0	7-0	11-0
Manchester City	Eng	Juventus	Ita	1-0	0-2	1-2
FC Tirol	Aut	IK Start	Nor	2-1	5-0	7-1
SV Salzburg	Aut	Adanaspor	Tur	5-0	0-2	5-2
Lokomotiv Plovdiv	Bul	Red Star Belgrade	Yug	2-1	1-4	3-5
Paralimni	Cyp	Kaiserslautern	FRG	1-3	0-8	1-11
Naestved IF	Den	RWD Molenbeek	Bel	0-3	0-4	0-7
Hibernian	Sco	Sochaux	Fra	1-0	0-0	1-0
Celtic	Sco	Wisla Kraków	Pol	2-2	0-2	2-4
Español	Esp	Nice	Fra	3-1	1-2	4-3
KuPS Kuopio	Fin	Öster SIF	Swe	3-2	0-2	3-4
AEK Athens	Gre	Dinamo Moscow	URS	2-0	1-2	3-2
Ujpesti Dózsa	Hun	Athletic Bilbao	Esp	1-0	0-5	1-5
Glentoran	Nir	FC Basle	Sui	3-2	0-3	3-5
Fram Reykjavik	Isl	Slovan Bratislava	Tch	0-3	0-5	0-8
Inter Milan	Ita	Honvéd	Hun	0-1	1-1	1-2
Red Boys Differdange	Lux	Lokeren	Bel	0-3	1-3	1-6
Ajax	Ned	Manchester United	Eng	1-0	0-2	1-2
Feyenoord	Ned	Djurgården SIF	Swe	3-0	1-2	4-2
Belenenses	Por	Barcelona	Esp	2-2	2-3	4-5
FC Porto	Por	Schalke 04	FRG	2-2	2-3	4-5
Eintracht Braunschweig	FRG	Holbaek BIF	Den	7-0	0-1	7-1
Cologne	FRG	GKS Tychy	Pol	2-0	1-1	3-1
Dinamo Bucharest	Rom	AC Milan	Ita	0-0	1-2	1-2
Sportul Studentesc Bucharest	Rom	Olympiakos Pireus	Gre	3-0	1-2	4-2
Tîrgu Mures ASA	Rom	Dinamo Zagreb	Yug	0-1	0-3	0-4
Grasshoppers Zürich	Sui	Hibernians	Mlt	7-0	2-0	9-0
Prague Slavia	Tch	Akademik Sofia	Bul	2-0	0-3	2-3
Fenerbahçe	Tur	Videoton	Hun	2-1	0-4	2-5
Shakhtyor Donetsk	URS	Dynamo Berlin	GDR	3-0	1-1	4-1
Magdeburg	GDR	Cesena	Ita	3-0	1-3	4-3

	Pts	P	W	D	L	F	A	Diff	Goals/P
Total	128	64	56	16	56	216	216	0	3.375

Second Round

Manchester United	Eng	Juventus	Ita	1-0	0-3	1-3
FC Tirol	Aut	Videoton	Hun	1-1	0-1	1- 2
SV Salzburg	Aut	Red Star Belgrade	Yug	2-1	0-1	2-2
Akademik Sofia	Bul	AC Milan	Ita	4-3	0-2	4-5
Hibernian	Sco	Öster SIF	Swe	2-0	1-4	3-4
Barcelona	Esp	Lokeren	Bel	2-0	1-2	3-2
AEK Athens	Gre	Derby County	Eng	2-0	3-2	5-2
Wisla Kraków	Pol	RWD Molenbeek	Bel	1-1	1-1	2-2
Eintracht Braunschweig	FRG	Español	Esp	2-1	0-2	2-3
Cologne	FRG	Grasshoppers Zürich	Sui	2-0	3-2	5-2
Kaiserslautern	FRG	Feyenoord	Ned	2-2	0-5	2-7
Sportul Studentesc Bucharest	Rom	Schalke 04	FRG	0-1	0-4	0-5
FC Basle	Sui	Athletic Bilbao	Esp	1-1	1-3	2-4
Slovan Bratislava	Tch	Queen's Park Rangers	Eng	3-3	2-5	5-8
Shakhtyor Donetsk	URS	Honvéd	Hun	3-0	3-2	6-2
Magdeburg	GDR	Dinamo Zagreb	Yug	2-0	2-2	4-2

	Pts	P	W	D	L	F	A	Diff	Goals/P
Total	64	32	25	14	25	102	102	0	3.188

Third Round

Queen's Park Rangers	Eng	Cologne	FRG	3-0	1-4	4-4
RWD Molenbeek	Bel	Schalke 04	FRG	1-0	1-1	2-1
Español	Esp	Feyenoord	Ned	0-1	0-2	0-3
Athletic Bilbao	Esp	AC Milan	Ita	4-1	1-3	5-4
AEK Athens	Gre	Red Star Belgrade	Yug	2-0	1-3	3-3
Juventus	Ita	Shakhtyor Donetsk	URS	3-0	0-1	3-1
Öster SIF	Swe	Barcelona	Esp	0-3	1-5	1-8
Magdeburg	GDR	Videoton	Hun	5-0	0-1	5-1

	Pts	P	W	D	L	F	A	Diff	Goals/P
Total	32	16	15	2	15	48	48	0	3.000

Quarter Finals

Queen's Park Rangers	Eng	AEK Athens	Gre	3-0	0-3	3-3
Athletic Bilbao	Esp	Barcelona	Esp	2-1	2-2	4-3
Feyenoord	Ned	RWD Molenbeek	Bel	0-0	1-2	1-2
Magdeburg	GDR	Juventus	Ita	1-3	0-1	1-4

	Pts	P	W	D	L	F	A	Diff	Goals/P
Total	16	8	6	4	6	21	21	0	2.625

Semi Finals

RWD Molenbeek	Bel	Athletic Bilbao	Esp	1-1	0-0	1-1
Juventus	Ita	AEK Athens	Gre	4-1	1-0	5-1

	Pts	P	W	D	L	F	A	Diff	Goals/P
Total	8	4	2	4	2	8	8	0	2.000

Final

Juventus	Ita	Athletic Bilbao	Esp	1-0	1-2	2-2

	Pts	P	W	D	L	F	A	Diff	Goals/P
Total	4	2	2	0	2	4	4	0	2.000

	Pts	P	W	D	L	F	A	Diff	Goals/P
Total	252	126	106	40	106	399	399	0	3.167

Pos'n	Club	Cnty	Pts	P	W	D	L	F	A	Diff	B	Pts/P	F/P
1	Juventus	Ita	19	12	8	0	4	19	7	12	3	1.583	1.583
2	Athletic Bilbao	Esp	17	12	5	4	3	21	13	8	3	1.417	1.750
3	RWD Molenbeek	Bel	16	10	4	6	0	14	5	9	2	1.600	1.400
4	Queen's Park Rangers	Eng	12	8	5	1	2	26	12	14	1	1.500	3.250
5	AEK Athens	Gre	12	10	5	0	5	15	15	0	2	1.200	1.500
6	Feyenoord	Ned	11	8	4	2	2	15	6	9	1	1.375	1.875
7	Barcelona	Esp	11	8	4	2	2	19	11	8	1	1.375	2.375
8	Cologne	FRG	9	6	4	1	1	12	7	5	0	1.500	2.000
9	Shakhtyor Donetsk	URS	9	6	4	1	1	11	6	5	0	1.500	1.833
10	Schalke 04	FRG	8	6	3	2	1	11	6	5	0	1.333	1.833
11	Magdeburg	GDR	8	8	3	1	4	14	10	4	1	1.000	1.750
12	AC Milan	Ita	7	6	3	1	2	11	10	1	0	1.167	1.833
13	Videoton	Hun	7	6	3	1	2	8	8	0	0	1.167	1.333
14	Lokeren	Bel	6	4	3	0	1	8	4	4	0	1.500	2.000
15	Red Star Belgrade	Yug	6	6	3	0	3	10	8	2	0	1.000	1.667
16	Kaiserslautern	FRG	5	4	2	1	1	13	8	5	0	1.250	3.250
–	Slovan Bratislava	Tch	5	4	2	1	1	13	8	5	0	1.250	3.250
18	FC Tirol	Aut	5	4	2	1	1	8	3	5	0	1.250	2.000
19	Wisla Kraków	Pol	5	4	1	3	0	6	4	2	0	1.250	1.500
–	Dinamo Zagreb	Yug	5	4	2	1	1	6	4	2	0	1.250	1.500
21	Hibernian	Sco	5	4	2	1	1	4	4	0	0	1.250	1.000
22	Derby County	Eng	4	4	2	0	2	18	6	12	0	1.000	4.500
23	Grasshoppers Zürich	Sui	4	4	2	0	2	11	5	6	0	1.000	2.750
24	Eintracht Braunschweig	FRG	4	4	2	0	2	9	4	5	0	1.000	2.250
25	SV Salzburg	Aut	4	4	2	0	2	7	4	3	0	1.000	1.750
26	Akademik Sofia	Bul	4	4	2	0	2	7	7	0	0	1.000	1.750
27	Español	Esp	4	6	2	0	4	7	8	-1	0	0.667	1.167
28	Manchester United	Eng	4	4	2	0	0	3	4	-1	0	1.000	0.750
29	Öster SIF	Swe	4	6	2	0	4	9	14	-5	0	0.667	1.500
30	FC Basle	Sui	3	4	1	1	2	7	7	0	0	0.750	1.750
31	Honvéd	Hun	3	4	1	1	2	4	7	-3	0	0.750	1.000
32	KUPS Kuopio	Fin	2	2	1	0	1	3	4	-1	0	1.000	1.500
–	Nice	Fra	2	2	1	0	1	3	4	-1	0	1.000	1.500
–	Cesena	Ita	2	2	1	0	1	3	4	-1	0	1.000	1.500
35	Slavia Prague	Tch	2	2	1	0	1	2	3	-1	0	1.000	1.000
–	Dinamo Moscow	URS	2	2	1	0	1	2	3	-1	0	1.000	1.000
37	Manchester City	Eng	2	2	1	0	1	1	2	-1	0	1.000	0.500
–	Ajax	Ned	2	2	1	0	1	1	2	-1	0	1.000	0.500
39	Lokomotiv Plovdiv	Bul	2	2	1	0	1	3	5	-2	0	1.000	1.500
–	Glentoran	Nir	2	2	1	0	1	3	5	-2	0	1.000	1.500
41	Olympiakos Pireus	Gre	2	2	1	0	1	2	4	-2	0	1.000	1.000
–	Djurgården SIF	Swe	2	2	1	0	1	2	4	-2	0	1.000	1.000
43	Sportul Studentesc Bucharest	Rom	2	4	1	0	3	4	7	-3	0	0.500	1.000
44	Adanaspor	Tur	2	2	1	0	1	2	5	-3	0	1.000	1.000
–	Fenerbahçe	Tur	2	2	1	0	1	2	5	-3	0	1.000	1.000
46	Ujpesti Dózsa	Hun	2	2	1	0	1	1	5	-4	0	1.000	0.500
47	Holbaek BIF	Den	2	2	1	0	1	1	7	-6	0	1.000	0.500
48	Belenenses	Por	1	2	0	1	1	4	5	-1	0	0.500	2.000
–	FC Porto	Por	1	2	0	1	1	4	5	-1	0	0.500	2.000
50	Inter Milan	Ita	1	2	0	1	1	1	2	-1	0	0.500	0.500
–	Dinamo Bucharest	Rom	1	2	0	1	1	1	2	-1	0	0.500	0.500
52	Sochaux	Fra	1	2	0	1	1	0	1	-1	0	0.500	0.000
53	Celtic	Sco	1	2	0	1	1	2	4	-2	0	0.500	1.000
54	GKS Tychy	Pol	1	2	0	1	1	1	3	-2	0	0.500	0.500
55	Dynamo Berlin	GDR	1	2	0	1	1	1	4	-3	0	0.500	0.500
56	ASA Tîrgu Mures	Rom	0	2	0	0	2	0	4	-4	0	0.000	0.000
57	Red Boys Differdange	Lux	0	2	0	0	2	1	6	-5	0	0.000	0.500
58	IK Start	Nor	0	2	0	0	2	1	7	-6	0	0.000	0.500
59	Naestved IF	Den	0	2	0	0	2	0	7	-7	0	0.000	0.000
60	Fram Reykjavik	Isl	0	2	0	0	2	0	8	-8	0	0.000	0.000
61	Hibernians	Mlt	0	2	0	0	2	0	9	-9	0	0.000	0.000
62	Paralimni	Cyp	0	2	0	0	2	1	11	-10	0	0.000	0.500
63	SK Brann	Nor	0	2	0	0	2	0	11	-11	0	0.000	0.000
61	Finn Harps	Irl	0	2	0	0	2	1	16	-15	0	0.000	0.500
	Total		**266**	**252**	**106**	**40**	**106**	**399**	**399**	**0**	**14**	**1.056**	**3.167**

National Performances by Points

1976-77

Pos'n	Cnty	Pts	P	W	D	L	F	A	Diff	B	Pts/P	F/P
1	FRG	65	44	25	8	11	93	47	46	7	1.477	2.114
2	Esp	50	38	18	8	12	62	44	18	6	1.316	1.632
3	Eng	48	33	21	1	11	86	37	49	5	1.455	2.606
4	Bel	47	31	16	9	6	50	27	23	6	1.516	1.613
5	Ita	47	34	18	6	10	47	30	17	5	1.382	1.382
6	URS	27	20	12	1	7	31	18	13	2	1.350	1.550
7	Hun	27	22	11	4	7	36	35	1	1	1.227	1.636
8	Sui	20	18	8	2	8	30	25	5	2	1.111	1.667
9	GDR	19	18	7	3	8	28	24	4	2	1.056	1.556
10	Gre	18	18	7	2	9	20	28	-8	2	1.000	1.111
11	Ned	17	16	6	4	6	26	15	11	1	1.063	1.625
12	Bul	16	14	7	1	6	34	22	12	1	1.143	2.429
13	Pol	16	14	5	5	4	18	13	5	1	1.143	1.286
14	Fra	14	12	5	3	4	9	13	-4	1	1.167	0.750
15	Yug	13	16	6	1	9	20	21	-1	0	0.813	1.250
16	Tur	13	12	6	1	5	16	28	-12	0	1.083	1.333
17	Aut	12	12	5	2	5	18	13	5	0	1.000	1.500
18	Tch	12	12	5	2	5	22	23	-1	0	1.000	1.833
19	Por	9	10	3	3	4	16	17	-1	0	0.900	1.600
20	Sco	9	12	3	3	6	15	21	-6	0	0.750	1.250
21	Swe	8	12	3	2	7	15	24	-9	0	0.667	1.250
22	Cyp	5	8	1	3	4	5	17	-12	0	0.625	0.625
23	Irl	5	8	2	1	5	5	28	-23	0	0.625	0.625
24	Wal	4	4	2	0	2	3	5	-2	0	1.000	0.750
25	Rom	4	12	1	2	9	9	21	-12	0	0.333	0.750
26	Nir	4	8	2	0	6	10	24	-14	0	0.500	1.250
27	Fin	4	8	2	0	6	8	28	-20	0	0.500	1.000
28	Lux	2	6	1	0	5	7	21	-14	0	0.333	1.167
29	Mlt	2	6	1	0	5	3	17	-14	0	0.333	0.500
30	Den	2	8	1	0	7	3	24	-21	0	0.250	0.375
–	Nor	2	8	1	0	7	3	24	-21	0	0.250	0.375
32	Isl	1	6	0	1	5	4	18	-14	0	0.167	0.667
	Total	**542**	**500**	**211**	**78**	**211**	**752**	**752**	**0**	**42**	**1.084**	**3.008**

1955-56 to 1976-77

1	Eng	946	637	349	133	155	1273	666	607	115	1.485	1.998
2	Esp	840	604	310	113	181	1181	754	427	107	1.391	1.955
3	FRG	795	574	302	106	166	1182	765	417	85	1.385	2.059
4	Ita	780	560	285	119	156	905	574	331	91	1.393	1.616
5	Sco	507	405	197	65	143	735	553	182	48	1.252	1.815
6	Ned	424	324	163	55	106	638	409	229	43	1.309	1.969
7	Yug	416	380	152	71	157	634	564	70	41	1.095	1.668
8	Por	398	342	147	72	123	591	455	136	32	1.164	1.728
9	Hun	389	320	148	54	118	608	463	145	39	1.216	1.900
10	Bel	380	336	152	44	140	545	476	69	32	1.131	1.622
11	Tch	294	253	114	43	96	402	345	57	23	1.162	1.589
12	GDR	294	268	108	56	104	391	338	53	22	1.097	1.459
13	Fra	261	267	97	48	122	386	421	-35	19	0.978	1.446
14	Pol	222	201	87	35	79	306	284	22	13	1.104	1.522
15	URS	209	153	84	27	42	240	149	91	14	1.366	1.569
16	Bul	204	201	81	31	89	336	311	25	11	1.015	1.672
17	Sui	184	231	67	37	127	347	493	-146	13	0.797	1.502
18	Rom	182	203	70	37	96	249	339	-90	5	0.897	1.227
19	Aut	176	208	65	38	105	256	353	-97	8	0.846	1.231
20	Gre	144	165	52	33	80	184	297	-113	7	0.873	1.115
21	Swe	131	160	46	34	80	214	301	-87	5	0.819	1.338
22	Tur	127	165	48	25	92	175	302	-127	6	0.770	1.061
23	Den	101	171	34	29	108	221	403	-182	4	0.591	1.292
24	Wal	65	60	21	18	21	80	74	6	5	1.083	1.333
25	Nor	58	118	22	13	83	119	326	-207	1	0.492	1.008
26	Nir	55	108	17	19	72	124	338	-214	2	0.509	1.148
27	Irl	52	120	17	18	85	103	330	-227	0	0.433	0.858
28	Lux	30	108	11	8	89	82	454	-372	0	0.278	0.759
29	Fin	29	84	10	9	65	66	278	-212	0	0.345	0.786
30	Mlt	29	88	10	9	69	44	288	-244	0	0.330	0.500
31	Alb	16	26	3	10	13	18	41	-23	0	0.615	0.692
32	Cyp	16	66	4	8	54	33	280	-247	0	0.242	0.500
33	Isl	13	70	2	9	59	41	285	-244	0	0.186	0.586
	Total	**8767**	**7976**	**3275**	**1426**	**3275**	**12709**	**12709**	**0**	**791**	**1.099**	**3.187**

1976-77

Pos'n	Cnty	Ave	Pts	P	W	D	L	F	A	Diff	B	No./T
1	Spain	10.000	50	38	18	8	12	62	44	18	6	5
2	Belgium	9.400	47	31	16	9	6	50	27	23	6	5
3	W. Germany	9.285	65	44	25	8	11	93	47	46	7	7
4	England	8.000	48	33	21	1	11	86	37	49	5	6
5	Italy	7.833	47	34	18	6	10	47	30	17	5	6
6	USSR	6.750	27	20	12	1	7	31	18	13	2	4
7	Hungary	5.400	27	22	11	4	7	36	35	1	1	5
8	Switzerland	5.000	20	18	8	2	8	30	25	5	2	4
9	E. Germany	4.750	19	18	7	3	8	28	24	4	2	4
10	Greece	4.500	18	18	7	2	9	20	28	-8	2	4
11	Netherlands	4.250	17	16	6	4	6	26	15	11	1	4
12	Bulgaria	4.000	16	14	7	1	6	34	22	12	1	4
–	Wales	4.000	4	4	2	0	2	3	5	-2	0	1
–	Poland	4.000	16	14	5	5	4	18	13	5	1	4
15	France	3.500	14	12	5	3	4	9	13	-4	1	4
16	Turkey	3.250	13	12	6	1	5	16	28	-12	0	4
–	Yugoslavia	3.250	13	16	6	1	9	20	21	-1	0	4
18	Austria	3.000	12	12	5	2	5	18	13	5	0	4
–	Czechoslovakia	3.000	12	12	5	2	5	22	23	-1	0	4
20	Scotland	2.250	9	12	3	3	6	15	21	-6	0	4
–	Portugal	2.250	9	10	3	3	4	16	17	-1	0	4
22	Sweden	2.000	8	12	3	2	7	15	24	-9	0	4
23	Cyprus	1.666	5	8	1	3	4	5	17	-12	0	3
–	Rep. of Ireland	1.666	5	8	2	1	5	5	28	-23	0	3
25	Finland	1.333	4	8	2	0	6	8	28	-20	0	3
–	N. Ireland	1.333	4	8	2	0	6	10	24	-14	0	3
27	Romania	0.800	4	12	1	2	9	9	21	-12	0	5
28	Luxembourg	0.666	2	6	1	0	5	7	21	-14	0	3
–	Malta	0.666	2	6	1	0	5	3	17	-14	0	3
30	Denmark	0.500	2	8	1	0	7	3	24	-21	0	4
–	Norway	0.500	2	8	1	0	7	3	24	-21	0	4
32	Iceland	0.333	1	6	0	1	5	4	18	-14	0	3
	Total		**542**	**500**	**211**	**78**	**211**	**752**	**752**	**0**	**42**	**3.008**

1955-56 to 1976-77

Pos'n	Cnty	Ave	Pts	P	W	D	L	F	A	Diff	B	No./T
1	England	9.274	946	637	349	133	155	1273	666	607	115	102
2	Spain	8.000	840	604	310	113	181	1181	754	427	107	105
3	Italy	7.572	780	560	285	119	156	905	574	331	91	103
4	W. Germany	7.361	795	574	302	106	166	1182	765	417	85	108
5	USSR	6.333	209	153	84	27	42	240	149	91	14	33
6	Netherlands	6.235	424	324	163	55	106	638	409	229	43	68
7	Hungary	6.078	389	320	148	54	118	608	463	145	39	64
8	Scotland	6.035	507	405	197	65	143	735	553	182	48	84
9	Belgium	4.871	380	336	152	44	140	545	476	69	32	78
10	Portugal	4.853	398	342	147	72	123	591	455	136	32	82
11	E. Germany	4.741	294	268	108	56	104	391	338	53	22	62
12	Yugoslavia	4.727	416	380	152	71	157	634	564	70	41	88
13	Czechoslovakia	4.593	294	253	114	43	96	402	345	57	23	64
14	Poland	4.352	222	201	87	35	79	306	284	22	13	51
15	Wales	4.062	65	60	21	18	21	80	74	6	5	16
16	Bulgaria	3.517	204	201	81	31	89	336	311	25	11	58
17	France	3.303	261	267	97	48	122	386	421	-35	19	79
18	Romania	2.935	182	203	70	37	96	249	339	-90	5	62
19	Austria	2.707	176	208	65	38	105	256	353	-97	8	65
20	Greece	2.526	144	165	52	33	80	184	297	-113	7	57
21	Sweden	2.425	131	160	46	34	80	214	301	-87	5	54
22	Switzerland	2.421	184	231	67	37	127	347	493	-146	13	76
23	Turkey	2.396	127	165	48	25	92	175	302	-127	6	53
24	Denmark	1.507	101	171	34	29	108	221	403	-182	4	67
25	Albania	1.454	16	26	3	10	13	18	41	-23	0	11
26	N. Ireland	1.195	55	108	17	19	72	124	338	-214	2	46
27	Norway	1.160	58	118	22	13	83	119	326	-207	1	50
28	Rep. of Ireland	1.019	52	120	17	18	85	103	330	-227	0	51
29	Finland	0.783	29	84	10	9	65	66	278	-212	0	37
30	Malta	0.707	29	88	10	9	69	44	288	-244	0	41
31	Luxembourg	0.588	30	108	11	8	89	82	454	-372	0	51
32	Cyprus	0.533	16	66	4	8	54	33	280	-247	0	30
33	Iceland	0.393	13	70	2	9	59	41	285	-244	0	33
	Total		**8767**	**7976**	**3275**	**1426**	**3275**	**12709**	**12709**	**0**	**791**	**3.187**

The Start of English Domination

Bayern Munich's long run of success in the Champions' Cup was at last brought to an end when they were beaten in the quarter-finals of the 1976-77 competition by former Cup-winners' Cup holders Dinamo Kiev. But there was a still a formidable German presence in the competition in the shape of three-time Bundesliga champions Borussia Mönchengladbach, now coached by former Bayern boss Udo Lattek. And they duly kept the German flag flying by knocking Kiev out in the following round and progressing through to their first Champions' Cup final. It was a reverse of the previous season when Borussia had been beaten by Real Madrid, only for Bayern to go on and beat them in the semi-final. But where Bayern had gone on to win the trophy, Borussia Mönchengladbach were to be outclassed in the final by the same team that had denied them in the UEFA Cup final of 1973, Liverpool.

The Reds, now managed by Bob Paisley, were having a magnificent season at home. Ultimately, they were denied an historic League and Cup double only by a fluke goal scored by Manchester United at Wembley in the FA Cup final. That match took place just a few days before the Champions' Cup final in Rome and might have been expected to sap the morale of some of the deflated Liverpool players. But in Rome it was the Germans who looked the wearier, and Liverpool, inspired by Kevin Keegan on his farewell European appearance for the club, took the Cup back to England for the first time in nine years with an outstanding performance of style and endeavour. Terry McDermott scored first, midway through the first half. Simonsen, the Dane, later to be voted European Footballer of the Year, equalised shortly after the break. But a bullet-like header from veteran defender Tommy Smith gave Liverpool the advantage once again and they cemented this lead with eight minutes left when Phil Neal converted a penalty after Keegan had been felled by his marker, Berti Vogts. Liverpool thus followed Manchester United into the history books as the second English winners of the Champions' Cup. The victory also began a spell of English domination in the competition that was to last for the next five years!

German consolation was to be found in the victory of Hamburg in the Cup-winners' Cup. It had been ten long years since a West German success in this competition (though Magdeburg, from the East, had triumphed in 1974), but Hamburg captured their first European trophy by defeating the holders Anderlecht 2-0 in the final, held, for the first time, in Amsterdam. Both goals came late. A penalty, converted by Volkert, in the 81st minute, followed by a second, from Felix Magath, in the dying seconds. Six years later, Magath would also be Hamburg's hero in the Champions' Cup final against Juventus. As for Anderlecht, their defeat meant that the jinx on Cup-winners' Cup holders successfully defending their trophy remained.

The UEFA Cup was won by Juventus – their first trophy success in four final appearances. They had a patchy campaign, losing all three of their away games in the first three rounds and relying entirely on home form to eliminate both Manchester clubs, City and United, and the Soviet Union side Shakhtyor Donetsk. The Italians' form picked up in the quarter and semi-finals, however, when they won all four matches against Magdeburg and AEK Athens. That took them into a final against an Athletic Bilbao side whose victims *en route* had included both AC Milan and Barcelona.

The final, as expected, was a closely contested affair. Juventus won the first leg with a single goal scored by Marco Tardelli, and it was one of his Italian national team colleagues, Roberto Bettega, who got the decisive goal for Juventus in Bilbao. The Spaniards won the match 2-1, but the Cup went to Juventus courtesy of the away goals rule. There was possibly some justice in this given that Juventus had themselves been victims of the rule in the 1971 Fairs' Cup final against Leeds United. But that was surely lost on the disappointed Spaniards who had never before, and have never since, come so close to winning a European trophy.

1977 - 1978

Liverpool

Anderlecht

PSV Eindhoven

European Cup 1977-78

First Round

Team 1	Cnty	Team 2	Cnty	1st leg	2nd leg	Agg
Levski Sofia	Bul	Slask Wroclaw	Pol	3-0	2-2	5-2
Omonia Nicosia	Cyp	Juventus	Ita	0-3	0-2	0-5
Celtic	Sco	Jeunesse Esch	Lux	5-0	6-1	11-1
KUPS Kuopio	Fin	Club Bruges	Bel	0-4	2-5	2-9
Vasas SC	Hun	Bor. Mönchengladbach	FRG	0-3	1-1	1-4
Valur Reykjavik	Isl	Glentoran	Nir	1-0	0-2	1-2
Floriana	Mlt	Panathinaikos	Gre	1-1	0-4	1-5
Lillestrøm SK	Nor	Ajax	Ned	2-0	0-4	2-4
Benfica	Por	Torpedo Moscow	URS	0-0	0-0	0-0
Dinamo Bucharest	Rom	Atlético Madrid	Esp	2-1	0-2	2-3
FC Basle	Sui	FC Tirol	Aut	1-3	1-0	2-3
Dukla Prague	Tch	Nantes	Fra	1-1	0-0	1-1
Trabzonspor	Tur	B 1903 Copenhagen	Den	1-0	0-2	1-2
Red Star Belgrade	Yug	Sligo Rovers	Irl	3-0	3-0	6-0
Dynamo Dresden	GDR	Halmstad SBK	Swe	2-0	1-2	3-2

	Pts	P	W	D	L	F	A	Diff	Goals/P
Total	60	30	23	14	23	81	81	0	2.700

Second Round

Liverpool	Eng	Dynamo Dresden	GDR	5-1	1-2	6-3
Club Bruges	Bel	Panathinaikos	Gre	2-0	0-1	2-1
Levski Sofia	Bul	Ajax	Ned	1-2	1-2	2-4
Celtic	Sco	FC Tirol	Aut	2-1	0-3	2- 4
Nantes	Fra	Atlético Madrid	Esp	1-1	1-2	2-3
Glentoran	Nir	Juventus	Ita	0-1	0-5	0-6
Benfica	Por	B 1903 Copenhagen	Den	1-0	1-0	2-0
Red Star Belgrade	Yug	Bor. Mönchengladbach	FRG	0-3	1-5	1- 8

	Pts	P	W	D	L	F	A	Diff	Goals/P
Total	32	16	15	2	15	46	46	0	2.875

Quarter Finals

FC Tirol	Aut	Bor. Mönchengladbach	FRG	3-1	0-2	3- 3
Club Bruges	Bel	Atlético Madrid	Esp	2-0	2-3	4-3
Ajax	Ned	Juventus	Ita	1-1	1-1	2-2
Benfica	Por	Liverpool	Eng	1-2	1-4	2-6

	Pts	P	W	D	L	F	A	Diff	Goals/P
Total	16	8	6	4	6	25	25	0	3.125

Semi Finals

Juventus	Ita	Club Bruges	Bel	1-0	0-2	1-2
Bor. Mönchengladbach	FRG	Liverpool	Eng	2-1	0-3	2-4

	Pts	P	W	D	L	F	A	Diff	Goals/P
Total	8	4	4	0	4	9	9	0	2.250

Final

Liverpool	Eng	Club Bruges	Bel	1-0	1-0

	Pts	P	W	D	L	F	A	Diff	Goals/P
Total	2	1	1	0	1	1	1	0	1.000

	Pts	P	W	D	L	F	A	Diff	Goals/P
Total	118	59	49	20	49	162	162	0	2.746

Pos'n	Club	Cnty	Pts	P	W	D	L	F	A	Diff	B	Pts/P	F/P
1	Juventus	Ita	14	8	5	2	1	14	4	10	2	1.750	1.750
2	Liverpool	Eng	13	7	5	0	2	17	7	10	3	1.857	2.429
3	Club Bruges	Bel	13	9	5	0	4	17	8	9	3	1.444	1.889
4	Bor. Mönchengladbach	FRG	13	8	5	1	2	17	9	8	2	1.625	2.125
5	Ajax	Ned	9	6	3	2	1	10	6	4	1	1.500	1.667
6	Atlético Madrid	Esp	8	6	3	1	2	9	8	1	1	1.333	1.500
7	FC Tirol	Aut	7	6	3	0	3	10	7	3	1	1.167	1.667
8	Benfica	Por	7	6	2	2	2	4	6	-2	1	1.167	0.667
9	Celtic	Sco	6	4	3	0	1	13	5	8	0	1.500	3.250
10	Panathinaikos	Gre	5	4	2	1	1	6	3	3	0	1.250	1.500
11	Red Star Belgrade	Yug	4	4	2	0	2	7	8	-1	0	1.000	1.750
12	Dynamo Dresden	GDR	4	4	2	0	2	6	8	-2	0	1.000	1.500
13	Levski Sofia	Bul	3	4	1	1	2	7	6	1	0	0.750	1.750
14	Nantes	Fra	3	4	0	3	1	3	4	-1	0	0.750	0.750
15	Dulka Prague	Tch	2	2	0	2	0	1	1	0	0	1.000	0.500
16	Torpedo Moscow	URS	2	2	0	2	0	0	0	0	0	1.000	0.000
17	B 1903 Copenhagen	Den	2	4	1	0	3	2	3	-1	0	0.500	0.500
–	Dinamo Bucharest	Rom	2	2	1	0	1	2	3	-1	0	1.000	1.000
–	Halmstad SBK	Swe	2	2	1	0	1	2	3	-1	0	1.000	1.000
–	FC Basle	Sui	2	2	1	0	1	2	3	-1	0	1.000	1.000
21	Valur Reykjavik	Isl	2	2	1	0	1	1	2	-1	0	1.000	0.500
–	Trabzonspor	Tur	2	2	1	0	1	1	2	-1	0	1.000	0.500
23	Lillestrøm SK	Nor	2	2	1	0	1	2	4	-2	0	1.000	1.000
24	Glentoran	Nir	2	4	1	0	3	2	7	-5	0	0.500	0.500
25	Slask Wroclaw	Pol	1	2	0	1	1	2	5	-3	0	0.500	1.000
26	Vasas SC	Hun	1	2	0	1	1	1	4	-3	0	0.500	0.500
27	Floriana	Mlt	1	2	0	1	1	1	5	-4	0	0.500	0.500
28	Omonia Nicosia	Cyp	0	2	0	0	2	0	5	-5	0	0.000	0.000
29	Sligo Rovers	Irl	0	2	0	0	2	0	6	-6	0	0.000	0.000
30	KuPS Kuopio	Fin	0	2	0	0	2	2	9	-7	0	0.000	1.000
31	Jeunesse Esch	Lux	0	2	0	0	2	1	11	-10	0	0.000	0.500
	Total		**132**	**118**	**49**	**20**	**49**	**162**	**162**	**0**	**14**	**1.119**	**2.746**

European Cup Winners Cup 1977-78

Preliminary Round

Team 1	Cnty	Team 2	Cnty	1st leg	2nd leg	Agg
Rangers	Sco	Young Boys Berne	Sui	1-0	2-2	3-2

	Pts	P	W	D	L	F	A	Diff	Goals/P
Total	4	2	1	2	1	5	5	0	2.500

First Round

Lokomotiv Sofia	Bul	Anderlecht	Bel	1-6	0-2	1-8
Olympiakos Nicosia	Cyp	Universitatea Craiova	Rom	1-6	0-2	1-8
Rangers	Sco	Twente Enschede	Ned	0-0	0-3	0-3
Dundalk	Irl	Hajduk Split	Yug	1-0	0-4	1-4
Real Betis	Esp	AC Milan	Ita	2-0	1-2	3-2
Saint-Etienne	Fra	Manchester United	Eng	1-1	0-2	1-3
Cardiff City	Wal	Austria Vienna	Aut	0-0	0-1	0-1
PAOK Salonika	Gre	Zaglebie Sosnowiec	Pol	2-0	2-0	4-0
Coleraine	Nir	Lokomotive Leipzig	GDR	1-4	2-2	3-6
Progrès Niedercorn	Lux	Vejle BK	Den	0-1	0-9	0-10
Valletta	Mlt	Dinamo Moscow	URS	0-2	0-5	0-7
SK Brann	Nor	IA Akranes	Isl	1-0	4-0	5-0
Cologne	FRG	FC Porto	Por	2-2	0-1	2-3
Hamburg	FRG	Reipas Lahti	Fin	8-1	5-2	13-3
Lokomotiv Kosice	Tch	Öster SIF	Swe	0-0	2-2	2-2
Besiktas	Tur	Diósgyöri VTK	Hun	2-0	0-5	2-5

	Pts	P	W	D	L	F	A	Diff	Goals/P
Total	64	32	25	14	25	103	103	0	3.219

Second Round

Austria Vienna	Aut	Lokomotiv Kosice	Tch	0-0	1-1	1-1
Vejle BK	Den	PAOK Salonika	Gre	3-0	1-2	4-2
Diósgyöri VTK	Hun	Hajduk Split	Yug	2-1	1-2	3-3
Twente Enschede	Ned	SK Brann	Nor	2-0	2-1	4-1
FC Porto	Por	Manchester United	Eng	4-0	2-5	6-5
Hamburg	FRG	Anderlecht	Bel	1-2	1-1	2-3
Dinamo Moscow	URS	Universitatea Craiova	Rom	2-0	0-2	2-2
Lokomotive Leipzig	GDR	Real Betis	Esp	1-1	1-2	2-3

	Pts	P	W	D	L	F	A	Diff	Goals/P
Total	32	16	12	8	12	44	44	0	2.750

Quarter Finals

Austria Vienna	Aut	Hajduk Split	Yug	1-1	1-1	2-2
Vejle BK	Den	Twente Enschede	Ned	0-3	0-4	0-7
Real Betis	Esp	Dinamo Moscow	URS	0-0	0-3	0-3
FC Porto	Por	Anderlecht	Bel	1-0	0-3	1-3

	Pts	P	W	D	L	F	A	Diff	Goals/P
Total	16	8	5	6	5	18	18	0	2.250

Semi Finals

Twente Enschede	Ned	Anderlecht	Bel	0-1	0-2	0-3
Dinamo Moscow	URS	Austria Vienna	Aut	2-1	1-2	3-3

	Pts	P	W	D	L	F	A	Diff	Goals/P
Total	8	4	4	0	4	9	9	0	2.250

Final

Anderlecht	Bel	Austria Vienna	Aut	4-0	4-0

	Pts	P	W	D	L	F	A	Diff	Goals/P
Total	2	1	1	0	1	4	4	0	4.000

	Pts	P	W	D	L	F	A	Diff	Goals/P
Total	126	63	48	30	48	183	183	0	2.905

Pos'n	Club	Cnty	Pts	P	W	D	L	F	A	Diff	B	Pts/P	F/P
1	Anderlecht	Bel	18	9	7	1	1	21	4	17	3	2.000	2.333
2	Dinamo Moscow	URS	13	8	5	1	2	15	5	10	2	1.625	1.875
3	Twente Enschede	Ned	13	8	5	1	2	14	4	10	2	1.625	1.750
–	Austria Vienna	Aut	12	9	2	5	2	7	10	-3	3	1.333	0.778
5	FC Porto	Por	8	6	3	1	2	10	10	0	1	1.333	1.667
6	Vejle BK	Den	7	6	3	0	3	14	9	5	1	1.167	2.333
7	Hajduk Split	Yug	7	6	2	2	2	9	6	3	1	1.167	1.500
8	Real Bétis	Esp	7	6	2	2	2	6	7	-1	1	1.167	1.000
9	Universitatea Craiova	Rom	6	4	3	0	1	10	3	7	0	1.500	2.500
10	PAOK Salonika	Gre	6	4	3	0	1	6	4	2	0	1.500	1.500
11	Hamburg	FRG	5	4	2	1	1	15	6	9	0	1.250	3.750
12	Manchester United	Eng	5	4	2	1	1	8	7	1	0	1.250	2.000
13	Diósgyöri VTK	Hun	4	4	2	0	2	8	5	3	0	1.000	2.000
14	Lokomotive Leipzig	GDR	4	4	1	2	1	8	6	2	0	1.000	2.000
15	SK Brann	Nor	4	4	2	0	2	6	4	2	0	1.000	1.500
16	Lokomotiv Kosice	Tch	4	4	0	4	0	3	3	0	0	1.000	0.750
17	Rangers	Sco	4	4	1	2	1	3	5	-2	0	1.000	0.750
18	Öster SIF	Swe	2	2	0	2	0	2	2	0	0	1.000	1.000
19	AC Milan	Ita	2	2	1	0	1	2	3	-1	0	1.000	1.000
20	Besiktas	Tur	2	2	1	0	1	2	5	-3	0	1.000	1.000
21	Dundalk	Irl	2	2	1	0	1	1	4	-3	0	1.000	0.500
22	Cologne	FRG	1	2	0	1	1	2	3	-1	0	0.500	1.000
–	Young Boys Berne	Sui	1	2	0	1	1	2	3	-1	0	0.500	1.000
24	Cardiff City	Wal	1	2	0	1	1	0	1	-1	0	0.500	0.000
25	Saint-Etienne	Fra	1	2	0	1	1	1	3	-2	0	0.500	0.500
26	Coleraine	Nir	1	2	0	1	1	3	6	-3	0	0.500	1.500
27	Zaglebie Sosnowiec	Pol	0	2	0	0	2	0	4	-4	0	0.000	0.000
28	IA Akranes	Isl	0	2	0	0	2	0	5	-5	0	0.000	0.000
29	Lokomotiv Sofia	Bul	0	2	0	0	2	1	8	-7	0	0.000	0.500
–	Olympiakos Nicosie	Cyp	0	2	0	0	2	1	8	-7	0	0.000	0.500
31	Valletta	Mlt	0	2	0	0	2	0	7	-7	0	0.000	0.000
32	Reipas Lahti	Fin	0	2	0	0	2	3	13	-10	0	0.000	1.500
33	Progrès Niedercorn	Lux	0	2	0	0	2	0	10	-10	0	0.000	0.000
	Total		**140**	**126**	**48**	**30**	**48**	**183**	**183**	**0**	**14**	**1.111**	**2.905**

UEFA Cup 1977-78

First Round

Team 1	Cnty	Team 2	Cnty	1st leg	2nd leg	Agg
Aston Villa	Eng	Fenerbahçe	Tur	4-0	2-0	6-0
Manchester City	Eng	Widzew Lódź	Pol	2-2	0-0	2-2
Linzer ASK	Aut	Ujpesti Dózsa	Hun	3-2	0-7	3-9
Rapid Vienna	Aut	Inter Bratislava	Tch	1-0	0-3	1-3
Standard Liège	Bel	Slavia Prague	Tch	1-0	2-3	3-3
RWD Molenbeek	Bel	Aberdeen	Sco	0-0	2-1	2-1
Marek Stanke Dimitrov	Bul	Ferencváros	Hun	3-0	0-2	3-2
BK Frem	Den	Grasshoppers Zürich	Sui	0-2	1-6	1-8
Dundee United	Sco	KB Copenhagen	Den	1-0	0-3	1-3
Bohemians	Irl	Newcastle United	Eng	0-0	0-4	0-4
Barcelona	Esp	Steaua Bucharest	Rom	5-1	3-1	8-2
Las Palmas	Esp	Sloboda Tuzla	Yug	5-0	3-4	8-4
Bastia	Fra	Sporting Lisbon	Por	3-2	2-1	5-3
Lens	Fra	Malmö FF	Swe	4-1	0-2	4-3
Olympiakos Pireus	Gre	Dinamo Zagreb	Yug	3-1	1-5	4-6
Glenavon	Nir	PSV Eindhoven	Ned	2-6	0-5	2-11
Fiorentina	Ita	Schalke 04	FRG	0-3	1-2	1-5
Inter Milan	Ita	Dinamo Tbilisi	URS	0-1	0-0	0-1
Torino	Ita	Apoel Nicosia	Cyp	3-0	1-1	4-1
IK Start	Nor	Fram Reykjavik	Isl	6-0	2-0	8-0
AZ'67 Alkmaar	Ned	Red Boys Differdange	Lux	11-1	5-0	16-1
Odra Opole	Pol	Magdeburg	GDR	1-2	1-1	2-3
Górnik Zabrze	Pol	Haka Valkeakoski	Fin	5-3	0-0	5-3
Boavista	Por	Lazio	Ita	1-0	0-5	1-5
Eintracht Frankfurt	FRG	Sliema Wanderers	Mlt	5-0	0-0	5-0
Bayern Munich	FRG	Mjøndalen IF	Nor	8-0	4-0	12-0
Tîrgu Mures ASA	Rom	AEK Athens	Gre	1-0	0-3	1-3
Landskrona BOIS	Swe	Ipswich Town	Eng	0-1	0-5	0-6
Servette	Sui	Athletic Bilbao	Esp	1-0	0-2	1-2
FC Zürich	Sui	CSKA Sofia	Bul	1-0	1-1	2-1
Dinamo Kiev	URS	Eintracht Braunschweig	FRG	1-1	0-0	1-1
Carl Zeiss Jena	GDR	Altay	Tur	5-1	1-4	6-5

	Pts	P	W	D	L	F	A	Diff	Goals/P
Total	128	64	52	24	52	219	219	0	3.422

Second Round

Aston Villa	Eng	Górnik Zabrze	Pol	2-0	1-1	3-1
Ipswich Town	Eng	Las Palmas	Esp	1-0	3-3	4-3
RWD Molenbeek	Bel	Carl Zeiss Jena	GDR	1-1	1-1	2-2
KB Copenhagen	Den	Dinamo Tbilisi	URS	1-4	1-2	2-6
Bastia	Fra	Newcastle United	Eng	2-1	3-1	5-2
AEK Athens	Gre	Standard Liège	Bel	2-2	1-4	3-6
Ujpesti Dózsa	Hun	Athletic Bilbao	Esp	2-0	0-3	2-3
Lazio	Ita	Lens	Fra	2-0	0-6	2-6
Torino	Ita	Dinamo Zagreb	Yug	3-1	0-1	3-2
IK Start	Nor	Eintracht Braunschweig	FRG	1-0	0-4	1-4
AZ'67 Alkmaar	Ned	Barcelona	Esp	1-1	1-1	2-2
Widzew Lódź	Pol	PSV Eindhoven	Ned	3-5	0-1	3-6
Bayern Munich	FRG	Marek Stanke Dimitrov	Bul	3-0	0-2	3- 2
FC Zürich	Sui	Eintracht Frankfurt	FRG	0-3	3-4	3-7
Inter Bratislava	Tch	Grasshoppers Zürich	Sui	1-0	1-5	2-5
Magdeburg	GDR	Schalke 04	FRG	4-2	3-1	7-3

	Pts	P	W	D	L	F	A	Diff	Goals/P
Total	64	32	25	14	25	107	107	0	3.344

Third Round

Aston Villa	Eng	Athletic Bilbao	Esp	2-0	1-1	3-1
Ipswich Town	Eng	Barcelona	Esp	3-0	0-3	3-3
Bastia	Fra	Torino	Ita	2-1	3-2	5-3
PSV Eindhoven	Ned	Eintracht Braunschweig	FRG	2-0	2-1	4-1
Eintracht Frankfurt	FRG	Bayern Munich	FRG	4-0	2-1	6-1
Dinamo Tbilisi	URS	Grasshoppers Zürich	Sui	1-0	0-4	1-4
Carl Zeiss Jena	GDR	Standard Liège	Bel	2-0	2-1	4-1
Magdeburg	GDR	Lens	Fra	4-0	0-2	4-2

	Pts	P	W	D	L	F	A	Diff	Goals/P
Total	32	16	15	2	15	46	46	0	2.875

Quarter Finals

Aston Villa	Eng	Barcelona	Esp	2-2	1-2	3-4
Bastia	Fra	Carl Zeiss Jena	GDR	7-2	2-4	9-6
Eintracht Frankfurt	FRG	Grasshoppers Zürich	Sui	3-2	0-1	3-3
Magdeburg	GDR	PSV Eindhoven	Ned	1-0	2-4	3-4

	Pts	P	W	D	L	F	A	Diff	Goals/P
Total	16	8	7	2	7	35	35	0	4.375

Semi Finals

PSV Eindhoven	Ned	Barcelona	Esp	3-0	1-3	4-3
Grasshoppers Zürich	Sui	Bastia	Fra	3-2	0-1	3-3

	Pts	P	W	D	L	F	A	Diff	Goals/P
Total	8	4	4	0	4	13	13	0	3.250

Final

Bastia	Fra	PSV Eindhoven	Ned	0-0	0-3	0-3

	Pts	P	W	D	L	F	A	Diff	Goals/P
Total	4	2	1	2	1	3	3	0	1.500

	Pts	P	W	D	L	F	A	Diff	Goals/P
Total	252	126	104	44	104	423	423	0	3.357

UEFA Cup 1977-78

Pos'n	Club	Cnty	Pts	P	W	D	L	F	A	Diff	B	Pts/P	F/P
1	PSV Eindhoven	Ned	22	12	9	1	2	32	12	20	3	1.833	2.667
2	Bastia	Fra	20	12	8	1	3	27	20	7	3	1.667	2.250
3	Barcelona	Esp	15	10	5	3	2	20	14	6	2	1.500	2.000
4	Eintracht Frankfurt	FRG	14	8	6	1	1	21	7	14	1	1.750	2.625
5	Grasshoppers Zürich	Sui	14	10	6	0	4	23	10	13	2	1.400	2.300
6	Aston Villa	Eng	12	8	4	3	1	15	6	9	1	1.500	1.875
7	Magdeburg	GDR	12	8	5	1	2	17	11	6	1	1.500	2.125
8	Carl Zeiss Jena	GDR	11	8	4	2	2	18	17	1	1	1.375	2.250
9	Ipswich Town	Eng	9	6	4	1	1	13	6	7	0	1.500	2.167
10	Dinamo Tbilisi	URS	9	6	4	1	1	8	6	2	0	1.500	1.333
11	AZ'67 Alkmaar	Ned	6	4	2	2	0	18	3	15	0	1.500	4.500
12	Bayern Munich	FRG	6	6	3	0	3	16	8	8	0	1.000	2.667
13	IK Start	Nor	6	4	3	0	1	9	4	5	0	1.500	2.250
14	Lens	Fra	6	6	3	0	3	12	9	3	0	1.000	2.000
15	Torino	Ita	5	6	2	1	3	10	8	2	0	0.833	1.667
16	RWD Molenbeek	Bel	5	4	1	3	0	4	3	1	0	1.250	1.000
17	Standard Liège	Bel	5	6	2	1	3	10	10	0	0	0.833	1.667
18	Athletic Bilbao	Esp	5	6	2	1	3	6	6	0	0	0.833	1.000
19	Ujpesti Dózsa	Hun	4	4	2	0	2	11	6	5	0	1.000	2.750
20	Dinamo Zagreb	Yug	4	4	2	0	2	8	7	1	0	1.000	2.000
21	Schalke 04	FRG	4	4	2	0	2	8	8	0	0	1.000	2.000
22	Lazio	Ita	4	4	2	0	2	7	7	0	0	1.000	1.750
23	Górnik Zabrze	Pol	4	4	1	2	1	6	6	0	0	1.000	1.500
–	Eintracht Braunschweig	FRG	4	6	1	2	3	6	6	0	0	0.667	1.000
25	Marek Stanke Dimitrov	Bul	4	4	2	0	2	5	5	0	0	1.000	1.250
26	Inter Bratislava	Tch	4	4	2	0	2	5	6	-1	0	1.000	1.250
27	Las Palmas	Esp	3	4	1	1	2	11	8	3	0	0.750	2.750
28	Newcastle United	Eng	3	4	1	1	2	6	5	1	0	0.750	1.500
29	AEK Athens	Gre	3	4	1	1	2	6	7	-1	0	0.750	1.500
30	FC Zürich	Sui	3	4	1	1	2	5	8	-3	0	0.750	1.250
31	Slavia Prague	Tch	2	2	1	0	1	3	3	0	0	1.000	1.500
32	Manchester City	Eng	2	2	0	2	0	2	2	0	0	1.000	1.000
33	Dinamo Kiev	URS	2	2	0	2	0	1	1	0	0	1.000	0.500
34	Altay	Tur	2	2	1	0	1	5	6	-1	0	1.000	2.500
35	Malmö FF	Swe	2	2	1	0	1	3	4	-1	0	1.000	1.500
36	Ferencváros	Hun	2	2	1	0	1	2	3	-1	0	1.000	1.000
37	Servette	Sui	2	2	1	0	1	1	2	-1	0	1.000	0.500
38	KB Copenhagen	Den	2	4	1	0	3	5	7	-2	0	0.500	1.250
39	Olympiakos Pireus	Gre	2	2	1	0	1	4	6	-2	0	1.000	2.000
40	Rapid Vienna	Aut	2	2	1	0	1	1	3	-2	0	1.000	0.500
–	Dundee United	Sco	2	2	1	0	1	1	3	-2	0	1.000	0.500
–	ASA Tîrgu Mures	Rom	2	2	1	0	1	1	3	-2	0	1.000	0.500
43	Widzew Lódź	Pol	2	4	0	2	2	5	8	-3	0	0.500	1.250
44	Sloboda Tuzla	Yug	2	2	1	0	1	4	8	-4	0	1.000	2.000
45	Boavista	Por	2	2	1	0	1	1	5	-4	0	1.000	0.500
46	Linzer ASK	Aut	2	2	1	0	1	3	9	-6	0	1.000	1.500
47	Odra Opole	Pol	1	2	0	1	1	2	3	-1	0	0.500	1.000
48	CSKA Sofia	Bul	1	2	0	1	1	1	2	-1	0	0.500	0.500
–	Aberdeen	Sco	1	2	0	1	1	1	2	-1	0	0.500	0.500
50	Inter Milan	Ita	1	2	0	1	1	0	1	-1	0	0.500	0.000
51	Haka Valkeakoski	Fin	1	2	0	1	1	3	5	-2	0	0.500	1.500
52	Apoel Nicosia	Cyp	1	2	0	1	1	1	4	-3	0	0.500	0.500
53	Bohemians	Irl	1	2	0	1	1	0	4	-4	0	0.500	0.000
54	Sliema Wanderers	Mlt	1	2	0	1	1	0	5	-5	0	0.500	0.000
55	Sporting Lisbon	Por	0	2	0	0	2	3	5	-2	0	0.000	1.500
56	Fiorentina	Ita	0	2	0	0	2	1	5	-4	0	0.000	0.500
57	Steaua Bucharest	Rom	0	2	0	0	2	2	8	-6	0	0.000	1.000
58	Landskrona BOIS	Swe	0	2	0	0	2	0	6	-6	0	0.000	0.000
–	Fenerbahçe	Tur	0	2	0	0	2	0	6	-6	0	0.000	0.000
60	BK Frem	Den	0	2	0	0	2	1	8	-7	0	0.000	0.500
61	Fram Reykjavik	Isl	0	2	0	0	2	0	8	-8	0	0.000	0.000
62	Glenavon	Nir	0	2	0	0	2	2	11	-9	0	0.000	1.000
63	Mjøndalen IF	Nor	0	2	0	0	2	0	12	-12	0	0.000	0.000
64	Red Boys Differdange	Lux	0	2	0	0	2	1	16	-15	0	0.000	0.500
	Total		**266**	**252**	**104**	**44**	**104**	**423**	**423**	**0**	**14**	**1.056**	**3.357**

1977-78

Pos'n	Cnty	Pts	P	W	D	L	F	A	Diff	B	Pts/P	F/P
1	Ned	50	30	19	6	5	74	25	49	6	1.667	2.467
2	FRG	47	38	19	6	13	85	47	38	3	1.237	2.237
3	Eng	44	31	16	8	7	61	33	28	4	1.419	1.968
4	Bel	41	28	15	5	8	52	25	27	6	1.464	1.857
5	Esp	38	32	13	8	11	52	43	9	4	1.188	1.625
6	GDR	31	24	12	5	7	49	42	7	2	1.292	2.042
7	Fra	30	24	11	5	8	43	36	7	3	1.250	1.792
8	URS	26	18	9	6	3	24	12	12	2	1.444	1.333
9	Ita	26	24	10	4	10	34	28	6	2	1.083	1.417
10	Aut	23	19	7	5	7	21	29	-8	4	1.211	1.105
11	Sui	22	20	9	2	9	33	26	7	2	1.100	1.650
12	Yug	17	16	7	2	7	28	29	-1	1	1.063	1.750
13	Por	17	16	6	3	7	18	26	-8	2	1.063	1.125
14	Gre	16	14	7	2	5	22	20	2	0	1.143	1.571
15	Sco	13	12	5	3	4	18	15	3	0	1.083	1.500
16	Tch	12	12	3	6	3	12	13	-1	0	1.000	1.000
17	Nor	12	12	6	0	6	17	24	-7	0	1.000	1.417
18	Hun	11	12	5	1	6	22	18	4	0	0.917	1.833
19	Den	11	16	5	0	11	22	27	-5	1	0.688	1.375
20	Rom	10	10	5	0	5	15	17	-2	0	1.000	1.500
21	Bul	8	12	3	2	7	14	21	-7	0	0.667	1.167
22	Pol	8	14	1	6	7	15	26	-11	0	0.571	1.071
23	Swe	6	8	2	2	4	7	15	-8	0	0.750	0.875
24	Tur	6	8	3	0	5	8	19	-11	0	0.750	1.000
25	Irl	3	6	1	1	4	1	14	-13	0	0.500	0.167
26	Nir	3	8	1	1	6	7	24	-17	0	0.375	0.875
27	Isl	2	6	1	0	5	1	15	-14	0	0.333	0.167
28	Mlt	2	6	0	2	4	1	17	-16	0	0.333	0.167
29	Wal	1	2	0	1	1	0	1	-1	0	0.500	0.000
30	Cyp	1	6	0	1	5	2	17	-15	0	0.167	0.333
31	Fin	1	6	0	1	5	8	27	-19	0	0.167	1.333
32	Lux	0	6	0	0	6	2	37	-35	0	0.000	0.333
	Total	**538**	**496**	**201**	**94**	**201**	**768**	**768**	**0**	**42**	**1.085**	**3.097**

1955-56 to 1977-78

1	Eng	990	668	365	141	162	1334	699	635	119	1.482	1.997
2	Esp	878	636	323	121	192	1233	797	436	111	1.381	1.939
3	FRG	842	612	321	112	179	1267	812	455	88	1.376	2.070
4	Ita	806	584	295	123	166	939	602	337	93	1.380	1.608
5	Sco	520	417	202	68	147	753	568	185	48	1.247	1.806
6	Ned	474	354	182	61	111	712	434	278	49	1.339	2.011
7	Yug	433	396	159	73	164	662	593	69	42	1.093	1.672
8	Bel	421	364	167	49	148	597	501	96	38	1.157	1.640
9	Por	415	358	153	75	130	609	481	128	34	1.159	1.701
10	Hun	400	332	153	55	124	630	481	149	39	1.205	1.898
11	GDR	325	292	120	61	111	440	380	60	24	1.113	1.507
12	Tch	306	265	117	49	99	414	358	56	23	1.155	1.562
13	Fra	291	291	108	53	130	429	457	-28	22	1.000	1.474
14	URS	235	171	93	33	45	264	161	103	16	1.374	1.544
15	Pol	230	215	88	41	86	321	310	11	13	1.070	1.493
16	Bul	212	213	84	33	96	350	332	18	11	0.995	1.643
17	Sui	206	251	76	39	136	380	519	-139	15	0.821	1.514
18	Aut	199	227	72	43	112	277	382	-105	12	0.877	1.220
19	Rom	192	213	75	37	101	264	356	-92	5	0.901	1.239
20	Gre	160	179	59	35	85	206	317	-111	7	0.894	1.151
21	Swe	137	168	48	36	84	221	316	-95	5	0.815	1.315
22	Tur	133	173	51	25	97	183	321	-138	6	0.769	1.058
23	Den	112	187	39	29	119	243	430	-187	5	0.599	1.299
24	Nor	70	130	28	13	89	136	350	-214	1	0.538	1.046
25	Wal	66	62	21	19	22	80	75	5	5	1.065	1.290
26	Nir	58	116	18	20	78	131	362	-231	2	0.500	1.129
27	Irl	55	126	18	19	89	104	344	-240	0	0.437	0.825
28	Mlt	31	94	10	11	73	45	305	-260	0	0.330	0.479
29	Fin	30	90	10	10	70	74	305	-231	0	0.333	0.822
30	Lux	30	114	11	8	95	84	491	-407	0	0.263	0.737
31	Cyp	17	72	4	9	59	35	297	-262	0	0.236	0.486
32	Alb	16	26	3	10	13	18	41	-23	0	0.615	0.692
33	Isl	15	76	3	9	64	42	300	-258	0	0.197	0.553
	Total	**9305**	**8472**	**3476**	**1520**	**3476**	**13477**	**13477**	**0**	**833**	**1.098**	**3.182**

National Performance by Index

1977-78

Pos'n	Cnty	Ave	Pts	P	W	D	L	F	A	Diff	B	No./T
1	Netherlands	12.500	50	30	19	6	5	74	25	49	6	4
2	Belgium	10.250	41	28	15	5	8	52	25	27	6	4
3	E. Germany	7.750	31	24	12	5	7	49	42	7	2	4
4	Spain	7.600	38	32	13	8	11	52	43	9	4	5
5	France	7.500	30	24	11	5	8	43	36	7	3	4
6	England	7.333	44	31	16	8	7	61	33	28	4	6
7	W. Germany	6.714	47	38	19	6	13	85	47	38	3	7
8	USSR	6.500	26	18	9	6	3	24	12	12	2	4
9	Austria	5.750	23	19	7	5	7	21	29	-8	4	4
10	Switzerland	4.400	22	20	9	2	9	33	26	7	2	5
11	Italy	4.333	26	24	10	4	10	34	28	6	2	6
12	Portugal	4.250	17	16	6	3	7	18	26	-8	2	4
–	Yugoslavia	4.250	17	16	7	2	7	28	29	-1	1	4
14	Greece	4.000	16	14	7	2	5	22	20	2	0	4
15	Scotland	3.250	13	12	5	3	4	18	15	3	0	4
16	Norway	3.000	12	12	6	0	6	17	24	-7	0	4
–	Czechoslovakia	3.000	12	12	3	6	3	12	13	-1	0	4
18	Denmark	2.750	11	16	5	0	11	22	27	-5	1	4
–	Hungary	2.750	11	12	5	1	6	22	18	4	0	4
20	Romania	2.500	10	10	5	0	5	15	17	-2	0	4
21	Bulgaria	2.000	8	12	3	2	7	14	21	-7	0	4
22	Poland	1.600	8	14	1	6	7	15	26	-11	0	5
23	Sweden	1.500	6	8	2	2	4	7	15	-8	0	4
–	Turkey	1.500	6	8	3	0	5	8	19	-11	0	4
25	Rep. of Ireland	1.000	3	6	1	1	4	1	14	-13	0	3
–	Wales	1.000	1	2	0	1	1	0	1	-1	0	1
–	N. Ireland	1.000	3	8	1	1	6	7	24	-17	0	3
28	Iceland	0.666	2	6	1	0	5	1	15	-14	0	3
–	Malta	0.666	2	6	0	2	4	1	17	-16	0	3
30	Cyprus	0.333	1	6	0	1	5	2	17	-15	0	3
–	Finland	0.333	1	6	0	1	5	8	27	-19	0	3
32	Luxembourg	0.000	0	6	0	0	6	2	37	-35	0	3
	Total		**538**	**496**	**201**	**94**	**201**	**768**	**768**	**0**	**42**	**3.097**

1955-56 to 1977-78

Pos'n	Cnty	Ave	Pts	P	W	D	L	F	A	Diff	B	No./T
1	England	9.166	990	668	365	141	162	1334	699	635	119	108
2	Spain	7.981	878	636	323	121	192	1233	797	436	111	110
3	Italy	7.394	806	584	295	123	166	939	602	337	93	109
4	W. Germany	7.321	842	612	321	112	179	1267	812	455	88	115
5	Netherlands	6.583	474	354	182	61	111	712	434	278	49	72
6	USSR	6.351	235	171	93	33	45	264	161	103	16	37
7	Scotland	5.909	520	417	202	68	147	753	568	185	48	88
8	Hungary	5.882	400	332	153	55	124	630	481	149	39	68
9	Belgium	5.134	421	364	167	49	148	597	501	96	38	82
10	E. Germany	4.924	325	292	120	61	111	440	380	60	24	66
11	Portugal	4.825	415	358	153	75	130	609	481	128	34	86
12	Yugoslavia	4.706	433	396	159	73	164	662	593	69	42	92
13	Czechoslovakia	4.500	306	265	117	49	99	414	358	56	23	68
14	Poland	4.107	230	215	88	41	86	321	310	11	13	56
15	Wales	3.882	66	62	21	19	22	80	75	5	5	17
16	France	3.506	291	291	108	53	130	429	457	-28	22	83
17	Bulgaria	3.419	212	213	84	33	96	350	332	18	11	62
18	Romania	2.909	192	213	75	37	101	264	356	-92	5	66
19	Austria	2.884	199	227	72	43	112	277	382	-105	12	69
20	Greece	2.622	160	179	59	35	85	206	317	-111	7	61
21	Switzerland	2.543	206	251	76	39	136	380	519	-139	15	81
22	Sweden	2.362	137	168	48	36	84	221	316	-95	5	58
23	Turkey	2.333	133	173	51	25	97	183	321	-138	6	57
24	Denmark	1.577	112	187	39	29	119	243	430	-187	5	71
25	Albania	1.454	16	26	3	10	13	18	41	-23	0	11
26	Norway	1.296	70	130	28	13	89	136	350	-214	1	54
27	N. Ireland	1.183	58	116	18	20	78	131	362	-231	2	49
28	Rep. of Ireland	1.018	55	126	18	19	89	104	344	-240	0	54
29	Finland	0.750	30	90	10	10	70	74	305	-231	0	40
30	Malta	0.704	31	94	10	11	73	45	305	-260	0	44
31	Luxembourg	0.555	30	114	11	8	95	84	491	-407	0	54
32	Cyprus	0.515	17	72	4	9	59	35	297	-262	0	33
33	Iceland	0.416	15	76	3	9	64	42	300	-258	0	36
	Total		**9305**	**8472**	**3476**	**1520**	**3476**	**13477**	**13477**	**0**	**833**	**3.182**

Unknowns Reach the Finals

Liverpool lost their star striker Kevin Keegan to Cup-winners' Cup holders Hamburg immediately after their 1977 Champions' Cup triumph, but, in Scotsman Kenny Dalglish, they bought wisely to replace him. And it was Dalglish, with a superbly taken goal served up for him by another Scottish newcomer to the side, Graeme Souness, who made Liverpool kings of Europe for the second year in succession.

The final, at Wembley, a repeat of the 1976 UEFA Cup final, with Belgian side Club Bruges again the opposition, could scarcely have been more of a contrast with the exciting match of a year earlier against Borussia Mönchengladbach. The Belgians, coached still by Ernst Happel, were surprise finalists. They had caused a big upset in the quarter-finals with the elimination of Atlético Madrid and an even bigger one in the following round when they came back from a first leg defeat to knock out Juventus after extra time. But at Wembley they came simply to defend, and the result was a dull, tedious match, livened up only by Dalglish's smartly-taken goal.

Liverpool thus completed an UEFA Cup and Champions' Cup final double over Bruges, just as they had done against Borussia Mönchengladbach the year before. Borussia were also defeated by Bob Paisley's men for a third time in 1977-78, on this occasion in the semi-finals. The Germans won the first leg in Düsseldorf 2-1, but they were visibly intimidated on their first visit to Anfield in the return and sank without trace to three goals from Ray Kennedy, Kenny Dalglish and Jimmy Case. It was Liverpool's third comprehensive home victory of the tournament after a 5-1 destruction of Dynamo Dresden in the first round and a 4-1 trouncing of once-mighty Benfica in the quarter-finals.

Bruges's defeat by Liverpool meant that Belgium was prevented from becoming the first country to win both the Champions' Cup and the Cup-winners' Cup in the same year – something which did not occur until Italy's grand slam season in 1989-90 – because a week earlier Anderlecht had regained the Cup-winners' Cup, destroying Austria Vienna 4-0 in the Paris final.

Like Bruges in the Champions' Cup, many felt that the Austrians had no right to be in the final. In their four previous ties, they had only scored more goals than their opponents once, in the first round, when a 1-0 aggregate victory saw off Cardiff City. The away goals rule had been necessary to dispose of Lokomotiv Kosice in the second round, and thereafter they had to resort to penalty kicks to eliminate both Hajduk Split and Dinamo Moscow. In the final, though, they got their come-uppance. Anderlecht, appearing in the Cup-winners' Cup final for a record third year in succession, won the match easily. Rensenbrink, their hero of 1976, scored two goals in a final yet again, with right-back Van Binst also scoring twice in the 4-0 win. The victory completed Anderlecht's revenge for their defeat by Hamburg in the previous season's final. It had begun in the second round when they put out their erstwhile conquerors 3-2 on aggregate after a 2-1 win in the Volksparkstadion – Hamburg's first home defeat in 31 European ties!

There was a new name on the UEFA Cup in 1978, with Dutch team PSV Eindhoven finally emerging from the shadows of Ajax and Feyenoord and adding their name to the European roll-of-honour for the first time.

As in the other two competitions, the beaten finalists were a relatively unknown quantity. Bastia, the Corsicans from the French First Division, were participating in only their second season of European competition and, given France's record in Europe, their presence in the UEFA Cup final had to rank as one of the most astonishing achievements in European Cup history. Their early victims included former winners Sporting Lisbon and Newcastle United, both of them beaten home and away, as were Torino in the third round. A 7-2 humbling of Carl Zeiss Jena followed in the quarter-finals, and only Grasshoppers, in the semi-finals, posed them any serious threat, when they had to resort to away goals to make further progress. But Bastia did meet their match in the final. Held 0-0 in Corsica, they lost 3-0 in Eindhoven, just as Barcelona had in the semi-finals, with Van der Kerkhof, Deijkers and Van der Kuyle scoring PSV's Cup-winning goals.

Nottingham Forest

Barcelona

Borussia Mönchengladbach

1978 – 1979

Preliminary Round

Team 1	Cnty	Team 2	Cnty	1st leg	2nd leg	Agg
Monaco	Fra	Steaua Bucharest	Rom	3-0	0-2	3-2

	Pts	P	W	D	L	F	A	Diff	Goals/P
Total	4	2	2	0	2	5	5	0	2.500

First Round

Team 1	Cnty	Team 2	Cnty	1st leg	2nd leg	Agg
Vllaznia Shkodër	Alb	Austria Vienna	Aut	2-0	1-4	3-4
Nottingham Forest	Eng	Liverpool	Eng	2-0	0-0	2-0
Club Bruges	Bel	Wisla Kraków	Pol	2-1	1-3	3-4
Omonia Nicosia	Cyp	Bohemians	Irl	2-1	0-1	2-2
OB Odense	Den	Lokomotiv Sofia	Bul	2-2	1-2	3-4
Real Madrid	Esp	Progrès Niedercorn	Lux	5-0	7-0	12-0
Haka Valkeakoski	Fin	Dinamo Kiev	URS	0-1	1-3	1-4
AEK Athens	Gre	FC Porto	Por	6-1	1-4	7-5
Linfield	Nir	Lillestrøm SK	Nor	0-0	0-1	0-1
Juventus	Ita	Rangers	Sco	1-0	0-2	1-2
Cologne	FRG	IA Akranes	Isl	4-1	1-1	5-2
Malmö FF	Swe	Monaco	Fra	0-0	1-0	1-0
Grasshoppers Zürich	Sui	Valletta	Mlt	8-0	5-3	13-3
Zbrojovka Brno	Tch	Ujpesti Dózsa	Hun	2-2	2-0	4-2
Fenerbahçe	Tur	PSV Eindhoven	Ned	2-1	1-6	3-7
Partizan Belgrade	Yug	Dynamo Dresden	GDR	2-0	0-2	2-2

	Pts	P	W	D	L	F	A	Diff	Goals/P
Total	64	32	26	12	26	104	104	0	3.250

Second Round

Team 1	Cnty	Team 2	Cnty	1st leg	2nd leg	Agg
Austria Vienna	Aut	Lillestrøm SK	Nor	4-1	0-0	4-1
Lokomotiv Sofia	Bul	Cologne	FRG	0-1	0-4	0-5
Rangers	Sco	PSV Eindhoven	Ned	0-0	3-2	3-2
Bohemians	Irl	Dynamo Dresden	GDR	0-0	0-6	0-6
Real Madrid	Esp	Grasshoppers Zürich	Sui	3-1	0-2	3-3
AEK Athens	Gre	Nottingham Forest	Eng	1-2	1-5	2-7
Zbrojovka Brno	Tch	Wisla Kraków	Pol	2-2	1-1	3-3
Dinamo Kiev	URS	Malmö FF	Swe	0-0	0-2	0-2

	Pts	P	W	D	L	F	A	Diff	Goals/P
Total	32	16	10	12	10	44	44	0	2.750

Quarter Finals

Team 1	Cnty	Team 2	Cnty	1st leg	2nd leg	Agg
Nottingham Forest	Eng	Grasshoppers Zürich	Sui	4-1	1-1	5-2
Austria Vienna	Aut	Dynamo Dresden	GDR	3-1	0-1	3-2
Wisla Kraków	Pol	Malmö FF	Swe	2-1	1-4	3-5
Cologne	FRG	Rangers	Sco	1-0	1-1	2-1

	Pts	P	W	D	L	F	A	Diff	Goals/P
Total	16	8	6	4	6	23	23	0	2.875

Semi Finals

Nottingham Forest	Eng	Cologne	FRG	3-3	1-0	4-3
Austria Vienna	Aut	Malmö FF	Swe	0-0	0-1	0-1

	Pts	P	W	D	L	F	A	Diff	Goals/P
Total	8	4	2	4	2	8	8	0	2.000

Final

Nottingham Forest	Eng	Malmö FF	Swe	1-0	1-0

	Pts	P	W	D	L	F	A	Diff	Goals/P
Total	2	1	1	0	1	1	1	0	1.000

	Pts	P	W	D	L	F	A	Diff	Goals/P
Total	126	63	47	32	47	185	185	0	2.937

Pos'n	Club	Cnty	Pts	P	W	D	L	F	A	Diff	B	Pts/P	F/P
1	Nottingham Forest	Eng	18	9	6	3	0	19	7	12	3	2.000	2.111
2	Malmö FF	Swe	14	9	4	3	2	9	4	5	3	1.556	1.000
3	Cologne	FRG	13	8	4	3	1	15	7	8	2	1.625	1.875
4	Austria Vienna	Aut	10	8	3	2	3	11	7	4	2	1.250	1.375
5	Grasshoppers Zürich	Sui	8	6	3	1	2	18	11	7	1	1.333	3.000
6	Dynamo Dresden	GDR	8	6	3	1	2	10	5	5	1	1.333	1.667
7	Rangers	Sco	7	6	2	2	2	6	5	1	1	1.167	1.000
8	Wisla Kraków	Pol	7	6	2	2	2	10	11	-1	1	1.167	1.667
9	Real Madrid	Esp	6	4	3	0	1	15	3	12	0	1.500	3.750
10	Zbrojovka Brno	Tch	5	4	1	3	0	7	5	2	0	1.250	1.750
11	Dinamo Kiev	URS	5	4	2	1	1	4	3	1	0	1.250	1.000
12	Lillestrøm SK	Nor	4	4	1	2	1	2	4	-2	0	1.000	0.500
13	PSV Eindhoven	Ned	3	4	1	1	2	9	6	3	0	0.750	2.250
14	Monaco	Fra	3	4	1	1	2	3	3	0	0	0.750	0.750
15	Lokomotiv Sofia	Bul	3	4	1	1	2	4	8	-4	0	0.750	1.000
16	Bohemians	Irl	3	4	1	1	2	2	8	-6	0	0.750	0.500
17	Omonia Nicosia	Cyp	2	2	1	0	1	2	2	0	0	1.000	1.000
–	Partizan Belgrade	Yug	2	2	1	0	1	2	2	0	0	1.000	1.000
19	Vllaznia Skhodër	Alb	2	2	1	0	1	3	4	-1	0	1.000	1.500
–	Club Bruges	Bel	2	2	1	0	1	3	4	-1	0	1.000	1.500
21	Steaua Bucharest	Rom	2	2	1	0	1	2	3	-1	0	1.000	1.000
22	Juventus	Ita	2	2	1	0	1	1	2	-1	0	1.000	0.500
23	FC Porto	Por	2	2	1	0	1	5	7	-2	0	1.000	2.500
24	AEK Athens	Gre	2	4	1	0	3	9	12	-3	0	0.500	2.250
25	Fenerbahçe	Tur	2	2	1	0	1	3	7	-4	0	1.000	1.500
26	OB Odense	Den	1	2	0	1	1	3	4	-1	0	0.500	1.500
27	Linfield	Nir	1	2	0	1	1	0	1	-1	0	0.500	0.000
28	Ujpesti Dózsa	Hun	1	2	0	1	1	2	4	-2	0	0.500	1.000
29	Liverpool	Eng	1	2	0	1	1	0	2	-2	0	0.500	0.000
30	IA Akranes	Isl	1	2	0	1	1	2	5	-3	0	0.500	1.000
31	Haka Valkeakoski	Fin	0	2	0	0	2	1	4	-3	0	0.000	0.500
32	Valletta	Mlt	0	2	0	0	2	3	13	-10	0	0.000	1.500
33	Progrès Niedercorn	Lux	0	2	0	0	2	0	12	-12	0	0.000	0.000
	Total		**140**	**126**	**47**	**32**	**47**	**185**	**185**	**0**	**14**	**1.111**	**2.937**

First Round

Team 1	Cnty	Team 2	Cnty	1st leg	2nd leg	Agg
Beveren	Bel	Ballymena United	Nir	3-0	3-0	6-0
Marek Stanke Dimitrov	Bul	Aberdeen	Sco	3-2	0-3	3-5
BK Frem	Den	Nantes	Fra	2-0	0-4	2-4
Shamrock Rovers	Irl	Apoel Nicosia	Cyp	2-0	1-0	3-0
Barcelona	Esp	Shakhtyor Donetsk	URS	3-0	1-1	4-1
PAOK Salonika	Gre	Servette	Sui	2-0	0-4	2-4
Ferencváros	Hun	Kalmar FF	Swe	2-0	2-2	4-2
Valur Reykjavik	Isl	Magdeburg	GDR	1-1	0-4	1-5
Floriana	Mlt	Inter Milan	Ita	1-3	0-5	1-8
SFK Bodø/Glimt	Nor	Union Luxembourg	Lux	4-1	0-1	4-2
AZ'67 Alkmaar	Ned	Ipswich Town	Eng	0-0	0-2	0-2
Zaglebie Sosnowiec	Pol	FC Tirol	Aut	2-3	1-1	3-4
Sporting Lisbon	Por	Banik Ostrava	Tch	0-1	0-1	0-2
Universitatea Craiova	Rom	Fortuna Düsseldorf	FRG	3-4	1-1	4-5
Rijeka	Yug	Wrexham	Wal	3-0	0-2	3-2

	Pts	P	W	D	L	F	A	Diff	Goals/P
Total	60	30	24	12	24	86	86	0	2.867

Second Round

Ipswich Town	Eng	FC Tirol	Aut	1-0	1-1	2-1
Anderlecht	Bel	Barcelona	Esp	3-0	0-3	3-3
Inter Milan	Ita	SFK Bodø/Glimt	Nor	5-0	2-1	7-1
Fortuna Düsseldorf	FRG	Aberdeen	Sco	3-0	0-2	3-2
Servette	Sui	Nantes	Fra	2-1	2-2	4-3
Banik Ostrava	Tch	Shamrock Rovers	Irl	3-0	3-1	6-1
Rijeka	Yug	Beveren	Bel	0-0	0-2	0-2
Magdeburg	GDR	Ferencváros	Hun	1-0	1-2	2-2

	Pts	P	W	D	L	F	A	Diff	Goals/P
Total	32	16	13	6	13	42	42	0	2.625

Quarter Finals

Ipswich Town	Eng	Barcelona	Esp	2-1	0-1	2-2
Inter Milan	Ita	Beveren	Bel	0-0	0-1	0-1
Fortuna Düsseldorf	FRG	Servette	Sui	0-0	1-1	1-1
Magdeburg	GDR	Banik Ostrava	Tch	2-1	2-4	4-5

	Pts	P	W	D	L	F	A	Diff	Goals/P
Total	16	8	5	6	5	16	16	0	2.000

Semi Finals

Barcelona	Esp	Beveren	Bel	1-0	1-0	2-0
Fortuna Düsseldorf	FRG	Banik Ostrava	Tch	3-1	1-2	4-3

	Pts	P	W	D	L	F	A	Diff	Goals/P
Total	8	4	4	0	4	9	9	0	2.250

European Cup Winners Cup 1978-79

Final

Barcelona	Esp	Fortuna Düsseldorf	FRG	4-3	4-3

	Pts	P	W	D	L	F	A	Diff	Goals/P
Total	2	1	1	0	1	7	7	0	7.000

	Pts	P	W	D	L	F	A	Diff	Goals/P
Total	118	59	47	24	47	160	160	0	2.712

Pos'n	Club	Cnty	Pts	P	W	D	L	F	A	Diff	B	Pts/P	F/P
1	Barcelona	Esp	16	9	6	1	2	15	9	6	3	1.778	1.667
2	Banik Ostrava	Tch	14	8	6	0	2	16	9	7	2	1.750	2.000
3	Beveren	Bel	12	8	4	2	2	9	2	7	2	1.500	1.125
4	Fortuna Düsseldorf	FRG	12	9	3	3	3	16	14	2	3	1.333	1.778
5	Inter Milan	Ita	10	6	4	1	1	15	3	12	1	1.667	2.500
6	Ipswich Town	Eng	9	6	3	2	1	6	3	3	1	1.500	1.000
7	Magdeburg	GDR	8	6	3	1	2	11	8	3	1	1.333	1.833
8	Servette	Sui	8	6	2	3	1	9	6	3	1	1.333	1.500
9	Ferencváros	Hun	5	4	2	1	1	6	4	2	0	1.250	1.500
10	Aberdeen	Sco	4	4	2	0	2	7	6	1	0	1.000	1.750
11	FC Tirol	Aut	4	4	1	2	1	5	5	0	0	1.000	1.250
12	Shamrock Rovers	Irl	4	4	2	0	2	4	6	-2	0	1.000	1.000
13	Nantes	Fra	3	4	1	1	2	7	6	1	0	0.750	1.750
14	Rijeka	Yug	3	4	1	1	2	3	4	-1	0	0.750	0.750
15	Anderlecht	Bel	2	2	1	0	1	3	3	0	0	1.000	1.500
16	Wrexham	Wal	2	2	1	0	1	2	3	-1	0	1.000	1.000
17	Marek Stanke Dimitrov	Bul	2	2	1	0	1	3	5	-2	0	1.000	1.500
18	BK Frem	Den	2	2	1	0	1	2	4	-2	0	1.000	1.000
–	PAOK Salonika	Gre	2	2	1	0	1	2	4	-2	0	1.000	1.000
–	US Rumelange	Lux	2	2	1	0	1	2	4	-2	0	1.000	1.000
21	SFK Bodø/Glimt	Nor	2	4	1	0	3	5	9	-4	0	0.500	1.250
22	Universitatea Craiova	Rom	1	2	0	1	1	4	5	-1	0	0.500	2.000
23	Zaglebie Sosnowiec	Pol	1	2	0	1	1	3	4	-1	0	0.500	1.500
24	Kalmar FF	Swe	1	2	0	1	1	2	4	-2	0	0.500	1.000
25	AZ'67 Alkmaar	Ned	1	2	0	1	1	0	2	-2	0	0.500	0.000
26	Shakhtyor Donetsk	URS	1	2	0	1	1	1	4	-3	0	0.500	0.500
27	Valur Reykjavik	Isl	1	2	0	1	1	1	5	-4	0	0.500	0.500
28	Sporting Lisbon	Por	0	2	0	0	2	0	2	-2	0	0.000	0.000
29	Apoel Nicosia	Cyp	0	2	0	0	2	0	3	-3	0	0.000	0.000
30	Ballymena United	Nir	0	2	0	0	2	0	6	-6	0	0.000	0.000
31	Floriana	Mlt	0	2	0	0	2	1	8	-7	0	0.000	0.500
	Total		**132**	**118**	**47**	**24**	**47**	**160**	**160**	**0**	**14**	**1.119**	**2.712**

First Round

Team 1	Cnty	Team 2	Cnty	1st leg	2nd leg	Agg
Arsenal	Eng	Lokomotive Leipzig	GDR	3-0	4-1	7-1
Standard Liège	Bel	Dundee United	Sco	1-0	0-0	1-0
CSKA Sofia	Bul	Valencia	Esp	2-1	1-4	3-5
Pezoporikos Larnaca	Cyp	Slask Wroclaw	Pol	2-2	1-5	3-7
Hibernian	Sco	IFK Norrköping	Swe	3-2	0-0	3-2
Finn Harps	Irl	Everton	Eng	0-5	0-5	0-10
Athletic Bilbao	Esp	Ajax	Ned	2-0	0-3	2-3
Sporting Gijón	Esp	Torino	Ita	3-0	0-1	3-1
KuPS Kuopio	Fin	B 1903 Copenhagen	Den	2-1	4-4	6-5
Nantes	Fra	Benfica	Por	0-2	0-0	0-2
Olympiakos Pireus	Gre	Levski Sofia	Bul	2-1	1-3	3-4
Honvéd	Hun	Adanaspor	Tur	6-0	2-2	8-2
IBV Vestmannaeyjar	Isl	Glentoran	Nir	0-0	1-1	1-1
AC Milan	Ita	Lokomotiv Kosice	Tch	1-0	0-1	1-1
Jeunesse Esch	Lux	Lausanne-Sports	Sui	0-0	0-2	0-2
IK Start	Nor	Esbjerg FB	Den	0-0	0-1	0-1
Twente Enschede	Ned	Manchester City	Eng	1-1	2-3	3-4
Sporting Braga	Por	Hibernians	Mlt	5-0	2-3	7-3
Hertha Berlin	FRG	Trakia Plovdiv	Bul	0-0	2-1	2-1
MSV Duisburg	FRG	Lech Poznań	Pol	5-0	5-2	10-2
Bor. Mönchengladbach	FRG	Sturm Graz	Aut	5-1	2-1	7-2
Arges Pitesti	Rom	Panathinaikos	Gre	3-0	2-1	5-1
Politehnica Timisoara	Rom	MTK-VM	Hun	2-0	1-2	3-2
IF Elfsborg	Swe	Strasbourg	Fra	2-0	1-4	3-4
FC Basle	Sui	VFB Stuttgart	FRG	2-3	1-4	3-7
Dukla Prague	Tch	Lanerossi Vicenza	Ita	1-0	1-1	2-1
Galatasaray	Tur	West Bromwich Albion	Eng	1-3	1-3	2-6
Torpedo Moscow	URS	Molde FK	Nor	4-0	3-3	7-3
Dinamo Tbilisi	URS	Napoli	Ita	2-0	1-1	3-1
Hajduk Split	Yug	Rapid Vienna	Aut	2-0	1-2	3-2
Dynamo Berlin	GDR	Red Star Belgrade	Yug	5-2	1-4	6-6
Carl Zeiss Jena	GDR	Lierse	Bel	1-0	2-2	3-2

	Pts	P	W	D	L	F	A	Diff	Goals/P
Total	128	64	48	32	48	204	204	0	3.188

Second Round

Everton	Eng	Dukla Prague	Tch	2-1	0-1	2-2
Manchester City	Eng	Standard Liège	Bel	4-0	0-2	4-2
Levski Sofia	Bul	AC Milan	Ita	1-1	0-3	1-4
Sporting Gijón	Esp	Red Star Belgrade	Yug	0-1	1-1	1-2
KuPS Kuopio	Fin	Esbjerg FB	Den	0-2	1-4	1-6
Strasbourg	Fra	Hibernian	Sco	2-0	0-1	2-1
Honvéd	Hun	Politehnica Timisoara	Rom	4-0	0-2	4-2
IBV Vestmannaeyjar	Isl	Slask Wroclaw	Pol	0-2	1-2	1-4
Ajax	Ned	Lausanne-Sports	Sui	1-0	4-0	5-0
Sporting Braga	Por	West Bromwich Albion	Eng	0-2	0-1	0-3
Benfica	Por	Bor. Mönchengladbach	FRG	0-0	0-2	0-2
Hertha Berlin	FRG	Dinamo Tbilisi	URS	2-0	0-1	2-1
Arges Pitesti	Rom	Valencia	Esp	2-1	2-5	4-6
Torpedo Moscow	URS	VFB Stuttgart	FRG	2-1	0-2	2-3
Hajduk Split	Yug	Arsenal	Eng	2-1	0-1	2-2
Carl Zeiss Jena	GDR	MSV Duisburg	FRG	0-0	0-3	0-3

	Pts	P	W	D	L	F	A	Diff	Goals/P
Total	64	32	28	8	28	74	74	0	2.313

Third Round

Esbjerg FB	Den	Hertha Berlin	FRG	2-1	0-4	2-5
Valencia	Esp	West Bromwich Albion	Eng	1-1	0-2	1-3
Strasbourg	Fra	MSV Duisburg	FRG	0-0	0-4	0-4
Honvéd	Hun	Ajax	Ned	4-1	0-2	4-3
AC Milan	Ita	Manchester City	Eng	2-2	0-3	2-5
Bor. Mönchengladbach	FRG	Slask Wroclaw	Pol	1-1	4-2	5-3
VFB Stuttgart	FRG	Dukla Prague	Tch	4-1	0-4	4-5
Red Star Belgrade	Yug	Arsenal	Eng	1-0	1-1	2-1

	Pts	P	W	D	L	F	A	Diff	Goals/P
Total	32	16	11	10	11	49	49	0	3.063

Quarter Finals

Manchester City	Eng	Bor. Mönchengladbach	FRG	1-1	1-3	2-4
Honvéd	Hun	MSV Duisburg	FRG	2-3	2-1	4-4
Hertha Berlin	FRG	Dukla Prague	Tch	1-1	2-1	3-2
Red Star Belgrade	Yug	West Bromwich Albion	Eng	1-0	1-1	2-1

	Pts	P	W	D	L	F	A	Diff	Goals/P
Total	16	8	5	6	5	22	22	0	2.750

Semi Finals

MSV Duisburg	FRG	Bor. Mönchengladbach	FRG	2-2	1-4	3-6
Red Star Belgrade	Yug	Hertha Berlin	FRG	1-0	1-2	2-2

	Pts	P	W	D	L	F	A	Diff	Goals/P
Total	8	4	3	2	3	13	13	0	3.250

Final

Red Star Belgrade	Yug	Bor. Mönchengladbach	FRG	1-1	0-1	1- 2

	Pts	P	W	D	L	F	A	Diff	Goals/P
Total	4	2	1	2	1	3	3	0	1.500

	Pts	P	W	D	L	F	A	Diff	Goals/P
Total	252	126	96	60	96	365	365	0	2.897

Pos'n	Club	Cnty	Pts	P	W	D	L	F	A	Diff	B	Pts/P	F/P
1	Bor. Mönchengladbach	FRG	22	12	7	5	0	26	11	15	3	1.833	2.167
2	Red Star Belgrade	Yug	17	12	5	4	3	15	13	2	3	1.417	1.250
3	MSV Duisburg	FRG	15	10	5	3	2	24	12	12	2	1.500	2.400
4	Hertha Berlin	FRG	14	10	5	2	3	14	8	6	2	1.400	1.400
5	West Bromwich Albion	Eng	13	8	5	2	1	13	5	8	1	1.625	1.625
6	Honvéd	Hun	10	8	4	1	3	20	11	9	1	1.250	2.500
7	Manchester City	Eng	10	8	3	3	2	15	11	4	1	1.250	1.875
8	Esbjerg FB	Den	9	6	4	1	1	9	6	3	0	1.500	1.500
9	Dulka Prague	Tch	9	8	3	2	3	11	10	1	1	1.125	1.375
10	Slask Wroclaw	Pol	8	6	3	2	1	14	9	5	0	1.333	2.333
11	Ajax	Ned	8	6	4	0	2	11	6	5	0	1.333	1.833
12	VFB Stuttgart	FRG	8	6	4	0	2	14	10	4	0	1.333	2.333
13	Arsenal	Eng	7	6	3	1	2	10	5	5	0	1.167	1.667
14	Everton	Eng	6	4	3	0	1	12	2	10	0	1.500	3.000
15	Arges Pitesh	Rom	6	4	3	0	1	9	7	2	0	1.500	2.250
16	AC Milan	Ita	6	6	2	2	2	7	7	0	0	1.000	1.167
17	Torpedo Moscow	URS	5	4	2	1	1	9	6	3	0	1.250	2.250
18	Valencia	Esp	5	6	2	1	3	12	10	2	0	0.833	2.000
19	Dinamo Tbilisi	URS	5	4	2	1	1	4	3	1	0	1.250	1.000
20	Hibernian	Sco	5	4	2	1	1	4	4	0	0	1.250	1.000
21	Standard Liège	Bel	5	4	2	1	1	3	4	-1	0	1.250	0.750
22	Strasbourg	Fra	5	6	2	1	3	6	8	-2	0	0.833	1.000
23	Hajduk Split	Yug	4	4	2	0	2	5	4	1	0	1.000	1.250
24	Benfica	Por	4	4	1	2	1	2	2	0	0	1.000	0.500
25	Politehnica Timisoara	Rom	4	4	2	0	2	5	6	-1	0	1.000	1.250
26	Carl Zeiss Jena	GDR	4	4	1	2	1	3	5	-2	0	1.000	0.750
27	Sporting Gijón	Esp	3	4	1	1	2	4	3	1	0	0.750	1.000
28	Levski Sofia	Bul	3	4	1	1	2	5	7	-2	0	0.750	1.250
29	Lausanne-Sports	Sui	3	4	1	1	2	2	5	-3	0	0.750	0.500
30	KuPS Kuopio	Fin	3	4	1	1	2	7	11	-4	0	0.750	1.750
31	Sporting Braga	Por	2	4	1	0	3	7	6	1	0	0.500	1.750
32	Dynamo Berlin	GDR	2	2	1	0	1	6	6	0	0	1.000	3.000
33	Glentoran	Nir	2	2	0	2	0	1	1	0	0	1.000	0.500
–	Lokomotiv Kosice	Tch	2	2	1	0	1	1	1	0	0	1.000	0.500
35	Olympiakos Pireus	Gre	2	2	1	0	1	3	4	-1	0	1.000	1.500
–	IF Elfsborg	Swe	2	2	1	0	1	3	4	-1	0	1.000	1.500
37	Rapid Vienna	Aut	2	2	1	0	1	2	3	-1	0	1.000	1.000
–	Athletic Bilbao	Esp	2	2	1	0	1	2	3	-1	0	1.000	1.000
–	MTK-VM	Hun	2	2	1	0	1	2	3	-1	0	1.000	1.000
40	CSKA Sofia	Bul	2	2	1	0	1	3	5	-2	0	1.000	1.500
41	Torino	Ita	2	2	1	0	1	1	3	-2	0	1.000	0.500
42	IBV Vestmannaeyjar	Isl	2	4	0	2	2	2	5	-3	0	0.500	0.500
43	Hibernians	Mlt	2	2	1	0	1	3	7	-4	0	1.000	1.500
44	B 1903 Copenhagen	Den	1	2	0	1	1	5	6	-1	0	0.500	2.500
45	Twente Enschede	Ned	1	2	0	1	1	3	4	-1	0	0.500	1.500
46	Lierse	Bel	1	2	0	1	1	2	3	-1	0	0.500	1.000
–	IFK Norrköping	Swe	1	2	0	1	1	2	3	-1	0	0.500	1.000
48	Trakia Plovdiv	Bul	1	2	0	1	1	1	2	-1	0	0.500	0.500
–	Lanerossi Vicenza	Ita	1	2	0	1	1	1	2	-1	0	0.500	0.500
50	Dundee	Sco	1	2	0	1	1	0	1	-1	0	0.500	0.000
–	IK Start	Nor	1	2	0	1	1	0	1	-1	0	0.500	0.000
52	Napoli	Ita	1	2	0	1	1	1	3	-2	0	0.500	0.500
53	Nantes	Fra	1	2	0	1	1	0	2	-2	0	0.500	0.000
–	Jeunesse Esch	Lux	1	2	0	1	1	0	2	-2	0	0.500	0.000
55	Pezoporikos Larnaca	Cyp	1	2	0	1	1	3	7	-4	0	0.500	1.500
–	Molde FK	Nor	1	2	0	1	1	3	7	-4	0	0.500	1.500
57	Adanaspor	Tur	1	2	0	1	1	2	8	-6	0	0.500	1.000
58	FC Basle	Sui	0	2	0	0	2	3	7	-4	0	0.000	1.500
59	Galatasaray	Tur	0	2	0	0	2	2	6	-4	0	0.000	1.000
60	Panathinaikos	Gre	0	2	0	0	2	1	5	-4	0	0.000	0.500
61	Sturm Graz	Aut	0	2	0	0	2	2	7	-5	0	0.000	1.000
62	Lokomotive Leipzig	GDR	0	2	0	0	2	1	7	-6	0	0.000	0.500
63	Lech Poznań	Pol	0	2	0	0	2	2	10	-8	0	0.000	1.000
64	Finn Harps	Irl	0	2	0	0	2	0	10	-10	0	0.000	0.000
	Total		**266**	**252**	**96**	**60**	**96**	**365**	**365**	**0**	**14**	**1.056**	**2.897**

1978-79

Pos'n	Cnty	Pts	P	W	D	L	F	A	Diff	B	Pts/P	F/P
1	FRG	84	55	28	16	11	109	62	47	12	1.527	1.982
2	Eng	64	43	23	12	8	75	35	40	6	1.488	1.744
3	Esp	32	25	13	3	9	48	28	20	3	1.280	1.920
4	Tch	30	22	11	5	6	35	25	10	3	1.364	1.591
5	Yug	26	22	9	5	8	25	23	2	3	1.182	1.136
6	Ita	22	20	8	5	7	26	20	6	1	1.100	1.300
7	Bel	22	18	8	4	6	20	16	4	2	1.222	1.111
8	GDR	22	20	8	4	8	31	31	0	2	1.100	1.550
9	Sui	19	18	6	5	7	32	29	3	2	1.056	1.778
10	Hun	18	16	7	3	6	30	22	8	1	1.125	1.875
11	Swe	18	15	5	5	5	16	15	1	3	1.200	1.067
12	Sco	17	16	6	4	6	17	16	1	1	1.063	1.063
13	URS	16	14	6	4	4	18	16	2	0	1.143	1.286
14	Aut	16	16	5	4	7	20	22	-2	2	1.000	1.250
15	Pol	16	16	5	5	6	29	34	-5	1	1.000	1.813
16	Ned	13	14	5	3	6	23	18	5	0	0.929	1.643
17	Rom	13	12	6	1	5	20	21	-1	0	1.083	1.667
18	Den	13	12	5	3	4	19	20	-1	0	1.083	1.583
19	Fra	12	16	4	4	8	16	19	-3	0	0.750	1.000
20	Bul	11	14	4	3	7	16	27	-11	0	0.786	1.143
21	Por	8	12	3	2	7	14	17	-3	0	0.667	1.167
22	Nor	8	12	2	4	6	10	21	-11	0	0.667	0.833
23	Irl	7	10	3	1	6	6	24	-18	0	0.700	0.600
24	Gra	6	10	3	0	7	15	25	-10	0	0.600	1.500
25	Isl	4	8	0	4	4	5	15	-10	0	0.500	0.625
26	Fin	3	6	1	1	4	8	15	-7	0	0.500	1.333
27	Cyp	3	6	1	1	4	5	12	-7	0	0.500	0.833
28	Nir	3	6	0	3	3	1	8	-7	0	0.500	0.167
29	Tur	3	6	1	1	4	7	21	-14	0	0.500	1.167
30	Lux	3	6	1	1	4	2	18	-16	0	0.500	0.333
31	Alb	2	2	1	0	1	3	4	-1	0	1.000	1.500
32	Wal	2	2	1	0	1	2	3	-1	0	1.000	1.000
33	Mlt	2	6	1	0	5	7	28	-21	0	0.333	1.167
	Total	**538**	**496**	**190**	**116**	**190**	**710**	**710**	**0**	**42**	**1.085**	**2.863**

1955-56 to 1978-79

Pos'n	Cnty	Pts	P	W	D	L	F	A	Diff	B	Pts/P	F/P
1	Eng	1054	711	388	153	170	1409	734	675	125	1.482	1.982
2	FRG	926	667	349	128	190	1376	874	502	100	1.388	2.063
3	Esp	910	661	336	124	201	1281	825	456	114	1.377	1.938
4	Ita	828	604	303	128	173	965	622	343	94	1.371	1.598
5	Sco	537	433	208	72	153	770	584	186	49	1.240	1.778
6	Ned	487	368	187	64	117	735	452	283	49	1.323	1.997
7	Yug	459	418	168	78	172	687	616	71	45	1.098	1.644
8	Bel	443	382	175	53	154	617	517	100	40	1.160	1.615
9	Por	423	370	156	77	137	623	498	125	34	1.143	1.684
10	Hun	418	348	160	58	130	660	503	157	40	1.201	1.897
11	GDR	347	312	128	65	119	471	411	60	26	1.112	1.510
12	Tch	336	287	128	54	105	449	383	66	26	1.171	1.564
13	Fra	303	307	112	57	138	445	476	-31	22	0.987	1.450
14	URS	251	185	99	37	49	282	177	105	16	1.357	1.524
15	Pol	246	231	93	46	92	350	344	6	14	1.065	1.515
16	Sui	225	269	82	44	143	412	548	-136	17	0.836	1.532
17	Bul	223	227	88	36	103	366	359	7	11	0.982	1.612
18	Aut	215	243	77	47	119	297	404	-107	14	0.885	1.222
19	Rom	205	225	81	38	106	284	377	-93	5	0.911	1.262
20	Gre	166	189	62	35	92	221	342	-121	7	0.878	1.169
21	Swe	155	183	53	41	89	237	331	-94	8	0.847	1.295
22	Tur	136	179	52	26	101	190	342	-152	6	0.760	1.061
23	Den	125	199	44	32	123	262	450	-188	5	0.628	1.317
24	Nor	78	142	30	17	95	146	371	-225	1	0.549	1.028
25	Wal	68	64	22	19	23	82	78	4	5	1.063	1.281
26	Irl	62	136	21	20	95	110	368	-258	0	0.456	0.809
27	Nir	61	122	18	23	81	132	370	-238	2	0.500	1.082
28	Fin	33	96	11	11	74	82	320	-238	0	0.344	0.854
29	Mlt	33	100	11	11	78	52	333	-281	0	0.330	0.520
30	Lux	33	120	12	9	99	86	509	-423	0	0.275	0.717
31	Cyp	20	78	5	10	63	40	309	-269	0	0.256	0.513
32	Isl	19	84	3	13	68	47	315	-268	0	0.226	0.560
33	Alb	18	28	4	10	14	21	45	-24	0	0.643	0.750
	Total	**9843**	**8968**	**3666**	**1636**	**3666**	**14187**	**14187**	**0**	**875**	**1.098**	**3.164**

1978-79

Pos'n	Cnty	Ave	Pts	P	W	D	L	F	A	Diff	B	No./T
1	W. Germany	14.000	84	55	28	16	11	109	62	47	12	6
2	England	9.142	64	43	23	12	8	75	35	40	6	7
3	Czechoslovakia	7.500	30	22	11	5	6	35	25	10	3	4
4	Yugoslavia	6.500	26	22	9	5	8	25	23	2	3	4
5	Spain	6.400	32	25	13	3	9	48	28	20	3	5
6	Switzerland	4.750	19	18	6	5	7	32	29	3	2	4
7	Hungary	4.500	18	16	7	3	6	30	22	8	1	4
–	Sweden	4.500	18	15	5	5	5	16	15	1	3	4
9	Belgium	4.400	22	18	8	4	6	20	16	4	2	5
–	E. Germany	4.400	22	20	8	4	8	31	31	0	2	5
11	Scotland	4.250	17	16	6	4	6	17	16	1	1	4
12	Austria	4.000	16	16	5	4	7	20	22	-2	2	4
–	Poland	4.000	16	16	5	5	6	29	34	-5	1	4
–	USSR	4.000	16	14	6	4	4	18	16	2	0	4
15	Italy	3.666	22	20	8	5	7	26	20	6	1	6
16	Denmark	3.250	13	12	5	3	4	19	20	-1	0	4
–	Netherlands	3.250	13	14	5	3	6	23	18	5	0	4
–	Romania	3.250	13	12	6	1	5	20	21	-1	0	4
19	France	3.000	12	16	4	4	8	16	19	-3	0	4
20	Rep. of Ireland	2.333	7	10	3	1	6	6	24	-18	0	3
21	Bulgaria	2.200	11	14	4	3	7	16	27	-11	0	5
22	Albania	2.000	2	2	1	0	1	3	4	-1	0	1
–	Wales	2.000	2	2	1	0	1	2	3	-1	0	1
–	Norway	2.000	8	12	2	4	6	10	21	-11	0	4
–	Portugal	2.000	8	12	3	2	7	14	17	-3	0	4
26	Finland	1.500	3	6	1	1	4	8	15	-7	0	2
–	Greece	1.500	6	10	3	0	7	15	25	-10	0	4
28	Iceland	1.333	4	8	0	4	4	5	15	-10	0	3
29	Cyprus	1.000	3	6	1	1	4	5	12	-7	0	3
–	N. Ireland	1.000	3	6	0	3	3	1	8	-7	0	3
–	Luxembourg	1.000	3	6	1	1	4	2	18	-16	0	3
–	Turkey	1.000	3	6	1	1	4	7	21	-14	0	3
33	Malta	0.666	2	6	1	0	5	7	28	-21	0	3
	Total		**538**	**496**	**190**	**116**	**190**	**710**	**710**	**0**	**42**	**2.863**

1955-56 to 1978-79

Pos'n	Cnty	Ave	Pts	P	W	D	L	F	A	Diff	B	No./T
1	England	9.165	1054	711	388	153	170	1409	734	675	125	115
2	Spain	7.913	910	661	336	124	201	1281	825	456	114	115
3	W. Germany	7.652	926	667	349	128	190	1376	874	502	100	121
4	Italy	7.200	828	604	303	128	173	965	622	343	94	115
5	Netherlands	6.407	487	368	187	64	117	735	452	283	49	76
6	USSR	6.121	251	185	99	37	49	282	177	105	16	41
7	Scotland	5.836	537	433	208	72	153	770	584	186	49	92
8	Hungary	5.805	418	348	160	58	130	660	503	157	40	72
9	Belgium	5.091	443	382	175	53	154	617	517	100	40	87
10	E. Germany	4.887	347	312	128	65	119	471	411	60	26	71
11	Yugoslavia	4.781	459	418	168	78	172	687	616	71	45	96
12	Portugal	4.700	423	370	156	77	137	623	498	125	34	90
13	Czechoslovakia	4.666	336	287	128	54	105	449	383	66	26	72
14	Poland	4.100	246	231	93	46	92	350	344	6	14	60
15	Wales	3.777	68	64	22	19	23	82	78	4	5	18
16	France	3.482	303	307	112	57	138	445	476	-31	22	87
17	Bulgaria	3.328	223	227	88	36	103	366	359	7	11	67
18	Austria	2.945	215	243	77	47	119	297	404	-107	14	73
19	Romania	2.928	205	225	81	38	106	284	377	-93	5	70
20	Switzerland	2.647	225	269	82	44	143	412	548	-136	17	85
21	Greece	2.553	166	189	62	35	92	221	342	-121	7	65
22	Sweden	2.500	155	183	53	41	89	237	331	-94	8	62
23	Turkey	2.266	136	179	52	26	101	190	342	-152	6	60
24	Denmark	1.666	125	199	44	32	123	262	450	-188	5	75
25	Albania	1.500	18	28	4	10	14	21	45	-24	0	12
26	Norway	1.344	78	142	30	17	95	146	371	-225	1	58
27	N. Ireland	1.173	61	122	18	23	81	132	370	-238	2	52
28	Rep. of Ireland	1.087	62	136	21	20	95	110	368	-258	0	57
29	Finland	0.785	33	96	11	11	74	82	320	-238	0	42
30	Malta	0.702	33	100	11	11	78	52	333	-281	0	47
31	Luxembourg	0.578	33	120	12	9	99	86	509	-423	0	57
32	Cyprus	0.555	20	78	5	10	63	40	309	-269	0	36
33	Iceland	0.487	19	84	3	13	68	47	315	-268	0	39
	Total		**9843**	**8968**	**3666**	**1636**	**3666**	**14187**	**14187**	**0**	**875**	**3.164**

Barcelona Back in Basle

Liverpool, going for a Champions' Cup hat-trick, were unfortunate enough to be drawn in the first round against another English team, Nottingham Forest, who, under the shrewd managership of Brian Clough, had run away with the League Championship title in their first season after promotion from Division Two.

The first leg took place at the City Ground, Nottingham, and was won, with some comfort, by the home side, 2-0. Liverpool, seeking to emulate the achievements of Ajax and Bayern Munich, had a mountain to climb at Anfield, and, sure enough, Clough's clever tactics, coupled with the brilliance of Peter Shilton in goal, kept the Merseysiders rooted at base camp, holding them to a 0-0 draw to qualify for the second round. Forest now carried the English flag alone, and they waved it proudly in the next two rounds. Firstly, against AEK Athens, and then, in the quarter-finals, against Grasshoppers Zürich, for whom Swiss international striker Claudio Sulser had scored a remarkable nine goals in the first two rounds, including all three which accounted for Spanish giants Real Madrid. Sulser was to score both of his team's goals against Forest, thus maintaining his amazing goal-a-game record, but Clough's men hit five and it was they who progressed into the semi-finals.

With teams such as Liverpool and Real Madrid being eliminated early on, this was an unusual tournament. Only Rangers, of the eight quarter-finalists, had ever won a European trophy before. But they were knocked out by Cologne and it was the Germans, in a European semi-final for the fourth time, whom Forest had to beat to reach the final.

When Cologne drew the first leg 3-3 in Nottingham, it looked odds on that they would at last exorcise their semi-final hoodoo and reach a European final for the first time. No English team had ever before won a European tie having failed to win the first leg at home. But Forest were to change all that, with Ian Bowyer stooping to head in the only goal of the game to give Forest the victory they required to return to Germany for the final in Munich against Malmö.

Malmö, coached by an Englishman, Bob Houghton, provided the same type of opposition for Forest that Liverpool had faced at Wembley, in the shape of Bruges, a year earlier. That is, they came to defend. Which, given that they had kept clean sheets in three of their four previous ties, was probably their best route to success. But the plan didn't work. Trevor Francis, making his European debut for Forest after an unprecedented £1 million move earlier in the year, headed in John Robertson's cross on the stroke of half-time and that was enough to keep the trophy in England for the third year in succession.

Ten years after their shock Cup-winners' Cup defeat in Basle by Slovan Bratislava, Barcelona returned to the Swiss city to capture the trophy for the first time. As in 1969, the final was an exciting, high-scoring match. Fortuna Düsseldorf, their opponents, were renowned for their all-out attacking play in the Bundesliga and with the two young Allofs brothers, Klaus and Thomas, in their strike force, they were sufficiently equipped to take the game to a Barcelona side which had its own star forwards in Rexach, Neeskens and the Austrian star of the 1978 World Cup, Hans Krankl. Four goals were scored in the first half, two apiece, and it stayed that way until extra-time when goals from Rexach and Krankl gave the Spaniards a decisive lead. Seel pulled one back for the Germans, but it wasn't enough and Barcelona, at last, had another European trophy to add to their three Fairs' Cups, the last of them won 13 years earlier, in 1966.

Borussia Mönchengladbach succeeded where Düsseldorf failed, however, and ensured that there would be no second successive year without a trophy for West German clubs by triumphing in the UEFA Cup. It was their second victory in the competition and one which was fully deserved, even if it needed a single Allan Simonsen penalty in the second leg of the final against Red Star Belgrade to secure the trophy. Borussia's particular merit was in remaining undefeated through all 12 of their matches, the first UEFA Cup winner to achieve that feat since Tottenham in the inaugural 1972 event.

1979 - 1980

Nottingham Forest

Valencia

Eintracht Frankfurt

Preliminary Round

Team 1	Cnty	Team 2	Cnty	1st leg	2nd leg	Agg
Dundalk	Irl	Linfield	Nir	1-1	2-0	3-1

	Pts	P	W	D	L	F	A	Diff	Goals/P
Total	4	2	1	2	1	4	4	0	2.000

First Round

Partizani Tirana	Alb	Celtic	Sco	1-0	1-4	2-4
Liverpool	Eng	Dinamo Tbilisi	URS	2-1	0-3	2-4
Nottingham Forest	Eng	Öster SIF	Swe	2-0	1-1	3-1
Levski Sofia	Bul	Real Madrid	Esp	0-1	0-2	0-3
Vejle BK	Den	Austria Vienna	Aut	3-2	1-1	4-3
Dundalk	Irl	Hibernians	Mlt	2-0	0-1	2-1
HJK Helsinki	Fin	Ajax	Ned	1-8	1-8	2-16
Ujpesti Dózsa	Hun	Dukla Prague	Tch	3-2	0-2	3-4
Valur Reykjavik	Isl	Hamburg	FRG	0-3	1-2	1-5
Red Boys Differdange	Lux	Omonia Nicosia	Cyp	2-1	1-6	3-7
IK Start	Nor	Strasbourg	Fra	1-2	0-4	1-6
FC Porto	Por	AC Milan	Ita	0-0	1-0	1-0
Arges Pitesti	Rom	AEK Athens	Gre	3-0	0-2	3-2
Servette	Sui	Beveren	Bel	3-1	1-1	4-2
Hajduk Split	Yug	Trabzonspor	Tur	1-0	1-0	2-0
Dynamo Berlin	GDR	Ruch Chorzów	Pol	4-1	0-0	4-1

	Pts	P	W	D	L	F	A	Diff	Goals/P
Total	64	32	27	10	27	96	96	0	3.000

Second Round

Nottingham Forest	Eng	Arges Pitesti	Rom	2-0	2-1	4-1
Vejle BK	Den	Hajduk Split	Yug	0-3	2-1	2-4
Celtic	Sco	Dundalk	Irl	3-2	0-0	3-2
Ajax	Ned	Omonia Nicosia	Cyp	10-0	0-4	10-4
FC Porto	Por	Real Madrid	Esp	2-1	0-1	2-2
Hamburg	FRG	Dinamo Tbilisi	URS	3-1	3-2	6-3
Dukla Prague	Tch	Strasbourg	Fra	1-0	0-2	1-2
Dynamo Berlin	GDR	Servette	Sui	2-1	2-2	4-3

	Pts	P	W	D	L	F	A	Diff	Goals/P
Total	32	16	14	4	14	53	53	0	3.313

Quarter Finals

Nottingham Forest	Eng	Dynamo Berlin	GDR	0-1	3-1	3-2
Celtic	Sco	Real Madrid	Esp	2-0	0-3	2-3
Strasbourg	Fra	Ajax	Ned	0-0	0-4	0-4
Hamburg	FRG	Hajduk Split	Yug	1-0	2-3	3-3

	Pts	P	W	D	L	F	A	Diff	Goals/P
Total	16	8	7	2	7	20	20	0	2.500

Semi Finals

Nottingham Forest	Eng	Ajax	Ned	2-0	0-1	2-1
Real Madrid	Esp	Hamburg	FRG	2-0	1-5	3-5

	Pts	P	W	D	L	F	A	Diff	Goals/P
Total	8	4	4	0	4	11	11	0	2.750

Final

Nottingham Forest	Eng	Hamburg	FRG	1-0		1-0

	Pts	P	W	D	L	F	A	Diff	Goals/P
Total	2	1	1	0	1	1	1	0	1.000

	Pts	P	W	D	L	F	A	Diff	Goals/P
Total	126	63	54	18	54	185	185	0	2.937

Pos'n	Club	Cnty	Pts	P	W	D	L	F	A	Diff	B	Pts/P	F/P
1	Nottingham Forest	Eng	16	9	6	1	2	13	5	8	3	1.778	1.444
2	Hamburg	FRG	15	9	6	0	3	19	11	8	3	1.667	2.111
3	Ajax	Ned	13	8	5	1	2	31	8	23	2	1.625	3.875
4	Real Madrid	Esp	12	8	5	0	3	11	9	2	2	1.500	1.375
5	Hajduk Split	Yug	9	6	4	0	2	9	5	4	1	1.500	1.500
6	Dynamo Berlin	GDR	9	6	3	2	1	10	7	3	1	1.500	1.667
7	Celtic	Sco	8	6	3	1	2	9	7	2	1	1.333	1.500
8	Strasbourg	Fra	8	6	3	1	2	8	6	2	1	1.333	1.333
9	Dundalk	Irl	6	6	2	2	2	7	5	2	0	1.000	1.167
10	FC Porto	Por	5	4	2	1	1	3	2	1	0	1.250	0.750
11	Vejle BK	Den	5	4	2	1	1	6	7	-1	0	1.250	1.500
12	Servette	Sui	4	4	1	2	1	7	6	1	0	1.000	1.750
13	Dulka Prague	Tch	4	4	2	0	2	5	5	0	0	1.000	1.250
14	Omonia Nicosia	Cyp	4	4	2	0	2	11	13	-2	0	1.000	2.750
15	Dinamo Tbilisi	URS	2	4	1	0	3	7	8	-1	0	0.500	1.750
16	Ujpesti Dózsa	Hun	2	2	1	0	1	3	4	-1	0	1.000	1.500
17	AEK Athens	Gre	2	2	1	0	1	2	3	-1	0	1.000	1.000
18	Hibernians	Mlt	2	2	1	0	1	1	2	-1	0	1.000	0.500
19	Arges Pitesti	Rom	2	4	1	0	3	4	6	-2	0	0.500	1.000
20	Partizani Tirana	Alb	2	2	1	0	1	2	4	-2	0	1.000	1.000
–	Liverpool	Eng	2	2	1	0	1	2	4	-2	0	1.000	1.000
22	Red Boys Differdange	Lux	2	2	1	0	1	3	7	-4	0	1.000	1.500
23	Austria Vienna	Aut	1	2	0	1	1	3	7	-1	0	0.500	1.500
24	AC Milan	Ita	1	2	0	1	1	0	1	-1	0	0.500	0.000
25	Beveren	Bel	1	2	0	1	1	2	4	-2	0	0.500	1.000
26	Linfield	Nir	1	2	0	1	1	1	3	-2	0	0.500	0.500
–	Öster SIF	Swe	1	2	0	1	1	1	3	-2	0	0.500	0.500
28	Ruch Chorzów	Pol	1	2	0	1	1	1	4	-3	0	0.500	0.500
29	Trabzonspor	Tur	0	2	0	0	2	0	2	-2	0	0.000	0.000
30	Levski Sofia	Bul	0	2	0	0	2	0	3	-3	0	0.000	0.000
31	Valur Reykjavik	Isl	0	2	0	0	2	1	5	-4	0	0.000	0.500
32	IK Start	Nor	0	2	0	0	2	1	6	-5	0	0.000	0.500
33	HJK Helsinki	Fin	0	2	0	0	2	2	16	-14	0	0.000	1.000
	Total		**140**	**126**	**54**	**18**	**54**	**185**	**185**	**0**	**14**	**1.111**	**2.937**

European Cup Winners Cup 1979-80

Preliminary Round

Team 1	Cnty	Team 2	Cnty	1st leg	2nd leg	Agg
B 1903 Copenhagen	Den	Apoel Nicosia	Cyp	6-0	1-0	7-0
Rangers	Sco	Lillestrøm SK	Nor	1-0	2-0	3-0

	Pts	P	W	D	L	F	A	Diff	Goals/P
Total	8	4	4	0	4	10	10	0	2.500

First Round

Arsenal	Eng	Fenerbahçe	Tur	2-0	0-0	2-0
FC Tirol	Aut	Lokomotiv Kosice	Tch	1-2	0-1	1-3
Beerschot	Bel	Rijeka	Yug	0-0	1-2	1-2
B 1903 Copenhagen	Den	Valencia	Esp	2-2	0-4	2-6
Rangers	Sco	Fortuna Düsseldorf	FRG	2-1	0-0	2-1
Reipas Lahti	Fin	Aris Bonnevoie	Lux	0-1	0-1	0-2
Wrexham	Wal	Magdeburg	GDR	3-2	2-5	5-7
Panionios	Gre	Twente Enschede	Ned	4-0	1-3	5-3
Cliftonville	Nir	Nantes	Fra	0-1	0-7	0-8
IA Akranes	Isl	Barcelona	Esp	0-1	0-5	0-6
Juventus	Ita	Rába ETO	Hun	2-0	1-2	3-2
Sliema Wanderers	Mlt	Boavista	Por	2-1	0-8	2-9
Arka Gdynia	Pol	Beroe Stara Zagora	Bul	3-2	0-2	3-4
IFK Gothenburg	Swe	Waterford United	Irl	1-0	1-1	2-1
Young Boys Berne	Sui	Steaua Bucharest	Rom	2-2	0-6	2-8

	Pts	P	W	D	L	F	A	Diff	Goals/P
Total	60	30	24	12	24	92	92	0	3.067

Second Round

Arsenal	Eng	Magdeburg	GDR	2-1	2-2	4-3
Beroe Stara Zagora	Bul	Juventus	Ita	1-0	0-3	1-3
Valencia	Esp	Rangers	Sco	1-1	3-1	4-2
Nantes	Fra	Steaua Bucharest	Rom	3-2	2-1	5-3
Panionios	Gre	IFK Gothenburg	Swe	1-0	0-2	1-2
Aris Bonnevoie	Lux	Barcelona	Esp	1-4	1-7	2-11
Lokomotiv Kosice	Tch	Rijeka	Yug	2-0	0-3	2-3
Dinamo Moscow	URS	Boavista	Por	0-0	1-1	1-1

	Pts	P	W	D	L	F	A	Diff	Goals/P
Total	32	16	12	8	12	48	48	0	3.000

Quarter Finals

Arsenal	Eng	IFK Gothenburg	Swe	5-1	0-0	5-1
Barcelona	Esp	Valencia	Esp	0-1	3-4	3-5
Dinamo Moscow	URS	Nantes	Fra	0-2	3-2	3-4
Rijeka	Yug	Juventus	Ita	0-0	0-2	0-2

	Pts	P	W	D	L	F	A	Diff	Goals/P
Total	16	8	6	4	6	23	23	0	2.875

Semi Finals

Arsenal	Eng	Juventus	Ita	1-1	1-0	2-1
Nantes	Fra	Valencia	Esp	2-1	0-4	2-5

	Pts	P	W	D	L	F	A	Diff	Goals/P
Total	8	4	3	2	3	10	10	0	2.500

Final

Valencia	Esp	Arsenal	Eng	0-0		0-0

	Pts	P	W	D	L	F	A	Diff	Goals/P
Total	2	1	0	2	0	0	0	0	0.000

	Pts	P	W	D	L	F	A	Diff	Goals/P
Total	126	63	49	28	49	183	183	0	2.905

Pos'n	Club	Cnty	Pts	P	W	D	L	F	A	Diff	B	Pts/P	F/P
1	Valencia	Esp	16	9	5	3	1	20	9	11	3	1.778	2.222
2	Arsenal	Eng	16	9	4	5	0	13	5	8	3	1.778	1.444
3	Nantes	Fra	14	8	6	0	2	19	11	8	2	1.750	2.375
4	Juventus	Ita	10	8	3	2	3	9	5	4	2	1.250	1.125
5	Barcelona	Esp	9	6	4	0	2	20	7	13	1	1.500	3.333
6	Rangers	Sco	8	6	3	2	1	7	5	2	0	1.333	1.167
7	Rijeka	Yug	7	6	2	2	2	5	5	0	1	1.167	0.833
8	IFK Gothenburg	Swe	7	6	2	2	2	5	7	-2	1	1.167	0.833
9	Lokomotiv Kosice	Tch	6	4	3	0	1	5	4	1	0	1.500	1.250
10	B 1903 Copenhagen	Den	5	4	2	1	1	9	6	3	0	1.250	2.250
11	Dinamo Moscow	URS	5	4	1	2	1	1	5	-1	1	1.250	1.000
12	Boavista	Por	4	4	1	2	1	10	3	7	0	1.000	2.500
13	Panionios	Gre	4	4	2	0	2	6	5	1	0	1.000	1.500
14	Beroe Stara Zagora	Bul	4	4	2	0	2	5	6	-1	0	1.000	1.250
15	Aris Bonnevoie	Lux	4	4	2	0	2	4	11	-7	0	1.000	1.000
16	Steaua Bucharest	Rom	3	4	1	1	2	11	7	4	0	0.750	2.750
17	Magdeburg	GDR	3	4	1	1	2	10	9	1	0	0.750	2.500
18	Arka Gdynia	Pol	2	2	1	0	1	3	4	-1	0	1.000	1.500
19	Rába ETO	Hun	2	2	1	0	1	2	3	-1	0	1.000	1.000
20	Wrexham	Wal	2	2	1	0	1	5	7	-2	0	1.000	2.500
21	Twente Enschede	Ned	2	2	1	0	1	3	5	-2	0	1.000	1.500
22	Sliema Wanderers	Mlt	2	2	1	0	1	2	9	-7	0	1.000	1.000
23	Beerschot	Bel	1	2	0	1	1	1	2	-1	0	0.500	0.500
–	Waterford United	Irl	1	2	0	1	1	1	2	-1	0	0.500	0.500
–	Fortuna Düsseldorf	FRG	1	2	0	1	1	1	2	-1	0	0.500	0.500
26	Fenerbahçe	Tur	1	2	0	1	1	0	2	-2	0	0.500	0.000
27	Young Boys Berne	Sui	1	2	0	1	1	2	8	-6	0	0.500	1.000
28	FC Tirol	Aut	0	2	0	0	2	1	3	-2	0	0.000	0.500
29	Reipas Lahti	Fin	0	2	0	0	2	0	2	-2	0	0.000	0.000
30	Lillestrøm SK	Nor	0	2	0	0	2	0	3	-3	0	0.000	0.000
31	IA Akranes	Isl	0	2	0	0	2	0	6	-6	0	0.000	0.000
32	Apoel Nicosia	Cyp	0	2	0	0	2	0	7	-7	0	0.000	0.000
33	Cliftonville	Nir	0	2	0	0	2	0	8	-8	0	0.000	0.000
	Total		**140**	**126**	**49**	**28**	**49**	**183**	**183**	**0**	**14**	**1.111**	**2.905**

First Round

Team 1	Cnty	Team 2	Cnty	1st leg	2nd leg	Agg
Rapid Vienna	Aut	Diósgyöri VTK	Hun	0-1	2-3	2-4
Wiener Sport-Club	Aut	Universitatea Craiova	Rom	0-0	1-3	1-3
Lokomotiv Sofia	Bul	Ferencváros	Hun	3-0	0-2	3-2
AGF Aarhus	Den	Stal Mielec	Pol	1-1	1-0	2-1
Aberdeen	Sco	Eintracht Frankfurt	FRG	1-1	0-1	1-2
Dundee United	Sco	Anderlecht	Bel	0-0	1-1	1-1
Sporting Gijón	Esp	PSV Eindhoven	Ned	0-0	0-1	0-1
Atlético Madrid	Esp	Dynamo Dresden	GDR	1-2	0-3	1-5
KuPS Kuopio	Fin	Malmö FF	Swe	1-2	0-2	1-4
Aris Salonika	Gre	Benfica	Por	3-1	1-2	4-3
Glenavon	Nir	Standard Liège	Bel	0-1	0-1	0-2
Inter Milan	Ita	Real Sociedad	Esp	3-0	0-2	3-2
Napoli	Ita	Olympiakos Pireus	Gre	2-0	0-1	2-1
Penigia	Ita	Dinamo Zagreb	Yug	1-0	0-0	1-0
Progrès Niedercorn	Lux	Grasshoppers Zürich	Sui	0-2	0-4	0-6
Valletta	Mlt	Leeds United	Eng	0-4	0-3	0-7
FK Skeid	Nor	Ipswich Town	Eng	1-3	0-7	1-10
Feyenoord	Ned	Everton	Eng	1-0	1-0	2-0
Widzew Lódź	Pol	Saint-Etienne	Fra	2-1	0-3	2-4
Sporting Lisbon	Por	Bohemians	Irl	2-0	0-0	2-0
Bor. Mönchengladbach	FRG	IL Viking	Nor	3-0	1-1	4-1
VFB Stuttgart	FRG	Torino	Ita	1-0	1-2	2-2
Dinamo Bucharest	Rom	Alki Larnaca	Cyp	3-0	9-0	12-0
Kalmar FF	Swe	IBK Keflavik	Isl	2-1	0-1	2-2
FC Zürich	Sui	Kaiserslautern	FRG	1-3	1-5	2-8
Zbrojovka Brno	Tch	Esbjerg FB	Den	6-0	1-1	7-1
Bohemians Prague	Tch	Bayern Munich	FRG	0-2	2-2	2-4
Galatasaray	Tur	Red Star Belgrade	Yug	0-0	1-3	1-3
Orduspor	Tur	Banik Ostrava	Tch	2-0	0-6	2-6
Shakhtyor Donetsk	URS	Monaco	Fra	2-1	0-2	2-3
Dinamo Kiev	URS	CSKA Sofia	Bul	2-1	1-1	3-2
Carl Zeiss Jena	GDR	West Bromwich Albion	Eng	2-0	2-1	4-1

	Pts	P	W	D	L	F	A	Diff	Goals/P
Total	128	64	51	26	51	163	163	0	2.547

Second Round

Standard Liège	Bel	Napoli	Ita	2-1	1-1	3-2
Lokomotiv Sofia	Bul	Monaco	Fra	4-2	1-2	5-4
AGF Aarhus	Den	Bayern Munich	FRG	1-2	1-3	2-5
Dundee United	Sco	Diósgyöri VTK	Hun	0-1	1-3	1-4
Aris Salonika	Gre	Penigia	Ita	1-1	3-0	4-1
PSV Eindhoven	Ned	Saint-Etienne	Fra	2-0	0-6	2-6
Feyenoord	Ned	Malmö FF	Swe	4-0	1-1	5-1
Sporting Lisbon	Por	Kaiserslautern	FRG	1-1	0-2	1-3
Bor. Mönchengladbach	FRG	Inter Milan	Ita	1-1	3-2	4-3
Dinamo Bucharest	Rom	Eintracht Frankfurt	FRG	2-0	0-3	2-3
Universitatea Craiova	Rom	Leeds United	Eng	2-0	2-0	4-0
Grasshoppers Zürich	Sui	Ipswich Town	Eng	0-0	1-1	1-1
Zbrojovka Brno	Tch	IBK Keflavik	Isl	3-1	2-1	5-2
Banik Ostrava	Tch	Dinamo Kiev	URS	1-0	0-2	1-2
Red Star Belgrade	Yug	Carl Zeiss Jena	GDR	3-2	3-2	6-4
Dynamo Dresden	GDR	VFB Stuttgart	FRG	1-1	0-0	1-1

	Pts	P	W	D	L	F	A	Diff	Goals/P
Total	64	32	23	18	23	89	89	0	2.781

Third Round

Standard Liège	Bel	Zbrojovka Brno	Tch	1-2	2-3	3-5
Lokomotiv Sofia	Bul	Dinamo Kiev	URS	1-0	1-2	2-2
Saint-Etienne	Fra	Aris Salonika	Gre	4-1	3-3	7-4
Diósgyöri VTK	Hun	Kaiserslautern	FRG	0-2	1-6	1-8
Eintracht Frankfurt	FRG	Feyenoord	Ned	4-1	0-1	4-2
Bayern Munich	FRG	Red Star Belgrade	Yug	2-0	2-3	4-3
Bor. Mönchengladbach	FRG	Universitatea Craiova	Rom	2-0	0-1	2-1
Grasshoppers Zürich	Sui	VFB Stuttgart	FRG	0-2	0-3	0-5

	Pts	P	W	D	L	F	A	Diff	Goals/P
Total	32	16	15	2	15	53	53	0	3.313

Quarter Finals

Saint-Etienne	Fra	Bor. Mönchengladbach	FRG	1-4	0-2	1-6
Eintracht Frankfurt	FRG	Zbrojovka Brno	Tch	4-1	2-3	6-4
Kaiserslautern	FRG	Bayern Munich	FRG	1-0	1-4	2-4
VFB Stuttgart	FRG	Lokomotiv Sofia	Bul	3-1	1-0	4-1

	Pts	P	W	D	L	F	A	Diff	Goals/P
Total	16	8	8	0	8	28	28	0	3.500

Semi Finals

Bayern Munich	FRG	Eintracht Frankfurt	FRG	2-0	1-5	3-5
VFB Stuttgart	FRG	Bor. Mönchengladbach	FRG	2-1	0-2	2-3

	Pts	P	W	D	L	F	A	Diff	Goals/P
Total	8	4	4	0	4	13	13	0	3.250

Final

Bor. Mönchengladbach	FRG	Eintracht Frankfurt	FRG	3-2	0-1	3-3

	Pts	P	W	D	L	F	A	Diff	Goals/P
Total	4	2	2	0	2	6	6	0	3.000

	Pts	P	W	D	L	F	A	Diff	Goals/P
Total	252	126	103	46	103	352	352	0	2.794

UEFA Cup 1979-80

Pos'n	Club	Cnty	Pts	P	W	D	L	F	A	Diff	B	Pts/P	F/P
1	Bor. Mönchengladbach	FRG	19	12	7	2	3	22	11	11	3	1.583	1.833
2	Eintracht Frankfurt	FRG	16	12	6	1	5	23	15	8	3	1.333	1.917
3	VFB Stuttgart	FRG	16	10	6	2	2	14	7	7	2	1.600	1.400
4	Bayern Munich	FRG	15	10	6	1	3	20	14	6	2	1.500	2.000
5	Kaiserslautern	FRG	14	8	6	1	1	21	8	13	1	1.750	2.625
6	Zbrojovka Brno	Tch	14	8	6	1	1	21	12	9	1	1.150	2.625
7	Universitatea Craiova	Rom	9	6	4	1	1	8	3	5	0	1.500	1.333
8	Feyenoord	Ned	9	6	4	1	1	9	5	4	0	1.500	1.500
9	Red Star Belgrade	Yug	9	6	4	1	1	12	9	3	0	1.500	2.000
10	Saint-Etienne	Fra	8	8	3	1	4	18	14	4	1	1.000	2.250
11	Diósgyöri VTK	Hun	8	6	4	0	2	9	11	-2	0	1.333	1.500
12	Dinamo Kiev	URS	7	6	3	1	2	7	5	2	0	1.167	1.167
13	Standard Liège	Bel	7	6	3	1	2	8	7	1	0	1.167	1.333
14	Lokomotiv Sofia	Bul	7	8	3	0	5	11	12	-1	1	0.875	1.375
15	Dinamo Bucharest	Rom	6	4	3	0	1	14	3	11	0	1.500	3.500
16	Ipswich Town	Eng	6	4	2	2	0	11	2	9	0	1.500	2.750
17	Dynamo Dresden	GDR	6	4	2	2	0	6	2	4	0	1.500	1.500
18	Aris Salonika	Gra	6	6	2	2	2	12	11	1	0	1.000	2.000
19	Grasshoppers Zürich	Sui	6	6	2	2	2	7	6	1	0	1.000	1.167
20	Malmö FF	Swe	5	4	2	1	1	5	6	-1	0	1.250	1.250
21	PSV Eindhoven	Ned	5	4	2	1	1	3	6	-3	0	1.250	0.750
22	Leeds United	Eng	4	4	2	0	2	7	4	3	0	1.000	1.750
–	Banik Ostrava	Tch	4	4	2	0	2	7	4	3	0	1.000	1.750
24	Carl Zeiss Jena	GDR	4	4	2	0	2	8	7	1	0	1.000	2.000
25	Monaco	Frs	4	4	2	0	2	7	7	0	0	1.000	1.750
26	Sporting Lisbon	Por	4	4	1	2	1	3	3	0	0	1.000	0.750
27	Penigia	Ita	4	4	1	2	1	2	4	-2	0	1.000	0.500
28	Inter Milan	Ita	3	4	1	1	2	6	6	0	0	0.750	1.500
29	Napoli	Ita	3	4	1	1	2	4	4	0	0	0.750	1.000
30	AGF Aarhus	Den	3	4	1	1	2	4	6	-2	0	0.750	1.000
31	Torino	Ita	2	2	1	0	1	2	2	0	0	1.000	1.000
–	Kalmar FF	Swe	2	2	1	0	1	2	2	0	0	1.000	1.000
33	Anderlecht	Bel	2	2	0	2	0	1	1	0	0	1.000	0.500
34	Benfica	Por	2	2	1	0	1	3	4	-1	0	1.000	1.500
35	Real Sociedad	Esp	2	2	1	0	1	2	3	-1	0	1.000	1.000
–	Ferencváros	Hun	2	2	1	0	1	2	3	-1	0	1.000	1.000
–	Shakhtyor Donetsk	URS	2	2	1	0	1	2	3	-1	0	1.000	1.000
38	Olympiakos Pireus	Gre	2	2	1	0	1	1	2	-1	0	1.000	0.500
39	Widzew Lódź	Pol	2	2	1	0	1	2	4	-2	0	1.000	1.000
40	IBK Keflavik	Isl	2	4	1	0	3	4	7	-3	0	0.500	1.000
41	Dundee	Sco	2	4	0	2	2	2	5	-3	0	0.500	0.500
42	Orduspor	Tur	2	2	1	0	1	2	6	-4	0	1.000	1.000
43	CSKA Sofia	Bul	1	2	0	1	1	2	3	-1	0	0.500	1.000
44	Aberdeen	Sco	1	2	0	1	1	1	2	-1	0	0.500	0.500
–	Stal Mielec	Pol	1	2	0	1	1	1	2	-1	0	0.500	0.500
46	Sporting Gijón	Esp	1	2	0	1	1	0	1	-1	0	0.500	0.000
–	Dinamo Zagreb	Yug	1	2	0	1	1	0	1	-1	0	0.500	0.000
48	Bohemians Prague	Tch	1	2	0	1	1	2	4	-2	0	0.500	1.000
49	Wiener Sport-Club	Aut	1	2	0	1	1	1	3	-2	0	0.500	0.500
–	Galatasaray	Tur	1	2	0	1	1	1	3	-2	0	0.500	0.500
51	Bohemians	Irl	1	2	0	1	1	0	2	-2	0	0.500	0.000
52	IL Viking	Nor	1	2	0	1	1	1	4	-3	0	0.500	0.500
53	Esbjerg FB	Den	1	2	0	1	1	1	7	-6	0	0.500	0.500
54	Rapid Vienna	Aut	0	2	0	0	2	2	4	-2	0	0.000	1.000
55	Everton	Eng	0	2	0	0	2	0	2	-2	0	0.000	0.000
–	Glenavon	Nir	0	2	0	0	2	0	2	-2	0	0.000	0.000
57	West Bromwich Albion	Eng	0	2	0	0	2	1	4	-3	0	0.000	0.500
–	KuPS Kuopio	Fin	0	2	0	0	2	1	4	-3	0	0.000	0.500
59	Atlético Madrid	Esp	0	2	0	0	2	1	5	-4	0	0.000	0.500
60	FC Zürich	Sui	0	2	0	0	2	2	8	-6	0	0.000	1.000
61	Progrès Niedercorn	Lux	0	2	0	0	2	0	6	-6	0	0.000	0.000
62	Valletta	Mal	0	2	0	0	2	0	7	-7	0	0.000	0.000
63	FK Skeid	Nor	0	2	0	0	2	1	10	-9	0	0.000	0.500
64	Alki Larnaca	Cyp	0	2	0	0	2	0	12	-12	0	0.000	0.000
	Total		**266**	**252**	**103**	**46**	**103**	**352**	**352**	**0**	**14**	**1.056**	**2.794**

1979-80

Pos'n	Cnty	Pts	P	W	D	L	F	A	Diff	B	Pts/P	F/P
1	FRG	96	63	37	8	18	120	68	52	14	1.524	1.905
2	Eng	44	32	15	8	9	47	26	21	6	1.375	1.469
3	Esp	40	29	15	4	10	54	34	20	6	1.379	1.862
4	Fra	34	26	14	2	10	52	38	14	4	1.308	2.000
5	Ned	29	20	12	3	5	46	24	22	2	1.450	2.300
6	Tch	29	22	13	2	7	40	29	11	1	1.318	1.818
7	Yug	26	20	10	4	6	26	20	6	2	1.300	1.300
8	Ita	23	24	7	7	10	23	22	1	2	0.958	0.958
9	GDR	22	18	8	5	5	34	25	9	1	1.222	1.889
10	Rom	20	18	9	2	7	37	19	18	0	1.111	2.056
11	Sco	19	18	6	6	6	19	19	0	1	1.056	1.056
12	URS	16	16	6	3	7	20	21	-1	1	1.000	1.250
13	Por	15	14	5	5	4	19	12	7	0	1.071	1.357
14	Swe	15	14	5	4	5	13	18	-5	1	1.071	0.929
15	Gre	14	14	6	2	6	21	21	0	0	1.000	1.500
16	Hun	14	12	7	0	5	16	21	-5	0	1.167	1.333
17	Den	14	14	5	4	5	20	26	-6	0	1.000	1.429
18	Bul	12	16	5	1	10	18	24	-6	1	0.750	1.125
19	Bel	11	12	3	5	4	12	14	-2	0	0.917	1.000
20	Sui	11	14	3	5	6	18	28	-10	0	0.786	1.286
21	Irl	8	10	2	4	4	8	9	-1	0	0.800	0.800
22	Pol	6	8	2	2	4	7	14	-7	0	0.750	0.875
23	Lux	6	8	3	0	5	7	24	-17	0	0.750	0.875
24	Tur	4	8	1	2	5	3	13	-10	0	0.500	0.375
25	Mlt	4	6	2	0	4	3	18	-15	0	0.667	0.500
26	Cyp	4	8	2	0	6	11	32	-21	0	0.500	1.375
27	Wal	2	2	1	0	1	5	7	-2	0	1.000	2.500
28	Alb	2	2	1	0	1	2	4	-2	0	1.000	1.000
29	Aut	2	8	0	2	6	7	14	-7	0	0.250	0.875
30	Isl	2	8	1	0	7	5	18	-13	0	0.250	0.625
31	Nir	1	6	0	1	5	1	13	-12	0	0.167	0.167
32	Nor	1	8	0	1	7	3	23	-20	0	0.125	0.375
33	Fin	0	6	0	0	6	3	22	-19	0	0.000	0.500
	Total	**546**	**504**	**206**	**92**	**206**	**720**	**720**	**0**	**42**	**1.083**	**2.857**

1955-56 to 1979-80

Pos'n	Cnty	Pts	P	W	D	L	F	A	Diff	B	Pts/P	F/P
1	Eng	1098	743	403	161	179	1456	760	696	131	1.478	1.960
2	FRG	1022	730	386	136	208	1496	942	554	114	1.400	2.049
3	Esp	950	690	351	128	211	1335	859	476	120	1.377	1.935
4	Ita	851	628	310	135	183	988	644	344	96	1.355	1.573
5	Sco	556	451	214	78	159	789	603	186	50	1.233	1.749
6	Ned	516	388	199	67	122	781	476	305	51	1.330	2.013
7	Yug	485	438	178	82	178	713	636	77	47	1.107	1.628
8	Bel	454	394	178	58	158	629	531	98	40	1.152	1.596
9	Por	438	384	161	82	141	642	510	132	34	1.141	1.672
10	Hun	432	360	167	58	135	676	524	152	40	1.200	1.878
11	GDR	369	330	136	70	124	505	436	69	27	1.118	1.530
12	Tch	365	309	141	56	112	489	412	77	27	1.181	1.583
13	Fra	337	333	126	59	148	497	514	-17	26	1.012	1.492
14	URS	267	201	105	40	56	302	198	104	17	1.328	1.502
15	Pol	252	239	95	48	96	357	358	-1	14	1.054	1.494
16	Sui	236	283	85	49	149	430	576	-146	17	0.834	1.519
17	Bul	235	243	93	37	113	384	383	1	12	0.967	1.580
18	Rom	225	243	90	40	113	321	396	-75	5	0.926	1.321
19	Aut	217	251	77	49	125	304	418	-114	14	0.865	1.211
20	Gre	180	203	68	37	98	242	363	-121	7	0.887	1.192
21	Swe	170	197	58	45	94	250	349	-99	9	0.863	1.269
22	Tur	140	187	53	28	106	193	355	-162	6	0.749	1.032
23	Den	139	213	49	36	128	282	476	-194	5	0.653	1.324
24	Nor	79	150	30	18	102	149	394	-245	1	0.527	0.993
25	Wal	70	66	23	19	24	87	85	2	5	1.061	1.318
26	Irl	70	146	23	24	99	118	377	-259	0	0.479	0.808
27	Nir	62	128	18	24	86	133	383	-250	2	0.484	1.039
28	Lux	39	128	15	9	104	93	533	-440	0	0.305	0.727
29	Mlt	37	106	13	11	82	55	351	-296	0	0.349	0.519
30	Fin	33	102	11	11	80	85	342	-257	0	0.324	0.833
31	Cyp	24	86	7	10	69	51	341	-290	0	0.279	0.593
32	Isl	21	92	4	13	75	52	333	-281	0	0.228	0.565
33	Alb	20	30	5	10	15	23	49	-26	0	0.667	0.767
	Total	**10389**	**9472**	**3872**	**1728**	**3872**	**14907**	**14907**	**0**	**917**	**1.097**	**3.148**

National Performance by Index

1979-80

Pos'n	Cnty	Ave	Pts	P	W	D	L	F	A	Diff	B	No./T
1	W. Germany	13.714	96	63	37	8	18	120	68	52	14	7
2	France	8.500	34	26	14	2	10	52	38	14	4	4
3	Netherlands	7.250	29	20	12	3	5	46	24	22	2	4
4	Spain	6.666	40	29	15	4	10	54	34	20	6	6
5	Yugoslavia	6.500	26	20	10	4	6	26	20	6	2	4
6	England	6.285	44	32	15	8	9	47	26	21	6	7
7	Czechoslovakia	5.800	29	22	13	2	7	40	29	11	1	5
8	E. Germany	5.500	22	18	8	5	5	34	25	9	1	4
9	Romania	5.000	20	18	9	2	7	37	19	18	0	4
10	Scotland	4.750	19	18	6	6	6	19	19	0	1	4
11	USSR	4.000	16	16	6	3	7	20	21	-1	1	4
12	Italy	3.833	23	24	7	7	10	23	22	1	2	6
13	Portugal	3.750	15	14	5	5	4	19	12	7	0	4
–	Sweden	3.750	15	14	5	4	5	13	18	-5	1	4
15	Denmark	3.500	14	14	5	4	5	20	26	-6	0	4
–	Greece	3.500	14	14	6	2	6	21	21	0	0	4
–	Hungary	3.500	14	12	7	0	5	16	21	-5	0	4
18	Bulgaria	3.000	12	16	5	1	10	18	24	-6	1	4
19	Belgium	2.750	11	12	3	5	4	12	14	-2	0	4
–	Switzerland	2.750	11	14	3	5	6	18	28	-10	0	4
21	Rep. of Ireland	2.666	8	10	2	4	4	8	9	-1	0	3
22	Albania	2.000	2	2	1	0	1	2	4	-2	0	1
–	Wales	2.000	2	2	1	0	1	5	7	-2	0	1
–	Luxembourg	2.000	6	8	3	0	5	7	24	-17	0	3
25	Poland	1.500	6	8	2	2	4	7	14	-7	0	4
26	Cyprus	1.333	4	8	2	0	6	11	32	-21	0	3
–	Malta	1.333	4	6	2	0	4	3	18	-15	0	3
28	Turkey	1.000	4	8	1	2	5	3	13	-10	0	4
29	Iceland	0.666	2	8	1	0	7	5	18	-13	0	3
30	Austria	0.500	2	8	0	2	6	7	14	-7	0	4
31	N. Ireland	0.333	1	6	0	1	5	1	13	-12	0	3
32	Norway	0.250	1	8	0	1	7	3	23	-20	0	4
33	Finland	0.000	0	6	0	0	6	3	22	-19	0	3
	Total		**546**	**504**	**206**	**92**	**206**	**720**	**720**	**0**	**42**	**2.857**

1955-56 to 1979-80

Pos'n	Cnty	Ave	Pts	P	W	D	L	F	A	Diff	B	No./T
1	England	9.000	1098	743	403	161	179	1456	760	696	131	122
2	W. Germany	7.984	1022	730	386	136	208	1496	942	554	114	128
3	Spain	7.851	950	690	351	128	211	1335	859	476	120	121
4	Italy	7.033	851	628	310	135	183	988	644	344	96	121
5	Netherlands	6.450	516	388	199	67	122	781	476	305	51	80
6	USSR	5.933	267	201	105	40	56	302	198	104	17	45
7	Scotland	5.791	556	451	214	78	159	789	603	186	50	96
8	Hungary	5.684	432	360	167	58	135	676	524	152	40	76
9	Belgium	4.989	454	394	178	58	158	629	531	98	40	91
10	E. Germany	4.920	369	330	136	70	124	505	436	69	27	75
11	Yugoslavia	4.850	485	438	178	82	178	713	636	77	47	100
12	Czechoslovakia	4.740	365	309	141	56	112	489	412	77	27	77
13	Portugal	4.659	438	384	161	82	141	642	510	132	34	94
14	Poland	3.937	252	239	95	48	96	357	358	-1	14	64
15	France	3.703	337	333	126	59	148	497	514	-17	26	91
16	Wales	3.684	70	66	23	19	24	87	85	2	5	19
17	Bulgaria	3.309	235	243	93	37	113	384	383	1	12	71
18	Romania	3.040	225	243	90	40	113	321	396	-75	5	74
19	Austria	2.818	217	251	77	49	125	304	418	-114	14	77
20	Switzerland	2.651	236	283	85	49	149	430	576	-146	17	89
21	Greece	2.608	180	203	68	37	98	242	363	-121	7	69
22	Sweden	2.575	170	197	58	45	94	250	349	-99	9	66
23	Turkey	2.187	140	187	53	28	106	193	355	-162	6	64
24	Denmark	1.759	139	213	49	36	128	282	476	-194	5	79
25	Albania	1.538	20	30	5	10	15	23	49	-26	0	13
26	Norway	1.274	79	150	30	18	102	149	394	-245	1	62
27	Rep. of Ireland	1.166	70	146	23	24	99	118	377	-259	0	60
28	N. Ireland	1.127	62	128	18	24	86	133	383	-250	2	55
29	Malta	0.740	37	106	13	11	82	55	351	-296	0	50
30	Finland	0.733	33	102	11	11	80	85	342	-257	0	45
31	Luxembourg	0.650	39	128	15	9	104	93	533	-440	0	60
32	Cyprus	0.615	24	86	7	10	69	51	341	-290	0	39
33	Iceland	0.500	21	92	4	13	75	52	333	-281	0	42
	Total		**10389**	**9472**	**3872**	**1728**	**3872**	**14907**	**14907**	**0**	**917**	**3.148**

Germans Win UEFA Full-House

Nottingham Forest retained the Champions' Cup, the seventh club – after Real Madrid, Benfica, Inter Milan, Ajax, Bayern Munich and Liverpool – to do so. Victory was achieved with a 1-0 defeat of pre-match favourites Hamburg in the Madrid final, with John Robertson scoring the only goal of the game in the 19th minute and Forest then packing their defence to keep the likes of Kaltz, Hrubesch, Magath and European Footballer of the Year Kevin Keegan at bay. Peter Shilton was the undisputed hero of the evening, showing all the athleticism and courage of one of the world's all-time great goalkeepers to deny the Hamburg attack time and again and help preserve the 1-0 scoreline.

Forest's defensive strategy for the final was in part due to the absence of their two star strikers, Tony Woodcock and Trevor Francis. Woodcock had gone to Cologne the previous autumn and Francis, having scored crucial goals in both the quarter-final against Dynamo Berlin and the semi-final against Ajax, ruptured his Achilles tendon in a domestic fixture shortly before the final, an injury that would also keep him out of England's European Championship side in Italy.

The early stages of the competition were notable for the first round eliminations of both AC Milan – beaten at home in Europe for the first time in 20 years, by FC Porto – and Liverpool, humbled by a Dynamo Tbilisi side that crashed out of the competition in the next round to Hamburg.

Hamburg, bidding to reclaim the Cup for West Germany after three years of English domination, were fortunate to get past Hajduk Split in the quarter-finals, but in the semi-finals they produced a memorable performance to knock out Real Madrid. Beaten 2-0 in the first leg at the Bernabéu, Hamburg crushed the Spaniards 5-1 in the return, with Kaltz and Hrubesch scoring two goals each. Their victory certainly did Nottingham Forest a favour. For it is doubtful whether even the brilliance of Shilton would have held up against a Real Madrid side playing the final before a partisan crowd in their own Bernabéu stadium.

There was, however, an Anglo-Spanish confrontation in the final of the Cup-winners' Cup. Valencia, coached by former Real idol Alfredo Di Stéfano and featuring World Cup winners past and present, Rainer Bonhof and Mario Kempes, against FA Cup holders Arsenal, starring the Irish triumvirate of Jennings, Brady and Stapleton.

Both teams had surpassed themselves to reach the final. Valencia, with wins at Ibrox and the Nou Camp, had eliminated former winners Glasgow Rangers and holders Barcelona, while Arsenal saved their best for the semi-final, putting out Juventus with a smash-and-grab 1-0 victory in Turin. The final, in Brussels, did not live up to expectations, however. 0-0 at the end of 90 minutes, it remained that way after extra-time, which meant that for the first time ever a European final had to be decided on a penalty shoot-out. Fortune was to favour the Spaniards, who ran out 5-4 winners when Arsenal's Graham Rix missed his decisive spot-kick. So, still no country had ever won the Champions' and Cup-winners' Cups in the same season.

But if English clubs had done well in the two premier competitions, they were totally eclipsed by West German clubs in the UEFA Cup. Not one of the four Football League representatives made it even into the third round, whereas the West Germans, with five teams, took all four semi-final places and one of the quarter-final spots – the maximum they could achieve! Bayern Munich, who knocked out Kaiserslautern in the quarter-finals, were eliminated in the next round by Eintracht Frankfurt, while holders Borussia Mönchengladbach reached their fifth European final in eight years by disposing of VFB Stuttgart. The final was a predictably hard-fought duel between two sides that knew each other inside out. Borussia, with two goals from Kulik and one from a teenage Lothar Matthäus, won the first leg 3-2. But those two away goals, scored by Karger and Hölzenbein, eventually proved to be decisive when Frankfurt won the second leg 1-0 with a goal from substitute Schaub. As in 1971 and 1977, the UEFA Cup final was decided on away goals, and Eintracht Frankfurt were the team to benefit, becoming the fifth West German club to win a European trophy.

Liverpool

Dinamo Tbilisi

Ipswich Town

1980 – 1981

Preliminary Round

Team 1	Cnty	Team 2	Cnty	1st leg	2nd leg	Agg
Honvéd	Hun	Valletta	Mlt	8-0	3-0	11-0

	Pts	P	W	D	L	F	A	Diff	Goals/P
Total	4	2	2	0	2	11	11	0	5.000

First Round

Team 1	Cnty	Team 2	Cnty	1st leg	2nd leg	Agg
Dinamo Tirana	Alb	Ajax	Ned	0-2	0-1	0-3
Club Bruges	Bel	FC Basle	Sui	0-1	1-4	1-5
CSKA Sofia	Bul	Nottingham Forest	Eng	1-0	1-0	2-0
Aberdeen	Sco	Austria Vienna	Aut	1-0	0-0	1-0
Limerick	Irl	Real Madrid	Esp	1-2	1-5	2-7
OPS Oulu	Fin	Liverpool	Eng	1-1	1-10	2-11
Olympiakos Pireus	Gre	Bayern Munich	FRG	2-4	0-3	2-7
Linfield	Nir	Nantes	Fra	0-1	0-2	0-3
IBV Vestmannaeyjar	Isl	Banik Ostrava	Tch	1-1	0-1	1-2
Inter Milan	Ita	Universitatea Craiova	Rom	2-0	1-1	3-1
Jeunesse Esch	Lux	Spartak Moscow	URS	0-5	0-4	0-9
IL Viking	Nor	Red Star Belgrade	Yug	2-3	1-4	3-7
Sporting Lisbon	Por	Honvéd	Hun	0-2	0-1	0-3
Halmstad SBK	Swe	Esbjerg FB	Den	0-0	2-3	2-3
Trabzonspor	Tur	Szombierki Bytom	Pol	2-1	0-3	2-4
Dynamo Berlin	GDR	Apoel Nicosia	Cyp	3-0	1-2	4-2

	Pts	P	W	D	L	F	A	Diff	Goals/P
Total	64	32	27	10	27	92	92	0	2.875

Second Round

Team 1	Cnty	Team 2	Cnty	1st leg	2nd leg	Agg
CSKA Sofia	Bul	Szombierki Bytom	Pol	4-0	1-0	5-0
Aberdeen	Sco	Liverpool	Eng	0-1	0-4	0-5
Real Madrid	Esp	Honvéd	Hun	1-0	2-0	3-0
Nantes	Fra	Inter Milan	Ita	1-2	1-1	2-3
Bayern Munich	FRG	Ajax	Ned	5-1	1-2	6-3
FC Basle	Sui	Red Star Belgrade	Yug	1-0	0-2	1-2
Banik Ostrava	Tch	Dynamo Berlin	GDR	0-0	1-1	1-1
Spartak Moscow	URS	Esbjerg FB	Den	3-0	0-2	3-2

	Pts	P	W	D	L	F	A	Diff	Goals/P
Total	32	16	13	6	13	37	37	0	2.313

Quarter Final

Team 1	Cnty	Team 2	Cnty	1st leg	2nd leg	Agg
Liverpool	Eng	CSKA Sofia	Bul	5-1	1-0	6-1
Inter Milan	Ita	Red Star Belgrade	Yug	1-1	1-0	2-1
Bayern Munich	FRG	Banik Ostrava	Tch	2-0	4-2	6-2
Spartak Moscow	URS	Real Madrid	Esp	0-0	0-2	0-2

	Pts	P	W	D	L	F	A	Diff	Goals/P
Total	16	8	6	4	6	20	20	0	2.500

Semi Finals

Liverpool	Eng	Bayern Munich	FRG	0-0	1-1	1-1
Real Madrid	Esp	Inter Milan	Ita	2-0	0-1	2-1

	Pts	P	W	D	L	F	A	Diff	Goals/P
Total	8	4	2	4	2	5	5	0	1.250

Final

Liverpool	Eng	Real Madrid	Esp	1-0	1-0

	Pts	P	W	D	L	F	A	Diff	Goals/P
Total	2	1	1	0	1	1	1	0	1.000

	Pts	P	W	D	L	F	A	Diff	Goals/P
Total	126	63	51	24	51	166	166	0	2.635

Pos'n	Club	Cnty	Pts	P	W	D	L	F	A	Diff	B	Pts/P	F/P
1	Liverpool	Eng	18	9	6	3	0	24	4	20	3	2.000	2.667
2	Real Madrid	Esp	16	9	6	1	2	14	4	10	3	1.778	1.556
3	Bayern Munich	FRG	14	8	5	2	1	20	8	12	2	1.750	2.500
4	Inter Milan	Ita	13	8	4	3	1	9	6	3	2	1.625	1.125
5	CSKA Sofia	Bul	9	6	4	0	2	8	6	2	1	1.500	1.333
6	Honvéd	Hun	8	6	4	0	2	14	3	11	0	1.333	2.333
7	Spartak Moscow	URS	8	6	3	1	2	12	4	8	1	1.333	2.000
8	Red Star Belgrade	Yug	8	6	3	1	2	10	6	4	1	1.333	1.667
9	FC Basle	Sui	6	4	3	0	1	6	3	3	0	1.500	1.500
10	Ajax	Ned	6	4	3	0	1	6	6	0	0	1.500	1.500
11	Banik Ostrava	Tch	6	6	1	3	2	5	8	-3	1	1.000	0.833
12	Nantes	Fra	5	4	2	1	1	5	3	2	0	1.250	1.250
13	Esbjerg FB	Den	5	4	2	1	1	5	5	0	0	1.250	1.250
14	Dynamo Berlin	GDR	4	4	1	2	1	5	3	2	0	1.000	1.250
15	Aberdeen	Sco	3	4	1	1	2	1	5	-4	0	0.750	0.250
16	Apoel Nicosia	Cyp	2	2	1	0	1	2	4	-2	0	1.000	1.000
–	Trabzonspor	Tur	2	2	1	0	1	2	4	-2	0	1.000	1.000
18	Szombierki Bytom	Pol	2	4	1	0	3	4	7	-3	0	0.500	1.000
19	Halmstad SBK	Swe	1	2	0	1	1	2	3	-1	0	0.500	1.000
20	IBV Vestmannaeyjar	Isl	1	2	0	1	1	1	2	-1	0	0.500	0.500
21	Austria Vienna	Aut	1	2	0	1	1	0	1	-1	0	0.500	0.000
22	Universitatea Craiova	Rom	1	2	0	1	1	1	3	-2	0	0.500	0.500
23	OPS Oulu	Fin	1	2	0	1	1	2	11	-9	0	0.500	1.000
24	Nottingham Forest	Eng	0	2	0	0	2	0	2	-2	0	0.000	0.000
25	Dinamo Tirana	Alb	0	2	0	0	2	0	3	-3	0	0.000	0.000
–	Linfield	Nir	0	2	0	0	2	0	3	-3	0	0.000	0.000
–	Sporting Lisbon	Por	0	2	0	0	2	0	3	-3	0	0.000	0.000
28	IL Viking	Nor	0	2	0	0	2	3	7	-4	0	0.000	1.500
29	Club Bruges	Bel	0	2	0	0	2	1	5	-4	0	0.000	0.500
30	Limerick	Irl	0	2	0	0	2	2	7	-5	0	0.000	1.000
–	Olympiakos Pireus	Gre	0	2	0	0	2	2	7	-5	0	0.000	1.000
32	Jeunesse Esch	Lux	0	2	0	0	2	0	9	-9	0	0.000	0.000
33	Valletta	Mlt	0	2	0	0	2	0	11	-11	0	0.000	0.000
	Total		**140**	**126**	**51**	**24**	**51**	**166**	**166**	**0**	**14**	**1.111**	**2.635**

Preliminary Round

Team 1	Cnty	Team 2	Cnty	1st leg	2nd leg	Agg
Celtic	Sco	Diósgyöri VTK	Hun	6-0	1-2	7-2
Altay	Tur	Benfica	Por	0-0	0-4	0-4

	Pts	P	W	D	L	F	A	Diff	Goals/P
Total	8	4	3	2	3	13	13	0	3.250

First Round

Slavia Sofia	Bul	Legia Warsaw	Pol	3-1	0-1	3-2
Omonia Nicosia	Cyp	Waterschei Thor	Bel	1-3	0-4	1-7
Hvidovre IF	Den	Fram Reykjavik	Isl	1-0	2-0	3-0
Celtic	Sco	Politehnica Timisoara	Rom	2-1	0-1	2-2
Castilla Madrid	Esp	West Ham United	Eng	3-1	1-5	4-6
Valencia	Esp	Monaco	Fra	2-0	3-3	5-3
Ilves Tampere	Fin	Feyenoord	Ned	1-3	2-4	3-7
Newport County	Wal	Crusaders	Nir	4-0	0-0	4-0
Kastoria	Gre	Dinamo Tbilisi	URS	0-0	0-2	0-2
Roma	Ita	Carl Zeiss Jena	GDR	3-0	0-4	3-4
Spora Luxembourg	Lux	Sparta Prague	Tch	0-6	0-6	0-12
Hibernians	Mlt	Waterford United	Irl	1-0	0-4	1-4
Fortuna Düsseldorf	FRG	SV Salzburg	Aut	5-0	3-0	8-0
Malmö FF	Swe	Partizani Tirana	Alb	1-0	0-0	1-0
Sion	Sui	Haugar FC	Nor	1-1	0-2	1-3
Dinamo Zagreb	Yug	Benfica	Por	0-0	0-2	0-2

	Pts	P	W	D	L	F	A	Diff	Goals/P
Total	64	32	26	12	26	93	93	0	2.906

Second Round

West Ham United	Eng	Politehnica Timisoara	Rom	4-0	0-1	4-1
Waterschei Thor	Bel	Fortuna Düsseldorf	FRG	0-0	0-1	0-1
Hvidovre IF	Den	Feyenoord	Ned	1-2	0-1	1-3
Waterford United	Irl	Dinamo Tbilisi	URS	0-1	0-4	0-5
Haugar FC	Nor	Newport County	Wal	0-0	0-6	0-6
Malmö FF	Swe	Benfica	Por	1-0	0-2	1-2
Sparta Prague	Tch	Slavia Sofia	Bul	2-0	0-3	2-3
Carl Zeiss Jena	GDR	Valencia	Esp	3-1	0-1	3-2

	Pts	P	W	D	L	F	A	Diff	Goals/P
Total	32	16	14	4	14	34	34	0	2.125

Quarter Finals

West Ham United	Eng	Dinamo Tbilisi	URS	1-4	1-0	2-4
Slavia Sofia	Bul	Feyenoord	Ned	3-2	0-4	3-6
Fortuna Düsseldorf	FRG	Benfica	Por	2-2	0-1	2-3
Carl Zeiss Jena	GDR	Newport County	Wal	2-2	1-0	3-2

	Pts	P	W	D	L	F	A	Diff	Goals/P
Total	16	8	6	4	6	25	25	0	3.125

European Cup Winners Cup 1980-81

Semi Finals

Dinamo Tbilisi	URS	Feyenoord	Ned	3-0	0-2	3-2
Carl Zeiss Jena	GDR	Benfica	Por	2-0	0-1	2-1

	Pts	P	W	D	L	F	A	Diff	Goals/P
Total	8	4	4	0	4	8	8	0	2.000

Final

Dinamo Tbilisi	URS	Carl Zeiss Jena	GDR	2-1	2-1

	Pts	P	W	D	L	F	A	Diff	Goals/P
Total	2	1	1	0	1	3	3	0	3.000

	Pts	P	W	D	L	F	A	Diff	Goals/P
Total	130	65	54	22	54	176	176	0	2.708

Pos'n	Club	Cnty	Pts	P	W	D	L	F	A	Diff	B	Pts/P	F/P
1	Dinamo Tbilisi	URS	16	9	6	1	2	16	5	11	3	1.778	1.778
2	Benfica	Por	15	10	5	3	2	12	5	7	2	1.500	1.200
3	Feyenoord	Ned	14	8	6	0	2	18	10	8	2	1.750	2.250
4	Carl Zeiss Jena	GDR	12	9	4	1	4	13	10	3	3	1.333	1.444
5	Fortuna Düsseldorf	FRG	9	6	3	2	1	11	3	8	1	1.500	1.833
6	Newport County	Wal	8	6	2	3	1	12	3	9	1	1.333	2.000
7	West Ham United	Eng	7	6	3	0	3	12	9	3	1	1.167	2.000
8	Slavia Sofia	Bul	7	6	3	0	3	9	10	-1	1	1.167	1.500
9	Sparta Prague	Tch	6	4	3	0	1	14	3	11	0	1.500	3.500
10	Waterschei Thor	Bel	5	4	2	1	1	7	2	5	0	1.250	1.750
11	Valencia	Esp	5	4	2	1	1	7	6	1	0	1.250	1.750
12	Malmö FF	Swe	5	4	2	1	1	2	2	0	0	1.250	0.500
13	Celtic	Sco	4	4	2	0	2	9	4	5	0	1.000	2.250
14	Hvidovre IF	Den	4	4	2	0	2	4	3	1	0	1.000	1.000
15	Politehnica Timisoara	Rom	4	4	2	0	2	3	6	-3	0	1.000	0.750
16	Haugar FC	Nor	4	4	1	2	1	3	7	-4	0	1.000	0.750
17	Roma	Ita	2	2	1	0	1	3	4	-1	0	1.000	1.500
18	Legia Warsaw	Pol	2	2	1	0	1	2	3	-1	0	1.000	1.000
19	Waterford United	Irl	2	4	1	0	3	4	6	-2	0	0.500	1.000
–	Castilla Madrid	Esp	2	2	1	0	1	4	6	-2	0	1.000	2.000
21	Hibernians	Mlt	2	2	1	0	1	1	4	-3	0	1.000	0.500
22	Diósgyöri VTK	Hun	2	2	1	0	1	2	7	-5	0	1.000	1.000
23	Partizani Tirana	Alb	1	2	0	1	1	0	1	-1	0	0.500	0.000
24	Monaco	Fra	1	2	0	1	1	3	5	-2	0	0.500	1.500
25	Sion	Sui	1	2	0	1	1	1	3	-2	0	0.500	0.500
26	Kastoria	Gre	1	2	0	1	1	0	2	-2	0	0.500	0.000
–	Dinamo Zagreb	Yug	1	2	0	1	1	0	2	-2	0	0.500	0.000
28	Crusaders	Nir	1	2	0	1	1	0	4	-4	0	0.500	0.000
–	Altay	Tur	1	2	0	1	1	0	4	-4	0	0.500	0.000
30	Fram Reykjavik	Isl	0	2	0	0	2	0	3	-3	0	0.000	0.000
31	Ilves Tampere	Fin	0	2	0	0	2	3	7	-4	0	0.000	1.500
32	Omonia Nicosia	Cyp	0	2	0	0	2	1	7	-6	0	0.000	0.500
33	SV Salzburg	Aut	0	2	0	0	2	0	8	-8	0	0.000	0.000
31	Spora Luxembourg	Lux	0	2	0	0	2	0	12	-12	0	0.000	0.000
	Total		**144**	**130**	**54**	**22**	**54**	**176**	**176**	**0**	**14**	**1.108**	**2.708**

First Round

Team 1	Cnty	Team 2	Cnty	1st leg	2nd leg	Agg
Ipswich Town	Eng	Aris Salonika	Gre	5-1	1-3	6-4
Manchester United	Eng	Widzew Lódź	Pol	1-1	0-0	1-1
Linzer ASK	Aut	Radnicki Nis	Yug	1-2	1-4	2-6
Standard Liège	Bel	Steaua Bucharest	Rom	1-1	2-1	3-2
Lokeren	Bel	Dinamo Moscow	URS	1-1	1-0	2-1
RWD Molenbeek	Bel	Torino	Ita	1-2	2-2	3-4
KuPS Kuopio	Fin	Saint-Etienne	Fra	0-7	0-7	0-14
Sochaux	Fra	Servette	Sui	2-0	1-2	3-2
Vasas SC	Hun	Boavista	Por	0-2	1-0	1-2
Ujpesti Dózsa	Hun	Real Sociedad	Esp	1-1	0-1	1-2
Ballymena United	Nir	Vorwärts Frankfurt/Oder	GDR	2-1	0-3	2-4
IA Akranes	Isl	Cologne	FRG	0-4	0-6	0-10
Juventus	Ita	Panathinaikos	Gre	4-0	2-4	6-4
Sliema Wanderers	Mlt	Barcelona	Esp	0-2	0-1	0-3
AZ'67 Alkmaar	Ned	Red Boys Differdange	Lux	6-0	4-0	10-0
PSV Eindhoven	Ned	Wolverhampton Wanderers	Eng	3-1	0-1	3-2
Twente Enschede	Ned	IFK Gothenburg	Swe	5-1	0-2	5-3
Slask Wroclaw	Pol	Dundee United	Sco	0-0	2-7	2-7
FC Porto	Por	Dundalk	Irl	1-0	0-0	1-0
Hamburg	FRG	Sarajevo	Yug	4-2	3-3	7-5
Kaiserslautern	FRG	Anderlecht	Bel	1-0	2-3	3-3
VFB Stuttgart	FRG	Pezoporikos Larnaca	Cyp	6-0	4-1	10-1
Arges Pitesti	Rom	Utrecht	Ned	0-0	0-2	0-2
IF Elfsborg	Swe	St. Mirren	Sco	1-2	0-0	1-2
Grasshoppers Zürich	Sui	KB Copenhagen	Den	3-1	5-2	8-3
Zbrojovka Brno	Tch	Vöest Linz	Aut	3-1	2-0	5-1
Bohemians Prague	Tch	Sporting Gijón	Esp	3-1	1-2	4-3
Fenerbahçe	Tur	Beroe Stara Zagora	Bul	0-1	1-2	1-3
Shakhtyor Donetsk	URS	Eintracht Frankfurt	FRG	1-0	0-3	1-3
Dinamo Kiev	URS	Levski Sofia	Bul	1-1	0-0	1-1
Dynamo Dresden	GDR	Napredak Krusevac	Yug	1-0	1-0	2-0
Magdeburg	GDR	Moss FK	Nor	2-1	3-2	5-3

	Pts	P	W	D	L	F	A	Diff	Goals/P
Total	128	64	51	26	51	200	200	0	3.125

Second Round

Ipswich Town	Eng	Bohemians Prague	Tch	3-0	0-2	3-2
Levski Sofia	Bul	AZ'67 Alkmaar	Ned	1-1	0-5	1-6
Beroe Stara Zagora	Bul	Radnicki Nis	Yug	0-1	1-2	1-3
Dundee United	Sco	Lokeren	Bel	1-1	0-0	1-1
St. Mirren	Sco	Saint-Etienne	Fra	0-0	0-2	0-2
Sochaux	Fra	Boavista	Por	2-2	1-0	3-2
Torino	Ita	Magdeburg	GDR	3-1	0-1	3-2
PSV Eindhoven	Ned	Hamburg	FRG	1-1	1-2	2-3
Twente Enschede	Ned	Dynamo Dresden	GDR	1-1	0-0	1-1
Utrecht	Ned	Eintracht Frankfurt	FRG	2-1	1-3	3-4
Widzew Lódź	Pol	Juventus	Ita	3-1	1-3	4-4
FC Porto	Por	Grasshoppers Zürich	Sui	2-0	0-3	2-3
Cologne	FRG	Barcelona	Esp	0-1	4-0	4-1
Kaiserslautern	FRG	Standard Liège	Bel	1-2	1-2	2-4
VFB Stuttgart	FRG	Vorwärts Frankfurt/Oder	GDR	5-1	2-1	7-2
Zbrojovka Brno	Tch	Real Sociedad	Esp	1-1	1-2	2-3

	Pts	P	W	D	L	F	A	Diff	Goals/P
Total	64	32	23	18	23	82	82	0	2.563

Third Round

Ipswich Town	Eng	Widzew Lódź	Pol	5-0	0-1	5-1
Standard Liège	Bel	Dynamo Dresden	GDR	1-1	4-1	5-2
Lokeren	Bel	Real Sociedad	Esp	1-0	2-2	3-2
Eintracht Frankfurt	FRG	Sochaux	Fra	4-2	0-2	4-4
Hamburg	FRG	Saint-Etienne	Fra	0-5	0-1	0-6
VFB Stuttgart	FRG	Cologne	FRG	3-1	1-4	4-5
Grasshoppers Zürich	Sui	Torino	Ita	2-1	1-2	3-3
Radnicki Nis	Yug	AZ'67 Alkmaar	Ned	2-2	0-5	2-7

	Pts	P	W	D	L	F	A	Diff	Goals/P
Total	32	16	13	6	13	56	56	0	3.500

Quarter Finals

Standard Liège	Bel	Cologne	FRG	0-0	2-3	2-3
Saint-Etienne	Fra	Ipswich Town	Eng	1-4	1-3	2-7
AZ'67 Alkmaar	Ned	Lokeren	Bel	2-0	0-1	2-1
Grasshoppers Zürich	Sui	Sochaux	Fra	0-0	1-2	1-2

	Pts	P	W	D	L	F	A	Diff	Goals/P
Total	16	8	6	4	6	20	20	0	2.500

Semi Finals

Ipswich Town	Eng	Cologne	FRG	1-0	1-0	2-0
Sochaux	Fra	AZ'67 Alkmaar	Ned	1-1	2-3	3-4

	Pts	P	W	D	L	F	A	Diff	Goals/P
Total	8	4	3	2	3	9	9	0	2.250

Final

Ipswich Town	Eng	AZ'67 Alkmaar	Ned	3-0	2-4	5-4

	Pts	P	W	D	L	F	A	Diff	Goals/P
Total	4	2	2	0	2	9	9	0	4.500

	Pts	P	W	D	L	F	A	Diff	Goals/P
Total	252	126	98	56	98	376	376	0	2.984

Pos'n	Club	Cnty	Pts	P	W	D	L	F	A	Diff	B	Pts/P	F/P
1	AZ'67 Alkmaar	Ned	20	12	7	3	2	33	12	21	3	1.667	2.750
2	Ipswich Town	Eng	19	12	8	0	4	28	13	15	3	1.583	2.333
3	Cologne	FRG	13	10	5	1	4	22	9	13	2	1.300	2.200
4	Sochaux	Fra	13	10	4	3	3	15	13	2	2	1.300	1.500
5	Saint-Etienne	Fra	12	8	5	1	2	24	7	17	1	1.500	3.000
6	Standard Liège	Bel	12	8	4	3	1	14	9	5	1	1.500	1.750
7	Lokeren	Bel	11	8	3	4	1	7	6	1	1	1.375	0.875
8	VFB Stuttgart	FRG	10	6	5	0	1	21	8	13	0	1.667	3.500
9	Grasshoppers Zürich	Sui	10	8	4	1	3	15	10	5	1	1.250	1.875
10	Radnicki Nis	Yug	9	6	4	1	1	11	10	1	0	1.500	1.833
11	Torino	Ita	7	6	3	1	2	10	8	2	0	1.167	1.667
12	Real Sociedad	Esp	7	6	2	3	1	7	6	1	0	1.167	1.167
13	Dynamo Dresden	GDR	7	6	2	3	1	5	6	-1	0	1.167	0.833
14	Eintracht Frankfurt	FRG	6	6	3	0	3	11	8	3	0	1.000	1.833
15	Magdeburg	GDR	6	4	3	0	1	7	6	1	0	1.500	1.750
16	Barcelona	Esp	6	4	3	0	1	4	4	0	0	1.500	1.000
17	Hamburg	FRG	6	6	2	2	2	10	13	-3	0	1.000	1.667
18	Widzew Lódź	Pol	6	6	2	2	2	6	10	-4	0	1.000	1.000
19	Dundee United	Sco	5	4	1	3	0	8	3	5	0	1.250	2.000
20	Zbrojovka Brno	Tch	5	4	2	1	1	7	4	3	0	1.250	1.750
21	Utrecht	Ned	5	4	2	1	1	5	4	1	0	1.250	1.250
22	FC Porto	Por	5	4	2	1	1	3	3	0	0	1.250	0.750
23	Juventus	Ita	4	4	2	0	2	10	8	2	0	1.000	2.500
24	Twente Enschede	Ned	4	4	1	2	1	6	4	2	0	1.000	1.500
25	Bohemians Prague	Tch	4	4	2	0	2	6	6	0	0	1.000	1.500
26	Boreo Stara Zagora	Bul	4	4	2	0	2	4	4	0	0	1.000	1.000
27	St. Mirren	Sco	4	4	1	2	1	2	3	-1	0	1.000	0.500
28	PSV Eindhoven	Ned	3	4	1	1	2	5	5	0	0	0.750	1.250
29	Boavista	Por	3	4	1	1	2	4	4	0	0	0.750	1.000
30	Levski Sofia	Bul	3	4	0	3	1	2	7	-5	0	0.750	0.500
31	Anderlecht	Bel	2	2	1	0	1	3	3	0	0	1.000	1.500
32	Manchester United	Eng	2	2	0	2	0	1	1	0	0	1.000	0.500
–	Dinamo Kiev	URS	2	2	0	2	0	1	1	0	0	1.000	0.500
34	Sporting Gijón	Esp	2	2	1	0	1	3	4	-1	0	1.000	1.500
35	Wolverhampton Wanderers	Eng	2	2	1	0	1	2	3	-1	0	1.000	1.000
–	Servette	Sui	2	2	1	0	1	2	3	-1	0	1.000	1.000
37	Vasas SC	Hun	2	2	1	0	1	1	2	-1	0	1.000	0.500
38	Kaiserslautern	FRG	2	4	1	0	3	5	7	-2	0	0.500	1.250
39	Panathinaikos	Gre	2	2	1	0	1	4	6	-2	0	1.000	2.000
–	Aris Salonika	Gre	2	2	1	0	1	4	6	-2	0	1.000	2.000
41	IFK Gothenburg	Swe	2	2	1	0	1	3	5	-2	0	1.000	1.500
42	Ballymena United	Nir	2	2	1	0	1	2	4	-2	0	1.000	1.000
43	Shakhtyor Donetsk	URS	2	2	1	0	1	1	3	-2	0	1.000	0.500
44	Vorwärts Frankfurt/Oder	GDR	2	4	1	0	3	6	9	-3	0	0.500	1.500
45	RWD Molenbeek	Bel	1	2	0	1	1	3	4	-1	0	0.500	1.500
46	Steaua Bucharest	Rom	1	2	0	1	1	2	3	-1	0	0.500	1.000
47	Ujpesti Dózsa	Hun	1	2	0	1	1	1	2	-1	0	0.500	0.500
–	IF Elfsborg	Swe	1	2	0	1	1	1	2	-1	0	0.500	0.500
–	Dinamo Moscow	URS	1	2	0	1	1	1	2	-1	0	0.500	0.500
50	Dundalk	Irl	1	2	0	1	1	0	1	-1	0	0.500	0.000
51	Sarajevo	Yug	1	2	0	1	1	5	7	-2	0	0.500	2.500
52	Arges Pitesti	Rom	1	2	0	1	1	0	2	-2	0	0.500	0.000
53	Slask Wroclaw	Pol	1	2	0	1	1	2	7	-5	0	0.500	1.000
54	Moss FK	Nor	0	2	0	0	2	3	5	-2	0	0.000	1.500
55	Fenerbahçe	Tur	0	2	0	0	2	1	3	-2	0	0.000	0.500
56	Napredak Krusevac	Yug	0	2	0	0	2	0	2	-2	0	0.000	0.000
57	Sliema Wanderers	Mlt	0	2	0	0	2	0	3	-3	0	0.000	0.000
58	Linzer ASK	Aut	0	2	0	0	2	2	6	-4	0	0.000	1.000
59	Vöest Linz	Aut	0	2	0	0	2	1	5	-4	0	0.000	0.500
60	KB Copenhagen	Den	0	2	0	0	2	3	8	-5	0	0.000	1.500
61	Pezoporikos Larnaca	Cyp	0	2	0	0	2	1	10	-9	0	0.000	0.500
62	IA Akranes	Isl	0	2	0	0	2	0	10	-10	0	0.000	0.000
–	Red Boys Differdange	Lux	0	2	0	0	2	0	10	-10	0	0.000	0.000
64	KuPS Kuopio	Fin	0	2	0	0	2	0	14	-14	0	0.000	0.000
	Total		**266**	**252**	**98**	**56**	**98**	**376**	**376**	**0**	**14**	**1.056**	**2.984**

National Performances by Points

1980-81

Pos'n	Cnty	Pts	P	W	D	L	F	A	Diff	B	Pts/P	F/P
1	FRG	60	46	24	7	15	100	56	44	5	1.304	2.174
2	Ned	52	36	20	7	9	73	41	32	5	1.444	2.028
3	Eng	48	33	18	5	10	67	32	35	7	1.455	2.030
4	Esp	38	27	15	5	7	39	30	9	3	1.407	1.444
5	Fra	31	24	11	6	7	47	28	19	3	1.292	1.958
6	Bel	31	26	10	9	7	35	29	6	2	1.192	1.346
7	GDR	31	27	11	6	10	36	34	2	3	1.148	1.333
8	URS	29	21	10	5	6	31	15	16	4	1.381	1.476
9	Ita	26	20	10	4	6	32	26	6	2	1.300	1.600
10	Por	23	20	8	5	7	19	15	4	2	1.150	0.950
11	Bul	23	20	9	3	8	23	27	-4	2	1.150	1.150
12	Tch	21	18	8	4	6	32	21	11	1	1.167	1.778
13	Sui	19	16	8	2	6	24	19	5	1	1.188	1.500
14	Yug	19	18	7	4	7	26	27	-1	1	1.056	1.444
15	Sco	16	16	5	6	5	20	15	5	0	1.000	1.250
16	Hun	13	12	6	1	5	18	14	4	0	1.083	1.500
17	Pol	11	14	4	3	7	14	27	-13	0	0.786	1.000
18	Den	9	10	4	1	5	12	16	-4	0	0.900	1.200
19	Swe	9	10	3	3	4	8	12	-4	0	0.900	0.800
20	Wal	8	6	2	3	1	12	3	9	1	1.333	2.000
21	Rom	7	10	2	3	5	6	14	-8	0	0.700	0.600
22	Gre	5	8	2	1	5	10	21	-11	0	0.625	1.250
23	Nor	4	8	1	2	5	9	19	-10	0	0.500	1.125
24	Irl	3	8	1	1	6	6	14	-8	0	0.375	0.750
25	Tur	3	6	1	1	4	3	11	-8	0	0.500	0.500
26	Nir	3	6	1	1	4	2	11	-9	0	0.500	0.333
27	Cyp	2	6	1	0	5	4	21	-17	0	0.333	0.667
28	Mlt	2	6	1	0	5	1	18	-17	0	0.333	0.167
29	Alb	1	4	0	1	3	0	4	-4	0	0.250	0.000
30	Isl	1	6	0	1	5	1	15	-14	0	0.167	0.167
31	Aut	1	8	0	1	7	3	20	-17	0	0.125	0.375
32	Fin	1	6	0	1	5	5	32	-27	0	0.167	0.833
33	Lux	0	6	0	0	6	0	31	-31	0	0.000	0.000
	Total	**550**	**508**	**203**	**102**	**203**	**718**	**718**	**0**	**42**	**1.083**	**2.827**

1955-56 to 1980-81

Pos'n	Cnty	Pts	P	W	D	L	F	A	Diff	B	Pts/P	F/P
1	Eng	1146	776	421	166	189	1523	792	731	138	1.477	1.963
2	FRG	1082	776	410	143	223	1596	998	598	119	1.394	2.057
3	Esp	988	717	366	133	218	1374	889	485	123	1.378	1.916
4	Ita	877	648	320	139	189	1020	670	350	98	1.353	1.574
5	Sco	572	467	219	84	164	809	618	191	50	1.225	1.732
6	Ned	568	424	219	74	131	854	517	337	56	1.340	2.014
7	Yug	504	456	185	86	185	739	663	76	48	1.105	1.621
8	Bel	485	420	188	67	165	664	560	104	42	1.155	1.581
9	Por	461	404	169	87	148	661	525	136	36	1.141	1.636
10	Hun	445	372	173	59	140	694	538	156	40	1.196	1.866
11	GDR	400	357	147	76	134	541	470	71	30	1.120	1.515
12	Tch	386	327	149	60	118	521	433	88	28	1.180	1.593
13	Fra	368	357	137	65	155	544	542	2	29	1.031	1.524
14	URS	296	222	115	45	62	333	213	120	21	1.333	1.500
15	Pol	263	253	99	51	103	371	385	-14	14	1.040	1.466
16	Bul	258	263	102	40	121	407	410	-3	14	0.981	1.548
17	Sui	255	299	93	51	155	454	595	-141	18	0.853	1.518
18	Rom	232	253	92	43	118	327	410	-83	5	0.917	1.292
19	Aut	218	259	77	50	132	307	438	-131	14	0.842	1.185
20	Gre	185	211	70	38	103	252	384	-132	7	0.877	1.194
21	Swe	179	207	61	48	98	258	361	-103	9	0.865	1.246
22	Den	148	223	53	37	133	294	492	-198	5	0.664	1.318
23	Tur	143	193	54	29	110	196	366	-170	6	0.741	1.016
24	Nor	83	158	31	20	107	158	413	-255	1	0.525	1.000
25	Wal	78	72	25	22	25	99	88	11	6	1.083	1.375
26	Irl	73	154	24	25	105	124	391	-267	0	0.474	0.805
27	Nir	65	134	19	25	90	135	394	-259	2	0.485	1.007
28	Mlt	39	112	14	11	87	56	369	-313	0	0.348	0.500
29	Lux	39	134	15	9	110	93	564	-471	0	0.291	0.694
30	Fin	34	108	11	12	85	90	374	-284	0	0.315	0.833
31	Cyp	26	92	8	10	74	55	362	-307	0	0.283	0.598
32	Isl	22	98	4	14	80	53	348	-295	0	0.224	0.541
33	Alb	21	34	5	11	18	23	53	-30	0	0.618	0.676
	Total	**10939**	**9980**	**4075**	**1830**	**4075**	**15625**	**15625**	**0**	**959**	**1.096**	**3.131**

1980-81

Pos'n	Cnty	Ave	Pts	P	W	D	L	F	A	Diff	B	No./T
1	Netherlands	8.666	52	36	20	7	9	73	41	32	5	6
2	W. Germany	8.571	60	46	24	7	15	100	56	44	5	7
3	England	8.000	48	33	18	5	10	67	32	35	7	6
–	Wales	8.000	8	6	2	3	1	12	3	9	1	1
5	France	7.750	31	24	11	6	7	47	28	19	3	4
6	Italy	6.500	26	20	10	4	6	32	26	6	2	4
7	Spain	6.333	38	27	15	5	7	39	30	9	3	6
8	E. Germany	6.200	31	27	11	6	10	36	34	2	3	5
9	USSR	5.800	29	21	10	5	6	31	15	16	4	5
10	Bulgaria	5.750	23	20	9	3	8	23	27	-4	2	4
–	Portugal	5.750	23	20	8	5	7	19	15	4	2	4
12	Czechoslovakia	5.250	21	18	8	4	6	32	21	11	1	4
13	Belgium	5.166	31	26	10	9	7	35	29	6	2	6
14	Switzerland	4.750	19	16	8	2	6	24	19	5	1	4
15	Scotland	4.000	16	16	5	6	5	20	15	5	0	4
16	Yugoslavia	3.800	19	18	7	4	7	26	27	-1	1	5
17	Hungary	3.250	13	12	6	1	5	18	14	4	0	4
18	Denmark	3.000	9	10	4	1	5	12	16	-4	0	3
19	Poland	2.750	11	14	4	3	7	14	27	-13	0	4
20	Sweden	2.250	9	10	3	3	4	8	12	-4	0	4
21	Romania	1.750	7	10	2	3	5	6	14	-8	0	4
22	Norway	1.333	4	8	1	2	5	9	19	-10	0	3
23	Greece	1.250	5	8	2	1	5	10	21	-11	0	4
24	Rep. of Ireland	1.000	3	8	1	1	6	6	14	-8	0	3
–	N. Ireland	1.000	3	6	1	1	4	2	11	-9	0	3
–	Turkey	1.000	3	6	1	1	4	3	11	-8	0	3
27	Cyprus	0.666	2	6	1	0	5	4	21	-17	0	3
–	Malta	0.666	2	6	1	0	5	1	18	-17	0	3
29	Albania	0.500	1	4	0	1	3	0	4	-4	0	2
30	Finland	0.333	1	6	0	1	5	5	32	-27	0	3
–	Iceland	0.333	1	6	0	1	5	1	15	-14	0	3
32	Austria	0.250	1	8	0	1	7	3	20	-17	0	4
33	Luxembourg	0.000	0	6	0	0	6	0	31	-31	0	3
	Total		**550**	**508**	**203**	**102**	**203**	**718**	**718**	**0**	**42**	**2.827**

1955-56 to 1980-81

Pos'n	Cnty	Ave	Pts	P	W	D	L	F	A	Diff	B	No./T
1	England	8.953	1146	776	421	166	189	1523	792	731	138	128
2	W. Germany	8.014	1082	776	410	143	223	1596	998	598	119	135
3	Spain	7.779	988	717	366	133	218	1374	889	485	123	127
4	Italy	7.016	877	648	320	139	189	1020	670	350	98	125
5	Netherlands	6.604	568	424	219	74	131	854	517	337	56	86
6	USSR	5.920	296	222	115	45	62	333	213	120	21	50
7	Scotland	5.720	572	467	219	84	164	809	618	191	50	100
8	Hungary	5.562	445	372	173	59	140	694	538	156	40	80
9	Belgium	5.000	485	420	188	67	165	664	560	104	42	97
–	E. Germany	5.000	400	357	147	76	134	541	470	71	30	80
11	Yugoslavia	4.800	504	456	185	86	185	739	663	76	48	105
12	Czechoslovakia	4.765	386	327	149	60	118	521	433	88	28	81
13	Portugal	4.704	461	404	169	87	148	661	525	136	36	98
14	Wales	3.900	78	72	25	22	25	99	88	11	6	20
15	France	3.873	368	357	137	65	155	544	542	2	29	95
16	Poland	3.867	263	253	99	51	103	371	385	-14	14	68
17	Bulgaria	3.440	258	263	102	40	121	407	410	-3	14	75
18	Romania	2.974	232	253	92	43	118	327	410	-83	5	78
19	Switzerland	2.741	255	299	93	51	155	454	595	-141	18	93
20	Austria	2.691	218	259	77	50	132	307	438	-131	14	81
21	Sweden	2.557	179	207	61	48	98	258	361	-103	9	70
22	Greece	2.534	185	211	70	38	103	252	384	-132	7	73
23	Turkey	2.134	143	193	54	29	110	196	366	-170	6	67
24	Denmark	1.804	148	223	53	37	133	294	492	-198	5	82
25	Albania	1.400	21	34	5	11	18	23	53	-30	0	15
26	Norway	1.276	83	158	31	20	107	158	413	-255	1	65
27	Rep. of Ireland	1.158	73	154	24	25	105	124	391	-267	0	63
28	N. Ireland	1.120	65	134	19	25	90	135	394	-259	2	58
29	Malta	0.735	39	112	14	11	87	56	369	-313	0	53
30	Finland	0.708	34	108	11	12	85	90	374	-284	0	48
31	Cyprus	0.619	26	92	8	10	74	55	362	-307	0	42
–	Luxembourg	0.619	39	134	15	9	110	93	564	-471	0	63
33	Iceland	0.488	22	98	4	14	80	53	348	-295	0	45
	Total		**10939**	**9980**	**4075**	**1830**	**4075**	**15625**	**15625**	**0**	**959**	**3.131**

Paisley Hat-trick, Robson's Arrival

For the fifth season in a row the Champions' Cup went to an English club. Not to Nottingham Forest, the holders, who were swiftly eliminated from the competition in the first round by Bulgarian champions CSKA Sofia, but to Liverpool, winners twice before, in 1977 and 1978. Liverpool's achievement meant that their manager, Bob Paisley, became the first man to lead a side to three Champions' Cup victories.

As Forest went out in the first round, Liverpool avoided a third successive opening-round elimination by annihilating Finnish side OPS 11-2 on aggregate, with ten of the goals coming in the return leg at Anfield. They were equally unforgiving in both the second round, when they defeated Aberdeen both home and away, and in the quarter-finals, when they disposed of Forest's conquerors CSKA in similar fashion, midfielder Graeme Souness notching his second hat-trick of the competition with three formidable long-range strikes in the 5-1 home victory.

The Merseysiders' first real test came in the semi-finals. They were drawn against Bayern Munich, but their task might have been equally difficult against either one of the other two teams left in the competition, Real Madrid and Inter Milan. Between them, these four teams had won over half of the previous 25 Champions' Cups. Liverpool looked to have blown their chance when they could only manage a 0-0 draw against Bayern at Anfield, but a fortnight later they pulled off one of their most remarkable European results by drawing 1-1 in Munich and qualifying for the final thanks to that lone away goal scored late in the game by midfielder Ray Kennedy.

It was to be another Kennedy, left-back Alan, who won the final for Liverpool in Paris. Yet again, the showpiece game of the season proved to be a massive let down. Real Madrid, in the final at last for the first time in 15 years and back in the stadium where they had won their first Champions' Cup a quarter of a century before, were a pale shadow of their once glorious side. Coached by the Yugoslav, Vujadin Boskov, they rarely threatened a Liverpool defence marshalled with poise and elegance by Thompson and Hansen. So it was that with just eight minutes to go, and extra-time imminent, Real were made to pay for their lack of ambition. A mistake in defence allowed Alan Kennedy to slip inside the penalty area and rifle home the winning goal from a narrow angle. For the fourth year running, the Champions' Cup final had been decided by a single goal.

The team that had knocked Liverpool out of the Champions' Cup with such style the previous season, Dinamo Tbilisi (pictured below), realised that potential with victory in the Cup-winners' Cup. An exciting

final in Düsseldorf against the East Germans of Carl Zeiss Jena was decided three minutes from time with a goal from Tbilisi forward Daraselia, but it was in the quarter-finals, against former winners West Ham, that the Georgians had produced their most memorable performance of the competition. Goals from Chivadze, Gutsaev and Shengelia (2) gave Tbilisi a resounding 4-1 victory at Upton Park, and one that earned a generous ovation from the West Ham fans. That the Hammers won the second leg 1-0 in Tbilisi was to their credit, but it mattered little in terms of the overall tie. Dinamo recovered their home form for the semi-finals with a decisive 3-0 victory over Feyenoord. Carl Zeiss Jena, who earlier had accounted for holders Valencia, joined them in an all-Eastern European final by causing another shock with a 2-1 aggregate victory over Benfica.

The Dutch Connection

Liverpool's Champions' Cup victory was accompanied by another English success in the UEFA Cup, where Ipswich Town, managed by Bobby Robson, made up for just missing out on the English League title by capturing the UEFA Cup. Ipswich's shaky away form in the early rounds gave a false indication of their true potential. That became evident when they thrashed Saint-Etienne 4-1 away in the quarter-final and then beat Cologne home and away to reach the final, prolonging the German club's semi-final agony in the process.

Ipswich faced another relative European novice, the Netherlands' AZ'67 Alkmaar, in the final. Victory appeared to be a formality after a first-leg 3-0 win at Portman Road. But AZ were a different proposition at home and gave Robson's men several frights in a 4-2 victory. Those two away goals, scored by John Wark and Frans Thijssen, were decisive, though, and Ipswich took the Cup on a 5-4 aggregate.

Left: Joy for Ipswich after Paul Mariner (both arms raised) had scored the third goal. Arnold Muhren congratulates Alan Brazil (10) for the pass that led to the goal.

1981 – 1982

Aston Villa

Barcelona

IFK Gothenburg

Preliminary Round

Team 1	Cnty	Team 2	Cnty	1st leg	2nd leg	Agg
Saint-Etienne	Fra	Dynamo Berlin	GDR	1-1	0-2	1-3

	Pts	P	W	D	L	F	A	Diff	Goals/P
Total	4	2	1	2	1	4	4	0	2.000

First Round

Aston Villa	Eng	Valur Reykjavik	Isl	5-0	2-0	7-0
Austria Vienna	Aut	Partizani Tirana	Alb	3-1	0-1	3-2
CSKA Sofia	Bul	Real Sociedad	Esp	1-0	0-0	1-0
B 93 Copenhagen	Den	Athlone Town	Irl	1-1	2-2	3-3
Celtic	Sco	Juventus	Ita	1-0	0-2	1-2
OPS Oulu	Fin	Liverpool	Eng	0-1	0-7	0-8
Ferencváros	Hun	Banik Ostrava	Tch	3-2	0-3	3-5
Progrès Niedercorn	Lux	Glentoran	Nir	1-1	0-4	1-5
Hibernians	Mlt	Red Star Belgrade	Yug	1-2	1-8	2-10
IK Start	Nor	AZ'67 Alkmaar	Ned	1-3	0-1	1-4
Widzew Lódź	Pol	Anderlecht	Bel	1-4	1-2	2-6
Benfica	Por	Omonia Nicosia	Cyp	3-0	1-0	4-0
Universitatea Craiova	Rom	Olympiakos Pireus	Gre	3-0	0-2	3-2
Öster SIF	Swe	Bayern Munich	FRG	0-1	0-5	0-6
Dinamo Kiev	URS	Trabzonspor	Tur	1-0	1-1	2-1
Dynamo Berlin	GDR	FC Zürich	Sui	2-0	1-3	3-3

	Pts	P	W	D	L	F	A	Diff	Goals/P
Total	64	32	27	10	27	93	93	0	2.906

Second Round

Austria Vienna	Aut	Dinamo Kiev	URS	0-1	1-1	1-2
Anderlecht	Bel	Juventus	Ita	3-1	1-1	4-2
CSKA Sofia	Bul	Glentoran	Nir	2-0	1-2	3-2
B 93 Copenhagen	Den	Universitatea Craiova	Rom	1-0	1-4	2-4
AZ'67 Alkmaar	Ned	Liverpool	Eng	2-2	2-3	4-5
Benfica	Por	Bayern Munich	FRG	0-0	1-4	1-4
Banik Ostrava	Tch	Red Star Belgrade	Yug	3-1	0-3	3-4
Dynamo Berlin	GDR	Aston Villa	Eng	1-2	1-0	2-2

	Pts	P	W	D	L	F	A	Diff	Goals/P
Total	32	16	12	8	12	45	45	0	2.813

Quarter Finals

Liverpool	Eng	CSKA Sofia	Bul	1-0	0-2	1-2
Anderlecht	Bel	Red Star Belgrade	Yug	2-1	2-1	4-2
Universitatea Craiova	Rom	Bayern Munich	FRG	0-2	1-1	1-3
Dinamo Kiev	URS	Aston Villa	Eng	0-0	0-2	0-2

	Pts	P	W	D	L	F	A	Diff	Goals/P
Total	16	8	6	4	6	15	15	0	1.875

Semi Finals

Aston Villa	Eng	Anderlecht	Bel	1-0	0-0		1-0
CSKA Sofia	Bul	Bayern Munich	FRG	4-3	0-4		4-7

	Pts	P	W	D	L	F	A	Diff	Goals/P
Total	8	4	3	2	3	12	12	0	3.000

Final

Aston Villa	Eng	Bayern Munich	FRG	1-0	1-0

	Pts	P	W	D	L	F	A	Diff	Goals/P
Total	2	1	1	0	1	1	1	0	1.000

	Pts	P	W	D	L	F	A	Diff	Goals/P
Total	126	63	50	26	50	170	170	0	2.698

Pos'n	Club	Cnty	Pts	P	W	D	L	F	A	Diff	B	Pts/P	F/P
1	Aston Villa	Eng	17	9	6	2	1	13	2	11	3	1.889	1.444
2	Bayern Munich	FRG	15	9	5	2	2	20	7	13	3	1.667	2.222
3	Anderlecht	Bel	14	8	5	2	1	14	7	7	2	1.750	1.750
4	CSKA Sofia	Bul	11	8	4	1	3	10	10	0	2	1.375	1.250
5	Liverpool	Eng	10	6	4	1	1	14	6	8	1	1.667	2.333
6	Dinamo Kiev	URS	8	6	2	3	1	4	4	0	1	1.333	0.667
7	Red Star Belgrade	Yug	7	6	3	0	3	16	9	7	1	1.167	2.667
8	Dynamo Berlin	GDR	7	6	3	1	2	8	6	2	0	1.167	1.333
9	Universitatea Craiova	Rom	6	6	2	1	3	8	7	1	1	1.000	1.333
10	Glentoran	Nir	5	4	2	1	1	7	4	3	0	1.250	1.750
11	AZ'67 Alkmaar	Ned	5	4	2	1	1	8	6	2	0	1.250	2.000
12	Benfica	Por	5	4	2	1	1	5	4	1	0	1.250	1.250
13	Banik Ostrava	Tch	4	4	2	0	2	8	7	1	0	1.000	2.000
14	B 93 Copenhagen	Den	4	4	1	2	1	5	7	-2	0	1.000	1.250
15	Austria Vienna	Aut	3	4	1	1	2	4	4	0	0	0.750	1.000
16	Juventus	Ita	3	4	1	1	2	4	5	-1	0	0.750	1.000
17	Athlone Town	Irl	2	2	0	2	0	3	3	0	0	1.000	1.500
–	FC Zürich	Sui	2	2	1	0	1	3	3	0	0	1.000	1.500
19	Partizani Tirana	Alb	2	2	1	0	1	2	3	-1	0	1.000	1.000
–	Olympiakos Pireus	Gre	2	2	1	0	1	2	3	-1	0	1.000	1.000
21	Celtic	Sco	2	2	1	0	1	1	2	-1	0	1.000	0.500
22	Ferencváros	Hun	2	2	1	0	1	3	5	-2	0	1.000	1.500
23	Trabzonspor	Tur	1	2	0	1	1	1	2	-1	0	0.500	0.500
24	Real Sociedad	Esp	1	2	0	1	1	0	1	-1	0	0.500	0.000
25	Saint-Etienne	Fra	1	2	0	1	1	1	3	-2	0	0.500	0.500
26	Progrès Niedercorn	Lux	1	2	0	1	1	1	5	-4	0	0.500	0.500
27	IK Start	Nor	0	2	0	0	2	1	4	-3	0	0.000	0.500
28	Widzew Lódź	Pol	0	2	0	0	2	2	6	-4	0	0.000	1.000
29	Omonia Nicosia	Cyp	0	2	0	0	2	0	4	-4	0	0.000	0.000
30	Öster SIF	Swe	0	2	0	0	2	0	6	-6	0	0.000	0.000
31	Valur Reykjavik	Isl	0	2	0	0	2	0	7	-7	0	0.000	0.000
32	Hibernians	Mlt	0	2	0	0	2	2	10	-8	0	0.000	1.000
33	OPS Oulu	Fin	0	2	0	0	2	0	8	-8	0	0.000	0.000
	Total		**140**	**126**	**50**	**26**	**50**	**170**	**170**	**0**	**14**	**1.111**	**2.698**

Preliminary Round

Team 1	Cnty	Team 2	Cnty	1st leg	2nd leg	Agg
Politehnica Timisoara	Rom	Lokomotive Leipzig	GDR	2-0	0-5	2-5

	Pts	P	W	D	L	F	A	Diff	Goals/P
Total	4	2	2	0	2	7	7	0	3.500

First Round

Team 1	Cnty	Team 2	Cnty	1st leg	2nd leg	Agg
Paralimni	Cyp	Vasas SC	Hun	1-0	0-8	1-8
Vejle BK	Den	FC Porto	Por	2-1	0-3	2-4
Barcelona	Esp	Trakia Plovdiv	Bul	4-1	0-1	4-2
KTP Kotka	Fin	Bastia	Fra	0-0	0-5	0-5
Swansea City	Wal	Lokomotive Leipzig	GDR	0-1	1-2	1-3
Ballymena United	Nir	Roma	Ita	0-2	0-4	0-6
Fram Reykjavik	Isl	Dundalk	Irl	2-1	0-4	2-5
Jeunesse Esch	Lux	Mostar Velez	Yug	1-1	1-6	2-7
Floriana	Mlt	Standard Liège	Bel	1-3	0-9	1-12
Vålerengen SIF	Nor	Legia Warsaw	Pol	2-2	1-4	3-6
Ajax	Ned	Tottenham Hotspur	Eng	1-3	0-3	1-6
Eintracht Frankfurt	FRG	PAOK Salonika	Gre	2-0	0-2	2-2
Lausanne-Sports	Sui	Kalmar FF	Swe	2-1	2-3	4-4
Dukla Prague	Tch	Rangers	Sco	3-0	1-2	4-2
SKA Rostov on Don	URS	Ankaragücü	Tur	3-0	2-0	5-0
Dinamo Tbilisi	URS	Grazer AK	Aut	2-0	2-2	4-2

	Pts	P	W	D	L	F	A	Diff	Goals/P
Total	64	32	28	8	28	110	110	0	3.438

Second Round

Team 1	Cnty	Team 2	Cnty	1st leg	2nd leg	Agg
Dundalk	Irl	Tottenham Hotspur	Eng	1-1	0-1	1-2
Bastia	Fra	Dinamo Tbilisi	URS	1-1	1-3	2-4
Vasas SC	Hun	Standard Liège	Bel	0-2	1-2	1-4
Legia Warsaw	Pol	Lausanne-Sports	Sui	2-1	1-1	3-2
FC Porto	Por	Roma	Ita	2-0	0-0	2-0
Dukla Prague	Tch	Barcelona	Esp	1-0	0-4	1-4
SKA Rostov on Don	URS	Eintracht Frankfurt	FRG	1-0	0-2	1-2
Lokomotive Leipzig	GDR	Mostar Velez	Yug	1-1	1-1	2-2

	Pts	P	W	D	L	F	A	Diff	Goals/P
Total	32	16	10	12	10	33	33	0	2.063

Quarter Finals

Team 1	Cnty	Team 2	Cnty	1st leg	2nd leg	Agg
Tottenham Hotspur	Eng	Eintracht Frankfurt	FRG	2-0	1-2	3-2
Standard Liège	Bel	FC Porto	Por	2-0	2-2	4-2
Legia Warsaw	Pol	Dinamo Tbilisi	URS	0-1	0-1	0-2
Lokomotive Leipzig	GDR	Barcelona	Esp	0-3	2-1	2-4

	Pts	P	W	D	L	F	A	Diff	Goals/P
Total	16	8	7	2	7	19	19	0	2.375

Semi Finals

Tottenham Hotspur	Eng	Barcelona	Esp	1-1	0-1	1-2
Dinamo Tbilisi	URS	Standard Liège	Bel	0-1	0-1	0-2

	Pts	P	W	D	L	F	A	Diff	Goals/P
Total	8	4	3	2	3	5	5	0	1.250

Final

Barcelona	Esp	Standard Liège	Bel	2-1	2-1

	Pts	P	W	D	L	F	A	Diff	Goals/P
Total	2	1	1	0	1	3	3	0	3.000

	Pts	P	W	D	L	F	A	Diff	Goals/P
Total	126	63	51	24	51	177	177	0	2.810

Pos'n	Club	Cnty	Pts	P	W	D	L	F	A	Diff	B	Pts/P	F/P
1	Standard Liège	Bel	18	9	7	1	1	23	6	17	3	2.000	2.556
2	Barcelona	Esp	14	9	5	1	3	16	7	9	3	1.556	1.778
3	Tottenham Hotspur	Eng	12	8	4	2	2	12	6	6	2	1.500	1.500
4	Dinamo Tbilisi	URS	12	8	4	2	2	10	6	4	2	1.500	1.250
5	Lokomotive Leipzig	GDR	11	8	4	2	2	12	9	3	1	1.375	1.500
6	Legia Warsaw	Pol	7	6	2	2	2	9	7	2	1	1.167	1.500
7	FC Porto	Por	7	6	2	2	2	8	6	2	1	1.167	1.333
8	Eintracht Frankfurt	FRG	7	6	3	0	3	6	6	0	1	1.167	1.000
9	SKA Rostov on Don	URS	6	4	3	0	1	6	2	4	0	1.500	1.500
10	Velez Mostar	Yug	5	4	1	3	0	9	4	5	0	1.250	2.250
11	Roma	Ita	5	4	2	1	1	6	2	4	0	1.250	1.500
12	Bastia	Fra	4	4	1	2	1	7	4	3	0	1.000	1.750
13	Dulka Prague	Tch	4	4	2	0	2	5	6	-1	0	1.000	1.250
14	Dundalk	Irl	3	4	1	1	2	6	4	2	0	0.750	1.500
15	Lausanne-Sports	Sui	3	4	1	1	2	6	7	-1	0	0.750	1.500
16	Vasas SC	Hun	2	4	1	0	3	9	5	4	0	0.500	2.250
17	Kalmar FF	Swe	2	2	1	0	1	4	4	0	0	1.000	2.000
18	PAOK Salonika	Gre	2	2	1	0	1	2	2	0	0	1.000	1.000
19	Trakia Plovdiv	Bul	2	2	1	0	1	2	4	-2	0	1.000	1.000
–	Vejle BK	Den	2	2	1	0	1	2	4	-2	0	1.000	1.000
–	Rangers	Sco	2	2	1	0	1	2	4	-2	0	1.000	1.000
22	Fram Reykjavik	Isl	2	2	1	0	1	2	5	-3	0	1.000	1.000
–	Politehnica Timisoara	Rom	2	2	1	0	1	2	5	-3	0	1.000	1.000
24	Paralimni	Cyp	2	2	1	0	1	1	8	-7	0	1.000	0.500
25	Grazer AK	Aut	1	2	0	1	1	2	4	-2	0	0.500	1.000
26	Vålerengen SIF	Nor	1	2	0	1	1	3	6	-3	0	0.500	1.500
27	Jeunesse Esch	Lux	1	2	0	1	1	2	7	-5	0	0.500	1.000
28	KTP Kotka	Fin	1	2	0	1	1	0	5	-5	0	0.500	0.000
29	Swansea Town	Wal	0	2	0	0	2	1	3	-2	0	0.000	0.500
30	Ajax	Ned	0	2	0	0	2	1	6	-5	0	0.000	0.500
31	Ankaragücü	Tur	0	2	0	0	2	0	5	-5	0	0.000	0.000
32	Ballymena United	Nir	0	2	0	0	2	0	6	-6	0	0.000	0.000
33	Floriana	Mlt	0	2	0	0	2	1	12	-11	0	0.000	0.500
	Total		**140**	**126**	**51**	**24**	**51**	**177**	**177**	**0**	**14**	**1.111**	**2.810**

First Round

Team 1	Cnty	Team 2	Cnty	1st leg	2nd leg	Agg
Dinamo Tirana	Alb	Carl Zeiss Jena	GDR	1-0	0-4	1-4
Ipswich Town	Eng	Aberdeen	Sco	1-1	1-3	2-4
Sturm Graz	Aut	CSKA Moscow	URS	1-0	1-2	2-2
Rapid Vienna	Aut	Videoton	Hun	2-2	2-0	4-2
Beveren	Bel	Linfield	Nir	3-0	5-0	8-0
Apoel Nicosia	Cyp	Arges Pitesti	Rom	1-1	0-4	1-5
Limerick	Irl	Southampton	Eng	0-3	1-1	1-4
Haka Valkeakoski	Fin	IFK Gothenburg	Swe	2-3	0-4	2-7
Monaco	Fra	Dundee United	Sco	2-5	2-1	4-6
Nantes	Fra	Lokeren	Bel	1-1	2-4	3-5
Panathinaikos	Gre	Arsenal	Eng	0-2	0-1	0-3
Aris Salonika	Gre	Sliema Wanderers	Mlt	4-0	4-2	8-2
Tatabánya	Hun	Real Madrid	Esp	2-1	0-1	2-2
Vikingur Reykjavik	Isl	Girondins Bordeaux	Fra	0-4	0-4	0-8
Napoli	Ita	Radnicki Nis	Yug	2-2	0-0	2-2
Bryne IL	Nor	Winterslag	Bel	0-2	2-1	2-3
PSV Eindhoven	Ned	Naestved IF	Den	7-0	1-2	8-2
Feyenoord	Ned	Szombierki Bytom	Pol	2-0	1-1	3-1
Sporting Lisbon	Por	Red Boys Differdange	Lux	4-0	7-0	11-0
Boavista	Por	Atlético Madrid	Esp	4-1	1-3	5-4
Hamburg	FRG	Utrecht	Ned	0-1	6-3	6-4
Kaiserslautern	FRG	Akademik Sofia	Bul	1-0	2-1	3-1
Dinamo Bucharest	Rom	Levski Sofia	Bul	3-0	1-2	4-2
Malmö FF	Swe	Wisla Kraków	Pol	2-0	3-1	5-1
Neuchâtel Xamax	Sui	Sparta Prague	Tch	4-0	2-3	6-3
Grasshoppers Zürich	Sui	West Bromwich Albion	Eng	1-0	3-1	4-1
Bohemians Prague	Tch	Valencia	Esp	0-1	0-1	0-2
Adanaspor	Tur	Inter Milan	Ita	1-3	1-4	2-7
Zenit Leningrad	URS	Dynamo Dresden	GDR	1-2	1-4	2-6
Spartak Moscow	URS	Club Bruges	Bel	3-1	3-1	6-2
Hajduk Split	Yug	VFB Stuttgart	FRG	3-1	2-2	5-3
Magdeburg	GDR	Bor. Mönchengladbach	FRG	3-1	0-2	3-3

	Pts	P	W	D	L	F	A	Diff	Goals/P
Total	128	64	55	18	55	216	216	0	3.375

Second Round

Southampton	Eng	Sporting Lisbon	Por	2-4	0-0	2-4
Graz Strum	Aut	IFK Gothenburg	Swe	2-2	2-3	4-5
Rapid Vienna	Aut	PSV Eindhoven	Ned	1-0	1-2	2-2
Beveren	Bel	Hajduk Split	Yug	2-3	2-1	4-4
Winterslag	Bel	Arsenal	Eng	1-0	1-2	2-2
Aberdeen	Sco	Arges Pitesti	Rom	3-0	2-2	5-2
Real Madrid	Esp	Carl Zeiss Jena	GDR	3-2	0-0	3-2
Valencia	Esp	Boavista	Por	2-0	0-1	2-1
Girondins Bordeaux	Fra	Hamburg	FRG	2-1	0-2	2-3
Aris Salonika	Gre	Lokeren	Bel	1-1	0-4	1-5
Inter Milan	Ita	Dinamo Bucharest	Rom	1-1	2-3	3-4
Feyenoord	Ned	Dynamo Dresden	GDR	2-1	1-1	3-2
Bor. Mönchengladbach	FRG	Dundee United	Sco	2-0	0-5	2-5
Malmö FF	Swe	Neuchâtel Xamax	Sui	0-1	0-1	0-2
Grasshoppers Zürich	Sui	Radnicki Nis	Yug	2-0	0-2	2-2
Spartak Moscow	URS	Kaiserslautern	FRG	2-1	0-4	2-5

	Pts	P	W	D	L	F	A	Diff	Goals/P
Total	64	32	25	14	25	89	89	0	2.781

Third Round

Rapid Vienna	Aut	Real Madrid	Esp	0-1	0-0	0-1
Lokeren	Bel	Kaiserslautern	FRG	1-0	1-4	2-4
Winterslag	Bel	Dundee United	Sco	0-0	0-5	0-5
Aberdeen	Sco	Hamburg	FRG	3-2	1-3	4-5
Valencia	Esp	Hajduk Split	Yug	5-1	1-4	6-5
Sporting Lisbon	Por	Neuchâtel Xamax	Sui	0-0	0-1	0-1
IFK Gothenburg	Swe	Dinamo Bucharest	Rom	3-1	1-0	4-1
Radnicki Nis	Yug	Feyenoord	Ned	2-0	0-1	2-1

	Pts	P	W	D	L	F	A	Diff	Goals/P
Total	32	16	13	6	13	41	41	0	2.563

Quarter Finals

Dundee Untied	Sco	Radnicki Nis	Yug	2-0	0-3	2-3
Real Madrid	Esp	Kaiserslautern	FRG	3-1	0-5	3-6
Valencia	Esp	IFK Gothenburg	Swe	2-2	0-2	2-4
Hamburg	FRG	Neuchâtel Xamax	Sui	3-2	0-0	3-2

	Pts	P	W	D	L	F	A	Diff	Goals/P
Total	16	8	6	4	6	25	25	0	3.125

Semi Finals

Kaiserslautern	FRG	IFK Gothenburg	Swe	1-1	1-2	2-3
Radnicki Nis	Yug	Hamburg	FRG	2-1	1-5	3-6

	Pts	P	W	D	L	F	A	Diff	Goals/P
Total	8	4	3	2	3	14	14	0	3.500

Final

IFK Gothenburg	Swe	Hamburg	FRG	1-0	3-0	4-0

	Pts	P	W	D	L	F	A	Diff	Goals/P
Total	4	2	2	0	2	4	4	0	2.000

	Pts	P	W	D	L	F	A	Diff	Goals/P
Total	252	126	104	44	104	389	389	0	3.087

Pos'n	Club	Cnty	Pts	P	W	D	L	F	A	Diff	B	Pts/P	F/P
1	IFK Gothenburg	Swe	24	12	9	3	0	27	11	16	3	2.000	2.250
2	Hamburg	FRG	14	12	5	1	6	23	19	1	3	1.167	1.917
3	Kaiserslautern	FRG	13	10	5	1	4	20	11	9	2	1.300	2 000
4	Radnicki Nis	Yug	12	10	4	2	4	12	13	-1	2	1.200	1.200
5	Neuchâtel Xamax	Sui	11	8	4	2	2	11	6	5	1	1.375	1.375
6	Real Madrid	Esp	11	8	1	2	2	9	10	-1	1	1.375	1.125
7	Dundee United	Sco	10	8	1	1	3	18	9	9	1	1.250	2.250
8	Valencia	Esp	10	8	4	1	3	12	10	2	1	1.250	1.500
9	Sporting Lisbon	Por	8	6	3	2	1	15	3	12	0	1.333	2.500
10	Aberdeen	Sco	8	6	3	2	1	13	9	4	0	1.333	2.167
11	Lokeren	Bel	8	6	3	2	1	12	8	4	0	1.333	2.000
12	Feyenoord	Ned	8	6	3	2	1	7	5	2	0	1.333	1.167
13	Hajduk Split	Yug	7	6	3	1	2	14	13	1	0	1.167	2.333
14	Beveren	Bel	6	4	3	0	1	12	4	8	0	1.500	3.000
15	Girondins Bordeaux	Fra	6	4	3	0	1	10	3	7	0	1.500	2.500
16	Grasshoppers Zürich	Sui	6	4	3	0	1	6	3	3	0	1.500	1.500
17	Arsenal	Eng	6	4	3	0	1	5	2	3	0	1.500	1.250
18	Spartak Moscow	URS	6	4	3	0	1	8	7	1	0	1.500	2.000
19	Rapid Vienna	Aut	6	6	2	2	2	6	5	1	0	1.000	1.000
20	Inter Milan	Ita	5	4	2	1	1	10	6	4	0	1.250	2.500
21	Dynamo Dresden	GDR	5	4	2	1	1	8	5	3	0	1.250	2.000
22	Aris Salonika	Gre	5	4	2	1	1	9	7	2	0	1.250	2.250
23	Dinamo Bucharest	Rom	5	6	2	1	3	9	9	0	0	0.833	1.500
24	Winterslag	Bel	5	6	2	1	3	5	9	-4	0	0.833	0.833
25	PSV Eindhoven	Ned	4	4	2	0	2	10	4	6	0	1.000	2.500
26	Malmö FF	Swe	4	4	2	0	2	5	3	2	0	1.000	1.250
27	Arges Pitesti	Rom	4	4	1	2	1	7	6	1	0	1.000	1.750
28	Southampton	Eng	4	4	1	2	1	6	5	1	0	1.000	1.500
29	Boavista	Por	4	4	2	0	2	6	6	0	0	1.000	1.500
30	Bor. Mönchengladbach	FRG	4	4	2	0	2	5	8	-3	0	1.000	1.250
31	Carl Zeiss Jena	GDR	3	4	1	1	2	6	4	2	0	0.750	1.500
32	Sturm Graz	Aut	3	1	1	1	2	6	7	-1	0	0.750	1.500
33	Magdeburg	GDR	2	2	1	0	1	3	3	0	0	1.000	1.500
34	Tatabánya	Hun	2	2	1	0	1	2	2	0	0	1.000	1.000
–	Napoli	Ita	2	2	0	2	0	2	2	0	0	1.000	1.000
–	CSKA Moscow	URS	2	2	1	0	1	2	2	0	0	1.000	1.000
37	Atlético Madrid	Esp	2	2	1	0	1	4	5	-1	0	1.000	2.000
38	Bryne IL	Nor	2	2	1	0	1	2	3	-1	0	1.000	1.000
39	Monaco	Fra	2	2	1	0	1	4	6	-2	0	1.000	2.000
–	Utrecht	Ned	2	2	1	0	1	4	6	-2	0	1.000	2.000
41	Levski Sofia	Bul	2	2	1	0	1	2	4	-2	0	1.000	1.000
42	Sparta Prague	Tch	2	2	1	0	1	3	6	-3	0	1.000	1.500
43	Dinamo Tirana	Alb	2	2	1	0	1	1	4	-3	0	1.000	0.500
44	Naestved IF	Den	2	2	1	0	1	2	8	-6	0	1.000	1.000
45	Nantes	Fra	1	2	0	1	1	3	5	-2	0	0.500	1.500
–	VFB Stuttgart	FRG	1	2	0	1	1	3	5	-2	0	0.500	1.500
47	Ipswich Town	Eng	1	2	0	1	1	2	4	-2	0	0.500	1.000
–	Videoton	Hun	1	2	0	1	1	2	4	-2	0	0.500	1.000
49	Szombierli Bytom	Pol	1	2	0	1	1	1	3	-2	0	0.500	0.500
50	Limerick	Irl	1	2	0	1	1	1	4	-3	0	0.500	0.500
51	Apoel Nicosia	Cyp	1	2	0	1	1	1	5	-4	0	0.500	0.500
52	Akademik Sofia	Bul	0	2	0	0	2	1	3	-2	0	0.000	0.500
53	Bohemians Prague	Tch	0	2	0	0	2	0	2	-2	0	0.000	0.000
54	West Bromwich Albion	Eng	0	2	0	0	2	1	4	-3	0	0.000	0.500
55	Panathinaikos	Gre	0	2	0	0	2	0	3	-3	0	0.000	0.000
56	Club Bruges	Bel	0	2	0	0	2	2	6	-4	0	0.000	1.000
–	Zenit Leningrad	URS	0	2	0	0	2	2	6	-4	0	0.000	1.000
58	Wisla Kraków	Pol	0	2	0	0	2	1	5	-4	0	0.000	0.500
59	Haka Valkeakoski	Fin	0	2	0	0	2	2	7	-5	0	0.000	1.000
–	Adanaspor	Tur	0	2	0	0	2	2	7	-5	0	0.000	1.000
61	Sliema Wanderers	Mlt	0	2	0	0	2	2	8	-6	0	0.000	1.000
62	Linfield	Nir	0	2	0	0	2	0	8	-8	0	0.000	0.000
–	Vikingur Reykjavik	Isl	0	2	0	0	2	0	8	-8	0	0.000	0.000
64	Red Boys Differdange	Lux	0	2	0	0	2	0	11	-11	0	0.000	0.000
	Total		**266**	**252**	**104**	**44**	**104**	**389**	**389**	**0**	**14**	**1.056**	**3.087**

1981-82

Pos'n	Cnty	Pts	P	W	D	L	F	A	Diff	B	Pts/P	F/P
1	FRG	54	43	20	5	18	77	56	21	9	1.256	1.791
2	Bel	51	35	20	6	9	68	40	28	5	1.457	1.943
3	Eng	50	35	18	8	9	53	29	24	6	1.429	1.514
4	Esp	38	29	14	5	10	41	33	8	5	1.310	1.414
5	URS	34	26	13	5	8	32	27	5	3	1.308	1.231
6	Yug	31	26	11	6	9	51	39	12	3	1.192	1.962
7	Swe	30	20	12	3	5	36	24	12	3	1.500	1.800
8	GDR	28	24	11	5	8	37	27	10	1	1.167	1.542
9	Por	24	20	9	5	6	34	19	15	1	1.200	1.700
10	Sco	22	18	9	3	6	34	24	10	1	1.222	1.889
11	Sui	22	18	9	3	6	26	19	7	1	1.222	1.444
12	Ned	19	18	8	3	7	30	27	3	0	1.056	1.667
13	Rom	17	18	6	4	8	26	27	-1	1	0.944	1.444
14	Ita	15	14	5	5	4	22	15	7	0	1.071	1.571
15	Bul	15	14	6	1	7	15	21	-6	2	1.071	1.071
16	Fra	14	14	5	4	5	25	21	4	0	1.000	1.786
17	Aut	13	16	4	5	7	18	20	-2	0	0.813	1.125
18	Tch	10	12	5	0	7	16	21	-5	0	0.833	1.333
19	Gre	9	10	4	1	5	13	15	-2	0	0.900	1.300
20	Pol	8	12	2	3	7	13	21	-8	1	0.667	1.083
21	Den	8	8	3	2	3	9	19	-10	0	1.000	1.125
22	Hun	7	10	3	1	6	16	16	0	0	0.700	1.600
23	Irl	6	8	1	4	3	10	11	-1	0	0.750	1.250
24	Nir	5	8	2	1	5	7	18	-11	0	0.625	0.875
25	Alb	4	4	2	0	2	3	7	-4	0	1.000	0.750
26	Nor	3	6	1	1	4	6	13	-7	0	0.500	1.000
27	Cyp	3	6	1	1	4	2	17	-15	0	0.500	0.333
28	Isl	2	6	1	0	5	2	20	-18	0	0.333	0.333
29	Lux	2	6	0	2	4	3	23	-20	0	0.333	0.500
30	Tur	1	6	0	1	5	3	14	-11	0	0.167	0.500
31	Fin	1	6	0	1	5	2	20	-18	0	0.167	0.333
32	Wal	0	2	0	0	2	1	3	-2	0	0.000	0.500
33	Mlt	0	6	0	0	6	5	30	-25	0	0.000	0.833
	Total	**546**	**504**	**205**	**94**	**205**	**736**	**736**	**0**	**42**	**1.083**	**2.921**

1955-56 to 1981-82

Pos'n	Cnty	Pts	P	W	D	L	F	A	Diff	B	Pts/P	F/P
1	Eng	1196	811	439	174	198	1576	821	755	144	1.475	1.943
2	FRG	1136	819	430	148	241	1673	1054	619	128	1.387	2.043
3	Esp	1026	746	380	138	228	1415	922	493	128	1.375	1.897
4	Ita	892	662	325	144	193	1042	685	357	98	1.347	1.574
5	Sco	594	485	228	87	170	843	642	201	51	1.225	1.738
6	Ned	587	442	227	77	138	884	544	340	56	1.328	2.000
7	Bel	536	455	208	73	174	732	600	132	47	1.178	1.609
8	Yug	535	482	196	92	194	790	702	88	51	1.110	1.639
9	Por	485	424	178	92	154	695	544	151	37	1.144	1.639
10	Hun	452	382	176	60	146	710	554	156	40	1.183	1.859
11	GDR	428	381	158	81	142	578	497	81	31	1.123	1.517
12	Tch	396	339	154	60	125	537	454	83	28	1.168	1.584
13	Fra	382	371	142	69	160	569	563	6	29	1.030	1.534
14	URS	330	248	128	50	70	365	240	125	24	1.331	1.472
15	Sui	277	317	102	54	161	480	614	-134	19	0.874	1.514
16	Bul	273	277	108	41	128	422	431	-9	16	0.986	1.523
17	Pol	271	265	101	54	110	384	406	-22	15	1.023	1.449
18	Rom	249	271	98	47	126	353	437	-84	6	0.919	1.303
19	Aut	231	275	81	55	139	325	458	-133	14	0.840	1.182
20	Swe	209	227	73	51	103	294	385	-91	12	0.921	1.295
21	Gre	194	221	74	39	108	265	399	-134	7	0.878	1.199
22	Den	156	231	56	39	136	303	511	-208	5	0.675	1.312
23	Tur	144	199	54	30	115	199	380	-181	6	0.724	1.000
24	Nor	86	164	32	21	111	164	426	-262	1	0.524	1.000
25	Irl	79	162	25	29	108	134	402	-268	0	0.488	0.827
26	Wal	78	74	25	22	27	100	91	9	6	1.054	1.351
27	Nir	70	142	21	26	95	142	412	-270	2	0.493	1.000
28	Lux	41	140	15	11	114	96	587	-491	0	0.293	0.686
29	Mlt	39	118	14	11	93	61	399	-338	0	0.331	0.517
30	Fin	35	114	11	13	90	92	394	-302	0	0.307	0.807
31	Cyp	29	98	9	11	78	57	379	-322	0	0.296	0.582
32	Alb	25	38	7	11	20	26	60	-34	0	0.658	0.684
33	Isl	24	104	5	14	85	55	368	-313	0	0.231	0.529
	Total	**11485**	**10484**	**4280**	**1924**	**4280**	**16361**	**16361**	**0**	**1001**	**1.095**	**3.121**

1981-82

Pos'n	Cnty	Ave	Pts	P	W	D	L	F	A	Diff	B	No./T
1	W. Germany	9.000	54	43	20	5	18	77	56	21	9	6
2	Belgium	8.500	51	35	20	6	9	68	40	28	5	6
3	Yugoslavia	7.750	31	26	11	6	9	51	39	12	3	4
4	Spain	7.600	38	29	14	5	10	41	33	8	5	5
5	Sweden	7.500	30	20	12	3	5	36	24	12	3	4
6	England	7.142	50	35	18	8	9	53	29	24	6	7
7	Portugal	6.000	24	20	9	5	6	34	19	15	1	4
8	USSR	5.666	34	26	13	5	8	32	27	5	3	6
9	E. Germany	5.600	28	24	11	5	8	37	27	10	1	5
10	Scotland	5.500	22	18	9	3	6	34	24	10	1	4
–	Switzerland	5.500	22	18	9	3	6	26	19	7	1	4
12	Romania	4.250	17	18	6	4	8	26	27	-1	1	4
13	Netherlands	3.800	19	18	8	3	7	30	27	3	0	5
14	Bulgaria	3.750	15	14	6	1	7	15	21	-6	2	4
–	Italy	3.750	15	14	5	5	4	22	15	7	0	4
16	Austria	3.250	13	16	4	5	7	18	20	-2	0	4
17	France	2.800	14	14	5	4	5	25	21	4	0	5
18	Denmark	2.666	8	8	3	2	3	9	19	-10	0	3
19	Czechoslovakia	2.500	10	12	5	0	7	16	21	-5	0	4
20	Greece	2.250	9	10	4	1	5	13	15	-2	0	4
21	Albania	2.000	4	4	2	0	2	3	7	-4	0	2
–	Rep. of Ireland	2.000	6	8	1	4	3	10	11	-1	0	3
–	Poland	2.000	8	12	2	3	7	13	21	-8	1	4
24	Hungary	1.750	7	10	3	1	6	16	16	0	0	4
25	N. Ireland	1.666	5	8	2	1	5	7	18	-11	0	3
26	Cyprus	1.000	3	6	1	1	4	2	17	-15	0	3
–	Norway	1.000	3	6	1	1	4	6	13	-7	0	3
28	Iceland	0.666	2	6	1	0	5	2	20	-18	0	3
–	Luxembourg	0.666	2	6	0	2	4	3	23	-20	0	3
30	Finland	0.333	1	6	0	1	5	2	20	-18	0	3
–	Turkey	0.333	1	6	0	1	5	3	14	-11	0	3
32	Wales	0.000	0	2	0	0	2	1	3	-2	0	1
–	Malta	0.000	0	6	0	0	6	5	30	-25	0	3
	Total		**546**	**504**	**205**	**94**	**205**	**736**	**736**	**0**	**42**	**2.921**

1955-56 to 1981-82

Pos'n	Cnty	Ave	Pts	P	W	D	L	F	A	Diff	B	No./T
1	England	8.859	1196	811	439	174	198	1576	821	755	144	135
2	W. Germany	8.056	1136	819	430	148	241	1673	1054	619	128	141
3	Spain	7.772	1026	746	380	138	228	1415	922	493	128	132
4	Italy	6.914	892	662	325	144	193	1042	685	357	98	129
5	Netherlands	6.450	587	442	227	77	138	884	544	340	56	91
6	USSR	5.892	330	248	128	50	70	365	240	125	24	56
7	Scotland	5.711	594	485	228	87	170	843	642	201	51	104
8	Hungary	5.380	452	382	176	60	146	710	554	156	40	84
9	Belgium	5.203	536	455	208	73	174	732	600	132	47	103
10	E. Germany	5.035	428	381	158	81	142	578	497	81	31	85
11	Yugoslavia	4.908	535	482	196	92	194	790	702	88	51	109
12	Portugal	4.754	485	424	178	92	154	695	544	151	37	102
13	Czechoslovakia	4.658	396	339	154	60	125	537	454	83	28	85
14	France	3.820	382	371	142	69	160	569	563	6	29	100
15	Poland	3.763	271	265	101	54	110	384	406	-22	15	72
16	Wales	3.714	78	74	25	22	27	100	91	9	6	21
17	Bulgaria	3.455	273	277	108	41	128	422	431	-9	16	79
18	Romania	3.036	249	271	98	47	126	353	437	-84	6	82
19	Switzerland	2.855	277	317	102	54	161	480	614	-134	19	97
20	Sweden	2.824	209	227	73	51	103	294	385	-91	12	74
21	Austria	2.717	231	275	81	55	139	325	458	-133	14	85
22	Greece	2.519	194	221	74	39	108	265	399	-134	7	77
23	Turkey	2.057	144	199	54	30	115	199	380	-181	6	70
24	Denmark	1.835	156	231	56	39	136	303	511	-208	5	85
25	Albania	1.470	25	38	7	11	20	26	60	-34	0	17
26	Norway	1.264	86	164	32	21	111	164	426	-262	1	68
27	Rep. of Ireland	1.196	79	162	25	29	108	134	402	-268	0	66
28	N. Ireland	1.147	70	142	21	26	95	142	412	-270	2	61
29	Malta	0.696	39	118	14	11	93	61	399	-338	0	56
30	Finland	0.686	35	114	11	13	90	92	394	-302	0	51
31	Cyprus	0.644	29	98	9	11	78	57	379	-322	0	45
32	Luxembourg	0.621	41	140	15	11	114	96	587	-491	0	66
33	Iceland	0.500	24	104	5	14	85	55	368	-313	0	48
	Total		**11485**	**10484**	**4280**	**1924**	**4280**	**16361**	**16361**	**0**	**1001**	**3.121**

Villa Beat Bayern in Thriller

In the year that the England national team returned to the World Cup finals after a 12-year absence, English club football was re-confirmed as the most powerful in Europe with its sixth Champions' Cup victory in a row. No nation had ever accomplished that feat before. The previous best had been Spain's run of five wins, all of them by Real Madrid, in the first five years of the competition. Furthermore, England's seventh victory also took it ahead of Spain (6) in the all-time Champions' Cup rankings.

The club responsible for this feat of record-breaking was not Liverpool, not even Nottingham Forest, but another Midlands club, Aston Villa.

Villa, who had won their first major honour for decades the previous season by lifting the English championship, were not generally expected to do much in European competition. They had only appeared in Europe twice before, both times in the UEFA Cup, and moreover had lost the man responsible for leading the team to the First Division title, manager Ron Saunders. Tony Barton, his assistant, took over for the Champions' Cup campaign, but the team, Saunders' team, by and large remained intact, and that unity and understanding proved to be its great strength over the course of the season.

Most English hopes initially rested on Liverpool, the holders. But after seeing off OPS of Finland and the previous season's UEFA Cup runners-up AZ'67 Alkmaar in the autumn, they came a cropper in the spring against the team that had eliminated Nottingham Forest the year before, but which Liverpool themselves had subsequently thrashed at Anfield, CSKA Sofia. This time Liverpool managed just a single goal at home, and the Bulgarians made them pay in the return, with two goals from left-winger Stoicho Mladenov, the second in extra-time, taking them into the semi-finals. Villa, meanwhile, had begun comfortably against Valur of Iceland. But in the next round they had to rely on away goals, both of them scored by winger Tony Morley, to get past the tricky East German side, Dynamo Berlin. Just as they had done against Forest two years earlier, Dynamo won 1-0 in England, but defeat at home sent them out. Villa then decisively knocked out Dinamo Kiev with goals from young striker Gary Shaw and defender Ken McNaught, and that put them into a semi-final confrontation with Anderlecht.

The Belgians, despite having appeared in four previous European finals, had never before reached the final of the Champions' Cup. It was becoming something of an obsession for them. But this was not to be their year. A single Tony Morley goal in Birmingham gave his team a first-leg lead, and Anderlecht, for all their huffing and puffing, couldn't blow the Villa down in the return. Villa's only real discomfort was caused by their unruly fans, whose idiotic behaviour almost led to the match being replayed. In the end, it merely caused the team's first-round match the following season to be played behind closed doors.

Villa were through to the final, but they would not be favourites. Bayern Munich, beaten in the semi-finals by Liverpool the previous season, were back in their first Champions' Cup final since 1976. The two outstanding players in the team now were Paul Breitner and Karl-Heinz Rummenigge, and they had each scored twice in the 4-0 semi-final second-leg victory over CSKA Sofia which took them through 7-4.

In Rotterdam, Aston Villa suffered an early blow when goalkeeper Jimmy Rimmer had to be substituted after only nine minutes. But his replacement, Nigel Spink, who had only ever appeared in the Villa first team once before, two and a half years earlier, proved to be the hero of the evening, saving time and again from Rummenigge and company to keep the scoreline blank. It was just after Villa had survived a lengthy bout of Bayern pressure midway through the second half that they broke away and scored. Morley, threatening as ever, teased the Bayern defence this way and that before crossing perfectly for Peter Withe in the centre. The finish was clumsy – off the knee and in via the post – but it counted, and Villa, to Bayern's astonishment, were 1-0 up. And so it remained, with more Bayern pressure coming to nothing in the last 20 minutes. So Villa, like Nottingham Forest before them, had succeeded in the Champions' Cup at the first time of asking, whereas Bayern, for the first time in their history, had been defeated in a Cup final.

The Champions' Cup final might have ended 1-0 yet again, but it was a distinct improvement on those of the previous four years. It was also a vastly superior game of football to the 1982 Cup-winners' Cup final, played between Barcelona and Standard Liège, in Barca's own Nou Camp stadium.

This was the first time that a Cup-winners' Cup final had been staged in the home stadium of one of the competing teams, but Barcelona didn't take advantage in the traditional way. Their game was one of intimidation and violence, especially after they went down to an early goal from Belgian international Guy Vandersmissen, and the result was one of the ugliest European finals on record. That they won the match was down almost entirely to the brilliance of their Danish forward Allan Simonsen, who scored their first goal and created the second for top-scoring centre-forward Quini with a quickly-taken free-kick. His goal meant that he had scored in the finals of all three European competitions, having previously found the net in both the Champions' and UEFA Cup finals for Borussia Mönchengladbach.

Barcelona had also been up to their dirty tricks in the semi-final against Tottenham Hotspur, fouling persistently throughout the two matches and more or less getting away with it thanks to poor refereeing. Standard, on the other hand, had performed admirably to defeat the much-fancied holders, Dinamo Tbilisi, both home and away and reach their first European final. Their coach Raymond Goethals was a highly experienced tactician, who knew how to grind out results with remarkable consistency. But in Barcelona, he could only sit and watch in frustration as the Spaniards bullied their way to victory, enabling their coach, Udo Lattek to become the first man to lead teams to victory in all three European Cups. He had previously won the Champions' Cup with Bayern Munich and the UEFA Cup with Borussia Mönchengladbach.

Above: Barcelona Captain Jose Vincente Sanchez holds the European Cup Winners' Cup aloft after the Spaniards had beaten Standard Liège 2-1.

The final of the 1981-82 UEFA Cup provided one of the biggest shocks the tournament had ever seen, with IFK Gothenburg becoming the first Swedish team to win a European trophy by beating Hamburg 4-0 on aggregate. The Swedes, coached by Sven Göran Eriksson, had been in excellent form throughout the competition, with strikers Torbjörn Nilsson and Dan Corneliusson scoring goals aplenty in an unbeaten ten-match run going into the final. Their semi-final victims were Kaiserslautern, the side that had inflicted on Real Madrid their heaviest ever defeat in Europe in the quarter-finals, but against Hamburg, few gave them much chance of success. Hamburg's appearance in the final made them the first West German to reach the finals of all three European Cups, but they certainly didn't live up to their reputation in the first leg, in Gothenburg. Clearly aiming to scramble a draw before finishing off the tie in Hamburg, they were caught out late in the game by a goal from Tord Holmgren. Psychologically, that goal swung the tie. The Germans never got going in the return, and Gothenburg shocked the 60,000 crowd with three breakaway goals, from Corneliusson, Nilsson and Fredriksson, to complete a sensational triumph.

Hamburg

Aberdeen

Anderlecht

1982 – 1983

Preliminary Round

Team 1	Cnty	Team 2	Cnty	1st leg	2nd leg	Agg
Dinamo Bucharest	Rom	Vålerengen SIF	Nor	3-1	1-2	4-3

	Pts	P	W	D	L	F	A	Diff	Goals/P
Total	4	2	2	0	2	7	7	0	3.500

First Round

17 Nëntori Tirana	Alb	Linfield	Nir	1-0	1-2	2-2
Aston Villa	Eng	Besiktas	Tur	3-1	0-0	3-1
Standard Liège	Bel	Rába ETO	Hun	5-0	0-3	5-3
Omonia Nicosia	Cyp	HJK Helsinki	Fin	2-0	0-3	2-3
Hvidovre IF	Den	Juventus	Ita	1-4	3-3	4-7
Celtic	Sco	Ajax	Ned	2-2	2-1	4-3
Dundalk	Irl	Liverpool	Eng	1-4	0-1	1-5
Monaco	Fra	CSKA Sofia	Bul	0-0	0-2	0-2
Olympiakos Pireus	Gre	Öster SIF	Swe	2-0	0-1	2-1
Vikingur Reykjavik	Isl	Real Sociedad	Esp	0-1	2-3	2-4
Avenir Beggen	Lux	Rapid Vienna	Aut	0-5	0-8	0-13
Hibernians	Mlt	Widzew Lódź	Pol	1-4	1-3	2-7
Dinamo Bucharest	Rom	Dukla Prague	Tch	2-0	1-2	3-2
Grasshoppers Zürich	Sui	Dinamo Kiev	URS	0-1	0-3	0-4
Dinamo Zagreb	Yug	Sporting Lisbon	Por	1-0	0-3	1-3
Dynamo Berlin	GDR	Hamburg	FRG	1-1	0-2	1-3

	Pts	P	W	D	L	F	A	Diff	Goals/P
Total	64	32	27	10	27	95	95	0	2.969

Second Round

Rapid Vienna	Aut	Widzew Lódź	Pol	2-1	3-5	5-6
Standard Liège	Bel	Juventus	Ita	1-1	0-2	1-3
CSKA Sofia	Bul	Sporting Lisbon	Por	2-2	0-0	2-2
Real Sociedad	Esp	Celtic	Sco	2-0	1-2	3-2
HJK Helsinki	Fin	Liverpool	Eng	1-0	0-5	1-5
Hamburg	FRG	Olympiakos Pireus	Gre	1-0	4-0	5-0
Dinamo Bucharest	Rom	Aston Villa	Eng	0-2	2-4	2-6

	Pts	P	W	D	L	F	A	Diff	Goals/P
Total	28	14	11	6	11	43	43	0	3.071

Quarter Finals

Aston Villa	Eng	Juventus	Ita	1-2	1-3	2-5
Widzew Lódź	Pol	Liverpool	Eng	2-0	2-3	4-3
Sporting Lisbon	Por	Real Sociedad	Esp	1-0	0-2	1-2
Dinamo Kiev	URS	Hamburg	FRG	0-3	2-1	2-4

	Pts	P	W	D	L	F	A	Diff	Goals/P
Total	16	8	8	0	8	23	23	0	2.875

Semi Finals

Real Sociedad	Esp	Hamburg	FRG	1-1	1-2	2-3
Juventus	Ita	Widzew Lódź	Pol	2-0	2-2	4-2

	Pts	P	W	D	L	F	A	Diff	Goals/P
Total	8	4	2	4	2	11	11	0	2.750

Final

Hamburg	FRG	Juventus	Ita	1-0	1-0

	Pts	P	W	D	L	F	A	Diff	Goals/P
Total	2	1	1	0	1	1	1	0	1.000

	Pts	P	W	D	L	F	A	Diff	Goals/P
Total	122	61	51	20	51	180	180	0	2.951

Pos'n	Club	Cnty	Pts	P	W	D	L	F	A	Diff	B	Pts/P	F/P
1	Hamburg	FRG	17	9	6	2	1	16	5	11	3	1.889	1.778
2	Juventus	Ita	16	9	5	3	1	19	10	9	3	1.778	2.111
3	Widzew Lódź	Pol	11	8	4	1	3	19	14	5	2	1.375	2.375
4	Real Sociedad	Esp	11	8	4	1	3	11	8	3	2	1.375	1.375
5	Liverpool	Eng	9	6	4	0	2	13	6	7	1	1.500	2.167
6	Aston Villa	Eng	8	6	3	1	2	11	8	3	1	1.333	1.833
7	Dinamo Kiev	URS	7	4	3	0	1	6	4	2	1	1.750	1.500
8	Sporting Lisbon	Por	7	6	2	2	2	6	5	1	1	1.167	1.000
9	Rapid Vienna	Aut	6	4	3	0	1	18	6	12	0	1.500	4.500
10	CSKA Sofia	Bul	5	4	1	3	0	4	2	2	0	1.250	1.000
11	Celtic	Sco	5	4	2	1	1	6	6	0	0	1.250	1.500
12	Dinamo Bucharest	Rom	4	6	2	0	1	9	11	-2	0	0.667	1.500
13	HJK Helsinki	Fin	4	4	2	0	2	4	7	-3	0	1.000	1.000
14	Standard Liège	Bel	3	4	1	1	2	6	6	0	0	0.750	1.500
15	17 Nëntori Tirana	Alb	2	2	1	0	1	2	2	0	0	1.000	1.000
–	Linfield	Nir	2	2	1	0	1	2	2	0	0	1.000	1.000
17	Vålerengen SIF	Nor	2	2	1	0	1	3	4	-1	0	1.000	1.500
18	Omonia Nicosia	Cyp	2	2	1	0	1	2	3	-1	0	1.000	1.000
–	Dulka Prague	Tch	2	2	1	0	1	2	3	-1	0	1.000	1.000
20	Öster SIF	Swe	2	2	1	0	1	1	2	-1	0	1.000	0.500
21	Rába ETO	Hun	2	2	1	0	1	3	5	-2	0	1.000	1.500
22	Dinamo Zagreb	Yug	2	2	1	0	1	1	3	-2	0	1.000	0.500
23	Olympiakos Pireus	Gre	2	4	1	0	3	2	6	-4	0	0.500	0.500
24	Ajax	Ned	1	2	0	1	1	3	4	-1	0	0.500	1.500
25	Besiktas	Tur	1	2	0	1	1	1	3	-2	0	0.500	0.500
–	Dynamo Berlin	GDR	1	2	0	1	1	1	3	-2	0	0.500	0.500
27	Monaco	Fra	1	2	0	1	1	0	2	-2	0	0.500	0.000
28	Hvidovre IF	Den	1	2	0	1	1	4	7	-3	0	0.500	2.000
29	Vikingur Reykjavik	Isl	0	2	0	0	2	2	1	-2	0	0.000	1.000
30	Dundalk	Irl	0	2	0	0	2	1	5	-4	0	0.000	0.500
31	Grasshoppers Zürich	Sui	0	2	0	0	2	0	4	-4	0	0.000	0.000
32	Hibernians	Mlt	0	2	0	0	2	2	7	-5	0	0.000	1.000
33	Avenir Beggen	Lux	0	2	0	0	2	0	13	-13	0	0.000	0.000
	Total		**136**	**122**	**51**	**20**	**51**	**180**	**180**	**0**	**14**	**1.115**	**2.951**

Preliminary Round

Team 1	Cnty	Team 2	Cnty	1st leg	2nd leg	Agg
Aberdeen	Sco	Sion	Sui	7-0	4-1	11-1
Swansea City	Wal	Sporting Braga	Por	3-0	0-1	3-1

	Pts	P	W	D	L	F	A	Diff	Goals/P
Total	8	4	4	0	4	16	16	0	4.000

First Round

Austria Vienna	Aut	Panathinaikos	Gre	2-0	1-2	3-2
Waterschei Thor	Bel	Red Boys Differdange	Lux	7-1	1-0	8-1
Lokomotiv Sofia	Bul	Paris Saint-Germain	Fra	1-0	1-5	2-5
Aberdeen	Sco	Dinamo Tirana	Alb	1-0	0-0	1-0
Limerick	Irl	AZ'67 Alkmaar	Ned	1-1	0-1	1-2
Barcelona	Esp	Apollon Limassol	Cyp	8-0	1-1	9-1
Swansea City	Wal	Sliema Wanderers	Mlt	12-0	5-0	17-0
Coleraine	Nir	Tottenham Hotspur	Eng	0-3	0-4	0-7
IBV Vestmannaeyjar	Isl	Lech Poznań	Pol	0-1	0-3	0-4
Inter Milan	Ita	Slovan Bratislava	Tch	2-0	1-2	3-2
Lillestrøm SK	Nor	Red Star Belgrade	Yug	0-4	0-3	0-7
Baia Mare	Rom	Real Madrid	Esp	0-0	2-5	2-5
IFK Gothenburg	Swe	Ujpesti Dózsa	Hun	1-1	1-3	2-4
Galatasaray	Tur	FC Kuusysi Lahti	Fin	2-1	1-1	3-2
Torpedo Moscow	URS	Bayern Munich	FRG	1-1	0-0	1-1
Dynamo Dresden	GDR	B 93 Copenhagen	Den	3-2	1-2	4-4

	Pts	P	W	D	L	F	A	Diff	Goals/P
Total	64	32	24	16	24	103	103	0	3.219

Second Round

Tottenham Hotspur	Eng	Bayern Munich	FRG	1-1	1-4	2-5
B 93 Copenhagen	Den	Waterschei Thor	Bel	0-2	1-4	1-6
Aberdeen	Sco	Lech Poznań	Pol	2-0	1-0	3-0
Real Madrid	Esp	Ujpesti Dózsa	Hun	3-1	1-0	4-1
Swansea City	Wal	Paris Saint-Germain	Fra	0-1	0-2	0-3
AZ'67 Alkmaar	Ned	Inter Milan	Ita	1-0	0-2	1-2
Galatasaray	Tur	Austria Vienna	Aut	2-4	1-0	3-4
Red Star Belgrade	Yug	Barcelona	Esp	2-4	1-2	3-6

	Pts	P	W	D	L	F	A	Diff	Goals/P
Total	32	16	15	2	15	44	44	0	2.750

Quarter Finals

Austria Vienna	Aut	Barcelona	Esp	0-0	1-1	1-1
Paris Saint-Germain	Fra	Waterschei Thor	Bel	2-0	0-3	2-3
Inter Milan	Ita	Real Madrid	Esp	1-1	1-2	2-3
Bayern Munich	FRG	Aberdeen	Sco	0-0	2-3	2-3

	Pts	P	W	D	L	F	A	Diff	Goals/P
Total	16	8	4	8	4	17	17	0	2.125

Semi Finals

Austria Vienna	Aut	Real Madrid	Esp	2-2	1-3	3-5
Aberdeen	Sco	Waterschei Thor	Bel	5-1	0-1	5-2

	Pts	P	W	D	L	F	A	Diff	Goals/P
Total	8	4	3	2	3	15	15	0	3.750

Final

Real Madrid	Esp	Aberdeen	Sco	1-2	1-2

	Pts	P	W	D	L	F	A	Diff	Goals/P
Total	2	1	1	0	1	3	3	0	3.000

	Pts	P	W	D	L	F	A	Diff	Goals/P
Total	130	65	51	28	51	198	198	0	3.046

Pos'n	Club	Cnty	Pts	P	W	D	L	F	A	Diff	B	Pts/P	F/P
1	Aberdeen	Sco	21	11	8	2	1	25	6	19	3	1.909	2.273
2	Real Madrid	Esp	16	9	5	3	1	18	10	8	3	1.778	2.000
3	Waterschei Thor	Bel	14	8	6	0	2	19	9	10	2	1.750	2.375
4	Barcelona	Esp	10	6	3	3	0	16	5	11	1	1.667	2.667
5	Paris Saint-Germain	Fra	9	6	4	0	2	10	5	5	1	1.500	1.667
6	Austria Vienna	Aut	9	8	2	3	3	11	11	0	2	1.125	1.375
7	Bayern Munich	FRG	7	6	1	4	1	8	6	2	1	1.167	1.333
8	Swansea Town	Wal	6	6	3	0	3	20	4	16	0	1.000	3.333
9	Inter Milan	Ita	6	6	2	1	3	7	6	1	1	1.000	1.167
10	Tottenham Hotspur	Eng	5	4	2	1	1	9	5	4	0	1.250	2.250
11	Galatasaray	Tur	5	4	2	1	1	6	6	0	0	1.250	1.500
12	AZ'67 Alkmaar	Ned	5	4	2	1	1	3	3	0	0	1.250	0.750
13	Red Star Belgrade	Yug	4	4	2	0	2	10	6	4	0	1.000	2.500
14	Lech Poznań	Pol	4	4	2	0	2	4	3	1	0	1.000	1.000
15	Ujpesti Dózsa	Hun	3	4	1	1	2	5	6	-1	0	0.750	1.250
16	Dynamo Dresden	GDR	2	2	1	0	1	4	4	0	0	1.000	2.000
17	Torpedo Moscow	URS	2	2	0	2	0	1	1	0	0	1.000	0.500
18	Panathinaikos	Gre	2	2	1	0	1	2	3	-1	0	1.000	1.000
–	Slovan Bratislava	Tch	2	2	1	0	1	2	3	-1	0	1.000	1.000
20	Sporting Braga	Por	2	2	1	0	1	1	3	-2	0	1.000	0.500
21	Lokomotiv Sofia	Bul	2	2	1	0	1	2	5	-3	0	1.000	1.000
22	B 93 Copenhagen	Den	2	4	1	0	3	5	10	-5	0	0.500	1.250
23	FC Kuusysi Lahti	Fin	1	2	0	1	1	2	3	-1	0	0.500	1.000
24	Limerick	Irl	1	2	0	1	1	1	2	-1	0	0.500	0.500
25	Dinamo Tirana	Alb	1	2	0	1	1	0	1	-1	0	0.500	0.000
26	IFK Gothenburg	Swe	1	2	0	1	1	2	4	-2	0	0.500	1.000
27	Baia Mare	Rom	1	2	0	1	1	2	5	-3	0	0.500	1.000
28	Apollon Limassol	Cyp	1	2	0	1	1	1	9	-8	0	0.500	0.500
29	IBV Vestmannaeyjar	Isl	0	2	0	0	2	0	4	-4	0	0.000	0.000
30	Red Boys Differdange	Lux	0	2	0	0	2	1	8	-7	0	0.000	0.500
31	Coleraine	Nir	0	2	0	0	2	0	7	-7	0	0.000	0.000
–	Lillestrøm SK	Nor	0	2	0	0	2	0	7	-7	0	0.000	0.000
33	Sion	Sui	0	2	0	0	2	1	11	-10	0	0.000	0.500
34	Sliema Wanderers	Mlt	0	2	0	0	2	0	17	-17	0	0.000	0.000
	Total		**144**	**130**	**51**	**28**	**51**	**198**	**198**	**0**	**14**	**1.108**	**3.046**

First Round

Team 1	Cnty	Team 2	Cnty	1st leg	2nd leg	Agg
Manchester United	Eng	Valencia	Esp	0-0	1-2	1-2
Southampton	Eng	IFK Norrköping	Swe	2-2	0-0	2-2
Grazer AK	Aut	Corvinul Hunedoara	Rom	1-1	0-3	1-4
Anderlecht	Bel	KuPS Kuopio	Fin	3-0	3-1	6-1
Slavia Sofia	Bul	Sarajevo	Yug	2-2	2-4	4-6
Pezoporikos Larnaca	Cyp	FC Zürich	Sui	2-2	0-1	2-3
Lyngby BK	Den	IK Brage	Swe	1-2	2-2	3-4
Dundee United	Sco	PSV Eindhoven	Ned	1-1	2-0	3-1
Seville	Esp	Levski Sofia	Bul	3-1	3-0	6-1
Saint-Etienne	Fra	Tatabánya	Hun	4-1	0-0	4-1
AEK Athens	Gre	Cologne	FRG	0-1	0-5	0-6
PAOK Salonika	Gre	Sochaux	Fra	1-0	1-2	2-2
Ferencváros	Hun	Athletic Bilbao	Esp	2-1	1-1	3-2
Glentoran	Nir	Banik Ostrava	Tch	1-3	0-1	1-4
Fram Reykjavik	Isl	Shamrock Rovers	Irl	0-3	0-4	0-7
Roma	Ita	Ipswich Town	Eng	3-0	1-3	4-3
Progrès Niedercorn	Lux	Servette	Sui	0-1	0-3	0-4
Zurrieq	Mlt	Hajduk Split	Yug	1-4	0-4	1-8
IL Viking	Nor	Leipzig Lokomitiv	GDR	1-0	2-3	3-3
Haarlem	Ned	Gent	Bel	2-1	3-3	5-4
Utrecht	Ned	FC Porto	Por	0-1	0-2	0-3
Stal Mielec	Pol	Lokeren	Bel	1-1	0-0	1-1
Slask Wroclaw	Pol	Dinamo Moscow	URS	2-2	1-0	3-2
Benfica	Por	Real Betis	Esp	2-1	2-1	4-2
Borussia Dortmund	FRG	Rangers	Sco	0-0	0-2	0-2
Kaiserslautern	FRG	Trabzonspor	Tur	3-0	3-0	6-0
Universitatea Craiova	Rom	Fiorentina	Ita	3-1	0-1	3-2
Bohemians Prague	Tch	Admira Wacker	Aut	5-0	2-1	7-1
Spartak Moscow	URS	Arsenal	Eng	3-2	5-2	8-4
Dinamo Tbilisi	URS	Napoli	Ita	2-1	0-1	2-2
Vorwärts Frankfurt/Oder	GDR	Werder Bremen	FRG	1-3	2-0	3-3
Carl Zeiss Jena	GDR	Girondins Bordeaux	Fra	3-1	0-5	3-6

	Pts	P	W	D	L	F	A	Diff	Goals/P
Total	128	64	49	30	49	187	187	0	2.922

Second Round

Anderlecht	Bel	FC Porto	Por	4-0	2-3	6-3
Rangers	Sco	Cologne	FRG	2-1	0-5	2-6
Shamrock Rovers	Irl	Universitatea Craiova	Rom	0-2	0-3	0-5
Valencia	Esp	Banik Ostrava	Tch	1-0	0-0	1-0
Saint-Etienne	Fra	Bohemians Prague	Tch	0-0	0-4	0-4
Salonika POAK	Gre	Seville	Esp	2-0	0-4	2-4
Ferencváros	Hun	FC Zürich	Sui	1-1	0-1	1-2
Napoli	Ita	Kaiserslautern	FRG	1-2	0-2	1-4
Roma	Ita	IFK Norrköping	Swe	1-0	0-1	1-1
IL Viking	Nor	Dundee United	Sco	1-3	0-0	1-3
Slask Wroclaw	Pol	Servette	Sui	0-2	1-5	1-7
Benfica	Por	Lokeren	Bel	2-0	2-1	4-1
Werder Bremen	FRG	IK Brage	Swe	2-0	6-2	8-2
Corvinul Hunedoara	Rom	Sarajevo	Yug	4-4	0-4	4-8
Spartak Moscow	URS	Haarlem	Ned	2-0	3-1	5-1
Hajduk Split	Yug	Girondins Bordeaux	Fra	4-1	0-4	4-5

	Pts	P	W	D	L	F	A	Diff	Goals/P
Total	64	32	27	10	27	97	97	0	3.031

Third Round

Anderlecht	Bel	Sarajevo	Yug	6-1	0-1	6-2
Dundee United	Sco	Werder Bremen	FRG	2-1	1-1	3-2
Seville	Esp	Kaiserslautern	FRG	1-0	0-4	1-4
Girondins Bordeaux	Fra	Craiova Unitversitatea	Rom	1-0	0-2	1-2
Cologne	FRG	Roma	Ita	1-0	0-2	1-2
Servette	Sui	Bohemians Prague	Tch	2-2	1-2	3-4
FC Zürich	Sui	Benfica	Por	1-1	0-4	1-5
Spartak Moscow	URS	Valencia	Esp	0-0	0-2	0-2

	Pts	P	W	D	L	F	A	Diff	Goals/P
Total	32	16	12	8	12	39	39	0	2.438

Quarter Finals

Valencia	Esp	Anderlecht	Bel	1-2	1-3	2-5
Roma	Ita	Benfica	Por	1-2	1-1	2-3
Kaiserslautern	FRG	Universitatea Craiova	Rom	3-2	0-1	3-3
Bohemians Prague	Tch	Dundee United	Sco	1-0	0-0	1-0

	Pts	P	W	D	L	F	A	Diff	Goals/P
Total	16	8	6	4	6	19	19	0	2.375

Semi Finals

Benfica	Por	Universitatea Craiova	Rom	0-0	1-1	1-1
Bohemians Prague	Tch	Anderlecht	Bel	0-1	1-3	1-4

	Pts	P	W	D	L	F	A	Diff	Goals/P
Total	8	4	2	4	2	7	7	0	1.750

Final

Anderlecht	Bel	Benfica	Por	1-0	1-1	2-1

	Pts	P	W	D	L	F	A	Diff	Goals/P
Total	4	2	1	2	1	3	3	0	1.500

	Pts	P	W	D	L	F	A	Diff	Goals/P
Total	252	126	97	58	97	352	352	0	2.794

Pos'n	Club	Cnty	Pts	P	W	D	L	F	A	Diff	B	Pts/P	F/P
1	Anderlecht	Bel	22	12	9	1	2	29	10	19	3	1.833	2.417
2	Benfica	Por	20	12	6	5	1	18	9	9	3	1.667	1.500
3	Bohemians Prague	Tch	15	10	5	3	2	17	8	9	2	1.500	1.700
4	Universitatea Craiova	Rom	14	10	5	2	3	14	7	7	2	1.400	1.400
5	Kaiserslautern	FRG	13	8	6	0	2	11	5	12	1	1.625	2.125
6	Dundee United	Sco	11	8	3	4	1	9	5	4	1	1.375	1.125
7	Valencia	Esp	10	8	3	3	2	7	6	1	1	1.250	0.875
8	Servette	Sui	9	6	4	1	1	14	5	9	0	1.500	2.333
9	Spartak Moscow	URS	9	6	4	1	1	13	7	6	0	1.500	2.167
10	Cologne	FRG	8	6	4	0	2	13	4	9	0	1.333	2.167
11	Seville	Esp	8	6	4	0	2	11	7	4	0	1.333	1.833
12	Sarajevo	Yug	8	6	3	2	1	16	14	2	0	1.333	2.667
13	Roma	Ita	8	8	3	1	4	9	8	1	1	1.000	1.125
14	Werder Bremen	FRG	7	6	3	1	2	13	8	5	0	1.167	2.167
15	FC Zürich	Sui	7	6	2	3	1	6	8	-2	0	1.167	1.000
16	Hajduk Split	Yug	6	4	3	0	1	12	6	6	0	1.500	3.000
17	Girondins Bordeaux	Fra	6	6	3	0	3	12	9	3	0	1.000	2.000
18	FC Porto	Por	6	4	3	0	1	6	6	0	0	1.500	1.500
19	Banik Ostrava	Tch	5	4	2	1	1	4	2	2	0	1.250	1.000
20	Rangers	Sco	5	4	2	1	1	4	6	-2	0	1.250	1.000
21	Shamrock Rovers	Irl	4	4	2	0	2	7	5	2	0	1.000	1.750
22	Ferencváros	Hun	4	4	1	2	1	4	4	0	0	1.000	1.000
23	IFK Norrköping	Swe	4	4	1	2	1	3	3	0	0	1.000	0.750
24	Corvinul Hunedoara	Rom	4	4	1	2	1	8	9	-1	0	1.000	2.000
25	Saint-Etienne	Fra	4	4	1	2	1	4	5	-1	0	1.000	1.000
26	PAOK Salonika	Gre	4	4	2	0	2	4	6	-2	0	1.000	1.000
27	IL Viking	Nor	3	4	1	1	2	4	6	-2	0	0.750	1.000
28	Haarlem	Ned	3	4	1	1	2	6	9	-3	0	0.750	1.500
29	IK Brage	Swe	3	4	1	1	2	6	11	-5	0	0.750	1.500
30	Slask Wroclaw	Pol	3	4	1	1	2	4	9	-5	0	0.750	1.000
31	Vorwärts Frankfurt/Oder	GDR	2	2	1	0	1	3	3	0	0	1.000	1.500
–	Lokomotive Leipzig	GDR	2	2	1	0	1	3	3	0	0	1.000	1.500
33	Southampton	Eng	2	2	0	2	0	2	2	0	0	1.000	1.000
–	Sochaux	Fra	2	2	1	0	1	2	2	0	0	1.000	1.000
–	Dinamo Tbilisi	URS	2	2	1	0	1	2	2	0	0	1.000	1.000
36	Stal Mielec	Pol	2	2	0	2	0	1	1	0	0	1.000	0.500
37	Ipswich Town	Eng	2	2	1	0	1	3	4	-1	0	1.000	1.500
38	Fiorentina	Ita	2	2	1	0	1	2	3	-1	0	1.000	1.000
39	Napoli	Ita	2	4	1	0	3	3	6	-3	0	0.500	0.750
–	Carl Zeiss Jena	GDR	2	2	1	0	1	3	6	-3	0	1.000	1.500
41	Lokeren	Bel	2	4	0	2	2	2	5	-3	0	0.500	0.500
42	Gent	Bel	1	2	0	1	1	4	5	-1	0	0.500	2.000
43	Lyngby BK	Den	1	2	0	1	1	3	4	-1	0	0.500	1.500
44	Pezoporikos Larnaca	Cyp	1	2	0	1	1	2	3	-1	0	0.500	1.000
–	Athletic Bilbao	Esp	1	2	0	1	1	2	3	-1	0	0.500	1.000
–	Dinamo Moscow	URS	1	2	0	1	1	2	3	-1	0	0.500	1.000
47	Manchester United	Eng	1	2	0	1	1	1	2	-1	0	0.500	0.500
48	Slavia Sofia	Bul	1	2	0	1	1	4	6	-2	0	0.500	2.000
49	PSV Eindhoven	Ned	1	2	0	1	1	1	3	-2	0	0.500	0.500
50	Borrusia Dortmund	FRG	1	2	0	1	1	0	2	-2	0	0.500	0.000
51	Grazer AK	Aut	1	2	0	1	1	1	4	-3	0	0.500	0.500
–	Tatabánya	Hun	1	2	0	1	1	1	4	-3	0	0.500	0.500
53	Real Betis	Esp	0	2	0	0	2	2	4	-2	0	0.000	1.000
54	Glentoran	Nir	0	2	0	0	2	1	4	-3	0	0.000	0.500
55	Utrecht	Ned	0	2	0	0	2	0	3	-3	0	0.000	0.000
56	Arsenal	Eng	0	2	0	0	2	4	8	-4	0	0.000	2.000
57	Progrès Niedercorn	Lux	0	2	0	0	2	0	4	-4	0	0.000	0.000
58	Levski Sofia	Bul	0	2	0	0	2	1	6	-5	0	0.000	0.500
–	KuPS Kuopio	Fin	0	2	0	0	2	1	6	-5	0	0.000	0.500
60	Admira Wacker	Aut	0	2	0	0	2	1	7	-6	0	0.000	0.500
61	AEK Athens	Gre	0	2	0	0	2	0	6	-6	0	0.000	0.000
–	Trabzonspur	Tur	0	2	0	0	2	0	6	-6	0	0.000	0.000
63	Zurrieq	Mlt	0	2	0	0	2	1	8	-7	0	0.000	0.500
64	Fram Reykjavik	Isl	0	2	0	0	2	0	7	-7	0	0.000	0.000
	Total		**266**	**252**	**97**	**58**	**97**	**352**	**352**	**0**	**14**	**1.056**	**2.794**

National Performances by Points

1982-83

Pos'n	Cnty	Pts	P	W	D	L	F	A	Diff	B	Pts/P	F/P
1	Esp	56	41	19	11	11	67	43	24	7	1.366	1.634
2	FRG	53	37	20	8	9	67	30	37	5	1.432	1.811
3	Bel	42	30	16	5	9	60	35	25	5	1.400	2.000
4	Sco	42	27	15	8	4	44	23	21	4	1.556	1.630
5	Por	34	24	12	7	5	31	23	8	3	1.417	1.292
6	Ita	34	29	12	5	12	40	33	7	5	1.172	1.379
7	Eng	27	24	10	5	9	43	35	8	2	1.125	1.792
8	Tch	24	18	9	4	5	25	16	9	2	1.333	1.389
9	Rom	24	22	8	5	9	33	32	1	3	1.091	1.500
10	Fra	22	20	9	3	8	28	23	5	1	1.100	1.400
11	URS	21	16	8	4	4	24	17	7	1	1.313	1.500
12	Yug	20	16	9	2	5	39	29	10	0	1.250	2.438
13	Pol	20	18	7	4	7	28	27	1	2	1.111	1.556
14	Aut	16	16	5	4	7	31	28	3	2	1.000	1.938
15	Sui	16	16	6	4	6	21	28	-7	0	1.000	1.313
16	Hun	10	12	3	4	5	13	19	-6	0	0.833	1.083
17	Swe	10	12	3	4	5	12	20	-8	0	0.833	1.000
18	Ned	10	14	3	4	7	13	22	-9	0	0.714	0.929
19	GDR	9	10	4	1	5	14	19	-5	0	0.900	1.400
20	Bul	8	10	2	4	4	11	19	-8	0	0.800	1.100
21	Gre	8	12	4	0	8	8	21	-13	0	0.667	0.667
22	Wal	6	6	3	0	3	20	4	16	0	1.000	3.333
23	Tur	6	8	2	2	4	7	15	-8	0	0.750	0.875
24	Irl	5	8	2	1	5	9	12	-3	0	0.625	1.125
25	Fin	5	8	2	1	5	7	16	-9	0	0.625	0.875
26	Nor	5	8	2	1	5	7	17	-10	0	0.625	0.875
27	Den	4	8	1	2	5	12	21	-9	0	0.500	1.500
28	Cyp	4	6	1	2	3	5	15	-10	0	0.667	0.833
29	Alb	3	4	1	1	2	2	3	-1	0	0.750	0.500
30	Nir	2	6	1	0	5	3	13	-10	0	0.333	0.500
31	Isl	0	6	0	0	6	2	15	-13	0	0.000	0.333
32	Lux	0	6	0	0	6	1	25	-24	0	0.000	0.167
33	Mlt	0	6	0	0	6	3	32	-29	0	0.000	0.500
	Total	**546**	**504**	**199**	**106**	**199**	**730**	**730**	**0**	**42**	**1.083**	**2.897**

1955-56 to 1982-83

1	Eng	1223	835	449	179	207	1619	856	763	146	1.465	1.939
2	FRG	1189	856	450	156	250	1740	1084	656	133	1.389	2.033
3	Esp	1082	787	399	149	239	1482	965	517	135	1.375	1.883
4	Ita	926	691	337	149	205	1082	718	364	103	1.340	1.566
5	Sco	636	512	243	95	174	887	665	222	55	1.242	1.732
6	Ned	597	456	230	81	145	897	566	331	56	1.309	1.967
7	Bel	578	485	224	78	183	792	635	157	52	1.192	1.633
8	Yug	555	498	205	94	199	829	731	98	51	1.114	1.665
9	Por	520	448	190	99	159	726	567	159	41	1.161	1.621
10	Hun	462	394	179	64	151	723	573	150	40	1.173	1.835
11	GDR	437	391	162	82	147	592	516	76	31	1.118	1.514
12	Tch	420	357	163	64	130	562	470	92	30	1.176	1.574
13	Fra	404	391	151	72	168	597	586	11	30	1.033	1.527
14	URS	351	264	136	54	74	389	257	132	25	1.330	1.473
15	Sui	293	333	108	58	167	501	642	-141	19	0.880	1.505
16	Pol	291	283	108	58	117	412	433	-21	17	1.028	1.456
17	Bul	281	287	110	45	132	433	450	-17	16	0.979	1.509
18	Rom	272	293	106	52	135	386	469	-83	8	0.928	1.317
19	Aut	247	291	86	59	146	356	486	-130	16	0.849	1.223
20	Swe	219	239	76	55	108	306	405	-99	12	0.916	1.280
21	Gre	202	233	78	39	116	273	420	-147	7	0.867	1.172
22	Den	160	239	57	41	141	315	532	-217	5	0.669	1.318
23	Tur	150	207	56	32	119	206	395	-189	6	0.725	0.995
24	Nor	91	172	34	22	116	171	443	-272	1	0.529	0.994
25	Wal	84	80	28	22	30	120	95	25	6	1.050	1.500
26	Irl	84	170	27	30	113	143	414	-271	0	0.494	0.841
27	Nir	72	148	22	26	100	145	425	-280	2	0.486	0.980
28	Lux	41	146	15	11	120	97	612	-515	0	0.281	0.664
29	Fin	40	122	13	14	95	99	410	-311	0	0.328	0.811
30	Mlt	39	124	14	11	99	64	431	-367	0	0.315	0.516
31	Cyp	33	104	10	13	81	62	394	-332	0	0.317	0.596
32	Alb	28	42	8	12	22	28	63	-35	0	0.667	0.667
33	Isl	24	110	5	14	91	57	383	-326	0	0.218	0.518
	Total	**12031**	**10988**	**4479**	**2030**	**4479**	**17091**	**17091**	**0**	**1043**	**1.095**	**3.111**

1982-83

Pos'n	Cnty	Ave	Pts	P	W	D	L	F	A	Diff	B	No./T
1	Scotland	10.500	42	27	15	8	4	44	23	21	4	4
2	W. Germany	8.833	53	37	20	8	9	67	30	37	5	6
3	Portugal	8.500	34	24	12	7	5	31	23	8	3	4
4	Belgium	8.400	42	30	16	5	9	60	35	25	5	5
5	Spain	8.000	56	41	19	11	11	67	43	24	7	7
6	Italy	6.800	34	29	12	5	12	40	33	7	5	5
7	Wales	6.000	6	6	3	0	3	20	4	16	0	1
–	Romania	6.000	24	22	8	5	9	33	32	1	3	4
–	Czechoslovakia	6.000	24	18	9	4	5	25	16	9	2	4
10	Poland	5.000	20	18	7	4	7	28	27	1	2	4
–	Yugoslavia	5.000	20	16	9	2	5	39	29	10	0	4
12	France	4.400	22	20	9	3	8	28	23	5	1	5
13	USSR	4.200	21	16	8	4	4	24	17	7	1	5
14	Austria	4.000	16	16	5	4	7	31	28	3	2	4
–	Switzerland	4.000	16	16	6	4	6	21	28	-7	0	4
16	England	3.857	27	24	10	5	9	43	35	8	2	7
17	Hungary	2.500	10	12	3	4	5	13	19	-6	0	4
–	Sweden	2.500	10	12	3	4	5	12	20	-8	0	4
19	Bulgaria	2.000	8	10	2	4	4	11	19	-8	0	4
–	Greece	2.000	8	12	4	0	8	8	21	-13	0	4
–	Netherlands	2.000	10	14	3	4	7	13	22	-9	0	5
–	Turkey	2.000	6	8	2	2	4	7	15	-8	0	3
23	E. Germany	1.800	9	10	4	1	5	14	19	-5	0	5
24	Rep. of Ireland	1.666	5	8	2	1	5	9	12	-3	0	3
–	Finland	1.666	5	8	2	1	5	7	16	-9	0	3
–	Norway	1.666	5	8	2	1	5	7	17	-10	0	3
27	Albania	1.500	3	4	1	1	2	2	3	-1	0	2
28	Cyprus	1.333	4	6	1	2	3	5	15	-10	0	3
–	Denmark	1.333	4	8	1	2	5	12	21	-9	0	3
30	N. Ireland	0.666	2	6	1	0	5	3	13	-10	0	3
31	Iceland	0.000	0	6	0	0	6	2	15	-13	0	3
–	Luxembourg	0.000	0	6	0	0	6	1	25	-24	0	3
–	Malta	0.000	0	6	0	0	6	3	32	-29	0	3
	Total		**546**	**504**	**199**	**106**	**199**	**730**	**730**	**0**	**42**	**2.897**

1955-56 to 1982-83

Pos'n	Cnty	Ave	Pts	P	W	D	L	F	A	Diff	B	No./T
1	England	8.612	1223	835	449	179	207	1619	856	763	146	142
2	W. Germany	8.088	1189	856	450	156	250	1740	1084	656	133	147
3	Spain	7.784	1082	787	399	149	239	1482	965	517	135	139
4	Italy	6.910	926	691	337	149	205	1082	718	364	103	134
5	Netherlands	6.218	597	456	230	81	145	897	566	331	56	96
6	Scotland	5.888	636	512	243	95	174	887	665	222	55	108
7	USSR	5.754	351	264	136	54	74	389	257	132	25	61
8	Belgium	5.351	578	485	224	78	183	792	635	157	52	108
9	Hungary	5.250	462	394	179	64	151	723	573	150	40	88
10	Yugoslavia	4.911	555	498	205	94	199	829	731	98	51	113
11	Portugal	4.905	520	448	190	99	159	726	567	159	41	106
12	E. Germany	4.855	437	391	162	82	147	592	516	76	31	90
13	Czechoslovakia	4.719	420	357	163	64	130	562	470	92	30	89
14	France	3.847	404	391	151	72	168	597	586	11	30	105
15	Poland	3.828	291	283	108	58	117	412	433	-21	17	76
16	Wales	3.818	84	80	28	22	30	120	95	25	6	22
17	Bulgaria	3.385	281	287	110	45	132	433	450	-17	16	83
18	Romania	3.162	272	293	106	52	135	386	469	-83	8	86
19	Switzerland	2.900	293	333	108	58	167	501	642	-141	19	101
20	Sweden	2.807	219	239	76	55	108	306	405	-99	12	78
21	Austria	2.775	247	291	86	59	146	356	486	-130	16	89
22	Greece	2.493	202	233	78	39	116	273	420	-147	7	81
23	Turkey	2.054	150	207	56	32	119	206	395	-189	6	73
24	Denmark	1.818	160	239	57	41	141	315	532	-217	5	88
25	Albania	1.473	28	42	8	12	22	28	63	-35	0	19
26	Norway	1.281	91	172	34	22	116	171	443	-272	1	71
27	Rep. of Ireland	1.217	84	170	27	30	113	143	414	-271	0	69
28	N. Ireland	1.125	72	148	22	26	100	145	425	-280	2	64
29	Finland	0.740	40	122	13	14	95	99	410	-311	0	54
30	Cyprus	0.687	33	104	10	13	81	62	394	-332	0	48
31	Malta	0.661	39	124	14	11	99	64	431	-367	0	59
32	Luxembourg	0.594	41	146	15	11	120	97	612	-515	0	69
33	Iceland	0.470	24	110	5	14	91	57	383	-326	0	51
	Total		**12031**	**10988**	**4479**	**2030**	**4479**	**17091**	**17091**	**0**	**1043**	**3.111**

Hamburg Surprise Star-studded Juventus

England's long reign in the Champions' Cup at last came to an end when both Aston Villa and Liverpool were eliminated at the quarter-final stage of the 1982-83 competition. Villa's exit was no surprise. They were simply outclassed by a Juventus side containing no fewer than six of Italy's World Cup-winning team, plus the remarkable midfield talents of Frenchman Michel Platini and Polish international Zbigniew Boniek. Liverpool, on the other hand, were expected to cruise through their tie with Boniek's former club, Widzew Lódź. But a couple of defensive errors in Poland left them with a lot of work to do at Anfield and, although they won the return 3-2 with a last-minute goal, they never really put themselves into a position to win the tie.

With Liverpool out of the way, Juventus were the clear favourites to win the trophy for the first time. Their star-studded line-up, coached by the highly successful Giovanni Trapattoni, succeeded where Bob Paisley's men failed by defeating Widzew in the semi-finals, 4-2 on aggregate, World Cup hero Paolo Rossi maintaining his record of scoring at least once in every round.

Juventus's opponents in the Athens final were the previous season's UEFA Cup runners-up, and the Champions' Cup losing finalists in 1980, Hamburg. Few experts gave them a chance of stopping the Italians in their glory bid, especially with the Olympic stadium almost entirely filled with Juventus supporters, black-and-white favours streaming down from every tier. But Hamburg had the wily old Ernst Happel as their coach, and his success rate against Italian teams was second to none. He had previously taken both Feyenoord and Club Bruges to Champions' Cup finals at the expense of Italian opposition, and at the 1978 World Cup he had led the Dutch national team to a crucial 2-1 victory over Enzo Bearzot's Italy.

In Athens, Happel triumphed again, outsmarting Trapattoni tactically and bringing the very best out of his supposedly inferior resources. Less than ten minutes were on the clock when Hamburg opened the scoring, through their influential West German international midfielder Felix Magath. It was some goal, struck with power and accuracy from fully 25 yards, the ball flying past Dino Zoff into the top corner.

From that moment on, Juventus were forced to chase the game, but for all the talent in their side, they simply couldn't get out of first gear. Platini had an anonymous game and Rossi was so out of sorts that he was substituted early in the second half. Hamburg continued to hold sway in the midfield, where Magath and Jürgen Milewski were outstanding, and they deservedly held on to their lead until the final whistle to take the Cup.

If the quarter-final defeats of Liverpool and Aston Villa in the Champions' Cup had been difficult to take for English fans so accustomed to European success, they were nothing compared to the astonishing fate that befell all four English teams in the UEFA Cup. Arsenal, Ipswich, Manchester United and Southampton were all bundled out in the very first round. Particularly galling was Arsenal's exit at the hands of Soviet side Spartak Moscow, who trounced them 5-2 at Highbury after a 3-2 victory in Moscow. Ipswich and Manchester United went out, respectively, to Roma and Valencia, and these two clubs went on to reach the quarter-finals before they, in turn, were knocked out by the eventual finalists, Benfica and Anderlecht.

Both the Portuguese and the Belgians were looking to win the UEFA Cup for the first time. Benfica reached the final by putting out the first ever Romanian semi-finalists in Europe, Universitatea Craiova, on the away goals rule, whilst Anderlecht kept up their impressive record of scoring at least three goals at home in every round to see off another Eastern European side, Bohemians Prague.

Two of Anderlecht's semi-final goals were scored by centre-forward Erwin Vandenbergh, the man whose goal had defeated Argentina in the opening match of the 1982 World Cup. He was one of several Belgian World Cup men in an Anderlecht side coached by former record international Paul Van Himst, the others being Munaron, Coeck, Vercauteren and Czerniatynski.

Van Himst's opposite number in the final was none other than Sven Göran Eriksson, the Swedish coach who had won the UEFA Cup with IFK Gothenburg the season before.

Eriksson went into the final with a remarkable record of 22 UEFA Cup matches undefeated. But that record went in the first leg, in Brussels, when Anderlecht's Danish striker Kenneth Brylle scored the only goal from close range after half an hour. The narrow 1-0 win left everything to play for in the second leg, and with 80,000 fans to cheer them on in the Stadium of Light, Benfica were marginal favourites. They did score first, through Sheu after 36 minutes, but then they relaxed and the Belgians took immediate advantage with an equaliser from their Spanish-born midfielder Juan Lozano. Benfica now had to score twice more to take the Cup, but they weren't up to it and the Anderlecht defence held firm through the second half to take the trophy. It was Anderlecht's third European triumph, taking them above Benfica, who, since their two Champions' Cup victories of 1961 and 1962, had now lost their last four European finals.

Real Madrid were another of the old guard to come away with runners-up medals in 1982-83. They had reached the Cup-winners' Cup final once before, in 1971, and lost to Chelsea, and now they were to go down yet again to British opposition in a match played in driving rain in Gothenburg.

This season's Cup-winners' Cup presented a strong field. In addition to Real, there were holders Barcelona, Champions' Cup runners-up Bayern Munich, plus strong Italian and English representation in the shape of Inter Milan and Tottenham Hotspur. But few would have predicted at the outset that Scottish Cup winners Aberdeen could emerge triumphant from such exalted company. Evidence of Aberdeen's lowly ranking was that they had to take part in the preliminary round. They made light work of that tie, hammering Swiss club Sion 11-1 on aggregate, and then forged their way into the quarter-finals with similar ease against Dinamo Tirana and Lech Poznań.

Now, though, came a true test of their pedigree. Paired with Bayern Munich, they played commendably well in the first leg, emerging from the Olympiastadion in Munich with a hard-earned 0-0 draw. But with less than 15 minutes left of the return leg at Pittodrie, they were 2-1 down, needing two goals to progress. Thanks to Alex McLeish and substitute John Hewitt they got them, to reach their first European semi-final. While Aberdeen were seeing off Bayern, Real Madrid renewed their age-old rivalry with Inter Milan and won the tie 3-2 on aggregate to also go 3-2 up in their overall meetings with the Italian club. Elsewhere, there were shocks, with Barcelona succumbing to Austria Vienna on away goals, and Paris Saint-Germain losing to Belgian outsiders Waterschei after extra-time.

The semi-finals, however, went to form. Aberdeen hammered five goals past Waterschei at home, while Real centre-forward Carlos Santillana took his goals total for the competition to nine with three more in his side's 5-3 aggregate win over Austria Vienna. In Gothenburg, that form book was to be turned on its head once again. Aberdeen scored early on, through Eric Black, only for Real to equalise within eight minutes from the penalty spot through Juanito. Aberdeen seemed to cope better with the wet conditions for the rest of the game, but as the score remained 1-1 deep into extra-time, a penalty shoot-out looked inevitable. Until, with barely five minutes left, Aberdeen's supersub Hewitt broke free in the centre and tucked away Mark McGhee's left-wing cross with a deft falling header. Aberdeen had won their first European trophy, becoming the first Scottish winners in Europe for 11 years.

Liverpool

Juventus

Tottenham Hotspur

1983 – 1984

First Round

Team 1	Cnty	Team 2	Cnty	1st leg	2nd leg	Agg
Rapid Vienna	Aut	Nantes	Fra	3-0	1-3	4-3
CSKA Sofia	Bul	Omonia Nicosia	Cyp	3-0	1-4	4-4
OB Odense	Den	Liverpool	Eng	0-1	0-5	0-6
Athlone Town	Irl	Standard Liège	Bel	2-3	2-8	4-11
FC Kuusysi Lahti	Fin	Dinamo Bucharest	Rom	0-1	0-3	0-4
Rába ETO	Hun	Vikingur Reykjavik	Isl	2-1	2-0	4-1
Roma	Ita	IFK Gothenburg	Swe	3-0	1-2	4-2
Hamrun Spartans	Mlt	Dundee United	Sco	0-3	0-3	0-6
Ajax	Ned	Olympiakos Pireus	Gre	0-0	0-2	0-2
Lech Poznań	Pol	Athletic Bilbao	Esp	2-0	0-4	2-4
Benfica	Por	Linfield	Nir	3-0	3-2	6-2
Fenerbahçe	Tur	Bohemians Prague	Tch	0-1	0-4	0-5
Dinamo Minsk	URS	Grasshoppers Zürich	Sui	1-0	2-2	3-2
Partizan Belgrade	Yug	IL Viking	Nor	5-1	0-0	5-1
Dynamo Berlin	GDR	Jeunesse Esch	Lux	4-1	2-0	6-1

	Pts	P	W	D	L	F	A	Diff	Goals/P
Total	60	30	27	6	27	96	96	0	3.200

Second Round

Liverpool	Eng	Athletic Bilbao	Esp	0-0	1-0	1-0
Standard Liège	Bel	Dundee United	Sco	0-0	0-4	0-4
CSKA Sofia	Bul	Roma	Ita	0-1	0-1	0-2
Olympiakos Pireus	Gre	Benfica	Por	1-0	0-3	1-3
Rába ETO	Hun	Dinamo Minsk	URS	3-6	1-3	4-9
Dinamo Bucharest	Rom	Hamburg	FRG	3-0	2-3	5-3
Bohemians Prague	Tch	Rapid Vienna	Aut	2-1	0-1	2-2
Dynamo Berlin	GDR	Partizan Belgrade	Yug	2-0	0-1	2-1

	Pts	P	W	D	L	F	A	Diff	Goals/P
Total	32	16	14	4	14	39	39	0	2.438

Quarter Finals

Liverpool	Eng	Benfica	Por	1-0	4-1	5-1
Rapid Vienna	Aut	Dundee United	Sco	2-1	0-1	2-2
Roma	Ita	Dynamo Berlin	GDR	3-0	1-2	4-2
Dinamo Minsk	URS	Dinamo Bucharest	Rom	1-1	0-1	1-2

	Pts	P	W	D	L	F	A	Diff	Goals/P
Total	16	8	7	2	7	19	19	0	2.375

Semi Finals

Liverpool	Eng	Dinamo Bucharest	Rom	1-0	2-1	3-1
Dundee United	Sco	Roma	Ita	2-0	0-3	2-3

	Pts	P	W	D	L	F	A	Diff	Goals/P
Total	8	4	4	0	4	9	9	0	2.250

Final

Roma	Ita	Liverpool	Eng	1-1	1-1

	Pts	P	W	D	L	F	A	Diff	Goals/P
Total	2	1	0	2	0	2	2	0	2.000

	Pts	P	W	D	L	F	A	Diff	Goals/P
Total	118	59	52	14	52	165	165	0	2.797

Pos'n	Club	Cnty	Pts	P	W	D	L	F	A	Diff	B	Pts/P	F/P
1	Liverpool	Eng	19	9	7	2	0	16	3	13	3	2.111	1.778
2	Roma	Ita	14	9	5	1	3	14	7	7	3	1.556	1.556
3	Dundee United	Sco	13	8	5	1	2	14	5	9	2	1.625	1.750
4	Dinamo Bucharest	Rom	11	8	4	1	3	12	7	5	2	1.375	1.500
5	Dinamo Minsk	URS	9	6	3	2	1	13	8	5	1	1.500	2.167
6	Dynamo Berlin	GDR	9	6	4	0	2	10	6	4	1	1.500	1.667
7	Benfica	Por	7	6	3	0	3	10	8	2	1	1.167	1.667
8	Rapid Vienna	Aut	7	6	3	0	3	8	7	1	1	1.167	1.333
9	Bohemians Prague	Tch	6	4	3	0	1	7	2	5	0	1.500	1.750
10	Standard Liège	Bel	5	4	2	1	1	11	8	3	0	1.250	2.750
11	Partizan Belgrade	Yug	5	4	2	1	1	6	3	3	0	1.250	1.500
12	Olympiakos Pireus	Gre	5	4	2	1	1	3	3	0	0	1.250	0.750
13	Rába ETO	Hun	4	4	2	0	2	8	10	-2	0	1.000	2.000
14	Athletic Bilbao	Esp	3	4	1	1	2	4	3	1	0	0.750	1.000
15	Omonia Nicosie	Cyp	2	2	1	0	1	4	4	0	0	1.000	2.000
16	Nantes	Fra	2	2	1	0	1	3	4	-1	0	1.000	1.500
17	CSKA Sofia	Bul	2	4	1	0	3	4	6	-2	0	0.500	1.000
18	Hamburg	FRG	2	2	1	0	1	3	5	-2	0	1.000	1.500
19	Lech Poznań	Pol	2	2	1	0	1	2	4	-2	0	1.000	1.000
–	IFK Gothenburg	Swe	2	2	1	0	1	2	4	-2	0	1.000	1.000
21	Grasshoppers Zürich	Sui	1	2	0	1	1	2	3	-1	0	0.500	1.000
22	Ajax	Ned	1	2	0	1	1	0	2	-2	0	0.500	0.000
23	IL Viking	Nor	1	2	0	1	1	1	5	-4	0	0.500	0.500
24	Vikingur Reykjavik	Isl	0	2	0	0	2	1	4	-3	0	0.000	0.500
25	Linfield	Nir	0	2	0	0	2	2	6	-4	0	0.000	1.000
26	FC Kuusysi Lahti	Fin	0	2	0	0	2	0	4	-4	0	0.000	0.000
27	Jeunesse Esch	Lux	0	2	0	0	2	1	6	-5	0	0.000	0.500
28	Fenerbahçe	Tur	0	2	0	0	2	0	5	-5	0	0 000	0.000
29	OB Odense	Den	0	2	0	0	2	0	6	-6	0	0.000	0.000
–	Hamrun Spartans	Mlt	0	2	0	0	2	0	6	-6	0	0.000	0.000
31	Athlone Town	Irl	0	2	0	0	2	4	11	-7	0	0.000	2.000
	Total		**132**	**118**	**52**	**14**	**52**	**165**	**165**	**0**	**14**	**1.119**	**2.797**

Preliminary Round

Team 1	Cnty	Team 2	Cnty	1st leg	2nd leg	Agg
Swansea City	Wal	Magdeburg	GDR	1-1	0-1	1-2

	Pts	P	W	D	L	F	A	Diff	Goals/P
Total	4	2	1	2	1	3	3	0	1.500

First Round

Manchester United	Eng	Dukla Prague	Tch	1-1	2-2	3-3
FC Tirol	Aut	Cologne	FRG	1-0	1-7	2-7
Paralimni	Cyp	Beveren	Bel	2-4	1-3	3-7
B 1901 Nykobing	Den	Shakhtyor Donetsk	URS	1-5	2-4	3-9
Sligo Rovers	Irl	Haka Valkeakoski	Fin	0-1	0-3	0-4
AEK Athens	Gre	Ujpesti Dózsa	Hun	2-0	1-4	3-4
Glentoran	Nir	Paris Saint-Germain	Fra	1-2	1-2	2-4
IA Akranes	Isl	Aberdeen	Sco	1-2	1-1	2-3
Juventus	Ita	Lechia Gdańsk	Pol	7-0	3-2	10-2
Valletta	Mlt	Rangers	Sco	0-8	0-10	0-18
NEC Nijmegen	Ned	SK Brann	Nor	1-1	1-0	2-1
Hammarby IF	Swe	17 Nëntori Tirana	Alb	4-0	1-2	5-2
Servette	Sui	Avenir Beggen	Lux	4-0	5-1	9-1
Mersin Idmanyurdu	Tur	Spartak Varna	Bul	0-0	0-1	0-1
Dinamo Zagreb	Yug	FC Porto	Por	2-1	0-1	2-2
Magdeburg	GDR	Barcelona	Esp	1-5	0-2	1-7

	Pts	P	W	D	L	F	A	Diff	Goals/P
Total	64	32	27	10	27	122	122	0	3.813

Second Round

Beveren	Bel	Aberdeen	Sco	0-0	1-4	1-4
Spartak Varna	Bul	Manchester United	Eng	1-2	0-2	1-4
Rangers	Sco	FC Porto	Por	2-1	0-1	2-2
Paris Saint-Germain	Fra	Juventus	Ita	2-2	0-0	2-2
Ujpesti Dózsa	Hun	Cologne	FRG	3-1	2-4	5-5
NEC Nijmegen	Ned	Barcelona	Esp	2-3	0-2	2-5
Hammarby IF	Swe	Haka Valkeakoski	Fin	1-1	1-2	2-3
Shakhtyor Donetsk	URS	Servette	Sui	1-0	2-1	3-1

	Pts	P	W	D	L	F	A	Diff	Goals/P
Total	32	16	12	8	12	44	44	0	2.750

Quarter Finals

Barcelona	Esp	Manchester United	Eng	2-0	0-3	2-3
Haka Valkeakoski	Fin	Juventus	Ita	0-1	0-1	0-2
Ujpesti Dózsa	Hun	Aberdeen	Sco	2-0	0-3	2-3
FC Porto	Por	Shakhtyor Donetsk	URS	3-2	1-1	4-3

	Pts	P	W	D	L	F	A	Diff	Goals/P
Total	16	8	7	2	7	19	19	0	2.375

Semi Finals

Manchester United	Eng	Juventus	Ita	1-1	1-2	2-3
FC Porto	Por	Aberdeen	Sco	1-0	1-0	2-0

	Pts	P	W	D	L	F	A	Diff	Goals/P
Total	8	4	3	2	3	7	7	0	1.750

Final

Juventus	Ita	FC Porto	Por	2-1	2-1

	Pts	P	W	D	L	F	A	Diff	Goals/P
Total	2	1	1	0	1	3	3	0	3.000

	Pts	P	W	D	L	F	A	Diff	Goals/P
Total	126	63	51	24	51	198	198	0	3.143

Pos'n	Club	Cnty	Pts	P	W	D	L	F	A	Diff	B	Pts/P	F/P
1	Juventus	Ita	18	9	6	3	0	19	7	12	3	2.000	2.111
2	FC Porto	Por	14	9	5	1	3	11	9	2	3	1.556	1.222
3	Barcelona	Esp	11	6	5	0	1	14	6	8	1	1.833	2.333
4	Manchester United	Eng	11	8	3	3	2	12	9	3	2	1.375	1.500
5	Shakhtyor Donetsk	URS	10	6	4	1	1	15	8	7	1	1.667	2.500
6	Aberdeen	Sco	10	8	3	2	3	10	7	3	2	1.250	1.250
7	Haka Valkeakoski	Fin	8	6	3	1	2	7	4	3	1	1.333	1.167
8	Ujpesti Dózsa	Hun	7	6	3	0	3	11	11	0	1	1.167	1.833
9	Rangers	Sco	6	4	3	0	1	20	2	18	0	1.500	5.000
10	Paris Saint-Germain	Fra	6	4	2	2	0	6	4	2	0	1.500	1.500
11	Beveren	Bel	5	4	2	1	1	8	7	1	0	1.250	2.000
12	Servette	Sui	4	4	2	0	2	10	4	6	0	1.000	2.500
13	Cologne	FRG	4	4	2	0	2	12	7	5	0	1.000	3.000
14	Hammarby IF	Swe	3	4	1	1	2	7	5	2	0	0.750	1.750
15	NEC Nijmegen	Ned	3	4	1	1	2	4	6	-2	0	0.750	1.000
16	Spartak Varna	Bul	3	4	1	1	2	2	4	-2	0	0.750	0.500
17	Magdeburg	GDR	3	4	1	1	2	3	8	-5	0	0.750	0.750
18	Dulka Prague	Tch	2	2	0	2	0	3	3	0	0	1.000	1.500
19	Dinamo Zagreb	Yug	2	2	1	0	1	2	2	0	0	1.000	1.000
20	AEK Athens	Gre	2	2	1	0	1	3	4	-1	0	1.000	1.500
21	17 Nëntori Tirana	Alb	2	2	1	0	1	2	5	-3	0	1.000	1.000
22	FC Tirol	Aut	2	2	1	0	1	2	7	-5	0	1.000	1.000
23	IA Akranes	Isl	1	2	0	1	1	2	3	-1	0	0.500	1.000
24	Swansea City	Wal	1	2	0	1	1	1	2	-1	0	0.500	0.500
–	SK Brann	Nor	1	2	0	1	1	1	2	-1	0	0.500	0.500
26	Mersin Idmanyurdu	Tur	1	2	0	1	1	0	1	-1	0	0.500	0.000
27	Glentoran	Nir	0	2	0	0	2	2	4	-2	0	0.000	1.000
28	Paralimni	Cyp	0	2	0	0	2	3	7	-4	0	0.000	1.500
29	Sligo Rovers	Irl	0	2	0	0	2	0	4	-4	0	0.000	0.000
30	B 1901 Nykobing	Den	0	2	0	0	2	3	9	-6	0	0.000	1.500
31	Lechia Gdańsk	Pol	0	2	0	0	2	2	10	-8	0	0.000	1.000
32	Avenir Beggen	Lux	0	2	0	0	2	1	9	-8	0	0.000	0.500
33	Valletta	Mlt	0	2	0	0	2	0	18	-18	0	0.000	0.000
	Total		**140**	**126**	**51**	**24**	**51**	**198**	**198**	**0**	**14**	**1.111**	**3.143**

First Round

Team 1	Cnty	Team 2	Cnty	1st leg	2nd leg	Agg
Nottingham Forest	Eng	Vorwärts Frankfurt/Oder	GDR	2-0	1-0	3-0
Gent	Bel	Lens	Fra	1-1	1-2	2-3
Lokomotiv Plovdiv	Bul	PAOK Salonika	Gre	1-2	1-3	2-5
Anorthosis Famagusta	Cyp	Bayern Munich	FRG	0-1	0-10	0-11
Celtic	Sco	AGF Aarhus	Den	1-0	4-1	5-1
St. Mirren	Sco	Feyenoord	Ned	0-1	0-2	0-3
Drogheda United	Irl	Tottenham Hotspur	Eng	0-6	0-8	0-14
Atlético Madrid	Esp	Groningen	Ned	2-1	0-3	2-4
Seville	Esp	Sporting Lisbon	Por	1-1	2-3	3-4
Girondins Bordeaux	Fra	Lokomotive Leipzig	GDR	2-3	0-4	2-7
Larissa	Gre	Honvéd	Hun	2-0	0-3	2-3
IBV Vestmannaeyjar	Isl	Carl Zeiss Jena	GDR	0-0	0-3	0-3
Verona	Ita	Red Star Belgrade	Yug	1-0	3-2	4-2
Aris Bonnevoie	Lux	Austria Vienna	Aut	0-5	0-10	0-15
Rabat Ajax	Mlt	Inter Bratislava	Tch	0-10	0-6	0-16
Bryne IL	Nor	Anderlecht	Bel	0-3	1-1	1-4
PSV Eindhoven	Ned	Ferencváros	Hun	4-2	2-0	6-2
Sparta Rotterdam	Ned	Coleraine	Nir	4-0	1-1	5-1
Widzew Lódź	Pol	IF Elfsborg	Swe	0-0	2-2	2-2
Vitória Guimarães	Por	Aston Villa	Eng	1-0	0-5	1-5
Werder Bremen	FRG	Malmö FF	Swe	1-1	2-1	3-2
Kaiserslautern	FRG	Watford	Eng	3-1	0-3	3-4
VFB Stuttgart	FRG	Levski Sofia	Bul	1-1	0-1	1-2
Sportul Studentesc Bucharest	Rom	Sturm Graz	Aut	1-2	0-0	1-2
Universitatea Craiova	Rom	Hajduk Split	Yug	1-0	0-1	1-1
FC Zürich	Sui	Antwerp	Bel	1-4	2-4	3-8
Banik Ostrava	Tch	B 1903 Copenhagen	Den	5-0	1-1	6-1
Sparta Prague	Tch	Real Madrid	Esp	3-2	1-1	4-3
Trabzonspor	Tur	Inter Milan	Ita	1-0	0-2	1-2
Dinamo Kiev	URS	Laval	Fra	0-0	0-1	0-1
Spartak Moscow	URS	HJK Helsinki	Fin	2-0	5-0	7-0
Radnicki Nis	Yug	St-Gallen	Sui	3-0	2-1	5-1

	Pts	P	W	D	L	F	A	Diff	Goals/P
Total	128	64	51	26	51	207	207	0	3.234

Second Round

Tottenham Hotspur	Eng	Feyenoord	Ned	4-2	2-0	6-2
Watford	Eng	Levski Sofia	Bul	1-1	3-1	4-2
Austria Vienna	Aut	Laval	Fra	2-0	3-3	5-3
Anderlecht	Bel	Banik Ostrava	Tch	2-0	2-2	4-2
Lens	Fra	Antwerp	Bel	2-2	3-2	5-4
PAOK Salonika	Gre	Bayern Munich	FRG	0-0	0-0	0-0
Honvéd	Hun	Hajduk Split	Yug	3-2	0-3	3-5
Verona	Ita	Sturm Graz	Aut	2-2	0-0	2-2
PSV Eindhoven	Ned	Nottingham Forest	Eng	1-2	0-1	1-3
Groningen	Ned	Inter Milan	Ita	2-0	1-5	3-5
Sparta Rotterdam	Ned	Carl Zeiss Jena	GDR	3-2	1-1	4-3
Widzew Lódź	Pol	Sparta Prague	Tch	1-0	0-3	1-3
Sporting Lisbon	Por	Celtic	Sco	2-0	0-5	2-5
Spartak Moscow	URS	Aston Villa	Eng	2-2	2-1	4-3
Radnicki Nis	Yug	Inter Bratislava	Tch	4-0	2-3	6-3
Lokomotive Leipzig	GDR	Werder Bremen	FRG	1-0	1-1	2-1

	Pts	P	W	D	L	F	A	Diff	Goals/P
Total	64	32	21	22	21	98	98	0	3.063

Third Round

Nottingham Forest	Eng	Celtic	Sco	0-0	2-1	2-1
Watford	Eng	Sparta Prague	Tch	2-3	0-4	2-7
Sturm Graz	Aut	Lokomotive Leipzig	GDR	2-0	0-1	2-1
Austria Vienna	Aut	Inter Milan	Ita	2-1	1-1	3-2
Lens	Fra	Anderlecht	Bel	1-1	0-1	1-2
Sparta Rotterdam	Ned	Spartak Moscow	URS	1-1	0-2	1-3
Bayern Munich	FRG	Tottenham Hotspur	Eng	1-0	0-2	1-2
Radnicki Nis	Yug	Hajduk Split	Yug	0-2	0-2	0-4

	Pts	P	W	D	L	F	A	Diff	Goals/P
Total	32	16	12	8	12	34	34	0	2.125

Quarter Finals

Tottenham Hotspur	Eng	Austria Vienna	Aut	2-0	2-2	4-2
Nottingham Forest	Eng	Sturm Graz	Aut	1-0	1-1	2-1
Anderlecht	Bel	Spartak Moscow	URS	4-2	0-1	4-3
Sparta Prague	Tch	Hajduk Split	Yug	1-0	0-2	1-2

	Pts	P	W	D	L	F	A	Diff	Goals/P
Total	16	8	6	4	6	19	19	0	2.375

Semi Finals

Nottingham Forest	Eng	Anderlecht	Bel	2-0	0-3	2-3
Hajduk Split	Yug	Tottenham Hotspur	Eng	2-1	0-1	2-2

	Pts	P	W	D	L	F	A	Diff	Goals/P
Total	8	4	4	0	4	9	9	0	2.250

Final

Anderlecht	Bel	Tottenham Hotspur	Eng	1-1	1-1	2-2

	Pts	P	W	D	L	F	A	Diff	Goals/P
Total	4	2	0	4	0	4	4	0	2.000

	Pts	P	W	D	L	F	A	Diff	Goals/P
Total	252	126	94	64	94	371	371	0	2.944

Pos'n	Club	Cnty	Pts	P	W	D	L	F	A	Diff	B	Pts/P	F/P
1	Tottenham Hotspur	Eng	20	12	7	3	2	30	9	21	3	1.667	2.500
2	Anderlecht	Bel	18	12	5	5	2	19	11	8	3	1.500	1.583
3	Nottingham Forest	Eng	18	10	7	2	1	12	6	6	2	1.800	1.200
4	Hajduk Split	Yug	14	10	6	0	4	14	7	7	2	1.400	1.400
5	Spartak Moscow	URS	13	8	5	2	1	17	8	9	1	1.625	2.125
6	Austria Vienna	Aut	12	8	4	3	1	25	9	16	1	1.500	3.125
7	Sparta Prague	Tch	12	8	5	1	2	15	8	7	1	1.500	1.875
8	Lokomotive Leipzig	GDR	9	6	4	1	1	10	5	5	0	1.500	1.667
9	Sturm Graz	Aut	9	8	2	4	2	7	6	1	1	1.125	0.875
10	Bayern Munich	FRG	8	6	3	2	1	12	2	10	0	1.333	2.000
11	Celtic	Sco	7	6	3	1	2	11	5	6	0	1.167	1.833
12	Sparta Rotterdam	Ned	7	6	2	3	1	10	7	3	0	1.167	1.667
13	Lens	Fra	7	6	2	3	1	9	8	1	0	1.167	1.500
14	Inter Bratislava	Tch	6	4	3	0	1	19	6	13	0	1.500	4.750
15	Radnicki Nis	Yug	6	6	3	0	3	11	8	3	0	1.000	1.833
16	PAOK Salonika	Gre	6	4	2	2	0	5	2	3	0	1.500	1.250
17	Verona	Ita	6	4	2	2	0	6	4	2	0	1.500	1.500
18	Antwerp	Bel	5	4	2	1	1	12	8	4	0	1.250	3.000
19	Inter Milan	Ita	5	6	2	1	3	9	7	2	0	0.833	1.500
20	Watford	Eng	5	6	2	1	3	10	12	-2	0	0.833	1.667
21	Sporting Lisbon	Por	5	4	2	1	1	6	8	-2	0	1.250	1.500
22	Banik Ostrava	Tch	4	4	1	2	1	8	5	3	0	1.000	2.000
23	PSV Eindhoven	Ned	4	4	2	0	2	7	5	2	0	1.000	1.750
24	Carl Zeiss Jena	GDR	4	4	1	2	1	6	4	2	0	1.000	1.500
25	Groningen	Ned	4	4	2	0	2	7	7	0	0	1.000	1.750
26	Werder Bremen	FRG	4	4	1	2	1	4	4	0	0	1.000	1.000
27	Honvéd	Hun	4	4	2	0	2	6	7	-1	0	1.000	1.500
28	Feyenoord	Ned	4	4	2	0	2	5	6	-1	0	1.000	1.250
29	Levski Sofia	Bul	4	4	1	2	1	4	5	-1	0	1.000	1.000
–	Laval	Fra	4	4	1	2	1	4	5	-1	0	1.000	1.000
31	Widzew Lódź	Pol	4	4	1	2	1	3	5	-2	0	1.000	0.750
32	Aston Villa	Eng	3	4	1	1	2	8	5	3	0	0.750	2.000
33	IF Elfsborg	Swe	2	2	0	2	0	2	2	0	0	1.000	1.000
34	Universitatea Craiova	Rom	2	2	1	0	1	1	1	0	0	1.000	0.500
35	Kaiserslautern	FRG	2	2	1	0	1	3	4	-1	0	1.000	1.500
36	Larissa	Gre	2	2	1	0	1	2	3	-1	0	1.000	1.000
37	Trabzonspor	Tur	2	2	1	0	1	1	2	-1	0	1.000	0.500
38	Atlético Madrid	Esp	2	2	1	0	1	2	4	-2	0	1.000	1.000
39	Vitória Guimarães	Por	2	2	1	0	1	1	5	-4	0	1.000	0.500
40	Real Madrid	Esp	1	2	0	1	1	3	4	-1	0	0.500	1.500
–	Seville	Esp	1	2	0	1	1	3	4	-1	0	0.500	1.500
42	Gent	Bel	1	2	0	1	1	2	3	-1	0	0.500	1.000
–	Malmö FF	Swe	1	2	0	1	1	2	3	-1	0	0.500	1.000
44	VFB Stuttgart	FRG	1	2	0	1	1	1	2	-1	0	0.500	0.500
–	Sportul Studentesc Bucharest	Rom	1	2	0	1	1	1	2	-1	0	0.500	0.500
46	Dinamo Kiev	URS	1	2	0	1	1	0	1	-1	0	0.500	0.000
47	Bryne IL	Nor	1	2	0	1	1	1	4	-3	0	0.500	0.500
48	IBV Vestmannaeyjar	Isl	1	2	0	1	1	0	3	-3	0	0.500	0.000
49	Coleraine	Nir	1	2	0	1	1	1	5	-4	0	0.500	0.500
50	B 1903 Copenhagen	Den	1	2	0	1	1	1	6	-5	0	0.500	0.500
51	Red Star Belgrade	Yug	0	2	0	0	2	2	4	-2	0	0.000	1.000
52	Lokomotiv Plovdiv	Bul	0	2	0	0	2	2	5	-3	0	0.000	1.000
53	St. Mirren	Sco	0	2	0	0	2	0	3	-3	0	0.000	0.000
–	Vorwärts Frankfurt/Oder	GDR	0	2	0	0	2	0	3	-3	0	0.000	0.000
55	Ferencváros	Hun	0	2	0	0	2	2	6	-4	0	0.000	1.000
56	AGF Aarhus	Den	0	2	0	0	2	1	5	-4	0	0.000	0.500
–	St-Gallen	Sui	0	2	0	0	2	1	5	-4	0	0.000	0.500
58	FC Zürich	Sui	0	2	0	0	2	3	8	-5	0	0.000	1.500
59	Girondins Bordeaux	Fra	0	2	0	0	2	2	7	-5	0	0.000	1.000
60	HJK Helsinki	Fin	0	2	0	0	2	0	7	-7	0	0.000	0.000
61	Anorthosis Famagusta	Cyp	0	2	0	0	2	0	11	-11	0	0.000	0.000
62	Drogheda United	Irl	0	2	0	0	2	0	14	-14	0	0.000	0.000
63	Aris Bonnevoie	Lux	0	2	0	0	2	0	15	-15	0	0.000	0.000
64	Rabat Ajax	Mlt	0	2	0	0	2	0	16	-16	0	0.000	0.000
	Total		**266**	**252**	**94**	**64**	**94**	**371**	**371**	**0**	**14**	**1.056**	**2.944**

1983-84

Pos'n	Cnty	Pts	P	W	D	L	F	A	Diff	B	Pts/P	F/P
1	Eng	76	49	27	12	10	88	44	44	10	1.551	1.796
2	Ita	43	28	15	7	6	48	25	23	6	1.536	1.714
3	Sco	36	28	14	4	10	55	22	33	4	1.286	1.964
4	Bel	34	26	11	9	6	52	37	15	3	1.308	2.000
5	URS	33	22	12	6	4	45	25	20	3	1.500	2.045
6	Tch	30	22	12	5	5	52	24	28	1	1.364	2.364
7	Aut	30	24	10	7	7	42	29	13	3	1.250	1.750
8	Por	28	21	11	2	8	28	30	-2	4	1.333	1.333
9	Yug	27	24	12	1	11	35	24	11	2	1.125	1.458
10	GDR	25	22	10	4	8	29	26	3	1	1.136	1.318
11	Ned	23	24	9	5	10	33	33	0	0	0.958	1.375
12	FRG	21	20	8	5	7	35	24	11	0	1.050	1.750
13	Fra	19	18	6	7	5	24	28	-4	0	1.056	1.333
14	Esp	18	16	7	3	6	26	21	5	1	1.125	1.625
15	Gre	15	12	6	3	3	13	12	1	0	1.250	1.083
16	Hun	15	16	7	0	9	27	34	-7	1	0.938	1.688
17	Rom	14	12	5	2	5	14	10	4	2	1.167	1.167
18	Bul	9	14	3	3	8	12	20	-8	0	0.643	0.857
19	Swe	8	10	2	4	4	13	14	-1	0	0.800	1.300
20	Fin	8	10	3	1	6	7	15	-8	1	0.800	0.700
21	Pol	6	8	2	2	4	7	19	-12	0	0.750	0.875
22	Sui	5	10	2	1	7	16	20	-4	0	0.500	1.600
23	Tur	3	6	1	1	4	1	8	-7	0	0.500	0.167
24	Nor	3	6	0	3	3	3	11	-8	0	0.500	0.500
25	Alb	2	2	1	0	1	2	5	-3	0	1.000	1.000
26	Isl	2	6	0	2	4	3	10	-7	0	0.333	0.500
27	Cyp	2	6	1	0	5	7	22	-15	0	0.333	1.167
28	Wal	1	2	0	1	1	1	2	-1	0	0.500	0.500
29	Nir	1	6	0	1	5	5	15	-10	0	0.167	0.833
30	Den	1	8	0	1	7	5	26	-21	0	0.125	0.625
31	Irl	0	6	0	0	6	4	29	-25	0	0.000	0.667
32	Lux	0	6	0	0	6	2	30	-28	0	0.000	0.333
33	Mlt	0	6	0	0	6	0	40	-40	0	0.000	0.000
	Total	**538**	**496**	**197**	**102**	**197**	**734**	**734**	**0**	**42**	**1.085**	**2.960**

1955-56 to 1983-84

Pos'n	Cnty	Pts	P	W	D	L	F	A	Diff	B	Pts/P	F/P
1	Eng	1299	884	476	191	217	1707	900	807	156	1.469	1.931
2	FRG	1210	876	458	161	257	1775	1108	667	133	1.381	2.026
3	Esp	1100	803	406	152	245	1508	986	522	136	1.370	1.878
4	Ita	969	719	352	156	211	1130	743	387	109	1.348	1.572
5	Sco	672	540	257	99	184	942	687	255	59	1.244	1.744
6	Ned	620	480	239	86	155	930	599	331	56	1.292	1.938
7	Bel	612	511	235	87	189	844	672	172	55	1.198	1.652
8	Yug	582	522	217	95	210	864	755	109	53	1.115	1.655
9	Por	548	469	201	101	167	754	597	157	45	1.168	1.608
10	Hun	477	410	186	64	160	750	607	143	41	1.163	1.829
11	GDR	462	413	172	86	155	621	542	79	32	1.119	1.504
12	Tch	450	379	175	69	135	614	494	120	31	1.187	1.620
13	Fra	423	409	157	79	173	621	614	7	30	1.034	1.518
14	URS	384	286	148	60	78	434	282	152	28	1.343	1.517
15	Sui	298	343	110	59	174	517	662	-145	19	0.869	1.507
16	Pol	297	291	110	60	121	419	452	-33	17	1.021	1.440
17	Bul	290	301	113	48	140	445	470	-25	16	0.963	1.478
18	Rom	286	305	111	54	140	400	479	-79	10	0.938	1.311
19	Aut	277	315	96	66	153	398	515	-117	19	0.879	1.263
20	Swe	227	249	78	59	112	319	419	-100	12	0.912	1.281
21	Gre	217	245	84	42	119	286	432	-146	7	0.886	1.167
22	Den	161	247	57	42	148	320	558	-238	5	0.652	1.296
23	Tur	153	213	57	33	123	207	403	-196	6	0.718	0.972
24	Nor	94	178	34	25	119	174	454	-280	1	0.528	0.978
25	Wal	85	82	28	23	31	121	97	24	6	1.037	1.476
26	Irl	84	176	27	30	119	147	443	-296	0	0.477	0.835
27	Nir	73	154	22	27	105	150	440	-290	2	0.474	0.974
28	Fin	48	132	16	15	101	106	425	-319	1	0.364	0.803
29	Lux	41	152	15	11	126	99	642	-543	0	0.270	0.651
30	Mlt	39	130	14	11	105	64	471	-407	0	0.300	0.492
31	Cyp	35	110	11	13	86	69	416	-347	0	0.318	0.627
32	Alb	30	44	9	12	23	30	68	-38	0	0.682	0.682
33	Isl	26	116	5	16	95	60	393	-333	0	0.224	0.517
	Total	**12569**	**11484**	**4676**	**2132**	**4676**	**17825**	**17825**	**0**	**1085**	**1.094**	**3.104**

1983-84

Pos'n	Cnty	Ave	Pts	P	W	D	L	F	A	Diff	B	No./T
1	England	12.666	76	49	27	12	10	88	44	44	10	6
2	Italy	10.750	43	28	15	7	6	48	25	23	6	4
3	USSR	8.250	33	22	12	6	4	45	25	20	3	4
4	Austria	7.500	30	24	10	7	7	42	29	13	3	4
5	Scotland	7.200	36	28	14	4	10	55	22	33	4	5
6	Portugal	7.000	28	21	11	2	8	28	30	-2	4	4
7	Belgium	6.800	34	26	11	9	6	52	37	15	3	5
8	Czechoslovakia	6.000	30	22	12	5	5	52	24	28	1	5
9	Yugoslavia	5.400	27	24	12	1	11	35	24	11	2	5
10	E. Germany	5.000	25	22	10	4	8	29	26	3	1	5
11	Romania	4.666	14	12	5	2	5	14	10	4	2	3
12	Netherlands	3.833	23	24	9	5	10	33	33	0	0	6
13	France	3.800	19	18	6	7	5	24	28	-4	0	5
14	Greece	3.750	15	12	6	3	3	13	12	1	0	4
–	Hungary	3.750	15	16	7	0	9	27	34	-7	1	4
16	Spain	3.600	18	16	7	3	6	26	21	5	1	5
17	W. Germany	3.500	21	20	8	5	7	35	24	11	0	6
18	Finland	2.666	8	10	3	1	6	7	15	-8	1	3
19	Bulgaria	2.250	9	14	3	3	8	12	20	-8	0	4
20	Albania	2.000	2	2	1	0	1	2	5	-3	0	1
–	Poland	2.000	6	8	2	2	4	7	19	-12	0	3
–	Sweden	2.000	8	10	2	4	4	13	14	-1	0	4
23	Switzerland	1.250	5	10	2	1	7	16	20	-4	0	4
24	Wales	1.000	1	2	0	1	1	1	2	-1	0	1
–	Norway	1.000	3	6	0	3	3	3	11	-8	0	3
–	Turkey	1.000	3	6	1	1	4	1	8	-7	0	3
27	Cyprus	0.666	2	6	1	0	5	7	22	-15	0	3
–	Iceland	0.666	2	6	0	2	4	3	10	-7	0	3
29	N. Ireland	0.333	1	6	0	1	5	5	15	-10	0	3
30	Denmark	0.250	1	8	0	1	7	5	26	-21	0	4
31	Rep. of Ireland	0.000	0	6	0	0	6	4	29	-25	0	3
–	Luxembourg	0.000	0	6	0	0	6	2	30	-28	0	3
–	Malta	0.000	0	6	0	0	6	0	40	-40	0	3
	Total		**538**	**496**	**197**	**102**	**197**	**734**	**734**	**0**	**42**	**2.960**

1955-56 to 1983-84

Pos'n	Cnty	Ave	Pts	P	W	D	L	F	A	Diff	B	No./T
1	England	8.777	1299	884	476	191	217	1707	900	807	156	148
2	W. Germany	7.908	1210	876	458	161	257	1775	1108	667	133	153
3	Spain	7.638	1100	803	406	152	245	1508	986	522	136	144
4	Italy	7.021	969	719	352	156	211	1130	743	387	109	138
5	Netherlands	6.078	620	480	239	86	155	930	599	331	56	102
6	Scotland	5.946	672	540	257	99	184	942	687	255	59	113
7	USSR	5.907	384	286	148	60	78	434	282	152	28	65
8	Belgium	5.415	612	511	235	87	189	844	672	172	55	113
9	Hungary	5.184	477	410	186	64	160	750	607	143	41	92
10	Portugal	4.981	548	469	201	101	167	754	597	157	45	110
11	Yugoslavia	4.932	582	522	217	95	210	864	755	109	53	118
12	E. Germany	4.863	462	413	172	86	155	621	542	79	32	95
13	Czechoslovakia	4.787	450	379	175	69	135	614	494	120	31	94
14	France	3.845	423	409	157	79	173	621	614	7	30	110
15	Poland	3.759	297	291	110	60	121	419	452	-33	17	79
16	Wales	3.695	85	82	28	23	31	121	97	24	6	23
17	Bulgaria	3.333	290	301	113	48	140	445	470	-25	16	87
18	Romania	3.213	286	305	111	54	140	400	479	-79	10	89
19	Austria	2.978	277	315	96	66	153	398	515	-117	19	93
20	Switzerland	2.838	298	343	110	59	174	517	662	-145	19	105
21	Sweden	2.768	227	249	78	59	112	319	419	-100	12	82
22	Greece	2.552	217	245	84	42	119	286	432	-146	7	85
23	Turkey	2.013	153	213	57	33	123	207	403	-196	6	76
24	Denmark	1.750	161	247	57	42	148	320	558	-238	5	92
25	Albania	1.500	30	44	9	12	23	30	68	-38	0	20
26	Norway	1.270	94	178	34	25	119	174	454	-280	1	74
27	Rep. of Ireland	1.166	84	176	27	30	119	147	443	-296	0	72
28	N. Ireland	1.089	73	154	22	27	105	150	440	-290	2	67
29	Finland	0.842	48	132	16	15	101	106	425	-319	1	57
30	Cyprus	0.686	35	110	11	13	86	69	416	-347	0	51
31	Malta	0.629	39	130	14	11	105	64	471	-407	0	62
32	Luxembourg	0.569	41	152	15	11	126	99	642	-543	0	72
33	Iceland	0.481	26	116	5	16	95	60	393	-333	0	54
	Total		**12569**	**11484**	**4676**	**2132**	**4676**	**17825**	**17825**	**0**	**1085**	**3.104**

Two out of Three on Penelties

Penalty shoot-outs decided the outcome of both Champions' Cup and UEFA Cup finals in 1983-84, and on both occasions it was an English team that emerged the winner.

The Champions' Cup marked the return to prominence of Liverpool, now under the managership of Joe Fagan after the retirement of Bob Paisley. Having been eliminated early from the competition the season before, when the Cup left England for the first time in seven years, the Merseysiders were determined to make their eighth consecutive Champions' Cup campaign a successful one. Added to their team now was young Welsh international striker Ian Rush, and he was to have a prolific season in front of goal both in domestic competition and in Europe. He didn't get on the scoresheet in Liverpool's easy first round victory over Danish side OB of Odense. But thereafter he was to be the team's prime asset in awkward-looking ties against Athletic Bilbao, Benfica and, conquerors of holders Hamburg, Dinamo Bucharest.

Liverpool were held 0-0 at home in the second round by Bilbao, but Rush came to the side's rescue in the return, scoring the only goal to take Liverpool into a quarter-final confrontation with Benfica. Again Rush saved Liverpool's blushes with the only goal in the home leg against the Portuguese champions, but Liverpool were rampant in the return and overwhelmed their hosts 4-1 in the Stadium of Light, with Rush adding another goal to his tally. In the semi-final, a solitary Sammy Lee goal was the slender advantage Liverpool had to take to Bucharest for the return, but once again Rush's opportunism averted the danger, and his two goals in the Romanian capital were sufficient to take his side into their fourth Champions' Cup final in eight seasons.

Unfortunately for Liverpool, their opponents in the final were Roma. Unfortunate because the final was scheduled for Roma's home ground, the Stadio Olimpico. Liverpool had of course won their first Champions' Cup on that ground seven years earlier, but the choice of venue was clearly in their opponents' favour.

Roma had made it to the final with a remarkable comeback in the semi- final against Dundee United. Down 2-0 from the first leg in Dundee, they triumphed 3-0 in the return, with star striker Roberto Pruzzo scoring two of the goals and the third coming from a Di Bartolomei penalty. Other key individuals in the Roma team were the Brazilian duo, Falcão and Toninho Cerezo, plus one of the Italian stars of the 1982 World Cup, right-winger Bruno Conti. The Roma coach was the veteran Swede, Nils Liedholm, once a fine player with AC Milan, a member of the team beaten in the 1958 final by Real Madrid.

Roma's home advantage made them the slight favourites to win the final and therefore become the first Italian winners for 15 years, but it was Liverpool who scored first, after 15 minutes, through right-back Phil Neal, scorer of Liverpool's third goal against Borussia Mönchengladbach on the same ground seven years earlier. There were doubts as to the validity of the goal, with Ronnie Whelan seeming to impede goalkeeper Tancredi as he went up for the ball just prior to Neal's shot, but the referee gave it, and Liverpool, much to the fury of the Romans in the crowd, were 1-0 up. They subsequently appeared to take a grip of the game, with Graeme Souness outplaying Falcão in midfield, but with 38 minutes gone, Roma pulled level with an excellent headed goal from Pruzzo. For the first time in seven years the Champions' Cup final had yielded more than a single goal.

Alas, there were to be no others, which meant that for the first time Europe's most prestigious club competition had to be decided on penalties. Steve Nicol missed first for Liverpool, but so did Conti for Roma. Neal, Souness and Rush, with his 50th goal of the season, put Liverpool 3-2 up before Graziani, another Italian international, fell prey to Grobbelaar's wobbly-knee antics on the goal line and blasted high over the bar. Now it was up to Alan Kennedy, Liverpool's final hero in 1981, and he duly slotted home the winning penalty to give Liverpool the Cup for the fourth time, putting them alone in second place behind Real Madrid in the all-time Champions' Cup roll-of-honour. Roma's defeat was particularly difficult for the Italians to swallow. Had they won, Italy would have become the first nation to lift both the Champions' and Cup-winners' Cups in the same season, because a fortnight earlier Juventus had recovered from their Champions' Cup nightmare of a year earlier to lift the Cup-winners' Cup with a 2-1 victory over FC Porto in Basle.

For the second year in a row, the Cup-winners' Cup had a strong cast. The first genuine heavyweight encounter took place in the quarter-finals between Barcelona and Manchester United. The Spaniards took the first match 2-0 in the Nou Camp, with Rojo adding a last-minute second to Graeme Hogg's own-goal. But United were inspired in the return, and Barcelona superstars Schuster and Maradona could do nothing to stop two-goal Bryan Robson leading the FA Cup holders to a brilliant 3-0 victory. Holders Aberdeen also came back from the dead in similar fashion to knock out Ujpesti Dózsa with a hat-trick from Mark McGhee, but in the semi-finals both British sides went out. The Dons surrendered their title with 1-0 defeats both home and away against FC Porto, while United endured the frustration of losing to a last-minute Paolo Rossi goal in their clash with Juventus.

In reaching the Cup-winners' Cup final, Juventus had become the first Italian club to contest the finals of all three European Cups, but their record of just one win in five previous finals was unimpressive. Porto, on the other hand, had never reached this stage of any of the three competitions. Juventus fielded nine of the players which had lost to Hamburg the previous year, but it was one of the two newcomers, Beniamino Vignola, who put them in front after 13 minutes with a strong, low shot from the edge of the area. Porto replied 15 minutes later, through Sousa, but this was to be Juventus's day and Zbigniew Boniek restored their lead shortly before half-time. A lead which would last right through to the final whistle, giving the Italians their second European trophy.

A week later, Tottenham Hotspur captured their third European trophy, defeating holders Anderlecht on a penalty shoot-out after two drawn games to win the UEFA Cup. Unlike Liverpool in the Champions' Cup, Tottenham were fortunate enough to stage the penalty competition on their own ground, having played the first leg in Brussels, and the fanatical support coming from the White Hart Lane terraces was certainly a contributory factor in their success.

Having achieved a 1-1 draw in Brussels, Tottenham might have felt that the most difficult part was over. But Anderlecht, who had staged a brilliant comeback against Nottingham Forest in the semi-finals, were not going to give up their trophy without a fight. An hour into the second leg, with Spurs leading on the away goals rule, the Belgians turned the tie around with an excellent goal from Alex Czerniatynski. Tottenham, without the injured Glenn Hoddle, who had earlier inspired them to a revenge victory over their 1974 conquerors, Feyenoord, now brought on another injury victim, the Argentinian Osvaldo Ardiles, and it was his industry that set up Tottenham skipper Graham Roberts for a dramatic late equaliser to send the match into extra-time. No further goals were scored, but Tottenham, with the crowd at fever pitch, had their tails up, and it was no surprise when they won the shoot-out, goalkeeper Tony Parks proving the hero with two fine saves from Morten Olsen and, decisively, the Icelandic forward, Arnor Gudjohnsen.

Above: Spurs goalie Tony Parks saves Anderlecht's fifth and final penalty, taken by Arnor Gudjohnsen, to give Spurs victory in the UEFA Cup final at White Hart Lane after a 2-2 aggregate draw.

Juventus

Everton

Real Madrid

1984 – 1985

First Round

Team 1	Cnty	Team 2	Cnty	1st leg	2nd leg	Agg
Labinoti Elbasan	Alb	Lyngby BK	Den	0-3	0-3	0-6
Austria Vienna	Aut	Valletta	Mlt	4-0	4-0	8-0
Levski Sofia	Bul	VFB Stuttgart	FRG	1-1	2-2	3-3
Aberdeen	Sco	Dynamo Berlin	GDR	2-1	1-2	3-3
Ilves Tampere	Fin	Juventus	Ita	0-4	1-2	1-6
Girondins Bordeaux	Fra	Athletic Bilbao	Esp	3-2	0-0	3-2
Linfield	Nir	Shamrock Rovers	Irl	0-0	1-1	1-1
IA Akranes	Isl	Beveren	Bel	2-2	0-5	2-7
Avenir Beggen	Lux	IFK Gothenburg	Swe	0-8	0-9	0-17
Vålerengen SIF	Nor	Sparta Prague	Tch	3-3	0-2	3-5
Feyenoord	Ned	Panathinaikos	Gre	0-0	1-2	1-2
Lech Poznań	Pol	Liverpool	Eng	0-1	0-4	0-5
Dinamo Bucharest	Rom	Omonia Nicosia	Cyp	4-1	1-2	5-3
Grasshoppers Zürich	Sui	Honvéd	Hun	3-1	1-2	4-3
Trabzonspor	Tur	Dnepr Dnepropetrovsk	URS	1-0	0-3	1-3
Red Star Belgrade	Yug	Benfica	Por	3-2	0-2	3-4

	Pts	P	W	D	L	F	A	Diff	Goals/P
Total	64	32	24	16	24	108	108	0	3.375

Second Round

Liverpool	Eng	Benfica	Por	3-1	0-1	3-2
Levski Sofia	Bul	Dnepr Dnepropetrovsk	URS	3-1	0-2	3-3
Girondins Bordeaux	Fra	Dinamo Bucharest	Rom	1-0	1-1	2-1
Panathinaikos	Gre	Linfield	Nir	2-1	3-3	5-4
Juventus	Ita	Grasshoppers Zürich	Sui	2-0	4-2	6-2
IFK Gothenburg	Swe	Beveren	Bel	1-0	1-2	2-2
Sparta Prague	Tch	Lyngby BK	Den	0-0	2-1	2-1
Dynamo Berlin	GDR	Austria Vienna	Aut	3-3	1-2	4-5

	Pts	P	W	D	L	F	A	Diff	Goals/P
Total	32	16	12	8	12	47	47	0	2.938

Quarter Finals

Austria Vienna	Aut	Liverpool	Eng	1-1	1-4	2-5
Girondins Bordeaux	Fra	Dnepr Dnepropetrovsk	URS	1-1	1-1	2-2
Juventus	Ita	Sparta Prague	Tch	3-0	0-1	3-1
IFK Gothenburg	Swe	Panathinaikos	Gre	0-1	2-2	2-3

	Pts	P	W	D	L	F	A	Diff	Goals/P
Total	16	8	4	8	4	20	20	0	2.500

Semi Finals

Liverpool	Eng	Panathinaikos	Gre	4-0	1-0	5-0
Juventus	Ita	Girondins Bordeaux	Fra	3-0	0-2	3-2

	Pts	P	W	D	L	F	A	Diff	Goals/P
Total	8	4	4	0	4	10	10	0	2.500

Final

Liverpool	Eng	Juventus	Ita	0-1	0-1

	Pts	P	W	D	L	F	A	Diff	Goals/P
Total	2	1	1	0	1	1	1	0	1.000

	Pts	P	W	D	L	F	A	Diff	Goals/P
Total	122	61	45	32	45	186	186	0	3.049

Pos'n	Club	Cnty	Pts	P	W	D	L	F	A	Diff	B	Pts/P	F/P
1	Juventus	Ita	17	9	7	0	2	19	6	13	3	1.889	2.111
2	Liverpool	Eng	16	9	6	1	2	18	5	13	3	1.778	2.000
3	Girondins Bordeaux	Fra	12	8	3	4	1	9	8	1	2	1.500	1.125
4	Panathinaikos	Gre	11	8	3	3	2	10	12	-2	2	1.375	1.250
5	Austria Vienna	Aut	9	6	3	2	1	15	9	6	1	1.500	2.500
6	Sparta Prague	Tch	9	6	3	2	1	8	7	1	1	1.500	1.333
7	IFK Gothenburg	Swe	8	6	3	1	2	21	5	16	1	1.333	3.500
8	Dnepr Dnepropetrovsk	URS	7	6	2	2	2	8	6	2	1	1.167	1.333
9	Beveren	Bel	5	4	2	1	1	9	4	5	0	1.250	2.250
10	Lyngby BK	Den	5	4	2	1	1	7	2	5	0	1.250	1.750
11	Levski Sofia	Bul	4	4	1	2	1	6	6	0	0	1.000	1.500
–	Benfica	Por	4	4	2	0	2	6	6	0	0	1.000	1.500
13	Dinamo Bucharest	Rom	3	4	1	1	2	6	5	1	0	0.750	1.500
14	Dynamo Berlin	GDR	3	4	1	1	2	7	8	-1	0	0.750	1.750
15	Linfield	Nir	3	4	0	3	1	5	6	-1	0	0.750	1.250
16	Aberdeen	Sco	2	2	1	0	1	3	3	0	0	1.000	1.500
–	VFB Stuttgart	FRG	2	2	0	2	0	3	3	0	0	1.000	1.500
18	Shamrock Rovers	Irl	2	2	0	2	0	1	1	0	0	1.000	0.500
19	Honvéd	Hun	2	2	1	0	1	3	4	-1	0	1.000	1.500
–	Red Star Belgrade	Yug	2	2	1	0	1	3	4	-1	0	1.000	1.500
21	Omonia Nicosia	Cyp	2	2	1	0	1	3	5	-2	0	1.000	1.500
22	Trabzonspor	Tur	2	2	1	0	1	1	3	-2	0	1.000	0.500
23	Grasshoppers Zürich	Sui	2	4	1	0	3	6	9	-3	0	0.500	1.500
24	Athletic Bilbao	Esp	1	2	0	1	1	2	3	-1	0	0.500	1.000
25	Feyenoord	Ned	1	2	0	1	1	1	2	-1	0	0.500	0.500
26	Vålerengen SIF	Nor	1	2	0	1	1	3	5	-2	0	0.500	1.500
27	IA Akranes	Isl	1	2	0	1	1	2	7	-5	0	0.500	1.000
28	Ilves Tampere	Fin	0	2	0	0	2	1	6	-5	0	0.000	0.500
29	Lech Poznań	Pol	0	2	0	0	2	0	5	-5	0	0.000	0.000
30	Labinoti Elbasan	Alb	0	2	0	0	2	0	6	-6	0	0.000	0.000
31	Valletta	Mlt	0	2	0	0	2	0	8	-8	0	0.000	0.000
32	Avenir Beggen	Lux	0	2	0	0	2	0	17	-17	0	0.000	0.000
	Total		**136**	**122**	**45**	**32**	**45**	**186**	**186**	**0**	**14**	**1.115**	**3.049**

First Round

Team 1	Cnty	Team 2	Cnty	1st leg	2nd leg	Agg
Everton	Eng	UCD	Irl	0-0	1-0	1-0
Rapid Vienna	Aut	Besiktas	Tur	4-1	1-1	5-2
Trakia Plovdiv	Bul	Union Luxembourg	Lux	4-0	1-1	5-1
Apoel Nicosia	Cyp	Servette	Sui	0-3	1-3	1-6
KB Copenhagen	Den	Fortuna Sittard	Ned	0-0	0-3	0-3
Celtic	Sco	Gent	Bel	0-1	3-0	3-1
Metz	Fra	Barcelona	Esp	2-4	4-1	6-5
Wrexham	Wal	FC Porto	Por	1-0	3-4	4-4
Siófok	Hun	Larissa	Gre	1-1	0-2	1-3
Roma	Ita	Steaua Bucharest	Rom	1-0	0-0	1-0
Hamrun Spartans	Mlt	Ballymena United	Nir	1-0	2-1	3-1
Wisla Kraków	Pol	IBV Vestmannaeyjar	Isl	4-2	3-1	7-3
Bayern Munich	FRG	Moss FK	Nor	4-1	2-1	6-2
Malmö FF	Swe	Dynamo Dresden	GDR	2-0	1-4	3-4
Inter Bratislava	Tch	FC Kuusysi Lahti	Fin	2-1	0-0	2-1
Dinamo Moscow	URS	Hajduk Split	Yug	1-0	5-2	6-2

	Pts	P	W	D	L	F	A	Diff	Goals/P
Total	64	32	25	14	25	92	92	0	2.875

Second Round

Team 1	Cnty	Team 2	Cnty	1st leg	2nd leg	Agg
Rapid Vienna	Aut	Celtic	Sco	3-1	1-0	4-1
Larissa	Gre	Servette	Sui	2-1	1-0	3-1
Roma	Ita	Wrexham	Wal	2-0	1-0	3-2
Fortuna Sittard	Ned	Wisla Kraków	Pol	2-0	1-2	3-2
Bayern Munich	FRG	Trakia Plovdiv	Bul	4-1	0-2	4-3
Inter Bratislava	Tch	Everton	Eng	0-1	0-3	0-4
Dinamo Moscow	URS	Hamrun Spartans	Mlt	5-0	1-0	6-0
Dynamo Dresden	GDR	Metz	Fra	3-1	0-0	3-1

	Pts	P	W	D	L	F	A	Diff	Goals/P
Total	32	16	15	2	15	38	38	0	2.375

Quarter Finals

Team 1	Cnty	Team 2	Cnty	1st leg	2nd leg	Agg
Everton	Eng	Fortuna Sittard	Ned	3-0	2-0	5-0
Larissa	Gre	Dinamo Moscow	URS	0-0	0-1	0-1
Bayern Munich	FRG	Roma	Ita	2-0	2-1	4-1
Dynamo Dresden	GDR	Rapid Vienna	Aut	3-0	0-5	3-5

	Pts	P	W	D	L	F	A	Diff	Goals/P
Total	16	8	7	2	7	19	19	0	2.375

Semi Finals

Team 1	Cnty	Team 2	Cnty	1st leg	2nd leg	Agg
Rapid Vienna	Aut	Dinamo Moscow	URS	3-1	1-1	4-2
Bayern Munich	FRG	Everton	Eng	0-0	1-3	1-3

	Pts	P	W	D	L	F	A	Diff	Goals/P
Total	8	4	2	4	2	10	10	0	2.500

Final

Everton	Eng	Rapid Vienna	Aut	3-1	3-1

	Pts	P	W	D	L	F	A	Diff	Goals/P
Total	2	1	1	0	1	4	4	0	4.000

	Pts	P	W	D	L	F	A	Diff	Goals/P
Total	122	61	50	22	50	163	163	0	2.672

Pos'n	Club	Cnty	Pts	P	W	D	L	F	A	Diff	B	Pts/P	F/P
1	Everton	Eng	19	9	7	2	0	16	2	14	3	2.111	1.778
2	Rapid Vienna	Aut	15	9	5	2	2	19	11	8	3	1.667	2.111
3	Dinamo Moscow	URS	14	8	5	2	1	15	6	9	2	1.750	1.875
4	Bayern Munich	FRG	13	8	5	1	2	15	9	6	2	1.625	1.875
5	Larissa	Gre	9	6	3	2	1	6	3	3	1	1.500	1.000
6	Dynamo Dresden	GDR	8	6	3	1	2	10	9	1	1	1.333	1.667
7	Roma	Ita	8	6	3	1	2	5	4	1	1	1.333	0.833
8	Wisla Kraków	Pol	6	4	3	0	1	9	6	3	0	1.500	2.250
9	Fortuna Sittard	Ned	6	6	2	1	3	6	7	-1	1	1.000	1.000
10	Trakia Plovdiv	Bul	5	4	2	1	1	8	5	3	0	1.250	2.000
11	Servette	Sui	4	4	2	0	2	7	4	3	0	1.000	1.750
12	Hamrun Spartans	Mlt	4	4	2	0	2	3	7	-4	0	1.000	0.750
13	Metz	Fra	3	4	1	1	2	7	8	-1	0	0.750	1.750
14	Inter Bratislava	Tch	3	4	1	1	2	2	5	-3	0	0.750	0.500
15	FC Porto	Por	2	2	1	0	1	4	4	0	0	1.000	2.000
16	Barcelona	Esp	2	2	1	0	1	5	6	-1	0	1.000	2.500
17	Celtic	Sco	2	4	1	0	3	4	5	-1	0	0.500	1.000
18	Malmö FF	Swe	2	2	1	0	1	3	4	-1	0	1.000	1.500
19	Gent	Bel	2	2	1	0	1	1	3	-2	0	1.000	0.500
20	Wrexham	Wal	2	4	1	0	3	4	7	-3	0	0.500	1.000
21	FC Kuusysi Lahti	Fin	1	2	0	1	1	1	2	-1	0	0.500	0.500
22	UCD	Irl	1	2	0	1	1	0	1	-1	0	0.500	0.000
–	Steaua Bucharest	Rom	1	2	0	1	1	0	1	-1	0	0.500	0.000
24	Siófok	Hun	1	2	0	1	1	1	3	-2	0	0.500	0.500
25	Besiktas	Tur	1	2	0	1	1	2	5	-3	0	0.500	1.000
26	KB Copenhagen	Den	1	2	0	1	1	0	3	-3	0	0.500	0.000
27	Union Luxembourg	Lux	1	2	0	1	1	1	5	-4	0	0.500	0.500
28	Ballymena United	Nir	0	2	0	0	2	1	3	-2	0	0.000	0.500
29	IBV Vestmannaeyjar	Isl	0	2	0	0	2	3	7	-4	0	0.000	1.500
30	Moss FK	Nor	0	2	0	0	2	2	6	-4	0	0.000	1.000
–	Hajduk Split	Yug	0	2	0	0	2	2	6	-4	0	0.000	1.000
32	Apoel Nicosia	Cyp	0	2	0	0	2	1	6	-5	0	0.000	0.500
	Total		**136**	**122**	**50**	**22**	**50**	**163**	**163**	**0**	**14**	**1.115**	**2.672**

First Round

Team 1	Cnty	Team 2	Cnty	1st leg	2nd leg	Agg
Manchester United	Eng	Rába ETO	Hun	3-0	2-2	5-2
Nottingham Forest	Eng	Club Bruges	Bel	0-0	0-1	0-1
Southampton	Eng	Hamburg	FRG	0-0	0-2	0-2
Anderlecht	Bel	Werder Bremen	FRG	1-0	1-2	2-2
Sliven	Bul	Zeljeznicar Sarajevo	Yug	1-0	1-5	2-5
OB Odense	Den	Spartak Moscow	URS	1-5	1-2	2-7
Bohemians	Irl	Rangers	Sco	3-2	0-2	3-4
Real Madrid	Esp	FC Tirol	Aut	5-0	0-2	5-2
Real Betis	Esp	Universitatea Craiova	Rom	1-0	0-1	1-1
Real Valladolid	Esp	Rijeka	Yug	1-0	1-4	2-4
Monaco	Fra	CSKA Sofia	Bul	2-2	1-2	3-4
Paris Saint-Germain	Fra	Heart of Midlothian	Sco	4-0	2-2	6- 2
Olympiakos Pireus	Gre	Neuchâtel Xamax	Sui	1-0	2-2	3-2
Videoton	Hun	Dukla Prague	Tch	1-0	0-0	1-0
Glentoran	Nir	Standard Liège	Bel	1-1	0-2	1-3
KR Reykjavik	Isl	Queen's Park Rangers	Eng	0-3	0-4	0-7
Red Boys Differdange	Lux	Ajax	Ned	0-0	0-14	0-14
Widzew Lódź	Pol	AGF Aarhus	Den	2-0	0-1	2-1
Sporting Braga	Por	Tottenham Hotspur	Eng	0-3	0-6	0-9
Sporting Lisbon	Por	Auxerre	Fra	2-0	2-2	4-2
Cologne	FRG	Pogon Szczecin	Pol	2-1	1-0	3-1
Sportul Studentesc Bucharest	Rom	Inter Milan	Ita	1-0	0-2	1-2
AIK	Swe	Dundee United	Sco	1-0	0-3	1-3
Öster SIF	Swe	Linzer ASK	Aut	0-1	0-1	0-2
Sion	Sui	Atlético Madrid	Esp	1-0	3-2	4-2
Dukla Banská Bystrica	Tch	Bor. Mönchengladbach	FRG	2-3	1-4	3-7
Bohemians Prague	Tch	Apollon Limassol	Cyp	6-1	2-2	8-3
Fenerbahçe	Tur	Fiorentina	Ita	0-1	0-2	0-3
Dinamo Minsk	URS	HJK Helsinki	Fin	4-0	6-0	10-0
Partizan Belgrade	Yug	Rabat Ajax	Mlt	2-0	2-0	4-0
Vorwärts Frankfurt/Oder	GDR	PSV Eindhoven	Ned	2-0	0-3	2-3
Lokomotive Leipzig	GDR	Lillestrøm SK	Nor	7-0	0-3	7-3

	Pts	P	W	D	L	F	A	Diff	Goals/P
Total	128	64	53	22	53	188	188	0	2.938

Second Round

Queen's Park Rangers	Eng	Partizan Belgrade	Yug	6-2	0-4	6-6
Linzer ASK	Aut	Dundee United	Sco	1-2	1-5	2-7
Club Bruges	Bel	Tottenham Hotspur	Eng	2-1	0-3	2-4
Standard Liège	Bel	Cologne	FRG	0-2	1-2	1-4
Paris Saint-Germain	Fra	Videoton	Hun	2-4	0-1	2-5
Fiorentina	Ita	Anderlecht	Bel	1-1	2-6	3-7
Inter Milan	Ita	Rangers	Sco	3-0	1-3	4-3
Ajax	Ned	Bohemians Prague	Tch	1-0	0-1	1-1
PSV Eindhoven	Ned	Manchester United	Eng	0-0	0-1	0-1
Sporting Lisbon	Por	Dinamo Minsk	URS	2-0	0-2	2-2
Hamburg	FRG	CSKA Sofia	Bul	4-0	2-1	6-1
Bor. Mönchengladbach	FRG	Widzew Lódź	Pol	3-2	0-1	3-3
Universitatea Craiova	Rom	Olympiakos Pireus	Gre	1-0	1-0	2-0
Rijeka	Yug	Real Madrid	Esp	3-1	0-3	3-4
Zeljeznicar Sarajevo	Yug	Sion	Sui	2-1	1-1	3-2
Lokomotive Leipzig	GDR	Spartak Moscow	URS	1-1	0-2	1-3

	Pts	P	W	D	L	F	A	Diff	Goals/P
Total	64	32	28	8	28	94	94	0	2.938

Third Round

Tottenham Hotspur	Eng	Bohemians Prague	Tch	2-0	1-1	3-1
Manchester United	Eng	Dundee United	Sco	2-2	3-2	5-4
Anderlecht	Bel	Real Madrid	Esp	3-0	1-6	4-6
Videoton	Hun	Partizan Belgrade	Yug	5-0	0-2	5-2
Widzew Lódź	Pol	Dinamo Minsk	URS	0-2	1-0	1-2
Hamburg	FRG	Inter Milan	Ita	2-1	0-1	2-2
Universitatea Craiova	Rom	Zeljeznicar Sarajevo	Yug	2-0	0-4	2-4
Spartak Moscow	URS	Cologne	FRG	1-0	0-2	1-2

	Pts	P	W	D	L	F	A	Diff	Goals/P
Total	32	16	14	4	14	46	46	0	2.875

Quarter Finals

Tottenham Hotspur	Eng	Real Madrid	Esp	0-1	0-0	0-1
Manchester United	Eng	Videoton	Hun	1-0	0-1	1-1
Inter Milan	Ita	Cologne	FRG	1-0	3-1	4-1
Zeljeznicar Sarajevo	Yug	Dinamo Minsk	URS	2-0	1-1	3-1

	Pts	P	W	D	L	F	A	Diff	Goals/P
Total	16	8	6	4	6	12	12	0	1.500

Semi Finals

Videoton	Hun	Zeljeznicar Sarajevo	Yug	3-1	1-2	4-3
Inter Milan	Ita	Real Madrid	Esp	2-0	0-3	2-3

	Pts	P	W	D	L	F	A	Diff	Goals/P
Total	8	4	4	0	4	12	12	0	3.000

Final

Videoton	Hun	Real Madrid	Esp	0-3	1-0	1-3

	Pts	P	W	D	L	F	A	Diff	Goals/P
Total	4	2	2	0	2	4	4	0	2.000

	Pts	P	W	D	L	F	A	Diff	Goals/P
Total	252	126	107	38	107	356	356	0	2.825

Pos'n	Club	Cnty	Pts	P	W	D	L	F	A	Diff	B	Pts/P	F/P
1	Videoton	Hun	18	12	7	1	4	17	11	6	3	1.500	1.417
2	Real Madrid	Esp	16	12	6	1	5	22	12	10	3	1.333	1.833
3	Zeljeznicar Sarajevo	Yug	14	10	5	2	3	18	11	7	2	1.400	1.800
4	Inter Milan	Ita	14	10	6	0	4	14	10	4	2	1.400	1.400
5	Manchester United	Eng	12	8	4	3	1	12	7	5	1	1.500	1.500
6	Tottenham Hotspur	Eng	11	8	4	2	2	16	4	12	1	1.375	2.000
7	Cologne	FRG	11	8	5	0	3	10	7	3	1	1.375	1.250
8	Dinamo Minsk	URS	10	8	4	1	3	15	6	9	1	1.250	1.875
9	Hamburg	FRG	9	6	4	1	1	10	3	7	0	1.500	1.667
10	Spartak Moscow	URS	9	6	4	1	1	11	5	6	0	1.500	1.833
11	Partizan Belgrade	Yug	8	6	4	0	2	12	11	1	0	1.333	2.000
12	Universitatea Craiova	Rom	8	6	4	0	2	5	5	0	0	1.333	0.833
13	Dundee United	Sco	7	6	3	1	2	14	8	6	0	1.167	2.333
14	Anderlecht	Bel	7	6	3	1	2	13	11	2	0	1.167	2.167
15	Queen's Park Rangers	Eng	6	4	3	0	1	13	6	7	0	1.500	3.250
16	Bor. Mönchengladbach	FRG	6	4	3	0	1	10	6	4	0	1.500	2.500
17	Bohemians Prague	Tch	6	6	2	2	2	10	7	3	0	1.000	1.667
18	Widzew Lódź	Pol	6	6	3	0	3	6	6	0	0	1.000	1.000
19	Ajax	Ned	5	4	2	1	1	15	1	14	0	1.250	3.750
20	Sporting Lisbon	Por	5	4	2	1	1	6	4	2	0	1.250	1.500
21	Sion	Sui	5	4	2	1	1	6	5	1	0	1.250	1.500
22	Fiorentina	Ita	5	4	2	1	1	6	7	-1	0	1.250	1.500
23	Club Bruges	Bel	5	4	2	1	1	3	4	-1	0	1.250	0.750
24	Rijeka	Yug	4	4	2	0	2	7	6	1	0	1.000	1.750
25	Rangers	Sco	4	4	2	0	2	7	7	0	0	1.000	1.750
26	Linzer ASK	Aut	4	4	2	0	2	4	7	-3	0	1.000	1.000
27	Lokomotive Leipzig	GDR	3	4	1	1	2	8	6	2	0	0.750	2.000
28	Paris Saint-Germain	Fra	3	4	1	1	2	8	7	1	0	0.750	2.000
29	PSV Eindhoven	Ned	3	4	1	1	2	3	3	0	0	0.750	0.750
30	Standard Liège	Bel	3	4	1	1	2	4	5	-1	0	0.750	1.000
31	Olympiakos Pireus	Gre	3	4	1	1	2	3	4	-1	0	0.750	0.750
32	CSKA Sofia	Bul	3	4	1	1	2	5	9	-4	0	0.750	1.250
33	Werder Bremen	FRG	2	2	1	0	1	2	2	0	0	1.000	1.000
34	Real Bétis	Esp	2	2	1	0	1	1	1	0	0	1.000	0.500
35	Bohemians	Irl	2	2	1	0	1	3	4	-1	0	1.000	1.500
36	Vorwärts Frankfurt/Oder	GDR	2	2	1	0	1	2	3	-1	0	1.000	1.000
37	AGF Aarhus	Den	2	2	1	0	1	1	2	-1	0	1.000	0.500
–	Sportul Studentesc Bucharest	Rom	2	2	1	0	1	1	2	-1	0	1.000	0.500
39	Real Valladolid	Esp	2	2	1	0	1	2	4	-2	0	1.000	1.000
40	AIK	Swe	2	2	1	0	1	1	3	-2	0	1.000	0.500
41	FC Tirol	Aut	2	2	1	0	1	2	5	-3	0	1.000	1.000
–	Sliven	Bul	2	2	1	0	1	2	5	-3	0	1.000	1.000
43	Lillestrøm SK	Nor	2	2	1	0	1	3	7	-4	0	1.000	1.500
44	Monaco	Fra	1	2	0	1	1	3	4	-1	0	0.500	1.500
45	Neuchâtel Xamax	Sui	1	2	0	1	1	2	3	-1	0	0.500	1.000
46	Nottingham Forest	Eng	1	2	0	1	1	0	1	-1	0	0.500	0.000
–	Dulka Prague	Tch	1	2	0	1	1	0	1	-1	0	0.500	0.000
48	Auxerre	Fra	1	2	0	1	1	2	4	-2	0	0.500	1.000
49	Glentoran	Nir	1	2	0	1	1	1	3	-2	0	0.500	0.500
50	Southampton	Eng	1	2	0	1	1	0	2	-2	0	0.500	0.000
51	Rába ETO	Hun	1	2	0	1	1	2	5	-3	0	0.500	1.000
52	Hearts of Midlothian	Sco	1	2	0	1	1	2	6	-4	0	0.500	1.000
53	Apollon Limassol	Cyp	1	2	0	1	1	3	8	-5	0	0.500	1.500
54	Red Boys Differdange	Lux	1	2	0	1	1	0	14	-14	0	0.500	0.000
55	Atlético Madrid	Esp	0	2	0	0	2	2	4	-2	0	0.000	1.000
56	Pogon Szczecin	Pol	0	2	0	0	2	1	3	-2	0	0.000	0.500
57	Öster SIF	Swe	0	2	0	0	2	0	2	-2	0	0.000	0.000
58	Fenerbahçe	Tur	0	2	0	0	2	0	3	-3	0	0.000	0.000
59	Dukla Banská Bystrica	Tch	0	2	0	0	2	3	7	-4	0	0.000	1.500
60	Rabat Ajax	Mlt	0	2	0	0	2	0	4	-4	0	0.000	0.000
61	OB Odense	Den	0	2	0	0	2	2	7	-5	0	0.000	1.000
62	KR Reykjavik	Isl	0	2	0	0	2	0	7	-7	0	0.000	0.000
63	Sporting Braga	Por	0	2	0	0	2	0	9	-9	0	0.000	0.000
64	HJK Helsinki	Fin	0	2	0	0	2	0	10	-10	0	0.000	0.000
	Total		**266**	**252**	**107**	**38**	**107**	**356**	**356**	**0**	**14**	**1.056**	**2.825**

National Performances by Points

1984-85

Pos'n	Cnty	Pts	P	W	D	L	F	A	Diff	B	Pts/P	F/P
1	Eng	66	42	24	10	8	75	27	48	8	1.571	1.786
2	Ita	44	29	18	2	9	44	27	17	6	1.517	1.517
3	FRG	43	30	18	4	8	50	30	20	3	1.433	1.667
4	URS	40	28	15	6	7	49	23	26	4	1.429	1.750
5	Aut	30	21	11	4	6	40	32	8	4	1.429	1.905
6	Yug	28	24	12	2	10	42	38	4	2	1.167	1.750
7	Esp	23	22	9	2	11	34	30	4	3	1.045	1.545
8	Gre	23	18	7	6	5	19	19	0	3	1.278	1.056
9	Bel	22	20	9	4	7	30	27	3	0	1.100	1.500
10	Hun	22	18	8	3	7	23	23	0	3	1.222	1.278
11	Fra	20	20	5	8	7	29	31	-2	2	1.000	1.450
12	Tch	19	20	6	6	8	23	27	-4	1	0.950	1.150
13	Sco	16	18	7	2	9	30	29	1	0	0.889	1.667
14	GDR	16	16	6	3	7	27	26	1	1	1.000	1.688
15	Ned	15	16	5	4	7	25	13	12	1	0.938	1.563
16	Rom	14	14	6	2	6	12	13	-1	0	1.000	0.857
17	Bul	14	14	5	4	5	21	25	-4	0	1.000	1.500
18	Swe	12	12	5	1	6	25	14	11	1	1.000	2.083
19	Sui	12	14	5	2	7	21	21	0	0	0.857	1.500
20	Pol	12	14	6	0	8	16	20	-4	0	0.857	1.143
21	Por	11	12	5	1	6	16	23	-7	0	0.917	1.333
22	Den	8	10	3	2	5	10	14	-4	0	0.800	1.000
23	Irl	5	6	1	3	2	4	6	-2	0	0.833	0.667
24	Nir	4	8	0	4	4	7	12	-5	0	0.500	0.875
25	Mlt	4	8	2	0	6	3	19	-16	0	0.500	0.375
26	Tur	3	6	1	1	4	3	11	-8	0	0.500	0.500
27	Nor	3	6	1	1	4	8	18	-10	0	0.500	1.333
28	Cyp	3	6	1	1	4	7	19	-12	0	0.500	1.167
29	Wal	2	4	1	0	3	4	7	-3	0	0.500	1.000
30	Lux	2	6	0	2	4	1	36	-35	0	0.333	0.167
31	Isl	1	6	0	1	5	5	21	-16	0	0.167	0.833
32	Fin	1	6	0	1	5	2	18	-16	0	0.167	0.333
33	Alb	0	2	0	0	2	0	6	-6	0	0.000	0.000
	Total	**538**	**496**	**202**	**92**	**202**	**705**	**705**	**0**	**42**	**1.085**	**2.843**

1955-56 to 1984-85

1	Eng	1365	926	500	201	225	1782	927	855	164	1.474	1.924
2	FRG	1253	906	476	165	265	1825	1138	687	136	1.383	2.014
3	Esp	1123	825	415	154	256	1542	1016	526	139	1.361	1.869
4	Ita	1013	748	370	158	220	1174	770	404	115	1.354	1.570
5	Sco	688	558	264	101	193	972	716	256	59	1.233	1.742
6	Ned	635	496	244	90	162	955	612	343	57	1.280	1.925
7	Bel	634	531	244	91	196	874	699	175	55	1.194	1.646
8	Yug	610	546	229	97	220	906	793	113	55	1.117	1.659
9	Por	559	481	206	102	173	770	620	150	45	1.162	1.601
10	Hun	499	428	194	67	167	773	630	143	44	1.166	1.806
11	GDR	478	429	178	89	162	648	568	80	33	1.114	1.510
12	Tch	469	399	181	75	143	637	521	116	32	1.175	1.596
13	Fra	443	429	162	87	180	650	645	5	32	1.033	1.515
14	URS	424	314	163	66	85	483	305	178	32	1.350	1.538
15	Sui	310	357	115	61	181	538	683	-145	19	0.868	1.507
16	Pol	309	305	116	60	129	435	472	-37	17	1.013	1.426
17	Aut	307	336	107	70	159	438	547	-109	23	0.914	1.304
18	Bul	304	315	118	52	145	466	495	-29	16	0.965	1.479
19	Rom	300	319	117	56	146	412	492	-80	10	0.940	1.292
20	Gre	240	263	91	48	124	305	451	-146	10	0.913	1.160
21	Swe	239	261	83	60	118	344	433	-89	13	0.916	1.318
22	Den	169	257	60	44	153	330	572	-242	5	0.658	1.284
23	Tur	156	219	58	34	127	210	414	-204	6	0.712	0.959
24	Nor	97	184	35	26	123	182	472	-290	1	0.527	0.989
25	Irl	89	182	28	33	121	151	449	-298	0	0.489	0.830
26	Wal	87	86	29	23	34	125	104	21	6	1.012	1.453
27	Nir	77	162	22	31	109	157	452	-295	2	0.475	0.969
28	Fin	49	138	16	16	106	108	443	-335	1	0.355	0.783
29	Mlt	43	138	16	11	111	67	490	-423	0	0.312	0.486
30	Lux	43	158	15	13	130	100	678	-578	0	0.272	0.633
31	Cyp	38	116	12	14	90	76	435	-359	0	0.328	0.655
32	Alb	30	46	9	12	25	30	74	-44	0	0.652	0.652
33	Isl	27	122	5	17	100	65	414	-349	0	0.221	0.533
	Total	**13107**	**11980**	**4878**	**2224**	**4878**	**18530**	**18530**	**0**	**1127**	**1.094**	**3.093**

1984-85

Pos'n	Cnty	Ave	Pts	P	W	D	L	F	A	Diff	B	No./T
1	Italy	11.000	44	29	18	2	9	44	27	17	6	4
2	USSR	10.000	40	28	15	6	7	49	23	26	4	4
3	England	9.428	66	42	24	10	8	75	27	48	8	7
4	Greece	7.666	23	18	7	6	5	19	19	0	3	3
5	Austria	7.500	30	21	11	4	6	40	32	8	4	4
6	W. Germany	7.166	43	30	18	4	8	50	30	20	3	6
7	Yugoslavia	5.600	28	24	12	2	10	42	38	4	2	5
8	Hungary	5.500	22	18	8	3	7	23	23	0	3	4
9	Belgium	4.400	22	20	9	4	7	30	27	3	0	5
10	France	4.000	20	20	5	8	7	29	31	-2	2	5
–	E. Germany	4.000	16	16	6	3	7	27	26	1	1	4
12	Spain	3.833	23	22	9	2	11	34	30	4	3	6
13	Czechoslovakia	3.800	19	20	6	6	8	23	27	-4	1	5
14	Netherlands	3.750	15	16	5	4	7	25	13	12	1	4
15	Bulgaria	3.500	14	14	5	4	5	21	25	-4	0	4
–	Romania	3.500	14	14	6	2	6	12	13	-1	0	4
17	Scotland	3.200	16	18	7	2	9	30	29	1	0	5
18	Poland	3.000	12	14	6	0	8	16	20	-4	0	4
–	Sweden	3.000	12	12	5	1	6	25	14	11	1	4
–	Switzerland	3.000	12	14	5	2	7	21	21	0	0	4
21	Portugal	2.750	11	12	5	1	6	16	23	-7	0	4
22	Denmark	2.000	8	10	3	2	5	10	14	-4	0	4
–	Wales	2.000	2	4	1	0	3	4	7	-3	0	1
24	Rep. of Ireland	1.666	5	6	1	3	2	4	6	-2	0	3
25	N. Ireland	1.333	4	8	0	4	4	7	12	-5	0	3
–	Malta	1.333	4	8	2	0	6	3	19	-16	0	3
27	Cyprus	1.000	3	6	1	1	4	7	19	-12	0	3
–	Norway	1.000	3	6	1	1	4	8	18	-10	0	3
–	Turkey	1.000	3	6	1	1	4	3	11	-8	0	3
30	Luxembourg	0.666	2	6	0	2	4	1	36	-35	0	3
31	Finland	0.333	1	6	0	1	5	2	18	-16	0	3
–	Iceland	0.333	1	6	0	1	5	5	21	-16	0	3
33	Albania	0.000	0	2	0	0	2	0	6	-6	0	1
	Total		**538**	**496**	**202**	**92**	**202**	**705**	**705**	**0**	**42**	**2.843**

1955-56 to 1984-85

Pos'n	Cnty	Ave	Pts	P	W	D	L	F	A	Diff	B	No./T
1	England	8.806	1365	926	500	201	225	1782	927	855	164	155
2	W. Germany	7.880	1253	906	476	165	265	1825	1138	687	136	159
3	Spain	7.486	1123	825	415	154	256	1542	1016	526	139	150
4	Italy	7.133	1013	748	370	158	220	1174	770	404	115	142
5	USSR	6.144	424	314	163	66	85	483	305	178	32	69
6	Netherlands	5.990	635	496	244	90	162	955	612	343	57	106
7	Scotland	5.830	688	558	264	101	193	972	716	256	59	118
8	Belgium	5.372	634	531	244	91	196	874	699	175	55	118
9	Hungary	5.197	499	428	194	67	167	773	630	143	44	96
10	Yugoslavia	4.959	610	546	229	97	220	906	793	113	55	123
11	Portugal	4.903	559	481	206	102	173	770	620	150	45	114
12	E. Germany	4.828	478	429	178	89	162	648	568	80	33	99
13	Czechoslovakia	4.737	469	399	181	75	143	637	521	116	32	99
14	France	3.852	443	429	162	87	180	650	645	5	32	115
15	Poland	3.722	309	305	116	60	129	435	472	-37	17	83
16	Wales	3.625	87	86	29	23	34	125	104	21	6	24
17	Bulgaria	3.340	304	315	118	52	145	466	495	-29	16	91
18	Romania	3.225	300	319	117	56	146	412	492	-80	10	93
19	Austria	3.164	307	336	107	70	159	438	547	-109	23	97
20	Switzerland	2.844	310	357	115	61	181	538	683	-145	19	109
21	Sweden	2.779	239	261	83	60	118	344	433	-89	13	86
22	Greece	2.727	240	263	91	48	124	305	451	-146	10	88
23	Turkey	1.974	156	219	58	34	127	210	414	-204	6	79
24	Denmark	1.760	169	257	60	44	153	330	572	-242	5	96
25	Albania	1.428	30	46	9	12	25	30	74	-44	0	21
26	Norway	1.259	97	184	35	26	123	182	472	-290	1	77
27	Rep. of Ireland	1.186	89	182	28	33	121	151	449	-298	0	75
28	N. Ireland	1.100	77	162	22	31	109	157	452	-295	2	70
29	Finland	0.816	49	138	16	16	106	108	443	-335	1	60
30	Cyprus	0.703	38	116	12	14	90	76	435	-359	0	54
31	Malta	0.661	43	138	16	11	111	67	490	-423	0	65
32	Luxembourg	0.573	43	158	15	13	130	100	678	-578	0	75
33	Iceland	0.473	27	122	5	17	100	65	414	-349	0	57
	Total		**13107**	**11980**	**4878**	**2224**	**4878**	**18530**	**18530**	**0**	**1127**	**3.093**

Football's European Tragedy

May 29th 1985 was, and remains, the saddest day in the history of European Cup football. The day that 39 people, most of them Italian, suffocated and died at the Heysel stadium in Brussels prior to the Champions' Cup final between Liverpool and Juventus.

Rampaging, drunken English hooligans were the cause of the disaster. They it was who charged and attacked the innocent Juventus supporters in the Z sector of the stadium, forcing them back against a wall, which then collapsed under the pressure, trapping and crushing the victims to death. But there were other parties responsible too. UEFA, for their absurd ticket allocation, for their ill-advised choice of venue; the Belgian police, for their unwillingness to intervene, their failure to appreciate the gravity of the situation. English football, however, was to pay the heaviest price. The Football Association swiftly moved to withdraw English teams from the following year's competition. UEFA, in turn, banned them indefinitely, adding three years on to the sentence for Liverpool. The ban would ultimately last five long years; in Liverpool's case, six.

As for the result of the Heysel final itself, that was of only incidental relevance in view of what had gone before. The match did take place the same evening. Arguments raged afterwards as to whether it was the right or wrong thing to do in the circumstances, but few who watched the match truly cared about the outcome.

Prior to the tragedy, the whole continent had been looking forward to the meeting of what were generally recognised to be the two finest teams in Europe. It was the perfect final, the Champions' Cup holders against the Cup-winners' Cup holders, the best of England against the best of Italy. But when the two teams finally stepped out on to the pitch, ringed now by heavily armed special policemen, no one was in the mood for football. In another year, on another day, Liverpool would have been up in arms in protest against the penalty decision which was erroneously awarded against them after 57 minutes and which produced the winning goal for Frenchman Michel Platini. But on this sad, sinister occasion there was not a flicker of dissent from the Liverpool players, resigned perhaps to the fate that awaited them in the days to come.

Juventus's triumph would enable them to go down in the record books as the first team to win all three European trophies. But, with 39 of their supporters dead or dying, this was not a night for celebration. Nothing, in fact, could have been farther from the minds of anyone that night.

The subsequent blanket ban on English clubs was particularly cruel on Liverpool's Merseyside rivals, Everton, whose supporters had behaved in exemplary fashion two weeks earlier at the European Cup-winners' Cup final in Rotterdam. Everton had just won the English First Division championship for the first time and were looking forward to taking part in the Champions' Cup with a team, managed by Howard Kendall, that was clearly going places. In fact they would win the Football League title a second time in 1987, only to be deprived of their Champions' Cup place once again with the European ban still in force.

But at least Everton bowed out of the European scene with their first victory. They were far and away the best side in the Cup-winners' Cup. They reached the final undefeated, striking peak form in the semi-finals against Bayern Munich. Bayern had knocked out the previous season's Champions' Cup runners-up, Roma, with victories home and away in the previous round, but Everton became the fourth English side to knock them out of Europe in five seasons when they drew 0-0 in Munich and then destroyed them with a brilliant second-half performance in the second leg at Goodison Park to reach their first European final.

Rapid Vienna were Everton's opponents in Rotterdam. Like Everton, they had never previously been in a European final. In fact, only one Austrian team had ever achieved that feat – Austria Vienna in the same tournament seven years earlier – so their presence was a considerable surprise. According to many, however, Rapid had no right to be there in Rotterdam, no right even to have reached the quarter-finals.

Rapid's second-round tie against Celtic was steeped in controversy. Rapid won the first leg soundly enough, 3-1 in Vienna, but in the return, at Celtic Park, there was menace in the air. As Rapid resorted to kicking opponents and wasting as much time as they could, Celtic played all the football to win the game 3-0. But one incident clouded the issue. The Celtic fans, incensed by Rapid's attitude, grew angry. A bottle flew onto the field of play and suddenly one of the Rapid players went down, as if hit. There was a long stoppage as the player was treated, then carried from the field, bandage wrapped around his head. Had the bottle struck him? Television evidence said no, but UEFA, astonishingly, said yes and ordered a replay, not in Glasgow, but in Manchester, at Old Trafford. Rapid went on to win that game, 1-0, but there was no holding the Celtic fans' rage, and two idiotic supporters escaped onto the field to deliver blows to Austrian players. Celtic were out of the competition, and those acts of hooliganism forced them to play their next European match behind closed doors.

So Rapid survived, went on to beat Dynamo Dresden and Dinamo Moscow, and faced Everton in Rotterdam. They had two fine strikers in Pacult and the ageing Krankl, but Everton were a team with international class in every department – from goalkeeper Southall, through centre-back Ratcliffe and midfielders Reid and Sheedy to the twin Scottish spearhead of Graeme Sharp and Andy Gray. They were the favourites, and although it took them almost an hour to score the first goal, through Gray, they were always in control. Trevor Steven and Kevin Sheedy scored further goals for Everton, with Krankl netting the Austrians' consolation. Remarkably, Everton's victory was the first English success in the Cup-winners' Cup for all of 14 years.

Real Madrid, meanwhile, had gone 19 long years without a European trophy. But that came to an end in 1984-85 with victory in the UEFA Cup. For the first time in years Real now had a team that could justly stand comparison with some of its great sides of the past. Santillana, the centre-forward, was still there, but he had been joined in attack by the precocious young forward, Emilio Butragueño. In midfield, there was another highly-rated newcomer, Míchel, and in defence, alongside veterans Stielike and Camacho, the promising Manuel Sanchis.

This season saw Real pull off some remarkable comebacks in the Bernabéu. The most amazing escape act came in the third round against Anderlecht. Beaten 3-0 in Brussels, they crushed the Belgians 6-1 in Madrid, with Butragueño scoring a hat-trick. Inter Milan, too, went the same way in the semi-final. Winners 2-0 at home, they went down 3-0 in Madrid. There was, however, a change of script for the final, against the surprising Hungarian side Videoton, who had earlier eliminated Manchester United on penalties. With the first leg held in Hungary, Real might have been expected to continue with the submissive approach they had adopted in previous away legs. But in Székesfehérvár they went for the win, and got it, three goals to nil, with Míchel the star of the show. Now, the return was a formality and although Butragueño treated the Madrid public to another virtuoso performance, he was the only person in the stadium who really seemed to care. Videoton, despite having little or none of the play, won the match, 1-0. It no doubt restored their pride, but, in terms of the overall scoreline, it mattered little. Real, in the first leg, had already won the Cup.

Steaua Bucharest

Dinamo Kiev

Real Madrid

1985 – 1986

First Round

Team 1	Cnty	Team 2	Cnty	1st leg	2nd leg	Agg
Vejle BK	Den	Steaua Bucharest	Rom	1-1	1-4	2-5
FC Kuusysi Lahti	Fin	Sarajevo	Yug	2-1	2-1	4-2
Girondins Bordeaux	Fra	Fenerbahçe	Tur	2-3	0-0	2-3
Honvéd	Hun	Shamrock Rovers	Irl	2-0	3-1	5-1
Linfield	Nir	Servette	Sui	2-2	1-2	3-4
IA Akranes	Isl	Aberdeen	Sco	1-3	1-4	2-7
Verona	Ita	PAOK Salonika	Gre	3-1	2-1	5-2
Jeunesse Esch	Lux	Juventus	Ita	0-5	0-4	0-9
Rabat Ajax	Mlt	Omonia Nicosia	Cyp	0-5	0-5	0-10
Górnik Zabrze	Pol	Bayern Munich	FRG	1-2	1-4	2-6
FC Porto	Por	Ajax	Ned	2-0	0-0	2-0
IFK Gothenburg	Swe	Trakia Plovdiv	Bul	3-2	2-1	5-3
Sparta Prague	Tch	Barcelona	Esp	1-2	1-0	2-2
Zenit Leningrad	URS	Vålerengen SIF	Nor	2-0	2-0	4-0
Dynamo Berlin	GDR	Austria Vienna	Aut	0-2	1-2	1-4

	Pts	P	W	D	L	F	A	Diff	Goals/P
Total	60	30	26	8	26	97	97	0	3.233

Second Round

Anderlecht	Bel	Omonia Nicosia	Cyp	1-0	3-1	4-1
Barcelona	Esp	FC Porto	Por	2-0	1-3	3-3
Honvéd	Hun	Steaua Bucharest	Rom	1-0	1-4	2-4
Verona	Ita	Juventus	Ita	0-0	0-2	0-2
Bayern Munich	FRG	Austria Vienna	Aut	4-2	3-3	7-5
IFK Gothenburg	Swe	Fenerbahçe	Tur	4-0	1-2	5-2
Servette	Sui	Aberdeen	Sco	0-0	0-1	0-1
Zenit Leningrad	URS	FC Kuusysi Lahti	Fin	2-1	1-3	3-4

	Pts	P	W	D	L	F	A	Diff	Goals/P
Total	32	16	13	6	13	46	46	0	2.875

Quarter Finals

Aberdeen	Sco	IFK Gothenburg	Swe	2-2	0-0	2-2
Barcelona	Esp	Juventus	Ita	1-0	1-1	2-1
Bayern Munich	FRG	Anderlecht	Bel	2-1	0-2	2-3
Steaua Bucharest	Rom	FC Kuusysi Lahti	Fin	0-0	1-0	1-0

	Pts	P	W	D	L	F	A	Diff	Goals/P
Total	16	8	4	8	4	13	13	0	1.625

Semi Finals

Anderlecht	Bel	Steaua Bucharest	Rom	1-0	0-3	1-3
IFK Gothenburg	Swe	Barcelona	Esp	3-0	0-3	3-3

	Pts	P	W	D	L	F	A	Diff	Goals/P
Total	8	4	4	0	4	10	10	0	2.500

Final

Steaua Bucharest	Rom	Barcelona	Esp	0-0	0-0

	Pts	P	W	D	L	F	A	Diff	Goals/P
Total	2	1	0	2	0	0	0	0	0.000

	Pts	P	W	D	L	F	A	Diff	Goals/P
Total	118	59	47	24	47	166	166	0	2.814

Pos'n	Club	Cnty	Pts	P	W	D	L	F	A	Diff	B	Pts/P	F/P
1	Steaua Bucharest	Rom	14	9	4	3	2	13	5	8	3	1.556	1.444
2	Barcelona	Esp	13	9	4	2	3	10	9	1	3	1 444	1.111
3	IFK Gothenburg	Swe	12	8	4	2	2	15	10	5	2	1.500	1.875
4	Aberdeen	Sco	10	6	3	3	0	10	4	6	1	1.667	1.667
5	Bayern Munich	FRG	10	6	4	1	1	15	10	5	1	1.667	2.500
6	Anderlecht	Bel	10	6	4	0	2	8	6	2	2	1.667	1.333
7	Juventus	Ita	9	6	3	2	1	12	2	10	1	1.500	2.000
8	FC Kuusysi Lahti	Fin	8	6	3	1	2	8	6	2	1	1.333	1.333
9	Zenit Leningrad	URS	6	4	3	0	1	7	4	3	0	1.500	1.750
10	Honvéd	Hun	6	4	3	0	1	7	5	2	0	1.500	1.750
11	FC Porto	Por	5	4	2	1	1	5	3	2	0	1.250	1.250
12	Austria Vienna	Aut	5	4	2	1	1	9	8	1	0	1.250	2.250
13	Verona	Ita	5	4	2	1	1	5	4	1	0	1.250	1.250
14	Fenerbahçe	Tur	5	4	2	1	1	5	7	-2	0	1.250	1.250
15	Omonia Nicosie	Cyp	4	4	2	0	2	11	4	7	0	1.000	2.750
16	Servette	Sui	4	4	1	2	1	4	4	0	0	1.000	1.000
17	Sparta Prague	Tch	2	2	1	0	1	2	2	0	0	1.000	1.000
18	Linfield	Nir	1	2	0	1	1	3	4	-1	0	0.500	1.500
19	Girondins Bordeaux	Fra	1	2	0	1	1	2	3	-1	0	0.500	1.000
20	Ajax	Ned	1	2	0	1	1	0	2	-2	0	0.500	0.000
21	Vejle BK	Den	1	2	0	1	1	2	5	-3	0	0.500	1.000
22	Trakia Plovdiv	Bul	0	2	0	0	2	3	5	-2	0	0.000	1.500
23	Sarajevo	Yug	0	2	0	0	2	2	4	-2	0	0.000	1.000
24	PAOK Salonika	Gre	0	2	0	0	2	2	5	-3	0	0.000	1.000
25	Dynamo Berlin	GDR	0	2	0	0	2	1	4	-3	0	0.000	0.500
26	Górmik Zabrze	Pol	0	2	0	0	2	2	6	-4	0	0.000	1.000
27	Shamrock Rovers	Irl	0	2	0	0	2	1	5	-4	0	0.000	0.500
28	Vålerengen SIF	Nor	0	2	0	0	2	0	4	-4	0	0.000	0.000
29	IA Akranes	Isl	0	2	0	0	2	2	7	-5	0	0.000	1.000
30	Jeunesse Esch	Lux	0	2	0	0	2	0	9	-9	0	0.000	0.000
31	Rabat Ajax	Mlt	0	2	0	0	2	0	10	-10	0	0.000	0.000
	Total		**132**	**118**	**47**	**24**	**47**	**166**	**166**	**0**	**14**	**1.119**	**2.814**

First Round

Team 1	Cnty	Team 2	Cnty	1st leg	2nd leg	Agg
Rapid Vienna	Aut	Tatabánya	Hun	5-0	1-1	6-1
Cercle Bruges	Bel	Dynamo Dresden	GDR	3-2	1-2	4-4
AEL Limassol	Cyp	Dukla Prague	Tch	2-2	0-4	2-6
Lyngby BK	Den	Galway United	Irl	1-0	3-2	4-2
Atlético Madrid	Esp	Celtic	Sco	1-1	2-1	3-2
HJK Helsinki	Fin	Flamurtari Vlorë	Alb	3-2	2-1	5-3
Monaco	Fra	Universitatea Craiova	Rom	2-0	0-3	2-3
Larissa	Gre	Sampdoria	Ita	1-1	0-1	1-2
Fram Reykjavik	Isl	Glentoran	Nir	3-1	0-1	3-2
Zurrieq	Mlt	Bayer Uerdingen	FRG	0-3	0-9	0-12
Utrecht	Ned	Dinamo Kiev	URS	2-1	1-4	3-5
AIK	Swe	Red Boys Differdange	Lux	8-0	5-0	13-0
Galatasaray	Tur	Widzew Lódź	Pol	1-0	1-2	2-2
Red Star Belgrade	Yug	Aarau	Sui	2-0	2-2	4-2

	Pts	P	W	D	L	F	A	Diff	Goals/P
Total	60	30	23	14	23	100	100	0	3.333

Second Round

Rapid Vienna	Aut	Fram Reykjavik	Isl	3-0	1-2	4-2
Lyngby BK	Den	Red Star Belgrade	Yug	2-2	1-3	3-5
HJK Helsinki	Fin	Dynamo Dresden	GDR	1-0	2-7	3-7
Bangor City	Wal	Atlético Madrid	Esp	0-2	0-1	0-3
Benfica	Por	Sampdoria	Ita	2-0	0-1	2-1
Bayer Uerdingen	FRG	Galatasaray	Tur	2-0	1-1	3-1
Universitatea Craiova	Rom	Dinamo Kiev	URS	2-2	0-3	2-5
Dukla Prague	Tch	AIK	Swe	1-0	2-2	3-2

	Pts	P	W	D	L	F	A	Diff	Goals/P
Total	32	16	12	8	12	46	46	0	2.875

Quarter Finals

Rapid Vienna	Aut	Dinamo Kiev	URS	1-4	1-5	2-9
Dukla Prague	Tch	Benfica	Por	1-0	1-2	2-2
Red Star Belgrade	Yug	Atlético Madrid	Esp	0-2	1-1	1-3
Dynamo Dresden	GDR	Bayer Uerdingen	FRG	2-0	3-7	5-7

	Pts	P	W	D	L	F	A	Diff	Goals/P
Total	16	8	7	2	7	31	31	0	3.875

Semi Finals

Atlético Madrid	Esp	Bayer Uerdingen	FRG	1-0	3-2	4-2
Dinamo Kiev	URS	Dukla Prague	Tch	3-0	1-1	4-1

	Pts	P	W	D	L	F	A	Diff	Goals/P
Total	8	4	3	2	3	11	11	0	2.750

Final

Dinamo Kiev	URS	Atlético Madrid	Esp	3-0	3-0

	Pts	P	W	D	L	F	A	Diff	Goals/P
Total	2	1	1	0	1	3	3	0	3.000

	Pts	P	W	D	L	F	A	Diff	Goals/P
Total	118	59	46	26	46	191	191	0	3.237

Pos'n	Club	Cnty	Pts	P	W	D	L	F	A	Diff	B	Pts/P	F/P
1	Dinamo Kiev	URS	17	9	6	2	1	26	8	18	3	1.889	2.889
2	Atlético Madrid	Esp	17	9	6	2	1	13	8	5	3	1.889	1.444
3	Bayer Uerdingen	FRG	11	8	4	1	3	24	10	14	2	1.375	3.000
4	Dulka Prague	Tch	11	8	3	3	2	12	10	2	2	1.375	1.500
5	Red Star Belgrade	Yug	8	6	2	3	1	10	8	2	1	1.333	1.667
6	Dynamo Dresden	GDR	7	6	3	0	3	16	14	2	1	1.167	2.667
7	Rapid Vienna	Aut	6	6	2	1	3	12	12	0	1	1.000	2.000
8	HJK Helsinki	Fin	6	4	3	0	1	8	10	-2	0	1.500	2.000
9	AIK	Swe	5	4	2	1	1	15	3	12	0	1.250	3.750
10	Benfica	Por	5	4	2	0	2	4	3	1	1	1.250	1.000
11	Lyngby BK	Den	5	4	2	1	1	7	7	0	0	1.250	1.750
12	Sampdoria	Ita	5	4	2	1	1	3	3	0	0	1.250	0.750
13	Fram Reykjavik	Isl	4	4	2	0	2	5	6	-1	0	1.000	1.250
14	Universitatea Craiova	Rom	3	4	1	1	2	5	7	-2	0	0.750	1.250
15	Galatasaray	Tur	3	4	1	1	2	3	5	-2	0	0.750	0.750
16	Cercle Bruges	Bel	2	2	1	0	1	4	4	0	0	1.000	2.000
17	Widzew Lódź	Pol	2	2	1	0	1	2	2	0	0	1.000	1.000
18	Fredrikstad FK	Nor	2	2	0	2	0	1	1	0	0	1.000	0.500
19	Monaco	Fra	2	2	1	0	1	2	3	-1	0	1.000	1.000
–	Glentoran	Nir	2	2	1	0	1	2	3	-1	0	1.000	1.000
21	Utrecht	Ned	2	2	1	0	1	3	5	-2	0	1.000	1.500
22	Bangor City	Wal	2	4	0	2	2	1	4	-3	0	0.500	0.250
23	Celtic	Sco	1	2	0	1	1	2	3	-1	0	0.500	1.000
24	Larissa	Gre	1	2	0	1	1	1	2	-1	0	0.500	0.500
25	Aarau	Sui	1	2	0	1	1	2	4	-2	0	0.500	1.000
26	AEL Limassol	Cyp	1	2	0	1	1	2	6	-4	0	0.500	1.000
27	Tatabánya	Hun	1	2	0	1	1	1	6	-5	0	0.500	0.500
28	Flamutari Vlorë	Alb	0	2	0	0	2	3	5	-2	0	0.000	1.500
29	Galway United	Irl	0	2	0	0	2	2	4	-2	0	0.000	1.000
30	Zurrieq	Mlt	0	2	0	0	2	0	12	-12	0	0.000	0.000
31	Red Boys Differdange	Lux	0	2	0	0	2	0	13	-13	0	0.000	0.000
	Total		**132**	**118**	**46**	**26**	**46**	**191**	**191**	**0**	**14**	**1.119**	**3.237**

First Round

Team 1	Cnty	Team 2	Cnty	1st leg	2nd leg	Agg
Dinamo Tirana	Alb	Hamrun Spartans	Mlt	1-0	0-0	1-0
Linzer ASK	Aut	Banik Ostrava	Tch	2-0	1-0	3-0
FC Liège	Bel	FC Tirol	Aut	1-0	3-1	4-1
Waregem	Bel	AGF Aarhus	Den	5-2	1-0	6-2
Pirin Blagoevgrad	Bul	Hammarby IF	Swe	1-3	0-4	1-7
Apoel Nicosia	Cyp	Lokomotiv Sofia	Bul	2-2	2-4	4-6
Rangers	Sco	Osasuna	Esp	1-0	0-2	1-2
Bohemians	Irl	Dundee United	Sco	2-5	2-2	4-7
Athletic Bilbao	Esp	Besiktas	Tur	4-1	1-0	5-1
Auxerre	Fra	AC Milan	Ita	3-1	0-3	3-4
AEK Athens	Gre	Real Madrid	Esp	1-0	0-5	1-5
Rába ETO	Hun	Bohemians Prague	Tch	3-1	1-4	4-5
Videoton	Hun	Malmö FF	Swe	1-0	2-3	3-3
Coleraine	Nir	Lokomotive Leipzig	GDR	1-1	0-5	1-6
Valur Reykjavik	Isl	Nantes	Fra	2-1	0-3	2-4
Inter Milan	Ita	St-Gallen	Sui	5-1	0-0	5-1
Torino	Ita	Panathinaikos	Gre	2-1	1-1	3-2
Avenir Beggen	Lux	PSV Eindhoven	Ned	0-2	0-4	0-6
Sparta Rotterdam	Ned	Hamburg	FRG	2-0	0-2	2-2
Legia Warsaw	Pol	IL Viking	Nor	3-0	1-1	4-1
Sporting Lisbon	Por	Feyenoord	Ned	3-1	1-2	4-3
Portimonense	Por	Partizan Belgrade	Yug	1-0	0-4	1-4
Boavista	Por	Club Bruges	Bel	4-3	1-3	5-6
Cologne	FRG	Sporting Gijón	Esp	0-0	2-1	2-1
Bor. Mönchengladbach	FRG	Lech Poznań	Pol	1-1	2-0	3-1
Dinamo Bucharest	Rom	Vardar Skoplje	Yug	2-1	0-1	2-2
Neuchâtel Xamax	Sui	Sportul Studentesc Bucharest	Rom	3-0	4-4	7-4
Prague Slavia	Tch	St. Mirren	Sco	1-0	0-3	1-3
Spartak Moscow	URS	TPS Turku	Fin	1-0	3-1	4-1
Chernomorets Odessa	URS	Werder Bremen	FRG	2-1	2-3	4-4
Hajduk Split	Yug	Metz	Fra	5-1	2-2	7-3
Wismut Aue	GDR	Dnepr Dnepropetrovsk	URS	1-3	1-2	2-5

	Pts	P	W	D	L	F	A	Diff	Goals/P
Total	128	64	53	22	53	201	201	0	3.141

Second Round

Dinamo Tirana	Alb	Sporting Lisbon	Por	0-0	0-1	0-1
Linzer ASK	Aut	Inter Milan	Ita	1-0	0-4	1-4
Waregem	Bel	Osasuna	Esp	2-0	1-2	3-2
Lokomotiv Sofia	Bul	Neuchâtel Xamax	Sui	1-1	0-0	1-1
Dundee United	Sco	Vardar Skoplje	Yug	2-0	1-1	3-1
Athletic Bilbao	Esp	FC Liège	Bel	1-0	3-1	4-1
Real Madrid	Esp	Chernomorets Odessa	URS	2-1	0-0	2-1
Videoton	Hun	Legia Warsaw	Pol	0-1	1-1	1-2
AC Milan	Ita	Lokomotive Leipzig	GDR	2-0	1-3	3-3
Torino	Ita	Hajduk Split	Yug	1-1	1-3	2-4
PSV Eindhoven	Ned	Dnepr Dnepropetrovsk	URS	2-2	0-1	2-3
Sparta Rotterdam	Ned	Bor. Mönchengladbach	FRG	1-1	1-5	2-6
Cologne	FRG	Bohemians Prague	Tch	4-0	4-2	8-2
Hammarby IF	Swe	St. Mirren	Sco	3-3	2-1	5-4
Spartak Moscow	URS	Club Bruges	Bel	1-0	3-1	4-1
Partizan Belgrade	Yug	Nantes	Fra	1-1	0-4	1-5

	Pts	P	W	D	L	F	A	Diff	Goals/P
Total	64	32	21	22	21	83	83	0	2.594

Third Round

Waregem	Bel	AC Milan	Ita	1-1	2-1	3-2
Dundee United	Sco	Neuchâtel Xamax	Sui	2-1	1-3	3-4
Athletic Bilbao	Esp	Sporting Lisbon	Por	2-1	0-3	2-4
Inter Milan	Ita	Legia Warsaw	Pol	0-0	1-0	1-0
Bor. Mönchengladbach	FRG	Real Madrid	Esp	5-1	0-4	5-5
Hammarby IF	Swe	Cologne	FRG	2-1	1-3	3-4
Dnepr Dnepropetrovsk	URS	Hajduk Split	Yug	0-1	0-2	0-3
Spartak Moscow	URS	Nantes	Fra	0-1	1-1	1-2

	Pts	P	W	D	L	F	A	Diff	Goals/P
Total	32	16	13	6	13	42	42	0	2.625

Quarter Finals

Real Madrid	Esp	Neuchâtel Xamax	Sui	3-0	0-2	3-2
Inter Milan	Ita	Nantes	Fra	3-0	3-3	6-3
Sporting Lisbon	Por	Cologne	FRG	1-1	0-2	1-3
Hajduk Split	Yug	Waregem	Bel	1-0	0-1	1-1

	Pts	P	W	D	L	F	A	Diff	Goals/P
Total	16	8	6	4	6	20	20	0	2.500

Semi Finals

Inter Milan	Ita	Real Madrid	Esp	3-1	1-5	4-6
Cologne	FRG	Waregem	Bel	4-0	3-3	7-3

	Pts	P	W	D	L	F	A	Diff	Goals/P
Total	8	4	3	2	3	20	20	0	5.000

Final

Real Madrid	Esp	Cologne	FRG	5-1	0-2	5-3

	Pts	P	W	D	L	F	A	Diff	Goals/P
Total	4	2	2	0	2	8	8	0	4.000

	Pts	P	W	D	L	F	A	Diff	Goals/P
Total	252	126	98	56	98	374	374	0	2.968

Pos'n	Club	Cnty	Pts	P	W	D	L	F	A	Diff	B	Pts/P	F/P
1	Cologne	FRG	20	12	7	3	2	27	15	12	3	1.667	2.250
2	Real Madrid	Esp	16	12	6	1	5	26	16	10	3	1.333	2.167
3	Inter Milan	Ita	15	10	5	3	2	20	11	9	2	1.500	2.000
4	Waregem	Bel	14	10	5	2	3	16	14	2	2	1.400	1.600
5	Hajduk Split	Yug	13	8	5	2	1	15	6	9	1	1.625	1.875
6	Athletic Bilbao	Esp	10	6	5	0	1	11	6	5	0	1.667	1.833
7	Nantes	Fra	10	8	3	3	2	14	10	4	1	1.250	1.750
8	Neuchâtel Xamax	Sui	10	8	3	3	2	14	11	3	1	1.250	1.750
9	Hammarby IF	Swe	9	6	4	1	1	15	9	6	0	1.500	2.500
10	Spartak Moscow	URS	9	6	4	1	1	9	4	5	0	1.500	1.500
11	Sporting Lisbon	Por	9	8	3	2	3	10	8	2	1	1.125	1.250
12	Bor. Mönchengladbach	FRG	8	6	3	2	1	14	8	6	0	1.333	2.333
13	Dundee United	Sco	8	6	3	2	1	13	9	4	0	1.333	2.167
14	Legia Warsaw	Pol	7	6	2	3	1	6	3	3	0	1.167	1.000
15	Dnepr Dnepropetrovsk	URS	7	6	3	1	2	8	7	1	0	1.167	1.333
16	Linzer ASK	Aut	6	4	3	0	1	4	4	0	0	1.500	1.000
17	Lokomotive Leipzig	GDR	5	4	2	1	1	9	4	5	0	1.250	2.250
18	PSV Eindhoven	Ned	5	4	2	1	1	8	3	5	0	1.250	2.000
19	Lokomotiv Sofia	Bul	5	4	1	3	0	7	5	2	0	1.250	1.750
20	AC Milan	Ita	5	6	2	1	3	9	9	0	0	0.833	1.500
21	FC Liège	Bel	4	4	2	0	2	5	5	0	0	1.000	1.250
22	Osasuna	Esp	4	4	2	0	2	4	4	0	0	1.000	1.000
23	Dinamo Tirana	Alb	4	4	1	2	1	1	1	0	0	1.000	0.250
24	Torino	Ita	4	4	1	2	1	5	6	-1	0	1.000	1.250
25	St. Mirren	Sco	3	4	1	1	2	7	6	1	0	0.750	1.750
26	Chernomorets Odessa	URS	3	4	1	1	2	5	6	-1	0	0.750	1.250
–	Partizan Belgrade	Yug	3	4	1	1	2	5	6	-1	0	0.750	1.250
28	Videoton	Hun	3	4	1	1	2	4	5	-1	0	0.750	1.000
29	Vardar Skoplje	Yug	3	4	1	1	2	3	5	-2	0	0.750	0.750
30	Sparta Rotterdam	Ned	3	4	1	1	2	4	8	-4	0	0.750	1.000
31	Werder Bremen	FRG	2	2	1	0	1	4	4	0	0	1.000	2.000
32	Malmö FF	Swe	2	2	1	0	1	3	3	0	0	1.000	1.500
33	Hamburg	FRG	2	2	1	0	1	2	2	0	0	1.000	1.000
–	Dinamo Bucharest	Rom	2	2	1	0	1	2	2	0	0	1.000	1.000
35	Boavista	Por	2	2	1	0	1	5	6	-1	0	1.000	2.500
36	Rába ETO	Hun	2	2	1	0	1	4	5	-1	0	1.000	2.000
37	Auxerre	Fra	2	2	1	0	1	3	4	-1	0	1.000	1.500
–	Feyenoord	Ned	2	2	1	0	1	3	4	-1	0	1.000	1.500
39	Rangers	Sco	2	2	1	0	1	1	2	-1	0	1.000	0.500
40	Club Bruges	Bel	2	4	1	0	3	7	9	-2	0	0.500	1.750
41	Valur Reykjavik	Isl	2	2	1	0	1	2	4	-2	0	1.000	1.000
42	Slavia Prague	Tch	2	2	1	0	1	1	3	-2	0	1.000	0.500
43	Poritimonense	Por	2	2	1	0	1	1	4	-3	0	1.000	0.500
44	AEK Athens	Gre	2	2	1	0	1	1	5	-4	0	1.000	0.500
45	Bohemians Prague	Tch	2	4	1	0	3	7	12	-5	0	0.500	1.750
46	Panathinaikos	Gre	1	2	0	1	1	2	3	-1	0	0.500	1.000
47	Sporting Gijón	Esp	1	2	0	1	1	1	2	-1	0	0.500	0.500
48	Hamrun Spartans	Mlt	1	2	0	1	1	0	1	-1	0	0.500	0.000
49	Apoel Nicosia	Cyp	1	2	0	1	1	4	6	-2	0	0.500	2.000
50	Lech Poznań	Pol	1	2	0	1	1	1	3	-2	0	0.500	0.500
51	Bohemians	Irl	1	2	0	1	1	4	7	-3	0	0.500	2.000
–	Sportul Studentesc Bucharest	Rom	1	2	0	1	1	4	7	-3	0	0.500	2.000
53	IL Viking	Nor	1	2	0	1	1	1	4	-3	0	0.500	0.500
54	Metz	Fra	1	2	0	1	1	3	7	-4	0	0.500	1.500
55	St-Gallen	Sui	1	2	0	1	1	1	5	-4	0	0.500	0.500
56	Coleraine	Nir	1	2	0	1	1	1	6	-5	0	0.500	0.500
57	Wismut Aue	RDA	0	2	0	0	2	2	5	-3	0	0.000	1.000
58	FC Tirol	Aut	0	2	0	0	2	1	4	-3	0	0.000	0.500
–	TPS Turku	Fin	0	2	0	0	2	1	4	-3	0	0.000	0.500
60	Banik Ostrava	Tch	0	2	0	0	2	0	3	-3	0	0.000	0.000
61	AGF Aarhus	Den	0	2	0	0	2	2	6	-4	0	0.000	1.000
62	Besiktas	Tur	0	2	0	0	2	1	5	-4	0	0.000	0.500
63	Pirin Blagoevgrad	Bul	0	2	0	0	2	1	7	-6	0	0.000	0.500
64	Avenir Beggen	Lux	0	2	0	0	2	0	6	-6	0	0.000	0.000
	Total		**266**	**252**	**98**	**56**	**98**	**374**	**374**	**0**	**14**	**1.056**	**2.968**

National Performances by Points

1985-86

Pos'n	Cnty	Pts	P	W	D	L	F	A	Diff	B	Pts/P	F/P
1	Esp	61	42	23	6	13	65	45	20	9	1.452	1.548
2	FRG	53	36	20	7	9	86	49	37	6	1.472	2.389
3	Ita	43	34	15	10	9	54	35	19	3	1.265	1.588
4	URS	42	29	17	5	7	55	29	26	3	1.448	1.897
5	Bel	32	26	13	2	11	40	38	2	4	1.231	1.538
6	Swe	28	20	11	4	5	48	25	23	2	1.400	2.400
7	Yug	27	24	9	7	8	35	29	6	2	1.125	1.458
8	Sco	24	20	8	7	5	33	24	9	1	1.200	1.650
9	Por	23	20	9	3	8	25	24	1	2	1.150	1.250
10	Rom	20	17	6	5	6	24	21	3	3	1.176	1.412
11	Aut	17	16	7	2	7	26	28	-2	1	1.063	1.625
12	Tch	17	18	6	3	9	22	30	-8	2	0.944	1.222
13	Fra	16	16	5	5	6	24	27	-3	1	1.000	1.500
14	Sui	16	16	4	7	5	21	24	-3	1	1.000	1.313
15	Fin	14	12	6	1	5	17	20	-3	1	1.167	1.417
16	Ned	13	14	5	3	6	18	22	-4	0	0.929	1.286
17	GDR	12	14	5	1	8	28	27	1	1	0.857	2.000
18	Hun	12	12	5	2	5	16	21	-5	0	1.000	1.333
19	Pol	10	12	3	4	5	11	14	-3	0	0.833	0.917
20	Tur	8	10	3	2	5	9	17	-8	0	0.800	0.900
21	Cyp	6	8	2	2	4	17	16	1	0	0.750	2.125
22	Den	6	8	2	2	4	11	18	-7	0	0.750	1.375
23	Isl	6	8	3	0	5	9	17	-8	0	0.750	1.125
24	Bul	5	8	1	3	4	11	17	-6	0	0.625	1.375
25	Alb	4	6	1	2	3	4	6	-2	0	0.667	0.667
26	Nir	4	6	1	2	3	6	13	-7	0	0.667	1.000
27	Gre	4	8	1	2	5	6	15	-9	0	0.500	0.750
28	Nor	3	6	0	3	3	2	9	-7	0	0.500	0.333
29	Wal	2	4	0	2	2	1	4	-3	0	0.500	0.250
30	Irl	1	6	0	1	5	7	16	-9	0	0.167	1.167
31	Mlt	1	6	0	1	5	0	23	-23	0	0.167	0.000
32	Lux	0	6	0	0	6	0	28	-28	0	0.000	0.000
	Total	**530**	**488**	**191**	**106**	**191**	**731**	**731**	**0**	**42**	**1.086**	**2.996**

1955-56 to 1985-86

1	Eng	1365	926	500	201	225	1782	927	855	164	1.474	1.924
2	FRG	1306	942	496	172	274	1911	1187	724	142	1.386	2.029
3	Esp	1184	867	438	160	269	1607	1061	546	148	1.366	1.854
4	Ita	1056	782	385	168	229	1228	805	423	118	1.350	1.570
5	Sco	712	578	272	108	198	1005	740	265	60	1.232	1.739
6	Bel	666	557	257	93	207	914	737	177	59	1.196	1.641
7	Ned	648	510	249	93	168	973	634	339	57	1.271	1.908
8	Yug	637	570	238	104	228	941	822	119	57	1.118	1.651
9	Por	582	501	215	105	181	795	644	151	47	1.162	1.587
10	Hun	511	440	199	69	172	789	651	138	44	1.161	1.793
11	GDR	490	443	183	90	170	676	595	81	34	1.106	1.526
12	Tch	486	417	187	78	152	659	551	108	34	1.165	1.580
13	URS	466	343	180	71	92	538	334	204	35	1.359	1.569
14	Fra	459	445	167	92	186	674	672	2	33	1.031	1.515
15	Sui	326	373	119	68	186	559	707	-148	20	0.874	1.499
16	Aut	324	352	114	72	166	464	575	-111	24	0.920	1.318
17	Rom	320	336	123	61	152	436	513	-77	13	0.952	1.298
18	Pol	319	317	119	64	134	446	486	-40	17	1.006	1.407
19	Bul	309	323	119	55	149	477	512	-35	16	0.957	1.477
20	Swe	267	281	94	64	123	392	458	-66	15	0.950	1.395
21	Gre	244	271	92	50	129	311	466	-155	10	0.900	1.148
22	Den	175	265	62	46	157	341	590	-249	5	0.660	1.287
23	Tur	164	229	61	36	132	219	431	-212	6	0.716	0.956
24	Nor	100	190	35	29	126	184	481	-297	1	0.526	0.968
25	Irl	90	188	28	34	126	158	465	-307	0	0.479	0.840
26	Wal	89	90	29	25	36	126	108	18	6	0.989	1.400
27	Nir	81	168	23	33	112	163	465	-302	2	0.482	0.970
28	Fin	63	150	22	17	111	125	463	-338	2	0.420	0.833
29	Cyp	44	124	14	16	94	93	451	-358	0	0.355	0.750
30	Mlt	44	144	16	12	116	67	513	-446	0	0.306	0.465
31	Lux	43	164	15	13	136	100	706	-606	0	0.262	0.610
32	Alb	34	52	10	14	28	34	80	-46	0	0.654	0.654
33	Isl	33	130	8	17	105	74	431	-357	0	0.254	0.569
	Total	**13637**	**12468**	**5069**	**2330**	**5069**	**19261**	**19261**	**0**	**1169**	**1.094**	**3.090**

1985-86

Pos'n	Cnty	Ave	Pts	P	W	D	L	F	A	Diff	B	No./T
1	Spain	10.166	61	42	23	6	13	65	45	20	9	6
2	W. Germany	8.833	53	36	20	7	9	86	49	37	6	6
3	USSR	8.400	42	29	17	5	7	55	29	26	3	5
4	Italy	7.166	43	34	15	10	9	54	35	19	3	6
5	Sweden	7.000	28	20	11	4	5	48	25	23	2	4
6	Belgium	6.400	32	26	13	2	11	40	38	2	4	5
7	Yugoslavia	5.400	27	24	9	7	8	35	29	6	22	5
8	Romania	5.000	20	17	6	5	6	24	21	3	3	4
9	Scotland	4.800	24	20	8	7	5	33	24	9	1	5
10	Finland	4.666	14	12	6	1	5	17	20	-3	1	3
11	Portugal	4.600	23	20	9	3	8	25	24	1	2	5
12	Austria	4.250	17	16	7	2	7	26	28	-2	1	4
13	Switzerland	4.000	16	16	4	7	5	21	24	-3	1	4
14	Czechoslovakia	3.400	17	18	6	3	9	22	30	-8	2	5
15	France	3.200	16	16	5	5	6	24	27	-3	1	5
16	Hungary	3.000	12	12	5	2	5	16	21	-5	0	4
–	E. Germany	3.000	12	14	5	1	8	28	27	1	1	4
18	Turkey	2.666	8	10	3	2	5	9	17	-8	0	3
19	Netherlands	2.600	13	14	5	3	6	18	22	-4	0	5
20	Poland	2.500	10	12	3	4	5	11	14	-3	0	4
21	Albania	2.000	4	6	1	2	3	4	6	-2	0	2
–	Cyprus	2.000	6	8	2	2	4	17	16	1	0	3
–	Denmark	2.000	6	8	2	2	4	11	18	-7	0	3
–	Wales	2.000	2	4	0	2	2	1	4	-3	0	1
–	Iceland	2.000	6	8	3	0	5	9	17	-8	0	3
26	Bulgaria	1.666	5	8	1	3	4	11	17	-6	0	3
27	N. Ireland	1.333	4	6	1	2	3	6	13	-7	0	3
28	Greece	1.000	4	8	1	2	5	6	15	-9	0	4
–	Norway	1.000	3	6	0	3	3	2	9	-7	0	3
30	Rep. of Ireland	0.333	1	6	0	1	5	7	16	-9	0	3
–	Malta	0.333	1	6	0	1	5	0	23	-23	0	3
32	Luxembourge	0.000	0	6	0	0	6	0	28	-28	0	3
	Total		**530**	**488**	**191**	**106**	**191**	**731**	**731**	**0**	**42**	**2.996**

1955-56 to 1985-86

Pos'n	Cnty	Ave	Pts	P	W	D	L	F	A	Diff	B	No./T
1	England	8.806	1365	926	500	201	225	1782	927	855	164	155
2	W. Germany	7.915	1306	942	496	172	274	1911	1187	724	142	165
3	Spain	7.589	1184	867	438	160	269	1607	1061	546	148	156
4	Italy	7.135	1056	782	385	168	229	1228	805	423	118	148
5	USSR	6.297	466	343	180	71	92	538	334	204	35	74
6	Netherlands	5.837	648	510	249	**930**	168	973	634	339	57	111
7	Scotland	5.788	712	578	272	108	198	1005	740	265	60	123
8	Belgium	5.414	666	557	257	93	207	914	737	177	59	123
9	Hungary	5.110	511	440	199	69	172	789	651	138	44	100
10	Yugoslavia	4.976	637	570	238	104	228	941	822	119	57	128
11	Portugal	4.890	582	501	215	105	181	795	644	151	47	119
12	E. Germany	4.757	490	443	183	90	170	676	595	81	34	103
13	Czechoslovakia	4.673	486	417	187	78	152	659	551	108	34	104
14	France	3.825	459	445	167	92	186	674	672	2	33	120
15	Poland	3.666	319	317	119	64	134	446	486	-40	17	87
16	Wales	3.560	89	90	29	25	36	126	108	18	6	25
17	Romania	3.298	320	336	123	**610**	152	436	513	-77	13	97
18	Bulgaria	3.287	309	323	119	55	149	477	512	-35	16	94
19	Austria	3.207	324	352	114	72	166	464	575	-111	24	101
20	Sweden	2.966	267	281	94	**640**	123	392	458	-66	15	90
21	Switzerland	2.884	326	373	119	68	186	559	707	-148	20	113
22	Greece	2.652	244	271	92	50	129	311	466	-155	10	92
23	Turkey	2.000	164	229	61	36	132	219	431	-212	6	82
24	Denmark	1.767	175	265	62	46	157	341	590	-249	5	99
25	Albania	1.478	34	52	10	14	28	34	80	-46	0	23
26	Norway	1.250	100	190	35	29	126	184	481	-297	1	80
27	Rep. of Ireland	1.153	90	188	28	34	126	158	465	-307	0	78
28	N. Ireland	1.109	81	168	23	33	112	163	465	-302	2	73
29	Finland	1.000	63	150	22	17	111	125	463	-338	2	63
30	Cyprus	0.771	44	124	14	16	94	93	451	-358	0	57
31	Malta	0.647	44	144	16	12	116	67	513	-446	0	68
32	Luxembourg	0.551	43	164	15	13	136	100	706	-606	0	78
33	Iceland	0.550	33	130	8	17	105	74	431	-357	0	60
	Total		**13637**	**12468**	**5069**	**2330**	**5069**	**19261**	**19261**	**0**	**1169**	**3.090**

First Victory for an East European Side

For the first time since the inaugural Champions' Cup event in 1955-56, the European season kicked off without the participation of any English clubs. This was the first year of the Heysel-induced ban, and one could not help feeling that the three competitions were all the poorer for the English clubs' absence.

But no English teams meant a better chance for others, and it was Spain, in particular, which thrived on their absence, with Spanish clubs reaching all three of the European finals for the first time since 1962. Given that the three Spanish finalists were the big three, namely Real Madrid, Barcelona and Atlético Madrid, there was considerable optimism in Spain that they could achieve the first ever European grand slam.

As it turned out, though, only one team, Real Madrid, succeeded in winning a trophy. They became the first club to retain the UEFA Cup. Barcelona and Valencia had successfully defended the old Fairs' Cup back in the '60s, but no team had ever carried off the new trophy two years in a row. Real's path to victory was plotted in much the same fashion as their 1984-85 win – losing the away legs and then thrashing the opposition at home in the Bernabéu.

The most spectacular Real comeback of this or any other season in their long European history came in the third round against UEFA Cup specialists Borussia Mönchengladbach. Down 5-1 from the first leg, Real did the impossible in the return, scoring four goals without reply, the fourth in the last minute from veteran striker Santillana, to take the tie on away goals. For the second season in succession, Inter Milan fell victim to Real's powers of recovery in the semi-finals. They won the first leg 3-1 in the San Siro, but Real, with two goals each from Hugo Sánchez and Santillana and another from Gordillo, knocked out their great Italian rivals yet again with a 5-1 victory in Madrid.

The winning margin was also 5-1 in the first leg of the final against Cologne. The Germans, who had at last won a European semi-final at the sixth attempt, actually scored first in the Bernabéu through Klaus Allofs, but, spurred on by 85,000 fanatical locals, Real quickly regained the initiative to take the lead at half-time through Sánchez and Gordillo and extend it with two goals from Valdano and a fifth from Santillana in the second half. Now it was Cologne's turn to show what they were made of. But crowd trouble in an earlier tie had led to a ban on their Müngersdorfer stadium, so they were forced to stage the return in Berlin. That they won the match was to their credit, but with only 15,000 fans present, the atmosphere was hardly conducive for a dramatic fightback, and in the end they could only score half the goals they required, through Bein and Geilenkirchen. As in 1985, the outcome of the final had been decided in the first leg, and Real, thanks to their brilliance in the Bernabéu, were able to add a record eighth European trophy to their collection. They would not be going for a UEFA Cup hat-trick, however, because victory in the Spanish championship – their first for six years – meant that they could return to the competition that meant most to them, the Champions' Cup.

But Real would be the only Spanish club to return to the Champions' Cup in 1986-87, because Barcelona, despite reaching the final for the first time in 25 years and despite the match being held in nearby Seville, could not win the Cup. It went instead to rank outsiders Steaua Bucharest, who thus became the first side from the East to win Europe's most prestigious club trophy.

Barcelona had won the Spanish championship in 1985 for the first time in over a decade, and although there were no English teams this season in Europe, there was considerable English interest in the man who had taken Barcelona to that triumph, Terry Venables. One of Venables' first moves at the club had been to sell off Diego Maradona, replacing him with the Scottish forward Steve Archibald, and it was Archibald who proved to be Barcelona's goalscoring saviour in both their second round tie with FC Porto, which, as in the first round against Sparta Prague, they won on away goals, and in the heavyweight quarter-final clash with holders Juventus. Barcelona won the first leg of that tie 1-0 in the Nou Camp, but saved their best form for the return in Turin, where Archibald's goal on the half hour, allied to some determined defending, proved conclusive.

But where the Catalan defence had held firm in Turin, it collapsed in the first leg of the semi-final against IFK Gothenburg, when the Swedes romped to a shock 3-0 victory. Barça had it all to do at home, especially with Archibald out injured, but they must have been studying videos of Real Madrid before the match, because they succeeded in staging a dramatic recovery of their own, with Archibald's replacement, Pichi Alonso, hitting a hat-trick to take the tie to extra-time and then penalties, which Barcelona won 5-4 after trailing 4-2!

With the final being staged in Seville, Barcelona were the hottest Champions' Cup favourites in history, especially as the only team left standing in their way were unfancied Steaua. They had become the first Romanian club to reach a European final, and the first Eastern European Champions' Cup finalists in 20 years, by defeating Anderlecht 3-1 on aggregate in the semi-final.

But in Seville, Barcelona wilted under the pressure. They were a pale shadow of the team that had put out Juventus and Gothenburg, unable at any stage of the game to put the Romanians under any concerted pressure. As for Steaua, they produced some delightful footwork and skilful inter-passing in midfield, but whenever they approached goal, they lost their heads and fired wildly into the crowd. It was almost as if they were afraid to score, afraid to gatecrash Barcelona's party. And yet Barça showed little inclination to score themselves, which meant that for the first time ever a Champions' Cup final ended goalless. The ensuing penalty shoot-out bordered on the farcical. Four kicks taken, and four kicks saved. It seemed as if no one would ever score, until Marius Lacatus, with Steaua's third penalty, at last found the net. But the Spaniards continued to find Steaua 'keeper Helmut Ducadam an insurmountable barrier. Two more players tried, and failed, which, with Balint scoring a second for Steaua, left the Romanians, against all the odds, as the new Champions of Europe.

More deserving of that particular title, however, were the winners of the Cup-winners' Cup, Dinamo Kiev. Their 3-0 victory in the Lyons final against Atlético Madrid was one of the finest exhibitions of football seen in European competition for years. Coached by Valery Lobanovsky, and containing almost a whole team full of Soviet internationals, later to star in the Mexico World Cup, Kiev had a relatively straightforward run to the final, losing just one match, their first, in Utrecht, and scoring no fewer than 15 goals in their four home games. Their most impressive display came in the quarter-finals, where they annihilated the previous season's runners-up, Rapid Vienna, 9-2 on aggregate. But few could have foreseen just how much they would outclass their opponents in the final. After all, Atlético had got there undefeated, winning all four of their away games in the process, including a semi-final victory away to Bayer Uerdingen, who had previously staged the comeback to beat all comebacks against Dynamo Dresden. But in Lyons, Kiev were irresistable. Man of the match Aleksandr Zavarov gave them an early lead after five minutes, but it was only the outstanding goalkeeping of Atlético's veteran Argentinian goalkeeper Ubaldo Fillol which kept the Ukrainians waiting until the 87th minute for their second. Scorer of that goal was another veteran, Oleg Blokhin, who had also scored a Cup-winners' Cup final goal on Kiev's previous appearance, in 1975. A third goal from Yevtushenko in the last minute rounded off the night in fitting style for Kiev, matching that 3-0 winning scoreline against Ferencváros 11 years earlier.

1986 – 1987

FC Porto

Ajax

IFK Gothenburg

First Round

Team 1	Cnty	Team 2	Cnty	1st leg	2nd leg	Agg
Anderlecht	Bel	Górnik Zabrze	Pol	2-0	1-1	3-1
Beroe Stara Zagora	Bul	Dinamo Kiev	URS	1-1	0-2	1-3
Apoel Nicosia	Cyp	HJK Helsinki	Fin	1-0	2-3	3-3
Brøndby IF	Den	Honvéd	Hun	4-1	2-2	6-3
Shamrock Rovers	Irl	Celtic	Sco	0-1	0-2	0-3
Paris Saint-Germain	Fra	TJ Vitkovice	Tch	2-2	0-1	2-3
Juventus	Ita	Valur Reykjavik	Isl	7-0	4-0	11-0
Avenir Beggen	Lux	Austria Vienna	Aut	0-3	0-3	0-6
Rosenborg BK	Nor	Linfield	Nir	1-0	1-1	2-1
PSV Eindhoven	Ned	Bayern Munich	FRG	0-2	0-0	0-2
FC Porto	Por	Rabat Ajax	Mlt	9-0	1-0	10-0
Örgryte IS	Swe	Dynamo Berlin	GDR	2-3	1-4	3-7
Young Boys Berne	Sui	Real Madrid	Esp	1-0	0-5	1-5
Besiktas	Tur	Dinamo Tirana	Alb	2-0	1-0	3-0
Red Star Belgrade	Yug	Panathinaikos	Gre	3-0	1-2	4- 2

	Pts	P	W	D	L	F	A	Diff	Goals/P
Total	60	30	24	12	24	88	88	0	2.933

Second Round

Anderlecht	Bel	Steaua Bucharest	Rom	3-0	0-1	3-1
Brøndby IF	Den	Dynamo Berlin	GDR	2-1	1-1	3-2
Celtic	Sco	Dinamo Kiev	URS	1-1	1-3	2-4
Real Madrid	Esp	Juventus	Ita	1-0	0-1	1-1
Rosenborg BK	Nor	Red Star Belgrade	Yug	0-3	1-4	1-7
Bayern Munich	FRG	Austria Vienna	Aut	2-0	1-1	3-1
TJ Vitkovice	Tch	FC Porto	Por	1-0	0-3	1-3

	Pts	P	W	D	L	F	A	Diff	Goals/P
Total	28	14	11	6	11	33	33	0	2.357

Quarter Finals

FC Porto	Por	Brøndby IF	Den	1-0	1-1	2-1
Bayern Munich	FRG	Anderlecht	Bel	5-0	2-2	7-2
Besiktas	Tur	Dinamo Kiev	URS	0-5	0-2	0-7
Red Star Belgrade	Yug	Real Madrid	Esp	4-2	0-2	4-4

	Pts	P	W	D	L	F	A	Diff	Goals/P
Total	16	8	6	4	6	27	27	0	3.375

Semi Finals

FC Porto	Por	Dinamo Kiev	URS	2-1	2-1	4-2
Bayern Munich	FRG	Real Madrid	Esp	4-1	0-1	4-2

	Pts	P	W	D	L	F	A	Diff	Goals/P
Total	8	4	4	0	4	12	12	0	3.000

Final

FC Porto	Por	Bayern Munich	FRG	2-1	2-1

	Pts	P	W	D	L	F	A	Diff	Goals/P
Total	2	1	1	0	1	3	3	0	3.000

	Pts	P	W	D	L	F	A	Diff	Goals/P
Total	114	57	46	22	46	163	163	0	2.860

Pos'n	Club	Cnty	Pts	P	W	D	L	F	A	Diff	B	Pts/P	F/P
1	FC Porto	Por	18	9	7	1	1	21	5	16	3	2.000	2.333
2	Bayern Munich	FRG	14	9	4	3	2	17	7	10	3	1.556	1.889
3	Dinamo Kiev	URS	12	8	4	2	2	16	7	9	2	1.500	2.000
4	Real Madrid	Esp	10	8	4	0	4	12	10	2	2	1.250	1.500
5	Red Star Belgrade	Yug	9	6	4	0	2	15	7	8	1	1.500	2.500
6	Brøndby IF	Den	8	6	2	3	1	10	7	3	1	1.333	1.667
7	Anderlecht	Bel	7	6	2	2	2	8	9	-1	1	1.167	1.333
8	Juventus	Ita	6	4	3	0	1	12	1	11	0	1.500	3.000
9	Austria Vienna	Aut	5	4	2	1	1	7	3	4	0	1.250	1.750
10	Dynamo Berlin	GDR	5	4	2	1	1	9	6	3	0	1.250	2.250
11	Celtic	Sco	5	4	2	1	1	5	4	1	0	1.250	1.250
12	TJ Vitkovice	Tch	5	4	2	1	1	4	5	-1	0	1.250	1.000
13	Besiktas	Tur	5	4	2	0	2	3	7	-4	1	1.250	0.750
14	Rosenborg BK	Nor	3	4	1	1	2	3	8	-5	0	0.750	0.750
15	Apoel Nicosia	Cyp	2	2	1	0	1	3	3	0	0	1.000	1.500
–	HJK Helsinki	Fin	2	2	1	0	1	3	3	0	0	1.000	1.500
17	Panathinaikos	Gre	2	2	1	0	1	2	4	-2	0	1.000	1.000
18	Steaua Bucharest	Rom	2	2	1	0	1	1	3	-2	0	1.000	0.500
19	Young Boys Berne	Sui	2	2	1	0	1	1	5	-4	0	1.000	0.500
20	Paris Saint-Germain	Fra	1	2	0	1	1	2	3	-1	0	0.500	1.000
21	Linfield	Nir	1	2	0	1	1	1	2	-1	0	0.500	0.500
22	Beroe Stara Zagora	Bul	1	2	0	1	1	1	3	-2	0	0.500	0.500
–	Górnik Zabrze	Pol	1	2	0	1	1	1	3	-2	0	0.500	0.500
24	PSV Eindhoven	Ned	1	2	0	1	1	0	2	-2	0	0.500	0.000
25	Honvéd	Hun	1	2	0	1	1	3	6	-3	0	0.500	1.500
26	Dinamo Tirana	Alb	0	2	0	0	2	0	3	-3	0	0.000	0.000
–	Shamrock Rovers	Irl	0	2	0	0	2	0	3	-3	0	0.000	0.000
28	Örgryte IS	Swe	0	2	0	0	2	3	7	-4	0	0.000	1.500
29	Avenir Beggen	Lux	0	2	0	0	2	0	6	-6	0	0.000	0.000
30	Rabat Ajax	Mlt	0	2	0	0	2	0	10	-10	0	0.000	0.000
31	Valur Reykjavik	Isl	0	2	0	0	2	0	11	-11	0	0.000	0.000
	Total		**128**	**114**	**46**	**22**	**46**	**163**	**163**	**0**	**14**	**1.123**	**2.860**

First Round

Team 1	Cnty	Team 2	Cnty	1st leg	2nd leg	Agg
17 Nëntori Tirana	Alb	Dinamo Bucharest	Rom	1-0	2-1	3-1
Rapid Vienna	Aut	Club Bruges	Bel	4-3	3-3	7-6
B 1903 Copenhagen	Den	Levski Sofia	Bul	1-0	0-2	1-2
Aberdeen	Sco	Sion	Sui	2-1	0-3	2-4
Waterford United	Irl	Girondins Bordeaux	Fra	1-2	0-4	1-6
Haka Valkeakoski	Fin	Torpedo Moscow	URS	2-2	1-3	3-5
Olympiakos Pireus	Gre	Union Luxembourg	Lux	3-0	3-0	6-0
Vasas SC	Hun	Mostar Velez	Yug	2-2	2-3	4-5
Glentoran	Nir	Lokomotive Leipzig	GDR	1-1	0-2	1-3
Fram Reykjavik	Isl	GKS Katowice	Pol	0-3	0-1	0-4
Roma	Ita	Real Zaragoza	Esp	2-0	0-2	2-2
Zurrieq	Mlt	Wrexham	Wal	0-3	0-4	0-7
Benfica	Por	Lillestrøm SK	Nor	2-0	2-1	4-1
VFB Stuttgart	FRG	Spartak Trnava	Tch	1-0	0-0	1-0
Malmö FF	Swe	Apollon Limassol	Cyp	6-0	1-2	7-2
Bursaspor	Tur	Ajax	Ned	0-2	0-5	0-7

	Pts	P	W	D	L	F	A	Diff	Goals/P
Total	64	32	27	10	27	97	97	0	3.031

Second Round

17 Nëntori Tirana	Alb	Malmö FF	Swe	0-3	0-0	0-3
Rapid Vienna	Aut	Lokomotive Leipzig	GDR	1-1	1-2	2-3
Levski Sofia	Bul	Velez Mostar	Yug	2-0	3-4	5-4
Real Zaragoza	Esp	Wrexham	Wal	0-0	2-2	2-2
Ajax	Ned	Olympiakos Pireus	Gre	4-0	1-1	5-1
GKS Katowice	Pol	Sion	Sui	2-2	0-3	2-5
Benfica	Por	Girondins Bordeaux	Fra	1-1	0-1	1-2
Torpedo Moscow	URS	VFB Stuttgart	FRG	2-0	5-3	7-3

	Pts	P	W	D	L	F	A	Diff	Goals/P
Total	32	16	9	14	9	47	47	0	2.938

Quarter Finals

Real Zaragoza	Esp	Levski Sofia	Bul	2-0	2-0	4-0
Girondins Bordeaux	Fra	Torpedo Moscow	URS	1-0	2-3	3-3
Malmö FF	Swe	Ajax	Ned	1-0	1-3	2-3
Lokomotive Leipzig	GDR	Sion	Sui	2-0	0-0	2-0

	Pts	P	W	D	L	F	A	Diff	Goals/P
Total	16	8	7	2	7	17	17	0	2.125

Semi Finals

Real Zaragoza	Esp	Ajax	Ned	2-3	0-3	2-6
Girondins Bordeaux	Fra	Lokomotive Leipzig	GDR	0-1	1-0	1-1

	Pts	P	W	D	L	F	A	Diff	Goals/P
Total	8	4	4	0	4	10	10	0	2.500

Final

Ajax	Ned	Lokomotive Leipzig	GDR	1-0	1-0

	Pts	P	W	D	L	F	A	Diff	Goals/P
Total	2	1	1	0	1	1	1	0	1.000

	Pts	P	W	D	L	F	A	Diff	Goals/P
Total	122	61	48	26	48	172	172	0	2.820

Pos'n	Club	Cnty	Pts	P	W	D	L	F	A	Diff	B	Pts/P	F/P
1	Ajax	Ned	18	9	7	1	1	22	5	17	3	2.000	2.444
2	Lokomotive Leipzig	GDR	14	9	4	3	2	9	5	4	3	1.556	1.000
3	Girondins Bordeaux	Fra	13	8	5	1	2	12	6	6	2	1.625	1.500
4	Torpedo Moscow	URS	10	6	4	1	1	15	9	6	1	1.667	2.500
5	Real Zaragoza	Esp	10	8	3	2	3	10	10	0	2	1.250	1.250
6	Malmö FF	Swe	8	6	3	1	2	12	5	7	1	1.333	2.000
7	Sion	Sui	7	6	2	2	2	9	6	3	1	1.167	1.500
8	Wrexham	Wal	6	4	2	2	0	9	2	7	0	1.500	2.250
9	Olympiakos Pireus	Gre	5	4	2	1	1	7	5	2	0	1.250	1.750
10	Benfica	Por	5	4	2	1	1	5	3	2	0	1.250	1.250
11	GKS Katowice	Pol	5	4	2	1	1	6	5	1	0	1.250	1.500
12	Velez Mostar	Yug	5	4	2	1	1	9	9	0	0	1.250	2.250
13	17 Nëntori Tirana	Alb	5	4	2	1	1	3	4	-1	0	1.250	0.750
14	Levski Sofia	Bul	5	6	2	0	4	7	9	-2	1	0.833	1.167
15	Rapid Vienna	Aut	4	4	1	2	1	9	9	0	0	1.000	2.250
16	VFB Stuttgart	FRG	3	4	1	1	2	4	7	-3	0	0.750	1.000
17	Roma	Ita	2	2	1	0	1	2	2	0	0	1.000	1.000
18	B 1903 Copenhagen	Den	2	2	1	0	1	1	2	-1	0	1.000	0.500
19	Aberdeen	Sco	2	2	1	0	1	2	4	-2	0	1.000	1.000
20	Apollon Limassol	Cyp	2	2	1	0	1	2	7	-5	0	1.000	1.000
21	Club Bruges	Bel	1	2	0	1	1	6	7	-1	0	0.500	3.000
22	Vasas SC	Hun	1	2	0	1	1	4	5	-1	0	0.500	2.000
23	Spartak Trnava	Tch	1	2	0	1	1	0	1	-1	0	0.500	0.000
24	Haka Valkeakoski	Fin	1	2	0	1	1	3	5	-2	0	0.500	1.500
25	Glentoran	Nir	1	2	0	1	1	1	3	-2	0	0.500	0.500
26	Dinamo Bucharest	Rom	0	2	0	0	2	1	3	-2	0	0.000	0.500
27	Lillestrøm SK	Nor	0	2	0	0	2	1	4	-3	0	0.000	0.500
28	Fram Reykjavik	Isl	0	2	0	0	2	0	4	-4	0	0.000	0.000
29	Waterford United	Irl	0	2	0	0	2	1	6	-5	0	0.000	0.500
30	Union Luxembourg	Lux	0	2	0	0	2	0	6	-6	0	0.000	0.000
31	Zurrieq	Mlt	0	2	0	0	2	0	7	-7	0	0.000	0.000
–	Bursaspor	Tur	0	2	0	0	2	0	7	-7	0	0.000	0.000
	Total		**136**	**122**	**48**	**26**	**48**	**172**	**172**	**0**	**14**	**1.115**	**2.820**

First Round

Team 1	Cnty	Team 2	Cnty	1st leg	2nd leg	Agg
Flamurtari Vlorë	Alb	Barcelona	Esp	1-1	0-0	1-1
FC Tirol	Aut	CSKA Sofia	Bul	3-0	0-2	3-2
Linzer ASK	Aut	Widzew Lódź	Pol	1-1	0-1	1-2
Beveren	Bel	Vålerengen SIF	Nor	1-0	0-0	1-0
Heart of Midlothian	Sco	Dukla Prague	Tch	3-2	0-1	3-3
Rangers	Sco	Ilves Tampere	Fin	4-0	0-2	4-2
Athletic Bilbao	Esp	Magdeburg	GDR	2-0	0-1	2-1
Atlético Madrid	Esp	Werder Bremen	FRG	2-0	1-2	3-2
Lens	Fra	Dundee United	Sco	1-0	0-2	1-2
Nantes	Fra	Torino	Ita	0-4	1-1	0-5
OFI Crete	Gre	Hajduk Split	Yug	1-0	0-4	1-4
Pécsi MSC	Hun	Feyenoord	Ned	1-0	0-2	1-2
Coleraine	Nir	Stahl Brandenburg	GDR	1-1	0-1	1-2
IA Akranes	Isl	Sporting Lisbon	Por	0-9	0-6	0-15
Fiorentina	Ita	Boavista	Por	1-0	0-1	1-1
Inter Milan	Ita	AEK Athens	Gre	2-0	1-0	3-0
Napoli	Ita	Toulouse	Fra	1-0	0-1	1-1
Jeunesse Esch	Lux	Gent	Bel	1-2	1-1	2-3
Hibernians	Mlt	Trakia Plovdiv	Bul	0-2	0-8	0-10
Groningen	Ned	Galway United	Irl	5-1	3-1	8-2
Legia Warsaw	Pol	Dnepr Dnepropetrovsk	URS	0-0	1-0	1-0
Bor. Mönchengladbach	FRG	Partizan Belgrade	Yug	1-0	3-1	4-1
Bayer Uerdingen	FRG	Carl Zeiss Jena	GDR	3-0	4-0	7-0
Sportul Studentesc Bucharest	Rom	Omonia Nicosia	Cyp	1-0	1-1	2-1
Universitatea Craiova	Rom	Galatasaray	Tur	2-0	1-2	3-2
Kalmar FF	Swe	Bayer Leverkusen	FRG	1-4	0-3	1-7
Neuchâtel Xamax	Sui	Lyngby BK	Den	2-0	3-1	5-1
Sigma Olomouc	Tch	IFK Gothenburg	Swe	1-1	0-4	1-5
Sparta Prague	Tch	Vitória Guimarães	Por	1-1	1-2	2-3
Dinamo Minsk	URS	Rába ETO	Hun	2-4	1-0	3-4
Spartak Moscow	URS	Lucerne	Sui	0-0	1-0	1-0
Rijeka	Yug	Standard Liège	Bel	0-1	1-1	1-2

	Pts	P	W	D	L	F	A	Diff	Goals/P
Total	128	64	51	26	51	155	155	0	2.422

Second Round

FC Tirol	Aut	Standard Liège	Bel	2-1	2-3	4-4
Beveren	Bel	Athletic Bilbao	Esp	3-1	1-2	4-3
Dundee United	Sco	Universitatea Craiova	Rom	3-0	0-1	3-1
Rangers	Sco	Boavista	Por	2-1	1-0	3-1
Barcelona	Esp	Sporting Lisbon	Por	1-0	1-2	2-2
Toulouse	Fra	Spartak Moscow	URS	3-1	1-5	4-6
Torino	Ita	Rába ETO	Hun	4-0	1-1	5-1
Groningen	Ned	Neuchâtel Xamax	Sui	0-0	1-1	1-1
Widzew Lódź	Pol	Bayer Uerdingen	FRG	0-0	0-2	0-2
Legia Warsaw	Pol	Inter Milan	Ita	3-2	0-1	3-3
Vitória Guimarães	Por	Atlético Madrid	Esp	2-0	0-1	2-1
Bor. Mönchengladbach	FRG	Feyenoord	Ned	5-1	0-2	5-3
Sportul Studentesc Bucharest	Rom	Gent	Bel	0-3	1-1	1-4
IFK Gothenburg	Swe	Stahl Brandenburg	GDR	2-0	1-1	3-1
Dukla Prague	Tch	Bayer Leverkusen	FRG	0-0	1-1	1-1
Hajduk Split	Yug	Trakia Plovdiv	Bul	3-1	2-2	5-3

	Pts	P	W	D	L	F	A	Diff	Goals/P
Total	64	32	23	18	23	83	83	0	2.594

Third Round

Gent	Bel	IFK Gothenburg	Swe	0-1	0-4	0-5
Dundee United	Sco	Hajduk Split	Yug	2-0	0-0	2-0
Rangers	Sco	Bor. Mönchengladbach	FRG	1-1	0-0	1-1
Torino	Ita	Beveren	Bel	2-1	1-0	3-1
Groningen	Ned	Vitória Guimarães	Por	0-1	0-3	0-4
Bayer Uerdingen	FRG	Barcelona	Esp	0-2	0-2	0-4
Dukla Prague	Tch	Inter Milan	Ita	0-1	0-0	0-1
Spartak Moscow	URS	FC Tirol	Aut	1-0	0-2	1-2

	Pts	P	W	D	L	F	A	Diff	Goals/P
Total	32	16	12	8	12	25	25	0	1.563

Quarter Finals

Dundee United	Sco	Barcelona	Esp	1-0	2-1	3-1
Torino	Ita	FC Tirol	Aut	0-0	1-2	1-2
Bor. Mönchengladbach	FRG	Vitória Guimarães	Por	3-0	2-2	5-2
IFK Gothenburg	Swe	Inter Milan	Ita	0-0	1-1	1-1

	Pts	P	W	D	L	F	A	Diff	Goals/P
Total	16	8	4	8	4	16	16	0	2.000

Semi Finals

Dundee United	Sco	Bor. Mönchengladbach	FRG	0-0	2-0	2-0
IFK Gothenburg	Swe	FC Tirol	Aut	4-1	1-0	5-1

	Pts	P	W	D	L	F	A	Diff	Goals/P
Total	8	4	3	2	3	8	8	0	2.000

Final

IFK Gothenburg	Swe	Dundee United	Sco	1-0	1-1	2-1

	Pts	P	W	D	L	F	A	Diff	Goals/P
Total	4	2	1	2	1	3	3	0	1.500

	Pts	P	W	D	L	F	A	Diff	Goals/P
Total	252	126	94	64	94	290	290	0	2.302

Pos'n	Club	Cnty	Pts	P	W	D	L	F	A	Diff	B	Pts/P	F/P
1	IFK Gothenburg	Swe	22	12	7	5	0	21	5	16	3	1.833	1 750
2	Dundee United	Sco	18	12	6	3	3	13	5	8	3	1.500	1.083
3	Bor. Moenchengladbach	FRG	14	10	4	4	2	15	9	6	2	1.400	1.500
4	Torino	Ita	12	8	4	3	1	14	5	9	1	1.500	1.750
5	Inter Milan	Ita	12	8	4	3	1	8	4	4	1	1.500	1.000
6	Vitória Guimarães	Por	11	8	4	2	2	11	8	3	1	1.375	1.375
7	FC Tirol	Aut	11	10	4	1	5	12	13	-1	2	1.100	1.200
8	Barcelona	Esp	9	8	3	2	3	8	6	2	1	1.125	1.000
9	Rangers	Sco	8	6	3	2	1	8	4	4	0	1.333	1.333
10	Bayer Uerdingen	FRG	7	6	3	1	2	9	4	5	0	1.167	1.500
11	Spartak Moscow	URS	7	6	3	1	2	8	6	2	0	1.167	1.333
12	Sporting Lisbon	Por	6	4	3	0	1	17	2	15	0	1.500	4.250
13	Bayer Leverkusen	FRG	6	4	2	2	0	8	2	6	0	1.500	2.000
14	Neuchâtel Xamax	Sui	6	4	2	2	0	6	2	4	0	1.500	1.500
15	Hajduk Split	Yug	6	6	2	2	2	9	6	3	0	1.000	1.500
16	Groningen	Ned	6	6	2	2	2	9	7	2	0	1.000	1.500
17	Gent	Bel	6	6	2	2	2	7	8	-1	0	1.000	1.167
18	Trakia Plovdiv	Bul	5	4	2	1	1	13	5	8	0	1.250	3.250
19	Standard Liège	Bel	5	4	2	1	1	6	5	1	0	1.250	1.500
20	Legia Warsaw	Pol	5	4	2	1	1	4	3	1	0	1.250	1.000
21	Beveren	Bel	5	6	2	1	3	6	6	0	0	0.833	1.000
22	Dulka Prague	Tch	5	6	1	3	2	4	5	-1	0	0.833	0.667
23	Athletic Bilbao	Esp	4	4	2	0	2	5	5	0	0	1.000	1.250
24	Atlético Madrid	Esp	4	4	2	0	2	4	4	0	0	1.000	1.000
25	Feyenoord	Ned	4	4	2	0	2	5	6	-1	0	1.000	1.250
26	Universitatea Craiova	Rom	4	4	2	0	2	4	5	-1	0	1.000	1.000
27	Stahl Brandenburg	GDR	4	4	1	2	1	3	4	-1	0	1.000	0.750
28	Widzew Lódź	Pol	4	4	1	2	1	2	3	-1	0	1.000	0.500
29	Toulouse	Fra	4	4	2	0	2	5	7	-2	0	1.000	1.250
30	Sportul Studentesc Bucharest	Rom	4	4	1	2	1	3	5	-2	0	1.000	0.750
31	Rába ETO	Hun	3	4	1	1	2	5	8	-3	0	0.750	1.250
32	Heart of Midlothian	Sco	2	2	1	0	1	3	3	0	0	1.000	1.500
33	Flamurtari Vlorë	Alb	2	2	0	2	0	1	1	0	0	1.000	0.500
–	Fiorentina	Ita	2	2	1	0	1	1	1	0	0	1.000	0.500
–	Napoli	Ita	2	2	1	0	1	1	1	0	0	1.000	0.500
36	Dinamo Minsk	URS	2	2	1	0	1	3	4	-1	0	1.000	1.500
37	CSKA Sofia	Bul	2	2	1	0	1	2	3	-1	0	1 000	1.000
–	Werder Bremen	FRG	2	2	1	0	1	2	3	-1	0	1.000	1.000
–	Galatasaray	Tur	2	2	1	0	1	2	3	-1	0	1.000	1.000
40	Lens	Fra	2	2	1	0	1	1	2	-1	0	1.000	0.500
–	Pécsi MSC	Hun	2	2	1	0	1	1	2	-1	0	1.000	0.500
–	Magdeburg	GDR	2	2	1	0	1	1	2	-1	0	1.000	0.500
43	Ilves Tampere	Fin	2	2	1	0	1	2	4	-2	0	1.000	1.000
–	Boavista	Por	2	4	1	0	3	2	4	-2	0	0.500	0.500
45	OFI Crete	Gre	2	2	1	0	1	1	4	-3	0	1.000	0.500
46	Jeunesse Esch	Lux	1	2	0	1	1	2	3	-1	0	0.500	1.000
–	Sparta Prague	Tch	1	2	0	1	1	2	3	-1	0	0.500	1.000
48	Linzer ASK	Aut	1	2	0	1	1	1	2	-1	0	0.500	0.500
–	Omonia Nicosia	Cyp	1	2	0	1	1	1	2	-1	0	0.500	0.500
–	Coleraine	Nir	1	2	0	1	1	1	2	-1	0	0.500	0.500
–	Rijeka	Yug	1	2	0	1	1	1	2	-1	0	0.500	0.500
52	Vålerengen SIF	Nor	1	2	0	1	1	0	1	-1	0	0.500	0.000
–	Lucerne	Sui	1	2	0	1	1	0	1	-1	0	0.500	0.000
–	Dnepr Dnepropetrovsk	URS	1	2	0	1	1	0	1	-1	0	0.500	0.000
55	Nantes	Fra	1	2	0	1	1	1	5	-4	0	0.500	0.500
–	Sigma Olomouc	Tch	1	2	0	1	1	1	5	-4	0	0.500	0.500
57	Partizan Belgrade	Yug	0	2	0	0	2	1	4	-3	0	0.000	0.500
58	AEK Athens	Gre	0	2	0	0	2	0	3	-3	0	0.000	0.000
59	Lyngby BK	Den	0	2	0	0	2	1	5	-4	0	0.000	0.500
60	Galway United	Irl	0	2	0	0	2	2	8	-6	0	0.000	1.000
61	Kalmar FF	Swe	0	2	0	0	2	1	7	-6	0	0.000	0.500
62	Carl Zeiss Jena	GDR	0	2	0	0	2	0	7	-7	0	0.000	0.000
63	Hibernians	Mlt	0	2	0	0	2	0	10	-10	0	0.000	0.000
64	IA Akranes	Isl	0	2	0	0	2	0	15	-15	0	0.000	0.000
	Total		**266**	**252**	**94**	**64**	**94**	**290**	**290**	**0**	**14**	**1.056**	**2.302**

1986-87

Pos'n	Cnty	Pts	P	W	D	L	F	A	Diff	B	Pts/P	F/P
1	FRG	48	35	16	11	8	57	30	27	5	1.371	1.629
2	Por	42	29	17	4	8	56	22	34	4	1.448	1.931
3	Esp	37	32	14	4	14	39	35	4	5	1.156	1.219
4	Ita	36	26	14	6	6	38	14	24	2	1.385	1.462
5	Sco	35	26	13	6	7	31	20	11	3	1.346	1.192
6	Swe	30	22	10	6	6	37	24	13	4	1.364	1.682
7	URS	30	24	11	5	8	40	29	11	3	1.250	1.667
8	Ned	29	21	11	4	6	36	20	16	3	1.381	1.714
9	GDR	25	21	8	6	7	22	24	-2	3	1.190	1.048
10	Bel	24	24	8	7	9	33	35	-2	1	1.000	1.375
11	Yug	21	20	8	4	8	35	28	7	1	1.050	1.750
12	Aut	21	20	7	5	8	29	27	2	2	1.050	1.450
13	Fra	21	18	8	3	7	21	23	-2	2	1.167	1.167
14	Sui	16	14	5	5	4	16	14	2	1	1.143	1.143
15	Pol	15	14	5	5	4	13	14	-1	0	1.071	0.929
16	Bul	13	14	5	2	7	23	20	3	1	0.929	1.643
17	Tch	13	16	3	7	6	11	19	-8	0	0.813	0.688
18	Den	10	10	3	3	4	12	14	-2	1	1.000	1.200
19	Rom	10	12	4	2	6	9	16	-7	0	0.833	0.750
20	Gre	9	10	4	1	5	10	16	-6	0	0.900	1.000
21	Alb	7	8	2	3	3	4	8	-4	0	0.875	0.500
22	Hun	7	10	2	3	5	13	21	-8	0	0.700	1.300
23	Tur	7	8	3	0	5	5	17	-12	1	0.875	0.625
24	Wal	6	4	2	2	0	9	2	7	0	1.500	2.250
25	Fin	5	6	2	1	3	8	12	-4	0	0.833	1.333
26	Cyp	5	6	2	1	3	6	12	-6	0	0.833	1.000
27	Nor	4	8	1	2	5	4	13	-9	0	0.500	0.500
28	Nir	3	6	0	3	3	3	7	-4	0	0.500	0.500
29	Lux	1	6	0	1	5	2	15	-13	0	0.167	0.333
30	Irl	0	6	0	0	6	3	17	-14	0	0.000	0.500
31	Mlt	0	6	0	0	6	0	27	-27	0	0.000	0.000
32	Isl	0	6	0	0	6	0	30	-30	0	0.000	0.000
	Total	**530**	**488**	**188**	**112**	**188**	**625**	**625**	**0**	**42**	**1.086**	**2.561**

1955-56 to 1986-87

Pos'n	Cnty	Pts	P	W	D	L	F	A	Diff	B	Pts/P	F/P
1	Eng	1365	926	500	201	225	1782	927	855	164	1.474	1.924
2	FRG	1352	977	511	183	283	1966	1219	747	147	1.384	2.012
3	Esp	1221	899	452	164	283	1646	1096	550	153	1.358	1.831
4	Ita	1092	808	399	174	235	1266	819	447	120	1.351	1.567
5	Sco	747	604	285	114	205	1036	760	276	63	1.237	1.715
6	Bel	690	581	265	100	216	947	772	175	60	1.188	1.630
7	Ned	677	531	260	97	174	1009	654	355	60	1.275	1.900
8	Yug	658	590	246	108	236	976	850	126	58	1.115	1.654
9	Por	624	530	232	109	189	851	666	185	51	1.177	1.606
10	Hun	518	450	201	72	177	802	672	130	44	1.151	1.782
11	GDR	515	464	191	96	177	698	619	79	37	1.110	1.504
12	Tch	499	433	190	85	158	670	570	100	34	1.152	1.547
13	URS	498	367	192	76	99	580	361	219	38	1.357	1.580
14	Fra	480	463	175	95	193	695	695	0	35	1.037	1.501
15	Aut	345	372	121	77	174	493	602	-109	26	0.927	1.325
16	Sui	342	387	124	73	190	575	721	-146	21	0.884	1.486
17	Pol	334	331	124	69	138	459	500	-41	17	1.009	1.387
18	Rom	330	348	127	63	158	445	529	-84	13	0.948	1.279
19	Bul	322	337	124	57	156	500	532	-32	17	0.955	1.484
20	Swe	297	303	104	70	129	429	482	-53	19	0.980	1.416
21	Gre	253	281	96	51	134	321	482	-161	10	0.900	1.142
22	Den	185	275	65	49	161	353	604	-251	6	0.673	1.284
23	Tur	171	237	64	36	137	224	448	-224	7	0.722	0.945
24	Nor	104	198	36	31	131	188	494	-306	1	0.525	0.949
25	Wal	95	94	31	27	36	135	110	25	6	1.011	1.436
26	Irl	90	194	28	34	132	161	482	-321	0	0.464	0.830
27	Nir	84	174	23	36	115	166	472	-306	2	0.483	0.954
28	Fin	68	156	24	18	114	133	475	-342	2	0.436	0.853
29	Cyp	49	130	16	17	97	99	463	-364	0	0.377	0.762
30	Mlt	44	150	16	12	122	67	540	-473	0	0.293	0.447
31	Lux	44	170	15	14	141	102	721	-619	0	0.259	0.600
32	Alb	41	60	12	17	31	38	88	-50	0	0.683	0.633
33	Isl	33	136	8	17	111	74	461	-387	0	0.243	0.544
	Total	**14167**	**12956**	**5257**	**2442**	**5257**	**19886**	**19886**	**0**	**1211**	**1.093**	**3.070**

1986-87

Pos'n	Cnty	Ave	Pts	P	W	D	L	F	A	Diff	B	No./T
1	Portugal	8.400	42	29	17	4	8	56	22	34	4	5
2	W. Germany	8.000	48	35	16	11	8	57	30	27	5	6
3	Sweden	7.500	30	22	10	6	6	37	24	13	4	4
4	Spain	7.400	37	32	14	4	14	39	35	4	5	5
5	Netherlands	7.250	29	21	11	4	6	36	20	16	3	4
6	Scotland	7.000	35	26	13	6	7	31	20	11	3	5
7	Wales	6.000	6	4	2	2	0	9	2	7	0	1
–	Italy	6.000	36	26	14	6	6	38	14	24	2	6
–	USSR	6.000	30	24	11	5	8	40	29	11	3	5
10	Austria	5.250	21	20	7	5	8	29	27	2	2	4
11	E. Germany	5.000	25	21	8	6	7	22	24	-2	3	5
12	Belgium	4.800	24	24	8	7	9	33	35	-2	1	5
13	France	4.200	21	18	8	3	7	21	23	-2	2	5
–	Yugoslavia	4.200	21	20	8	4	8	35	28	7	1	5
15	Switzerland	4.000	16	14	5	5	4	16	14	2	1	4
16	Poland	3.750	15	14	5	5	4	13	14	-1	0	4
17	Denmark	3.333	10	10	3	3	4	12	14	-2	1	3
18	Bulgaria	3.250	13	14	5	2	7	23	20	3	1	4
19	Czechoslovakia	2.600	13	16	3	7	6	11	19	-8	0	5
20	Romania	2.500	10	12	4	2	6	9	16	-7	0	4
21	Albania	2.333	7	8	2	3	3	4	8	-4	0	3
–	Turkey	2.333	7	8	3	0	5	5	17	-12	1	3
23	Greece	2.250	9	10	4	1	5	10	16	-6	0	4
24	Hungary	1.750	7	10	2	3	5	13	21	-8	0	4
25	Cyprus	1.666	5	6	2	1	3	6	12	-6	0	3
–	Finland	1.666	5	6	2	1	3	8	12	-4	0	3
27	Norway	1.333	4	8	1	2	5	4	13	-9	0	3
28	N. Ireland	1.000	3	6	0	3	3	3	7	-4	0	3
29	Luxembourg	0.333	1	6	0	1	5	2	15	-13	0	3
30	Rep. of Ireland	0.000	0	6	0	0	6	3	17	-14	0	3
–	Iceland	0.000	0	6	0	0	6	0	30	-30	0	3
–	Malta	0.000	0	6	0	0	6	0	27	-27	0	3
	Total		**530**	**488**	**188**	**112**	**188**	**625**	**625**	**0**	**42**	**2.561**

1955-56 to 1986-87

Pos'n	Cnty	Ave	Pts	P	W	D	L	F	A	Diff	B	No./T
1	England	8.806	1365	926	500	201	225	1782	927	855	164	155
2	W. Germany	7.906	1352	977	511	183	283	1966	1219	747	147	171
3	Spain	7.583	1221	899	452	164	283	1646	1096	550	153	161
4	Italy	7.090	1092	808	399	174	235	1266	819	447	120	154
5	USSR	6.303	498	367	192	76	99	580	361	219	38	79
6	Netherlands	5.886	677	531	260	97	174	1009	654	355	60	115
7	Scotland	5.835	747	604	285	114	205	1036	760	276	63	128
8	Belgium	5.390	690	581	265	100	216	947	772	175	60	128
9	Portugal	5.032	624	530	232	109	189	851	666	185	51	124
10	Hungary	4.980	518	450	201	72	177	802	672	130	44	104
11	Yugoslavia	4.947	658	590	246	108	236	976	850	126	58	133
12	E. Germany	4.768	515	464	191	96	177	698	619	79	37	108
13	Czechoslovakia	4.577	499	433	190	85	158	670	570	100	34	109
14	France	3.840	480	463	175	95	193	695	695	0	35	125
15	Poland	3.670	334	331	124	69	138	459	500	-41	17	91
16	Wales	3.653	95	94	31	27	36	135	110	25	6	26
17	Austria	3.285	345	372	121	77	174	493	602	-109	26	105
–	Bulgaria	3.285	322	337	124	57	156	500	532	-32	17	98
19	Romania	3.267	330	348	127	63	158	445	529	-84	13	101
20	Sweden	3.159	297	303	104	70	129	429	482	-53	19	94
21	Switzerland	2.923	342	387	124	73	190	575	721	-146	21	117
22	Greece	2.635	253	281	96	51	134	321	482	-161	10	96
23	Turkey	2.011	171	237	64	36	137	224	448	-224	7	85
24	Denmark	1.813	185	275	65	49	161	353	604	-251	6	102
25	Albania	1.576	41	60	12	17	31	38	88	-50	0	26
26	Norway	1.253	104	198	36	31	131	188	494	-306	1	83
27	Rep. of Ireland	1.111	90	194	28	34	132	161	482	-321	0	81
28	N. Ireland	1.105	84	174	23	36	115	166	472	-306	2	76
29	Finland	1.030	68	156	24	18	114	133	475	-342	2	66
30	Cyprus	0.816	49	130	16	17	97	99	463	-364	0	60
31	Malta	0.619	44	150	16	12	122	67	540	-473	0	71
32	Luxembourg	0.543	44	170	15	14	141	102	721	-619	0	81
33	Iceland	0.523	33	136	8	17	111	74	461	-387	0	63
	Total		**14167**	**12956**	**5257**	**2442**	**5257**	**19886**	**19886**	**0**	**1211**	**3.070**

Football Triumphs Over Glamour

The 1986-87 European Cups, still devoid of English participation, sprang up a number of surprises. First prizes in all three competitions went to clubs from less fashionable nations – Portugal, the Netherlands and Sweden – whilst the usual dominant forces of Spain, Italy, West Germany and, from afar, England could only look on in envy. The Italians, in particular, had a dreadful season, losing all six of their representatives before the semi-finals, four of them after unsuccessful penalty shoot-outs. As for the Spanish, after providing finalists in all three Cups the season before, they couldn't manage one this year.

Of the so-called European giants, Bayern Munich were the only team to impress consistently. They reached the final of the Champions' Cup for the fifth time, despatching on the way top-quality opponents in the shape of PSV Eindhoven, Austria Vienna, Anderlecht and Real Madrid. They gave a marvellous performance in freezing conditions to beat Anderlecht 5-0 in the first leg of the quarter-final, but their classiest and most courageous display was reserved for the semi-final against Real.

The Spaniards, back in the competition for the first time in six years, had scraped through the early stages, sandwiching a penalty shoot-out elimination of Juventus between two by now customary second-leg comebacks in the Bernabéu against Young Boys Berne and Red Star Belgrade. Their form away from Madrid was poor, and Bayern duly took advantage of this, inflicting on Real a fourth successive away defeat with a dramatic 4-1 victory in Munich. It was a match which had everything – goals, penalties, controversial refereeing decisions and two sendings-off – but left the Spaniards needing to pull off another of their great escape acts to stay in the competition. This time, however, they could not make up the deficit, scoring just once, through Santillana, in a game marred by the disgraceful behaviour of the Madrid fans, who bombarded the German players, and in particular their Belgian goalkeeper Jean-Marie Pfaff, with an assortment of projectiles throughout the 90 minutes.

So Real had lost for the first time in 16 European ties and it was Bayern who went through to the final in Vienna. Expected to meet them there were Cup-winners' Cup holders Dinamo Kiev, but they suffered a major upset in the semi-finals, beaten 2-1 in both legs by Portuguese underdogs, FC Porto, who thus made it through to their second European final in three years.

And what a final it was! The best, certainly, for a decade and, in terms of sheer excitement at the end, one of the best, perhaps, of all time. For the second year in a row, the form book was turned completely on its head. Two late goals for Porto, from Algerian striker Rabah Madjer and Brazilian substitute Juary, completely transformed a match which Bayern appeared, very cautiously, to be on the way to winning after a header from winger Ludwig Kögl had given them a 26th-minute lead. The Germans played reasonably well in the opening period and deserved their lead. But the second half saw a complete reversal of roles, with Bayern seemingly content to hold on to what they had, and Porto, with Juary on as an extra attacker, suddenly controlling the play. Whilst Madjer, with his nonchalantly back-heeled equaliser and his superb run and cross for the second goal, was the undisputed match-winner, Porto's real crowd-pleaser was young Paulo Futre, who constantly mesmerised the Bayern defence. One particularly astonishing run from the halfway line was reminiscent of Maradona at his best.

As for the little Argentinian maestro himself, fresh from his world-beating triumph in Mexico, he did not enjoy the best of starts to his European career with Napoli. His penalty miss sent Napoli crashing out of the first round of the UEFA Cup against French side Toulouse. That was just the first in a long list of upsets that were to figure in this season's UEFA Cup. There was almost another in the first round for Maradona's old club Barcelona, who needed a last-minute away goal to put out Albanian novices Flamurtari Vlorë.

Barcelona did survive as far as the quarter-finals, along with other pre-tournament favourites Inter

Milan, Torino and Borussia Mönchengladbach. But that was when the real shocks arrived, with only the Germans, of that quartet, surviving into the semi-finals. Barcelona were beaten both home and away by Scotland's Dundee United; Torino went down to Austrian surprise package FC Tirol; and Inter, seeking to reach the semi-finals for the third season in a row, succumbed on the away goals rule to the astonishing IFK Gothenburg, winners of the trophy in 1982 and now unbeaten in 21 successive UEFA Cup matches.

Gothenburg prolonged that sequence by two in the next round, winning both legs against Tirol. But there was yet another upset in the other tie, in which Dundee United, held at home to a goalless draw in the first leg, pulled off a gallant 2-0 victory in Mönchengladbach to reach their first ever European final.

The first leg of the final, in Gothenburg, was won by the home side 1-0 thanks to a headed goal after 38 minutes from striker Stefan Pettersson. United's high hopes of ending the Swedes' undefeated record and, more importantly, winning the Cup received a severe setback just 20 minutes into the return at Tannadice when Lennart Nilsson extended Gothenburg's aggregate lead. The Scots now required three goals. They got one back, on the hour, from centre-half turned centre-forward John Clark, but with the formidable partnership of Glenn Hysén and Peter Larsson masterminding the Gothenburg rearguard, there was no further breakthrough. The Swedes, for the second time in five years, lifted the trophy, and the sporting Scottish supporters applauded them around the ground on their lap of honour – a gesture later recognised by FIFA, who awarded them with their Fair Play trophy for 1987.

If the UEFA Cup had received a breath of fresh air with the success of several hitherto unfancied clubs, the Cup-winners' Cup welcomed the triumphant return of one of European football's most admired and respected names of the past, Ajax. Since reaching the semi-finals of the Champions' Cup in 1980, the famous Amsterdam club had won just two ties in six years of European competition. But with the great Johan Cruijff guiding the team from the bench, Ajax burst into form again in 1986-87 to win the Cup-winners' Cup in a style that bore all the familiar hallmarks of the Ajax of old.

There was talent in abundance in the side – Frank Rijkaard in defence, Jan Wouters in midfield and the twin attacking strike force of John Bosman and captain Marco van Basten up front. Bosman scored five goals to Van Basten's two in the first-round destruction of Turkish side Bursaspor. And both men were again on target against Olympiakos in the next round. Ajax were unfortunate to lose their first match of the competition to a highly debatable penalty in the first leg of the quarter-finals, against Malmö, but Van Basten saw them through again in Amsterdam with two goals in a 3-0 win. The team's best performance of all came in the semi-final, where they revived memories of the club's glorious *total football* past with two three-goal victories over Real Zaragoza.

The final, against Lokomotive Leipzig in Athens, proved to be something of a let down. Ajax won the game, with a typically spectacular Van Basten header midway through the first half, but there was disappointment that they could not repeat their semi-final form and put on a display worthy of either Dinamo Kiev a year earlier or their own predecessors from the early '70s. The opposition, of course, had much to do with it. The East Germans, who had only got to Athens after a penalty shoot-out victory over Bordeaux in the semi-final, persisted with their dull, defensive tactics even after Ajax had taken the lead. Clearly, having never reached a European final before, they were just happy to be there.

1987 – 1988

PSV Eindhoven

KV Mechelen

Bayer Leverkusen

First Round

Team 1	Cnty	Team 2	Cnty	1st leg	2nd leg	Agg
Rapid Vienna	Aut	Hamrun Spartans	Mlt	6-0	1-0	7-0
AGF Aarhus	Den	Jeunesse Esch	Lux	4-1	0-1	4-2
Shamrock Rovers	Irl	Omonia Nicosia	Cyp	0-1	0-0	0-1
Real Madrid	Esp	Napoli	Ita	2-0	1-1	3-1
Girondins Bordeaux	Fra	Dynamo Berlin	GDR	2-0	2-0	4-0
Olympiakos Pireus	Gre	Górnik Zabrze	Pol	1-1	1-2	2-3
Fram Reykjavik	Isl	Sparta Prague	Tch	0-2	0-8	0-10
Lillestrøm SK	Nor	Linfield	Nir	1-1	4-2	5-3
PSV Eindhoven	Ned	Galatasaray	Tur	3-0	0-2	3-2
Benfica	Por	Partizani Tirana	Alb	4-0		4-0
FC Porto	Por	Vardar Skoplje	Yug	3-0	3-0	6-0
Bayern Munich	FRG	CSKA Sofia	Bul	4-0	1-0	5-0
Steaua Bucharest	Rom	MTK-VM	Hun	4-0	0-2	4-2
Malmö FF	Swe	Anderlecht	Bel	0-1	1-1	1-2
Neuchâtel Xamax	Sui	FC Kuusysi Lahti	Fin	5-0	1-2	6-2
Dinamo Kiev	URS	Rangers	Sco	1-0	0-2	1-2

	Pts	P	W	D	L	F	A	Diff	Goals/P
Total	62	31	26	10	26	85	85	0	2.742

Second Round

Rapid Vienna	Aut	PSV Eindhoven	Ned	1-2	0-2	1-4
AGF Aarhus	Den	Benfica	Por	0-0	0-1	0-1
Rangers	Sco	Górnik Zabrze	Pol	3-1	1-1	4-2
Real Madrid	Esp	FC Porto	Por	2-1	2-1	4-2
Lillestrøm SK	Nor	Girondins Bordeaux	Fra	0-0	0-1	0-1
Steaua Bucharest	Rom	Omonia Nicosia	Cyp	3-1	2-0	5-1
Neuchâtel Xamax	Sui	Bayern Munich	FRG	2-1	0-2	2-3
Sparta Prague	Tch	Anderlecht	Bel	1-2	0-1	1-3

	Pts	P	W	D	L	F	A	Diff	Goals/P
Total	32	16	13	6	13	34	34	0	2.125

Quarter Finals

Girondins Bordeaux	Fra	PSV Eindhoven	Ned	1-1	0-0	1-1
Benfica	Por	Anderlecht	Bel	2-0	0-1	2-1
Bayern Munich	FRG	Real Madrid	Esp	3-2	0-2	3-4
Steaua Bucharest	Rom	Rangers	Sco	2-0	1-2	3-2

	Pts	P	W	D	L	F	A	Diff	Goals/P
Total	16	8	6	4	6	17	17	0	2.125

Semi Finals

Real Madrid	Esp	PSV Eindhoven	Ned	1-1	0-0	1-1
Steaua Bucharest	Rom	Benfica	Por	0-0	0-2	0-2

	Pts	P	W	D	L	F	A	Diff	Goals/P
Total	8	4	1	6	1	4	4	0	1.000

Final

PSV Eindhoven	Ned	Benfica	Por	0-0	0-0

	Pts	P	W	D	L	F	A	Diff	Goals/P
Total	2	1	0	2	0	0	0	0	0.000

	Pts	P	W	D	L	F	A	Diff	Goals/P
Total	120	60	46	28	46	140	140	0	2.333

Pos'n	Club	Cnty	Pts	P	W	D	L	F	A	Diff	B	Pts/P	F/P
1	Benfica	Por	14	8	4	3	1	9	1	8	3	1.750	1.125
2	PSV Eindhoven	Ned	14	9	3	5	1	9	5	4	3	1.556	1.000
3	Real Madrid	Esp	13	8	4	3	1	12	7	5	2	1.625	1.500
4	Steaua Bucharest	Rom	11	8	4	1	3	12	7	5	2	1.375	1.500
5	Girondins Bordeaux	Fra	10	6	3	3	0	6	1	5	1	1.667	1.000
6	Anderlecht	Bel	10	6	4	1	1	6	4	2	1	1.667	1.000
7	Bayern Munich	FRG	9	6	4	0	2	11	6	5	1	1.500	1.833
8	Rangers	Sco	8	6	3	1	2	8	6	2	1	1.333	1.333
9	Sparta Prague	Tch	4	4	2	0	2	11	3	8	0	1.000	2.750
10	Rapid Vienna	Aut	4	4	2	0	2	8	4	4	0	1.000	2.000
–	FC Porto	Por	4	4	2	0	2	8	4	4	0	1.000	2.000
12	Neuchâtel Xamax	Sui	4	4	2	0	2	8	5	3	0	1.000	2.000
13	Lillestrøm SK	Nor	4	4	1	2	1	5	4	1	0	1.000	1.250
14	Górnik Zabrze	Pol	4	4	1	2	1	5	6	-1	0	1.000	1.250
15	AGF Aarhus	Den	3	4	1	1	2	4	3	1	0	0.750	1.000
16	Omonia Nicosia	Cyp	3	4	1	1	2	2	5	-3	0	0.750	0.500
17	Galatasaray	Tur	2	2	1	0	1	2	3	-1	0	1.000	1.000
18	Dinamo Kiev	URS	2	2	1	0	1	1	2	-1	0	1.000	0.500
19	MTK-VM	Hun	2	2	1	0	1	2	4	-2	0	1.000	1.000
–	Jeunesse Esch	Lux	2	2	1	0	1	2	4	-2	0	1.000	1.000
21	FC Kuusysi Lahti	Fin	2	2	1	0	1	2	6	-4	0	1.000	1.000
22	Olympiakos Pireus	Gre	1	2	0	1	1	2	3	-1	0	0.500	1.000
23	Malmö FF	Swe	1	2	0	1	1	1	2	-1	0	0.500	0.500
24	Shamrock Rovers	Irl	1	2	0	1	1	0	1	-1	0	0.500	0.000
25	Linfield	Nir	1	2	0	1	1	3	5	-2	0	0.500	1.500
26	Napoli	Ita	1	2	0	1	1	1	3	-2	0	0.500	0.500
27	Partizani Tirana	Alb	0	1	0	0	1	0	4	-4	0	0.000	0.000
–	Dynamo Berlin	GDR	0	2	0	0	2	0	4	-4	0	0.000	0.000
29	CSKA Sofia	Bul	0	2	0	0	2	0	5	-5	0	0.000	0.000
30	Vardar Skoplje	Yug	0	2	0	0	2	0	6	-6	0	0.000	0.000
31	Hamrun Spartans	Mlt	0	2	0	0	2	0	7	-7	0	0.000	0.000
32	Fram Reykjavik	Isl	0	2	0	0	2	0	10	-10	0	0.000	0.000
	Total		**134**	**120**	**46**	**28**	**46**	**140**	**140**	**0**	**14**	**1.117**	**2.333**

Preliminary Round

Team 1	Cnty	Team 2	Cnty	1st leg	2nd leg	Agg
AEL Limassol	Cyp	DAC Dunajská Streda	Tch	0-1	0-5	0-6

	Pts	P	W	D	L	F	A	Diff	Goals/P
Total	4	2	2	0	2	6	6	0	3.000

First Round

Vllaznia Shkodër	Alb	Sliema Wanderers	Mlt	2-0	4-0	6-0
KV Mechelen	Bel	Dinamo Bucharest	Rom	1-0	2-0	3-0
Levski Sofia	Bul	OFI Crete	Gre	1-0	1-3	2-3
AaB Aalborg	Den	Hajduk Split	Yug	1-0	0-1	1-1
St. Mirren	Sco	Tromsø IL	Nor	1-0	0-0	1-0
Real Sociedad	Esp	Slask Wroclaw	Pol	0-0	2-0	2-0
RoPS Rovaniemi	Fin	Glentoran	Nir	0-0	1-1	1-1
Merthyr Tydfil	Wal	Atalanta	Ita	2-1	0-2	2-3
Ujpesti Dózsa	Hun	FC Den Haag	Ned	1-0	1-3	2-3
IA Akranes	Isl	Kalmar FF	Swe	0-0	0-1	0-1
Avenir Beggen	Lux	Hamburg	FRG	0-5	0-3	0-8
Ajax	Ned	Dundalk	Irl	4-0	2-0	6-0
Sporting Lisbon	Por	FC Tirol	Aut	4-0	2-4	6-4
DAC Dunajská Streda	Tch	Young Boys Berne	Sui	2-1	1-3	3-4
Dinamo Minsk	URS	Gençlerbirligi	Tur	2-0	2-1	4-1
Lokomotive Leipzig	GDR	Olympique Marseille	Fra	0-0	0-1	0-1

	Pts	P	W	D	L	F	A	Diff	Goals/P
Total	64	32	26	12	26	69	69	0	2.156

Second Round

Vllaznia Shkodër	Alb	RoPS Rovaniemi	Fin	0-1	0-1	0-2
KV Mechelen	Bel	St. Mirren	Sco	0-0	2-0	2-0
Real Sociedad	Esp	Dinamo Minsk	URS	1-1	0-0	1-1
Olympique Marseille	Fra	Hajduk Split	Yug	4-0	3-0	7-0
OFI Crete	Gre	Atalanta	Ita	1-0	0-2	1-2
FC Den Haag	Ned	Young Boys Berne	Sui	2-1	0-1	2-2
Hamburg	FRG	Ajax	Ned	0-1	0-2	0-3
Kalmar FF	Swe	Sporting Lisbon	Por	1-0	0-5	1-5

	Pts	P	W	D	L	F	A	Diff	Goals/P
Total	32	16	13	6	13	29	29	0	1.813

Quarter Finals

KV Mechelen	Bel	Dinamo Minsk	URS	1-0	1-1	2-1
RoPS Rovaniemi	Fin	Olympique Marseille	Fra	0-1	0-3	0-4
Atalanta	Ita	Sporting Lisbon	Por	2-0	1-1	3-1
Young Boys Berne	Sui	Ajax	Ned	0-1	0-1	0-2

	Pts	P	W	D	L	F	A	Diff	Goals/P
Total	16	8	6	4	6	13	13	0	1.625

Semi Finals

KV Mechelen	Bel	Atalanta	Ita	2-1	2-1		4-2
Olympique Marseille	Fra	Ajax	Ned	0-3	2-1		2-4

	Pts	P	W	D	L	F	A	Diff	Goals/P
Total	8	4	4	0	4	12	12	0	3.000

Final

KV Mechelen	Bel	Ajax	Ned	1-0	1-0

	Pts	P	W	D	L	F	A	Diff	Goals/P
Total	2	1	1	0	1	1	1	0	1.000

	Pts	P	W	D	L	F	A	Diff	Goals/P
Total	126	63	52	22	52	130	130	0	2.063

Pos'n	Club	Cnty	Pts	P	W	D	L	F	A	Diff	B	Pts/P	F/P
1	KV Mechelen	Bel	19	9	7	2	0	12	3	9	3	2.111	1.333
2	Ajax	Ned	17	9	7	0	2	15	3	12	3	1.889	1.667
3	Olympique Marseille	Fra	15	8	6	1	1	14	4	10	2	1.875	1.750
4	Atalanta	Ita	9	8	3	1	4	10	8	2	2	1.125	1.250
5	Dinamo Minsk	URS	8	6	2	3	1	6	4	2	1	1.333	1.000
6	RoPS Rovaniemi	Fin	7	6	2	2	2	3	5	-2	1	1.167	0.500
7	DAC Dunajská Streda	Tch	6	4	3	0	1	9	4	5	0	1.500	2.250
8	Sporting Lisbon	Por	6	6	2	1	3	12	8	1	1	1.000	2.000
9	Real Sociedad	Esp	5	4	1	3	0	3	1	2	0	1.250	0.750
10	Young Boys Berne	Sui	5	6	2	0	4	6	7	-1	1	0.833	1.000
11	Kalmar FF	Swe	5	4	2	1	1	2	5	-3	0	1.250	0.500
12	Hamburg	FRG	4	4	2	0	2	8	3	5	0	1.000	2.000
13	Vllaznia Skhodër	Alb	4	4	2	0	2	6	2	4	0	1.000	1.500
14	FC Den Haag	Ned	4	4	2	0	2	5	4	1	0	1.000	1.250
15	OFI Crete	Gre	4	4	2	0	2	4	4	0	0	1.000	1.000
16	St. Mirren	Sco	4	4	1	2	1	1	2	-1	0	1.000	0.250
17	AaB Aalborg	Den	2	2	1	0	1	1	1	0	0	1.000	0.500
–	Glentoran	Nir	2	2	0	2	0	1	1	0	0	1.000	0.500
19	Levski Sofia	Bul	2	2	1	0	1	2	3	-1	0	1.000	1.000
–	Merthyr Tydfil	Wal	2	2	1	0	1	2	3	-1	0	1.000	1.000
–	Ujpesti Dózsa	Hun	2	2	1	0	1	2	3	-1	0	1.000	1.000
22	FC Tirol	Aut	2	2	1	0	1	4	6	-2	0	1.000	2.000
23	Hajduk Split	Yug	2	4	1	0	3	1	8	-7	0	0.500	0.250
24	IA Akranes	Isl	1	2	0	1	1	0	1	-1	0	0.500	0.000
–	Tromsø IL	Nor	1	2	0	1	1	0	1	-1	0	0.500	0.000
–	Lokomotive Leipzig	GDR	1	2	0	1	1	0	1	-1	0	0.500	0.000
27	Slask Wroclaw	Pol	1	2	0	1	1	0	2	-2	0	0.500	0.000
28	Gençlerbirligi	Tur	0	2	0	0	2	1	4	-3	0	0.000	0.500
29	Dinamo Bucharest	Rom	0	2	0	0	2	0	3	-3	0	0.000	0.000
30	AEL Limassol	Cyp	0	2	0	0	2	0	6	-6	0	0.000	0.000
–	Dundalk	Irl	0	2	0	0	2	0	6	-6	0	0.000	0.000
–	Sliema Wanderers	Mlt	0	2	0	0	2	0	6	-6	0	0.000	0.000
33	Avenir Beggen	Lux	0	2	0	0	2	0	8	-8	0	0.000	0.000
	Total		**140**	**126**	**52**	**22**	**52**	**130**	**130**	**0**	**14**	**1.111**	**2.063**

First Round

Team 1	Cnty	Team 2	Cnty	1st leg	2nd leg	Agg
Flamurtari Vlorë	Alb	Partizan Belgrade	Yug	2-0	1-2	3-2
Linzer ASK	Aut	Utrecht	Ned	0-0	0-2	0-2
Austria Vienna	Aut	Bayer Leverkusen	FRG	0-0	1-5	1-5
Beveren	Bel	Bohemians Prague	Tch	2-0	0-1	2-1
Lokomotiv Sofia	Bul	Dinamo Tbilisi	URS	3-1	0-3	3-4
EPA Larnaca	Cyp	Victoria Bucharest	Rom	0-1	0-3	0-4
Brøndby IF	Den	IFK Gothenburg	Swe	2-1	0-0	2-1
Celtic	Sco	Borussia Dortmund	FRG	2-1	0-2	2-3
Bohemians	Irl	Aberdeen	Sco	0-0	0-1	0-1
Barcelona	Esp	Belenenses	Por	2-0	0-1	2-1
Sporting Gijón	Esp	AC Milan	Ita	1-0	0-3	1-3
TPS Turku	Fin	Admira Wacker	Aut	0-1	2-0	2-1
Toulouse	Fra	Panionios	Gre	5-1	1-0	6-1
Panathinaikos	Gre	Auxerre	Fra	2-0	2-3	4-3
Honvéd	Hun	Lokeren	Bel	1-0	0-0	1-0
Tatabánya	Hun	Vitória Guimarães	Por	1-1	0-1	1-2
Coleraine	Nir	Dundee United	Sco	0-1	1-3	1-4
Valletta	Mlt	Juventus	Ita	0-4	0-3	0-7
Mjøndalen IF	Nor	Werder Bremen	FRG	0-5	1-0	1-5
Feyenoord	Ned	Spora Luxembourg	Lux	5-0	5-2	10-2
Pogon Szczecin	Pol	Verona	Ita	1-1	1-3	2-4
Bor. Mönchengladbach	FRG	Español	Esp	0-1	1-4	1-5
Sportul Studentesc Bucharest	Rom	GKS Katowice	Pol	1-0	2-1	3-1
Universitatea Craiova	Rom	Chaves	Por	3-2	1-2	4-4
Grasshoppers Zürich	Sui	Dinamo Moscow	URS	0-4	0-1	0-5
TJ Vitkovice	Tch	AIK	Swe	1-1	2-0	3-1
Besiktas	Tur	Inter Milan	Ita	0-0	1-3	1-3
Zenit Leningrad	URS	Club Bruges	Bel	2-0	0-5	2-5
Spartak Moscow	URS	Dynamo Dresden	GDR	3-0	0-1	3-1
Red Star Belgrade	Yug	Trakia Plovdiv	Bul	3-0	2-2	5-2
Velez Mostar	Yug	Sion	Sui	5-0	0-3	5-3
Wismut Aue	GDR	Valur Reykjavik	Isl	0-0	1-1	1-1

	Pts	P	W	D	L	F	A	Diff	Goals/P
Total	128	64	52	24	52	159	159	9	2.484

Second Round

Brøndby IF	Den	Sportul Studentesc Bucharest	Rom	3-0	0-3	3-3
Aberdeen	Sco	Feyenoord	Ned	2-1	0-1	2-2
Dundee United	Sco	TJ Vitkovice	Tch	1-2	1-1	2-3
Barcelona	Esp	Dinamo Moscow	URS	2-0	0-0	2-0
Toulouse	Fra	Bayer Leverkusen	FRG	1-1	0-1	1-2
Panathinaikos	Gre	Juventus	Ita	1-0	2-3	3-3
AC Milan	Ita	Español	Esp	0-2	0-0	0-2
Inter Milan	Ita	TPS Turku	Fin	0-1	2-0	2-1
Utrecht	Ned	Verona	Ita	1-1	1-2	2-3
Chaves	Por	Honvéd	Hun	1-2	1-3	2-5
Vitória Guimarães	Por	Beveren	Bel	1-0	0-1	1-1
Borussia Dortmund	FRG	Velez Mostar	Yug	2-0	1-2	3-2
Victoria Bucharest	Rom	Dinamo Tbilisi	URS	1-2	0-0	1-2
Spartak Moscow	URS	Werder Bremen	FRG	4-1	2-6	6-7
Red Star Belgrade	Yug	Club Bruges	Bel	3-1	0-4	3-5
Wismut Aue	GDR	Flamurtari Vlorë	Alb	1-0	0-2	1-2

	Pts	P	W	D	L	F	A	Diff	Goals/P
Total	64	32	26	12	26	77	77	0	2.406

Third Round

Barcelona	Esp	Flamurtari Vlorë	Alb	4-1	0-1	4-2
Honvéd	Hun	Panathinaikos	Gre	5-2	1-5	6-7
Inter Milan	Ita	Español	Esp	1-1	0-1	1-2
Verona	Ita	Sportul Studentesc Bucharest	Rom	3-1	1-0	4-1
Feyenoord	Ned	Bayer Leverkusen	FRG	2-2	0-1	2-3
Vitória Guimarães	Por	TJ Vitkovice	Tch	2-0	0-2	2-2
Werder Bremen	FRG	Dinamo Tbilisi	URS	2-1	1-1	3-2
Borussia Dortmund	FRG	Club Bruges	Bel	3-0	0-5	3-5

	Pts	P	W	D	L	F	A	Diff	Goals/P
Total	32	16	13	6	13	49	49	0	3.063

Quarter Finals

Español	Esp	TJ Vitkovice	Tch	2-0	0-0	2-0
Panathinaikos	Gre	Club Bruges	Bel	2-2	0-1	2-3
Verona	Ita	Werder Bremen	FRG	0-1	1-1	1-2
Bayer Leverkusen	FRG	Barcelona	Esp	0-0	1-0	1-0

	Pts	P	W	D	L	F	A	Diff	Goals/P
Total	16	8	4	8	4	11	11	0	1.375

Semi Finals

Club Bruges	Bel	Español	Esp	2-0	0-3	2-3
Bayer Leverkusen	FRG	Werder Bremen	FRG	1-0	0-0	1-0

	Pts	P	W	D	L	F	A	Diff	Goals/P
Total	8	4	3	2	3	6	6	0	1.5000

Final

Español	Esp	Bayer Leverkusen	FRG	3-0	0-3	3-3

	Pts	P	W	D	L	F	A	Diff	Goals/P
Total	4	2	2	0	2	6	6	0	3.000

	Pts	P	W	D	L	F	A	Diff	Goals/P
Total	252	126	100	52	100	308	308	0	2.444

Pos'n	Club	Cnty	Pts	P	W	D	L	F	A	Diff	B	Pts/P	F/P
1	Español	Esp	20	12	7	3	2	17	7	10	3	1.667	1.417
2	Bayer Leverkusen	FRG	20	12	6	5	1	15	7	8	3	1.667	1.250
3	Club Bruges	Bel	13	10	5	1	4	20	13	7	2	1.300	2.000
4	Werder Bremen	FRG	13	10	4	3	3	17	11	6	2	1.300	1.700
5	Verona	Ita	12	8	4	3	1	12	7	5	1	1.500	1.500
6	TJ Vitkovice	Tch	10	8	3	3	2	8	7	1	1	1.250	1.000
7	Barcelona	Esp	9	8	3	2	3	8	4	4	1	1.125	1.000
8	Honvéd	Hun	9	6	4	1	1	12	9	3	0	1.500	2.000
9	Panathinaikos	Gre	8	8	3	1	4	16	15	1	1	1.000	2.000
10	Feyenoord	Ned	7	6	3	1	2	14	7	7	0	1.167	2.333
11	Vitória Guimarães	Por	7	6	3	1	2	5	4	1	0	1.167	0.833
12	Juventus	Ita	6	4	3	0	1	10	3	7	0	1.500	2.500
13	Inter Milan	Ita	6	6	2	2	2	6	4	2	0	1.000	1.000
14	Dinamo Tbilisi	URS	6	6	2	2	2	8	7	1	0	1.000	1.333
15	Borrusia Dortmund	FRG	6	6	3	0	3	9	9	0	0	1.000	1.500
16	Flamutari Vlorë	Alb	6	6	3	0	3	7	7	0	0	1.000	1.167
17	Sportul Studentesc Bucharest	Rom	6	6	3	0	3	7	8	-1	0	1.000	1.167
18	Toulouse	Fra	5	4	2	1	1	7	3	4	0	1.250	1.750
19	Victoria Bucharest	Rom	5	4	2	1	1	5	2	3	0	1.250	1.250
–	Dinamo Moscow	URS	5	4	2	1	1	5	2	3	0	1.250	1.250
21	Dundee United	Sco	5	4	2	1	1	6	4	2	0	1.250	1.500
22	Red Star Belgrade	Yug	5	4	2	1	1	8	7	1	0	1.250	2.000
23	Brøndby IF	Den	5	4	2	1	1	5	4	1	0	1.250	1.250
24	Aberdeen	Sco	5	4	2	1	1	3	2	1	0	1.250	0.750
25	Spartak Moscow	URS	4	4	2	0	2	9	8	1	0	1.000	2.250
26	Velez Mostar	Yug	4	4	2	0	2	7	6	1	0	1.000	1.750
27	Utrecht	Ned	4	4	1	2	1	4	3	1	0	1.000	1.000
28	Beveren	Bel	4	4	2	0	2	3	2	1	0	1.000	0.750
29	TPS Turku	Fin	4	4	2	0	2	3	3	0	0	1.000	0.750
30	Wismut Aue	GDR	4	4	1	2	1	2	3	-1	0	1.000	0.500
31	AC Milan	Ita	3	4	1	1	2	3	3	0	0	0.750	0.750
32	Universitatea Craiova	Rom	2	2	1	0	1	4	4	0	0	1.000	2.000
33	Valur Reykjavik	Isl	2	2	0	2	0	1	1	0	0	1.000	0.500
34	Lokomotiv Sofia	Bul	2	2	1	0	1	3	4	-1	0	1.000	1.500
–	Auxerre	Fra	2	2	1	0	1	3	4	-1	0	1.000	1.500
36	Celtic	Sco	2	2	1	0	1	2	3	-1	0	1.000	1.000
–	Partizan Belgrade	Yug	2	2	1	0	1	2	3	-1	0	1.000	1.000
38	Admira Wacker	Aut	2	2	1	0	1	1	2	-1	0	1.000	0.500
–	Belenenses	Por	2	2	1	0	1	1	2	-1	0	1.000	0.500
–	Bohemians Prague	Tch	2	2	1	0	1	1	2	-1	0	1.000	0.500
41	Sion	Sui	2	2	1	0	1	3	5	-2	0	1.000	1.500
42	Sporting Gijón	Esp	2	2	1	0	1	1	3	-2	0	1.000	0.500
–	Dynamo Dresden	GDR	2	2	1	0	1	1	3	-2	0	1.000	0.500
44	Chaves	Por	2	4	1	0	3	6	9	-3	0	0.500	1.500
45	Zenit Leningrad	URS	2	2	1	0	1	2	5	-3	0	1.000	1.000
46	Mjøndalen IF	Nor	2	2	1	0	1	1	5	-4	0	1.000	0.500
47	Tatabánya	Hun	1	2	0	1	1	1	2	-1	0	0.500	0.500
–	IFK Gothenburg	Swe	1	2	0	1	1	1	2	-1	0	0.500	0.500
49	Lokeren	Bel	1	2	0	1	1	0	1	-1	0	0.500	0.000
–	Bohemians	Irl	1	2	0	1	1	0	1	-1	0	0.500	0.000
51	Pogon Szczecin	Pol	1	2	0	1	1	2	4	-2	0	0.500	1.000
52	AIK	Swe	1	2	0	1	1	1	3	-2	0	0.500	0.500
–	Besiktas	Tur	1	2	0	1	1	1	3	-2	0	0.500	0.500
54	Linzer ASK	Aut	1	2	0	1	1	0	2	-2	0	0.500	0.000
55	Trakia Plovdiv	Bul	1	2	0	1	1	2	5	-3	0	0.500	1.000
56	Austria Vienna	Aut	1	2	0	1	1	1	5	-4	0	0.500	0.500
57	GKS Katowice	Pol	0	2	0	0	2	1	3	-2	0	0.000	0.500
58	Coleraine	Nir	0	2	0	0	2	1	4	-3	0	0.000	0.500
59	Bor. Mönchengladbach	FRG	0	2	0	0	2	1	5	-4	0	0.000	0.500
60	EPA Larnaca	Cyp	0	2	0	0	2	0	4	-4	0	0.000	0.000
61	Panionios	Gre	0	2	0	0	2	1	6	-5	0	0.000	0.500
62	Grasshoppers Zürich	Sui	0	2	0	0	2	0	5	-5	0	0.000	0.000
63	Valletta	Mlt	0	2	0	0	2	0	7	-7	0	0.000	0.000
64	Spora Luxembourg	Lux	0	2	0	0	2	2	10	-8	0	0.000	1.000
	Total		**266**	**252**	**100**	**52**	**100**	**308**	**308**	**0**	**14**	**1.056**	**2.444**

1987-88

Pos'n	Cnty	Pts	P	W	D	L	F	A	Diff	B	Pts/P	F/P
1	FRG	52	40	19	8	13	61	41	20	6	1.300	1.525
2	Esp	49	34	16	11	7	41	22	19	6	1.441	1.206
3	Bel	47	31	18	5	8	41	23	18	6	1.516	1.323
4	Ned	46	32	16	8	8	47	22	25	6	1.438	1.469
5	Ita	37	32	13	8	11	42	28	14	3	1.156	1.313
6	Por	35	30	13	5	12	41	28	13	4	1.167	1.367
7	Fra	32	20	12	5	3	30	12	18	3	1.600	1.500
8	URS	27	24	10	6	8	31	28	3	1	1.125	1.292
9	Rom	24	22	10	2	10	28	24	4	2	1.091	1.273
10	Sco	24	20	9	5	6	20	17	3	1	1.200	1.000
11	Tch	22	18	9	3	6	29	16	13	1	1.222	1.611
12	Hun	14	12	6	2	4	17	18	-1	0	1.167	1.417
13	Gre	13	16	5	2	9	23	28	-5	1	0.813	1.438
14	Fin	13	12	5	2	5	8	14	-6	1	1.083	0.667
15	Yug	13	16	6	1	9	18	30	-12	0	0.813	1.125
16	Sui	11	14	5	0	9	17	22	-5	1	0.786	1.214
17	Den	10	10	4	2	4	10	8	2	0	1.000	1.000
18	Alb	10	11	5	0	6	13	13	0	0	0.909	1.182
19	Aut	10	12	4	2	6	14	19	-5	0	0.833	1.167
20	Swe	8	10	2	4	4	5	12	-7	0	0.800	0.500
21	Nor	7	8	2	3	3	6	10	-4	0	0.875	0.750
22	GDR	7	10	2	3	5	3	11	-8	0	0.700	0.300
23	Pol	6	10	1	4	5	8	15	-7	0	0.600	0.800
24	Bul	5	8	2	1	5	7	17	-10	0	0.625	0.875
25	Nir	3	6	0	3	3	5	10	-5	0	0.500	0.833
26	Tur	3	6	1	1	4	4	10	-6	0	0.500	0.667
27	Isl	3	6	0	3	3	1	12	-11	0	0.500	0.167
28	Cyp	3	8	1	1	6	2	15	-13	0	0.375	0.250
29	Wal	2	2	1	0	1	2	3	-1	0	1.000	1.000
30	Irl	2	6	0	2	4	0	8	-8	0	0.333	0.000
31	Lux	2	6	1	0	5	4	22	-18	0	0.333	0.667
32	Mlt	0	6	0	0	6	0	20	-20	0	0.000	0.000
	Total	**540**	**498**	**198**	**102**	**198**	**578**	**578**	**0**	**42**	**1.084**	**2.321**

1955-56 to 1987-88

1	FRG	1404	1017	530	191	296	2027	1260	767	153	1.381	1.993
2	Eng	1365	926	500	201	225	1782	927	855	164	1.474	1.924
3	Esp	1270	933	468	175	290	1687	1118	569	159	1.361	1.808
4	Ita	1129	840	412	182	246	1308	847	461	123	1.344	1.557
5	Sco	771	624	294	119	211	1056	777	279	64	1.236	1.692
6	Bel	737	612	283	105	224	988	795	193	66	1.204	1.614
7	Ned	723	563	276	105	182	1056	676	380	66	1.284	1.876
8	Yug	671	606	252	109	245	994	880	114	58	1.107	1.640
9	Por	659	560	245	114	201	892	694	198	55	1.177	1.593
10	Hun	532	462	207	74	181	819	690	129	44	1.152	1.773
11	URS	525	391	202	82	107	611	389	222	39	1.343	1.563
12	GDR	522	474	193	99	182	701	630	71	37	1.101	1.479
13	Tch	521	451	199	88	164	699	586	113	35	1.155	1.550
14	Fra	512	483	187	100	196	725	707	18	38	1.060	1.501
15	Aut	355	384	125	79	180	507	621	-114	26	0.924	1.320
16	Rom	354	370	137	65	168	473	553	-80	15	0.957	1.278
17	Sui	353	401	129	73	199	592	743	-151	22	0.880	1.476
18	Pol	340	341	125	73	143	467	515	-48	17	0.997	1.370
19	Bul	327	345	126	58	161	507	549	-42	17	0.948	1.470
20	Swe	305	313	106	74	133	434	494	-60	19	0.974	1.387
21	Gre	266	297	101	53	143	344	510	-166	11	0.896	1.158
22	Den	195	285	69	51	165	363	612	-249	6	0.684	1.274
23	Tur	174	243	65	37	141	228	458	-230	7	0.716	0.938
24	Nor	111	206	38	34	134	194	504	-310	1	0.539	0.942
25	Wal	97	96	32	27	37	137	113	24	6	1.010	1.427
26	Irl	92	200	28	36	136	161	490	-329	0	0.460	0.805
27	Nir	87	180	23	39	118	171	482	-311	2	0.483	0.950
28	Fin	81	168	29	20	119	141	489	-348	3	0.482	0.839
29	Cyp	52	138	17	18	103	101	478	-377	0	0.377	0.732
30	Alb	51	71	17	17	37	51	101	-50	0	0.718	0.718
31	Lux	46	176	16	14	146	106	743	-637	0	0.261	0.602
32	Mlt	44	156	16	12	128	67	560	-493	0	0.282	0.429
33	Isl	36	142	8	20	114	75	473	-398	0	0.254	0.528
	Total	**14707**	**13454**	**5455**	**2544**	**5455**	**20464**	**20464**	**0**	**1253**	**1.093**	**3.042**

1987-88

Pos'n	Cnty	Ave	Pts	P	W	D	L	F	A	Diff	B	No./T
1	Spain	9.800	49	34	16	11	7	41	22	19	6	5
2	Belgium	9.400	47	31	18	5	8	41	23	18	6	5
3	Netherlands	9.200	46	32	16	8	8	47	22	25	6	5
4	W. Germany	8.666	52	40	19	8	13	61	41	20	6	6
5	France	8.000	32	20	12	5	3	30	12	18	3	4
6	Italy	6.166	37	32	13	8	11	42	28	14	3	6
7	Portugal	5.833	35	30	13	5	12	41	28	13	4	6
8	Czechoslovakia	5.500	22	18	9	3	6	29	16	13	1	4
9	Scotland	4.800	24	20	9	5	6	20	17	3	1	5
–	Romania	4.800	24	22	10	2	10	28	24	4	2	5
11	USSR	4.500	27	24	10	6	8	31	28	3	1	6
12	Finland	4.333	13	12	5	2	5	8	14	-6	1	3
13	Hungary	3.500	14	12	6	2	4	17	18	-1	0	4
14	Albania	3.333	10	11	5	0	6	13	13	0	0	3
–	Denmark	3.333	10	10	4	2	4	10	8	2	0	3
16	Greece	3.250	13	16	5	2	9	23	28	-5	1	4
17	Switzerland	2.750	11	14	5	0	9	17	22	-5	1	4
18	Yugoslavia	2.600	13	16	6	1	9	18	30	-12	0	5
19	Norway	2.333	7	8	2	3	3	6	10	-4	0	3
20	Austria	2.000	10	12	4	2	6	14	19	-5	0	5
–	Wales	2.000	2	2	1	0	1	2	3	-1	0	1
–	Sweden	2.000	8	10	2	4	4	5	12	-7	0	4
23	E. Germany	1.750	7	10	2	3	5	3	11	-8	0	4
24	Poland	1.500	6	10	1	4	5	8	15	-7	0	4
25	Bulgaria	1.250	5	8	2	1	5	7	17	-10	0	4
26	Cyprus	1.000	3	8	1	1	6	2	15	-13	0	3
–	N. Ireland	1.000	3	6	0	3	3	5	10	-5	0	3
–	Iceland	1.000	3	6	0	3	3	1	12	-11	0	3
–	Turkey	1.000	3	6	1	1	4	4	10	-6	0	3
30	Rep. of Ireland	0.666	2	6	0	2	4	0	8	-8	0	3
–	Luxembourg	0.666	2	6	1	0	5	4	22	-18	0	3
32	Malta	0.000	0	6	0	0	6	0	20	-20	0	3
	Total		**540**	**498**	**198**	**102**	**198**	**578**	**578**	**0**	**42**	**2.321**

1955-56 to 1987-88

Pos'n	Cnty	Ave	Pts	P	W	D	L	F	A	Diff	B	No./T
1	England	8.806	1365	926	500	201	225	1782	927	855	164	155
2	W. Germany	7.932	1404	1017	530	191	296	2027	1260	767	153	177
3	Spain	7.650	1270	933	468	175	290	1687	1118	569	159	166
4	Italy	7.056	1129	840	412	182	246	1308	847	461	123	160
5	USSR	6.176	525	391	202	82	107	611	389	222	39	85
6	Netherlands	6.025	723	563	276	105	182	1056	676	380	66	120
7	Scotland	5.796	771	624	294	119	211	1056	777	279	64	133
8	Belgium	5.541	737	612	283	105	224	988	795	193	66	133
9	Portugal	5.069	659	560	245	114	201	892	694	198	55	130
10	Hungary	4.925	532	462	207	74	181	819	690	129	44	108
11	Yugoslavia	4.862	671	606	252	109	245	994	880	114	58	138
12	E. Germany	4.660	522	474	193	99	182	701	630	71	37	112
13	Czechoslovakia	4.610	521	451	199	88	164	699	586	113	35	113
14	France	3.968	512	483	187	100	196	725	707	18	38	129
15	Wales	3.592	97	96	32	27	37	137	113	24	6	27
16	Poland	3.578	340	341	125	73	143	467	515	-48	17	95
17	Romania	3.339	354	370	137	65	168	473	553	-80	15	106
18	Austria	3.227	355	384	125	79	180	507	621	-114	26	110
19	Bulgaria	3.205	327	345	126	58	161	507	549	-42	17	102
20	Sweden	3.112	305	313	106	74	133	434	494	-60	19	98
21	Switzerland	2.917	353	401	129	73	199	592	743	-151	22	121
22	Greece	2.660	266	297	101	53	143	344	510	-166	11	100
23	Turkey	1.977	174	243	65	37	141	228	458	-230	7	88
24	Denmark	1.857	195	285	69	51	165	363	612	-249	6	105
25	Albania	1.758	51	71	17	17	37	51	101	-50	0	29
26	Norway	1.290	111	206	38	34	134	194	504	-310	1	86
27	Finland	1.173	81	168	29	20	119	141	489	-348	3	69
28	N. Ireland	1.101	87	180	23	39	118	171	482	-311	2	79
29	Rep. of Ireland	1.095	92	200	28	36	136	161	490	-329	0	84
30	Cyprus	0.825	52	138	17	18	103	101	478	-377	0	63
31	Malta	0.594	44	156	16	12	128	67	560	-493	0	74
32	Luxembourg	0.547	46	176	16	14	146	106	743	-637	0	84
33	Iceland	0.545	36	142	8	20	114	75	473	-398	0	66
	Total		**14707**	**13454**	**5455**	**2544**	**5455**	**20464**	**20464**	**0**	**1253**	**3.042**

Double Dutch Delight

In the year that the Netherlands' national team lifted the European Championship trophy, PSV Eindhoven made it a double Dutch success by winning the European Champions' Cup for the first time. They also completed a rare *treble* by winning both their national League and Cup as well – something only Ajax, of all the Champions' Cup winners, had ever previously managed, back in 1972.

PSV's triumph was unique in that it was achieved with only three victories in their nine matches, and none at all from the quarter-finals onwards! They benefitted from the away goals rule to eliminate both Bordeaux in the quarter-finals and Real Madrid in the semis, scoring not a single goal in either of their home matches. As for the final itself, that was to follow the trend set two years earlier between Steaua Bucharest and Barcelona and be decided with a penalty shoot-out after two hours of largely unremarkable goalless football.

PSV's opponents in the Stuttgart final were Benfica, who had lost on their three previous visits to the Champions' Cup final, in 1963, 1965 and 1968. That sorry sequence was to extend to four as their Portuguese international full-back Veloso saw his decisive penalty saved by PSV's Hans van Breukelen. The PSV 'keeper was one of five players in the side who were to add the European Championship trophy to the Champions' Cup the following month. The others were defenders Ronald Koeman and Berry van Aerle, midfielder Gerald Vanenburg and centre-forward Wim Kieft.

PSV's semi-final victims, Real Madrid, were generally considered to have been the best team in the competition. After all, they had been drawn against extremely tough opponents in every single round – Italian champions Napoli, holders FC Porto and their semi-final conquerors of the previous season, Bayern Munich – and, furthermore, due to UEFA disciplinary action against their supporters, they had been compelled to play their first round home leg (against Napoli) behind closed doors and their second round home fixture (against Porto) in Valencia. Of all their impressive displays during the competition, their proudest achievement was in eliminating Bayern, as it was the first time that Real had ever knocked the German side out of a European competition. Sadly, though, Real's determined quest for that elusive seventh Champions' Cup triumph was again to end in failure when they were narrowly eliminated by PSV in the semi-final. Held at home 1-1 in the Bernabéu, they had more of the play in the Eindhoven return, but a combination of poor finishing and the brilliance of PSV 'keeper Van Breukelen left them beaten semi-finalists for the second season in a row.

If the Champions' Cup largely went to form – Bordeaux were the only one of the eight quarter-finalists never to have previously won a European Cup – there were to be a whole host of shocks and surprises in the other two competitions.

KV Mechelen won the Cup-winners' Cup in their very first season of European competition! Not only that, but in doing so they remained unbeaten in all nine of their matches, conceding just three goals in the process. It was a remarkable achievement for a club which four years earlier had been hidden in the depths of the Belgian Second Division.

The odds were heavily on PSV's domestic rivals, Ajax, to become the first side to retain the Cup-winners' Cup when they lined up against debutants Mechelen in the Strasbourg final. The side no longer boasted the two heroes of the previous season's final, Marco van Basten and Frank Rijkaard, nor coach Johan Cruijff, who had quit in acrimonious circumstances in mid-season. But they had come through their four previous ties with relative ease, conceding not a single goal until the second leg of the semi-final against Olympique Marseille, by which stage they were already virtually certain of making progress thanks to a first-leg 3-0 win in France where winger Rob Witschge had been the match-winner with two goals.

But in Strasbourg, the sending-off of Ajax defender Danny Blind early on in the final handed the initiative to the Belgian underdogs and they took advantage of their good fortune by scoring the only

Above: Mechelen's Eliahu Ohana, Pascal de Wilde, Erwin Koeman and goalscorer Pieter den Boer hold the Cup Winners' Cup after beating Ajax 1-0.

goal of the match through their Dutch centre-forward Piet den Boer, who converted a cross from Israeli international Eliahu Ohana eight minutes into the second half. Another Dutchman on the winning side was Mechelen boss Aad de Mos – a former coach at Ajax, who had been sacked from his post to make room for Johan Cruijff two years earlier!

Mechelen's triumph was an enormous surprise, but there might have been an even more sensational outcome to the competition had they not disposed of Italian side Atalanta in the semi-final. For Atalanta had made it into the last four despite spending the season in the Italian Second Division. Their run to the semis made them the most successful Divison Two representatives in European competition since Cardiff City reached the same stage of the Cup-winners' Cup 20 years earlier.

In direct contrast to the Champions' Cup, the quarter-finals of the UEFA Cup contained just one club which had previously won a European trophy. So when that club, Barcelona, was surprisingly eliminated by West German side Bayer Leverkusen, it meant that a new name was bound to be added to the European roll-of-honour.

After two closely contested semi-finals, it was Leverkusen, conquerors of fellow Germans and Bundesliga champions-elect Werder Bremen, and Barcelona's city rivals, Español, extra-time winners against home-leg specialists Club Bruges, who came face to face in the final. It was the first time that a UEFA Cup final was to be disputed between two teams who had never won their own national championship.

Both finalists had their rightful claim to this particular trophy, however. Leverkusen, in dismissing Austria Vienna, Toulouse and Feyenoord as well as Barcelona and Bremen, had set a new record in going through their first 13 UEFA Cup matches undefeated (beating Valencia's 25-year-old record set in the old Fairs' Cup), whereas Español had claimed the prestigious scalps of both Milan clubs on their way to the final.

An exciting competition, and an enthralling final, alas reached the same unsatisfactory conclusion as the Champions' Cup when Leverkusen, showing typical German resilience, somehow managed to claw back the 3-0 deficit they had conceded in the first leg with three second-half goals in the return to take the tie into a penalty shoot-out. Tita, Götz and South Korean Cha Bum Kun were Leverkusen's scorers, cancelling out the goals scored by Losada (2) and Soler for Español in the first leg.

With the home crowd behind them, Leverkusen continued their comeback to take the Cup 3-2 on penalties thanks to both the histrionics and the agility of their goalkeeper, Rüdiger Vollborn, and become the third West German club – after Borussia Mönchengladbach (1975, 1979) and Eintracht Frankfurt (1980) – to have their name engraved on the trophy. No team had ever previously won the trophy after conceding a three-goal advantage in the first leg.

1988 – 1989

AC Milan

Barcelona

Napoli

First Round

Team 1	Cnty	Team 2	Cnty	1st leg	2nd leg	Agg
Rapid Vienna	Aut	Galatasaray	Tur	2-1	0-2	2-3
Club Bruges	Bel	Brøndby IF	Den	1-0	1-2	2-2
Levski Sofia	Bul	AC Milan	Ita	0-2	2-5	2-7
Pezoporikos Larnaca	Cyp	IFK Gothenburg	Swe	1-2	1-5	2-7
Dundalk	Irl	Red Star Belgrade	Yug	0-5	0-3	0-8
Real Madrid	Esp	Moss FK	Nor	3-0	1-0	4-0
Larissa	Gre	Neuchâtel Xamax	Sui	2-1	1-2	3-3
Honvéd	Hun	Celtic	Sco	1-0	0-4	1-4
Valur Reykjavik	Isl	Monaco	Fra	1-0	0-2	1-2
Hamrun Spartans	Mlt	17 Nëntori Tirana	Alb	2-1	0-2	2-3
Górnik Zabrze	Pol	Jeunesse Esch	Lux	3-0	4-1	7-1
FC Porto	Por	HJK Helsinki	Fin	3-0	0-2	3-2
Sparta Prague	Tch	Steaua Bucharest	Rom	1-5	2-2	3-7
Spartak Moscow	URS	Glentoran	Nir	2-0	1-1	3-1
Dynamo Berlin	GDR	Werder Bremen	FRG	3-0	0-5	3-5

	Pts	P	W	D	L	F	A	Diff	Goals/P
Total	60	30	28	4	28	93	93	0	3.100

Second Round

Team 1	Cnty	Team 2	Cnty	1st leg	2nd leg	Agg
17 Nëntori Tirana	Alb	IFK Gothenburg	Swe	0-3	0-1	0-4
Club Bruges	Bel	Monaco	Fra	1-0	1-6	2-6
Celtic	Sco	Werder Bremen	FRG	0-1	0-0	0-1
AC Milan	Ita	Red Star Belgrade	Yug	1-1	1-1	2-2
PSV Eindhoven	Ned	FC Porto	Por	5-0	0-2	5-2
Górnik Zabrze	Pol	Real Madrid	Esp	0-1	2-3	2-4
Steaua Bucharest	Rom	Spartak Moscow	URS	3-0	2-1	5-1
Neuchâtel Xamax	Sui	Galatasaray	Tur	3-0	0-5	3-5

	Pts	P	W	D	L	F	A	Diff	Goals/P
Total	32	16	13	6	13	44	44	0	2.750

Quarter Finals

Team 1	Cnty	Team 2	Cnty	1st leg	2nd leg	Agg
Monaco	Fra	Galatasaray	Tur	0-1	1-1	1-2
PSV Eindhoven	Ned	Real Madrid	Esp	1-1	1-2	2-3
Werder Bremen	FRG	AC Milan	Ita	0-0	0-1	0-1
IFK Gothenburg	Swe	Steaua Bucharest	Rom	1-0	1-5	2-5

	Pts	P	W	D	L	F	A	Diff	Goals/P
Total	16	8	5	6	5	16	16	90	2.000

Semi Finals

Team 1	Cnty	Team 2	Cnty	1st leg	2nd leg	Agg
Real Madrid	Esp	AC Milan	Ita	1-1	0-5	1-6
Steaua Bucharest	Rom	Galatasaray	Tur	4-0	1-1	5-1

	Pts	P	W	D	L	F	A	Diff	Goals/P
Total	8	4	2	4	2	13	13	0	3.250

Final

AC Milan	Ita	Steaua Bucharest	Rom	4-0		4-0

	Pts	P	W	D	L	F	A	Diff	Goals/P
Total	2	1	1	0	1	4	4	0	4.000

	Pts	P	W	D	L	F	A	Diff	Goals/P
Total	118	59	49	20	49	170	170	0	2.881

Pos'n	Club	Cnty	Pts	P	W	D	L	F	A	Diff	B	Pts/P	F/P
1	AC Milan	Ita	17	9	5	4	0	20	5	15	3	1.889	2.222
2	Steaua Bucharest	Rom	15	9	5	2	2	22	11	11	3	1.667	2.444
3	Real Madrid	Esp	14	8	5	2	1	12	10	2	2	1.750	1.500
4	IFK Gothenburg	Swe	11	6	5	0	1	13	7	6	1	1.833	2.167
5	Galatasaray	Tur	10	8	3	2	3	11	11	0	2	1.250	1.375
6	Werder Bremen	FRG	7	6	2	2	2	6	4	2	1	1.167	1.000
7	Red Star Belgrade	Yug	6	4	2	2	0	10	2	8	0	1.500	2.500
8	Monaco	Fra	6	6	2	1	3	9	5	4	1	1.000	1.500
9	Górnik Zabrze	Pol	4	4	2	0	2	9	5	4	0	1.000	2.250
10	PSV Eindhoven	Ned	4	4	1	1	2	7	5	2	1	1.000	1.750
11	Neuchâtel Xamax	Sui	4	4	2	0	2	6	8	-2	0	1.000	1.500
12	FC Porto	Por	4	4	2	0	2	5	7	-2	0	1.000	1.250
13	Club Bruges	Bel	4	4	2	0	2	4	8	-4	0	1.000	1.000
14	Celtic	Sco	3	4	1	1	2	4	2	2	0	0.750	1.000
15	Spartak Moscow	URS	3	4	1	1	2	4	6	-2	0	0.750	1.000
16	Larissa	Gre	2	2	1	0	1	3	3	0	0	1.000	1.500
17	Brøndby IF	Den	2	2	1	0	1	2	2	0	0	1.000	1.000
18	Rapid Vienna	Aut	2	2	1	0	1	2	3	-1	0	1.000	1.000
–	HJK Helsinki	Fin	2	2	1	0	1	2	3	-1	0	1.000	1.000
–	Hamrun Spartans	Mlt	2	2	1	0	1	2	3	-1	0	1.000	1.000
21	Valur Reykjavik	Isl	2	2	1	0	1	1	2	-1	0	1.000	0.500
22	Dynamo Berlin	GDR	2	2	1	0	1	3	5	-2	0	1.000	1.500
23	17 Nëntori Tirana	Alb	2	4	1	0	3	3	6	-3	0	0.500	0.750
24	Honvéd	Hun	2	2	1	0	1	1	4	-3	0	1.000	0.500
25	Glentoran	Nir	1	2	0	1	1	1	3	-2	0	0.500	0.500
26	Sparta Prague	Tch	1	2	0	1	1	3	7	-4	0	0.500	1.500
27	Moss FK	Nor	0	2	0	0	2	0	4	-4	0	0.000	0.000
28	Levski Sofia	Bul	0	2	0	0	2	2	7	-5	0	0.000	1.000
–	Pezoporikos Larnaca	Cyp	0	2	0	0	2	2	7	-5	0	0.000	1.000
30	Jeunesse Esch	Lux	0	2	0	0	2	1	7	-6	0	0.000	0.500
31	Dundalk	Irl	0	2	0	0	2	0	8	-8	0	0.000	0.000
	Total		**132**	**118**	**49**	**20**	**49**	**170**	**170**	**0**	**14**	**1.119**	**2.881**

Preliminary Round

Team 1	Cnty	Team 2	Cnty	1st leg	2nd leg	Agg
Békéscsaba	Hun	Bryne IL	Nor	3-0	1-2	4-2

	Pts	P	W	D	L	F	A	Diff	Goals/P
Total	4	2	2	0	2	6	6	0	3.000

First Round

Flamurtari Vlorë	Alb	Lech Poznań	Pol	2-3	0-1	2-4
KV Mechelen	Bel	Avenir Beggen	Lux	5-0	3-1	8-1
Omonia Nicosia	Cyp	Panathinaikos	Gre	0-1	0-2	0-3
Derry City	Irl	Cardiff City	Wal	0-0	0-4	0-4
Metz	Fra	Anderlecht	Bel	1-3	0-2	1-5
Glenavon	Nir	AGF Aarhus	Den	1-4	1-3	2-7
Fram Reykjavik	Isl	Barcelona	Esp	0-2	0-5	0-7
Floriana	Mlt	Dundee United	Sco	0-0	0-1	0-1
Roda JC	Ned	Vitória Guimarães	Por	2-0	0-1	2-1
Dinamo Bucharest	Rom	FC Kuusysi Lahti	Fin	3-0	3-0	6-0
IFK Norrköping	Swe	Sampdoria	Ita	2-1	0-2	2-3
Grasshoppers Zürich	Sui	Eintracht Frankfurt	FRG	0-0	0-1	0-1
Inter Bratislava	Tch	CSKA Sofia	Bul	2-3	0-5	2-8
Sakaryaspor	Tur	Békéscsaba	Hun	2-0	0-1	2-1
Borac Banja Luka	Yug	Metallist Kharkov	URS	2-0	0-4	2-4
Carl Zeiss Jena	GDR	Krems	Aut	5-0	0-1	5-1

	Pts	P	W	D	L	F	A	Diff	Goals/P
Total	64	32	29	6	29	85	85	0	2.656

Second Round

KV Mechelen	Bel	Anderlecht	Bel	1-0	2-0	3-0
CSKA Sofia	Bul	Panathinaikos	Gre	2-0	1-0	3-0
Dundee United	Sco	Dinamo Bucharest	Rom	0-1	1-1	1-2
Barcelona	Esp	Lech Poznań	Pol	1-1	1-1	2-2
Cardiff City	Wal	AGF Aarhus	Den	1-2	0-4	1-6
Roda JC	Ned	Metallist Kharkov	URS	1-0	0-0	1-0
Eintracht Frankfurt	FRG	Sakaryaspor	Tur	3-1	3-0	6-1
Carl Zeiss Jena	GDR	Sampdoria	Ita	1-1	1-3	2-4

	Pts	P	W	D	L	F	A	Diff	Goals/P
Total	32	16	11	10	11	34	34	0	2.125

Quarter Finals

CSKA Sofia	Bul	Roda JC	Ned	2-1	1-2	3-3
AGF Aarhus	Den	Barcelona	Esp	0-1	0-0	0-1
Eintracht Frankfurt	FRG	KV Mechelen	Bel	0-0	0-1	0-1
Dinamo Bucharest	Rom	Sampdoria	Ita	1-1	0-0	1-1

	Pts	P	W	D	L	F	A	Diff	Goals/P
Total	16	8	4	8	4	10	10	0	1.250

European Cup Winners Cup 1988-89

Semi Finals

KV Mechelen	Bel	Sampdoria	Ita	2-1	0-3	2-4
Barcelona	Esp	CSKA Sofia	Bul	4-2	2-1	6-3

	Pts	P	W	D	L	F	A	Diff	Goals/P
Total	8	4	4	0	4	15	15	0	3.750

Final

Barcelona	Esp	Sampdoria	Ita	2-0	2-0

	Pts	P	W	D	L	F	A	Diff	Goals/P
Total	2	1	1	0	1	2	2	0	2.000

	Pts	P	W	D	L	F	A	Diff	Goals/P
Total	126	63	51	24	51	152	152	0	2.413

Pos'n	Club	Cnty	Pts	P	W	D	L	F	A	Diff	B	Pts/P	F/P
1	Barcelona	Esp	18	9	6	3	0	18	5	13	3	2.000	2.000
2	KV Mechelen	Bel	15	8	6	1	1	14	5	9	2	1.875	1.750
3	CSKA Sofia	Bul	12	8	5	0	3	17	11	6	2	1.500	2.125
4	Sampdoria	Ita	12	9	3	3	3	12	9	3	3	1.333	1.333
5	AGF Aarhus	Den	10	6	4	1	1	13	4	9	1	1.667	2.167
6	Dinamo Bucharest	Rom	10	6	3	3	0	9	2	7	1	1.667	1.500
7	Eintracht Frankfurt	FRG	9	6	3	2	1	7	2	5	1	1.500	1.167
8	Roda JC	Ned	8	6	3	1	2	6	4	2	1	1.333	1.000
9	Lech Poznań	Pol	6	4	2	2	0	6	4	2	0	1.500	1.500
10	Anderlecht	Bel	4	4	2	0	2	5	4	1	0	1.000	1.250
–	Békécsaba	Hun	4	4	2	0	2	5	4	1	0	1.000	1.250
12	Panathinaikos	Gre	4	4	2	0	2	3	3	0	0	1.000	0.750
13	Dundee United	Sco	4	4	1	2	1	2	2	0	0	1.000	0.500
14	Carl Zeiss Jena	GDR	3	4	1	1	2	7	5	2	0	0.750	1.750
15	Metallist Kharkov	URS	3	4	1	1	2	4	3	1	0	0.750	1.000
16	Cardiff City	Wal	3	4	1	1	2	5	6	-1	0	0.750	1.250
17	IFK Norrköping	Swe	2	2	1	0	1	2	3	-1	0	1.000	1.000
18	Vitória Guimarães	Por	2	2	1	0	1	1	2	-1	0	1.000	0.500
19	Bryne IL	Nor	2	2	1	0	1	2	4	-2	0	1.000	1.000
–	Borac Banja Luka	Yug	2	2	1	0	1	2	4	-2	0	1.000	1.000
21	Sakaryaspor	Tur	2	4	1	0	3	3	7	-4	0	0.500	0.750
22	Krems	Aut	2	2	1	0	1	1	5	-4	0	1.000	0.500
23	Floriana	Mlt	1	2	0	1	1	0	1	-1	0	0.500	0.000
–	Grasshoppers Zürich	Sui	1	2	0	1	1	0	1	-1	0	0.500	0.000
25	Derry City	Nir	1	2	0	1	1	0	4	-4	0	0.500	0.000
26	Flamutari Vlorë	Alb	0	2	0	0	2	2	4	-2	0	0.000	1.000
27	Omonia Nicosia	Cyp	0	2	0	0	2	0	3	-3	0	0.000	0.000
28	Metz	Fra	0	2	0	0	2	1	5	-4	0	0.000	0.500
29	Glenavon	Nir	0	2	0	0	2	2	7	-5	0	0.000	1.000
30	Inter Bratislava	Tch	0	2	0	0	2	2	8	-6	0	0.000	1.000
31	FC Kuusysi Lahti	Fin	0	2	0	0	2	0	6	-6	0	0.000	0.000
32	Avenir Beggen	Lux	0	2	0	0	2	1	8	-7	0	0.000	0.500
33	Fram Reykjavik	Isl	0	2	0	0	2	0	7	-7	0	0.000	0.000
	Total		**140**	**126**	**51**	**24**	**51**	**152**	**152**	**0**	**14**	**1.111**	**2.413**

First Round

Team 1	Cnty	Team 2	Cnty	1st leg	2nd leg	Agg
First Vienna	Aut	Ikast FS	Den	1-0	1-2	2-2
Antwerp	Bel	Cologne	FRG	2-4	1-2	3-6
Trakia Plovdiv	Bul	Dinamo Minsk	URS	1-2	0-0	1-2
Aberdeen	Sco	Dynamo Dresden	GDR	0-0	0-2	0-2
Rangers	Sco	GKS Katowice	Pol	1-0	4-2	5-2
St. Patrick's Athletic	Irl	Heart of Midlothian	Sco	0-2	0-2	0-4
Real Sociedad	Esp	Dukla Prague	Tch	2-1	2-3	4-4
TPS Turku	Fin	Linfield	Nir	0-0	1-1	1-1
Montpellier	Fra	Benfica	Por	0-3	1-3	1-6
AEK Athens	Gre	Athletic Bilbao	Esp	1-0	0-2	1-2
IA Akranes	Isl	Ujpesti Dózsa	Hun	0-0	1-2	1-2
Inter Milan	Ita	IK Brage	Swe	2-1	2-1	4-2
Napoli	Ita	PAOK Salonika	Gre	1-0	1-1	2-1
Roma	Ita	Nuremberg	FRG	1-2	3-1	4-3
Union Luxembourg	Lux	FC Liège	Bel	1-7	0-4	1-11
Sliema Wanderers	Mlt	Victoria Bucharest	Rom	0-2	1-6	1-8
Molde FK	Nor	Waregem	Bel	0-0	1-5	1-5
Groningen	Ned	Athlético Madrid	Esp	1-0	1-2	2-2
Sporting Lisbon	Por	Ajax	Ned	4-2	2-1	6-3
Bayer Leverkusen	FRG	Belenenses	Por	0-1	0-1	0-2
Bayern Munich	FRG	Legia Warsaw	Pol	3-1	7-3	10-4
VFB Stuttgart	FRG	Tatabánya	Hun	2-0	1-2	3-2
CSU Galati	Rom	Juventus	Ita	1-0	0-5	1-5
Malmö FF	Swe	Torpedo Moscow	URS	2-0	1-2	3-2
Öster SIF	Swe	DAC Dunajská Streda	Tch	2-0	0-6	2-6
Aarau	Sui	Lokomotive Leipzig	GDR	0-3	0-4	0-7
Servette	Sui	Sturm Graz	Aut	1-0	0-0	1-0
Besiktas	Tur	Dinamo Zagreb	Yug	1-0	0-2	1-2
Dnepr Dnepropetrovsk	URS	Girondins Bordeaux	Fra	1-1	1-2	2-3
Zhalgiris Vilnius	URS	Austria Vienna	Aut	2-0	2-5	4-5
Partizan Belgrade	Yug	Slavia Sofia	Bul	5-0	5-0	10-0
Velez Mostar	Yug	Apoel Nicosia	Cyp	1-0	5-2	6-2

	Pts	P	W	D	L	F	A	Diff	Goals/P
Total	128	64	55	18	55	191	191	0	2.984

Second Round

First Vienna	Aut	TPS Turku	Fin	2-1	0-1	2-2
FC Liège	Bel	Benfica	Por	2-1	1-1	3-2
Heart of Midlothian	Sco	Austria Vienna	Aut	0-0	1-0	1-0
Ujpesti Dózsa	Hun	Girondins Bordeaux	Fra	0-1	0-1	0-2
Juventus	Ita	Athletic Bilbao	Esp	5-1	2-3	7-4
Groningen	Ned	Servette	Sui	2-0	1-1	3-1
Sporting Lisbon	Por	Real Sociedad	Esp	1-2	0-0	1-2
Cologne	FRG	Rangers	Sco	2-0	1-1	3-1
Bayern Munich	FRG	DAC Dunajská Streda	Tch	3-1	2-0	5-1
Malmö FF	Swe	Inter Milan	Ita	0-1	1-1	1-2
Dinamo Minsk	URS	Victoria Bucharest	Rom	2-1	0-1	2-2
Partizan Belgrade	Yug	Roma	Ita	4-2	0-2	4-4
Velez Mostar	Yug	Belenenses	Por	0-0	0-0	0-0
Dinamo Zagreb	Yug	VFB Stuttgart	FRG	1-3	1-1	2-4
Dynamo Dresden	GDR	Waregem	Bel	4-1	1-2	5-3
Lokomotive Leipzig	GDR	Napoli	Ita	1-1	0-2	1-3

UEFA Cup 1988-89

	Pts	P	W	D	L	F	A	Diff	Goals/P
Total	64	32	22	20	22	73	73	0	2.281

Third Round

FC Liège	Bel	Juventus	Ita	0-1	0-1	0-2
Heart of Midlothian	Sco	Velez Mostar	Yug	3-0	1-2	4-2
Real Sociedad	Esp	Cologne	FRG	1-0	2-2	3-2
Girondins Bordeaux	Fra	Napoli	Ita	0-1	0-0	0-1
Groningen	Ned	VFB Stuttgart	FRG	1-3	0-2	1-5
Bayern Munich	FRG	Inter Milan	Ita	0-2	3-1	3-3
Victoria Bucharest	Rom	TPS Turku	Fin	1-0	2-3	3-3
Dynamo Dresden	GDR	Roma	Ita	2-0	2-0	4-0

	Pts	P	W	D	L	F	A	Diff	Goals/P
Total	32	16	14	4	14	36	36	0	2.250

Quarter Finals

Heart of Midlothian	Sco	Bayern Munich	FRG	1-0	0-2	1-2
Juventus	Ita	Napoli	Ita	2-0	0-3	2-3
VFB Stuttgart	FRG	Real Sociedad	Esp	1-0	0-1	1-1
Victoria Bucharest	Rom	Dynamo Dresden	GDR	1-1	0-4	1-5

	Pts	P	W	D	L	F	A	Diff	Goals/P
Total	16	8	7	2	7	16	16	0	2.000

Semi Finals

Napoli	Ita	Bayern Munich	FRG	2-0	2-2	4-2
VFB Stuttgart	FRG	Dynamo Dresden	GDR	1-0	1-1	2-1

	Pts	P	W	D	L	F	A	Diff	Goals/P
Total	8	4	2	4	2	9	9	0	2.250

Final

Napoli	Ita	VFB Stuttgart	FRG	2-1	3-3	5-4

	Pts	P	W	D	L	F	A	Diff	Goals/P
Total	4	2	1	2	1	9	9	0	4.500

	Pts	P	W	D	L	F	A	Diff	Goals/P
Total	252	126	101	50	101	334	334	0	2.651

Pos'n	Club	Cnty	Pts	P	W	D	L	F	A	Diff	B	Pts/P	F/P
1	Napoli	Ita	20	12	6	5	1	18	10	8	3	1.667	1.500
2	VFB Stuttgart	FRG	18	12	6	3	3	19	12	7	3	1.500	1.583
3	Dynamo Dresden	GDR	15	10	5	3	2	17	6	11	2	1.500	1.700
4	Bayern Munich	FRG	15	10	6	1	3	22	13	9	2	1.500	2.200
5	Heart of Midlothian	Sco	12	8	5	1	2	10	4	6	1	1.500	1.250
6	Juventus	Ita	11	8	5	0	3	16	8	8	1	1.375	2.000
7	Real Sociedad	Esp	11	8	4	2	2	10	8	2	1	1.375	1.250
8	Victoria Bucharest	Rom	10	8	4	1	3	14	11	3	1	1.250	1.750
9	Inter Milan	Ita	9	6	4	1	1	9	6	3	0	1.500	1.500
10	Cologne	FRG	8	6	3	2	1	11	7	4	0	1.333	1.833
11	Velez Mostar	Yug	8	6	3	2	1	8	6	2	0	1.333	1.333
12	Girondins Bordeaux	Fra	8	6	3	2	1	5	3	2	0	1.333	0.833
13	FC Liège	Bel	7	6	3	1	2	14	5	9	0	1.167	2.333
14	Partizan Belgrade	Yug	6	4	3	0	1	14	4	10	0	1.500	3.500
15	Belenenses	Por	6	4	2	2	0	2	0	2	0	1.500	0.500
16	TPS Turku	Fin	6	6	2	2	2	6	6	0	0	1.000	1.000
17	Lokomotive Leipzig	GDR	5	4	2	1	1	8	3	5	0	1.250	2.000
18	Benfica	Por	5	4	2	1	1	8	4	4	0	1.250	2.000
19	Waregem	Bel	5	4	2	1	1	8	6	2	0	1.250	2.000
20	Sporting Lisbon	Por	5	4	2	1	1	7	5	2	0	1.250	1.750
21	Rangers	Sco	5	4	2	1	1	6	5	1	0	1.250	1.500
22	Dinamo Minsk	URS	5	4	2	1	1	4	3	1	0	1.250	1.000
23	Groningen	Ned	5	6	2	1	3	6	8	-2	0	0.833	1.000
24	First Vienna	Aut	4	4	2	0	2	4	4	0	0	1.000	1.000
25	Servette	Sui	4	4	1	2	1	2	3	-1	0	1.000	0.500
26	Athletic Bilbao	Esp	4	4	2	0	2	6	8	-2	0	1.000	1.500
27	Roma	Ita	4	6	2	0	4	8	11	-3	0	0.667	1.333
28	Austria Vienna	Aut	3	4	1	1	2	5	5	0	0	0.750	1.250
29	Malmö FF	Swe	3	4	1	1	2	4	4	0	0	0.750	1.000
30	Dinamo Zagreb	Yug	3	4	1	1	2	4	5	-1	0	0.750	1.000
31	Ujpesti Dózsa	Hun	3	4	1	1	2	2	3	-1	0	0.750	0.500
32	DAC Dunajská Streda	Tch	2	4	1	0	3	7	7	0	0	0.500	1.750
33	Dulka Prague	Tch	2	2	1	0	1	4	4	0	0	1.000	2.000
34	Ikast FS	Den	2	2	1	0	1	2	2	0	0	1.000	1.000
–	Atlético Madrid	Esp	2	2	1	0	1	2	2	0	0	1.000	1.000
36	Linfield	Nir	2	2	0	2	0	1	1	0	0	1.000	0.500
37	Zhalgiris Vilnius	URS	2	2	1	0	1	4	5	-1	0	1.000	2.000
38	Nuremberg	FRG	2	2	1	0	1	3	4	-1	0	1.000	1.500
39	Tatabánya	Hun	2	2	1	0	1	2	3	-1	0	1.000	1.000
–	Torpedo Moscow	URS	2	2	1	0	1	2	3	-1	0	1.000	1.000
41	AEK Athens	Gre	2	2	1	0	1	1	2	-1	0	1.000	0.500
–	Besiktas	Tur	2	2	1	0	1	1	2	-1	0	1.000	0.500
43	Öster SIF	Swe	2	2	1	0	1	2	6	-4	0	1.000	1.000
44	CSU Galati	Rom	2	2	1	0	1	1	5	-4	0	1.000	0.500
45	Dnepr Dnepropetrovsk	URS	1	2	0	1	1	2	3	-1	0	0.500	1.000
46	Trakia Plovdiv	Bul	1	2	0	1	1	1	2	-1	0	0.500	0.500
–	PAOK Salonika	Gre	1	2	0	1	1	1	2	-1	0	0.500	0.500
–	IA Akranes	Isl	1	2	0	1	1	1	2	-1	0	0.500	0.500
49	Sturm Graz	Aut	1	2	0	1	1	0	1	-1	0	0.500	0.000
50	Aberdeen	Sco	1	2	0	1	1	0	2	-2	0	0.500	0.000
51	Molde FK	Nor	1	2	0	1	1	1	5	-4	0	0.500	0.500
52	IK Brage	Swe	0	2	0	0	2	2	4	-2	0	0.000	1.000
53	Bayer Leverkusen	FRG	0	2	0	0	2	0	2	-2	0	0.000	0.000
54	Antwerp	Bel	0	2	0	0	2	3	6	-3	0	0.000	1.500
–	Ajax	Ned	0	2	0	0	2	3	6	-3	0	0.000	1.500
56	GKS Katowice	Pol	0	2	0	0	2	2	5	-3	0	0.000	1.000
57	Apoel Nicosia	Cyp	0	2	0	0	2	2	6	-4	0	0.000	1.000
58	St. Patrick's Athletic	Irl	0	2	0	0	2	0	4	-4	0	0.000	0.000
59	Montpellier	Fra	0	2	0	0	2	1	6	-5	0	0.000	0.500
60	Legia Warsaw	Pol	0	2	0	0	2	4	10	-6	0	0.000	2.000
61	Sliema Wanderers	Mlt	0	2	0	0	2	1	8	-7	0	0.000	0.500
62	Aarau	Sui	0	2	0	0	2	0	7	-7	0	0.000	0.000
63	Union Luxembourg	Lux	0	2	0	0	2	1	11	-10	0	0.000	0.500
64	Slavia Sofia	Bul	0	2	0	0	2	0	10	-10	0	0.000	0.000
	Total		**266**	**252**	**101**	**50**	**101**	**334**	**334**	**0**	**14**	**1.056**	**2.651**

1988-89

Pos'n	Cnty	Pts	P	W	D	L	F	A	Diff	B	Pts/P	F/P
1	Ita	73	50	25	13	12	83	50	33	10	1.460	1.660
2	FRG	59	44	21	10	13	68	44	24	7	1.341	1.545
3	Esp	49	31	18	7	6	48	33	15	6	1.581	1.548
4	Rom	37	25	13	6	6	46	29	17	5	1.480	1.840
5	Bel	35	28	15	3	10	48	34	14	2	1.250	1.714
6	Yug	25	20	10	5	5	38	21	17	0	1.250	1.900
7	GDR	25	20	9	5	6	36	19	17	2	1.250	1.800
8	Sco	25	22	9	6	7	22	15	7	1	1.136	1.000
9	Por	22	18	9	4	5	23	18	5	0	1.222	1.278
10	Swe	18	16	8	1	7	23	24	-1	1	1.125	1.438
11	Ned	17	18	6	3	9	22	23	-1	2	0.944	1.222
12	URS	16	18	6	4	8	20	23	-3	0	0.889	1.111
13	Den	14	10	6	1	3	17	8	9	1	1.400	1.700
14	Fra	14	16	5	3	8	16	19	-3	1	0.875	1.000
15	Tur	14	14	5	2	7	15	20	-5	2	1.000	1.071
16	Bul	13	14	5	1	8	20	30	-10	2	0.929	1.429
17	Aut	12	14	5	2	7	12	18	-6	0	0.857	0.857
18	Hun	11	12	5	1	6	10	14	-4	0	0.917	0.833
19	Pol	10	12	4	2	6	21	24	-3	0	0.833	1.750
20	Gre	9	10	4	1	5	8	10	-2	0	0.900	0.800
21	Sui	9	12	3	3	6	8	19	-11	0	0.750	0.667
22	Fin	8	10	3	2	5	8	15	-7	0	0.800	0.800
23	Tch	5	10	2	1	7	16	26	-10	0	0.500	1.600
24	Wal	3	4	1	1	2	5	6	-1	0	0.750	1.250
25	Nir	3	6	0	3	3	4	11	-7	0	0.500	0.667
26	Mlt	3	6	1	1	4	3	12	-9	0	0.500	0.500
27	Isl	3	6	1	1	4	2	11	-9	0	0.500	0.333
28	Nor	3	6	1	1	4	3	13	-10	0	0.500	0.500
29	Alb	2	6	1	0	5	5	10	-5	0	0.333	0.833
30	Irl	1	6	0	1	5	0	16	-16	0	0.167	0.000
31	Cyp	0	6	0	0	6	4	16	-12	0	0.000	0.667
32	Lux	0	6	0	0	6	3	26	-23	0	0.000	0.500
	Total	**538**	**496**	**201**	**94**	**201**	**657**	**657**	**0**	**42**	**1.085**	**2.649**

1955-56 to 1988-89

Pos'n	Cnty	Pts	P	W	D	L	F	A	Diff	B	Pts/P	F/P
1	FRG	1463	1061	551	201	309	2095	1304	791	160	1.379	1.975
2	Eng	1365	926	500	201	225	1782	927	855	164	1.474	1.924
3	Esp	1319	964	486	182	296	1735	1151	584	165	1.368	1.800
4	Ita	1202	890	437	195	258	1391	896	495	133	1.351	1.563
5	Sco	796	646	303	125	218	1078	792	286	65	1.232	1.669
6	Bel	772	640	298	108	234	1036	829	207	68	1.206	1.619
7	Ned	740	581	282	108	191	1078	699	379	68	1.274	1.855
8	Yug	696	626	262	114	250	1032	901	131	58	1.112	1.649
9	Por	681	578	254	118	206	915	712	203	55	1.178	1.583
10	GDR	547	494	202	104	188	736	649	87	39	1.107	1.490
11	Hun	543	474	212	75	187	829	704	125	44	1.146	1.749
12	URS	541	409	208	86	115	631	412	219	39	1.323	1.543
13	Tch	526	461	201	89	171	715	612	103	35	1.141	1.551
14	Fra	526	499	192	103	204	741	726	15	39	1.054	1.485
15	Rom	391	395	150	71	174	519	582	-63	20	0.990	1.314
16	Aut	367	398	130	81	187	519	639	-120	26	0.922	1.304
17	Sui	362	413	132	76	205	600	762	-162	22	0.877	1.453
18	Pol	350	353	129	75	149	488	539	-51	17	0.992	1.382
19	Bul	340	359	131	59	169	527	579	-52	19	0.947	1.468
20	Swe	323	329	114	75	140	457	518	-61	20	0.982	1.389
21	Gre	275	307	105	54	148	352	520	-168	11	0.896	1.147
22	Den	209	295	75	52	168	380	620	-240	7	0.708	1.288
23	Tur	188	257	70	39	148	243	478	-235	9	0.732	0.946
24	Nor	114	212	39	35	138	197	517	-320	1	0.538	0.929
25	Wal	100	100	33	28	39	142	119	23	6	1.000	1.420
26	Irl	93	206	28	37	141	161	506	-345	0	0.451	0.782
27	Nir	90	186	23	42	121	175	493	-318	2	0.484	0.941
28	Fin	89	178	32	22	124	149	504	-355	3	0.500	0.837
29	Alb	53	77	18	17	42	56	111	-55	0	0.688	0.727
30	Cyp	52	144	17	18	109	105	494	-389	0	0.361	0.729
31	Mlt	47	162	17	13	132	70	572	-502	0	0.290	0.432
32	Lux	46	182	16	14	152	109	769	-660	0	0.253	0.599
33	Isl	39	148	9	21	118	77	484	-407	0	0.264	0.520
	Total	**15245**	**13950**	**5656**	**2638**	**5656**	**21120**	**21120**	**0**	**1295**	**1.093**	**3.028**

1988-89

Pos'n	Cnty	Ave	Pts	P	W	D	L	F	A	Diff	B	No./T
1	Italy	12.166	73	50	25	13	12	83	50	33	10	6
2	Spain	9.800	49	31	18	7	6	48	33	15	6	5
3	Romania	9.250	37	25	13	6	6	46	29	17	5	4
4	W. Germany	8.428	59	44	21	10	13	68	44	24	7	7
5	E. Germany	6.250	25	20	9	5	6	36	19	17	2	4
6	Belgium	5.833	35	28	15	3	10	48	34	14	2	6
7	Scotland	5.000	25	22	9	6	7	22	15	7	1	5
–	Yugoslavia	5.000	25	20	10	5	5	38	21	17	0	5
9	Denmark	4.666	14	10	6	1	3	17	8	9	1	3
–	Turkey	4.666	14	14	5	2	7	15	20	-5	2	3
11	Portugal	4.400	22	18	9	4	5	23	18	5	0	5
12	Netherlands	4.250	17	18	6	3	9	22	23	-1	2	4
13	Sweden	3.600	18	16	8	1	7	23	24	-1	1	5
14	France	3.500	14	16	5	3	8	16	19	-3	1	4
15	Bulgaria	3.250	13	14	5	1	8	20	30	-10	2	4
16	Wales	3.000	3	4	1	1	2	5	6	-1	0	1
17	Hungary	2.750	11	12	5	1	6	10	14	-4	0	4
18	Finland	2.666	8	10	3	2	5	8	15	-7	0	3
–	USSR	2.666	16	18	6	4	8	20	23	-3	0	6
20	Poland	2.500	10	12	4	2	6	21	24	-3	0	4
21	Austria	2.400	12	14	5	2	7	12	18	-6	0	5
22	Greece	2.250	9	10	4	1	5	8	10	-2	0	4
–	Switzerland	2.250	9	12	3	3	6	8	19	-11	0	4
24	Czechoslovakia	1.250	5	10	2	1	7	16	26	-10	0	4
25	Albania	1.000	2	6	1	0	5	5	10	-5	0	2
–	N. Ireland	1.000	3	6	0	3	3	4	11	-7	0	3
–	Iceland	1.000	3	6	1	1	4	2	11	-9	0	3
–	Malta	1.000	3	6	1	1	4	3	12	-9	0	3
–	Norway	1.000	3	6	1	1	4	3	13	-10	0	3
30	Rep. of Ireland	0.333	1	6	0	1	5	0	16	-16	0	3
31	Cyprus	0.000	0	6	0	0	6	4	16	-12	0	3
–	Luxembourg	0.000	0	6	0	0	6	3	26	-23	0	3
	Total		**538**	**496**	**201**	**94**	**201**	**657**	**657**	**0**	**42**	**2.649**

1955-56 to 1988-89

1	England	8.806	1365	926	500	201	225	1782	927	855	164	155
2	W. Germany	7.951	1463	1061	551	201	309	2095	1304	791	160	184
3	Spain	7.713	1319	964	486	182	296	1735	1151	584	165	171
4	Italy	7.240	1202	890	437	195	258	1391	896	495	133	166
5	Netherlands	5.967	740	581	282	108	191	1078	699	379	68	124
6	USSR	5.945	541	409	208	86	115	631	412	219	39	91
7	Scotland	5.768	796	646	303	125	218	1078	792	286	65	138
8	Belgium	5.553	772	640	298	108	234	1036	829	207	68	139
9	Portugal	5.044	681	578	254	118	206	915	712	203	55	135
10	Yugoslavia	4.867	696	626	262	114	250	1032	901	131	58	143
11	Hungary	4.848	543	474	212	75	187	829	704	125	44	112
12	E. Germany	4.715	547	494	202	104	188	736	649	87	39	116
13	Czechoslovakia	4.495	526	461	201	89	171	715	612	103	35	117
14	France	3.954	526	499	192	103	204	741	726	15	39	133
15	Wales	3.571	100	100	33	28	39	142	119	23	6	28
16	Romania	3.554	391	395	150	71	174	519	582	-63	20	110
17	Poland	3.535	350	353	129	75	149	488	539	-51	17	99
18	Bulgaria	3.207	340	359	131	59	169	527	579	-52	19	106
19	Austria	3.191	367	398	130	81	187	519	639	-120	26	115
20	Sweden	3.135	323	329	114	75	140	457	518	-61	20	103
21	Switzerland	2.896	362	413	132	76	205	600	762	-162	22	125
22	Greece	2.644	275	307	105	54	148	352	520	-168	11	104
23	Turkey	2.065	188	257	70	39	148	243	478	-235	9	91
24	Denmark	1.935	209	295	75	52	168	380	620	-240	7	108
25	Albania	1.709	53	77	18	17	42	56	111	-55	0	31
26	Norway	1.280	114	212	39	35	138	197	517	-320	1	89
27	Finland	1.236	89	178	32	22	124	149	504	-355	3	72
28	N. Ireland	1.097	90	186	23	42	121	175	493	-318	2	82
29	Rep. of Ireland	1.068	93	206	28	37	141	161	506	-345	0	87
30	Cyprus	0.787	52	144	17	18	109	105	494	-389	0	66
31	Malta	0.610	47	162	17	13	132	70	572	-502	0	77
32	Iceland	0.565	39	148	9	21	118	77	484	-407	0	69
33	Luxembourg	0.528	46	182	16	14	152	109	769	-660	0	87
	Total		**15245**	**13950**	**5656**	**2638**	**5656**	**21120**	**21120**	**0**	**1295**	**3.028**

Italian Imports Hit Form

After two miserable seasons in Europe, Italian clubs returned to dominate all three competitions in 1988-89. AC Milan, inspired by their Dutch triumvirate of Ruud Gullit, Marco van Basten and Frank Rijkaard, won the Champions' Cup; Napoli, boasting South American stars Maradona and Careca, enjoyed their first ever European success in the UEFA Cup; and Sampdoria came close to completing a first ever grand slam by reaching the final of the Cup-winners' Cup, only to lose in Berne to Johan Cruijff's Barcelona.

Milan's third Champions' Cup triumph came after one of the most one-sided finals in the history of the competition. Steaua Bucharest, the Romanian team that had shocked the continent by winning the trophy in 1986, reached the final again after several impressive performances, especially at home, in previous ties with Sparta Prague, Spartak Moscow, IFK Gothenburg and the first-ever Turkish semi-finalists, Galatasaray. But in a Nou Camp stadium filled with an estimated 80,000 Italians, their game went to pieces. Visibly intimidated by both the occasion and the quality of players that faced them, they simply froze, enabling Milan to do pretty much what they wanted with them.

The Italians, on the other hand, relishing the atmosphere and the setting, took full advantage of their opponents' discomfiture to produce a display of the highest quality. With each player in the team performing to the height of his ability, Milan played like true champions and, after the turgid stalemate of a year before between PSV and Benfica, restored at last to Europe's premier club competition a standard of football which its final deserved.

Milan's particular heroes on the night were the Dutchmen Gullit and Van Basten, both of whom scored twice in the 4-0 victory. But it was the tactical disposition of the team, masterminded by coach Arrigo Sacchi, that really caught the eye. Steaua, quite simply, could not get out of their own half, and every time one of their defenders or midfielders dwelled on the ball, there was Donadoni or Rijkaard or Ancelotti biting at his heels to win the ball back. Such was their dominance that, had they wished to, Milan could easily have gone on from being 4-0 up just after half-time to run up the biggest margin of victory in Champions' Cup final history. But after their inspiration, Gullit, left the field to tumultuous applause on the hour, it was as if the motor had stalled and all they had to do was freewheel to victory.

Remarkable though it may appear, Milan's display in the final was not in fact their best of the competition. That had come in the second leg of the semi-final against Real Madrid, when Sacchi's men destroyed Real with some truly spectacular football, to which the Spaniards simply had no answer. Ceaseless Milan attacks brought five spectacular goals from Ancelotti, Rijkaard, Gullit, Van Basten and Donadoni, knocking Real out of the semi-finals for the third year in a row and in a manner which hinted that the Spanish club had reached the end of an era.

Real had looked somewhat shaky in earlier rounds, needing two late goals at home to see off Górnik Zabrze in the second round and then extra-time to eliminate holders PSV Eindhoven in the quarter-finals. But Milan, too, had been far from convincing in those rounds. In a dramatic second-round tie with Red Star Belgrade, the Italian champions eventually won through on a penalty shoot-out, but only after a 1-1 draw in Milan, a second leg in Belgrade abandoned due to fog after an hour with the Yugoslavs 1-0 ahead, and another 1-1 draw the following day in an extraordinarily eventful replay. Their quarter-final encounter against Werder Bremen was equally tight, with only a single, hotly-disputed Van Basten penalty seeing them through.

Van Basten, with ten goals in the Champions' Cup, was the top scorer in Europe during the season, but another world-class foreign striker in the Italian First Division, the Brazilian Careca, also came up with a plentiful supply of goals for Napoli on their way to winning the UEFA Cup.

Careca also had a formidable attacking partner in Diego Maradona, and these two were Napoli's outstanding players throughout an exciting run which took the side into their first European final against West Germany's VFB Stuttgart.

Napoli's first defeat of the competition came in the first leg of the quarter-final against another Italian club, Juventus, but they recovered in dramatic fashion in the return leg, with defender Alessandro Renica scoring Napoli's vital third goal in the very last minute of extra-time amidst understandable scenes of euphoria in the sold-out Stadio San Paolo. That put Maradona and company into an intriguing semi-final pairing with Bayern Munich, who had previously pulled off the most remarkable European performance of the season in the third round, coming back from a 0-2 home defeat to runaway Italian League leaders Inter Milan to pull off a sensational 3-1 win in the San Siro!

Maradona and Careca together, though, were to deny Bayern a second Italian scalp. Bringing a 2-0 lead from the first match in the San Paolo, Napoli controlled most of the return match in the Olympiastadion, with Maradona giving a vintage performance and supplying Careca with the two goals that earned the draw they needed to progress into the final. The scenario was much the same against Stuttgart, themselves, like Napoli, in a European final for the first time, although the Germans were extremely unlucky to lose the first leg in Naples after Maradona had again used his *Hand of God* to dupe the referee into awarding the Italian side a penalty. But, that incident apart, Napoli were certainly the stronger team over both legs. A late Careca winner gave them the first leg 2-1, and they were the dominant team again in Stuttgart, leading 3-1 through goals from Alemão, Ferrara and Careca before two defensive errors allowed the Germans to draw on the night and reduce Napoli's winning aggregate to 5-4.

Sampdoria, in only their third European campaign, reached the final of the Cup-winners' Cup to keep Italy's treble hopes alive. They were fortunate to overcome an exciting Dinamo Bucharest side on away goals in the quarter-finals, and then needed three late goals in the second leg of the semi-final to put out holders Mechelen. It was the Belgian club's first defeat in 17 European matches.

Sampdoria's opponents in the Berne final were former two-time winners, Barcelona. They too had lived dangerously in earlier ties, notably in the second round when penalties were required to knock out Polish side Lech Poznań. Midfielder Roberto, with five goals in the first two rounds, was their early star, but in the spring matches it was Englishman Gary Lineker who supplied the crucial goals against AGF of Denmark and CSKA Sofia. The Bulgarians themselves possessed the competition's leading scorer in Christo Stoichkov. He scored all three of his side's goals against Barcelona, and was to join the Catalan giants a year or so later.

And so to Berne for the final, an all-Mediterranean affair between two sides whose reputations had been built on attacking football. In the event, the match was no classic, but both teams at least tried to go forward and win the game rather than sitting back and waiting for the counter-attack, as had become the norm for so many Latin teams. Barcelona won the game 2-0 with goals from Julio Salinas in the fourth minute and substitute Lopez Rekarte in the 81st to give coach Johan Cruijff his second Cup-winners' Cup triumph in three years. Victory gave them the trophy for a record third time, enabling them to edge closer to Real Madrid's record grand total of eight European trophies. The triumph in Berne was Barcelona's sixth, putting them second equal with Liverpool in the all-time league table of European Cup victories.

AC Milan

Sampdoria

Juventus

1989 – 1990

First Round

Team 1	Cnty	Team 2	Cnty	1st leg	2nd leg	Agg
FC Tirol	Aut	Omonia Nicosia	Cyp	6-0	3-2	9-2
Rangers	Sco	Bayern Munich	FRG	1-3	0-0	1-3
Derry City	Irl	Benfica	Por	1-2	0-4	1-6
Olympique Marseille	Fra	Brøndby IF	Den	3-0	1-1	4-1
Honvéd	Hun	Vojvodina Novi Sad	Yug	1-0	1-2	2-2
Linfield	Nir	Dnepr Dnepropetrovsk	URS	1-2	0-1	1-3
AC Milan	Ita	HJK Helsinki	Fin	4-0	1-0	5-0
Spora Luxembourg	Lux	Real Madrid	Esp	0-3	0-6	0-9
Sliema Wanderers	Mlt	17 Nëntori Tirana	Alb	1-0	0-5	1-5
Rosenborg BK	Nor	KV Mechelen	Bel	0-0	0-5	0-5
PSV Eindhoven	Ned	Lucerne	Sui	3-0	2-0	5-0
Ruch Chorzów	Pol	CSKA Sofia	Bul	1-1	1-5	2-6
Steaua Bucharest	Rom	Fram Reykjavik	Isl	4-0	1-0	5-0
Malmö FF	Swe	Inter Milan	Ita	1-0	1-1	2-1
Sparta Prague	Tch	Fenerbahçe	Tur	3-1	2-1	5-2
Dynamo Dresden	GDR	AEK Athens	Gre	1-0	3-5	4-5

	Pts	P	W	D	L	F	A	Diff	Goals/P
Total	64	32	27	10	27	97	97	0	3.031

Second Round

Olympique Marseille	Fra	AEK Athens	Gre	2-0	1-1	3-1
Honvéd	Hun	Benfica	Por	0-2	0-7	0-9
AC Milan	Ita	Real Madrid	Esp	2-0	0-1	2-1
Bayern Munich	FRG	17 Nëntori Tirana	Alb	3-1	3-0	6-1
Steaua Bucharest	Rom	PSV Eindhoven	Ned	1-0	1-5	2-5
Malmö FF	Swe	KV Mechelen	Bel	0-0	1-4	1-4
Sparta Prague	Tch	CSKA Sofia	Bul	2-2	0-3	2-5
Dnepr Dnepropetrovsk	URS	FC Tirol	Aut	2-0	2-2	4-2

	Pts	P	W	D	L	F	A	Diff	Goals/P
Total	32	16	12	8	12	48	48	0	3.000

Quarter Finals

KV Mechelen	Bel	AC Milan	Ita	0-0	0-2	0-2
CSKA Sofia	Bul	Olympique Marseille	Fra	0-1	1-3	1-4
Benfica	Por	Dnepr Dnepropetrovsk	URS	1-0	3-0	4-0
Bayern Munich	FRG	PSV Eindhoven	Ned	2-1	1-0	3-1

	Pts	P	W	D	L	F	A	Diff	Goals/P
Total	16	8	7	2	7	15	15	0	1.875

Semi Finals

Olympique Marseille	Fra	Benfica	Por	2-1	0-1	2-2
AC Milan	Ita	Bayern Munich	FRG	1-0	1-2	2-2

	Pts	P	W	D	L	F	A	Diff	Goals/P
Total	8	4	4	0	4	8	8	0	2.000

Final

AC Milan	Ita	Benfica	Por	1-0		1-0

	Pts	P	W	D	L	F	A	Diff	Goals/P
Total	2	1	1	0	1	1	1	0	1.000

	Pts	P	W	D	L	F	A	Diff	Goals/P
Total	122	61	51	20	51	169	169	0	2.770

Pos'n	Club	Cnty	Pts	P	W	D	L	F	A	Diff	B	Pts/P	F/P
1	Benfica	Por	17	9	7	0	2	21	4	17	3	1.889	2.333
2	AC Milan	Ita	16	9	6	1	2	12	3	9	3	1.778	1.333
3	Bayern Munich	FRG	15	8	6	1	1	14	5	9	2	1.875	1.750
4	Olympique Marseille	Fra	14	8	5	2	1	13	5	8	2	1.750	1.625
5	KV Mechelen	Bel	8	6	2	3	1	9	3	6	1	1.333	1.500
6	Dnepr Dnepropetrovsk	URS	8	6	3	1	2	7	7	0	1	1.333	1.167
7	PSV Eindhoven	Ned	7	6	3	0	3	11	5	6	1	1.167	1.833
8	CSKA Sofia	Bul	7	6	2	2	2	12	8	4	1	1.167	2.000
9	Real Madrid	Esp	6	4	3	0	1	10	2	8	0	1.500	2.500
10	Steaua Bucharest	Rom	6	4	3	0	1	7	5	2	0	1.500	1.750
11	FC Tirol	Aut	5	4	2	1	1	11	6	5	0	1.250	2.750
12	Sparta Prague	Tch	5	4	2	1	1	7	7	0	0	1.250	1.750
13	Malmö FF	Swe	4	4	1	2	1	3	5	-2	0	1.000	0.750
14	AEK Athens	Gre	3	4	1	1	2	6	7	-1	0	0.750	1.500
15	Vojvodina Novi Sad	Yug	2	2	1	0	1	2	2	0	0	1.000	1.000
16	17 Nëntori Tirana	Alb	2	4	1	0	3	6	7	-1	0	0.500	1.500
17	Dynamo Dresden	GDR	2	2	1	0	1	4	5	-1	0	1.000	2.000
18	Sliema Wanderers	Mlt	2	2	1	0	1	1	5	-4	0	1.000	0.500
19	Honvéd	Hun	2	4	1	0	3	2	11	-9	0	0.500	0.500
20	Inter Milan	Ita	1	2	0	1	1	1	2	-1	0	0.500	0.500
21	Rangers	Sco	1	2	0	1	1	1	3	-2	0	0.500	0.500
22	Brøndby IF	Den	1	2	0	1	1	1	4	-3	0	0.500	0.500
23	Ruch Chorzów	Pol	1	2	0	1	1	2	6	-4	0	0.500	1.000
24	Rosenborg BK	Nor	1	2	0	1	1	0	5	-5	0	0.500	0.000
25	Linfield	Nir	0	2	0	0	2	1	3	-2	0	0.000	0.500
26	Fenerbahçe	Tur	0	2	0	0	2	2	5	-3	0	0.000	1.000
27	Derry City	Nir	0	2	0	0	2	1	6	-5	0	0.000	0.500
28	HJK Helsinki	Fin	0	2	0	0	2	0	5	-5	0	0.000	0.000
–	Fram Reykjavik	Isl	0	2	0	0	2	0	5	-5	0	0.000	0.000
–	Lucerne	Sui	0	2	0	0	2	0	5	-5	0	0 000	0 000
31	Omonia Nicosia	Cyp	0	2	0	0	2	2	9	-7	0	0.000	1.000
32	Spora Luxembourg	Lux	0	2	0	0	2	0	9	-9	0	0.000	0.000
	Total		**136**	**122**	**51**	**20**	**51**	**169**	**169**	**0**	**14**	**1.115**	**2.770**

Preliminary Round

Team 1	Cnty	Team 2	Cnty	1st leg	2nd leg	Agg
Chernomorets Bourgas	Bul	Dinamo Tirana	Alb	3-1	0-4	3-5

	Pts	P	W	D	L	F	A	Diff	Goals/P
Total	4	2	2	0	2	8	8	0	4.000

First Round

Dinamo Tirana	Alb	Dinamo Bucharest	Rom	1-0	0-2	1-2
Admira Wacker	Aut	AEL Limassol	Cyp	3-0	0-1	3-1
Anderlecht	Bel	Ballymena United	Nir	6-0	4-0	10-0
Barcelona	Esp	Legia Warsaw	Pol	1-1	1-0	2-1
Real Valladolid	Esp	Hamrun Spartans	Mlt	5-0	1-0	6-0
Panathinaikos	Gre	Swansea City	Wal	3-2	3-3	6-5
Ferencváros	Hun	Haka Valkeakoski	Fin	5-1	1-1	6-2
Valur Reykjavik	Isl	Dynamo Berlin	GDR	1-2	1-2	2-4
Union Luxembourg	Lux	Djurgården SIF	Swe	0-0	0-5	0-5
SK Brann	Nor	Sampdoria	Ita	0-2	0-1	0-3
Groningen	Ned	Ikast FS	Den	1-0	2-1	3-1
Belenenses	Por	Monaco	Fra	1-1	0-3	1-4
Slovan Bratislava	Tch	Grasshoppers Zürich	Sui	3-0	0-4	3-4
Besiktas	Tur	Borussia Dortmund	FRG	0-1	1-2	1-3
Torpedo Moscow	URS	Cork City	Irl	5-0	1-0	6-0
Partizan Belgrade	Yug	Celtic	Sco	2-1	4-5	6-6

	Pts	P	W	D	L	F	A	Diff	Goals/P
Total	64	32	27	10	27	97	97	0	3.031

Second Round

Admira Wacker	Aut	Ferencváros	Hun	1-0	1-0	2-0
Anderlecht	Bel	Barcelona	Esp	2-0	1-2	3-2
Real Valladolid	Esp	Djurgården SIF	Swe	2-0	2-2	4-2
Monaco	Fra	Dynamo Berlin	GDR	0-0	1-1	1-1
Panathinaikos	Gre	Dinamo Bucharest	Rom	0-2	1-6	1-8
Groningen	Ned	Partizan Belgrade	Yug	4-3	1-3	5-6
Borussia Dortmund	FRG	Sampdoria	Ita	1-1	0-2	1-3
Torpedo Moscow	URS	Grasshoppers Zürich	Sui	1-1	0-3	1-4

	Pts	P	W	D	L	F	A	Diff	Goals/P
Total	32	16	11	10	11	44	44	0	2.750

Quarter Finals

Anderlecht	Bel	Admira Wacker	Aut	2-0	1-1	3-1
Real Valladolid	Esp	Monaco	Fra	0-0	0-0	0-0
Sampdoria	Ita	Grasshoppers Zürich	Sui	2-0	2-1	4-1
Dinamo Bucharest	Rom	Partizan Belgrade	Yug	2-1	2-0	4-1

	Pts	P	W	D	L	F	A	Diff	Goals/P
Total	16	8	5	6	5	14	14	0	1.750

Semi Finals

Anderlecht	Bel	Dinamo Bucharest	Rom	1-0	1-0	2-0
Monaco	Fra	Sampdoria	Ita	2-2	0-2	2-4

	Pts	P	W	D	L	F	A	Diff	Goals/P
Total	8	4	3	2	3	8	8	0	2.000

Final

Sampdoria	Ita	Anderlecht	Bel	2-0	2-0

	Pts	P	W	D	L	F	A	Diff	Goals/P
Total	2	1	1	0	1	2	2	0	2.000

	Pts	P	W	D	L	F	A	Diff	Goals/P
Total	126	63	49	28	49	173	173	0	2.746

Pos'n	Club	Cnty	Pts	P	W	D	L	F	A	Diff	B	Pts/P	F/P
1	Sampdoria	Ita	19	9	7	2	0	16	4	12	3	2.111	1.778
2	Anderlecht	Bel	16	9	6	1	2	18	5	13	3	1.778	2.000
3	Dinamo Bucharest	Rom	12	8	5	0	3	14	5	9	2	1.500	1.750
4	Real Valladolid	Esp	10	6	3	3	0	10	2	8	1	1.667	1.667
5	Monaco	Fra	10	8	1	6	1	7	6	1	2	1.250	0.875
6	Admira Wacker	Aut	8	6	3	1	2	6	4	2	1	1.333	1.000
7	Dynamo Berlin	GDR	6	4	2	2	0	5	3	2	0	1.500	1.250
8	Grasshoppers Zürich	Sui	6	6	2	1	3	9	8	1	1	1.000	1.500
9	Groningen	Ned	6	4	3	0	1	8	7	1	0	1.500	2.000
10	Torpedo Moscow	URS	5	4	2	1	1	7	4	3	0	1.250	1.750
11	Barcelona	Esp	5	4	2	1	1	4	4	0	0	1.250	1.000
–	Borrusia Dortmund	FRG	5	4	2	1	1	4	4	0	0	1.250	1.000
13	Partizan Belgrade	Yug	5	6	2	0	4	13	15	-2	1	0.833	2.167
14	Djurgården SIF	Swe	4	4	1	2	1	7	4	3	0	1.000	1.750
15	Dinamo Tirana	Alb	4	4	2	0	2	6	5	1	0	1.000	1.500
16	Ferencváros	Hun	3	4	1	1	2	6	4	2	0	0.750	1.500
17	Panathinaikos	Gre	3	4	1	1	2	7	13	-6	0	0.750	1.750
18	Celtic	Sco	2	2	1	0	1	6	6	0	0	1.000	3.000
19	Slovan Bratislava	Tch	2	2	1	0	1	3	4	-1	0	1.000	1.500
20	Chernomorets Bourgas	Bul	2	2	1	0	1	3	5	-2	0	1.000	1.500
21	AEL Limassol	Cyp	2	2	1	0	1	1	3	-2	0	1.000	0.500
22	Swansea City	Wal	1	2	0	1	1	5	6	-1	0	0.500	2.500
23	Legia Warsaw	Pol	1	2	0	1	1	1	2	-1	0	0.500	0.500
24	Belenenses	Por	1	2	0	1	1	1	4	-3	0	0.500	0.500
25	Haka Valkeakoski	Fin	1	2	0	1	1	2	6	-4	0	0.500	1.000
26	Union Luxembourg	Lux	1	2	0	1	1	0	5	-5	0	0.500	0.000
27	Valur Reykjavik	Isl	0	2	0	0	2	2	4	-2	0	0.000	1.000
28	Ikast FS	Den	0	2	0	0	2	1	3	-2	0	0.000	0.500
–	Besiktas	Tur	0	2	0	0	2	1	3	-2	0	0.000	0.500
30	SK Brann	Nor	0	2	0	0	2	0	3	-3	0	0.000	0.000
31	Cork City	Irl	0	2	0	0	2	0	6	-6	0	0.000	0.000
–	Hamrun Spartans	Mlt	0	2	0	0	2	0	6	-6	0	0.000	0.000
33	Ballymena United	Nir	0	2	0	0	2	0	10	-10	0	0.000	0.000
	Total		**140**	**126**	**49**	**28**	**49**	**173**	**173**	**0**	**14**	**1.111**	**2.746**

First Round

Team 1	Cnty	Team 2	Cnty	1st leg	2nd leg	Agg
Austria Vienna	Aut	Ajax	Ned	1-0	3-0	4-0
Levski Sofia	Bul	Antwerp	Bel	0-0	3-4	3-4
Apollon Limassol	Cyp	Real Zaragoza	Esp	0-3	1-1	1-4
Aberdeen	Sco	Rapid Vienna	Aut	2-1	0-1	2-2
Hibernian	Sco	Videoton	Hon	1-0	3-0	4-0
Atlético Madrid	Esp	Fiorentina	Ita	1-0	0-1	1-1
Valencia	Esp	Victoria Bucharest	Rom	3-1	1-1	4-2
FC Kuusysi Lahti	Fin	Paris Saint-Germain	Fra	0-0	2-3	2-3
RoPS Rovaniemi	Fin	GKS Katowice	Pol	1-1	0-1	2-1
Auxerre	Fra	Apolonia Fier	Alb	5-0	3-0	8-0
Sochaux	Fra	Jeunesse Esch	Lux	7-0	5-0	12-0
Iraklis	Gre	Sion	Sui	1-0	0-2	1-2
Glentoran	Nir	Dundee United	Sco	1-3	0-2	1-5
IA Akranes	Isl	FC Liège	Bel	0-2	1-4	1-6
Atalanta	Ita	Spartak Moscow	URS	0-0	0-2	0-2
Valletta	Mlt	First Vienna	Aut	1-4	0-3	1-7
Lillestrøm SK	Nor	Werder Bremen	FRG	1-3	0-2	1-5
Twente Enschede	Ned	Club Bruges	Bel	0-0	1-4	1-4
Gornik Zabrze	Pol	Juventus	Ita	0-1	2-4	2-5
Sporting Lisbon	Por	Napoli	Ita	0-0	0-0	0-0
FC Porto	Por	Flacara Moreni	Rom	2-0	2-1	4-1
Cologne	FRG	Plastika Nitra	Tch	4-1	1-0	5-1
VFB Stuttgart	FRG	Feyenoord	Ned	2-0	1-2	3-2
Örgryte IS	Swe	Hamburg	FRG	1-2	1-5	2-7
Wettingen	Sui	Dundalk	Irl	3-0	2-0	5-0
Galatasaray	Tur	Red Star Belgrade	Yug	1-1	0-2	1-3
Dinamo Kiev	URS	MTK-VM	Hun	4-0	2-1	6-1
Zenit Leningrad	URS	Naestved IF	Den	3-1	0-0	3-1
Zhalgiris Vilnius	URS	IFK Gothenburg	Swe	2-0	0-1	2-1
Rad Belgrade	Yug	Olympiakos Pireus	Gre	2-1	0-2	2-3
Karl-Marx-Stadt	GDR	Boavista	Por	1-0	2-2	3-2
Hansa Rostock	GDR	Banik Ostrava	Tch	2-3	0-4	2-7

	Pts	P	W	D	L	F	A	Diff	Goals/P
Total	128	64	52	24	52	171	171	0	2.672

Second Round

First Vienna	Aut	Olympiakos Pireus	Gre	2-2	1-1	3-3
Antwerp	Bel	Dundee United	Sco	4-0	2-3	6-3
Club Bruges	Bel	Rapid Vienna	Aut	1-2	3-4	4-6
Hibernian	Sco	FC Liège	Bel	0-0	0-1	0-1
Real Zaragoza	Esp	Hamburg	FRG	1-0	0-2	1-2
RoPS Rovaniemi	Fin	Auxerre	Fra	0-5	0-3	0-8
Paris Saint-Germain	Fra	Juventus	Ita	0-1	1-2	1-3
Fiorentina	Ita	Sochaux	Fra	0-0	1-1	1-1
FC Porto	Por	Valencia	Esp	3-1	2-3	5-4
Werder Bremen	FRG	Austria Vienna	Aut	5-0	0-2	5-2
Cologne	FRG	Spartak Moscow	URS	3-1	0-0	3-1
Sion	Sui	Karl-Marx-Stadt	GDR	2-1	1-4	3-5
Wettingen	Sui	Napoli	Ita	0-0	1-2	1-2
Dinamo Kiev	URS	Banik Ostrava	Tch	3-0	1-1	4-1
Zenit Leningrad	URS	VFB Stuttgart	FRG	0-1	0-5	0-6
Red Star Belgrade	You	Zhalgiris Vilnius	URS	4-1	1-0	5-1

	Pts	P	W	D	L	F	A	Diff	Goals/P
Total	64	32	24	16	24	91	91	0	2.844

Third Round

Rapid Vienna	Aut	FC Liège	Bel	1-0	1-3	2-3
Antwerp	Bel	VFB Stuttgart	FRG	1-0	1-1	2-1
Olympiakos Pireus	Gre	Auxerre	Fra	1-1	0-0	1-1
Fiorentina	Ita	Dinamo Kiev	URS	1-0	0-0	1-0
Napoli	Ita	Werder Bremen	FRG	2-3	1-5	3-8
Juventus	Ita	Karl-Marx-Stadt	GDR	2-1	1-0	3-1
Hamburg	FRG	FC Porto	Por	1-0	1-2	2-2
Red Star Belgrade	You	Cologne	FRG	2-0	0-3	2-3

	Pts	P	W	D	L	F	A	Diff	Goals/P
Total	32	16	12	8	12	35	35	0	2.188

Quarter Finals

FC Liège	Bel	Werder Bremen	FRG	1-4	2-0	3-4
Fiorentina	Ita	Auxerre	Fra	1-0	1-0	2-0
Cologne	FRG	Antwerp	Bel	2-0	0-0	2-0
Hamburg	FRG	Juventus	Ita	0-2	2-1	2-3

	Pts	P	W	D	L	F	A	Diff	Goals/P
Total	16	8	7	2	7	16	16	0	2.000

Semi Finals

Juventus	Ita	Cologne	FRG	3-2	0-0	3-2
Werder Bremen	FRG	Fiorentina	Ita	1-1	0-0	1-1

	Pts	P	W	D	L	F	A	Diff	Goals/P
Total	8	4	1	6	1	7	7	0	1.750

Final

Juventus	Ita	Fiorentina	I ta	3-1	0-0	3-1

	Pts	P	W	D	L	F	A	Diff	Goals/P
Total	4	2	1	2	1	4	4	0	2.000

	Pts	P	W	D	L	F	A	Diff	Goals/P
Total	252	126	97	58	97	324	324	0	2.571

Pos'n	Club	Cnty	Pts	P	W	D	L	F	A	Diff	B	Pts/P	F/P
1	Juventus	Ita	23	12	9	2	1	20	9	11	3	1.917	1.667
2	Fiorentina	Ita	17	12	4	6	2	7	6	1	3	1.417	0.583
3	Werder Bremen	FRG	16	10	6	2	2	23	10	13	2	1.600	2.300
4	Cologne	FRG	15	10	5	3	2	15	7	8	2	1.500	1.500
5	FC Liège	Bel	12	8	5	1	2	13	7	6	1	1.500	1.625
6	Auxerre	Fra	11	8	4	2	2	17	3	14	1	1.375	2.125
7	Hamburg	FRG	11	8	5	0	3	13	8	5	1	1.375	1.625
8	Antwerp	Bel	10	8	3	3	2	12	9	3	1	1.250	1.500
9	Red Star Belgrade	Yug	9	6	4	1	1	10	5	5	0	1.500	1.667
10	Dinamo Kiev	URS	8	6	3	2	1	10	3	7	0	1.333	1.667
11	FC Porto	Por	8	6	4	0	2	11	7	4	0	1.333	1.833
12	Rapid Vienna	Aut	8	6	4	0	2	10	9	1	0	1.333	1.667
13	VFB Stuttgart	FRG	7	6	3	1	2	10	4	6	0	1.167	1.667
14	Sochaux	Fra	6	4	2	2	0	13	1	12	0	1.500	3.250
15	First Vienna	Aut	6	4	2	2	0	10	4	6	0	1.500	2.500
16	Dundee United	Sco	6	4	3	0	1	8	7	1	0	1.500	2.000
17	Olympiakos Pireus	Gre	6	6	1	4	1	7	6	1	0	1.000	1.167
18	Austria Vienna	Aut	6	4	3	0	1	6	5	1	0	1.500	1.500
19	Wettingen	Sui	5	4	2	1	1	6	2	4	0	1.250	1.500
20	Hibernian	Sco	5	4	2	1	1	4	1	3	0	1.250	1.000
21	Banik Ostrava	Tch	5	4	2	1	1	8	6	2	0	1.250	2.000
22	Real Zaragoza	Esp	5	4	2	1	1	5	3	2	0	1.250	1.250
23	Karl-Marx-Stadt	GDR	5	6	2	1	3	9	8	1	0	0.833	1.500
24	Valencia	Esp	5	4	2	1	1	8	7	1	0	1.250	2.000
25	Napoli	Ita	5	6	1	3	2	5	9	-4	0	0.833	0.833
26	Spartak Moscow	URS	4	4	1	2	1	3	3	0	0	1.000	0.750
27	Sion	Sui	4	4	2	0	2	5	6	-1	0	1.000	1.250
28	Club Bruges	Bel	3	4	1	1	2	8	7	1	0	0.750	2.000
29	Paris Saint-Germain	Fra	3	4	1	1	2	4	5	-1	0	0.750	1.000
30	Zenit Leningrad	URS	3	4	1	1	2	3	7	-4	0	0.750	0.750
31	RoPS Rovaniemi	Fin	3	4	1	1	2	2	9	-7	0	0.750	0.500
32	Aberdeen	Sco	2	2	1	0	1	2	2	0	0	1.000	1.000
33	Atlético Madrid	Esp	2	2	1	0	1	1	1	0	0	1.000	0.500
34	Sporting Lisbon	Por	2	2	0	2	0	0	0	0	0	1.000	0.000
35	Feyenoord	Ned	2	2	1	0	1	2	3	-1	0	1.000	1.000
–	Rad Belgrade	Yug	2	2	1	0	1	2	3	-1	0	1.000	1.000
37	Iraklis	Gre	2	2	1	0	1	1	2	-1	0	1.000	0.500
–	IFK Gothenburg	Swe	2	2	1	0	1	1	2	-1	0	1.000	0.500
39	Zhalgiris Vilnius	URS	2	4	1	0	3	3	6	-3	0	0.500	0.750
40	Levski Sofia	Bul	1	2	0	1	1	3	4	-1	0	0.500	1.500
41	FC Kuusysi Lahti	Fin	1	2	0	1	1	2	3	-1	0	0.500	1.000
–	Boavista	Por	1	2	0	1	1	2	3	-1	0	0.500	1.000
43	GKS Katowice	Pol	1	2	0	1	1	1	2	-1	0	0.500	0.500
44	Victoria Bucharest	Rom	1	2	0	1	1	2	4	-2	0	0.500	1.000
45	Naestved IF	Den	1	2	0	1	1	1	3	-2	0	0.500	0.500
–	Galatasaray	Tur	1	2	0	1	1	1	3	-2	0	0.500	0.500
47	Atalanta	Ita	1	2	0	1	1	0	2	-2	0	0.500	0.000
48	Apollon Limassol	Cyp	1	2	0	1	1	1	4	-3	0	0.500	0.500
–	Twente Enschede	Ned	1	2	0	1	1	1	4	-3	0	0.500	0.500
50	Górmik Zabrze	Pol	0	2	0	0	2	2	5	-3	0	0.000	1.000
51	Flacara Moreni	Rom	0	2	0	0	2	1	4	-3	0	0.000	0.500
52	Glentoran	Nir	0	2	0	0	2	1	5	-4	0	0.000	0.500
–	Lillestrøm SK	Nor	0	2	0	0	2	1	5	-4	0	0.000	0.500
–	Plastika Nitra	Tch	0	2	0	0	2	1	5	-4	0	0.000	0.500
55	Videoton	Hun	0	2	0	0	2	0	4	-4	0	0.000	0.000
–	Ajax	Ned	0	2	0	0	2	0	4	-4	0	0.000	0.000
57	Örgryte IS	Swe	0	2	0	0	2	2	7	-5	0	0.000	1.000
–	Hansa Rostock	GDR	0	2	0	0	2	2	7	-5	0	0.000	1.000
59	MTK-VM	Hun	0	2	0	0	2	1	6	-5	0	0.000	0.500
–	IA Akranes	Isl	0	2	0	0	2	1	6	-5	0	0.000	0.500
61	Dundalk	Irl	0	2	0	0	2	0	5	-5	0	0.000	0.000
62	Valletta	Mlt	0	2	0	0	2	1	7	-6	0	0.000	0.500
63	Apollonia Fier	Alb	0	2	0	0	2	0	8	-8	0	0.000	0.000
64	Jeunesse Esch	Lux	0	2	0	0	2	0	12	-12	0	0.000	0.000
	Total		**266**	**252**	**97**	**58**	**97**	**324**	**324**	**0**	**14**	**1.056**	**2.571**

1989-90

Pos'n	Cnty	Pts	P	W	D	L	F	A	Diff	B	Pts/P	F/P
1	Ita	82	52	27	16	9	61	35	26	12	1.577	1.173
2	FRG	69	46	27	8	11	79	38	41	7	1.500	1.717
3	Bel	49	35	17	9	9	60	31	29	6	1.400	1.714
4	Fra	44	32	13	13	6	54	20	34	5	1.375	1.688
5	Esp	33	24	13	6	5	38	19	19	1	1.375	1.583
6	Aut	33	24	14	4	6	43	28	15	1	1.375	1.792
7	URS	30	28	11	7	10	33	30	3	1	1.071	1.179
8	Por	29	21	11	4	6	35	18	17	3	1.381	1.667
9	Rom	19	16	8	1	7	24	18	6	2	1.188	1.500
10	Yug	18	16	8	1	7	27	25	2	1	1.125	1.688
11	Sco	16	14	7	2	5	21	19	2	0	1.143	1.500
12	Ned	16	16	7	1	8	22	23	-1	1	1.000	1.375
13	Sui	15	16	6	2	8	20	21	-1	1	0.938	1.250
14	Gre	14	16	4	6	6	21	28	-7	0	0.875	1.313
15	GDR	13	14	5	3	6	20	23	-3	0	0.929	1.429
16	Tch	12	12	5	2	5	19	22	-3	0	1.000	1.583
17	Bul	10	10	3	3	4	18	17	1	1	1.000	1.800
18	Swe	10	12	3	4	5	13	18	-5	0	0.833	1.083
19	Alb	6	10	3	0	7	12	20	-8	0	0.600	1.200
20	Hun	5	12	2	1	9	9	25	-16	0	0.417	0.750
21	Fin	5	10	1	3	6	6	23	-17	0	0.500	0.600
22	Pol	3	8	0	3	5	6	15	-9	0	0.375	0.750
23	Cyp	3	6	1	1	4	4	16	-12	0	0.500	0.667
24	Den	2	6	0	2	4	3	10	-7	0	0.333	0.500
25	Mlt	2	6	1	0	5	2	18	-16	0	0.333	0.333
26	Wal	1	2	0	1	1	5	6	-1	0	0.500	2.500
27	Tur	1	6	0	1	5	4	11	-7	0	0.167	0.667
28	Nor	1	6	0	1	5	1	13	-12	0	0.167	0.167
29	Lux	1	6	0	1	5	0	26	-26	0	0.167	0.000
30	Isl	0	6	0	0	6	3	15	-12	0	0.000	0.500
31	Nir	0	6	0	0	6	2	18	-16	0	0.000	0.333
32	Irl	0	6	0	0	6	1	17	-16	0	0.000	0.167
	Total	**542**	**500**	**197**	**106**	**197**	**666**	**666**	**0**	**42**	**1.084**	**2.664**

1955-56 to 1989-90

Pos'n	Cnty	Pts	P	W	D	L	F	A	Diff	B	Pts/P	F/P
1	FRG	1532	1107	578	209	320	2174	1342	832	167	1.384	1.964
2	Eng	1365	926	500	201	225	1782	927	855	164	1.474	1.924
3	Esp	1352	988	499	188	301	1773	1170	603	166	1.368	1.795
4	Ita	1284	942	464	211	267	1452	931	521	145	1.363	1.541
5	Bel	821	675	315	117	243	1096	860	236	74	1.216	1.624
6	Sco	812	660	310	127	223	1099	811	288	65	1.230	1.665
7	Ned	756	597	289	109	199	1100	722	378	69	1.266	1.843
8	Yug	714	642	270	115	257	1059	926	133	59	1.112	1.650
9	Por	710	599	265	122	212	950	730	220	58	1.185	1.586
10	URS	571	437	219	93	125	664	442	222	40	1.307	1.519
11	Fra	570	531	205	116	210	795	746	49	44	1.073	1.497
12	GDR	560	508	207	107	194	756	672	84	39	1.102	1.488
13	Hun	548	486	214	76	196	838	729	109	44	1.128	1.724
14	Tch	538	473	206	91	176	734	634	100	35	1.137	1.552
15	Rom	410	411	158	72	181	543	600	-57	22	0.998	1.321
16	Aut	400	422	144	85	193	562	667	-105	27	0.948	1.332
17	Sui	377	429	138	78	213	620	783	-163	23	0.879	1.445
18	Pol	353	361	129	78	154	494	554	-60	17	0.978	1.368
19	Bul	350	369	134	62	173	545	596	-51	20	0.949	1.477
20	Swe	333	341	117	79	145	470	536	-66	20	0.977	1.378
21	Gre	289	323	109	60	154	373	548	-175	11	0.895	1.155
22	Den	211	301	75	54	172	383	630	-247	7	0.701	1.272
23	Tur	189	263	70	40	153	247	489	-242	9	0.719	0.939
24	Nor	115	218	39	36	143	198	530	-332	1	0.528	0.908
25	Wal	101	102	33	29	40	147	125	22	6	0.990	1.441
26	Fin	94	188	33	25	130	155	527	-372	3	0.500	0.824
27	Irl	93	212	28	37	147	162	523	-361	0	0.439	0.764
28	Nir	90	192	23	42	127	177	511	-334	2	0.469	0.922
29	Alb	59	87	21	17	49	68	131	-63	0	0.678	0.782
30	Cyp	55	150	18	19	113	109	510	-401	0	0.367	0.727
31	Mlt	49	168	18	13	137	72	590	-518	0	0.292	0.429
32	Lux	47	188	16	15	157	109	795	-686	0	0.250	0.580
33	Isl	39	154	9	21	124	80	499	-419	0	0.253	0.519
	Total	**15787**	**14450**	**5853**	**2744**	**5853**	**21786**	**21786**	**0**	**1337**	**1.093**	**3.015**

1989-90

Pos'n	Cnty	Ave	Pts	P	W	D	L	F	A	Diff	B	No./T
1	Italy	11.714	82	52	27	16	9	61	35	26	12	7
2	W. Germany	11.500	69	46	27	8	11	79	38	41	7	6
3	Belgium	9.800	49	35	17	9	9	60	31	29	6	5
4	France	8.800	44	32	13	13	6	54	20	34	5	5
5	Austria	6.600	33	24	14	4	6	43	28	15	1	5
6	Portugal	5.800	29	21	11	4	6	35	18	17	3	5
7	Spain	5.500	33	24	13	6	5	38	19	19	1	6
8	USSR	5.000	30	28	11	7	10	33	30	3	1	6
9	Romania	4.750	19	16	8	1	7	24	18	6	2	4
10	Yugoslavia	4.500	18	16	8	1	7	27	25	2	1	4
11	Switzerland	3.750	15	16	6	2	8	20	21	-1	1	4
12	Greece	3.500	14	16	4	6	6	21	28	-7	0	4
13	Bulgaria	3.333	10	10	3	3	4	18	17	1	1	3
14	E. Germany	3.250	13	14	5	3	6	20	23	-3	0	4
15	Scotland	3.200	16	14	7	2	5	21	19	2	0	5
–	Netherlands	3.200	16	16	7	1	8	22	23	-1	1	5
17	Czechoslovakia	3.000	12	12	5	2	5	19	22	-3	0	4
18	Sweden	2.500	10	12	3	4	5	13	18	-5	0	4
19	Albania	2.000	6	10	3	0	7	12	20	-8	0	3
20	Finland	1.250	5	10	1	3	6	6	23	-17	0	4
–	Hungary	1.250	5	12	2	1	9	9	25	-16	0	4
22	Cyprus	1.000	3	6	1	1	4	4	16	-12	0	3
–	Wales	1.000	1	2	0	1	1	5	6	-1	0	1
24	Poland	0.750	3	8	0	3	5	6	15	-9	0	4
25	Denmark	0.666	2	6	0	2	4	3	10	-7	0	3
–	Malta	0.666	2	6	1	0	5	2	18	-16	0	3
27	Luxembourg	0.333	1	6	0	1	5	0	26	-26	0	3
–	Norway	0.333	1	6	0	1	5	1	13	-12	0	3
–	Turkey	0.333	1	6	0	1	5	4	11	-7	0	3
30	Rep. of Ireland	0.000	0	6	0	0	6	1	17	-16	0	3
–	N. Ireland	0.000	0	6	0	0	6	2	18	-16	0	3
–	Iceland	0.000	0	6	0	0	6	3	15	-12	0	3
	Total		**542**	**500**	**197**	**106**	**197**	**666**	**666**	**0**	**42**	**2.664**

1955-56 to 1989-90

Pos'n	Cnty	Ave	Pts	P	W	D	L	F	A	Diff	B	No./T
1	England	8.806	1365	926	500	201	225	1782	927	855	164	155
2	W. Germany	8.063	1532	1107	578	209	320	2174	1342	832	167	190
3	Spain	7.638	1352	988	499	188	301	1773	1170	603	166	177
4	Italy	7.421	1284	942	464	211	267	1452	931	521	145	173
5	USSR	5.886	571	437	219	93	125	664	442	222	40	97
6	Netherlands	5.860	756	597	289	109	199	1100	722	378	69	129
7	Belgium	5.701	821	675	315	117	243	1096	860	236	74	144
8	Scotland	5.678	812	660	310	127	223	1099	811	288	65	143
9	Portugal	5.071	710	599	265	122	212	950	730	220	58	140
10	Yugoslavia	4.857	714	642	270	115	257	1059	926	133	59	147
11	Hungary	4.724	548	486	214	76	196	838	729	109	44	116
12	E. Germany	4.666	560	508	207	107	194	756	672	84	39	120
13	Czechoslovakia	4.446	538	473	206	91	176	734	634	100	35	121
14	France	4.130	570	531	205	116	210	795	746	49	44	138
15	Romania	3.596	410	411	158	72	181	543	600	-57	22	114
16	Wales	3.482	101	102	33	29	40	147	125	22	6	29
17	Poland	3.427	353	361	129	78	154	494	554	-60	17	103
18	Austria	3.333	400	422	144	85	193	562	667	-105	27	120
19	Bulgaria	3.211	350	369	134	62	173	545	596	-51	20	109
20	Sweden	3.112	333	341	117	79	145	470	536	-66	20	107
21	Switzerland	2.922	377	429	138	78	213	620	783	-163	23	129
22	Greece	2.675	289	323	109	60	154	373	548	-175	11	108
23	Turkey	2.010	189	263	70	40	153	247	489	-242	9	94
24	Denmark	1.900	211	301	75	54	172	383	630	-247	7	111
25	Albania	1.735	59	87	21	17	49	68	131	-63	0	34
26	Norway	1.250	115	218	39	36	143	198	530	-332	1	92
27	Finland	1.236	94	188	33	25	130	155	527	-372	3	76
28	N. Ireland	1.058	90	192	23	42	127	177	511	-334	2	85
29	Rep. of Ireland	1.033	93	212	28	37	147	162	523	-361	0	90
30	Cyprus	0.797	55	150	18	19	113	109	510	-401	0	69
31	Malta	0.612	49	168	18	13	137	72	590	-518	0	80
32	Iceland	0.541	39	154	9	21	124	80	499	-419	0	72
33	Luxembourg	0.522	47	188	16	15	157	109	795	-686	0	90
	Total		**15787**	**14450**	**5853**	**2744**	**5853**	**21786**	**21786**	**0**	**1337**	**3.015**

Italian Triumvirate

In the year that Italy hosted the World Cup, its clubs pulled off an unprecedented treble with victories in all three European competitions – AC Milan in the Champions' Cup, Sampdoria in the Cup-winners' Cup and Juventus in the UEFA Cup.

The so-called grand slam would have been achieved a year earlier had Sampdoria not gone down to Barcelona in the Cup-winners' Cup final in Berne. But this time the Genoese club made up for that disappointment by capturing the trophy in Gothenburg after a 2-0 victory over the Belgians of Anderlecht.

Sampdoria's hero in Gothenburg, and throughout the tournament, was Italian international striker Gianluca Vialli. He was the top scorer in the competition coming into the final, having scored five goals to help Sampdoria come undefeated through their earlier ties with Brann, Borussia Dortmund, Grasshoppers and Monaco. For the first, largely unforgettable 90 minutes in Gothenburg, Vialli was barely seen. But in extra-time he suddenly burst into life with two goals in a four-minute spell either side of the interval that left Anderlecht dead and buried and their coach Aad de Mos, who had won the Cup for Mechelen two years earlier, reflecting on the merits of the excessively cautious game plan he had advocated for his team in normal time. For Sampdoria, and their Yugoslav coach Vujadin Boskov, Vialli's double strike meant a first European trophy for the club and hooded revenge on their previous season's conquerors Barcelona, who had been eliminated by Anderlecht in the second round.

The second leg of the Italian treble, the UEFA Cup, was already secure after the semi-finals, with Juventus and Fiorentina seeing off West German opponents to qualify for the first all-Italian final in European Cup history.

Napoli, the Italian winners in 1988-89, narrowly avoided becoming the third UEFA holders in a row to be knocked out in the opening round when they beat Sporting Lisbon on penalties after two goalless draws. And there was further torment for the holders in the second round when only a late disputed penalty took them through against Swiss debutants, and rank outsiders, Wettingen.

But where Sporting and Wettingen had chipped away resolutely at Napoli's defence of the trophy, Werder Bremen, in the third round, smashed it to smithereens, destroying Maradona's side with a 3-2 win in Naples followed by a 5-1 success in Bremen. But in four Italy v West Germany confrontations during the course of the tournament, that was the only one which would go the Germans' way. Juventus gained revenge for their 1983 Champions' Cup final defeat by eliminating Hamburg in the quarter-finals, and then went on to bury Cologne's eternal UEFA Cup hopes once again in the semis. Fiorentina, meanwhile, avenged Napoli's conquerors by reaching the final at the expense of Werder Bremen on the away goals rule.

The all-Italian final brought together two of European football's oldest and most bitter rivals. Juventus were clear favourites to take the trophy. Not only had they been the most consistent team in the tournament, but they had also won the Italian Cup the week before and finished a respectable third in the Italian championship. Fiorentina, on the other hand, had only just escaped relegation and had managed to prolong their European campaign only by taking full advantage of both penalty shoot-outs and the away goals rule, scoring a bare minimum of six goals along the way. Even second-leg home advantage had been denied to Fiorentina after crowd misbehaviour during their semi-final against Bremen, so the second leg had to be switched to Avellino from their adopted home of Perugia, where they had played their previous ties due to World Cup reconstruction work on their own stadium in Florence.

But Fiorentina at least made a go of it in the first leg in Turin. Buso equalised an early Juventus goal from Galia and only the splendid form of Juventus goalkeeper Tacconi prevented Fiorentina's star forward Roberto Baggio from giving the visitors the lead in the first half. After the interval, though, Fiorentina faded and Juventus were able to establish a healthy two-goal cushion thanks to further goals from Casiraghi and De Agostini. The 3-1 scoreline meant that Fiorentina had conceded as many goals in that one match as they had during all ten of their previous matches in the competition. It was also a reassuring lead for Juventus, who, remarkably, had not conceded an away goal in any of their previous five ties. That record was to remain in the second leg, with 0-0 the inevitable outcome of a rather dreary encounter that had *foregone conclusion* written all over it. Still, the draw meant a second UEFA Cup victory for Juventus and a clear conscience for coach Dino Zoff, whose last game this was before his enforced departure to Lazio.

So the pressure was on AC Milan to cement the third leg of the Italian grand slam with a second successive victory in the Champions' Cup. The onus had fallen on them after the shock first-round elimination of their city rivals Inter, beaten 2-1 on aggregate by Swedish champions Malmö FF. Milan themselves, had better success against Scandinavian opposition in the shape of HJK Helsinki in the opening round, but they then had the misfortune of being drawn against Real Madrid. After their 5-0 demolition of the Spaniard giants a year earlier, Arrigo Sacchi's men might have been expected to lick their lips at the prospect of facing Real yet again. But for the past two seasons Real had made a habit of defeating the clubs which had eliminated them from the semi-finals of the competition the previous year, so the Italians had to be on their guard.

But it was to be third time unlucky for Real. Milan's 2-1 aggregate margin of victory was deceptive – in reality, the Italians had proved themselves once again to be far and away the better side. The next two rounds, however, were to offer severe tests of Milan's pedigree. Extra-time was required to defeat an impressive KV Mechelen, and then both extra-time and the away goals rule came to their rescue in a high-quality semi-final confrontation with Bayern Munich.

The other semi-final, between Marseille and Benfica, was steeped in controversy. The French champions, appearing in the tournament for the first time in 17 years, had torn Benfica apart in the first leg, but could only emerge with a 2-1 victory. And that slim margin of victory was to prove decisive in the second leg when, with just seven minutes left, the Portuguese scored the one goal they needed through a blatantly handled effort from Angolan striker Vata. Despite heated protests, the Belgian referee refused even to consult his linesman and gave the goal that deprived Marseille, and their wealthy president Bernard Tapie, of an amply merited first ever place in the Champions' Cup final.

Certainly, Marseille would have provided a more courageous opponent to Milan in the final than did Benfica. In the same Vienna Prater stadium where, three years earlier, FC Porto had triumphed so dramatically against Bayern Munich, Benfica gave a performance that was just as uninspired as their 1988 display in Stuttgart against PSV. And once again, they paid for it. This time, thankfully, there was no penalty shoot-out. The only goal of the game, and the one which secured the first Champions' Cup defence since Nottingham Forest's achievement ten years earlier, was scored midway through the first half by Dutchman Frank Rijkaard, who, running on to a deft flick from his compatriot Van Basten, steered the ball confidently past the Benfica 'keeper Silvino with the outside of his right foot.

Benfica had thus lost their fifth Champions' Cup final in a row, whereas Milan joined Liverpool in joint second place behind Real Madrid in the all-time Champions' Cup honours list with four victories.

Red Star Belgrade

Manchester United

Inter Milan

1990 – 1991

First Round

Team 1	Cnty	Team 2	Cnty	1st leg	2nd leg	Agg
FC Tirol	Aut	FC Kuusysi Lahti	Fin	5-0	2-1	7-1
Apoel Nicosia	Cyp	Bayern Munich	FRG	2-3	0-4	2-7
OB Odense	Den	Real Madrid	Esp	1-4	0-6	1-10
Olympique Marseille	Fra	Dinamo Tirana	Alb	5-1	0-0	5-1
IBA Akureyri	Isl	CSKA Sofia	Bul	1-0	0-3	1-3
Napoli	Ita	Ujpesti Dósza	Hun	3-0	2-0	5-0
Union Luxembourg	Lux	Dynamo Dresden	GDR	1-3	0-3	1-6
Valletta	Mlt	Rangers	Sco	0-4	0-6	0-10
Lillestrøm SK	Nor	Club Bruges	Bel	1-1	0-2	1-3
Lech Poznań	Pol	Panathinaikos	Gre	3-0	2-1	5-1
FC Porto	Por	Portadown	Nir	5-0	8-1	13-1
Dinamo Bucarest	Rom	St. Patrick's Athletic	Irl	4-0	1-1	5-1
Malmö FF	Swe	Besiktas	Tur	3-2	2-2	5-4
Sparta Prague	Tch	Spartak Moscow	URS	0-2	0-2	0-4
Red Star Belgrade	Yug	Grasshoppers Zürich	Sui	1-1	4-1	5-2

	Pts	P	W	D	L	F	A	Diff	Goals/P
Total	60	30	25	10	25	110	110	0	3.667

Second Round

Real Madrid	Esp	FC Tirol	Aut	9-1	2-2	11-3
AC Milan	Ita	Club Bruges	Bel	0-0	1-0	1-0
Napoli	Ita	Spartak Moscow	URS	0-0	0-0	0-0
Lech Poznań	Pol	Olympique Marseille	Fra	3-2	1-6	4-8
Bayern Munich	FRG	CSKA Sofia	Bul	4-0	3-0	7-0
Dinamo Bucarest	Rom	FC Porto	Por	0-0	0-4	0-4
Red Star Belgrade	You	Rangers	Sco	3-0	1-1	4-1
Dynamo Dresden	GDR	Malmö FF	Swe	1-1	1-1	2-2

	Pts	P	W	D	L	F	A	Diff	Goals/P
Total	32	16	8	16	8	47	47	0	2.938

Quarter Finals

AC Milan	Ita	Olympique Marseille	Fra	1-1	0-1	1-2
Bayern Munich	FRG	FC Porto	Por	1-1	2-0	3-1
Spartak Moscow	URS	Real Madrid	Esp	0-0	3-1	3-1
Red Star Belgrade	You	Dynamo Dresden	GDR	3-0	2-1	5-1

	Pts	P	W	D	L	F	A	Diff	Goals/P
Total	16	8	5	6	5	17	17	0	2.125

Semi Finals

Bayern Munich	RFA	Red Star Belgrade	You	1-2	2-2	3-4
Spartak Moscow	URS	Olympique Marseille	Fra	1-3	1-2	2-5

	Pts	P	W	D	L	F	A	Diff	Goals/P
Total	8	4	3	2	3	14	14	0	3.500

Final

Olympique Marseille	Fra	Red Star Belgrade	Yug	0-0	0-0

	Pts	P	W	D	L	F	A	Diff	Goals/P
Total	2	1	0	2	0	0	0	0	0.000

	Pts	P	W	D	L	F	A	Diff	Goals/P
Total	118	59	41	36	41	188	188	0	3.186

Pos'n	Club	Cnty	Pts	P	W	D	L	F	A	Diff	B	Pts/P	F/P
1	Red Star Belgrade	Yug	17	9	5	4	0	18	7	11	3	1.889	2.000
2	Olympique Marseille	Fra	16	9	5	3	1	20	8	12	3	1.778	2.222
3	Bayern Munich	FRG	14	8	5	2	1	20	7	13	2	1.750	2.500
4	Spartak Moscow	URS	11	8	3	3	2	9	6	3	2	1.375	1.125
5	Real Madrid	Esp	9	6	3	2	1	22	7	15	1	1.500	3.667
6	FC Porto	Por	9	6	3	2	1	18	4	14	1	1.500	3.000
7	Dynamo Dresden	GDR	7	6	2	2	2	9	8	1	1	1.167	1.500
8	Napoli	Ita	6	4	2	2	0	5	0	5	0	1.500	1.250
9	Lech Poznań	Pol	6	4	3	0	1	9	9	0	0	1.500	2.250
10	Rangers	Sco	5	4	2	1	1	11	4	7	0	1.250	2.750
11	Malmö FF	Swe	5	4	1	3	0	7	6	1	0	1.250	1.750
12	AC Milan	Ita	5	4	1	2	1	2	2	0	1	1.250	0.500
13	FC Tirol	Aut	5	4	2	1	1	10	12	-2	0	1.250	2.500
14	Club Bruges	Bel	4	4	1	2	1	3	2	1	0	1.000	0.750
15	Dinamo Bucarest	Rom	4	4	1	2	1	5	5	0	0	1.000	1.250
16	IBA Akureyri	Isl	2	2	1	0	1	1	3	-2	0	1.000	0.500
17	CSKA Sofia	Bul	2	4	1	0	3	3	8	-5	0	0.500	0.750
18	Besiktas	Tur	1	2	0	1	1	4	5	-1	0	0.500	2.000
19	Lillestrøm SK	Nor	1	2	0	1	1	1	3	-2	0	0.500	0.500
20	Grasshoppers Zürich	Sui	1	2	0	1	1	2	5	-3	0	0.500	1.000
21	Dinamo Tirana	Alb	1	2	0	1	1	1	5	-4	0	0.500	0.500
–	St. Patrick's Athletic	Irl	1	2	0	1	1	1	5	-4	0	0.500	0.500
23	Panathinaikos	Gre	0	2	0	0	2	1	5	-4	0	0.000	0.500
24	Sparta Prague	Tch	0	2	0	0	2	0	4	-4	0	0.000	0.000
25	Apoel Nicosia	Cyp	0	2	0	0	2	2	7	-5	0	0.000	1.000
26	Union Luxembourg	Lux	0	2	0	0	2	1	6	-5	0	0.000	0.500
27	Ujpesti Dósza	Hun	0	2	0	0	2	0	5	-5	0	0.000	0.000
28	FC Kuusysi Lahti	Fin	0	2	0	0	2	1	7	-6	0	0.000	0.500
29	OB Odense	Den	0	2	0	0	2	1	10	-9	0	0.000	0.500
30	Valletta	Mlt	0	2	0	0	2	0	10	-10	0	0.000	0.000
31	Portadown	Nir	0	2	0	0	2	1	13	-12	0	0.000	0.500
	Total		**132**	**118**	**41**	**36**	**41**	**188**	**188**	**0**	**14**	**1.119**	**3.186**

Preliminary Round

Team 1	Cnty	Team 2	Cnty	1st leg	2nd leg	Agg
Bray Wanderers	Irl	Trabzonspor	Tur	1-1	0-2	1-3

	Pts	P	W	D	L	F	A	Diff	Goals/P
Total	4	2	1	2	1	4	4	0	2.000

First Roun

Manchester United	Eng	Pécsi MSC	Hun	2-0	1-0	3-0
Sliven	Bul	Juventus	Ita	0-2	1-6	1-8
NEA Salamina Famagusta	Cyp	Aberdeen	Sco	0-2	0-3	0-5
KuPS Kuopio	Fin	Dinamo Kiev	URS	2-2	0-4	2-6
Montpellier	Fra	PSV Eindhoven	Ned	1-0	0-0	1-0
Wrexham	Wal	Lynghy BK	Den	0-0	1-0	1-0
Olympiakos Pireus	Gre	Flamurtari Vlorë	Alb	3-1	2-0	5-1
Glentoran	Nir	Steaua Bucharest	Rom	1-1	0-5	1-6
Fram Reykjavik	Isl	Djurgården SIF	Swe	3-0	1-1	4-1
Sliema Wanderers	Mal	Dukla Prague	Tch	1-2	0-2	1-4
IL Viking	Nor	FC Liège	Bel	0-2	0-3	0-5
Legia Warsaw	Pol	Swift Hesperange	Lux	3-0	3-0	6-0
Estrela Amadora	Por	Neuchâtel Xamax	Sui	1-1	1-1	2-2
Kaiserslautern	FRG	Sampdoria	Ita	1-0	0-2	1-2
Trabzonspor	Tur	Barcelona	Esp	1-0	2-7	3-7
PSV Schwerin	GDR	Austria Vienna	Aut	0-2	0-0	0-2

	Pts	P	W	D	L	F	A	Diff	Goals/P
Total	64	32	24	16	24	80	80	0	2.500

Second Round

Manchester United	Eng	Wrexham	Wal	3-0	2-0	5-0
Austria Vienna	Aut	Juventus	Ita	0-4	0-4	0-8
FC Liège	Bel	Estrela Amadora	Por	2-0	0-1	2-1
Aberdeen	Sco	Legia Warsaw	Pol	0-0	0-1	0-1
Montpellier	Fra	Steaua Bucharest	Rom	5-0	3-0	8-0
Olympiakos Pireus	Gre	Sampdoria	Ita	0-1	1-3	1-4
Fram Reykjavik	Isl	Barcelona	Esp	1-2	0-3	1-5
Dinamo Kiev	URS	Dukla Prague	Tch	1-0	2-2	3-2

	Pts	P	W	D	L	F	A	Diff	Goals/P
Total	32	16	14	4	14	41	41	0	2.563

Quarter Finals

Manchester United	Eng	Montpellier	Fra	1-1	2-0	3-1
FC Liège	Bel	Juventus	Ita	1-3	0-3	1-6
Legia Warsaw	Pol	Sampdoria	Ita	1-0	2-2	3-2
Dinamo Kiev	URS	Barcelona	Esp	2-3	1-1	3-4

	Pts	P	W	D	L	F	A	Diff	Goals/P
Total	16	8	5	6	5	23	23	0	2.875

Semi Finals

Barcelona	Esp	Juventus	Ita	3-1	0-1	3-2
Legia Warsaw	Pol	Manchester United	Eng	1-3	1-1	2-4

	Pts	P	W	D	L	F	A	Diff	Goals/P
Total	8	4	3	2	3	11	11	0	2.750

Final

Manchester United	Eng	Barcelona	Esp	2-1	2-1

	Pts	P	W	D	L	F	A	Diff	Goals/P
Total	2	1	1	0	1	3	3	0	3.000

	Pts	P	W	D	L	F	A	Diff	Goals/P
Total	126	63	48	30	48	162	162	0	2.571

Pos'n	Club	Cnty	Pts	P	W	D	L	F	A	Diff	B	Pts/P	F/P
1	Manchester United	Eng	19	9	7	2	0	17	4	13	3	2.111	1.889
2	Juventus	Ita	16	8	7	0	1	24	5	19	2	2.000	3.000
3	Barcelona	Esp	14	9	5	1	3	20	11	9	3	1.556	2.222
4	Legia Warsaw	Pol	13	8	4	3	1	12	6	6	2	1.625	1.500
5	Montpellier	Fra	9	6	3	2	1	10	3	7	1	1.500	1.667
6	Dinamo Kiev	URS	8	6	2	3	1	12	8	4	1	1.333	2.000
7	Sampdoria	Ita	8	6	3	1	2	8	5	3	1	1.333	1.333
8	FC Liège	Bel	7	6	3	0	3	8	7	1	1	1.167	1.333
9	Aberdeen	Sco	5	4	2	1	1	5	1	4	0	1.250	1.250
10	Dukla Prague	Tch	5	4	2	1	1	6	4	2	0	1.250	1.500
11	Trabzonspor	Tur	5	4	2	1	1	6	8	-2	0	1.250	1.500
12	Olympiakos Pireus	Gre	4	4	2	0	2	6	5	1	0	1.000	1.500
13	Estrela Amadora	Por	4	4	1	2	1	3	4	-1	0	1.000	0.750
14	Fram Reykjavik	Isl	3	4	1	1	2	5	6	-1	0	0.750	1.250
15	Steaua Bucharest	Rom	3	4	1	1	2	6	9	-3	0	0.750	1.500
16	Wrexham	Wal	3	4	1	1	2	1	5	-4	0	0.750	0.250
17	Austria Vienna	Aut	3	4	1	1	2	2	8	-6	0	0.750	0.500
18	Neuchâtel Xamax	Sui	2	2	0	2	0	2	2	0	0	1.000	1.000
19	Kaiserslautern	FRG	2	2	1	0	1	1	2	-1	0	1.000	0.500
21	Lyngby BK	Den	1	2	0	1	1	0	1	-1	0	0.500	0.000
–	PSV Eindhoven	Ned	1	2	0	1	1	0	1	-1	0	0.500	0.000
22	Bray Wanderers	Irl	1	2	0	1	1	1	3	-2	0	0.500	0.500
23	PSV Schwerin	GDR	1	2	0	1	1	0	2	-2	0	0.500	0.000
24	Djurgården SIF	Swe	1	2	0	1	1	1	4	-3	0	0.500	0.500
25	KuPS Kuopio	Fin	1	2	0	1	1	2	6	-4	0	0.500	1.000
26	Glentoran	Nir	1	2	0	1	1	1	6	-5	0	0.500	0.500
27	Sliema Wanderers	Mlt	0	2	0	0	2	1	4	-3	0	0.000	0.500
28	Pécsi MSC	Hun	0	2	0	0	2	0	3	-3	0	0.000	0.000
29	Flamurtari Vlorë	Alb	0	2	0	0	2	1	5	-4	0	0.000	0.500
30	NEA Salamina Famagusta	Cyp	0	2	0	0	2	0	5	-5	0	0.000	0.000
–	IL Viking	Nor	0	2	0	0	2	0	5	-5	0	0.000	0.000
32	Swift Hesperange	Lux	0	2	0	0	2	0	6	-6	0	0.000	0.000
33	Sliven	Bul	0	2	0	0	2	1	8	-7	0	0.000	0.500
	Tolal		**140**	**126**	**48**	**30**	**48**	**162**	**162**	**0**	**14**	**1.111**	**2.571**

First Round

Team 1	Cnty	Team 2	Cnty	1st leg	2nd leg	Agg
Partizani Tirana	Alb	Universitatea Craiova	Rom	0-1	0-1	0-2
Aston Villa	Eng	Banik Ostrava	Tch	3-1	2-1	5-2
Rapid Vienna	Aut	Inter Milan	Ita	2-1	1-3	3-4
Anderlecht	Bel	Petrolul Ploiesti	Rom	2-0	2-0	4-0
Antwerp	Bel	Ferencváros	Hun	0-0	1-3	1-3
Sofia Slavia	Bul	Omonia Nicosia	Cyp	2-1	2-4	4-5
Brøndby IF	Den	Eintracht Frankfurt	FRG	5-0	1-4	6-4
Vejle BK	Den	Admira Wacker	Aut	0-1	0-3	0-4
Derry City	Irl	Vitesse	Ned	0-1	0-0	0-1
Seville	Esp	PAOK Salonika	Gre	0-0	0-0	0-0
Iraklis	Gre	Valencia	Esp	0-0	0-2	0-2
MTK-VM	Hun	Lucerne	Sui	1-1	1-2	2-3
Glenavon	Nir	Girondins Bordeaux	Fra	0-0	0-2	0-2
FH Hafnarfjördhur	Isl	Dundee United	Sco	1-3	2-2	3-5
Atalanta	Ita	Dinamo Zagreb	Yug	0-0	1-1	1-1
Roma	Ita	Benfica	Por	1-0	1-0	2-0
Avenir Beggen	Lux	Inter Bratislava	Tch	2-1	0-5	2-6
Hibernians	Mal	Partizan Belgrade	Yug	0-3	0-2	0-5
Roda JC	Ned	Monaco	Fra	1-3	1-3	2-6
GKS Katowice	Pol	TPS Turku	Fin	3-0	1-0	4-0
Zaglebie Lubin	Pol	Bologna	Ita	0-1	0-1	0-2
Sporting Lisbon	Por	KV Mechelen	Bel	1-0	2-2	3-2
Borussia Dortmund	FRG	Karl-Marx-Stadt	GDR	2-0	2-0	4-0
Bayer Leverkusen	FRG	Twente Enschede	Ned	1-0	1-1	2-1
Politehnica Timisoara	Rom	Atlético Madrid	Esp	2-0	0-1	2-1
IFK Norrköping	Swe	Cologne	FRG	0-0	1-3	1-3
Lausanne-Sports	Sui	Real Sociedad	Esp	3-2	0-1	3-3
Fenerbahçe	Tur	Vitória Guimarães	Por	3-0	3-2	6-2
Dnepr Dnepropetrovsk	URS	Heart of Midlothian	Sco	1-1	1-3	2-4
Torpedo Moscow	URS	GAIS	Swe	4-1	1-1	5-2
Chernomorets Odessa	URS	Rosenborg BK	Nor	3-1	1-2	4-3
Magdeburg	GDR	RoPS Rovaniemi	Fin	0-0	1-0	1-0

	Pts	P	W	D	L	F	A	Diff	Goals/P
Total	128	64	48	32	48	150	150	0	2.344

Second Round

Aston Villa	Eng	Inter Milan	Ita	2-0	0-3	2-3
Omonia Nicosia	Cyp	Anderlecht	Bel	1-1	0-3	1-4
Brøndby IF	Den	Ferencváros	Hun	3-0	1-0	4-0
Heart of Midlothian	Sco	Bologna	Ita	3-1	0-3	3-4
Real Sociedad	Esp	Partizan Belgrade	Yug	1-0	0-1	1-1
Valencia	Esp	Roma	Ita	1-1	1-2	2-3
Vitesse	Ned	Dundee United	Sco	1-0	4-0	5-0
GKS Katowice	Pol	Bayer Leverkusen	FRG	1-2	0-4	1-6
Sporting Lisbon	Por	Politehnica Timisoara	Rom	7-0	0-2	7-2
Cologne	FRG	Inter Bratislava	Tch	0-1	2-0	2-1
Universitatea Craiova	Rom	Borussia Dortmund	FRG	0-3	0-1	0-4
Lucerne	Sui	Admira Wacker	Aut	0-1	1-1	1-2
Fenerbahçe	Tur	Atalanta	Ita	0-1	1-4	1-5
Torpedo Moscow	URS	Seville	Esp	3-1	1-2	4-3
Chernomorets Odessa	URS	Monaco	Fra	0-0	0-1	0-1
Magdeburg	GDR	Girondins Bordeaux	Fra	0-1	0-1	0-2

	Pts	P	W	D	L	F	A	Diff	Goals/P
Total	64	32	28	8	28	75	75	0	2.344

Third Round

Admira Wacker	Aut	Bologna	Ita	3-0	0-3	3-3
Anderlecht	Bel	Borussia Dortmund	FRG	1-0	1-2	2-2
Brøndby IF	Den	Bayer Leverkusen	FRG	3-0	0-0	3-0
Inter Milan	Ita	Partizan Belgrade	Yug	3-0	1-1	4-1
Roma	Ita	Girondins Bordeaux	Fra	5-0	2-0	7-0
Vitesse	Ned	Sporting Lisbon	Por	0-2	1-2	1-4
Cologne	FRG	Atalanta	Ita	1-1	0-1	1-2
Torpedo Moscow	URS	Monaco	Fra	2-1	2-1	4-2

	Pts	P	W	D	L	F	A	Diff	Goals/P
Total	32	16	13	6	13	39	39	0	2.438

Quarter Finals

Brøndby IF	Den	Torpedo Moscow	URS	1-0	0-1	1-1
Atalanta	Ita	Inter Milan	Ita	0-0	0-2	0-2
Bologna	Ita	Sporting Lisbon	Por	1-1	0-2	1-3
Roma	Ita	Anderlecht	Bel	3-0	3-2	6-2

	Pts	P	W	D	L	F	A	Diff	Goals/P
Total	16	8	6	4	6	16	16	0	2.000

Semi Finals

Brøndby IF	Den	Roma	Ita	0-0	1-2	1-2
Sporting Lisbon	Por	Inter Milan	Ita	0-0	0-2	0-2

	Pts	P	W	D	L	F	A	Diff	Goals/P
Total	8	4	2	4	2	5	5	0	1.250

Final

Inter Milan	Ita	Roma	Ita	2-0	0-1	2-1

	Pts	P	W	D	L	F	A	Diff	Goals/P
Total	4	2	2	0	2	3	3	0	1.500

	Pts	P	W	D	L	F	A	Diff	Goals/P
Total	252	126	99	54	99	288	288	0	2.286

Pos'n	Club	Cnty	Pts	P	W	D	L	F	A	Diff	B	Pts/P	F/P
1	Roma	Ita	23	12	9	2	1	21	7	14	3	1.917	1.750
2	Inter Milan	Ita	18	12	6	3	3	17	7	10	3	1.500	1.417
3	Sporting Lisbon	Por	15	10	5	3	2	17	8	9	2	1.500	1.700
4	Brøndby IF	Den	14	10	5	2	3	15	7	8	2	1.400	1.500
5	Torpedo Moscow	URS	12	8	5	1	2	14	8	6	1	1.500	1.750
6	Atalanta	Ita	11	8	3	4	1	8	5	3	1	1.375	1.000
7	Borrusia Dortmund	FRG	10	6	5	0	1	10	2	8	0	1.667	1.667
8	Anderlecht	Bel	10	8	4	1	3	12	9	3	1	1.250	1.500
9	Bologna	Ita	10	8	4	1	3	10	9	1	1	1.250	1.250
10	Admira Wacker	Aut	9	6	4	1	1	9	4	5	0	1.500	1.500
11	Bayer Leverkusen	FRG	8	6	3	2	1	8	5	3	0	1.333	1.333
12	Monaco	Fra	7	6	3	1	2	9	6	3	0	1.167	1.500
13	Vitesse	Ned	7	6	3	1	2	7	4	3	0	1.167	1.167
14	Partizan Belgrade	Yug	7	6	3	1	2	7	5	2	0	1.167	1.167
15	Girondins Bordeaux	Fra	7	6	3	1	2	4	7	-3	0	1.167	0.667
16	Aston Villa	Eng	6	4	3	0	1	7	5	2	0	1.500	1.750
17	Cologne	FRG	6	6	2	2	2	6	4	2	0	1.000	1.000
18	Hearts of Midlothian	Sco	5	4	2	1	1	7	6	1	0	1.250	1.750
19	Inter Bratislava	Tch	4	4	2	0	2	7	4	3	0	1.000	1.750
20	Valencia	Esp	4	4	1	2	1	4	3	1	0	1.000	1.000
21	Fenerbahçe	Tur	4	4	2	0	2	7	7	0	0	1.000	1.750
22	Real Sociedad	Esp	4	4	2	0	2	4	4	0	0	1.000	1.000
–	Lucerne	Sui	4	4	1	2	1	4	4	0	0	1.000	1.000
24	GKS Katowice	Pol	4	4	2	0	2	5	6	-1	0	1.000	1.250
25	Seville	Esp	4	4	1	2	1	3	4	-1	0	1.000	0.750
26	Universitatea Craiova	Rom	4	4	2	0	2	2	4	-2	0	1.000	0.500
27	Politehnica Timisoara	Rom	4	4	2	0	2	4	8	-4	0	1.000	1.000
28	Chernomorets Odessa	URS	3	4	1	1	2	4	4	0	0	0.750	1.000
29	Magdeburg	GDR	3	4	1	1	2	1	2	-1	0	0.750	0.250
30	Omonia Nicosie	Cyp	3	4	1	1	2	6	8	-2	0	0.750	1.500
31	Ferencváros	Hun	3	4	1	1	2	3	5	-2	0	0.750	0.750
32	Dundee United	Sco	3	4	1	1	2	5	8	-3	0	0.750	1.250
33	Lausanne-Sports	Sui	2	2	1	0	1	3	3	0	0	1.000	1.500
34	Dinamo Zagreb	Yug	2	2	0	2	0	1	1	0	0	1.000	0.500
35	PAOK Salonika	Gre	2	2	0	2	0	0	0	0	0	1.000	0.000
36	Slavia Sofia	Bul	2	2	1	0	1	4	5	-1	0	1.000	2.000
37	Rapid Vienna	Aut	2	2	1	0	1	3	4	-1	0	1.000	1.500
–	Rosenborg BK	Nor	2	2	1	0	1	3	4	-1	0	1.000	1.500
39	Atlético Madrid	Esp	2	2	1	0	1	1	2	-1	0	1.000	0.500
40	Eintracht Frankfurt	FRG	2	2	1	0	1	4	6	-2	0	1.000	2.000
41	Avenir Beggen	Lux	2	2	1	0	1	2	6	-4	0	1.000	1.000
42	KV Mechelen	Bel	1	2	0	1	1	2	3	-1	0	0.500	1.000
–	MTK-VM	Hun	1	2	0	1	1	2	3	-1	0	0.500	1.000
44	Twente Enschede	Ned	1	2	0	1	1	1	2	-1	0	0.500	0.500
45	Derry City	Nir	1	2	0	1	1	0	1	-1	0	0.500	0.000
–	RoPS Rovaniemi	Fin	1	2	0	1	1	0	1	-1	0	0.500	0.000
47	FH Hafnarfjördhur	Isl	1	2	0	1	1	3	5	-2	0	0.500	1.500
48	Dnepr Dnepropetrovsk	URS	1	2	0	1	1	2	4	-2	0	0.500	1.000
49	Antwerp	Bel	1	2	0	1	1	1	3	-2	0	0.500	0.500
–	IFK Norrköping	Swe	1	2	0	1	1	1	3	-2	0	0.500	0.500
51	Iraklis	Gre	1	2	0	1	1	0	2	-2	0	0.500	0.000
–	Glenavon	Nir	1	2	0	1	1	0	2	-2	0	0.500	0.000
53	GAIS	Swe	1	2	0	1	1	2	5	-3	0	0.500	1.000
54	Partizani Tirana	Alb	0	2	0	0	2	0	2	-2	0	0.000	0.000
–	Zaglebie Lubin	Pol	0	2	0	0	2	0	2	-2	0	0.000	0.000
–	Benfica	Por	0	2	0	0	2	0	2	-2	0	0.000	0.000
57	Banik Ostrava	Tch	0	2	0	0	2	2	5	-3	0	0.000	1.000
58	Roda JC	Ned	0	2	0	0	2	2	6	-4	0	0.000	1.000
–	Vitória Guimarães	Por	0	2	0	0	2	2	6	-4	0	0.000	1.000
60	Vejle BK	Den	0	2	0	0	2	0	4	-4	0	0.000	0.000
–	TPS Turku	Fin	0	2	0	0	2	0	4	-4	0	0.000	0.000
–	Petrolul Ploiesti	Rom	0	2	0	0	2	0	4	-4	0	0.000	0.000
–	Karl-Marx-Stadt	GDR	0	2	0	0	2	0	4	-4	0	0.000	0.000
64	Hibernians	Mlt	0	2	0	0	2	0	5	-5	0	0.000	0.000
	Total		**266**	**252**	**99**	**54**	**99**	**288**	**288**	**0**	**14**	**1.056**	**2.286**

National Performances by Points

1990-91

Pos'n	Cnty	Pts	P	W	D	L	F	A	Diff	B	Pts/P	F/P
1	Ita	97	62	35	15	12	95	40	55	12	1.565	1.532
2	FRG	42	30	17	6	7	49	26	23	2	1.400	1.633
3	Fra	39	27	14	7	6	43	24	19	4	1.444	1.593
4	Esp	37	29	13	7	9	54	31	23	4	1.276	1.862
5	URS	35	28	11	9	8	41	30	11	4	1.250	1.464
6	Por	28	24	9	7	8	40	24	16	3	1.167	1.667
7	Yug	26	17	8	7	2	26	13	13	3	1.529	1.529
8	Eng	25	13	10	2	1	24	9	15	3	1.923	1.846
9	Pol	23	18	9	3	6	26	23	3	2	1.278	1.444
10	Bel	23	22	8	5	9	26	24	2	2	1.045	1.182
11	Aut	19	16	8	3	5	24	28	-4	0	1.188	1.500
12	Sco	18	16	7	4	5	28	19	9	0	1.125	1.750
13	Den	15	16	5	3	8	16	22	-6	2	0.938	1.000
14	Rom	15	18	6	3	9	17	30	-13	0	0.833	0.944
15	GDR	11	14	3	4	7	10	16	-6	1	0.786	0.714
16	Tur	10	10	4	2	4	17	20	-3	0	1.000	1.700
17	Tch	9	12	4	1	7	15	17	-2	0	0.750	1.250
18	Sui	9	10	2	5	3	11	14	-3	0	0.900	1.100
19	Ned	9	12	3	3	6	10	13	-3	0	0.750	0.833
20	Swe	8	10	1	6	3	11	18	-7	0	0.800	1.100
21	Gre	7	10	2	3	5	7	12	-5	0	0.700	0.700
22	Isl	6	8	2	2	4	9	14	-5	0	0.750	1.125
23	Hun	4	10	1	2	7	5	16	-11	0	0.400	0.500
24	Bul	4	8	2	0	6	8	21	-13	0	0.500	1.000
25	Wal	3	4	1	1	2	1	5	-4	0	0.750	0.250
26	Irl	3	6	0	3	3	2	9	-7	0	0.500	0.333
27	Nor	3	6	1	1	4	4	12	-8	0	0.500	0.667
28	Cyp	3	8	1	1	6	8	20	-12	0	0.375	1.000
29	Fin	2	8	0	2	6	3	18	-15	0	0.250	0.375
–	Lux	2	6	1	0	5	3	18	-15	0	0.333	0.500
31	Nir	2	6	0	2	4	2	21	-19	0	0.333	0.333
32	Alb	1	6	0	1	5	2	12	-10	0	0.167	0.333
33	Mlt	0	6	0	0	6	1	19	-18	0	0.000	0.167
	Total	**538**	**496**	**188**	**120**	**188**	**638**	**638**	**0**	**42**	**1.085**	**2.573**

1955-56 to 1990-91

Pos'n	Cnty	Pts	P	W	D	L	F	A	Diff	B	Pts/P	F/P
1	FRG	1574	1137	595	215	327	2223	1368	855	169	1.384	1.955
2	Eng	1390	939	510	203	226	1806	936	870	167	1.480	1.923
3	Esp	1389	1017	512	195	310	1827	1201	626	170	1.366	1.796
4	Ita	1381	1004	499	226	279	1547	971	576	157	1.375	1.541
5	Bel	844	697	323	122	252	1122	884	238	76	1.211	1.610
6	Sco	830	676	317	131	228	1127	830	297	65	1.228	1.667
7	Ned	765	609	292	112	205	1110	735	375	69	1.256	1.823
8	Yug	740	659	278	122	259	1085	939	146	62	1.123	1.646
9	Por	738	623	274	129	220	990	754	236	61	1.185	1.589
10	Fra	609	558	219	123	216	838	770	68	48	1.091	1.502
11	URS	606	465	230	102	133	705	472	233	44	1.303	1.516
12	GDR	571	522	210	111	201	766	688	78	40	1.094	1.467
13	Hun	552	496	215	78	203	843	745	98	44	1.113	1.700
14	Tch	547	485	210	92	183	749	651	98	35	1.128	1.544
15	Rom	425	429	164	75	190	560	630	-70	22	0.991	1.305
16	Aut	419	438	152	88	198	586	695	-109	27	0.957	1.338
17	Sui	386	439	140	83	216	631	797	-166	23	0.879	1.437
18	Pol	376	379	138	81	160	520	577	-57	19	0.992	1.372
19	Bul	354	377	136	62	179	553	617	-64	20	0.939	1.467
20	Swe	341	351	118	85	148	481	554	-73	20	0.972	1.370
21	Gre	296	333	111	63	159	380	560	-180	11	0.889	1.141
22	Den	226	317	80	57	180	399	652	-253	9	0.713	1.259
23	Tur	199	273	74	42	157	264	509	-245	9	0.729	0.967
24	Nor	118	224	40	37	147	202	542	-340	1	0.527	0.902
25	Wal	104	106	34	30	42	148	130	18	6	0.981	1.396
26	Irl	96	218	28	40	150	164	532	-368	0	0.440	0.752
27	Fin	96	196	33	27	136	158	545	-387	3	0.490	0.806
28	Nir	92	198	23	44	131	179	532	-353	2	0.465	0.904
29	Alb	60	93	21	18	54	70	143	-73	0	0.645	0.753
30	Cyp	58	158	19	20	119	117	530	-413	0	0.367	0.741
31	Mlt	49	174	18	13	143	73	609	-536	0	0.282	0.420
32	Lux	49	194	17	15	162	112	813	-701	0	0.253	0.577
33	Isl	45	162	11	23	128	89	513	-424	0	0.278	0.549
	Total	**16325**	**14946**	**6041**	**2864**	**6041**	**22424**	**22424**	**0**	**1379**	**1.092**	**3.001**

1990-91

Pos'n	Cnty	Ave	Pts	P	W	D	L	F	A	Diff	B	No./T
1	England	12.500	25	13	10	2	1	24	9	15	3	2
2	Italy	12.125	97	62	35	15	12	95	40	55	12	8
3	France	9.750	39	27	14	7	6	43	24	19	4	4
4	Yugoslavia	8.666	26	17	8	7	2	26	13	13	3	3
5	W. Germany	7.000	42	30	17	6	7	49	26	23	2	6
–	USSR	7.000	35	28	11	9	8	41	30	11	4	5
7	Spain	6.166	37	29	13	7	9	54	31	23	4	6
8	Poland	5.750	23	18	9	3	6	26	23	3	2	4
9	Portugal	5.600	28	24	9	7	8	40	24	16	3	5
10	Austria	4.750	19	16	8	3	5	24	28	-4	0	4
11	Belgium	4.600	23	22	8	5	9	26	24	2	2	5
12	Scotland	4.500	18	16	7	4	5	28	19	9	0	4
13	Denmark	3.750	15	16	5	3	8	16	22	-6	2	4
14	Turkey	3.333	10	10	4	2	4	17	20	-3	0	3
15	Wales	3.000	3	4	1	1	2	1	5	-4	0	1
–	Romania	3.000	15	18	6	3	9	17	30	-13	0	5
17	E. Germany	2.750	11	14	3	4	7	10	16	-6	1	4
18	Netherlands	2.250	9	12	3	3	6	10	13	-3	0	4
–	Switzerland	2.250	9	10	2	5	3	11	14	-3	0	4
–	Czechoslovakia	2.250	9	12	4	1	7	15	17	-2	0	4
21	Iceland	2.000	6	8	2	2	4	9	14	-5	0	3
–	Sweden	2.000	8	10	1	6	3	11	18	-7	0	4
23	Greece	1.750	7	10	2	3	5	7	12	-5	0	4
24	Bulgaria	1.333	4	8	2	0	6	8	21	-13	0	3
25	Cyprus	1.000	3	8	1	1	6	8	20	-12	0	3
–	Rep. of Ireland	1.000	3	6	0	3	3	2	9	-7	0	3
–	Hungary	1.000	4	10	1	2	7	5	16	-11	0	4
–	Norway	1.000	3	6	1	1	4	4	12	-8	0	3
29	N. Ireland	0.666	2	6	0	2	4	2	21	-19	0	3
–	Luxembourg	0.666	2	6	1	0	5	3	18	-15	0	3
31	Finland	0.500	2	8	0	2	6	3	18	-15	0	4
32	Albania	0.333	1	6	0	1	5	2	12	-10	0	3
33	Malta	0.000	0	6	0	0	6	1	19	-18	0	3
	Total		**538**	**496**	**188**	**120**	**188**	**638**	**638**	**0**	**42**	**2.573**

1955-56 to 1990-91

1	England	8.853	1390	939	510	203	226	1806	936	870	167	157
2	W. Germany	8.030	1574	1137	595	215	327	2223	1368	855	169	196
3	Italy	7.629	1381	1004	499	226	279	1547	971	576	157	181
4	Spain	7.590	1389	1017	512	195	310	1827	1201	626	170	183
5	USSR	5.941	606	465	230	102	133	705	472	233	44	102
6	Netherlands	5.751	765	609	292	112	205	1110	735	375	69	133
7	Belgium	5.664	844	697	323	122	252	1122	884	238	76	149
8	Scotland	5.646	830	676	317	131	228	1127	830	297	65	147
9	Portugal	5.089	738	623	274	129	220	990	754	236	61	145
10	Yugoslavia	4.933	740	659	278	122	259	1085	939	146	62	150
11	E. Germany	4.604	571	522	210	111	201	766	688	78	40	124
12	Hungary	4.600	552	496	215	78	203	843	745	98	44	120
13	Czechoslovakia	4.376	547	485	210	92	183	749	651	98	35	125
14	France	4.288	609	558	219	123	216	838	770	68	48	142
15	Romania	3.571	425	429	164	75	190	560	630	-70	22	119
16	Poland	3.514	376	379	138	81	160	520	577	-57	19	107
17	Wales	3.466	104	106	34	30	42	148	130	18	6	30
18	Austria	3.379	419	438	152	88	198	586	695	-109	27	124
19	Bulgaria	3.160	354	377	136	62	179	553	617	-64	20	112
20	Sweden	3.072	341	351	118	85	148	481	554	-73	20	111
21	Switzerland	2.902	386	439	140	83	216	631	797	-166	23	133
22	Greece	2.642	296	333	111	63	159	380	560	-180	11	112
23	Turkey	2.051	199	273	74	42	157	264	509	-245	9	97
24	Denmark	1.965	226	317	80	57	180	399	652	-253	9	115
25	Albania	1.621	60	93	21	18	54	70	143	-73	0	37
26	Norway	1.242	118	224	40	37	147	202	542	-340	1	95
27	Finland	1.200	96	196	33	27	136	158	545	-387	3	80
28	N. Ireland	1.045	92	198	23	44	131	179	532	-353	2	88
29	Rep. of Ireland	1.032	96	218	28	40	150	164	532	-368	0	93
30	Cyprus	0.805	58	158	19	20	119	117	530	-413	0	72
31	Iceland	0.600	45	162	11	23	128	89	513	-424	0	75
32	Malta	0.590	49	174	18	13	143	73	609	-536	0	83
33	Luxembourg	0.526	49	194	17	15	162	112	813	-701	0	93
	Total		**16325**	**14946**	**6041**	**2864**	**6041**	**22424**	**22424**	**0**	**1379**	**3.001**

Manchester Signals England's Return

The 1990-91 season marked the long-awaited return of English clubs to European competition. For this first season back, however, only two teams were permitted to take part – Manchester United in the Cup-winners' Cup and Aston Villa in the UEFA Cup. The five-year ban had reduced England's UEFA Cup allocation to just one team, and with Liverpool, the Football League champions, kept out for a further year, there was no English representative in the Champions' Cup.

But, despite the restricted entry, English football returned to Europe in triumphant style, and, perhaps more importantly, with impeccably behaved supporters. Aston Villa left the UEFA Cup early, but Manchester United went all the way to the Cup-winners' Cup final, where they beat Barcelona 2-1 in Rotterdam to give England a record 23nd European trophy.

To be sure, United enjoyed the advantage of a fairly straightforward run to the final. Pecs and Wrexham held little fear for them in the first two rounds, and although Montpellier had reached the quarter-finals at the expense of recent Champions' Cup winners PSV Eindhoven and Steaua Bucharest, the French side betrayed their European inexperience in the second leg against United, losing 0-2 at home after a 1-1 draw at Old Trafford. United's luck was certainly in for the semi-finals when they were drawn against Polish outsiders, Legia Warsaw. Legia had caused the upset of the season in the previous round by putting out holders Sampdoria, but for the first leg against the English Cup holders they were missing several key players and that contributed greatly to United's 3-1 victory in Warsaw, which effectively sealed their place in the final.

Barcelona reached their fifth Cup-winners' Cup final by defeating UEFA Cup holders Juventus 3-2 on aggregate in the other semi-final. This was an epic confrontation in the grand European tradition. Barcelona won the first leg 3-1 in the Nou Camp, but had to withstand ferocious Juventus pressure to restrict the Italians to a 1-0 win in Turin. Juventus's goal was scored by the world's most expensive footballer, Roberto Baggio, and was his ninth of the tournament, but his world-class display that evening was matched by that of Barcelona's goalkeeper Andoni Zubizarreta, who saved his team on numerous occasions.

But Zubizarreta, cautioned for a second time in Turin, was to miss the game in Rotterdam along with team-mates Amor and Stoichkov. Manchester United, though, had no problems with team selection and they confirmed their early superiority in the final by taking a 2-0 lead midway through the second half, with both goals being credited to former Barcelona player, Mark Hughes. Dutchman Ronald Koeman reduced the deficit late in the game with a typical free-kick, but United deservedly held on to win the match and give their manager Alex Ferguson his second Cup-winners' Cup – he had led Aberdeen to their triumph back in 1983.

Aston Villa could not make it two wins out of two for England, but they provided Inter Milan with their toughest test on the way to winning the UEFA Cup. Inter, featuring West German World Cup winners in Lothar Matthäus, Andreas Brehme and Jürgen Klinsmann, reached their first European final in 19 years thanks to some brilliant displays in the San Siro. They failed to win any of their away legs against Rapid Vienna, Villa, Partizan Belgrade, Atalanta and Sporting Lisbon, but they maintained a 100% record at home, scoring 13 goals in the process.

Inter's opponents in the final were Roma, which meant that for the second year running the UEFA Cup final was an all-Italian affair. Roma had produced a scintillating run of ten matches without defeat to get there, and in each round they had been paired against difficult opponents – Champions' Cup runners-up Benfica, followed by Valencia, Bordeaux, Anderlecht and the surprise package of the tournament, Brøndby, the first Danish team ever to reach a European semi-final. Brøndby it was who came closest to putting Roma out, with Rudi Völler saving the Italians' blushes with a late winner in the Stadio Olimpico – his tenth goal of the competition.

The first leg of the final saw Roma concede their first defeat. A fiercely-struck penalty from Matthäus opened the scoring in the San Siro after 55 minutes and was followed ten minutes later by a second from Nicola Berti. That gave Inter a 2-0 first-leg cushion and, predictably, they packed their defence in the second leg in an attempt to cling onto that lead. It was a policy that worked for 80 minutes until Ruggiero Rizzitelli at last broke the deadlock for Roma. But the home side could not find a second goal to take the tie into extra-time and so Inter, coached by ex-Juventus chief Giovanni Trapattoni, stepped up to collect their first European trophy for 26 years.

That was the 99th European Cup final, and the 100th also took place in Italy, a week later, when Red Star Belgrade and Olympique Marseille faced each other for the Champions' Cup showdown in Bari.

The form of both teams throughout the competition had led many to believe that this 100th European final would be one to savour. Red Star and Marseille had both produced football of outstanding quality to reach the final. They each possessed in their ranks a world-class attacking trio – Dejan Savicevic, Robert Prosinecki and Darko Pancev for the Yugoslavs, Chris Waddle, Abedi Pelé and Jean-Pierre Papin for the French – and there was no doubt whatsoever that these were the best two teams in the competition. But in Bari, inexplicably and inexcusably, neither side came out to play. The result was arguably the poorest European final of all time, decided, yet again, after 120 minutes of uneventful goalless football, by the lottery of a penalty shoot-out.

Prior to Bari, though, both teams had been in brilliant form. Red Star eclipsed Grasshoppers, Rangers and Dynamo Dresden before putting on a truly outstanding performance in the first leg of the semi-final, away to Bayern Munich. Two breathtaking goals from Pancev and Savicevic enabled the Yugoslavs, wth a 2-1 win, to become the first foreign side to defeat Bayern at home in European competition. The Germans staged a dramatic comeback in the return, but Klaus Augenthaler's agonising last-minute own-goal sent Red Star through to the final and left Bayern beaten semi-finalists for the second year in succession.

Marseille, meanwhile, saw off Dinamo Tirana and Lech Poznań with high-scoring home victories in the first two rounds before facing the might of holders AC Milan in the quarter-finals. A 1-1 draw in the first leg at the San Siro flattered the holders, and Marseille completed the job with a single Waddle goal in the return – or at least they thought they had. A floodlight failure in the last minute of the game prompted a mass walk-off by the Milan players. It was a petulant act, and one which was rightly punished by UEFA when they awarded the match 3-0 to Marseille and banned Milan from Europe for a year. Next up for Marseille came Spartak Moscow, surprise earlier conquerors of both Napoli and Real Madrid. But against the brilliance of Pelé, Waddle and Papin, the Soviets had no answer. Marseille won the first leg 3-1 in Moscow and completed the job with a comfortable 2-1 victory at home to reach their first European final.

It is difficult to believe, however, that the much-anticipated 100th European Cup final actually took place. Certainly, very little football was played in Bari. But in the end there had to be a winner, and it was Red Star who took the Cup when Marseille's Manuel Amoros missed his team's first penalty and everybody else scored theirs. It provided Yugoslavia, in its year of civil unrest, with a first ever Champions' Cup, and left France, after 100 attempts, still awaiting a first European triumph, not just in the Champions' Cup, but in all three competitions!

The individual merits of club and country come more fully under the spotlight in this second half of *100 European Cups* which is arranged as four sections, three of which deal with each European cup individually, concluding with a look at the same information as an accumulation of all three competitions – a 100 European Cups.

The information in each of these sections follows a very similar pattern so to avoid repeating ourselves we will provide an outline of the first of these which covers the major competition – the European Cup itself. We will leave you to draw your own complete comparisons for the other competitions.

36 Years of the Champions' Cup – Spain Under Threat

The first part of the European Champions' Cup contains various league tables organised over various periods of time (starting on page 412). Perhaps the most significant of these is the all-time league table (shown in part below) by country established over 36 years of the European Champions' Cup. It shows us that Spain leads the way with a total of 423 points, that Spain has been represented, in number, by 42 clubs in the Champions' Cup, who have played 278 matches (154 victories, 49 draws and 75 defeats). Spanish clubs have also accumulated a total of 66 bonus points.

Pos	Cnty	Ave	Pts	P	W	D	L	F	A	Diff	N	Teams
1	Spain	10.071	423	278	154	49	75	585	307	278	66	42
2	England	10.057	352	222	130	39	53	458	210	248	53	35
3	W. Germany	9.179	358	234	127	52	55	498	271	227	52	39
4	Italy	8.853	363	239	126	54	59	398	214	184	57	41
5	Netherlands	6.810	252	179	90	39	50	350	191	159	33	37

These figures combine to give Spain an average performance index (number of points divided by the number of participating clubs) of 10.071. Spain owes this position at the top of the table above all to the six victories achieved in the first ten years of the competition by Real Madrid (1956, 57, 58, 59, 60, 66), but also to the consistent performances of Real and her two domestic rivals, Barcelona and Atlético Madrid. It is interesting to note, however, that despite Real Madrid's early success in the competition, no other Spanish club has ever won the Champions' Cup trophy since Real's sixth win in 1966!

In five appearances Atlético Madrid have only once reached the final, in 1974 (beaten 4-0 by Bayern Munich in a replay after a 1-1 draw), and, also from five appearances, Barcelona have made it into two finals, both of which they lost, in 1961 to Benfica (2-3) and in 1986 on penalties against Steaua Bucharest, even though the final was played in front of 55,000 Catalan supporters in Seville.

It is interesting to note that although Barcelona are top of the all-time Cup-winners' Cup listings (three wins) and second behind Cologne in the Fairs'/UEFA Cup table (also three wins), they never managed to lift the Champions' Cup during the first 36 years.

To a certain extent, Spanish clubs have rested on their laurels in the Champions' Cup since Real's early dominance, and although they still retain top spot after 36 years, they are under serious threat from England (average co-efficient 10.057) and West Germany (9.179).

The performance of England over 36 years is significant because it has taken 352 points from only 222 matches, of which 53 are bonus points, an enormous figure given that it has had only 35 participants! And let us not forget that English clubs were missing from the Champions' Cup for six years following the Heysel disaster. England's extraordinary figures are explained by the eight victories achieved by Manchester United (1968), Liverpool (1977, 78, 81, 84), Nottingham Forest (1979, 80) and Aston Villa (1982), two runners-up Leeds (1975), Liverpool (1985) and several appearances in the semi-finals.

The Anglo-German Factor

Top of the table over 36 years, Spain does not fare nearly so well when observed over the last 10 years of the competition. Spain's decline is sharp, with a drop to fifth place, a long way behind England, whose exceptional co-efficient of 13.166 is the highest in all four of the tables shown, and West Germany.

From 1971, when Ajax won the first of their three trophies, right through to the mid '80s, it is evident that the clubs from the Northern European nations achieved almost complete domination of the Champions' Cup, with English and German clubs leading the way in the latter years of the competition.

From 1971-72 to 1988, England had seven winners and two runners-up. West Germany had four winners and four runners-up. The Netherlands recorded four victories.

It was not until 1985, with Juventus' 1-0 success over Liverpool, that the Latin countries, and those in Eastern Europe, began to dominate the competition again with three wins for Italy (Juventus 1985, AC Milan 1989 and 1990), one for Romania (Steaua Bucharest 1986) and one for Yugoslavia (Red Star 1991).

This is a period, of course, which coincides with the absence of English clubs and which one might have been led to believe would be particularly fruitful for Italy. But the facts show that over the last five years of the Champions' Cup, despite the double success of AC Milan and despite having a record seven clubs engaged in the competition, Italy is only classified in sixth place, having figured in fourth place over 36 years and in third place over 10.

The explanation is simple: Italy, despite its seven clubs, could not take advantage of this increased representation, recording only seven bonus points in five years! Both Inter Milan, champions of Italy in 1989, and Napoli, title winners in 1987 and 1990, failed to make an impression, leaving AC Milan to score all of the bonus points themselves. With the performance index being calculated on the basis of the number of points gained and the number of clubs taking part, Italy could only manage a modest 7.428 over the last five seasons. All that glitters is not gold, as they say!

Portugal and France: A Leap Forward

Two countries, on the other hand, who have made a giant leap forward towards the end of the first 100 European Cups are Portugal and France. In the case of Portugal there is nothing especially illogical as this is a country which established itself early on in Champions' Cup history with back-to-back wins for Benfica in 1961 and 1962. But the progress made by France is quite a surprise given that French clubs were (and still are) chasing their first European trophy.

Over 36 years of the Champions' Cup, Portugal is in eighth place. Over 10 years it is ranked fourth and over five years it has moved up to second! This improvement is in a large part due to the victory of FC Porto in 1987 (2-1 against Bayern Munich) and to the two finals reached by Benfica in 1988 and 1990. In contrast to Italy, Portugal has taken advantage of its six Champions' Cup entrants

Above: Altafini (9) is congratulated by his team mates after scoring Benfica's second goal against Milan in the 1962-63 Champions' Cup Final.

in the last five years, pocketing 10 bonus points (as against Italy's seven points for seven clubs). With a co-efficient of 11.000 Portugal is right behind West Germany (11.800), the six Portuguese clubs having accumulated 66 points from 40 matches, by far the biggest total recorded between 1986-87 and 1990-91.

France has also taken its place in the leading group after lying low in eighth and ninth places over 36 and 10 years. Fourth over the last five years, it owes this high ranking to the performances of Olympique Marseille during the last two seasons (runners-up in 1991, semi-finalist in 1990) and to the quarter-final placing of Monaco in 1989.

The presence of France in the upper reaches of the five-year table is one of the most interesting observations to be made from this classification by country, together with the continued good health of German football and the rising fortunes of the Portuguese. Whatever, as a new Champions' Cup is born, our tables over 36, 10 and 5 years give a perfect insight into the changing trends and should offer an interesting guide to the respective values of the eight teams left in the final phase of the 1991-92 competition.

Performance Records

The next set of tables lists the club performances by the total number of points gained over the last 36, 10 and 5 years (pages 414) and by the national cumulative indices over the same period (page 433).

Club Participation Records

Listed alphabetically by country we next find the playing records of each club listed with their accumulative playing record and this is summed to provide a full country by country record. The entry for England (page 426) shows that Liverpool have represented their nation in the Champions' Cup on no less than 12 occasions winning 48 of their 77 ties.

Who Against Who?

This is without doubt one of the most fascinating sections of our statistical study (pages 438). Cup by cup and country by country, as well as over all three competitions, we have drawn up tables of the points won by a country against all the other countries that it has played against since the first season of European Cup competition. Listed in alphabetical order, our tables will be extremely useful when comparing the strengths of two clubs drawn against each other.

Thus, in the Champions' Cup, over the entire duration of the European competitions, English clubs have been drawn against opponents from 29 different countries and twice against other English teams. The most common opponents are those from West Germany. In meetings between these two nations, English clubs have taken 30 points from 21 matches (seven wins, ten draws, four defeats and six bonus points). In 12 ties English clubs have qualified nine times, with three being eliminated. A particularly impressive success rate of 75%!

In contrast, English clubs have had very little success when drawn against Italian clubs in 36 years of the Champions' Cup: only one qualifier as against eight teams eliminated!

Even more interesting is the outcome of Anglo-Belgian confrontations in the Champions' Cup, for no Belgian club has ever knocked out an English team in this competition. English clubs have amassed from these encounters a total of 28 points from 13 matches (11 victories, one draw, one defeat and five bonus points), with a perfect record of seven qualifiers from seven into the bargain!

Qualifiers and Eliminators

The Comparative Country v Country Performance Chart (page 455) is a most useful tool if you are looking to gauge the chances of a club from any one country against that from another. The chart shows us for instance, that English clubs have been pitted against Belgium clubs on no less than seven occasions and have qualified every time! The English record is not so good against the Italians where they have been eliminated on eight occasions and only qualified once!

Second Leg Outcomes

Here we have listed second leg outcomes by first leg results (page 459). The number of times a particular second leg score has occurred is listed, the score of the first leg home side being shown first. For example, if the first leg of a tie was goaless then the most common outcome of the return leg was a 2-0 win for the team at home in the second leg – this happened on no less than 16 occasions during the course of the European Champions' Cup up until 1991. Equally as interesting is that the second most common result was a 1-0 win from either side, which happened on nine occasions!

The Home Match statistics at the end of this section (page 467) show that the 2-0 score line was the most common with an amazing 201 occurrancies during those first 35 years of competition.

Above: FC Bruges midfield player Julien Cools shoots to score their second goal in the first leg of the 1975-76 UEFA Cup Final against Liverpool at Anfield.

The Finals

1955-56	Real Madrid	4	Stade Reims	3
1956-57	Real Madrid	2	Fiorentina	0
1957-58	Real Madrid	3	AC Milan	2
1958-59	Real Madrid	2	Stade Reims	0
1959-60	Real Madrid	7	Eintract Frankfurt	3
1960-61	Benfica	3	Barcelona	2
1961-62	Benfica	5	Real Madrid	3
1962-63	AC Milan	2	Benfica	1
1963-64	Inter Milan	3	Real Madrid	1
1964-65	Inter Milan	1	Benfica	0
1965-66	Real Madrid	2	Partizan Belgrade	1
1966-67	Celtic	2	Inter Milan	1
1967-68	Manchester United	4	Benfica	1
1968-69	AC Milan	4	Ajax	1
1969-70	Feyenoord	2	Celtic	1
1970-71	Ajax	2	Panathinaikos	0
1971-72	Ajax	2	Inter Milan	0
1972-73	Ajax	1	Juventus	0
1973-74	Bayern Munich	4	Atlético Madrid	0
1974-75	Bayern Munich	2	Leeds United	0
1975-76	Bayern Munich	1	Saint-Etienne	0
1976-77	Liverpool	3	Borussia Mönchengladbach	1
1977-78	Liverpool	1	Club Bruges	0
1978-79	Nottingham Forest	1	Malmö FF	0
1979-80	Nottingham Forest	1	Hamburg	0
1980-81	Liverpool	1	Real Madrid	0
1981-82	Aston Villa	1	Bayern Munich	0
1982-83	Hamburg	1	Juventus	0
1983-84	Liverpool †	1	Roma	1
1984-85	Juventus	1	Liverpool	0
1985-86	Steaua Bucharest †	0	Barcelona	0
1986-87	FC Porto	2	Bayern Munich	1
1987-88	PSV Endhoven †	0	Benfica	0
1988-89	AC Milan	4	Steaua Bucharest	0
1989-90	AC Millan	1	Benfica	0
1990-91	Red Star Belgrade †	0	Olympique Marseille	0

† won on penalty kicks

National Performances by Index

1955-56 to 1990-91

Pos'n	Cnty	Ave	Pts	P	W	D	L	F	A	Diff	B	No./T
1	Spain	10.071	423	278	154	49	75	585	307	278	66	42
2	England	10.057	352	222	130	39	53	458	210	248	53	35
3	West Germany	9.179	358	234	127	52	55	498	271	227	52	39
4	Italy	8.853	363	239	126	54	59	398	214	184	57	41
5	Netherlands	6.810	252	179	90	39	50	350	191	159	33	37
6	USSR	6.458	155	116	57	26	33	165	105	60	15	24
7	Scotland	6.416	231	175	87	31	57	300	217	83	26	36
8	Portugal	6.410	250	188	91	35	62	354	223	131	33	39
9	France	5.638	203	162	70	38	54	258	195	63	25	36
10	Czechoslovakia	5.342	187	147	69	35	43	235	191	44	14	35
11	Belgium	5.305	191	161	74	24	63	270	234	36	19	36
12	Yugoslavia	5.138	185	150	71	23	56	283	208	75	20	36
13	Hungary	4.342	152	133	60	21	52	257	227	30	11	35
14	Romania	3.970	135	131	51	22	58	191	194	-3	11	34
15	Austria	3.916	141	138	53	24	61	219	214	5	11	36
16	E. Germany	3.848	127	127	50	19	58	197	185	12	8	33
17	Poland	3.714	130	122	52	18	52	184	200	-16	8	35
18	Bulgaria	3.470	118	124	44	22	58	182	200	-18	8	34
19	Switzerland	3.333	120	123	45	21	57	196	225	-29	9	36
20	Sweden	3.250	117	119	42	23	54	163	195	-32	10	36
21	Greece	2.593	83	99	27	23	49	119	163	-44	6	32
22	Turkey	2.441	83	98	31	16	51	98	171	-73	5	34
23	Denmark	2.277	82	107	27	26	54	136	212	-76	2	36
24	N. Ireland	1.156	37	74	8	20	46	77	191	-114	1	32
25	Cyprus	1.115	29	60	13	3	44	58	191	-133	0	26
26	Albania	1.111	20	39	7	6	26	25	68	-43	0	18
27	Finland	1.000	32	76	13	5	58	59	237	-178	1	32
–	Norway	1.000	31	72	9	13	50	61	177	-116	0	31
29	Rep. of Ireland	0.823	28	77	8	12	57	58	222	-164	0	34
30	Malta	0.633	19	62	7	5	50	29	216	-187	0	30
31	Luxembourg	0.600	21	76	8	5	63	61	317	-256	0	35
32	Iceland	0.555	15	58	4	7	47	42	195	-153	0	27

1981-82 to 1990-91

Pos'n	Cnty	Ave	Pts	P	W	D	L	F	A	Diff	B	No./T
1	England	13.166	79	45	30	7	8	85	30	55	12	6
2	West Germany	10.500	105	65	37	15	13	125	59	66	16	10
3	Italy	8.923	116	75	40	19	16	126	50	76	17	13
4	Portugal	8.545	94	64	36	10	18	114	51	63	12	11
5	Spain	8.100	81	59	28	13	18	95	60	35	12	10
6	Romania	7.600	76	60	27	11	22	95	66	29	11	10
7	USSR	7.300	73	54	25	14	15	75	54	21	9	10
8	Belgium	7.000	70	52	25	13	14	78	57	21	7	10
9	France	6.400	64	47	19	17	11	65	42	23	9	10
10	Scotland	5.400	54	42	20	10	12	63	39	24	4	10
11	Austria	5.100	51	42	21	7	14	92	62	30	2	10
12	Yugoslavia	5.000	50	39	19	7	13	73	47	26	5	10
13	Sweden	4.500	45	38	16	9	13	66	54	12	4	10
14	Netherlands	3.888	35	33	9	12	12	39	33	6	5	9
15	Czechoslovakia	3.800	38	34	16	5	13	52	47	5	1	10
16	E. Germany	3.600	36	36	14	6	16	52	55	-3	2	10
17	Bulgaria	3.200	32	38	10	9	19	45	60	-15	3	10

18	Poland	2.900	29	32	11	5	16	51	64	-13	2	10
19	Greece	2.800	28	32	10	6	16	33	51	-18	2	10
20	Turkey	2.700	27	30	9	6	15	30	51	-21	3	10
21	Denmark	2.500	25	30	7	10	13	36	53	-17	1	10
22	Hungary	2.300	23	26	11	1	14	32	59	-27	0	10
23	Switzerland	2.000	20	28	8	4	16	32	51	-19	0	10
24	Finland	1.800	18	26	8	1	17	21	55	-34	1	10
25	Cyprus	1.500	15	24	7	1	16	31	51	-20	0	10
26	N. Ireland	1.400	14	24	3	8	13	26	48	-22	0	10
27	Norway	1.300	13	24	3	7	14	17	46	-29	0	10
28	Albania	1.125	9	19	4	1	14	14	36	-22	0	8
29	Rep. of Ireland	0.600	6	20	0	6	14	12	48	-36	0	10
30	Iceland	0.500	5	20	2	1	17	9	60	-51	0	10
31	Malta	0.400	4	20	2	0	18	7	76	-69	0	10
32	Luxembourg	0.300	3	20	1	1	18	6	82	-76	0	10

1986-87 to 1990-91

Pos'n	Cnty	Ave	Pts	P	W	D	L	F	A	Diff	B	No./T
1	West Germany	11.800	59	37	21	8	8	68	29	39	9	5
2	Portugal	11.000	66	40	25	6	9	82	25	57	10	6
3	Spain	10.400	52	34	19	7	8	68	36	32	7	5
4	France	9.400	47	31	15	10	6	50	22	28	7	5
5	Romania	7.600	38	27	14	5	8	47	31	16	5	5
6	Italy	7.428	52	34	17	11	6	53	16	37	7	7
7	USSR	7.200	36	28	12	7	9	37	28	9	5	5
8	Yugoslavia	6.800	34	23	12	6	5	45	24	21	4	5
9	Belgium	6.600	33	26	11	8	7	30	26	4	3	5
10	Netherlands	6.500	26	21	7	7	7	27	17	10	5	4
11	Scotland	4.400	22	20	8	5	7	29	19	10	1	5
12	Austria	4.200	21	18	9	3	6	38	28	10	0	5
–	Sweden	4.200	21	18	7	6	5	27	27	0	1	5
14	Turkey	3.600	18	18	6	3	9	22	31	-9	3	5
15	Poland	3.200	16	16	6	4	6	26	29	-3	0	5
–	E. Germany	3.200	16	16	6	3	7	25	28	-3	1	5
17	Czechoslovakia	3.000	15	16	6	3	7	25	26	-1	0	5
18	Denmark	2.800	14	16	4	5	7	18	26	-8	1	5
19	Switzerland	2.200	11	14	5	1	8	17	28	-11	0	5
20	Bulgaria	2.000	10	16	3	3	10	18	31	-13	1	5
21	Norway	1.800	9	14	2	5	7	9	24	-15	0	5
22	Greece	1.600	8	12	3	2	7	14	22	-8	0	5
23	Hungary	1.400	7	12	3	1	8	8	30	-22	0	5
24	Finland	1.200	6	10	3	0	7	8	24	-16	0	5
25	Albania	1.000	5	13	2	1	10	10	25	-15	0	5
–	Cyprus	1.000	5	12	2	1	9	11	31	-20	0	5
27	Iceland	0.800	4	10	2	0	8	2	31	-29	0	5
–	Malta	0.800	4	10	2	0	8	3	35	-32	0	5
29	N. Ireland	0.600	3	10	0	3	7	7	26	-19	0	5
30	Rep. of Ireland	0.400	2	10	0	2	8	2	23	-21	0	5
–	Luxembourg	0.400	2	10	1	0	9	4	32	-28	0	5

Summary Totals

	Pts	P	W	D	L	F	A	D	B	F/P
1955-56 to 1990-91	**4670**	**4166**	**1705**	**756**	**1705**	**6566**	**6566**	**0**	**504**	**3.152**
1981-82 to 1990-91	**1338**	**1198**	**478**	**242**	**478**	**1697**	**1697**	**0**	**140**	**2.833**
1986-87 to 1990-91	**662**	**592**	**233**	**126**	**233**	**830**	**830**	**0**	**70**	**2.804**

Club Performance by Points

1955-56 to 1990-91

Pos'n	Club	Cnty	Pts	P	W	D	L	F	A	Diff	B	Pts/P	F/P
1	Real Madrid	Esp	271	170	101	25	44	401	187	214	44	1.594	2.359
2	Benfica	Por	179	123	63	25	35	244	134	110	28	1.455	1.984
3	Bayern Munich	FRG	159	94	58	18	18	210	87	123	25	1.691	2.234
4	Liverpool	Eng	128	77	48	13	16	159	64	95	19	1.662	2.065
5	Ajax	Ned	116	75	42	15	18	141	74	67	17	1.547	1.880
6	Celtic	Sco	112	78	42	15	21	143	73	70	13	1.436	1.833
7	Juventus	Ita	112	77	41	15	21	124	70	54	15	1.455	1.610
8	AC Milan	Ita	108	68	38	13	17	150	70	80	19	1.588	2.206
9	Red Star Belgrade	Rom	103	76	39	13	24	164	103	61	12	1.355	2.158
10	CSKA Sofia	Bul	93	86	35	15	36	124	125	-1	8	1.081	1.442
11	Inter Milan	Ita	84	51	27	14	10	74	38	36	16	1.647	1.451
12	Anderlecht	Bel	82	70	31	11	28	120	115	5	9	1.171	1.714
13	Dinamo Kiev	URS	75	52	28	11	13	72	42	30	8	1.442	1.385
14	Manchester United	Eng	70	41	26	7	8	100	45	55	11	1.707	2.439
15	Rangers	Sco	64	55	25	8	22	92	90	2	6	1.164	1.673
16	Dukla Prague	Tch	59	45	22	10	13	75	58	17	5	1.311	1.667
17	PSV Eindhoven	Ned	58	45	19	12	14	79	43	36	8	1.289	1.756
18	Atlético Madrid	Esp	57	39	21	7	11	65	39	26	8	1.462	1.667
19	Rapid Vienna	Aut	57	49	24	4	21	89	69	20	5	1.163	1.816
20	Feyenoord	Ned	56	39	20	10	9	90	41	49	6	1.436	2.308
21	Barcelona	Esp	56	35	19	8	8	71	34	37	10	1.600	2.029
22	Steaua Bucharest	Rom	56	43	20	8	15	68	52	16	8	1.302	1.581
23	Standard Liège	Bel	54	40	23	3	14	72	47	25	5	1.350	1.800
24	Dinamo Bucharest	Rom	52	52	21	8	23	84	83	1	2	1.000	1.615
25	Saint-Etienne	Fra	51	41	19	7	15	50	44	6	6	1.244	1.220
26	Austria Vienna	Aut	50	49	18	11	20	73	70	3	3	1.020	1.490
27	Górnik Zabrze	Pol	49	43	21	6	16	70	64	6	1	1.140	1.628
28	FC Porto	Por	47	37	19	5	13	69	41	28	4	1.270	1.865
29	Bor. Mönchengladbach	FRG	46	31	15	10	6	69	31	38	6	1.484	2.226
30	Ujpesti Dózsa	Hun	46	40	17	8	15	65	63	2	4	1.150	1.625
31	Malmö FF	Swe	45	41	15	11	15	45	58	-13	4	1.098	1.098
32	Hamburg	FRG	43	27	16	3	8	53	31	22	8	1.593	1.963
33	IFK Gothenburg	Swe	42	36	17	4	15	75	62	13	4	1.167	2.083
34	Panathinaikos	Gre	41	43	12	12	19	53	63	-10	5	0.953	1.233
35	Dynamo Berlin	GDR	40	38	15	8	15	54	52	2	2	1.053	1.421
36	Stade Reims	Fra	38	24	14	3	7	63	30	33	7	1.583	2.625
37	Sparta Prague	Tch	38	32	14	7	11	53	48	5	3	1.188	1.656
38	Galatasaray	Tur	38	35	13	8	14	45	52	-7	4	1.086	1.286
39	Spartak Trnava	Tch	37	24	13	7	4	44	20	24	4	1.542	1.833
40	Club Bruges	Bel	37	31	14	5	12	51	39	12	4	1.194	1.645
41	Olympique Marseille	Fra	35	23	12	6	5	39	24	15	5	1.522	1.696
42	Partizan Belgrade	Yug	35	33	13	4	16	55	52	3	5	1.061	1.667
43	Nottingham Forest	Eng	34	20	12	4	4	32	14	18	6	1.700	1.600
44	Vasas SC	Hun	33	27	12	6	9	62	34	28	3	1.222	2.296
45	Dynamo Dresden	GDR	33	30	12	6	12	49	43	6	3	1.100	1.633
46	Leeds United	Eng	30	17	12	1	4	42	11	31	5	1.765	2.471
47	Hajduk Split	Yug	28	18	12	2	4	41	18	23	2	1.556	2.278
48	FC Zürich	Sui	28	27	11	2	14	36	49	-13	4	1.037	1.333
49	Legia Warsaw	Pol	27	18	11	2	5	29	16	13	3	1.500	1.611
50	Aston Villa	Eng	25	15	9	3	3	24	10	14	4	1.667	1.600
51	Cologne	FRG	25	17	7	8	2	27	19	8	3	1.471	1.588
52	Spartak Moscow	URS	24	20	8	5	7	29	20	9	3	1.200	1.450
53	Sporting Lisbon	Por	24	28	9	5	14	41	48	-7	1	0.857	1.464

Pos'n	Club	Cnty	Pts	P	W	D	L	F	A	Diff	B	Pts/P	F/P
54	Omonia Nicosia	Cyp	24	36	11	2	23	44	87	-43	0	0.667	1.222
55	Girondins Bordeaux	Fra	23	16	6	8	2	17	12	5	3	1.438	1.063
56	FC Basle	Sui	23	22	10	2	10	43	40	3	1	1.045	1.955
57	Borussia Dortmund	FRG	22	18	8	3	7	44	30	14	3	1.222	2.444
58	Vorwärts Frankfurt/Oder	GDR	22	23	10	1	12	37	34	3	1	0.957	1.609
59	Fiorentina	Ita	22	13	7	4	2	14	11	3	4	1.692	1.077
60	Honvéd	Hun	22	22	10	2	10	35	39	-4	0	1.000	1.591
61	Fenerbahçe	Tur	22	33	9	4	20	30	70	-40	0	0.667	0.909
62	Ferencváros	Hun	21	18	9	2	7	39	35	4	1	1.167	2.167
63	Young Boys Berne	Sui	21	17	7	5	5	29	31	-2	2	1.235	1.706
64	Linfield	Nir	21	39	4	12	23	43	83	-40	1	0.538	1.103
65	Olympiakos Pireus	Gre	20	28	7	6	15	25	43	-18	0	0.714	0.893
66	Grasshoppers Zürich	Sui	19	24	6	5	13	42	44	-2	2	0.792	1.750
67	Nice	Fra	18	14	7	2	5	29	25	4	2	1.286	2.071
68	FC Tirol	Aut	18	22	7	3	12	34	46	-12	1	0.818	1.545
69	AGF Aarhus	Den	17	18	6	4	8	23	25	-2	1	0.944	1.278
70	Rába ETO	Hun	17	14	7	1	6	27	30	-3	2	1.214	1.929
71	AEK Athenes	Gre	17	20	6	4	10	33	42	-9	1	0.850	1.650
72	Derby County	Eng	16	12	6	2	4	18	12	6	2	1.333	1.500
73	Servette	Sui	16	17	6	4	7	27	30	-3	0	0.941	1.588
74	Nantes	Fra	16	18	5	6	7	25	28	-3	0	0.889	1.389
75	Dnepr Dnepropetrovsk	URS	15	12	5	3	4	15	13	2	2	1.250	1.250
76	Aberdeen	Sco	15	12	5	4	3	14	12	2	1	1.250	1.167
77	Karl-Marx-Stadt	GDR	15	18	5	4	9	28	28	0	1	0.833	1.556
78	Ruch Chorzów	Pol	15	14	5	4	5	20	25	-5	1	1.071	1.429
79	Jeunesse Esch	Lux	15	39	6	3	30	41	132	-91	0	0.385	1.051
80	Roma	Ita	14	9	5	1	3	14	7	7	3	1.556	1.556
81	Wiener Sport-Club	Aut	14	12	4	4	4	21	18	3	2	1.167	1.750
82	Athletic Bilbao	Esp	14	12	5	3	4	22	20	2	1	1.167	1.833
83	Banik Ostrava	Tch	14	14	5	3	6	18	23	-5	1	1.000	1.286
84	Werder Bremen	FRG	13	10	5	2	3	17	7	10	1	1.300	1.700
85	Dundee United	Sco	13	8	5	1	2	14	5	9	2	1.625	1.750
86	Eintracht Frankfurt	FRG	13	7	4	2	1	23	15	8	3	1.857	3.286
87	Monaco	Fra	13	18	4	4	10	25	23	2	1	0.722	1.389
88	Slovan Bratislava	Tch	13	12	6	1	5	17	19	-2	0	1.083	1.417
89	Trabzonspor	Tur	13	14	6	1	7	12	19	-7	0	0.929	0.857
90	Dundee	Sco	12	8	5	0	3	20	14	6	2	1.500	2.500
91	MTK-VM	Hun	12	10	5	1	4	26	22	4	1	1.200	2.600
92	Nuremberg	FRG	12	8	5	1	2	16	14	2	1	1.500	2.000
93	Real Sociedad	Esp	12	10	4	2	4	11	9	2	2	1.200	1.100
94	Vojvodina Novi Sad	Yug	12	9	5	1	3	10	9	1	1	1.333	1.111
95	Levski Sofia	Bul	12	20	4	4	12	30	40	-10	0	0.600	1.500
96	Glentoran	Nir	12	18	3	6	9	18	29	-11	0	0.667	1.000
97	Ararat Erevan	URS	11	6	5	0	1	14	5	9	1	1.833	2.333
98	Tottenham Hotspur	Eng	11	8	4	1	3	21	13	8	2	1.375	2.625
99	Widzew Lódź	Pol	11	10	4	1	5	21	20	1	2	1.100	2.100
100	Carl Zeiss Jena	GDR	11	8	5	0	3	12	11	1	1	1.375	1.500
101	Brøndby IF	Den	11	10	3	4	3	13	13	0	1	1.100	1.300
102	Lillestrøm SK	Nor	11	12	3	5	4	10	15	-5	0	0.917	0.833
103	FC Amsterdam	Ned	10	6	4	1	1	13	4	9	1	1.667	2.167
104	Everton	Eng	10	8	2	5	1	12	6	6	1	1.250	1.500
105	KB Copenhagen	Den	10	13	4	2	7	19	25	-6	0	0.769	1.462
106	Vejle BK	Den	10	12	3	4	5	13	22	-9	0	0.833	1.083
107	FC Kuusysi Lahti	Fin	10	12	4	1	7	11	23	-12	1	0.833	0.917
108	Besiktas	Tur	10	16	3	3	10	11	30	-19	1	0.625	0.688
109	HJK Helsinki	Fin	10	18	5	0	13	17	49	-32	0	0.556	0.944
110	Arsenal	Eng	9	6	4	0	2	13	4	9	1	1.500	2.167

Pos'n	Club	Cnty	Pts	P	W	D	L	F	A	Diff	B	Pts/P	F/P
111	Dinamo Minsk	URS	9	6	3	2	1	13	8	5	1	1.500	2.167
112	Hibernian	Sco	9	6	3	1	2	9	5	4	2	1.500	1.500
113	Schalke 04	FRG	9	7	3	2	2	13	13	0	1	1.286	1.857
114	Åtvidaberg SFF	Swe	9	8	4	0	4	12	12	0	1	1.125	1.500
115	Universitatea Craiova	Rom	9	10	3	2	5	12	14	-2	1	0.900	1.200
116	IFK Norrköping	Swe	9	12	2	5	5	14	20	-6	0	0.750	1.167
117	17 Nëntori Tirana	Alb	9	16	3	3	10	14	24	-10	0	0.563	0.875
118	Esbjerg FB	Den	9	12	3	3	6	11	28	-17	0	0.750	0.917
119	Dundalk	Irl	9	16	3	3	10	12	38	-26	0	0.563	0.750
120	Sliema Wanderers	Mlt	9	16	4	1	11	11	41	-30	0	0.563	0.688
121	KV Mechelen	Bel	8	6	2	3	1	9	3	6	1	1.333	1.500
122	Arges Pitesti	Rom	8	8	4	0	4	13	10	3	0	1.000	1.625
123	Strasbourg	Fra	8	6	3	1	2	8	6	2	1	1.333	1.333
124	Neuchâtel Xamax	Sui	8	8	4	0	4	14	13	1	0	1.000	1.750
125	Lech Poznań	Pol	8	8	4	0	4	11	18	-7	0	1.000	1.375
126	Partizani Tirana	Alb	8	13	3	2	8	7	23	-16	0	0.615	0.538
127	Napoli	Ita	7	6	2	3	1	6	3	3	0	1.167	1.000
128	Sparta Rotterdam	Ned	7	6	3	0	3	12	11	1	1	1.167	2.000
129	Wisla Kraków	Pol	7	6	2	2	2	10	11	-1	1	1.167	1.667
130	Lokomotiv Sofia	Bul	7	8	3	1	4	19	21	-2	0	0.875	2.375
131	Wolverhampton Wanderers	Eng	7	8	2	2	4	12	16	-4	1	0.875	1.500
132	Seville	Esp	7	6	2	2	2	9	13	-4	1	1.167	1.500
133	Valur Reykjavik	Isl	7	16	2	3	11	9	50	-41	0	0.438	0.563
134	Ipswich Town	Eng	6	4	3	0	1	16	5	11	0	1.500	4.000
135	1860 Munich	FRG	6	4	3	0	1	12	4	8	0	1.500	3.000
136	Bohemians Prague	Tch	6	4	3	0	1	7	2	5	0	1.500	1.750
137	Magdeburg	GDR	6	8	3	0	5	15	11	4	0	0.750	1.875
138	Beveren	Bel	6	6	2	2	2	11	8	3	0	1.000	1.833
139	Zenit Leningrad	URS	6	4	3	0	1	7	4	3	0	1.500	1.750
140	Valencia	Esp	6	6	2	2	2	6	5	1	0	1.000	1.000
141	Hvidovre IF	Den	6	8	1	4	3	13	19	-6	0	0.750	1.625
142	Djurgården SIF	Swe	6	8	2	1	5	7	16	-9	1	0.750	0.875
143	Reipas Lahti	Fin	6	8	2	2	4	8	30	-22	0	0.750	1.000
144	Waterford United	Irl	6	14	3	0	11	15	47	-32	0	0.429	1.071
145	Lyngby BK	Den	5	4	2	1	1	7	2	5	0	1.250	1.750
146	Inter Bratislava	Tch	5	4	2	1	1	8	6	2	0	1.250	2.000
147	AZ'67 Alkmaar	Ned	5	4	2	1	1	8	6	2	0	1.250	2.000
148	Zbrojovka Brno	Tch	5	4	1	3	0	7	5	2	0	1.250	1.750
149	CSKA Moscow	URS	5	4	2	1	1	5	3	2	0	1.250	1.250
150	Zaria Voroshilovgrad	URS	5	4	2	1	1	3	1	2	0	1.250	0.750
151	Verona	Ita	5	4	2	1	1	5	4	1	0	1.250	1.250
152	Burnley	Eng	5	4	2	0	2	8	8	0	1	1.250	2.000
153	Eintracht Brunschweig	FRG	5	5	2	0	3	5	5	0	1	1.000	1.000
154	TJ Vitkovice	Tch	5	4	2	1	1	4	5	-1	0	1.250	1.000
155	Trakia Plovdiv	Bul	5	8	2	1	5	8	11	-3	0	0.625	1.000
156	Spartak Hradec Králové	Tch	5	4	1	2	1	2	5	-3	1	1.250	0.500
157	B 1903 Copenhagen	Den	5	8	2	1	5	7	11	-4	0	0.625	0.875
158	Petrolul Ploiesti	Rom	5	8	2	1	5	8	15	-7	0	0.625	1.000
159	IA Akranes	Isl	5	14	1	3	10	14	36	-22	0	0.357	1.000
160	Rosenborg BK	Nor	5	12	1	3	8	9	31	-22	0	0.417	0.750
161	Cagliari	Ita	4	4	2	0	2	5	5	0	0	1.000	1.250
162	Torino	Ita	4	4	1	2	1	4	4	0	0	1.000	1.000
163	Sarajevo	Yug	4	6	1	2	3	8	9	-1	0	0.667	1.333
164	Gwardia Warsaw	Pol	4	5	1	2	2	6	9	-3	0	0.800	1.200
165	RWD Molenbeek	Bel	4	4	2	0	2	6	9	-3	0	1.000	1.500
166	Kilmarnock	Sco	4	4	1	2	1	4	7	-3	0	1.000	1.000
167	La Chaux-de-Fonds	Sui	4	4	1	2	1	5	9	-4	0	1.000	1.250

Pos'n	Club	Cnty	Pts	P	W	D	L	F	A	Diff	B	Pts/P	F/P
168	Polonia Bytom	Pol	4	6	2	0	4	7	13	-6	0	0.667	1.167
169	B 1913 Odense	Den	4	6	2	0	4	16	24	-8	0	0.667	2.667
170	Bohemians	Irl	4	6	1	2	3	4	13	-9	0	0.667	0.667
171	Vålerengens SIF	Nor	4	8	1	2	5	8	18	-10	0	0.500	1.000
172	Apoel Nicosia	Cyp	4	10	2	0	8	7	27	-20	0	0.400	0.700
173	Shamrock Rovers	Irl	4	14	0	4	10	7	28	-21	0	0.286	0.500
174	SFK Lyn	Nor	4	10	2	0	8	13	40	-27	0	0.400	1.300
175	Hibernians	Mlt	4	12	1	2	9	8	36	-28	0	0.333	0.667
176	Rapid Bucharest	Rom	3	4	1	1	2	3	3	0	0	0.750	0.750
177	Bologna	Ita	3	3	1	1	1	2	2	0	0	1.000	0.667
178	AB Copenhagen	Den	3	4	1	1	2	4	5	-1	0	0.750	1.000
179	Torpedo Moscow	URS	3	4	0	3	1	0	1	-1	0	0.750	0.000
180	Halmstad SBK	Swe	3	4	1	1	2	4	6	-2	0	0.750	1.000
181	Dinamo Zagreb	Yug	3	4	1	1	2	4	7	-3	0	0.750	1.000
182	PAOK Salonika	Gre	3	6	1	1	4	5	12	-7	0	0.500	0.833
183	Öester SIF	Swe	3	8	1	1	6	3	14	-11	0	0.375	0.375
184	Fredrikstad FK	Nor	3	8	1	1	6	6	22	-16	0	0.375	0.750
185	IL Viking	Nor	3	12	1	1	10	11	28	-17	0	0.250	0.917
186	VFB Stuttgart	FRG	2	2	0	2	0	3	3	0	0	1.000	1.500
187	Larissa	Gre	2	2	1	0	1	3	3	0	0	1.000	1.500
188	Dinamo Tbilisi	URS	2	4	1	0	3	7	8	-1	0	0.500	1.750
189	Vllaznia Shkodër	Alb	2	2	1	0	1	3	4	-1	0	1.000	1.500
190	Saarbrücken	FRG	2	2	1	0	1	5	7	-2	0	1.000	2.500
191	IBA Akureyri	Isl	2	2	1	0	1	1	3	-2	0	1.000	0.500
192	Szombierki Bytom	Pol	2	4	1	0	3	4	7	-3	0	0.500	1.000
193	Red Boys Differdange	Lux	2	2	1	0	1	3	7	-4	0	1.000	1.500
194	LKS Lódź	Pol	2	2	1	0	1	2	6	-4	0	1.000	1.000
195	Athlone Town	Irl	2	4	0	2	2	7	14	-7	0	0.500	1.750
196	Heart of Midlothian	Sco	2	4	1	0	3	4	11	-7	0	0.500	1.000
197	Derry City	Irl	2	5	1	0	4	9	21	-12	0	0.400	1.800
198	UT Arad	Rom	2	6	0	2	4	3	17	-14	0	0.333	0.500
199	Hamrun Spartans	Mlt	2	6	1	0	5	2	16	-14	0	0.333	0.333
200	Haka Valkeakoski	Fin	2	8	1	0	7	7	28	-21	0	0.250	0.875
201	Drumcondra	Irl	2	7	1	0	6	4	27	-23	0	0.286	0.571
202	TPS Turku	Fin	2	10	1	0	9	4	28	-24	0	0.200	0.400
203	Spora Luxembourg	Lux	2	7	1	0	6	7	36	-29	0	0.286	1.000
204	Floriana	Mlt	2	12	0	2	10	3	49	-46	0	0.167	0.250
205	Valletta	Mlt	2	12	1	0	11	5	54	-49	0	0.167	0.417
206	Csepel	Hun	1	2	0	1	1	3	4	-1	0	0.500	1.500
207	Paris Saint-Germain	Fra	1	2	0	1	1	2	3	-1	0	0.500	1.000
208	FK Skeid	Nor	1	2	0	1	1	1	2	-1	0	0.500	0.500
209	Manchester City	Eng	1	2	0	1	1	1	2	-1	0	0.500	0.500
210	IBV Vestmannaeyjar	Isl	1	2	0	1	1	1	2	-1	0	0.500	0.500
211	Admira Wacker	Aut	1	2	0	1	1	0	1	-1	0	0.500	0.000
212	Beroe Stara Zagora	Bul	1	2	0	1	1	1	3	-2	0	0.500	0.500
213	Slask Wroclaw	Pol	1	2	0	1	1	2	5	-3	0	0.500	1.000
214	Glenavon	Nir	1	2	0	1	1	0	3	-3	0	0.500	0.000
215	Rot-Weiss Essen	FRG	1	2	0	1	1	1	5	-4	0	0.500	0.500
216	St. Patrick's Athletic	Irl	1	2	0	1	1	1	5	-4	0	0.500	0.500
217	Lausanne-Sports	Sui	1	2	0	1	1	0	4	-4	0	0.500	0.000
218	Distillery	Nir	1	2	0	1	1	3	8	-5	0	0.500	1.500
219	Vöest Linz	Aut	1	2	0	1	1	0	5	-5	0	0.500	0.000
220	OB Odense	Den	1	4	0	1	3	3	10	-7	0	0.250	0.750
221	Dinamo Tirana	Alb	1	6	0	1	5	1	11	-10	0	0.167	0.167
222	B 1909 Odense	Den	1	6	0	1	5	6	21	-15	0	0.167	1.000
223	Progrès Niedercorn	Lux	1	4	0	1	3	1	17	-16	0	0.250	0.250
224	KuPS Kuopio	Fin	1	6	0	1	5	4	21	-17	0	0.167	0.667

Pos'n	Club	Cnty	Pts	P	W	D	L	F	A	Diff	B	Pts/P	F/P
225	OPS Oulu	Fin	1	4	0	1	3	2	19	-17	0	0.250	0.500
226	Aris Bonnevoie	Lux	1	6	0	1	5	6	25	-19	0	0.167	1.000
227	Olympiakos Nicosia	Cyp	1	6	0	1	5	4	36	-32	0	0.167	0.667
228	Utrecht	Ned	0	2	0	0	2	4	6	-2	0	0.000	2.000
229	Roda JC	Ned	0	2	0	0	2	3	6	-3	0	0.000	1.500
230	Linzer ASK	Aut	0	2	0	0	2	2	5	-3	0	0.000	1.000
231	Zeljeznicar Sarajevo	Yug	0	2	0	0	2	1	4	-3	0	0.000	0.500
232	Örgryte IS	Swe	0	2	0	0	2	3	7	-4	0	0.000	1.500
233	Chemie Leipzig	GDR	0	2	0	0	2	2	6	-4	0	0.000	1.000
234	Stal Mielec	Pol	0	4	0	0	4	2	6	-4	0	0.000	0.500
235	Moss FK	Nor	0	2	0	0	2	0	4	-4	0	0.000	0.000
236	Vikingur Reykjavik	Isl	0	4	0	0	4	3	8	-5	0	0.000	0.750
237	Pezoporikos Larnaca	Cyp	0	2	0	0	2	2	7	-5	0	0.000	1.000
238	Anorthosis Famagousta	Cyp	0	2	0	0	2	1	6	-5	0	0.000	0.500
239	Ilves Tampere	Fin	0	2	0	0	2	1	6	-5	0	0.000	0.500
240	Lierse	Bel	0	2	0	0	2	0	5	-5	0	0.000	0.000
241	Lucerne	Sui	0	2	0	0	2	0	5	-5	0	0.000	0.000
242	Shelbourne	Irl	0	2	0	0	2	1	7	-6	0	0.000	0.500
243	Strømgodset IF	Nor	0	2	0	0	2	1	7	-6	0	0.000	0.500
244	Cork Hibernians	Irl	0	2	0	0	2	1	7	-6	0	0.000	0.500
245	Cork Celtic	Irl	0	2	0	0	2	1	7	-6	0	0.000	0.500
246	Køge BK	Den	0	2	0	0	2	1	7	-6	0	0.000	0.500
247	Sligo Rovers	Irl	0	2	0	0	2	0	6	-6	0	0.000	0.000
248	Labinoti Elbasan	Alb	0	2	0	0	2	0	6	-6	0	0.000	0.000
249	Vardar Skoplje	Yug	0	2	0	0	2	0	6	-6	0	0.000	0.000
250	HIFK Helsinki	Fin	0	4	0	0	4	5	12	-7	0	0.000	1.250
251	Ards	Nir	0	2	0	0	2	3	10	-7	0	0.000	1.500
252	Antwerp	Bel	0	2	0	0	2	1	8	-7	0	0.000	0.500
253	HPS Helsinki	Fin	0	2	0	0	2	0	7	-7	0	0.000	0.000
254	IK Start	Nor	0	4	0	0	4	2	10	-8	0	0.000	0.500
255	Coleraine	Nir	0	2	0	0	2	1	11	-10	0	0.000	0.500
256	Portadown	Nir	0	2	0	0	2	1	13	-12	0	0.000	0.500
257	AEL Limassol	Cyp	0	2	0	0	2	0	12	-12	0	0.000	0.000
258	Limerick	Irl	0	4	0	0	4	4	17	-13	0	0.000	1.000
259	KPV Kokkola	Fin	0	2	0	0	2	0	14	-14	0	0.000	0.000
260	EPA Larnaca	Cyp	0	2	0	0	2	0	16	-16	0	0.000	0.000
261	Crusaders	Nir	0	4	0	0	4	0	19	-19	0	0.000	0.000
262	Rabat Ajax	Mlt	0	4	0	0	4	0	20	-20	0	0.000	0.000
263	Union Luxembourg	Lux	0	6	0	0	6	2	24	-22	0	0.000	0.333
264	Fram Reykjavik	Isl	0	6	0	0	6	2	26	-24	0	0.000	0.333
265	KR Reykjavik	Isl	0	6	0	0	6	7	35	-28	0	0.000	1.167
266	IBK Keflavik	Isl	0	8	0	0	8	5	35	-30	0	0.000	0.625
267	Stade Dudelange	Lux	0	4	0	0	4	1	32	-31	0	0.000	0.250
268	Avenir Beggen	Lux	0	8	0	0	8	0	44	-44	0	0.000	0.000
	Total		**4670**	**4166**	**1705**	**756**	**1705**	**6566**	**6566**	**0**	**504**	**1.121**	**3.152**

Club Performance by Points

1981-82 to 1990-91

Pos'n	Club	Cnty	Pts	P	W	D	L	F	A	Diff	B	Pts/P	F/P
1	Bayern Munich	FRG	77	46	28	9	9	97	42	55	12	1.674	2.109
2	Liverpool	Eng	54	30	21	4	5	61	20	41	8	1.800	2.033
3	Real Madrid	Esp	52	34	19	7	8	68	36	32	7	1.529	2.000
4	Juventus	Ita	51	32	19	6	7	66	24	42	7	1.594	2.063
5	Steaua Bucharest	Rom	48	32	17	6	9	55	31	24	8	1.500	1.719
6	Benfica	Por	47	31	18	4	9	51	23	28	7	1.516	1.645
7	Red Star Belgrade	Yug	41	27	15	6	6	62	29	33	5	1.519	2.296
8	Anderlecht	Bel	41	26	15	5	6	36	26	10	6	1.577	1.385
9	FC Porto	Por	40	27	16	4	7	57	23	34	4	1.481	2.111
10	AC Milan	Ita	38	22	12	7	3	34	10	24	7	1.727	1.545
11	IFK Gothenburg	Swe	33	22	13	3	6	51	26	25	4	1.500	2.318
12	Olympique Marseille	Fra	30	17	10	5	2	33	13	20	5	1.765	1.941
13	Dinamo Kiev	URS	29	20	10	5	5	27	17	10	4	1.450	1.350
14	Dynamo Berlin	GDR	27	28	11	4	13	39	42	-3	1	0.964	1.393
15	CSKA Sofia	Bul	27	28	9	6	13	33	39	-6	3	0 964	1.179
16	PSV Eindhoven	Ned	26	21	7	7	7	27	17	10	5	1.238	1.286
17	Aston Villa	Eng	25	15	9	3	3	24	10	14	4	1.667	1.600
18	Girondins Bordeaux	Fra	23	16	6	8	2	17	12	5	3	1.438	1.063
19	Austria Vienna	Aut	22	18	8	5	5	35	24	11	1	1.222	1.944
20	Dinamo Bucharest	Rom	22	22	8	4	10	32	28	4	2	1.000	1.455
21	Sparta Prague	Tch	21	20	8	4	8	31	30	1	1	1.050	1.550
22	Rapid Vienna	Aut	19	16	9	0	7	36	20	16	1	1.188	2.250
23	Hamburg	FRG	19	11	7	2	2	19	10	9	3	1.727	1.727
24	Celtic	Sco	15	14	6	3	5	16	14	2	0	1.071	1.143
25	Dnepr Dnepropetrovsk	URS	15	12	5	3	4	15	13	2	2	1.250	1.250
26	Rangers	Sco	14	12	5	3	4	20	13	7	1	1.167	1.667
27	Roma	Ita	14	9	5	1	3	14	7	7	3	1.556	1.556
28	Spartak Moscow	URS	14	12	4	4	4	13	12	1	2	1.167	1.083
29	Dundee United	Sco	13	8	5	1	2	14	5	9	2	1.625	1.750
30	Barcelona	Esp	13	9	4	2	3	10	9	1	3	1.444	1.111
31	Panathinaikos	Gre	13	12	4	3	5	13	21	-8	2	1.083	1.083
32	Omonia Nicosia	Cyp	13	18	6	1	11	24	34	-10	0	0.722	1.333
33	Honvéd	Hun	13	14	6	1	7	16	30	-14	0	0.929	1.143
34	Aberdeen	Sco	12	8	4	3	1	13	7	6	1	1.500	1.625
35	Real Sociedad	Esp	12	10	4	2	4	11	9	2	2	1.200	1.100
36	Galatasaray	Tur	12	10	4	2	4	13	14	-1	2	1.200	1.300
37	Widzew Lódź	Pol	11	10	4	1	5	21	20	1	2	1.100	2.100
38	Brøndby IF	Den	11	10	3	4	3	13	13	0	1	1.100	1.300
39	FC Tirol	Aut	10	8	4	2	2	21	18	3	0	1.250	2.625
40	Malmö FF	Swe	10	10	2	6	2	11	13	-2	0	1.000	1.100
41	Olympiakos Pireus	Gre	10	12	4	2	6	9	15	-6	0	0.833	0.750
42	FC Kuusysi Lahti	Fin	10	12	4	1	7	11	23	-12	1	0.833	0.917
43	Dinamo Minsk	URS	9	6	3	2	1	13	8	5	1	1.500	2.167
44	Dynamo Dresden	GDR	9	8	3	2	3	13	13	0	1	1.125	1.625
45	Górnik Zabrze	Pol	9	12	3	3	6	17	20	-3	0	0.750	1.417
46	KV Mechelen	Bel	8	6	2	3	1	9	3	6	1	1.333	1.500
47	Standard Liège	Bel	8	8	3	2	3	17	14	3	0	1.000	2.125
48	Neuchâtel Xamax	Sui	8	8	4	0	4	14	13	1	0	1.000	1.750
49	Club Bruges	Bel	8	8	3	2	3	7	10	-3	0	1.000	0.875
50	Lech Poznań	Pol	8	8	4	0	4	11	18	-7	0	1.000	1.375
51	HJK Helsinki	Fin	8	10	4	0	6	9	18	-9	0	0.800	0.900
52	Linfield	Nir	8	16	1	6	9	17	28	-11	0	0.500	1.063
53	Napoli	Ita	7	6	2	3	1	6	3	3	0	1.167	1.000

Pos'n	Club	Cnty	Pts	P	W	D	L	F	A	Diff	B	Pts/P	F/P
54	Monaco	Fra	7	8	2	2	4	9	7	2	1	0 875	1.125
55	Werder Bremen	FRG	7	6	2	2	2	6	4	2	1	1.167	1.000
56	Sporting Lisbon	Por	7	6	2	2	2	6	5	1	1	1.167	1.000
57	Besiktas	Tur	7	8	2	2	4	8	15	-7	1	0.875	1.000
58	Bohemians Prague	Tch	6	4	3	0	1	7	2	5	0	1.500	1.750
59	Zenit Leningrad	URS	6	4	3	0	1	7	4	3	0	1.500	1.750
60	Universitatea Craiova	Rom	6	6	2	1	3	8	7	1	1	1.000	1.333
61	Glentoran	Nir	6	6	2	2	2	8	7	1	0	1.000	1.333
62	Rába ETO	Hun	6	6	3	0	3	11	15	-4	0	1.000	1.833
63	17 Nëntori Tirana	Alb	6	10	3	0	7	11	15	-4	0	0.600	1.100
64	Beveren	Bel	5	4	2	1	1	9	4	5	0	1.250	2.250
65	Lyngby BK	Den	5	4	2	1	1	7	2	5	0	1.250	1.750
66	Partizan Belgrade	Yug	5	4	2	1	1	6	3	3	0	1.250	1.500
67	AZ'67 Alkmaar	Ned	5	4	2	1	1	8	6	2	0	1.250	2.000
68	Verona	Ita	5	4	2	1	1	5	4	1	0	1.250	1.250
69	Lillestrøm SK	Nor	5	6	1	3	2	6	7	-1	0	0.833	1.000
70	TJ Vitkovice	Tch	5	4	2	1	1	4	5	-1	0	1.250	1.000
71	Fenerbahçe	Tur	5	8	2	1	5	7	17	-10	0	0.625	0.875
72	Banik Ostrava	Tch	4	4	2	0	2	8	7	1	0	1.000	2.000
73	Athletic Bilbao	Esp	4	6	1	2	3	6	6	0	0	0.667	1.000
74	Servette	Sui	4	4	1	2	1	4	4	0	0	1.000	1.000
75	KB Copenhagen	Den	4	4	1	2	1	5	7	-2	0	1.000	1.250
76	Levski Sofia	Bul	4	6	1	2	3	8	13	-5	0	0.667	1.333
77	Rosenborg BK	Nor	4	6	1	2	3	3	13	-10	0	0.667	0.500
78	Grasshoppers Zürich	Sui	4	10	1	2	7	10	21	-11	0	0.400	1.000
79	AGF Aarhus	Den	3	4	1	1	2	4	3	1	0	0.750	1.000
80	AEK Athens	Gre	3	4	1	1	2	6	7	-1	0	0.750	1.500
81	Trabzonspor	Tur	3	4	1	1	2	2	5	-3	0	0.750	0.500
82	Ajax	Ned	3	6	0	3	3	3	8	-5	0	0.500	0.500
83	Vålerengen SIF	Nor	3	6	1	1	4	6	13	-7	0	0.500	1.000
84	Shamrock Rovers	Irl	3	8	0	3	5	2	10	-8	0	0.375	0.250
85	FC Zürich	Sui	2	2	1	0	1	3	3	0	0	1.000	1.500
86	VFB Stuttgart	FRG	2	2	0	2	0	3	3	0	0	1.000	1.500
87	Larissa	Gre	2	2	1	0	1	3	3	0	0	1.000	1.500
88	Vojvodina Novi Sad	Yug	2	2	1	0	1	2	2	0	0	1.000	1.000
89	Nantes	Fra	2	2	1	0	1	3	4	-1	0	1.000	1.500
90	Dukla Prague	Tch	2	2	1	0	1	2	3	-1	0	1.000	1.000
91	Ferencváros	Hun	2	2	1	0	1	3	5	-2	0	1.000	1.500
92	MTK-VM	Hun	2	2	1	0	1	2	4	-2	0	1.000	1.000
93	Dinamo Zagreb	Yug	2	2	1	0	1	1	3	-2	0	1.000	0.500
94	IBA Akureyri	Isl	2	2	1	0	1	1	3	-2	0	1.000	0.500
95	Young Boys Berne	Sui	2	2	1	0	1	1	5	-4	0	1.000	0.500
96	Sliema Wanderers	Mlt	2	2	1	0	1	1	5	-4	0	1.000	0.500
97	Apoel Nicosia	Cyp	2	4	1	0	3	5	10	-5	0	0.500	1.250
98	Partizani Tirana	Alb	2	3	1	0	2	2	7	-5	0	0.667	0.667
99	Athlone Town	Irl	2	4	0	2	2	7	14	-7	0	0.500	1.750
100	Öester SIF	Swe	2	4	1	0	3	1	8	-7	0	0.500	0.250
101	Hamrun Spartans	Mlt	2	6	1	0	5	2	16	-14	0	0.333	0.333
102	Valur Reykjavik	Isl	2	6	1	0	5	1	20	-19	0	0.333	0.167
103	Jeunesse Esch	Lux	2	8	1	0	7	4	26	-22	0	0.250	0.500
104	Paris Saint-Germain	Fra	1	2	0	1	1	2	3	-1	0	0.500	1.000
105	Feyenoord	Ned	1	2	0	1	1	1	2	-1	0	0.500	0.500
106	Inter Milan	Ita	1	2	0	1	1	1	2	-1	0	0.500	0.500
107	Saint-Etienne	Fra	1	2	0	1	1	1	3	-2	0	0.500	0.500
108	Beroe Stara Zagora	Bul	1	2	0	1	1	1	3	-2	0	0.500	0.500
109	Hvidovre IF	Den	1	2	0	1	1	4	7	-3	0	0.500	2.000
110	Vejle BK	Den	1	2	0	1	1	2	5	-3	0	0.500	1.000

Pos'n	Club	Cnty	Pts	P	W	D	L	F	A	Diff	B	Pts/P	F/P
111	Ruch Chorzów	Pol	1	2	0	1	1	2	6	-4	0	0.500	1.000
112	Progrès Niedercorn	Lux	1	2	0	1	1	1	5	-4	0	0.500	0.500
113	IL Viking	Nor	1	2	0	1	1	1	5	-4	0	0.500	0.500
114	St. Patrick's Athletic	Irl	1	2	0	1	1	1	5	-4	0	0.500	0.500
115	Dinamo Tirana	Alb	1	4	0	1	3	1	8	-7	0	0.250	0.250
116	IA Akranes	Isl	1	4	0	1	3	4	14	-10	0	0.250	1.000
117	Trakia Plovdiv	Bul	0	2	0	0	2	3	5	-2	0	0.000	1.500
118	Sarajevo	Yug	0	2	0	0	2	2	4	-2	0	0.000	1.000
119	PAOK Salonika	Gre	0	2	0	0	2	2	5	-3	0	0.000	1.000
120	IK Start	Nor	0	2	0	0	2	1	4	-3	0	0.000	0.500
121	Örgryte IS	Swe	0	2	0	0	2	3	7	-4	0	0.000	1.500
122	Moss FK	Nor	0	2	0	0	2	0	4	-4	0	0.000	0.000
123	Vikingur Reykjavik	Isl	0	4	0	0	4	3	8	-5	0	0.000	0.750
124	Pezoporikos Larnaca	Cyp	0	2	0	0	2	2	7	-5	0	0.000	1.000
125	Ilves Tampere	Fin	0	2	0	0	2	1	6	-5	0	0.000	0.500
126	Derry City	Irl	0	2	0	0	2	1	6	-5	0	0.000	0.500
127	Union Luxembourg	Lux	0	2	0	0	2	1	6	-5	0	0.000	0.500
128	Lucerne	Sui	0	2	0	0	2	0	5	-5	0	0.000	0.000
129	Ujpesti Dózsa	Hun	0	2	0	0	2	0	5	-5	0	0.000	0.000
130	OB Odense	Den	0	2	0	0	2	0	6	-6	0	0.000	0.000
131	Labinoti Elbasan	Alb	0	2	0	0	2	0	6	-6	0	0.000	0.000
132	Vardar Skoplje	Yug	0	2	0	0	2	0	6	-6	0	0.000	0.000
133	OPS Oulu	Fin	0	2	0	0	2	0	8	-8	0	0.000	0.000
134	B 1913 Odense	Den	0	2	0	0	2	1	10	-9	0	0.000	0.500
135	Spora Luxembourg	Lux	0	2	0	0	2	0	9	-9	0	0.000	0.000
136	Portadown	Nir	0	2	0	0	2	1	13	-12	0	0.000	0.500
137	Dundalk	Irl	0	4	0	0	4	1	13	-12	0	0.000	0.250
138	Hibernians	Mlt	0	4	0	0	4	4	17	-13	0	0.000	1.000
139	Fram Reykjavik	Isl	0	4	0	0	4	0	15	-15	0	0.000	0.000
140	Valletta	Mlt	0	4	0	0	4	0	18	-18	0	0.000	0.000
141	Rabat Ajax	Mlt	0	4	0	0	4	0	20	-20	0	0.000	0.000
142	Avenir Beggen	Lux	0	6	0	0	6	0	36	-36	0	0.000	0.000
	Total		**1338**	**1198**	**478**	**242**	**478**	**1697**	**1697**	**0**	**140**	**1.117**	**2.833**

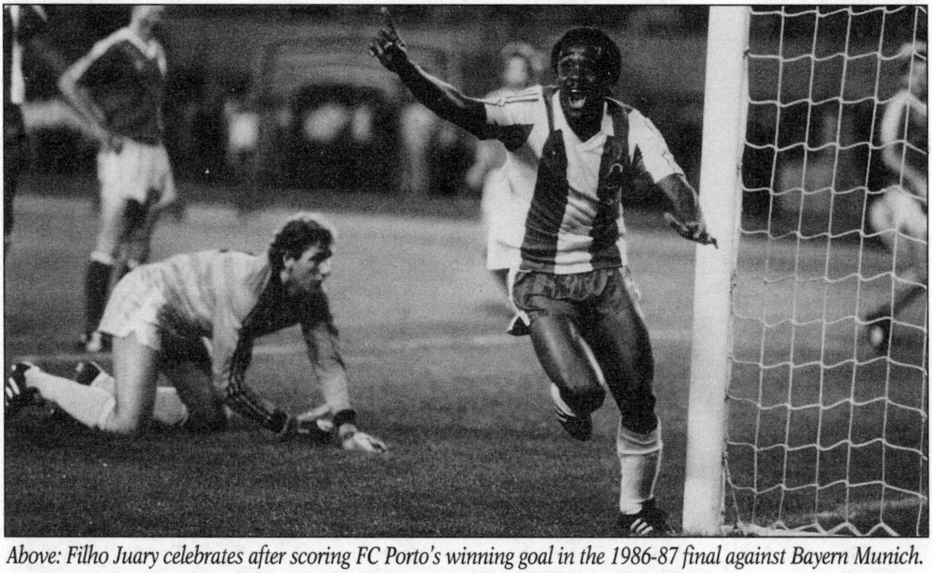

Above: Filho Juary celebrates after scoring FC Porto's winning goal in the 1986-87 final against Bayern Munich.

Club Performance by Points

1986-87 to 1990-91

Pos'n	Club	Cnty	Pts	P	W	D	L	F	A	Diff	B	Pts/P	F/P
1	Bayern Munich	FRG	52	31	19	6	6	62	25	37	8	1.677	2.000
2	Real Madrid	Esp	52	34	19	7	8	68	36	32	7	1.529	2.000
3	AC Milan	Ita	38	22	12	7	3	34	10	24	7	1.727	1.545
4	FC Porto	Por	35	23	14	3	6	52	20	32	4	1.522	2.261
5	Steaua Bucharest	Rom	34	23	13	3	7	42	26	16	5	1.478	1.826
6	Red Star Belgrade	Yug	32	19	11	6	2	43	16	27	4	1.684	2.263
7	Benfica	Por	31	17	11	3	3	30	5	25	6	1.824	1.765
8	Olympique Marseille	Fra	30	17	10	5	2	33	13	20	5	1.765	1.941
9	PSV Eindhoven	Ned	26	21	7	7	7	27	17	10	5	1.238	1.286
10	Anderlecht	Bel	17	12	6	3	3	14	13	1	2	1.417	1.167
11	Dinamo Kiev	URS	14	10	5	2	3	17	9	8	2	1.400	1.700
12	Rangers	Sco	14	12	5	3	4	20	13	7	1	1.167	1.667
13	Spartak Moscow	URS	14	12	4	4	4	13	12	1	2	1.167	1.083
14	Galatasaray	Tur	12	10	4	2	4	13	14	-1	2	1.200	1.300
15	IFK Gothenburg	Swe	11	6	5	0	1	13	7	6	1	1.833	2.167
16	Brøndby IF	Den	11	10	3	4	3	13	13	0	1	1.100	1.300
17	Girondins Bordeaux	Fra	10	6	3	3	0	6	1	5	1	1.667	1.000
18	FC Tirol	Aut	10	8	4	2	2	21	18	3	0	1.250	2.625
19	Sparta Prague	Tch	10	12	4	2	6	21	21	0	0	0.833	1.750
20	Malmö FF	Swe	10	10	2	6	2	11	13	-2	0	1.000	1.100
21	Górnik Zabrze	Pol	9	10	3	3	4	15	14	1	0	0.900	1.500
22	Dynamo Dresden	GDR	9	8	3	2	3	13	13	0	1	1.125	1.625
23	CSKA Sofia	Bul	9	12	3	2	7	15	21	-6	1	0.750	1.250
24	KV Mechelen	Bel	8	6	2	3	1	9	3	6	1	1.333	1.500
25	Celtic	Sco	8	8	3	2	3	9	6	3	0	1.000	1.125
26	Neuchâtel Xamax	Sui	8	8	4	0	4	14	13	1	0	1.000	1.750
27	Dnepr Dnepropetrovsk	URS	8	6	3	1	2	7	7	0	1	1.333	1.167
28	Club Bruges	Bel	8	8	3	2	3	7	10	-3	0	1.000	0.875
29	Napoli	Ita	7	6	2	3	1	6	3	3	0	1.167	1.000
30	Werder Bremen	FRG	7	6	2	2	2	6	4	2	1	1.167	1.000
31	Dynamo Berlin	GDR	7	8	3	1	4	12	15	-3	0	0.875	1.500
32	Juventus	Ita	6	4	3	0	1	12	1	11	0	1.500	3.000
33	Monaco	Fra	6	6	2	1	3	9	5	4	1	1.000	1.500
34	Rapid Vienna	Aut	6	6	3	0	3	10	7	3	0	1.000	1.667
35	Lech Poznań	Pol	6	4	3	0	1	9	9	0	0	1.500	2.250
36	Besiktas	Tur	6	6	2	1	3	7	12	-5	1	1.000	1.167
37	Austria Vienna	Aut	5	4	2	1	1	7	3	4	0	1.250	1.750
38	Lillestrøm SK	Nor	5	6	1	3	2	6	7	-1	0	0.833	1.000
39	TJ Vitkovice	Tch	5	4	2	1	1	4	5	-1	0	1.250	1.000
40	Honvéd	Hun	5	8	2	1	5	6	21	-15	0	0.625	0.750
41	Dinamo Bucharest	Rom	4	4	1	2	1	5	5	0	0	1.000	1.250
42	17 Nëntori Tirana	Alb	4	8	2	0	6	9	13	-4	0	0.500	1.125
43	HJK Helsinki	Fin	4	6	2	0	4	5	11	-6	0	0.667	0.833
44	Rosenborg BK	Nor	4	6	1	2	3	3	13	-10	0	0.667	0.500
45	AGF Aarhus	Den	3	4	1	1	2	4	3	1	0	0.750	1.000
46	AEK Athenes	Gre	3	4	1	1	2	6	7	-1	0	0.750	1.500
47	Omonia Nicosia	Cyp	3	6	1	1	4	4	14	-10	0	0.500	0.667
48	Larissa	Gre	2	2	1	0	1	3	3	0	0	1.000	1.500
49	Vojvodina Novi Sad	Yug	2	2	1	0	1	2	2	0	0	1.000	1.000
50	MTK-VM	Hun	2	2	1	0	1	2	4	-2	0	1.000	1.000
51	IBA Akureyri	Isl	2	2	1	0	1	1	3	-2	0	1.000	0.500
52	Young Boys Berne	Sui	2	2	1	0	1	1	5	-4	0	1.000	0.500
53	Sliema Wanderers	Mlt	2	2	1	0	1	1	5	-4	0	1.000	0.500

Pos'n	Club	Cnty	Pts	P	W	D	L	F	A	Diff	B	Pts/P	F/P
54	Apoel Nicosia	Cyp	2	4	1	0	3	5	10	-5	0	0.500	1.250
55	Linfield	Nir	2	6	0	2	4	5	10	-5	0	0.333	0.833
56	Panathinaikos	Gre	2	4	1	0	3	3	9	-6	0	0.500	0.750
57	Jeunesse Esch	Lux	2	4	1	0	3	3	11	-8	0	0.500	0.750
58	Hamrun Spartans	Mlt	2	4	1	0	3	2	10	-8	0	0.500	0.500
59	FC Kuusysi Lahti	Fin	2	4	1	0	3	3	13	-10	0	0.500	0.750
60	Valur Reykjavik	Isl	2	4	1	0	3	1	13	-12	0	0.500	0.250
61	Paris Saint-Germain	Fra	1	2	0	1	1	2	3	-1	0	0.500	1.000
62	Olympiakos Pireus	Gre	1	2	0	1	1	2	3	-1	0	0.500	1.000
63	Inter Milan	Ita	1	2	0	1	1	1	2	-1	0	0.500	0.500
64	Boreo Stara Zagora	Bul	1	2	0	1	1	1	3	-2	0	0.500	0.500
65	Glentoran	Nir	1	2	0	1	1	1	3	-2	0	0.500	0.500
66	Grasshoppers Zürich	Sui	1	2	0	1	1	2	5	-3	0	0.500	1.000
67	Ruch Chorzów	Pol	1	2	0	1	1	2	6	-4	0	0.500	1.000
68	St. Patrick's Athletic	Irl	1	2	0	1	1	1	5	-4	0	0.500	0.500
69	Shamrock Rovers	Irl	1	4	0	1	3	0	4	-4	0	0.250	0.000
70	Dinamo Tirana	Alb	1	4	0	1	3	1	8	-7	0	0.250	0.250
71	Fenerbahçe	Tur	0	2	0	0	2	2	5	-3	0	0.000	1.000
72	Örgryte IS	Swe	0	2	0	0	2	3	7	-4	0	0.000	1.500
73	Partizani Tirana	Alb	0	1	0	0	1	0	4	-4	0	0.000	0.000
74	Moss FK	Nor	0	2	0	0	2	0	4	-4	0	0.000	0.000
75	Levski Sofia	Bul	0	2	0	0	2	2	7	-5	0	0.000	1.000
76	Pezoporikos Larnaca	Cyp	0	2	0	0	2	2	7	-5	0	0.000	1.000
77	Derry City	Irl	0	2	0	0	2	1	6	-5	0	0.000	0.500
78	Union Luxembourg	Lux	0	2	0	0	2	1	6	-5	0	0.000	0.500
79	Lucerne	Sui	0	2	0	0	2	0	5	-5	0	0.000	0.000
80	Ujpesti Dózsa	Hun	0	2	0	0	2	0	5	-5	0	0.000	0.000
81	Avenir Beggen	Lux	0	2	0	0	2	0	6	-6	0	0.000	0.000
82	Vardar Skoplje	Yug	0	2	0	0	2	0	6	-6	0	0.000	0.000
83	Dundalk	Irl	0	2	0	0	2	0	8	-8	0	0.000	0.000
84	B1903 Odense	Den	0	2	0	0	2	1	10	-9	0	0.000	0.500
85	Spora Luxembourg	Lux	0	2	0	0	2	0	9	-9	0	0.000	0.000
86	Rabat Ajax	Mlt	0	2	0	0	2	0	10	-10	0	0.000	0.000
87	Valletta	Mlt	0	2	0	0	2	0	10	-10	0	0.000	0.000
88	Portadown	Nir	0	2	0	0	2	1	13	-12	0	0.000	0.500
89	Fram Reykjavik	Isl	0	4	0	0	4	0	15	-15	0	0.000	0.000
	Total		**662**	**592**	**233**	**126**	**233**	**830**	**830**	**0**	**70**	**1.118**	**2.804**

Participation Details 1955-56 to 1990-91 by Club

Albania

Club	Seasons Entered	Pts	P	W	D	L	F	A	Diff	B
Labinoti Elbasan	84-85	0	2	0	0	2	0	6	-6	–
Vllaznia Shkodër	78-79	2	2	1	0	1	3	4	-1	–
Dinamo Tirana	80-81, 86-87, 90-91	1	6	0	1	5	1	11	-10	–
17 Nëntori Tirana	65-66, 69-70, 70-71, 82-83, 88-89, 89-90	9	16	3	3	10	14	24	-10	–
Partizani Tirana	62-63, 63-64, 64-65, 71-72, 79-80, 81-82, 87-88	8	13	3	2	8	7	23	-16	–
Total times entered	**18** **Total**	**20**	**39**	**7**	**6**	**26**	**25**	**68**	**-43**	**–**

Austria

Club	Seasons Entered	Pts	P	W	D	L	F	A	Diff	B
FC Tirol	71-72, 72-73, 73-74, 75-76, 77-78, 89-90, 90-91	18	22	7	3	12	34	46	-12	1
Linzer ASK	65-66	0	2	0	0	2	2	5	-3	–
Vöest Linz	74-75	1	2	0	1	1	0	5	-5	–
Admira Wacker	66-67	1	2	0	1	1	0	1	-1	–
Austria Vienna	61-62, 62-63, 63-64, 69-70, 70-71, 76-77, 78-79, 79-80, 80-81, 81-82, 84-85, 85-86, 86-87	50	49	18	11	20	73	70	3	3
Rapid Vienna	55-56, 56-57, 57-58, 60-61, 64-65, 67-68, 68-69, 82-83, 83-84, 87-88, 88-89	57	49	24	4	21	89	69	20	5
Wiener Sport-Club	58-59, 59-60	14	12	4	4	4	21	18	3	2
Total times entered	**36** **Total**	**141**	**138**	**53**	**24**	**61**	**219**	**214**	**5**	**11**

Belgium

Club	Seasons Entered	Pts	P	W	D	L	F	A	Diff	B
Anderlecht	55-56, 56-57, 59-60, 62-63, 64-65, 65-66, 66-67,67-68, 68-69, 72-73, 74-75, 81-82, 85-86, 86-87, 87-88	82	70	31	11	28	120	115	5	9
Antwerp	57-58	0	2	0	0	2	1	8	-7	–
Beveren	79-80, 84-85	6	6	2	2	2	11	8	3	–
Club Bruges	73-74, 76-77, 77-78, 78-79, 80-81, 88-89, 90-91	37	31	14	5	12	51	39	12	4
Standard Liège	58-59, 61-62, 63-64, 69-70, 70-71, 71-72, 82-83, 83-84	54	40	23	3	14	72	47	25	5
Lierse	60-61	0	2	0	0	2	0	5	-5	–
KV Mechelen	89-90	8	6	2	3	1	9	3	6	1
RWD Molenbeek	75-76	4	4	2	0	2	6	9	-3	–
Total times entered	**36** **Total**	**191**	**161**	**74**	**24**	**63**	**270**	**234**	**36**	**19**

Bulgaria

Club	Seasons Entered	Pts	P	W	D	L	F	A	Diff	B
Trakia Plovdiv	63-64, 67-68, 85-86	5	8	2	1	5	8	11	-3	–
CSKA Sofia	56-57, 57-58, 58-59, 59-60, 60-61, 61-62, 62-63, 66-67, 69-70, 71-72, 72-73, 73-74, 75-76, 76-77, 80-81, 81-82, 82-83, 83-84, 87-88, 89-90, 90-91	93	86	35	15	36	124	125	-1	8
Levski Sofia	65-66, 70-71, 74-75, 77-78, 79-80, 84-85, 88-89	12	20	4	4	12	30	40	-10	–

Lokomotiv Sofia	64-65, 78-79		7	8	3	1	4	19	21	-2	–
Beroe Stara Zagora	86-87		1	2	0	1	1	1	3	-2	–
Total times entered	**34**	**Total**	**118**	**124**	**44**	**22**	**58**	**182**	**200**	**-18**	**8**

Cyprus

Club	Seasons Entered		Pts	P	W	D	L	F	A	Diff	B
Anorthosis Famagusta	63-64		0	2	0	0	2	1	6	-5	–
EPA Larnaca	70-71		0	2	0	0	2	0	16	-16	–
Pezoporikos Larnaca	88-89		0	2	0	0	2	2	7	-5	–
AEL Limassol	68-69		0	2	0	0	2	0	12	-12	–
Apoel Nicosia	65-66, 73-74, 80-81, 86-87, 90-91		4	10	2	0	8	7	27	-20	–
Olympiakos Nicosia	67-68, 69-70, 71-72		1	6	0	1	5	4	36	-32	–
Omonia Nicosia	66-67, 72-73, 75-76, 76-77, 77-78, 78-79, 79-80, 81-82, 82-83, 83-84, 84-85, 85-86, 87-88, 89-90		24	36	11	2	23	44	87	-43	–
Total times entered	**26**	**Total**	**29**	**60**	**13**	**3**	**44**	**58**	**191**	**-133**	**–**

Czechoslovakia

Club	Seasons Entered		Pts	P	W	D	L	F	A	Diff	B
Inter Bratislava	59-60		5	4	2	1	1	8	6	2	–
Slovan Bratislava	56-57, 70-71, 74-75, 75-76		13	12	6	1	5	17	19	-2	–
Zbrojovka Brno	78-79		5	4	1	3	0	7	5	2	–
Spartak Hradec Králové	60-61		5	4	1	2	1	2	5	-3	1
Banik Ostrava	76-77, 80-81, 81-82		14	14	5	3	6	18	23	-5	1
Bohemians Prague	83-84		6	4	3	0	1	7	2	5	–
Dukla Prague	57-58, 58-59, 61-62, 62-63, 63-64, 64-65, 66-67, 77-78, 79-80, 82-83		59	45	22	10	13	75	58	17	5
Sparta Prague	65-66, 67-68, 84-85, 85-86, 87-88, 88-89, 89-90, 90-91		38	32	14	7	11	53	48	5	3
Spartak Trnava	68-69, 69-70, 71-72, 72-73, 73-74		37	24	13	7	4	44	20	24	4
TJ Vitkovice	86-87		5	4	2	1	1	4	5	-1	–
Total times entered	**35**	**Total**	**187**	**147**	**69**	**35**	**43**	**235**	**191**	**44**	**14**

Denmark

Club	Seasons Entered		Pts	P	W	D	L	F	A	Diff	B
AGF Aarhus	55-56, 56-57, 57-58, 60-61, 87-88		17	18	6	4	8	23	25	-2	1
AB Copenhagen	68-69		3	4	1	1	2	4	5	-1	–
B 1903 Copenhagen	70-71, 71-72, 77-78		5	8	2	1	5	7	11	-4	–
KB Copenhagen	58-59, 69-70, 75-76, 81-82		10	13	4	2	7	19	25	-6	–
Brøndby IF	86-87, 88-89, 89-90		11	10	3	4	3	13	13	0	1
Hvidovre IF	67-68, 74-75, 82-83		6	8	1	4	3	13	19	-6	–
Esbjerg FB	62-63, 63-64, 66-67, 80-81		9	12	3	3	6	11	28	-17	–
Køge BK	76-77		0	2	0	0	2	1	7	-6	–
Lyngby BK	84-85		5	4	2	1	1	7	2	5	–
OB Odense	78-79, 83-84		1	4	0	1	3	3	10	-7	–
B 1909 Odense	59-60, 64-65, 65-66		1	6	0	1	5	6	21	-15	–
B 1913 Odense	61-62, 90-91		4	6	2	0	4	16	24	-8	–
Vejle BK	72-73, 73-74, 79-80, 85-86		10	12	3	4	5	13	22	-9	–
Total times entered	**36**	**Total**	**82**	**107**	**27**	**26**	**54**	**136**	**212**	**-76**	**2**

East Germany

Club	Seasons Entered		Pts	P	W	D	L	F	A	Diff	B
Dynamo Berlin	79-80, 80-81, 81-82, 82-83, 83-84, 84-85, 85-86, 86-87, 87-88, 88-89		40	38	15	8	15	54	52	2	2
Karl-Marx-Stadt	57-58, 58-59, 60-61, 67-68		15	18	5	4	9	28	28	0	1

Dynamo Dresden	71-72, 73-74, 76-77, 77-78, 78-79, 89-90, 90-91		33	30	12	6	12	49	43	6	3
Vorwärts Frankfurt/Oder	59-60, 61-62, 62-63, 65-66, 66-67, 69-70		22	23	10	1	12	37	34	3	1
Carl Zeiss Jena	63-64, 70-71		11	8	5	0	3	12	11	1	1
Chemie Leipzig	64-65		0	2	0	0	2	2	6	-4	–
Magdeburg	72-73, 74-75, 75-76		6	8	3	0	5	15	11	4	–
Total times entered	**33**	**Total**	**127**	**127**	**50**	**19**	**58**	**197**	**185**	**12**	**8**

England

Club	Seasons Entered		Pts	P	W	D	L	F	A	Diff	B
Aston Villa	81-82, 82-83		25	15	9	3	3	24	10	14	4
Burnley	60-61		5	4	2	0	2	8	8	0	1
Derby County	72-73, 75-76		16	12	6	2	4	18	12	6	2
Ipswich Town	62-63		6	4	3	0	1	16	5	11	–
Leeds United	69-70, 74-75		30	17	12	1	4	42	11	31	5
Everton	63-64, 70-71		10	8	2	5	1	12	6	6	1
Liverpool	64-65, 66-67, 73-74, 76-77, 77-78, 78-79, 79-80, 80-81, 81-82, 82-83, 83-84, 84-85		128	77	48	13	16	159	64	95	19
Arsenal	71-72		9	6	4	0	2	13	4	9	1
Tottenham Hotspur	61-62		11	8	4	1	3	21	13	8	2
Manchester City	68-69		1	2	0	1	1	1	2	-1	–
Manchester United	56-57, 57-58, 65-66, 67-68, 68-69		70	41	26	7	8	100	45	55	11
Nottingham Forest	78-79, 79-80, 80-81		34	20	12	4	4	32	14	18	6
Wolverhampton Wanderers	58-59, 59-60		7	8	2	2	4	12	16	-4	1
Total times entered	**35**	**Total**	**352**	**222**	**130**	**39**	**53**	**458**	**210**	**248**	**53**

Finland

Club	Seasons Entered		Pts	P	W	D	L	F	A	Diff	B
HIFK Helsinki	60-61, 62-63		0	4	0	0	4	5	12	-7	–
HJK Helsinki	65-66, 74-75, 79-80, 82-83, 86-87, 88-89, 89-90		10	18	5	0	13	17	49	-32	–
HPS Helsinki	58-59		0	2	0	0	2	0	7	-7	–
KPV Kokkola	70-71		0	2	0	0	2	0	14	-14	–
KuPS Kuopio	67-68, 75-76, 77-78		1	6	0	1	5	4	21	-17	–
FC Kuusysi Lahti	83-84, 85-86, 87-88, 90-91		10	12	4	1	7	11	23	-12	1
Reipas Lahti	64-65, 68-69, 71-72		6	8	2	2	4	8	30	-22	–
OPS Oulu	80-81, 81-82		1	4	0	1	3	2	19	-17	–
Ilves Tampere	84-85		0	2	0	0	2	1	6	-5	–
TPS Turku	69-70, 72-73, 73-74, 76-77		2	10	1	0	9	4	28	-24	–
Haka Valkeakoski	61-62, 63-64, 66-67, 78-79		2	8	1	0	7	7	28	-21	–
Total times entered	**32**	**Total**	**32**	**76**	**13**	**5**	**58**	**59**	**237**	**-178**	**1**

France

Club	Seasons Entered		Pts	P	W	D	L	F	A	Diff	B
Girondins Bordeaux	84-85, 85-86, 87-88		23	16	6	8	2	17	12	5	3
Olympique Marseille	71-72, 72-73, 89-90, 90-91		35	23	12	6	5	39	24	15	5
Monaco	61-62, 63-64, 78-79, 82-83, 88-89		13	18	4	4	10	25	23	2	1
Nantes	65-66, 66-67, 73-74, 77-78, 80-81, 83-84		16	18	5	6	7	25	28	-3	–
Nice	56-57, 59-60		18	14	7	2	5	29	25	4	2
Paris Saint-Germain	86-87		1	2	0	1	1	2	3	-1	–
Stade Reims	55-56, 58-59, 60-61, 62-63		38	24	14	3	7	63	30	33	7
Saint-Etienne	57-58, 64-65, 67-68, 68-69, 69-70, 70-71, 74-75, 75-76, 76-77, 81-82		51	41	19	7	15	50	44	6	6

Strasbourg	70-80		8	6	3	1	2	8	6	2	1
Total times entered	**36**	**Total**	**203**	**162**	**70**	**38**	**54**	**258**	**195**	**63**	**25**

Greece

Club	Seasons Entered		Pts	P	W	D	L	F	A	Diff	B
AEK Athenes	63-64, 68-69, 71-72, 78-79, 79-80, 89-90		17	20	6	4	10	33	42	-9	1
Panathinaikos	60-61, 61-62, 62-63, 64-65, 65-66, 69-70, 70-71,72-73, 77-78, 84-85, 86-87, 90-91		41	43	12	12	19	53	63	-10	5
Larissa	88-89		2	2	1	0	1	3	3	0	–
Olympiakos Pireus	59-60, 66-67, 67-68, 73-74, 74-75, 75-76, 80-81, 81-82, 82-83, 83-84, 87-88		20	28	7	6	15	25	43	-18	–
PAOK Salonika	76-77, 85-86		3	6	1	1	4	5	12	-7	–
Total times entered	**32**	**Total**	**83**	**99**	**27**	**23**	**49**	**119**	**163**	**-44**	**6**

Hungary

Club	Seasons Entered		Pts	P	W	D	L	F	A	Diff	B
Csepel	59-60		1	2	0	1	1	3	4	-1	–
Ferencváros	63-64, 65-66, 69-70, 76-77, 81-82		21	18	9	2	7	39	35	4	1
Honvéd	56-57, 80-81, 84-85, 85-86, 86-87, 88-89, 89-90		22	22	10	2	10	35	39	-4	–
MTK-VM	55-56, 58-59, 87-88		12	10	5	1	4	26	22	4	1
Vasas SC	57-58, 61-62, 62-63, 66-67, 67-68, 77-78		33	27	12	6	9	62	34	28	3
Rába ETO	64-65, 82-83, 83-84		17	14	7	1	6	27	30	-3	2
Ujpesti Dózsa	60-61, 70-71, 71-72, 72-73, 73-74, 74-75, 75-76, 78-79, 79-80, 90-91		46	40	17	8	15	65	63	2	4
Total times entered	**35**	**Total**	**152**	**133**	**60**	**21**	**52**	**257**	**227**	**30**	**11**

Iceland

Club	Seasons Entered		Pts	P	W	D	L	F	A	Diff	B
IA Akranes	71-72, 75-76, 76-77, 78-79, 84-85, 85-86		5	14	1	3	10	14	36	-22	–
IBA Akureyri	90-91		2	2	1	0	1	1	3	-2	–
IBK Keflavik	65-66, 70-71, 72-73, 74-75		0	8	0	0	8	5	35	-30	–
Fram Reykjavik	73-74, 87-88, 89-90		0	6	0	0	6	2	26	-24	–
KR Reykjavik	64-65, 66-67, 69-70		0	6	0	0	6	7	35	-28	–
Valur Reykjavik	67-68, 68-69, 77-78, 79-80, 81-82, 86-87, 88-89		7	16	2	3	11	9	50	-41	–
Vikingur Reykjavik	82-83, 83-84		0	4	0	0	4	3	8	-5	–
IBV Vestmannaeyjar	80-81		1	2	0	1	1	1	2	-1	–
Total times entered	**27**	**Total**	**15**	**58**	**4**	**7**	**47**	**42**	**195**	**-153**	**–**

Italy

Club	Seasons Entered		Pts	P	W	D	L	F	A	Diff	B
Bologna	64-65		3	3	1	1	1	2	2	0	–
Cagliari	70-71		4	4	2	0	2	5	5	0	–
Fiorentina	56-57, 69-70		22	13	7	4	2	14	11	3	4
AC Milan	55-56, 57-58, 59-60, 62-63, 63-64, 68-69, 69-70, 79-80, 88-89, 89-90, 90-91		108	68	38	13	17	150	70	80	19

Inter Milan	63-64, 64-65, 65-66, 66-67, 71-72, 80-81, 89-90	84	51	27	14	10	74	38	36	16
Napoli	87-88, 90-91	7	6	2	3	1	6	3	3	–
Roma	83-84	14	9	5	1	3	14	7	7	3
Torino	76-77	4	4	1	2	1	4	4	0	–
Juventus	58-59, 60-61, 61-62, 67-68, 72-73, 73-74, 75-76, 77-78, 78-79, 81-82, 82-83, 84-85, 85-86, 86-87	112	77	41	15	21	124	70	54	15
Verona	85-86	5	4	2	1	1	5	4	1	–
Total times entered	**41** **Total**	**363**	**239**	**126**	**54**	**59**	**398**	**214**	**184**	**57**

Luxembourg

Club	Seasons Entered	Pts	P	W	D	L	F	A	Diff	B
Avenir Beggen	69-70, 82-83, 84-85, 86-87	0	8	0	0	8	0	44	-44	–
Aris Bonnevoie	64-65, 66-67, 72-73	1	6	0	1	5	6	25	-19	–
Red Boys Differdange	79-80	2	2	1	0	1	3	7	-4	–
Stade Dudelange	57-58, 65-66	0	4	0	0	4	1	32	-31	–
Jeunesse Esch	58-59, 59-60, 60-61, 63-64, 67-68, 68-69, 70-71, 73-74, 74-75, 75-76, 76-77, 77-78, 80-81, 83-84, 85-86, 87-88, 88-89	15	39	6	3	30	41	132	-91	–
Spora Luxembourg	56-57, 61-62, 89-90	2	7	1	0	6	7	36	-29	–
Union Luxembourg	62-63, 71-72, 90-91	0	6	0	0	6	2	24	-22	–
Progrès Niedercorn	78-79, 81-82	1	4	0	1	3	1	17	-16	–
Total times entered	**35** **Total**	**21**	**76**	**8**	**5**	**63**	**61**	**317**	**-256**	**–**

Malta

Club	Seasons Entered	Pts	P	W	D	L	F	A	Diff	B
Hamrun Spartans	83-84, 87-88, 88-89	2	6	1	0	5	2	16	-14	–
Valletta	63-64, 74-75, 78-79, 80-81, 84-85, 90-91	2	12	1	0	11	5	54	-49	–
Floriana	62-63, 68-69, 70-71, 73-74, 75-76, 77-78	2	12	0	2	10	3	49	-46	–
Hibernians	61-62, 67-68, 69-70, 79-80, 81-82, 82-83	4	12	1	2	9	8	36	-28	–
Rabat Ajax	85-86, 86-87	0	4	0	0	4	0	20	-20	–
Sliema Wanderers	64-65, 65-66, 66-67, 71-72, 72-73, 76-77, 89-90	9	16	4	1	11	11	41	-30	–
Total times entered	**30** **Total**	**19**	**62**	**7**	**5**	**50**	**29**	**216**	**-187**	**–**

Northern Ireland

Club	Seasons Entered	Pts	P	W	D	L	F	A	Diff	B
Crusaders	73-74, 76-77	0	4	0	0	4	0	19	-19	–
Distillery	63-64	1	2	0	1	1	3	8	-5	–
Glentoran	64-65, 67-68, 68-69, 70-71, 77-78, 81-82, 88-89	12	18	3	6	9	18	29	-11	–
Linfield	59-60, 61-62, 62-63, 66-67, 69-70, 71-72, 75-76, 78-79, 79-80, 80-81, 82-83, 83-84, 84-85, 85-86, 86-87, 87-88, 89-90	21	39	4	12	23	43	83	-40	1
Coleraine	74-75	0	2	0	0	2	1	11	-10	–
Glenavon	57-58	1	2	0	1	1	0	3	-3	–
Ards	58-59	0	2	0	0	2	3	10	-7	–
Portadown	90-91	0	2	0	0	2	1	13	-12	–
Derry City*	65-66	2	3	1	0	2	8	15	-7	–
Total times entered	**32** **Total**	**37**	**74**	**8**	**20**	**46**	**77**	**191**	**-114**	**1**

Norway

Club	Seasons Entered	Pts	P	W	D	L	F	A	Diff	B
Strømgodset IF	71-72,	0	2	0	0	2	1	7	-6	–
Fredrikstad FK	60-61, 61-62, 62-63	3	8	1	1	6	6	22	-16	–
IK Start	79-80, 81-82	0	4	0	0	4	2	10	-8	–
Lillestrøm SK	77-78, 78-79, 87-88, 90-91	11	12	3	5	4	10	15	-5	–
Moss FK	88-89	0	2	0	0	2	0	4	-4	–
FK Skeid	67-68	1	2	0	1	1	1	2	-1	–
SFK Lyn	63-64, 64-65, 65-66, 69-70	4	10	2	0	8	13	40	-27	–
Vålerengen SIF	66-67, 82-83, 84-85, 85-86	4	8	1	2	5	8	18	-10	–
IL Viking	73-74, 74-75, 75-76, 76-77, 80-81, 83-84	3	12	1	1	10	11	28	-17	–
Rosenborg BK	68-69, 70-71, 72-73, 86-87, 89-90	5	12	1	3	8	9	31	-22	–
Total times entered	**31** **Total**	**31**	**72**	**9**	**13**	**50**	**61**	**177**	**-116**	**–**

Netherlands

Club	Seasons Entered	Pts	P	W	D	L	F	A	Diff	B
AZ'67 Alkmaar	81-82	5	4	2	1	1	8	6	2	–
Ajax	57-58, 60-61, 66-67, 67-68, 68-69, 70-71, 71-72, 72-73, 73-74, 77-78, 79-80, 80-81, 82-83, 83-84, 85-86	116	75	42	15	18	141	74	67	17
FC Amsterdam	64-65	10	6	4	1	1	13	4	9	1
PSV Eindhoven	55-56, 63-64, 75-76, 76-77, 78-79, 86-87, 87-88, 88-89, 89-90	58	45	19	12	14	79	43	36	8
Haarlem	56-57	0	2	0	0	2	3	6	-3	–
Feyenoord	61-62, 62-63, 65-66, 69-70, 70-71, 71-72, 74-75, 84-85	56	39	20	10	9	90	41	49	6
Sparta Rotterdam	59-60	7	6	3	0	3	12	11	1	1
Utrecht	58-59	0	2	0	0	2	4	6	-2	–
Total times entered	**37** **Total**	**252**	**179**	**90**	**39**	**50**	**350**	**191**	**159**	**33**

Poland

Club	Seasons Entered	Pts	P	W	D	L	F	A	Diff	B
Polonia Bytom	58-59, 62-63	4	6	2	0	4	7	13	-6	–
Szombierki Bytom	80-81	2	4	1	0	3	4	7	-3	–
Ruch Chorzów	74-75, 75-76, 79-80, 89-90	15	14	5	4	5	20	25	-5	1
Wisla Kraków	78-79	7	6	2	2	2	10	11	-1	1
LKS Lódź	59-60	2	2	1	0	1	2	6	-4	–
Widzew Lódź	81-82, 82-83	11	10	4	1	5	21	20	1	2
Stal Mielec	73-74, 76-77	0	4	0	0	4	2	6	-4	–
Lech Poznań	83-84, 84-85, 90-91	8	8	4	0	4	11	18	-7	–
Gwardia Warsaw	55-56, 57-58	4	5	1	2	2	6	9	-3	–
Legia Warsaw	56-57, 60-61, 69-70, 70-71	27	18	11	2	5	29	16	13	3
Slask Wroclaw	77-78	1	2	0	1	1	2	5	-3	–
Górnik Zabrze	61-62, 63-64, 64-65, 65-66, 66-67, 67-68, 71-72, 72-73, 85-86, 86-87, 87-88, 88-89	49	43	21	6	16	70	64	-6	1
Total times entered	**35** **Total**	**130**	**122**	**52**	**18**	**52**	**184**	**200**	**-16**	**8**

Portugal

Club	Seasons Entered	Pts	P	W	D	L	F	A	Diff	B
Benfica	57-58, 60-61, 61-62, 62-63, 63-64, 64-65, 65-66, 67-68, 68-69, 69-70, 71-72, 72-73, 73-74, 75-76, 76-77, 77-78, 81-82, 83-84, 84-85, 87-88,	179	123	63	25	35	244	134	110	28

Club	Seasons Entered	Pts	P	W	D	L	F	A	Diff	B
	89-90									
Sporting Lisbon	55-56, 58-59, 61-62, 62-63, 66-67, 70-71, 74-75, 80-81, 82-83	24	28	9	5	14	41	48	-7	1
FC Porto	56-57, 59-60, 78-79, 79-80, 85-86, 86-87, 87-88, 88-89, 90-91	47	37	19	5	13	69	41	28	4
Total times entered	**39** **Total**	**250**	**188**	**91**	**35**	**62**	**354**	**223**	**131**	**33**

Republic of Ireland

Club	Seasons Entered	Pts	P	W	D	L	F	A	Diff	B
Athlone Town	81-82, 83-84	2	4	0	2	2	7	14	-7	–
Cork Celtic	74-75	0	2	0	0	2	1	7	-6	–
Cork Hibernians	71-72	0	2	0	0	2	1	7	-6	–
Derry City*	89-90	0 2 } 2	2 3 } 5	0 1 } 1	0 0 } 0	2 2 } 4	1 8 } 9	6 13 } 19	-5 -7 } -12	– – } –
Bohemians	75-76, 78-79	4	6	1	2	3	4	13	-9	–
Drumcondra	58-59, 61-62, 65-66	2	7	1	0	6	4	27	-23	–
Shamrock Rovers	57-58, 59-60, 64-65, 84-85, 85-86, 86-87, 87-88	4	14	0	4	10	7	28	-21	–
Shelbourne	62-63	0	2	0	0	2	1	7	-6	–
St. Patrick's Athletic	90-91	1	2	0	1	1	1	5	-4	–
Dundalk	63-64, 67-68, 76-77, 79-80, 82-83, 88-89	9	16	3	3	10	12	38	-26	–
Limerick	60-61, 80-81	0	4	0	0	4	4	17	-13	–
Sligo Rovers	77-78	0	2	0	0	2	0	6	-6	–
Waterford United	66-67, 68-69, 69-70, 70-71, 72-73, 73-74	6	14	3	0	11	15	47	-32	–
Total times entered	**34** **Total**	**28**	**77**	**8**	**12**	**57**	**58**	**222**	**-164**	**–**

Romania

Club	Seasons Entered	Pts	P	W	D	L	F	A	Diff	B
UT Arad	69-70, 70-71	2	6	0	2	4	3	17	-14	–
Dinamo Bucharest	56-57, 62-63, 63-64, 64-65, 65-66, 71-72, 73-74, 75-76, 77-78, 82-83, 83-84, 84-85, 90-91	52	52	21	8	23	84	83	1	2
Rapid Bucharest	67-68	3	4	1	1	2	3	3	0	–
Steaua Bucharest	57-58, 61-62, 68-69, 76-77, 78-79, 85-86, 86-87, 87-88, 88-89, 89-90	56	43	20	8	15	68	52	16	8
Universitatea Craiova	74-75, 80-81, 81-82	9	10	3	2	5	12	14	-2	1
Arges Pitesti	72-73, 79-80	8	8	4	0	4	13	10	3	–
Petrolul Ploiesti	58-59, 59-60, 66-67	5	8	2	1	5	8	15	-7	–
Total times entered	**34** **Total**	**135**	**131**	**51**	**22**	**58**	**191**	**194**	**-3**	**11**

Scotland

Club	Seasons Entered	Pts	P	W	D	L	F	A	Diff	B
Aberdeen	80-81, 84-85, 85-86	15	12	5	4	3	14	12	2	1
Dundee	62-63	12	8	5	0	3	20	14	6	2
Dundee United	83-84	13	8	5	1	2	14	5	9	2
Heart of Midlothian	58-59, 60-61	2	4	1	0	3	4	11	-7	–
Hibernian	55-56	9	6	3	1	2	9	5	4	2
Celtic	66-67, 67-68, 68-69, 69-70, 70-71, 71-72, 72-73, 73-74, 74-75, 77-78, 79-80, 81-82, 82-83, 86-87, 88-89	112	78	42	15	21	143	73	70	13
Rangers	56-57, 57-58, 59-60, 61-62, 63-64, 64-65, 75-76, 76-77, 78-79, 87-88, 89-90, 90-91	64	55	25	8	22	92	90	2	6
Kilmarnock	65-66	4	4	1	2	1	4	7	-3	–

Total times entered	**36**	**Total**	**231**	**175**	**87**	**31**	**57**	**300**	**217**	**83**	**26**

Spain

Club	Seasons Entered		Pts	P	W	D	L	F	A	Diff	B
Barcelona	59-60, 60-61, 74-75, 85-86		56	35	19	8	8	71	34	37	10
Athletic Bilbao	56-57, 83-84, 84-85		14	12	5	3	4	22	20	2	1
Atlético Madrid	58-59, 66-67, 70-71, 73-74, 77-78		57	39	21	7	11	65	39	26	8
Real Madrid	55-56, 56-57, 57-58, 58-59, 59-60, 60-61, 61-62, 62-63, 63-64, 64-65, 65-66, 66-67, 67-68, 68-69, 69-70, 72-73, 75-76, 76-77, 78-79, 79-80, 80-81, 86-87, 87-88, 88-89, 89-90, 90-91		271	170	101	25	44	401	187	214	44
Real Sociedad	81-82, 82-83		12	10	4	2	4	11	9	2	2
Seville	57-58		7	6	2	2	2	9	13	-4	1
Valencia	71-72		6	6	2	2	2	6	5	1	–
Total times entered	**42**	**Total**	**423**	**278**	**154**	**49**	**75**	**585**	**307**	**278**	**66**

Sweden

Club	Seasons Entered		Pts	P	W	D	L	F	A	Diff	B
Åtvidaberg FF	73-74, 74-75		9	8	4	0	4	12	12	0	1
IFK Gothenburg	58-59, 59-60, 61-62, 70-71, 83-84, 84-85, 85-86, 88-89		42	36	17	4	15	75	62	13	4
Örgryte IS	86-87		0	2	0	0	2	3	7	-4	–
Halmstad SBK	77-78, 80-81		3	4	1	1	2	4	6	-2	–
Malmö FF	60-61, 64-65, 66-67, 68-69, 71-72, 72-73, 75-76, 76-77, 78-79, 87-88, 89-90, 90-91		45	41	15	11	15	45	58	-13	4
IFK Norrköping	56-57, 57-58, 62-63, 63-64		9	12	2	5	5	14	20	-6	–
Djurgården SIF	55-56, 65-66, 67-68		6	8	2	1	5	7	16	-9	1
Öster SIF	69-70, 79-80, 81-82, 82-83		3	8	1	1	6	3	14	-11	–
Total times entered	**36**	**Total**	**117**	**119**	**42**	**23**	**54**	**163**	**195**	**-32**	**10**

Switzerland

Club	Seasons Entered		Pts	P	W	D	L	F	A	Diff	B
FC Basle	67-68, 69-70, 70-71, 72-73, 73-74, 77-78, 80-81		23	22	10	2	10	43	40	3	1
Young Boys Berne	57-58, 58-59, 59-60, 60-61, 86-87		21	17	7	5	5	29	31	-2	2
Servette	55-56, 61-62, 62-63, 79-80, 85-86		16	17	6	4	7	27	30	-3	–
La Chaux-de-Fonds	64-65		4	4	1	2	1	5	9	-4	–
Lausanne-Sports	65-66		1	2	0	1	1	0	4	-4	–
Lucerne	89-90		0	2	0	0	2	0	5	-5	–
Neuchâtel Xamax	87-88, 88-89		8	8	4	0	4	14	13	1	–
FC Zürich	63-64, 66-67, 68-69, 74-75, 75-76, 76-77, 81-82		28	27	11	2	14	36	49	-13	4
Grasshoppers Zürich	56-57, 71-72, 78-79, 82-83, 83-84, 84-85, 90-91		19	24	6	5	13	42	44	-2	2
Total times entered	**36**	**Total**	**120**	**123**	**45**	**21**	**57**	**196**	**225**	**-29**	**9**

Turkey

Club	Seasons Entered		Pts	P	W	D	L	F	A	Diff	B
Besiktas	58-59, 60-61, 66-67, 67-68, 82-83, 86-87, 90-91		10	16	3	3	10	11	30	-19	1
Fenerbahçe	59-60, 61-62, 64-65, 65-66, 68-69, 70-71, 74-75, 75-76, 78-79, 83-84,		22	33	9	4	20	30	70	-40	–

Club	Seasons Entered		Pts	P	W	D	L	F	A	Diff	B
	85-86, 89-90										
Galatasaray	56-57, 62-63, 63-64, 69-70, 71-72, 72-73, 73-74, 87-88, 88-89		38	35	13	8	14	45	52	-7	4
Trabzonspor	76-77, 77-78, 79-80, 80-81, 81-82, 84-85		13	14	6	1	7	12	19	-7	–
Total times entered	**34**	**Total**	**83**	**98**	**31**	**16**	**51**	**98**	**171**	**-73**	**5**

USSR

Club	Seasons Entered		Pts	P	W	D	L	F	A	Diff	B
Dnepr Dnepropetrovsk	84-85, 89-90		15	12	5	3	4	15	13	2	2
Ararat Erevan	74-75		11	6	5	0	1	14	5	9	1
Dinamo Kiev	67-68, 69-70, 72-73, 75-76, 76-77, 78-79, 81-82, 82-83, 86-87, 87-88		75	52	28	11	13	72	42	30	8
Zenit Leningrad	85-86		6	4	3	0	1	7	4	3	–
Dinamo Minsk	83-84		9	6	3	2	1	13	8	5	1
CSKA Moscow	71-72		5	4	2	1	1	5	3	2	–
Spartak Moscow	70-71, 80-81, 88-89, 90-91		24	20	8	5	7	29	20	9	3
Torpedo Moscow	66-67, 77-78		3	4	0	3	1	0	1	-1	–
Dinamo Tbilisi	79-80		2	4	1	0	3	7	8	-1	–
Zaria Voroshilovgrad	73-74		5	4	2	1	1	3	1	2	–
Total times entered	**24**	**Total**	**155**	**116**	**57**	**26**	**33**	**165**	**105**	**60**	**15**

West Germany

Club	Seasons Entered		Pts	P	W	D	L	F	A	Diff	B
Werder Bremen	65-66, 88-89		13	10	5	2	3	17	7	10	1
Eintracht Braunschweig	67-68		5	5	2	0	3	5	5	0	1
Cologne	62-63, 64-65, 78-79		25	17	7	8	2	27	19	8	3
Borussia Dortmund	56-57, 57-58, 63-64		22	18	8	3	7	44	30	14	3
Rot-Weiss Essen	55-56		1	2	0	1	1	1	5	-4	–
Eintracht Frankfurt	59-60		13	7	4	2	1	23	15	8	3
Schalke 04	58-59		9	7	3	2	2	13	13	0	1
Hamburg	60-61, 79-80, 82-83, 83-84		43	27	16	3	8	53	31	22	8
Bor. Mönchengladbach	70-71, 71-72, 75-76, 76-77, 77-78		46	31	15	10	6	69	31	38	6
Bayern Munich	69-70, 72-73, 73-74, 74-75, 75-76, 76-77, 80-81, 81-82, 85-86, 86-87, 87-88, 89-90, 90-91		159	94	58	18	18	210	87	123	25
1860 Munich	66-67		6	4	3	0	1	12	4	8	–
Nuremberg	61-62, 68-69		12	8	5	1	2	16	14	2	1
Saarbrücken	55-56		2	2	1	0	1	5	7	-2	–
VFB Stuttgart	84-85		2	2	0	2	0	3	3	0	–
Total times entered	**39**	**Total**	**358**	**234**	**127**	**52**	**55**	**498**	**271**	**227**	**52**

Yugoslavia

Club	Seasons Entered		Pts	P	W	D	L	F	A	Diff	B
Red Star Belgrade	56-57, 57-58, 59-60, 60-61, 64-65, 68-69, 69-70, 70-71, 73-74, 77-78, 80-81, 81-82, 84-85, 86-87, 88-89, 90-91		103	76	39	13	24	164	103	61	12
Partizan Belgrade	55-56, 61-62, 62-63, 63-64, 65-66, 76-77, 78-79, 83-84		35	33	13	4	16	55	52	3	5
Vojvodina Novi Sad	66-67, 89-90		12	9	5	1	3	10	9	1	1
Sarajevo	67-68, 85-86		4	6	1	2	3	8	9	-1	–
Zeljeznicar Sarajevo	72-73		0	2	0	0	2	1	4	-3	–
Vardar Skoplje	87-88		0	2	0	0	2	0	6	-6	2
Hajduk Split	71-72, 74-75, 75-76, 79-80		28	18	12	2	4	41	18	23	–
Dinamo Zagreb	58-59, 82-83		3	4	1	1	2	4	7	-3	–
Total times entered	**36**	**Total**	**185**	**150**	**71**	**23**	**56**	**283**	**208**	**75**	**20**

National Classification by Cumulative Year-by-Year Index

1955-56 to 1990-91

Pos	Cnty	Total	5556	5657	5758	5859	5960	6061	6162	6263	6364	6465	6566	6667	6768	6869	6970
1	Esp	357.000	13.000	13.000	10.500	15.000	14.000	9.000	19.000	1.000	17.000	10.000	15.000	4.500	11.000	6.000	4.000
2	FRG	332.500	1.5000	5.000	6.000	9.000	13.000	9.000	11.000	2.000	11.000	10.000	6.000	6.000	5.000	1.000	2.000
3	Ita	313.500	9.000	12.000	16.000	2.000	3.000	2.000	10.000	17.000	12.500	8.000	8.000	18.000	12.000	12.000	8.000
4	Eng	295.500	–	12.000	13.000	1.000	6.000	5.000	11.000	6.000	1.000	15.000	16.000	5.000	16.000	7.000	14.000
5	Sco	231.000	9.000	2.000	2.000	2.000	13.000	0.000	11.000	12.000	0.000	11.000	4.000	18.000	1.000	7.000	14.000
6	Ned	228.000	2.000	0.000	6.000	0.000	7.000	1.000	5.000	14.000	10.000	10.000	2.000	9.000	1.000	16.000	16.000
7	Por	225.500	1.000	0.000	1.000	4.000	0.000	18.000	6.500	9.000	5.000	16.000	8.000	0.000	14.000	6.000	6.000
8	Fra	203.000	13.000	8.000	2.000	15.000	10.000	6.000	0.000	4.000	3.000	1.000	1.000	4.000	6.000	2.000	2.000
9	Bel	191.000	0.000	0.000	0.000	9.000	0.000	0.000	12.000	7.000	2.000	3.000	8.000	4.000	5.000	5.000	8.000
10	Tch	187.000	–	4.000	2.000	5.000	5.000	5.000	8.000	9.000	9.000	4.000	8.000	14.000	9.000	13.000	5.000
11	Yug	185.000	6.000	9.000	9.000	1.000	1.000	0.000	3.000	0.000	7.000	2.000	12.000	10.000	4.000	1.000	6.000
12	URS	155.000	–	–	–	–	–	–	–	–	–	–	–	1.000	4.000	–	5.000
13	Hun	152.000	6.000	1.000	12.000	4.000	1.000	6.000	0.000	6.000	2.000	11.000	9.000	4.000	10.000	–	2.000
14	Aut	141.000	4.000	2.000	2.000	6.000	8.000	13.000	4.000	6.000	2.000	4.000	0.000	1.000	6.000	7.000	0.000
15	Rom	135.000	–	4.000	2.000	2.000	1.000	–	1.000	1.000	4.000	4.000	6.000	2.000	3.000	2.000	0.000
16	Pol	130.000	1.000	2.000	3.000	0.000	2.000	2.000	2.000	4.000	6.000	3.000	6.000	6.000	10.000	–	14.000
17	GDR	127.000	–	–	3.000	10.000	2.000	2.000	2.000	0.000	0.000	0.000	4.000	6.000	0.000	–	8.000
18	Sui	120.000	0.000	4.000	1.000	12.000	1.000	5.000	6.000	2.000	9.000	4.000	1.000	0.000	1.000	2.000	1.000
19	Bul	118.000	–	5.000	2.000	2.000	1.000	3.000	1.000	5.000	3.000	4.000	3.000	15.000	2.000	–	2.000
20	Swe	117.000	4.000	1.000	1.000	5.000	4.000	8.000	0.000	4.000	3.000	2.000	2.000	0.000	0.000	2.000	0.000
21	Gre	83.000	–	–	–	–	1.000	1.000	1.000	0.000	1.000	4.000	3.000	2.000	1.000	7.000	1.000
–	Tur	83.000	–	2.000	–	1.000	5.000	2.000	0.000	8.000	5.000	0.000	1.000	0.000	0.000	3.000	8.000
23	Den	82.000	1.000	1.000	5.000	2.000	1.000	7.000	4.000	4.000	0.000	0.000	0.000	0.000	4.000	3.000	4.000
24	Nir	37.000	–	–	1.000	0.000	2.000	–	0.000	1.000	1.000	1.000	2.000	8.000	2.000	1.000	0.000
25	Fin	32.000	–	–	–	0.000	–	0.000	0.000	0.000	2.000	2.000	0.000	0.000	0.000	3.000	0.000
26	Nor	31.000	–	–	–	–	–	3.000	0.000	0.000	0.000	2.000	2.000	1.000	1.000	1.000	0.000
27	Cyp	29.000	–	–	–	–	–	–	–	–	0.000	–	0.000	0.000	1.000	0.000	0.000
28	Irl	28.000	–	–	0.000	0.000	1.000	0.000	0.000	0.000	2.000	0.000	2.000	0.000	0.000	0.000	0.000
29	Lux	21.000	–	2.000	0.000	2.000	2.000	0.000	0.000	0.000	4.000	0.000	0.000	1.000	2.000	2.000	0.000
30	Alb	20.000	–	–	–	–	–	–	–	1.000	2.000	1.000	1.000	–	–	–	1.000
31	Mlt	19.000	–	–	–	–	–	–	0.000	0.000	0.000	0.000	2.000	0.000	1.000	1.000	1.000
32	Isl	15.000	–	–	–	–	–	–	–	–	–	0.000	0.000	0.000	2.000	1.000	0.000

	Pts	P	W	D	L	F	A	Diff	B	F/P
Total	4670	4166	1705	756	1705	6566	6566	0	504	3.152

1955-56 to 1990-91

Pos	Cnty	Total	7071	7172	7273	7374	7475	7576	7677	7778	7879	7980	8081	8182	8283	8384	8485
1	Esp	357.000	12.000	6.000	11.000	16.000	13.000	9.000	5.000	8.000	6.000	12.000	16.000	1.000	11.000	3.000	1.000
2	FRG	332.500	6.000	5.000	10.000	16.000	14.000	13.000	11.000	13.000	13.000	15.000	14.000	15.000	17.000	2.000	2.000
3	Ita	313.500	4.000	12.000	14.000	2.000	–	3.000	4.000	14.000	2.000	1.000	13.000	3.000	16.000	14.000	17.000
4	Eng	295.500	9.000	9.000	12.000	3.000	16.000	4.000	17.000	13.000	9.500	9.000	9.000	13.500	8.500	19.000	16.000
5	Sco	231.000	11.000	13.000	6.000	12.000	1.000	3.000	1.000	6.000	7.000	8.000	3.000	2.000	5.000	13.000	2.000
6	Ned	228.000	9.000	15.000	15.000	2.000	5.000	13.000	4.000	9.000	3.000	13.000	6.000	5.000	1.000	1.000	1.000
7	Por	225.500	4.000	12.000	3.000	5.000	1.000	6.000	1.000	7.000	2.000	5.000	0.000	5.000	7.000	7.000	4.000
8	Fra	203.000	2.000	3.000	2.000	1.000	10.000	16.000	9.000	3.000	3.000	8.000	5.000	1.000	1.000	2.000	12.000
9	Bel	191.000	6.000	9.000	4.000	6.000	5.000	4.000	8.000	13.000	2.000	1.000	0.000	14.000	3.000	5.000	5.000
10	Tch	187.000	5.000	2.000	7.000	10.000	2.000	2.000	4.000	2.000	5.000	4.000	6.000	4.000	2.000	6.000	9.000
11	Yug	185.000	12.000	2.000	0.000	10.000	6.000	11.000	0.000	4.000	2.000	9.000	8.000	7.000	2.000	5.000	2.000
12	URS	155.000	2.000	5.000	8.000	5.000	11.000	10.000	14.000	2.000	5.000	2.000	8.000	8.000	7.000	9.000	7.000
13	Hun	152.000	2.000	8.000	7.000	12.000	4.000	4.000	6.000	1.000	1.000	2.000	8.000	2.000	2.000	4.000	2.000
14	Aut	141.000	2.000	0.000	0.000	0.000	1.000	1.000	2.000	7.000	10.000	1.000	1.000	3.000	6.000	7.000	9.000
15	Rom	135.000	2.000	2.000	6.000	5.000	2.000	2.000	1.000	2.000	2.000	2.000	1.000	6.000	4.000	11.000	3.000
16	Pol	130.000	9.000	1.000	6.000	0.000	10.000	3.000	0.000	1.000	7.000	1.000	2.000	0.000	11.000	2.000	0.000
17	GDR	127.000	11.000	1.000	4.000	3.000	0.000	2.000	8.000	4.000	8.000	9.000	4.000	7.000	1.000	9.000	3.000
18	Sui	120.000	2.000	3.000	2.000	9.000	2.000	2.000	11.000	2.000	8.000	4.000	6.000	2.000	0.000	1.000	2.000
19	Bul	118.000	2.000	5.000	4.000	9.000	0.000	2.000	1.000	3.000	3.000	0.000	9.000	11.000	5.000	2.000	4.000
20	Swe	117.000	0.000	2.000	2.000	2.000	7.000	4.000	1.000	2.000	14.000	1.000	1.000	0.000	2.000	2.000	8.000
21	Gre	83.000	13.000	2.000	0.000	0.000	5.000	1.000	3.000	5.000	2.000	2.000	0.000	2.000	2.000	5.000	11.000
–	Tur	83.000	0.000	1.000	1.000	1.000	4.000	2.000	6.000	2.000	2.000	0.000	2.000	1.000	1.000	0.000	2.000
23	Den	82.000	1.000	2.000	0.000	4.000	1.000	0.000	0.000	2.000	1.000	5.000	5.000	4.000	1.000	0.000	5.000
24	Nir	37.000	0.000	0.000	–	0.000	0.000	0.000	0.000	2.000	1.000	1.000	0.000	5.000	2.000	0.000	3.000
25	Fin	32.000	0.000	1.000	0.000	0.000	2.000	1.000	2.000	0.000	0.000	0.000	1.000	0.000	4.000	0.000	0.000
26	Nor	31.000	0.000	0.000	0.000	0.000	0.000	0.000	2.000	2.000	4.000	0.000	0.000	0.000	2.000	1.000	1.000
27	Cyp	29.000	0.000	0.000	2.000	0.000	–	2.000	1.000	0.000	2.000	4.000	2.000	0.000	2.000	2.000	2.000
28	Irl	28.000	4.000	0.000	2.000	0.000	0.000	1.000	1.000	0.000	3.000	6.000	0.000	2.000	0.000	0.000	2.000
29	Lux	21.000	0.000	0.000	0.000	1.000	0.000	0.000	0.000	0.000	0.000	2.000	0.000	1.000	0.000	0.000	0.000
30	Alb	20.000	1.000	0.000	–	–	–	–	–	–	2.000	2.000	0.000	2.000	2.000	–	0.000
31	Mlt	19.000	0.000	3.000	0.000	0.000	2.000	0.000	2.000	1.000	0.000	2.000	0.000	0.000	0.000	0.000	0.000
32	Isl	15.000	0.000	1.000	0.000	0.000	0.000	2.000	0.000	2.000	1.000	0.000	1.000	0.000	0.000	0.000	1.000

	Pts	P	W	D	L	F	A	Diff	B	F/P
Total	**4670**	**4166**	**1705**	**756**	**1705**	**6566**	**6566**	**0**	**504**	**3.152**

1955-56 to 1990-91

Pos	Cnty	Total	8586	8687	8788	8889	8990	9091
1	Esp	357.000	13.000	10.000	13.000	14.000	6.000	9.000
2	FRG	332.500	10.000	14.000	9.000	7.000	15.000	14.000
3	Ita	313.500	7.000	6.000	1.000	17.000	8.500	5.500
4	Eng	295.500	–	–	–	–	–	–
5	Sco	231.000	10.000	5.000	8.000	3.000	1.000	5.000
6	Ned	228.000	1.000	1.000	14.000	4.000	7.000	–
7	Por	225.500	5.000	18.000	9.000	4.000	17.000	9.000
8	Fra	203.000	1.000	1.000	10.000	6.000	14.000	16.000
9	Bel	191.000	10.000	7.000	10.000	4.000	8.000	4.000
10	Tch	187.000	2.000	5.000	4.000	1.000	5.000	0.000
11	Yug	185.000	0.000	9.000	0.000	6.000	2.000	17.000
12	URS	155.000	6.000	12.000	2.000	3.000	8.000	11.000
13	Hun	152.000	6.000	1.000	2.000	2.000	2.000	0.000
14	Aut	141.000	5.000	5.000	4.000	2.000	5.000	5.000
15	Rom	135.000	14.000	2.000	11.000	15.000	6.000	4.000
16	Pol	130.000	0.000	1.000	4.000	4.000	1.000	6.000
17	GDR	127.000	0.000	5.000	0.000	2.000	2.000	7.000
18	Sui	120.000	4.000	2.000	4.000	4.000	0.000	1.000
19	Bul	118.000	0.000	1.000	0.000	0.000	7.000	2.000
20	Swe	117.000	12.000	0.000	1.000	11.000	4.000	5.000
21	Gre	83.000	0.000	2.000	1.000	2.000	3.000	0.000
–	Tur	83.000	5.000	5.000	2.000	10.000	0.000	1.000
23	Den	82.000	1.000	8.000	3.000	2.000	1.000	0.000
24	Nir	37.000	1.000	1.000	1.000	1.000	0.000	0.000
25	Fin	32.000	8.000	2.000	2.000	2.000	0.000	0.000
26	Nor	31.000	0.000	3.000	4.000	0.000	1.000	1.000
27	Cyp	29.000	4.000	2.000	3.000	0.000	0.000	0.000
28	Irl	28.000	0.000	0.000	1.000	0.000	0.000	1.000
29	Lux	21.000	0.000	0.000	2.000	0.000	0.000	0.000
30	Alb	20.000	–	0.000	0.000	2.000	2.000	1.000
31	Mlt	19.000	0.000	0.000	0.000	2.000	2.000	0.000
32	Isl	15.000	0.000	0.000	0.000	2.000	0.000	2.000

	Pts	P	W	D	L	F	A	Diff	B	F/P
Total	**4670**	**4166**	**1705**	**756**	**1705**	**6566**	**6566**	**0**	**504**	**3.152**

National Classification by Cumulative Year-by-Year Index

1981-82 to 1990-91

Pos	Cnty	Total	8182	8283	8384	8485	8586	8687	8788	8889	8990	9091
1	FRG	105.000	15.000	17.000	2.000	2.000	10.000	14.000	9.000	7.000	15.000	14.000
2	Ita	95.000	3.000	16.000	14.000	17.000	7.000	6.000	1.000	17.000	8.500	5.500
3	Por	85.000	5.000	7.000	7.000	4.000	5.000	18.000	9.000	4.000	17.000	9.000
4	Esp	81.000	1.000	11.000	3.000	1.000	13.000	10.000	13.000	14.000	6.000	9.000
5	Rom	76.000	6.000	4.000	11.000	3.000	14.000	2.000	11.000	15.000	6.000	4.000
6	URS	73.000	8.000	7.000	9.000	7.000	6.000	12.000	2.000	3.000	8.000	11.000
7	Bel	70.000	14.000	3.000	5.000	5.000	10.000	7.000	10.000	4.000	8.000	4.000
8	Fra	64.000	1.000	1.000	2.000	12.000	1.000	1.000	10.000	6.000	14.000	16.000
9	Eng	57.000	13.500	8.500	19.000	16.000	–	–	–	–	–	–
10	Sco	54.000	2.000	5.000	13.000	2.000	10.000	5.000	8.000	3.000	1.000	5.000
11	Aut	51.000	3.000	6.000	7.000	9.000	5.000	5.000	4.000	2.000	5.000	5.000
12	Yug	50.000	7.000	2.000	5.000	2.000	0.000	9.000	0.000	6.000	2.000	17.000
13	Swe	45.000	0.000	2.000	2.000	8.000	12.000	0.000	1.000	11.000	4.000	5.000
14	Tch	38.000	4.000	2.000	6.000	9.000	2.000	5.000	4.000	1.000	5.000	0.000
15	GDR	36.000	7.000	1.000	9.000	3.000	0.000	5.000	0.000	2.000	2.000	7.000
16	Ned	35.000	5.000	1.000	1.000	1.000	1.000	1.000	14.000	4.000	7.000	–
17	Bul	32.000	11.000	5.000	2.000	4.000	0.000	1.000	0.000	0.000	7.000	2.000
18	Pol	29.000	0.000	11.000	2.000	0.000	0.000	1.000	4.000	4.000	1.000	6.000
19	Gre	28.000	2.000	2.000	5.000	11.000	0.000	2.000	1.000	2.000	3.000	0.000
20	Tur	27.000	1.000	1.000	0.000	2.000	5.000	5.000	2.000	10.000	0.000	1.000
21	Den	25.000	4.000	1.000	0.000	5.000	1.000	8.000	3.000	2.000	1.000	0.000
22	Hun	23.000	2.000	2.000	4.000	2.000	6.000	1.000	2.000	2.000	2.000	0.000
23	Sui	20.000	2.000	0.000	1.000	2.000	4.000	2.000	4.000	4.000	0.000	1.000
24	Fin	18.000	0.000	4.000	0.000	0.000	8.000	2.000	2.000	2.000	0.000	0.000
25	Cyp	15.000	0.000	2.000	2.000	2.000	4.000	2.000	3.000	0.000	0.000	0.000
26	Nir	14.000	5.000	2.000	0.000	3.000	1.000	1.000	1.000	1.000	0.000	0.000
27	Nor	13.000	0.000	2.000	1.000	1.000	0.000	3.000	4.000	0.000	1.000	1.000
28	Alb	9.000	2.000	2.000	–	0.000	–	0.000	0.000	2.000	2.000	1.000
29	Irl	6.000	2.000	0.000	0.000	2.000	0.000	0.000	1.000	0.000	0.000	1.000
30	Isl	5.000	0.000	0.000	0.000	1.000	0.000	0.000	0.000	2.000	0.000	2.000
31	Mlt	4.000	0.000	0.000	0.000	0.000	0.000	0.000	0.000	2.000	2.000	0.000
32	Lux	3.000	1.000	0.000	0.000	0.000	0.000	0.000	2.000	0.000	0.000	0.000

	Pts	P	W	D	L	F	A	Diff	B	F/P
Total	**1338**	**1198**	**478**	**242**	**478**	**1697**	**1697**	**0**	**140**	**2.833**

National Classification by Cumulative Year–by–Year Index

1986–87 to 1990–91

Pos	Cnty	Total	8687	8788	8889	8990	9091
1	FRG	59.000	14.000	9.000	7.000	15.000	14.000
2	Por	57.000	18.000	9.000	4.000	17.000	9.000
3	Esp	52.000	10.000	13.000	14.000	6.000	9.000
4	Fra	47.000	1.000	10.000	6.000	14.000	16.000
5	Ita	38.000	6.000	1.000	17.000	8.500	5.500
–	Rom	38.000	2.000	11.000	15.000	6.000	4.000
7	URS	36.000	12.000	2.000	3.000	8.000	11.000
8	Yug	34.000	9.000	0.000	6.000	2.000	17.000
9	Bel	33.000	7.000	10.000	4.000	8.000	4.000
10	Ned	26.000	1.000	14.000	4.000	7.000	–
11	Sco	22.000	5.000	8.000	3.000	1.000	5.000
12	Aut	21.000	5.000	4.000	2.000	5.000	5.000
–	Swe	21.000	0.000	1.000	11.000	4.000	5.000
14	Tur	18.000	5.000	2.000	10.000	0.000	1.000
15	Pol	16.000	1.000	4.000	4.000	1.000	6.000
–	GDR	16.000	5.000	0.000	2.000	2.000	7.000
17	Tch	15.000	5.000	4.000	1.000	5.000	0.000
18	Den	14.000	8.000	3.000	2.000	1.000	0.000
19	Sui	11.000	2.000	4.000	4.000	0.000	1.000
20	Bul	10.000	1.000	0.000	0.000	7.000	2.000
21	Nor	9.000	3.000	4.000	0.000	1.000	1.000
22	Gre	8.000	2.000	1.000	2.000	3.000	0.000
23	Hun	7.000	1.000	2.000	2.000	2.000	0.000
24	Fin	6.000	2.000	2.000	2.000	0.000	0.000
25	Alb	5.000	0.000	0.000	2.000	2.000	1.000
–	Cyp	5.000	2.000	3.000	0.000	0.000	0.000
27	Isl	4.000	0.000	0.000	2.000	0.000	2.000
–	Mlt	4.000	0.000	0.000	2.000	2.000	0.000
29	Nir	3.000	1.000	1.000	1.000	0.000	0.000
30	Irl	2.000	0.000	1.000	0.000	0.000	1.000
–	Lux	2.000	0.000	2.000	0.000	0.000	0.000

	Pts	P	W	D	L	F	A	Diff	B	F/P
Total	**662**	**592**	**233**	**126**	**233**	**830**	**830**	**0**	**70**	**2.804**

Country Records – Points Gained 1955-56 to 1990-91

Albania

Pos'n	Cnty	Pts	P	W	D	L	F	A	Diff	B	Pts/P	Q	E
1	Malta	4	4	2	0	2	8	3	5	0	1.000	2	0
2	Austria	4	4	2	0	2	5	7	-2	0	1.000	0	2
3	Scotland	3	4	1	1	2	2	5	-3	0	0.750	0	2
4	Northern Ireland	2	2	1	0	1	2	2	0	0	1.000	1	0
5	Bulgaria	2	4	1	0	3	2	7	-5	0	0.500	0	2
6	Belgium	1	2	0	1	1	1	4	-3	0	0.500	0	1
7	France	1	2	0	1	1	1	5	-4	0	0.500	0	1
8	Netherlands	1	4	0	1	3	2	7	-5	0	0.250	0	2
9	Sweden	1	4	0	1	3	1	7	-6	0	0.250	0	2
10	West Germany	1	4	0	1	3	1	8	-7	0	0.250	0	2
11	Turkey	0	2	0	0	2	0	3	-3	0	0.000	0	1
12	Portugal	0	1	0	0	1	0	4	-4	0	0.000	0	1
13	Denmark	0	2	0	0	2	0	6	-6	0	0.000	0	1
	Total	**20**	**39**	**7**	**6**	**26**	**25**	**68**	**-43**	**0**	**0.513**	**3**	**17**

Austria

Pos'n	Cnty	Pts	P	W	D	L	F	A	Diff	B	Pts/P	Q	E
1	East Germany	16	9	6	1	2	16	10	6	3	1.778	4	0
2	West Germany	10	14	3	4	7	15	28	-13	0	0.714	0	7
3	Luxembourg	8	4	4	0	0	19	0	19	0	2.000	2	0
4	Malta	8	4	4	0	0	15	0	15	0	2.000	2	0
5	Finland	8	4	4	0	0	14	4	10	0	2.000	2	0
6	Turkey	8	6	4	0	2	10	4	6	0	1.333	2	1
7	Spain	8	13	2	3	8	12	36	-24	1	0.615	1	5
8	Norway	7	4	2	2	0	10	5	5	1	1.750	2	0
9	Romania	6	4	2	2	0	4	1	3	0	1.500	2	0
–	Sweden	6	4	2	1	1	4	1	3	1	1.500	1	1
11	Czechoslovakia	6	4	2	0	2	5	4	1	2	1.500	2	0
12	Scotland	6	8	2	1	5	6	8	-2	1	0.750	1	3
13	Denmark	5	4	1	2	1	8	6	2	1	1.250	1	1
14	Italy	5	7	2	1	4	19	21	-2	0	0.714	1	2
15	Cyprus	4	2	2	0	0	9	2	7	0	2.000	1	0
16	Republic of Ireland	4	2	2	0	0	5	0	5	0	2.000	1	0
17	Albania	4	4	2	0	2	7	5	2	0	1.000	2	0
18	France	4	4	2	0	2	7	10	-3	0	1.000	1	1
19	Poland	4	7	2	0	5	9	14	-5	0	0.571	0	3
20	Netherlands	3	4	1	0	3	7	6	1	1	0.750	1	1
21	Switzerland	2	2	1	0	1	3	2	1	0	1.000	1	0
22	Bulgaria	2	4	1	0	3	4	7	-3	0	0.500	1	1
23	England	2	4	0	2	2	2	8	-6	0	0.500	0	2
24	USSR	2	8	0	2	6	5	14	-9	0	0.250	0	4
25	Portugal	2	6	0	2	4	4	17	-13	0	0.333	0	3
26	Yugoslavia	1	2	0	1	1	0	1	-1	0	0.500	0	1
	Total	**141**	**138**	**53**	**24**	**61**	**219**	**214**	**5**	**11**	**1.022**	**31**	**36**

Belgium

Pos'n	Cnty	Pts	P	W	D	L	F	A	Diff	B	Pts/P	Q	E
1	Norway	18	10	8	2	0	23	4	19	0	1.800	5	0
2	Spain	17	16	6	2	8	18	31	-13	3	1.063	4	4
3	Italy	15	15	4	5	6	11	13	-2	2	1.000	3	4
4	Finland	13	6	6	0	0	28	4	24	1	2.167	3	0

5	Poland	11	8	5	1	2	13	9	4	0	1.375	2	2
6	Sweden	11	8	4	2	2	9	6	3	1	1.375	2	2
7	Northern Ireland	10	5	4	1	0	19	4	15	1	2.000	3	0
8	Romania	8	6	3	1	2	7	6	1	1	1.333	2	1
9	Czechoslovakia	8	10	3	1	6	15	20	-5	1	0.800	2	3
10	Portugal	7	4	3	0	1	7	4	3	1	1.750	1	1
11	Denmark	6	4	3	0	1	9	4	5	0	1.500	2	0
12	Greece	6	4	2	0	2	7	5	2	2	1.500	2	0
13	Scotland	6	10	2	1	7	14	23	-9	1	0.600	2	3
14	Cyprus	5	2	2	0	0	4	1	3	1	2.500	1	0
15	Yugoslavia	5	4	2	0	2	6	9	-3	1	1.250	1	1
16	West Germany	5	6	1	2	3	7	12	-5	1	0.833	1	2
17	Malta	4	2	2	0	0	10	0	10	0	2.000	1	0
18	Republic of Ireland	4	2	2	0	0	11	4	7	0	2.000	1	0
19	East Germany	4	2	2	0	0	5	2	3	0	2.000	1	0
20	Bulgaria	4	2	1	1	0	4	2	2	1	2.000	1	0
21	France	4	4	2	0	2	4	9	-5	0	1.000	0	2
22	Iceland	3	2	1	1	0	7	2	5	0	1.500	1	0
23	Turkey	3	2	1	1	0	5	1	4	0	1.500	1	0
24	Albania	3	2	1	1	0	4	1	3	0	1.500	1	0
25	USSR	3	2	1	0	1	2	1	1	1	1.500	1	0
26	Switzerland	3	6	1	1	4	9	16	-7	0	0.500	0	3
27	England	3	13	1	1	11	3	28	-25	0	0.231	0	7
28	Hungary	2	4	1	0	3	9	13	-4	0	0.500	1	1
	Total	**191**	**161**	**74**	**24**	**63**	**270**	**234**	**36**	**19**	**1.186**	**45**	**36**

Bulgaria

Pos'n	Cnty	Pts	P	W	D	L	F	A	Diff	B	Pts/P	Q	E
1	Poland	14	8	5	2	1	20	7	13	2	1.750	4	0
2	Northern Ireland	7	4	2	1	1	6	4	2	2	1.750	2	0
3	England	7	6	3	0	3	5	7	-2	1	1.167	2	1
4	Albania	6	4	3	0	1	7	2	5	0	1.500	2	0
5	Greece	6	4	3	0	1	7	3	4	0	1.500	2	0
6	Yugoslavia	6	4	3	0	1	9	6	3	0	1.500	1	1
7	Austria	6	4	3	0	1	7	4	3	0	1.500	1	1
8	Italy	6	11	2	2	7	10	18	-8	0	0.545	1	4
9	Spain	6	9	2	2	5	8	16	-8	0	0.667	1	3
10	Hungary	6	8	3	0	5	14	27	-13	0	0.750	0	4
11	West Germany	6	12	2	2	8	10	32	-22	0	0.500	1	5
12	Sweden	5	8	2	1	5	19	14	5	0	0.625	2	2
13	Romania	5	4	2	0	2	12	7	5	1	1.250	1	1
14	Czechoslovakia	5	4	1	2	1	10	8	2	1	1.250	1	1
15	Malta	4	2	2	0	0	6	1	5	0	2.000	1	0
16	Portugal	4	6	0	4	2	7	9	-2	0	0.667	0	3
17	France	4	6	1	2	3	3	5	-2	0	0.667	1	2
18	Netherlands	4	8	1	1	6	5	12	-7	1	0.500	1	3
19	Denmark	3	2	1	1	0	4	3	1	0	1.500	1	0
20	USSR	3	4	1	1	2	4	6	-2	0	0.750	0	2
21	Iceland	2	2	1	0	1	3	1	2	0	1.000	1	0
22	Cyprus	2	2	1	0	1	4	4	0	0	1.000	1	0
23	Belgium	1	2	0	1	1	2	4	-2	0	0.500	0	1
	Total	**118**	**124**	**44**	**22**	**58**	**182**	**200**	**-18**	**8**	**0.952**	**27**	**34**

Cyprus

Pos'n	Cnty	Pts	P	W	D	L	F	A	Diff	B	Pts/P	Q	E
1	Republic of Ireland	7	6	3	1	2	6	4	2	0	1.1.67	2	1

2	Malta	4	2	2	0	0	10	0	10	0	2.000	1	0
3	Finland	4	4	2	0	2	5	6	-1	0	1.000	1	1
4	Luxembourg	2	2	1	0	1	7	3	4	0	1.000	1	0
5	Bulgaria	2	2	1	0	1	4	4	0	0	1.000	0	1
6	East Germany	2	2	1	0	1	2	4	-2	0	1.000	0	1
7	Iceland	2	2	1	0	1	2	5	-3	0	1.000	0	1
8	Romania	2	4	1	0	3	4	10	-6	0	0.500	0	2
9	Netherlands	2	4	1	0	3	4	27	-23	0	0.500	0	2
10	Greece	1	2	0	1	1	1	3	-2	0	0.500	0	1
11	Yugoslavia	1	4	0	1	3	4	11	-7	0	0.250	0	2
12	Belgium	0	2	0	0	2	1	4	-3	0	0.000	0	1
13	USSR	0	2	0	0	2	0	3	-3	0	0.000	0	1
14	Portugal	0	2	0	0	2	0	4	-4	0	0.000	0	1
15	Sweden	0	2	0	0	2	2	7	-5	0	0.000	0	1
16	Italy	0	2	0	0	2	0	5	-5	0	0.000	0	1
17	Austria	0	2	0	0	2	2	9	-7	0	0.000	0	1
18	Spain	0	4	0	0	4	1	26	-25	0	0.000	0	2
19	West Germany	0	10	0	0	10	3	56	-53	0	0.000	0	5
	Total	**29**	**60**	**13**	**3**	**44**	**58**	**191**	**-133**	**0**	**0.483**	**5**	**25**

Czechoslovakia

Pos'n	Cnty	Pts	P	W	D	L	F	A	Diff	B	Pts/P	Q	E
1	Belgium	16	10	6	1	3	20	15	5	3	1.600	3	2
2	Denmark	15	8	5	3	0	17	4	13	2	1.875	4	0
3	Poland	13	11	4	3	4	19	14	5	2	1.182	4	1
4	Norway	12	8	5	2	1	13	7	6	0	1.500	4	0
5	Turkey	10	6	5	0	1	11	3	8	0	1.667	2	1
6	Greece	10	6	3	2	1	6	6	0	2	1.667	2	1
7	Hungary	9	8	3	3	2	15	10	5	0	1.125	3	1
8	Switzerland	8	6	3	1	2	10	6	4	1	1.333	2	1
9	England	8	8	4	0	4	5	12	-7	0	1.000	0	4
10	Malta	7	4	3	1	0	14	2	12	0	1.750	2	0
11	Iceland	7	4	3	1	0	12	1	11	0	1.750	2	0
12	East Germany	7	4	2	2	0	5	1	4	1	1.750	2	0
13	Portugal	7	6	3	1	2	6	6	0	0	1.167	1	2
14	France	7	6	2	3	1	5	5	0	0	1.1.67	1	2
15	Yugoslavia	7	6	3	1	2	11	13	-2	0	1.167	1	2
16	Romania	7	8	2	3	3	12	15	-3	0	0.875	1	3
17	Netherlands	6	4	2	1	1	5	5	0	1	1.500	1	1
18	Spain	6	8	2	2	4	7	17	-10	0	0.750	0	4
19	Finland	5	2	2	0	0	16	2	14	1	2.500	1	0
20	Austria	4	4	2	0	2	4	5	-1	0	1.000	0	2
21	Bulgaria	4	4	1	2	1	8	10	-2	0	1.000	1	1
22	USSR	4	4	1	1	2	1	4	-3	1	1.000	1	1
23	West Germany	4	6	2	0	4	7	17	-10	0	0.667	0	3
24	Italy	2	2	1	0	1	1	3	-2	0	1.000	0	1
25	Scotland	2	4	0	2	2	5	8	-3	0	0.500	0	2
	Total	**187**	**147**	**69**	**35**	**43**	**235**	**191**	**44**	**14**	**1.272**	**38**	**35**

Denmark

Pos'n	Cnty	Pts	P	W	D	L	F	A	Diff	B	Pts/P	Q	E
1	Luxembourg	6	4	3	0	1	19	4	15	0	1.500	2	0
2	Northern Ireland	6	4	2	2	0	5	1	4	0	1.500	2	0
3	France	6	10	1	4	5	9	21	-12	0	0.600	1	4
4	Norway	5	2	2	0	0	4	0	4	1	2.500	1	0
5	Switzerland	5	4	2	1	1	9	7	2	0	1.250	2	0

6	Albania	4	2	2	0	0	6	0	6	0	2.000	1	0
7	Finland	4	2	2	0	0	5	0	5	0	2.000	1	0
8	East Germany	4	2	1	1	0	3	2	1	1	2.000	1	0
9	Austria	4	4	1	2	1	6	8	-2	0	1.000	1	1
10	Hungary	3	2	1	1	0	6	3	3	0	1.500	1	0
11	Poland	3	4	1	1	2	4	3	1	0	0.750	1	1
12	Sweden	3	2	1	1	0	3	2	1	0	1.500	1	0
13	Scotland	3	4	1	1	2	2	5	-3	0	0.750	0	2
14	Romania	3	6	1	1	4	6	16	-10	0	0.500	0	3
15	Czechoslovakia	3	8	0	3	5	4	17	-13	0	0.375	0	4
16	Spain	3	10	1	1	8	8	41	-33	0	0.300	0	5
17	Turkey	2	2	1	0	1	2	1	1	0	1.000	1	0
18	Republic of Ireland	2	2	0	2	0	3	3	0	0	1.000	1	0
19	USSR	2	2	1	0	1	2	3	-1	0	1.000	0	1
20	Yugoslavia	2	2	1	0	1	2	4	-2	0	1.000	0	1
21	Belgium	2	4	1	0	3	4	9	-5	0	0.500	0	2
22	West Germany	2	5	1	0	4	7	15	-8	0	0.400	0	2
23	Portugal	2	10	0	2	8	6	17	-11	0	0.200	0	5
24	Bulgaria	1	2	0	1	1	3	4	-1	0	0.500	0	1
25	Greece	1	2	0	1	1	0	2	-2	0	0.500	0	1
26	Italy	1	2	0	1	1	4	7	-3	0	0.500	0	1
27	England	0	2	0	0	2	0	6	-6	0	0.000	0	1
28	Netherlands	0	2	0	0	2	4	11	-7	0	0.000	0	1
	Total	**82**	**107**	**27**	**26**	**54**	**136**	**212**	**-76**	**2**	**0.766**	**17**	**36**

East Germany

Pos'n	Cnty	Pts	P	W	D	L	F	A	Diff	B	Pts/P	Q	E
1	Sweden	15	10	5	3	2	21	12	9	2	1.500	4	1
2	Republic of Ireland	12	7	5	1	1	23	3	20	1	1.714	3	0
3	Switzerland	10	9	3	3	3	14	14	0	1	1.111	2	2
4	Yugoslavia	10	10	4	0	6	12	18	-6	2	1.000	3	2
5	Luxembourg	8	4	4	0	0	12	2	10	0	2.000	2	0
6	Portugal	8	4	3	1	0	6	2	4	1	2.000	2	0
7	Poland	8	8	3	2	3	13	12	1	0	1.000	2	1
8	England	8	10	4	0	6	10	19	-9	0	0.800	0	5
9	Greece	5	4	2	1	1	7	6	1	0	1.250	1	1
10	Austria	5	9	2	1	6	10	16	-6	0	0.556	0	4
11	Finland	4	2	2	0	0	9	1	8	0	2.000	1	0
12	Turkey	4	2	2	0	0	5	0	5	0	2.000	1	0
13	Romania	4	5	2	0	3	8	7	1	0	0.800	1	1
14	Italy	4	6	2	0	4	6	9	-3	0	0.667	1	2
15	West Germany	4	8	1	2	5	13	20	-7	0	0.500	0	4
16	Hungary	3	4	1	0	3	6	7	-1	1	0.750	1	1
17	France	3	4	1	1	2	3	5	-2	0	0.750	1	1
18	Netherlands	3	6	1	1	4	2	8	-6	0	0.500	0	3
19	Northern Ireland	2	1	1	0	0	3	0	3	0	2.000	1	0
20	Cyprus	2	2	1	0	1	4	2	2	0	1.000	1	0
21	Scotland	2	4	1	0	3	5	9	-4	0	0.500	1	1
22	Czechoslovakia	2	4	0	2	2	1	5	-4	0	0.500	0	2
23	Denmark	1	2	0	1	1	2	3	-1	0	0.500	0	1
24	Belgium	0	2	0	0	2	2	5	-3	0	0.000	0	1
	Total	**127**	**127**	**50**	**19**	**58**	**197**	**185**	**12**	**8**	**1.000**	**28**	**33**

England

Pos'n	Cnty	Pts	P	W	D	L	F	A	Diff	B	Pts/P	Q	E
1	West Germany	30	21	7	10	4	28	24	4	6	1.429	9	3
2	Belgium	28	13	11	1	1	28	3	25	5	2.154	7	0
3	Portugal	26	13	10	1	2	32	13	19	5	2.000	6	1
4	Spain	20	15	6	4	5	25	30	-5	4	1.333	5	3
5	Romania	19	9	8	0	1	18	7	11	3	2.111	4	0
6	Yugoslavia	18	12	6	3	3	18	13	5	3	1.500	4	2
7	Switzerland	16	8	6	1	1	21	6	15	3	2.000	4	0
8	East Germany	16	10	6	0	4	19	10	9	4	1.600	5	0
9	Finland	14	8	6	1	1	33	5	28	1	1.750	4	0
10	Iceland	12	6	6	0	0	27	3	24	0	2.000	3	0
11	Republic of Ireland	12	6	6	0	0	24	5	19	0	2.000	3	0
12	Greece	12	6	4	2	0	13	3	10	2	2.000	2	1
13	Netherlands	12	10	3	3	4	15	17	-2	3	1.200	3	2
14	Poland	11	8	5	0	3	20	10	10	1	1.375	3	1
15	Czechoslovakia	11	8	4	0	4	12	5	7	3	1.375	4	0
16	Italy	11	16	4	3	9	12	26	-14	0	0.688	1	8
17	Hungary	10	4	4	0	0	11	1	10	2	2.500	2	0
18	Norway	8	4	4	0	0	23	1	22	0	2.000	2	0
19	Austria	8	4	2	2	0	8	2	6	2	2.000	2	0
20	Malta	7	4	3	1	0	18	1	17	0	1.750	2	0
21	Turkey	7	6	2	2	2	7	4	3	1	1.167	2	1
22	Bulgaria	7	6	3	0	3	7	5	2	1	1.167	1	2
23	France	6	4	2	0	2	7	5	2	2	1.500	2	0
24	USSR	6	4	2	1	1	4	4	0	1	1.500	1	1
25	Scotland	5	4	2	0	2	6	3	3	1	1.250	1	1
26	Sweden	5	3	2	1	0	4	1	3	0	1.667	2	0
27	Northern Ireland	4	2	2	0	0	7	0	7	0	2.000	1	0
28	Denmark	4	2	2	0	0	6	0	6	0	2.000	1	0
29	England	4	4	1	2	1	2	2	0	0	1.000	1	1
30	Luxembourg	3	2	1	1	0	3	1	2	0	1.500	1	0
	Total	**352**	**222**	**130**	**39**	**53**	**458**	**210**	**248**	**53**	**1.586**	**88**	**27**

Finland

Pos'n	Cnty	Pts	P	W	D	L	F	A	Diff	B	Pts/P	Q	E
1	Malta	7	6	3	1	2	9	5	4	0	1.167	3	0
2	Yugoslavia	4	2	2	0	0	4	2	2	0	2.000	1	0
3	Cyprus	4	4	2	0	2	6	5	1	0	1.000	1	1
4	USSR	3	4	1	0	3	6	7	-2	1	0.750	1	1
5	Switzerland	3	6	1	1	4	3	18	-15	0	0.500	0	3
6	England	3	8	1	1	6	5	33	-28	0	0.375	0	4
7	Luxembourg	2	2	1	0	1	4	5	-1	0	1.000	0	1
8	Portugal	2	2	1	0	1	2	3	-1	0	1.000	0	1
9	Norway	2	2	1	0	1	2	4	-2	0	1.000	0	1
10	Poland	1	2	0	1	1	2	7	-5	0	0.500	0	1
11	Romania	1	4	0	1	3	0	5	-5	0	0.250	0	2
12	Denmark	0	2	0	0	2	0	5	-5	0	0.000	0	1
13	Sweden	0	4	0	0	4	2	9	-7	0	0.000	0	2
14	East Germany	0	2	0	0	2	1	9	-8	0	0.000	0	1
15	Austria	0	4	0	0	4	4	14	-10	0	0.000	0	2
16	Italy	0	4	0	0	4	1	11	-10	0	0.000	0	2
17	France	0	4	0	0	4	0	12	-12	0	0.000	0	2
18	Netherlands	0	2	0	0	2	2	16	-14	0	0.000	0	1
–	Czechoslovakia	0	2	0	0	2	2	16	-14	0	0.000	0	1
20	Scotland	0	4	0	0	4	1	23	-22	0	0.000	0	2

21	Belgium	0	6	0	0	6	4	28	-24	0	0.000	0	3
	Total	**32**	**76**	**13**	**5**	**58**	**59**	**237**	**-178**	**1**	**0.421**	**6**	**32**

France

Pos'n	Cnty	Pts	P	W	D	L	F	A	Diff	B	Pts/P	Q	E
1	Scotland	19	15	8	0	7	24	25	-1	3	1.267	3	4
2	Denmark	15	10	5	4	1	21	9	12	1	1.500	4	1
3	Netherlands	12	12	2	6	4	6	13	-7	2	1.000	2	4
4	USSR	11	6	3	2	1	10	6	4	3	1.833	3	0
5	Italy	11	12	4	2	6	9	17	-8	1	0.917	1	5
6	Finland	9	4	4	0	0	12	0	12	1	2.250	2	0
7	Poland	9	8	3	1	4	16	12	4	2	1.125	3	1
8	Bulgaria	9	6	3	2	1	5	3	2	1	1.500	2	1
9	Northern Ireland	8	4	4	0	0	13	3	10	0	2.000	2	0
10	Norway	8	4	3	1	0	7	1	6	1	2.000	2	0
11	Greece	7	4	2	2	0	11	4	7	1	1.750	2	0
12	Turkey	7	7	2	2	3	11	9	2	1	1.000	1	2
13	Portugal	7	6	3	1	2	6	5	1	0	1.167	1	2
14	Iceland	6	4	3	0	1	10	5	5	0	1.500	2	0
15	Belgium	6	4	2	0	2	9	4	5	2	1.500	2	0
16	Romania	6	4	2	1	1	5	3	2	1	1.500	2	0
17	Czechoslovakia	6	6	1	3	2	5	5	0	1	1.000	2	1
18	Spain	6	10	2	2	6	13	23	-10	0	0.600	1	5
19	Austria	5	4	2	0	2	10	7	3	1	1.250	1	1
20	East Germany	5	4	2	1	1	5	3	2	0	1.250	1	1
21	Yugoslavia	5	5	1	2	2	8	9	-1	1	1.000	1	2
22	Luxembourg	4	2	2	0	0	11	1	10	0	2.000	1	0
23	Hungary	4	2	1	1	0	8	6	2	1	2.000	1	0
24	Switzerland	4	4	1	1	2	6	5	1	1	1.000	1	1
25	England	4	4	2	0	2	5	7	-2	0	1.000	0	2
26	Albania	3	2	1	1	0	5	1	4	0	1.500	1	0
27	Republic of Ireland	3	2	1	1	0	4	3	1	0	1.500	1	0
28	West Germany	3	5	1	1	3	3	5	-2	0	0.600	1	2
29	Sweden	1	2	0	1	1	0	1	-1	0	0.500	0	1
	Total	**203**	**162**	**70**	**38**	**54**	**258**	**195**	**63**	**25**	**1.253**	**46**	**36**

Greece

Pos'n	Cnty	Pts	P	W	D	L	F	A	Diff	B	Pts/P	Q	E
1	Northern Ireland	7	4	2	2	0	10	8	2	1	1.750	2	0
2	Luxembourg	6	4	3	0	1	12	4	8	0	1.500	2	0
3	Sweden	6	4	2	1	1	5	3	2	1	1.500	2	0
4	Netherlands	6	5	2	2	1	4	3	1	0	1.200	2	1
5	Malta	5	4	2	1	1	9	3	6	0	1.250	2	0
6	Czechoslovakia	5	6	1	2	3	6	6	0	1	0.833	1	2
7	Yugoslavia	5	4	2	0	2	6	8	-2	1	1.250	1	1
8	Italy	5	10	1	3	6	11	21	-10	0	0.500	0	5
9	Denmark	4	2	1	1	0	2	0	2	1	2.000	1	0
10	Portugal	4	6	2	0	4	8	10	-2	0	0.667	1	2
11	Belgium	4	4	2	0	2	5	7	-2	0	1.000	0	2
12	Romania	4	4	2	0	2	4	6	-2	0	1.000	0	2
13	Cyprus	3	2	1	1	0	3	1	2	0	1.500	1	0
–	Scotland	3	2	1	1	0	3	1	2	0	1.500	1	0
15	East Germany	3	4	1	1	2	6	7	-1	0	0.750	1	1
16	England	3	6	0	2	4	3	13	-10	1	0.500	1	2
17	Switzerland	2	2	1	0	1	3	3	0	0	1.000	0	1
18	Bulgaria	2	4	1	0	3	3	7	-4	0	0.500	0	2

19	France	2	4	0	2	2	4	11	-7	0	0.500	0	2
20	Hungary	1	2	0	1	1	1	3	-2	0	0.500	0	1
21	USSR	1	4	0	1	3	2	9	-7	0	0.250	0	2
22	Poland	1	6	0	1	5	5	14	-9	0	0.167	0	3
23	West Germany	1	6	0	1	5	4	15	-11	0	0.167	0	3
	Total	**83**	**99**	**27**	**23**	**49**	**119**	**163**	**-44**	**6**	**0.838**	**18**	**32**

Hungary

Pos'n	Cnty	Pts	P	W	D	L	F	A	Diff	B	Pts/P	Q	E
1	Portugal	17	16	7	2	7	22	31	-9	1	1.063	3	5
2	Iceland	13	6	6	0	0	28	4	24	1	2.167	3	0
3	Republic of Ireland	12	6	6	0	0	20	4	16	0	2.000	3	0
4	Bulgaria	11	8	5	0	3	27	14	13	1	1.375	4	0
5	Netherlands	10	7	2	4	1	11	7	4	2	1.429	2	1
6	Switzerland	10	10	4	1	5	17	20	-3	1	1.000	3	2
7	Yugoslavia	8	6	4	0	2	9	7	2	0	1.333	2	1
8	Czechoslovakia	8	8	2	3	3	10	15	-5	1	1.000	1	3
9	Spain	8	10	3	1	6	11	19	-8	1	0.800	1	4
10	Belgium	7	4	3	0	1	13	9	4	1	1.750	1	1
11	East Germany	6	4	3	0	1	7	6	1	0	1.500	1	1
12	Scotland	6	6	2	1	3	7	9	-2	1	1.000	1	2
13	Malta	4	2	2	0	0	11	0	11	0	2.000	1	0
14	Norway	4	2	2	0	0	11	1	10	0	2.000	1	0
15	Luxembourg	4	2	2	0	0	11	3	8	0	2.000	1	0
16	Poland	4	2	2	0	0	6	0	6	0	2.000	1	0
17	Greece	4	2	1	1	0	3	1	2	1	2.000	1	0
18	Romania	4	4	2	0	2	4	8	-4	0	1.000	0	2
19	Turkey	3	4	1	1	2	5	10	-5	0	0.750	0	2
20	Italy	3	8	0	3	5	4	16	-12	0	0.375	0	4
21	Sweden	2	2	1	0	1	4	1	3	0	1.000	1	0
22	West Germany	2	4	0	2	2	2	8	-6	0	0.500	0	2
23	France	1	2	0	1	1	6	8	-2	0	0.500	0	1
24	Denmark	1	2	0	1	1	3	6	-3	0	0.500	0	1
25	USSR	0	2	0	0	2	4	9	-5	0	0.000	0	1
26	England	0	4	0	0	4	1	11	-10	0	0.000	0	2
	Total	**152**	**133**	**60**	**21**	**52**	**257**	**227**	**30**	**11**	**1.143**	**31**	**35**

Iceland

Pos'n	Cnty	Pts	P	W	D	L	F	A	Diff	B	Pts/P	Q	E
1	Cyprus	2	2	1	0	1	5	2	3	0	1.000	1	0
2	Luxembourg	2	2	0	2	0	4	4	0	0	1.000	1	0
3	Northern Ireland	2	2	1	0	1	1	2	-1	0	1.000	0	1
4	Bulgaria	2	2	1	0	1	1	3	-2	0	1.000	0	1
5	France	2	4	1	0	3	5	10	-5	0	0.500	0	2
6	Malta	1	2	0	1	1	0	4	-4	0	0.500	0	1
7	Belgium	1	2	0	1	1	2	7	-5	0	0.500	0	1
8	West Germany	1	4	0	1	3	3	10	-7	0	0.250	0	2
9	Portugal	1	2	0	1	1	1	8	-7	0	0.500	0	1
10	Czechoslovakia	1	4	0	1	3	1	12	-11	0	0.250	0	2
11	Turkey	0	2	0	0	2	3	6	-3	0	0.000	0	1
12	Scotland	0	2	0	0	2	2	7	-5	0	0.000	0	1
13	Romania	0	2	0	0	2	0	5	-5	0	0.000	0	1
–	USSR	0	2	0	0	2	0	5	-5	0	0.000	0	1
15	Spain	0	4	0	0	4	2	8	-6	0	0.000	0	2
16	Yugoslavia	0	2	0	0	2	1	9	-8	0	0.000	0	1
17	Switzerland	0	2	0	0	2	2	11	-9	0	0.000	0	1

18	Italy	0	2	0	0	2	0	11	-11	0	0.000	0	1
19	Netherlands	0	2	0	0	2	2	16	-14	0	0.000	0	1
20	Hungary	0	6	0	0	6	4	28	-24	0	0.000	0	3
21	England	0	6	0	0	6	3	27	-24	0	0.000	0	3
	Total	**15**	**58**	**4**	**7**	**47**	**42**	**195**	**-153**	**0**	**0.259**	**2**	**27**

Italy

Pos'n	Cnty	Pts	P	W	D	L	F	A	Diff	B	Pts/P	Q	E
1	West Germany	29	20	8	6	6	30	23	7	7	1.450	7	3
2	Spain	29	30	11	4	15	33	42	-9	3	0.967	4	12
3	England	27	16	9	3	4	26	12	14	6	1.688	8	1
4	Scotland	27	19	9	3	7	23	15	8	6	1.421	7	3
5	Yugoslavia	21	10	6	4	0	16	5	11	5	2.100	5	0
6	Sweden	21	14	7	4	3	24	14	10	3	1.500	6	1
7	Belgium	21	15	6	5	4	13	11	2	4	1.400	4	3
8	Bulgaria	18	11	7	2	2	18	10	8	2	1.636	4	1
9	Romania	17	9	6	2	1	18	3	15	3	1.889	5	0
10	France	17	12	6	2	4	17	9	8	3	1.417	5	1
11	Hungary	16	8	5	3	0	16	4	12	3	2.000	4	0
12	Greece	15	10	6	3	1	21	11	10	0	1.500	5	0
13	Luxembourg	12	6	6	0	0	31	0	31	0	2.000	3	0
14	East Germany	10	6	4	0	2	9	6	3	2	1.667	2	1
15	Austria	10	7	4	1	2	21	19	2	1	1.429	2	1
16	Switzerland	9	4	3	1	0	11	5	6	2	2.250	2	0
17	USSR	9	6	2	4	0	3	1	2	1	1.500	2	1
18	Finland	8	4	4	0	0	11	1	10	0	2.000	2	0
19	Netherlands	7	7	2	2	3	7	8	-1	1	1.000	2	3
20	Portugal	7	7	3	1	3	4	5	-1	0	1.000	3	2
21	Turkey	5	2	2	0	0	8	1	7	1	2.500	1	0
22	Northern Ireland	5	2	2	0	0	6	0	6	1	2.500	1	0
23	Italy	5	4	1	2	1	2	2	0	1	1.250	1	1
24	Iceland	4	2	2	0	0	11	0	11	0	2.000	1	0
25	Cyprus	4	2	2	0	0	5	0	5	0	2.000	1	0
26	Poland	4	2	1	1	0	4	2	2	1	2.000	1	0
27	Denmark	3	2	1	1	0	7	4	3	0	1.500	1	0
28	Czechoslovakia	3	2	1	0	1	3	1	2	1	1.500	1	0
	Total	**363**	**239**	**126**	**54**	**59**	**398**	**214**	**184**	**57**	**1.519**	**90**	**34**

Luxembourg

Pos'n	Cnty	Pts	P	W	D	L	F	A	Diff	B	Pts/P	Q	E
1	Finland	2	2	1	0	1	5	4	1	0	1.000	1	0
2	Iceland	2	2	0	2	0	4	4	0	0	1.000	0	1
3	Poland	2	4	1	0	3	7	9	-2	0	0.500	1	1
4	Cyprus	2	2	1	0	1	3	7	-4	0	1.000	0	1
5	Greece	2	4	1	0	3	4	12	-8	0	0.500	0	2
6	Northern Ireland	2	4	0	2	2	5	14	-9	0	0.500	0	2
7	West Germany	2	5	1	0	4	6	20	-14	0	0.400	0	2
8	Denmark	2	4	1	0	3	4	19	-15	0	0.500	0	2
9	Yugoslavia	2	4	1	0	3	5	21	-16	0	0.500	0	2
10	Sweden	2	5	1	0	4	3	24	-21	0	0.400	0	2
11	England	1	2	0	1	1	1	3	-2	0	0.500	0	1
12	Turkey	0	2	0	0	2	2	5	-3	0	0.000	0	1
13	Romania	0	2	0	0	2	0	6	-6	0	0.000	0	1
14	Hungary	0	2	0	0	2	3	11	-8	0	0.000	0	1
15	USSR	0	2	0	0	2	0	9	-9	0	0.000	0	1
16	East Germany	0	4	0	0	4	2	12	-10	0	0.000	0	2

17	Scotland	0	2	0	0	2	1	11	-10	0	0.000	0	1
–	France	0	2	0	0	2	1	11	-10	0	0.000	0	1
19	Austria	0	4	0	0	4	0	19	-19	0	0.000	0	2
20	Portugal	0	4	0	0	4	2	28	-26	0	0.000	0	2
21	Italy	0	6	0	0	6	0	31	-31	0	0.000	0	3
22	Spain	0	8	0	0	8	3	37	-34	0	0.000	0	4
	Total	**21**	**76**	**8**	**5**	**63**	**61**	**317**	**-256**	**0**	**0.276**	**2**	**35**

Malta

Pos'n	Cnty	Pts	P	W	D	L	F	A	Diff	B	Pts/P	Q	E
1	Finland	5	6	2	1	3	5	9	-4	0	0.833	0	3
2	Albania	4	4	2	0	2	3	8	-5	0	1.000	0	2
3	Iceland	3	2	1	1	0	4	0	4	0	1.500	1	0
4	Greece	3	4	1	1	2	3	9	-6	0	0.750	0	2
5	Republic of Ireland	2	2	1	0	1	1	2	-1	0	1.000	0	1
6	Czechoslovakia	1	4	0	1	3	2	14	-12	0	0.250	0	2
7	England	1	4	0	1	3	1	18	-17	0	0.250	0	2
8	Bulgaria	0	2	0	0	2	1	6	-5	0	0.000	0	1
9	Romania	0	2	0	0	2	0	7	-7	0	0.000	0	1
10	Belgium	0	2	0	0	2	0	10	-10	0	0.000	0	1
–	Cyprus	0	2	0	0	2	0	10	-10	0	0.000	0	1
12	Hungary	0	2	0	0	2	0	11	-11	0	0.000	0	1
13	Poland	0	4	0	0	4	2	17	-15	0	0.000	0	2
14	Austria	0	4	0	0	4	0	15	-15	0	0.000	0	2
15	Switzerland	0	4	0	0	4	4	20	-16	0	0.000	0	2
16	Yugoslavia	0	4	0	0	4	2	18	-16	0	0.000	0	2
17	Portugal	0	4	0	0	4	0	19	-19	0	0.000	0	2
18	Scotland	0	6	0	0	6	1	23	-22	0	0.000	0	3
	Total	**19**	**62**	**7**	**5**	**50**	**29**	**216**	**-187**	**0**	**0.306**	**1**	**30**

Netherlands

Pos'n	Cnty	Pts	P	W	D	L	F	A	Diff	B	Pts/P	Q	E
1	France	18	12	4	6	2	13	6	7	4	1.500	4	2
2	Turkey	17	10	8	0	2	22	7	15	1	1.700	5	0
3	Portugal	17	16	5	4	7	20	22	-2	3	1.063	4	4
4	Bulgaria	16	8	6	1	1	12	5	7	3	2.000	3	1
5	Spain	16	14	4	5	5	13	18	-5	3	1.143	3	4
6	Switzerland	15	9	7	0	2	19	9	10	1	1.667	3	1
7	England	13	10	4	3	3	17	15	2	2	1.300	2	3
8	Norway	12	8	5	1	2	19	8	11	1	1.500	3	1
9	East Germany	11	6	4	1	1	8	2	6	2	1.833	3	0
10	Romania	10	6	3	2	1	11	3	8	2	1.667	2	1
11	Sweden	9	5	4	0	1	18	7	11	1	1.800	2	0
12	Poland	9	4	3	1	0	9	1	8	2	2.250	2	0
13	Italy	9	7	3	2	2	8	7	1	1	1.286	3	2
14	Scotland	9	10	3	2	5	15	15	0	1	0.900	2	3
15	West Germany	9	10	3	2	5	14	14	0	1	0.900	2	3
16	Northern Ireland	8	4	4	0	0	21	2	19	0	2.000	2	0
17	Cyprus	7	4	3	0	1	27	4	23	1	1.750	2	0
18	Albania	7	4	3	1	0	7	2	5	0	1.750	2	0
19	Austria	7	4	3	0	1	6	7	-1	1	1.750	1	1
20	Hungary	7	7	1	4	2	7	11	-4	1	1.000	1	2
21	Finland	4	2	2	0	0	16	2	14	0	2.000	1	0
–	Iceland	4	2	2	0	0	16	2	14	0	2.000	1	0
23	Denmark	4	2	2	0	0	11	4	7	0	2.000	1	0
24	Czechoslovakia	4	4	1	1	2	5	5	0	1	1.000	1	1

25	Greece	4	5	1	2	2	3	4	-1	0	0.800	1	2
26	Republic of Ireland	3	2	1	1	0	7	1	6	0	1.500	1	0
27	Yugoslavia	3	4	1	0	3	6	8	-2	1	0.750	1	1
	Total	**252**	**179**	**90**	**39**	**50**	**350**	**191**	**159**	**33**	**1.408**	**58**	**32**

Northern Ireland

Pos'n	Cnty	Pts	P	W	D	L	F	A	Diff	B	Pts/P	Q	E
1	Norway	9	10	2	4	4	17	16	1	1	0.900	2	3
2	Luxembourg	6	4	2	2	0	14	5	9	0	1.500	2	0
3	Bulgaria	3	4	1	1	2	4	6	-2	0	0.750	0	2
4	Republic of Ireland	3	6	0	3	3	3	8	-5	0	0.500	1	2
5	Portugal	3	8	0	3	5	7	28	-21	0	0.375	0	4
6	Iceland	2	2	1	0	1	2	1	1	0	1.000	1	0
7	Albania	2	2	1	0	1	2	2	0	0	1.000	0	1
8	Greece	2	4	0	2	2	8	10	-2	0	0.500	0	2
9	Sweden	2	2	1	0	1	3	7	-4	0	1.000	0	1
10	Denmark	2	4	0	2	2	1	5	-4	0	0.500	0	2
11	Switzerland	1	2	0	1	1	3	4	-1	0	0.500	0	1
12	USSR	1	4	0	1	3	2	6	-4	0	0.250	0	2
13	Belgium	1	5	0	1	4	4	19	-15	0	0.200	0	3
14	East Germany	0	1	0	0	1	0	3	-3	0	0.000	0	1
15	Italy	0	2	0	0	2	0	6	-6	0	0.000	0	1
16	England	0	2	0	0	2	0	7	-7	0	0.000	0	1
17	France	0	4	0	0	4	3	13	-10	0	0.000	0	2
18	Yugoslavia	0	2	0	0	2	2	12	-10	0	0.000	0	1
19	Romania	0	2	0	0	2	0	12	-12	0	0.000	0	1
20	Netherlands	0	4	0	0	4	2	21	-19	0	0.000	0	2
	Total	**37**	**74**	**8**	**20**	**46**	**77**	**191**	**-114**	**1**	**0.500**	**6**	**32**

Norway

Pos'n	Cnty	Pts	P	W	D	L	F	A	Diff	B	Pts/P	Q	E
1	Northern Ireland	12	10	4	4	2	16	17	-1	0	1.200	3	2
2	Netherlands	5	8	2	1	5	8	19	-11	0	0.625	1	3
3	Czechoslovakia	4	8	1	2	5	7	13	-6	0	0.500	0	4
4	Finland	2	2	1	0	1	4	2	2	0	1.000	1	0
5	Romania	2	2	1	0	1	3	4	-1	0	1.000	0	1
6	Austria	2	4	0	2	2	5	10	-5	0	0.500	0	2
7	Belgium	2	10	0	2	8	4	23	-19	0	0.200	0	5
8	France	1	4	0	1	3	1	7	-6	0	0.250	0	2
9	Yugoslavia	1	6	0	1	5	5	19	-14	0	0.167	0	3
10	Scotland	0	2	0	0	2	2	5	-3	0	0.000	0	1
11	West Germany	0	2	0	0	2	2	6	-4	0	0.000	0	1
12	Denmark	0	2	0	0	2	0	4	-4	0	0.000	0	1
–	Spain	0	2	0	0	2	0	4	-4	0	0.000	0	1
14	USSR	0	4	0	0	4	2	10	-8	0	0.000	0	2
15	Hungary	0	2	0	0	2	1	11	-10	0	0.000	0	1
16	England	0	4	0	0	4	1	23	-22	0	0.000	0	2
	Total	**31**	**72**	**9**	**13**	**50**	**61**	**177**	**-116**	**0**	**0.431**	**5**	**31**

Poland

Pos'n	Cnty	Pts	P	W	D	L	F	A	Diff	B	Pts/P	Q	E
1	Czechoslovakia	12	11	4	3	4	14	19	-5	1	1.091	1	4
2	Greece	11	6	5	1	0	14	5	9	0	1.833	3	0
3	Austria	11	7	5	0	2	14	9	5	1	1.571	3	0
4	Sweden	11	8	5	1	2	14	10	4	0	1.375	2	2
5	Turkey	11	8	4	1	3	12	9	3	2	1.375	3	1

6	France	10	8	4	1	3	12	16	-4	1	1.250	1	3
7	Malta	8	4	4	0	0	17	2	15	0	2.000	2	0
8	East Germany	8	8	3	2	3	12	13	-1	0	1.000	1	2
9	England	7	8	3	0	5	10	20	-10	1	0.875	1	3
10	Luxembourg	6	4	3	0	1	9	7	2	0	1.500	1	1
11	USSR	6	4	2	1	1	5	5	0	1	1.500	1	1
12	Belgium	6	8	2	1	5	9	13	-4	1	0.750	2	2
13	Denmark	5	4	2	1	1	3	4	-1	0	1.250	1	1
14	Romania	4	2	2	0	0	10	1	9	0	2.000	1	0
15	Spain	4	8	2	0	6	7	13	-6	0	0.500	0	4
16	Bulgaria	4	8	1	2	5	7	20	-13	0	0.500	0	4
17	Finland	3	2	1	1	0	7	2	5	0	1.500	1	0
18	Scotland	1	2	0	1	1	2	4	-2	0	0.500	0	1
–	Italy	1	2	0	1	1	2	4	-2	0	0.500	0	1
20	Netherlands	1	4	0	1	3	1	9	-8	0	0.250	0	2
21	Yugoslavia	0	2	0	0	2	1	3	-2	0	0.000	0	1
22	West Germany	0	2	0	0	2	2	6	-4	0	0.000	0	1
23	Hungary	0	2	0	0	2	0	6	-6	0	0.000	0	1
	Total	**130**	**122**	**52**	**18**	**52**	**184**	**200**	**-16**	**8**	**1.066**	**24**	**35**

Portugal

Pos'n	Cnty	Pts	P	W	D	L	F	A	Diff	B	Pts/P	Q	E
1	Denmark	22	10	8	2	0	17	6	11	4	2.200	5	0
2	Hungary	21	16	7	2	7	31	22	9	5	1.313	5	3
3	Netherlands	20	16	7	4	5	22	20	2	2	1.250	4	4
4	Spain	14	16	6	1	9	26	27	-1	1	0.875	3	6
5	Northern Ireland	13	8	5	3	0	28	7	21	0	1.625	4	0
6	Austria	12	6	4	2	0	17	4	13	2	2.000	3	0
7	USSR	12	6	4	2	0	8	2	6	2	2.000	3	0
8	Bulgaria	11	6	2	4	0	9	7	2	3	1.833	3	0
9	Yugoslavia	10	10	4	2	4	19	15	4	0	1.000	3	2
10	West Germany	10	11	3	3	5	14	23	-9	1	0.909	2	4
11	Greece	9	6	4	0	2	10	8	2	1	1.500	2	1
12	Luxembourg	8	4	4	0	0	28	2	26	0	2.000	2	0
13	Malta	8	4	4	0	0	19	0	19	0	2.000	2	0
14	Republic of Ireland	8	4	4	0	0	13	2	11	0	2.000	2	0
15	Romania	8	4	2	2	0	6	0	6	2	2.000	2	0
16	Scotland	8	6	4	0	2	10	8	2	0	1.333	1	2
17	Italy	8	7	3	1	3	5	4	1	1	1.143	2	3
18	Czechoslovakia	7	6	2	1	3	6	6	0	2	1.167	2	1
19	France	7	6	2	1	3	5	6	-1	2	1.167	2	1
20	Sweden	6	4	2	1	1	10	4	6	1	1.500	2	0
21	England	6	13	2	1	10	13	32	-19	1	0.462	1	6
22	Iceland	4	2	1	1	0	8	1	7	1	2.000	1	0
23	Switzerland	4	2	1	1	0	6	1	5	1	2.000	1	0
24	Cyprus	4	2	2	0	0	4	0	4	0	2.000	1	0
25	Belgium	3	4	1	0	3	4	7	-3	1	0.750	1	1
26	Turkey	2	2	1	0	1	7	1	6	0	1.000	1	0
27	Albania	2	1	1	0	0	4	0	4	0	2.000	1	0
28	Finland	2	2	1	0	1	3	2	1	0	1.000	1	0
29	East Germany	1	4	0	1	3	2	6	-4	0	0.250	0	2
	Total	**250**	**188**	**91**	**35**	**62**	**354**	**223**	**131**	**33**	**1.330**	**62**	**36**

Republic of Ireland

Pos'n	Cnty	Pts	P	W	D	L	F	A	Diff	B	Pts/P	Q	E
1	Northern Ireland	9	6	3	3	0	8	3	5	0	1.500	2	1
2	Cyprus	5	6	2	1	3	4	6	-2	0	0.833	1	2
3	East Germany	3	7	1	1	5	3	23	-20	0	0.429	0	3
4	Malta	2	2	1	0	1	2	1	1	0	1.000	1	0
5	Denmark	2	2	0	2	0	3	3	0	0	1.000	0	1
6	Switzerland	2	4	1	0	3	4	14	-10	0	0.500	0	2
7	Scotland	2	8	0	2	6	6	21	-15	0	0.250	0	4
8	France	1	2	0	1	1	3	4	-1	0	0.500	0	1
9	Romania	1	2	0	1	1	1	5	-4	0	0.500	0	1
10	Netherlands	1	2	0	1	1	1	7	-6	0	0.500	0	1
11	Turkey	0	2	0	0	2	2	5	-3	0	0.000	0	1
12	Austria	0	2	0	0	2	0	5	-5	0	0.000	0	1
13	USSR	0	2	0	0	2	1	7	-6	0	0.000	0	1
14	Belgium	0	2	0	0	2	4	11	-7	0	0.000	0	1
15	Portugal	0	4	0	0	4	2	13	-11	0	0.000	0	2
16	West Germany	0	4	0	0	4	2	16	-14	0	0.000	0	2
17	Yugoslavia	0	4	0	0	4	0	14	-14	0	0.000	0	2
18	Hungary	0	6	0	0	6	4	20	-16	0	0.000	0	3
19	Spain	0	4	0	0	4	3	20	-17	0	0.000	0	2
20	England	0	6	0	0	6	5	24	-19	0	0.000	0	3
	Total	**28**	**77**	**8**	**12**	**57**	**58**	**222**	**-164**	**0**	**0.364**	**4**	**34**

Romania

Pos'n	Cnty	Pts	P	W	D	L	F	A	Diff	B	Pts/P	Q	E
1	Denmark	10	6	4	1	1	16	6	10	1	1.667	3	0
2	USSR	9	4	3	1	0	7	2	5	2	2.250	2	0
3	Czechoslovakia	9	8	3	3	2	15	12	3	0	1.125	3	1
4	Finland	8	4	3	1	0	5	0	5	1	2.000	2	0
5	Spain	8	11	3	2	6	13	23	-10	0	0.727	1	5
6	Cyprus	7	4	3	0	1	10	4	6	1	1.750	2	0
7	Turkey	7	6	2	2	2	10	8	2	1	1.167	2	1
8	East Germany	6	5	3	0	2	7	8	-1	0	1.200	1	1
9	Belgium	6	6	2	1	3	6	7	-1	1	1.000	1	2
10	West Germany	6	7	2	1	4	12	14	-2	1	0.857	1	2
11	Hungary	5	4	2	0	2	8	4	4	1	1.250	2	0
12	Sweden	5	4	2	0	2	8	6	2	1	1.250	1	1
13	Northern Ireland	4	2	2	0	0	12	0	12	0	2.000	1	0
14	Malta	4	2	2	0	0	7	0	7	0	2.000	1	0
15	Luxembourg	4	2	2	0	0	6	0	6	0	2.000	1	0
16	Iceland	4	2	2	0	0	5	0	5	0	2.000	1	0
17	Greece	4	4	2	0	2	6	4	2	0	1.000	2	0
18	Bulgaria	4	4	2	0	2	7	12	-5	0	1.000	1	1
19	Netherlands	4	6	1	2	3	3	11	-8	0	0.667	1	2
20	Italy	4	9	1	2	6	3	18	-15	0	0.444	0	5
21	Republic of Ireland	3	2	1	1	0	5	1	4	0	1.500	1	0
22	Scotland	3	2	1	0	1	3	2	1	1	1.500	1	0
23	France	3	4	1	1	2	3	5	-2	0	0.750	0	2
24	Norway	2	2	1	0	1	4	3	1	0	1.000	1	0
25	Austria	2	4	0	2	2	1	4	-3	0	0.500	0	2
26	Portugal	2	4	0	2	2	0	6	-6	0	0.500	0	2
27	England	2	9	1	0	8	7	18	-11	0	0.222	0	4
28	Yugoslavia	0	2	0	0	2	1	6	-5	0	0.000	0	1
29	Poland	0	2	0	0	2	1	10	-9	0	0.000	0	1
	Total	**135**	**131**	**51**	**22**	**58**	**191**	**194**	**-3**	**11**	**1.031**	**32**	**33**

Scotland

Pos'n	Cnty	Pts	P	W	D	L	F	A	Diff	B	Pts/P	Q	E
1	Italy	18	19	7	3	9	15	23	-8	1	0.947	3	7
2	Belgium	17	10	7	1	2	23	14	9	2	1.700	3	2
3	Republic of Ireland	16	8	6	2	0	21	6	15	2	2.000	4	0
4	Switzerland	15	10	5	3	2	15	7	8	2	1.500	4	1
5	France	15	15	7	0	8	25	24	1	1	1.000	4	3
6	Netherlands	14	10	5	2	3	15	15	0	2	1.400	3	2
7	Malta	13	6	6	0	0	23	1	22	1	2.167	3	0
8	Austria	13	8	5	1	2	8	6	2	2	1.625	3	1
9	Yugoslavia	12	9	4	2	3	17	13	4	2	1.333	3	1
10	West Germany	9	12	2	4	6	19	24	-5	1	0.750	2	4
11	Finland	8	4	4	0	0	23	1	22	0	2.000	2	0
12	Czechoslovakia	8	4	2	2	0	8	5	3	2	2.000	2	0
13	Hungary	8	6	3	1	2	9	7	2	1	1.333	2	1
14	East Germany	7	4	3	0	1	9	5	4	1	1.750	1	1
15	Sweden	7	4	2	2	0	6	3	3	1	1.750	1	1
16	Denmark	6	4	2	1	1	5	2	3	1	1.500	2	0
17	Portugal	6	6	2	0	4	8	10	-2	2	1.000	2	1
18	Spain	6	10	2	2	6	7	22	-15	0	0.600	0	5
19	Albania	5	4	2	1	1	5	2	3	0	1.250	2	0
20	England	5	4	2	0	2	3	6	-3	1	1.250	1	1
21	Luxembourg	4	2	2	0	0	11	1	10	0	2.000	1	0
22	Iceland	4	2	2	0	0	7	2	5	0	2.000	1	0
23	Norway	4	2	2	0	0	5	2	3	0	2.000	1	0
24	Poland	4	2	1	1	0	4	2	2	1	2.000	1	0
25	USSR	4	6	1	2	3	6	8	-2	0	0.667	1	2
26	Romania	2	2	1	0	1	2	3	-1	0	1.000	0	1
27	Greece	1	2	0	1	1	1	3	-2	0	0.500	0	1
	Total	**231**	**175**	**87**	**31**	**57**	**300**	**217**	**83**	**26**	**1.320**	**52**	**35**

Spain

Pos'n	Cnty	Pts	P	W	D	L	F	A	Diff	B	Pts/P	Q	E
1	Italy	43	30	15	4	11	42	33	9	9	1.433	12	4
2	West Germany	27	22	8	6	8	33	34	-1	5	1.227	6	5
3	Portugal	23	16	9	1	6	27	26	1	4	1.438	6	3
4	Austria	22	13	8	3	2	36	12	24	3	1.692	5	1
5	Spain	22	18	7	4	7	35	35	0	4	1.222	4	4
6	Belgium	21	16	8	2	6	31	18	13	3	1.313	4	4
7	Denmark	20	10	8	1	1	41	8	33	3	2.000	5	0
8	Scotland	18	10	6	2	2	22	7	15	4	1.800	5	0
9	Luxembourg	17	8	8	0	0	37	3	34	1	2.125	4	0
10	France	17	10	6	2	2	23	13	10	3	1.700	5	1
–	Romania	17	11	6	2	3	23	13	10	3	1.545	5	1
12	England	17	15	5	4	6	30	25	5	3	1.133	3	5
13	Netherlands	17	14	5	5	4	18	13	5	2	1.214	4	3
14	Hungary	16	10	6	1	3	19	11	8	3	1.600	4	1
15	Yugoslavia	16	12	5	3	4	18	15	3	3	1.333	5	1
16	Switzerland	14	8	6	0	2	23	5	18	2	1.750	3	1
17	Poland	14	8	6	0	2	13	7	6	2	1.750	4	0
18	Czechoslovakia	13	8	4	2	2	17	7	10	3	1.625	4	0
19	Bulgaria	13	9	5	2	2	16	8	8	1	1.444	3	1
20	Sweden	12	6	5	0	1	13	4	9	2	2.000	3	0
21	USSR	9	6	2	3	1	6	3	3	2	1.500	2	1
22	Cyprus	8	4	4	0	0	26	1	25	0	2.000	2	0
23	Republic of Ireland	8	4	4	0	0	20	3	17	0	2.000	2	0
24	Iceland	8	4	4	0	0	8	2	6	0	2.000	2	0

25	Turkey	7	4	2	2	0	4	1	3	1	1.750	2	0
26	Norway	4	2	2	0	0	4	0	4	0	2.000	1	0
	Total	**423**	**278**	**154**	**49**	**75**	**585**	**307**	**278**	**66**	**1.522**	**105**	**36**

Sweden

Pos'n	Cnty	Pts	P	W	D	L	F	A	Diff	B	Pts/P	Q	E
1	Bulgaria	12	8	5	1	2	14	19	-5	1	1.500	2	2
2	Italy	10	14	3	4	7	14	24	-10	0	0.714	1	6
3	Finland	9	4	4	0	0	9	2	7	1	2.250	2	0
4	Luxembourg	8	5	4	0	1	24	3	21	0	1.600	2	0
5	Albania	8	4	3	1	0	7	1	6	1	2.000	2	0
6	Belgium	7	8	2	2	4	6	9	-3	1	0.875	2	2
7	Poland	7	8	2	1	5	10	14	-4	2	0.875	2	2
8	East Germany	7	10	2	3	5	12	21	-9	0	0.700	1	4
9	Turkey	6	4	2	1	1	10	6	4	1	1.500	2	0
10	Cyprus	4	2	2	0	0	7	2	5	0	2.000	1	0
11	USSR	4	2	1	1	0	2	0	2	1	2.000	1	0
12	Romania	4	4	2	0	2	6	8	-2	0	1.000	1	1
13	Austria	4	4	1	1	2	1	4	-3	1	1.000	1	1
14	West Germany	4	6	2	0	4	5	12	-7	0	0.667	0	3
15	France	3	2	1	1	0	1	0	1	0	1.500	1	0
16	Greece	3	4	1	1	2	3	5	-2	0	0.750	0	2
17	Scotland	3	4	0	2	2	3	6	-3	1	0.750	1	1
18	Portugal	3	4	1	1	2	4	10	-6	0	0.750	0	2
19	Northern Ireland	2	2	1	0	1	7	3	4	0	1.000	1	0
20	Hungary	2	2	1	0	1	1	4	-3	0	1.000	0	1
21	Spain	2	6	1	0	5	4	13	-9	0	0.333	0	3
22	Netherlands	2	5	1	0	4	7	18	-11	0	0.400	0	2
23	Yugoslavia	1	2	0	1	1	3	4	-1	0	0.500	0	1
24	Denmark	1	2	0	1	1	2	3	-1	0	0.500	0	1
25	England	1	3	0	1	2	1	4	-3	0	0.333	0	2
	Total	**117**	**119**	**42**	**23**	**54**	**163**	**195**	**-32**	**10**	**0.983**	**23**	**36**

Switzerland

Pos'n	Cnty	Pts	P	W	D	L	F	A	Diff	B	Pts/P	Q	E
1	Hungary	12	10	5	1	4	20	17	3	1	1.200	2	3
2	East Germany	11	9	3	3	3	14	14	0	2	1.222	2	2
3	Finland	10	6	4	1	1	18	3	15	1	1.667	3	0
4	Belgium	10	6	4	1	1	16	9	7	1	1.667	3	0
5	Malta	8	4	4	0	0	20	4	16	0	2.000	2	0
6	Scotland	7	10	2	3	5	7	15	-8	0	0.700	1	4
7	Republic of Ireland	6	4	3	0	1	14	4	10	0	1.500	2	0
8	Turkey	6	5	2	1	2	7	9	-2	1	1.200	1	1
9	Czechoslovakia	6	6	2	1	3	6	10	-4	1	1.000	1	2
10	France	5	4	2	1	1	5	6	-1	0	1.250	1	1
11	Netherlands	5	9	2	0	7	9	19	-10	1	0.556	1	3
12	Spain	5	8	2	0	6	5	23	-18	1	0.625	1	3
13	Iceland	4	2	2	0	0	11	2	9	0	2.000	1	0
14	West Germany	4	6	1	2	3	7	16	-9	0	0.667	0	3
15	Northern Ireland	3	2	1	1	0	4	3	1	0	1.500	1	0
16	Denmark	3	4	1	1	2	7	9	-2	0	0.750	0	2
17	Yugoslavia	3	4	1	1	2	3	7	-4	0	0.750	0	2
18	USSR	3	6	1	1	4	6	11	-5	0	0.500	1	2
19	England	3	8	1	1	6	6	21	-15	0	0.375	0	4
20	Greece	2	2	1	0	1	3	3	0	0	1.000	1	0
21	Austria	2	2	1	0	1	2	3	-1	0	1.000	0	1

22	Portugal	1	2	0	1	1	1	6	-5	0	0.500	0	1
23	Italy	1	4	0	1	3	5	11	-6	0	0.250	0	2
	Total	**120**	**123**	**45**	**21**	**57**	**196**	**225**	**-29**	**9**	**0.976**	**24**	**36**

Turkey

Pos'n	Cnty	Pts	P	W	D	L	F	A	Diff	B	Pts/P	Q	E
1	France	9	7	3	2	2	9	11	-2	1	1.286	2	1
2	Poland	8	8	3	1	4	9	12	-3	1	1.000	1	3
3	Switzerland	6	5	2	1	2	9	7	2	1	1.200	1	1
4	Romania	6	6	2	2	2	8	10	-2	0	1.000	1	2
5	England	6	6	2	2	2	4	7	-3	0	1.000	1	2
6	Hungary	5	4	2	1	1	10	5	5	0	1.250	2	0
7	Albania	5	2	2	0	0	3	0	3	1	2.500	1	0
8	Iceland	4	2	2	0	0	6	3	3	0	2.000	1	0
9	Republic of Ireland	4	2	2	0	0	5	2	3	0	2.000	1	0
–	Luxembourg	4	2	2	0	0	5	2	3	0	2.000	1	0
11	Austria	4	6	2	0	4	4	10	-6	0	0.667	1	2
12	USSR	4	8	1	2	5	3	16	-13	0	0.500	0	4
13	Netherlands	4	10	2	0	8	7	22	-15	0	0.400	0	5
14	Sweden	3	4	1	1	2	6	10	-4	0	0.750	0	2
15	Czechoslovakia	3	6	1	0	5	3	11	-8	1	0.500	1	2
16	Denmark	2	2	1	0	1	1	2	-1	0	1.000	0	1
17	Spain	2	4	0	2	2	1	4	-3	0	0.500	0	2
18	Portugal	2	2	1	0	1	1	7	-6	0	1.000	0	1
19	Belgium	1	2	0	1	1	1	5	-4	0	0.500	0	1
20	West Germany	1	4	0	1	3	2	10	-8	0	0.250	0	2
21	Yugoslavia	0	2	0	0	2	0	2	-2	0	0.000	0	1
22	East Germany	0	2	0	0	2	0	5	-5	0	0.000	0	1
23	Italy	0	2	0	0	2	1	8	-7	0	0.000	0	1
	Total	**83**	**98**	**31**	**16**	**51**	**98**	**171**	**-73**	**5**	**0.847**	**14**	**34**

USSR

Pos'n	Cnty	Pts	P	W	D	L	F	A	Diff	B	Pts/P	Q	E
1	Austria	16	8	6	2	0	14	5	9	2	2.000	4	0
2	Turkey	13	8	5	2	1	16	3	13	1	1.625	4	0
3	Switzerland	10	6	4	1	1	11	6	5	1	1.667	2	1
4	Scotland	9	6	3	2	1	8	6	2	1	1.500	2	1
5	West Germany	9	10	4	0	6	9	15	-6	1	0.900	1	4
6	Norway	8	4	4	0	0	10	2	8	0	2.000	2	0
7	Greece	8	4	3	1	0	9	2	7	1	2.000	2	0
8	Northern Ireland	7	4	3	1	0	6	2	4	0	1.750	2	0
9	Finland	6	4	3	0	1	7	5	2	0	1.500	1	1
10	Bulgaria	6	4	2	1	1	6	4	2	1	1.500	2	0
11	Spain	6	6	1	3	2	3	6	-3	1	1.000	1	2
12	Republic of Ireland	5	2	2	0	0	7	1	6	1	2.500	1	0
13	Hungary	5	2	2	0	0	9	4	5	1	2.500	1	0
14	Iceland	5	2	2	0	0	5	0	5	1	2.500	1	0
15	Czechoslovakia	5	4	2	1	1	4	1	3	0	1.250	1	1
16	Italy	5	6	0	4	2	1	3	-2	1	0.833	1	2
17	Luxembourg	4	2	2	0	0	9	0	9	0	2.000	1	0
18	Yugoslavia	4	2	2	0	0	5	0	5	0	2.000	1	0
19	Cyprus	4	2	2	0	0	3	0	3	0	2.000	1	0
20	Poland	4	4	1	1	2	5	5	0	1	1.000	1	1
21	France	4	6	1	2	3	6	10	-4	0	0.667	0	3
22	Denmark	3	2	1	0	1	3	2	1	1	1.500	1	0
23	England	3	4	1	1	2	4	4	0	0	0.750	1	1

24	Belgium	2	2	1	0	1	1	2	-1	0	1.000	0	1
25	Portugal	2	6	0	2	4	2	8	-6	0	0.333	0	3
26	Sweden	1	2	0	1	1	0	2	-2	0	0.500	0	1
27	Romania	1	4	0	1	3	2	7	-5	0	0.250	0	2
	Total	**155**	**116**	**57**	**26**	**33**	**165**	**105**	**60**	**15**	**1.336**	**34**	**24**

West Germany

Pos'n	Cnty	Pts	P	W	D	L	F	A	Diff	B	Pts/P	Q	E
1	Spain	26	22	8	6	8	34	33	1	4	1.182	5	6
2	Austria	23	14	7	4	3	28	15	13	5	1.643	7	0
3	Bulgaria	22	12	8	2	2	32	10	22	4	1.833	5	1
4	Cyprus	21	10	10	0	0	56	3	53	1	2.100	5	0
5	England	20	21	4	10	7	24	28	-4	2	0.952	3	9
6	Italy	20	20	6	6	8	23	30	-7	2	1.000	3	7
7	Scotland	19	12	6	4	2	24	19	5	3	1.583	4	2
8	Portugal	17	11	5	3	3	23	14	9	4	1.545	4	2
9	USSR	16	10	6	0	4	15	9	6	4	1.600	4	1
10	East Germany	14	8	5	2	1	20	13	7	2	1.750	4	0
11	Netherlands	14	10	5	2	3	14	14	0	2	1.400	3	2
12	Greece	13	6	5	1	0	15	4	11	2	2.167	3	0
13	Czechoslovakia	11	6	4	0	2	17	7	10	3	1.833	3	0
14	Switzerland	11	6	3	2	1	16	7	9	3	1.833	3	0
15	Yugoslavia	11	8	4	1	3	15	11	4	2	1.375	2	2
16	Romania	11	7	4	1	2	14	12	2	2	1.571	2	1
17	Belgium	10	6	3	2	1	12	7	5	2	1.667	2	1
18	Sweden	9	6	4	0	2	12	5	7	1	1.500	3	0
19	Luxembourg	8	5	4	0	1	20	6	14	0	1.600	2	0
20	Republic of Ireland	8	4	4	0	0	16	2	14	0	2.000	2	0
21	Denmark	8	5	4	0	1	15	7	8	0	1.600	2	0
22	Turkey	8	4	3	1	0	10	2	8	1	2.000	2	0
23	Albania	8	4	3	1	0	8	1	7	1	2.000	2	0
24	France	8	5	3	1	1	5	3	2	1	1.600	2	1
25	Iceland	7	4	3	1	0	10	3	7	0	1.750	2	0
26	Hungary	7	4	2	2	0	8	2	6	1	1.750	2	0
27	Norway	4	2	2	0	0	6	2	4	0	2.000	1	0
–	Poland	4	2	2	0	0	6	2	4	0	2.000	1	0
	Total	**358**	**234**	**127**	**52**	**55**	**498**	**271**	**227**	**52**	**1.530**	**83**	**35**

Yugoslavia

Pos'n	Cnty	Pts	P	W	D	L	F	A	Diff	B	Pts/P	Q	E
1	East Germany	14	10	6	0	4	18	12	6	2	1.400	2	3
2	Norway	12	6	5	1	0	19	5	14	1	2.000	3	0
3	Spain	12	12	4	3	5	15	18	-3	1	1.000	1	5
4	Portugal	11	10	4	2	4	15	19	-4	1	1.100	2	3
5	England	11	12	3	3	6	13	18	-5	2	0.917	2	4
6	Scotland	9	9	3	2	4	13	17	-4	1	1.000	1	3
7	West Germany	9	8	3	1	4	11	15	-4	2	1.125	2	2
8	Malta	8	4	4	0	0	18	2	16	0	2.000	2	0
9	Republic of Ireland	8	4	4	0	0	14	0	14	0	2.000	2	0
10	Luxembourg	7	4	3	0	1	21	5	16	1	1.750	2	0
11	Cyprus	7	4	3	1	0	11	4	7	0	1.750	2	0
12	Czechoslovakia	7	6	2	1	3	13	11	2	2	1.167	2	1
13	Netherlands	7	4	3	0	1	8	6	2	1	1.750	1	1
14	Switzerland	6	4	2	1	1	7	3	4	1	1.500	2	0
15	France	6	5	2	2	1	9	8	1	0	1.200	2	1
16	Romania	5	2	2	0	0	6	1	5	1	2.500	1	0

17	Belgium	5	4	2	0	2	9	6	3	1	1.250	1	1
18	Northern Ireland	4	2	2	0	0	12	2	10	0	2.000	1	0
19	Iceland	4	2	2	0	0	9	1	8	0	2.000	1	0
20	Greece	4	4	2	0	2	8	6	2	0	1.000	1	1
21	Poland	4	2	2	0	0	3	1	2	0	2.000	1	0
22	Turkey	4	2	2	0	0	2	0	2	0	2.000	1	0
23	Sweden	4	2	1	1	0	4	3	1	1	2.000	1	0
24	Hungary	4	6	2	0	4	7	9	-2	0	0.667	1	2
25	Italy	4	10	0	4	6	5	16	-11	0	0.400	0	5
26	Denmark	3	2	1	0	1	4	2	2	1	1.500	1	0
27	Austria	3	2	1	1	0	1	0	1	0	1.500	1	0
28	Bulgaria	3	4	1	0	3	6	9	-3	1	0.750	1	1
29	Finland	0	2	0	0	2	2	4	-2	0	0.000	0	1
30	USSR	0	2	0	0	2	0	5	-5	0	0.000	0	1
	Total	**185**	**150**	**71**	**23**	**56**	**283**	**208**	**75**	**20**	**1.233**	**40**	**35**

Below: Steaua Bucharest's Anghel Jordanescu (left) and goalkeeper Helmut Ducadam with the European Champions' Cup after beating Barcelona 2-0 on penalties in the 1985-86 final in Seville.

Comparative Country v. Country Performance Chart

1955-56 to 1990-91

	Total		%	No.	Albania		Austria		Belgium		Bulgaria		Cyprus		Czechoslovacia		Denmark		E. Germany	
	Q	E	Qual	Adv	Q	E	Q	E	Q	E	Q	E	Q	E	Q	E	Q	E	Q	E
Albania	3	17	15.00%	13	–	–	0	2	0	1	0	2	–	–	–	–	0	1	–	–
Austria	31	36	46.30%	26	2	0	–	–	–	–	1	1	1	0	2	0	1	1	4	0
Belgium	45	36	55.60%	28	1	0	–	–	–	–	1	0	1	0	2	3	2	0	1	0
Bulgaria	27	34	44.30%	23	2	0	1	1	0	1	–	–	1	0	1	1	1	0	–	–
Cyprus	5	25	16.70%	19	–	–	0	1	0	1	0	1	–	–	–	–	–	–	0	1
Czechoslovakia	38	35	52.10%	25	–	–	0	2	3	2	1	1	–	–	–	–	4	0	2	0
Denmark	17	36	32.10%	28	1	0	1	1	0	2	0	1	–	–	0	4	–	–	1	0
East Germany	28	33	45.90%	24	–	–	0	4	0	1	–	–	1	0	0	2	0	1	–	–
England	88	27	76.50%	30	–	–	2	0	7	0	1	2	–	–	4	0	1	0	5	0
Finland	6	32	15.80%	21	–	–	0	2	0	3	–	–	1	1	0	1	0	1	0	1
France	46	36	56.10%	29	1	0	1	1	2	0	2	1	–	–	2	1	4	1	1	1
Greece	18	32	36.00%	23	–	–	–	–	0	2	0	2	1	0	1	2	1	0	1	1
Hungary	31	35	47.00%	26	–	–	–	–	1	1	4	0	–	–	1	3	0	1	1	1
Iceland	2	27	6.90%	21	–	–	–	–	0	1	0	1	1	0	0	2	–	–	–	–
Italy	90	34	72.60%	28	–	–	2	1	4	3	4	1	1	0	1	0	1	0	2	1
Luxembourg	2	35	5.40%	22	–	–	0	2	–	–	–	–	0	1	–	–	0	2	0	2
Malta	1	30	3.20%	18	0	2	0	2	0	1	0	1	0	1	0	2	–	–	–	–
Netherlands	58	32	64.40%	27	2	0	1	1	–	–	3	1	2	0	1	1	1	0	3	0
Northern Ireland	6	32	15.80%	20	0	1	–	–	0	3	0	2	–	–	–	–	0	2	0	1
Norway	5	31	13.90%	16	–	–	0	2	0	5	–	–	–	–	0	4	0	1	–	–
Poland	24	35	40.70%	23	–	–	3	0	2	2	0	4	–	–	1	4	1	1	1	2
Portugal	62	36	63.30%	29	1	0	3	0	1	1	3	0	1	0	2	1	5	0	0	2
Rep. of Ireland	4	34	10.50%	20	–	–	0	1	0	1	–	–	1	2	–	–	0	1	0	3
Romania	32	33	49.20%	29	–	–	0	2	1	2	1	1	2	0	3	1	3	0	1	1
Scotland	52	35	59.80%	27	2	0	3	1	3	2	–	–	–	–	2	0	2	0	1	1
Spain	105	36	74.50%	26	–	–	5	1	4	4	3	1	2	0	4	0	5	0	–	–
Sweden	23	36	39.00%	25	2	0	1	1	2	2	2	2	1	0	–	–	0	1	1	4
Switzerland	24	36	40.00%	23	–	–	0	1	3	0	–	–	–	–	1	2	0	2	2	2
Turkey	14	34	29.20%	23	1	0	1	2	0	1	–	–	–	–	1	2	0	1	0	1
USSR	34	24	58.60%	27	–	–	4	0	0	1	2	0	1	0	1	1	1	0	–	–
West Germany	83	35	70.30%	28	2	0	7	0	2	1	5	1	5	0	3	0	2	0	4	0
Yugoslavia	40	35	53.30%	30	–	–	1	0	1	1	1	1	2	0	2	1	1	0	2	3
					Elim	Qual	Elim	Qual	Elim	Qual	Elim	Qual	Elim	Qual	Elim	Qual	Elim	Qual	Elim	Qual
Total	**1044**	**1044**	**50.00%**		**17**	**3**	**36**	**31**	**36**	**45**	**34**	**27**	**25**	**5**	**35**	**38**	**36**	**17**	**33**	**28**

	England		Finland		France		Greece		Hungary		Iceland		Italy		Luxembourg		Malta		Netherlands	
	Q	E	Q	E	Q	E	Q	E	Q	E	Q	E	Q	E	Q	E	Q	E	Q	E
Albania	–	–	–	–	0	1	–	–	–	–	–	–	–	–	–	–	2	0	0	2
Austria	0	2	2	0	1	1	–	–	–	–	–	–	1	2	2	0	2	0	1	1
Belgium	0	7	3	0	0	2	2	0	1	1	1	0	3	4	–	–	1	0	–	–
Bulgaria	2	1	–	–	1	2	2	0	0	4	1	0	1	4	–	–	1	0	1	3
Cyprus	–	–	1	1	–	–	0	1	–	–	0	1	0	1	1	0	1	0	0	2
Czechoslovakia	0	4	1	0	1	2	2	1	3	1	2	0	0	1	–	–	2	0	1	1
Denmark	0	1	1	0	1	4	0	1	1	0	–	–	0	1	2	0	–	–	0	1
East Germany	0	5	1	0	1	1	1	1	1	1	–	–	1	2	2	0	–	–	0	3
England	1	1	4	0	2	0	2	1	2	0	3	0	1	8	1	0	2	0	3	2
Finland	0	4	–	–	0	2	–	–	–	–	–	–	0	2	0	1	3	0	0	1
France	0	2	2	0	–	–	2	0	1	0	2	0	1	5	1	0	–	–	2	4
Greece	1	2	–	–	0	2	–	–	0	1	–	–	0	5	2	0	2	0	2	1
Hungary	0	2	–	–	0	1	1	0	–	–	3	0	0	4	1	0	1	0	2	1
Iceland	0	3	–	–	0	2	–	–	0	3	–	–	0	1	1	0	0	1	0	1
Italy	8	1	2	0	5	1	5	0	4	0	1	0	1	1	3	0	–	–	2	3
Luxembourg	0	1	1	0	0	1	0	2	0	1	0	1	0	3	–	–	–	–	–	–
Malta	0	2	0	3	–	–	0	2	0	1	1	0	–	–	–	–	–	–	–	–
Netherlands	2	3	1	0	4	2	1	2	1	2	1	0	3	2	–	–	–	–	–	–
Northern Ireland	0	1	–	–	0	2	0	2	–	–	1	0	0	1	2	0	–	–	0	2
Norway	0	2	1	0	0	2	–	–	0	1	–	–	–	–	–	–	–	–	1	3
Poland	1	3	1	0	1	3	3	0	0	1	–	–	0	1	1	1	2	0	0	2
Portugal	1	6	1	0	2	1	2	1	5	3	1	0	2	3	2	0	2	0	4	4
Rep. of Ireland	0	3	–	–	0	1	–	–	0	3	–	–	–	–	–	–	1	0	0	1
Romania	0	4	2	0	0	2	2	0	2	0	1	0	0	5	1	0	1	0	1	2
Scotland	1	1	2	0	4	3	0	1	2	1	1	0	3	7	1	0	3	0	3	2
Spain	3	5	–	–	5	1	–	–	4	1	2	0	12	4	4	0	–	–	4	3
Sweden	0	2	2	0	1	0	0	2	0	1	–	–	1	6	2	0	–	–	0	2
Switzerland	0	4	3	0	1	1	1	0	2	3	1	0	0	2	–	–	2	0	1	3
Turkey	1	2	–	–	2	1	–	–	2	0	1	0	0	1	1	0	–	–	0	5
USSR	1	1	1	1	0	3	2	0	1	0	1	0	1	2	1	0	–	–	–	–
West Germany	3	9	–	–	2	1	3	0	2	0	2	0	3	7	2	0	–	–	3	2
Yugoslavia	2	4	0	1	2	1	1	1	1	2	1	0	0	5	2	0	2	0	1	1
	Elim	**Qual**	**Elim**	**Qual**	**Elim**	**Qual**	**Elim**	**Qual**	**Elim**	**Qual**	**Elim**	**Qual**	**Elim**	**Qual**	**Elim**	**Qual**	**Elim**	**Qual**	**Elim**	**Qual**
Total	**27**	**88**	**32**	**6**	**36**	**46**	**32**	**18**	**35**	**31**	**27**	**2**	**34**	**90**	**35**	**2**	**30**	**1**	**32**	**58**

1955-56 to 1990-91

	N. Ireland		Norway		Poland		Portugal		Rep. of Ire.		Romania		Scotland		Spain		Sweden		Switzerland	
	Q	E	Q	E	Q	E	Q	E	Q	E	Q	E	Q	E	Q	E	Q	E	Q	E
Albania	1	0	–	–	–	–	0	1	–	–	–	–	0	2	–	–	0	2	–	–
Austria	–	–	2	0	0	3	0	3	1	0	2	0	1	3	1	5	1	1	1	0
Belgium	3	0	5	0	2	2	1	1	1	0	2	1	2	3	4	4	2	2	0	3
Bulgaria	2	0	–	–	4	0	0	3	–	–	1	1	–	–	1	3	2	2	–	–
Cyprus	–	–	–	–	–	–	0	1	2	1	0	2	–	–	0	2	0	1	–	–
Czechoslovakia	–	–	4	0	4	1	1	2	–	–	1	3	0	2	0	4	–	–	2	1
Denmark	2	0	1	0	1	1	0	5	1	0	0	3	0	2	0	5	1	0	2	0
East Germany	1	0	–	–	2	1	2	0	3	0	1	1	1	1	–	–	4	1	2	2
England	1	0	2	0	3	1	6	1	3	0	4	0	1	1	5	3	2	0	4	0
Finland	–	–	0	1	0	1	0	1	–	–	0	2	0	2	–	–	0	2	0	3
France	2	0	2	0	3	1	1	2	1	0	2	0	3	4	1	5	0	1	1	1
Greece	2	0	–	–	0	3	1	2	–	–	0	2	1	0	–	–	2	0	0	1
Hungary	–	–	1	0	1	0	3	5	3	0	0	2	1	2	1	4	1	0	3	2
Iceland	0	1	–	–	–	–	0	1	–	–	0	1	0	1	0	2	–	–	0	1
Italy	1	0	–	–	1	0	3	2	–	–	5	0	7	3	4	12	6	1	2	0
Luxembourg	0	2	–	–	1	1	0	2	–	–	0	1	0	1	0	4	0	2	–	–
Malta	–	–	–	–	0	2	0	2	0	1	0	1	0	3	–	–	–	–	0	2
Netherlands	2	0	3	1	2	0	4	4	1	0	2	1	2	3	3	4	2	0	3	1
Northern Ireland	–	–	2	3	–	–	0	4	1	2	0	1	–	–	–	–	0	1	0	1
Norway	3	2	–	–	–	–	–	–	–	–	0	1	0	1	0	1	–	–	–	–
Poland	–	–	–	–	–	–	–	–	–	–	1	0	0	1	0	4	2	2	–	–
Portugal	4	0	–	–	–	–	–	–	2	0	2	0	1	2	3	6	2	0	1	0
Rep. of Ireland	2	1	–	–	–	–	0	2	–	–	0	1	0	4	0	2	–	–	0	2
Romania	1	0	1	0	0	1	0	2	1	0	–	–	1	0	1	5	1	1	–	–
Scotland	–	–	1	0	1	0	2	1	4	0	0	1	–	–	0	5	1	1	4	1
Spain	–	–	1	0	4	0	6	3	2	0	5	1	5	0	4	4	3	0	3	1
Sweden	1	0	–	–	2	2	0	2	–	–	1	1	1	1	0	3	–	–	–	–
Switzerland	1	0	–	–	–	–	0	1	2	0	–	–	1	4	1	3	–	–	–	–
Turkey	–	–	–	–	1	3	0	1	1	0	1	2	–	–	0	2	0	2	1	1
USSR	2	0	2	0	1	1	0	3	1	0	0	2	2	1	1	2	0	1	2	1
West Germany	–	–	1	0	1	0	4	2	2	0	2	1	4	2	5	6	3	0	3	0
Yugoslavia	1	0	3	0	1	0	2	3	2	0	1	0	1	3	1	5	1	0	2	0
	Elim	**Qual**	**Elim**	**Qual**	**Elim**	**Qual**	**Elim**	**Qual**	**Elim**	**Qual**	**Elim**	**Qual**	**Elim**	**Qual**	**Elim**	**Qual**	**Elim**	**Qual**	**Elim**	**Qual**
Total	**32**	**6**	**31**	**5**	**35**	**24**	**36**	**62**	**34**	**4**	**33**	**32**	**35**	**52**	**36**	**105**	**36**	**23**	**36**	**24**

1955-56 to 1990-91

	Turkey		USSR		W. Germany		Yugoslavia	
	Q	E	Q	E	Q	E	Q	E
Albania	0	1	–	–	0	2	–	–
Austria	2	1	0	4	0	7	0	1
Belgium	1	0	1	0	1	2	1	1
Bulgaria	–	–	0	2	1	5	1	1
Cyprus	–	–	0	1	0	5	0	2
Czechoslovakia	2	1	1	1	0	3	1	2
Denmark	1	0	0	1	0	2	0	1
East Germany	1	0	–	–	0	4	3	2
England	2	1	1	1	9	3	4	2
Finland	–	–	1	1	–	–	1	0
France	1	2	3	0	1	2	1	2
Greece	–	–	0	2	0	3	1	1
Hungary	0	2	0	1	0	2	2	1
Iceland	0	1	0	1	0	2	0	1
Italy	1	0	2	1	7	3	5	0
Luxembourg	0	1	0	1	0	2	0	2
Malta	–	–	–	–	–	–	0	2
Netherlands	5	0	–	–	2	3	1	1
Northern Ireland	–	–	0	2	–	–	0	1
Norway	–	–	0	2	0	1	0	3
Poland	3	1	1	1	0	1	0	1
Portugal	1	0	3	0	2	4	3	2
Rep. of Ireland	0	1	0	1	0	2	0	2
Romania	2	1	2	0	1	2	0	1
Scotland	–	–	1	2	2	4	3	1
Spain	2	0	2	1	6	5	5	1
Sweden	2	0	1	0	0	3	0	1
Switzerland	1	1	1	2	0	3	0	2
Turkey	–	–	0	4	0	2	0	1
USSR	4	0	–	–	1	4	1	0
West Germany	2	0	4	1	–	–	2	2
Yugoslavia	1	0	0	1	2	2	–	–
	Elim	**Qual**	**Elim**	**Qual**	**Elim**	**Qual**	**Elim**	**Qual**
Total	**34**	**14**	**24**	**34**	**35**	**83**	**35**	**40**

Below: Peter Withe beats Bayern Munich 'keeper Manfred Müller to score Aston Villa's goal in the 1981-82 European Champions's Cup Final in Rotterdam.

Second-leg Outcomes 1955-56 to 1990-91

First-leg: 0-0

Second-leg	1-0	2-0	3-0	4-0	5-0	2-1	3-1	4-1	5-1	3-2	4-2	5-2	4-3
	9	1	1	0	0	2	2	1	0	1	0	0	0
Second-leg	5-3	5-4	0-0	1-1	2-2	3-3	4-4	5-5	0-1	0-2	0-3	0-4	0-5
	0	0	4	4	2	0	0	0	9	16	3	4	3
Second-leg	1-2	1-3	1-4	1-5	2-3	2-4	2-5	3-4	3-5	4-5	5>	<5	
	4	1	2	2	1	0	0	0	0	0	0	3	

First-leg: 1-0

Second-leg	1-0	2-0	3-0	4-0	5-0	2-1	3-1	4-1	5-1	3-2	4-2	5-2	4-3
	6	3	1	1	0	2	2	1	0	1	0	0	0
Second-leg	5-3	5-4	0-0	1-1	2-2	3-3	4-4	5-5	0-1	0-2	0-3	0-4	0-5
	0	0	9	9	1	1	0	0	3	24	12	2	3
Second-leg	1-2	1-3	1-4	1-5	2-3	2-4	2-5	3-4	3-5	4-5	5>	<5	
	11	4	7	3	2	1	0	0	1	0	0	1	

First-leg: 2-0

Second-leg	1-0	2-0	3-0	4-0	5-0	2-1	3-1	4-1	5-1	3-2	4-2	5-2	4-3
	6	4	4	0	1	5	1	0	0	3	2	0	0
Second-leg	5-3	5-4	0-0	1-1	2-2	3-3	4-4	5-5	0-1	0-2	0-3	0-4	0-5
	0	0	4	12	4	0	0	0	13	2	8	4	0
Second-leg	1-2	1-3	1-4	1-5	2-3	2-4	2-5	3-4	3-5	4-5	5>	<5	
	6	3	3	1	5	0	0	0	0	0	0	0	

First-leg: 3-0

Second-leg	1-0	2-0	3-0	4-0	5-0	2-1	3-1	4-1	5-1	3-2	4-2	5-2	4-3
	9	5	3	0	0	4	2	1	0	2	0	0	0
Second-leg	5-3	5-4	0-0	1-1	2-2	3-3	4-4	5-5	0-1	0-2	0-3	0-4	0-5
	0	0	2	5	2	0	0	0	8	8	2	0	2
Second-leg	1-2	1-3	1-4	1-5	2-3	2-4	2-5	3-4	3-5	4-5	5>	<5	
	8	2	1	0	2	0	1	0	0	0	0	0	

First-leg: 1-1

Second-leg	1-0	2-0	3-0	4-0	5-0	2-1	3-1	4-1	5-1	3-2	4-2	5-2	4-3
	2	2	0	0	0	0	0	1	0	1	1	0	0
Second-leg	5-3	5-4	0-0	1-1	2-2	3-3	4-4	5-5	0-1	0-2	0-3	0-4	0-5
	0	0	6	7	3	1	0	0	5	11	4	3	2
Second-leg	1-2	1-3	1-4	1-5	2-3	2-4	2-5	3-4	3-5	4-5	5>	<5	
	9	1	3	4	0	0	1	0	0	0	1	5	

First-leg: 2-1

Second-leg	1-0	2-0	3-0	4-0	5-0	2-1	3-1	4-1	5-1	3-2	4-2	5-2	4-3
	5	6	0	0	0	6	1	2	0	0	0	0	0
Second-leg	5-3	5-4	0-0	1-1	2-2	3-3	4-4	5-5	0-1	0-2	0-3	0-4	0-5
	0	0	2	7	2	2	0	0	8	10	8	2	2
Second-leg	1-2	1-3	1-4	1-5	2-3	2-4	2-5	3-4	3-5	4-5	5>	<5	
	6	4	3	0	2	0	0	0	1	0	0	8	

First-leg: 3-1

Second-leg	1-0	2-0	3-0	4-0	5-0	2-1	3-1	4-1	5-1	3-2	4-2	5-2	4-3
	3	1	1	0	0	2	0	0	0	1	1	0	0
Second-leg	5-3	5-4	0-0	1-1	2-2	3-3	4-4	5-5	0-1	0-2	0-3	0-4	0-5
	0	0	4	3	2	0	0	0	6	5	3	1	0
Second-leg	1-2	1-3	1-4	1-5	2-3	2-4	2-5	3-4	3-5	4-5	5>	<5	
	6	3	1	0	0	1	0	0	0	0	0	2	

First-leg: 4-1

Second-leg	1-0	2-0	3-0	4-0	5-0	2-1	3-1	4-1	5-1	3-2	4-2	5-2	4-3
	1	1	0	0	0	1	0	0	0	0	0	0	0
Second-leg	5-3	5-4	0-0	1-1	2-2	3-3	4-4	5-5	0-1	0-2	0-3	0-4	0-5
	0	0	2	3	1	0	0	0	4	2	2	1	1
Second-leg	1-2	1-3	1-4	1-5	2-3	2-4	2-5	3-4	3-5	4-5	5>	<5	
	3	0	0	2	1	0	1	0	0	0	0	0	

First-leg: 5-1

Second-leg	1-0	2-0	3-0	4-0	5-0	2-1	3-1	4-1	5-1	3-2	4-2	5-2	4-3
	1	1	0	0	0	0	0	0	0	0	0	0	0
Second-leg	5-3	5-4	0-0	1-1	2-2	3-3	4-4	5-5	0-1	0-2	0-3	0-4	0-5
	0	0	2	1	1	0	0	0	1	0	1	0	0
Second-leg	1-2	1-3	1-4	1-5	2-3	2-4	2-5	3-4	3-5	4-5	5>	<5	
	4	0	0	0	0	0	0	0	0	0	1	0	

First-leg: 2-2

Second-leg	1-0	2-0	3-0	4-0	5-0	2-1	3-1	4-1	5-1	3-2	4-2	5-2	4-3
	2	1	0	0	0	1	0	0	0	0	0	0	0
Second-leg	5-3	5-4	0-0	1-1	2-2	3-3	4-4	5-5	0-1	0-2	0-3	0-4	0-5
	0	0	3	2	0	0	0	0	3	3	1	3	1
Second-leg	1-2	1-3	1-4	1-5	2-3	2-4	2-5	3-4	3-5	4-5	5>	<5	
	7	2	1	1	3	0	0	0	0	0	0	1	

First-leg: 3-2

Second-leg	1-0	2-0	3-0	4-0	5-0	2-1	3-1	4-1	5-1	3-2	4-2	5-2	4-3
	1	0	0	0	0	2	1	0	1	0	0	0	0
Second-leg	5-3	5-4	0-0	1-1	2-2	3-3	4-4	5-5	0-1	0-2	0-3	0-4	0-5
	0	0	3	2	1	2	0	0	1	4	1	2	1
Second-leg	1-2	1-3	1-4	1-5	2-3	2-4	2-5	3-4	3-5	4-5	5>	<5	
	1	0	0	0	0	1	0	0	0	0	0	1	

First-leg: 4-2

Second-leg	1-0	2-0	3-0	4-0	5-0	2-1	3-1	4-1	5-1	3-2	4-2	5-2	4-3
	0	0	1	0	0	0	0	0	0	0	0	0	0
Second-leg	5-3	5-4	0-0	1-1	2-2	3-3	4-4	5-5	0-1	0-2	0-3	0-4	0-5
	0	0	1	0	0	1	1	0	0	2	0	0	0
Second-leg	1-2	1-3	1-4	1-5	2-3	2-4	2-5	3-4	3-5	4-5	5>	<5	
	1	3	0	0	0	0	0	0	0	0	0	1	

First-leg: 5-2

Second-leg	1-0	2-0	3-0	4-0	5-0	2-1	3-1	4-1	5-1	3-2	4-2	5-2	4-3
	0	1	0	0	0	0	0	0	0	0	0	0	0
Second-leg	5-3	5-4	0-0	1-1	2-2	3-3	4-4	5-5	0-1	0-2	0-3	0-4	0-5
	0	0	0	0	0	0	0	0	0	0	0	0	0
Second-leg	1-2	1-3	1-4	1-5	2-3	2-4	2-5	3-4	3-5	4-5	5>	<5	
	0	1	0	0	0	0	0	0	0	0	0	0	

First-leg: 6-2

Second-leg	1-0	2-0	3-0	4-0	5-0	2-1	3-1	4-1	5-1	3-2	4-2	5-2	4-3
	0	0	1	0	0	0	0	0	0	0	0	0	0
Second-leg	5-3	5-4	0-0	1-1	2-2	3-3	4-4	5-5	0-1	0-2	0-3	0-4	0-5
	0	0	0	0	0	0	0	0	0	0	0	0	0
Second-leg	1-2	1-3	1-4	1-5	2-3	2-4	2-5	3-4	3-5	4-5	5>	<5	
	1	0	0	0	0	0	0	0	0	0	0	0	

First-leg: 3-3

Second-leg	1-0	2-0	3-0	4-0	5-0	2-1	3-1	4-1	5-1	3-2	4-2	5-2	4-3
	1	0	0	0	0	0	0	0	0	0	0	0	0
Second-leg	5-3	5-4	0-0	1-1	2-2	3-3	4-4	5-5	0-1	0-2	0-3	0-4	0-5
	0	0	0	0	0	0	0	0	1	1	0	0	1
Second-leg	1-2	1-3	1-4	1-5	2-3	2-4	2-5	3-4	3-5	4-5	5>	<5	
	1	0	0	0	0	0	1	0	0	0	0	1	

First-leg: 4-3

Second-leg	1-0	2-0	3-0	4-0	5-0	2-1	3-1	4-1	5-1	3-2	4-2	5-2	4-3
	0	0	0	0	0	0	0	0	0	0	0	0	0
Second-leg	5-3	5-4	0-0	1-1	2-2	3-3	4-4	5-5	0-1	0-2	0-3	0-4	0-5
	0	0	1	1	0	1	0	0	0	1	0	1	0
Second-leg	1-2	1-3	1-4	1-5	2-3	2-4	2-5	3-4	3-5	4-5	5>	<5	
	1	0	0	0	0	0	0	0	0	0	0	0	

First-leg: 5-3

Second-leg	1-0	2-0	3-0	4-0	5-0	2-1	3-1	4-1	5-1	3-2	4-2	5-2	4-3
	0	1	0	0	0	0	0	0	0	0	0	0	0
Second-leg	5-3	5-4	0-0	1-1	2-2	3-3	4-4	5-5	0-1	0-2	0-3	0-4	0-5
	0	0	0	0	0	0	0	0	0	0	1	0	0
Second-leg	1-2	1-3	1-4	1-5	2-3	2-4	2-5	3-4	3-5	4-5	5>	<5	
	0	0	0	1	0	0	0	1	0	0	0	0	

First-leg: 0-1

Second-leg	1-0	2-0	3-0	4-0	5-0	2-1	3-1	4-1	5-1	3-2	4-2	5-2	4-3
	1	0	0	0	0	0	1	0	0	0	0	0	0
Second-leg	5-3	5-4	0-0	1-1	2-2	3-3	4-4	5-5	0-1	0-2	0-3	0-4	0-5
	0	0	5	5	1	0	0	0	2	4	3	6	3
Second-leg	1-2	1-3	1-4	1-5	2-3	2-4	2-5	3-4	3-5	4-5	5>	<5	
	2	2	1	0	2	0	0	0	0	0	0	4	

First-leg: 0-2

Second-leg	1-0	2-0	3-0	4-0	5-0	2-1	3-1	4-1	5-1	3-2	4-2	5-2	4-3
	0	0	0	0	0	0	0	0	0	0	0	0	0
Second-leg	5-3	5-4	0-0	1-1	2-2	3-3	4-4	5-5	0-1	0-2	0-3	0-4	0-5
	0	0	2	2	2	0	0	0	2	1	1	2	3
Second-leg	1-2	1-3	1-4	1-5	2-3	2-4	2-5	3-4	3-5	4-5	5>	<5	
	2	4	0	2	0	3	1	0	0	0	0	3	

First-leg: 1-2

Second-leg	1-0	2-0	3-0	4-0	5-0	2-1	3-1	4-1	5-1	3-2	4-2	5-2	4-3
	3	0	0	0	0	0	0	0	0	0	0	0	0
Second-leg	5-3	5-4	0-0	1-1	2-2	3-3	4-4	5-5	0-1	0-2	0-3	0-4	0-5
	0	0	3	5	0	1	0	0	5	1	3	3	3
Second-leg	1-2	1-3	1-4	1-5	2-3	2-4	2-5	3-4	3-5	4-5	5>	<5	
	1	2	5	3	1	0	0	0	0	0	0	5	

First-leg: 1-3

Second-leg	1-0	2-0	3-0	4-0	5-0	2-1	3-1	4-1	5-1	3-2	4-2	5-2	4-3
	1	0	0	0	0	1	2	0	0	0	0	0	0
Second-leg	5-3	5-4	0-0	1-1	2-2	3-3	4-4	5-5	0-1	0-2	0-3	0-4	0-5
	0	0	1	1	0	1	0	0	3	0	3	2	1
Second-leg	1-2	1-3	1-4	1-5	2-3	2-4	2-5	3-4	3-5	4-5	5>	<5	
	4	1	1	0	1	0	0	0	1	0	0	1	

First-leg: 2-4

Second-leg	1-0	2-0	3-0	4-0	5-0	2-1	3-1	4-1	5-1	3-2	4-2	5-2	4-3
	0	0	0	0	0	0	0	0	0	0	0	0	0
Second-leg	5-3	5-4	0-0	1-1	2-2	3-3	4-4	5-5	0-1	0-2	0-3	0-4	0-5
	0	0	0	0	0	0	0	0	0	1	1	0	0
Second-leg	1-2	1-3	1-4	1-5	2-3	2-4	2-5	3-4	3-5	4-5	5>	<5	
	0	0	0	0	0	0	0	0	0	0	0	0	

First-leg: 3-4

Second-leg	1-0	2-0	3-0	4-0	5-0	2-1	3-1	4-1	5-1	3-2	4-2	5-2	4-3
	0	0	0	0	0	0	0	1	0	0	0	0	0
Second-leg	5-3	5-4	0-0	1-1	2-2	3-3	4-4	5-5	0-1	0-2	0-3	0-4	0-5
	0	0	0	0	0	0	0	0	0	1	0	0	0
Second-leg	1-2	1-3	1-4	1-5	2-3	2-4	2-5	3-4	3-5	4-5	5>	<5	
	1	0	0	0	0	0	0	0	0	0	0	1	

Qualification/Eliminations after First-leg Score

First-leg Score	No. Matches	Qualifications No.	Qualifications %	Eliminations No.	Eliminations %
0-0	75	25	33.33 %	50	66.67 %
1-0	111	51	45.95 %	60	54.05 %
2-0	91	74	81.32 %	17	18.68 %
3-0	69	65	94.20 %	4	5.80 %
1-1	73	16	21.92%	57	78.08 %
2-1	87	39	44.83%	48	55.17 %
3-1	46	35	76.09 %	11	23.91 %
4-1	26	21	80.77 %	5	19.23 %
5-1	13	13	100.00 %	0	0.00 %
2-2	35	5	14.29 %	30	85.71 %
3-2	25	13	52.00 %	12	48.00 %
4-2	11	8	72.73 %	3	27.27 %
5-2	2	2	100.00 %	0	0.00 %
6-2	2	2	100.00 %	0	0.00 %
3-3	7	1	14.29 %	6	85.71 %
4-3	6	4	66.67 %	2	33.33 %
5-3	4	2	50.00 %	2	50.00 %
0-1	42	1	2.38 %	41	97.62 %
0-2	30	0	0.00 %	30	100.00 %
1-2	44	0	0.00 %	44	100.00 %
1-3	25	1	4.00 %	24	96.00 %
2-4	2	0	0.00 %	2	100.00 %
3-4	4	1	25.00 %	3	75.00 %

Home Match Statistics

	1-0	2-0	3-0	4-0	5-0	2-1	3-1	4-1	5-1	3-2	4-2	5-2	4-3
Number	194	201	139	74	48	178	83	59	35	49	18	9	7
	5-3	5-4	0-0	1-1	2-2	3-3	4-4	5-5	0-1	0-2	0-3	0-4	0-5
Number	7	0	132	151	64	19	2	0	102	64	37	14	18
	1-2	1-3	1-4	1-5	2-3	2-4	2-5	3-4	3-5	4-5	5>	<5	
Number	77	40	23	5	24	7	3	4	1	0	100	25	
	1-0	2-0	3-0	4-0	5-0	2-1	3-1	4-1	5-1	3-2	4-2	5-2	4-3
Percent	10	10	7	4	2	9	4	3	2	2	1	0	0
	5-3	5-4	0-0	1-1	2-2	3-3	4-4	5-5	0-1	0-2	0-3	0-4	0-5
Percent	0	0	7	8	3	1	0	0	5	3	2	1	1
	1-2	1-3	1-4	1-5	2-3	2-4	2-5	3-4	3-5	4-5	5>	<5	
Percent	4	2	1	0	1	0	0	0	0	0	5	1	

Number of matches: 2013

Roll of Honour – the Winners and the Runners-up

The Winners

1.	England	8
2.	Itlay	7
3.	Spain	6
4.	Netherlands	5
5.	West Germany	4
6.	Portugal	3
7.	Scotland	1
8.	Romania	1
9.	Yugoslavia	1
	Total	**36**

The Runners-up

1.	Italy	7
2.	Spain	6
3.	West Germany	5
4.	Portugal	5
5.	France	4
6.	England	2
7.	Yugoslavia	1
8.	Netherlands	1
9.	Scotland	1
10.	Greece	1
11.	Belgium	1
12.	Sweden	1
13.	Romania	1
	Total	**36**

No. of Appearances in the Final

1.	Italy	14
2.	Spain	12
3.	England	10
4.	West Germany	9
5.	Portugal	8
6.	Netherlands	6
7.	France	4
8.	Scotland	2
9.	Romania	2
10.	Yugoslavia	2
11.	Greece	1
12.	Belgium	1
13.	Sweden	1
	Total	**72**

The Winners – Classification by Country

Country	Appearances	Winning Teams
Albania	–	–
Austria	–	–
Belgium	–	–
Bulgaria	–	–
Cyprus	–	–
Czechoslovakia	–	–
Denmark	–	–
East Germany	–	–
England	8	Manchester United (1968), Liverpool (1977, 1978, 1981, 1984), Nottingham Forest (1979), 1980), Aston Villa (1982)
Finland	–	–
France	–	–
Greece	–	–
Hungary	–	–
Iceland	–	–
Italy	7	AC Milan (1963, 1969, 1989, 1990), Inter Milan (1964, 1965), Juventus (1985)
Luxembourg	–	–
Malta	–	–
Netherlands	5	Feyenoord (1970), Ajax (1971, 1972, 1973), PSV Eindhoven (1988)
Northern Ireland	–	–
Norway	–	–
Poland	–	–
Portugal	3	Benfica (1961, 1962), FC Porto (1987)
Republic of Ireland	–	–
Romania	1	Steaua Bucharest (1986)
Scotland	1	Celtic (1967)
Spain	6	Real Madrid (1956, 1957, 1958, 1959, 1960, 1966)
Sweden	–	–
Switzerland	–	–
Turkey	–	–
USSR	–	–
West Germany	4	Bayern Munich (1974, 1975, 1976), Hamburg (1983)
Yugoslavia	1	Red Star Belgrade (1991)

The Winners – Classification by Results

Pos'n	Club	Cnty	Wins	Years
1	Real Madrid	Esp	6	1956, 1957, 1958, 1959, 1960, 1966
2	AC Milan	Ita	4	1963, 1969, 1989, 1990
3	Liverpool	Eng	4	1977, 1978, 1981, 1984
4	Ajax	Ned	3	1971, 1972, 1973
5	Bayern Munich	FRG	3	1974, 1975, 1976
6	Benfica	Por	2	1961, 1962
7	Inter Milan	Ita	2	1964, 1965
8	Nottingham Forest	Eng	2	1979, 1980
9	Celtic	Sco	1	1967
10	Manchester United	Eng	1	1968
11	Feyenoord	Ned	1	1970
12	Aston Villa	Eng	1	1982
13	Hamburg	FRG	1	1983
14	Juventus	Ita	1	1985
15	Steaua Bucharest	Rom	1	1986
16	FC Porto	Por	1	1987
17	PSV Eindhoven	Ned	1	1988
18	Red Star Belgrade	Yug	1	1991

The Runners-up — Classification by Country

Country	Appearances	Winning Teams
Albania	–	–
Austria	–	–
Belgium	1	Club Bruges (1978)
Bulgaria	–	–
Cyprus	–	–
Czechoslovakia	–	–
Denmark	–	–
East Germany	–	–
England	2	Leeds United (1975), Liverpool (1985)
Finland	–	–
France	3	Stade Reims (1956, 1959), Saint-Etienne (1976), Olympique Marseille (1991)
Greece	1	Panathiniakos (1971)
Hungary	–	–
Iceland	–	–
Italy	7	Fiorentina (1957), AC Milan (1958), Inter Milan (1967, 1972) Juventus (1973, 1983), Roma (1984)
Luxembourg	–	–
Malta	–	–
Netherlands	1	Ajax (1969)
Northern Ireland	–	–
Norway	–	–
Poland	–	–
Portugal	5	Benfica (1963, 1965, 1968, 1988, 1990)
Republic of Ireland	–	–
Romania	1	Steaua Bucharest (1989)
Scotland	1	Celtic (1970)
Spain	6	Real Madrid (1962, 1964, 1981), Barcelona (1961, 1986), Atlético Madrid (1974)
Sweden	1	Malmö FF (1979)

Switzerland	–	–
Turkey	–	–
USSR	–	–
West Germany	5	Eintracht Frankfurt (1960), Borussia Mönchengladbach (1977) Hamburg (1980), Bayern Munich (1982, 1987)
Yugoslavia	1	Partizan Belgrade (1966)

The European Cup Finalists

Pos'n	Club	Cnty	Appearances	Wins
1	Real Madrid	Esp	9	6
2	Benfica	Por	7	2
3	AC Milan	Ita	5	4
4	Liverpool	Eng	5	4
5	Ajax	Ned	4	3
6	Bayern Munich	FRG	5	3
7	Inter Milan	Ita	4	3
8	Juventus	Ita	3	1
9	Nottingham Forest	Eng	2	2
10	Celtic	Sco	2	1
11	Hamburg	FRG	2	1
12	Steaua Bucharest	Rom	2	1
13	Stade Reims	Fra	2	0
14	Barcelona	Esp	2	0
15	Manchester United	Eng	1	1
16	Feyenoord	Ned	1	1
17	Aston Villa	Eng	1	1
18	FC Porto	Por	1	1
19	PSV Eindhoven	Ned	1	1
20	Red Star Belgrade	Yug	1	1
21	Fiorentina	Ita	1	0
22	Eintracht Frankfurt	FRG	1	0
23	Partizan Belgrade	Yug	1	0
24	Panithaniakos	Gre	1	0
25	Atlético Madrid	Esp	1	0
26	Leeds United	Eng	1	0
27	Saint-Etienne	Fra	1	0
28	Borussia Mönchengladbach	FRG	1	0
29	Club Bruges	Bel	1	0
30	Malmö FF	Swe	1	0
31	Roma	Ita	1	0
32	Olympique Marseille	Fra	1	0
	Total		**72**	**36**

The Finals

1960-61	Rangers	1	Fiorentina ∞	4
1961-62	Atlético Madrid≈	4	Fiorentina	1
1962-63	Tottenham Hotspur	5	Atlético Madrid	1
1963-64	Sporting Lisbon≈	4	MTK-VM	3
1964-65	West Ham United	2	1860 Munich	0
1965-66	Borussia Dortmund	2	Liverpool	1
1966-67	Bayern Munich	1	Rangers	0
1967-68	AC Milan	2	Hamburg	0
1968-69	Slovan Bratislava	3	Barcelona	2
1969-70	Manchester City	2	Górnik Zabrze	1
1970-71	Chelsea≈	3	Real Madrid	2
1971-72	Rangers	3	Dinamo Moscow	2
1972-73	AC Milan	1	Leeds United	0
1973-74	Magdeburg	2	AC Milan	0
1974-75	Dinamo Kiev	3	Ferencváros	0
1975-76	Anderlecht	4	West Ham United	2
1976-77	Hamburg	2	Anderlecht	0
1977-78	Anderlecht	4	Austria Vienna	0
1978-79	Barcelona	4	Fortuna Düsseldorf	3
1979-80	Valencia†	0	Arsenal	0
1980-81	Dinamo Tbilisi	2	Carl Zeiss Jena	1
1981-82	Barcelona	2	Standard Liège	1
1982-83	Real Madrid	1	Aberdeen	2
1983-84	Juventus	2	FC Porto	1
1984-85	Everton	3	Rapid Vienna	1
1985-86	Dinamo Kiev	3	Atlético Madrid	0
1986-87	Ajax	1	Lokomotive Leipzig	0
1987-88	KV Mechelen	1	Ajax	0
1988-89	Barcelona	2	Sampdoria	0
1989-90	Sampdoria	2	Anderlecht	0
1990-91	Manchester United	2	Barcelona	1

† won on penalty kicks

∞ Scores shown are aggregate scores for the two legs of the final

≈ Scores shown are aggregate scores for the final and replay if the final ended in a draw

National Performances by Index

1960-61 to 1990-91

Pos'n	Cnty	Ave	Pts	P	W	D	L	F	A	Diff	B	No./T
1	England	10.033	301	192	107	43	42	362	178	184	44	30
2	Spain	9.485	332	216	116	52	48	401	223	178	48	35
3	Italy	9.031	289	191	102	43	46	300	158	142	42	32
4	W. Germany	8.941	304	203	109	43	51	400	219	181	43	34
5	USSR	7.884	205	141	71	37	33	241	129	112	26	26
6	Belgium	7.433	223	153	88	18	47	273	158	115	29	30
7	Scotland	6.625	212	161	80	29	52	307	171	136	23	32
8	E. Germany	5.933	178	144	56	45	43	211	169	42	21	30
9	Portugal	5.612	174	141	61	35	45	222	160	62	17	31
10	Netherlands	5.451	169	130	67	18	45	207	150	57	17	31
11	France	4.700	141	124	48	32	44	177	156	21	13	30
12	Czechoslovakia	4.625	148	123	57	21	45	187	154	33	13	32
13	Poland	4.370	118	103	43	23	37	157	137	20	9	27
14	Hungary	4.366	131	121	48	23	50	208	172	36	12	30
15	Yugoslavia	4.333	130	126	46	24	56	191	188	3	14	30
16	Bulgaria	3.964	111	105	45	11	49	176	156	20	10	28
17	Austria	3.806	118	121	36	34	51	149	194	-45	12	31
18	Sweden	3.478	80	78	24	28	26	112	94	18	4	23
19	Wales	3.466	104	106	34	30	42	148	130	18	6	30
20	Romania	3.172	92	94	34	19	41	114	135	-21	5	29
21	Switzerland	2.967	92	105	31	23	51	143	175	-32	7	31
22	Greece	2.931	85	87	33	17	37	100	128	-28	2	29
23	Denmark	2.400	72	86	28	12	46	112	144	-32	4	30
24	Turkey	2.296	62	85	21	17	47	81	143	-62	3	27
25	Albania	2.000	26	36	9	8	19	35	52	-17	0	13
26	Finland	1.500	39	66	11	15	40	58	176	-118	2	26
27	Norway	1.428	40	70	15	9	46	69	157	-88	1	28
28	Rep. of Ireland	1.233	37	72	12	13	47	56	132	-76	0	30
29	N. Ireland	0.896	26	64	7	11	46	52	186	-134	1	29
30	Malta	0.800	24	66	9	6	51	30	227	-197	0	30
31	Cyprus	0.666	18	58	5	8	45	30	206	-176	0	27
32	Iceland	0.615	16	56	5	6	45	30	172	-142	0	26
33	Luxembourg	0.566	17	62	6	5	51	34	244	-210	0	30

1981-82 to 1990-91

Pos'n	Cnty	Ave	Pts	P	W	D	L	F	A	Diff	B	No./T
1	England	13.200	66	38	23	10	5	66	26	40	10	5
2	Spain	11.000	132	81	45	22	14	147	75	72	20	12
3	Italy	9.818	108	71	39	14	18	112	55	57	16	11
4	Belgium	9.363	103	63	41	7	15	118	60	58	14	11
5	USSR	8.636	95	63	33	18	12	117	59	58	11	11
6	France	7.100	71	52	24	15	13	76	48	28	8	10
7	W. Germany	6.500	65	52	24	10	18	89	56	33	7	10
8	Netherlands	6.363	70	52	28	6	18	73	51	22	8	11
9	E. Germany	5.600	56	47	19	12	16	66	60	6	6	10
10	Scotland	5.363	59	47	22	10	15	79	42	37	5	11
11	Austria	5.200	52	45	17	11	17	68	77	-9	7	10
12	Portugal	4.800	48	41	17	8	16	50	46	4	6	10
13	Poland	4.500	45	38	16	10	12	51	47	4	3	10
14	Bulgaria	3.666	33	32	14	2	16	44	54	-10	3	9
–	Yugoslavia	3.666	33	34	12	7	15	58	62	-4	2	9
16	Greece	3.600	36	34	15	5	14	41	44	-3	1	10
–	Czechoslovakia	3.600	36	34	13	8	13	44	48	-4	2	10

18	Romania	3.555	32	32	11	7	14	39	40	-1	3	9
19	Sweden	3.300	33	32	12	8	12	55	41	14	1	10
–	Switzerland	3.300	33	38	11	8	19	52	54	-2	3	10
21	Finland	2.700	27	30	8	9	13	28	52	-24	2	10
22	Wales	2.600	26	34	9	8	17	49	42	7	0	10
23	Denmark	2.500	25	28	10	4	14	33	44	-11	1	10
24	Hungary	2.400	24	32	9	5	18	44	50	-6	1	10
25	Albania	2.000	16	22	7	2	13	23	31	-8	0	8
26	Turkey	1.700	17	28	6	5	17	22	51	-29	0	10
27	Iceland	1.100	11	24	4	3	17	19	47	-28	0	10
28	Cyprus	0.800	8	20	3	2	15	11	60	-49	0	10
29	Rep. of Ireland	0.700	7	22	1	5	16	11	40	-29	0	10
–	Norway	0.700	7	20	1	5	14	10	39	-29	0	10
31	N. Ireland	0.600	6	20	1	4	15	10	50	-40	0	10
32	Malta	0.500	5	22	2	1	19	5	90	-85	0	10
33	Luxembourg	0.300	3	20	0	3	17	6	75	-69	0	10

1986-87 to 1990-91

Pos'n	Cnty	Ave	Pts	P	W	D	L	F	A	Diff	B	No./T
1	England	19.000	19	9	7	2	0	17	4	13	3	1
2	Italy	11.000	66	42	24	7	11	72	33	39	11	6
3	Belgium	10.333	62	38	24	5	9	63	31	32	9	6
–	Spain	10.333	62	40	20	13	7	65	33	32	9	6
5	France	9.400	47	32	15	10	7	44	24	20	7	5
6	Netherlands	9.000	54	34	22	3	9	56	24	32	7	6
7	USSR	6.800	34	26	11	9	6	44	28	16	3	5
8	Poland	5.200	26	20	8	8	4	25	19	6	2	5
9	Romania	5.000	25	22	9	4	9	30	22	8	3	5
–	E. Germany	5.000	25	21	7	8	6	21	16	5	3	5
11	W. Germany	4.600	23	20	9	4	7	24	18	6	1	5
12	Bulgaria	4.200	21	20	9	0	11	30	36	-6	3	5
–	Switzerland	4.200	21	22	6	6	10	26	24	2	3	5
14	Greece	4.000	20	20	9	2	9	27	30	-3	0	5
–	Sweden	4.000	20	18	7	5	6	24	21	3	1	5
16	Austria	3.800	19	18	7	4	7	22	32	-10	1	5
17	Portugal	3.600	18	18	6	5	7	22	21	1	1	5
18	Yugoslavia	3.500	14	16	6	1	9	25	36	-11	1	4
19	Scotland	3.400	17	16	6	5	5	16	15	1	0	5
20	Denmark	3.000	15	14	6	2	6	16	11	5	1	5
–	Wales	3.000	15	16	5	5	6	22	22	0	0	5
22	Czechoslovakia	2.800	14	14	6	2	6	20	21	-1	0	5
23	Albania	2.600	13	16	6	1	9	18	20	-2	0	5
24	Finland	2.000	10	14	2	5	7	10	28	-18	1	5
–	Hungary	2.000	10	14	4	2	8	17	19	-2	0	5
26	Turkey	1.400	7	14	3	1	10	11	29	-18	0	5
27	Cyprus	0.800	4	10	2	0	8	3	24	-21	0	5
–	N. Ireland	0.800	4	10	0	4	6	5	27	-22	0	5
–	Iceland	0.800	4	12	1	2	9	7	22	-15	0	5
30	Norway	0.600	3	10	1	1	8	3	17	-14	0	5
31	Rep. of Ireland	0.400	2	10	0	2	8	2	25	-23	0	5
32	Luxembourg	0.200	1	10	0	1	9	1	33	-32	0	5
–	Malta	0.200	1	10	0	1	9	1	24	-23	0	5

Summary Totals	**Pts**	**P**	**W**	**D**	**L**	**F**	**A**	**Diff**	**B**	**F/P**
1955-56 to 1990-91	**4114**	**3686**	**1464**	**758**	**1464**	**5373**	**5373**	**0**	**428**	**2.915**
1981-82 to 1990-91	**1388**	**1248**	**497**	**254**	**497**	**1716**	**1716**	**0**	**140**	**2.750**
1986-87 to 1990-91	**696**	**626**	**248**	**130**	**248**	**789**	**789**	**0**	**70**	**2.521**

Club Performance by Points

1960-61 to 1990-91

Pos'n	Club	Cnty	Pts	P	W	D	L	F	A	Diff	B	Pts/P	F/P
1	Barcelona	Esp	122	76	45	14	17	164	82	82	18	1.605	2.158
2	Atlético Madrid	Esp	79	48	28	11	9	85	46	39	12	1.646	1.771
3	Rangers	Sco	74	54	27	11	16	100	62	38	9	1.370	1.852
4	Anderlecht	Bel	73	44	29	3	12	86	34	52	12	1.659	1.955
5	Bayern Munich	FRG	62	39	19	14	6	67	36	31	10	1.590	1.718
6	Dinamo Kiev	URS	54	30	20	6	4	72	27	45	8	1.800	2.400
7	Hamburg	FRG	54	34	20	7	7	81	39	42	7	1.588	2.382
8	AC Milan	Ita	53	30	17	10	3	47	20	27	9	1.767	1.567
9	Aberdeen	Sco	50	35	20	5	10	69	32	37	5	1.429	1.971
10	Cardiff City	Wal	49	45	16	13	16	62	50	12	4	1.089	1.378
11	Rapid Vienna	Aut	48	43	14	15	14	72	68	4	5	1.116	1.674
12	Celtic	Sco	47	34	19	4	11	68	31	37	5	1.382	2.000
13	Magdeburg	GDR	47	36	15	12	9	57	41	16	5	1.306	1.583
14	Juventus	Ita	46	27	17	5	5	53	19	34	7	1.704	1.963
15	Sporting Lisbon	Por	46	36	16	8	12	76	44	32	6	1.278	2.111
16	Dinamo Moscow	URS	46	29	15	8	6	46	25	21	8	1.586	1.586
17	Standard Liège	Bel	45	32	17	5	10	60	36	24	6	1.406	1.875
18	West Ham United	Eng	45	30	15	6	9	58	42	16	9	1.500	1.933
19	Sampdoria	Ita	44	28	15	7	6	39	21	18	7	1.571	1.393
20	Manchester United	Eng	43	27	15	7	5	52	31	21	6	1.593	1.926
21	FC Porto	Por	41	31	15	6	10	43	38	5	5	1.323	1.387
22	Tottenham Hotspur	Eng	40	25	16	3	6	58	31	27	5	1.600	2.320
23	Real Madrid	Esp	40	25	13	7	5	46	20	26	7	1.600	1.840
24	Legia Warsaw	Pol	40	33	13	10	10	47	35	12	4	1.212	1.424
25	Benfica	Por	38	28	13	8	7	42	19	23	4	1.357	1.500
26	Ajax	Ned	37	22	15	1	6	41	18	23	6	1.682	1.864
27	Slovan Bratislava	Tch	36	25	14	3	8	40	28	12	5	1.440	1.600
28	Eintracht Frankfurt	FRG	35	24	14	3	7	41	23	18	4	1.458	1.708
29	Austria Vienna	Aut	35	35	9	12	14	36	52	-16	5	1.000	1.029
30	Fiorentina	Ita	34	20	14	1	5	44	20	24	5	1.700	2.200
31	KV Mechelen	Bel	34	17	13	3	1	26	8	18	5	2.000	1.529
32	Carl Zeiss Jena	GDR	34	29	10	9	10	51	35	16	5	1.172	1.759
33	Steaua Bucharest	Rom	34	34	12	9	13	42	49	-7	1	1.000	1.235
34	PSV Eindhoven	Ned	33	22	13	3	6	45	17	28	4	1.500	2.045
35	Lokomotive Leipzig	GDR	32	25	10	8	7	32	26	6	4	1.280	1.280
36	Red Star Belgrade	Yug	30	24	10	6	8	51	32	19	4	1.250	2.125
37	Dinamo Tbilisi	URS	30	21	11	3	7	30	17	13	5	1.429	1.429
38	Torpedo Moscow	URS	30	23	10	8	5	32	20	12	2	1.304	1.391
39	Real Zaragoza	Esp	30	22	10	5	7	36	26	10	5	1.364	1.636
40	Roma	Ita	30	23	10	7	6	26	18	8	3	1.304	1.130
41	Valencia	Esp	29	19	10	5	4	39	20	19	4	1.526	2.053
42	Manchester City	Eng	29	18	11	2	5	32	13	19	5	1.611	1.778
43	Ujpesti Dózsa	Hun	29	25	11	4	10	50	38	12	3	1.160	2.000
44	Ferencváros	Hun	29	23	10	6	7	40	28	12	3	1.261	1.739
45	Dukla Prague	Tch	29	24	10	7	7	33	29	4	2	1.208	1.375
46	Dinamo Zagreb	Yug	29	29	10	6	13	28	34	-6	3	1.000	0.966
47	Levski Sofia	Bul	28	24	11	3	10	52	34	18	3	1.167	2.167
48	Servette	Sui	28	24	11	4	9	36	25	11	2	1.167	1.500
49	Wrexham	Wal	28	26	10	7	9	34	34	0	1	1.077	1.308
50	Olympiakos Pireus	Gre	28	27	12	4	11	37	42	-5	0	1.037	1.370
51	Malmö FF	Swe	27	22	9	7	6	35	18	17	2	1.227	1.591
52	Górnik Zabrze	Pol	26	17	9	4	4	38	20	18	4	1.529	2.235
53	Torino	Ita	26	19	9	4	6	28	17	11	4	1.368	1.474

Pos'n	Club	Cnty	Pts	P	W	D	L	F	A	Diff	B	Pts/P	F/P
54	Olympique Lyon	Fra	26	22	9	5	8	31	28	3	3	1.182	1.409
55	Chelsea	Eng	25	14	9	4	1	39	7	32	3	1.786	2.786
56	Napoli	Ita	25	17	9	4	4	23	16	7	3	1.471	1.353
57	MTK-VM	Hun	25	19	8	5	6	27	22	5	4	1.316	1.421
58	Borussia Dortmund	FRG	24	15	9	3	3	32	15	17	3	1.600	2.133
59	Everton	Eng	24	13	9	3	1	19	5	14	3	1.846	1.462
60	Slavia Sofia	Bul	24	25	9	3	13	31	31	0	3	0.960	1.240
61	Liverpool	Eng	23	17	8	4	5	29	12	17	3	1.353	1.706
62	Dinamo Bucharest	Rom	23	20	8	4	8	25	18	7	3	1.150	1.250
63	Schalke 04	FRG	23	14	9	2	3	21	14	7	3	1.643	1.500
64	CSKA Sofia	Bul	22	18	10	0	8	36	22	14	2	1.222	2.000
65	Fortuna Düsseldorf	FRG	22	17	6	6	5	28	19	9	4	1.294	1.647
66	PAOK Salonika	Gre	22	18	8	5	5	24	23	1	1	1.222	1.333
67	Hajduk Split	Yug	22	26	8	3	15	29	38	-9	3	0.846	1.115
68	Sparta Prague	Tch	21	18	9	1	8	46	20	26	2	1.167	2.556
69	FC Den Haag	Ned	20	16	9	1	6	26	18	8	1	1.250	1.625
70	Banik Ostrava	Tch	20	12	9	0	3	21	13	8	2	1.667	1.750
71	Olympique Marseille	Fra	20	14	8	2	4	19	13	6	2	1.429	1.357
72	Dunfermline Athletic	Sco	19	14	7	2	5	34	14	20	3	1.357	2.429
73	Waterschei Thor	Bel	19	12	8	1	3	26	11	15	2	1.583	2.167
74	Dynamo Berlin	GDR	19	12	5	7	0	19	11	8	2	1.583	1.583
75	Cologne	FRG	18	14	7	2	5	30	19	11	2	1.286	2.143
76	Galatasaray	Tur	18	22	6	6	10	25	44	-19	0	0.818	1.136
77	1860 Munich	FRG	17	10	6	2	2	21	6	15	3	1.700	2.100
78	Beveren	Bel	17	12	6	3	3	17	9	8	2	1.417	1.417
79	Dynamo Dresden	GDR	17	14	7	1	6	30	27	3	2	1.214	2.143
80	Inter Milan	Ita	16	12	6	2	4	22	9	13	2	1.333	1.833
81	Leeds United	Eng	16	9	5	3	1	13	3	10	3	1.778	1.444
82	Arsenal	Eng	16	9	4	5	0	13	5	8	3	1.778	1.444
83	Nantes	Fra	16	12	7	0	5	28	21	7	2	1.333	2.333
84	Rába ETO	Hun	15	12	6	2	4	23	14	9	1	1.250	1.917
85	Twente Enschede	Ned	15	10	6	1	3	17	9	8	2	1.500	1.700
86	Paris Saint-Germain	Fra	15	10	6	2	2	16	9	7	1	1.500	1.600
87	Trakia Plovdiv	Bul	15	12	6	2	4	23	18	5	1	1.250	1.917
88	Girondins Bordeaux	Fra	15	10	6	1	3	14	10	4	2	1.500	1.400
89	Lausanne-Sports	Sui	15	17	6	2	9	26	28	-2	1	0.882	1.529
90	Bor. Mönchengladbach	FRG	14	10	6	0	4	29	17	12	2	1.400	2.900
91	Boavista	Por	14	12	5	4	3	22	11	11	0	1.167	1.833
92	Feyenoord	Ned	14	8	6	0	2	18	10	8	2	1.750	2.250
93	AGF Åarhus	Den	14	12	6	1	5	19	14	5	1	1.167	1.583
94	Monaco	Fra	14	14	2	8	4	14	19	-5	2	1.000	1.000
95	FC Tirol	Aut	14	14	6	2	6	18	26	-8	0	1.000	1.286
96	Glentoran	Nir	14	18	3	7	8	16	33	-17	1	0.778	0.889
97	FC Zürich	Sui	13	12	4	4	4	24	16	8	1	1.083	2.000
98	Sachsenning Zwickau	GDR	13	12	4	3	5	6	10	-4	2	1.083	0.500
99	Sion	Sui	13	16	4	4	8	21	34	-13	1	0.813	1.313
100	Beroe Stara Zagora	Bul	12	10	5	1	4	20	11	9	1	1.200	2.000
101	Honvéd	Hun	12	12	5	1	6	25	17	8	1	1.000	2.083
102	Spartak Moscow	URS	12	10	4	3	3	14	10	4	1	1.200	1.400
103	Shamrock Rovers	Irl	12	16	5	2	9	19	27	-8	0	0.750	1.188
104	Haka Valkeakoski	Fin	12	16	4	3	9	15	33	-18	1	0.750	0.938
105	Bayer Uerdingen	FRG	11	8	4	1	3	24	10	14	2	1.375	3.000
106	Nuremberg	FRG	11	6	4	1	1	12	3	9	2	1.833	2.000
107	Sparta Rotterdam	Ned	11	10	4	3	3	17	12	5	0	1.100	1.700
108	Slask Wroclaw	Pol	11	8	4	2	2	10	5	5	1	1.375	1.250
109	Shakhtyor Donetsk	URS	11	8	4	2	2	16	12	4	1	1.375	2.000
110	Atalanta	Ita	11	11	4	1	6	14	14	0	2	1.000	1.273

Pos'n	Club	Cnty	Pts	P	W	D	L	F	A	Diff	B	Pts/P	F/P
111	OFK Belgrade	Yug	11	11	4	1	6	21	22	-1	2	1.000	1.909
112	Fram Reykjavik	Isl	11	20	5	1	14	14	42	-28	0	0.550	0.700
113	Real Valladolid	Esp	10	6	3	3	0	10	2	8	1	1.667	1.667
114	Velez Mostar	Yug	10	8	3	4	1	18	13	5	0	1.250	2.250
115	SK Brann	Nor	10	12	4	2	6	18	13	5	0	0.833	1.500
116	Wisla Kraków	Pol	10	8	5	0	3	17	12	5	0	1.250	2.125
117	Swansea City	Wal	10	16	3	4	9	31	27	4	0	0.625	1.938
118	Universitatea Craiova	Rom	10	10	4	2	4	19	15	4	0	1.000	1.900
119	Göztepe	Tur	10	10	4	1	5	14	10	4	1	1.000	1.400
120	IFK Norrköping	Swe	10	10	4	2	4	16	13	3	0	1.000	1.600
121	Lech Pozna ´n	Pol	10	8	4	2	2	10	7	3	0	1.250	1.250
122	Larissa	Gre	10	8	3	3	2	7	5	2	1	1.250	0.875
123	Randers Freja FC	Den	10	10	4	1	5	16	15	1	1	1.000	1.600
124	Lokomotiv Kosice	Tch	10	8	3	4	1	8	7	1	0	1.250	1.000
125	Club Bruges	Bel	10	10	4	1	5	18	19	-1	1	1.000	1.800
126	Rijeka	Yug	10	10	3	3	4	8	9	-1	1	1.000	0.800
127	Panathinaikos	Gre	10	14	4	2	8	13	28	-15	0	0.714	0.929
128	Southampton	Eng	9	6	4	0	2	16	8	8	1	1.500	2.667
129	Montpellier	Fra	9	6	3	2	1	10	3	7	1	1.500	1.667
130	Ipswich Town	Eng	9	6	3	2	1	6	3	3	1	1.500	1.000
131	B 1909 Odense	Den	9	8	3	2	3	19	17	2	1	1.125	2.375
132	Vejle BK	Den	9	10	4	0	6	16	17	-1	1	0.900	1.600
133	Vorwärts Frankfurt/Oder	GDR	9	8	3	2	3	6	8	-2	1	1.125	0.750
134	Sliema Wanderers	Mlt	9	18	4	1	13	10	57	-47	0	0.500	0.556
135	Hibernian	Sco	8	6	3	1	2	19	10	9	1	1.333	3.167
136	Borac Banja Luka	Yug	8	6	4	0	2	17	8	9	0	1.333	2.833
137	Newport County	Wal	8	6	2	3	1	12	3	9	1	1.333	2.000
138	Dinamo Minsk	URS	8	6	2	3	1	6	4	2	1	1.333	1.000
139	Fenerbahçe	Tur	8	9	3	1	5	11	11	0	1	0.889	1.222
140	Roda JC	Ned	8	8	3	1	4	9	9	0	1	1.000	1.125
141	Admira Wacker	Aut	8	8	3	1	4	7	8	-1	1	1.000	0.875
142	Sporting Braga	Por	8	6	4	0	2	7	8	-1	0	1.333	1.167
143	Åtvidaberg SFF	Swe	8	8	1	5	2	9	12	-3	1	1.000	1.125
144	Rapid Bucharest	Rom	8	8	3	1	4	9	13	-4	1	1.000	1.125
145	IFK Gothenburg	Swe	8	8	2	3	3	7	11	-4	1	1.000	0.875
146	Kalmar FF	Swe	8	8	3	2	3	8	13	-5	0	1.000	1.000
147	West Bromwich Albion	Eng	7	6	2	2	2	8	5	3	1	1.167	1.333
148	B 1903 Copenhagen	Den	7	6	3	1	2	10	8	2	0	1.167	1.667
149	FC Liège	Bel	7	6	3	0	3	8	7	1	1	1.167	1.333
150	Dynamo Zilina	Tch	7	4	3	0	1	7	6	1	1	1.750	1.750
151	Academica Coimbra	Por	7	6	2	2	2	3	2	1	1	1.167	0.500
152	Leixões	Por	7	6	2	2	2	11	11	0	1	1.167	1.833
153	Grasshoppers Zürich	Sui	7	8	2	2	4	9	9	0	1	0.875	1.125
154	Dundee United	Sco	7	8	2	3	3	5	5	0	0	0.875	0.625
155	Real Betis	Esp	7	6	2	2	2	6	7	-1	1	1.167	1.000
156	RoPS Rovaniemi	Fin	7	6	2	2	2	3	5	-2	1	1.167	0.500
157	Fortuna Sittard	Ned	7	8	2	2	4	9	12	-3	1	0.875	1.125
158	17 Nëntori Tirana	Alb	7	6	3	1	2	5	9	-4	0	1.167	0.833
159	Bursaspor	Tur	7	8	2	2	4	5	12	-7	1	0.875	0.625
160	Young Boys Berne	Sui	7	10	2	2	6	10	18	-8	1	0.700	1.000
161	AIK	Swe	6	6	2	2	2	17	6	11	0	1.000	2.833
162	DAC Dunajská Streda	Tch	6	4	3	0	1	9	4	5	0	1.500	2.250
163	SKA Rostov on Don	URS	6	4	3	0	1	6	2	4	0	1.500	1.500
164	Sunderland	Eng	6	4	3	0	1	5	3	2	0	1.500	1.250
165	Groningen	Ned	6	4	3	0	1	8	7	1	0	1.500	2.000
166	Werder Bremen	FRG	6	4	2	1	1	7	6	1	1	1.500	1.750
167	Lierse	Bel	6	6	3	0	3	12	12	0	0	1.000	2.000

Pos'n	Club	Cnty	Pts	P	W	D	L	F	A	Diff	B	Pts/P	F/P
168	Sturm Graz	Aut	6	6	2	1	3	6	6	0	1	1.000	1.000
169	Djurgården SIF	Swe	6	8	1	4	3	10	11	-1	0	0.750	1.250
170	Dinamo Tirana	Alb	6	8	2	2	4	7	8	-1	0	0.750	0.875
171	Lyngby BK	Den	6	6	2	2	2	7	8	-1	0	1.000	1.167
172	Diósgyöri VTK	Hun	6	6	3	0	3	10	12	-2	0	1.000	1.667
173	Partizani Tirana	Alb	6	8	2	2	4	8	10	-2	0	0.750	1.000
174	AZ'67 Alkmaar	Ned	6	6	2	2	2	3	5	-2	0	1.000	0.500
175	Athletic Bilbao	Esp	6	6	2	2	2	6	9	-3	0	1.000	1.000
176	NAC Breda	Ned	6	6	2	2	2	5	8	-3	0	1.000	0.833
177	Vitória Setúbal	Por	6	8	2	2	4	13	17	-4	0	0.750	1.625
178	SFK Lyn	Nor	6	8	2	1	5	13	19	-6	1	0.750	1.625
179	Politehnica Timisoara	Rom	6	6	3	0	3	5	11	-6	0	1.000	0.833
180	HJK Helsinki	Fin	6	6	3	0	3	9	18	-9	0	1.000	1.500
181	Aris Bonnevoie	Lux	6	8	3	0	5	8	20	-12	0	0.750	1.000
182	Hibernians	Mlt	6	10	2	2	6	4	17	-13	0	0.600	0.400
183	Union Luxembourg	Lux	6	16	2	2	12	8	48	-40	0	0.375	0.500
184	Apoel Nicosia	Cyp	6	18	2	2	14	13	61	-48	0	0.333	0.722
185	Stal Rzeszów	Pol	5	4	2	1	1	9	4	5	0	1.250	2.250
186	Beerschot	Bel	5	6	2	1	3	11	8	3	0	0.833	1.833
187	Leicester City	Eng	5	4	2	1	1	8	5	3	0	1.250	2.000
188	Chemie Leipzig	GDR	5	4	2	1	1	7	4	3	0	1.250	1.750
189	Bastia	Fra	5	6	1	3	2	8	6	2	0	0.833	1.333
190	Real Sociedad	Esp	5	4	1	3	0	3	1	2	0	1.250	0.750
191	TJ Gottwaldov	Tch	5	4	2	1	1	6	5	1	0	1.250	1.500
192	GKS Katowice	Pol	5	4	2	1	1	6	5	1	0	1.250	1.500
193	Strasbourg	Fra	5	4	2	1	1	3	3	0	0	1.250	0.750
194	Cork Hibernians	Irl	5	6	2	1	3	7	8	-1	0	0.833	1.167
195	Partizan Belgrade	Yug	5	6	2	0	4	13	15	-2	1	0.833	2.167
196	Trabzonspor	Tur	5	4	2	1	1	6	8	-2	0	1.250	1.500
197	Saint-Etienne	Fra	5	6	1	3	2	5	7	-2	0	0.833	0.833
198	Bohemians	Irl	5	6	2	1	3	6	9	-3	0	0.833	1.000
199	Dundalk	Irl	5	8	2	1	5	7	14	-7	0	0.625	0.875
200	Zaglebie Sosnowiec	Pol	5	11	1	3	7	9	22	-13	0	0.455	0.818
201	Reipas Lahti	Fin	5	16	1	3	12	15	63	-48	0	0.313	0.938
202	Ararat Erevan	URS	4	4	1	2	1	12	5	7	0	1.000	3.000
203	Haladás	Hun	4	4	1	2	1	9	4	5	0	1.000	2.250
204	Vllaznia Shkodër	Alb	4	4	2	0	2	6	2	4	0	1.000	1.500
205	Wolverhampton Wanderers	Eng	4	4	1	1	2	6	5	1	1	1.000	1.500
206	Panionios	Gre	4	4	2	0	2	6	5	1	0	1.000	1.500
207	Békéscaba	Hun	4	4	2	0	2	5	4	1	0	1.000	1.250
208	Hvidovre IF	Den	4	4	2	0	2	4	3	1	0	1.000	1.000
209	Bologna	Ita	4	4	1	2	1	4	4	0	0	1.000	1.000
210	OFI Crete	Gre	4	4	2	0	2	4	4	0	0	1.000	1.000
211	Rosenborg BK	Nor	4	4	2	0	2	7	8	-1	0	1.000	1.750
212	Linfield	Nir	4	4	2	0	2	5	6	-1	0	1.000	1.250
213	Zbrojovka Brno	Tch	4	4	1	1	2	3	4	-1	1	1.000	0.750
214	Estrela Amadora	Por	4	4	1	2	1	3	4	-1	0	1.000	0.750
215	St. Mirren	Sco	4	4	1	2	1	1	2	-1	0	1.000	0.250
216	BK Frem	Den	4	4	2	0	2	4	6	-2	0	1.000	1.000
217	Universitatea Cluj	Rom	4	4	2	0	2	3	6	-3	0	1.000	0.750
218	AEK Athenes	Gre	4	6	2	0	4	7	11	-4	0	0.667	1.167
219	Bangor City	Wal	4	7	1	2	4	5	9	-4	0	0.571	0.714
220	Haugar FC	Nor	4	4	1	2	1	3	7	-4	0	1.000	0.750
221	Spartak Varna	Bul	4	6	1	2	3	4	9	-5	0	0.667	0.667
222	Altay	Tur	4	6	1	2	3	6	12	-6	0	0.667	1.000
223	Spartak Trnava	Tch	4	8	1	2	5	5	13	-8	0	0.500	0.625
224	FK Skeid	Nor	4	6	2	0	4	6	15	-9	0	0.667	1.000

Pos'n	Club	Cnty	Pts	P	W	D	L	F	A	Diff	B	Pts/P	F/P
225	Hamrun Spartans	Mlt	4	6	2	0	4	3	13	-10	0	0.667	0.500
226	Floriana	Mlt	4	18	1	2	15	11	71	-60	0	0.222	0.611
227	Lens	Fra	3	4	1	1	2	10	7	3	0	0.750	2.500
228	Hammarby IF	Swe	3	4	1	1	2	7	5	2	0	0.750	1.750
229	Eskisehirspor	Tur	3	4	1	1	2	4	2	2	0	0.750	1.000
230	Nancy	Fra	3	4	1	1	2	7	6	1	0	0.750	1.750
231	Metallist Kharkov	URS	3	4	1	1	2	4	3	1	0	0.750	1.000
232	Vasas SC	Hun	3	8	1	1	6	13	13	0	0	0.375	1.625
233	Linzer ASK	Aut	3	3	1	1	1	2	2	0	0	1.000	0.667
234	NEC Nijmegen	Ned	3	4	1	1	2	4	6	-2	0	0.750	1.000
235	Borough United	Wal	3	4	1	1	2	2	4	-2	0	0.750	0.500
236	VFB Stuttgart	FRG	3	4	1	1	2	4	7	-3	0	0.750	1.000
237	Gent	Bel	3	4	1	1	2	2	5	-3	0	0.750	0.500
238	St-Gallen	Sui	3	4	1	1	2	2	6	-4	0	0.750	0.500
239	Metz	Fra	3	6	1	1	4	8	13	-5	0	0.500	1.333
240	Besa Kavajë	Alb	3	4	0	3	1	3	9	-6	0	0.750	0.750
241	Waterford United	Irl	3	8	1	1	6	6	14	-8	0	0.375	0.750
242	MP Mikkeli	Fin	3	4	1	1	2	4	12	-8	0	0.750	1.000
243	Inter Bratislava	Tch	3	6	1	1	4	4	13	-9	0	0.500	0.667
244	AaB Aalborg	Den	3	6	1	1	4	3	12	-9	0	0.500	0.500
245	AEL Limassol	Cyp	3	6	1	1	4	3	15	-12	0	0.500	0.500
246	Besiktas	Tur	3	8	1	1	6	5	19	-14	0	0.375	0.625
247	Apollon Limassol	Cyp	3	8	1	1	6	4	31	-27	0	0.375	0.500
248	Cercle Bruges	Bel	2	2	1	0	1	4	4	0	0	1.000	2.000
249	Öster SIF	Swe	2	2	0	2	0	2	2	0	0	1.000	1.000
250	Widzew Lódź	Pol	2	2	1	0	1	2	2	0	0	1.000	1.000
251	Neuchâtel Xamax	Sui	2	2	0	2	0	2	2	0	0	1.000	1.000
–	BK Fremad Amager	Den	2	2	0	2	0	1	1	0	0	1.000	0.500
253	Slavia Prague	Tch	2	2	1	0	1	1	1	0	0	1.000	0.500
254	La Chaux-de-Fonds	Sui	2	2	1	0	1	6	7	-1	0	1.000	3.000
255	Arka Gdynia	Pol	2	2	1	0	1	3	4	-1	0	1.000	1.500
256	Borovo	Yug	2	2	1	0	1	2	3	-1	0	1.000	1.000
257	Kickers Offenbach	FRG	2	2	1	0	1	2	3	-1	0	1.000	1.000
258	Jiul Petrosani	Rom	2	2	1	0	1	2	3	-1	0	1.000	1.000
259	Merthyr Tydfil	Wal	2	2	1	0	1	2	3	-1	0	1.000	1.000
260	Vitória Guimarães	Por	2	2	1	0	1	1	2	-1	0	1.000	0.500
261	Kaiserslautern	FRG	2	2	1	0	1	1	2	-1	0	1.000	0.500
262	Castilla Madrid	Esp	2	2	1	0	1	4	6	-2	0	1.000	2.000
263	Waregem	Bel	2	2	1	0	1	3	5	-2	0	1.000	1.500
264	Marek Stanke Dimitrov	Bul	2	2	1	0	1	3	5	-2	0	1.000	1.500
265	Utrecht	Ned	2	2	1	0	1	3	5	-2	0	1.000	1.500
266	Chernonorets Bourgas	Bul	2	2	1	0	1	3	5	-2	0	1.000	1.500
267	Seville	Esp	2	2	1	0	1	2	4	-2	0	1.000	1.000
268	Petrolul Ploiesti	Rom	2	2	1	0	1	2	4	-2	0	1.000	1.000
269	Bryne IL	Nor	2	2	1	0	1	2	4	-2	0	1.000	1.000
270	Landskrona BOIS	Swe	2	2	1	0	1	1	3	-2	0	1.000	0.500
271	Heart of Midlothian	Sco	2	4	1	0	3	8	11	-3	0	0.500	2.000
272	Portadown	Nir	2	2	1	0	1	4	7	-3	0	1.000	2.000
273	Vardar Skopje	Yug	2	2	1	0	1	2	5	-3	0	1.000	1.000
274	Stade Rennes	Fra	2	4	0	2	2	1	4	-3	0	0.500	0.250
275	Komló	Hun	2	2	1	0	1	4	8	-4	0	1.000	2.000
276	Sakaryaspor	Tur	2	4	1	0	3	3	7	-4	0	0.500	0.750
277	Krems	Aut	2	2	1	0	1	1	5	-4	0	1.000	0.500
278	Carrick Rangers	Nir	2	4	1	0	3	7	12	-5	0	0.500	1.750
279	B 93 Copenhagen	Den	2	4	1	0	3	5	10	-5	0	0.500	1.250
280	KuPS Kuopio	Fin	2	4	0	2	2	2	7	-5	0	0.500	0.500
281	Gjøvik/Lyn	Nor	2	2	1	0	1	1	6	-5	0	1.000	0.500

Pos'n	Club	Cnty	Pts	P	W	D	L	F	A	Diff	B	Pts/P	F/P
282	SFK Bodø/Glimt	Nor	2	6	1	0	5	5	12	-7	0	0.333	0.833
283	Gwardia Warsaw	Pol	2	4	1	0	3	4	11	-7	0	0.500	1.000
284	Fredrikstad FK	Nor	2	6	0	2	4	3	10	-7	0	0.333	0.500
285	FC Kuusysi Lahti	Fin	2	6	0	2	4	3	11	-8	0	0.333	0.500
2a6	Grazer AK	Aut	2	6	0	2	4	7	16	-9	0	0.333	1.167
287	Lokomotiv Sofia	Bul	2	4	1	0	3	3	13	-10	0	0.500	0.750
288	Paralimni	Cyp	2	4	1	0	3	4	15	-11	0	0.500	1.000
289	Crusaders	Nir	2	6	0	2	4	5	18	-13	0	0.333	0.833
290	US Rumelange	Lux	2	4	1	0	3	3	16	-13	0	0.500	0.750
291	IA Akranes	Isl	2	8	0	2	6	2	15	-13	0	0.250	0.250
292	Alliance Dudelange	Lux	2	4	0	2	2	4	18	-14	0	0.500	1.000
293	Strømgodset IF	Nor	2	4	1	0	3	3	19	-16	0	0.500	0.750
294	Valur Reykjavik	Isl	2	8	0	2	6	5	27	-22	0	0.250	0.625
295	Pezoporikos Larnaca	Cyp	2	6	0	2	4	2	25	-23	0	0.333	0.333
296	Dundee	Sco	1	2	0	1	1	3	4	-1	0	0.500	1.500
–	Tatran Presov	Tch	1	2	0	1	1	3	4	-1	0	0.500	1.500
–	Karpaty Lvov	URS	1	2	0	1	1	3	4	-1	0	0.500	1.500
299	TPS Turku	Fin	1	2	0	1	1	2	3	-1	0	0.500	1.000
300	Progresul Bucharest	Rom	1	2	0	1	1	1	2	-1	0	0.500	0.500
301	Mersin Idmanyurdu	Tur	1	2	0	1	1	0	1	-1	0	0.500	0.000
–	UCD	Irl	1	2	0	1	1	0	1	-1	0	0.500	0.000
–	Tromsø IL	Nor	1	2	0	1	1	0	1	-1	0	0.500	0.000
304	Chemie Halle	GDR	1	2	0	1	1	3	5	-2	0	0.500	1.500
305	Chimia Râmnicu Vâlcea	Rom	1	2	0	1	1	2	4	-2	0	0.500	1.000
306	Finn Harps	Irl	1	2	0	1	1	2	4	-2	0	0.500	1.000
307	Aarau	Sui	1	2	0	1	1	2	4	-2	0	0.500	1.000
308	Cork Celtic	Irl	1	2	0	1	1	1	3	-2	0	0.500	0.500
309	Siófok	Hun	1	2	0	1	1	1	3	-2	0	0.500	0.500
310	Bray Wanderers	Irl	1	2	0	1	1	1	3	-2	0	0.500	0.500
311	Iraklis	Gre	1	2	0	1	1	0	2	-2	0	0.500	0.000
312	Kastoria	Gre	1	2	0	1	1	0	2	-2	0	0.500	0.000
313	PSV Schwerin	GDR	1	2	0	1	1	0	2	-2	0	0.500	0.000
314	Vålerengens SIF	Nor	1	2	0	1	1	3	6	-3	0	0.500	1.500
315	Baia Mare	Rom	1	2	0	1	1	2	5	-3	0	0.500	1.000
316	Esbjerg FB	Den	1	4	0	1	3	1	4	-3	0	0.250	0.250
317	IBK Keflavik	Isl	1	2	0	1	1	1	4	-3	0	0.500	0.500
318	Belenenses	Por	1	2	0	1	1	1	4	-3	0	0.500	0.500
319	KB Copenhagen	Den	1	2	0	1	1	0	3	-3	0	0.500	0.000
320	Aris Salonika	Gre	1	2	0	1	1	2	6	-4	0	0.500	1.000
321	Willem II	Ned	1	2	0	1	1	2	7	-5	0	0.500	1.000
322	Jeunesse Esch	Lux	1	2	0	1	1	2	7	-5	0	0.500	1.000
323	Tatabánya	Hun	1	2	0	1	1	1	6	-5	0	0.500	0.500
324	KTP Kotka	Fin	1	2	0	1	1	0	5	-5	0	0.500	0.000
325	Home Farm	Irl	1	2	0	1	1	1	7	-6	0	0.500	0.500
326	Olimpija Ljubljana	Yug	1	2	0	1	1	2	9	-7	0	0.500	1.000
327	Limerick	Irl	1	6	0	1	5	2	11	-9	0	0.167	0.333
328	Derry City	Irl	1	4	0	1	3	0	9	-9	0	0.250	0.000
329	FC Basle	Sui	1	4	0	1	3	3	13	-10	0	0.250	0.750
330	Omonia Nicosia	Cyp	1	6	0	1	5	2	12	-10	0	0.167	0.333
331	Ankaragücü	Tur	1	6	0	1	5	1	13	-12	0	0.167	0.167
332	Ards	Nir	1	4	0	1	3	2	17	-15	0	0.250	0.500
333	Anorthosis Famagusta	Cyp	1	4	0	1	3	1	18	-17	0	0.250	0.250
334	Coleraine	Nir	1	8	0	1	7	7	34	-27	0	0.125	0.875
335	Valletta	Mlt	1	8	0	1	7	2	41	-39	0	0.125	0.250
336	Galway United	Irl	0	2	0	0	2	2	4	-2	0	0.000	1.000
337	Ikast FS	Den	0	2	0	0	2	1	3	-2	0	0.000	0.500
338	CSU Galati	Rom	0	2	0	0	2	2	5	-3	0	0.000	1.000

Pos'n	Club	Cnty	Pts	P	W	D	L	F	A	Diff	B	Pts/P	F/P
339	Genclerbirligi	Tur	0	2	0	0	2	1	4	-3	0	0.000	0.500
340	Wiener Neustadt	Aut	0	2	0	0	2	0	3	-3	0	0.000	0.000
341	Pécsi MSC	Hun	0	2	0	0	2	0	3	-3	0	0.000	0.000
342	Sedan	Fra	0	2	0	0	2	3	7	-4	0	0.000	1.500
343	Ilves Tampere	Fin	0	2	0	0	2	3	7	-4	0	0.000	1.500
344	B 1913 Odense	Den	0	2	0	0	2	2	6	-4	0	0.000	1.000
345	Moss FK	Nor	0	2	0	0	2	2	6	-4	0	0.000	1.000
346	Shelbourne	Irl	0	2	0	0	2	1	5	-4	0	0.000	0.500
347	Lugano	Sui	0	2	0	0	2	0	4	-4	0	0.000	0.000
348	Sligo Rovers	Irl	0	2	0	0	2	0	4	-4	0	0.000	0.000
349	IL Viking	Nor	0	2	0	0	2	0	5	-5	0	0.000	0.000
350	NEA Salamina Famagusta	Cyp	0	2	0	0	2	0	5	-5	0	0.000	0.000
351	B 1901 Nykobing	Den	0	2	0	0	2	3	9	-6	0	0.000	1.500
352	Skoda Plzen	Tch	0	2	0	0	2	1	7	-6	0	0.000	0.500
353	Distillery	Nir	0	2	0	0	2	1	7	-6	0	0.000	0.500
354	Cork City	Irl	0	2	0	0	2	0	6	-6	0	0.000	0.000
355	Swift Hesperange	Lux	0	2	0	0	2	0	6	-6	0	0.000	0.000
356	Lucerne	Sui	0	2	0	0	2	2	9	-7	0	0.000	1.000
357	St. Patrick's Athletic	Irl	0	2	0	0	2	1	8	-7	0	0.000	0.500
358	Vanløse IF	Den	0	2	0	0	2	1	8	-7	0	0.000	0.500
359	Olympiakos Nicosia	Cyp	0	2	0	0	2	1	8	-7	0	0.000	0.500
360	Sliven	Bul	0	2	0	0	2	1	8	-7	0	0.000	0.500
361	Go Ahead Eagles	Ned	0	2	0	0	2	0	7	-7	0	0.000	0.000
362	Flamurtari Vlorë	Alb	0	6	0	0	6	6	14	-8	0	0.000	1.000
363	Lechia Gdańsk	Pol	0	2	0	0	2	2	10	-8	0	0.000	1.000
364	Cliftonville	Nir	0	2	0	0	2	0	8	-8	0	0.000	0.000
365	SV Salzburg	Aut	0	2	0	0	2	0	8	-8	0	0.000	0.000
366	Gzira United	Mlt	0	2	0	0	2	0	9	-9	0	0.000	0.000
367	Glenavon	Nir	0	4	0	0	4	4	14	-10	0	0.000	1.000
368	HPS Helsinki	Fin	0	2	0	0	2	2	12	-10	0	0.000	1.000
369	Mjøndalen IF	Nor	0	2	0	0	2	2	12	-10	0	0.000	1.000
370	Fola Esch	Lux	0	2	0	0	2	1	11	-10	0	0.000	0.500
371	Progrès Niedercorn	Lux	0	2	0	0	2	0	10	-10	0	0.000	0.000
372	Vikingur Reykjavik	Isl	0	2	0	0	2	0	11	-11	0	0.000	0.000
373	IBA Akureyri	Isl	0	2	0	0	2	1	14	-13	0	0.000	0.500
374	Lillestrøm SK	Nor	0	6	0	0	6	1	14	-13	0	0.000	0.167
375	Anorthosis Nicosia	Cyp	0	2	0	0	2	0	16	-16	0	0.000	0.000
376	Zurrieq	Mlt	0	4	0	0	4	0	19	-19	0	0.000	0.000
377	KR Reykjavik	Isl	0	6	0	0	6	3	24	-21	0	0.000	0.500
378	Spora Luxembourg	Lux	0	6	0	0	6	2	23	-21	0	0.000	0.333
379	Jeunesse Hautcharage	Lux	0	2	0	0	2	0	21	-21	0	0.000	0.000
380	Ballymena United	Nir	0	8	0	0	8	1	25	-24	0	0.000	0.125
381	Red Boys Differdange	Lux	0	6	0	0	6	2	28	-26	0	0 000	0.333
382	IBV Vestmannaeyjar	Isl	0	8	0	0	8	4	35	-31	0	0.000	0.500
383	Avenir Beggen	Lux	0	8	0	0	8	4	36	-32	0	0.000	0.500
	Total		**4114**	**3686**	**1464**	**758**	**1464**	**5373**	**5373**	**0**	**428**	**1.116**	**2.915**

Club Performance by Points

1981-82 to 1990-91

Pos'n	Club	Cnty	Pts	P	W	D	L	F	A	Diff	B	Pts/P	F/P
1	Barcelona	Esp	74	45	27	9	9	93	44	49	11	1.644	2.067
2	Sampdoria	Ita	44	28	15	7	6	39	21	18	7	1.571	1.393
3	Aberdeen	Sco	38	25	14	5	6	42	18	24	5	1.520	1.680
4	Ajax	Ned	35	20	14	1	5	38	14	24	6	1.750	1.900
5	Juventus	Ita	34	17	13	3	1	43	12	31	5	2.000	2.529
6	KV Mechelen	Bel	34	17	13	3	1	26	8	18	5	2.000	1.529
7	Manchester United	Eng	30	17	10	5	2	29	13	16	5	1.765	1.706
8	Lokomotive Leipzig	GDR	26	19	8	6	5	21	15	6	4	1.368	1.105
9	Dinamo Kiev	URS	25	15	8	5	2	38	16	22	4	1.667	2.533
10	Rapid Vienna	Aut	25	19	8	5	6	40	32	8	4	1.316	2.105
11	FC Porto	Por	23	17	8	3	6	23	19	4	4	1.353	1.353
12	Dinamo Bucharest	Rom	22	18	8	3	7	24	13	11	3	1.222	1.333
13	Dukla Prague	Tch	22	18	7	6	5	26	23	3	2	1.222	1.444
14	Legia Warsaw	Pol	21	16	6	6	4	22	15	7	3	1.313	1.375
15	Anderlecht	Bel	20	13	8	1	4	23	9	14	3	1.538	1.769
16	Bayern Munich	FRG	20	14	6	5	3	23	15	8	3	1.429	1.643
17	Everton	Eng	19	9	7	2	0	16	2	14	3	2.111	1.778
18	Standard Liège	Bel	18	9	7	1	1	23	6	17	3	2.000	2.556
19	Tottenham Hotspur	Eng	17	12	6	3	3	21	11	10	2	1.417	1.750
20	Torpedo Moscow	URS	17	12	6	4	2	23	14	9	1	1.417	1.917
21	Atlético Madrid	Esp	17	9	6	2	1	13	8	5	3	1.889	1.444
22	Dynamo Dresden	GDR	17	14	7	1	6	30	27	3	2	1.214	2.143
23	Real Madrid	Esp	16	9	5	3	1	18	10	8	3	1.778	2.000
24	Eintracht Frankfurt	FRG	16	12	6	2	4	13	8	5	2	1.333	1.083
25	Olympique Marseille	Fra	15	8	6	1	1	14	4	10	2	1.875	1.750
26	Paris Saint-Germain	Fra	15	10	6	2	2	16	9	7	1	1.500	1.600
27	Roma	Ita	15	12	6	2	4	13	8	5	1	1.250	1.083
28	Waterschei Thor	Bel	14	8	6	0	2	19	9	10	2	1.750	2.375
29	Dinamo Moscow	URS	14	8	5	2	1	15	6	9	2	1.750	1.875
30	Girondins Bordeaux	Fra	13	8	5	1	2	12	6	6	2	1.625	1.500
31	Red Star Belgrade	Yug	12	10	4	3	3	20	14	6	1	1.200	2.000
32	CSKA Sofia	Bul	12	8	5	0	3	17	11	6	2	1.500	2.125
33	Dinamo Tbilisi	URS	12	8	4	2	2	10	6	4	2	1.500	1.250
34	Monaco	Fra	12	10	2	6	2	9	9	0	2	1.200	0.900
35	Ujpesti Dózsa	Hun	12	12	5	1	6	18	20	-2	1	1.000	1.500
36	Austria Vienna	Aut	12	12	3	4	5	13	19	-6	2	1.000	1.083
37	Bayer Uerdingen	FRG	11	8	4	1	3	24	10	14	2	1.375	3.000
38	Wrexham	Wal	11	12	4	3	5	14	14	0	0	0.917	1.167
39	AGF Åarhus	Den	10	6	4	1	1	13	4	9	1	1.667	2.167
40	Real Valladolid	Esp	10	6	3	3	0	10	2	8	1	1.667	1.667
41	Shakhtyor Donetsk	URS	10	6	4	1	1	15	8	7	1	1.667	2.500
42	Malmö FF	Swe	10	8	4	1	3	15	9	6	1	1.250	1.875
43	Velez Mostar	Yug	10	8	3	4	1	18	13	5	0	1.250	2.250
44	Lech Poznań	Pol	10	8	4	2	2	10	7	3	0	1.250	1.250
45	Benfica	Por	10	8	4	1	3	9	6	3	1	1.250	1.125
46	Larissa	Gre	10	8	3	3	2	7	5	2	1	1.250	0.875
47	Real Zaragoza	Esp	10	8	3	2	3	10	10	0	2	1.250	1.250
48	Haka Valkeakoski	Fin	10	10	3	3	4	12	15	-3	1	1.000	1.200
49	Montpellier	Fra	9	6	3	2	1	10	3	7	1	1.500	1.667
50	Olympiakos Pireus	Gre	9	8	4	1	3	13	10	3	0	1.125	1.625
51	Atalanta	Ita	9	8	3	1	4	10	8	2	2	1.125	1.250
52	Panathinaikos	Gre	9	10	4	1	5	12	19	-7	0	0.900	1.200
53	Fram Reykjavik	Isl	9	14	4	1	9	12	28	-16	0	0.643	0.857

Pos'n	Club	Cnty	Pts	P	W	D	L	F	A	Diff	B	Pts/P	F/P
54	Rangers	Sco	8	6	4	0	2	22	6	16	0	1.333	3.667
55	Swansea City	Wal	8	12	3	2	7	27	15	12	0	0.667	2.250
56	Servette	Sui	8	8	4	0	4	17	8	9	0	1.000	2.125
57	Dinamo Minsk	URS	8	6	2	3	1	6	4	2	1	1.333	1.000
58	Roda JC	Ned	8	6	3	1	2	6	4	2	1	1.333	1.000
59	Admira Wacker	Aut	8	6	3	1	2	6	4	2	1	1.333	1.000
60	Galatasaray	Tur	8	8	3	2	3	9	11	-2	0	1.000	1.125
61	Trakia Plovdiv	Bul	7	6	3	1	2	10	9	1	0	1.167	1.667
62	FC Liège	Bel	7	6	3	0	3	8	7	1	1	1.167	1.333
63	Grasshoppers Zürich	Sui	7	8	2	2	4	9	9	0	1	0.875	1.125
64	RoPS Povaniemi	Fin	7	6	2	2	2	3	5	-2	1	1.167	0.500
65	Levski Sofia	Bul	7	8	3	0	5	9	12	-3	1	0.875	1.125
66	Kalmar FF	Swe	7	6	3	1	2	6	9	-3	0	1.167	1.000
67	17 Nëntori Tirana	Alb	7	6	3	1	2	5	9	-4	0	1.167	0.833
68	Sion	Sui	7	8	2	2	4	10	17	-7	1	0.875	1.250
69	DAC Dunajská Streda	Tch	6	4	3	0	1	9	4	5	0	1.500	2.250
70	Sporting Lisbon	Por	6	6	2	1	3	12	8	4	1	1.000	2.000
71	SKA Rostov on Don	URS	6	4	3	0	1	6	2	4	0	1.500	1.500
72	Wisla Kraków	Pol	6	4	3	0	1	9	6	3	0	1.500	2.250
73	Dynamo Berlin	GDR	6	4	2	2	0	5	3	2	0	1.500	1.250
74	Groningen	Ned	6	4	3	0	1	8	7	1	0	1.500	2.000
75	Inter Milan	Ita	6	6	2	1	3	7	6	1	1	1.000	1.167
76	Lyngby BK	Den	6	6	2	2	2	7	8	-1	0	1.000	1.167
77	Fortuna Sittard	Ned	6	6	2	1	3	6	7	-1	1	1.000	1.000
78	HJK Helsinki	Fin	6	4	3	0	1	8	10	-2	0	1.500	2.000
79	Glentoran	Nir	6	10	1	4	5	7	17	-10	0	0.600	0.700
80	AIK	Swe	5	4	2	1	1	15	3	12	0	1.250	3.750
81	Real Sociedad	Esp	5	4	1	3	0	3	1	2	0	1.250	0.750
82	Beveren	Bel	5	4	2	1	1	8	7	1	0	1.250	2.000
83	GKS Katowice	Pol	5	4	2	1	1	6	5	1	0	1.250	1.500
84	Djurgården SIF	Swe	5	6	1	3	2	8	8	0	0	0.833	1.333
85	Dinamo Tirana	Alb	5	6	2	1	3	6	6	0	0	0.833	1.000
86	Borussia Dortmund	FRG	5	4	2	1	1	4	4	0	0	1.250	1.000
87	AZ'67 Alkmaar	Ned	5	4	2	1	1	3	3	0	0	1.250	0.750
88	Young Boys Berne	Sui	5	6	2	0	4	6	7	-1	1	0.833	1.000
89	Partizan Belgrade	Yug	5	6	2	0	4	13	15	-2	1	0.833	2.167
90	Celtic	Sco	5	8	2	1	5	12	14	-2	0	0.625	1.500
91	Trabzonspor	Tur	5	4	2	1	1	6	8	-2	0	1.250	1.500
92	Cologne	FRG	4	4	2	0	2	12	7	5	0	1.000	3.000
93	Hamburg	FRG	4	4	2	0	2	8	3	5	0	1.000	2.000
94	Vllaznia Shkodër	Alb	4	4	2	0	2	6	2	4	0	1.000	1.500
95	Bastia	Fra	4	4	1	2	1	7	4	3	0	1.000	1.750
96	FC Den Haag	Ned	4	4	2	0	2	5	4	1	0	1.000	1.250
97	Békéscsaba	Hun	4	4	2	0	2	5	4	1	0	1.000	1.250
98	OFI Crete	Gre	4	4	2	0	2	4	4	0	0	1.000	1.000
99	Dundee United	Sco	4	4	1	2	1	2	2	0	0	1.000	0.500
100	Estrela Amadora	Por	4	4	1	2	1	3	4	-1	0	1.000	0.750
101	St. Mirren	Sco	4	4	1	2	1	1	2	-1	0	1.000	0.250
102	Slovan Bratislava	Tch	4	4	2	0	2	5	7	-2	0	1.000	1.250
103	Steaua Bucharest	Rom	4	6	1	2	3	6	10	-4	0	0.667	1.000
104	FC Tirol	Aut	4	4	2	0	2	6	13	-7	0	1.000	1.500
105	Hamrun Spartans	Mlt	4	6	2	0	4	3	13	-10	0	0.667	0.500
106	Vasas SC	Hun	3	6	1	1	4	13	10	3	0	0.500	2.167
107	Hammarby IF	Swe	3	4	1	1	2	7	5	2	0	0.750	1.750
108	Carl Zeiss Jena	GDR	3	4	1	1	2	7	5	2	0	0.750	1.750
109	Ferencváros	Hun	3	4	1	1	2	6	4	2	0	0.750	1.500
110	Metallist Kharkov	URS	3	4	1	1	2	4	3	1	0	0.750	1.000

Pos'n	Club	Cnty	Pts	P	W	D	L	F	A	Diff	B	Pts/P	F/P
111	Lausanne-Sports	Sui	3	4	1	1	2	6	7	-1	0	0.750	1.500
112	Cardiff City	Wal	3	4	1	1	2	5	6	-1	0	0.750	1.250
113	Universitatea Craiova	Rom	3	4	1	1	2	5	7	-2	0	0.750	1.250
114	NEC Nijmegen	Ned	3	4	1	1	2	4	6	-2	0	0.750	1.000
115	Spartak Varna	Bul	3	4	1	1	2	2	4	-2	0	0.750	0.500
116	VFB Stuttgart	FRG	3	4	1	1	2	4	7	-3	0	0.750	1.000
117	Dundalk	Irl	3	6	1	1	4	6	10	-4	0	0.500	1.000
118	Metz	Fra	3	6	1	1	4	8	13	-5	0	0.500	1.333
119	Magdeburg	GDR	3	4	1	1	2	3	8	-5	0	0.750	0.750
120	Inter Bratislava	Tch	3	6	1	1	4	4	13	-9	0	0.500	0.667
121	AEL Limassol	Cyp	3	6	1	1	4	3	15	-12	0	0.500	0.500
122	Apollon Limassol	Cyp	3	4	1	1	2	3	16	-13	0	0.750	0.750
123	Cercle Bruges	Bel	2	2	1	0	1	4	4	0	0	1.000	2.000
124	PAOK Salonika	Gre	2	2	1	0	1	2	2	0	0	1.000	1.000
125	Dinamo Zagreb	Yug	2	2	1	0	1	2	2	0	0	1.000	1.000
126	Widzew Lódź	Pol	2	2	1	0	1	2	2	0	0	1.000	1.000
127	Neuchâtel Xamax	Sui	2	2	0	2	0	2	2	0	0	1.000	1.000
128	Fredrikstad FK	Nor	2	2	0	2	0	1	1	0	0	1.000	0.500
129	AaB Aalborg	Den	2	2	1	0	1	1	1	0	0	1.000	0.500
130	AEK Athenes	Gre	2	2	1	0	1	3	4	-1	0	1.000	1.500
131	Merthyr Tydfil	Wal	2	2	1	0	1	2	3	-1	0	1.000	1.000
132	IFK Norrköping	Swe	2	2	1	0	1	2	3	-1	0	1.000	1.000
133	B 1903 Copenhagen	Den	2	2	1	0	1	1	2	-1	0	1.000	0.500
134	Vitória Guimarães	Por	2	2	1	0	1	1	2	-1	0	1.000	0.500
135	Kaiserslautern	FRG	2	2	1	0	1	1	2	-1	0	1.000	0.500
136	Utrecht	Ned	2	2	1	0	1	3	5	-2	0	1.000	1.500
137	Chernomorets Bourgas	Bul	2	2	1	0	1	3	5	-2	0	1.000	1.500
138	Vejle BK	Den	2	2	1	0	1	2	4	-2	0	1.000	1.000
139	IA Akranes	Isl	2	4	0	2	2	2	4	-2	0	0.500	0.500
140	Bryne IL	Nor	2	2	1	0	1	2	4	-2	0	1.000	1.000
141	Borac Banja Luka	Yug	2	2	1	0	1	2	4	-2	0	1.000	1.000
142	Sporting Braga	Por	2	2	1	0	1	1	3	-2	0	1.000	0.500
143	Gent	Bel	2	2	1	0	1	1	3	-2	0	1.000	0.500
144	Politehnica Timisoara	Rom	2	2	1	0	1	2	5	-3	0	1.000	1.000
145	Lokomotiv Sofia	Bul	2	2	1	0	1	2	5	-3	0	1.000	1.000
146	Bangor City	Wal	2	4	0	2	2	1	4	-3	0	0.500	0.250
147	Sakaryaspor	Tur	2	4	1	0	3	3	7	-4	0	0.500	0.750
148	Krems	Aut	2	2	1	0	1	1	5	-4	0	1.000	0.500
149	B 93 Copenhagen	Den	2	4	1	0	3	5	10	-5	0	0.500	1.250
150	FC Kuusysi Lahti	Fin	2	6	0	2	4	3	11	-8	0	0.333	0.500
151	Paralimni	Cyp	2	4	1	0	3	4	15	-11	0	0.500	1.000
152	Hajduk Split	Yug	2	6	1	0	5	3	14	-11	0	0.333	0.500
153	Union Luxembourg	Lux	2	6	0	2	4	1	16	-15	0	0.333	0.167
154	Club Bruges	Bel	1	2	0	1	1	6	7	-1	0	0.500	3.000
155	Limerick	Irl	1	2	0	1	1	1	2	-1	0	0.500	0.500
156	Mersin Idmanyurdu	Tur	1	2	0	1	1	0	1	-1	0	0.500	0.000
157	UCD	Irl	1	2	0	1	1	0	1	-1	0	0.500	0.000
158	Spartak Trnava	Tch	1	2	0	1	1	0	1	-1	0	0.500	0.000
159	Tromsø IL	Nor	1	2	0	1	1	0	1	-1	0	0.500	0.000
160	PSV Eindhoven	Ned	1	2	0	1	1	0	1	-1	0	0.500	0.000
161	Grazer AK	Aut	1	2	0	1	1	2	4	-2	0	0.500	1.000
162	IFK Gothenburg	Swe	1	2	0	1	1	2	4	-2	0	0.500	1.000
163	Aarau	Sui	1	2	0	1	1	2	4	-2	0	0.500	1.000
164	Siófok	Hun	1	2	0	1	1	1	3	-2	0	0.500	0.500
165	Bray Wanderers	Irl	1	2	0	1	1	1	3	-2	0	0.500	0.500
166	Slask Wroclaw	Pol	1	2	0	1	1	0	2	-2	0	0.500	0.000
167	PSV Schwerin	GDR	1	2	0	1	1	0	2	-2	0	0.500	0.000

Pos'n	Club	Cnty	Pts	P	W	D	L	F	A	Diff	B	Pts/P	F/P
168	Vålerengen SIF	Nor	1	2	0	1	1	3	6	-3	0	0.500	1.500
169	Baia Mare	Rom	1	2	0	1	1	2	5	-3	0	0.500	1.000
170	Belenenses	Por	1	2	0	1	1	1	4	-3	0	0.500	0.500
171	KB Copenhagen	Den	1	2	0	1	1	0	3	-3	0	0.500	0.000
172	KuPS Kuopio	Fin	1	2	0	1	1	2	6	-4	0	0.500	1.000
173	SK Brann	Nor	1	4	0	1	3	1	5	-4	0	0.250	0.250
174	Derry City	Irl	1	2	0	1	1	0	4	-4	0	0.500	0.000
175	Besiktas	Tur	1	4	0	1	3	3	8	-5	0	0.250	0.750
176	Jeunesse Esch	Lux	1	2	0	1	1	2	7	-5	0	0.500	1.000
177	Tatabánya	Hun	1	2	0	1	1	1	6	-5	0	0.500	0.500
178	KTP Kotka	Fin	1	2	0	1	1	0	5	-5	0	0.500	0.000
179	Floriana	Mlt	1	4	0	1	3	1	13	-12	0	0.250	0.250
180	Galway United	Irl	0	2	0	0	2	2	4	-2	0	0.000	1.000
181	Valur Reykjavik	Isl	0	2	0	0	2	2	4	-2	0	0.000	1.000
182	Ikast FS	Den	0	2	0	0	2	1	3	-2	0	0.000	0.500
183	Gençlerbirligi	Tur	0	2	0	0	2	1	4	-3	0	0.000	0.500
184	Omonia Nicosia	Cyp	0	2	0	0	2	0	3	-3	0	0.000	0.000
185	Pécsi MSC	Hun	0	2	0	0	2	0	3	-3	0	0.000	0.000
186	Moss FK	Nor	0	2	0	0	2	2	6	-4	0	0.000	1.000
187	Sligo Rovers	Irl	0	2	0	0	2	0	4	-4	0	0.000	0.000
188	Glenavon	Nir	0	2	0	0	2	2	7	-5	0	0.000	1.000
189	Apoel Nicosia	Cyp	0	2	0	0	2	1	6	-5	0	0.000	0.500
190	Waterford United	Irl	0	2	0	0	2	1	6	-5	0	0.000	0.500
191	Ankaragücü	Tur	0	2	0	0	2	0	5	-5	0	0.000	0.000
192	NEA Salamina Famagousta	Cyp	0	2	0	0	2	0	5	-5	0	0.000	0.000
193	IL Viking	Nor	0	2	0	0	2	0	5	-5	0	0.000	0.000
194	B 1901 Nykobing	Den	0	2	0	0	2	3	9	-6	0	0.000	1.500
195	Cork City	Irl	0	2	0	0	2	0	6	-6	0	0.000	0.000
196	Swift Hesperange	Lux	0	2	0	0	2	0	6	-6	0	0.000	0.000
197	Sliven	Bul	0	2	0	0	2	1	8	-7	0	0.000	0.500
198	Coleraine	Nir	0	2	0	0	2	0	7	-7	0	0.000	0.000
199	Bursaspor	Tur	0	2	0	0	2	0	7	-7	0	0.000	0.000
200	Flamurtari Vlorë	Alb	0	6	0	0	6	6	14	-8	0	0.000	1.000
201	IBV Vestmannaeyjar	Isl	0	4	0	0	4	3	11	-8	0	0.000	0.750
202	Lechia Gdańsk	Pol	0	2	0	0	2	2	10	-8	0	0.000	1.000
203	Lillestrøm SK	Nor	0	4	0	0	4	1	11	-10	0	0.000	0.250
204	Ballymena United	Nir	0	6	0	0	6	1	19	-18	0	0.000	0.167
205	Valletta	Mlt	0	2	0	0	2	0	18	-18	0	0.000	0.000
206	Zurrieq	Mlt	0	4	0	0	4	0	19	-19	0	0.000	0.000
207	Red Boys Differdange	Lux	0	4	0	0	4	1	21	-20	0	0.000	0.250
208	Avenir Beggen	Lux	0	6	0	0	6	2	25	-23	0	0.000	0.333
209	Sliema Wanderers	Mlt	0	6	0	0	6	1	27	-26	0	0.000	0.167
	Total		**1388**	**1248**	**497**	**254**	**497**	**1716**	**1716**	**0**	**140**	**1.112**	**2.750**

Club Performance by Points

1986-87 to 1990-91

Pos'n	Club	Cnty	Pts	P	W	D	L	F	A	Diff	B	Pts/P	F/P
1	Sampdoria	Ita	39	24	13	6	5	36	18	18	7	1.625	1.500
2	Barcelona	Esp	37	22	13	5	4	42	20	22	6	1.682	1.909
3	Ajax	Ned	35	18	14	1	3	37	8	29	6	1.944	2.056
4	KV Mechelen	Bel	34	17	13	3	1	26	8	18	5	2.000	1.529
5	Dinamo Bucharest	Rom	22	18	8	3	7	24	13	11	3	1.222	1.333
6	Anderlecht	Bel	20	13	8	1	4	23	9	14	3	1.538	1.769
7	Manchester United	Eng	19	9	7	2	0	17	4	13	3	2.111	1.889
8	Juventus	Ita	16	8	7	0	1	24	5	19	2	2.000	3.000
9	Olympique Marseille	Fra	15	8	6	1	1	14	4	10	2	1.875	1.750
10	Torpedo Moscow	URS	15	10	6	2	2	22	13	9	1	1.500	2.200
11	Lokomotive Leipzig	GDR	15	11	4	4	3	9	6	3	3	1.364	0.818
12	Legia Warsaw	Pol	14	10	4	4	2	13	8	5	2	1.400	1.300
13	Girondins Bordeaux	Fra	13	8	5	1	2	12	6	6	2	1.625	1.500
14	CSKA Sofia	Bul	12	8	5	0	3	17	11	6	2	1.500	2.125
15	AGF Åarhus	Den	10	6	4	1	1	13	4	9	1	1.667	2.167
16	Real Valladolid	Esp	10	6	3	3	0	10	2	8	1	1.667	1.667
17	Monaco	Fra	10	8	1	6	1	7	6	1	2	1.250	0.875
18	Real Zaragoza	Esp	10	8	3	2	3	10	10	0	2	1.250	1.250
19	Montpellier	Fra	9	6	3	2	1	10	3	7	1	1.500	1.667
20	Eintracht Frankfurt	FRG	9	6	3	2	1	7	2	5	1	1.500	1.167
21	Olympiakos Pireus	Gre	9	8	4	1	3	13	10	3	0	1.125	1.625
22	Wrexham	Wal	9	8	3	3	2	10	7	3	0	1.125	1.250
23	Atalanta	Ita	9	8	3	1	4	10	8	2	2	1.125	1.250
24	Malmö FF	Swe	8	6	3	1	2	12	5	7	1	1.333	2.000
25	Dinamo Kiev	URS	8	6	2	3	1	12	8	4	1	1.333	2.000
26	Dinamo Minsk	URS	8	6	2	3	1	6	4	2	1	1.333	1.000
27	Roda JC	Ned	8	6	3	1	2	6	4	2	1	1.333	1.000
28	Admira Wacker	Aut	8	6	3	1	2	6	4	2	1	1.333	1.000
29	Sion	Sui	7	6	2	2	2	9	6	3	1	1.167	1.500
30	Aberdeen	Sco	7	6	3	1	2	7	5	2	0	1.167	1.167
31	FC Liège	Bel	7	6	3	0	3	8	7	1	1	1.167	1.333
32	Grasshoppers Zürich	Sui	7	8	2	2	4	9	9	0	1	0.875	1.125
33	RoPS Rovaniemi	Fin	7	6	2	2	2	3	5	-2	1	1.167	0.500
34	Levski Sofia	Bul	7	8	3	0	5	9	12	-3	1	0.875	1.125
35	Panathinaikos	Gre	7	8	3	1	4	10	16	-6	0	0.875	1.250
36	DAC Dunajská Streda	Tch	6	4	3	0	1	9	4	5	0	1.500	2.250
37	Sporting Lisbon	Por	6	6	2	1	3	12	8	4	1	1.000	2.000
38	Lech Poznań	Pol	6	4	2	2	0	6	4	2	0	1.500	1.500
39	Dynamo Berlin	GDR	6	4	2	2	0	5	3	2	0	1.500	1.250
40	Groningen	Ned	6	4	3	0	1	8	7	1	0	1.500	2.000
41	Dukla Prague	Tch	5	4	2	1	1	6	4	2	0	1.250	1.500
42	Benfica	Por	5	4	2	1	1	5	3	2	0	1.250	1.250
43	Real Sociedad	Esp	5	4	1	3	0	3	1	2	0	1.250	0.750
44	GKS Katowice	Pol	5	4	2	1	1	6	5	1	0	1.250	1.500
45	Velez Mostar	Yug	5	4	2	1	1	9	9	0	0	1.250	2.250
46	Djurgården SIF	Swe	5	6	1	3	2	8	8	0	0	0.833	1.333
47	Borussia Dortmund	FRG	5	4	2	1	1	4	4	0	0	1.250	1.000
48	Young Boys Berne	Sui	5	6	2	0	4	6	7	-1	1	0.833	1.000
49	17 Nëntori Tirana	Alb	5	4	2	1	1	3	4	-1	0	1.250	0.750
50	Partizan Belgrade	Yug	5	6	2	0	4	13	15	-2	1	0.833	2.167
51	Trabzonspor	Tur	5	4	2	1	1	6	8	-2	0	1.250	1.500
52	Kalmar FF	Swe	5	4	2	1	1	2	5	-3	0	1.250	0.500
53	Hamburg	FRG	4	4	2	0	2	8	3	5	0	1.000	2.000

Pos'n	Club	Cnty	Pts	P	W	D	L	F	A	Diff	B	Pts/P	F/P
54	Vllaznia Shkodër	Alb	4	4	2	0	2	6	2	4	0	1.000	1.500
55	Dinamo Tirana	Alb	4	4	2	0	2	6	5	1	0	1.000	1.500
56	FC Den Haag	Ned	4	4	2	0	2	5	4	1	0	1.000	1.250
57	Békécsaba	Hun	4	4	2	0	2	5	4	1	0	1.000	1.250
58	Rapid Vienna	Aut	4	4	1	2	1	9	9	0	0	1.000	2.250
59	OFI Crete	Gre	4	4	2	0	2	4	4	0	0	1.000	1.000
60	Dundee United	Sco	4	4	1	2	1	2	2	0	0	1.000	0.500
61	Estrela Amadora	Por	4	4	1	2	1	3	4	-1	0	1.000	0.750
62	St. Mirren	Sco	4	4	1	2	1	1	2	-1	0	1.000	0.250
63	Glentoran	Nir	4	6	0	4	2	3	10	-7	0	0.667	0.500
64	Carl Zeiss Jena	GDR	3	4	1	1	2	7	5	2	0	0.750	1.750
65	Ferencváros	Hun	3	4	1	1	2	6	4	2	0	0.750	1.500
66	Metallist Kharkov	URS	3	4	1	1	2	4	3	1	0	0.750	1.000
67	Cardiff City	Wal	3	4	1	1	2	5	6	-1	0	0.750	1.250
68	Steaua Bucharest	Rom	3	4	1	1	2	6	9	-3	0	0.750	1.500
69	VFB Stuttgart	FRG	3	4	1	1	2	4	7	-3	0	0.750	1.000
70	Austria Vienna	Aut	3	4	1	1	2	2	8	-6	0	0.750	0.500
71	Fram Reykjavik	Isl	3	8	1	1	6	5	17	-12	0	0.375	0.625
72	Celtic	Sco	2	2	1	0	1	6	6	0	0	1.000	3.000
73	Roma	Ita	2	2	1	0	1	2	2	0	0	1.000	1.000
74	Neuchâtel Xamax	Sui	2	2	0	2	0	2	2	0	0	1.000	1.000
75	AaB Aalborg	Den	2	2	1	0	1	1	1	0	0	1.000	0.500
76	Slovan Bratislava	Tch	2	2	1	0	1	3	4	-1	0	1.000	1.500
77	Merthyr Tydfil	Wal	2	2	1	0	1	2	3	-1	0	1.000	1.000
78	Ujpesti Dózsa	Hun	2	2	1	0	1	2	3	-1	0	1.000	1.000
79	IFK Norrköping	Swe	2	2	1	0	1	2	3	-1	0	1.000	1.000
80	B 1903 Copenhagen	Den	2	2	1	0	1	1	2	-1	0	1.000	0.500
81	Vitória Guimarães	Por	2	2	1	0	1	1	2	-1	0	1.000	0.500
82	Kaiserslautern	FRG	2	2	1	0	1	1	2	-1	0	1.000	0.500
83	FC Tirol	Aut	2	2	1	0	1	4	6	-2	0	1.000	2.000
84	Chernomorets Bourgas	Bul	2	2	1	0	1	3	5	-2	0	1.000	1.500
85	Bryne IL	Nor	2	2	1	0	1	2	4	-2	0	1.000	1.000
86	Borac Banja Luka	Yug	2	2	1	0	1	2	4	-2	0	1.000	1.000
87	Sakaryaspor	Tur	2	4	1	0	3	3	7	-4	0	0.500	0.750
88	Krems	Aut	2	2	1	0	1	1	5	-4	0	1.000	0.500
89	Apollon Limassol	Cyp	2	2	1	0	1	2	7	-5	0	1.000	1.000
90	Haka Valkeakoski	Fin	2	4	0	2	2	5	11	-6	0	0.500	1.250
91	Hajduk Split	Yug	2	4	1	0	3	1	8	-7	0	0.500	0.250
92	AEL Limassol	Cyp	2	4	1	0	3	1	9	-8	0	0.500	0.250
93	Club Bruges	Bel	1	2	0	1	1	6	7	-1	0	0.500	3.000
94	Swansea City	Wal	1	2	0	1	1	5	6	-1	0	0.500	2.500
95	Vasas SC	Hun	1	2	0	1	1	4	5	-1	0	0.500	2.000
96	Spartak Trnava	Tch	1	2	0	1	1	0	1	-1	0	0.500	0.000
97	IA Akranes	Isl	1	2	0	1	1	0	1	-1	0	0.500	0.000
98	Tromsø IL	Nor	1	2	0	1	1	0	1	-1	0	0.500	0.000
99	Floriana	Mlt	1	2	0	1	1	0	1	-1	0	0.500	0.000
100	Lyngby BK	Den	1	2	0	1	1	0	1	-1	0	0.500	0.000
101	PSV Eindhoven	Ned	1	2	0	1	1	0	1	-1	0	0.500	0.000
102	Bray Wanderers	Nir	1	2	0	1	1	1	3	-2	0	0.500	0.500
103	Slask Wroclaw	Pol	1	2	0	1	1	0	2	-2	0	0.500	0.000
104	PSV Schwerin	GDR	1	2	0	1	1	0	2	-2	0	0.500	0.000
105	Belenenses	Por	1	2	0	1	1	1	4	-3	0	0.500	0.500
106	KuPS Kuopio	Fin	1	2	0	1	1	2	6	-4	0	0.500	1.000
107	Derry City	Nir	1	2	0	1	1	0	4	-4	0	0.500	0.000
108	Union Luxembourg	Lux	1	4	0	1	3	0	11	-11	0	0.250	0.000
109	Valur Reykjavik	Isl	0	2	0	0	2	2	4	-2	0	0.000	1.000
110	Ikast FS	Den	0	2	0	0	2	1	3	-2	0	0.000	0.500

Pos'n	Club	Cnty	Pts	P	W	D	L	F	A	Diff	B	Pts/P	F/P
111	Besiktas	Tur	0	2	0	0	2	1	3	-2	0	0.000	0.500
112	Lillestrøm SK	Nor	0	2	0	0	2	1	4	-3	0	0.000	0.500
113	Gençlerbirligi	Tur	0	2	0	0	2	1	4	-3	0	0.000	0.500
114	Omonia Nicosia	Cyp	0	2	0	0	2	0	3	-3	0	0.000	0.000
115	SK Brann	Nor	0	2	0	0	2	0	3	-3	0	0.000	0.000
116	Pécsi MSC	Hun	0	2	0	0	2	0	3	-3	0	0.000	0.000
117	Metz	Fra	0	2	0	0	2	1	5	-4	0	0.000	0.500
118	Glenavon	Nir	0	2	0	0	2	2	7	-5	0	0.000	1.000
119	Waterford United	Nir	0	2	0	0	2	1	6	-5	0	0.000	0.500
120	NEA Salamina Famagusta	Cyp	0	2	0	0	2	0	5	-5	0	0.000	0.000
121	IL Viking	Nor	0	2	0	0	2	0	5	-5	0	0.000	0.000
122	Flamurtari Vlorë	Alb	0	4	0	0	4	3	9	-6	0	0.000	0.750
123	Inter Bratislava	Tch	0	2	0	0	2	2	8	-6	0	0.000	1.000
124	Dundalk	Nir	0	2	0	0	2	0	6	-6	0	0.000	0.000
125	FC Kuusysi Lahti	Fin	0	2	0	0	2	0	6	-6	0	0.000	0.000
126	Cork City	Nir	0	2	0	0	2	0	6	-6	0	0.000	0.000
127	Hamrun Spartans	Mlt	0	2	0	0	2	0	6	-6	0	0.000	0.000
128	Swift Hesperange	Lux	0	2	0	0	2	0	6	-6	0	0.000	0.000
129	Sliven	Bul	0	2	0	0	2	1	8	-7	0	0.000	0.500
130	Zurrieq	Mlt	0	2	0	0	2	0	7	-7	0	0.000	0.000
131	Bursaspor	Tur	0	2	0	0	2	0	7	-7	0	0.000	0.000
132	Sliema Wanderers	Mlt	0	4	0	0	4	1	10	-9	0	0.000	0.250
133	Ballymena United	Nir	0	2	0	0	2	0	10	-10	0	0.000	0.000
134	Avenir Beggen	Lux	0	4	0	0	4	1	16	-15	0	0.000	0.250
	Total		**696**	**626**	**248**	**130**	**248**	**789**	**789**	**0**	**70**	**1.112**	**2.521**

Everton defender Gary Stevens (left) is challenged by Rapid Vienna's Peter Hrstic in the 1984-85 final.

Participation Details 1960-61 to 1990-91 by Club

Albania

Club	Seasons Entered		Pts	P	W	D	L	F	A	Diff	B
Besa Kavajë	72-73		3	4	0	3	1	3	9	-6	–
Vllaznia Shkodër	87-88		4	4	2	0	2	6	2	4	–
Dinamo Tirana	71-72, 82-83, 89-90		6	8	2	2	4	7	8	-1	–
17 Nëntori Tirana	83-84, 86-87		7	6	3	1	2	5	9	-4	–
Partizani Tirana	68-69, 70-71, 80-81		6	8	2	2	4	8	10	-2	–
Flamurtari Vlorë	85-86, 88-89, 90-91		0	6	0	0	6	6	14	-8	–
Total times entered	**13**	**Total**	**26**	**36**	**9**	**8**	**19**	**35**	**52**	**-17**	–

Austria

Club	Seasons Entered		Pts	P	W	D	L	F	A	Diff	B
Grazer AK	62-63, 68-69, 81-82		2	6	0	2	4	7	16	-9	1
Sturm Graz	75-76		6	6	2	1	3	6	6	0	–
FC Tirol	70-71, 78-79, 79-80, 83-84, 87-88		14	14	6	2	6	18	26	-8	–
Krems	88-89		2	2	1	0	1	1	5	-4	–
Linzer ASK	63-64		3	3	1	1	1	2	2	0	–
SV Salzburg	80-81		0	2	0	0	2	0	8	-8	–
Admira Wacker	64-65, 89-90		8	8	3	1	4	7	8	-1	1
Austria Vienna	60-61, 67-68, 71-72, 74-75, 77-78, 82-83, 90-91		35	35	9	12	14	36	52	-16	5
Rapid Vienna	61-62, 66-67, 69-70, 72-73, 73-74, 76-77, 84-85, 85-86, 86-87		48	43	14	15	14	72	68	4	5
Wiener Neustadt	65-66		0	2	0	0	2	0	3	-3	–
Total times entered	**31**	**Total**	**118**	**121**	**36**	**34**	**51**	**149**	**194**	**-45**	**12**

Belgium

Club	Seasons Entered		Pts	P	W	D	L	F	A	Diff	B
Anderlecht	73-74, 75-76, 76-77, 77-78, 78-79, 88-89, 89-90		73	44	29	3	12	86	34	52	12
Beerschot	71-72, 79-80		5	6	2	1	3	11	8	3	–
Beveren	78-79, 83-84		17	12	6	3	3	17	9	8	2
Cercle Bruges	85-86		2	2	1	0	1	4	4	0	–
Club Bruges	68-69, 70-71, 86-87		10	10	4	1	5	18	19	-1	1
Gent	64-65, 84-85		3	4	1	1	2	2	5	-3	–
FC Liège	90-91		7	6	3	0	3	8	7	1	1
Standard Liège	65-66, 66-67, 67-68, 72-73, 81-82		45	32	17	5	10	60	36	24	6
Lierse	69-70, 76-77		6	6	3	0	3	12	12	0	–
KV Mechelen	87-88, 88-89		34	17	13	3	1	26	8	18	5
Waregem	74-75		2	2	1	0	1	3	5	-2	–
Waterschei Thor	80-81, 82-83		19	12	8	1	3	26	11	15	2
Total times entered	**30**	**Total**	**223**	**153**	**88**	**18**	**47**	**273**	**158**	**115**	**29**

Bulgaria

Club	Seasons Entered		Pts	P	W	D	L	F	A	Diff	B
Chernomorets Bourgas	89-90		2	2	1	0	1	3	5	-2	–
Trakia Plovdiv	62-63, 81-82, 84-85		15	12	6	2	4	23	18	5	1
Sliven	90-91		0	2	0	0	2	1	8	-7	–
CSKA Sofia	65-66, 70-71, 74-75, 88-89		22	18	10	0	8	36	22	14	2
Levski Sofia	67-68, 69-70, 71-72, 76-77, 86-87, 87-88		28	24	11	3	10	52	34	18	3
Lokomotiv Sofia	77-78, 82-83		2	4	1	0	3	3	13	-10	–

		Pts	P	W	D	L	F	A	Diff	B
Slavia Sofia	63-64, 64-65, 66-67, 72-73, 75-76, 80-81	24	25	9	3	13	31	31	0	3
Marek Stanke Dimitrov	78-79	2	2	1	0	1	3	5	-2	–
Beroe Stara Zagora	73-74, 79-80	12	10	5	1	4	20	11	9	–
Spartak Varna	61-62, 83-84	4	6	1	2	3	4	9	-5	–
Total times entered	**28** **Total**	**111**	**105**	**45**	**11**	**49**	**176**	**156**	**20**	–

Cyprus

Club	Seasons Entered	Pts	P	W	D	L	F	A	Diff	B
Anorthosis Famagusta	71-72, 75-76	1	4	0	1	3	1	18	-17	–
Paralimni	81-82, 83-84	2	4	1	0	3	4	15	-11	–
NEA Salamina Famagusta	90-91	0	2	0	0	2	0	5	-5	–
Pezoporikos Larnaca	70-71, 72-73, 73-74	2	6	0	2	4	2	25	-23	–
AEL Limassol	85-86, 87-88, 89-90	3	6	1	1	4	3	15	-12	–
Apollon Limassol	66-67, 67-68, 82-83, 86-87	3	8	1	1	6	4	31	-27	–
Anorthosis Nicosia	64-65	0	2	0	0	2	0	16	-16	–
Apoel Nicosia	63-64, 68-69, 69-70, 76-77, 78-79, 79-80, 84-85	6	18	2	2	14	13	61	-48	–
Olympiakos Nicosia	77-78	0	2	0	0	2	1	8	-7	–
Omonia Nicosia	65-66, 80-81, 88-89	1	6	0	1	5	2	12	-10	–
Total times entered	**27** **Total**	**18**	**58**	**5**	**8**	**45**	**30**	**206**	**-176**	–

Czechslovakia

Club	Seasons Entered	Pts	P	W	D	L	F	A	Diff	B
Inter Bratislava	84-85, 88-89	3	6	1	1	4	4	13	-9	–
Slovan Bratislava	62-63, 63-64, 68-69, 69-70, 82-83, 89-90	36	25	14	3	8	40	28	12	5
Zbrojovka Brno	60-61	4	4	1	1	2	3	4	-1	1
DAC Dunajská Streda	87-88	6	4	3	0	1	9	4	5	–
TJ Gottwaldov	70-71	5	4	2	1	1	6	5	1	–
Lokomotiv Kosice	77-78, 79-80	10	8	3	4	1	8	7	1	–
Banik Ostrava	73-74, 78-79	20	12	9	0	3	21	13	8	2
Skoda Plzen	71-72	0	2	0	0	2	1	7	-6	–
Dukla Prague	65-66, 69-70, 81-82, 83-84, 85-86, 90-91	29	24	10	7	7	33	29	4	2
Slavia Prague	74-75	2	2	1	0	1	1	1	0	–
Sparta Prague	64-65, 72-73, 76-77, 80-81	21	18	9	1	8	46	20	26	2
Tatran Presov	66-67	1	2	0	1	1	3	4	-1	–
Spartak Trnava	67-68, 75-76, 86-87	4	8	1	2	5	5	13	-8	–
Dynamo Zilina	61-62	7	4	3	0	1	7	6	1	1
Total times entered	**32** **Total**	**148**	**123**	**57**	**21**	**45**	**187**	**154**	**33**	**13**

Denmark

Club	Seasons Entered	Pts	P	W	D	L	F	A	Diff	B
AaB Aalborg	66-67, 70-71, 87-88	3	6	1	1	4	3	12	-9	–
BK Fremad Amager	72-73	2	2	0	2	0	1	1	0	–
AGF Åarhus	61-62, 65-66, 88-89	14	12	6	1	5	19	14	5	1
AB Copenhagen	84-85	1	2	0	1	1	0	3	-3	–
B 1903 Copenhagen	79-80, 86-87	7	6	3	1	2	10	8	2	–
B 93 Copenhagen	82-83	2	4	1	0	3	5	10	-5	–
BK Frem	69-70, 78-79	4	4	2	0	2	4	6	-2	–
Hvidovre IF	80-81	4	4	2	0	2	4	3	1	–
Esbjerg FB	64-65, 76-77	1	4	0	1	3	1	4	-3	–
Ikast FS	89-90	0	2	0	0	2	1	3	-2	–
Lyngby BK	85-86, 90-91	6	6	2	2	2	7	8	-1	–
B 1901 Nykobing	83-84	0	2	0	0	2	3	9	-6	–

B 1909 Odense	62-63, 71-72		9	8	3	2	3	19	17	2	1
B 1913 Odense	63-64		0	2	0	0	2	2	6	-4	–
Randers Freja FC	67-68, 68-69, 73-74		10	10	4	1	5	16	15	1	1
Vanløse IF	74-75		0	2	0	0	2	1	8	-7	–
Vejle BK	75-76, 77-78, 81-82		9	10	4	0	6	16	17	-1	1
Total times entered	**30**	**Total**	**72**	**86**	**28**	**12**	**46**	**112**	**144**	**-32**	**4**

East Germany

Club	Seasons Entered		Pts	P	W	D	L	F	A	Diff	B
Dynamo Berlin	71-72, 89-90		19	12	5	7	0	19	11	8	2
Dynamo Dresden	82-83, 84-85, 85-86		17	14	7	1	6	30	27	3	2
Vorwärts Frankfurt/Oder	60-61, 70-71		9	8	3	2	3	6	8	-2	1
Chemie Halle	62-63		1	2	0	1	1	3	5	-2	–
Carl Zeiss Jena	61-62, 72-73, 74-75, 80-81, 88-89		34	29	10	9	10	51	35	16	5
Chemie Leipzig	66-67		5	4	2	1	1	7	4	3	–
Lokomotive Leipzig	76-77, 77-78, 81-82, 86-87, 87-88		32	25	10	8	7	32	26	6	4
Magdeburg	64-65, 65-66, 69-70, 73-74, 78-79, 79-80, 83-84		47	36	15	12	9	57	41	16	5
PSV Schwerin	90-91		1	2	0	1	1	0	2	-2	–
Sachsenning Zwickau	63-64, 67-68, 75-76		13	12	4	3	5	6	10	-4	2
Total times entered	**30**	**Total**	**178**	**144**	**56**	**45**	**43**	**211**	**169**	**42**	**21**

England

Club	Seasons Entered		Pts	P	W	D	L	F	A	Diff	B
Ipswich Town	78-79		9	6	3	2	1	6	3	3	1
Leeds United	72-73		16	9	5	3	1	13	3	10	3
Leicester City	61-62		5	4	2	1	1	8	5	3	–
Everton	66-67, 84-85		24	13	9	3	1	19	5	14	3
Liverpool	65-66, 71-72, 74-75		23	17	8	4	5	29	12	17	3
Arsenal	79-80		16	9	4	5	0	13	5	8	3
Chelsea	70-71, 71-72		25	14	9	4	1	39	7	32	3
Tottenham Hotspur	62-63, 63-64, 67-68, 81-82, 82-83		40	25	16	3	6	58	31	27	5
West Ham United	64-65, 65-66, 75-76, 80-81		45	30	15	6	9	58	42	16	9
Manchester City	69-70, 70-71		29	18	11	2	5	32	13	19	5
Manchester United	63-64, 77-78, 83-84, 90-91		43	27	15	7	5	52	31	21	6
Southampton	76-77		9	6	4	0	2	16	8	8	1
Sunderland	73-74		6	4	3	0	1	5	3	2	–
West Bromwich Albion	68-69		7	6	2	2	2	8	5	3	1
Wolverhampton Wanderers	60-61		4	4	1	1	2	6	5	1	1
Total times entered	**30**	**Total**	**301**	**192**	**107**	**43**	**42**	**362**	**178**	**184**	**44**

Finland

Club	Seasons Entered		Pts	P	W	D	L	F	A	Diff	B
HJK Helsinki	67-68, 85-86		6	6	3	0	3	9	18	-9	–
HPS Helsinki	63-64		0	2	0	0	2	2	12	-10	–
KTP Kotka	81-82		1	2	0	1	1	0	5	-5	–
KuPS Kuopio	69-70, 90-91		2	4	0	2	2	2	7	-5	–
FC Kuusysi Lahti	82-83, 84-85, 88-89		2	6	0	2	4	3	11	-8	–
Reipas Lahti	65-66, 73-74, 74-75, 75-76, 76-77, 77-78, 79-80		5	16	1	3	12	15	63	-48	–
MP Mikkeli	71-72, 72-73		3	4	1	1	2	4	12	-8	–
RoPS Rovaniemi	87-88		7	6	2	2	2	3	5	-2	1
Ilves Tampere	80-81		0	2	0	0	2	3	7	-4	–
TPS Turku	66-67		1	2	0	1	1	2	3	-1	–
Haka Valkeakoski	64-65, 70-71, 83-84, 86-87, 89-90		12	16	4	3	9	15	33	-18	1
Total times entered	**26**	**Total**	**39**	**66**	**11**	**15**	**40**	**58**	**176**	**-118**	**2**

France

Club	Seasons Entered		Pts	P	W	D	L	F	A	Diff	B
Bastia	72-73, 81-82		5	6	1	3	2	8	6	2	–
Girondins Bordeaux	68-69, 86-87		15	10	6	1	3	14	10	4	2
Lens	75-76		3	4	1	1	2	10	7	3	–
Olympique Lyon	63-64, 64-65, 67-68, 73-74		26	22	9	5	8	31	28	3	3
Olympique Marseille	69-70, 76-77, 87-88		20	14	8	2	4	19	13	6	2
Metz	84-85, 88-89		3	6	1	1	4	8	13	-5	–
Monaco	74-75, 80-81, 85-86, 89-90		14	14	2	8	4	14	19	-5	2
Montpellier	90-91		9	6	3	2	1	10	3	7	1
Nancy	78-79		3	4	1	1	2	7	6	1	–
Nantes	70-71, 79-80		16	12	7	0	5	28	21	7	2
Paris Saint-Germain	82-83, 83-84		15	10	6	2	2	16	9	7	1
Stade Rennes	65-66, 71-72		2	4	0	2	2	1	4	-3	–
Saint-Etienne	62-63, 77-78		5	6	1	3	2	5	7	-2	–
Sedan	61-62		0	2	0	0	2	3	7	-4	–
Strasbourg	66-67		5	4	2	1	1	3	3	0	–
Total times entered	**30**	**Total**	**141**	**124**	**48**	**32**	**44**	**177**	**156**	**21**	**13**

Greece

Club	Seasons Entered		Pts	P	W	D	L	F	A	Diff	B
AEK Athenes	64-65, 66-67, 83-84		4	6	2	0	4	7	11	-4	–
Panathinaikos	67-68, 75-76, 82-83, 88-89, 89-90		10	14	4	2	8	13	28	-15	–
Panionios	79-80		4	4	2	0	2	6	5	1	–
OFI Crete	87-88		4	4	2	0	2	4	4	0	–
Kastoria	80-81		1	2	0	1	1	0	2	-2	–
Larissa	84-85, 85-86		10	8	3	3	2	7	5	2	1
Olympiakos Pireus	61-62, 63-64, 65-66, 68-69, 69-70, 71-72, 86-87, 90-91		28	27	12	4	11	37	42	-5	–
Aris Salonika	70-71		1	2	0	1	1	2	6	-4	–
Iraklis	76-77		1	2	0	1	1	0	2	-2	–
PAOK Salonika	72-73, 73-74, 74-75, 77-78, 78-79, 81-82		22	18	8	5	5	24	23	1	1
Total times entered	**29**	**Total**	**85**	**87**	**33**	**17**	**37**	**100**	**128**	**-28**	**2**

Hungary

Club	Seasons Entered		Pts	P	W	D	L	F	A	Diff	B
Békéscsaba	88-89		4	4	2	0	2	5	4	1	–
Ferencváros	60-61, 72-73, 74-75, 78-79, 89-90		29	23	10	6	7	40	28	12	3
Honvéd	64-65, 65-66, 70-71		12	12	5	1	6	25	17	8	1
MTK-VM	63-64, 69-70, 76-77		25	19	8	5	6	27	22	5	4
Vasas SC	73-74, 81-82, 86-87		3	8	1	1	6	13	13	0	–
Diósgyöri VTK	77-78, 80-81		6	6	3	0	3	10	12	-2	–
Rába ETO	66-67, 67-68, 79-80		15	12	6	2	4	23	14	9	1
Komló	71-72		2	2	1	0	1	4	8	-4	–
Pécsi MSC	90-91		0	2	0	0	2	0	3	-3	–
Siófok	84-85		1	2	0	1	1	1	3	-2	–
Haladás	75-76		4	4	1	2	1	9	4	5	–
Tatabánya	85-86		1	2	0	1	1	1	6	-5	–
Ujpesti Dózsa	61-62, 62-63, 82-83, 83-84, 87-88		29	25	11	4	10	50	38	12	3
Total times entered	**30**	**Total**	**131**	**121**	**48**	**23**	**50**	**208**	**172**	**36**	**12**

Iceland

Club	Seasons Entered	Pts	P	W	D	L	F	A	Diff	B
IA Akranes	77-78, 79-80, 83-84, 87-88	2	8	0	2	6	2	15	-13	–

IBA Akureyri	70-71	0	2	0	0	2	1	14	-13	–
IBK Keflavik	76-77	1	2	0	1	1	1	4	-3	–
Fram Reykjavik	71-72, 74-75, 80-81, 81-82, 85-86, 86-87, 88-89, 90-91	11	20	5	1	14	14	42	-28	–
KR Reykjavik	65-66, 67-68, 68-69	0	6	0	0	6	3	24	-21	–
Valur Reykjavik	66-67, 75-76, 78-79, 89-90	2	8	0	2	6	5	27	-22	–
Vikingur Reykjavik	72-73	0	2	0	0	2	0	11	-11	–
IBV Vestmannaeyjar	69-70, 73-74, 82-83, 84-85	0	8	0	0	8	4	35	-31	–
Total times entered	**26** **Total**	**16**	**56**	**5**	**6**	**45**	**30**	**172**	**-142**	**–**

Italy

Club	Seasons Entered	Pts	P	W	D	L	F	A	Diff	B
Atalanta	63-64, 87-88	11	11	4	1	6	14	14	0	2
Bologna	70-71, 74-75	4	4	1	2	1	4	4	0	–
Fiorentina	60-61, 61-62, 66-67, 75-76	34	20	14	1	5	44	20	24	5
Sampdoria	85-86, 88-89, 89-90, 90-91	44	28	15	7	6	39	21	18	7
AC Milan	67-68, 72-73, 73-74, 77-78	53	30	17	10	3	47	20	27	9
Inter Milan	78-79, 82-83	16	12	6	2	4	22	9	13	2
Napoli	62-63, 76-77	25	17	9	4	4	23	16	7	3
Roma	69-70, 80-81, 81-82, 84-85, 86-87	30	23	10	7	6	26	18	8	3
Torino	64-65, 68-69, 71-72	26	19	9	4	6	28	17	11	4
Juventus	65-66, 79-80, 83-84, 90-91	46	27	17	5	5	53	19	34	7
Total times entered	**32** **Total**	**289**	**191**	**102**	**43**	**46**	**300**	**158**	**142**	**42**

Luxembourg

Club	Seasons Entered	Pts	P	W	D	L	F	A	Diff	B
Avenir Beggen	74-75, 83-84, 87-88, 88-89	0	8	0	0	8	4	36	-32	–
Aris Bonnevoie	67-68, 76-77, 79-80	6	8	3	0	5	8	20	-12	–
Red Boys Differdange	72-73, 82-83, 85-86	0	6	0	0	6	2	28	-26	–
Alliance Dudelange	61-62, 62-63	2	4	0	2	2	4	18	-14	–
Fola Esch	73-74	0	2	0	0	2	1	11	-10	–
Jeunesse Esch	81-82	1	2	0	1	1	2	7	-5	–
Jeunesse Hautcharage	71-72	0	2	0	0	2	0	21	-21	–
Swift Hesperange	90-91	0	2	0	0	2	0	6	-6	–
Spora Luxembourg	65-66, 66-67, 80-81	0	6	0	0	6	2	23	-21	–
Union Luxembourg	63-64, 64-65, 69-70, 70-71, 78-79, 84-85, 86-87, 89-90	6	16	2	2	12	8	48	-40	–
Progrès Niedercorn	77-78	0	2	0	0	2	0	10	-10	–
US Rumelange	68-69, 75-76	2	4	1	0	3	3	16	-13	–
Total times entered	**30** **Total**	**17**	**62**	**6**	**5**	**51**	**34**	**244**	**-210**	**–**

Malta

Club	Seasons Entered	Pts	P	W	D	L	F	A	Diff	B
Gzira United	73-74	0	2	0	0	2	0	9	-9	–
Hamrun Spartans	84-85, 89-90	4	6	2	0	4	3	13	-10	–
Valletta	64-65, 75-76, 77-78, 83-84	1	8	0	1	7	2	41	-39	–
Floriana	61-62, 65-66, 66-67, 67-68, 72-73, 76-77, 78-79, 81-82, 88-89	4	18	1	2	15	11	71	-60	–
Hibernians	62-63, 70-71, 71-72, 80-81	6	10	2	2	6	4	17	-13	–
Sliema Wanderers	63-64, 68-69, 69-70, 74-75, 79-80, 82-83, 87-88, 90-91	9	18	4	1	13	10	57	-47	–
Zurrieq	85-86, 86-87	0	4	0	0	4	0	19	-19	–
Total times entered	**30** **Total**	**24**	**66**	**9**	**6**	**51**	**30**	**227**	**-197**	**–**

Netherlands

Club	Seasons Entered		Pts	P	W	D	L	F	A	Diff	B
AZ'67 Alkmaar	78-79, 82-83		6	6	2	2	2	3	5	-2	–
Ajax	61-62, 81-82, 86-87, 87-88		37	22	15	1	6	41	18	23	6
NAC Breda	67-68, 73-74		6	6	2	2	2	5	8	-3	–
Go Ahead Eagles	65-66		0	2	0	0	2	0	7	-7	–
PSV Eindhoven	69-70, 70-71, 74-75, 90-91		33	22	13	3	6	45	17	28	4
Twente Enschede	77-78, 79-80		15	10	6	1	3	17	9	8	2
Groningen	89-90		6	4	3	0	1	8	7	1	–
Roda JC	76-77, 88-89		8	8	3	1	4	9	9	0	1
FC Den Haag	68-69, 72-73, 75-76, 87-88		20	16	9	1	6	26	18	8	1
NEC Nijmegen	83-84		3	4	1	1	2	4	6	-2	–
Feyenoord	80-81		14	8	6	0	2	18	10	8	2
Sparta Rotterdam	62-63, 66-67, 71-72		11	10	4	3	3	17	12	5	–
Fortuna Sittard	64-65, 84-85		7	8	2	2	4	9	12	-3	1
Willem II	63-64		1	2	0	1	1	2	7	-5	–
Utrecht	85-86		2	2	1	0	1	3	5	-2	–
Total times entered	**31**	**Total**	**169**	**130**	**67**	**18**	**45**	**207**	**150**	**57**	**17**

Northern Ireland

Club	Seasons Entered		Pts	P	W	D	L	F	A	Diff	B
Ballymena United	78-79, 81-82, 84-85, 89-90		0	8	0	0	8	1	25	-24	–
Cliftonville	79-80		0	2	0	0	2	0	8	-8	–
Crusaders	67-68, 68-69, 80-81		2	6	0	2	4	5	18	-13	–
Distillery	71-72		0	2	0	0	2	1	7	-6	–
Glentoran	66-67, 73-74, 83-84, 85-86, 86-87, 87-88, 90-91		14	18	3	7	8	16	33	-17	1
Linfield	63-64, 70-71		4	4	2	0	2	5	6	-1	–
Carrick Rangers	76-77		2	4	1	0	3	7	12	-5	–
Coleraine	65-66, 75-76, 77-78, 82-83		1	8	0	1	7	7	34	-27	–
Glenavon	61-62, 88-89		0	4	0	0	4	4	14	-10	–
Ards	69-70, 74-75		1	4	0	1	3	2	17	-15	–
Portadown	62-63		2	2	1	0	1	4	7	-3	–
Derry City	64-65		0	2	0	0	2	0	5	-5	–
Total times entered	**29**	**Total**	**26**	**64**	**7**	**11**	**46**	**52**	**186**	**-134**	**1**

Norway

Club	Seasons Entered		Pts	P	W	D	L	F	A	Diff	B
SK Brann	73-74, 77-78, 83-84, 89-90		10	12	4	2	6	18	13	5	–
SFK Bodø/Glimt	76-77, 78-79		2	6	1	0	5	5	12	-7	–
Bryne IL	88-89		2	2	1	0	1	2	4	-2	–
Strømgodset IF	70-71, 74-75		2	4	1	0	3	3	19	-16	–
Fredrikstad FK	67-68, 72-73, 85-86		2	6	0	2	4	3	10	-7	–
Gjøvik/Lyn	63-64		2	2	1	0	1	1	6	-5	–
Haugar FC	80-81		4	4	1	2	1	3	7	-4	–
Lillestrøm SK	79-80, 82-83, 86-87		0	6	0	0	6	1	14	-13	–
Mjøndalen IF	69-70		0	2	0	0	2	2	12	-10	–
Moss FK	84-85		0	2	0	0	2	2	6	-4	–
FK Skeid	64-65, 66-67, 75-76		4	6	2	0	4	6	15	-9	–
SFK Lyn	68-69, 71-72		6	8	2	1	5	13	19	-6	1
Vålerengen SIF	81-82		1	2	0	1	1	3	6	-3	–
IL Viking	90-91		0	2	0	0	2	0	5	-5	–
Tromsø IL	87-88		1	2	0	1	1	0	1	-1	–
Rosenborg BK	65-66		4	4	2	0	2	7	8	-1	–
Total times entered	**28**	**Total**	**40**	**70**	**15**	**9**	**46**	**69**	**157**	**-88**	**1**

Poland

Club	Seasons Entered		Pts	P	W	D	L	F	A	Diff	B
Wisla Kraków	67-68, 84-85		10	8	5	0	3	17	12	5	–
Lechia Gdańsk	83-84		0	2	0	0	2	2	10	-8	–
Arka Gdynia	79-80		2	2	1	0	1	3	4	-1	–
GKS Katowice	86-87		5	4	2	1	1	6	5	1	–
Widzew Lódź	85-86		2	2	1	0	1	2	2	0	–
Lech Poznań	82-83, 88-89		10	8	4	2	2	10	7	3	–
Stal Rzeszów	75-76		5	4	2	1	1	9	4	5	–
Zaglebie Sosnowiec	62-63, 63-64, 71-72, 77-78, 78-79		5	11	1	3	7	9	22	-13	–
Gwardia Warsaw	74-75		2	4	1	0	3	4	11	-7	–
Legia Warsaw	64-65, 66-67, 72-73, 73-74, 80-81, 81-82, 89-90, 90-91		40	33	13	10	10	47	35	12	4
Slask Wroclaw	76-77, 87-88		11	8	4	2	2	10	5	5	1
Górnik Zabrze	69-70, 70-71		26	17	9	4	4	38	20	18	4
Total times entered	**27**	**Total**	**118**	**103**	**43**	**23**	**37**	**157**	**137**	**20**	**9**

Portugal

Club	Seasons Entered		Pts	P	W	D	L	F	A	Diff	B
Estrela Amadora	90-91		4	4	1	2	1	3	4	-1	–
Sporting Braga	66-67, 82-83		8	6	4	0	2	7	8	-1	–
Academica Coimbra	69-70		7	6	2	2	2	3	2	1	1
Vitória Guimarães	88-89		2	2	1	0	1	1	2	-1	–
Belenenses	89-90		1	2	0	1	1	1	4	-3	–
Benfica	70-71, 74-75, 80-81, 85-86, 86-87		38	28	13	8	7	42	19	23	4
Sporting Lisbon	63-64, 64-65, 71-72, 72-73, 73-74, 78-79, 87-88		46	36	16	8	12	76	44	32	6
Leixões	61-62		7	6	2	2	2	11	11	0	1
Portimonense	75-76, 76-77, 79-80		14	12	5	4	3	22	11	11	–
FC Porto	64-65, 68-69, 77-78, 81-82, 83-84, 84-85		41	31	15	6	10	43	38	5	5
Vitória Setúbal	62-63, 65-66, 67-68		6	8	2	2	4	13	17	-4	–
Total times entered	**31**	**Total**	**174**	**141**	**61**	**35**	**45**	**222**	**160**	**62**	**17**

Republic of Ireland

Club	Seasons Entered		Pts	P	W	D	L	F	A	Diff	B
Finn Harps	74-75		1	2	0	1	1	2	4	-2	–
Bray Wanderers	90-91		1	2	0	1	1	1	3	-2	–
Cork Celtic	64-65		1	2	0	1	1	1	3	-2	–
Cork City	89-90		0	2	0	0	2	0	6	-6	–
Cork Hibernians	72-73, 73-74		5	6	2	1	3	7	8	-1	–
Derry City*	88-89		1, 0 } 1	2, 2 } 4	0, 0 } 0	1, 0 } 1	1, 2 } 3	0, 0 } 0	4, 5 } 9	-4, -5 } -9	–, – } –
Bohemians	70-71, 76-77		5	6	2	1	3	6	9	-3	–
Home Farm	75-76		1	2	0	1	1	1	7	-6	–
St. Patrick's Athletic	61-62		0	2	0	0	2	1	8	-7	–
Shamrock Rovers	62-63, 66-67, 67-68, 68-69, 69-70, 78-79		12	16	5	2	9	19	27	-8	–
Shelbourne	63-64		0	2	0	0	2	1	5	-4	–
UCD	84-85		1	2	0	1	1	0	1	-1	–
Dundalk	77-78, 81-82, 87-88		5	8	2	1	5	7	14	-7	–
Galway United	85-86		0	2	0	0	2	2	4	-2	–
Limerick	65-66, 71-72, 82-83		1	6	0	1	5	2	11	-9	–
Sligo Rovers	83-84		0	2	0	0	2	0	4	-4	–
Waterford United	79-80, 80-81, 86-87		3	8	1	1	6	6	14	-8	–
Total times entered	**30**	**Total**	**37**	**72**	**12**	**13**	**47**	**56**	**132**	**-76**	**–**

Romania

Club	Seasons Entered		Pts	P	W	D	L	F	A	Diff	B
Baia Mare	82-83		1	2	0	1	1	2	5	-3	–
Dinamo Bucharest	68-69, 86-87, 87-88, 88-89, 89-90		23	20	8	4	8	25	18	7	3
Progresul Bucharest	61-62		1	2	0	1	1	1	2	-1	–
Rapid Bucharest	72-73, 75-76		8	8	3	1	4	9	13	-4	1
Steaua Bucharest	62-63, 64-65, 66-67, 67-68, 69-70, 70-71, 71-72, 79-80, 84-85, 90-91		34	34	12	9	13	42	49	-7	1
Universitatea Cluj	65-66		4	4	2	0	2	3	6	-3	–
Universitatea Craiova	77-78, 78-79, 85-86		10	10	4	2	4	19	15	4	–
CSU Galati	76-77		0	2	0	0	2	2	5	-3	–
Jiul Petrosani	74-75		2	2	1	0	1	2	3	-1	–
Petrolul Ploiesti	63-64		2	2	1	0	1	2	4	-2	–
Chimia Râmnicu Vâlcea	73-74		1	2	0	1	1	2	4	-2	–
Politehnica Timisoara	80-81, 81-82		6	6	3	0	3	5	11	-6	–
Total times entered	**29**	**Total**	**92**	**94**	**34**	**19**	**41**	**114**	**135**	**-21**	**5**

Scotland

Club	Seasons Entered		Pts	P	W	D	L	F	A	Diff	B
Aberdeen	67-68, 70-71, 78-79, 82-83, 83-84, 86-87, 90-91		50	35	20	5	10	69	32	37	5
Dundee	64-65		1	2	0	1	1	3	4	-1	–
Dundee United	74-75, 88-89		7	8	2	3	3	5	5	0	–
Dunfermline Athletic	61-62, 68-69		19	14	7	2	5	34	14	20	3
Heart of Midlothian	76-77		2	4	1	0	3	8	11	-3	–
Hibernian	72-73		8	6	3	1	2	19	10	9	1
Celtic	63-64, 65-66, 75-76, 80-81, 84-85, 85-86, 89-90		47	34	19	4	11	68	31	37	5
Rangers	60-61, 62-63, 66-67, 69-70, 71-72, 73-74, 77-78, 79-80, 81-82, 83-84		74	54	27	11	16	100	62	38	9
St. Mirren	87-88		4	4	1	2	1	1	2	-1	–
Total times entered	**32**	**Total**	**212**	**161**	**80**	**29**	**52**	**307**	**171**	**136**	**23**

Spain

Club	Seasons Entered		Pts	P	W	D	L	F	A	Diff	B
Barcelona	63-64, 68-69, 71-72, 78-79, 79-80, 81-82, 82-83, 83-84, 84-85, 88-89, 89-90, 90-91		122	76	45	14	17	164	82	82	18
Athletic Bilbao	69-70, 73-74		6	6	2	2	2	6	9	-3	12
Atlético Madrid	61-62, 62-63, 65-66, 72-73, 75-76, 76-77, 85-86		79	48	28	11	9	85	46	39	–
Castilla Madrid	80-81		2	2	1	0	1	4	6	-2	–
Real Madrid	70-71, 74-75, 82-83		40	25	13	7	5	46	20	26	7
Real Sociedad	87-88		5	4	1	3	0	3	1	2	–
Real Zaragoza	64-65, 66-67, 86-87		30	22	10	5	7	36	26	10	5
Real Betis	77-78		7	6	2	2	2	6	7	-1	1
Seville	62-63		2	2	1	0	1	2	4	-2	–
Valencia	67-68, 79-80, 80-81		29	19	10	5	4	39	20	19	4
Real Valladolid	89-90		10	6	3	3	0	10	2	8	1
Total times entered	**35**	**Total**	**332**	**216**	**116**	**52**	**48**	**401**	**223**	**178**	**48**

Sweden

Club	Seasons Entered	Pts	P	W	D	L	F	A	Diff	B
Åtvidaberg SFF	70-71, 71-72	8	8	1	5	2	9	12	-3	1
IFK Gothenburg	79-80, 82-83	8	8	2	3	3	7	11	-4	1

Hammarby IF	83-84		3	4	1	1	2	7	5	2	–
Kalmar FF	78-79, 81-82, 87-88		8	8	3	2	3	8	13	-5	–
Landskrona BOIS	72-73		2	2	1	0	1	1	3	-2	–
Malmö FF	73-74, 74-75, 80-81, 84-85, 86-87		27	22	9	7	6	35	18	17	2
IFK Norrköping	68-69, 69-70, 88-89		10	10	4	2	4	16	13	3	–
AIK	76-77, 85-86		6	6	2	2	2	17	6	11	–
Djurgården SIF	75-76, 89-90, 90-91		6	8	1	4	3	10	11	-1	–
Öster SIF	77-78		2	2	0	2	0	2	2	0	–
Total times entered	**23**	**Total**	**80**	**78**	**24**	**28**	**26**	**112**	**94**	**18**	**4**

Switzerland

Club	Seasons Entered		Pts	P	W	D	L	F	A	Diff	B
Aarau	85-86		1	2	0	1	1	2	4	-2	–
FC Basle	63-64, 75-76		1	4	0	1	3	3	13	-10	–
Young Boys Berne	77-78, 79-80, 87-88		7	10	2	2	6	10	18	-8	1
Servette	66-67, 71-72, 76-77, 78-79, 83-84, 84-85		28	24	11	4	9	36	25	11	2
La Chaux-de-Fonds	61-62		2	2	1	0	1	6	7	-1	–
Lausanne-Sports	62-63, 64-65, 67-68, 81-82		15	17	6	2	9	26	28	-2	1
Lucerne	60-61		0	2	0	0	2	2	9	-7	–
Lugano	68-69		0	2	0	0	2	0	4	-4	–
Neuchâtel Xamax	90-91		2	2	0	2	0	2	2	0	–
St-Gallen	69-70		3	4	1	1	2	2	6	-4	–
Sion	65-66, 74-75, 80-81, 82-83, 86-87		13	16	4	4	8	21	34	-13	1
FC Zürich	70-71, 72-73, 73-74		13	12	4	4	4	24	16	8	1
Grasshoppers Zürich	88-89, 89-90		7	8	2	2	4	9	9	0	1
Total times entered	**31**	**Total**	**92**	**105**	**31**	**23**	**51**	**143**	**175**	**-32**	**7**

Turkey

Club	Seasons Entered		Pts	P	W	D	L	F	A	Diff	B
Sakaryaspor	88-89		2	4	1	0	3	3	7	-4	–
Gençlerbirligi	87-88		0	2	0	0	2	1	4	-3	–
Ankaragücü	72-73, 73-74, 81-82		1	6	0	1	5	1	13	-12	–
Bursaspor	74-75, 86-87		7	8	2	2	4	5	12	-7	1
Eskisehirspor	71-72		3	4	1	1	2	4	2	2	–
Besiktas	75-76, 77-78, 84-85, 89-90		3	8	1	1	6	5	19	-14	–
Fenerbahçe	63-64, 79-80		8	9	3	1	5	11	11	0	1
Galatasaray	64-65, 65-66, 66-67, 76-77, 82-83, 85-86		18	22	6	6	10	25	44	-19	–
Altay	67-68, 68-69, 80-81		4	6	1	2	3	6	12	-6	–
Göztepe	69-70, 70-71		10	10	4	1	5	14	10	4	1
Mersin Idmanyurdu	83-84		1	2	0	1	1	0	1	-1	–
Trabzonspor	90-91		5	4	2	1	1	6	8	-2	–
Total times entered	**27**	**Total**	**62**	**85**	**21**	**17**	**47**	**81**	**143**	**-62**	**3**

USSR

Club	Seasons Entered	Pts	P	W	D	L	F	A	Diff	B
Shakhtyor Donetsk	78-79, 83-84	11	8	4	2	2	16	12	4	1
Ararat Erevan	75-76	4	4	1	2	1	12	5	7	–
Metallist Kharkov	88-89	3	4	1	1	2	4	3	1	–
Dinamo Kiev	65-66, 74-75, 85-86, 90-91	54	30	20	6	4	72	27	45	8
Karpaty Lvov	70-71	1	2	0	1	1	3	4	-1	–
Dinamo Minsk	87-88	8	6	2	3	1	6	4	2	1
Dinamo Moscow	71-72, 77-78, 79-80, 84-85	46	29	15	8	6	46	25	21	8
Spartak Moscow	66-67, 72-73	12	10	4	3	3	14	10	4	1
Torpedo Moscow	67-68, 69-70, 73-74, 82-83, 86-87,	30	23	10	8	5	32	20	12	2

	89-90										
SKA Rostov on Don	81-82		6	4	3	0	1	6	2	4	–
Dinamo Tbilisi	76-77, 80-81, 81-82		30	21	11	3	7	30	17	13	5
Total times entered	**26**	**Total**	**205**	**141**	**71**	**37**	**33**	**241**	**129**	**112**	**26**

Wales

Club	Seasons Entered		Pts	P	W	D	L	F	A	Diff	B
Bangor City	62-63, 85-86		4	7	1	2	4	5	9	-4	–
Cardiff City	64-65, 65-66, 67-68, 68-69, 69-70, 70-71, 71-72, 73-74, 74-75, 76-77, 77-78, 88-89		49	45	16	13	16	62	50	12	4
Borough United	63-64		3	4	1	1	2	2	4	-2	–
Merthyr Tydfil	87-88		2	2	1	0	1	2	3	-1	–
Newport County	80-81		8	6	2	3	1	12	3	9	1
Swansea Town	61-62, 66-67, 81-82, 82-83, 83-84, 89-90		10	16	3	4	9	31	27	4	–
Wrexham	72-73, 75-76, 78-79, 79-80, 84-85, 86-87, 90-91		28	26	10	7	9	34	34	0	1
Total times entered	**30**	**Total**	**104**	**106**	**34**	**30**	**42**	**148**	**130**	**18**	**6**

West Germany

Club	Seasons Entered		Pts	P	W	D	L	F	A	Diff	B
Werder Bremen	61-62		6	4	2	1	1	7	6	1	1
Cologne	68-69, 77-78, 83-84		18	14	7	2	5	30	19	11	2
Borussia Dortmund	65-66, 66-67, 89-90		24	15	9	3	3	32	15	17	3
Fortuna Düsseldorf	78-79, 79-80, 80-81		22	17	6	6	5	28	19	9	4
Eintracht Frankfurt	74-75, 75-76, 81-82, 88-89		35	24	14	3	7	41	23	18	4
Schalke 04	69-70, 72-73		23	14	9	2	3	21	14	7	3
Hamburg	63-64, 67-68, 76-77, 77-78, 87-88		54	34	20	7	7	81	39	42	7
Kaiserslautern	90-91		2	2	1	0	1	1	2	-1	–
Borussia Mönchengladbach	60-61, 73-74		14	10	6	0	4	29	17	12	2
Bayern Munich	66-67, 67-68, 71-72, 82-83, 84-85		62	39	19	14	6	67	36	31	10
1860 Munich	64-65		17	10	6	2	2	21	6	15	3
Nuremberg	62-63		11	6	4	1	1	12	3	9	2
Kickers Offenbach	70-71		2	2	1	0	1	2	3	-1	–
VFB Stuttgart	86-87		3	4	1	1	2	4	7	-3	–
Bayer Uerdingen	85-86		11	8	4	1	3	24	10	14	2
Total times entered	**34**	**Total**	**304**	**203**	**109**	**43**	**51**	**400**	**219**	**181**	**43**

Yugoslavia

Club	Seasons Entered		Pts	P	W	D	L	F	A	Diff	B
Borac Banja Luka	75-76, 88-89		8	6	4	0	2	17	8	9	–
Red Star Belgrade	71-72, 74-75, 82-83, 85-86		30	24	10	6	8	51	32	19	4
OFK Belgrade	62-63, 66-67		11	11	4	1	6	21	22	-1	2
Partizan Belgrade	89-90		5	6	2	0	4	13	15	-2	1
Borovo	68-69		2	2	1	0	1	2	3	-1	–
Olimpija Ljubljana	70-71		1	2	0	1	1	2	9	-7	–
Velez Mostar	81-82, 86-87		10	8	3	4	1	18	13	5	–
Rijeka	78-79, 79-80		10	10	3	3	4	8	9	-1	1
Vardar Skoplje	61-62		2	2	1	0	1	2	5	-3	–
Hajduk Split	67-68, 72-73, 76-77, 77-78, 84-85, 87-88		22	26	8	3	15	29	38	-9	3
Dinamo Zagreb	60-61, 63-64, 64-65, 65-66, 69-70, 73-74, 80-81, 83-84		29	29	10	6	13	28	34	-6	3
Total times entered	**30**	**Total**	**130**	**126**	**46**	**24**	**56**	**191**	**188**	**3**	**14**

Notes:
*** In 1988-89 Derry City left the Irish League (Northern Ireland) and joined the League of Ireland (Republic of Ireland).**

Above: Real Madrid's Uli Stielike strokes the ball past Aberdeen's Neil Simpson as Mark McGhee moves away in the 1982-83 final. Aberdeen won 2-1 in Gothenburg.

Below: Pat Holland of West Ham follows up his shot as he scores the first goal in the 1975-76 final against Anderlecht.

National Classification by Cumulative Year-by-Year Index

1960-61 to 1990-91

Pos	Cnty	Total	6061	6162	6263	6364	6465	6566	6667	6768	6869	6970	7071	7172	7273	7374	7475
1	Esp	288.500	–	19.000	7.000	6.000	13.000	10.000	7.000	8.000	13.000	1.000	14.000	4.000	5.000	5.000	10.000
2	Ita	277.000	12.000	14.000	11.000	2.000	14.000	2.000	2.000	17.000	3.000	13.000	2.000	9.000	19.000	15.000	2.000
3	FRG	276.500	0.000	6.000	11.000	10.000	17.000	18.000	9.000	15.500	13.000	13.000	2.000	12.000	10.000	14.000	3.000
4	Eng	265.000	4.000	5.000	15.000	5.000	17.000	11.000	5.000	6.000	7.000	17.000	15.500	4.500	16.000	6.000	6.000
5	Sco	204.000	12.000	7.000	2.000	14.000	1.000	15.000	15.000	6.000	12.000	3.000	2.000	16.000	8.000	6.000	3.000
6	Bel	198.000	–	–	–	–	1.000	4.000	13.000	8.000	2.000	4.000	7.000	4.000	2.000	2.000	2.000
7	URS	196.000	–	–	–	–	–	10.000	5.000	10.000	–	2.000	1.000	14.000	7.000	1.000	19.000
8	GDR	178.000	2.000	12.000	1.000	2.000	3.000	9.000	5.000	1.000	–	5.000	7.000	13.000	3.000	16.000	4.000
9	Por	171.000	–	7.000	1.000	20.000	3.000	0.000	6.000	5.000	5.000	7.000	5.000	6.000	2.000	11.000	8.000
10	Ned	158.500	–	2.000	2.000	1.000	1.000	0.000	5.000	5.000	4.000	6.000	11.000	4.000	1.000	1.000	15.000
11	Tch	146.500	4.000	7.000	6.000	9.000	6.000	5.000	1.000	2.000	16.000	1.500	5.000	0.000	8.000	6.000	2.000
12	Fra	141.000	–	0.000	4.000	13.000	0.000	1.000	5.000	9.000	2.000	3.000	2.000	1.000	1.000	4.000	1.000
13	Hun	131.000	2.000	12.000	5.000	15.000	2.000	8.000	7.000	6.000	–	1.000	2.000	2.000	4.000	0.000	15.000
14	Yug	130.000	6.000	2.000	11.000	5.000	8.000	0.000	0.000	0.000	2.000	7.000	1.000	7.000	11.000	0.000	11.000
15	Aut	118.000	2.000	3.000	1.000	3.000	0.000	0.000	10.000	0.000	0.000	2.000	6.000	6.000	3.000	4.000	3.000
–	Pol	118.000	–	–	1.000	2.000	10.000	–	1.000	4.000	–	15.000	11.000	1.000	5.000	1.000	2.000
17	Bul	111.000	–	1.000	8.000	1.000	5.000	6.000	9.000	1.000	–	10.000	4.000	1.000	0.000	8.000	0.000
18	Wal	104.000	–	1.000	2.000	3.000	8.000	0.000	1.000	13.000	1.000	6.000	10.000	2.000	5.000	1.000	0.000
19	Rom	92.000	–	1.000	2.000	2.000	4.000	4.000	1.000	6.000	1.000	1.000	3.000	10.000	6.000	1.000	2.000
–	Sui	92.000	0.000	2.000	3.000	0.000	7.000	3.000	8.000	2.000	0.000	3.000	6.000	2.000	1.000	6.000	2.000
21	Gre	85.000	–	0.000	–	6.000	2.000	4.000	0.000	0.000	6.000	1.000	1.000	2.000	2.000	8.000	2.000
22	Swe	80.000	–	–	–	–	–	–	–	–	5.000	3.000	1.000	7.000	2.000	5.000	7.000
23	Den	72.000	–	0.000	7.000	0.000	1.000	4.000	1.000	0.000	9.000	2.000	0.000	2.000	2.000	1.000	0.000
24	Tur	62.000	–	–	–	7.000	5.000	2.000	0.000	1.000	2.000	8.000	2.000	3.000	1.000	0.000	7.000
25	Nor	40.000	–	–	–	2.000	2.000	4.000	2.000	0.000	6.000	0.000	2.000	0.000	0.000	5.000	0.000
26	Fin	39.000	–	–	–	0.000	2.000	0.000	1.000	0.000	–	1.000	0.000	1.000	2.000	1.000	3.000
27	Irl	37.000	–	0.000	0.000	0.000	1.000	0.000	5.000	1.000	0.000	2.000	1.000	0.000	5.000	0.000	1.000
28	Alb	26.000	–	–	–	–	–	–	–	–	2.000	–	3.000	1.000	3.000	–	–
–	Nir	26.000	–	0.000	2.000	2.000	0.000	0.000	1.000	0.000	1.000	1.000	2.000	0.000	–	7.000	0.000
30	Mlt	24.000	–	0.000	0.000	1.000	0.000	0.000	1.000	0.000	2.000	2.000	1.000	3.000	2.000	0.000	2.000
31	Cyp	18.000	–	–	–	2.000	0.000	1.000	0.000	0.000	0.000	0.000	1.000	0.000	0.000	1.000	–
32	Lux	17.000	–	1.000	1.000	0.000	0.000	0.000	0.000	0.000	2.000	0.000	2.000	0.000	0.000	0.000	0.000
33	Isl	16.000	–	–	–	–	–	0.000	1.000	0.000	0.000	0.000	0.000	2.000	0.000	0.000	0.000

	Pts	P	W	D	L	F	A	Diff	B	F/P
Total	**4114**	**3686**	**1464**	**758**	**1464**	**5373**	**5373**	**0**	**428**	**2.915**

Pos	Cnty	Total	7576	7677	7778	7879	7980	8081	8182	8283	8384	8485	8586	8687	8788	8889	8990	9091
1	Esp	288.500	3.000	13.000	7.000	16.000	12.500	3.500	14.000	13.000	11.000	2.000	17.000	10.000	5.000	18.000	7.500	14.000
2	Ita	277.000	6.000	14.000	2.000	10.000	10.000	2.000	5.000	6.000	18.000	8.000	5.000	2.000	9.000	12.000	19.000	12.000
3	FRG	276.500	16.000	17.000	3.000	12.000	1.000	9.000	7.000	7.000	4.000	13.000	11.000	3.000	4.000	9.000	5.000	2.000
4	Eng	265.000	13.000	9.000	5.000	9.000	16.000	7.000	12.000	5.000	11.000	19.000	–	–	–	–	–	19.000
5	Sco	204.000	9.000	2.000	4.000	4.000	8.000	4.000	2.000	21.000	8.000	2.000	1.000	2.000	4.000	4.000	2.000	5.000
6	Bel	198.000	16.000	8.500	18.000	7.000	1.000	5.000	18.000	14.000	5.000	2.000	2.000	1.000	19.000	9.500	16.000	7.000
7	URS	196.000	4.000	2.000	13.000	1.000	5.000	16.000	9.000	2.000	10.000	14.000	17.000	10.000	8.000	3.000	5.000	8.000
8	GDR	178.000	10.000	2.000	4.000	8.000	3.000	12.000	11.000	2.000	3.000	8.000	7.000	14.000	1.000	3.000	6.000	1.000
9	Por	171.000	4.000	6.000	8.000	0.000	4.000	15.000	7.000	2.000	14.000	2.000	5.000	5.000	6.000	2.000	1.000	4.000
10	Ned	158.500	11.000	0.000	13.000	1.000	2.000	14.000	0.000	5.000	3.000	6.000	2.000	18.000	10.500	8.000	6.000	1.000
11	Tch	146.500	1.000	1.000	4.000	14.000	6.000	6.000	4.000	2.000	2.000	3.000	11.000	1.000	6.000	0.000	2.000	5.000
12	Fra	141.000	3.000	2.000	1.000	3.000	14.000	1.000	4.000	9.000	6.000	3.000	2.000	13.000	15.000	0.000	10.000	9.000
13	Hun	131.000	4.000	9.000	4.000	5.000	2.000	2.000	2.000	3.000	7.000	1.000	1.000	1.000	2.000	4.000	3.000	0.000
14	Yug	130.000	6.000	2.000	7.000	3.000	7.000	1.000	5.000	4.000	2.000	0.000	8.000	5.000	2.000	2.000	5.000	–
15	Aut	118.000	6.000	1.000	12.000	4.000	0.000	0.000	1.000	9.000	2.000	15.000	6.000	4.000	2.000	2.000	8.000	3.000
–	Pol	118.000	5.000	10.000	0.000	1.000	2.000	2.000	7.000	4.000	0.000	6.000	2.000	5.000	1.000	6.000	1.000	13.000
17	Bul	111.000	2.000	9.000	0.000	2.000	4.000	7.000	2.000	2.000	3.000	5.000	–	5.000	2.000	12.000	2.000	0.000
18	Wal	104.000	8.000	4.000	1.000	2.000	2.000	8.000	0.000	6.000	1.000	2.000	2.000	6.000	2.000	3.000	1.000	3.000
19	Rom	92.000	2.000	0.000	6.000	1.000	3.000	4.000	2.000	1.000	–	1.000	3.000	0.000	0.000	10.000	12.000	3.000
–	Sui	92.000	1.000	2.000	1.000	8.000	1.000	1.000	3.000	0.000	4.000	4.000	1.000	7.000	5.000	1.000	6.000	2.000
21	Gre	85.000	1.000	1.000	6.000	2.000	4.000	1.000	2.000	2.000	2.000	9.000	1.000	5.000	4.000	4.000	3.000	4.000
22	Swe	80.000	1.000	1.000	2.000	1.000	7.000	5.000	2.000	1.000	3.000	2.000	5.000	8.000	5.000	2.000	4.000	1.000
23	Den	72.000	0.000	0.000	7.000	2.000	5.000	4.000	2.000	2.000	0.000	1.000	5.000	2.000	2.000	10.000	0.000	1.000
24	Tur	62.000	0.000	3.000	2.000	–	1.000	1.000	0.000	5.000	1.000	1.000	3.000	0.000	0.000	2.000	0.000	5.000
25	Nor	40.000	0.000	0.000	4.000	2.000	0.000	4.000	1.000	0.000	1.000	0.000	2.000	0.000	1.000	2.000	0.000	0.000
26	Fin	39.000	1.000	0.000	0.000	–	0.000	0.000	1.000	1.000	8.000	1.000	6.000	1.000	7.000	0.000	1.000	1.000
27	Irl	37.000	1.000	4.000	2.000	4.000	1.000	2.000	3.000	1.000	0.000	1.000	0.000	0.000	0.000	1.000	0.000	1.000
28	Alb	26.000	–	–	–	–	–	1.000	–	1.000	2.000	–	0.000	5.000	4.000	0.000	4.000	0.000
–	Nir	26.000	0.000	2.000	1.000	0.000	0.000	1.000	0.000	0.000	0.000	0.000	2.000	1.000	2.000	0.000	0.000	1.000
30	Mlt	24.000	1.000	0.000	0.000	0.000	2.000	2.000	0.000	0.000	0.000	4.000	0.000	0.000	0.000	1.000	0.000	0.000
31	Cyp	18.000	1.000	4.000	0.000	0.000	0.000	0.000	2.000	1.000	0.000	0.000	1.000	2.000	0.000	0.000	2.000	0.000
32	Lux	17.000	0.000	2.000	0.000	2.000	4.000	0.000	1.000	0.000	0.000	1.000	0.000	0.000	0.000	0.000	1.000	0.000
33	Isl	16.000	0.000	1.000	0.000	1.000	0.000	0.000	2.000	0.000	1.000	0.000	4.000	0.000	1.000	0.000	0.000	3.000

	Pts	P	W	D	L	F	A	Diff	B	F/P
Total	**4114**	**3686**	**1464**	**758**	**1464**	**5373**	**5373**	**0**	**428**	**2.915**

National Classification by Cumulative Year-by-Year Index

1981-82 to 1990-91

Pos	Cnty	Total	8182	8283	8384	8485	8586	8687	8788	8889	8990	9091
1	Esp	111.500	14.000	13.000	11.000	2.000	17.000	10.000	5.000	18.000	7.500	14.000
2	Ita	96.000	5.000	6.000	18.000	8.000	5.000	2.000	9.000	12.000	19.000	12.000
3	Bel	93.500	18.000	14.000	5.000	2.000	2.000	1.000	19.000	9.500	16.000	7.000
4	URS	86.000	9.000	2.000	10.000	14.000	17.000	10.000	8.000	3.000	5.000	8.000
5	Fra	71.000	4.000	9.000	6.000	3.000	2.000	13.000	15.000	0.000	10.000	9.000
6	Eng	66.000	12.000	5.000	11.000	19.000	–	–	–	–	–	19.000
7	FRG	65.000	7.000	7.000	4.000	13.000	11.000	3.000	4.000	9.000	5.000	2.000
8	Ned	59.500	0.000	5.000	3.000	6.000	2.000	18.000	10.500	8.000	6.000	1.000
9	GDR	56.000	11.000	2.000	3.000	8.000	7.000	14.000	1.000	3.000	6.000	1.000
10	Aut	52.000	1.000	9.000	2.000	15.000	6.000	4.000	2.000	2.000	8.000	3.000
11	Sco	51.000	2.000	21.000	8.000	2.000	1.000	2.000	4.000	4.000	2.000	5.000
12	Por	48.000	7.000	2.000	14.000	2.000	5.000	5.000	6.000	2.000	1.000	4.000
13	Pol	45.000	7.000	4.000	0.000	6.000	2.000	5.000	1.000	6.000	1.000	13.000
14	Gre	36.000	2.000	2.000	2.000	9.000	1.000	5.000	4.000	4.000	3.000	4.000
–	Tch	36.000	4.000	2.000	2.000	3.000	11.000	1.000	6.000	0.000	2.000	5.000
16	Bul	33.000	2.000	2.000	3.000	5.000	–	5.000	2.000	12.000	2.000	0.000
–	Swe	33.000	2.000	1.000	3.000	2.000	5.000	8.000	5.000	2.000	4.000	1.000
–	Sui	33.000	3.000	0.000	4.000	4.000	1.000	7.000	5.000	1.000	6.000	2.000
–	Yug	33.000	5.000	4.000	2.000	0.000	8.000	5.000	2.000	2.000	5.000	–
20	Rom	32.000	2.000	1.000	–	1.000	3.000	0.000	0.000	10.000	12.000	3.000
21	Fin	27.000	1.000	1.000	8.000	1.000	6.000	1.000	7.000	0.000	1.000	1.000
22	Wal	26.000	0.000	6.000	1.000	2.000	2.000	6.000	2.000	3.000	1.000	3.000
23	Den	25.000	2.000	2.000	0.000	1.000	5.000	2.000	2.000	10.000	0.000	1.000
24	Hun	24.000	2.000	3.000	7.000	1.000	1.000	1.000	2.000	4.000	3.000	0.000
25	Tur	17.000	0.000	5.000	1.000	1.000	3.000	0.000	0.000	2.000	0.000	5.000
26	Alb	16.000	–	1.000	2.000	–	0.000	5.000	4.000	0.000	4.000	0.000
27	Isl	11.000	2.000	0.000	1.000	0.000	4.000	0.000	1.000	0.000	0.000	3.000
28	Cyp	8.000	2.000	1.000	0.000	0.000	1.000	2.000	0.000	0.000	2.000	0.000
29	Irl	7.000	3.000	1.000	0.000	1.000	0.000	0.000	0.000	1.000	0.000	1.000
–	Nor	7.000	1.000	0.000	1.000	0.000	2.000	0.000	1.000	2.000	0.000	0.000
31	Nir	6.000	0.000	0.000	0.000	0.000	2.000	1.000	2.000	0.000	0.000	1.000
32	Mlt	5.000	0.000	0.000	0.000	4.000	0.000	0.000	0.000	1.000	0.000	0.000
33	Lux	3.000	1.000	0.000	0.000	1.000	0.000	0.000	0.000	0.000	1.000	0.000

	Pts	P	W	D	L	F	A	Diff	B	F/P
Total	**1388**	**1248**	**497**	**254**	**497**	**1716**	**1716**	**0**	**140**	**2.750**

National Classification by Cumulative Year–by–Year Index

1986–87 to 1990–91

Pos	Cnty	Total	8687	8788	8889	8990	9091
1	Esp	54.500	10.000	5.000	18.000	7.500	14.000
2	Ita	54.000	2.000	9.000	12.000	19.000	12.000
3	Bel	52.500	1.000	19.000	9.500	16.000	7.000
4	Fra	47.000	13.000	15.000	0.000	10.000	9.000
5	Ned	43.500	18.000	10.500	8.000	6.000	1.000
6	URS	34.000	10.000	8.000	3.000	5.000	8.000
7	Pol	26.000	5.000	1.000	6.000	1.000	13.000
8	Rom	25.000	0.000	0.000	10.000	12.000	3.000
–	GDR	25.000	14.000	1.000	3.000	6.000	1.000
10	FRG	23.000	3.000	4.000	9.000	5.000	2.000
11	Bul	21.000	5.000	2.000	12.000	2.000	0.000
–	Sui	21.000	7.000	5.000	1.000	6.000	2.000
13	Gre	20.000	5.000	4.000	4.000	3.000	4.000
–	Swe	20.000	8.000	5.000	2.000	4.000	1.000
15	Eng	19.000	–	–	–	–	19.000
–	Aut	19.000	4.000	2.000	2.000	8.000	3.000
17	Por	18.000	5.000	6.000	2.000	1.000	4.000
18	Sco	17.000	2.000	4.000	4.000	2.000	5.000
19	Den	15.000	2.000	2.000	10.000	0.000	1.000
–	Wal	15.000	6.000	2.000	3.000	1.000	3.000
21	Tch	14.000	1.000	6.000	0.000	2.000	5.000
–	Yug	14.000	5.000	2.000	2.000	5.000	–
23	Alb	13.000	5.000	4.000	0.000	4.000	0.000
24	Fin	10.000	1.000	7.000	0.000	1.000	1.000
–	Hun	10.000	1.000	2.000	4.000	3.000	0.000
26	Tur	7.000	0.000	0.000	2.000	0.000	5.000
27	Cyp	4.000	2.000	0.000	0.000	2.000	0.000
–	Nir	4.000	1.000	2.000	0.000	0.000	1.000
–	Isl	4.000	0.000	1.000	0.000	0.000	3.000
30	Nor	3.000	0.000	1.000	2.000	0.000	0.000
31	Irl	2.000	0.000	0.000	1.000	0.000	1.000
32	Lux	1.000	0.000	0.000	0.000	1.000	0.000
–	Mlt	1.000	0.000	0.000	1.000	0.000	0.000

	Pts	P	W	D	L	F	A	Diff	B	F/P
Total	**696**	**626**	**248**	**130**	**248**	**789**	**789**	**0**	**70**	**2.521**

Country Records – Points Gained 1960-61 to 1990-91

Albania

Pos'n	Cnty	Pts	P	W	D	L	F	A	Diff	B	Pts/P	Q	E
1	Sweden	7	8	2	3	3	5	10	-5	0	0.875	1	3
2	Romania	6	4	3	0	1	4	3	1	0	1.500	1	1
3	Malta	4	2	2	0	0	6	0	6	0	2.000	1	0
4	Bulgaria	2	2	1	0	1	5	3	2	0	1.000	1	0
5	Denmark	2	2	0	2	0	1	1	0	0	1.000	1	0
6	Italy	2	2	1	0	1	2	3	-1	0	1.000	0	1
7	Scotland	2	4	0	2	2	2	9	-7	0	0.500	0	2
8	Austria	1	4	0	1	3	4	7	-3	0	0.250	0	2
9	Poland	0	2	0	0	2	2	4	-2	0	0.000	0	1
10	Finland	0	4	0	0	4	3	7	-4	0	0.000	0	2
11	Greece	0	2	0	0	2	1	5	-4	0	0.000	0	1
	Total	**26**	**36**	**9**	**8**	**19**	**35**	**52**	**-17**	**0**	**0.722**	**5**	**13**

Austria

Pos'n	Cnty	Pts	P	W	D	L	F	A	Diff	B	Pts/P	Q	E
1	USSR	14	12	3	5	4	14	20	-6	3	1.167	4	2
2	Hungary	12	6	4	2	0	11	2	9	2	2.000	3	0
3	Turkey	10	6	4	1	1	18	8	10	1	1.667	3	0
4	East Germany	9	8	3	2	3	10	11	-1	1	1.125	2	2
5	Spain	8	10	1	5	4	9	16	-7	1	0.800	1	4
6	Albania	7	4	3	1	0	7	4	3	0	1.750	2	0
7	Yugoslavia	6	5	1	3	1	4	4	0	1	1.200	1	1
8	Denmark	6	6	2	2	2	10	11	-1	0	1.000	2	1
9	Belgium	6	7	2	2	3	13	16	-3	0	0.857	2	2
10	Bulgaria	5	4	2	1	1	8	4	4	0	1.250	2	0
11	Scotland	5	2	2	0	0	4	1	3	1	2.500	1	0
12	Greece	4	4	1	2	1	5	4	1	0	1.000	2	0
13	West Germany	4	8	2	0	6	3	20	-17	0	0.500	0	4
14	Iceland	3	2	1	0	1	4	2	2	1	1.500	1	0
15	Wales	3	2	1	1	0	1	0	1	0	1.500	1	0
16	Poland	3	4	1	1	2	5	7	-2	0	0.750	1	1
17	Czechoslovakia	3	4	0	2	2	2	4	-2	1	0.750	1	1
18	England	3	5	1	1	3	4	10	-6	0	0.600	0	3
19	Cyprus	2	2	1	0	1	3	1	2	0	1.000	1	0
20	Portugal	2	2	1	0	1	4	6	-2	0	1.000	0	1
21	Italy	2	8	0	2	6	3	20	-17	0	0.250	0	4
22	Romania	1	6	0	1	5	3	11	-8	0	0.167	0	3
23	Netherlands	0	4	0	0	4	4	12	-8	0	0.000	0	2
	Total	**118**	**121**	**36**	**34**	**51**	**149**	**194**	**-45**	**12**	**0.975**	**30**	**31**

Belgium

Pos'n	Cnty	Pts	P	W	D	L	F	A	Diff	B	Pts/P	Q	E
1	Cyprus	20	10	10	0	0	39	6	33	0	2.000	5	0
2	Italy	16	14	5	3	6	12	19	-7	3	1.143	3	4
3	Scotland	12	10	4	2	4	9	14	-5	2	1.200	2	3
4	Netherlands	11	5	5	0	0	9	3	6	1	2.200	3	0
5	Romania	11	6	5	0	1	7	1	6	1	1.833	3	0
6	West Germany	11	11	3	3	5	8	12	-4	2	1.000	3	3
7	Portugal	10	6	3	1	2	9	4	5	3	1.667	3	0
8	East Germany	10	8	4	0	4	13	12	1	2	1.250	2	2
9	Yugoslavia	10	8	3	2	3	7	6	1	2	1.250	2	2

10	England	10	13	4	1	8	15	26	-11	1	0.769	2	5
11	Austria	9	7	3	2	2	16	13	3	1	1.286	2	2
12	USSR	9	4	3	1	0	4	1	3	2	2.250	2	0
13	Northern Ireland	8	4	4	0	0	16	0	16	0	2.000	2	0
14	Luxembourg	8	4	4	0	0	16	2	14	0	2.000	2	0
15	Turkey	8	4	3	1	0	13	4	9	1	2.000	2	0
16	Hungary	8	4	3	0	1	7	3	4	2	2.000	2	0
17	Wales	8	4	3	1	0	5	2	3	1	2.000	2	0
18	France	7	4	3	0	1	8	3	5	1	1.750	2	0
19	Denmark	5	2	2	0	0	6	1	5	1	2.500	1	0
20	Switzerland	5	4	2	0	2	7	6	1	1	1.250	1	1
21	Belgium	5	4	2	0	2	3	3	0	1	1.250	1	1
22	Spain	5	7	2	0	5	7	9	-2	1	0.714	1	3
23	Malta	4	2	2	0	0	12	1	11	0	2.000	1	0
24	Bulgaria	4	2	2	0	0	8	1	7	0	2.000	1	0
25	Norway	4	2	2	0	0	5	0	5	0	2.000	1	0
26	Iceland	3	2	1	1	0	9	2	7	0	1.500	1	0
27	Czechoslovakia	2	2	1	0	1	3	4	-1	0	1.000	0	1
	Total	**223**	**153**	**88**	**18**	**47**	**273**	**158**	**115**	**29**	**1.458**	**52**	**27**

Bulgaria

Pos'n	Cnty	Pts	P	W	D	L	F	A	Diff	B	Pts/P	Q	E
1	Rep. of Ireland	12	6	5	1	0	12	2	10	1	2.000	3	0
2	Switzerland	9	7	3	1	3	11	6	5	2	1.286	2	1
3	Finland	8	4	4	0	0	30	4	26	0	2.000	2	0
4	Spain	8	12	3	1	8	11	23	-12	1	0.667	1	5
5	Luxembourg	7	4	3	1	0	16	2	14	0	1.750	2	0
6	Czechoslovakia	7	4	3	0	1	11	4	7	1	1.750	2	0
7	Greece	7	4	3	0	1	5	3	2	1	1.750	1	1
8	Poland	6	6	3	0	3	11	9	2	0	1.000	2	1
9	Netherlands	6	6	2	1	3	7	12	-5	1	1.000	1	2
10	France	5	4	2	0	2	4	6	-2	1	1.250	1	1
11	Iceland	4	2	2	0	0	8	0	8	0	2.000	1	0
12	West Germany	4	6	2	0	4	9	14	-5	0	0.667	0	3
13	Wales	3	2	1	1	0	5	1	4	0	1.500	1	0
14	Yugoslavia	3	2	1	0	1	5	4	1	1	1.500	1	0
15	Turkey	3	2	1	1	0	1	0	1	0	1.500	1	0
16	Portugal	3	2	1	0	1	3	3	0	1	1.500	1	0
17	Austria	3	4	1	1	2	4	8	-4	0	0.750	0	2
18	Italy	3	6	1	1	4	4	17	-13	0	0.500	0	3
19	Romania	2	2	1	0	1	7	4	3	0	1.000	1	0
20	Denmark	2	2	1	0	1	2	1	1	0	1.000	1	0
21	Albania	2	2	1	0	1	3	5	-2	0	1.000	0	1
22	Scotland	2	4	1	0	3	3	7	-4	0	0.500	0	2
23	Hungary	1	2	0	1	1	1	2	-1	0	0.500	0	1
24	East Germany	1	2	0	1	1	1	3	-2	0	0.500	0	1
25	USSR	0	2	0	0	2	0	2	-2	0	0.000	0	1
26	England	0	4	0	0	4	1	6	-5	0	0.000	0	2
27	Belgium	0	2	0	0	2	1	8	-7	0	0.000	0	1
	Total	**111**	**105**	**45**	**11**	**49**	**176**	**156**	**20**	**10**	**1.057**	**24**	**28**

Cyprus

Pos'n	Cnty	Pts	P	W	D	L	F	A	Diff	B	Pts/P	Q	E
1	Greece	4	6	1	2	3	3	5	-2	0	0.667	1	2
2	Sweden	3	4	1	1	2	2	18	-16	0	0.750	0	2
3	Norway	2	2	1	0	1	6	1	5	0	1.000	1	0

4	Austria	2	2	1	0	1	1	3	-2	0	1.000	0	1
5	Hungary	2	4	1	0	3	1	17	-16	0	0.500	0	2
6	Italy	1	2	0	1	1	1	3	-2	0	0.500	0	1
7	Spain	1	2	0	1	1	1	9	-8	0	0.500	0	1
8	Wales	1	2	0	1	1	0	8	-8	0	0.500	0	1
9	USSR	1	2	0	1	1	1	10	-9	0	0.500	0	1
10	Czechoslovakia	1	6	0	1	5	2	28	-26	0	0.167	0	3
11	Switzerland	0	2	0	0	2	1	6	-5	0	0.000	0	1
12	Rep. of Ireland	0	4	0	0	4	2	9	-7	0	0.000	0	2
13	Romania	0	2	0	0	2	1	8	-7	0	0.000	0	1
14	Denmark	0	2	0	0	2	0	7	-7	0	0.000	0	1
15	Scotland	0	4	0	0	4	1	17	-16	0	0.000	0	2
16	Portugal	0	2	0	0	2	1	18	-17	0	0.000	0	1
17	Belgium	0	10	0	0	10	6	39	-33	0	0.000	0	5
	Total	**18**	**58**	**5**	**8**	**45**	**30**	**206**	**-176**	**0**	**0.310**	**2**	**27**

Czechoslovakia

Pos'n	Cnty	Pts	P	W	D	L	F	A	Diff	B	Pts/P	Q	E
1	Rep. of Ireland	12	6	5	1	0	13	5	8	1	2.000	3	0
2	Cyprus	11	6	5	1	0	28	2	26	0	1.833	3	0
3	Portugal	11	8	4	1	3	8	6	2	2	1.375	3	1
4	East Germany	10	8	4	0	4	11	10	1	2	1.250	2	2
5	Switzerland	10	8	4	1	3	12	12	0	1	1.250	2	2
6	Italy	9	8	4	0	4	8	10	-2	1	1.125	1	3
7	Finland	7	4	3	1	0	14	3	11	0	1.750	2	0
8	West Germany	7	10	2	2	6	11	18	-7	1	0.700	1	4
9	Austria	6	4	2	2	0	4	2	2	0	1.500	1	1
10	Scotland	6	6	2	1	3	6	5	1	1	1.000	2	1
11	Sweden	6	4	1	3	0	5	4	1	1	1.500	2	0
12	Hungary	6	6	2	1	3	10	11	-1	1	1.000	1	2
13	Yugoslavia	6	8	2	2	4	5	10	-5	0	0.750	1	3
14	England	6	8	2	2	4	7	16	-9	0	0.750	0	4
15	Wales	5	2	2	0	0	4	0	4	1	2.500	1	0
16	Greece	5	2	2	0	0	4	2	2	1	2.500	1	0
17	France	5	4	2	1	1	3	2	1	0	1.250	1	1
18	Luxembourg	4	2	2	0	0	12	0	12	0	2.000	1	0
19	Malta	4	2	2	0	0	4	1	3	0	2.000	1	0
20	Spain	4	3	2	0	1	4	6	-2	0	1.333	1	1
21	Belgium	2	2	1	0	1	4	3	1	0	1.000	1	0
22	Netherlands	2	2	1	0	1	2	2	0	0	1.000	0	1
23	Bulgaria	2	4	1	0	3	4	11	-7	0	0.500	0	2
24	USSR	2	6	0	2	4	4	13	-9	0	0.333	0	3
	Total	**148**	**123**	**57**	**21**	**45**	**187**	**154**	**33**	**13**	**1.203**	**31**	**31**

Denmark

Pos'n	Cnty	Pts	P	W	D	L	F	A	Diff	B	Pts/P	Q	E
1	Rep. of Ireland	8	6	4	0	2	8	6	2	0	1.333	2	1
2	Luxembourg	7	4	3	1	0	19	2	17	0	1.750	2	0
3	Wales	7	6	2	2	2	6	3	3	1	1.167	1	2
4	Austria	7	6	2	2	2	11	10	1	1	1.167	1	2
5	Portugal	6	6	3	0	3	7	14	-7	0	1.000	1	2
6	Malta	5	2	2	0	0	8	0	8	1	2.500	1	0
7	Cyprus	4	2	2	0	0	7	0	7	0	2.000	1	0
8	Northern Ireland	4	2	2	0	0	7	2	5	0	2.000	1	0
9	Iceland	4	2	2	0	0	3	0	3	0	2.000	1	0
10	Greece	3	2	1	0	1	4	2	2	1	1.500	1	0

11	Yugoslavia	3	4	1	1	2	4	6	-2	0	0.750	0	2
12	East Germany	2	2	1	0	1	4	4	0	0	1.000	1	0
13	Switzerland	2	2	1	0	1	2	2	0	0	1.000	0	1
14	Albania	2	2	0	2	0	1	1	0	0	1.000	0	1
15	Bulgaria	2	2	1	0	1	1	2	-1	0	1.000	0	1
16	Spain	2	4	0	2	2	2	7	-5	0	0.500	0	2
17	France	2	4	1	0	3	4	10	-6	0	0.500	0	2
18	England	1	2	0	1	1	1	2	-1	0	0.500	0	1
19	Netherlands	1	10	0	1	9	2	20	-18	0	0.100	0	5
20	Scotland	0	2	0	0	2	0	3	-3	0	0.000	0	1
21	Belgium	0	2	0	0	2	1	6	-5	0	0.000	0	1
22	USSR	0	2	0	0	2	3	9	-6	0	0.000	0	1
23	Poland	0	2	0	0	2	1	9	-8	0	0.000	0	1
24	West Germany	0	8	0	0	8	6	24	-18	0	0.000	0	4
	Total	**72**	**86**	**28**	**12**	**46**	**112**	**144**	**-32**	**4**	**0.837**	**13**	**30**

East Germany

Pos'n	Cnty	Pts	P	W	D	L	F	A	Diff	B	Pts/P	Q	E
1	Wales	18	12	6	5	1	24	14	10	1	1.500	6	0
2	Portugal	18	12	5	4	3	13	10	3	4	1.500	4	2
3	Italy	10	9	3	3	3	10	9	1	1	1.111	4	1
4	France	10	8	2	4	2	5	4	1	2	1.250	2	2
5	Austria	9	8	3	2	3	11	10	1	1	1.125	2	2
6	Belgium	9	8	4	0	4	12	13	-1	1	1.125	2	2
7	Czechoslovakia	9	8	4	0	4	10	11	-1	1	1.125	2	2
8	Luxembourg	8	4	3	1	0	12	2	10	1	2.000	2	0
9	Switzerland	8	4	2	2	0	12	3	9	2	2.000	2	0
10	Hungary	8	6	3	1	2	5	5	0	1	1.333	2	1
11	Iceland	7	4	3	1	0	9	3	6	0	1.750	2	0
12	Spain	7	10	2	2	6	9	21	-12	1	0.700	1	4
13	Northern Ireland	6	4	2	2	0	9	4	5	0	1.500	2	0
14	Sweden	6	4	2	1	1	8	5	3	1	1.500	2	0
15	Scotland	6	4	2	1	1	5	6	-1	1	1.500	1	1
16	Finland	5	4	2	0	2	15	7	8	1	1.250	2	0
17	Netherlands	5	5	2	1	2	3	3	0	0	1.000	1	2
18	Bulgaria	4	2	1	1	0	3	1	2	1	2.000	1	0
19	Yugoslavia	4	4	0	3	1	5	7	-2	1	1.000	1	1
20	Poland	3	2	1	1	0	5	2	3	0	1.500	1	0
21	Greece	3	2	1	1	0	2	0	2	0	1.500	1	0
22	Turkey	3	3	0	3	0	3	3	0	0	1.000	0	1
23	USSR	3	5	0	3	2	3	5	-2	0	0.600	0	3
24	England	3	6	0	3	3	4	8	-4	0	0.500	0	3
25	Romania	2	2	1	0	1	5	2	3	0	1.000	1	0
26	Denmark	2	2	1	0	1	4	4	0	0	1.000	0	1
27	West Germany	2	2	1	0	1	5	7	-2	0	1.000	0	1
	Total	**178**	**144**	**56**	**45**	**43**	**211**	**169**	**42**	**21**	**1.236**	**44**	**29**

England

Pos'n	Cnty	Pts	P	W	D	L	F	A	Diff	B	Pts/P	Q	E
1	Spain	26	21	9	6	6	33	24	9	2	1.238	7	5
2	Belgium	20	13	8	1	4	26	15	11	3	1.538	5	2
3	Hungary	19	10	7	3	0	12	1	11	2	1.900	4	1
4	Netherlands	18	10	7	2	1	25	8	17	2	1.800	5	0
5	West Germany	17	16	5	3	8	23	23	0	4	1.063	5	4
6	Northern Ireland	15	8	7	0	1	25	7	18	1	1.875	4	0
7	Czechoslovakia	13	8	4	2	2	16	7	9	3	1.625	4	0

8	Yugoslavia	13	6	5	1	0	12	5	7	2	2.167	3	0
9	Romania	12	6	4	1	1	17	3	14	3	2.000	3	0
10	East Germany	12	6	3	3	0	8	4	4	3	2.000	3	0
11	France	11	8	4	2	2	15	8	7	1	1.375	3	1
12	Poland	11	6	4	1	1	11	6	5	2	1.833	3	0
13	Bulgaria	10	4	4	0	0	6	1	5	2	2.500	2	0
14	Scotland	10	8	3	2	3	11	9	2	2	1.250	2	2
15	England	10	8	4	0	4	9	9	0	2	1.250	2	2
16	Portugal	10	8	4	1	3	12	15	-3	1	1.250	1	3
17	Austria	9	5	3	1	1	10	4	6	2	1.800	3	0
18	Greece	7	4	2	2	0	12	4	8	1	1.750	2	0
19	Switzerland	7	4	3	0	1	9	6	3	1	1.750	2	0
20	Rep. of Ireland	7	4	2	2	0	3	1	2	1	1.750	2	0
21	Italy	7	7	2	2	3	6	6	0	1	1.000	2	2
22	Sweden	6	4	1	3	0	6	2	4	1	1.500	1	1
23	Turkey	6	4	2	2	0	4	1	3	0	1.500	2	0
24	USSR	6	4	2	1	1	6	6	0	1	1.500	1	1
25	Wales	5	2	2	0	0	5	0	5	1	2.500	1	0
26	Luxembourg	4	2	2	0	0	21	0	21	0	2.000	1	0
27	Norway	4	2	2	0	0	12	0	12	0	2.000	1	0
28	Finland	3	2	1	1	0	5	2	3	0	1.500	1	0
29	Denmark	3	2	1	1	0	2	1	1	0	1.500	1	0
	Total	**301**	**192**	**107**	**43**	**42**	**362**	**178**	**184**	**44**	**1.568**	**76**	**24**

Finland

Pos'n	Cnty	Pts	P	W	D	L	F	A	Diff	B	Pts/P	Q	E
1	Albania	9	4	4	0	0	7	3	4	1	2.250	2	0
2	Sweden	5	4	1	2	1	4	5	-1	1	1.250	1	1
3	Rep. of Ireland	4	2	2	0	0	4	0	4	0	2.000	1	0
4	East Germany	4	4	2	0	2	7	15	-8	0	1.000	0	2
5	Malta	2	2	1	0	1	4	3	1	0	1.000	1	0
6	Norway	2	2	1	0	1	2	1	1	0	1.000	1	0
7	Northern Ireland	2	2	0	2	0	1	1	0	0	1.000	1	0
8	Turkey	2	4	0	2	2	2	7	-5	0	0.500	0	2
9	USSR	2	4	0	2	2	5	11	-6	0	0.500	0	2
10	France	2	6	0	2	4	0	11	-11	0	0.333	0	3
11	Switzerland	1	2	0	1	1	2	3	-1	0	0.500	0	1
12	Portugal	1	2	0	1	1	0	1	-1	0	0.500	0	1
13	England	1	2	0	1	1	2	5	-3	0	0.500	0	1
14	Czechoslovakia	1	4	0	1	3	3	14	-11	0	0.250	0	2
15	Hungary	1	4	0	1	3	4	22	-18	0	0.250	0	2
16	Luxembourg	0	2	0	0	2	0	2	-2	0	0.000	0	1
17	Netherlands	0	2	0	0	2	3	7	-4	0	0.000	0	1
18	Romania	0	2	0	0	2	0	6	-6	0	0.000	0	1
19	Poland	0	2	0	0	2	1	8	-7	0	0.000	0	1
20	Italy	0	4	0	0	4	0	8	-8	0	0.000	0	2
21	West Germany	0	2	0	0	2	3	13	-10	0	0.000	0	1
22	Bulgaria	0	4	0	0	4	4	30	-26	0	0.000	0	2
	Total	**39**	**66**	**11**	**15**	**40**	**58**	**176**	**-118**	**2**	**0.591**	**7**	**26**

France

Pos'n	Cnty	Pts	P	W	D	L	F	A	Diff	B	Pts/P	Q	E
1	Romania	15	8	6	1	1	17	7	10	2	1.875	3	1
2	Portugal	12	11	3	5	3	11	9	2	1	1.091	3	2
3	Finland	11	6	4	2	0	11	0	11	1	1.833	3	0
4	West Germany	10	11	3	3	5	9	17	-8	1	0.909	1	4

5	East Germany	9	8	2	4	2	4	5	-1	1	1.125	2	2
6	Spain	9	12	2	4	6	15	24	-9	1	0.750	2	4
7	Northern Ireland	8	4	4	0	0	12	2	10	0	2.000	2	0
8	Rep. of Ireland	7	4	3	1	0	13	2	11	0	1.750	2	0
9	USSR	7	6	2	1	3	9	10	-1	2	1.167	2	1
10	England	7	8	2	2	4	8	15	-7	1	0.875	1	3
11	Denmark	6	4	3	0	1	10	4	6	0	1.500	2	0
12	Yugoslavia	6	4	2	1	1	8	3	5	1	1.500	1	1
13	Wales	5	4	2	0	2	5	7	-2	1	1.250	1	1
14	Netherlands	5	6	2	1	3	6	10	-4	0	0.833	1	2
15	Luxembourg	4	2	2	0	0	5	1	4	0	2.000	1	0
16	Bulgaria	4	4	2	0	2	6	4	2	0	1.000	1	1
17	Greece	4	4	1	1	2	8	10	-2	1	1.000	1	1
18	Czechoslovakia	3	4	1	1	2	2	3	-1	0	0.750	1	1
19	Italy	3	4	0	3	1	4	6	-2	0	0.750	0	2
20	Norway	2	2	1	0	1	7	3	4	0	1.000	1	0
21	Belgium	2	4	1	0	3	3	8	-5	0	0.500	0	2
22	Switzerland	1	2	0	1	1	3	4	-1	0	0.500	0	1
23	Scotland	1	2	0	1	1	1	2	-1	0	0.500	0	1
	Total	**141**	**124**	**48**	**32**	**44**	**177**	**156**	**21**	**13**	**1.137**	**31**	**30**

Greece

Pos'n	Cnty	Pts	P	W	D	L	F	A	Diff	B	Pts/P	Q	E
1	Poland	12	9	5	2	2	12	10	2	0	1.333	3	1
2	Cyprus	8	6	3	2	1	5	3	2	0	1.333	2	1
3	Switzerland	7	4	3	0	1	5	5	0	1	1.750	1	1
4	France	6	4	2	1	1	10	8	2	1	1.500	1	1
5	Hungary	5	4	2	1	1	6	5	1	0	1.250	1	1
6	Luxembourg	4	2	2	0	0	6	0	6	0	2.000	1	0
7	Albania	4	2	2	0	0	5	1	4	0	2.000	1	0
8	Iceland	4	2	2	0	0	4	0	4	0	2.000	1	0
9	Austria	4	4	1	2	1	4	5	-1	0	1.000	0	2
10	Yugoslavia	4	4	2	0	2	3	5	-2	0	1.000	0	2
11	USSR	4	6	1	2	3	2	6	-4	0	0.667	0	3
12	Italy	4	8	1	2	5	5	13	-8	0	0.500	0	4
13	Wales	3	2	1	1	0	6	5	1	0	1.500	1	0
14	Netherlands	3	4	1	1	2	6	8	-2	0	0.750	1	1
15	Scotland	2	2	1	0	1	3	4	-1	0	1.000	0	1
16	Sweden	2	2	1	0	1	1	2	-1	0	1.000	0	1
17	Bulgaria	2	4	1	0	3	3	5	-2	0	0.500	1	1
18	Denmark	2	2	1	0	1	2	4	-2	0	1.000	0	1
19	West Germany	2	4	1	0	3	3	9	-6	0	0.500	0	2
20	England	2	4	0	2	2	4	12	-8	0	0.500	0	2
21	East Germany	1	2	0	1	1	0	2	-2	0	0.500	0	1
22	Portugal	0	2	0	0	2	2	4	-2	0	0.000	0	1
–	Czechoslovakia	0	2	0	0	2	2	4	-2	0	0.000	0	1
24	Romania	0	2	0	0	2	1	8	-7	0	0.000	0	1
	Total	**85**	**87**	**33**	**17**	**37**	**100**	**128**	**-28**	**2**	**0.977**	**14**	**29**

Hungary

Pos'n	Cnty	Pts	P	W	D	L	F	A	Diff	B	Pts/P	Q	E
1	Scotland	16	12	7	0	5	21	25	-4	2	1.333	3	3
2	Sweden	10	6	3	3	0	12	6	6	1	1.667	3	0
3	Malta	9	6	4	1	1	29	6	23	0	1.500	3	0
4	Turkey	9	7	4	0	3	10	7	3	1	1.286	2	1
5	Yugoslavia	9	8	3	2	3	15	19	-4	1	1.125	1	3

6	Czechoslovakia	8	6	3	1	2	11	10	1	1	1.333	2	1
7	Italy	8	11	2	4	5	12	17	-5	0	0.727	1	4
8	Finland	7	4	3	1	0	22	4	18	0	1.750	2	0
9	Cyprus	6	4	3	0	1	17	1	16	0	1.500	2	0
10	East Germany	6	6	2	1	3	5	5	0	1	1.000	1	2
11	USSR	5	3	2	0	1	5	4	1	1	1.667	1	1
12	Netherlands	5	4	2	0	2	6	6	0	1	1.250	1	1
13	Wales	4	2	2	0	0	6	1	5	0	2.000	1	0
14	Portugal	4	4	1	1	2	6	6	0	1	1.000	1	1
15	West Germany	4	4	1	1	2	7	10	-3	1	1.000	1	1
16	England	4	10	0	3	7	1	12	-11	1	0.400	1	4
17	Poland	3	2	1	1	0	5	0	5	0	1.500	1	0
18	Bulgaria	3	2	1	1	0	2	1	1	0	1.500	1	0
19	Greece	3	4	1	1	2	5	6	-1	0	0.750	1	1
20	Norway	2	2	1	0	1	4	2	2	0	1.000	1	0
21	Switzerland	2	2	1	0	1	1	2	-1	0	1.000	0	1
22	Belgium	2	4	1	0	3	3	7	-4	0	0.500	0	2
23	Austria	2	6	0	2	4	2	11	-9	0	0.333	0	3
24	Spain	0	2	0	0	2	1	4	-3	0	0.000	0	1
	Total	**131**	**121**	**48**	**23**	**50**	**208**	**172**	**36**	**12**	**1.083**	**30**	**30**

Iceland

Pos'n	Cnty	Pts	P	W	D	L	F	A	Diff	B	Pts/P	Q	E
1	Sweden	4	4	1	2	1	4	2	2	0	1.000	1	1
2	Northern Ireland	2	2	1	0	1	3	2	1	0	1.000	1	0
3	Malta	2	2	1	0	1	2	3	-1	0	1.000	0	1
4	Austria	2	2	1	0	1	2	4	-2	0	1.000	0	1
5	Rep. of Ireland	2	2	1	0	1	2	5	-3	0	1.000	0	1
6	East Germany	1	4	0	1	3	3	9	-6	0	0.250	0	2
7	Belgium	1	2	0	1	1	2	9	-7	0	0.500	0	1
8	West Germany	1	4	0	1	3	2	20	-18	0	0.250	0	2
9	Scotland	1	6	0	1	5	3	26	-23	0	0.167	0	3
10	Denmark	0	2	0	0	2	0	3	-3	0	0.000	0	1
11	Greece	0	2	0	0	2	0	4	-4	0	0.000	0	1
12	Bulgaria	0	2	0	0	2	0	8	-8	0	0.000	0	1
13	Norway	0	4	0	0	4	2	11	-9	0	0.000	0	2
14	Switzerland	0	2	0	0	2	1	14	-13	0	0.000	0	1
15	Poland	0	8	0	0	8	3	26	-23	0	0.000	0	4
16	Spain	0	8	0	0	8	1	26	-25	0	0.000	0	4
	Total	**16**	**56**	**5**	**6**	**45**	**30**	**172**	**-142**	**0**	**0.286**	**2**	**26**

Italy

Pos'n	Cnty	Pts	P	W	D	L	F	A	Diff	B	Pts/P	Q	E
1	Austria	18	8	6	2	0	20	3	17	4	2.250	4	0
2	Poland	18	13	5	6	2	24	14	10	2	1.385	3	3
3	Belgium	18	14	6	3	5	19	12	7	3	1.286	4	3
4	Yugoslavia	17	11	6	2	3	17	11	6	3	1.545	4	1
5	Hungary	17	11	5	4	2	17	12	5	3	1.545	4	1
6	West Germany	17	14	6	2	6	15	12	3	3	1.214	5	2
7	Greece	15	8	5	2	1	13	5	8	3	1.875	4	0
8	Norway	13	6	6	0	0	13	1	12	1	2.167	3	0
9	Wales	11	7	5	0	2	11	6	5	1	1.571	3	0
10	Portugal	11	10	4	2	4	10	12	-2	1	1.100	2	3
11	Bulgaria	10	6	4	1	1	17	4	13	1	1.667	3	0
12	Switzerland	10	4	4	0	0	13	3	10	2	2.500	2	0
13	Finland	10	4	4	0	0	8	0	8	2	2.500	2	0

14	Czechoslovakia	10	8	4	0	4	10	8	2	2	1.250	3	1
15	East Germany	10	9	3	3	3	9	10	-1	1	1.111	1	4
16	Netherlands	9	6	3	1	2	8	5	3	2	1.500	3	0
17	England	9	7	3	2	2	6	6	0	1	1.286	2	2
18	Turkey	8	4	3	1	0	8	0	8	1	2.000	2	0
19	Spain	8	11	3	2	6	9	17	-8	0	0.727	0	6
20	Northern Ireland	7	4	3	1	0	9	1	8	0	1.750	2	0
21	France	7	4	1	3	0	6	4	2	2	1.750	2	0
22	Romania	6	4	1	3	0	2	1	1	1	1.500	2	0
23	Scotland	5	4	2	1	1	5	3	2	0	1.250	1	1
24	Malta	4	2	2	0	0	8	1	7	0	2.000	1	0
25	Luxembourg	4	2	2	0	0	7	1	6	0	2.000	1	0
26	Rep. of Ireland	4	2	2	0	0	5	0	5	0	2.000	1	0
27	Cyprus	4	2	1	1	0	3	1	2	1	2.000	1	0
28	USSR	4	2	1	1	0	2	1	1	1	2.000	1	0
29	Albania	3	2	1	0	1	3	2	1	1	1.500	1	0
30	Sweden	2	2	1	0	1	3	2	1	0	1.000	1	0
	Total	**289**	**191**	**102**	**43**	**46**	**300**	**158**	**142**	**42**	**1.513**	**68**	**27**

Luxembourg

Pos'n	Cnty	Pts	P	W	D	L	F	A	Diff	B	Pts/P	Q	E
1	Finland	4	2	2	0	0	2	0	2	0	2.000	1	0
2	Malta	2	2	1	0	1	2	2	0	0	1.000	0	1
3	Northern Ireland	2	2	1	0	1	3	4	-1	0	1.000	0	1
4	Norway	2	2	1	0	1	2	4	-2	0	1.000	0	1
5	Turkey	2	4	1	0	3	3	11	-8	0	0.500	0	2
6	East Germany	1	4	0	1	3	2	12	-10	0	0.250	0	2
7	Bulgaria	1	4	0	1	3	2	16	-14	0	0.250	0	2
8	Denmark	1	4	0	1	3	2	19	-17	0	0.250	0	2
9	Sweden	1	4	0	1	3	0	18	-18	0	0.250	0	2
10	Yugoslavia	1	6	0	1	5	5	32	-27	0	0.167	0	3
11	France	0	2	0	0	2	1	5	-4	0	0.000	0	1
12	Rep. of Ireland	0	2	0	0	2	2	8	-6	0	0.000	0	1
13	Italy	0	2	0	0	2	1	7	-6	0	0.000	0	1
14	Greece	0	2	0	0	2	0	6	-6	0	0.000	0	1
–	Poland	0	2	0	0	2	0	6	-6	0	0.000	0	1
16	Switzerland	0	2	0	0	2	1	9	-8	0	0.000	0	1
17	Spain	0	2	0	0	2	2	11	-9	0	0.000	0	1
18	Czechoslovakia	0	2	0	0	2	0	12	-12	0	0.000	0	1
19	Belgium	0	4	0	0	4	2	16	-14	0	0.000	0	2
20	England	0	2	0	0	2	0	21	-21	0	0.000	0	1
21	West Germany	0	6	0	0	6	2	25	-23	0	0.000	0	3
	Total	**17**	**62**	**6**	**5**	**51**	**34**	**244**	**-210**	**0**	**0.274**	**1**	**30**

Malta

Pos'n	Cnty	Pts	P	W	D	L	F	A	Diff	B	Pts/P	Q	E
1	Northern Ireland	4	2	2	0	0	3	1	2	0	2.000	1	0
2	Hungary	3	6	1	1	4	6	29	-23	0	0.500	0	3
3	Iceland	2	2	1	0	1	3	2	1	0	1.000	1	0
4	Luxembourg	2	2	1	0	1	2	2	0	0	1.000	1	0
5	Finland	2	2	1	0	1	3	4	-1	0	1.000	0	1
6	Sweden	2	2	1	0	1	2	5	-3	0	1.000	0	1
7	Rep. of Ireland	2	2	1	0	1	1	4	-3	0	1.000	0	1
8	Portugal	2	2	1	0	1	2	9	-7	0	1.000	0	1
9	Romania	1	2	0	1	1	0	1	-1	0	0.500	0	1
10	Netherlands	1	4	0	1	3	2	10	-8	0	0.250	0	2

11	Scotland	1	4	0	1	3	0	19	-19	0	0.250	0	2
12	Spain	1	8	0	1	7	1	24	-23	0	0.125	0	4
13	Wales	1	6	0	1	5	0	26	-26	0	0.167	0	3
14	Czechoslovakia	0	2	0	0	2	1	4	-3	0	0.000	0	1
15	Poland	0	2	0	0	2	1	6	-5	0	0.000	0	1
16	Albania	0	2	0	0	2	0	6	-6	0	0.000	0	1
17	Italy	0	2	0	0	2	1	8	-7	0	0.000	0	1
18	Denmark	0	2	0	0	2	0	8	-8	0	0.000	0	1
19	Norway	0	2	0	0	2	0	9	-9	0	0.000	0	1
20	Belgium	0	2	0	0	2	1	12	-11	0	0.000	0	1
21	USSR	0	4	0	0	4	0	13	-13	0	0.000	0	2
22	West Germany	0	4	0	0	4	1	25	-24	0	0.000	0	2
	Total	**24**	**66**	**9**	**6**	**51**	**30**	**227**	**-197**	**0**	**0.364**	**3**	**30**

Netherlands

Pos'n	Cnty	Pts	P	W	D	L	F	A	Diff	B	Pts/P	Q	E
1	Denmark	21	10	9	1	0	20	2	18	2	2.100	5	0
2	Switzerland	11	8	5	0	3	9	9	0	1	1.375	1	3
3	USSR	11	10	4	2	4	8	13	-5	1	1.100	1	4
4	France	9	6	3	1	2	10	6	4	2	1.500	2	1
5	Austria	8	4	4	0	0	12	4	8	0	2.000	2	0
6	Poland	8	4	3	0	1	11	3	8	2	2.000	2	0
7	Bulgaria	8	6	3	1	2	12	7	5	1	1.333	2	1
8	Norway	8	4	3	1	0	6	2	4	1	2.000	2	0
9	Malta	7	4	3	1	0	10	2	8	0	1.750	2	0
10	Rep. of Ireland	7	4	3	1	0	8	1	7	0	1.750	2	0
11	Greece	6	4	2	1	1	8	6	2	1	1.500	1	1
12	Portugal	6	4	2	1	1	4	2	2	1	1.500	2	0
13	Spain	6	6	2	1	3	9	9	0	1	1.000	1	2
14	East Germany	6	5	2	1	2	3	3	0	1	1.200	2	1
15	Romania	5	2	2	0	0	7	0	7	1	2.500	1	0
16	West Germany	5	4	2	0	2	3	4	-1	1	1.250	1	1
17	Italy	5	6	2	1	3	5	8	-3	0	0.833	0	3
18	Northern Ireland	4	2	2	0	0	14	1	13	0	2.000	1	0
19	Turkey	4	2	2	0	0	7	0	7	0	2.000	1	0
20	Finland	4	2	2	0	0	7	3	4	0	2.000	1	0
21	Hungary	4	4	2	0	2	6	6	0	0	1.000	1	1
22	England	4	10	1	2	7	8	25	-17	0	0.400	0	5
23	Sweden	3	2	1	0	1	3	2	1	1	1.500	1	0
24	Yugoslavia	3	4	1	1	2	7	9	-2	0	0.750	0	2
25	Scotland	3	4	1	1	2	3	7	-4	0	0.750	1	1
26	Czechoslovakia	2	2	1	0	1	2	2	0	0	1.000	1	0
27	Wales	1	2	0	1	1	2	5	-3	0	0.500	0	1
28	Belgium	0	5	0	0	5	3	9	-6	0	0.000	0	3
	Total	**169**	**130**	**67**	**18**	**45**	**207**	**150**	**57**	**17**	**1.300**	**36**	**30**

Northern Ireland

Pos'n	Cnty	Pts	P	W	D	L	F	A	Diff	B	Pts/P	Q	E
1	Norway	4	2	1	1	0	4	2	2	1	2.000	1	0
2	Romania	4	6	1	2	3	5	13	-8	0	0.667	1	2
3	Luxembourg	2	2	1	0	1	4	3	1	0	1.000	1	0
4	Finland	2	2	0	2	0	1	1	0	0	1.000	0	1
5	Turkey	2	2	1	0	1	3	4	-1	0	1.000	0	1
6	Iceland	2	2	1	0	1	2	3	-1	0	1.000	0	1
7	Yugoslavia	2	2	1	0	1	4	7	-3	0	1.000	0	1
8	East Germany	2	4	0	2	2	4	9	-5	0	0.500	0	2

9	England	2	8	1	0	7	7	25	-18	0	0.250	0	4
10	Sweden	1	2	0	1	1	3	6	-3	0	0.500	0	1
11	Scotland	1	2	0	1	1	1	5	-4	0	0.500	0	1
12	Wales	1	2	0	1	1	0	4	-4	0	0.500	0	1
13	Italy	1	4	0	1	3	1	9	-8	0	0.250	0	2
14	Malta	0	2	0	0	2	1	3	-2	0	0.000	0	1
15	Denmark	0	2	0	0	2	2	7	-5	0	0.000	0	1
16	USSR	0	2	0	0	2	1	10	-9	0	0.000	0	1
17	France	0	4	0	0	4	2	12	-10	0	0.000	0	2
18	Spain	0	4	0	0	4	3	15	-12	0	0.000	0	2
19	Netherlands	0	2	0	0	2	1	14	-13	0	0.000	0	1
20	West Germany	0	4	0	0	4	3	18	-15	0	0.000	0	2
21	Belgium	0	4	0	0	4	0	16	-16	0	0.000	0	2
	Total	**26**	**64**	**7**	**11**	**46**	**52**	**186**	**-134**	**1**	**0.406**	**3**	**29**

Norway

Pos'n	Cnty	Pts	P	W	D	L	F	A	Diff	B	Pts/P	Q	E
1	Iceland	8	4	4	0	0	11	2	9	0	2.000	2	0
2	Malta	4	2	2	0	0	9	0	9	0	2.000	1	0
3	Switzerland	3	2	1	1	0	3	1	2	0	1.500	1	0
4	Sweden	3	2	1	0	1	4	3	1	1	1.500	1	0
5	Spain	3	4	1	1	2	8	10	-2	0	0.750	0	2
6	Wales	3	6	0	3	3	3	19	-16	0	0.500	0	3
7	Luxembourg	2	2	1	0	1	4	2	2	0	1.000	1	0
8	Turkey	2	2	1	0	1	5	4	1	0	1.000	1	0
9	Finland	2	2	1	0	1	1	2	-1	0	1.000	0	1
10	Hungary	2	2	1	0	1	2	4	-2	0	1.000	0	1
11	France	2	2	1	0	1	3	7	-4	0	1.000	0	1
12	Cyprus	2	2	1	0	1	1	6	-5	0	1.000	0	1
13	Northern Ireland	1	2	0	1	1	2	4	-2	0	0.500	0	1
14	Netherlands	1	4	0	1	3	2	6	-4	0	0.250	0	2
15	Scotland	1	4	0	1	3	0	4	-4	0	0.250	0	2
16	Poland	1	4	0	1	3	4	14	-10	0	0.250	0	2
17	West Germany	0	2	0	0	2	2	6	-4	0	0.000	0	1
18	USSR	0	2	0	0	2	1	6	-5	0	0.000	0	1
19	Belgium	0	2	0	0	2	0	5	-5	0	0.000	0	1
20	Yugoslavia	0	4	0	0	4	0	9	-9	0	0.000	0	2
21	Italy	0	6	0	0	6	1	13	-12	0	0.000	0	3
22	England	0	2	0	0	2	0	12	-12	0	0.000	0	1
23	Portugal	0	6	0	0	6	3	18	-15	0	0.000	0	3
	Total	**40**	**70**	**15**	**9**	**46**	**69**	**157**	**-88**	**1**	**0.571**	**7**	**28**

Poland

Pos'n	Cnty	Pts	P	W	D	L	F	A	Diff	B	Pts/P	Q	E
1	Iceland	16	8	8	0	0	26	3	23	0	2.000	4	0
2	Turkey	12	7	5	0	2	9	4	5	2	1.714	2	1
3	Italy	12	13	2	6	5	14	24	-10	2	0.923	3	3
4	Scotland	9	6	3	1	2	7	5	2	2	1.500	2	1
5	Norway	7	4	3	1	0	14	4	10	0	1.750	2	0
6	Bulgaria	7	6	3	0	3	9	11	-2	1	1.167	1	2
7	Greece	6	9	2	2	5	10	12	-2	0	0.667	1	3
8	Rep. of Ireland	5	2	2	0	0	4	0	4	1	2.500	1	0
9	Austria	5	4	2	1	1	7	5	2	0	1.250	1	1
10	Switzerland	5	4	1	2	1	5	7	-2	1	1.250	1	1
11	Denmark	4	2	2	0	0	9	1	8	0	2.000	1	0
12	Finland	4	2	2	0	0	8	1	7	0	2.000	1	0

13	Luxembourg	4	2	2	0	0	6	0	6	0	2.000	1	0
14	Malta	4	2	2	0	0	6	1	5	0	2.000	1	0
15	Albania	4	2	2	0	0	4	2	2	0	2.000	1	0
16	Spain	4	6	0	4	2	3	6	-3	0	0.667	0	3
17	England	3	6	1	1	4	6	11	-5	0	0.500	0	3
18	Netherlands	2	4	1	0	3	3	11	-8	0	0.500	0	2
19	Sweden	1	2	0	1	1	4	5	-1	0	0.500	0	1
20	Wales	1	2	0	1	1	1	3	-2	0	0.500	0	1
21	East Germany	1	2	0	1	1	2	5	-3	0	0.500	0	1
22	Hungary	1	2	0	1	1	0	5	-5	0	0.500	0	1
23	West Germany	1	4	0	1	3	0	9	-9	0	0.250	0	2
24	USSR	0	2	0	0	2	0	2	-2	0	0.000	0	1
	Total	**118**	**103**	**43**	**23**	**37**	**157**	**137**	**20**	**9**	**1.146**	**23**	**27**

Portugal

Pos'n	Cnty	Pts	P	W	D	L	F	A	Diff	B	Pts/P	Q	E
1	Scotland	13	10	5	1	4	14	18	-4	2	1.300	2	3
2	Norway	12	6	6	0	0	18	3	15	0	2.000	3	0
3	Italy	12	10	4	2	4	12	10	2	2	1.200	3	2
4	France	12	11	3	5	3	9	11	-2	1	1.091	2	3
5	East Germany	12	12	3	4	5	10	13	-3	2	1.000	2	4
6	Wales	11	10	4	3	3	12	12	0	0	1.100	2	3
7	England	10	8	3	1	4	15	12	3	3	1.250	3	1
8	West Germany	9	8	2	4	2	10	13	-3	1	1.125	2	2
9	Yugoslavia	8	6	3	2	1	13	4	9	0	1.333	3	0
10	Switzerland	8	6	2	3	1	13	9	4	1	1.333	3	0
11	Romania	8	4	3	1	0	7	3	4	1	2.000	2	0
12	Czechoslovakia	7	8	3	1	4	6	8	-2	0	0.875	1	3
13	Denmark	6	6	3	0	3	14	7	7	0	1.000	2	1
14	Sweden	6	4	2	0	2	7	2	5	2	1.500	2	0
15	USSR	6	4	1	3	0	5	4	1	1	1.500	1	1
16	Cyprus	5	2	2	0	0	18	1	17	1	2.500	1	0
17	Hungary	5	4	2	1	1	6	6	0	0	1.250	1	1
18	Belgium	5	6	2	1	3	4	9	-5	0	0.833	0	3
19	Greece	4	2	2	0	0	4	2	2	0	2.000	1	0
20	Turkey	3	2	1	1	0	4	0	4	0	1.500	1	0
21	Finland	3	2	1	1	0	1	0	1	0	1.500	1	0
22	Netherlands	3	4	1	1	2	2	4	-2	0	0.750	0	2
23	Malta	2	2	1	0	1	9	2	7	0	1.000	1	0
24	Austria	2	2	1	0	1	6	4	2	0	1.000	1	0
25	Bulgaria	2	2	1	0	1	3	3	0	0	1.000	0	1
	Total	**174**	**141**	**61**	**35**	**45**	**222**	**160**	**62**	**17**	**1.234**	**40**	**30**

Republic of Ireland

Pos'n	Cnty	Pts	P	W	D	L	F	A	Diff	B	Pts/P	Q	E
1	Cyprus	8	4	4	0	0	9	2	7	0	2.000	2	0
2	Luxembourg	4	2	2	0	0	8	2	6	0	2.000	1	0
3	Denmark	4	6	2	0	4	6	8	-2	0	0.667	1	2
4	West Germany	4	6	1	2	3	5	11	-6	0	0.667	0	3
5	Iceland	2	2	1	0	1	5	2	3	0	1.000	1	0
6	Malta	2	2	1	0	1	4	1	3	0	1.000	1	0
7	England	2	4	0	2	2	1	3	-2	0	0.500	0	2
8	Yugoslavia	2	2	1	0	1	1	4	-3	0	1.000	0	1
9	Turkey	2	4	0	2	2	3	7	-4	0	0.500	0	2
10	Wales	2	4	0	2	2	1	7	-6	0	0.500	0	2
11	Sweden	1	2	0	1	1	1	2	-1	0	0.500	0	1

12	Netherlands	1	4	0	1	3	1	8	-7	0	0.250	0	2
13	Czechoslovakia	1	6	0	1	5	5	13	-8	0	0.167	0	3
14	Bulgaria	1	6	0	1	5	2	12	-10	0	0.167	0	3
15	France	1	4	0	1	3	2	13	-11	0	0.250	0	2
16	Spain	0	2	0	0	2	1	5	-4	0	0.000	0	1
17	Finland	0	2	0	0	2	0	4	-4	0	0.000	0	1
–	Poland	0	2	0	0	2	0	4	-4	0	0.000	0	1
19	Italy	0	2	0	0	2	0	5	-5	0	0.000	0	1
20	Scotland	0	2	0	0	2	1	8	-7	0	0.000	0	1
21	USSR	0	4	0	0	4	0	11	-11	0	0.000	0	2
	Total	**37**	**72**	**12**	**13**	**47**	**56**	**132**	**-76**	**0**	**0.514**	**6**	**30**

Romania

Pos'n	Cnty	Pts	P	W	D	L	F	A	Diff	B	Pts/P	Q	E
1	Austria	12	6	5	1	0	11	3	8	1	2.000	3	0
2	Scotland	9	8	3	2	3	6	8	-2	1	1.125	2	2
3	Northern Ireland	8	6	3	2	1	13	5	8	0	1.333	2	1
4	Spain	8	8	3	1	4	6	15	-9	1	1.000	1	3
5	USSR	6	6	2	2	2	8	10	-2	0	1.000	1	2
6	Greece	5	2	2	0	0	8	1	7	1	2.500	1	0
7	Yugoslavia	5	4	2	0	2	5	6	-1	1	1.250	1	1
8	Cyprus	4	2	2	0	0	8	1	7	0	2.000	1	0
9	Finland	4	2	2	0	0	6	0	6	0	2.000	1	0
10	Switzerland	3	2	1	1	0	8	2	6	0	1.500	1	0
11	Malta	3	2	1	1	0	1	0	1	0	1.500	1	0
12	West Germany	3	4	0	3	1	5	6	-1	0	0.750	0	2
13	Italy	3	4	0	3	1	1	2	-1	0	0.750	0	2
14	France	3	8	1	1	6	7	17	-10	0	0.375	1	3
15	England	3	6	1	1	4	3	17	-14	0	0.500	0	3
16	Sweden	2	2	1	0	1	3	1	2	0	1.000	1	0
17	Albania	2	4	1	0	3	3	4	-1	0	0.500	1	1
18	Turkey	2	2	1	0	1	2	4	-2	0	1.000	0	1
19	Bulgaria	2	2	1	0	1	4	7	-3	0	1.000	0	1
20	East Germany	2	2	1	0	1	2	5	-3	0	1.000	0	1
21	Belgium	2	6	1	0	5	1	7	-6	0	0.333	0	3
22	Portugal	1	4	0	1	3	3	7	-4	0	0.250	0	2
23	Netherlands	0	2	0	0	2	0	7	-7	0	0.000	0	1
	Total	**92**	**94**	**34**	**19**	**41**	**114**	**135**	**-21**	**5**	**0.979**	**18**	**29**

Scotland

Pos'n	Cnty	Pts	P	W	D	L	F	A	Diff	B	Pts/P	Q	E
1	West Germany	24	17	8	4	5	29	22	7	4	1.412	5	4
2	Switzerland	13	8	6	1	1	26	8	18	0	1.625	3	1
3	Belgium	12	10	4	2	4	14	9	5	2	1.200	3	2
4	Hungary	12	12	5	0	7	25	21	4	2	1.000	3	3
5	Iceland	11	6	5	1	0	26	3	23	0	1.833	3	0
6	Portugal	11	10	4	1	5	18	14	4	2	1.100	3	2
7	Yugoslavia	10	8	4	0	4	19	15	4	2	1.250	2	2
8	Spain	10	11	3	3	5	15	16	-1	1	0.909	3	3
9	England	10	8	3	2	3	9	11	-2	2	1.250	2	2
10	Cyprus	8	4	4	0	0	17	1	16	0	2.000	2	0
11	Romania	8	8	3	2	3	8	6	2	0	1.000	2	2
12	Czechoslovakia	8	6	3	1	2	5	6	-1	1	1.333	1	2
13	Malta	7	4	3	1	0	19	0	19	0	1.750	2	0
14	Albania	7	4	2	2	0	9	2	7	1	1.750	2	0
15	Bulgaria	7	4	3	0	1	7	3	4	1	1.750	2	0

16	Norway	7	4	3	1	0	4	0	4	0	1.750	2	0
17	USSR	6	3	2	1	0	7	3	4	1	2.000	2	0
18	Poland	6	6	2	1	3	5	7	-2	1	1.000	1	2
19	Turkey	5	4	2	1	1	6	1	5	0	1.250	1	1
20	Netherlands	5	4	2	1	1	7	3	4	0	1.250	1	1
21	Denmark	5	2	2	0	0	3	0	3	1	2.500	1	0
22	Rep. of Ireland	4	2	2	0	0	8	1	7	0	2.000	1	0
23	Italy	4	4	1	1	2	3	5	-2	1	1.000	1	1
24	Northern Ireland	3	2	1	1	0	5	1	4	0	1.500	1	0
25	East Germany	3	4	1	1	2	6	5	1	0	0.750	1	1
26	Greece	3	2	1	0	1	4	3	1	1	1.500	1	0
27	France	3	2	1	1	0	2	1	1	0	1.500	1	0
28	Austria	0	2	0	0	2	1	4	-3	0	0.000	0	1
	Total	**212**	**161**	**80**	**29**	**52**	**307**	**171**	**136**	**23**	**1.317**	**52**	**30**

Spain

Pos'n	Cnty	Pts	P	W	D	L	F	A	Diff	B	Pts/P	Q	E
1	West Germany	24	20	7	6	7	33	30	3	4	1.200	5	5
2	England	22	21	6	6	9	24	33	-9	4	1.048	5	7
3	Bulgaria	21	12	8	1	3	23	11	12	4	1.750	5	1
4	Yugoslavia	20	10	8	1	1	19	7	12	3	2.000	4	1
5	Iceland	17	8	8	0	0	26	1	25	1	2.125	4	0
6	East Germany	17	10	6	2	2	21	9	12	3	1.700	4	1
7	France	17	12	6	4	2	24	15	9	1	1.417	4	2
8	Malta	16	8	7	1	0	24	1	23	1	2.000	4	0
9	Italy	16	11	6	2	3	17	9	8	2	1.455	6	0
10	Austria	16	10	4	5	1	16	9	7	3	1.600	4	1
11	Wales	15	8	4	3	1	10	5	5	4	1.875	4	0
12	Scotland	15	11	5	3	3	16	15	1	2	1.364	3	3
13	USSR	15	13	4	6	3	16	16	0	1	1.154	3	4
14	Belgium	12	7	5	0	2	9	7	2	2	1.714	3	1
15	Romania	11	8	4	1	3	15	6	9	2	1.375	3	1
16	Poland	9	6	2	4	0	6	3	3	1	1.500	3	0
17	Netherlands	9	6	3	1	2	9	9	0	2	1.500	2	1
18	Northern Ireland	8	4	4	0	0	15	3	12	0	2.000	2	0
19	Switzerland	8	4	3	1	0	7	2	5	1	2.000	2	0
20	Denmark	7	4	2	2	0	7	2	5	1	1.750	2	0
21	Norway	6	4	2	1	1	10	8	2	1	1.500	2	0
22	Luxembourg	5	2	2	0	0	11	2	9	1	2.500	1	0
23	Hungary	5	2	2	0	0	4	1	3	1	2.500	1	0
24	Spain	5	4	2	0	2	8	8	0	1	1.250	1	1
25	Rep. of Ireland	4	2	2	0	0	5	1	4	0	2.000	1	0
26	Sweden	4	2	1	1	0	4	2	2	1	2.000	1	0
27	Cyprus	3	2	1	1	0	9	1	8	0	1.500	1	0
28	Czechoslovakia	3	3	1	0	2	6	4	2	1	1.000	1	1
29	Turkey	2	2	1	0	1	7	3	4	0	1.000	1	0
	Total	**332**	**216**	**116**	**52**	**48**	**401**	**223**	**178**	**48**	**1.537**	**82**	**30**

Sweden

Pos'n	Cnty	Pts	P	W	D	L	F	A	Diff	B	Pts/P	Q	E
1	Albania	10	8	3	3	2	10	5	5	1	1.250	3	1
2	Luxembourg	7	4	3	1	0	18	0	18	0	1.750	2	0
3	Switzerland	6	6	2	2	2	6	6	0	0	1.000	1	2
4	Cyprus	5	4	2	1	1	18	2	16	0	1.250	2	0
5	Finland	5	4	1	2	1	5	4	1	1	1.250	1	1
6	Iceland	4	4	1	2	1	2	4	-2	0	1.000	1	1

7	England	4	4	0	3	1	2	6	-4	1	1.000	1	1
8	Portugal	4	4	2	0	2	2	7	-5	0	1.000	0	2
9	Northern Ireland	3	2	1	1	0	6	3	3	0	1.500	1	0
10	Poland	3	2	1	1	0	5	4	1	0	1.500	1	0
11	Rep. of Ireland	3	2	1	1	0	2	1	1	0	1.500	1	0
–	Greece	3	2	1	0	1	2	1	1	1	1.500	1	0
13	Czechoslovakia	3	4	0	3	1	4	5	-1	0	0.750	0	2
14	East Germany	3	4	1	1	2	5	8	-3	0	0.750	0	2
15	Hungary	3	6	0	3	3	6	12	-6	0	0.500	0	3
16	Malta	2	2	1	0	1	5	2	3	0	1.000	1	0
17	Norway	2	2	1	0	1	3	4	-1	0	1.000	0	1
18	Italy	2	2	1	0	1	2	3	-1	0	1.000	0	1
–	Netherlands	2	2	1	0	1	2	3	-1	0	1.000	0	1
20	Romania	2	2	1	0	1	1	3	-2	0	1.000	0	1
21	Wales	1	2	0	1	1	2	3	-1	0	0.500	0	1
–	Turkey	1	2	0	1	1	2	3	-1	0	0.500	0	1
23	West Germany	1	2	0	1	1	0	1	-1	0	0.500	0	1
24	Spain	1	2	0	1	1	2	4	-2	0	0.500	0	1
	Total	**80**	**78**	**24**	**28**	**26**	**112**	**94**	**18**	**4**	**1.026**	**16**	**23**

Switzerland

Pos'n	Cnty	Pts	P	W	D	L	F	A	Diff	B	Pts/P	Q	E
1	Netherlands	8	8	3	0	5	9	9	0	2	1.000	3	1
2	Bulgaria	8	7	3	1	3	6	11	-5	1	1.143	1	2
3	Czechoslovakia	7	8	3	1	4	12	12	0	0	0.875	2	2
4	Sweden	7	6	2	2	2	6	6	0	1	1.167	2	1
5	Poland	5	4	1	2	1	7	5	2	1	1.250	1	1
6	Portugal	5	6	1	3	2	9	13	-4	0	0.833	0	3
7	Iceland	4	2	2	0	0	14	1	13	0	2.000	1	0
8	Luxembourg	4	2	2	0	0	9	1	8	0	2.000	1	0
9	Cyprus	4	2	2	0	0	6	1	5	0	2.000	1	0
10	USSR	4	4	1	1	2	5	4	1	1	1.000	1	1
11	France	4	2	1	1	0	4	3	1	1	2.000	1	0
12	Belgium	4	4	2	0	2	6	7	-1	0	1.000	1	1
13	Finland	3	2	1	1	0	3	2	1	0	1.500	1	0
14	Wales	3	4	1	1	2	4	5	-1	0	0.750	0	2
15	West Germany	3	4	0	3	1	1	2	-1	0	0.750	0	2
16	Scotland	3	8	1	1	6	8	26	-18	0	0.375	1	3
17	Turkey	2	2	1	0	1	6	3	3	0	1.000	1	0
18	Hungary	2	2	1	0	1	2	1	1	0	1.000	1	0
19	Greece	2	4	1	0	3	5	5	0	0	0.500	1	1
20	Denmark	2	2	1	0	1	2	2	0	0	1.000	1	0
21	England	2	4	1	0	3	6	9	-3	0	0.500	0	2
22	East Germany	2	4	0	2	2	3	12	-9	0	0.500	0	2
23	Yugoslavia	1	2	0	1	1	2	4	-2	0	0.500	0	1
24	Norway	1	2	0	1	1	1	3	-2	0	0.500	0	1
25	Spain	1	4	0	1	3	2	7	-5	0	0.250	0	2
26	Romania	1	2	0	1	1	2	8	-6	0	0.500	0	1
27	Italy	0	4	0	0	4	3	13	-10	0	0.000	0	2
	Total	**92**	**105**	**31**	**23**	**51**	**143**	**175**	**-32**	**7**	**0.876**	**21**	**31**

Turkey

Pos'n	Cnty	Pts	P	W	D	L	F	A	Diff	B	Pts/P	Q	E
1	Luxembourg	6	4	3	0	1	11	3	8	0	1.500	2	0
2	Finland	6	4	2	2	0	7	2	5	0	1.500	2	0
3	Rep. of Ireland	6	4	2	2	0	7	3	4	0	1.500	2	0

4	Hungary	6	7	3	0	4	7	10	-3	0	0.857	1	2
5	Poland	4	7	2	0	5	4	9	-5	0	0.571	1	2
6	Scotland	4	4	1	1	2	1	6	-5	1	1.000	1	1
7	Wales	3	2	1	0	1	3	1	2	1	1.500	1	0
8	Northern Ireland	3	2	1	0	1	4	3	1	1	1.500	1	0
9	Sweden	3	2	1	1	0	3	2	1	0	1.500	1	0
10	East Germany	3	3	0	3	0	3	3	0	0	1.000	1	0
11	Austria	3	6	1	1	4	8	18	-10	0	0.500	0	3
12	Romania	2	2	1	0	1	4	2	2	0	1.000	1	0
13	Norway	2	2	1	0	1	4	5	-1	0	1.000	0	1
14	Switzerland	2	2	1	0	1	3	6	-3	0	1.000	0	1
15	England	2	4	0	2	2	1	4	-3	0	0.500	0	2
16	Spain	2	2	1	0	1	3	7	-4	0	1.000	0	1
17	Bulgaria	1	2	0	1	1	0	1	-1	0	0.500	0	1
18	Portugal	1	2	0	1	1	0	4	-4	0	0.500	0	1
19	Italy	1	4	0	1	3	0	8	-8	0	0.250	0	2
20	Belgium	1	4	0	1	3	4	13	-9	0	0.250	0	2
21	West Germany	1	6	0	1	5	3	12	-9	0	0.167	0	3
22	Netherlands	0	2	0	0	2	0	7	-7	0	0.000	0	1
23	USSR	0	8	0	0	8	1	14	-13	0	0.000	0	4
	Total	**62**	**85**	**21**	**17**	**47**	**81**	**143**	**-62**	**3**	**0.729**	**14**	**27**

USSR

Pos'n	Cnty	Pts	P	W	D	L	F	A	Diff	B	Pts/P	Q	E
1	Turkey	18	8	8	0	0	14	1	13	2	2.250	4	0
2	Spain	15	13	3	6	4	16	16	0	3	1.154	4	3
3	Yugoslavia	14	8	6	1	1	19	7	12	1	1.750	4	0
4	Austria	14	12	4	5	3	20	14	6	1	1.167	2	4
5	West Germany	14	8	5	2	1	14	9	5	2	1.750	2	2
6	Czechoslovakia	13	6	4	2	0	13	4	9	3	2.167	3	0
7	Netherlands	12	10	4	2	4	13	8	5	2	1.200	4	1
8	Malta	9	4	4	0	0	13	0	13	1	2.250	2	0
9	Rep. of Ireland	9	4	4	0	0	11	0	11	1	2.250	2	0
10	Greece	9	6	3	2	1	6	2	4	1	1.500	3	0
11	Romania	8	6	2	2	2	10	8	2	2	1.333	2	1
12	East Germany	8	5	2	3	0	5	3	2	1	1.600	3	0
13	France	8	6	3	1	2	10	9	1	1	1.333	1	2
14	Finland	6	4	2	2	0	11	5	6	0	1.500	2	0
15	Switzerland	6	4	2	1	1	4	5	-1	1	1.500	1	1
16	Norway	5	2	2	0	0	6	1	5	1	2.500	1	0
17	Poland	5	2	2	0	0	2	0	2	1	2.500	1	0
18	Northern Ireland	4	2	2	0	0	10	1	9	0	2.000	1	0
19	Denmark	4	2	2	0	0	9	3	6	0	2.000	1	0
20	Bulgaria	4	2	2	0	0	2	0	2	0	2.000	1	0
21	Wales	4	5	2	0	3	4	3	1	0	0.800	1	1
22	England	4	4	1	1	2	6	6	0	1	1.000	1	1
23	Portugal	4	4	0	3	1	4	5	-1	1	1.000	1	1
24	Cyprus	3	2	1	1	0	10	1	9	0	1.500	1	0
25	Hungary	2	3	1	0	2	4	5	-1	0	0.667	1	1
26	Italy	1	2	0	1	1	1	2	-1	0	0.500	0	1
27	Belgium	1	4	0	1	3	1	4	-3	0	0.250	0	2
28	Scotland	1	3	0	1	2	3	7	-4	0	0.333	0	2
	Total	**205**	**141**	**71**	**37**	**33**	**241**	**129**	**112**	**26**	**1.454**	**49**	**23**

Wales

Pos'n	Cnty	Pts	P	W	D	L	F	A	Diff	B	Pts/P	Q	E
1	Malta	11	6	5	1	0	26	0	26	0	1.833	3	0
2	Norway	10	6	3	3	0	19	3	16	1	1.667	3	0
3	Portugal	10	10	3	3	4	12	12	0	1	1.000	3	2
4	USSR	7	5	3	0	2	3	4	-1	1	1.400	1	1
5	East Germany	7	12	1	5	6	14	24	-10	0	0.583	0	6
6	Rep. of Ireland	6	4	2	2	0	7	1	6	0	1.500	2	0
7	Denmark	6	6	2	2	2	3	6	-3	0	1.000	2	1
8	France	5	4	2	0	2	7	5	2	1	1.250	1	1
9	Switzerland	5	4	2	1	1	5	4	1	0	1.250	2	0
10	Spain	5	8	1	3	4	5	10	-5	0	0.625	0	4
11	Netherlands	4	2	1	1	0	5	2	3	1	2.000	1	0
12	Poland	4	2	1	1	0	3	1	2	1	2.000	1	0
13	Yugoslavia	4	4	2	0	2	5	6	-1	0	1.000	0	2
14	Italy	4	7	2	0	5	6	11	-5	0	0.571	0	3
15	Cyprus	3	2	1	1	0	8	0	8	0	1.500	1	0
16	Northern Ireland	3	2	1	1	0	4	0	4	0	1.500	1	0
17	Sweden	3	2	1	1	0	3	2	1	0	1.500	1	0
18	Turkey	2	2	1	0	1	1	3	-2	0	1.000	0	1
19	Greece	1	2	0	1	1	5	6	-1	0	0.500	0	1
20	West Germany	1	2	0	1	1	3	4	-1	0	0.500	0	1
21	Austria	1	2	0	1	1	0	1	-1	0	0.500	0	1
22	Belgium	1	4	0	1	3	2	5	-3	0	0.250	0	2
23	Bulgaria	1	2	0	1	1	1	5	-4	0	0.500	0	1
24	Czechoslovakia	0	2	0	0	2	0	4	-4	0	0.000	0	1
25	Hungary	0	2	0	0	2	1	6	-5	0	0.000	0	1
26	England	0	2	0	0	2	0	5	-5	0	0.000	0	1
	Total	**104**	**106**	**34**	**30**	**42**	**148**	**130**	**18**	**6**	**0.981**	**22**	**30**

West Germany

Pos'n	Cnty	Pts	P	W	D	L	F	A	Diff	B	Pts/P	Q	E
1	Spain	25	20	7	6	7	30	33	-3	5	1.250	5	5
2	England	22	16	8	3	5	23	23	0	3	1.375	4	5
3	Denmark	19	8	8	0	0	24	6	18	3	2.375	4	0
4	Scotland	17	17	5	4	8	22	29	-7	3	1.000	4	5
5	Italy	16	14	6	2	6	12	15	-3	2	1.143	2	5
6	France	15	11	5	3	3	17	9	8	2	1.364	4	1
7	Czechoslovakia	15	10	6	2	2	18	11	7	1	1.500	4	1
8	Belgium	15	11	5	3	3	12	8	4	2	1.364	3	3
9	Austria	14	8	6	0	2	20	3	17	2	1.750	4	0
10	Turkey	13	6	5	1	0	12	3	9	2	2.167	3	0
11	Luxembourg	12	6	6	0	0	25	2	23	0	2.000	3	0
12	Rep. of Ireland	10	6	3	2	1	11	5	6	2	1.667	3	0
1 3	Bulgaria	10	6	4	0	2	14	9	5	2	1.667	3	0
14	Portugal	10	8	2	4	2	13	10	3	2	1.250	2	2
15	Northern Ireland	9	4	4	0	0	18	3	15	1	2.250	2	0
16	Poland	9	4	3	1	0	9	0	9	2	2.250	2	0
17	Malta	8	4	4	0	0	25	1	24	0	2.000	2	0
18	Iceland	7	4	3	1	0	20	2	18	0	1.750	2	0
19	Greece	6	4	3	0	1	9	3	6	0	1.500	2	0
20	Hungary	6	4	2	1	1	10	7	3	1	1.500	1	1
21	Romania	6	4	1	3	0	6	5	1	1	1.500	2	0
22	Switzerland	6	4	1	3	0	2	1	1	1	1.500	2	0
23	Yugoslavia	5	2	2	0	0	4	1	3	1	2.500	1	0
24	Netherlands	5	4	2	0	2	4	3	1	1	1.250	1	1

25	USSR	5	8	1	2	5	9	14	-5	1	0.625	2	2
26	Finland	4	2	2	0	0	13	3	10	0	2.000	1	0
27	Norway	4	2	2	0	0	6	2	4	0	2.000	1	0
28	Wales	4	2	1	1	0	4	3	1	1	2.000	1	0
29	Sweden	4	2	1	1	0	1	0	1	1	2.000	1	0
30	East Germany	3	2	1	0	1	7	5	2	1	1.500	1	0
	Total	**304**	**203**	**109**	**43**	**51**	**400**	**219**	**181**	**43**	**1.498**	**72**	**31**

Yugoslavia

Pos'n	Cnty	Pts	P	W	D	L	F	A	Diff	B	Pts/P	Q	E
1	Luxembourg	12	6	5	1	0	32	5	27	1	2.000	3	0
2	Czechoslovakia	12	8	4	2	2	10	5	5	2	1.500	3	1
3	Hungary	9	8	3	2	3	19	15	4	1	1.125	3	1
4	Scotland	9	8	4	0	4	15	19	-4	1	1.125	2	2
5	Italy	9	11	3	2	6	11	17	-6	1	0.818	1	4
6	Norway	8	4	4	0	0	9	0	9	0	2.000	2	0
7	Belgium	8	8	3	2	3	6	7	-1	0	1.000	2	2
8	Netherlands	7	4	2	1	1	9	7	2	2	1.750	2	0
9	Denmark	6	4	2	1	1	6	4	2	1	1.500	2	0
10	East Germany	5	4	1	3	0	7	5	2	0	1.250	1	1
11	Wales	5	4	2	0	2	6	5	1	1	1.250	2	0
–	Romania	5	4	2	0	2	6	5	1	1	1.250	1	1
13	Austria	5	5	1	3	1	4	4	0	0	1.000	1	1
14	Greece	4	4	2	0	2	5	3	2	0	1.000	2	0
15	France	4	4	1	1	2	3	8	-5	1	1.000	1	1
16	Portugal	4	6	1	2	3	4	13	-9	0	0.667	0	3
17	Spain	4	10	1	1	8	7	19	-12	1	0.400	1	4
18	Northern Ireland	3	2	1	0	1	7	4	3	1	1.500	1	0
19	Switzerland	3	2	1	1	0	4	2	2	0	1.500	1	0
20	USSR	3	8	1	1	6	7	19	-12	0	0.375	0	4
21	Rep. of Ireland	2	2	1	0	1	4	1	3	0	1.000	1	0
22	Bulgaria	2	2	1	0	1	4	5	-1	0	1.000	0	1
23	England	1	6	0	1	5	5	12	-7	0	0.167	0	3
24	West Germany	0	2	0	0	2	1	4	-3	0	0.000	0	1
	Total	**130**	**126**	**46**	**24**	**56**	**191**	**188**	**3**	**14**	**1.032**	**32**	**30**

Comparative Country v. Country Performance Chart

1960-61 to 1990-91

	Total		%	No.	Albania		Austria		Belgium		Bulgaria		Cyprus		Czechoslovacia		Denmark		E. Germany	
	Q	E	Qual	Adv	Q	E	Q	E	Q	E	Q	E	Q	E	Q	E	Q	E	Q	E
Albania	5	13	27.8%	11	–	–	0	2	–	–	1	0	–	–	–	–	1	0	–	–
Austria	30	31	49.2%	23	2	0	–	–	2	2	2	0	1	0	1	1	2	1	2	2
Belgium	52	27	65.8%	27	–	–	2	2	1	1	1	0	5	0	0	1	1	0	2	2
Bulgaria	24	28	46.2%	27	0	1	0	2	0	1	–	–	–	–	2	0	1	0	0	1
Cyprus	2	27	6.9%	17	–	–	0	1	0	5	–	–	–	–	0	3	0	1	–	–
Czechoslovakia	31	31	50.0%	24	–	–	1	1	1	0	0	2	3	0	–	–	–	–	2	2
Denmark	13	30	30.2%	24	0	1	1	2	0	1	0	1	1	0	–	–	–	–	1	0
East Germany	44	29	60.3%	27	–	–	2	2	2	2	1	0	–	–	2	2	0	1	–	–
England	76	24	76.0%	29	–	–	3	0	5	2	2	0	–	–	4	0	1	0	3	0
Finland	7	26	21.2%	22	2	0	–	–	–	–	0	2	–	–	0	2	–	–	0	2
France	31	30	50.8%	23	–	–	–	–	0	2	1	1	–	–	1	1	2	0	2	2
Greece	14	29	32.6%	24	1	0	0	2	–	–	1	1	2	1	0	1	0	1	0	1
Hungary	30	30	50.0%	24	–	–	0	3	0	2	1	0	2	0	2	1	–	–	1	2
Iceland	2	26	7.1%	16	–	–	0	1	0	1	0	1	–	–	–	–	0	1	0	2
Italy	68	27	71.6%	30	1	0	4	0	4	3	3	0	1	0	3	1	–	–	1	4
Luxembourg	1	30	3.2%	21	–	–	–	–	0	2	0	2	–	–	0	1	0	2	0	2
Malta	3	30	9.1%	22	0	1	–	–	0	1	–	–	–	–	0	1	0	1	–	–
Netherlands	36	30	54.5%	28	–	–	2	0	0	3	2	1	–	–	1	0	5	0	2	1
Northern Ireland	3	29	9.4%	21	–	–	–	–	0	2	–	–	–	–	–	–	0	1	0	2
Norway	7	28	20.0%	23	–	–	–	–	0	1	–	–	0	1	–	–	–	–	–	–
Poland	23	27	46.0%	24	1	0	1	1	–	–	1	2	–	–	–	–	1	0	0	1
Portugal	40	30	57.1%	25	–	–	1	0	0	3	0	1	1	0	1	3	2	1	2	4
Rep. of Ireland	6	30	16.7%	21	–	–	–	–	–	–	0	3	2	0	0	3	1	2	–	–
Romania	18	29	38.3%	23	1	1	3	0	0	3	0	1	1	0	–	–	–	–	0	1
Scotland	52	30	63.4%	28	2	0	0	1	3	2	2	0	2	0	1	2	1	0	1	1
Spain	82	30	73.2%	29	–	–	4	1	3	1	5	1	1	0	1	1	2	0	4	1
Sweden	16	23	41.0%	24	3	1	–	–	–	–	–	–	2	0	0	2	–	–	0	2
Switzerland	21	31	40.4%	27	–	–	–	–	1	1	1	2	1	0	2	2	1	0	0	2
Turkey	14	27	34.1%	23	–	–	0	3	0	2	0	1	–	–	–	–	–	–	1	0
USSR	49	23	68.1%	28	–	–	2	4	0	2	1	0	1	0	3	0	1	0	3	0
Wales	22	30	42.3%	26	–	–	0	1	0	2	0	1	1	0	0	1	2	1	0	6
West Germany	72	31	69.9%	30	–	–	4	0	3	3	3	0	–	–	4	1	4	0	1	0
Yugoslavia	32	30	51.6%	24	–	–	1	1	2	2	0	1	–	–	3	1	2	0	1	1
					Elim	Qual	Elim	Qual	Elim	Qual	Elim	Qual	Elim	Qual	Elim	Qual	Elim	Qual	Elim	Qual
Total	**926**	**926**	**50.0%**		**13**	**5**	**31**	**30**	**27**	**52**	**28**	**24**	**27**	**2**	**31**	**31**	**30**	**13**	**29**	**44**

1960-61 to 1990-91

	England		Finland		France		Greece		Hungary		Iceland		Italy		Luxembourg		Malta		Netherlands	
	Q	E	Q	E	Q	E	Q	E	Q	E	Q	E	Q	E	Q	E	Q	E	Q	E
Albania	–	–	0	2	–	–	0	1	–	–	–	–	0	1	–	–	1	0	–	–
Austria	0	3	–	–	–	–	2	0	3	0	1	0	0	4	–	–	–	–	0	2
Belgium	2	5	–	–	2	0	–	–	2	0	1	0	3	4	2	0	1	0	3	0
Bulgaria	0	2	2	0	1	1	1	1	0	1	1	0	0	3	2	0	–	–	1	2
Cyprus	–	–	–	–	–	–	1	2	0	2	–	–	0	1	–	–	–	–	–	–
Czechoslovakia	0	4	2	0	1	1	1	0	1	2	–	–	1	3	1	0	1	0	0	1
Denmark	0	1	–	–	0	2	1	0	–	–	1	0	–	–	2	0	1	0	0	5
East Germany	0	3	2	0	2	2	1	0	2	1	2	0	4	1	2	0	–	–	1	2
England	2	2	1	0	3	1	2	0	4	1	–	–	2	2	1	0	–	–	5	0
Finland	0	1	–	–	0	3	–	–	0	2	–	–	0	2	0	1	1	0	0	1
France	1	3	3	0	–	–	1	1	–	–	–	–	0	2	1	0	–	–	1	2
Greece	0	2	–	–	1	1	–	–	1	1	1	0	0	4	1	0	–	–	1	1
Hungary	1	4	2	0	–	–	1	1	–	–	–	–	1	4	–	–	3	0	1	1
Iceland	–	–	–	–	–	–	0	1	–	–	–	–	–	–	–	–	0	1	–	–
Italy	2	2	2	0	2	0	4	0	4	1	–	–	–	–	1	0	1	0	3	0
Luxembourg	0	1	1	0	0	1	0	1	–	–	–	–	0	1	–	–	0	1	–	–
Malta	–	–	0	1	–	–	–	–	0	3	1	0	0	1	1	0	–	–	0	2
Netherlands	0	5	1	0	2	1	1	1	1	1	–	–	0	3	–	–	2	0	–	–
Northern Ireland	0	4	0	1	0	2	–	–	–	–	0	1	0	2	1	0	0	1	0	1
Norway	0	1	0	1	0	1	–	–	0	1	2	0	0	3	1	0	1	0	0	2
Poland	0	3	1	0	–	–	1	3	0	1	4	0	3	3	1	0	1	0	0	2
Portugal	3	1	1	0	2	3	1	0	1	1	–	–	3	2	–	–	1	0	0	2
Rep. of Ireland	0	2	0	1	0	2	–	–	–	–	1	0	0	1	1	0	1	0	0	2
Romania	0	3	1	0	1	3	1	0	–	–	–	–	0	2	–	–	1	0	0	1
Scotland	2	2	–	–	1	0	1	0	3	3	3	0	1	1	–	–	2	0	1	1
Spain	5	7	–	–	4	2	–	–	1	0	4	0	6	0	1	0	4	0	2	1
Sweden	1	1	1	1	–	–	1	0	0	3	1	1	0	1	2	0	1	0	0	1
Switzerland	0	2	1	0	1	0	1	1	1	0	1	0	0	2	1	0	–	–	3	1
Turkey	0	2	2	0	–	–	–	–	1	2	–	–	0	2	2	0	–	–	0	1
USSR	1	1	2	0	1	2	3	0	1	1	–	–	0	1	–	–	2	0	4	1
Wales	0	1	–	–	1	1	0	1	0	1	–	–	0	3	–	–	3	0	1	0
West Germany	4	5	1	0	4	1	2	0	1	1	2	0	2	5	3	0	2	0	1	1
Yugoslavia	0	3	–	–	1	1	2	0	3	1	–	–	1	4	3	0	–	–	2	0
	Elim	**Qual**	**Elim**	**Qual**	**Elim**	**Qual**	**Elim**	**Qual**	**Elim**	**Qual**	**Elim**	**Qual**	**Elim**	**Qual**	**Elim**	**Qual**	**Elim**	**Qual**	**Elim**	**Qual**
Total	**24**	**76**	**26**	**7**	**30**	**31**	**29**	**14**	**30**	**30**	**26**	**2**	**27**	**68**	**30**	**1**	**30**	**3**	**30**	**36**

	N. Ireland		Norway		Poland		Portugal		Rep. of Ire.		Romania		Scotland		Spain		Sweden		Switzerland	
	Q	E	Q	E	Q	E	Q	E	Q	E	Q	E	Q	E	Q	E	Q	E	Q	E
Albania	–	–	–	–	0	1	–	–	–	–	1	1	0	2	–	–	1	3	–	–
Austria	–	–	–	–	1	1	0	1	–	–	0	3	1	0	1	4	–	–	–	–
Belgium	2	0	1	0	–	–	3	0	–	–	3	0	2	3	1	3	–	–	1	1
Bulgaria	–	–	–	–	2	1	1	0	3	0	1	0	0	2	1	5	–	–	2	1
Cyprus	–	–	1	0	–	–	0	1	0	2	0	1	0	2	0	1	0	2	0	1
Czechoslovakia	–	–	–	–	–	–	3	1	3	0	–	–	2	1	1	1	2	0	2	2
Denmark	1	0	–	–	0	1	1	2	2	1	–	–	0	1	0	2	–	–	0	1
East Germany	2	0	–	–	1	0	4	2	–	–	1	0	1	1	1	4	2	0	2	0
England	4	0	1	0	3	0	1	3	2	0	3	0	2	2	7	5	1	1	2	0
Finland	1	0	1	0	0	1	0	1	1	0	0	1	–	–	–	–	1	1	0	1
France	2	0	1	0	–	–	3	2	2	0	3	1	0	1	2	4	–	–	0	1
Greece	–	–	–	–	3	1	0	1	–	–	0	1	0	1	–	–	0	1	1	1
Hungary	–	–	1	0	1	0	1	1	–	–	–	–	3	3	0	1	3	0	0	1
Iceland	1	0	0	2	0	4	–	–	0	1	–	–	0	3	0	4	1	1	0	1
Italy	2	0	3	0	3	3	2	3	1	0	2	0	1	1	0	6	1	0	2	0
Luxembourg	0	1	0	1	0	1	–	–	0	1	–	–	–	–	0	1	0	2	0	1
Malta	1	0	0	1	0	1	0	1	0	1	0	1	0	2	0	4	0	1	–	–
Netherlands	1	0	2	0	2	0	2	0	2	0	1	0	1	1	1	2	1	0	1	3
Northern Ireland	–	–	1	0	–	–	–	–	–	–	1	2	0	1	0	2	0	1	–	–
Norway	0	1	–	–	0	2	0	3	–	–	–	–	0	2	0	2	1	0	1	0
Poland	–	–	2	0	–	–	–	–	1	0	–	–	2	1	0	3	0	1	1	1
Portugal	–	–	3	0	–	–	–	–	–	–	2	0	2	3	–	–	2	0	3	0
Rep. of Ireland	–	–	–	–	0	1	–	–	–	–	–	–	0	1	0	1	0	1	–	–
Romania	2	1	–	–	–	–	0	2	–	–	–	–	2	2	1	3	1	0	1	0
Scotland	1	0	2	0	1	2	3	2	1	0	2	2	–	–	3	3	–	–	3	1
Spain	2	0	2	0	3	0	–	–	1	0	3	1	3	3	1	1	1	0	2	0
Sweden	1	0	0	1	1	0	0	2	1	0	0	1	–	–	0	1	–	–	1	2
Switzerland	–	–	0	1	1	1	0	3	–	–	0	1	1	3	0	2	2	1	–	–
Turkey	1	0	0	1	1	2	0	1	2	0	1	0	1	1	0	1	1	0	0	1
USSR	1	0	1	0	1	0	1	1	2	0	2	1	0	2	4	3	–	–	1	1
Wales	1	0	3	0	1	0	3	2	2	0	–	–	–	–	0	4	1	0	2	0
West Germany	2	0	1	0	2	0	2	2	3	0	2	0	4	5	5	5	1	0	2	0
Yugoslavia	1	0	2	0	–	–	0	3	1	0	1	1	2	2	1	4	–	–	1	0
	Elim	**Qual**	**Elim**	**Qual**	**Elim**	**Qual**	**Elim**	**Qual**	**Elim**	**Qual**	**Elim**	**Qual**	**Elim**	**Qual**	**Elim**	**Qual**	**Elim**	**Qual**	**Elim**	**Qual**
Total	**29**	**3**	**28**	**7**	**27**	**23**	**30**	**40**	**30**	**6**	**29**	**18**	**30**	**52**	**30**	**82**	**23**	**16**	**31**	**21**

1960-61 to 1990-91

	Turkey		USSR		Wales		W. Germany		Yugoslavia	
	Q	E	Q	E	Q	E	Q	E	Q	E
Albania	–	–	–	–	–	–	–	–	–	–
Austria	3	0	4	2	1	0	0	4	1	1
Belgium	2	0	2	0	2	0	3	3	2	2
Bulgaria	1	0	0	1	1	0	0	3	1	0
Cyprus	–	–	0	1	0	1	–	–	–	–
Czechoslovakia	–	–	0	3	1	0	1	4	1	3
Denmark	–	–	0	1	1	2	0	4	0	2
East Germany	0	1	0	3	6	0	0	1	1	1
England	2	0	1	1	1	0	5	4	3	0
Finland	0	2	0	2	–	–	0	1	–	–
France	–	–	2	1	1	1	1	4	1	1
Greece	–	–	0	3	1	0	0	2	0	2
Hungary	2	1	1	1	1	0	1	1	1	3
Iceland	–	–	–	–	–	–	0	2	–	–
Italy	2	0	1	0	3	0	5	2	4	1
Luxembourg	0	2	–	–	–	–	0	3	0	3
Malta	–	–	0	2	0	3	0	2	–	–
Netherlands	1	0	1	4	0	1	1	1	0	2
Northern Ireland	0	1	0	1	0	1	0	2	0	1
Norway	1	0	0	1	0	3	0	1	0	2
Poland	2	1	0	1	0	1	0	2	–	–
Portugal	1	0	1	1	2	3	2	2	3	0
Rep. of Ireland	0	2	0	2	0	2	0	3	0	1
Romania	0	1	1	2	–	–	0	2	1	1
Scotland	1	1	2	0	–	–	5	4	2	2
Spain	1	0	3	4	4	0	5	5	4	1
Sweden	0	1	–	–	0	1	0	1	–	–
Switzerland	1	0	1	1	0	2	0	2	0	1
Turkey	–	–	0	4	1	0	0	3	–	–
USSR	4	0	–	–	1	1	2	2	4	0
Wales	0	1	1	1	–	–	0	1	0	2
West Germany	3	0	2	2	1	0	–	–	1	0
Yugoslavia	–	–	0	4	2	0	0	1	–	–
	Elim	**Qual**	**Elim**	**Qual**	**Elim**	**Qual**	**Elim**	**Qual**	**Elim**	**Qual**
Total	**27**	**14**	**23**	**49**	**30**	**22**	**31**	**72**	**30**	**32**

Above: Juventus' Michel Platini is held by FC Porto's Jaime Pacheco during the 1983-84 final in Basle.

Second-leg Outcomes 1960-61 to 1990-91

First-leg: 0-0

Second-leg	1-0	2-0	3-0	4-0	5-0	2-1	3-1	4-1	5-1	3-2	4-2	5-2	4-3
	5	3	0	0	0	1	0	0	0	0	0	1	0
Second-leg	5-3	5-4	0-0	1-1	2-2	3-3	4-4	5-5	0-1	0-2	0-3	0-4	0-5
	0	0	1	11	3	0	0	0	16	16	6	3	3
Second-leg	1-2	1-3	1-4	1-5	2-3	2-4	2-5	3-4	3-5	4-5	5>	<5	
	5	4	1	0	1	0	1	0	0	0	0	2	

First-leg: 1-0

Second-leg	1-0	2-0	3-0	4-0	5-0	2-1	3-1	4-1	5-1	3-2	4-2	5-2	4-3
	9	5	0	1	0	6	0	0	0	2	0	1	0
Second-leg	5-3	5-4	0-0	1-1	2-2	3-3	4-4	5-5	0-1	0-2	0-3	0-4	0-5
	0	0	10	8	4	0	0	0	7	20	5	4	1
Second-leg	1-2	1-3	1-4	1-5	2-3	2-4	2-5	3-4	3-5	4-5	5>	<5	
	6	4	0	2	1	2	0	2	0	0	0	5	

First-leg: 2-0

Second-leg	1-0	2-0	3-0	4-0	5-0	2-1	3-1	4-1	5-1	3-2	4-2	5-2	4-3
	6	3	0	1	0	5	1	1	0	1	0	0	0
Second-leg	5-3	5-4	0-0	1-1	2-2	3-3	4-4	5-5	0-1	0-2	0-3	0-4	0-5
	1	0	7	7	5	2	0	0	10	8	8	4	3
Second-leg	1-2	1-3	1-4	1-5	2-3	2-4	2-5	3-4	3-5	4-5	5>	<5	
	9	5	5	1	2	0	0	1	0	0	0	2	

First-leg: 3-0

Second-leg	1-0	2-0	3-0	4-0	5-0	2-1	3-1	4-1	5-1	3-2	4-2	5-2	4-3
	2	4	4	0	0	0	2	0	0	1	0	0	0
Second-leg	5-3	5-4	0-0	1-1	2-2	3-3	4-4	5-5	0-1	0-2	0-3	0-4	0-5
	0	0	1	6	4	0	0	0	7	8	1	3	1
Second-leg	1-2	1-3	1-4	1-5	2-3	2-4	2-5	3-4	3-5	4-5	5>	<5	
	7	0	0	0	1	2	0	0	0	0	0	0	

First-leg: 1-1

Second-leg	1-0	2-0	3-0	4-0	5-0	2-1	3-1	4-1	5-1	3-2	4-2	5-2	4-3
	4	1	1	0	0	3	2	0	0	1	0	0	0
Second-leg	5-3	5-4	0-0	1-1	2-2	3-3	4-4	5-5	0-1	0-2	0-3	0-4	0-5
	0	0	8	9	2	0	0	0	17	14	2	6	1
Second-leg	1-2	1-3	1-4	1-5	2-3	2-4	2-5	3-4	3-5	4-5	5>	<5	
	9	7	3	1	2	0	0	0	1	0	0	7	

First-leg: 2-1

Second-leg	1-0	2-0	3-0	4-0	5-0	2-1	3-1	4-1	5-1	3-2	4-2	5-2	4-3
	2	1	1	0	0	2	1	1	0	1	0	0	0
Second-leg	5-3	5-4	0-0	1-1	2-2	3-3	4-4	5-5	0-1	0-2	0-3	0-4	0-5
	0	0	3	4	3	0	0	0	11	9	6	2	0
Second-leg	1-2	1-3	1-4	1-5	2-3	2-4	2-5	3-4	3-5	4-5	5>	<5	
	4	3	2	0	1	1	0	0	0	1	0	2	

First-leg: 3-1

Second-leg	1-0	2-0	3-0	4-0	5-0	2-1	3-1	4-1	5-1	3-2	4-2	5-2	4-3
	3	1	1	0	0	1	2	0	0	0	0	0	0
Second-leg	5-3	5-4	0-0	1-1	2-2	3-3	4-4	5-5	0-1	0-2	0-3	0-4	0-5
	0	0	2	2	1	0	0	0	5	3	1	1	0
Second-leg	1-2	1-3	1-4	1-5	2-3	2-4	2-5	3-4	3-5	4-5	5>	<5	
	2	1	1	1	0	1	0	0	0	0	1	0	

First-leg: 4-1

Second-leg	1-0	2-0	3-0	4-0	5-0	2-1	3-1	4-1	5-1	3-2	4-2	5-2	4-3
	0	1	0	1	0	1	0	1	0	0	0	0	0
Second-leg	5-3	5-4	0-0	1-1	2-2	3-3	4-4	5-5	0-1	0-2	0-3	0-4	0-5
	0	0	0	1	0	0	0	0	3	2	0	0	1
Second-leg	1-2	1-3	1-4	1-5	2-3	2-4	2-5	3-4	3-5	4-5	5>	<5	
	1	0	0	0	0	0	0	0	0	0	0	0	

First-leg: 5-1

Second-leg	1-0	2-0	3-0	4-0	5-0	2-1	3-1	4-1	5-1	3-2	4-2	5-2	4-3
	1	0	0	0	0	1	0	0	1	0	0	0	0
Second-leg	5-3	5-4	0-0	1-1	2-2	3-3	4-4	5-5	0-1	0-2	0-3	0-4	0-5
	0	0	1	2	0	0	0	0	2	0	0	0	0
Second-leg	1-2	1-3	1-4	1-5	2-3	2-4	2-5	3-4	3-5	4-5	5>	<5	
	1	0	0	0	1	0	0	0	0	0	1	0	

First-leg: 2-2

Second-leg	1-0	2-0	3-0	4-0	5-0	2-1	3-1	4-1	5-1	3-2	4-2	5-2	4-3
	1	0	0	0	0	0	0	0	0	0	0	0	0
Second-leg	5-3	5-4	0-0	1-1	2-2	3-3	4-4	5-5	0-1	0-2	0-3	0-4	0-5
	0	0	1	1	0	0	0	0	2	2	3	3	1
Second-leg	1-2	1-3	1-4	1-5	2-3	2-4	2-5	3-4	3-5	4-5	5>	<5	
	2	3	3	1	1	0	0	0	0	0	0	1	

First-leg: 3-2

Second-leg	1-0	2-0	3-0	4-0	5-0	2-1	3-1	4-1	5-1	3-2	4-2	5-2	4-3
	0	0	0	0	0	3	1	0	0	0	0	0	0
Second-leg	5-3	5-4	0-0	1-1	2-2	3-3	4-4	5-5	0-1	0-2	0-3	0-4	0-5
	0	0	0	1	1	1	0	0	1	3	1	1	0
Second-leg	1-2	1-3	1-4	1-5	2-3	2-4	2-5	3-4	3-5	4-5	5>	<5	
	3	1	0	1	0	0	1	1	0	0	0	0	

First-leg: 4-2

Second-leg	1-0	2-0	3-0	4-0	5-0	2-1	3-1	4-1	5-1	3-2	4-2	5-2	4-3
	0	0	0	0	0	1	1	1	0	0	0	0	0
Second-leg	5-3	5-4	0-0	1-1	2-2	3-3	4-4	5-5	0-1	0-2	0-3	0-4	0-5
	0	0	1	0	0	0	0	0	0	1	1	0	0
Second-leg	1-2	1-3	1-4	1-5	2-3	2-4	2-5	3-4	3-5	4-5	5>	<5	
	1	1	0	0	0	0	0	0	0	0	0	0	

First-leg: 5-2

Second-leg	1-0	2-0	3-0	4-0	5-0	2-1	3-1	4-1	5-1	3-2	4-2	5-2	4-3
	0	0	0	0	0	0	0	0	0	1	0	0	0
Second-leg	5-3	5-4	0-0	1-1	2-2	3-3	4-4	5-5	0-1	0-2	0-3	0-4	0-5
	0	0	0	0	0	0	0	0	0	0	0	0	0
Second-leg	1-2	1-3	1-4	1-5	2-3	2-4	2-5	3-4	3-5	4-5	5>	<5	
	0	0	0	0	0	0	0	0	0	0	0	0	

First-leg: 6-2

Second-leg	1-0	2-0	3-0	4-0	5-0	2-1	3-1	4-1	5-1	3-2	4-2	5-2	4-3
	0	0	0	0	0	0	0	0	0	0	0	0	0
Second-leg	5-3	5-4	0-0	1-1	2-2	3-3	4-4	5-5	0-1	0-2	0-3	0-4	0-5
	0	0	0	1	0	0	0	0	0	0	0	0	1
Second-leg	1-2	1-3	1-4	1-5	2-3	2-4	2-5	3-4	3-5	4-5	5>	<5	
	0	0	0	0	0	0	0	0	0	0	0	0	

First-leg: 3-3

Second-leg	1-0	2-0	3-0	4-0	5-0	2-1	3-1	4-1	5-1	3-2	4-2	5-2	4-3
	0	0	0	0	0	0	0	0	0	0	0	0	0
Second-leg	5-3	5-4	0-0	1-1	2-2	3-3	4-4	5-5	0-1	0-2	0-3	0-4	0-5
	0	0	0	0	0	0	0	0	0	0	1	1	0
Second-leg	1-2	1-3	1-4	1-5	2-3	2-4	2-5	3-4	3-5	4-5	5>	<5	
	0	0	0	0	0	0	0	0	0	0	0	0	

First-leg: 4-3

Second-leg	1-0	2-0	3-0	4-0	5-0	2-1	3-1	4-1	5-1	3-2	4-2	5-2	4-3
	1	0	0	0	0	0	0	0	0	0	0	0	0
Second-leg	5-3	5-4	0-0	1-1	2-2	3-3	4-4	5-5	0-1	0-2	0-3	0-4	0-5
	0	0	0	0	0	1	0	0	0	0	0	0	0
Second-leg	1-2	1-3	1-4	1-5	2-3	2-4	2-5	3-4	3-5	4-5	5>	<5	
	0	1	0	0	0	0	0	0	0	0	0	0	

First-leg: 5-3

Second-leg	1-0	2-0	3-0	4-0	5-0	2-1	3-1	4-1	5-1	3-2	4-2	5-2	4-3
	0	1	0	0	0	0	0	0	0	0	0	0	0
Second-leg	5-3	5-4	0-0	1-1	2-2	3-3	4-4	5-5	0-1	0-2	0-3	0-4	0-5
	0	0	0	0	0	0	0	0	0	0	0	0	0
Second-leg	1-2	1-3	1-4	1-5	2-3	2-4	2-5	3-4	3-5	4-5	5>	<5	
	0	0	0	0	0	0	0	0	0	0	0	0	

First-leg: 0-1

Second-leg	1-0	2-0	3-0	4-0	5-0	2-1	3-1	4-1	5-1	3-2	4-2	5-2	4-3
	1	1	1	0	0	0	0	0	0	0	0	0	0
Second-leg	5-3	5-4	0-0	1-1	2-2	3-3	4-4	5-5	0-1	0-2	0-3	0-4	0-5
	0	0	1	5	1	1	0	0	10	8	8	3	3
Second-leg	1-2	1-3	1-4	1-5	2-3	2-4	2-5	3-4	3-5	4-5	5>	<5	
	4	1	0	0	1	0	0	1	0	0	0	5	

First-leg: 0-2

Second-leg	1-0	2-0	3-0	4-0	5-0	2-1	3-1	4-1	5-1	3-2	4-2	5-2	4-3
	0	0	0	0	0	1	0	0	0	1	0	0	0
Second-leg	5-3	5-4	0-0	1-1	2-2	3-3	4-4	5-5	0-1	0-2	0-3	0-4	0-5
	0	0	1	2	1	0	0	0	5	1	2	3	4
Second-leg	1-2	1-3	1-4	1-5	2-3	2-4	2-5	3-4	3-5	4-5	5>	<5	
	3	1	1	0	0	0	0	1	0	0	0	6	

First-leg: 1-2

Second-leg	1-0	2-0	3-0	4-0	5-0	2-1	3-1	4-1	5-1	3-2	4-2	5-2	4-3
	0	0	0	0	0	0	0	0	0	0	0	0	0
Second-leg	5-3	5-4	0-0	1-1	2-2	3-3	4-4	5-5	0-1	0-2	0-3	0-4	0-5
	0	0	1	6	1	0	0	0	6	3	1	2	0
Second-leg	1-2	1-3	1-4	1-5	2-3	2-4	2-5	3-4	3-5	4-5	5>	<5	
	2	2	0	0	0	1	0	1	0	0	0	0	

First-leg: 1-3

Second-leg	1-0	2-0	3-0	4-0	5-0	2-1	3-1	4-1	5-1	3-2	4-2	5-2	4-3
	0	0	0	0	0	0	0	0	0	0	0	0	0
Second-leg	5-3	5-4	0-0	1-1	2-2	3-3	4-4	5-5	0-1	0-2	0-3	0-4	0-5
	0	0	0	2	0	0	0	0	2	2	3	2	1
Second-leg	1-2	1-3	1-4	1-5	2-3	2-4	2-5	3-4	3-5	4-5	5>	<5	
	0	2	0	0	0	1	0	0	0	0	0	1	

First-leg: 2-4

Second-leg	1-0	2-0	3-0	4-0	5-0	2-1	3-1	4-1	5-1	3-2	4-2	5-2	4-3
	1	0	0	0	0	0	0	1	0	0	0	0	0
Second-leg	5-3	5-4	0-0	1-1	2-2	3-3	4-4	5-5	0-1	0-2	0-3	0-4	0-5
	0	0	0	0	0	0	0	0	0	0	0	0	0
Second-leg	1-2	1-3	1-4	1-5	2-3	2-4	2-5	3-4	3-5	4-5	5>	<5	
	1	1	0	0	0	0	0	0	0	0	0	0	

First-leg: 3-4

Second-leg	1-0	2-0	3-0	4-0	5-0	2-1	3-1	4-1	5-1	3-2	4-2	5-2	4-3
	0	0	0	0	0	1	0	0	0	0	0	0	0
Second-leg	5-3	5-4	0-0	1-1	2-2	3-3	4-4	5-5	0-1	0-2	0-3	0-4	0-5
	0	0	0	2	0	0	0	0	0	0	0	0	0
Second-leg	1-2	1-3	1-4	1-5	2-3	2-4	2-5	3-4	3-5	4-5	5>	<5	
	0	0	0	0	0	0	0	0	0	0	0	0	

Qualification/Eliminations after First-leg Score

First-leg Score	No. Matches	Qualifications No.	Qualifications %	Eliminations No.	Eliminations %
0-0	83	23	27.71%	60	72.29%
1-0	105	57	54.29%	48	45.71%
2-0	98	68	69.39%	30	30.61%
3-0	54	49	90.74%	5	9.26%
1-1	101	19	18.81%	82	81.19%
2-1	61	25	40.98%	36	59.02%
3-1	30	22	73.33%	8	26.67%
4-1	12	11	91.67%	1	8.33%
5-1	11	11	100.00%	0	0.00%
2-2	25	1	4.00%	24	96.00%
3-2	20	8	40.00%	12	60.00%
4-2	8	5	62.50%	3	37.50%
5-2	1	1	100.00%	0	0.00%
6-2	2	1	50.00%	1	50.00%
3-3	2	0	0.00%	2	100.00%
4-3	3	2	66.67%	1	33.33%
5-3	1	1	100.00%	0	0.00%
0-1	55	2	3.64%	53	96.36%
0-2	33	0	0.00%	33	100.00%
1-2	26	0	0.00%	26	100.00%
1-3	16	0	0.00%	16	100.00%
2-4	4	1	25.00%	3	75.00%
3-4	3	0	0.00%	3	100.00%

Home Match Statistics

	1-0	2-0	3-0	4-0	5-0	2 -1	3-1	4-1	5-1	3-2	4-2	5-2	4-3
Number	219	208	110	70	38	128	71	30	22	32	18	4	10
	5-3	5-4	0-0	1-1	2-2	3-3	4-4	5-5	0-1	0-2	0-3	0-4	0-5
Number	2	1	129	180	55	7	1	0	102	58	29	11	4
	1-2	1-3	1-4	1-5	2-3	2-4	2-5	3-4	3-5	4-5	5>	<5	
Number	59	28	23	9	23	5	5	3	2	0	79	17	
	1-0	2-0	3-0	4-0	5-0	2-1	3-1	4-1	5-1	3-2	4-2	5-2	4-3
Percent	12	12	6	4	2	7	4	2	1	2	1	0	1
	5-3	5-4	0-0	1-1	2-2	3-3	4-4	5-5	0-1	0-2	0-3	0-4	0-5
Percent	0	0	7	10	3	0	0	0	6	3	2	1	0
	1-2	1-3	1-4	1-5	2-3	2-4	2-5	3-4	3-5	4-5	5>	<5	
Percent	3	2	1	1	1	0	0	0	0	0	4	1	

Number of matches 1792

Roll of Honour – the Winners and the Runners-up

The Winners

1.	England	6
2.	Italy	5
3.	Spain	5
4.	West Germany	3
5.	USSR	3
6.	Belgium	3
7.	Scotland	2
8.	Portugal	1
9.	Czechoslovakia	1
10.	East Germany	1
11.	Netherlands	1
	Total	**31**

The Runners-up

1.	Spain	6
2.	England	4
3.	Italy	3
4.	West Germany	3
5.	Belgium	3
6.	Scotland	2
7.	Hungary	2
8.	Austria	2
9.	East Germany	2
10.	Poland	1
11.	USSR	1
12.	Portugal	1
13.	Netherlands	1
	Total	**31**

No. of Appearances in the Final

1.	Spain	11
2.	England	10
3.	Italy	9
4.	West Germany	6
5.	Belgium	5
6.	Scotland	4
7.	USSR	4
8.	East Germany	3
9.	Portugal	2
10.	Hungary	2
11.	Austria	2
12.	Netherlands	2
13.	Czechoslovakia	1
14.	Poland	1
	Total	**62**

The Winners – Classification by Country

Country	Appearances	Winning Teams
Albania	–	–
Austria	–	–
Belgium	3	Anderlecht (1976, 1978), KV Mechelen (1988)
Bulgaria	–	–
Cyprus	–	–
Czechoslovakia	1	Slovan Bratislava (1969)
Denmark	–	–
East Germany	1	Magdeburg (1974)
England	6	Tottenham Hotspur (1963), West Ham United (1965), Manchester City (1970), Chelsea (1971), Everton (1985), Manchester United (1991)
Finland	–	–
France	–	–
Greece	–	–
Hungary	–	–
Iceland	–	–
Italy	5	Fiorentina (1961), AC Milan (1968, 1973), Juventus (1984), Sampdoria (1990)
Luxembourg	–	–
Malta	–	–
Netherlands	1	Ajax (1987)
Northern Ireland	–	–
Norway	–	–
Poland	–	–
Portugal	1	Sporting Lisbon (1964)
Republic of Ireland	–	–
Romania	–	–
Scotland	2	Rangers (1972), Aberdeen (1983)
Spain	5	Atlético Madrid (1962), Barcelona (1979, 1982, 1989), Valencia (1980)
Sweden	–	–
Switzerland	–	–
Turkey	–	–
USSR	3	Dinamo Kiev (1975, 1986), Dinamo Tbilisi (1981)
Wales	–	–
West Germany	3	Borussia Dortmund (1966), Bayern Munich (1967), Hamburg (1977)
Yugoslavia	–	–

The Winners – classification by Results

Pos'n	Club	Cnty	Wins	Years
1	Barcelona	Esp	3	1979, 1982, 1989
2	AC Milan	Ita	2	1968, 1973
3	Dinamo Kiev	URS	2	1975, 1986
4	Anderlecht	Bel	2	1976, 1978
5	Fiorentina	Ita	1	1961
6	Atlético Madrid	Esp	1	1962
7	Tottenham Hotspur	Eng	1	1963
8	Sporting Lisbon	Por	1	1964
9	West Ham United	Eng	1	1965
10	Borussia Dortmund	FRG	1	1966
11	Bayern Munich	FRG	1	1967
12	Slovan Bratislava	Tch	1	1969
13	Manchester City	Eng	1	1970
14	Chelsea	Eng	1	1971
15	Rangers	Sco	1	1972
16	Magdeburg	GDR	1	1974
17	Hamburg	FRG	1	1977
18	Valencia	Esp	1	1980
19	Dinamo Tbilisi	URS	1	1981
20	Aberdeen	Sco	1	1983
21	Juventus	Ita	1	1984
22	Everton	Eng	1	1985
23	Ajax	Ned	1	1987
24	KV Mechelen	Bel	1	1988
25	Sampdoria	Ita	1	1990
26	Manchester United	Eng	1	1991

The Runners-up – Classification by Country

Country	Appearances	Winning Teams
Albania	–	–
Austria	2	Austria Vienna (1978), Rapid Vienna (1985)
Belgium	3	Anderlecht (1977, 1990), Standard Liège (1982)
Bulgaria	–	–
Cyprus	–	–
Czechoslovakia	–	–
Denmark	–	–
East Germany	2	Carl Zeiss Jena (1981), Lokomotive Leipzig (1987)
England	4	Liverpool (1966), Leeds United (1973), West Ham United (1976), Arsenal (1980)
Finland	–	–
France	–	–
Greece	–	–
Hungary	2	MTK-VM (1964), Ferencváros (1975)
Iceland	–	–
Italy	3	Fiorentina (1962), AC Milan (1974), Sampdoria (1989)
Luxembourg	–	–
Malta	–	–
Netherlands	1	Ajax (1988)
Northern Ireland	–	–
Norway	–	–
Poland	1	Górnik Zabrze (1970)
Portugal	1	FC Porto (1984)

Republic of Ireland	–	–
Romania	–	–
Scotland	2	Rangers (1961, 1967)
Spain	5	Atlético Madrid (1963, 1986), Barcelona (1969, 1991), Real Madrid (1971, 1983)
Sweden	–	–
Switzerland	–	–
Turkey	–	–
USSR	1	Dinamo Moscow (1972)
Wales	–	–
West Germany	3	1860 Munich (1965), Hamburg (1968), Fortuna Düsseldorf (1979)
Yugoslavia	–	–

The European Cup Winners' Cup Finalists

Pos'n	Club	Cnty	Appearances	Wins
1	Barcelona	Esp	5	3
2	Anderlecht	Bel	4	2
3	AC Milan	Ita	3	2
4	Atlético Madrid	Esp	3	1
5	Rangers	Sco	3	1
6	Dinamo Kiev	URS	2	2
7	Fiorentina	Ita	2	1
8	West Ham United	Eng	2	1
9	Hamburg	Eng	2	1
10	Ajax	Ned	2	1
11	Sampdoria	Ita	2	1
12	Real Madrid	Esp	2	0
13	Tottenham Hotspur	Eng	1	1
14	Sporting Lisbon	Por	1	1
15	Borussia Dortmund	FRG	1	1
16	Bayern Munich	FRG	1	1
17	Slovan Bratislava	Tch	1	1
18	Manchester City	Eng	1	1
19	Chelsea	Eng	1	1
20	Magdeburg	GDR	1	1
21	Valencia	Esp	1	1
22	Dinamo Tbilisi	URS	1	1
23	Aberdeen	Sco	1	1
24	Juventus	Ita	1	1
25	Everton	Eng	1	1
26	KV Mechelen	Bel	1	1
27	Manchester United	Eng	1	1
28	MTK-VM	Hun	1	0
29	1860 Munich	FRG	1	0
30	Liverpool	Eng	1	0
31	Górnik Zabrze	Pol	1	0
32	Dinamo Moscow	URS	1	0
33	Leeds United	Eng	1	0
34	Ferencváros	Hun	1	0
35	Austria Vienna	Aut	1	0
36	Fortuna Düsseldorf	FRG	1	0
37	Arsenal	Eng	1	0
38	Carl Zeiss Jena	GDR	1	0
39	Standard Liège	Bel	1	0
40	FC Porto	Por	1	0
41	Rapid Vienna	Aut	1	0
41	Lokomotive Leipzig	GDR	1	0
	Total		**62**	**31**

Above:
Dossena of Sampdoria is stopped by Barcelona striker Julio Salinas (left) during the 1988-89 final in Berne. Barcelona won 2-0.

Left:
Real Madrid captain Santillana uses an over head kick to beat Aberdeen's Willie Miller during extra time. The Dons won 2-1.

The Finals

1956-58	Chelsea	2	Barcelona	8
1958-60	Barcelona	5	Birmingham City	2
1960-61	Roma	4	Birmingham City	2
1961-62	Valencia	7	Barcelona	3
1962-63	Valencia	4	Dinamo Zagreb	1
1963-64	Real Zaragoza	2	Valencia	1
1964-65	Juventus	0	Ferencváros	1
1965-66	Barcelona	4	Real Zaragoza	3
1966-67	Dinamo Zagreb	2	Leeds United	0
1967-68	Leeds United	1	Ferencváros	0
1968-69	Newcastle United	6	Ujpesti Dózsa	2
1969-70	Anderlecht	3	Arsenal	4
1970-71	Leeds United‡	3	Juventus	3
1971-72	Wolverhampton Wanderers	2	Tottenham Hotspur	3
1972-73	Liverpool	3	Borussia Mönchengladbach	2
1973-74	Tottenham Hotspur	2	Feyenoord	4
1974-75	Borussia Mönchengladbach	5	Twente Enschede	1
1975-76	Liverpool	4	Club Bruges	3
1976-77	Juventus‡	2	Athletic Bilbao	2
1977-78	Bastia	0	PSV Eindhoven	3
1978-79	Red Star Belgrade	1	Borussia Mönchengladbach	2
1979-80	Borussia Mönchengladbach	3	Eintracht Frankfurt‡	3
1980-81	Ipswich Town	5	AZ'67 Alkmaar	4
1981-82	IFK Gothenburg	4	Hamburg	0
1982-83	Anderlecht	2	Benfica	1
1983-84	Anderlecht	2	Tottenham Hotspur†	2
1984-85	Videoton	1	Real Madrid	3
1985-86	Real Madrid	5	Cologne	3
1986-87	IFK Gothenburg	2	Dundee United	1
1987-88	Español	3	Bayer Leverkusen†	3
1988-89	Napoli	5	VFB Stuttgart	4
1989-90	Juventus	3	Fiorentina	1
1990-91	Inter Milan	2	Roma	1

‡won on away goals rule
† won on penalty kicks
Scores shown are the aggregate scores for the two legs of the final.

National Performances by Index

1956-58 to 1990-91

Pos'n	Cnty	Ave	Pts	P	W	D	L	F	A	Diff	B	No./T
1	England	8.010	737	525	273	121	131	986	548	438	70	92
2	W. Germany	7.414	912	700	359	120	221	1325	878	447	74	123
3	Italy	6.750	729	574	271	129	174	849	599	250	58	108
4	Spain	5.981	634	523	242	94	187	841	671	170	56	106
5	Netherlands	5.292	344	300	135	55	110	553	394	159	19	65
6	Belgium	5.180	430	383	161	80	142	579	492	87	28	83
7	Yugoslavia	5.059	425	383	161	75	147	611	543	68	28	84
8	Scotland	4.898	387	340	150	71	119	520	442	78	16	79
9	Hungary	4.890	269	242	107	34	101	378	346	32	21	55
10	USSR	4.730	246	208	102	39	67	299	238	61	3	52
11	E. Germany	4.360	266	251	104	47	100	358	334	24	11	61
12	Portugal	4.186	314	294	122	59	113	414	371	43	11	75
13	Czechoslovakia	3.655	212	215	84	36	95	327	306	21	8	58
14	Romania	3.535	198	204	79	34	91	255	301	-46	6	56
15	France	3.486	265	272	101	53	118	403	419	-16	10	76
16	Poland	2.844	128	154	43	40	71	179	240	-61	2	45
17	Austria	2.807	160	179	63	30	86	218	287	-69	4	57
18	Sweden	2.769	144	154	52	34	68	206	265	-59	6	52
19	Switzerland	2.636	174	211	64	39	108	292	397	-105	7	66
20	Greece	2.509	128	147	51	23	73	161	269	-108	3	51
21	Bulgaria	2.500	125	148	47	29	72	195	261	-66	2	50
22	Albania	2.333	14	18	5	4	9	10	23	-13	0	6
23	Turkey	1.500	54	90	22	9	59	85	195	-110	1	36
24	Denmark	1.469	72	124	25	19	80	151	296	-145	3	49
25	Norway	1.305	47	82	16	15	51	72	208	-136	0	36
26	Finlande	1.136	25	54	9	7	38	41	132	-91	0	22
27	N. Ireland	1.074	29	60	8	13	39	50	155	-105	0	27
28	Rep. of Ireland	1.068	31	69	8	15	46	50	178	-128	0	29
29	Iceland	0.636	14	48	2	10	36	17	146	-129	0	22
30	Cyprus	0.578	11	40	1	9	30	29	133	-104	0	19
31	Luxembourg	0.392	11	56	3	5	48	17	252	-235	0	28
32	Malta	0.260	6	46	2	2	42	14	166	-152	0	23

1981-82 to 1990-91

Pos'n	Cnty	Ave	Pts	P	W	D	L	F	A	Diff	B	No./T
1	Italy	8.750	280	210	100	54	56	289	196	93	26	32
2	W. Germany	7.853	322	244	124	47	73	413	255	158	27	41
3	Belgium	6.000	186	162	69	35	58	262	207	55	13	31
4	Yugoslavia	5.884	153	130	62	22	46	215	167	48	7	26
5	Scotland	5.576	145	120	56	27	37	176	131	45	6	26
6	Spain	5.529	188	160	73	27	60	211	177	34	15	34
7	England	5.500	99	80	36	20	24	132	88	44	7	18
8	Portugal	5.192	135	114	52	24	38	165	132	33	7	26
9	USSR	4.580	142	126	57	25	44	180	146	34	3	31
10	Austria	4.260	98	92	37	20	35	119	118	1	4	23
11	Sweden	4.000	84	74	29	20	25	102	98	4	6	21
12	France	3.925	106	102	39	26	37	153	138	15	2	27
13	Switzerland	3.900	78	74	28	20	26	93	97	-4	2	20
14	Romania	3.863	85	84	34	14	36	99	114	-15	3	22
15	Czechoslovakia	3.625	87	90	32	19	39	132	123	9	4	24
16	Netherlands	3.407	92	100	36	20	44	144	134	10	0	27
17	E. Germany	3.291	79	82	30	17	35	107	103	4	2	24

18	Hungary	3.000	60	66	22	13	31	73	98	-25	3	20
19	Greece	2.473	47	56	16	14	26	54	81	-27	1	19
20	Albania	2.333	14	18	5	4	9	10	23	-13	0	6
21	Denmark	2.153	28	36	10	6	20	36	63	-27	2	13
22	Poland	2.052	39	56	12	15	29	47	81	-34	0	19
23	Bulgaria	1.722	31	44	10	11	23	57	93	-36	0	18
24	Norway	1.500	15	22	5	5	12	17	44	-27	0	10
25	Finlande	1.416	17	32	6	5	21	19	64	-45	0	12
26	Turkey	1.200	12	22	5	2	15	16	41	-25	0	10
27	Rep. of Ireland	1.000	10	22	3	4	15	17	53	-36	0	10
28	Cyprus	0.900	9	22	1	7	14	20	57	-37	0	10
29	N. Ireland	0.700	7	20	0	7	13	8	40	-32	0	10
30	Iceland	0.700	7	20	1	5	14	8	58	-50	0	10
31	Luxembourg	0.400	4	20	1	2	17	7	92	-85	0	10
32	Malta	0.100	1	20	0	1	19	5	74	-69	0	10

1986-87 to 1990-91

Pos'n	Cnty	Ave	Pts	P	W	D	L	F	A	Diff	B	No./T
1	Italy	10.350	207	146	73	40	33	194	117	77	21	20
2	W. Germany	8.857	186	138	69	31	38	220	134	86	17	21
3	England	6.000	6	4	3	0	1	7	5	2	0	1
4	Spain	5.687	91	76	35	15	26	87	71	16	6	16
5	Scotland	5.642	79	62	31	13	18	77	56	21	4	14
6	Belgium	5.533	83	76	31	16	29	115	90	25	5	15
7	Portugal	4.800	72	64	28	13	23	91	64	27	3	15
8	France	4.666	56	50	22	11	17	70	52	18	1	12
9	Austria	4.230	55	50	22	9	19	62	60	2	2	13
10	Yugoslavia	4.230	55	50	22	11	17	74	57	17	0	13
11	USSR	3.888	70	68	27	15	26	86	82	4	1	18
12	Denmark	3.666	22	22	8	4	10	24	25	-1	2	6
13	E. Germany	3.636	40	42	14	10	18	44	49	-5	2	11
14	Romania	3.500	42	44	18	5	21	47	64	-17	1	12
15	Netherlands	3.083	37	44	14	9	21	54	60	-6	0	12
16	Sweden	3.000	33	34	10	10	14	38	48	-10	3	11
17	Czechoslovakia	2.909	32	38	11	9	18	45	53	-8	1	11
18	Switzerland	2.800	28	30	10	8	12	29	38	-9	0	10
19	Finland	2.428	17	22	6	5	11	15	30	-15	0	7
20	Greece	2.400	24	30	7	9	14	28	42	-14	1	10
21	Hungary	2.400	24	30	9	6	15	29	45	-16	0	10
22	Albania	2.000	8	12	3	2	7	8	18	-10	0	4
23	Turkey	2.000	10	12	4	2	6	12	18	-6	0	5
24	Bulgaria	1.750	14	18	5	4	9	28	38	-10	0	8
25	Poland	1.500	15	26	5	5	16	23	43	-20	0	10
26	Norway	1.200	6	10	2	2	6	6	20	-14	0	5
27	Cyprus	1.000	5	12	1	3	8	10	24	-14	0	5
28	N. Ireland	0.800	4	10	0	4	6	4	14	-10	0	5
29	Iceland	0.800	4	10	0	4	6	6	29	-23	0	5
30	Luxembourg	0.600	3	10	1	1	8	7	42	-35	0	5
31	Rep. of Ireland	0.400	2	10	0	2	8	2	19	-17	0	5
32	Malta	0.000	0	10	0	0	10	2	37	-35	0	5

Summary Totals	**Pts**	**P**	**W**	**D**	**L**	**F**	**A**	**Diff**	**B**	**F/P**
1955-56 to 1990-91	**7541**	**7094**	**2872**	**1350**	**2872**	**10485**	**10485**	**0**	**447**	**2.956**
1981-82 to 1990-91	**2660**	**2520**	**991**	**538**	**991**	**3386**	**3386**	**0**	**140**	**2.687**
1986-87 to 1990-91	**1330**	**1260**	**491**	**278**	**491**	**1544**	**1544**	**0**	**70**	**2.451**

Club Performance by Points

1956-58 to 1990-91

Pos'n	Club	Cnty	Pts	P	W	D	L	F	A	Diff	B	Pts/P	F/P
1	Cologne	FRG	180	134	72	20	42	261	157	104	16	1.343	1.948
2	Barcelona	Esp	164	122	59	27	36	228	144	84	19	1.344	1.869
3	Juventus	Ita	161	104	64	16	24	191	81	104	17	1.548	1.837
4	Inter Milan	Ita	147	115	54	25	36	187	114	73	14	1.278	1.626
5	Bor. Mönchengladbach	FRG	121	74	46	15	13	161	79	82	14	1.635	2.176
6	Valencia	Esp	114	86	42	19	25	160	110	50	11	1.326	1.860
7	Dundee United	Sco	107	86	39	22	25	130	88	42	7	1.244	1.512
8	Leeds United	Eng	98	65	33	20	12	110	53	57	12	1.508	1.692
9	Roma	Ita	95	70	36	12	22	114	76	38	11	1.357	1.629
10	Anderlecht	Bel	91	62	35	11	16	129	75	54	10	1.468	2.081
11	Tottenham Hotspur	Eng	90	54	33	12	9	129	40	89	12	1.667	2.389
12	VFB Stuttgart	FRG	87	64	33	14	17	121	67	54	7	1.359	1.891
13	Sporting Lisbon	Por	86	71	32	19	20	126	77	49	3	1.211	1.775
14	Hamburg	FRG	85	64	34	10	20	118	77	41	7	1.328	1.844
15	Ferencváros	Hun	83	67	31	11	25	109	79	30	10	1.239	1.627
16	Red Star Belgrade	Yug	83	67	33	11	23	108	87	21	6	1.239	1.612
17	Athletic Bilbao	Esp	83	68	33	11	24	93	82	11	6	1.221	1.368
18	Feyenoord	Ned	75	58	31	9	18	112	69	43	4	1.293	1.931
19	Spartak Moscow	URS	75	56	32	10	14	91	62	29	1	1.339	1.625
20	Liverpool	Eng	73	46	28	9	9	90	30	60	8	1.587	1.957
21	Dinamo Zagreb	Yug	73	67	24	18	25	101	85	16	7	1.090	1.507
22	Napoli	Ita	72	62	25	19	18	73	70	3	3	1.161	1.177
23	Hibernian	Sco	69	58	28	11	19	97	84	13	2	1.190	1.672
24	Eintracht Frankfurt	FRG	68	54	27	8	19	106	75	31	6	1.259	1.963
25	Dynamo Dresden	GDR	68	54	23	18	13	77	51	26	4	1.259	1.426
26	Lokomotive Leipzig	GDR	68	69	28	9	32	103	99	4	3	0.986	1.493
27	Real Zaragoza	Esp	62	48	25	6	17	93	72	21	6	1.292	1.938
28	Bayern Munich	FRG	61	45	24	7	14	95	52	43	6	1.356	2.111
29	AC Milan	Ita	59	53	22	12	19	71	57	14	3	1.113	1.340
30	Carl Zeiss Jena	GDR	59	50	24	9	17	77	68	9	2	1.180	1.540
31	Ipswich Town	Eng	57	40	23	7	10	78	43	35	4	1.425	1.950
32	Twente Enschede	Ned	57	48	20	11	17	86	60	26	6	1.188	1.792
33	Vitória Setúbal	Por	57	48	24	5	19	77	55	22	4	1.188	1.604
34	Kaiserslautern	FRG	56	44	24	3	17	91	59	32	5	1.273	2.068
35	Fiorentina	Ita	56	48	21	11	16	54	50	4	3	1.167	1.125
36	Hajduk Split	Yug	54	42	23	5	14	74	46	28	3	1.286	1.762
37	FC Porto	Por	54	50	23	8	19	70	61	9	0	1.080	1.400
38	FC Liège	Bel	53	42	22	6	14	60	41	19	3	1.262	1.429
39	Grasshoppers Zürich	Sui	53	50	22	6	22	84	75	9	3	1.060	1.680
40	IFK Gothenburg	Swe	51	30	18	9	3	53	25	28	6	1.700	1.767
41	PSV Eindhoven	Ned	51	42	21	6	15	73	48	25	3	1.214	1.738
42	Real Madrid	Esp	51	40	19	6	15	67	48	19	7	1.275	1.675
43	Club Bruges	Bel	51	48	20	6	22	83	77	6	5	1.063	1.729
44	Universitatea Craiova	Rom	50	42	21	6	15	44	40	4	2	1.190	1.048
45	Arsenal	Eng	48	36	19	6	11	66	33	33	4	1.333	1.833
46	Hertha Berlin	FRG	48	36	20	5	11	54	42	12	3	1.333	1.500
47	Upjesti Dózsa	Hun	47	40	18	6	16	73	57	16	5	1.175	1.825
48	Rangers	Sco	47	38	18	8	12	53	41	12	3	1.237	1.395
49	Werder Bremen	FRG	46	36	17	8	11	65	42	23	4	1.278	1.806
50	Bologna	Ita	46	32	16	10	6	49	30	19	4	1.438	1.531
51	Standard Liège	Bel	45	40	17	10	13	61	51	10	1	1.125	1.525
52	Honvéd	Hun	44	36	19	5	12	66	55	11	1	1.222	1.833
53	Español	Esp	44	34	18	3	13	49	41	8	5	1.294	1.441

Pos'n	Club	Cnty	Pts	P	W	D	L	F	A	Diff	B	Pts/P	F/P
54	Ajax	Ned	43	38	19	3	16	80	41	39	2	1.132	2.105
55	OFK Belgrade	Yug	43	38	16	7	15	69	68	1	4	1.132	1.816
56	Atlético Madrid	Esp	43	43	19	4	20	60	59	1	1	1.000	1.395
57	Birmingham City	Eng	41	25	14	6	5	52	39	13	7	1.640	2.080
58	Partizan Belgrade	Yug	41	38	17	7	14	64	55	9	0	1.079	1.684
59	Newcastle United	Eng	39	28	14	7	7	43	26	17	4	1.393	1.536
60	Chelsea	Eng	39	28	14	6	8	47	37	10	5	1.393	1.679
61	Zbrojovka Brno	Tch	38	33	16	4	13	55	43	12	2	1.152	1.667
62	Girondins Bordeaux	Fra	38	38	17	4	17	52	59	-7	0	1.000	1.368
63	Antwerp	Bel	37	38	14	8	16	53	55	-2	1	0.974	1.395
64	Manchester United	Eng	36	27	12	9	6	46	24	22	3	1.333	1.704
65	Dunfermline Athletic	Sco	36	28	16	3	9	49	31	18	1	1.286	1.750
66	Benfica	Por	36	28	12	9	7	38	26	12	3	1.286	1.357
67	Torino	Ita	36	36	13	9	14	49	46	3	1	1.000	1.361
68	Bayer Leverkusen	FRG	34	24	11	9	4	31	16	15	3	1.417	1.292
69	Magdeburg	GDR	33	28	14	3	11	43	34	9	2	1.179	1.536
70	RWD Molenbeek	Bel	33	30	10	11	9	36	30	6	2	1.100	1.200
71	Aberdeen	Sco	33	32	12	9	11	42	42	0	0	1.031	1.313
72	Rapid Vienna	Aut	33	36	13	7	16	40	49	-9	0	0.917	1.111
73	Wolverhampton Wanderers	Eng	32	20	13	3	4	41	23	18	3	1.600	2.050
74	Heart of Midlothian	Sco	32	28	12	7	9	44	41	3	1	1.143	1.571
75	Dinamo Tbilisi	URS	31	26	13	5	8	39	32	7	0	1.192	1.500
76	Bohemians Prague	Tch	31	32	11	7	14	45	44	1	2	0.969	1.406
77	Dinamo Kiev	URS	30	24	11	8	5	29	15	14	0	1.250	1.208
78	Videoton	Hun	30	28	11	5	12	32	35	-3	3	1.071	1.143
79	Banik Ostrava	Tch	29	30	11	6	13	41	33	8	1	0.967	1.367
80	Dinamo Bucharest	Rom	28	28	11	6	11	48	32	16	0	1.000	1.714
81	Torpedo Moscow	URS	28	20	12	3	5	40	25	15	1	1.400	2.000
82	Neuchâtel Xamax	Sui	28	22	9	8	5	33	22	11	2	1.273	1.500
83	Lokeren	Bel	28	24	9	9	6	29	24	5	1	1.167	1.208
84	Vitória Guimarães	Por	28	26	11	5	10	31	38	-7	1	1.077	1.192
85	Levski Sofia	Bul	28	30	10	7	13	44	57	-13	1	0.933	1.467
86	Radnicki Nis	Yug	27	22	11	3	8	34	31	3	2	1.227	1.545
87	Vojvodina Novi Sad	Yug	27	27	9	7	11	29	33	-4	2	1.000	1.074
88	AEK Athenes	Gre	27	32	11	3	18	34	54	-20	2	0.844	1.063
89	Utrecht	Ned	27	32	10	7	15	41	62	-21	0	0.844	1.281
90	AZ'67 Alkmaar	Ned	26	16	9	5	2	51	15	36	3	1.625	3.188
91	Lokomotiv Plovdiv	Bul	26	30	10	6	14	40	50	-10	0	0.867	1.333
92	Real Sociedad	Esp	26	26	9	7	10	28	39	-11	1	1.000	1.077
93	Saint-Etienne	Fra	25	22	9	5	8	48	29	19	2	1.136	2.182
94	Legia Warsaw	Pol	25	24	9	7	8	34	30	4	0	1.042	1.417
95	Nottingham Forest	Eng	25	18	10	3	5	20	16	4	2	1.389	1.111
96	Dukla Prague	Tch	24	24	8	7	9	30	32	-2	1	1.000	1.250
97	Widzew Lódź	Pol	24	26	8	8	10	24	36	-12	0	0.923	0.923
98	Everton	Eng	23	20	10	3	7	34	20	14	0	1.150	1.700
99	Beveren	Bel	23	20	10	3	7	28	17	11	0	1.150	1.400
100	Zeljeznicar Sarajevo	Yug	23	20	8	4	8	40	31	9	3	1.150	2.000
101	Waregem	Bel	23	18	9	3	6	27	24	3	2	1.278	1.500
102	Velez Mostar	Yug	23	20	9	4	7	29	27	2	1	1.150	1.450
103	Olympiakos Pireus	Gre	23	22	9	5	8	24	31	-7	0	1.045	1.091
104	Aris Salonika	Gre	23	26	9	5	12	39	55	-16	0	0.885	1.500
105	Inter Bratislava	Tch	22	18	11	0	7	43	23	20	0	1.222	2.389
106	Sochaux	Fra	22	20	7	6	7	32	22	10	2	1.100	1.600
107	Austria Vienna	Aut	22	20	8	5	7	38	34	4	1	1.100	1.900
108	Nantes	Fra	22	22	6	9	7	25	28	-3	1	1.000	1.136
109	Servette	Sui	22	26	8	6	12	34	48	-14	0	0.846	1.308
110	MSV Duisburg	FRG	21	14	8	3	3	38	19	19	2	1.500	2.714

Pos'n	Club	Cnty	Pts	P	W	D	L	F	A	Diff	B	Pts/P	F/P
111	Aston Villa	Eng	21	18	8	4	6	31	21	10	1	1.167	1.722
112	Kilmarnock	Sco	21	20	8	3	9	34	32	2	2	1.050	1.700
113	Sparta Prague	Tch	21	22	8	4	10	31	37	-6	1	0.955	1.409
114	FC Tirol	Aut	21	22	8	3	11	27	34	-7	2	0.955	1.227
115	Bastia	Fra	20	12	8	1	3	27	20	7	3	1.667	2.250
116	Brøndby IF	Den	19	14	7	3	4	20	11	9	2	1.357	1.429
117	FC Amsterdam	Ned	19	18	7	4	7	30	28	2	1	1.056	1.667
118	Petrolul Ploiesti	Rom	19	15	9	0	6	14	15	-1	1	1.267	0.933
119	Borussia Dortmund	FRG	19	18	9	1	8	24	26	-2	0	1.056	1.333
120	Sturm Graz	Aut	19	22	6	6	10	23	29	-6	1	0.864	1.045
121	Strasbourg	Fra	19	20	6	6	8	22	34	-12	1	0.950	1.100
122	FC Zürich	Sui	19	24	7	4	13	28	44	-16	1	0.792	1.167
123	PAOK Salonika	Gre	19	20	7	5	8	17	33	-16	0	0.950	0.850
124	Queen's Park Rangers	Eng	18	12	8	1	3	39	18	21	1	1.500	3.250
125	Sparta Rotterdam	Ned	18	16	7	4	5	35	21	14	0	1.125	2.188
126	Verona	Ita	18	12	6	5	1	18	11	7	1	1.500	1.500
127	Belenenses	Por	18	22	5	8	9	23	29	-6	0	0.818	1.045
128	Arges Pitesti	Rom	18	18	6	6	6	25	32	-7	0	1.000	1.389
129	Panathinaikos	Gre	18	24	7	3	14	30	40	-10	1	0.750	1.250
130	Malmö FF	Swe	18	26	7	4	15	26	47	-21	0	0.692	1.000
131	Dinamo Minsk	URS	17	14	7	2	5	22	13	9	1	1.214	1.571
132	1860 Munich	FRG	17	16	6	4	6	37	32	5	1	1.063	2.313
133	MTK-VM	Hun	17	15	7	1	7	32	30	2	2	1.133	2.133
134	Slask Wroclaw	Pol	17	18	6	5	7	29	36	-7	0	0.944	1.611
135	Auxerre	Fra	16	14	6	3	5	25	15	10	1	1.143	1.786
136	Eintracht Braunschweig	FRG	16	16	6	4	6	29	20	9	0	1.000	1.813
137	Victoria Bucharest	Rom	16	14	6	3	5	21	17	4	1	1.143	1.500
138	Southampton	Eng	16	16	4	8	4	21	18	3	0	1.000	1.313
139	West Bromwich Albion	Eng	16	16	6	3	7	22	22	0	1	1.000	1.375
140	Seville	Esp	16	16	6	4	6	21	22	-1	0	1.000	1.313
141	Sportul Studentesc Bucharest	Rom	16	20	6	4	10	20	31	-11	0	0.800	1.000
142	Lausanne-Sports	Sui	16	28	6	3	19	42	75	-33	1	0.571	1.500
143	Lens	Fra	15	14	6	3	5	22	19	3	0	1.071	1.571
144	Celtic	Sco	15	16	5	5	6	24	22	2	0	0.938	1.500
145	Manchester City	Eng	15	14	4	6	4	21	19	2	1	1.071	1.500
146	Groningen	Ned	15	16	6	3	7	22	22	0	0	0.938	1.375
147	Admira Wacker	Aut	15	14	7	1	6	15	19	-4	0	1.071	1.071
148	AIK	Swe	15	16	5	5	6	20	26	-6	0	0.938	1.250
149	Wiener Sport-Club	Aut	15	21	7	1	13	25	40	-15	0	0.714	1.190
150	Hanover 96	FRG	15	21	6	3	12	30	50	-20	0	0.714	1.429
151	Linzer ASK	Aut	15	18	6	3	9	16	36	-20	0	0.833	0.889
152	Monaco	Fra	14	14	6	2	6	23	23	0	0	1.000	1.643
153	Lokomotiv Sofia	Bul	14	14	5	3	6	21	21	0	1	1.000	1.500
154	Boavista	Por	14	18	6	2	10	20	28	-8	0	0.778	1.111
155	Rába ETO	Hun	14	16	6	2	8	23	32	-9	0	0.875	1.438
156	Fenerbahçe	Tur	14	20	6	2	12	21	37	-16	0	0.700	1.050
157	Göztepe	Tur	14	20	6	1	13	22	39	-17	1	0.700	1.100
158	Shakhtyor Donetsk	URS	13	10	6	1	3	14	12	2	0	1.300	1.400
159	Stal Mielec	Pol	13	12	4	4	4	9	8	1	1	1.083	0.750
160	Dinamo Moscow	URS	13	14	5	3	6	15	15	0	0	0.929	1.071
161	Sion	Sui	13	12	6	1	5	17	20	-3	0	1.083	1.417
162	Vasas SC	Hun	13	16	6	1	9	19	23	-4	0	0.813	1.188
163	Ruch Chorzów	Pol	13	18	5	2	11	29	35	-6	1	0.722	1.611
164	Slavia Sofia	Bul	13	16	5	3	8	18	35	-17	0	0.813	1.125
165	Derby County	Eng	12	10	5	2	3	32	17	15	0	1.200	3.200
166	Burnley	Eng	12	8	4	3	1	16	5	11	1	1.500	2.000
167	Schalke 04	FRG	12	10	5	2	3	19	14	5	0	1.200	1.900

Pos'n	Club	Cnty	Pts	P	W	D	L	F	A	Diff	B	Pts/P	F/P
168	Olympique Marseille	Fra	12	12	6	0	6	21	19	2	0	1.000	1.750
169	Atalanta	Ita	12	10	3	5	2	8	7	1	1	1.200	0.800
170	Fortuna Düsseldorf	FRG	12	12	5	2	5	17	17	0	0	1.000	1.417
171	Union St-Gilloise	Bel	12	17	4	2	11	23	30	-7	2	0.706	1.353
172	Öster SIF	Swe	12	18	6	0	12	24	34	-10	0	0.667	1.333
113	Gent	Bel	12	18	3	6	9	18	31	-13	0	0.667	1.000
174	Beroe Stara Zagora	Bul	11	10	5	1	4	18	9	9	0	1.100	1.800
175	Sheffield Wednesday	Eng	11	10	5	0	5	25	18	7	1	1.100	2.500
176	Las Palmas	Esp	11	12	4	3	5	20	17	3	0	0.917	1.667
177	Toulouse	Fra	11	10	5	1	4	16	15	1	0	1.100	1.600
178	Slavia Prague	Tch	11	12	5	1	6	17	19	-2	0	0.917	1.417
179	IFK Norrköping	Swe	11	12	3	5	4	12	14	-2	0	0.917	1.000
180	Trakia Plovdiv	Bul	11	16	3	5	8	22	27	-5	0	0.688	1.375
181	Lazio	Ita	11	14	5	1	8	20	28	-8	0	0.786	1.429
182	Nice	Fra	11	14	5	1	8	16	25	-9	0	0.786	1.143
183	Olympique Lyon	Fra	11	16	5	1	10	28	41	-13	0	0.688	1.750
184	Slovan Bratislava	Tch	10	8	4	2	2	23	12	11	0	1.250	2.875
185	First Vienna	Aut	10	8	4	2	2	14	8	6	0	1.250	1.750
186	Ararat Erevan	URS	10	6	5	0	1	11	5	6	0	1.667	1.833
187	TJ Vitkovice	Tch	10	8	3	3	2	8	7	1	1	1.250	1.000
188	Dnepr Dnepropetrovsk	URS	10	12	3	4	5	12	15	-3	0	0.833	1.000
189	Esbjerg FB	Den	10	8	4	2	2	10	13	-3	0	1.250	1.250
190	Barreirense	Por	10	11	5	0	6	11	16	-5	0	0.909	1.000
191	Rosenborg BK	Nor	10	10	5	0	5	15	22	-7	0	1.000	1.500
192	TPS Turku	Fin	10	14	4	2	8	10	17	-7	0	0.714	0.714
193	IL Viking	Nor	10	12	3	4	5	9	23	-14	0	0.833	0.750
194	KB Copenhagen	Den	10	20	3	3	14	39	66	-27	1	0.500	1.950
195	FC Basle	Sui	10	29	3	4	22	39	82	-43	0	0.345	1.345
196	Hammarby IF	Swe	9	6	4	1	1	15	9	6	0	1.500	2.500
197	NK Zagreb	Yug	9	12	3	3	6	20	18	2	0	0.750	1.667
198	Lierse	Bel	9	10	3	2	5	15	13	2	1	0.900	1.500
199	Bacau	Rom	9	8	3	2	3	12	11	1	1	1.125	1.500
200	Sarajevo	Yug	9	8	3	3	2	21	21	0	0	1.125	2.625
201	Gwardia Warsaw	Pol	9	8	4	1	3	8	8	0	0	1.125	1.000
202	UT Arad	Rom	9	10	3	2	5	13	14	-1	1	0.900	1.300
203	Dynamo Berlin	GDR	9	10	3	3	4	14	17	-3	0	0.900	1.400
204	Sporting Gijón	Esp	9	12	3	3	6	9	13	-4	0	0.750	0.750
205	CSKA Sofia	Bul	9	12	3	3	6	13	22	-9	0	0.750	1.083
206	Flamurtari Vlorë	Alb	8	8	3	2	3	8	8	0	0	1.000	1.000
207	Diósgyöri VTK	Hun	8	6	4	0	2	9	11	-2	0	1.333	1.500
208	Chernomorets Odessa	URS	8	10	3	2	5	10	13	-3	0	0.800	1.000
209	Dundee	Sco	8	10	4	0	6	17	21	-4	0	0.800	1.700
210	Hansa Rostock	GDR	8	10	4	0	6	15	19	-4	0	0.800	1.500
211	Politehnica Timisoara	Rom	8	8	4	0	4	9	14	-5	0	1.000	1.125
212	Vorwärts Frankfurt/Oder	GDR	8	12	4	0	8	13	22	-9	0	0.667	1.083
213	Djurgården SIF	Swe	8	12	3	2	7	17	28	-11	0	0.667	1.417
214	Coleraine	Nir	8	16	2	4	10	19	40	-21	0	0.500	1.188
215	Glentoran	Nir	8	22	2	4	16	16	61	-45	0	0.364	0.727
216	Bayer Uerdingen	FRG	7	6	3	1	2	9	4	5	0	1.167	1.500
217	Vitesse	Ned	7	6	3	1	2	7	4	3	0	1.167	1.167
218	St. Mirren	Sco	7	10	2	3	5	9	12	-3	0	0.700	0.900
219	IK Start	Nor	7	10	3	1	6	11	19	-8	0	0.700	1.100
220	Red Flag Brasov	Rom	7	11	3	1	7	14	25	-11	0	0.636	1.273
221	Charleroi	Bel	6	4	3	0	1	8	5	3	0	1.500	2.000
222	SV Salzburg	Aut	6	6	3	0	3	11	9	2	0	1.000	1.833
223	Coventry City	Eng	6	4	3	0	1	9	8	1	0	1.500	2.250
224	Paris Saint-Germain	Fra	6	8	2	2	4	12	12	0	0	0.750	1.500

Pos'n	Club	Cnty	Pts	P	W	D	L	F	A	Diff	B	Pts/P	F/P
225	Shamrock Rovers	Irl	6	8	2	2	4	11	11	0	0	0.750	1.375
226	St. Johnstone	Sco	6	6	3	0	3	8	8	0	0	1.000	1.333
227	Partick Thistle	Sco	6	6	3	0	3	10	11	-1	0	1.000	1.667
228	Sampdoria	Ita	6	4	3	0	1	4	6	-2	0	1.500	1.000
229	Dinamo Tirana	Alb	6	6	2	2	2	2	5	-3	0	1.000	0.333
230	Tatabánya	Hun	6	8	2	2	4	6	11	-5	0	0.750	0.750
231	Rapid Bucharest	Rom	6	10	3	0	7	12	22	-10	0	0.600	1.200
232	Galatasaray	Tur	6	12	2	2	8	11	24	-13	0	0.500	0.917
233	Bohemians	Irl	6	14	1	4	9	8	27	-19	0	0.429	0.571
234	Wettingen	Sui	5	4	2	1	1	6	2	4	0	1.250	1.500
235	Zaglebie Walbrzych	Pol	5	4	2	1	1	6	5	1	0	1.250	1.500
236	Rijeka	Yug	5	6	2	1	3	8	8	0	0	0.833	1.333
237	Rouen	Fra	5	6	2	1	3	5	5	0	0	0.833	0.833
238	Stade Français	Fra	5	6	1	3	2	3	3	0	0	0.833	0.500
239	Lucerne	Sui	5	6	1	3	2	4	5	-1	0	0.833	0.667
240	Watford	Eng	5	6	2	1	3	10	12	-2	0	0.833	1.667
241	Wisla Kraków	Pol	5	6	1	3	2	7	9	-2	0	0.833	1.167
242	Shelbourne	Irl	5	7	1	3	3	4	6	-2	0	0.714	0.571
243	Karl-Marx-Stadt	GDR	5	8	2	1	5	9	12	-3	0	0.625	1.125
244	Winterslag	Bel	5	6	2	1	3	5	9	-4	0	0.833	0.833
245	Panahaiki	Gre	5	4	2	1	1	4	9	-5	0	1.250	1.000
246	Górnik Zabrze	Pol	5	8	1	3	4	10	16	-6	0	0.625	1.250
247	IF Elfsborg	Swe	5	8	1	3	4	8	15	-7	0	0.625	1.000
248	Besiktas	Tur	5	8	2	1	5	5	13	-8	0	0.625	0.625
249	GKS Katowice	Pol	5	12	2	1	9	11	20	-9	0	0.417	0.917
250	AGF Aarhus	Den	5	10	2	1	7	8	19	-11	0	0.500	0.800
251	FK Skeid	Nor	5	8	1	3	4	7	18	-11	0	0.625	0.875
252	Zenit Leningrad	URS	5	8	2	1	5	7	18	-11	0	0.625	0.875
253	Valur Reykjavik	Isl	5	8	1	3	4	4	15	-11	0	0.625	0.500
254	Örgryte IS	Swe	5	8	1	3	4	9	21	-12	0	0.625	1.125
255	Eskisehirspor	Tur	5	10	2	1	7	9	24	-15	0	0.500	0.900
256	B 1903 Copenhagen	Den	5	12	1	3	8	14	31	-17	0	0.417	1.167
257	Iraklis	Gre	5	8	2	1	5	5	23	-18	0	0.625	0.625
258	BK Frem	Den	5	12	2	1	9	13	37	-24	0	0.417	1.083
259	KuPS Kuopio	Fin	5	12	2	1	9	12	39	-27	0	0.417	1.000
260	Marek Stanke Dimitrov	Bul	4	4	2	0	2	5	5	0	0	1.000	1.250
261	Osasuna	Esp	4	4	2	0	2	4	4	0	0	1.000	1.000
262	AB Copenhagen	Den	4	6	2	0	4	13	14	-1	0	0.667	2.167
263	Corvinul Hunedoara	Rom	4	4	1	2	1	8	9	-1	0	1.000	2.000
264	Pécs Dózsa	Hun	4	6	2	0	4	6	7	-1	0	0.667	1.000
265	Athlone Town	Irl	4	4	1	2	1	4	5	-1	0	1.000	1.000
266	Laval	Fra	4	4	1	2	1	4	5	-1	0	1.000	1.000
267	Stahl Brandenburg	GDR	4	4	1	2	1	3	4	-1	0	1.000	0.750
268	Akademik Sofia	Bul	4	6	2	0	4	8	10	-2	0	0.667	1.333
269	Stoke City	Eng	4	4	1	2	1	4	6	-2	0	1.000	1.000
270	Penigia	Ita	4	4	1	2	1	2	4	-2	0	1.000	0.500
271	Omonia Nicosia	Cyp	4	6	1	2	3	7	10	-3	0	0.667	1.167
272	Ilves Tampere	Fin	4	4	2	0	2	6	9	-3	0	1.000	1.500
273	Spartak Trnava	Tch	4	6	2	0	4	5	8	-3	0	0.667	0.833
274	VSS Kosice	Tch	4	4	2	0	2	5	8	-3	0	1.000	1.250
275	Zhalgiris Vilnius	URS	4	6	2	0	4	7	11	-4	0	0.667	1.167
276	Wismut Aue	GDR	4	6	1	2	3	4	8	-4	0	0.667	0.667
277	Portadown	Nir	4	4	1	2	1	3	7	-4	0	1.000	0.750
278	IBV Vestmannaeyjar	Isl	4	8	0	4	4	2	9	-7	0	0.500	0.250
279	RoPS Rovaniemi	Fin	4	6	1	2	3	2	10	-8	0	0.667	0.333
280	Drumcondra	Irl	4	6	2	0	4	8	19	-11	0	0.667	1.333
281	Panionios	Gre	4	7	2	0	5	5	17	-12	0	0.571	0.714

Pos'n	Club	Cnty	Pts	P	W	D	L	F	A	Diff	B	Pts/P	F/P
282	Molde FK	Nor	4	6	1	2	3	5	18	-13	0	0.667	0.833
283	Naestved IF	Den	4	8	1	2	5	5	21	-16	0	0.500	0.625
284	Linfield	Nir	4	8	1	2	5	4	20	-16	0	0.500	0.500
285	Jeunesse Esch	Lux	4	8	1	2	5	5	23	-18	0	0.500	0.625
286	Dundalk	Irl	4	10	1	2	7	4	31	-27	0	0.400	0.400
287	FC Den Haag	Ned	3	4	1	1	2	8	9	-1	0	0.750	2.000
288	Tatran Presov	Tch	3	4	1	1	2	9	11	-2	0	0.750	2.250
289	Cagliari	Ita	3	6	1	1	4	5	7	-2	0	0.500	0.833
290	Vardar Skopje	Yug	3	4	1	1	2	3	5	-2	0	0.750	0.750
291	Haarlem	Ned	3	4	1	1	2	6	9	-3	0	0.750	1.500
292	Leixões	Por	3	4	0	3	1	2	5	-3	0	0.750	0.500
293	GAIS	Swe	3	4	1	1	2	6	10	-4	0	0.750	1.500
294	Real Betis	Esp	3	6	1	1	4	4	8	-4	0	0.500	0.667
295	Bryne IL	Nor	3	4	1	1	2	3	7	-4	0	0.750	0.750
296	Nuremberg	FRG	3	6	1	1	4	5	10	-5	0	0.500	0.833
297	IK Brage	Swe	3	6	1	1	4	8	15	-7	0	0.500	1.333
298	Vöest Linz	Aut	3	6	1	1	4	5	13	-8	0	0.500	0.833
299	ASA Tîrgu Mures	Rom	3	6	1	1	4	4	13	-9	0	0.500	0.667
300	Altay	Tur	3	6	1	1	4	8	20	-12	0	0.500	1.333
301	Apoel Nicosia	Cyp	3	8	0	3	5	8	21	-13	0	0.375	1.000
302	Adanaspor	Tur	3	6	1	1	4	6	20	-14	0	0.500	1.000
303	IBK Keflavik	Isl	3	10	1	1	8	6	31	-25	0	0.300	0.600
304	DAC Dunajská Streda	Tch	2	4	1	0	3	7	7	0	0	0.500	1.750
305	CSKA Moscow	URS	2	2	1	0	1	2	2	0	0	1.000	1.000
306	Ikast FS	Den	2	2	1	0	1	2	2	0	0	1.000	1.000
307	Randers Freja FC	Den	2	2	0	2	0	1	1	0	0	1.000	0.500
308	Lokomotiv Kosice	Tch	2	2	1	0	1	1	1	0	0	1.000	0.500
309	Universitatea Cluj	Rom	2	2	1	0	1	5	6	-1	0	1.000	2.500
310	Åtvidaberg SFF	Swe	2	2	1	0	1	5	6	-1	0	1.000	2.500
311	Angoulême	Fra	2	2	1	0	1	3	4	-1	0	1.000	1.500
312	Cesena	Ita	2	2	1	0	1	3	4	-1	0	1.000	1.500
313	Larissa	Gre	2	2	1	0	1	2	3	-1	0	1.000	1.000
314	Rad Belgrade	Yug	2	2	1	0	1	2	3	-1	0	1.000	1.000
315	Dunav Ruse	Bul	2	2	1	0	1	1	2	-1	0	1.000	0.500
316	Pécsi MSC	Hun	2	2	1	0	1	1	2	-1	0	1.000	0.500
317	Wuppertal	FRG	2	2	1	0	1	6	8	-2	0	1.000	3.000
318	Viktoria Cologne	FRG	2	2	1	0	1	5	7	-2	0	1.000	2.500
319	Nîmes Olympique	Fra	2	4	1	0	3	4	6	-2	0	0.500	1.000
320	Sabadell	Esp	2	2	1	0	1	3	5	-2	0	1.000	1.500
321	Ballymena United	Nir	2	2	1	0	1	2	4	-2	0	1.000	1.000
322	Real Valladolid	Esp	2	2	1	0	1	2	4	-2	0	1.000	1.000
323	Chaves	Por	2	4	1	0	3	6	9	-3	0	0.500	1.500
324	Sedan	Fra	2	2	1	0	1	2	5	-3	0	1.000	1.000
325	Sliven	Bul	2	2	1	0	1	2	5	-3	0	1.000	1.000
326	Portimonense	Por	2	2	1	0	1	1	4	-3	0	1.000	0.500
327	OFI Crete	Gre	2	2	1	0	1	1	4	-3	0	1.000	0.500
328	Ards	Nir	2	2	1	0	1	4	8	-4	0	1.000	2.000
329	Sloboda Tuzla	Yug	2	2	1	0	1	4	8	-4	0	1.000	2.000
330	Zaglebie Sosnowiec	Pol	2	2	1	0	1	2	6	-4	0	1.000	1.000
331	Orduspor	Tur	2	2	1	0	1	2	6	-4	0	1.000	1.000
332	CSU Galati	Rom	2	2	1	0	1	1	5	-4	0	1.000	0.500
333	Floriana	Mlt	2	2	1	0	1	1	6	-5	0	1.000	0.500
334	Kalmar FF	Swe	2	4	1	0	3	3	9	-6	0	0.500	0.750
335	Academica Coimbra	Por	2	4	1	0	3	2	8	-6	0	0.500	0.500
336	Trabzonspor	Tur	2	4	1	0	3	1	8	-7	0	0.500	0.250
337	Sporting Braga	Por	2	6	1	0	5	7	15	-8	0	0.333	1.167
338	Lillestrøm SK	Nor	2	4	1	0	3	4	12	-8	0	0.500	1.000

Pos'n	Club	Cnty	Pts	P	W	D	L	F	A	Diff	B	Pts/P	F/P
339	Apollon Limassol	Cyp	2	4	0	2	2	4	12	-8	0	0.500	1.000
340	Holbaek BIF	Den	2	4	1	0	3	2	10	-8	0	0.500	0.500
341	Metz	Fra	2	6	0	2	4	8	17	-9	0	0.333	1.333
342	B 1913 Odense	Den	2	6	1	0	5	6	16	-10	0	0.333	1.000
343	Vålerengen SIF	Nor	2	8	0	2	6	7	18	-11	0	0.250	0.875
344	Pezoporikos Larnaca	Cyp	2	6	0	2	4	6	20	-14	0	0.333	1.000
345	Mjøndalen IF	Nor	2	4	1	0	3	1	17	-16	0	0.500	0.250
346	Avenir Beggen	Lux	2	6	1	0	5	2	22	-20	0	0.333	0.333
347	Spora Luxembourg	Lux	2	6	1	0	5	3	28	-25	0	0.333	0.500
348	Aris Bonnevoie	Lux	2	8	0	2	6	2	27	-25	0	0.250	0.250
349	Hibernians	Mlt	2	12	1	0	11	3	50	-47	0	0.167	0.250
350	Angers	Fra	1	2	0	1	1	2	3	-1	0	0.500	1.000
351	Odra Opole	Pol	1	2	0	1	1	2	3	-1	0	0.500	1.000
352	FC Kuusysi Lahti	Fin	1	2	0	1	1	2	3	-1	0	0.500	1.000
353	KV Mechelen	Bel	1	2	0	1	1	2	3	-1	0	0.500	1.000
354	Lanerossi Vicenza	Ita	1	2	0	1	1	1	2	-1	0	0.500	0.500
355	Hamrun Spartans	Mlt	1	2	0	1	1	0	1	-1	0	0.500	0.000
356	Derry City	Irl	1	2	0	1	1	0	1	-1	0	0.500	0.000
357	FH Hafnarfjördhur	Isl	1	2	0	1	1	3	5	-2	0	0.500	1.500
358	Salgótarján	Hun	1	2	0	1	1	2	4	-2	0	0.500	1.000
359	Young Boys Berne	Sui	1	2	0	1	1	2	4	-2	0	0.500	1.000
360	Lugano	Sui	1	2	0	1	1	1	3	-2	0	0.500	0.500
361	GKS Tychy	Pol	1	2	0	1	1	1	3	-2	0	0.500	0.500
362	Szombierki Bytom	Pol	1	2	0	1	1	1	3	-2	0	0.500	0.500
363	Limerick	Irl	1	2	0	1	1	1	4	-3	0	0.500	0.500
364	Etar Veliko Turnovo	Bul	1	2	0	1	1	0	3	-3	0	0.500	0.000
365	Pogon Szczecin	Pol	1	4	0	1	3	3	7	-4	0	0.250	0.750
366	Sigma Olomouc	Tch	1	2	0	1	1	1	5	-4	0	0.500	0.500
367	Lyngby BK	Den	1	4	0	1	3	4	9	-5	0	0.250	1.000
368	Beerschot	Bel	1	4	0	1	3	2	7	-5	0	0.250	0.500
369	Strømgodset IF	Nor	1	2	0	1	1	2	7	-5	0	0.500	1.000
370	Haka Valkeakoski	Fin	1	4	0	1	3	5	12	-7	0	0.250	1.250
371	Olimpija Ljubljana	Yug	1	4	0	1	3	4	11	-7	0	0.250	1.000
372	Steaua Bucharest	Rom	1	4	0	1	3	4	11	-7	0	0.250	1.000
373	St-Gallen	Sui	1	4	0	1	3	2	10	-8	0	0.250	0.500
374	Lech Poznań	Pol	1	4	0	1	3	3	13	-10	0	0.250	0.750
375	SFK Lyn	Nor	1	4	0	1	3	3	14	-11	0	0.250	0.750
376	Hvidovre IF	Den	1	6	0	1	5	5	17	-12	0	0.167	0.833
377	Grazer AK	Aut	1	6	0	1	5	4	16	-12	0	0.167	0.667
378	Glenavon	Nir	1	6	0	1	5	2	15	-13	0	0.167	0.333
379	Sliema Wanderers	Mlt	1	14	0	1	13	7	42	-35	0	0.071	0.500
380	IA Akranes	Isl	1	10	0	1	9	2	48	-46	0	0.100	0.200
381	Red Boys Differdange	Lux	1	12	0	1	11	3	68	-65	0	0.083	0.250
382	Tasmania Berlin	FRG	0	2	0	0	2	3	5	-2	0	0.000	1.500
383	Moss FK	Nor	0	2	0	0	2	3	5	-2	0	0.000	1.500
384	Racing Club Paris	Fra	0	2	0	0	2	2	4	-2	0	0.000	1.000
385	Union Teplice	Tch	0	2	0	0	2	2	4	-2	0	0.000	1.000
386	Napredak Krusevac	Yug	0	2	0	0	2	0	2	-2	0	0.000	0.000
387	Zaglebie Lubin	Pol	0	2	0	0	2	0	2	-2	0	0.000	0.000
388	Partizan Tirana	Alb	0	2	0	0	2	0	2	-2	0	0.000	0.000
389	Tresnjevka Zagreb	Yug	0	2	0	0	2	1	4	-3	0	0.000	0.500
390	Flacara Moreni	Rom	0	2	0	0	2	1	4	-3	0	0.000	0.500
391	Celta Vigo	Esp	0	2	0	0	2	0	3	-3	0	0.000	0.000
392	Dukla Banská Bystrica	Tch	0	2	0	0	2	3	7	-4	0	0.000	1.500
393	B 1909 Odense	Den	0	2	0	0	2	2	6	-4	0	0.000	1.000
394	SK Frigg	Nor	0	2	0	0	2	2	6	-4	0	0.000	1.000
395	Roda JC	Ned	0	2	0	0	2	2	6	-4	0	0.000	1.000

Pos'n	Club	Cnty	Pts	P	W	D	L	F	A	Diff	B	Pts/P	F/P
396	Plastika Nitra	Tch	0	2	0	0	2	1	5	-4	0	0.000	0.500
397	HIFK Helsinki	Fin	0	2	0	0	2	0	4	-4	0	0.000	0.000
398	Boluspor	Tur	0	2	0	0	2	0	4	-4	0	0.000	0.000
399	Vejle BK	Den	0	2	0	0	2	0	4	-4	0	0.000	0.000
400	B 1901 Nykobing	Den	0	2	0	0	2	3	8	-5	0	0.000	1.500
401	Cork Hibernian	Irl	0	2	0	0	2	1	6	-5	0	0.000	0.500
402	Montpellier	Fra	0	2	0	0	2	1	6	-5	0	0.000	0.500
403	Fredrikstad FK	Nor	0	2	0	0	2	0	5	-5	0	0.000	0.000
404	Morton	Sco	0	2	0	0	2	3	9	-6	0	0.000	1.500
405	Botev Vratsa	Bul	0	2	0	0	2	2	8	-6	0	0.000	1.000
406	Galway United	Irl	0	2	0	0	2	2	8	-6	0	0.000	1.000
407	Pirin Blagoevgrad	Bul	0	2	0	0	2	1	7	-6	0	0.000	0.500
408	IF Sarpsborg	Nor	0	2	0	0	2	0	6	-6	0	0.000	0.000
409	MP Mikkeli	Fin	0	2	0	0	2	0	6	-6	0	0.000	0.000
410	EPA Larnaca	Cyp	0	4	0	0	4	0	6	-6	0	0.000	0.000
411	Landskrona BOIS	Swe	0	2	0	0	2	0	6	-6	0	0.000	0.000
412	OB Odense	Den	0	4	0	0	4	4	11	-7	0	0.000	1.000
413	KPV Kokkola	Fin	0	2	0	0	2	2	9	-7	0	0.000	1.000
414	Zurrieq	Mlt	0	2	0	0	2	1	8	-7	0	0.000	0.500
415	Akritas Morphou	Cyp	0	2	0	0	2	0	7	-7	0	0.000	0.000
416	KR Reykjavik	Isl	0	2	0	0	2	0	7	-7	0	0.000	0.000
417	Aarau	Sui	0	2	0	0	2	0	7	-7	0	0.000	0.000
418	Vikingur Reykjavik	Isl	0	2	0	0	2	0	8	-8	0	0.000	0.000
419	Apolonia Fier	Alb	0	2	0	0	2	0	8	-8	0	0.000	0.000
420	St. Patrick's Athletic	Irl	0	4	0	0	4	4	13	-9	0	0.000	1.000
421	Progrès Niedercorn	Lux	0	4	0	0	4	0	10	-10	0	0.000	0.000
422	Marsa	Mlt	0	2	0	0	2	0	11	-11	0	0.000	0.000
423	SK Brann	Nor	0	2	0	0	2	0	11	-11	0	0.000	0.000
424	Anorthosis Famagusta	Cyp	0	2	0	0	2	0	11	-11	0	0.000	0.000
425	Alki Larnaca	Cyp	0	2	0	0	2	0	12	-12	0	0.000	0.000
426	Olympiakos Nicosia	Cyp	0	2	0	0	2	0	13	-13	0	0.000	0.000
427	Drogheda United	Irl	0	2	0	0	2	0	14	-14	0	0.000	0.000
428	Paralimni	Cyp	0	4	0	0	4	4	21	-17	0	0.000	1.000
429	Rabat Ajax	Mlt	0	4	0	0	4	0	20	-20	0	0.000	0.000
430	HJK Helsinki	Fin	0	6	0	0	6	2	23	-21	0	0.000	0.333
431	Fram Reykjavik	Isl	0	6	0	0	6	0	23	-23	0	0.000	0.000
432	Valletta	Mlt	0	8	0	0	8	2	28	-26	0	0.000	0.250
433	Finn Harps	Irl	0	6	0	0	6	3	33	-30	0	0.000	0.500
434	US Rumelange	Lux	0	4	0	0	4	0	32	-32	0	0.000	0.000
435	Union Luxembourg	Lux	0	8	0	0	8	2	42	-40	0	0.000	0.250
	Total		**7541**	**7094**	**2872**	**1350**	**2872**	**10485**	**10485**	**0**	**447**	**1.063**	**2.956**

Club Performance by Points

1981-82 to 1990-91

Pos'n	Club	Cnty	Pts	P	W	D	L	F	A	Diff	B	Pts/P	F/P
1	Inter Milan	Ita	84	62	31	14	17	93	55	38	8	1.355	1.500
2	Cologne	FRG	68	48	26	10	12	82	44	38	6	1.417	1.708
3	Dundee United	Sco	68	52	25	13	14	86	55	31	5	1.308	1.654
4	Spartak Moscow	URS	61	44	26	8	10	78	48	30	1	1.386	1.773
5	Anderlecht	Bel	57	38	21	8	9	73	41	32	7	1.500	1.921
6	Sporting Lisbon	Por	55	42	20	12	10	78	38	40	3	1.310	1.857
7	IFK Gothenburg	Swe	49	28	17	9	2	50	20	30	6	1.750	1.786
8	Hajduk Split	Yug	46	34	19	5	10	64	38	26	3	1.353	1.882
9	Werder Bremen	FRG	46	36	17	8	11	65	42	23	4	1.278	1.806
10	Real Madrid	Esp	44	34	16	5	13	60	42	18	7	1.294	1.765
11	Juventus	Ita	40	24	17	2	5	46	20	26	4	1.667	1.917
12	Hamburg	FRG	36	28	15	2	11	48	32	16	4	1.286	1.714
13	Roma	Ita	35	26	14	3	9	38	26	12	4	1.346	1.462
14	Bayer Leverkusen	FRG	34	24	11	9	4	31	16	15	3	1.417	1.292
15	Universitatea Craiova	Rom	34	28	15	2	11	30	26	4	2	1.214	1.071
16	Bor. Mönchengladbach	FRG	32	26	12	6	8	45	36	9	2	1.231	1.731
17	Tottenham Hotspur	Eng	31	20	11	5	4	46	13	33	4	1.550	2.300
18	Napoli	Ita	31	26	9	10	7	29	28	1	3	1.192	1.115
19	Valencia	Esp	29	24	10	7	7	31	26	5	2	1.208	1.292
20	Kaiserslautern	FRG	28	20	12	1	7	40	20	20	3	1.400	2.000
21	Neuchâtel Xamax	Sui	28	22	9	8	5	33	22	11	2	1.273	1.500
22	VFB Stuttgart	FRG	27	22	9	6	7	33	23	10	3	1.227	1.500
23	Feyenoord	Ned	27	24	12	3	9	36	31	5	0	1.125	1.500
24	Girondins Bordeaux	Fra	27	24	12	3	9	33	29	4	0	1.125	1.375
25	Partizan Belgrade	Yug	26	24	12	2	10	41	33	8	0	1.083	1.708
26	Fiorentina	Ita	26	20	8	7	5	16	17	-1	3	1.300	0.800
27	Benfica	Por	25	18	8	6	4	26	15	11	3	1.389	1.444
28	Bohemians Prague	Tch	25	24	9	5	10	35	31	4	2	1.042	1.458
29	Lokomotive Leipzig	GDR	24	20	10	4	6	38	21	17	0	1.200	1.900
30	Rangers	Sco	24	20	10	4	6	26	24	2	0	1.200	1.300
31	Bayern Munich	FRG	23	16	9	3	4	34	15	19	2	1.438	2.125
32	FC Liège	Bel	23	18	10	2	6	32	17	15	1	1.278	1.778
33	Club Bruges	Bel	23	24	9	3	12	40	39	1	2	0.958	1.667
34	Austria Vienna	Aut	22	18	8	5	5	37	24	13	1	1.222	2.056
35	Dynamo Dresden	GDR	22	16	8	4	4	26	14	12	2	1.375	1.625
36	Videoton	Hun	22	20	8	3	9	23	24	-1	3	1.100	1.150
37	Español	Esp	20	12	7	3	2	17	7	10	3	1.667	1.417
38	Heart of Midlothian	Sco	20	16	8	3	5	22	19	3	1	1.250	1.375
39	Vitória Guimarães	Por	20	18	8	3	7	19	23	-4	1	1.111	1.056
40	Brøndby IF	Den	19	14	7	3	4	20	11	9	2	1.357	1.429
41	Nottingham Forest	Eng	19	12	7	3	2	12	7	5	2	1.583	1.000
42	Waregem	Bel	19	14	7	3	4	24	20	4	2	1.357	1.714
43	Athletic Bilbao	Esp	19	16	9	1	6	24	22	2	0	1.188	1.500
44	Verona	Ita	18	12	6	5	1	18	11	7	1	1.500	1.500
45	Barcelona	Esp	18	16	6	4	6	16	10	6	2	1.125	1.000
46	Radnicki Nis	Yug	18	16	7	2	7	23	21	2	2	1.125	1.438
47	PSV Eindhoven	Ned	17	18	7	3	8	29	18	11	0	0.944	1.611
48	Dinamo Minsk	URS	17	14	7	2	5	22	13	9	1	1.214	1.571
49	Borussia Dortmund	FRG	17	14	8	1	5	19	13	6	0	1.214	1.357
50	Auxerre	Fra	16	14	6	3	5	25	15	10	1	1.143	1.786
51	Torino	Ita	16	12	5	5	2	19	11	8	1	1.333	1.583
52	Victoria Bucharest	Rom	16	14	6	3	5	21	17	4	1	1.143	1.500
53	Aberdeen	Sco	16	14	6	4	4	18	15	3	0	1.143	1.286
54	Antwerp	Bel	16	16	5	5	6	28	26	2	1	1.000	1.750

Pos'n	Club	Cnty	Pts	P	W	D	L	F	A	Diff	B	Pts/P	F/P
55	Rapid Vienna	Aut	16	14	7	2	5	19	18	1	0	1.143	1.357
56	Beveren	Bel	15	14	7	1	6	21	12	9	0	1.071	1.500
57	Sparta Prague	Tch	15	12	6	2	4	20	17	3	1	1.250	1.667
58	Real Sociedad	Esp	15	12	6	2	4	14	12	2	1	1.250	1.167
59	Groningen	Ned	15	16	6	3	7	22	22	0	0	0.938	1.375
60	Zaljeznicar Sarajevo	Yug	14	10	5	2	3	18	11	7	2	1.400	1.800
61	Torpedo Moscow	URS	14	10	6	1	3	16	11	5	1	1.400	1.600
62	Red Star Belgrade	Yug	14	12	6	2	4	20	16	4	0	1.167	1.667
63	FC Porto	Por	14	10	7	0	3	17	13	4	0	1.400	1.700
64	Banik Ostrava	Tch	14	16	5	4	7	22	21	1	0	0.875	1.375
65	Widzew Lódź	Pol	14	14	5	4	5	11	14	-3	0	1.000	0.786
66	Atlético Madrid	Esp	14	16	7	0	9	16	22	-6	0	0.875	1.000
67	Sportul Studentesc Bucharest	Rom	14	16	5	4	7	16	24	-8	0	0.875	1.000
68	Servette	Sui	13	10	5	3	2	16	8	8	0	1.300	1.600
69	Manchester United	Eng	13	10	4	4	2	13	9	4	1	1.300	1.300
70	Honvéd	Hun	13	10	6	1	3	18	16	2	0	1.300	1.800
71	Seville	Esp	13	12	5	3	4	17	15	2	0	1.083	1.417
72	PAOK Salonika	Gre	13	12	4	5	3	10	10	0	0	1.083	0.833
73	Sturm Graz	Aut	13	14	3	6	5	13	14	-1	1	0.929	0.929
74	FC Tirol	Aut	13	14	5	1	8	15	22	-7	2	0.929	1.071
75	Velez Mostar	Yug	12	10	5	2	3	15	12	3	0	1.200	1.500
76	Atalanta	Ita	12	10	3	5	2	8	7	1	1	1.200	0.800
77	Nantes	Fra	12	12	3	5	4	18	20	-2	1	1.000	1.500
78	Legia Warsaw	Pol	12	12	4	4	4	14	16	-2	0	1.000	1.167
79	Linzer ASK	Aut	12	12	5	2	5	9	15	-6	0	1.000	0.750
80	Lokeren	Bel	11	12	3	5	4	14	14	0	0	0.917	1.167
81	Sion	Sui	11	10	5	1	4	14	16	-2	0	1.100	1.400
82	Admira Wacker	Aut	11	10	5	1	4	11	13	-2	0	1.100	1.100
83	Inter Bratislava	Tch	10	8	5	0	3	26	10	16	0	1.250	3.250
84	First Vienna	Aut	10	8	4	2	2	14	8	6	0	1.250	1.750
85	Malmö FF	Swe	10	12	4	2	6	14	13	1	0	0.833	1.167
86	Bologna	Ita	10	8	4	1	3	10	9	1	1	1.250	1.250
87	TJ Vitkovice	Tch	10	8	3	3	2	8	7	1	1	1.250	1.000
88	Monaco	Fra	10	10	4	2	4	16	16	0	0	1.000	1.600
89	Sparta Rotterdam	Ned	10	10	3	4	3	14	15	-1	0	1.000	1.400
90	Dnepr Dnepropetrovsk	URS	10	12	3	4	5	12	15	-3	0	0.833	1.000
91	TPS Turku	Fin	10	14	4	2	8	10	17	-7	0	0.714	0.714
92	Hammarby IF	Swe	9	6	4	1	1	15	9	6	0	1.500	2.500
93	Dinamo Kiev	URS	9	8	3	3	2	10	4	6	0	1.125	1.250
94	Aston Villa	Eng	9	8	4	1	3	15	10	5	0	1.125	1.875
95	Celtic	Sco	9	8	4	1	3	13	8	5	0	1.125	1.625
96	Toulouse	Fra	9	8	4	1	3	12	10	2	0	1.125	1.500
97	Lens	Fra	9	8	3	3	2	10	10	0	0	1.125	1.250
98	Olympiakos Pireus	Gre	9	10	2	5	3	10	10	0	0	0.900	1.000
99	Panathinaikos	Gre	9	12	3	2	7	18	21	-3	1	0.750	1.500
100	Boavista	Por	9	12	4	1	7	15	19	-4	0	0.750	1.250
101	Carl Zeiss Jena	GDR	9	12	3	3	6	15	21	-6	0	0.750	1.250
102	Sochaux	Fra	8	6	3	2	1	15	3	12	0	1.333	2.500
103	Sarajevo	Yug	8	6	3	2	1	16	14	2	0	1.333	2.667
104	Dinamo Tbilisi	URS	8	8	3	2	3	10	9	1	0	1.000	1.250
105	Belenenses	Por	8	6	3	2	1	3	2	1	0	1.333	0.500
106	AC Milan	Ita	8	10	3	2	5	12	12	0	0	0.800	1.200
107	Standard Liège	Bel	8	8	3	2	3	10	10	0	0	1.000	1.250
108	Flamurtari Vlorë	Alb	8	8	3	2	3	8	8	0	0	1.000	1.000
109	Dukla Prague	Tch	8	10	2	4	4	8	10	-2	0	0.800	0.800
110	Gent	Bel	8	10	2	4	4	13	16	-3	0	0.800	1.300
111	Bayer Uerdingen	FRG	7	6	3	1	2	9	4	5	0	1.167	1.500

Pos'n	Club	Cnty	Pts	P	W	D	L	F	A	Diff	B	Pts/P	F/P
112	Trakia Plovdiv	Bul	7	8	2	3	3	16	12	4	0	0.875	2.000
113	Vitesse	Ned	7	6	3	1	2	7	4	3	0	1.167	1.167
114	Lokomotiv Sofia	Bul	7	6	2	3	1	10	9	1	0	1.167	1.667
115	Dinamo Bucarest	Rom	7	8	3	1	4	11	11	0	0	0.875	1.375
116	Southampton	Eng	7	8	1	5	2	8	9	-1	0	0.875	1.000
117	Magdeburg	GDR	7	8	3	1	4	5	7	-2	0	0.875	0.625
118	Ferencváros	Hun	7	10	2	3	5	9	15	-6	0	0.700	0.900
119	FC Zürich	Sui	7	8	2	3	3	9	16	-7	0	0.875	1.125
120	Levski Sofia	Bul	7	10	2	3	5	10	19	-9	0	0.700	1.000
121	Queen's Park Rangers	Eng	6	4	3	0	1	13	6	7	0	1.500	3.250
122	Dinamo Moscow	URS	6	6	2	2	2	7	5	2	0	1.000	1.167
123	Paris Saint-Germain	Fra	6	8	2	2	4	12	12	0	0	0.750	1.500
124	Arsenal	Eng	6	6	3	0	3	9	10	-1	0	1.000	1.500
125	Chernomorets Odessa	URS	6	8	2	2	4	9	10	-1	0	0.750	1.125
126	Grasshoppers Zürich	Sui	6	6	3	0	3	6	8	-2	0	1.000	1.000
127	Dinamo Tirana	Alb	6	6	2	2	2	2	5	-3	0	1.000	0.333
128	Utrecht	Ned	6	8	2	2	4	8	12	-4	0	0.750	1.000
129	Tatabánya	Hun	6	8	2	2	4	6	11	-5	0	0.750	0.750
130	Rába ETO	Hun	6	8	2	2	4	11	18	-7	0	0.750	1.375
131	Ajax	Ned	5	8	2	1	5	18	11	7	0	0.625	2.250
132	Wettingen	Sui	5	4	2	1	1	6	2	4	0	1.250	1.500
133	Hibernian	Sco	5	4	2	1	1	4	1	3	0	1.250	1.000
134	Aris Salonika	Gre	5	4	2	1	1	9	7	2	0	1.250	2.250
135	Real Zaragoza	Esp	5	4	2	1	1	5	3	2	0	1.250	1.250
136	Rijeka	Yug	5	6	2	1	3	8	8	0	0	0.833	1.333
137	Dinamo Zagreb	Yug	5	6	1	3	2	5	6	-1	0	0.833	0.833
138	Lucerne	Sui	5	6	1	3	2	4	5	-1	0	0.833	0.667
139	Watford	Eng	5	6	2	1	3	10	12	-2	0	0.833	1.667
140	IFK Norrköping	Swe	5	6	1	3	2	4	6	-2	0	0.833	0.667
141	Karl-Marx-Stadt	GDR	5	8	2	1	5	9	12	-3	0	0.625	1.125
142	Winterslag	Bel	5	6	2	1	3	5	9	-4	0	0.833	0.833
143	CSKA Sofia	Bul	5	6	2	1	3	7	12	-5	0	0.833	1.167
144	GKS Katowice	Pol	5	10	2	1	7	9	16	-7	0	0.500	0.900
145	Zenit Leningrad	URS	5	8	2	1	5	7	18	-11	0	0.625	0.875
146	Shamrock Rovers	Irl	4	4	2	0	2	7	5	2	0	1.000	1.750
147	Arges Pitesti	Rom	4	4	1	2	1	7	6	1	0	1.000	1.750
148	Osasuna	Esp	4	4	2	0	2	4	4	0	0	1.000	1.000
149	Corvinul Hunedoara	Rom	4	4	1	2	1	8	9	-1	0	1.000	2.000
150	Saint-Etienne	Fra	4	4	1	2	1	4	5	-1	0	1.000	1.000
151	Laval	Fra	4	4	1	2	1	4	5	-1	0	1.000	1.000
152	Stahl Brandenburg	GDR	4	4	1	2	1	3	4	-1	0	1.000	0.750
153	Valur Reykjavik	Isl	4	4	1	2	1	3	5	-2	0	1.000	0.750
154	Fenerbahçe	Tur	4	6	2	0	4	7	10	-3	0	0.667	1.167
155	Omonia Nicosia	Cyp	4	6	1	2	3	7	10	-3	0	0.667	1.167
156	Zhalgiris Vilnius	URS	4	6	2	0	4	7	11	-4	0	0.667	1.167
157	Vorwärts Frankfurt/Oder	GDR	4	6	2	0	4	5	9	-4	0	0.667	0.833
158	Wismut Aue	GDR	4	6	1	2	3	4	8	-4	0	0.667	0.667
159	Politehnica Timisoara	Rom	4	4	2	0	2	4	8	-4	0	1.000	1.000
160	Bohemians	Irl	4	6	1	2	3	7	12	-5	0	0.667	1.167
161	IL Viking	Nor	4	6	1	2	3	5	10	-5	0	0.667	0.833
162	RoPS Rovaniemi	Fin	4	6	1	2	3	2	10	-8	0	0.667	0.333
163	AEK Athenes	Gre	4	8	2	0	6	2	16	-14	0	0.500	0.250
164	Ujpesti Dózsa	Hun	3	4	1	1	2	2	3	-1	0	0.750	0.500
165	St. Mirren	Sco	3	6	1	1	4	7	9	-2	0	0.500	1.167
166	Vardar Skopje	Yug	3	4	1	1	2	3	5	-2	0	0.750	0.750
167	Haarlem	Ned	3	4	1	1	2	6	9	-3	0	0.750	1.500
168	Ipswich Town	Eng	3	4	1	1	2	5	8	-3	0	0.750	1.250

Pos'n	Club	Cnty	Pts	P	W	D	L	F	A	Diff	B	Pts/P	F/P
169	Galatasaray	Tur	3	4	1	1	2	3	6	-3	0	0.750	0.750
170	Sporting Gijón	Esp	3	4	1	1	2	2	5	-3	0	0.750	0.500
171	Iraklis	Gre	3	4	1	1	2	1	4	-3	0	0.750	0.250
172	Bryne IL	Nor	3	4	1	1	2	3	7	-4	0	0.750	0.750
173	AIK	Swe	3	4	1	1	2	2	6	-4	0	0.750	0.500
174	Slask Wroclaw	Pol	3	4	1	1	2	4	9	-5	0	0.750	1.000
175	IK Brage	Swe	3	6	1	1	4	8	15	-7	0	0.500	1.333
176	Besiktas	Tur	3	6	1	1	4	3	10	-7	0	0.500	0.500
177	Naestved IF	Den	3	4	1	1	2	3	11	-8	0	0.750	0.750
178	Slavia Sofia	Bul	3	6	1	1	4	8	21	-13	0	0.500	1.333
179	Coleraine	Nir	3	8	0	3	5	4	17	-13	0	0.375	0.500
180	DAC Dunajská Streda	Tch	2	4	1	0	3	7	7	0	0	0.500	1.750
181	Lausanne-Sports	Sui	2	2	1	0	1	3	3	0	0	1.000	1.500
182	CSKA Moscow	URS	2	2	1	0	1	2	2	0	0	1.000	1.000
183	IF Elfsborg	Swe	2	2	0	2	0	2	2	0	0	1.000	1.000
184	Ikast FS	Den	2	2	1	0	1	2	2	0	0	1.000	1.000
185	Stal Mielec	Pol	2	2	0	2	0	1	1	0	0	1.000	0.500
186	Nuremberg	FRG	2	2	1	0	1	3	4	-1	0	1.000	1.500
187	Rosenborg BK	Nor	2	2	1	0	1	3	4	-1	0	1.000	1.500
188	Larissa	Gre	2	2	1	0	1	2	3	-1	0	1.000	1.000
189	Rad Belgrade	Yug	2	2	1	0	1	2	3	-1	0	1.000	1.000
190	Pécsi MSC	Hun	2	2	1	0	1	1	2	-1	0	1.000	0.500
191	Eintracht Frankfurt	FRG	2	2	1	0	1	4	6	-2	0	1.000	2.000
192	Real Betis	Esp	2	4	1	0	3	3	5	-2	0	0.500	0.750
193	Real Valladolid	Esp	2	2	1	0	1	2	4	-2	0	1.000	1.000
194	Ilves Tampere	Fin	2	2	1	0	1	2	4	-2	0	1.000	1.000
195	Slavia Prague	Tch	2	2	1	0	1	1	3	-2	0	1.000	0.500
196	Chaves	Por	2	4	1	0	3	6	9	-3	0	0.500	1.500
197	Sliven	Bul	2	2	1	0	1	2	5	-3	0	1.000	1.000
198	Portimonense	Por	2	2	1	0	1	1	4	-3	0	1.000	0.500
199	OFI Crete	Gre	2	2	1	0	1	1	4	-3	0	1.000	0.500
200	Twente Enschede	Ned	2	4	0	2	2	2	6	-4	0	0.500	0.500
201	Mjøndalen IF	Nor	2	2	1	0	1	1	5	-4	0	1.000	0.500
202	CSU Galati	Rom	2	2	1	0	1	1	5	-4	0	1.000	0.500
203	Öster SIF	Swe	2	4	1	0	3	2	8	-6	0	0.500	0.500
204	Trabzonspor	Tur	2	4	1	0	3	1	8	-7	0	0.500	0.250
205	Lillestrøm SK	Nor	2	4	1	0	3	4	12	-8	0	0.500	1.000
206	Apollon Limassol	Cyp	2	4	0	2	2	4	12	-8	0	0.500	1.000
207	Linfield	Nir	2	4	0	2	2	1	9	-8	0	0.500	0.250
208	AGF Aarhus	Den	2	6	1	0	5	4	13	-9	0	0.333	0.667
209	Apoel Nicosia	Cyp	2	6	0	2	4	7	17	-10	0	0.333	1.167
210	Avenir Beggen	Lux	2	4	1	0	3	2	12	-10	0	0.500	0.500
211	Pezoporikos Larnaca	Cyp	1	2	0	1	1	2	3	-1	0	0.500	1.000
212	FC Kuusysi Lahti	Fin	1	2	0	1	1	2	3	-1	0	0.500	1.000
213	KV Mechelen	Bel	1	2	0	1	1	2	3	-1	0	0.500	1.000
214	Hamrun Spartans	Mlt	1	2	0	1	1	0	1	-1	0	0.500	0.000
215	Vålerengen SIF	Nor	1	2	0	1	1	0	1	-1	0	0.500	0.000
216	Derry City	Irl	1	2	0	1	1	0	1	-1	0	0.500	0.000
217	FH Hafnarfjördhur	Isl	1	2	0	1	1	3	5	-2	0	0.500	1.500
218	Szombierki Bytom	Pol	1	2	0	1	1	1	3	-2	0	0.500	0.500
219	Lech Poznań	Pol	1	2	0	1	1	1	3	-2	0	0.500	0.500
220	Glenavon	Nir	1	2	0	1	1	0	2	-2	0	0.500	0.000
221	GAIS	Swe	1	2	0	1	1	2	5	-3	0	0.500	1.000
222	Limerick	Irl	1	2	0	1	1	1	4	-3	0	0.500	0.500
223	Grazer AK	Aut	1	2	0	1	1	1	4	-3	0	0.500	0.500
224	IBV Vestmannaeyjar	Isl	1	2	0	1	1	0	3	-3	0	0.500	0.000
225	Pogon Szczecin	Pol	1	4	0	1	3	3	7	-4	0	0.250	0.750

Pos'n	Club	Cnty	Pts	P	W	D	L	F	A	Diff	B	Pts/P	F/P
226	Metz	Fra	1	2	0	1	1	3	7	-4	0	0.500	1.500
227	Sigma Olomouc	Tch	1	2	0	1	1	1	5	-4	0	0.500	0.500
228	Molde FK	Nor	1	2	0	1	1	1	5	-4	0	0.500	0.500
229	Lyngby BK	Den	1	4	0	1	3	4	9	-5	0	0.250	1.000
230	B 1903 Copenhagen	Den	1	2	0	1	1	1	6	-5	0	0.500	0.500
231	MTK-VM	Hun	1	4	0	1	3	3	9	-6	0	0.250	0.750
232	St-Gallen	Sui	1	4	0	1	3	2	10	-8	0	0.250	0.500
233	Glentoran	Nir	1	6	0	1	5	3	12	-9	0	0.167	0.500
234	Jeunesse Esch	Lux	1	4	0	1	3	2	15	-13	0	0.250	0.500
235	IA Akranes	Isl	1	6	0	1	5	2	23	-21	0	0.167	0.333
236	Red Boys Differdange	Lux	1	4	0	1	3	0	25	-25	0	0.250	0.000
237	Akademik Sofia	Bul	0	2	0	0	2	1	3	-2	0	0.000	0.500
238	Zaglebie Lubin	Pol	0	2	0	0	2	0	2	-2	0	0.000	0.000
239	Partizan Tirana	Alb	0	2	0	0	2	0	2	-2	0	0.000	0.000
240	Lokomotiv Plovdiv	Bul	0	2	0	0	2	2	5	-3	0	0.000	1.000
241	Górnik Zabrze	Pol	0	2	0	0	2	2	5	-3	0	0.000	1.000
242	West Bromwich Albion	Eng	0	2	0	0	2	1	4	-3	0	0.000	0.500
243	Flacara Moreni	Rom	0	2	0	0	2	1	4	-3	0	0.000	0.500
244	Dukla Banská Bystrica	Tch	0	2	0	0	2	3	7	-4	0	0.000	1.500
245	Roda JC	Ned	0	2	0	0	2	2	6	-4	0	0.000	1.000
246	Wisla Kraków	Pol	0	2	0	0	2	1	5	-4	0	0.000	0.500
247	Plastika Nitra	Tch	0	2	0	0	2	1	5	-4	0	0.000	0.500
248	Progrès Niedercorn	Lux	0	2	0	0	2	0	4	-4	0	0.000	0.000
249	EPA Larnaca	Cyp	0	2	0	0	2	0	4	-4	0	0.000	0.000
250	St. Patrick's Athletic	Irl	0	2	0	0	2	0	4	-4	0	0.000	0.000
251	Petrolul Ploiesti	Rom	0	2	0	0	2	0	4	-4	0	0.000	0.000
252	Vejle BK	Den	0	2	0	0	2	0	4	-4	0	0.000	0.000
253	Adanaspor	Tur	0	2	0	0	2	2	7	-5	0	0.000	1.000
254	Haka Valkeakoski	Fin	0	2	0	0	2	2	7	-5	0	0.000	1.000
255	OB Odense	Den	0	2	0	0	2	2	7	-5	0	0.000	1.000
256	Hansa Rostock	GDR	0	2	0	0	2	2	7	-5	0	0.000	1.000
257	Örgryte IS	Swe	0	2	0	0	2	2	7	-5	0	0.000	1.000
258	KuPS Kuopio	Fin	0	2	0	0	2	1	6	-5	0	0.000	0.500
259	Panionios	Gre	0	2	0	0	2	1	6	-5	0	0.000	0.500
260	Montpellier	Fra	0	2	0	0	2	1	6	-5	0	0.000	0.500
261	Dundalk	Irl	0	2	0	0	2	0	5	-5	0	0.000	0.000
262	Galway United	Irl	0	2	0	0	2	2	8	-6	0	0.000	1.000
263	Pirin Blagoevgrad	Bul	0	2	0	0	2	1	7	-6	0	0.000	0.500
264	Kalmar FF	Swe	0	2	0	0	2	1	7	-6	0	0.000	0.500
265	Zurrieq	Mlt	0	2	0	0	2	1	8	-7	0	0.000	0.500
266	Fram Reykjavik	Isl	0	2	0	0	2	0	7	-7	0	0.000	0.000
267	KR Reykjavik	Isl	0	2	0	0	2	0	7	-7	0	0.000	0.000
268	Aarau	Sui	0	2	0	0	2	0	7	-7	0	0.000	0.000
269	Spora Luxembourg	Lux	0	2	0	0	2	2	10	-8	0	0.000	1.000
270	Vikingur Reykjavik	Isl	0	2	0	0	2	0	8	-8	0	0.000	0.000
271	Apolonia Fier	Alb	0	2	0	0	2	0	8	-8	0	0.000	0.000
272	Sporting Braga	Por	0	2	0	0	2	0	9	-9	0	0.000	0.000
273	Union Luxembourg	Lux	0	2	0	0	2	1	11	-10	0	0.000	0.500
274	Anorthosis Famagusta	Cyp	0	2	0	0	2	0	11	-11	0	0.000	0.000
275	Sliema Wanderers	Mlt	0	4	0	0	4	3	16	-13	0	0.000	0.750
276	Valletta	Mlt	0	4	0	0	4	1	14	-13	0	0.000	0.250
277	Drogheda United	Irl	0	2	0	0	2	0	14	-14	0	0.000	0.000
278	Aris Bonnevoie	Lux	0	2	0	0	2	0	15	-15	0	0.000	0.000
279	Hibernians	Mlt	0	4	0	0	4	0	15	-15	0	0.000	0.000
280	HJK Helsinki	Fin	0	4	0	0	4	0	17	-17	0	0.000	0.000
281	Rabat Ajax	Mlt	0	4	0	0	4	0	20	-20	0	0.000	0.000
	Total		**2660**	**2520**	**991**	**538**	**991**	**3386**	**3386**	**0**	**140**	**1.056**	**2.687**

Club Performance by Points

1986-87 to 1990-91

Pos'n	Club	Cnty	Pts	P	W	D	L	F	A	Diff	B	Pts/P	F/P
1	Inter Milan	Ita	45	32	16	9	7	40	21	19	4	1.406	1.250
2	Juventus	Ita	40	24	17	2	5	46	20	26	4	1.667	1.917
3	Bayer Leverkusen	FRG	34	24	11	9	4	31	16	15	3	1.417	1.292
4	Dundee United	Sco	32	24	12	5	7	32	24	8	3	1.333	1.333
5	Werder Bremen	FRG	31	22	11	5	6	42	24	18	4	1.409	1.909
6	Cologne	FRG	29	22	10	7	5	32	18	14	2	1.318	1.455
7	Sporting Lisbon	Por	28	20	10	6	4	41	15	26	2	1.400	2.050
8	Roma	Ita	27	18	11	2	5	29	18	11	3	1.500	1.611
9	Napoli	Ita	27	20	8	8	4	24	20	4	3	1.350	1.200
10	IFK Gothenburg	Swe	25	16	8	6	2	23	9	14	3	1.563	1.438
11	VFB Stuttgart	FRG	25	18	9	4	5	29	16	13	3	1.389	1.611
12	Español	Esp	20	12	7	3	2	17	7	10	3	1.667	1.417
13	FC Liège	Bel	19	14	8	2	4	27	12	15	1	1.357	1.929
14	Brøndby IF	Den	19	14	7	3	4	20	11	9	2	1.357	1.429
15	Heart of Midlothian	Sco	19	14	8	2	4	20	13	7	1	1.357	1.429
16	Fiorentina	Ita	19	14	5	6	3	8	7	1	3	1.357	0.571
17	Barcelona	Esp	18	16	6	4	6	16	10	6	2	1.125	1.000
18	Vitória Guimarães	Por	18	16	7	3	6	18	18	0	1	1.125	1.125
19	Dynamo Dresden	GDR	17	12	6	3	3	18	9	9	2	1.417	1.500
20	Club Bruges	Bel	16	14	6	2	6	28	20	8	2	1.143	2.000
21	Borussia Dortmund	FRG	16	12	8	0	4	19	11	8	0	1.333	1.583
22	Victoria Bucharest	Rom	16	14	6	3	5	21	17	4	1	1.143	1.500
23	Bayern Munich	FRG	15	10	6	1	3	22	13	9	2	1.500	2.200
24	Partizan Belgrade	Yug	15	14	7	1	6	24	16	8	0	1.071	1.714
25	Spartak Moscow	URS	15	14	6	3	5	20	17	3	0	1.071	1.429
26	Real Sociedad	Esp	15	12	6	2	4	14	12	2	1	1.250	1.167
27	Girondins Bordeaux	Fra	15	12	6	3	3	9	10	-1	0	1.250	0.750
28	Red Star Belgrade	Yug	14	10	6	2	2	18	12	6	0	1.400	1.800
29	Torpedo Moscow	URS	14	10	6	1	3	16	11	5	1	1.400	1.600
30	Bor. Mönchengladbach	FRG	14	12	4	4	4	16	14	2	2	1.167	1.333
31	Auxerre	Fra	13	10	5	2	3	20	7	13	1	1.300	2.000
32	Feyenoord	Ned	13	12	6	1	5	21	16	5	0	1.083	1.750
33	Rangers	Sco	13	10	5	3	2	14	9	5	0	1.300	1.400
34	Torino	Ita	12	8	4	3	1	14	5	9	1	1.500	1.750
35	Verona	Ita	12	8	4	3	1	12	7	5	1	1.500	1.500
36	Velez Mostar	Yug	12	10	5	2	3	15	12	3	0	1.200	1.500
37	Atalanta	Ita	12	10	3	5	2	8	7	1	1	1.200	0.800
38	Hamburg	FRG	11	8	5	0	3	13	8	5	1	1.375	1.625
39	Admira Wacker	Aut	11	8	5	1	2	10	6	4	0	1.375	1.250
40	Groningen	Ned	11	12	4	3	5	15	15	0	0	0.917	1.250
41	FC Tirol	Aut	11	10	4	1	5	12	13	-1	2	1.100	1.200
42	Antwerp	Bel	11	12	3	4	5	16	18	-2	1	0.917	1.333
43	First Vienna	Aut	10	8	4	2	2	14	8	6	0	1.250	1.750
44	Anderlecht	Bel	10	8	4	1	3	12	9	3	1	1.250	1.500
45	Bologna	Ita	10	8	4	1	3	10	9	1	1	1.250	1.250
46	TJ Vitkovice	Tch	10	8	3	3	2	8	7	1	1	1.250	1.000
47	Rapid Vienna	Aut	10	8	5	0	3	13	13	0	0	1.250	1.625
48	Atlético Madrid	Esp	10	10	5	0	5	8	9	-1	0	1.000	0.800
49	Austria Vienna	Aut	10	10	4	2	4	12	15	-3	0	1.000	1.200
50	Sportul Studentesc Bucharest	Rom	10	10	4	2	4	10	13	-3	0	1.000	1.000
51	Universitatea Craiova	Rom	10	10	5	0	5	10	13	-3	0	1.000	1.000
52	TPS Turku	Fin	10	12	4	2	6	9	13	-4	0	0.833	0.750
53	Honvéd	Hun	9	6	4	1	1	12	9	3	0	1.500	2.000

Pos'n	Club	Cnty	Pts	P	W	D	L	F	A	Diff	B	Pts/P	F/P
54	Toulouse	Fra	9	8	4	1	3	12	10	2	0	1.125	1.500
55	Valencia	Esp	9	8	3	3	2	12	10	2	0	1.125	1.500
56	Beveren	Bel	9	10	4	1	5	9	8	1	0	0.900	0.900
57	Dinamo Kiev	URS	8	6	3	2	1	10	3	7	0	1.333	1.667
58	FC Porto	Por	8	6	4	0	2	11	7	4	0	1.333	1.833
59	Panathinaikos	Gre	8	8	3	1	4	16	15	1	1	1.000	2.000
60	Belenenses	Por	8	6	3	2	1	3	2	1	0	1.333	0.500
61	Flamurtari Vlorë	Alb	8	8	3	2	3	8	8	0	0	1.000	1.000
62	Aberdeen	Sco	8	8	3	2	3	5	6	-1	0	1.000	0.625
63	Athletic Bilbao	Esp	8	8	4	0	4	11	13	-2	0	1.000	1.375
64	Bayer Uerdingen	FRG	7	6	3	1	2	9	4	5	0	1.167	1.500
65	Trakia Plovdiv	Bul	7	8	2	3	3	16	12	4	0	0.875	2.000
66	Monaco	Fra	7	6	3	1	2	9	6	3	0	1.167	1.500
67	Vitesse	Ned	7	6	3	1	2	7	4	3	0	1.167	1.167
68	Dinamo Minsk	URS	7	6	3	1	2	7	7	0	0	1.167	1.167
69	Dukla Prague	Tch	7	8	2	3	3	8	9	-1	0	0.875	1.000
70	Sochaux	Fra	6	4	2	2	0	13	1	12	0	1.500	3.250
71	Neuchâtel Xamax	Sui	6	4	2	2	0	6	2	4	0	1.500	1.500
72	Hajduk Split	Yug	6	6	2	2	2	9	6	3	0	1.000	1.500
73	Aston Villa	Eng	6	4	3	0	1	7	5	2	0	1.500	1.750
74	Dinamo Tbilisi	URS	6	6	2	2	2	8	7	1	0	1.000	1.333
75	Olympiakos Pireus	Gre	6	6	1	4	1	7	6	1	0	1.000	1.167
76	Gent	Bel	6	6	2	2	2	7	8	-1	0	1.000	1.167
77	Sion	Sui	6	6	3	0	3	8	11	-3	0	1.000	1.333
78	Lokomotive Leipzig	GDR	5	4	2	1	1	8	3	5	0	1.250	2.000
79	Wettingen	Sui	5	4	2	1	1	6	2	4	0	1.250	1.500
80	Dinamo Moscow	URS	5	4	2	1	1	5	2	3	0	1.250	1.250
81	Hibernian	Sco	5	4	2	1	1	4	1	3	0	1.250	1.000
82	Waregem	Bel	5	4	2	1	1	8	6	2	0	1.250	2.000
83	Benfica	Por	5	6	2	1	3	8	6	2	0	0.833	1.333
84	Real Zaragoza	Esp	5	4	2	1	1	5	3	2	0	1.250	1.250
85	Standard Liège	Bel	5	4	2	1	1	6	5	1	0	1.250	1.500
86	Banik Ostrava	Tch	5	6	2	1	3	10	11	-1	0	0.833	1.667
87	Dinamo Zagreb	Yug	5	6	1	3	2	5	6	-1	0	0.833	0.833
88	Lucerne	Sui	5	6	1	3	2	4	5	-1	0	0.833	0.667
89	Magdeburg	GDR	5	6	2	1	3	2	4	-2	0	0.833	0.333
90	Karl-Marx-Stadt	GDR	5	8	2	1	5	9	12	-3	0	0.625	1.125
91	Legia Warsaw	Pol	5	6	2	1	3	8	13	-5	0	0.833	1.333
92	GKS Katowice	Pol	5	10	2	1	7	9	16	-7	0	0.500	0.900
93	Zenit Leningrad	URS	5	6	2	1	3	5	12	-7	0	0.833	0.833
94	Inter Bratislava	Tch	4	4	2	0	2	7	4	3	0	1.000	1.750
95	Utrecht	Ned	4	4	1	2	1	4	3	1	0	1.000	1.000
96	Fenerbahçe	Tur	4	4	2	0	2	7	7	0	0	1.000	1.750
97	Stahl Brandenburg	GDR	4	4	1	2	1	3	4	-1	0	1.000	0.750
98	Seville	Esp	4	4	1	2	1	3	4	-1	0	1.000	0.750
99	Widzew Lódź	Pol	4	4	1	2	1	2	3	-1	0	1.000	0.500
100	Wismut Aue	GDR	4	4	1	2	1	2	3	-1	0	1.000	0.500
101	Servette	Sui	4	4	1	2	1	2	3	-1	0	1.000	0.500
102	Omonia Nicosia	Cyp	4	6	1	2	3	7	10	-3	0	0.667	1.167
103	Zhalgiris Vilnius	URS	4	6	2	0	4	7	11	-4	0	0.667	1.167
104	Politehnica Timisoara	Rom	4	4	2	0	2	4	8	-4	0	1.000	1.000
105	RoPS Rovaniemi	Fin	4	6	1	2	3	2	10	-8	0	0.667	0.333
106	Malmö FF	Swe	3	4	1	1	2	4	4	0	0	0.750	1.000
107	Chernomorets Odessa	URS	3	4	1	1	2	4	4	0	0	0.750	1.000
108	AC Milan	Ita	3	4	1	1	2	3	3	0	0	0.750	0.750
109	Paris Saint-Germain	Fra	3	4	1	1	2	4	5	-1	0	0.750	1.000
110	Ujpesti Dózsa	Hun	3	4	1	1	2	2	3	-1	0	0.750	0.500

Pos'n	Club	Cnty	Pts	P	W	D	L	F	A	Diff	B	Pts/P	F/P
111	PAOK Salonika	Gre	3	4	0	3	1	1	2	-1	0	0.750	0.250
112	Tatabánya	Hun	3	4	1	1	2	3	5	-2	0	0.750	0.750
113	Ferencváros	Hun	3	4	1	1	2	3	5	-2	0	0.750	0.750
114	Rába ETO	Hun	3	4	1	1	2	5	8	-3	0	0.750	1.250
115	Boavista	Por	3	6	1	1	4	4	7	-3	0	0.500	0.667
116	Galatasaray	Tur	3	4	I	1	2	3	6	-3	0	0.750	0.750
117	Besiktas	Tur	3	4	1	1	2	2	5	-3	0	0.750	0.500
118	Iraklis	Gre	3	4	1	1	2	1	4	-3	0	0.750	0.250
119	Dnepr Dnepropetrovsk	URS	3	6	0	3	3	4	8	-4	0	0.500	0.667
120	DAC Dunajská Streda	Tch	2	4	1	0	3	7	7	0	0	0.500	1.750
121	Lausanne-Sports	Sui	2	2	1	0	1	3	3	0	0	1.000	1.500
122	Ikast FS	Den	2	2	1	0	1	2	2	0	0	1.000	1.000
123	Valur Reykjavik	Isl	2	2	0	2	0	1	1	0	0	1.000	0.500
124	Linfield	Nir	2	2	0	2	0	1	1	0	0	1.000	0.500
125	Lokomotiv Sofia	Bul	2	2	1	0	1	3	4	-1	0	1.000	1.500
126	Nuremberg	FRG	2	2	1	0	1	3	4	-1	0	1.000	1.500
127	Rosenborg BK	Nor	2	2	1	0	1	3	4	-1	0	1.000	1.500
128	CSKA Sofia	Bul	2	2	1	0	1	2	3	-1	0	1.000	1.000
129	Celtic	Sco	2	2	1	0	1	2	3	-1	0	1.000	1.000
130	Rad Belgrade	Yug	2	2	1	0	1	2	3	-1	0	1.000	1.000
131	Pécsi MSC	Hun	2	2	1	0	1	1	2	-1	0	1.000	0.500
132	Lens	Fra	2	2	1	0	1	1	2	-1	0	1.000	0.500
133	Bohemians Prague	Tch	2	2	1	0	1	1	2	-1	0	1.000	0.500
134	Eintracht Frankfurt	FRG	2	2	1	0	1	4	6	-2	0	1.000	2.000
135	Ilves Tampere	Fin	2	2	1	0	1	2	4	-2	0	1.000	1.000
136	Sporting Gijón	Esp	2	2	1	0	1	1	3	-2	0	1.000	0.500
137	Chaves	Por	2	4	1	0	3	6	9	-3	0	0.500	1.500
138	OFI Crete	Gre	2	2	1	0	1	1	4	-3	0	1.000	0.500
139	Linzer ASK	Aut	2	4	0	2	2	1	4	-3	0	0.500	0.250
140	Öster SIF	Swe	2	2	1	0	1	2	6	-4	0	1.000	1.000
141	Twente Enschede	Ned	2	4	0	2	2	2	6	-4	0	0.500	0.500
142	Avenir Beggen	Lux	2	2	1	0	1	2	6	-4	0	1.000	1.000
143	AEK Athens	Gre	2	4	1	0	3	1	5	-4	0	0.500	0.250
144	Mjøndalen IF	Nor	2	2	1	0	1	1	5	-4	0	1.000	0.500
145	CSU Galati	Rom	2	2	1	0	1	1	5	-4	0	1.000	0.500
146	Slavia Sofia	Bul	2	4	1	0	3	4	15	-11	0	0.500	1.000
147	Levski Sofia	Bul	1	2	0	1	1	3	4	-1	0	0.500	1.500
148	Sparta Prague	Tch	1	2	0	1	1	2	3	-1	0	0.500	1.000
149	FC Kuusysi Lahti	Fin	1	2	0	1	1	2	3	-1	0	0.500	1.000
150	KV Mechelen	Bel	1	2	0	1	1	2	3	-1	0	0.500	1.000
151	Rijeka	Yug	1	2	0	1	1	1	2	-1	0	0.500	0.500
152	Vålerengen SIF	Nor	1	2	0	1	1	0	1	-1	0	0.500	0.000
153	Lokeren	Bel	1	2	0	1	1	0	1	-1	0	0.500	0.000
154	Bohemians	Irl	1	2	0	1	1	0	1	-1	0	0.500	0.000
155	Sturm Graz	Aut	1	2	0	1	1	0	1	-1	0	0.500	0.000
156	Derry City	Irl	1	2	0	1	1	0	1	-1	0	0.500	0.000
157	FH Hafnarfjördhur	Isl	1	2	0	1	1	3	5	-2	0	0.500	1.500
158	Pogon Szczecin	Pol	1	2	0	1	1	2	4	-2	0	0.500	1.000
159	AIK	Swe	1	2	0	1	1	1	3	-2	0	0.500	0.500
160	Naestved IF	Den	1	2	0	1	1	1	3	-2	0	0.500	0.500
161	IFK Norrköping	Swe	1	2	0	1	1	1	3	-2	0	0.500	0.500
162	Glenavon	Nir	1	2	0	1	1	0	2	-2	0	0.500	0.000
163	GAIS	Swe	1	2	0	1	1	2	5	-3	0	0.500	1.000
164	Apollon Limassol	Cyp	1	2	0	1	1	1	4	-3	0	0.500	0.500
165	Coleraine	Nir	1	4	0	1	3	2	6	-4	0	0.250	0.500
166	Sigma Olomouc	Tch	1	2	0	1	1	1	5	-4	0	0.500	0.500
167	Nantes	Fra	1	2	0	1	1	1	5	-4	0	0.500	0.500

Pos'n	Club	Cnty	Pts	P	W	D	L	F	A	Diff	B	Pts/P	F/P
168	Molde FK	Nor	1	2	0	1	1	1	5	-4	0	0.500	0.500
169	MTK-VM	Hun	1	4	0	1	3	3	9	-6	0	0.250	0.750
170	Jeunesse Esch	Lux	1	4	0	1	3	2	15	-13	0	0.250	0.500
171	IA Akranes	Isl	1	6	0	1	5	2	23	-21	0	0.167	0.333
172	IK Brage	Swe	0	2	0	0	2	2	4	-2	0	0.000	1.000
173	Zaglebie Lubin	Pol	0	2	0	0	2	0	2	-2	0	0.000	0.000
174	Partizani Tirana	Alb	0	2	0	0	2	0	2	-2	0	0.000	0.000
175	Górnik Zabrze	Pol	0	2	0	0	2	2	5	-3	0	0.000	1.000
176	Flacara Moreni	Rom	0	2	0	0	2	1	4	-3	0	0.000	0.500
177	Apoel Nicosia	Cyp	0	2	0	0	2	2	6	-4	0	0.000	1.000
178	Roda JC	Ned	0	2	0	0	2	2	6	-4	0	0.000	1.000
179	Lyngby BK	Den	0	2	0	0	2	1	5	-4	0	0.000	0.500
180	Plastika Nitra	Tch	0	2	0	0	2	1	5	-4	0	0.000	0.500
181	Lillestrøm SK	Nor	0	2	0	0	2	1	5	-4	0	0.000	0.500
182	Glentoran	Nir	0	2	0	0	2	1	5	-4	0	0.000	0.500
183	EPA Larnaca	Cyp	0	2	0	0	2	0	4	-4	0	0.000	0.000
184	St. Patrick's Athletic	Irl	0	2	0	0	2	0	4	-4	0	0.000	0.000
185	Videoton	Hun	0	2	0	0	2	0	4	-4	0	0.000	0.000
186	Petrolul Ploiesti	Rom	0	2	0	0	2	0	4	-4	0	0.000	0.000
187	Vejle BK	Den	0	2	0	0	2	0	4	-4	0	0.000	0.000
188	Hansa Rostock	GDR	0	2	0	0	2	2	7	-5	0	0.000	1.000
189	Örgryte IS	Swe	0	2	0	0	2	2	7	-5	0	0.000	1.000
190	Panionios	Gre	0	2	0	0	2	1	6	-5	0	0.000	0.500
191	Montpellier	Fra	0	2	0	0	2	1	6	-5	0	0.000	0.500
192	Grasshoppers Zürich	Sui	0	2	0	0	2	0	5	-5	0	0.000	0.000
193	Dundalk	Irl	0	2	0	0	2	0	5	-5	0	0.000	0.000
194	Galway United	Irl	0	2	0	0	2	2	8	-6	0	0.000	1.000
195	Kalmar FF	Swe	0	2	0	0	2	1	7	-6	0	0.000	0.500
196	Ajax	Ned	0	4	0	0	4	3	10	-7	0	0.000	0.750
197	Sliema Wanderers	Mlt	0	2	0	0	2	1	8	-7	0	0.000	0.500
198	Carl Zeiss Jena	GDR	0	2	0	0	2	0	7	-7	0	0.000	0.000
199	Aarau	Sui	0	2	0	0	2	0	7	-7	0	0.000	0.000
200	Spora Luxembourg	Lux	0	2	0	0	2	2	10	-8	0	0.000	1.000
201	Apolonia Fier	Alb	0	2	0	0	2	0	8	-8	0	0.000	0.000
202	Union Luxembourg	Lux	0	2	0	0	2	1	11	-10	0	0.000	0.500
203	Valletta	Mlt	0	4	0	0	4	1	14	-13	0	0.000	0.250
204	Hibernians	Mlt	0	4	0	0	4	0	15	-15	0	0.000	0.000
	Total		**1330**	**1260**	**491**	**278**	**491**	**1544**	**1544**	**0**	**70**	**1.056**	**2.451**

Participation Details 1956-58 to 1990-91 by Club

Albania

Club	Seasons Entered		Pts	P	W	D	L	F	A	Diff	B
Apolonia Fier	89-90		0	2	0	0	2	0	8	-8	–
Dinamo Tirana	81-80, 85-86		6	6	2	2	2	2	5	-3	–
Partizani Tirana	90-91		0	2	0	0	2	0	2	-2	–
Flamurtari Vlorë	86-87, 87-88		8	8	3	2	3	8	8	0	–
Total times entered	**6**	**Total**	**14**	**18**	**5**	**4**	**9**	**10**	**23**	**-13**	**–**

Austria

Club	Seasons Entered		Pts	P	W	D	L	F	A	Diff	B
Grazer AK	64-65, 73-74, 82-83		1	6	0	1	5	4	16	-12	–
Sturm Graz	70-71, 74-75, 78-79, 81-82, 83-84, 88-89		19	22	6	6	10	23	29	-6	1
FC Tirol	68-69, 74-75, 76-77, 84-85, 85-86, 86-87		21	22	8	3	11	27	34	-7	2
Linzer ASK	69-70, 77-78, 80-81, 84-85, 85-86, 86-87, 87-88		15	18	6	3	9	16	36	-20	–
Vöest Linz	72-73, 75-76, 80-81		3	6	1	1	4	5	13	-8	–
SV Salzburg	71-72, 76-77		6	6	3	0	3	11	9	2	–
Admira Wacker	73-74, 82-83, 87-88, 90-91		15	14	7	1	6	15	19	-4	–
Austria Vienna	72-73, 83-84, 87-88, 88-89, 89-90		22	20	8	5	7	38	34	4	1
First Vienna	88-89, 89-90		10	8	4	2	2	14	8	6	–
Rapid Vienna	62-63, 63-64, 71-72, 74-75, 75-76, 77-78, 78-79, 79-80, 81-82, 89-90, 90-91		33	36	13	7	16	40	49	-9	–
Wiener Sport-Club	64-65, 65-66, 66-67, 67-68, 68-69, 69-70, 70-71, 79-80		15	21	7	1	13	25	40	-15	–
Total times entered	**57**	**Total**	**160**	**179**	**63**	**30**	**86**	**218**	**287**	**-69**	**4**

Belgium

Club	Seasons Entered	Pts	P	W	D	L	F	A	Diff	B
Anderlecht	69-70, 70-71, 71-72, 79-80, 80-81, 82-83, 83-84, 84-85, 90-91	91	62	35	11	16	129	75	54	10
Beerschot	68-69, 73-74	1	4	0	1	3	2	7	-5	–
Antwerp	64-65, 65-66, 66-67, 67-68, 74-75, 75-76, 83-84, 88-89, 89-90, 90-91	37	38	14	8	16	53	55	-2	1
Beveren	70-71, 81-82, 86-87, 87-88	23	20	10	3	7	28	17	11	–
Club Bruges	67-68, 69-70, 71-72, 72-73, 75-76, 81-82, 84-85, 85-86, 87-88, 89-90	51	48	20	6	22	83	77	6	5
Charleroi	69-70	6	4	3	0	1	8	5	3	–
Gent	63-64, 66-67, 70-71, 82-83, 83-84, 86-87	12	18	3	6	9	18	31	-13	–
FC Liège	63-64, 64-65, 65-66, 66-67, 67-68, 85-86, 88-89, 89-90	53	42	22	6	14	60	41	19	3
Standard Liège	68-69, 73-74, 77-78, 78-79, 79-80, 80-81, 84-85, 86-87	45	40	17	10	13	61	51	10	1
Lierse	71-72, 78-79	9	10	3	2	5	15	13	2	1
Lokeren	76-77, 80-81, 81-82, 82-83, 87-88	28	24	9	9	6	29	24	5	1
KV Mechelen	90-91	1	2	0	1	1	2	3	-1	–
RWD Molenbeek	65-66, 68-69, 72-73, 73-74, 74-75, 76-77, 77-78, 80-81	33	30	10	11	9	36	30	6	2
Union St-Gilloise	58-60, 60-61, 61-62, 62-63, 64-65	12	17	4	2	11	23	30	-7	2
Waregem	68-69, 85-86, 88-89	23	18	9	3	6	27	24	3	2

Club	Seasons Entered		Pts	P	W	D	L	F	A	Diff	B
Winterslag	81-82		5	6	2	1	3	5	9	-4	–
Total times entered	**83**	**Total**	**430**	**383**	**161**	**80**	**142**	**579**	**492**	**87**	**28**

Bulgaria

Club	Seasons Entered		Pts	P	W	D	L	F	A	Diff	B
Pirin Blagoevgrad	85-86		0	2	0	0	2	1	7	-6	–
Lokomotiv Plovdiv	63-64, 64-65, 65-66, 67-68, 69-70, 71-72, 73-74, 74-75, 76-77, 83-84		26	30	10	6	14	40	50	-10	–
Trakia Plovdiv	66-67, 68-69, 70-71, 78-79, 86-87, 87-88, 88-89		11	16	3	5	8	22	27	-5	–
Dunav Ruse	75-76		2	2	1	0	1	1	2	-1	–
Sliven	84-85		2	2	1	0	1	2	5	-3	–
Akademik Sofia	76-77, 81-82		4	6	2	0	4	8	10	-2	–
CSKA Sofia	77-78, 78-79, 79-80, 84-85, 86-87		9	12	3	3	6	13	22	-9	–
Levski Sofia	72-73, 75-76, 78-79, 80-81, 81-82, 82-83, 83-84, 89-90		28	30	10	7	13	44	57	-13	1
Lokomotiv Sofia	79-80, 85-86, 87-88		14	14	5	3	6	21	21	0	1
Slavia Sofia	68-69, 69-70, 70-71, 73-74, 82-83, 88-89, 90-91		13	16	5	3	8	18	35	-17	–
Marek Stanke Dimitrov	77-78		4	4	2	0	2	5	5	0	–
Beroe Stara Zagora	72-73, 80-81		11	10	5	1	4	18	9	9	–
Etar Veliko Tarnovo	74-75		1	2	0	1	1	0	3	-3	–
Botev Vratsa	71-72		0	2	0	0	2	2	8	-6	–
Total times entered	**50**	**Total**	**125**	**148**	**47**	**29**	**72**	**195**	**261**	**-66**	**2**

Cyprus

Club	Seasons Entered		Pts	P	W	D	L	F	A	Diff	B
Paralimni	75-76, 76-77		0	4	0	0	4	4	21	-17	–
Alki Larnaca	79-80		0	2	0	0	2	0	12	-12	–
EPA Larnaca	72-73, 87-88		0	4	0	0	4	0	6	-6	–
Pezoporikos Larnaca	78-79, 80-81, 82-83		2	6	0	2	4	6	20	-14	–
Apollon Limassol	84-85, 89-90		2	4	0	2	2	4	12	-8	–
Akritas Morphou	71-72		0	2	0	0	2	0	7	-7	–
Apoel Nicosia	77-78, 81-82, 85-86, 88-89		3	8	0	3	5	8	21	-13	–
Olympiakos Nicosia	73-74		0	2	0	0	2	0	13	-13	–
Omonia Nicosia	86-87, 90-91		4	6	1	2	3	7	10	-3	–
Anorthosis Famagusta	83-84		0	2	0	0	2	0	11	-11	–
Total times entered	**19**	**Total**	**11**	**40**	**1**	**9**	**30**	**29**	**133**	**-104**	**–**

Czechslovakia

Club	Seasons Entered		Pts	P	W	D	L	F	A	Diff	B
Dukla Banská Bystrica	84-85		0	2	0	0	2	3	7	-4	–
Inter Bratislava	75-76, 77-78, 83-84, 90-91		22	18	11	0	7	43	23	20	–
Slovan Bratislava	72-73, 76-77		10	8	4	2	2	23	12	11	–
Zbrojovka Brno	61-62, 62-63, 63-64, 64-65, 65-66, 66-67, 79-80, 80-81		38	33	16	4	13	55	43	12	2
DAC Dunajská Streda	88-89		2	4	1	0	3	7	7	0	–
Lokomotiv Kosice	78-79		2	2	1	0	1	1	1	0	–
VSS Kosice	71-72, 73-74		4	4	2	0	2	5	8	-3	–
Plastika Nitra	89-90		0	2	0	0	2	1	5	-4	–
Sigma Olomouc	86-87		1	2	0	1	1	1	5	-4	–
Banik Ostrava	69-70, 74-75, 79-80, 82-83, 83-84, 85-86, 89-90, 90-91		29	30	11	6	13	41	33	8	1
Bohemians Prague	75-76, 79-80, 80-81, 81-82, 82-83, 84-85, 85-86, 87-88		31	32	11	7	14	45	44	1	2
Dukla Prague	72-73, 74-75, 78-79, 84-85, 86-87,		24	24	8	7	9	30	32	-2	1

	88-89										
Slavia Prague	67-68, 68-69, 76-77, 77-78, 85-86		11	12	5	1	6	17	19	-2	–
Sparta Prague	66-67, 69-70, 70-71, 81-82, 83-84, 86-87		21	22	8	4	10	31	37	-6	1
Tatran Presov	73-74		3	4	1	1	2	9	11	-2	–
Union Teplice	71-72		0	2	0	0	2	2	4	-2	–
Spartak Trnava	70-71		4	6	2	0	4	5	8	-3	–
TJ Vitkovice	87-88		10	8	3	3	2	8	7	1	1
Total times entered	**58**	**Total**	**212**	**215**	**84**	**36**	**95**	**327**	**306**	**21**	**8**

Denmark

Club	Seasons Entered		Pts	P	W	D	L	F	A	Diff	B
AGF Aarhus	79-80, 83-84, 84-85, 85-86		5	10	2	1	7	8	19	-11	–
AB Copenhagen	70-71, 71-72		4	6	2	0	4	13	14	-1	–
B 1903 Copenhagen	65-66, 73-74, 75-76, 78-79, 83-84		5	12	1	3	8	14	31	-17	–
KB Copenhagen	60-61, 61-62, 62-63, 63-64, 64-65, 74-75, 77-78, 80-81		10	20	3	3	14	39	66	-27	1
Brøndby IF	87-88, 90-91		19	14	7	3	4	20	11	9	2
BK Frem	56-58, 58-60, 67-68, 72-73, 77-78		5	12	2	1	9	13	37	-24	–
Hvidovre IF	66-67, 69-70, 72-73		1	6	0	1	5	5	17	-12	–
Esbjerg FB	78-79, 79-80		10	8	4	2	2	10	13	-3	–
Holbaek BIF	75-76, 76-77		2	4	1	0	3	2	10	-8	–
Ikast FS	88-89		2	2	1	0	1	2	2	0	–
Lyngby BK	82-83, 86-87		1	4	0	1	3	4	9	-5	–
Naestved IF	73-74, 76-77, 81-82, 89-90		4	8	1	2	5	5	21	-16	–
B 1901 Nykobing	70-71		0	2	0	0	2	3	8	-5	–
OB Odense	68-69, 84-85		0	4	0	0	4	4	11	-7	–
B 1909 Odense	66-67		0	2	0	0	2	2	6	-4	–
B 1913 Odense	62-63, 64-65, 69-70		2	6	1	0	5	6	16	-10	–
Randers Freja FC	74-75		2	2	0	2	0	1	1	0	–
Vejle BK	90-91		0	2	0	0	2	0	4	-4	–
Total times entered	**49**	**Total**	**72**	**124**	**25**	**19**	**80**	**151**	**296**	**-145**	**3**

East Germany

Club	Seasons Entered		Pts	P	W	D	L	F	A	Diff	B
Wismut Aue	85-86, 87-88		4	6	1	2	3	4	8	-4	–
Dynamo Berlin	72-73, 76-77, 78-79		9	10	3	3	4	14	17	-3	–
Stahl Brandenburg	86-87		4	4	1	2	1	3	4	-1	–
Karl-Marx-Stadt	89-90, 90-91		5	8	2	1	5	9	12	-3	–
Dynamo Dresden	67-68, 70-71, 72-73, 74-75, 75-76, 79-80, 80-81, 81-82, 87-88, 88-89		68	54	23	18	13	77	51	26	4
Vorwärts Frankfurt/Oder	74-75, 80-81, 82-83, 83-84, 84-85		8	12	4	0	8	13	22	-9	–
Carl Zeiss Jena	69-70, 71-72, 73-74, 75-76, 77-78, 78-79, 79-80, 81-82, 82-83, 83-84, 86-87		59	50	24	9	17	77	68	9	2
Lokomotive Leipzig	56-58, 58-60, 60-61, 61-62, 62-63, 63-64, 64-65, 65-66, 66-67, 67-68, 68-69, 73-74, 78-79, 82-83, 83-84, 84-85, 85-86, 88-89		68	69	28	9	32	103	99	4	3
Magdeburg	76-77, 77-78, 80-81, 81-82, 86-87, 90-91		33	28	14	3	11	43	34	9	2
Hansa Rostock	68-69, 69-70, 89-90		8	10	4	0	6	15	19	-4	–
Total times entered	**61**	**Total**	**266**	**251**	**104**	**47**	**100**	**358**	**334**	**24**	**11**

England

Club	Seasons Entered		Pts	P	W	D	L	F	A	Diff	B
Aston Villa	75-76, 77-78, 83-84, 90-91		21	18	8	4	6	31	21	10	1
Birmingham City	56-58, 58-60, 60-61, 61-62		41	25	14	6	5	52	39	13	7
Burnley	66-67		12	8	4	3	1	16	5	11	1
Coventry City	70-71		6	4	3	0	1	9	8	1	–
Derby County	74-75, 76-77		12	10	5	2	3	32	17	15	–
Ipswich Town	73-74, 74-75, 75-76, 77-78, 79-80, 80-81, 81-82, 82-83		57	40	23	7	10	78	43	35	4
Leeds United	65-66, 66-67, 67-68, 68-69, 70-71, 71-72, 73-74, 79-80		98	65	33	20	12	110	53	57	12
Everton	62-63, 64-65, 65-66, 75-76, 78-79, 79-80		23	20	10	3	7	34	20	14	–
Liverpool	67-68, 68-69, 69-70, 70-71, 72-73, 75-76		73	46	28	9	9	90	30	60	8
Arsenal	63-64, 69-70, 70-71, 78-79, 81-82, 82-83		48	36	19	6	11	66	33	33	4
Chelsea	56-58, 58-60, 65-66, 68-69		39	28	14	6	8	47	37	10	5
Queen's Park Rangers	76-77, 84-85		18	12	8	1	3	39	18	21	1
Tottenham Hotspur	71-72, 72-73, 73-74, 83-84, 84-85		90	54	33	12	9	129	40	89	12
Manchester City	72-73, 76-77, 77-78, 78-79		15	14	4	6	4	21	19	2	1
Manchester United	64-65, 76-77, 80-81, 82-83, 84-85		36	27	12	9	6	46	24	22	3
Newcastle United	68-69, 69-70, 70-71, 77-78		39	28	14	7	7	43	26	17	4
Nottingham Forest	61-62, 67-68, 83-84, 84-85		25	18	10	3	5	20	16	4	2
Sheffield Wednesday	61-62, 63-64		11	10	5	0	5	25	18	7	1
Southampton	69-70, 71-72, 81-82, 82-83, 84-85		16	16	4	8	4	21	18	3	–
Stoke City	72-73, 74-75		4	4	1	2	1	4	6	-2	–
Watford	83-84		5	6	2	1	3	10	12	-2	–
West Bromwich Albion	66-67, 78-79, 79-80, 81-82		16	16	6	3	7	22	22	0	1
Wolverhampton Wanderers	71-72, 73-74, 74-75, 80-81		32	20	13	3	4	41	23	18	3
Total times entered	**92**	**Total**	**737**	**525**	**273**	**121**	**131**	**986**	**548**	**438**	**70**

Finland

Club	Seasons Entered		Pts	P	W	D	L	F	A	Diff	B
HIFK Helsinki	71-72		0	2	0	0	2	0	4	-4	–
HJK Helsinki	75-76, 83-84, 84-85		0	6	0	0	6	2	23	-21	–
KPV Kokkola	74-75		0	2	0	0	2	2	9	-7	–
KuPS Kuopio	76-77, 78-79, 79-80, 80-81, 82-83		5	12	2	1	9	12	39	-27	–
FC Kuusysi Lahti	89-90		1	2	0	1	1	2	3	-1	–
MP Mikkeli	73-74		0	2	0	0	2	0	6	-6	–
RoPS Rovaniemi	89-90, 90-91		4	6	1	2	3	2	10	-8	–
Ilves Tampere	70-71, 86-87		4	4	2	0	2	6	9	-3	–
TPS Turku	85-86, 87-88, 88-89, 90-91		10	14	4	2	8	9	17	-8	–
Haka Valkeakoski	77-78, 81-82		1	4	0	1	3	5	12	-7	–
Total times entered	**22**	**Total**	**25**	**54**	**9**	**7**	**38**	**41**	**132**	**-91**	**–**

France

Club	Seasons Entered	Pts	P	W	D	L	F	A	Diff	B
Angers	72-73	1	2	0	1	1	2	3	-1	–
Angoulême	70-71	2	2	1	0	1	3	4	-1	–
Auxerre	84-85, 85-86, 87-88, 89-90	16	14	6	3	5	25	15	10	1
Bastia	77-78	20	12	8	1	3	27	20	7	3
Girondins Bordeaux	64-65, 65-66, 66-67, 67-68, 69-70, 81-82, 82-83, 83-84, 88-89, 90-91	38	38	17	4	17	52	59	-7	–
Laval	83-84	4	4	1	2	1	4	5	-1	–
Lens	77-78, 83-84, 86-87	15	14	6	3	5	22	19	3	–

Olympique Lyon	58-60, 60-61, 61-62, 68-69, 74-75, 75-76	11	16	5	1	10	28	41	-13	–
Olympique Marseille	62-63, 68-69, 70-71, 73-74, 75-76	12	12	6	0	6	21	19	2	–
Metz	68-69, 69-70, 85-86	2	6	0	2	4	8	17	-9	–
Monaco	79-80, 81-82, 84-85, 90-91	14	14	6	2	6	23	23	0	–
Montpellier	88-89	0	2	0	0	2	1	6	-5	–
Nantes	71-72, 74-75, 78-79, 81-82, 85-86, 86-87	22	22	6	9	7	25	28	-3	1
Nice	66-67, 67-68, 68-69, 73-74, 76-77	11	14	5	1	8	16	25	-9	–
Nîmes Olympique	71-72, 72-73	2	4	1	0	3	4	6	-2	–
Racing Club Paris	63-64	0	2	0	0	2	2	4	-2	–
Paris Saint-Germain	84-85, 89-90	6	8	2	2	4	12	12	0	–
Stade Français	64-65, 65-66	5	6	1	3	2	3	3	0	–
Rouen	69-70	5	6	2	1	3	5	5	0	–
Saint-Etienne	71-72, 79-80, 80-81, 82-83	25	22	9	5	8	48	29	19	2
Sedan	70-71	2	2	1	0	1	2	5	-3	–
Sochaux	72-73, 76-77, 80-81, 82-83, 89-90	22	20	7	6	7	32	22	10	2
Strasbourg	61-62, 64-65, 65-66, 78-79	19	20	6	6	8	22	34	-12	1
Toulouse	66-67, 86-87, 87-88	11	10	5	1	4	16	15	1	–
Total times entered	**76** **Total**	**265**	**272**	**101**	**53**	**118**	**403**	**419**	**-16**	**10**

Greece

Club	Seasons Entered	Pts	P	W	D	L	F	A	Diff	B
AEK Athenes	70-71, 72-73, 75-76, 76-77, 77-78, 82-83, 85-86, 86-87, 88-89	27	32	11	3	18	34	54	-20	2
Panathinaikos	68-69, 73-74, 74-75, 78-79, 80-81, 81-82, 85-86, 87-88	18	24	7	3	14	30	40	-10	1
Panionios	69-70, 71-72, 87-88	4	7	2	0	5	5	17	-12	–
OFI Crete	86-87	2	2	1	0	1	1	4	-3	–
Larissa	83-84	2	2	1	0	1	2	3	-1	–
Panahaiki	73-74	5	4	2	1	1	4	9	-5	–
Olympiakos Pireus	72-73, 76-77, 77-78, 78-79, 79-80, 84-85, 89-90	23	22	9	5	8	24	31	-7	–
Aris Salonika	64-65, 65-66, 66-67, 68-69, 69-70, 74-75, 79-80, 80-81, 81-82	23	26	9	5	12	39	55	-16	–
Iraklis	61-62, 63-64, 89-90, 90-91	5	8	2	1	5	5	23	-18	–
PAOK Salonika	65-66, 67-68, 70-71, 75-76, 82-83, 83-84, 88-89, 90-91	19	20	7	5	8	17	33	-16	–
Total times entered	**51** **Total**	**128**	**147**	**51**	**23**	**73**	**161**	**269**	**-108**	**3**

Hungary

Club	Seasons Entered	Pts	P	W	D	L	F	A	Diff	B
Ferencváros	62-63, 64-65, 66-67, 67-68, 70-71, 71-72, 73-74, 77-78, 79-80, 82-83, 83-84, 90-91	83	67	31	11	25	109	79	30	10
Honvéd	72-73, 73-74, 75-76, 76-77, 78-79, 83-84, 87-88	44	36	19	5	12	66	55	11	1
MTK-VM	61-62, 78-79, 89-90, 90-91	17	15	7	1	7	32	30	2	2
Vasas SC	58-60, 60-61, 71-72, 75-76, 80-81	13	16	6	1	9	19	23	-4	–
Diósgyöri VTK	79-80	8	6	4	0	2	9	11	-2	–
Rába ETO	69-70, 74-75, 84-85, 85-86, 86-87	14	16	6	2	8	23	32	-9	–
Pécs Dózsa	70-71	4	6	2	0	4	6	7	-1	–
Pécsi MSC	86-87	2	2	1	0	1	1	2	-1	–
Salgótarján	72-73	1	2	0	1	1	2	4	-2	–
Videoton	74-75, 76-77, 81-82, 84-85, 85-86, 89-90	30	28	11	5	12	32	35	-3	3

Tatabánya	81-82, 82-83, 87-88, 88-89	6	8	2	2	4	6	11	-5	–
Ujpesti Dózsa	63-64, 65-66, 68-69, 69-70, 76-77, 77-78, 80-81, 88-89	47	40	18	6	16	73	57	16	5
Total times entered	**55** **Total**	**269**	**242**	**107**	**34**	**101**	**378**	**346**	**32**	**21**

Iceland

Club	**Seasons Entered**	**Pts**	**P**	**W**	**D**	**L**	**F**	**A**	**Diff**	**B**
IA Akranes	70-71, 80-81, 86-87, 88-89, 89-90	1	10	0	1	9	2	48	-46	–
FH Hafnarfjördhur	90-91	1	2	0	1	1	3	5	-2	–
IBK Keflavik	71-72, 73-74, 75-76, 79-80	3	10	1	1	8	6	31	-25	–
Fram Reykjavik	76-77, 77-78, 82-83	0	6	0	0	6	0	23	-23	–
KR Reykjavik	84-85	0	2	0	0	2	0	7	-7	–
Valur Reykjavik	69-70, 74-75, 85-86, 87-88	5	8	1	3	4	4	15	-11	–
Vikingur Reykjavik	81-82	0	2	0	0	2	0	8	-8	–
IBV Vestmannaeyjar	72-73, 78-79, 83-84	4	8	0	4	4	2	9	-7	–
Total times entered	**22** **Total**	**14**	**48**	**2**	**10**	**36**	**17**	**146**	**-129**	**–**

Italy

Club	**Seasons Entered**	**Pts**	**P**	**W**	**D**	**L**	**F**	**A**	**Diff**	**B**
Atalanta	89-90, 90-91	12	10	3	5	2	8	7	1	1
Bologna	66-67, 67-68, 68-69, 71-72, 90-91	46	32	16	10	6	49	30	19	4
Cagliari	69-70, 72-73	3	6	1	1	4	5	7	-2	–
Cesena	76-77	2	2	1	0	1	3	4	-1	–
Fiorentina	64-65, 65-66, 67-68, 68-69, 70-71, 72-73, 73-74, 77-78, 82-83, 84-85, 86-87, 89-90	56	48	21	11	16	54	50	4	3
Sampdoria	62-63	6	4	3	0	1	4	6	-2	–
AC Milan	61-62, 64-65, 65-66, 71-72, 75-76, 76-77, 78-79, 85-86, 87-88	59	53	22	12	19	71	57	14	3
Inter Milan	56-58, 58-60, 60-61, 61-62, 69-70, 70-71, 72-73, 73-74, 74-75, 76-77, 77-78, 79-80, 81-82, 83-84, 84-85, 85-86, 86-87, 87-88, 88-89, 90-91	147	115	54	25	36	187	114	73	14
Napoli	66-67, 67-68, 68-69, 69-70, 71-72, 74-75, 75-76, 78-79, 79-80, 81-82, 82-83, 86-87, 88-89, 89-90	72	62	25	19	18	73	70	3	3
Penigia	79-80	4	4	1	2	1	2	4	-2	–
Roma	58-60, 60-61, 61-62, 62-63, 63-64, 64-65, 65-66, 75-76, 82-83, 88-89, 90-91	95	70	36	12	22	114	76	38	11
Lazio	70-71, 73-74, 75-76, 77-78	11	14	5	1	8	20	28	-8	–
Torino	65-66, 72-73, 73-74, 74-75, 77-78, 78-79, 79-80, 80-81, 85-86, 86-87	36	36	13	9	14	49	46	3	1
Juventus	63-64, 64-65, 66-67, 68-69, 69-70, 70-71, 71-72, 74-75, 76-77, 80-81, 87-88, 88-89, 89-90	161	104	64	16	24	191	87	104	17
Verona	83-84, 87-88	18	12	6	5	1	18	11	7	1
Lanerossi Vicenza	78-79	1	2	0	1	1	1	2	-1	–
Total times entered	**108** **Total**	**729**	**574**	**271**	**129**	**174**	**849**	**599**	**250**	**58**

Luxembourg

Club	**Seasons Entered**	**Pts**	**P**	**W**	**D**	**L**	**F**	**A**	**Diff**	**B**
Avenir Beggen	75-76, 85-86, 90-91	2	6	1	0	5	2	22	-20	–
Aris Bonnevoie	62-63, 63-64, 71-72, 83-84	2	8	0	2	6	2	27	-25	–
Red Boys Differdange	74-75, 76-77, 77-78, 80-81, 81-82, 84-85	1	12	0	1	11	3	68	-65	–

Jeunesse Esch	69-70, 78-79, 86-87, 89-90		4	8	1	2	5	5	23	-18	–
Spora Luxembourg	64-65, 67-68, 87-88		2	6	1	0	5	3	28	-25	–
Union Luxembourg	65-66, 66-67, 73-74, 88-89		0	8	0	0	8	2	42	-40	–
Progrès Niedercorn	79-80, 82-83		0	4	0	0	4	0	10	-10	–
US Rumelange	70-71, 72-73		0	4	0	0	4	0	32	-32	–
Total times entered	**28**	**Total**	**11**	**56**	**3**	**5**	**48**	**17**	**252**	**-235**	**–**

Malta

Club	Seasons Entered		Pts	P	W	D	L	F	A	Diff	B
Hamrun Spartans	85-86		1	2	0	1	1	0	1	-1	–
Valletta	72-73, 79-80, 87-88, 89-90		0	8	0	0	8	2	28	-26	–
Floriana	69-70		2	2	1	0	1	1	6	-5	–
Hibernians	68-69, 74-75, 76-77, 78-79, 86-87, 90-91		2	12	1	0	11	3	50	-47	–
Marsa	71-72		0	2	0	0	2	0	11	-11	–
Rabat Ajax	83-84, 84-85		0	4	0	0	4	0	20	-20	–
Sliema Wanderers	70-71, 73-74, 75-76, 77-78, 80-81, 81-82, 88-89		1	14	0	1	13	7	42	-35	–
Zurrieq	82-83		0	2	0	0	2	1	8	-7	–
Total times entered	**23**	**Total**	**6**	**46**	**2**	**2**	**42**	**14**	**166**	**-152**	**–**

Netherlands

Club	Seasons Entered		Pts	P	W	D	L	F	A	Diff	B
AZ'67 Alkmaar	77-78, 80-81		26	16	9	5	2	51	15	36	3
Ajax	69-70, 74-75, 75-76, 76-77, 78-79, 84-85, 88-89, 89-90		43	38	19	3	16	80	41	39	2
FC Amsterdam	66-67, 67-68, 68-69, 74-75		19	18	7	4	7	30	28	2	1
Vitesse	90-91		7	6	3	1	2	7	4	3	–
PSV Eindhoven	71-72, 77-78, 79-80, 80-81, 81-82, 82-83, 83-84, 84-85, 85-86		51	42	21	6	15	73	48	25	3
Twente Enschede	69-70, 70-71, 72-73, 73-74, 74-75, 78-79, 80-81, 89-90, 90-91		57	48	20	11	17	86	60	26	6
Groningen	83-84, 86-87, 88-89		15	16	6	3	7	22	22	0	–
Haarlem	82-83		3	4	1	1	2	6	9	-3	–
Roda JC	90-91		0	2	0	0	2	2	6	-4	–
FC Den Haag	71-72		3	4	1	1	2	8	9	-1	–
Feyenoord	68-69, 72-73, 73-74, 75-76, 76-77, 79-80, 81-82, 83-84, 85-86, 86-87, 87-88, 89-90		75	58	31	9	18	112	69	43	4
Sparta Rotterdam	70-71, 83-84, 85-86		18	16	7	4	5	35	21	14	–
Utrecht	62-63, 63-64, 64-65, 65-66, 66-67, 67-68, 68-69, 80-81, 81-82, 82-83, 87-88		27	32	10	7	15	41	62	-21	–
Total times entered	**65**	**Total**	**344**	**300**	**135**	**55**	**110**	**553**	**394**	**159**	**19**

Northern Ireland

Club	Seasons Entered	Pts	P	W	D	L	F	A	Diff	B
Ballymena United	80-81	2	2	1	0	1	2	4	-2	–
Glentoran	62-63, 63-64, 65-66, 69-70, 71-72, 75-76, 76-77, 78-79, 82-83, 84-85, 89-90	8	22	2	4	16	16	61	-45	–
Linfield	67-68, 68-69, 81-82, 88-89	4	8	1	2	5	4	20	-16	–
Coleraine	69-70, 70-71, 83-84, 85-86, 86-87, 87-88	8	16	2	4	10	19	40	-21	–
Glenavon	77-78, 79-80, 90-91	1	6	0	1	5	2	15	-13	–
Ards	73-74	2	2	1	0	1	4	8	-4	–

Club	Seasons Entered		Pts	P	W	D	L	F	A	Diff	B
Portadown	74-75		4	4	1	2	1	3	7	-4	–
Total times entered	**27**	**Total**	**29**	**60**	**8**	**13**	**39**	**50**	**155**	**-105**	**–**

Norway

Club	Seasons Entered		Pts	P	W	D	L	F	A	Diff	B
SK Brann	76-77		0	2	0	0	2	0	11	-11	–
Bryne IL	81-82, 83-84		3	4	1	1	2	3	7	-4	–
Strømgodset IF	73-74		1	2	0	1	1	2	7	-5	–
Fredrikstad FK	73-74		0	2	0	0	2	0	5	-5	–
IK Start	74-75, 76-77, 77-78, 78-79		7	10	3	1	6	11	19	-8	–
Lillestrøm SK	84-85, 89-90		2	4	1	0	3	4	12	-8	–
Mjøndalen IF	77-78, 87-88		2	4	1	0	3	1	17	-16	–
Molde FK	75-76, 78-79, 88-89		4	6	1	2	3	5	18	-13	–
Moss FK	80-81		0	2	0	0	2	3	5	-2	–
SK Frigg	66-67		0	2	0	0	2	2	6	-4	–
FK Skeid	68-69, 69-70, 79-80		5	8	1	3	4	7	18	-11	–
SFK Lyn	67-68, 72-73		1	4	0	1	3	3	14	-11	–
Vålerengen SIF	64-65, 65-66, 75-76, 86-87		2	8	0	2	6	7	18	-11	–
IF Sarpsborg	70-71		0	2	0	0	2	0	6	-6	–
IL Viking	72-73, 79-80, 82-83, 85-86		10	12	3	4	5	9	23	-14	–
Rosenborg BK	69-70, 71-72, 74-75, 90-91		10	10	5	0	5	15	22	-7	–
Total times entered	**36**	**Total**	**47**	**82**	**16**	**15**	**51**	**72**	**208**	**-136**	**–**

Poland

Club	Seasons Entered		Pts	P	W	D	L	F	A	Diff	B
Szombierki Bytom	81-82		1	2	0	1	1	1	3	-2	–
Ruch Chorzów	69-70, 70-71, 72-73, 73-74		13	18	5	2	11	29	35	-6	1
Wisla Kraków	76-77, 81-82		5	6	1	3	2	7	9	-2	–
GKS Katowice	70-71, 87-88, 88-89, 89-90, 90-91		5	12	2	1	9	11	20	-9	–
Widzew Lódź	77-78, 79-80, 80-81, 83-84, 84-85, 86-87		24	26	8	8	10	24	36	-12	–
Zaglebie Lubin	90-91		0	2	0	0	2	0	2	-2	–
Stal Mielec	75-76, 79-80, 82-83		13	12	4	4	4	9	8	1	1
Odra Opole	77-78		1	2	0	1	1	2	3	-1	–
Lech Poznań	78-79, 85-86		1	4	0	1	3	3	13	-10	–
Zaglebie Sosnowiec	72-73		2	2	1	0	1	2	6	-4	–
Pogon Szczecin	84-85, 87-88		1	4	0	1	3	3	7	-4	–
GKS Tychy	76-77		1	2	0	1	1	1	3	-2	–
Gwardia Warsaw	69-70, 73-74		9	8	4	1	3	8	8	0	–
Legia Warsaw	68-69, 71-72, 74-75, 85-86, 86-87, 88-89		25	24	9	7	8	34	30	4	–
Zaglebie Walbrzych	71-72		5	4	2	1	1	6	5	1	–
Slask Wroclaw	75-76, 78-79, 80-81, 82-83		17	18	6	5	7	29	36	-7	–
Górnik Zabrze	74-75, 77-78, 89-90		5	8	1	3	4	10	16	-6	–
Total times entered	**45**	**Total**	**128**	**154**	**43**	**40**	**71**	**179**	**240**	**-61**	**2**

Portugal

Club	Seasons Entered		Pts	P	W	D	L	F	A	Diff	B
Barreirense	65-66, 67-68, 70-71, 72-73		10	11	5	0	6	11	16	-5	–
Sporting Braga	78-79, 84-85		2	6	1	0	5	7	15	-8	–
Chaves	87-88		2	4	1	0	3	6	9	-3	–
Academica Coimbra	68-69, 71-72		2	4	1	0	3	2	8	-6	–
Vitória Guimarães	69-70, 70-71, 83-84, 86-87, 87-88, 90-91		28	26	11	5	10	31	38	-7	1
Belenenses	61-62, 62-63, 63-64, 64-65, 73-74, 76-77, 87-88, 88-89		18	22	5	8	9	23	29	-6	–

Benfica	66-67, 78-79, 79-80, 82-83, 88-89, 90-91	36	28	12	9	7	38	26	12	3
Sporting Lisbon	65-66, 67-68, 68-69, 69-70, 75-76, 77-78, 79-80, 81-82, 83-84, 84-85, 85-86, 86-87, 88-89, 89-90, 90-91	86	71	32	19	20	126	77	49	3
Leixões	64-65, 68-69	3	4	0	3	1	2	5	-3	–
Portimonense	85-86	2	2	1	0	1	1	4	-3	–
Boavista	77-78, 80-81, 81-82, 85-86, 86-87, 89-90	14	18	6	2	10	20	28	-8	–
FC Porto	62-63, 63-64, 65-66, 66-67, 67-68, 69-70, 71-72, 72-73, 74-75, 75-76, 76-77, 80-81, 82-83, 89-90	54	50	23	8	19	70	61	9	–
Vitória Setúbal	66-67, 68-69, 69-70, 70-71, 71-72, 72-73, 73-74, 74-75	57	48	24	5	19	77	55	22	4
Total times entered	**75** **Total**	**314**	**294**	**122**	**59**	**113**	**414**	**371**	**43**	**11**

Republic of Ireland

Club	Seasons Entered	Pts	P	W	D	L	F	A	Diff	B
Athlone Town	75-76	4	4	1	2	1	4	5	-1	–
Finn Harps	73-74, 76-77, 78-79	0	6	0	0	6	3	33	-30	–
Cork Hibernians	70-71	0	2	0	0	2	1	6	-5	–
Derry City	90-91	1	2	0	1	1	0	1	-1	–
Drogheda United	83-84	0	2	0	0	2	0	14	-14	–
Bohemians	72-73, 74-75, 77-78, 79-80, 84-85, 85-86, 87-88	6	14	1	4	9	8	27	-19	–
Drumcondra	62-63, 66-67	4	6	2	0	4	8	19	-11	–
Shamrock Rovers	63-64, 65-66, 82-83	6	8	2	2	4	11	11	0	–
St. Patrick's Athletic	67-68, 88-89	0	4	0	0	4	4	13	-9	–
Shelbourne	64-65, 71-72	5	7	1	3	3	4	6	-2	–
Dundalk	68-69, 69-70, 80-81, 89-90	4	10	1	2	7	4	31	-27	–
Galway United	86-87	0	2	0	0	2	2	8	-6	–
Limerick	81-82	1	2	0	1	1	1	4	-3	–
Total times entered	**29** **Total**	**31**	**69**	**8**	**15**	**46**	**50**	**178**	**-128**	–

Romania

Club	Seasons Entered	Pts	P	W	D	L	F	A	Diff	B
UT Arad	71-72, 72-73	9	10	3	2	5	13	14	-1	1
Bacau	69-70	9	8	3	2	3	12	11	1	1
Red Flag Brasov	63-64, 65-66, 74-75	7	11	3	1	7	14	25	-11	–
Dinamo Bucharest	66-67, 70-71, 74-75, 76-77, 79-80, 81-82, 85-86	28	28	11	6	11	48	32	16	–
Rapid Bucharest	68-69, 69-70, 71-72	6	10	3	0	7	12	22	-10	–
Sportul Studentesc Bucharest	76-77, 83-84, 84-85, 85-86, 86-87, 87-88	16	20	6	4	10	20	31	-11	–
Steaua Bucharest	77-78, 80-81	1	4	0	1	3	4	11	-7	–
Victoria Bucharest	87-88, 88-89, 89-90	16	14	6	3	5	21	17	4	1
Universitatea Cluj	72-73	2	2	1	0	1	5	6	-1	–
Universitatea Craiova	70-71, 73-74, 75-76, 79-80, 82-83, 83-84, 84-85, 86-87, 87-88, 90-91	50	42	21	6	15	44	40	4	2
CSU Galati	88-89	2	2	1	0	1	1	5	-4	–
Corvinul Hunedoara	82-83	4	4	1	2	1	8	9	-1	–
Flacara Moreni	89-90	0	2	0	0	2	1	4	-3	–
Arges Pitesti	67-68, 68-69, 73-74, 78-79, 80-81, 81-82	18	18	6	6	6	25	32	-7	–
Petrolul Ploiesti	62-63, 64-65, 67-68, 90-91	19	15	9	0	6	14	15	-1	1
Politehnica Timisoara	78-79, 90-91	8	8	4	0	4	9	14	-5	–

ASA Tîrgu Mures	75-76, 76-77, 77-78		3	6	1	1	4	4	13	-9	–
Total times entered	**56**	**Total**	**198**	**204**	**79**	**34**	**91**	**255**	**301**	**-46**	**6**

Scotland

Club	Seasons Entered		Pts	P	W	D	L	F	A	Diff	B
Aberdeen	68-69, 71-72, 72-73, 73-74, 77-78, 79-80, 81-82, 87-88, 88-89, 89-90		33	32	12	9	11	42	42	0	–
Dundee	71-72, 73-74, 74-75		8	10	4	0	6	17	21	-4	–
Dundee United	66-67, 67-68, 69-70, 70-71, 75-76, 77-78, 78-79, 79-80, 80-81, 81-82, 82-83, 84-85, 85-86, 86-87, 87-88, 89-90, 90-91		107	86	39	22	25	130	88	42	7
Dunfermline Athletic	62-63, 64-65, 65-66, 66-67, 69-70		36	28	16	3	9	49	31	18	1
Heart of Midlothian	61-62, 63-64, 65-66, 84-85, 86-87, 88-89, 90-91		32	28	12	7	9	44	41	3	1
Hibernian	60-61, 61-62, 62-63, 65-66, 67-68, 68-69, 70-71, 73-74, 74-75, 75-76, 76-77, 78-79, 89-90		69	58	28	11	19	97	84	13	2
Celtic	62-63, 64-65, 76-77, 83-84, 87-88		15	16	5	5	6	24	22	2	–
Rangers	67-68, 68-69, 70-71, 82-83, 84-85, 85-86, 86-87, 88-89		47	38	18	8	12	53	41	12	3
Morton	68-69		0	2	0	0	2	3	9	-6	–
Kilmarnock	64-65, 66-67, 69-70, 70-71		21	20	8	3	9	34	32	2	2
St. Mirren	80-81, 83-84, 85-86		7	10	2	3	5	9	12	-3	–
St. Johnstone	71-72		6	6	3	0	3	8	8	0	–
Partick Thistle	63-64, 72-73		6	6	3	0	3	10	11	-1	–
Total times entered	**79**	**Total**	**387**	**340**	**150**	**71**	**119**	**520**	**442**	**78**	**16**

Spain

Club	Seasons Entered		Pts	P	W	D	L	F	A	Diff	B
Español	61-62, 65-66, 73-74, 76-77, 87-88		44	34	18	3	13	49	41	8	5
Barcelona	56-58, 58-60, 60-61, 61-62, 62-63, 64-65, 65-66, 66-67, 67-68, 69-70, 70-71, 72-73, 73-74, 75-76, 76-77, 77-78, 80-81, 86-87, 87-88		164	122	59	27	36	228	144	84	19
Athletic Bilbao	64-65, 66-67, 67-68, 68-69, 70-71, 71-72, 76-77, 77-78, 78-79, 82-83, 85-86, 86-87, 88-89		83	68	33	11	24	93	82	11	6
Sporting Gijón	78-79, 79-80, 80-81, 85-86, 87-88		9	12	3	3	6	9	13	-4	–
Las Palmas	69-70, 72-73, 77-78		11	12	4	3	5	20	17	3	–
Atlético Madrid	63-64, 64-65, 67-68, 68-69, 71-72, 74-75, 79-80, 81-82, 83-84, 84-85, 86-87, 88-89, 89-90, 90-91		43	43	19	4	20	60	59	1	1
Real Madrid	71-72, 73-74, 81-82, 83-84, 84-85, 85-86		51	40	19	6	15	67	48	19	7
Osasuna	85-86		4	4	2	0	2	4	4	0	–
Sabadell	69-70		2	2	1	0	1	3	5	-2	–
Real Sociedad	74-75, 75-76, 79-80, 80-81, 88-89, 90-91		26	26	9	7	10	28	39	-11	1
Real Zaragoza	62-63, 63-64, 65-66, 67-68, 68-69, 74-75, 75-76, 89-90		62	48	25	6	17	93	72	21	6
Real Betis	64-65, 82-83, 84-85		3	6	1	1	4	4	8	-4	–
Seville	66-67, 70-71, 82-83, 83-84, 90-91		16	16	6	4	6	21	22	-1	–
Valencia	61-62, 62-63, 63-64, 64-65, 65-66, 66-67, 68-69, 69-70, 70-71, 72-73, 78-79, 81-82, 82-83, 89-90, 90-91		114	86	42	19	25	160	110	50	11

Real Valladolid	84-85		2	2	1	0	1	2	4	-2	–
Celta Vigo	71-72		0	2	0	0	2	0	3	-3	–
Total times entered	**106**	**Total**	**634**	**523**	**242**	**94**	**187**	**841**	**671**	**170**	**56**

Sweden

Club	Seasons Entered		Pts	P	W	D	L	F	A	Diff	B
Åtvidaberg SFF	72-73		2	2	1	0	1	5	6	-1	–
IF Elfsborg	71-72, 78-79, 80-81, 83-84		5	8	1	3	4	8	15	-7	–
IK Brage	82-83, 88-89		3	6	1	1	4	8	15	-7	–
GAIS	75-76, 90-91		3	4	1	1	2	6	10	-4	–
IFK Gothenburg	80-81, 81-82, 86-87, 87-88, 89-90		51	30	18	9	3	53	25	28	6
Örgryte IS	64-65, 66-67, 89-90		5	8	1	3	4	9	21	-12	–
Hammarby IF	85-86		9	6	4	1	1	15	9	6	–
Kalmar FF	79-80, 86-87		2	4	1	0	3	3	9	-6	–
Landskrona BOIS	77-78		0	2	0	0	2	0	6	-6	–
Malmö FF	65-66, 67-68, 69-70, 70-71, 77-78, 79-80, 81-82, 83-84, 85-86, 88-89		18	26	7	4	15	26	47	-21	–
IFK Norrköping	72-73, 78-79, 82-83, 90-91		11	12	3	5	4	12	14	-2	–
AIK	65-66, 68-69, 73-74, 75-76, 84-85, 87-88		15	16	5	5	6	20	26	-6	–
Djurgården SIF	64-65, 66-67, 71-72, 74-75, 76-77		8	12	3	2	7	17	28	-11	–
Öster SIF	73-74, 74-75, 75-76, 76-77, 84-85, 88-89		12	18	6	0	12	24	34	-10	–
Total times entered	**52**	**Total**	**144**	**154**	**52**	**34**	**68**	**206**	**265**	**-59**	**6**

Switzerland

Club	Seasons Entered		Pts	P	W	D	L	F	A	Diff	B
Aarau	88-89		0	2	0	0	2	0	7	-7	–
FC Basle	56-58, 58-60, 60-61, 61-62, 62-63, 64-65, 65-66, 66-67, 68-69, 71-72, 76-77, 78-79		10	29	3	4	22	39	82	-43	–
Young Boys Berne	75-76		1	2	0	1	1	2	4	-2	–
Servette	63-64, 64-65, 65-66, 67-68, 74-75, 77-78, 80-81, 82-83, 88-89		22	26	8	6	12	34	48	-14	–
Lausanne-Sports	56-58, 58-60, 61-62, 63-64, 66-67, 68-69, 69-70, 70-71, 72-73, 78-79, 90-91		16	28	6	3	19	42	75	-33	1
Lucerne	86-87, 90-91		5	6	1	3	2	4	5	-1	–
Lugano	71-72		1	2	0	1	1	1	3	-2	–
Neuchâtel Xamax	81-82, 84-85, 85-86, 86-87		28	22	9	8	5	33	22	11	2
St-Gallen	83-84, 85-86		1	4	0	1	3	2	10	-8	–
Sion	73-74, 84-85, 87-88, 89-90		13	12	6	1	5	17	20	-3	–
Wettingen	89-90		5	4	2	1	1	6	2	4	–
FC Zürich	67-68, 69-70, 77-78, 79-80, 82-83, 83-84		19	24	7	4	13	28	44	-16	1
Grasshoppers Zürich	68-69, 70-71, 72-73, 73-74, 74-75, 75-76, 76-77, 77-78, 79-80, 80-81, 81-82, 87-88		53	50	22	6	22	84	75	9	3
Total times entered	**66**	**Total**	**174**	**211**	**64**	**39**	**108**	**292**	**397**	**-105**	**7**

Turkey

Club	Seasons Entered		Pts	P	W	D	L	F	A	Diff	B
Adanaspor	76-77, 78-79, 81-82		3	6	1	1	4	6	20	-14	–
Boluspor	74-75		0	2	0	0	2	0	4	-4	–
Eskisehirspor	70-71, 72-73, 73-74, 75-76		5	10	2	1	7	9	24	-15	–
Besiktas	74-75, 85-86, 87-88, 88-89		5	8	2	1	5	5	13	-8	–

Fenerbahçe	71-72, 72-73, 73-74, 76-77, 77-78, 80-81, 84-85, 90-91	14	20	6	2	12	21	37	-16	–
Galatasaray	75-76, 78-79, 79-80, 86-87, 89-90	6	12	2	2	8	11	24	-13	–
Altay	62-63, 69-70, 77-78	3	6	1	1	4	8	20	-12	–
Göztepe	64-65, 65-66, 66-67, 67-68, 68-69	14	20	6	1	13	22	39	-17	1
Orduspor	79-80	2	2	1	0	1	2	6	-4	–
Trabzonspor	82-83, 83-84	2	4	1	0	3	1	8	-7	–
Total times entered	**36** **Total**	**54**	**90**	**22**	**9**	**59**	**85**	**195**	**-110**	**1**

USSR

Club	Seasons Entered	Pts	P	W	D	L	F	A	Diff	B
Dnepr Dnepropetrovsk	85-86, 86-87, 88-89, 90-91	10	12	3	4	5	12	15	-3	–
Shakhtyor Donetsk	76-77, 79-80, 80-81	13	10	6	1	3	14	12	2	–
Ararat Erevan	72-73	10	6	5	0	1	11	5	6	–
Dinamo Kiev	73-74, 77-78, 79-80, 80-81, 83-84, 89-90	30	24	11	8	5	29	15	14	–
Zenit Leningrad	81-82, 87-88, 89-90	5	8	2	1	5	7	18	-11	–
Dinamo Minsk	84-85, 86-87, 88-89	17	14	7	2	5	22	13	9	1
CSKA Moscow	81-82	2	2	1	0	1	2	2	0	–
Dinamo Moscow	74-75, 76-77, 80-81, 82-83, 87-88	13	14	5	3	6	15	15	0	–
Spartak Moscow	71-72, 74-75, 75-76, 81-82, 82-83, 83-84, 84-85, 85-86, 86-87, 87-88, 89-90	75	56	32	10	14	91	61	30	1
Torpedo Moscow	75-76, 78-79, 88-89, 90-91	28	20	12	3	5	40	25	15	1
Chernomorets Odessa	75-76, 85-86, 90-91	8	10	3	2	5	10	13	-3	–
Dinamo Tbilisi	72-73, 73-74, 77-78, 78-79, 82-83, 87-88	31	26	13	5	8	39	32	7	–
Zhalgiris Vilnius	88-89, 89-90	4	6	2	0	4	7	11	-4	–
Total times entered	**52** **Total**	**246**	**208**	**102**	**39**	**67**	**299**	**238**	**61**	**3**

West Germany

Club	Seasons Entered	Pts	P	W	D	L	F	A	Diff	B
Hertha Berlin	61-62, 63-64, 64-65, 69-70, 70-71, 71-72, 75-76, 78-79	48	36	20	5	11	54	42	12	3
Tasmania Berlin	62-63	0	2	0	0	2	3	5	-2	–
Werder Bremen	82-83, 83-84, 84-85, 85-86, 86-87, 87-88, 89-90	46	36	17	8	11	65	42	23	4
Eintracht Braunschweig	71-72, 76-77, 77-78	16	16	6	4	6	29	20	9	–
Cologne	58-60, 60-61, 61-62, 63-64, 65-66, 67-68, 70-71, 71-72, 72-73, 73-74, 74-75, 75-76, 76-77, 80-81, 82-83, 84-85, 85-86, 88-89, 89-90, 90-91	180	134	72	20	42	261	157	104	16
Viktoria Cologne	62-63	2	2	1	0	1	5	7	-2	–
Borussia Dortmund	64-65, 82-83, 87-88, 90-91	19	18	9	1	8	24	26	-2	–
MSV Duisburg	75-76, 78-79	21	14	8	3	3	38	19	19	2
Fortuna Düsseldorf	73-74, 74-75	12	12	5	2	5	17	17	0	–
Eintracht Frankfurt	56-58, 64-65, 66-67, 67-68, 68-69, 72-73, 77-78, 79-80, 80-81, 90-91	68	54	27	8	19	106	75	31	6
Schalke 04	76-77, 77-78	12	10	5	2	3	19	14	5	–
Hamburg	68-69, 70-71, 71-72, 74-75, 75-76, 80-81, 81-82, 84-85, 85-86, 89-90	85	64	34	10	20	118	77	41	7
Hannover 96	58-60, 60-61, 61-62, 65-66, 67-68, 68-69, 69-70	15	21	6	3	12	30	50	-20	–
Kaiserslautern	72-73, 76-77, 79-80, 80-81, 81-82, 82-83, 83-84	56	44	24	3	17	91	59	32	5
Bayer Leverkusen	86-87, 87-88, 88-89, 90-91	34	24	11	9	4	31	16	15	3
Bor. Mönchengladbach	72-73, 74-75, 78-79, 79-80, 81-82,	121	74	46	15	13	161	79	82	14

	84-85, 85-86, 86-87, 87-88									
Bayern Munich	62-63, 70-71, 77-78, 79-80, 83-84, 88-89	61	45	24	7	14	95	52	43	6
1860 Munich	65-66, 67-68, 68-69, 69-70	17	16	6	4	6	37	32	5	1
Nuremberg	65-66, 66-67, 88-89	3	6	1	1	4	5	10	-5	–
VFB Stuttgart	64-65, 66-67, 69-70, 73-74, 78-79, 79-80, 80-81, 81-82, 83-84, 88-89, 89-90	87	64	33	14	17	121	67	54	7
Bayer Uerdingen	86-87	7	6	3	1	2	9	4	5	–
Wuppertal	73-74	2	2	1	0	1	6	8	-2	–
Total times entered	**123** **Total**	**912**	**700**	**359**	**120**	**221**	**1325**	**878**	**447**	**74**

Yugoslavia

Club	Seasons Entered	Pts	P	W	D	L	F	A	Diff	B
Red Star Belgrade	61-62, 62-63, 65-66, 66-67, 72-73, 75-76, 76-77, 78-79, 79-80, 83-84, 87-88, 89-90	83	67	33	11	23	108	87	21	6
OFK Belgrade	58-60, 60-61, 63-64, 64-65, 68-69, 71-72, 72-73, 73-74	43	38	16	7	15	69	68	1	4
Partizan Belgrade	67-68, 69-70, 70-71, 74-75, 84-85, 85-86, 86-87, 87-88, 88-89, 90-91	41	38	17	7	14	64	55	9	–
Rad Belgrade	89-90	2	2	1	0	1	2	3	-1	–
Napredak Krusevac	80-81	0	2	0	0	2	0	2	-2	–
Olimpija Ljubljana	66-67, 68-69	1	4	0	1	3	4	11	-7	–
Velez Mostar	73-74, 74-75, 87-88, 88-89	23	20	9	4	7	29	27	2	1
Radnicki Nis	80-81, 81-82, 83-84	27	22	11	3	8	34	31	3	2
Vojvodina Novi Sad	61-62, 62-63, 64-65, 67-68, 68-69, 69-70, 72-73, 75-76	27	27	9	7	11	29	33	-4	2
Rijeka	84-85, 86-87	5	6	2	1	3	8	8	0	–
Sarajevo	80-81, 82-83	9	8	3	3	2	21	21	0	–
Zeljeznicar Sarajevo	70-71, 71-72, 84-85	23	20	8	4	8	40	31	9	3
Vardar Skoplje	85-86	3	4	1	1	2	3	5	-2	–
Hajduk Split	70-71, 78-79, 81-82, 82-83, 83-84, 85-86, 86-87	54	42	23	5	14	74	46	28	3
Sloboda Tuzla	77-78	2	2	1	0	1	4	8	-4	–
Dinamo Zagreb	56-58, 58-60, 61-62, 62-63, 66-67, 67-68, 68-69, 70-71, 71-72, 76-77, 77-78, 79-80, 88-89, 90-91	73	67	24	18	25	101	85	16	7
NK Zagreb	60-61, 64-65, 65-66, 69-70	9	12	3	3	6	20	18	2	–
Tresnjevka Zagreb	63-64	0	2	0	0	2	1	4	-3	–
Total times entered	**84** **Total**	**425**	**383**	**161**	**75**	**147**	**611**	**543**	**68**	**28**

National Classification by Cumulative Year-by-Year Index

1956-58 to 1990-91

Pos	Cnty	Total	5556	5657	5758	5859	5960	6061	6162	6263	6364	6465	6566	6667	6768	6869	6970
1	FRG	230.915	–	–	4.000	–	1.000	3.500	1.333	2.666	6.500	2.750	6.250	5.666	2.750	5.250	4.750
2	Eng	227.332	–	–	10.500	–	10.500	15.000	3.000	2.000	4.500	13.000	12.000	10.333	11.333	9.250	11.000
3	Ita	225.582	–	–	5.000	–	4.500	12.500	4.333	10.000	10.500	6.750	4.500	11.666	7.333	5.250	7.750
4	Esp	209.943	–	–	12.000	–	17.000	5.000	13.666	9.333	12.000	7.200	14.250	3.000	5.250	5.250	3.250
5	Hun	186.000	–	–	–		2.000	0.000	14.000	8.000	9.000	23.000	6.000	8.000	19.000	18.000	4.000
6	Yug	165.493	–	–	0.000	–	6.500	4.000	7.666	9.666	1.000	2.666	1.500	7.000	6.666	2.500	1.000
7	Bel	162.911	–	–	–	–	7.000	1.000	0.000	4.000	7.500	3.666	2.666	2.666	2.000	2.000	9.666
8	Ned	149.914	–	–	–	–	–	–	–	4.000	0.000	4.000	1.000	2.000	2.000	2.666	8.000
9	Sco	146.413	–	–	–	–	–	6.000	3.500	5.333	4.000	4.666	6.000	8.333	8.333	7.500	4.333
10	GDR	143.166	–	–	2.000	–	2.000	2.000	5.000	4.000	1.000	0.000	1.000	12.000	2.000	2.000	9.000
11	Por	120.829	–	–	–	–	–	–	1.000	1.500	2.500	1.500	4.333	2.333	3.333	5.000	5.000
12	Fra	111.495	–	–	–	–	1.000	0.000	1.000	2.000	0.000	5.666	1.333	2.000	2.000	1.500	2.666
13	Rom	108.999	–	–	–	–	–	–	–	11.000	0.000	6.000	5.000	6.000	2.000	3.000	4.500
14	Tch	107.165	–	–	–	–	–	–	1.000	0.000	9.000	2.000	5.000	1.500	1.000	4.000	0.500
15	URS	98.497	–	–	–	–	–	–	–	–	–	–	–	–	–	–	–
16	Sui	83.999	–	–	3.500	–	0.000	1.000	0.500	0.000	2.000	1.500	1.500	0.500	4.000	0.666	1.000
17	Aut	78.498	–	–	–	–	–	–	–	1.000	5.000	3.000	4.000	0.000	0.000	1.500	1.500
18	Swe	72.999	–	–	–	–	–	–	–	–	–	1.000	2.500	2.000	0.000	5.000	1.000
19	Bul	71.500	–	–	–	–	–	–	–	–	5.000	8.000	2.000	1.000	1.000	1.500	2.500
20	Pol	68.333	–	–	–	–	–	–	–	–	–	–	–	–	–	7.000	2.500
21	Gre	68.000	–	–	–	–	–	–	2.000	–	0.000	1.000	2.000	0.000	0.000	3.500	1.500
22	Den	45.000	–	–	1.000	–	0.000	5.000	1.000	1.000	0.000	0.000	0.000	0.500	0.000	0.000	0.000
23	Tur	43.000	–	–	–	–	–	–	–	0.000	–	0.000	2.000	0.000	5.000	7.000	1.000
24	Nor	35.000	–	–	–	–	–	–	–	–	–	0.000	0.000	0.000	1.000	1.000	3.000
25	Irl	31.000	–	–	–	–	–	–	–	4.000	1.000	4.000	1.000	0.000	0.000	3.000	0.000
26	Nir	27.000	–	–	–	–	–	–	–	0.000	0.000	–	1.000	–	2.000	0.000	2.000
27	Fin	22.500	–	–	–	–	–	–	–	–	–	–	–	–	–	–	–
28	Alb	14.000	–	–	–	–	–	–	–	–	–	–	–	–	–	–	–
–	Isl	14.000	–	–	–	–	–	–	–	–	–	–	–	–	–	–	0.000
30	Cyp	11.000	–	–	–	–	–	–	–	–	–	–	–	–	–	–	–
–	Lux	11.000	–	–	–	–	–	–	–	0.000	1.000	2.000	0.000	0.000	0.000	–	2.000
32	Mlt	6.000	–	–	–	–	–	–	–	–	–	–	–	–	–	0.000	2.000

	Pts	P	W	D	L	F	A	Diff	B	F/P
Total	7541	7094	2872	1350	2872	10485	10485	0	447	2.956

1956-58 to 1990-91

Pos	Cnty	Total	7071	7172	7273	7374	7475	7576	7677	7778	7879	7980	8081	8182	8283	8384	8485	8586
1	FRG	230.915	9.500	5.250	9.750	8.250	14.250	7.500	6.500	7.000	14.750	16.000	7.400	8.000	7.250	3.750	7.000	8.000
2	Eng	227.332	11.800	12.250	9.500	11.750	3.500	7.250	5.500	6.500	9.000	2.500	7.666	2.750	1.250	11.500	6.200	–
3	Ita	225.582	7.000	8.500	4.250	1.750	6.500	4.500	7.250	2.500	2.500	3.000	5.500	3.500	4.000	5.500	9.500	8.000
4	Esp	209.943	3.000	2.750	3.333	1.666	3.000	5.666	10.666	7.666	3.333	1.000	5.000	7.666	4.750	1.333	5.000	7.750
5	Hun	186.000	2.500	9.000	3.500	4.000	2.500	4.000	4.000	3.000	6.000	5.000	1.500	1.500	2.500	2.000	9.500	2.500
6	Yug	165.493	2.500	6.333	6.333	1.500	9.000	2.500	5.500	3.000	10.500	5.000	3.333	9.500	7.000	6.666	8.666	6.333
7	Bel	162.911	6.000	3.666	2.000	3.666	4.000	11.000	11.000	5.000	3.000	4.500	6.500	4.750	8.333	8.000	5.000	6.666
8	Ned	149.914	9.500	3.500	9.000	13.500	12.000	4.000	6.500	14.000	4.500	7.000	8.000	4.666	1.333	4.750	4.000	3.333
9	Sco	146.413	3.250	6.333	0.000	3.333	2.000	3.500	3.000	1.500	3.000	1.500	4.500	9.000	8.000	3.500	4.000	4.333
10	GDR	143.166	5.000	5.000	9.000	9.000	3.500	8.000	4.500	11.500	2.000	5.000	5.000	3.333	2.000	4.333	2.500	2.500
11	Por	120.829	5.333	2.666	7.000	5.000	1.500	7.500	1.000	1.000	3.000	3.000	4.000	6.000	13.000	3.500	2.500	4.333
12	Fra	111.495	2.000	2.333	0.333	6.000	4.500	1.000	1.500	13.000	3.000	6.000	12.500	3.000	4.000	3.666	1.666	4.333
13	Rom	108.999	2.500	6.500	1.000	2.500	3.500	1.000	1.000	1.000	5.000	7.500	1.000	4.500	9.000	1.500	5.000	1.500
14	Tch	107.165	4.500	1.000	3.000	2.500	8.000	4.500	3.500	3.000	5.500	6.333	4.500	1.000	10.000	7.333	2.333	1.333
15	URS	98.497	–	3.000	6.000	8.500	3.000	6.666	5.500	5.500	5.000	4.500	1.666	2.666	4.000	7.000	9.500	6.333
16	Sui	83.999	0.500	0.500	3.000	1.000	2.000	1.500	3.500	6.333	1.500	3.000	6.000	8.500	8.000	0.000	3.000	5.500
17	Aut	78.498	2.000	2.000	0.500	2.000	2.333	2.000	4.500	2.000	1.000	0.500	0.000	4.500	0.500	10.500	3.000	3.000
18	Swe	72.999	0.000	0.500	3.500	0.500	3.000	2.333	3.000	1.000	1.500	3.500	1.500	14.000	3.500	1.500	1.000	5.500
19	Bul	71.500	1.000	1.000	5.500	3.000	1.500	6.500	3.000	2.500	2.000	4.000	3.500	1.000	0.500	2.000	2.500	2.500
20	Pol	68.333	0.500	5.000	2.000	7.000	1.000	7.500	3.000	2.333	4.000	1.500	3.500	0.500	2.500	4.000	3.000	4.000
21	Gre	68.000	1.000	2.000	4.500	3.500	2.000	3.500	7.000	2.500	1.000	4.000	2.000	2.500	2.000	4.000	3.000	1.500
22	Den	45.000	2.000	0.000	2.000	2.000	2.000	0.000	1.000	1.000	5.000	2.000	0.000	2.000	1.000	0.500	1.000	0.000
23	Tur	43.000	4.000	1.000	1.000	3.000	1.000	1.000	2.000	1.000	0.500	1.500	0.000	0.000	0.000	2.000	0.000	0.000
24	Nor	35.000	0.000	6.000	2.500	0.500	0.000	1.500	0.000	3.000	1.000	0.500	0.000	2.000	3.000	1.000	2.000	1.000
25	Irl	31.000	0.000	1.000	0.000	0.000	0.000	4.000	0.000	1.000	0.000	1.000	1.000	1.000	4.000	0.000	2.000	1.000
26	Nir	27.000	3.000	0.000	–	2.000	4.000	0.000	2.000	0.000	2.000	0.000	2.000	0.000	0.000	1.000	1.000	1.000
27	Fin	22.500	2.000	0.000	–	0.000	0.000	0.000	2.000	1.000	3.000	0.000	0.000	0.000	0.000	0.000	0.000	0.000
28	Alb	14.000	–	–	–	–	–	–	–	–	–	–	–	2.000	–	–	–	4.000
–	Isl	14.000	0.000	0.000	1.000	1.000	1.000	0.000	0.000	0.000	2.000	2.000	0.000	0.000	0.000	1.000	0.000	2.000
30	Cyp	11.000	–	0.000	0.000	0.000	–	0.000	0.000	1.000	1.000	0.000	0.000	1.000	1.000	0.000	1.000	1.000
–	Lux	11.000	0.000	1.000	0.000	0.000	0.000	0.000	0.000	0.000	1.000	0.000	0.000	0.000	0.000	0.000	1.000	0.000
32	Mlt	6.000	0.000	0.000	0.000	0.000	0.000	0.000	0.000	1.000	2.000	0.000	0.000	0.000	0.000	0.000	0.000	1.000

	Pts	P	W	D	L	F	A	Diff	B	F/P
Total	**7541**	**7094**	**2872**	**1350**	**2872**	**10485**	**10485**	**0**	**447**	**2.956**

National Classification by Cumulative Year-by-Year Index

1956-58 to 1990-91

Pos	Cnty	Total	8687	8788	8889	8990	9091
1	FRG	230.915	7.250	9.750	8.600	12.250	6.500
2	Eng	227.332	–	–	–	–	6.000
3	Ita	225.582	7.000	6.750	11.000	11.500	15.500
4	Esp	209.943	5.666	10.333	5.666	4.000	3.500
5	Hun	186.000	2.500	5.000	2.500	0.000	2.000
6	Yug	165.493	2.333	3.666	5.666	5.500	4.500
7	Bel	162.911	5.333	6.000	4.000	8.333	4.000
8	Ned	149.914	5.000	5.500	2.500	1.000	2.666
9	Sco	146.413	9.333	4.000	6.000	4.333	4.000
10	GDR	143.166	2.000	3.000	10.000	2.500	1.500
11	Por	120.829	6.333	3.666	5.333	3.666	5.000
12	Fra	111.495	2.333	3.500	4.000	6.666	7.000
13	Rom	108.999	4.000	4.333	6.000	0.500	2.666
14	Tch	107.165	2.333	6.000	2.000	2.500	2.000
15	URS	98.497	3.333	4.250	2.500	4.250	5.333
16	Sui	83.999	3.500	1.000	2.000	4.500	3.000
17	Aut	78.498	6.000	1.333	2.666	6.666	5.500
18	Swe	72.999	11.000	1.000	1.666	1.000	1.000
19	Bul	71.500	3.500	1.500	0.500	1.000	2.000
20	Pol	68.333	4.500	0.500	0.000	0.500	2.000
21	Gre	68.000	1.000	4.000	1.500	4.000	1.500
22	Den	45.000	0.000	5.000	2.000	1.000	7.000
23	Tur	43.000	2.000	1.000	2.000	1.000	4.000
24	Nor	35.000	1.000	2.000	1.000	0.000	2.000
25	Irl	31.000	0.000	1.000	0.000	0.000	1.000
26	Nir	27.000	1.000	0.000	2.000	0.000	1.000
27	Fin	22.500	2.000	4.000	6.000	2.000	0.500
28	Alb	14.000	2.000	6.000	–	0.000	0.000
–	Isl	14.000	0.000	2.000	1.000	0.000	1.000
30	Cyp	11.000	1.000	0.000	0.000	1.000	3.000
–	Lux	11.000	1.000	0.000	0.000	0.000	2.000
32	Mlt	6.000	0.000	0.000	0.000	0.000	0.000

	Pts	P	W	D	L	F	A	Diff	B	F/P
Total	**7541**	**7094**	**2872**	**1350**	**2872**	**10485**	**10485**	**0**	**447**	**2.956**

National Classification by Cumulative Year-by-Year Index

1981-82 to 1990-91

Pos	Cnty	Total	8182	8283	8384	8485	8586	8687	8788	8889	8990	9091
1	Ita	82.250	3.500	4.000	5.500	9.500	8.000	7.000	6.750	11.000	11.500	15.500
2	FRG	78.350	8.000	7.250	3.750	7.000	8.000	7.250	9.750	8.600	12.250	6.500
3	Bel	60.415	4.750	8.333	8.000	5.000	6.666	5.333	6.000	4.000	8.333	4.000
4	Yug	59.830	9.500	7.000	6.666	8.666	6.333	2.333	3.666	5.666	5.500	4.500
5	Sco	56.499	9.000	8.000	3.500	4.000	4.333	9.333	4.000	6.000	4.333	4.000
6	Esp	55.664	7.666	4.750	1.333	5.000	7.750	5.666	10.333	5.666	4.000	3.500
7	Por	53.331	6.000	13.000	3.500	2.500	4.333	6.333	3.666	5.333	3.666	5.000
8	URS	49.165	2.666	4.000	7.000	9.500	6.333	3.333	4.250	2.500	4.250	5.333
9	Aut	43.665	4.500	0.500	10.500	3.000	3.000	6.000	1.333	2.666	6.666	5.500
10	Swe	41.166	14.000	3.500	1.500	1.000	5.500	11.000	1.000	1.666	1.000	1.000
11	Fra	40.164	3.000	4.000	3.666	1.666	4.333	2.333	3.500	4.000	6.666	7.000
12	Sui	39.000	8.500	8.000	0.000	3.000	5.500	3.500	1.000	2.000	4.500	3.000
13	Rom	38.999	4.500	9.000	1.500	5.000	1.500	4.000	4.333	6.000	0.500	2.666
14	Tch	36.832	1.000	10.000	7.333	2.333	1.333	2.333	6.000	2.000	2.500	2.000
15	Ned	34.748	4.666	1.333	4.750	4.000	3.333	5.000	5.500	2.500	1.000	2.666
16	GDR	33.666	3.333	2.000	4.333	2.500	2.500	2.000	3.000	10.000	2.500	1.500
17	Hun	30.000	1.500	2.500	2.000	9.500	2.500	2.500	5.000	2.500	0.000	2.000
18	Eng	27.700	2.750	1.250	11.500	6.200	–	–	–	–	–	6.000
19	Gre	25.000	2.500	2.000	4.000	3.000	1.500	1.000	4.000	1.500	4.000	1.500
20	Pol	21.500	0.500	2.500	4.000	3.000	4.000	4.500	0.500	0.000	0.500	2.000
21	Den	19.500	2.000	1.000	0.500	1.000	0.000	0.000	5.000	2.000	1.000	7.000
22	Bul	17.000	1.000	0.500	2.000	2.500	2.500	3.500	1.500	0.500	1.000	2.000
23	Nor	15.000	2.000	3.000	1.000	2.000	1.000	1.000	2.000	1.000	0.000	2.000
24	Fin	14.500	0.000	0.000	0.000	0.000	0.000	2.000	4.000	6.000	2.000	0.500
25	Alb	14.000	2.000	–	–	–	4.000	2.000	6.000	–	0.000	0.000
26	Tur	12.000	0.000	0.000	2.000	0.000	0.000	2.000	1.000	2.000	1.000	4.000
27	Irl	10.000	1.000	4.000	0.000	2.000	1.000	0.000	1.000	0.000	0.000	1.000
28	Cyp	9.000	1.000	1.000	0.000	1.000	1.000	1.000	0.000	0.000	1.000	3.000
29	Nir	7.000	0.000	0.000	1.000	1.000	1.000	1.000	0.000	2.000	0.000	1.000
–	Isl	7.000	0.000	0.000	1.000	0.000	2.000	0.000	2.000	1.000	0.000	1.000
31	Lux	4.000	0.000	0.000	0.000	1.000	0.000	1.000	0.000	0.000	0.000	2.000
32	Mlt	1.000	0.000	0.000	0.000	0.000	1.000	0.000	0.000	0.000	0.000	0.000

	Pts	P	W	D	L	F	A	Diff	B	F/P
Total	**2660**	**2520**	**991**	**538**	**991**	**3386**	**3386**	**0**	**140**	**2.687**

National Classification by Cumulative Year–by–Year Index

1986–87 to 1990–91

Pos'n	Cnty	Total	8687	8788	8889	8990	9091
1	Ita	51.750	7.000	6.750	11.000	11.500	15.500
2	FRG	44.350	7.250	9.750	8.600	12.250	6.500
3	Esp	29.165	5.666	10.333	5.666	4.000	3.500
4	Bel	27.666	5.333	6.000	4.000	8.333	4.000
–	Sco	27.666	9.333	4.000	6.000	4.333	4.000
6	Por	23.998	6.333	3.666	5.333	3.666	5.000
7	Fra	23.499	2.333	3.500	4.000	6.666	7.000
8	Aut	22.165	6.000	1.333	2.666	6.666	5.500
9	Yug	21.665	2.333	3.666	5.666	5.500	4.500
10	URS	19.666	3.333	4.250	2.500	4.250	5.333
11	GDR	19.000	2.000	3.000	10.000	2.500	1.500
12	Rom	17.499	4.000	4.333	6.000	0.500	2.666
13	Ned	16.666	5.000	5.500	2.500	1.000	2.666
14	Swe	15.666	11.000	1.000	1.666	1.000	1.000
15	Den	15.000	0.000	5.000	2.000	1.000	7.000
16	Tch	14.833	2.333	6.000	2.000	2.500	2.000
17	Fin	14.500	2.000	4.000	6.000	2.000	0.500
18	Sui	14.000	3.500	1.000	2.000	4.500	3.000
19	Gre	12.000	1.000	4.000	1.500	4.000	1.500
–	Hun	12.000	2.500	5.000	2.500	0.000	2.000
21	Tur	10.000	2.000	1.000	2.000	1.000	4.000
22	Bul	8.500	3.500	1.500	0.500	1.000	2.000
23	Alb	8.000	2.000	6.000	–	0.000	0.000
24	Pol	7.500	4.500	0.500	0.000	0.500	2.000
25	Eng	6.000	–	–	–	–	6.000
–	Nor	6.000	1.000	2.000	1.000	0.000	2.000
27	Cyp	5.000	1.000	0.000	0.000	1.000	3.000
28	Nir	4.000	1.000	0.000	2.000	0.000	1.000
–	Isl	4.000	0.000	2.000	1.000	0.000	1.000
30	Lux	3.000	1.000	0.000	0.000	0.000	2.000
31	Irl	2.000	0.000	1.000	0.000	0.000	1.000
32	Mlt	0.000	0.000	0.000	0.000	0.000	0.000

	Pts	P	W	D	L	F	A	Diff	B	F/P
Total	**1330**	**1260**	**491**	**278**	**491**	**1544**	**1544**	**0**	**70**	**2.451**

Country Records – Points Gained 1956-58 to 1990-91

Albania

Pos'n	Cnty	Pts	P	W	D	L	F	A	Diff	B	Pts/P	Q	E
1	Spain	4	4	1	2	1	3	5	-2	0	1.000	0	2
–	East Germany	4	4	2	0	2	3	5	-2	0	1.000	1	1
3	Malta	3	2	1	1	0	1	0	1	0	1.500	1	0
4	Yugoslavia	2	2	1	0	1	3	2	1	0	1.000	1	0
5	Portugal	1	2	0	1	1	0	1	-1	0	0.500	0	1
6	Romania	0	2	0	0	2	0	2	-2	0	0.000	0	1
7	France	0	2	0	0	2	0	8	-8	0	0.000	0	1
	Total	**14**	**18**	**5**	**4**	**9**	**10**	**23**	**-13**	**0**	**0.778**	**3**	**6**

Austria

Pos'n	Cnty	Pts	P	W	D	L	F	A	Diff	B	Pts/P	Q	E
1	Italy	18	18	6	4	8	19	28	-9	2	1.000	4	5
2	Belgium	10	12	5	0	7	15	22	-7	0	0.833	2	4
3	Hungary	10	13	4	2	7	14	25	-11	0	0.769	1	5
4	East Germany	8	6	3	1	2	7	6	1	1	1.333	2	1
5	Czechoslovakia	8	10	4	0	6	7	20	-13	0	0.800	1	4
6	Yugoslavia	8	14	2	4	8	12	26	-14	0	0.571	1	6
7	West Germany	8	12	3	2	7	11	30	-19	0	0.667	0	6
8	France	7	4	3	1	0	9	5	4	0	1.750	2	0
9	USSR	7	6	3	0	3	9	7	2	1	1.167	3	0
10	Netherlands	7	6	3	1	2	6	4	2	0	1.167	2	1
11	Romania	7	8	2	3	3	8	13	-5	0	0.875	1	3
12	Greece	6	8	2	2	4	14	10	4	0	0.750	2	2
13	Denmark	6	4	3	0	1	6	2	4	0	1.500	2	0
14	Finland	6	6	3	0	3	8	8	0	0	1.000	1	2
15	England	6	8	2	2	4	5	10	-5	0	0.750	0	4
16	Sweden	5	6	2	1	3	7	10	-3	0	0.833	1	2
17	Luxembourg	4	2	2	0	0	15	0	15	0	2.000	1	0
18	Malta	4	2	2	0	0	7	1	6	0	2.000	1	0
–	Norway	4	2	2	0	0	7	1	6	0	2.000	1	0
20	Turkey	4	4	2	0	2	7	5	2	0	1.000	1	1
21	Switzerland	4	4	1	2	1	2	2	0	0	1.000	1	1
22	Spain	4	8	1	2	5	7	16	-9	0	0.500	0	4
23	Poland	3	4	1	1	2	6	8	-2	0	0.750	0	2
24	Scotland	3	6	1	1	4	4	10	-6	0	0.500	1	2
25	Bulgaria	2	4	1	0	3	4	12	-8	0	0.500	1	1
26	Portugal	1	2	0	1	1	2	6	-4	0	0.500	0	1
	Total	**160**	**179**	**63**	**30**	**86**	**218**	**287**	**-69**	**4**	**0.894**	**32**	**57**

Belgium

Pos'n	Cnty	Pts	P	W	D	L	F	A	Diff	B	Pts/P	Q	E
1	Spain	39	37	16	5	16	47	48	-1	2	1.054	9	9
2	West Germany	36	36	12	7	17	42	59	-17	5	1.000	8	10
3	England	34	32	12	7	13	44	48	-4	3	1.063	8	8
4	Italy	29	30	8	8	14	32	38	-6	5	0.967	7	8
5	Yugoslavia	27	21	12	1	8	40	31	9	2	1.286	6	4
6	Scotland	23	26	7	8	11	26	39	-13	1	0.885	7	6
7	Netherlands	22	20	8	4	8	27	21	6	2	1.100	4	6
8	Northern Ireland	20	12	9	2	1	38	12	26	0	1.667	6	0
9	Portugal	20	26	8	4	14	30	39	-9	0	0.769	4	9
10	Luxembourg	18	10	8	2	0	24	4	20	0	1.800	5	0

11	France	18	16	6	5	5	27	22	5	1	1.125	5	3
12	Czechoslovakia	17	13	7	1	5	19	14	5	2	1.308	5	1
13	Greece	16	10	6	3	1	21	11	10	1	1.600	4	1
14	Austria	15	12	7	0	5	22	15	7	1	1.250	4	2
15	Romania	13	8	5	3	0	14	4	10	0	1.625	4	0
16	Norway	13	10	5	3	2	17	8	9	0	1.300	5	0
17	East Germany	13	14	3	5	6	19	19	0	2	0.929	2	5
18	Denmark	12	6	6	0	0	20	3	17	0	2.000	3	0
19	Iceland	8	4	4	0	0	14	1	13	0	2.000	2	0
20	USSR	8	10	3	1	6	14	16	-2	1	0.800	3	2
21	Poland	7	8	1	5	2	6	8	-2	0	0.875	2	2
22	Switzerland	4	2	2	0	0	8	3	5	0	2.000	1	0
23	Finland	4	2	2	0	0	6	1	5	0	2.000	1	0
24	Hungary	4	6	1	2	3	6	9	-3	0	0.667	0	3
25	Cyprus	3	2	1	1	0	4	1	3	0	1.500	1	0
26	Bulgaria	3	2	1	1	0	4	3	1	0	1.500	1	0
27	Sweden	3	6	1	1	4	7	13	-6	0	0.500	1	2
28	Turkey	1	2	0	1	1	1	2	-1	0	0.500	0	1
	Total	**430**	**383**	**161**	**80**	**142**	**579**	**492**	**87**	**28**	**1.123**	**108**	**82**

Bulgaria

Pos'n	Cnty	Pts	P	W	D	L	F	A	Diff	B	Pts/P	Q	E
1	Yugoslavia	15	25	4	7	14	25	61	-36	0	0.600	1	11
2	USSR	11	12	3	4	5	12	16	-4	1	0.917	2	4
3	Romania	10	8	5	0	3	15	12	3	0	1.250	3	1
4	Hungary	9	12	4	1	7	19	19	0	0	0.750	3	3
5	Spain	9	10	4	1	5	15	23	-8	0	0.900	1	4
6	Malta	8	4	4	0	0	13	0	13	0	2.000	2	0
7	Turkey	8	4	4	0	0	10	2	8	0	2.000	2	0
8	West Germany	8	14	3	2	9	12	23	-11	0	0.571	2	5
9	Italy	8	13	2	4	7	11	23	-12	0	0.615	0	6
10	Austria	6	4	3	0	1	12	4	8	0	1.500	1	1
11	France	5	4	2	1	1	9	7	2	0	1.250	2	0
12	Cyprus	5	4	2	1	1	10	9	1	0	1.250	1	1
13	Czechoslovakia	4	4	2	0	2	4	4	0	0	1.000	1	1
14	East Germany	4	4	2	0	2	5	7	-2	0	1.000	0	2
15	Netherlands	4	4	1	1	2	4	9	-5	1	1.000	1	1
16	Switzerland	3	4	0	3	1	2	3	-1	0	0.750	0	2
17	Scotland	3	4	1	1	2	3	6	-3	0	0.750	0	2
18	Greece	2	4	1	0	3	6	8	-2	0	0.500	1	1
19	Belgium	1	2	0	1	1	3	4	-1	0	0.500	0	1
20	Portugal	1	2	0	1	1	1	4	-3	0	0.500	0	1
21	England	1	4	0	1	3	3	10	-7	0	0.250	0	2
22	Sweden	0	2	0	0	2	1	7	-6	0	0.000	0	1
	Total	**125**	**148**	**47**	**29**	**72**	**195**	**261**	**-66**	**2**	**0.845**	**23**	**50**

Cyprus

Pos'n	Cnty	Pts	P	W	D	L	F	A	Diff	B	Pts/P	Q	E
1	Bulgaria	3	4	1	1	2	9	10	-1	0	0.750	1	1
2	Romania	2	8	0	2	6	2	23	-21	0	0.250	0	4
3	Switzerland	1	2	0	1	1	2	3	-1	0	0.500	0	1
4	Belgium	1	2	0	1	1	1	4	-3	0	0.500	0	1
–	Spain	1	2	0	1	1	1	4	-3	0	0.500	0	1
6	Poland	1	2	0	1	1	3	7	-4	0	0.500	0	1
7	Czechoslovakia	1	2	0	1	1	3	8	-5	0	0.500	0	1
8	Italy	1	4	0	1	3	1	11	-10	0	0.250	0	2

9	USSR	0	2	0	0	2	0	2	-2	0	0.000	0	1
10	Yugoslavia	0	2	0	0	2	2	6	-4	0	0.000	0	
11	West Germany	0	10	0	0	10	5	55	-50	0	0.000	0	5
	Total	**11**	**40**	**1**	**9**	**30**	**29**	**133**	**-104**	**0**	**0.275**	**1**	**19**

Czechoslovakia

Pos'n	Cnty	Pts	P	W	D	L	F	A	Diff	B	Pts/P	Q	E
1	Spain	22	22	8	6	8	32	24	8	0	1.000	5	6
2	Scotland	17	14	6	3	5	17	15	2	2	1.214	5	2
3	West Germany	16	32	5	5	22	36	72	-36	1	0.500	3	13
4	Yugoslavia	14	12	6	2	4	22	19	3	0	1.167	2	4
5	Italy	13	14	4	4	6	13	14	-1	1	0.929	3	4
6	Austria	12	10	6	0	4	20	7	13	0	1.200	4	1
7	Switzerland	12	8	5	1	2	16	15	1	1	1.500	2	2
8	Belgium	12	13	5	1	7	14	19	-5	1	0.923	1	5
9	England	11	14	4	2	8	21	32	-11	1	0.786	2	5
10	Sweden	10	8	4	2	2	15	9	6	0	1.250	3	1
11	Iceland	8	4	4	0	0	13	2	11	0	2.000	2	0
12	Hungary	8	10	3	2	5	11	15	-4	0	0.800	1	4
13	France	7	6	3	1	2	8	3	5	0	1.167	3	0
14	Denmark	6	4	2	2	0	13	2	11	0	1.500	2	0
15	East Germany	5	4	2	1	1	10	8	2	0	1.250	1	1
16	Portugal	5	6	1	2	3	5	7	-2	1	0.833	1	2
17	USSR	5	6	2	1	3	4	9	-5	0	0.833	0	3
18	Malta	4	2	2	0	0	16	0	16	0	2.000	1	0
19	Northern Ireland	4	2	2	0	0	4	1	3	0	2.000	1	0
20	Bulgaria	4	4	2	0	2	4	4	0	0	1.000	1	1
21	Poland	4	6	2	0	4	6	7	-1	0	0.667	1	2
22	Netherlands	4	4	2	0	2	4	7	-3	0	1.000	1	1
23	Cyprus	3	2	1	1	0	8	3	5	0	1.500	1	0
24	Eux	2	2	1	0	1	6	2	4	0	1.000	1	0
–	Turkey	2	2	1	0	1	6	2	4	0	1.000	1	0
26	Greece	2	2	1	0	1	3	3	0	0	1.000	1	0
27	Romania	0	2	0	0	2	0	5	-5	0	0.000	0	1
	Total	**212**	**215**	**84**	**36**	**95**	**327**	**306**	**21**	**8**	**0.986**	**49**	**58**

Denmark

Pos'n	Cnty	Pts	P	W	D	L	F	A	Diff	B	Pts/P	Q	E
1	West Germany	12	24	4	3	17	28	58	-30	1	0.500	2	10
2	Sweden	7	6	2	3	1	8	7	1	0	1.167	2	1
3	Finland	5	4	2	1	1	11	7	4	0	1.250	1	1
2	Poland	5	6	2	1	3	4	6	-2	0	0.833	1	2
5	Malta	4	2	2	0	0	10	2	8	0	2.000	1	0
6	Hungary	4	2	2	0	0	4	0	4	0	2.000	1	0
7	France	4	2	2	0	0	5	2	3	0	2.000	1	0
8	Switzerland	4	8	1	1	6	16	25	-9	1	0.500	1	3
9	USSR	4	10	1	1	8	7	20	-13	1	0.400	1	4
10	Norway	3	2	1	1	0	1	0	1	0	1.500	1	0
11	Spain	3	8	1	1	6	8	23	-15	0	0.375	0	4
12	Romania	2	2	1	0	1	3	3	0	0	1.000	0	1
13	East Germany	2	2	0	2	0	1	1	0	0	1.000	0	1
14	Rep. of Ireland	2	2	1	0	1	5	6	-1	0	1.000	0	1
15	Austria	2	4	1	0	3	2	6	-4	0	0.500	0	2
16	Czechoslovakia	2	4	0	2	2	2	13	-11	0	0.500	0	2
17	Scotland	2	10	1	0	9	10	27	-17	0	0.200	1	4
18	Netherlands	2	6	1	0	5	6	23	-17	0	0.333	0	3

Pos'n	Cnty	Pts	P	W	D	L	F	A	Diff	B	Pts/P	Q	E
19	Yugoslavia	1	2	0	1	1	4	9	-5	0	0.500	0	1
20	Italy	1	4	0	1	3	3	8	-5	0	0.250	0	2
21	England	1	6	0	1	5	9	26	-17	0	0.167	0	3
22	Portugal	0	2	0	0	2	1	4	-3	0	0.000	0	1
23	Belgium	0	6	0	0	6	3	20	-17	0	0.000	0	3
	Total	**72**	**124**	**25**	**19**	**80**	**151**	**296**	**-145**	**3**	**0.581**	**13**	**49**

East Germany

Pos'n	Cnty	Pts	P	W	D	L	F	A	Diff	B	Pts/P	Q	E
1	Italy	26	24	12	1	11	31	33	-2	1	1.083	4	8
2	Yugoslavia	20	19	8	4	7	35	26	9	0	1.053	5	4
3	France	20	16	9	1	6	31	25	6	1	1.250	5	3
4	West Germany	19	24	6	6	12	26	42	-16	1	0.792	3	9
5	Belgium	18	14	6	5	3	19	19	0	1	1.286	5	2
6	Hungary	14	11	5	2	4	17	11	6	2	1.273	3	2
7	England	14	24	5	3	16	16	36	-20	1	0.583	3	9
8	USSR	13	14	5	2	7	16	21	-5	1	0.929	3	4
9	Portugal	11	6	4	1	1	10	6	4	2	1.833	3	0
10	Poland	11	8	5	1	2	9	6	3	0	1.375	2	2
11	Northern Ireland	10	8	4	2	2	17	6	11	0	1.250	4	0
12	Netherlands	10	12	3	4	5	15	21	-6	0	0.833	1	5
13	Romania	9	7	3	2	2	12	6	6	1	1.286	2	1
14	Switzerland	8	6	4	0	2	21	13	8	0	1.333	2	1
15	Norway	8	6	4	0	2	15	9	6	0	1.333	2	1
16	Finland	7	4	3	1	0	7	0	7	0	1.750	2	0
17	Spain	7	6	3	1	2	8	6	2	0	1.167	1	2
18	Scotland	6	8	2	2	4	6	9	-3	0	0.750	1	3
19	Iceland	5	4	1	3	0	4	1	3	0	1.250	2	0
20	Turkey	5	4	2	1	1	7	5	2	0	1.250	2	0
21	Sweden	5	4	2	1	1	6	5	1	0	1.250	1	1
22	Austria	5	6	2	1	3	6	7	-1	0	0.833	1	2
23	Bulgaria	4	4	2	0	2	7	5	2	0	1.000	2	0
24	Albania	4	4	2	0	2	5	3	2	0	1.000	1	1
25	Czechoslovakia	3	4	1	1	2	8	10	-2	0	0.750	1	1
26	Greece	2	2	1	0	1	3	2	1	0	1.000	1	0
27	Denmark	2	2	0	2	0	1	1	0	0	1.000	1	0
	Total	**266**	**251**	**104**	**47**	**100**	**358**	**334**	**24**	**11**	**1.060**	**63**	**61**

England

Pos'n	Cnty	Pts	P	W	D	L	F	A	Diff	B	Pts/P	Q	E
1	West Germany	67	48	25	9	14	87	54	33	8	1.396	16	8
2	Italy	62	47	20	14	13	63	52	11	8	1.319	16	7
3	Spain	57	53	18	15	20	71	84	-13	6	1.075	11	15
4	Netherlands	56	40	22	10	8	72	37	35	2	1.400	14	6
5	Scotland	55	32	18	11	3	51	24	27	8	1.719	14	2
6	Portugal	47	32	19	6	7	64	31	33	3	1.469	12	4
7	East Germany	40	24	16	3	5	36	16	20	5	1.667	9	3
8	Belgium	35	32	13	7	12	48	44	4	2	1.094	8	8
9	Hungary	34	27	13	5	9	37	30	7	3	1.259	7	6
10	Yugoslavia	29	24	10	5	9	31	31	0	4	1.208	6	6
11	Norway	25	14	12	1	1	57	11	46	0	1.786	7	0
12	Switzerland	24	16	10	2	4	36	14	22	2	1.500	5	3
13	England	24	20	5	10	5	17	17	0	4	1.200	5	5
14	Rep. of Ireland	22	12	10	2	0	62	2	60	0	1.833	6	0
15	Czechoslovakia	20	14	8	2	4	32	21	11	2	1.429	5	2
16	France	18	12	6	3	3	23	13	10	3	1.500	5	1

17	Romania	17	10	6	2	2	21	7	14	3	1.700	4	1
18	Poland	15	10	4	5	1	16	6	10	2	1.500	3	2
19	Greece	14	12	7	0	5	24	14	10	0	1.167	4	2
20	Denmark	13	6	5	1	0	26	9	17	2	2.167	3	0
21	Sweden	13	8	5	3	0	19	5	14	0	1.625	3	1
22	Austria	12	8	4	2	2	10	5	5	2	1.500	4	0
23	Iceland	8	4	4	0	0	22	1	21	0	2.000	2	0
24	Turkey	8	4	4	0	0	12	2	10	0	2.000	2	0
25	Bulgaria	7	4	3	1	0	10	3	7	0	1.750	2	0
26	USSR	5	6	1	2	3	13	14	-1	1	0.833	1	2
27	Luxembourg	4	2	2	0	0	16	0	16	0	2.000	1	0
28	Malta	4	2	2	0	0	7	0	7	0	2.000	1	0
29	Northern Ireland	2	2	1	0	1	3	1	2	0	1.000	1	0
	Total	**737**	**525**	**273**	**121**	**131**	**986**	**548**	**438**	**70**	**1.404**	**176**	**84**

Finland

Pos'n	Cnty	Pts	P	W	D	L	F	A	Diff	B	Pts/P	Q	E
1	Austria	6	6	3	0	3	8	8	0	0	1.000	2	1
2	Poland	4	6	1	2	3	5	10	-5	0	0.667	1	2
3	Denmark	3	4	1	1	2	7	11	-4	0	0.750	1	1
4	Romania	2	2	1	0	1	3	3	0	0	1.000	0	1
5	Northern Ireland	2	2	0	2	0	1	1	0	0	1.000	1	0
6	Italy	2	2	1	0	1	1	2	-1	0	1.000	0	1
7	Scotland	2	2	1	0	1	2	4	-2	0	1.000	0	1
8	Sweden	2	6	1	0	5	6	15	-9	0	0.333	0	3
9	East Germany	1	4	0	1	3	0	7	-7	0	0.250	0	2
10	France	1	6	0	1	5	2	25	-23	0	0.167	0	3
11	Norway	0	2	0	0	2	0	4	-4	0	0.000	0	1
12	Belgium	0	2	0	0	2	1	6	-5	0	0.000	0	1
13	West Germany	0	4	0	0	4	4	15	-11	0	0.000	0	2
14	USSR	0	6	0	0	6	1	21	-20	0	0.000	0	3
	Total	**25**	**54**	**9**	**7**	**38**	**41**	**132**	**-91**	**0**	**0.463**	**5**	**22**

France

Pos'n	Cnty	Pts	P	W	D	L	F	A	Diff	B	Pts/P	Q	E
1	Italy	24	35	7	9	19	29	56	-27	1	0.686	4	13
2	Portugal	21	26	8	5	13	25	46	-21	0	0.808	5	8
3	West Germany	21	28	8	3	17	31	59	-28	2	0.750	2	12
4	USSR	17	14	6	4	4	16	15	1	1	1.214	5	2
5	Greece	15	10	5	3	2	19	12	7	2	1.500	3	2
6	Scotland	15	14	6	3	5	17	16	1	0	1.071	3	4
7	Belgium	15	16	5	5	6	22	27	-5	0	0.938	3	5
8	East Germany	14	16	6	1	9	25	31	-6	1	0.875	3	5
9	Switzerland	13	10	5	1	4	16	12	4	2	1.300	4	1
10	Luxembourg	12	6	6	0	0	35	2	33	0	2.000	3	0
11	Finland	11	6	5	1	0	25	2	23	0	1.833	3	0
12	Spain	11	11	3	4	4	12	13	-1	1	1.000	3	2
13	Netherlands	10	10	4	2	4	17	12	5	0	1.000	3	2
14	England	9	12	3	3	6	13	23	-10	0	0.750	1	5
15	Hungary	7	8	3	1	4	11	19	-8	0	0.875	2	2
16	Iceland	6	4	3	0	1	12	2	10	0	1.500	2	0
17	Yugoslavia	6	6	2	2	2	13	12	1	0	1.000	2	1
18	Poland	5	4	2	1	1	7	4	3	0	1.250	2	0
19	Sweden	5	6	2	1	3	11	10	1	0	0.833	2	1
20	Czechoslovakia	5	6	2	1	3	3	8	-5	0	0.833	0	3
21	Albania	4	2	2	0	0	8	0	8	0	2.000	1	0

22	Rep. of Ireland	4	2	2	0	0	9	4	5	0	2.000	1	0
23	Turkey	4	4	2	0	2	6	4	2	0	1.000	1	1
24	Romania	4	4	2	0	2	5	7	-2	0	1.000	0	2
25	Northern Ireland	3	2	1	1	0	2	0	2	0	1.500	1	0
26	Bulgaria	3	4	1	1	2	7	9	-2	0	0.750	0	2
27	Austria	1	4	0	1	3	5	9	-4	0	0.250	0	2
28	Denmark	0	2	0	0	2	2	5	-3	0	0.000	0	1
	Total	**265**	**272**	**101**	**53**	**118**	**403**	**419**	**-16**	**10**	**0.974**	**59**	**76**

Greece

Pos'n	Cnty	Pts	P	W	D	L	F	A	Diff	B	Pts/P	Q	E
1	Italy	17	24	6	5	13	20	40	-20	0	0.708	3	9
2	Yugoslavia	16	14	7	1	6	19	28	-9	1	1.143	3	4
3	Spain	14	18	5	4	9	9	31	-22	0	0.778	1	8
4	England	11	12	5	0	7	14	24	-10	1	0.917	2	4
5	Austria	10	8	4	2	2	10	14	-4	0	1.250	2	2
6	Malta	8	4	4	0	0	15	2	13	0	2.000	2	0
7	Hungary	8	9	3	1	5	15	28	-13	1	0.889	2	3
8	Switzerland	7	6	3	1	2	6	7	-1	0	1.167	1	2
9	France	7	10	2	3	5	12	19	-7	0	0.700	2	3
10	Bulgaria	6	4	3	0	1	8	6	2	0	1.500	1	1
11	Romania	6	10	3	0	7	7	17	-10	0	0.600	1	4
12	Belgium	5	10	1	3	6	11	21	-10	0	0.500	1	4
13	West Germany	4	6	1	2	3	2	9	-7	0	0.667	0	3
14	Portugal	2	2	1	0	1	4	3	1	0	1.000	1	0
15	USSR	2	2	1	0	1	3	2	1	0	1.000	1	0
16	Czechoslovakia	2	2	1	0	1	3	3	0	0	1.000	0	1
17	East Germany	2	2	1	0	1	2	3	-1	0	1.000	0	1
18	Netherlands	1	4	0	1	3	1	12	-11	0	0.250	0	2
	Total	**128**	**147**	**51**	**23**	**73**	**161**	**269**	**-108**	**3**	**0.871**	**23**	**51**

Hungary

Pos'n	Cnty	Pts	P	W	D	L	F	A	Diff	B	Pts/P	Q	E
1	England	27	27	9	5	13	30	37	-7	4	1.000	6	7
2	Spain	26	27	11	2	14	34	48	-14	2	0.963	1	9
3	Yugoslavia	23	18	9	1	8	34	27	7	4	1.278	6	3
4	Italy	19	15	6	4	5	19	18	1	3	1.267	5	3
5	West Germany	17	16	7	1	8	31	34	-3	2	1.063	3	5
6	Austria	16	13	7	2	4	25	14	11	0	1.231	5	1
7	Bulgaria	16	12	7	1	4	19	19	0	1	1.333	3	3
8	Turkey	13	8	5	2	1	25	7	18	1	1.625	4	0
9	Czechoslovakia	12	10	5	2	3	15	11	4	0	1.200	4	1
10	Greece	11	9	5	1	3	28	15	13	0	1.222	3	2
11	Romania	11	10	5	0	5	17	11	6	1	1.100	4	1
12	East Germany	11	11	4	2	5	11	17	-6	1	1.000	2	3
13	Scotland	10	8	5	0	3	9	7	2	0	1.250	2	2
14	France	9	8	4	1	3	19	11	8	0	1.125	2	2
15	Portugal	9	8	4	1	3	11	9	2	0	1.125	2	2
16	Belgium	8	6	3	2	1	9	6	3	0	1.333	3	0
17	Poland	7	8	2	2	4	7	12	-5	1	0.875	1	3
18	Switzerland	6	6	2	2	2	7	7	0	0	1.000	1	2
19	Sweden	5	4	2	1	1	10	4	6	0	1.250	2	0
20	Netherlands	5	6	2	0	4	7	11	-4	1	0.833	1	2
21	Rep. of Ireland	3	2	1	1	0	2	1	1	0	1.500	1	0
–	Iceland	3	2	1	1	0	2	1	1	0	1.500	1	0
23	USSR	2	6	1	0	5	7	15	-8	0	0.333	1	2

24	Denmark	0	2	0	0	2	0	4	-4	0	0.000	0	1
	Total	**269**	**242**	**107**	**34**	**101**	**378**	**346**	**32**	**21**	**1.112**	**66**	**54**

Iceland

Pos'n	Cnty	Pts	P	W	D	L	F	A	Diff	B	Pts/P	Q	E
1	Northern Ireland	3	4	0	3	1	2	3	-1	0	0.750	1	1
2	East Germany	3	4	0	3	1	1	4	-3	0	0.750	0	2
3	Sweden	2	2	1	0	1	2	2	0	0	1.000	1	0
4	Scotland	2	6	0	2	4	4	14	-10	0	0.333	0	3
5	France	2	4	1	0	3	2	12	-10	0	0.500	0	2
6	Hungary	1	2	0	1	1	1	2	-1	0	0.500	0	1
7	Norway	1	4	0	1	3	0	9	-9	0	0.250	0	2
8	Poland	0	2	0	0	2	1	4	-3	0	0.000	0	1
9	Rep. of Ireland	0	2	0	0	2	0	7	-7	0	0.000	0	1
10	West Germany	0	2	0	0	2	0	10	-10	0	0.000	0	1
11	Czechoslovakia	0	4	0	0	4	2	13	-11	0	0.000	0	2
12	Belgium	0	4	0	0	4	1	14	-13	0	0.000	0	2
13	Netherlands	0	2	0	0	2	0	15	-15	0	0.000	0	1
–	Portugal	0	2	0	0	2	0	15	-15	0	0.000	0	1
15	England	0	4	0	0	4	1	22	-21	0	0.000	0	2
	Total	**14**	**48**	**2**	**10**	**36**	**17**	**146**	**-129**	**0**	**0.292**	**2**	**22**

Italy

Pos'n	Cnty	Pts	P	W	D	L	F	A	Diff	B	Pts/P	Q	E
1	West Germany	86	68	28	16	24	107	86	21	14	1.265	21	12
2	Yugoslavia	57	43	18	16	9	60	39	21	5	1.326	15	6
3	Spain	54	49	22	6	21	65	78	-13	4	1.102	11	13
4	France	52	35	19	9	7	56	29	27	5	1.486	13	4
5	Belgium	41	30	14	8	8	38	32	6	5	1.367	8	7
6	England	41	47	13	14	20	52	63	-11	1	0.872	7	16
7	Portugal	40	31	16	6	9	33	23	10	2	1.290	8	7
8	Greece	32	24	13	5	6	40	20	20	1	1.333	9	3
9	Turkey	29	16	14	1	1	43	11	32	0	1.813	8	0
10	Scotland	29	19	11	3	5	45	23	22	4	1.526	8	1
11	East Germany	25	24	11	1	12	33	31	2	2	1.042	8	4
12	Poland	22	14	9	3	2	22	12	10	1	1.571	6	1
13	Austria	22	18	8	4	6	28	19	9	2	1.222	5	4
14	Switzerland	20	14	9	2	3	27	12	15	0	1.429	6	1
15	Bulgaria	19	13	7	4	2	23	11	12	1	1.462	6	0
16	Romania	18	16	7	3	6	19	14	5	1	1.125	4	4
17	Italy	18	16	6	4	6	14	14	0	2	1.125	4	4
18	USSR	18	18	5	5	8	16	17	-1	3	1.000	5	4
19	Czechoslovakia	17	14	6	4	4	14	13	1	1	1.214	4	3
20	Sweden	16	12	6	4	2	14	8	6	0	1.333	5	1
21	Hungary	15	15	5	4	6	18	19	-1	1	1.000	3	5
22	Netherlands	15	14	5	3	6	17	19	-2	2	1.071	4	3
23	Malta	12	6	6	0	0	25	1	24	0	2.000	3	0
24	Luxembourg	8	4	4	0	0	14	0	14	0	2.000	2	0
25	Denmark	8	4	3	1	0	8	3	5	1	2.000	2	0
26	Cyprus	7	4	3	1	0	11	1	10	0	1.750	2	0
27	Rep. of Ireland	3	2	1	1	0	3	0	3	0	1.500	1	0
28	Norway	3	2	1	1	0	2	0	2	0	1.500	1	0
29	Finland	2	2	1	0	1	2	1	1	0	1.000	1	0
	Total	**729**	**574**	**271**	**129**	**174**	**849**	**599**	**250**	**58**	**1.270**	**180**	**103**

Luxembourg

Pos'n	Cnty	Pts	P	W	D	L	F	A	Diff	B	Pts/P	Q	E
1	Switzerland	3	8	1	1	6	1	14	-13	0	0.375	0	4
2	Northern Ireland	2	2	1	0	1	3	6	-3	0	1.000	0	1
3	Czechoslovakia	2	2	1	0	1	2	6	-4	0	1.000	0	1
4	Belgium	2	10	0	2	8	4	24	-20	0	0.200	0	5
5	Netherlands	2	14	0	2	12	5	84	-79	0	0.143	0	7
6	Italy	0	4	0	0	4	0	14	-14	0	0.000	0	2
7	Austria	0	2	0	0	2	0	15	-15	0	0.000	0	1
8	England	0	2	0	0	2	0	16	-16	0	0.000	0	1
9	West Germany	0	2	0	0	2	0	17	-17	0	0.000	0	1
10	Portugal	0	4	0	0	4	0	21	-21	0	0.000	0	2
11	France	0	6	0	0	6	2	35	-33	0	0.000	0	3
	Total	**11**	**56**	**3**	**5**	**48**	**17**	**252**	**-235**	**0**	**0.196**	**0**	**28**

Malta

Pos'n	Cnty	Pts	P	W	D	L	F	A	Diff	B	Pts/P	Q	E
1	Portugal	2	4	1	0	3	5	12	-7	0	0.500	0	2
2	Romania	2	4	1	0	3	2	14	-12	0	0.500	0	2
3	Albania	1	2	0	1	1	0	1	-1	0	0.500	0	1
4	West Germany	1	2	0	1	1	0	5	-5	0	0.500	0	1
5	Spain	0	2	0	0	2	0	3	-3	0	0.000	0	1
6	Austria	0	2	0	0	2	1	7	-6	0	0.000	0	1
7	England	0	2	0	0	2	0	7	-7	0	0.000	0	1
8	Denmark	0	2	0	0	2	2	10	-8	0	0.000	0	1
9	Switzerland	0	2	0	0	2	0	9	-9	0	0.000	0	1
10	Netherlands	0	2	0	0	2	0	12	-12	0	0.000	0	1
11	Greece	0	4	0	0	4	2	15	-13	0	0.000	0	2
12	Bulgaria	0	4	0	0	4	0	13	-13	0	0.000	0	2
13	Yugoslavia	0	6	0	0	6	1	17	-16	0	0.000	0	3
14	Czechoslovakia	0	2	0	0	2	0	16	-16	0	0.000	0	1
15	Italy	0	6	0	0	6	1	25	-24	0	0.000	0	3
	Total	**6**	**46**	**2**	**2**	**42**	**14**	**166**	**-152**	**0**	**0.130**	**0**	**23**

Netherlands

Pos'n	Cnty	Pts	P	W	D	L	F	A	Diff	B	Pts/P	Q	E
1	West Germany	42	44	16	7	21	64	80	-16	3	0.955	8	14
2	Spain	27	22	10	4	8	31	28	3	3	1.227	8	3
3	Luxembourg	26	14	12	2	0	84	5	79	0	1.857	7	0
4	England	26	40	8	10	22	37	72	-35	0	0.650	6	14
5	Belgium	22	20	8	4	8	21	27	-6	2	1.100	6	4
6	Yugoslavia	18	12	6	2	4	22	15	7	4	1.500	4	2
7	Poland	17	10	7	2	1	25	9	16	1	1.700	5	0
8	Scotland	17	16	8	1	7	22	19	3	0	1.063	4	4
9	Italy	17	14	6	3	5	19	17	2	2	1.214	3	4
10	East Germany	16	12	5	4	3	21	15	6	2	1.333	5	1
11	Northern Ireland	15	8	7	1	0	34	5	29	0	1.875	4	0
12	Switzerland	12	8	4	4	0	13	5	8	0	1.500	4	0
13	Sweden	11	8	5	1	2	19	8	11	0	1.375	4	0
14	France	11	10	4	2	4	12	17	-5	1	1.100	2	3
15	Denmark	10	6	5	0	1	23	6	17	0	1.667	3	0
16	Rep. of Ireland	8	6	3	2	1	11	5	6	0	1.333	2	1
17	Hungary	8	6	4	0	2	11	7	4	0	1.333	2	1
18	Greece	7	4	3	1	0	12	1	11	0	1.750	2	0
19	Bulgaria	5	4	2	1	1	9	4	5	0	1.250	1	1
20	Czechoslovakia	5	4	2	0	2	7	4	3	1	1.250	1	1

21	Austria	5	6	2	1	3	4	6	-2	0	0.833	1	2
22	Iceland	4	2	2	0	0	15	0	15	0	2.000	1	0
23	Malta	4	2	2	0	0	12	0	12	0	2.000	1	0
24	USSR	4	8	1	2	5	8	14	-6	0	0.500	1	3
25	Romania	3	2	1	1	0	2	0	2	0	1.500	1	0
26	Turkey	2	2	1	0	1	8	4	4	0	1.000	1	0
27	Portugal	2	10	1	0	9	7	21	-14	0	0.200	0	5
	Total	**344**	**300**	**135**	**55**	**110**	**553**	**394**	**159**	**19**	**1.147**	**87**	**63**

Northern Ireland

Pos'n	Cnty	Pts	P	W	D	L	F	A	Diff	B	Pts/P	Q	E
1	East Germany	6	8	2	2	4	6	17	-11	0	0.750	0	4
2	Iceland	5	4	1	3	0	3	2	1	0	1.250	1	1
3	Belgium	4	12	1	2	9	12	38	-26	0	0.333	0	6
4	Scotland	3	8	1	1	6	7	19	-12	0	0.375	1	3
5	Luxembourg	2	2	1	0	1	6	3	3	0	1.000	1	0
6	Finland	2	2	0	2	0	1	1	0	0	1.000	0	1
7	Switzerland	2	2	1	0	1	3	5	-2	0	1.000	0	1
8	England	2	2	1	0	I	1	3	-2	0	1.000	0	1
9	France	1	2	0	1	1	0	2	-2	0	0.500	0	1
10	Yugoslavia	1	2	0	1	1	1	6	-5	0	0.500	0	1
11	Netherlands	1	8	0	1	7	5	34	-29	0	0.125	0	4
12	Czechoslovakia	0	2	0	0	2	1	4	-3	0	0.000	0	1
13	Portugal	0	2	0	0	2	1	6	-5	0	0.000	0	1
14	Spain	0	2	0	0	2	2	8	-6	0	0.000	0	1
15	West Germany	0	2	0	0	2	1	7	-6	0	0.000	0	1
	Total	**29**	**60**	**8**	**13**	**39**	**50**	**155**	**-105**	**0**	**0.483**	**3**	**27**

Norway

Pos'n	Cnty	Pts	P	W	D	L	F	A	Diff	B	Pts/P	Q	E
1	West Germany	10	14	4	2	8	10	42	-32	0	0.714	1	6
2	Iceland	7	4	3	1	0	9	0	9	0	1.750	2	0
3	Belgium	7	10	2	3	5	8	17	-9	0	0.700	0	5
4	Finland	4	2	2	0	0	4	0	4	0	2.000	1	0
5	East Germany	4	6	2	0	4	9	15	-6	0	0.667	1	2
6	USSR	3	6	1	1	4	6	16	-10	0	0.500	0	3
7	Sweden	3	6	1	1	4	4	16	-12	0	0.500	0	3
8	England	3	14	1	1	12	11	57	-46	0	0.214	0	7
9	Denmark	1	2	0	1	1	0	1	-1	0	0.500	0	1
10	Rep. of Ireland	1	2	0	1	1	2	4	-2	0	0.500	0	1
11	Italy	1	2	0	1	1	0	2	-2	0	0.500	0	1
–	Romania	1	2	0	1	1	0	2	-2	0	0.500	0	1
13	Poland	1	2	0	1	1	1	4	-3	0	0.500	0	1
14	Scotland	1	8	0	1	7	7	25	-18	0	0.125	0	4
15	Austria	0	2	0	0	2	1	7	-6	0	0.000	0	1
	Total	**47**	**82**	**16**	**15**	**51**	**72**	**208**	**-136**	**0**	**0.573**	**5**	**36**

Poland

Pos'n	Cnty	Pts	P	W	D	L	F	A	Diff	B	Pts/P	Q	E
1	West Germany	13	24	4	5	15	34	55	-21	0	0.542	3	9
2	Hungary	11	8	4	2	2	12	7	5	1	1.375	3	1
3	Belgium	9	8	2	5	1	8	6	2	0	1.125	2	2
4	Czechoslovakia	9	6	4	0	2	7	6	1	1	1.500	2	1
5	Finland	8	6	3	2	1	10	5	5	0	1.333	2	1
6	USSR	8	6	3	2	1	5	4	1	0	1.333	2	1
7	Denmark	7	6	3	1	2	6	4	2	0	1.167	2	1

8	Italy	7	14	2	3	9	12	22	-10	0	0.500	1	6
9	England	7	10	1	5	4	6	16	-10	0	0.700	2	3
10	Austria	5	4	2	1	1	8	6	2	0	1.250	2	0
11	East Germany	5	8	2	1	5	6	9	-3	0	0.625	2	2
12	Iceland	4	2	2	0	0	4	1	3	0	2.000	1	0
13	Yugoslavia	4	4	1	2	1	4	6	-2	0	1.000	1	1
14	Sweden	4	6	1	2	3	8	11	-3	0	0.667	2	1
15	Scotland	4	8	1	2	5	9	17	-8	0	0.500	1	3
16	Netherlands	4	10	1	2	7	9	25	-16	0	0.400	0	5
17	Cyprus	3	2	1	1	0	7	3	4	0	1.500	1	0
18	Norway	3	2	1	1	0	4	1	3	0	1.500	1	0
19	France	3	4	1	1	2	4	7	-3	0	0.750	0	2
20	Switzerland	3	4	1	1	2	4	8	-4	0	0.750	1	1
21	Romania	3	6	1	1	4	5	10	-5	0	0.500	0	3
22	Turkey	2	2	1	0	1	3	1	2	0	1.000	1	0
23	Portugal	2	2	1	0	1	2	6	-4	0	1.000	0	1
24	Spain	0	2	0	0	2	2	4	-2	0	0.000	0	1
	Total	**128**	**154**	**43**	**40**	**71**	**179**	**240**	**-61**	**2**	**0.831**	**32**	**45**

Portugal

Pos'n	Cnty	Pts	P	W	D	L	F	A	Diff	B	Pts/P	Q	E
1	Spain	36	36	14	7	15	54	53	1	1	1.000	8	9
2	Belgium	33	26	14	4	8	39	30	9	1	1.269	9	4
3	France	31	26	13	5	8	46	25	21	0	1.192	8	5
4	Italy	28	31	9	6	16	23	33	-10	4	0.903	7	8
5	England	21	32	7	6	19	31	64	-33	1	0.656	4	12
6	Netherlands	20	10	9	0	1	21	7	14	2	2.000	5	0
7	Romania	19	14	7	4	3	25	14	11	1	1.357	5	2
8	West Germany	19	24	6	7	11	21	37	-16	0	0.792	1	11
9	Switzerland	13	10	5	2	3	12	9	3	1	1.300	2	3
10	Yugoslavia	13	14	5	3	6	13	19	-6	0	0.929	2	5
11	Scotland	11	14	4	3	7	16	27	-11	0	0.786	1	6
12	Luxembourg	8	4	4	0	0	21	0	21	0	2.000	2	0
13	Czechoslovakia	8	6	3	2	1	7	5	2	0	1.333	2	1
14	Rep. of Ireland	8	7	2	4	1	5	3	2	0	1.143	2	1
15	Hungary	7	8	3	1	4	9	11	-2	0	0.875	2	2
16	Malta	6	4	3	0	1	12	5	7	0	1.500	2	0
17	USSR	5	4	2	1	1	6	2	4	0	1.250	1	1
18	Iceland	4	2	2	0	0	15	0	15	0	2.000	1	0
19	Northern Ireland	4	2	2	0	0	6	1	5	0	2.000	1	0
20	Denmark	4	2	2	0	0	4	1	3	0	2.000	1	0
21	Austria	3	2	1	1	0	6	2	4	0	1.500	1	0
22	Bulgaria	3	2	1	1	0	4	1	3	0	1.500	1	0
23	Albania	3	2	1	1	0	1	0	1	0	1.500	1	0
24	East Germany	3	6	1	1	4	6	10	-4	0	0.500	0	3
25	Poland	2	2	1	0	1	6	2	4	0	1.000	1	0
26	Greece	2	2	1	0	1	3	4	-1	0	1.000	0	1
27	Turkey	0	2	0	0	2	2	6	-4	0	0.000	0	1
	Total	**314**	**294**	**122**	**59**	**113**	**414**	**371**	**43**	**11**	**1.068**	**70**	**75**

Republic of Ireland

Pos'n	Cnty	Pts	P	W	D	L	F	A	Diff	B	Pts/P	Q	E
1	Portugal	6	7	1	4	2	3	5	-2	0	0.857	1	2
2	Iceland	4	2	2	0	0	7	0	7	0	2.000	1	0
3	Netherlands	4	6	1	2	3	5	11	-6	0	0.667	1	2
4	Scotland	4	12	1	2	9	10	32	-22	0	0.333	0	6

5	Norway	3	2	1	1	0	4	2	2	0	1.500	1	0
6	Denmark	2	2	1	0	1	6	5	1	0	1.000	1	0
7	Spain	2	8	0	2	6	5	14	-9	0	0.250	0	4
8	West Germany	2	8	1	0	7	3	23	-20	0	0.250	0	4
9	England	2	12	0	2	10	2	62	-60	0	0.167	0	6
10	Hungary	1	2	0	1	1	1	2	-1	0	0.500	0	1
11	Italy	1	2	0	1	1	0	3	-3	0	0.500	0	1
12	France	0	2	0	0	2	4	9	-5	0	0.000	0	1
13	Romania	0	2	0	0	2	0	5	-5	0	0.000	0	1
–	Switzerland	0	2	0	0	2	0	5	-5	0	0.000	0	1
	Total	**31**	**69**	**8**	**15**	**46**	**50**	**178**	**-128**	**0**	**0.449**	**5**	**29**

Romania

Pos'n	Cnty	Pts	P	W	D	L	F	A	Diff	B	Pts/P	Q	E
1	Yugoslavia	16	20	6	4	10	20	38	-18	0	0.800	1	9
2	Turkey	15	12	7	1	4	18	16	2	0	1.250	4	2
3	Italy	15	16	6	3	7	14	19	-5	0	0.938	4	4
4	Cyprus	14	8	6	2	0	23	2	21	0	1.750	4	0
5	Greece	14	10	7	0	3	17	7	10	0	1.400	4	1
6	Spain	12	15	5	2	8	20	28	-8	0	0.800	3	4
7	Portugal	11	14	3	4	7	14	25	-11	1	0.786	2	5
8	Hungary	10	10	5	0	5	11	17	-6	0	1.000	1	4
9	Austria	9	8	3	3	2	13	8	5	0	1.125	3	1
10	Poland	9	6	4	1	1	10	5	5	0	1.500	3	0
11	West Germany	8	14	3	1	10	10	31	-21	1	0.571	1	6
12	Scotland	7	6	2	2	2	6	9	-3	1	1.167	1	2
13	East Germany	7	7	2	2	3	6	12	-6	1	1.000	1	2
14	Malta	6	4	3	0	1	14	2	12	0	1.500	2	0
15	Bulgaria	6	8	3	0	5	12	15	-3	0	0.750	1	3
16	England	6	10	2	2	6	7	21	-14	0	0.600	1	4
17	France	5	4	2	0	2	7	5	2	1	1.250	2	0
18	Rep. of Ireland	4	2	2	0	0	5	0	5	0	2.000	1	0
–	Czechoslovakia	4	2	2	0	0	5	0	5	0	2.000	1	0
20	Albania	4	2	2	0	0	2	0	2	0	2.000	1	0
21	Norway	3	2	1	1	0	2	0	2	0	1.500	1	0
22	Finland	3	2	1	0	1	3	3	0	1	1.500	1	0
23	USSR	3	4	1	1	2	3	4	-1	0	0.750	1	1
24	Belgium	3	8	0	3	5	4	14	-10	0	0.375	0	4
25	Denmark	2	2	1	0	1	3	3	0	0	1.000	1	0
26	Netherlands	1	2	0	1	1	0	2	-2	0	0.500	0	1
27	Switzerland	1	2	0	1	1	4	7	-3	0	0.500	0	1
28	Sweden	0	4	0	0	4	2	8	-6	0	0.000	0	2
	Total	**198**	**204**	**79**	**34**	**91**	**255**	**301**	**-46**	**6**	**0.971**	**45**	**56**

Scotland

Pos'n	Cnty	Pts	P	W	D	L	F	A	Diff	B	Pts/P	Q	E
1	West Germany	40	38	14	9	15	51	52	-1	3	1.053	9	10
2	Spain	38	34	15	5	14	49	57	-8	3	1.118	5	10
3	Belgium	33	26	11	8	7	39	26	13	3	1.269	6	7
4	Yugoslavia	22	18	9	2	7	24	22	2	2	1.222	5	4
5	Rep. of Ireland	20	12	9	2	1	32	10	22	0	1.667	6	0
6	Sweden	19	16	7	5	4	29	19	10	0	1.188	5	3
7	Denmark	18	10	9	0	1	27	10	17	0	1.800	4	1
8	Portugal	17	14	7	3	4	27	16	11	0	1.214	6	1
9	Netherlands	17	16	7	1	8	19	22	-3	2	1.063	4	4
10	England	17	32	3	11	18	24	51	-27	0	0.531	2	14

11	Norway	15	8	7	1	0	25	7	18	0	1.875	4	0
12	Switzerland	14	11	5	3	3	21	19	2	1	1.273	3	2
13	Czechoslovakia	14	14	5	3	6	15	17	-2	1	1.000	2	5
14	Northern Ireland	13	8	6	1	1	19	7	12	0	1.625	3	1
15	France	13	14	5	3	6	16	17	-1	0	0.929	4	3
16	Italy	13	19	5	3	11	23	45	-22	0	0.684	1	8
17	Poland	12	8	5	2	1	17	9	8	0	1.500	3	1
18	East Germany	11	8	4	2	2	9	6	3	1	1.375	3	1
19	Iceland	10	6	4	2	0	14	4	10	0	1.667	3	0
20	Austria	9	6	4	1	1	10	4	6	0	1.500	2	1
21	Romania	6	6	2	2	2	9	6	3	0	1.000	2	1
22	Hungary	6	8	3	0	5	7	9	-2	0	0.750	2	2
23	Bulgaria	5	4	2	1	1	6	3	3	0	1.250	2	0
24	USSR	3	2	1	1	0	4	2	2	0	1.500	1	0
25	Finland	2	2	1	0	1	4	2	2	0	1.000	1	0
	Total	**387**	**340**	**150**	**71**	**119**	**520**	**442**	**78**	**16**	**1.138**	**88**	**79**

Spain

Pos'n	Cnty	Pts	P	W	D	L	F	A	Diff	B	Pts/P	Q	E
1	England	63	53	20	15	18	84	71	13	8	1.189	15	10
2	West Germany	59	49	23	7	19	63	61	2	6	1.204	13	11
3	Italy	56	49	21	6	22	78	65	13	8	1.143	13	11
4	Yugoslavia	44	35	17	5	13	61	54	7	5	1.257	10	7
5	Belgium	42	37	16	5	16	48	47	1	5	1.135	9	9
6	Switzerland	40	27	16	4	7	62	35	27	4	1.481	12	2
7	Scotland	38	34	14	5	15	57	49	8	5	1.118	10	5
8	Portugal	37	36	15	7	14	53	54	-1	0	1.028	9	8
9	Hungary	33	27	14	2	11	48	34	14	3	1.222	9	4
10	Czechoslovakia	23	22	8	6	8	24	32	-8	1	1.045	6	5
11	Greece	22	18	9	4	5	31	9	22	0	1.222	8	1
12	Spain	20	18	7	4	7	29	29	0	2	1.111	5	5
13	Netherlands	20	22	8	4	10	28	31	-3	0	0.909	3	8
14	Romania	19	15	8	2	5	28	20	8	1	1.267	4	3
15	Denmark	14	8	6	1	1	23	8	15	1	1.750	4	0
16	Austria	14	8	5	2	1	16	7	9	2	1.750	4	0
17	Rep. of Ireland	14	8	6	2	0	14	5	9	0	1.750	4	0
18	France	13	11	4	4	3	13	12	1	1	1.182	2	3
19	Bulgaria	12	10	5	1	4	23	15	8	1	1.200	4	1
20	USSR	12	8	4	3	1	9	5	4	1	1.500	3	1
21	Turkey	8	6	4	0	2	9	7	2	0	1.333	1	2
22	Sweden	6	4	2	1	1	10	5	5	1	1.500	1	1
23	Albania	5	4	1	2	1	5	3	2	1	1.250	2	0
24	East Germany	5	6	2	1	3	6	8	-2	0	0.833	2	1
25	Northern Ireland	4	2	2	0	0	8	2	6	0	2.000	1	0
26	Malta	4	2	2	0	0	3	0	3	0	2.000	1	0
27	Poland	4	2	2	0	0	4	2	2	0	2.000	1	0
28	Cyprus	3	2	1	1	0	4	1	3	0	1.500	1	0
	Total	**634**	**523**	**242**	**94**	**187**	**841**	**671**	**170**	**56**	**1.212**	**157**	**98**

Sweden

Pos'n	Cnty	Pts	P	W	D	L	F	A	Diff	B	Pts/P	Q	E
1	West Germany	15	24	5	4	15	27	59	-32	1	0.625	2	10
2	Scotland	13	16	4	5	7	19	29	-10	0	0.813	3	5
3	Finland	10	6	5	0	1	15	6	9	0	1.667	3	0
4	Belgium	10	6	4	1	1	13	7	6	1	1.667	2	1
5	Norway	9	6	4	1	1	16	4	12	0	1.500	3	0

6	Romania	9	4	4	0	0	8	2	6	1	2.250	2	0
7	Italy	9	12	2	4	6	8	14	-6	1	0.750	1	5
8	Poland	8	6	3	2	1	11	8	3	0	1.333	1	2
9	Austria	8	6	3	1	2	10	7	3	1	1.333	2	1
10	USSR	8	10	3	2	5	11	15	-4	0	0.800	1	4
11	France	7	6	3	1	2	10	11	-1	0	1.167	1	2
12	Czechoslovakia	6	8	2	2	4	9	15	-6	0	0.750	1	3
13	Denmark	5	6	1	3	2	7	8	-1	0	0.833	1	2
14	Netherlands	5	8	2	1	5	8	19	-11	0	0.625	0	4
15	Bulgaria	4	2	2	0	0	7	1	6	0	2.000	1	0
16	Spain	4	4	1	1	2	5	10	-5	1	1.000	1	1
17	East Germany	3	4	1	1	2	5	6	-1	0	0.750	1	1
18	Hungary	3	4	1	1	2	4	10	-6	0	0.750	0	2
19	England	3	8	0	3	5	5	19	-14	0	0.375	1	3
20	Iceland	2	2	1	0	1	2	2	0	0	1.000	0	1
21	Switzerland	2	4	1	0	3	3	7	-4	0	0.500	0	2
22	Yugoslavia	1	2	0	1	1	3	6	-3	0	0.500	0	1
	Total	**144**	**154**	**52**	**34**	**68**	**206**	**265**	**-59**	**6**	**0.935**	**27**	**50**

Switzerland

Pos'n	Cnty	Pts	P	W	D	L	F	A	Diff	B	Pts/P	Q	E
1	Spain	18	27	7	4	16	35	62	-27	0	0.667	2	12
2	Luxembourg	13	8	6	1	1	14	1	13	0	1.625	4	0
3	Denmark	13	8	6	1	1	25	16	9	0	1.625	3	1
4	Scotland	10	11	3	3	5	19	21	-2	1	0.909	2	3
5	Portugal	10	10	3	2	5	9	12	-3	2	1.000	3	2
6	England	10	16	4	2	10	14	36	-22	0	0.625	3	5
7	France	9	10	4	1	5	12	16	-4	0	0.900	1	4
8	Italy	9	14	3	2	9	12	27	-15	1	0.643	1	6
9	West Germany	9	23	2	4	17	28	63	-35	1	0.391	2	10
10	Yugoslavia	8	14	3	2	9	18	38	-20	0	0.571	0	7
11	Sweden	6	4	3	0	1	7	3	4	0	1.500	2	0
12	Hungary	6	6	2	2	2	7	7	0	0	1.000	2	1
13	Poland	5	4	2	1	1	8	4	4	0	1.250	1	1
14	Greece	5	6	2	1	3	7	6	1	0	0.833	2	1
15	Bulgaria	5	4	1	3	0	3	2	1	0	1.250	2	0
16	Czechoslovakia	5	8	2	1	5	15	16	-1	0	0.625	2	2
17	East Germany	5	6	2	0	4	13	21	-8	1	0.833	1	2
18	Malta	4	2	2	0	0	9	0	9	0	2.000	1	0
19	Rep. of Ireland	4	2	2	0	0	5	0	5	0	2.000	1	0
20	Austria	4	4	1	2	1	2	2	0	0	1.000	1	1
21	USSR	4	8	1	1	6	7	14	-7	1	0.500	1	3
22	Netherlands	4	8	0	4	4	5	13	-8	0	0.500	0	4
23	Romania	3	2	1	1	0	7	4	3	0	1.500	1	0
24	Cyprus	3	2	1	1	0	3	2	1	0	1.500	1	0
25	Northern Ireland	2	2	1	0	1	5	3	2	0	1.000	1	0
26	Belgium	0	2	0	0	2	3	8	-5	0	0.000	0	1
	Total	**174**	**211**	**64**	**39**	**108**	**292**	**397**	**-105**	**7**	**0.825**	**40**	**66**

Turkey

Pos'n	Cnty	Pts	P	W	D	L	F	A	Diff	B	Pts/P	Q	E
1	Romania	9	12	4	1	7	16	18	-2	0	0.750	2	4
2	Yugoslavia	7	10	2	2	6	6	13	-7	1	0.700	1	4
3	Portugal	4	2	2	0	0	6	2	4	0	2.000	1	0
4	Spain	4	6	2	0	4	7	9	-2	0	0.667	2	1
5	Austria	4	4	2	0	2	5	7	-2	0	1.000	1	1

6	France	4	4	2	0	2	4	6	-2	0	1.000	1	1
7	Hungary	4	8	1	2	5	7	25	-18	0	0.500	0	4
8	Belgium	3	2	1	1	0	2	1	1	0	1.500	1	0
9	East Germany	3	4	1	1	2	5	7	-2	0	0.750	0	2
10	West Germany	3	6	1	1	4	3	18	-15	0	0.500	0	3
11	Italy	3	16	1	1	14	11	43	-32	0	0.188	0	8
12	Poland	2	2	1	0	1	1	3	-2	0	1.000	0	1
13	Netherlands	2	2	1	0	1	4	8	-4	0	1.000	0	1
14	Czechoslovakia	2	2	1	0	1	2	6	-4	0	1.000	0	1
15	USSR	0	2	0	0	2	2	7	-5	0	0.000	0	1
16	Bulgaria	0	4	0	0	4	2	10	-8	0	0.000	0	2
17	England	0	4	0	0	4	2	12	-10	0	0.000	0	2
	Total	**54**	**90**	**22**	**9**	**59**	**85**	**195**	**-110**	**1**	**0.600**	**9**	**36**

USSR

Pos'n	Cnty	Pts	P	W	D	L	F	A	Diff	B	Pts/P	Q	E
1	West Germany	26	28	11	4	13	28	44	-16	0	0.929	2	12
2	Italy	21	18	8	5	5	17	16	1	0	1.167	4	5
3	Denmark	17	10	8	1	1	20	7	13	0	1.700	4	1
4	East Germany	16	14	7	2	5	21	16	5	0	1.143	4	3
5	Bulgaria	14	12	5	4	3	16	12	4	0	1.167	4	2
6	Switzerland	13	8	6	1	1	14	7	7	0	1.625	3	1
7	Netherlands	13	8	5	2	1	14	8	6	1	1.625	3	1
8	Belgium	13	10	6	1	3	16	14	2	0	1.300	2	3
9	France	13	14	4	4	6	15	16	-1	1	0.929	2	5
10	Finland	12	6	6	0	0	21	1	20	0	2.000	3	0
11	Sweden	12	10	5	2	3	15	11	4	0	1.200	4	1
12	Hungary	10	6	5	0	1	15	7	8	0	1.667	2	1
13	Norway	9	6	4	1	1	16	6	10	0	1.500	3	0
14	England	8	6	3	2	1	14	13	1	0	1.333	2	1
15	Czechoslovakia	7	6	3	1	2	9	4	5	0	1.167	3	0
16	Yugoslavia	7	10	3	1	6	13	15	-2	0	0.700	1	4
17	Austria	6	6	3	0	3	7	9	-2	0	1.000	0	3
18	Romania	5	4	2	1	1	4	3	1	0	1.250	1	1
19	Poland	5	6	1	2	3	4	5	-1	1	0.833	1	2
20	Spain	5	8	1	3	4	5	9	-4	0	0.625	1	3
21	Turkey	4	2	2	0	0	7	2	5	0	2.000	1	0
22	Cyprus	4	2	2	0	0	2	0	2	0	2.000	1	0
23	Portugal	3	4	1	1	2	2	6	-4	0	0.750	1	1
24	Greece	2	2	1	0	1	2	3	-1	0	1.000	0	1
25	Scotland	1	2	0	1	1	2	4	-2	0	0.500	0	1
	Total	**246**	**208**	**102**	**39**	**67**	**299**	**238**	**61**	**3**	**1.183**	**52**	**52**

West Germany

Pos'n	Cnty	Pts	P	W	D	L	F	A	Diff	B	Pts/P	Q	E
1	Italy	68	68	24	16	28	86	107	-21	4	1.000	12	21
2	Netherlands	55	44	21	7	16	80	64	16	6	1.250	14	8
3	West Germany	54	44	19	6	19	72	72	0	10	1.227	11	11
4	Czechoslovakia	53	32	22	5	5	72	36	36	4	1.656	13	3
5	Spain	50	49	19	7	23	61	63	-2	5	1.020	11	13
6	Belgium	46	36	17	7	12	59	42	17	5	1.278	10	8
7	Scotland	42	38	15	9	14	52	51	1	3	1.105	10	9
8	Switzerland	41	23	17	4	2	63	28	35	3	1.783	10	2
9	France	41	28	17	3	8	59	31	28	4	1.464	12	2
10	England	41	48	14	9	25	54	87	-33	4	0.854	8	16
11	Denmark	38	24	17	3	4	58	28	30	1	1.583	10	2

12	Yugoslavia	38	30	14	6	10	53	41	12	4	1.267	10	5
13	Poland	37	24	15	5	4	55	34	21	2	1.542	9	3
14	Sweden	35	24	15	4	5	59	27	32	1	1.458	10	2
15	Portugal	35	24	11	7	6	37	21	16	6	1.458	11	1
16	USSR	34	28	13	4	11	44	28	16	4	1.214	12	2
17	East Germany	32	24	12	6	6	42	26	16	2	1.333	9	3
18	Romania	22	14	10	1	3	31	10	21	1	1.571	6	1
19	Bulgaria	21	14	9	2	3	23	12	11	1	1.500	5	2
20	Cyprus	20	10	10	0	0	55	5	50	0	2.000	5	0
21	Hungary	20	16	8	1	7	34	31	3	3	1.250	5	3
22	Norway	18	14	8	2	4	42	10	32	0	1.286	6	1
23	Austria	16	12	7	2	3	30	11	19	0	1.333	6	0
24	Rep. of Ireland	15	8	7	0	1	23	3	20	1	1.875	4	0
25	Turkey	9	6	4	1	1	18	3	15	0	1.500	3	0
26	Finland	8	4	4	0	0	15	4	11	0	2.000	2	0
27	Greece	8	6	3	2	1	9	2	7	0	1.333	3	0
28	Luxembourg	4	2	2	0	0	17	0	17	0	2.000	1	0
29	Iceland	4	2	2	0	0	10	0	10	0	2.000	1	0
30	Northern Ireland	4	2	2	0	0	7	1	6	0	2.000	1	0
31	Malta	3	2	1	1	0	5	0	5	0	1.500	1	0
	Total	**912**	**700**	**359**	**120**	**221**	**1325**	**878**	**447**	**74**	**1.303**	**231**	**118**

Yugoslavia

Pos'n	Cnty	Pts	P	W	D	L	F	A	Diff	B	Pts/P	Q	E
1	Bulgaria	36	25	14	7	4	61	25	36	1	1.440	11	1
2	Italy	35	43	9	16	18	39	60	-21	1	0.814	6	15
3	Spain	33	35	13	5	17	54	61	-7	2	0.943	7	10
4	West Germany	29	30	10	6	14	41	53	-12	3	0.967	5	10
5	England	27	24	9	5	10	31	31	0	4	1.125	6	6
6	Romania	26	20	10	4	6	38	20	18	2	1.300	9	1
7	Switzerland	21	14	9	2	3	38	18	20	1	1.500	7	0
8	Austria	20	14	8	4	2	26	12	14	0	1.429	6	1
9	Scotland	19	18	7	2	9	22	24	-2	3	1.056	4	5
10	Hungary	19	18	8	1	9	27	34	-7	2	1.056	3	6
11	East Germany	19	19	7	4	8	26	35	-9	1	1.000	4	5
12	Belgium	18	21	8	1	12	31	40	-9	1	0.857	4	6
13	Turkey	15	10	6	2	2	13	6	7	1	1.500	4	1
14	Portugal	15	14	6	3	5	19	13	6	0	1.071	5	2
15	USSR	15	10	6	1	3	15	13	2	2	1.500	4	1
16	Greece	14	14	6	1	7	28	19	9	1	1.000	4	3
17	Malta	12	6	6	0	0	17	1	16	0	2.000	3	0
18	Czechoslovakia	11	12	4	2	6	19	22	-3	1	0.917	4	2
19	Netherlands	11	12	4	2	6	15	22	-7	1	0.917	2	4
20	France	6	6	2	2	2	12	13	-1	0	1.000	1	2
21	Yugoslavia	5	4	2	0	2	4	4	0	1	1.250	1	1
22	Cyprus	4	2	2	0	0	6	2	4	0	2.000	1	0
23	Poland	4	4	1	2	1	6	4	2	0	1.000	1	1
24	Denmark	3	2	1	1	0	9	4	5	0	1.500	1	0
25	Northern Ireland	3	2	1	1	0	6	1	5	0	1.500	1	0
26	Sweden	3	2	1	1	0	6	3	3	0	1.500	1	0
27	Albania	2	2	1	0	1	2	3	-1	0	1.000	0	1
	Total	**425**	**383**	**161**	**75**	**147**	**611**	**543**	**68**	**28**	**1.110**	**105**	**84**

Comparative Country v Country Performance Charts

1956-58 to 1990-91

	Total		%	Albania		Austria		Belgium		Bulgaria		Cyprus		Czechoslovac		Denmark		E. Germany	
	Q	E	Qual	Q	E	Q	E	Q	E	Q	E	Q	E	Q	E	Q	E	Q	E
Albania	3	6	33.3%	–	–	–	–	–	–	–	–	–	–	–	–	–	–	1	1
Austria	32	57	36.0%	–	–	–	–	2	4	1	1	–	–	1	4	2	0	2	1
Belgium	108	82	56.8%	–	–	4	2	–	–	1	0	1	0	5	1	3	0	2	5
Bulgaria	23	50	31.5%	–	–	1	1	0	1	–	–	1	1	1	1	–	–	0	2
Cyprus	1	19	5.0%	–	–	–	–	0	1	1	1	–	–	0	1	–	–	–	–
Czechoslovakia	49	58	45.8%	–	–	4	1	1	5	1	1	1	0	–	–	2	0	1	1
Denmark	13	49	21.0%	–	–	0	2	0	3	–	–	–	–	0	2	–	–	0	1
East Germany	63	61	50.8%	1	1	1	2	5	2	2	0	–	–	1	1	1	0	–	–
England	176	84	67.7%	–	–	4	0	8	8	2	0	–	–	5	2	3	0	9	3
Finland	5	22	18.5%	–	–	2	1	0	1	–	–	–	–	–	–	1	1	0	2
France	59	76	43.7%	1	0	0	2	3	5	0	2	–	–	0	3	0	1	3	5
Greece	23	51	31.1%	–	–	2	2	1	4	1	1	–	–	0	1	–	–	0	1
Hungary	66	54	55.0%	–	–	5	1	3	0	3	3	–	–	4	1	0	1	2	3
Iceland	2	22	8.3%	–	–	–	–	0	2	–	–	–	–	0	2	–	–	0	2
Italy	180	103	63.6%	–	–	5	4	8	7	6	0	2	0	4	3	2	0	8	4
Luxembourg	0	28	0.0%	–	–	0	1	0	5	–	–	–	–	0	1	–	–	–	–
Malta	0	23	0.0%	0	1	0	1	–	–	0	2	–	–	0	1	0	1	–	–
Netherlands	87	63	58.0%	–	–	1	2	6	4	1	1	–	–	1	1	3	0	5	1
N. Ireland	3	27	10.0%	–	–	–	–	0	6	–	–	–	–	0	1	–	–	0	4
Norway	5	36	12.2%	–	–	0	1	0	5	–	–	–	–	–	–	0	1	1	2
Poland	32	45	41.6%	–	–	2	0	2	2	–	–	1	0	2	1	2	1	2	2
Portugal	70	75	48.3%	1	0	1	0	9	4	1	0	–	–	2	1	1	0	0	3
Rep. of Ireland	5	29	14.7%	–	–	–	–	–	–	–	–	–	–	–	–	1	0	–	–
Romania	45	56	44.6%	1	0	3	1	0	4	1	3	4	0	1	0	1	0	1	2
Scotland	88	79	52.7%	–	–	2	1	6	7	2	0	–	–	2	5	4	1	3	1
Spain	157	98	61.6%	2	0	4	0	9	9	4	1	1	0	6	5	4	0	2	1
Sweden	27	50	35.1%	–	–	2	1	2	1	1	0	–	–	1	3	1	2	1	1
Switzerland	40	66	37.7%	–	–	1	1	0	1	2	0	1	0	2	2	3	1	1	2
Turkey	9	36	20.0%	–	–	1	1	1	0	0	2	–	–	0	1	–	–	0	2
USSR	52	52	50.0%	–	–	0	3	2	3	4	2	1	0	3	0	4	1	4	3
West Germany	231	118	66.2%	–	–	6	0	10	8	5	2	5	0	13	3	10	2	9	3
Yugoslavia	105	84	55.6%	0	1	6	1	4	6	11	1	1	0	4	2	1	0	4	5
				Elim	**Qual**	**Elim**	**Qual**	**Elim**	**Qual**	**Elim**	**Qual**	**Elim**	**Qual**	**Elim**	**Qual**	**Elim**	**Qual**	**Elim**	**Qual**
Totaux	**1759**	**1759**	**50.0%**	**6**	**3**	**57**	**32**	**82**	**108**	**50**	**23**	**19**	**1**	**58**	**49**	**49**	**13**	**61**	**63**

1956-58 to 1990-91

	England		Finland		France		Greece		Hungary		Iceland		Italy		Luxmbrg		Malta		Netherlands	
	Q	E	Q	E	Q	E	Q	E	Q	E	Q	E	Q	E	Q	E	Q	E	Q	E
Albania	–	–	–	–	0	1	–	–	–	–	–	–	–	–	–	–	1	0	–	–
Austria	0	4	1	2	2	0	2	2	1	5	–	–	4	5	1	0	1	0	2	1
Belgium	8	8	1	0	5	3	4	1	0	3	2	0	7	8	5	0	–	–	4	6
Bulgaria	0	2	–	–	2	0	1	1	3	3	–	–	0	6	–	–	2	0	1	1
Cyprus	–	–	–	–	–	–	–	–	–	–	–	–	0	2	–	–	–	–	–	–
Czechoslovakia	2	5	–	–	3	0	1	0	1	4	2	0	3	4	1	0	1	0	1	1
Denmark	0	3	1	1	1	0	–	–	1	0	–	–	0	2	–	–	1	0	0	3
East Germany	3	9	2	0	5	3	1	0	3	2	2	0	4	8	–	–	–	–	1	5
England	5	5	–	–	5	1	4	2	7	6	2	0	16	7	1	0	1	0	14	6
Finland	–	–	–	–	0	3	–	–	–	–	–	–	0	1	–	–	–	–	–	–
France	1	5	3	0	–	–	3	2	2	2	2	0	4	13	3	0	–	–	3	2
Greece	2	4	–	–	2	3	–	–	2	3	–	–	3	9	–	–	2	0	0	2
Hungary	6	7	–	–	2	2	3	2	–	–	1	0	5	3	–	–	–	–	1	2
Iceland	0	2	–	–	0	2	–	–	0	1	–	–	–	–	–	–	–	–	0	1
Italy	7	16	1	0	13	4	9	3	3	5	–	–	4	4	2	0	3	0	4	3
Luxembourg	0	1	–	–	0	3	–	–	–	–	–	–	0	2	–	–	–	–	0	7
Malta	0	1	–	–	–	–	0	2	–	–	–	–	0	3	–	–	–	–	0	1
Netherlands	6	14	–	–	2	3	2	0	2	1	1	0	3	4	7	0	1	0	–	–
N. Ireland	0	1	0	1	0	1	–	–	–	–	1	1	–	–	1	0	–	–	0	4
Norway	0	7	1	0	–	–	–	–	–	–	2	0	0	1	–	–	–	–	–	–
Poland	2	3	2	1	0	2	–	–	3	1	1	0	1	6	–	–	–	–	0	5
Portugal	4	12	–	–	8	5	0	1	2	2	1	0	7	8	2	0	2	0	5	0
Rep. of Ireland	0	6	–	–	0	1	–	–	0	1	1	0	0	1	–	–	–	–	1	2
Romania	1	4	1	0	2	0	4	1	1	4	–	–	4	4	–	–	2	0	0	1
Scotland	2	14	1	0	4	3	–	–	2	2	3	0	1	8	–	–	–	–	4	4
Spain	15	10	–	–	2	3	8	1	9	4	–	–	13	11	–	–	1	0	3	8
Sweden	1	3	3	0	1	2	–	–	0	2	0	1	1	5	–	–	–	–	0	4
Switzerland	3	5	–	–	1	4	2	1	2	1	–	–	1	6	4	0	1	0	0	4
Turkey	0	2	–	–	1	1	–	–	0	4	–	–	0	8	–	–	–	–	0	1
USSR	2	1	3	0	2	5	0	1	2	1	–	–	4	5	–	–	–	–	3	1
West Germany	8	16	2	0	12	2	3	0	5	3	1	0	12	21	1	0	1	0	14	8
Yugoslavia	6	6	–	–	1	2	4	3	3	6	–	–	6	15	–	–	3	0	2	4
	Elim	**Qual**	**Elim**	**Qual**	**Elim**	**Qual**	**Elim**	**Qual**	**Elim**	**Qual**	**Elim**	**Qual**	**Elim**	**Qual**	**Elim**	**Qual**	**Elim**	**Qual**	**Elim**	**Qual**
Total	**84**	**176**	**22**	**5**	**76**	**59**	**51**	**23**	**54**	**66**	**22**	**2**	**103**	**180**	**28**	**0**	**23**	**0**	**63**	**87**

	N. Ireland		Norway		Poland		Portugal		Rep. of Ire.		Romania		Scotland		Spain		Sweden		Switzerland	
	Q	E	Q	E	Q	E	Q	E	Q	E	Q	E	Q	E	Q	E	Q	E	Q	E
Albania	–	–	–	–	–	–	0	1	–	–	0	1	–	–	0	2	–	–	–	–
Austria	–	–	1	0	0	2	0	1	–	–	1	3	1	2	0	4	1	2	1	1
Belgium	6	0	5	0	2	2	4	9	–	–	4	0	7	6	9	9	1	2	1	0
Bulgaria	–	–	–	–	–	–	0	1	–	–	3	1	0	2	1	4	0	1	0	2
Cyprus	–	–	–	–	0	1	–	–	–	–	0	4	–	–	0	1	–	–	0	1
Czechoslovakia	1	0	–	–	1	2	1	2	–	–	0	1	5	2	5	6	3	1	2	2
Denmark	–	–	1	0	1	2	0	1	0	1	0	1	1	4	0	4	2	1	1	3
East Germany	4	0	2	1	2	2	3	0	–	–	2	1	1	3	1	2	1	1	2	1
England	1	0	7	0	3	2	12	4	6	0	4	1	14	2	10	15	3	1	5	3
Finland	1	0	0	1	1	2	–	–	–	–	0	1	0	1	–	–	0	3	–	–
France	1	0	–	–	2	0	5	8	1	0	0	2	3	4	3	2	2	1	4	1
Greece	–	–	–	–	–	–	1	0	–	–	1	4	–	–	1	8	–	–	1	2
Hungary	–	–	–	–	1	3	2	2	1	0	4	1	2	2	4	9	2	0	1	2
Iceland	1	1	0	2	0	1	0	1	0	1	–	–	0	3	–	–	1	0	–	–
Italy	–	–	1	0	6	1	8	7	1	0	4	4	8	1	11	13	5	1	6	1
Luxembourg	0	1	–	–	–	–	0	2	–	–	–	–	–	–	–	–	–	–	0	4
Malta	–	–	–	–	–	–	0	2	–	–	0	2	–	–	0	1	–	–	0	1
Netherlands	4	0	–	–	5	0	0	5	2	1	1	0	4	4	8	3	4	0	4	0
Northern Ireland	–	–	–	–	–	–	0	1	–	–	–	–	1	3	0	1	–	–	0	1
Norway	–	–	–	–	0	1	–	–	0	1	0	1	0	4	–	–	0	3	–	–
Poland	–	–	1	0	–	–	0	1	–	–	0	3	1	3	0	1	2	1	1	1
Portugal	1	0	–	–	1	0	–	–	2	1	5	2	1	6	8	9	–	–	2	3
Rep. of Ireland	–	–	1	0	–	–	1	2	–	–	0	1	0	6	0	4	–	–	0	1
Romania	–	–	1	0	3	0	2	5	1	0	–	–	1	2	3	4	0	2	0	1
Scotland	3	1	4	0	3	1	6	1	6	0	2	1	–	–	5	10	5	3	3	2
Spain	1	0	–	–	1	0	9	8	4	0	4	3	10	5	5	5	1	1	12	2
Sweden	–	–	3	0	1	2	–	–	–	–	2	0	3	5	1	1	–	–	0	2
Switzerland	1	0	–	–	1	1	3	2	1	0	1	0	2	3	1	12	2	0	–	–
Turkey	–	–	–	–	0	1	1	0	–	–	2	4	–	–	2	1	–	–	–	–
USSR	–	–	3	0	1	2	1	1	–	–	1	1	0	1	1	3	4	1	3	1
West Germany	1	0	6	1	9	3	11	1	4	0	6	1	10	9	11	13	10	2	10	2
Yugoslavia	1	0	–	–	1	1	5	2	–	–	9	1	4	5	7	10	1	0	7	0
	Elim	**Qual**	**Elim**	**Qual**	**Elim**	**Qual**	**Elim**	**Qual**	**Elim**	**Qual**	**Elim**	**Qual**	**Elim**	**Qual**	**Elim**	**Qual**	**Elim**	**Qual**	**Elim**	**Qual**
Total	**27**	**3**	**36**	**5**	**45**	**32**	**75**	**70**	**29**	**5**	**56**	**45**	**79**	**88**	**98**	**157**	**50**	**27**	**66**	**40**

1956-58 to 1990-91

	Turkey		USSR		W. Germany		Yugoslavia	
	Q	E	Q	E	Q	E	Q	E
Albania	–	–	–	–	–	–	1	0
Austria	1	1	3	0	0	6	1	6
Belgium	0	1	3	2	8	10	6	4
Bulgaria	2	0	2	4	2	5	1	11
Cyprus	–	–	0	1	0	5	0	1
Czechoslovakia	1	0	0	3	3	13	2	4
Denmark	–	–	1	4	2	10	0	1
East Germany	2	0	3	4	3	9	5	4
England	2	0	1	2	16	8	6	6
Finland	–	–	0	3	0	2	–	–
France	1	1	5	2	2	12	2	1
Greece	–	–	1	0	0	3	3	4
Hungary	4	0	1	2	3	5	6	3
Iceland	–	–	–	–	0	1	–	–
Italy	8	0	5	4	21	12	15	6
Luxembourg	–	–	–	–	0	1	–	–
Malta	–	–	–	–	0	1	0	3
Netherlands	1	0	1	3	8	14	4	2
Northern Ireland	–	–	–	–	0	1	0	1
Norway	–	–	0	3	1	6	–	–
Poland	1	0	2	1	3	9	1	1
Portugal	0	1	1	1	1	11	2	5
Rep. of Ireland	–	–	–	–	0	4	–	–
Romania	4	2	1	1	1	6	1	9
Scotland	–	–	1	0	9	10	5	4
Spain	1	2	3	1	13	11	10	7
Sweden	–	–	1	4	2	10	0	1
Switzerland	–	–	1	3	2	10	0	7
Turkey	–	–	0	1	0	3	1	4
USSR	1	0	–	–	2	12	1	4
West Germany	3	0	12	2	11	11	10	5
Yugoslavia	4	1	4	1	5	10	1	1
	Elim	**Qual**	**Elim**	**Qual**	**Elim**	**Qual**	**Elim**	**Qual**
Total	**36**	**9**	**52**	**52**	**118**	**231**	**84**	**105**

IFK Gothenburg celebrate their 2-1 aggregate win over Dundee United in the 1986-87 final.

Second-leg Outcomes 1956-58 to 1990-91

First-leg: 0-0

Second-leg	1-0	2-0	3-0	4-0	5-0	2-1	3-1	4-1	5-1	3-2	4-2	5-2	4-3
	7	4	0	0	0	5	2	0	1	0	0	0	0

Second-leg	5-3	5-4	0-0	1-1	2-2	3-3	4-4	5-5	0-1	0-2	0-3	0-4	0-5
	0	0	6	13	2	0	0	0	20	21	6	4	

Second-leg	1-2	1-3	1-4	1-5	2-3	2-4	2-5	3-4	3-5	4-5	5>	<5
	12	7	2	2	5	1	0	1	0	0	0	5

First-leg: 1-0

Second-leg	1-0	2-0	3-0	4-0	5-0	2-1	3-1	4-1	5-1	3-2	4-2	5-2	4-3
	14	1	5	2	0	8	9	1	0	4	2	2	0

Second-leg	5-3	5-4	0-0	1-1	2-2	3-3	4-4	5-5	0-1	0-2	0-3	0-4	0-5
	0	0	20	23	8	2	0	0	21	35	11	10	6

Second-leg	1-2	1-3	1-4	1-5	2-3	2-4	2-5	3-4	3-5	4-5	5>	<5
	28	6	5	4	8	2	1	0	0	0	1	4

First-leg: 2-0

Second-leg	1-0	2-0	3-0	4-0	5-0	2-1	3-1	4-1	5-1	3-2	4-2	5-2	4-3
	7	7	0	0	1	7	4	0	1	3	0	0	0

Second-leg	5-3	5-4	0-0	1-1	2-2	3-3	4-4	5-5	0-1	0-2	0-3	0-4	0-5
	0	0	10	20	11	2	0	0	28	15	18	5	4

Second-leg	1-2	1-3	1-4	1-5	2-3	2-4	2-5	3-4	3-5	4-5	5>	<5
	21	4	2	3	2	0	1	0	0	0	1	6

First-leg: 3-0

Second-leg	1-0	2-0	3-0	4-0	5-0	2-1	3-1	4-1	5-1	3-2	4-2	5-2	4-3
	6	2	2	1	1	4	5	3	1	4	0	0	0

Second-leg	5-3	5-4	0-0	1-1	2-2	3-3	4-4	5-5	0-1	0-2	0-3	0-4	0-5
	0	0	3	10	4	1	1	0	14	13	6	2	1

Second-leg	1-2	1-3	1-4	1-5	2-3	2-4	2-5	3-4	3-5	4-5	5>	<5
	8	11	2	2	2	1	0	0	0	0	1	1

First-leg: 1-1

Second-leg	1-0	2-0	3-0	4-0	5-0	2-1	3-1	4-1	5-1	3-2	4-2	5-2	4-3
	5	5	1	0	0	7	2	2	0	2	1	0	0

Second-leg	5-3	5-4	0-0	1-1	2-2	3-3	4-4	5-5	0-1	0-2	0-3	0-4	0-5
	0	0	16	7	1	0	0	0	21	14	5	9	2

Second-leg	1-2	1-3	1-4	1-5	2-3	2-4	2-5	3-4	3-5	4-5	5>	<5
	19	11	3	2	5	1	2	1	0	0	0	3

First-leg: 2-1

Second-leg	1-0	2-0	3-0	4-0	5-0	2-1	3-1	4-1	5-1	3-2	4-2	5-2	4-3
	12	0	1	0	1	4	4	0	0	2	0	0	1

Second-leg	5-3	5-4	0-0	1-1	2-2	3-3	4-4	5-5	0-1	0-2	0-3	0-4	0-5
	0	0	4	15	4	2	1	0	21	12	17	3	3

Second-leg	1-2	1-3	1-4	1-5	2-3	2-4	2-5	3-4	3-5	4-5	5>	<5
	6	6	4	1	3	3	1	1	0	0	0	3

First-leg: 3-1

Second-leg	1-0	2-0	3-0	4-0	5-0	2-1	3-1	4-1	5-1	3-2	4-2	5-2	4-3
	9	3	1	0	0	3	1	3	0	0	0	1	0
Second-leg	5-3	5-4	0-0	1-1	2-2	3-3	4-4	5-5	0-1	0-2	0-3	0-4	0-5
	1	0	6	5	2	0	0	0	9	7	6	4	3
Second-leg	1-2	1-3	1-4	1-5	2-3	2-4	2-5	3-4	3-5	4-5	5>	<5	
	10	3	3	4	1	1	0	0	0	0	1	1	

First-leg: 4-1

Second-leg	1-0	2-0	3-0	4-0	5-0	2-1	3-1	4-1	5-1	3-2	4-2	5-2	4-3
	6	1	0	0	0	3	2	0	0	0	0	0	0
Second-leg	5-3	5-4	0-0	1-1	2-2	3-3	4-4	5-5	0-1	0-2	0-3	0-4	0-5
	0	0	3	3	2	1	0	0	2	8	1	2	1
Second-leg	1-2	1-3	1-4	1-5	2-3	2-4	2-5	3-4	3-5	4-5	5>	<5	
	2	5	0	1	1	1	0	0	0	1	0	1	

First-leg: 5-1

Second-leg	1-0	2-0	3-0	4-0	5-0	2-1	3-1	4-1	5-1	3-2	4-2	5-2	4-3
	1	0	0	0	0	3	3	1	0	1	0	0	0
Second-leg	5-3	5-4	0-0	1-1	2-2	3-3	4-4	5-5	0-1	0-2	0-3	0-4	0-5
	0	0	1	2	3	0	0	0	2	3	0	1	0
Second-leg	1-2	1-3	1-4	1-5	2-3	2-4	2-5	3-4	3-5	4-5	5>	<5	
	0	2	2	0	2	0	0	0	0	0	0	1	

First-leg: 2-2

Second-leg	1-0	2-0	3-0	4-0	5-0	2-1	3-1	4-1	5-1	3-2	4-2	5-2	4-3
	4	3	0	0	0	1	0	0	0	2	0	0	0
Second-leg	5-3	5-4	0-0	1-1	2-2	3-3	4-4	5-5	0-1	0-2	0-3	0-4	0-5
	0	0	5	3	1	0	1	0	8	4	4	1	2
Second-leg	1-2	1-3	1-4	1-5	2-3	2-4	2-5	3-4	3-5	4-5	5>	<5	
	8	1	4	1	3	2	0	0	0	0	1	1	

First-leg: 3-2

Second-leg	1-0	2-0	3-0	4-0	5-0	2-1	3-1	4-1	5-1	3-2	4-2	5-2	4-3
	2	1	0	0	0	4	0	0	0	1	0	1	0
Second-leg	5-3	5-4	0-0	1-1	2-2	3-3	4-4	5-5	0-1	0-2	0-3	0-4	0-5
	0	0	6	3	1	0	0	0	11	5	2	4	0
Second-leg	1-2	1-3	1-4	1-5	2-3	2-4	2-5	3-4	3-5	4-5	5>	<5	
	5	3	0	0	0	0	0	0	0	0	2	3	

First-leg: 4-2

Second-leg	1-0	2-0	3-0	4-0	5-0	2-1	3-1	4-1	5-1	3-2	4-2	5-2	4-3
	1	2	0	0	0	1	1	0	0	0	1	1	0
Second-leg	5-3	5-4	0-0	1-1	2-2	3-3	4-4	5-5	0-1	0-2	0-3	0-4	0-5
	0	0	2	1	1	1	0	0	3	4	1	0	0
Second-leg	1-2	1-3	1-4	1-5	2-3	2-4	2-5	3-4	3-5	4-5	5>	<5	
	2	0	1	0	0	0	2	0	0	0	0	0	

First-leg: 5-2

Second-leg	1-0	2-0	3-0	4-0	5-0	2-1	3-1	4-1	5-1	3-2	4-2	5-2	4-3
	2	0	0	0	0	1	0	0	0	0	0	0	0
Second-leg	5-3	5-4	0-0	1-1	2-2	3-3	4-4	5-5	0-1	0-2	0-3	0-4	0-5
	0	0	0	0	0	0	0	0	1	0	1	0	0
Second-leg	1-2	1-3	1-4	1-5	2-3	2-4	2-5	3-4	3-5	4-5	5>	<5	
	0	1	2	1	0	0	0	0	0	0	0	0	

First-leg: 6-2

Second-leg	1-0	2-0	3-0	4-0	5-0	2-1	3-1	4-1	5-1	3-2	4-2	5-2	4-3
	0	0	0	0	0	0	0	0	0	0	0	0	0
Second-leg	5-3	5-4	0-0	1-1	2-2	3-3	4-4	5-5	0-1	0-2	0-3	0-4	0-5
	0	0	0	2	0	0	0	0	0	0	0	1	0
Second-leg	1-2	1-3	1-4	1-5	2-3	2-4	2-5	3-4	3-5	4-5	5>	<5	
	0	0	0	0	0	0	0	0	0	0	0	0	

First-leg: 3-3

Second-leg	1-0	2-0	3-0	4-0	5-0	2-1	3-1	4-1	5-1	3-2	4-2	5-2	4-3
	0	0	0	0	0	1	0	0	0	0	0	0	0
Second-leg	5-3	5-4	0-0	1-1	2-2	3-3	4-4	5-5	0-1	0-2	0-3	0-4	0-5
	0	0	0	1	2	0	0	0	1	0	1	0	0
Second-leg	1-2	1-3	1-4	1-5	2-3	2-4	2-5	3-4	3-5	4-5	5>	<5	
	0	0	0	1	0	0	1	0	0	0	0	0	

First-leg: 4-3

Second-leg	1-0	2-0	3-0	4-0	5-0	2-1	3-1	4-1	5-1	3-2	4-2	5-2	4-3
	0	0	0	0	0	0	0	0	0	0	0	0	0
Second-leg	5-3	5-4	0-0	1-1	2-2	3-3	4-4	5-5	0-1	0-2	0-3	0-4	0-5
	0	0	0	0	0	0	0	0	1	1	1	0	0
Second-leg	1-2	1-3	1-4	1-5	2-3	2-4	2-5	3-4	3-5	4-5	5>	<5	
	1	1	1	0	0	0	0	0	0	0	0	0	

First-leg: 5-3

Second-leg	1-0	2-0	3-0	4-0	5-0	2-1	3-1	4-1	5-1	3-2	4-2	5-2	4-3
	0	0	0	0	0	0	0	0	0	0	0	0	0
Second-leg	5-3	5-4	0-0	1-1	2-2	3-3	4-4	5-5	0-1	0-2	0-3	0-4	0-5
	0	0	1	0	0	0	0	0	0	0	0	0	0
Second-leg	1-2	1-3	1-4	1-5	2-3	2-4	2-5	3-4	3-5	4-5	5>	<5	
	0	0	0	0	0	0	0	0	0	0	0	0	

First-leg: 0-1

Second-leg	1-0	2-0	3-0	4-0	5-0	2-1	3-1	4-1	5-1	3-2	4-2	5-2	4-3
	0	4	0	1	0	0	0	0	0	0	1	0	0
Second-leg	5-3	5-4	0-0	1-1	2-2	3-3	4-4	5-5	0-1	0-2	0-3	0-4	0-5
	0	0	8	10	2	0	0	0	12	10	11	8	4
Second-leg	1-2	1-3	1-4	1-5	2-3	2-4	2-5	3-4	3-5	4-5	5>	<5	
	6	4	3	0	2	1	0	0	0	0	1	4	

First-leg: 0-2

Second-leg	1-0	2-0	3-0	4-0	5-0	2-1	3-1	4-1	5-1	3-2	4-2	5-2	4-3
	3	0	0	1	0	2	1	0	0	0	0	0	0
Second-leg	5-3	5-4	0-0	1-1	2-2	3-3	4-4	5-5	0-1	0-2	0-3	0-4	0-5
	0	0	2	3	1	0	0	0	5	4	3	3	1
Second-leg	1-2	1-3	1-4	1-5	2-3	2-4	2-5	3-4	3-5	4-5	5>	<5	
	8	1	2	1	0	0	0	0	0	0	0	7	

First-leg: 1-2

Second-leg	1-0	2-0	3-0	4-0	5-0	2-1	3-1	4-1	5-1	3-2	4-2	5-2	4-3
	1	0	0	0	0	1	1	0	0	0	0	0	0
Second-leg	5-3	5-4	0-0	1-1	2-2	3-3	4-4	5-5	0-1	0-2	0-3	0-4	0-5
	0	0	9	9	2	0	0	0	5	8	5	1	1
Second-leg	1-2	1-3	1-4	1-5	2-3	2-4	2-5	3-4	3-5	4-5	5>	<5	
	7	7	2	2	1	0	0	1	0	0	0	2	

First-leg: 1-3

Second-leg	1-0	2-0	3-0	4-0	5-0	2-1	3-1	4-1	5-1	3-2	4-2	5-2	4-3
	1	1	0	0	0	0	0	0	0	0	0	0	0
Second-leg	5-3	5-4	0-0	1-1	2-2	3-3	4-4	5-5	0-1	0-2	0-3	0-4	0-5
	0	0	2	2	1	1	0	0	4	4	0	3	1
Second-leg	1-2	1-3	1-4	1-5	2-3	2-4	2-5	3-4	3-5	4-5	5>	<5	
	5	3	1	2	0	2	0	0	0	0	0	5	

First-leg: 2-4

Second-leg	1-0	2-0	3-0	4-0	5-0	2-1	3-1	4-1	5-1	3-2	4-2	5-2	4-3
	1	0	0	0	0	0	0	0	0	0	0	0	0
Second-leg	5-3	5-4	0-0	1-1	2-2	3-3	4-4	5-5	0-1	0-2	0-3	0-4	0-5
	0	0	1	0	0	0	0	0	1	0	1	1	0
Second-leg	1-2	1-3	1-4	1-5	2-3	2-4	2-5	3-4	3-5	4-5	5>	<5	
	2	0	1	0	0	0	0	0	0	0	0	0	

First-leg: 3-4

Second-leg	1-0	2-0	3-0	4-0	5-0	2-1	3-1	4-1	5-1	3-2	4-2	5-2	4-3
	0	0	0	0	0	0	0	0	0	0	0	0	0
Second-leg	5-3	5-4	0-0	1-1	2-2	3-3	4-4	5-5	0-1	0-2	0-3	0-4	0-5
	0	0	0	0	0	0	0	0	0	0	0	0	0
Second-leg	1-2	1-3	1-4	1-5	2-3	2-4	2-5	3-4	3-5	4-5	5>	<5	
	0	0	0	0	1	0	0	0	0	1	0	0	

Qualification/Eliminations after First-leg Score

First-leg Score	No. Matches	Qualifications No.	Qualifications %	Eliminations No.	Eliminations %
0-0	128	37	28.91%	91	71.09%
1-0	243	146	60.08%	97	39.92%
2-0	183	136	74.32%	47	25.68%
3-0	112	101	90.18%	11	9.82%
1-1	147	29	19.73%	118	80.27%
2-1	135	59	43.70%	76	56.30%
3-1	88	58	65.91%	30	34.09%
4-1	47	41	87.23%	6	12.77%
5-1	28	26	92.86%	2	7.14%
2-2	60	13	21.67%	47	78.33%
3-2	54	22	40.74%	32	59.26%
4-2	25	17	68.00%	8	32.00%
5-2	9	5	55.56%	4	44.44%
6-2	3	2	66.67%	1	33.33%
3-3	8	2	25.00%	6	75.00%
4-3	6	0	0.00%	6	100.00%
5-3	1	1	100.00%	0	0.00%
0-1	92	8	8.70%	84	91.30%
0-2	48	2	4.17%	46	95.83%
1-2	65	2	3.08%	63	96.92%
1-3	38	0	0.00%	38	100.00%
2-4	8	0	0.00%	8	100.00%
3-4	2	0	0.00%	2	100.00%

Home Match Statistics

	1-0	2-0	3-0	4-0	5-0	2-1	3-1	4-1	5-1	3-2	4-2	5-2	4-3
Number	451	371	221	124	70	298	169	93	57	97	44	17	13
	5-3	5-4	0-0	1-1	2-2	3-3	4-4	5-5	0-1	0-2	0-3	0-4	0-5
Number	1	3	236	293	115	21	6	0	179	89	38	19	15
	1-2	1-3	1-4	1-5	2-3	2-4	2-5	3-4	3-5	4-5	5>	<5	
Number	135	74	28	5	39	18	10	4	4	0	122	29	
	1-0	2-0	3-0	4-0	5-0	2-1	3-1	4-1	5-1	3-2	4-2	5-2	4-3
Percent	13	11	6	4	2	8	5	3	2	3	1	0	0
	5-3	5-4	0-0	1-1	2-2	3-3	4-4	5-5	0-1	0-2	0-3	0-4	0-5
Percent	0	0	7	8	3	1	0	0	5	3	1	1	0
	1-2	1-3	1-4	1-5	2-3	2-4	2-5	3-4	3-5	4-5	5>	<5	
Percent	4	2	1	0	1	1	0	0	0	0	3	1	

Number of matches **3508**

Roll of Honour – the Winners and the Runners-up

The Winners

1.	England	9
2.	Spain	8
3.	Italy	5
4.	W. Germany	4
5.	Netherlands	2
6.	Sweden	2
7.	Hungary	1
8.	Portugal	1
9.	Belgium	1
Total		**33**

The Runners-up

1.	England	6
2.	Spain	5
3.	W. Germany	5
4.	Italy	4
5.	Hungary	3
6.	Belgium	3
7.	Yugoslavia	2
8.	Netherlands	2
9.	France	1
10.	Portugal	1
11.	Scotland	1
	Total	**33**

No. of Appearances in the Final

1.	England	15
2.	Spain	13
3.	W. Germany	9
4.	Italy	9
5.	Hungary	4
6.	Belgium	4
7.	Netherlands	4
8.	Yugoslavia	3
9.	Sweden	2
10.	France	1
11.	Portugal	1
12.	Scotland	1
	Total	**66**

The Winners – Classification by Country

Country	Appearances	Winning Teams
Albania	–	–
Austria	–	–
Belgium	1	Anderlecht (1983)
Bulgaria	–	–
Cyprus	–	–
Czechoslovakia	–	–
Denmark	–	–
East Germany	–	–
England	9	Leeds United (1968, 1971), Newcastle United (1969), Arsenal (1970), Tottenham Hotspur (1972, 1984), Liverpool (1973, 1976), Ipswich Town (1981)
Finland	–	–
France	–	–
Greece	–	–
Hungary	1	Ferencváros (1965)
Iceland	–	–
Italy	4	Roma (1961), Juventus (1977, 1990), Napoli (1989), Inter Milan (1991)
Luxembourg	–	–
Malta	–	–
Netherlands	2	Feyenoord (1974), PSV Eindhoven (1978)
Northern Ireland	–	–
Norway	–	–
Poland	–	–
Portugal	–	–
Republic of Ireland	–	–
Romania	–	–
Scotland	–	–
Spain	8	Barcelona (1958, 1960, 1966), Valencia (1962, 1963), Real Zaragoza (1964), Real Madrid (1985, 1986)
Sweden	1	IFK Gothenburg (1982, 1987)
Switzerland	–	–
Turkey	–	–
USSR	–	–
Wales	–	–
West Germany	4	Borussia Mönchengladbach (1975, 1979), Eintracht Frankfurt (1980), Bayer Leverkusen (1988)
Yugoslavia	1	Dinamo Zagreb (1967)

The Winners – Classification by Results

Pos'n	Club	Cnty	Wins	Years
1	Barcelona	Esp	3	1958, 1960, 1966
2	Valencia	Esp	2	1962, 1963
3	Leeds United	Eng	2	1968, 1971
4	Tottenham Hotspur	Eng	2	1972, 1984
5	Liverpool	Eng	2	1973, 1976
6	Borussia Mönchengladbach	FRG	2	1975, 1979
7	Juventus	Ita	2	1977, 1990
8	IFK Gothenburg	Swe	2	1982, 1987
9	Real Madrid	Esp	2	1985, 1986
10	Roma	Ita	1	1961
11	Real Zaragoza	Esp	1	1964
12	Ferencváros	Hun	1	1965
13	Dinamo Zagreb	Yug	1	1967
14	Newcastle United	Eng	1	1969
15	Arsenal	Eng	1	1970
16	Feyenoord	Ned	1	1974
17	PSV Eindhoven	Ned	1	1978
18	Eintracht Frankfurt	FRG	1	1980
19	Ipswich Town	Eng	1	1981
20	Anderlecht	Bel	1	1983
21	Bayer Leverkusen	FRG	1	1988
22	Napoli	Ita	1	1989
23	Inter Milan	Ita	1	1991
	Total		**33**	

The Runners-up – Classification by Country

Country	Appearances	Winning Teams
Albania	–	–
Austria	–	–
Belgium	3	Anderlecht (1970, 1984), Club Bruges (1976)
Bulgaria	–	–
Cyprus	–	–
Czechoslovakia	–	–
Denmark	–	–
East Germany	–	–
England	6	Chelsea (1958), Birmingham (1960, 1961), Leeds United (1967), Wolverhampton Wanderers (1972), Tottenham Hotspur (1974)
Finland	–	–
France	1	Bastia (1978)
Greece	–	–
Hungary	3	Ujpesti Dózsa (1969), Ferencváros (1968), Videoton (1985)
Iceland	–	–
Italy	3	Juventus (1965, 1971), Fiorentina (1990), Roma (1991)
Luxembourg	–	–
Malta	–	–
Netherlands	2	Twente Enschede (1975), AZ'67 Alkmaar (1981)
Northern Ireland	–	–
Norway	–	–
Poland	–	–
Portugal	1	Benfica (1983)
Republic of Ireland	–	–
Romania	–	–

Scotland	1	Dundee United (1987)
Spain	5	Barcelona (1962), Valencia (1964), Real Zaragoza (1966), Athletic Bilbao (1977), Español (1988)
Sweden	–	–
Switzerland	–	–
Turkey	–	–
USSR	–	–
West Germany	5	Borussia Mönchengladbach (1973, 1980), Hamburg (1982), Cologne (1986), VFB Stuttgart (1989)
Yugoslavia	2	Dinamo Zagreb (1963), Red Star Belgrade (1979)

The UEFA Cup Finalists

Pos'n	Club	Cnty	Appearances	Wins
1	Barcelona	Esp	4	3
2	Borussia Mönchengladbach	FRG	4	2
3	Juventus	Ita	4	2
4	Valencia	Esp	3	2
5	Leeds United	Eng	3	2
6	Tottenham Hotspur	Eng	3	2
7	Anderlecht	Bel	3	1
8	Liverpool	Eng	2	2
9	IFK Gothenburg	Swe	2	2
10	Real Madrid	Esp	2	2
11	Roma	Ita	2	1
12	Real Zaragoza	Esp	2	1
13	Ferencváros	Hun	2	1
14	Dinamo Zagreb	Yug	2	1
15	Birmingham City	Eng	2	0
16	Newcastle United	Eng	1	1
17	Arsenal	Eng	1	1
18	Feyenoord	Ned	1	1
19	PSV Eindhoven	Ned	1	1
20	Eintracht Frankfurt	FRG	1	1
21	Ipswich Town	Eng	1	1
22	Bayer Leverkusen	FRG	1	1
23	Napoli	Ita	1	1
24	Inter Milan	Ita	1	1
25	Chelsea	Eng	1	0
26	Ujpesti Dózsa	Hun	1	0
27	Wolverhampton Wanderers	Eng	1	0
28	Twente Enschede	Ned	1	0
29	Club Bruges	Bel	1	0
30	Athletic Bilbao	Esp	1	0
31	Bastia	Fra	1	0
32	Red Star Belgrade	Yug	1	0
33	AZ'67 Alkmaar	Ned	1	0
34	Hamburg	FRG	1	0
35	Benfica	Por	1	0
36	Videoton	Hun	1	0
37	Cologne	FRG	1	0
38	Dundee United	Sco	1	0
39	Español	Esp	1	0
40	VFB Stuttgart	FRG	1	0
41	Fiorentina	Ita	1	0
	Total		**66**	**33**

Above: Feynoord's Theo De Jong (centre) explodes past Spur's Mike England in the 1973-74 final first-leg. Below: VFB Stuttgart's Srecko Katanec is challenged by Napoli's De Napoli (right) and Ferrara in the 1988-89 final second-leg.

The Reign of the English

If Spain leads the all-time table over 36 years in the Champions' Cup, they are denied top spot in the same table over all three competitions (page 600). That honour goes instead to England, despite the enforced absence of all English clubs during the period 1985-86 to 1989-90. Since the creation of the European Cups, England has entered 157 clubs in the three competitions. These clubs have played 939 matches, recording 510 victories, 203 draws and 226 defeats. And they have scored almost twice as many goals as they have conceded: 1806 for, 936 against.

During the same period English clubs have amassed a total of 1390 points, including a bonus point total of 157. A remarkable figure when compared to the West German total of 169 from 196 clubs entered since 1955-56. With an overall average performance index of 8.853, England leads West Germany (8.030) in this classification too. All this is not surprising given the actual number of trophies won by English clubs:

Champions' Cup

8 winners	1968, 1977, 1978, 1979, 1980, 1981, 1982, 1984
2 runners-up	1975, 1985

Cup Winners' Cup

6 winners	1963, 1965, 1970, 1971, 1985, 1991
4 runners-up	1966, 1973, 1976, 1980

Fairs'/UEFA Cup

9 winners	1968, 1969, 1970, 1971, 1972, 1973, 1976, 1981, 1984
6 runners-up	1958, 1960, 1961, 1967, 1972, 1974

As we can see, there has been a considerable domination in the Champions' Cup, with four wins and one runners-up spot for Liverpool alone, and also in the Fairs' and UEFA Cups, where English clubs were victorious six years in a row from 1968 to 1973 (Leeds United, Newcastle United, Arsenal, Leeds again, Tottenham Hotspur and Liverpool!) It is also interesting to note that England has had 17 different clubs represented in these 35 European Cup finals. Conversely, West Germany has had only nine different clubs in their 22 finals.

The German elite from 1974 to 1983 consisted of just three clubs: Bayern Munich, Hamburg and Borussia Mönchengladbach. Between 1973 and 1980 Mönchengladbach won the UEFA Cup twice and played in two other finals. What is particularly interesting about West Germany's record is Cologne's first place in the all-time table for the Fairs'/UEFA Cup. This club has never won either the Fairs' or the UEFA Cups, nor for that matter any European trophy. But Cologne have been in so many quarter-finals and semi-finals that they have accumulated an impressive total, bonus points excluded, of 174 points (72 victories, 20 draws, 42 defeats), giving them a better aggregate in this competition than such giants as Barcelona, Juventus and Inter Milan!

Italians on the March

On the subject of Italian clubs, the all-time classification of countries over all three competitions shows Italy in an honourable third place behind England and West Germany, a position that seems logical in view of the exceptional performances of Italian clubs in the three competitions over the past five years:

Champions' Cup	2 winners	AC Milan in 1989 and 1990
Cup-winners' Cup	1 winner	Sampdoria in 1990
	1 runner-up	Sampdoria in 1989
UEFA Cup	3 winners	Napoli 1989, Juventus 1990, Inter Milan 1991
	2 runners-up	Fiorentina 1990 and Roma 1991

This contributes to Italy's index of 7.629, behind England and West Germany, over 36 years, but makes Italy the number one power in Europe over the past five years. Spain, ranked fourth over 36 years in all three competitions, owes its position above all to Real Madrid's early domination of the Champions' Cup, but also to the trio of Barcelona-Valencia-Zaragoza which had the Fairs' Cup virtually all to themselves in the period 1958 to 1966. Barcelona have also added three Cup-winners' Cup victories to their three Fairs' Cup wins, with Valencia adding the Cup-winners' Cup to their two Fairs' Cup triumphs with a victory over Arsenal on penalty-kicks in the 1980 final.

The Champions' Cup table for the last five years enabled us to look at the spectacular progress made by both Portugal and France, positioned respectively second and fourth over this period. But in the all-time classification over 36 years in all three competitions Portugal finds itself in ninth spot (evidence of the country's mediocre record in the Cup-winners' and UEFA Cups) with France much further down the table in 14th position. The reason for France's poor ranking is quite simple: French clubs have never won a single European trophy and have only ever contested five finals: four in the Champions' Cup – Reims (1956, 59), Saint-Etienne (1976), Marseille (1991) and one in the UEFA Cup – Bastia (1978). Fifth place in the general all-time classification belongs to the Soviet Union, regularly placed in the top six bracket in virtually all of the various tables. They are closely followed by the Netherlands (sixth) and Belgium (seventh). These two countries have both enjoyed their own particular periods of success, notably with Feyenoord, Ajax and PSV in the Champions' Cup for the Dutch and Anderlecht in the Cup-winners' and UEFA Cups for the Belgians.

Finally, it is worth noting the excellent performance of Wales. As we have mentioned, Wales is only represented in one competition, with the winner of the Welsh Cup going into the Cup-winners' Cup. Usually this team comes from one of the lower divisions of the English League, yet Wales occupies a very praiseworthy 17th place in the all-time classification. And this with only 30 clubs having participated over 35 years! An honourable performance in all respects.

Real, Barcelona, Juventus – The Magic Trio

One of the most interesting sections in our entire statistical work is the all-time general classification of clubs in all three competitions (pages 602 to 611). All 538 clubs which have played in European competition at least once have been indexed and classified on the basis of the number of points they have accumulated in 36 years, bonus points included.

We have already mentioned Cologne's exceptional case in our earlier study of the all-time classification of nations. There we saw that West Germany was ranked second, a position made possible not only by the excellent performances of Bayern Munich (fourth-ranked club in the all-time list), Hamburg and Borussia Mönchengladbach, but also by the consistency of Cologne. The Rhinelanders are the second-ranked West German club in the all-time table, with a total of 223 points gained from 165 matches (86 victories, 30 draws, 40 defeats), including 21 bonus points, which gives a good indication of how often Cologne have reached the latter stages of the competitions they have entered, without, however, a single trophy to show for their efforts!

This all-time club ranking is nevertheless dominated by the magic trio of Real Madrid, Barcelona and Juventus. These are the only three clubs to have passed the 300-point barrier: 362 points for Real Madrid, 342 for Barcelona and 319 for Juventus. Juventus have the proud record of being the only European club to have won all three competitions: Champions' Cup in 1985, Cup-winners' Cup in 1984, UEFA Cup in 1977 and 1990. And there are some Juventus players who have winner's medals from all three cups – Brio, Tacconi, Tardelli and the late Gaetano Scirea.

The Turin club's record over the last decade is particularly impressive. Under the inspired leadership of Frenchman Michel Platini (European Footballer of the Year in 1983, 1984 and 1985) Juventus were runners-up in the Champions' Cup in 1983 (beaten 1-0 by Hamburg), winners of the Cup-winners' Cup in 1984 (2-1 v FC Porto) and winners of the Champions' Cup in 1985 (1-0 against Liverpool). More recently, in 1990, they captured the UEFA Cup, defeating another Italian club, Fiorentina, 3-1 and 0-0 in the two-legged final. It is therefore no surprise to see *Juve* in third place behind the two Spanish giants, Real and Barcelona.

In pole-position with 362 points, Real Madrid have contested 235 European

Cup matches in a run which has remained unbroken since 1955-56. Their record from these matches is 133 victories, 38 draws and 64 defeats! Thanks to their frequent participation in finals, semi-finals and quarter-finals, Real have also earned themselves a grand total of 58 bonus points! To give an idea of what such a figure represents, it is worth having another look at the all-time country table. Here we can see that Real have earned 10 bonus points more than all the French clubs put together (page 600)! As for Barcelona, they also have a considerable bonus point total of 47. It is not surprising, then, to find the two Spanish clubs at the top of the table, whereas the first French club, Saint-Etienne, is in 57th place with 81 points, eight of them bonus points, and Olympique Marseille, Champions' Cup runners-up in 1991 and semi-finalists in 1990, are only 72nd, headed by Girondins Bordeaux in 63rd place. But once again it is important to note that French clubs have only really begun to make a name for themselves *en masse* (Marseille, Monaco, Bordeaux, Auxerre, Sochaux) over the last 5-10 years.

Of particular note in the case of French clubs is their lack of consistency. There was a gap of almost 20 years between Stade Reims' two appearances in European finals (1956 and 1959 Champions' Cup) and the next two by French clubs – Saint-Etienne, beaten 1-0 by Bayern Munich in the 1976 Champions' Cup final, and Bastia, defeated 0-0, 3-0 by PSV Eindhoven in the final of the 1978 UEFA Cup. If Saint-Etienne's success played a leading role in the resurgence of the French national team, it hardly had a similar inspirational success on French clubs, because 15 long years were to pass before Olympique Marseille reached the 1991 Champions' Cup final, where, of course, they were to suffer the same disappointment as their predecessors.

Red Star Belgrade, conquerors of Marseille in Bari, are placed 11th in the all-time general classification. The Yugoslavs, whose win in Bari gave them their first trophy, have played 167 European matches (as against only 49 for Marseille), registering 82 victories, 30 draws, 55 defeats and 22 bonus points. An old proverb running through the history of the European Cups tells us that "The big clubs never die". Looking at the results in the three European competitions over the past 36 years shows us that the big teams in the '60s and '70s are still the ones to beat in the '80s and '90s. This explains why we find a concentration of clubs from a select few countries in the leading positions of the all-time classification. The following list illustrates the distribution by country of those clubs ranked in the top 30:

SPAIN	Real Madrid (1st), Barcelona (2nd), Atlético Madrid (16th), Valencia (21st)
ITALY	Juventus (3rd), Inter Milan (6th), AC Milan (10th), Roma (28th)
WEST GERMANY	Bayern Munich (4th), Cologne (9th), Hamburg (14th),

	Borussia Mönchengladbach (15th)
BELGIUM	Anderlecht (7th), Standard Liège (24th)
ENGLAND	Liverpool (8th), Manchester United (20th), Leeds United (23rd), Tottenham Hotspur (27th)
PORTUGAL	Benfica (5th), Sporting Lisbon (19th), FC Porto (26th)
SCOTLAND	Rangers (13th), Celtic (17th)
NETHERLANDS	Ajax (12th), Feyenoord (22nd), PSV Eindhoven (25th)

It is clear from this list that, with one or two possible exceptions ('Gladbach and Leeds), most of the clubs ranked in the top 30 are still representing their countries regularly in the '80s and '90s. And, what is more, there are only four clubs in the top 30 who do not belong to the countries mentioned above: Red Star Belgrade, the top Yugoslav club, in 11th place; Dinamo Kiev, regular Soviet Union representatives every season, in 18th; Rapid Vienna, from Austria, in 29th; and Hungarian club Ferencváros one place lower in 30th.

Above: AC Milan's Ruud Gullit holds the European Champions' Cup aloft after the Italians had beaten Steaua Bucharest 4-0 in the 1988-89 final in Barcelona.

National Performances by Index

1955-56 to 1990-91

Pos'n	Cnty	Ave	Pts	P	W	D	L	F	A	Diff	B	No./T
1	England	8.853	1390	939	510	203	226	1806	936	870	167	157
2	W. Germany	8.030	1574	1137	595	215	327	2223	136	855	169	196
3	Italy	7.629	1381	1004	499	226	279	1547	971	576	157	181
4	Spain	7.590	1389	1017	512	195	310	1827	1201	626	170	183
5	USSR	5.941	606	465	230	102	133	705	472	233	44	102
6	Netherlands	5.751	765	609	292	112	205	1110	735	375	69	133
7	Belgium	5.664	844	697	323	122	252	1122	884	238	76	149
8	Scotland	5.646	830	676	317	131	228	1127	830	297	65	147
9	Portugal	5.089	738	623	274	129	220	990	754	236	61	145
10	Yugoslavia	4.933	740	659	278	122	259	1085	939	146	62	150
11	E. Germany	4.604	571	522	210	111	201	766	688	78	40	124
12	Hungary	4.600	552	496	215	78	203	843	745	98	44	120
13	Czechoslovakia	4.376	547	485	210	92	183	749	651	98	35	125
14	France	4.288	609	558	219	123	216	838	770	68	48	142
15	Romania	3.571	425	429	164	75	190	560	630	-70	22	119
16	Poland	3.514	376	379	138	81	160	520	577	-57	19	107
17	Wales	3.466	104	106	34	30	42	148	130	18	6	30
18	Austria	3.379	419	438	152	88	198	586	695	-109	27	124
19	Bulgaria	3.160	354	377	136	62	179	553	617	-64	20	112
20	Sweden	3.072	341	351	118	85	148	481	554	-73	20	111
21	Switzerland	2.902	386	439	140	83	216	631	797	-166	23	133
22	Greece	2.642	296	333	111	63	159	380	560	-180	11	112
23	Turkey	2.051	199	273	74	42	157	264	509	-245	9	97
24	Denmark	1.965	226	317	80	57	180	399	652	-253	9	115
25	Albania	1.621	60	93	21	18	54	70	143	-73	0	37
26	Norway	1.242	118	224	40	37	147	202	542	-340	1	95
27	Finland	1.200	96	196	33	27	136	158	545	-387	3	80
28	N. Ireland	1.045	92	198	23	44	131	179	532	-353	2	88
29	Rep. of Ireland	1.032	96	218	28	40	150	164	532	-368	0	93
30	Cyprus	0.805	58	158	19	20	119	117	530	-413	0	72
31	Iceland	0.600	45	162	11	23	128	89	513	-424	0	75
32	Malta	0.590	49	174	18	13	143	73	609	-536	0	83
33	Luxembourg	0.526	49	194	17	15	162	112	813	-701	0	93

1981-82 to 1990-91

Pos'n	Cnty	Ave	Pts	P	W	D	L	F	A	Diff	B	No./T
1	Italy	9.000	504	356	179	87	90	527	301	226	59	56
2	England	8.413	244	163	89	37	37	283	144	139	29	29
3	W. Germany	8.065	492	361	185	72	104	627	370	257	50	61
4	Spain	7.160	401	300	146	62	92	453	312	141	47	56
5	Belgium	6.903	359	277	135	55	87	458	324	134	34	52
6	USSR	5.961	310	243	115	57	71	372	259	113	23	52
7	Portugal	5.893	277	219	105	42	72	329	229	100	25	47
8	Scotland	5.489	258	209	98	47	64	318	212	106	15	47
9	Yugoslavia	5.244	236	203	93	36	74	346	276	70	14	45
10	France	5.127	241	201	82	58	61	294	228	66	19	47
11	Romania	4.707	193	176	72	32	72	233	220	13	17	41
12	Austria	4.674	201	179	75	38	66	279	257	22	13	43
13	Netherlands	4.191	197	185	73	38	74	256	218	38	13	47
14	Sweden	3.951	162	144	57	37	50	223	193	30	11	41
15	E. Germany	3.886	171	165	63	35	67	225	218	7	10	44
16	Czechoslovakia	3.659	161	158	61	32	65	228	218	10	7	44
17	Switzerland	3.275	131	140	47	32	61	177	202	-25	5	40

18	Poland	2.897	113	126	39	30	57	149	192	-43	5	39
19	Greece	2.846	111	122	41	25	56	128	176	-48	4	39
20	Hungary	2.675	107	124	42	19	63	149	207	-58	4	40
21	Wales	2.600	26	34	9	8	17	49	42	7	0	10
22	Bulgaria	2.594	96	114	34	22	58	146	207	-61	6	37
23	Denmark	2.363	78	94	27	20	47	105	160	-55	4	33
24	Finland	1.937	62	88	22	15	51	68	171	-103	3	32
25	Turkey	1.866	56	80	20	13	47	68	143	-75	3	30
26	Albania	1.772	39	59	16	7	36	47	90	-43	0	22
27	Norway	1.166	35	66	9	17	40	44	129	-85	0	30
28	Cyprus	1.066	32	66	11	10	45	62	168	-106	0	30
29	N. Ireland	0.900	27	64	4	19	41	44	138	-94	0	30
30	Rep. of Ireland	0.766	23	64	4	15	45	40	141	-101	0	30
–	Iceland	0.766	23	64	7	9	48	36	165	-129	0	30
32	Luxembourg	0.333	10	60	2	6	52	19	249	-230	0	30
–	Malta	0.333	10	62	4	2	56	17	240	-223	0	30

1986-87 to 1990-91

Pos'n	Cnty	Ave	Pts	P	W	D	L	F	A	Diff	B	No./T
1	England	12.500	25	13	10	2	1	24	9	15	3	2
2	Italy	9.848	325	222	114	58	50	319	166	153	39	33
3	W. Germany	8.645	268	195	99	43	53	312	181	131	27	31
4	Spain	7.592	205	150	74	35	41	220	140	80	22	27
5	Belgium	6.846	178	140	66	29	45	208	147	61	17	26
6	France	6.818	150	113	52	31	30	164	98	66	15	22
7	Portugal	6.000	156	122	59	24	39	195	110	85	14	26
8	Netherlands	5.318	117	99	43	19	37	137	101	36	12	22
9	USSR	5.000	140	122	50	31	41	167	138	29	9	28
10	Scotland	4.916	118	98	45	23	30	122	90	32	5	24
11	Romania	4.772	105	93	41	14	38	124	117	7	9	22
12	Yugoslavia	4.681	103	89	40	18	31	144	117	27	5	22
13	Austria	4.130	95	86	38	16	32	122	120	2	3	23
14	E. Germany	3.857	81	79	27	21	31	90	93	-3	6	21
15	Sweden	3.523	74	70	24	21	25	89	96	-7	5	21
16	Denmark	3.187	51	52	18	11	23	58	62	-4	4	16
17	Wales	3.000	15	16	5	5	6	22	22	0	0	5
–	Switzerland	3.000	60	66	21	15	30	72	90	-18	3	20
19	Czechoslovakia	2.904	61	68	23	14	31	90	100	-10	1	21
20	Poland	2.850	57	62	19	17	26	74	91	-17	2	20
21	Greece	2.600	52	62	19	13	30	69	94	-25	1	20
22	Bulgaria	2.500	45	54	17	7	30	76	105	-29	4	18
23	Turkey	2.333	35	44	13	6	25	45	78	-33	3	15
24	Hungary	2.050	41	56	16	9	31	54	94	-40	0	20
25	Finland	1.941	33	46	11	10	25	33	82	-49	1	17
26	Albania	1.857	26	41	11	4	26	36	63	-27	0	14
27	Norway	1.200	18	34	5	8	21	18	61	-43	0	15
28	Cyprus	0.933	14	34	5	4	25	24	79	-55	0	15
29	Iceland	0.800	12	32	3	6	23	15	82	-67	0	15
30	N. Ireland	0.733	11	30	0	11	19	16	67	-51	0	15
31	Rep. of Ireland	0.400	6	30	0	6	24	6	67	-61	0	15
–	Luxembourg	0.400	6	30	2	2	26	12	107	-95	0	15
33	Malta	0.333	5	30	2	1	27	6	96	-90	0	15

Summary Totals	Pts	P	W	D	L	F	A	Diff	B	F/P
1955-56 to 1990-91	**16325**	**14946**	**6041**	**2864**	**6041**	**22424**	**22424**	**0**	**1379**	**3.001**
1981-82 to 1990-91	**5386**	**4966**	**1966**	**1034**	**1966**	**6799**	**6799**	**0**	**420**	**2.738**
1986-87 to 1990-91	**2688**	**2478**	**972**	**534**	**972**	**3163**	**3163**	**0**	**210**	**2.553**

Club Performance by Points

1955-56 to 1990-91

Pos'n	Club	Cnty	Pts	P	W	D	L	F	A	Diff	B	Pts/P	F/P
1	Real Madrid	Esp	362	235	133	38	64	514	255	259	58	1.540	2.187
2	Barcelona	Esp	342	233	123	49	61	463	260	203	47	1.468	1.987
3	Juventus	Ita	319	208	122	36	50	368	176	192	39	1.534	1.769
4	Bayern Munich	FRG	282	178	101	39	38	372	175	197	41	1.584	2.090
5	Benfica	Por	253	179	88	42	49	324	179	145	35	1.413	1.810
6	Inter Milan	Ita	247	178	87	41	50	283	161	122	32	1.388	1.590
7	Anderlecht	Bel	246	176	95	25	56	335	224	111	31	1.398	1.903
8	Liverpool	Eng	224	140	84	26	30	278	106	172	30	1.600	1.986
9	Cologne	FRG	223	165	86	30	49	318	195	123	21	1.352	1.927
10	AC Milan	Ita	220	151	77	35	39	268	147	121	31	1.457	1.775
11	Red Star Belgrade	Yug	216	167	82	30	55	323	222	101	22	1.293	1.934
12	Ajax	Ned	196	135	76	19	40	262	133	129	25	1.452	1.941
13	Rangers	Sco	185	147	70	27	50	245	193	52	18	1.259	1.667
14	Hamburg	FRG	182	125	70	20	35	252	147	105	22	1.456	2.016
15	Bor. Mönchengladbach	FRG	181	115	67	25	23	259	127	132	22	1.574	2.252
16	Atlético Madrid	Esp	179	130	68	22	40	210	144	66	21	1.377	1.615
17	Celtic	Sco	174	128	66	24	38	235	126	10	18	1.359	1.836
18	Dinamo Kiev	URS	159	106	59	25	22	173	84	89	16	1.500	1.632
19	Sporting Lisbon	Por	156	135	57	32	46	243	169	74	10	1.156	1.800
20	Manchester United	Eng	149	95	53	23	19	198	100	98	20	1.568	2.084
21	Valencia	Esp	149	111	54	26	31	205	135	70	15	1.342	1.847
22	Feyenoord	Ned	145	105	57	19	29	220	120	100	12	1.381	2.095
23	Leeds United	Eng	144	91	50	24	17	165	67	98	20	1.582	1.813
24	Standard Liège	Bel	144	112	57	18	37	193	134	59	12	1.286	1.723
25	PSV Eindhoven	Ned	142	109	53	21	35	197	108	89	15	1.303	1.807
26	FC Porto	Por	142	118	57	19	42	182	140	42	9	1.203	1.542
27	Tottenham Hotspur	Eng	141	87	53	16	18	208	84	124	19	1.621	2.391
28	Roma	Ita	139	102	51	20	31	154	101	53	17	1.363	1.510
29	Rapid Vienna	Aut	138	128	51	26	51	201	186	15	10	1.078	1.570
30	Ferencváros	Hun	133	108	50	19	39	188	142	46	14	1.231	1.741
31	Dundee United	Sco	127	102	46	26	30	149	98	51	9	1.245	1.461
32	CSKA Sofia	Bul	124	116	48	18	50	173	169	4	10	1.069	1.491
33	Ujpesti Dózsa	Hun	122	105	46	18	41	188	158	30	12	1.162	1.790
34	Dynamo Dresden	GDR	118	98	42	25	31	156	121	35	9	1.204	1.592
35	Eintracht Frankfurt	FRG	116	85	45	13	27	170	113	57	13	1.365	2.000
36	Fiorentina	Ita	112	81	42	16	23	112	81	31	12	1.383	1.383
37	Dukla Prague	Tch	112	93	40	24	29	138	119	19	8	1.204	1.484
38	Spartak Moscow	URS	111	86	44	18	24	134	92	42	5	1.291	1.558
39	Austria Vienna	Aut	107	104	35	28	41	147	156	-9	9	1.029	1.413
40	Dinamo Zagreb	Yug	105	100	35	25	40	133	126	7	10	1.050	1.330
41	Hajduk Split	Yug	104	86	43	10	33	144	102	42	8	1.209	1.674
42	Carl Zeiss Jena	GDR	104	87	39	18	30	140	114	26	8	1.195	1.609
43	Napoli	Ita	104	85	36	26	23	102	89	13	6	1.224	1.200
44	Dinamo Bucharest	Rom	103	100	40	18	42	157	133	24	5	1.030	1.570
45	Athletic Bilbao	Esp	103	86	40	16	30	121	111	10	7	1.198	1.407
46	IFK Gothenburg	Swe	101	74	37	16	21	135	98	37	11	1.365	1.824
47	Lokomotive Leipzig	GDR	100	94	38	17	39	135	125	10	7	1.064	1.436
48	Aberdeen	Sco	98	79	37	18	24	125	86	39	6	1.241	1.582
49	Club Bruges	Bel	98	89	38	12	39	152	135	11	10	1.101	1.708
50	VFB Stuttgart	FRG	92	70	34	17	19	128	77	51	7	1.314	1.829
51	Real Zaragoza	Esp	92	70	35	11	24	129	98	31	11	1.314	1.843
52	Legia Warsaw	Pol	92	75	33	19	23	110	81	29	7	1.227	1.467
53	Steaua Bucharest	Rom	91	81	32	18	31	114	112	2	9	1.123	1.407

Pos'n	Club	Cnty	Pts	P	W	D	L	F	A	Diff	B	Pts/P	F/P
54	Malmö FF	Swe	90	89	31	22	36	106	123	-17	6	1.011	1.191
55	Magdeburg	GDR	86	72	32	15	25	115	86	29	7	1.194	1.597
56	Hibernian	Sco	86	70	34	13	23	125	99	26	5	1.229	1.786
57	Saint-Etienne	Fra	81	69	29	15	25	103	80	23	8	1.174	1.493
58	Partizan Belgrade	Yug	81	77	32	11	34	132	122	10	6	1.052	1.714
59	Sparta Prague	Tch	80	72	31	12	29	130	105	25	6	1.111	1.806
60	Górnik Zabrze	Pol	80	68	31	13	24	118	100	18	5	1.176	1.735
61	Grasshoppers Zürich	Sui	79	82	30	13	39	135	128	7	6	0.963	1.646
62	Honvéd	Hun	78	70	34	8	28	126	111	15	2	1.114	1.800
63	Girondins Bordeaux	Fra	76	64	29	13	22	83	81	2	5	1.188	1.297
64	Arsenal	Eng	73	51	27	11	13	92	42	50	8	1.431	1.804
65	Ipswich Town	Eng	72	50	29	9	12	100	51	49	5	1.440	2.000
66	Twente Enschede	Ned	72	58	26	12	20	103	69	34	8	1.241	1.776
67	Olympiakos Pireus	Gre	71	77	28	15	34	86	116	-30	0	0.922	1.177
68	Universitatea Craiova	Rom	69	62	28	10	24	75	69	6	3	1.113	1.210
69	Panathinaikos	Gre	69	81	23	17	41	96	131	-35	6	0.852	1.185
70	Dynamo Berlin	GDR	68	60	23	18	19	87	80	7	4	1.133	1.450
71	Levski Sofia	Bul	68	74	25	14	35	126	131	-5	4	0.919	1.703
72	Olympique Marseille	Fra	67	49	26	8	15	79	56	23	7	1.367	1.612
73	Torino	Ita	66	59	23	15	21	81	67	14	5	1.119	1.373
74	Servette	Sui	66	67	25	14	28	97	103	-6	2	0.985	1.448
75	Werder Bremen	FRG	65	50	24	11	15	89	55	34	6	1.300	1.780
76	Borussia Dortmund	FRG	65	51	26	7	18	100	71	29	6	1.275	1.961
77	Chelsea	Eng	64	42	23	10	9	86	44	42	8	1.524	2.048
78	Dinamo Tbilisi	URS	63	51	25	8	18	76	57	19	5	1.235	1.490
79	Vitória Setúbal	Por	63	56	26	7	23	90	72	18	4	1.125	1.607
80	Banik Ostrava	Tch	63	56	25	9	22	80	69	11	4	1.125	1.429
81	Galatasaray	Tur	62	69	21	16	32	81	120	-39	4	0.899	1.174
82	Torpedo Moscow	URS	61	47	22	14	11	72	46	26	3	1.298	1.532
83	FC Liège	Bel	60	48	25	6	17	68	48	20	4	1.250	1.417
84	FC Zürich	Sui	60	63	22	10	31	88	109	-21	6	0.952	1.397
85	Nottingham Forest	Eng	59	38	22	7	9	52	30	22	8	1.553	1.368
86	Slovan Bratislava	Tch	59	45	24	6	15	80	59	21	5	1.311	1.778
87	Dinamo Moscow	URS	59	43	20	11	12	61	40	21	8	1.372	1.419
88	Kaiserslautern	FRG	58	46	21	3	18	92	61	31	5	1.261	2.000
89	Everton	Eng	57	41	21	11	9	65	31	34	4	1.390	1.585
90	Dunfermline Athletic	Sco	55	42	23	5	14	83	45	38	4	1.310	1.976
91	MTK-VM	Hun	54	44	20	7	17	85	74	11	7	1.227	1.932
92	Nantes	Fra	54	52	18	15	19	78	77	1	3	1.038	1.500
93	OFK Belgrade	Yug	54	49	20	8	21	90	90	0	6	1.102	1.837
94	Bologna	Ita	53	39	18	13	8	55	36	19	4	1.359	1.410
95	FC Tirol	Aut	53	58	21	8	29	79	106	-27	3	0.914	1.362
96	Sampdoria	Ita	50	32	18	7	7	43	27	16	7	1.563	1.344
97	Vasas SC	Hun	49	51	19	8	24	94	70	24	3	0.961	1.843
98	Cardiff City	Wal	49	45	16	13	16	62	50	12	4	1.089	1.378
99	Hertha Berlin	FRG	48	36	20	5	11	54	42	12	3	1.333	1.500
100	AEK Athenes	Gre	48	58	19	7	32	74	107	-33	3	0.828	1.276
101	Zbrojovka Brno	Tch	47	41	18	8	15	65	52	13	3	1.146	1.585
102	Aston Villa	Eng	46	33	17	7	9	55	31	24	5	1.394	1.667
103	Beveren	Bel	46	38	18	8	12	56	34	22	2	1.211	1.474
104	Rába ETO	Hun	46	42	19	5	18	73	76	-3	3	1.095	1.738
105	Manchester City	Eng	45	34	15	9	10	54	34	20	6	1.324	1.588
106	West Ham United	Eng	45	30	15	6	9	58	42	16	9	1.500	1.933
107	Spartak Trnava	Tch	45	38	16	9	13	54	41	13	4	1.184	1.421
108	Schalke 04	FRG	44	31	17	6	8	53	41	12	4	1.419	1.710
109	Español	Esp	44	34	18	3	13	49	41	8	5	1.294	1.411
110	PAOK Salonika	Gre	44	44	16	11	17	46	68	-22	1	1.000	1.045

Pos'n	Club	Cnty	Pts	P	W	D	L	F	A	Diff	B	Pts/P	F/P
111	Fenerbahçe	Tur	44	62	18	7	37	62	118	-56	1	0.710	1.000
112	KV Mechelen	Bel	43	25	15	7	3	37	14	23	6	1.720	1.480
113	Wolverhampton Wanderers	Eng	43	32	16	6	10	59	44	15	5	1.344	1.844
114	Real Sociedad	Esp	43	40	14	12	14	42	49	-7	3	1.075	1.050
115	Birmingham City	Eng	41	25	14	6	5	52	39	13	7	1.640	2.080
116	Monaco	Fra	41	46	12	14	20	62	65	-3	3	0.891	1.348
117	1860 Munich	FRG	40	30	15	6	9	70	42	28	4	1.333	2.333
118	Newcastle United	Eng	39	28	14	7	7	13	26	17	1	1.393	1.536
119	Vojvodina Novi Sad	Yug	39	36	14	8	14	39	42	-3	3	1.083	1.083
120	Vorwärts Frankfurt/Oder	GDR	39	43	17	3	23	56	64	-8	2	0.907	1.302
121	Stade Reims	Fra	38	24	14	3	7	63	30	33	7	1.583	2.625
122	Neuchâtel Xamax	Sui	38	32	13	10	9	49	37	12	2	1.188	1.531
123	AZ'67 Alkmaar	Ned	37	26	13	8	5	62	26	36	3	1.423	2.385
124	Bohemians Prague	Tch	37	36	14	7	15	52	46	6	2	1.028	1.444
125	RWD Molenbeek	Bel	37	34	12	11	11	42	39	3	2	1.088	1.235
126	Antwerp	Bel	37	40	14	8	18	54	63	-9	1	0.925	1.350
127	Olympique Lyon	Fra	37	38	14	6	18	59	69	-10	3	0.974	1.553
128	Widzew Lódź	Pol	37	38	13	9	16	47	58	-11	2	0.974	1.237
129	Slavia Sofia	Bul	37	41	14	6	21	49	66	-17	3	0.902	1.195
130	Sparta Rotterdam	Ned	36	32	14	7	11	64	44	20	1	1.125	2.000
131	Heart of Midlothian	Sco	36	36	14	7	15	56	63	-7	1	1.000	1.556
132	AGF Aarhus	Den	36	40	14	6	20	50	58	-8	2	0.900	1.250
133	Dinamo Minsk	URS	34	26	12	7	7	41	25	16	3	1.308	1.577
134	Bayer Leverkusen	FRG	34	24	11	9	4	31	16	15	3	1.417	1.292
135	Fortuna Düsseldorf	FRG	34	29	11	8	10	45	36	9	4	1.172	1.552
136	FC Basle	Sui	34	55	13	7	35	85	135	-50	1	0.618	1.545
137	Glentoran	Nir	34	58	8	17	33	50	123	-73	1	0.586	0.862
138	Velez Mostar	Yug	33	28	12	8	8	47	40	7	1	1.179	1.679
139	Strasbourg	Fra	32	30	11	8	11	33	43	-10	2	1.067	1.100
140	Lausanne-Sports	Sui	32	47	12	6	29	68	107	-39	2	0.681	1.447
141	Trakia Plovdiv	Bul	31	36	11	8	17	53	56	-3	1	0.861	1.472
142	Inter Bratislava	Tch	30	28	14	2	12	55	42	13	0	1.071	1.964
143	Brøndby IF	Den	30	24	10	7	7	33	24	9	3	1.250	1.375
144	Videoton	Hun	30	28	11	5	12	32	35	-3	3	1.071	1.143
145	IFK Norrköping	Swe	30	34	9	12	13	42	47	-5	0	0.882	1.235
146	Vitória Guimarães	Por	30	28	12	5	11	32	40	-8	1	1.071	1.143
147	FC Amsterdam	Ned	29	24	11	5	8	43	32	11	2	1.208	1.792
148	Nice	Fra	29	28	12	3	13	45	50	-5	2	1.036	1.607
149	Slask Wroclaw	Pol	29	28	10	8	10	41	46	-5	1	1.036	1.464
150	Wiener Sport-Club	Aut	29	33	11	5	17	46	58	-12	2	0.879	1.394
151	Young Boys Berne	Sui	29	29	9	8	12	41	53	-12	3	1.000	1.414
152	Utrecht	Ned	29	36	11	7	18	48	73	-25	0	0.806	1.333
153	Omonia Nicosia	Cyp	29	48	12	5	31	53	109	-56	0	0.604	1.104
154	Linfield	Nir	29	51	7	14	30	52	109	-57	1	0.569	1.020
155	Derby County	Eng	28	22	11	4	7	50	29	21	2	1.273	2.273
156	Lokeren	Bel	28	24	9	9	6	29	24	5	1	1.167	1.208
157	Boavista	Por	28	30	11	6	13	42	39	3	0	0.933	1.400
158	Wrexham	Wal	28	26	10	7	9	34	34	0	1	1.077	1.308
159	Ruch Chorzów	Pol	28	32	10	6	16	49	60	-11	2	0.875	1.531
160	Radnicki Nis	Yug	27	22	11	3	8	34	31	3	2	1.227	1.545
161	Nuremberg	FRG	26	20	10	3	7	33	21	6	3	1.300	1.650
162	Arges Pitesti	Rom	26	26	10	6	10	38	42	-4	0	1.000	1.462
163	Lokomotiv Plovdiv	Bul	26	30	10	6	14	40	50	-10	0	0.867	1.333
164	Petrolul Ploiesti	Rom	26	25	12	1	12	24	34	-10	1	1.040	0.960
165	Sion	Sui	26	28	10	5	13	38	54	-16	1	0.929	1.357
166	Ararat Erevan	URS	25	16	11	2	3	37	15	22	1	1.563	2.313
167	Southampton	Eng	25	22	8	8	6	37	26	11	1	1.136	1.682

Pos'n	Club	Cnty	Pts	P	W	D	L	F	A	Diff	B	Pts/P	F/P
168	Bastia	Fra	25	18	9	4	5	35	26	9	3	1.389	1.944
169	Waregem	Bel	25	20	10	3	7	30	29	1	2	1.250	1.500
170	Kilmarnock	Sco	25	24	9	5	10	38	39	-1	2	1.042	1 583
171	Dnepr Dnepropetrovsk	URS	25	24	8	7	9	27	28	-1	2	1.042	1.125
172	Sturm Graz	Aut	25	28	8	7	13	29	35	-6	2	0.893	1.036
173	Seville	Esp	25	24	9	6	9	32	39	-7	1	1.042	1.333
174	Beroe Stara Zagora	Bul	24	22	10	3	9	39	23	16	1	1.091	1.773
175	Shakhtyor Donetsk	URS	24	18	10	3	5	30	24	6	1	1.333	1.667
176	Admira Wacker	Aut	24	24	10	3	11	22	28	-6	1	1.000	0.917
177	Göztepe	Tur	24	30	10	2	18	36	49	-13	2	0.800	1.200
178	Aris Salonika	Gre	24	28	9	6	13	41	61	-20	0	0.857	1.464
179	Verona	Ita	23	16	8	6	2	23	15	8	1	1.438	1.438
180	FC Den Haag	Ned	23	20	10	2	8	34	27	7	1	1.150	1.700
181	Zeljeznicar Sarajevo	Yug	23	22	8	4	10	41	35	6	3	1.045	1.864
182	West Bromwich Albion	Eng	23	22	85	9	30	30	27	3	2	1.045	1.364
183	Atalanta	Ita	23	21	7	6	8	22	21	1	3	1.095	1.048
184	Lokomotiv Sofia	Bul	23	26	9	4	13	43	55	-12	1	0.885	1.654
185	Sochaux	Fra	22	20	7	6	7	32	11	10	2	1.100	1.600
186	Paris Saint-Germain	Fra	22	20	8	5	7	30	24	6	1	1.100	1.500
187	Wisla Kraków	Pol	22	20	8	5	7	34	32	2	1	1.100	1.700
188	Shamrock Rovers	Irl	22	38	7	8	23	37	66	-29	0	0.579	0.974
189	MSV Duisburg	FRG	21	14	8	3	3	38	19	19	2	1.500	2.714
190	Eintracht Braunschweig	FRG	21	21	8	4	9	34	25	9	1	1.000	1.619
191	AIK	Swe	21	22	7	7	8	37	32	5	0	0.955	1.682
192	Dundee	Sco	21	20	9	1	10	40	39	1	2	1.050	2.000
193	Groningen	Ned	21	20	9	3	8	30	29	1	0	1.050	1.500
194	KB Copenhagen	Den	21	35	7	6	22	58	94	-36	1	0.600	1.657
195	Karl-Marx-Stadt	GDR	20	26	7	5	14	37	40	-3	1	0.769	1.423
196	Trabzonspor	Tur	20	22	9	2	11	19	35	-16	0	0.909	0.864
197	Djurgården SIF	Swe	20	28	6	7	15	34	55	-21	1	0.714	1.214
198	Esbjerg FB	Den	20	24	7	6	11	22	45	-23	0	0.833	0.917
199	Jeunesse Esch	Lux	20	49	7	6	36	48	162	-114	0	0.408	0.980
200	Waterschei Thor	Bel	19	12	8	1	3	26	11	15	2	1.583	2.167
201	Åtvidaberg SFF	Swe	19	18	6	5	7	26	30	-4	2	1.056	1.444
202	Belenenses	Por	19	24	5	9	10	24	33	-9	0	0.792	1.000
203	Vejle BK	Den	19	24	7	4	13	29	43	-14	1	0.792	1.208
204	Lech Poznań	Pol	19	20	8	3	9	24	38	-14	0	0.950	1.200
205	Rosenborg BK	Nor	19	26	8	3	15	31	61	-30	0	0.731	1.192
206	Sliema Wanderers	Mlt	19	48	8	3	37	28	140	-112	0	0.396	0.583
207	Queen's Park Rangers	Eng	18	12	8	1	3	39	18	21	1	1.500	3.250
208	Bayer Uerdingen	FRG	18	14	7	2	5	33	14	19	2	1.286	2.357
209	Lens	Fra	18	18	7	4	7	32	26	6	0	1.000	1.778
210	Linzer ASK	Aut	18	23	7	4	12	20	43	-23	0	0.783	0.870
211	Besiktas	Tur	18	32	6	5	21	21	62	-41	1	0.563	0.656
212	Dundalk	Irl	18	34	6	6	22	23	83	-60	0	0.529	0.676
213	Burnley	Eng	17	12	6	3	3	24	13	11	2	1.417	2.000
214	Rapid Bucharest	Rom	17	22	7	2	13	24	38	-14	1	0.773	1.091
215	B 1903 Copenhagen	Den	17	26	6	5	15	31	50	-19	0	0.654	1.192
216	Öster SIF	Swe	17	28	7	3	18	29	50	-21	0	0.607	1.036
217	Auxerre	Fra	16	14	6	3	5	25	15	10	1	1.143	1.786
218	Victoria Bucharest	Rom	16	14	6	3	5	21	17	4	1	1.143	1.500
219	Sportul Studentesc Bucharest	Rom	16	20	6	4	10	20	31	-11	0	0.800	1.000
220	17 Nëntori Tirana	Alb	16	22	6	4	12	19	33	-14	0	0.727	0.864
221	HJK Helsinki	Fin	16	30	8	0	22	28	90	-62	0	0.533	0.933
222	TJ Vitkovice	Tch	15	12	5	4	3	12	12	0	1	1.250	1.000
223	Rijeka	Yug	15	16	5	4	7	16	17	-1	1	0.938	1.000
224	Lierse	Bel	15	18	6	2	10	27	30	-3	1	0.833	1.500

Pos'n	Club	Cnty	Pts	P	W	D	L	F	A	Diff	B	Pts/P	F/P
225	Gwardia Warsaw	Pol	15	17	6	3	8	18	28	-10	0	0.882	1.059
226	Gent	Bel	15	22	4	7	11	20	36	-16	0	0.682	0.909
227	Hannover 96	FRG	15	21	6	3	12	30	50	-20	0	0.714	1.429
228	Bohemians	Irl	15	26	4	7	15	18	49	-31	0	0.577	0.692
229	Haka Valkeakoski	Fin	14	28	5	4	19	27	73	-46	1	0.536	0.964
230	Larissa	Gre	14	12	5	3	4	12	11	1	1	1.167	1.000
231	Diósgyöri VTK	Hun	14	12	7	0	5	19	23	-4	0	1.167	1.583
232	Politehnica Timisoara	Rom	14	14	7	0	7	14	25	-11	0	1.000	1.000
233	Partizani Tirana	Alb	14	23	5	4	14	15	35	-20	0	0.609	0.652
234	Valur Reykjavik	Isl	14	32	3	8	21	18	92	-74	0	0.438	0.563
235	Sarajevo	Yug	13	14	4	5	5	29	30	-1	0	0.929	2.071
236	Slavia Prague	Tch	13	14	6	1	7	18	20	-2	0	0.929	1.286
237	Stal Mielec	Pol	13	16	4	4	8	11	14	-3	1	0.813	0.688
238	Sachsenning Zwickau	GDR	13	12	4	3	5	6	10	-4	2	1.083	0.500
239	Dinamo Tirana	Alb	13	20	4	5	11	10	24	-14	0	0.650	0.500
240	FC Kuusysi Lahti	Fin	13	20	4	4	12	16	37	-21	1	0.650	0.800
241	Lillestrøm SK	Nor	13	22	4	5	13	15	41	-26	0	0.591	0.682
242	TPS Turku	Fin	13	26	5	3	18	16	48	-32	0	0.500	0.615
243	IL Viking	Nor	13	26	4	5	17	20	56	-36	0	0.500	0.769
244	Apoel Nicosia	Cyp	13	36	4	5	27	28	109	-81	0	0.361	0.778
245	Hammarby IF	Swe	12	10	5	2	3	22	14	8	0	1.200	2.200
246	Real Valladolid	Esp	12	8	4	3	1	12	6	6	1	1.500	1.500
247	Randers Freja FC	Den	12	12	4	3	5	17	16	1	1	1.000	1.417
248	Lokomotiv Kosice	Tch	12	10	4	4	2	9	8	1	0	1.200	0.900
249	Lyngby BK	Den	12	14	4	4	6	18	19	-1	0	0.857	1.286
250	Union St-Gilloise	Bel	12	17	4	2	11	23	30	-7	2	0.706	1.353
251	Hibernians	Mlt	12	34	4	4	26	15	103	-88	0	0.353	0.441
252	Sheffield Wednesday	Eng	11	10	5	0	5	25	18	7	1	1.100	2.500
253	Las Palmas	Esp	11	12	4	3	5	20	17	3	0	0.917	1.667
254	Toulouse	Fra	11	10	5	1	4	16	15	1	0	1.100	1.600
255	St. Mirren	Sco	11	14	3	5	6	10	14	-4	0	0.786	0.714
256	Lazio	Ita	11	14	5	1	8	20	28	-8	0	0.786	1.429
257	Zenit Leningrad	URS	11	12	5	1	6	14	22	-8	0	0.917	1.167
258	RoPS Rovaniemi	Fin	11	12	3	4	5	5	15	-10	1	0.917	0.417
259	UT Arad	Rom	11	16	3	4	9	16	31	-15	1	0.688	1.000
260	Hvidovre IF	Den	11	18	3	5	10	22	39	-17	0	0.611	1.222
261	SFK Lyn	Nor	11	22	4	2	16	29	73	-44	1	0.500	1.318
262	Reipas Lahti	Fin	11	24	3	5	16	23	93	-70	0	0.458	0.958
263	Fram Reykjavik	Isl	11	32	5	1	26	16	91	-75	0	0.344	0.500
264	First Vienna	Aut	10	8	4	2	2	14	8	6	0	1.250	1.750
265	Swansea City	Wal	10	16	3	4	9	31	27	4	0	0.625	1.938
266	Leixões	Por	10	10	2	5	3	13	16	-3	1	1.000	1.300
267	Barreirense	Por	10	11	5	0	6	11	16	-5	0	0.909	1.000
268	Real Betis	Esp	10	12	3	3	6	10	15	-5	1	0.833	0.833
269	SK Brann	Nor	10	14	4	2	8	18	24	-6	0	0.714	1.286
270	GKS Katowice	Pol	10	16	4	2	10	17	25	-8	0	0.625	1.063
271	Sporting Braga	Por	10	12	5	0	7	14	23	-9	0	0.833	1.167
272	Kalmar FF	Swe	10	12	4	2	6	11	22	-11	0	0.833	0.917
273	B 1909 Odense	Den	10	16	3	3	10	27	44	-17	1	0.625	1.888
274	FK Skeid	Nor	10	16	3	4	9	14	35	-21	0	0.625	0.875
275	NK Zagreb	Yug	9	12	3	3	6	20	18	2	0	0.750	1.667
276	Montpellier	Fra	9	8	3	2	3	11	9	2	1	1.125	1.375
277	Bacau	Rom	9	8	3	2	3	12	11	1	1	1.125	1.500
278	Sporting Gijón	Esp	9	12	3	3	6	9	13	-4	0	0.750	0.750
279	Academica Coimbra	Por	9	10	3	2	5	5	10	-5	1	0.900	0.500
280	BK Frem	Den	9	16	4	1	11	17	43	-26	0	0.563	1.063
281	Waterford United	Irl	9	22	4	1	17	21	61	-40	0	0.409	0.955

Pos'n	Club	Cnty	Pts	P	W	D	L	F	A	Diff	B	Pts/P	F/P
282	Aris Bonnevoie	Lux	9	22	3	3	16	16	72	-56	0	0.409	0.727
283	Coleraine	Nir	9	26	2	5	19	27	85	-58	0	0.346	1.038
284	Borac Banja Luka	Yug	8	6	4	0	2	17	8	9	0	1.333	2.833
285	Newport County	Wal	8	6	2	3	1	12	3	9	1	1.333	2.000
286	DAC Dunajská Streda	Tch	8	8	4	0	4	16	11	5	0	1.000	2.000
287	Chernomorets Odessa	URS	8	10	3	2	5	10	13	-3	0	0.800	1.000
288	Hansa Rostock	GDR	8	10	4	0	6	15	19	-4	0	0.800	1.500
289	Roda JC	Ned	8	12	3	1	8	14	21	-7	1	0.667	1.167
290	Flamurtari Vlorë	Alb	8	14	3	2	9	14	22	-8	0	0.571	1.000
291	Panionios	Gre	8	11	4	0	7	11	22	-11	0	0.727	1.000
292	Eskisehirspor	Tur	8	14	3	2	9	13	26	-13	0	0.571	0.929
293	KuPS Kuopio	Fin	8	22	2	4	16	18	67	-49	0	0.364	0.818
294	IA Akranes	Isl	8	32	1	6	25	18	99	-81	0	0.250	0.563
295	Floriana	Mlt	8	32	2	4	26	15	126	-11	1	0.250	0.469
296	Vitesse	Ned	7	6	3	1	2	7	4	3	0	1.167	1.167
297	CSKA Moscow	URS	7	6	3	1	2	7	5	2	0	1.167	1.167
298	Dynamo Zilina	Tch	7	4	3	0	1	7	6	1	1	1.750	1.750
299	AB Copenhagen	Den	7	10	3	1	6	17	19	-2	0	0.700	1.700
300	Cagliari	Ita	7	10	3	1	6	10	12	-2	0	0.700	1.000
301	Fortuna Sittard	Ned	7	8	2	2	4	9	12	-3	1	0.875	1.125
302	Bursaspor	Tur	7	8	2	2	4	5	12	-7	1	0.875	0.625
303	Tatabánya	Hun	7	10	2	3	5	7	17	-10	0	0.700	0.700
304	Red Flag Brasov	Rom	7	11	3	1	7	14	25	-11	0	0.636	1.273
305	IK Start	Nor	7	14	3	1	10	13	29	-16	0	0.500	0.929
306	Zaglebie Sosnowiec	Pol	7	13	2	3	8	11	28	-17	0	0.538	0.846
307	Altay	Tur	7	12	2	3	7	14	32	-18	0	0.583	1.167
308	Vålerengen SIF	Nor	7	18	1	5	12	18	42	-24	0	0.389	1.000
309	Hamrun Spartans	Mlt	7	14	3	1	10	5	30	-25	0	0.500	0.357
310	SKA Rostov on Don	URS	6	4	3	0	1	6	2	4	0	1.500	1.500
311	Vllaznia Shkodër	Alb	6	6	3	0	3	9	6	3	0	1.000	1.500
312	Charleroi	Bel	6	4	3	0	1	8	5	3	0	1.500	2.000
313	Sunderland	Eng	6	4	3	0	1	5	3	2	0	1.500	1.250
314	Coventry City	Eng	6	4	3	0	1	9	8	1	0	1.500	2.250
315	St. Johnstone	Sco	6	6	3	0	3	8	8	0	0	1.000	1.333
316	Partick Thistle	Sco	6	6	3	0	3	10	11	-1	0	1.000	1.667
317	Beerschot	Bel	6	10	2	2	6	13	15	-2	0	0.600	1.300
318	Marek Stanke Dimitrov	Bul	6	6	3	0	3	8	10	-2	0	1.000	1.333
319	NAC Breda	Ned	6	6	2	2	2	5	8	-3	0	1.000	0.833
320	OFI Crete	Gre	6	6	3	0	3	5	8	-3	0	1.000	0.833
321	Universitatea Cluj	Rom	6	6	3	0	3	8	12	-4	0	1.000	1.333
322	La Chaux-de-Fonds	Sui	6	6	2	2	2	11	16	-5	0	1.000	1.833
323	SV Salzburg	Aut	6	8	3	0	5	11	17	-6	0	0.750	1.375
324	Athlone Town	Irl	6	8	1	4	3	11	19	-8	0	0.750	1.375
325	Portadown	Nir	6	8	2	2	4	8	27	-19	0	0.750	1.000
326	Iraklis	Gre	6	10	2	2	6	5	25	-20	0	0.600	0.500
327	B 1913 Odense	Den	6	14	3	0	11	24	46	-22	0	0.429	1.714
328	Drumcondra	Irl	6	13	3	0	10	12	46	-34	0	0.462	0.923
329	Union Luxembourg	Lux	6	30	2	2	26	12	114	-102	0	0.200	0.400
330	Stal Rzeszów	Pol	5	4	2	1	1	9	4	5	0	1.250	2.250
331	Wettingen	Sui	5	4	2	1	1	6	2	4	0	1.250	1.500
332	Leicester City	Eng	5	4	2	1	1	8	5	3	0	1.250	2.000
333	Zaria Voroshilovgrad	URS	5	4	2	1	1	3	1	2	0	1.250	0.750
334	TJ Gottwaldov	Tch	5	4	2	1	1	6	5	1	0	1.250	1.500
335	Zaglebie Walbrzych	Pol	5	4	2	1	1	6	5	1	0	1.250	1.500
336	Rouen	Fra	5	6	2	1	3	5	5	0	0	0.833	0.833
337	Stade Français	Fra	5	6	1	3	2	3	3	0	0	0.833	0.500
338	Chemie Leipzig	GDR	5	6	2	1	3	9	10	-1	0	0.833	1.500

Pos'n	Club	Cnty	Pts	P	W	D	L	F	A	Diff	B	Pts/P	F/P
339	Watford	Eng	5	6	2	1	3	10	12	-2	0	0.833	1.667
340	Spartak Hradec Králové	Tch	5	4	1	2	1	2	5	-3	1	1.250	0.500
341	Winterslag	Bel	5	6	2	1	3	5	9	-4	0	0.833	0.833
342	Panahaiki	Gre	5	4	2	1	1	4	9	-5	0	1.250	1.000
343	Bryne IL	Nor	5	6	2	1	3	5	11	-6	0	0.833	0.833
344	IF Elfsborg	Swe	5	8	1	3	4	8	15	-7	0	0.625	1.000
345	Vardar Skoplje	Yug	5	8	2	1	5	5	16	-11	0	0.625	0.625
346	Cork Hibernians	Irl	5	10	2	1	7	9	21	-12	0	0.500	0.900
347	Shelbourne	Irl	5	11	1	3	7	6	18	-12	0	0.455	0.545
348	Lucerne	Sui	5	10	1	3	6	6	19	-13	0	0.500	0.600
349	Metz	Fra	5	12	1	3	8	16	30	-14	0	0.417	1.333
350	Örgryte IS	Swe	5	10	1	3	6	12	28	-16	0	0.500	1.200
351	Fredrikstad FK	Nor	5	16	1	3	12	9	37	-28	0	0.313	0.563
352	Apollon Limassol	Cyp	5	12	1	3	8	8	43	-35	0	0.417	0.667
353	IBV Vestmannaeyjar	Isl	5	18	0	5	13	7	46	-39	0	0.278	0.389
354	Haladás	Hun	4	4	1	2	1	9	4	5	0	1.000	2.250
355	Békéscsaba	Hun	4	4	2	0	2	5	4	1	0	1.000	1.250
356	Osasuna	Esp	4	4	2	0	2	4	4	0	0	1.000	1.000
357	Corvinul Hunedoara	Rom	4	4	1	2	1	8	9	-1	0	1.000	2.000
358	Pécs Dózsa	Hun	4	6	2	0	4	6	7	-1	0	0.667	1.000
359	Laval	Fra	4	4	1	2	1	4	5	-1	0	1.000	1.000
360	Stahl Brandenburg	GDR	4	4	1	2	1	3	4	-1	0	1.000	0.750
361	Estrela Amadora	Por	4	4	1	2	1	3	4	-1	0	1.000	0.750
362	Akademik Sofia	Bul	4	6	2	0	4	8	10	-2	0	0.667	1.333
363	Stoke City	Eng	4	4	1	2	1	4	6	-2	0	1.000	1.000
364	Penigia	Ita	4	4	1	2	1	2	4	-2	0	1.000	0.500
365	Tatran Presov	Tch	4	6	1	2	3	12	15	-3	0	0.667	2.000
366	VSS Kosice	Tch	4	4	2	0	2	5	8	-3	0	1.000	1.250
367	Zhalgiris Vilnius	URS	4	6	2	0	4	7	11	-4	0	0.667	1.167
368	Bangor City	Wal	4	7	1	2	4	5	9	-4	0	0.571	0.714
369	Wismut Aue	GDR	4	6	1	2	3	4	8	-4	0	0.667	0.667
370	Haugar FC	Nor	4	4	1	2	1	3	7	-4	0	1.000	0.750
371	Spartak Varna	Bul	4	6	1	2	3	4	9	-5	0	0.667	0.667
372	Polonia Bytom	Pol	4	6	2	0	4	7	13	-6	0	0.667	1.167
373	Ilves Tampere	Fin	4	8	2	0	6	10	22	-12	0	0.500	1.250
374	St-Gallen	Sui	4	8	1	2	5	4	16	-12	0	0.500	0.500
375	Vöest Linz	Aut	4	8	1	2	5	5	18	-13	0	0.500	0.625
376	Molde FK	Nor	4	6	1	2	3	5	18	-13	0	0.667	0.833
377	Naestved IF	Den	4	8	1	2	5	5	21	-16	0	0.500	0.625
378	Derry City	Irl	4	11	1	2	8	9	31	-22	0	0.364	0.818
379	Pezoporikos Larnaca	Cyp	4	14	0	4	10	10	52	-42	0	0.286	0.714
380	IBK Keflavik	Isl	4	20	1	2	17	12	70	-58	0	0.200	0.600
381	Spora Luxembourg	Lux	4	19	2	0	17	12	87	-75	0	0.211	0.632
382	Nancy	Fra	3	4	1	1	2	7	6	1	0	0.750	1.750
383	Metallist Kharkov	URS	3	4	1	1	2	4	3	1	0	0.750	1.000
384	Halmstad SBK	Swe	3	4	1	1	2	4	6	-2	0	0.750	1.000
385	NEC Nijmegen	Ned	3	4	1	1	2	4	6	-2	0	0.750	1.000
386	Borough United	Wal	3	4	1	1	2	2	4	-2	0	0.750	0.500
387	Haarlem	Ned	3	4	1	1	2	6	9	-3	0	0.750	1.500
388	GAIS	Swe	3	4	1	1	2	6	10	-4	0	0.750	1.500
389	Szombierki Bytom	Pol	3	6	1	1	4	5	10	-5	0	0.500	0.833
390	Besa Kavajë	Alb	3	4	0	3	1	3	9	-6	0	0.750	0.750
391	IK Brage	Swe	3	6	1	1	4	8	15	-7	0	0.500	1.333
392	ASA Tîrgu Mures	Rom	3	6	1	1	4	4	13	-9	0	0.500	0.667
393	AaB Aalborg	Den	3	6	1	1	4	3	12	-9	0	0.500	0.500
394	Adanaspor	Tur	3	6	1	1	4	6	20	-14	0	0.500	1.000
395	MP Mikkeli	Fin	3	6	1	1	4	4	18	-14	0	0.500	0 667

Pos'n	Club	Cnty	Pts	P	W	D	L	F	A	Diff	B	Pts/P	F/P
396	Grazer AK	Aut	3	12	0	3	9	11	32	-21	0	0.250	0.917
397	AEL Limassol	Cyp	3	8	1	1	6	3	27	-24	0	0.375	0.375
398	Ards	Nir	3	8	1	1	6	9	35	-26	0	0.375	1.125
399	Strømgodset IF	Nor	3	8	1	1	6	6	33	-27	0	0.375	0.750
400	Red Boys Differdange	Lux	3	20	1	1	18	8	103	-95	0	0.150	0.400
401	Valletta	Mlt	3	28	1	1	26	9	123	-114	0	0.107	0.321
402	Cercle Bruges	Bel	2	2	1	0	1	4	4	0	0	1.000	2.000
403	BK Fremad Amager	Den	2	2	0	2	0	1	1	0	0	1.000	0.500
404	Angoulême	Fra	2	2	1	0	1	3	4	-1	0	1.000	1.500
405	Cesena	Ita	2	2	1	0	1	3	4	-1	0	1.000	1.500
406	Arka Gdynia	Pol	2	2	1	0	1	3	4	-1	0	1.000	1.500
407	Borovo	Yug	2	2	1	0	1	2	3	-1	0	1.000	1.000
408	Kickers Offenbach	FRG	2	2	1	0	1	2	3	-1	0	1.000	1.000
409	Jiul Petrosani	Rom	2	2	1	0	1	2	3	-1	0	1.000	1.000
410	Merthyr Tydfil	Wal	2	2	1	0	1	2	3	-1	0	1.000	1.000
411	Rad Belgrade	Yug	2	2	1	0	1	2	3	-1	0	1.000	1.000
412	Dunav Ruse	Bul	2	2	1	0	1	1	2	-1	0	1.000	0.500
413	Wuppertal	FRG	2	2	1	0	1	6	8	-2	0	1.000	3.000
414	Saarbrücken	FRG	2	2	1	0	1	5	7	-2	0	1.000	2.500
415	Viktoria Cologne	FRG	2	2	1	0	1	5	7	-2	0	1.000	2.500
416	Nîmes Olympique	Fra	2	4	1	0	3	4	6	-2	0	0.500	1.000
417	Castilla Madrid	Esp	2	2	1	0	1	4	6	-2	0	1.000	2.000
418	Sabadell	Esp	2	2	1	0	1	3	5	-2	0	1.000	1.500
419	Ikast FS	Den	2	4	1	0	3	3	5	-2	0	0.500	0.750
420	Chernomorets Bourgas	Bul	2	2	1	0	1	3	5	-2	0	1.000	1.500
421	Chaves	Por	2	4	1	0	3	6	9	-3	0	0.500	1.500
422	Stade Rennes	Fra	2	4	0	2	2	1	4	-3	0	0.500	0.250
423	Portimonense	Por	2	2	1	0	1	1	4	-3	0	1.000	0.500
424	Komló	Hun	2	2	1	0	1	4	8	-4	0	1.000	2.000
425	Sloboda Tuzla	Yug	2	2	1	0	1	4	8	-4	0	1.000	2.000
426	Sakaryaspor	Tur	2	4	1	0	3	3	7	-4	0	0.500	0.750
427	LKS Lódź	Pol	2	2	1	0	1	2	6	-4	0	1.000	1.000
428	Orduspor	Tur	2	2	1	0	1	2	6	-4	0	1.000	1.000
429	Pécsi MSC	Hun	2	4	1	0	3	1	5	-4	0	0.500	0.250
430	Krems	Aut	2	2	1	0	1	1	5	-4	0	1.000	0.500
431	Carrick Rangers	Nir	2	4	1	0	3	7	12	-5	0	0.500	1.750
432	B 93 Copenhagen	Den	2	4	1	0	3	5	10	-5	0	0.500	1.250
433	Gjøvik/Lyn	Nor	2	2	1	0	1	1	6	-5	0	1.000	0.500
434	Sedan	Fra	2	4	1	0	3	5	12	-7	0	0.500	1.250
435	SFK Bodø/Glimt	Nor	2	6	1	0	5	5	12	-7	0	0.333	0.833
436	CSU Galati	Rom	2	4	1	0	3	3	10	-7	0	0.500	0.750
437	Holbaek BIF	Den	2	4	1	0	3	2	10	-8	0	0.500	0.500
438	Landskrona BOIS	Swe	2	4	1	0	3	1	9	-8	0	0.500	0.250
439	Sliven	Bul	2	4	1	0	3	3	13	-10	0	0.500	0.750
440	Olimpija Ljubljana	Yug	2	6	0	2	4	6	20	-14	0	0.333	1.000
441	Alliance Dudelange	Lux	2	4	0	2	2	4	18	-14	0	0.500	1.000
442	IBA Akureyri	Isl	2	4	1	0	3	2	17	-15	0	0.500	0.500
443	Limerick	Irl	2	12	0	2	10	7	32	-25	0	0.167	0.583
444	Glenavon	Nir	2	12	0	2	10	6	32	-26	0	0.167	0.500
445	Mjøndalen IF	Nor	2	6	1	0	5	3	29	-26	0	0.333	0.500
446	Ballymena United	Nir	2	10	1	0	9	3	29	-26	0	0.200	0.300
447	Paralimni	Cyp	2	8	1	0	7	8	36	-28	0	0.250	1.000
448	Crusaders	Nir	2	10	0	2	8	5	37	-32	0	0.200	0.500
449	US Rumelange	Lux	2	8	1	0	7	3	48	-45	0	0.250	0.375
450	Avenir Beggen	Lux	2	22	1	0	21	6	102	-96	0	0.091	0.273
451	Csepel	Hun	1	2	0	1	1	3	4	-1	0	0.500	1.500
452	Karpaty Lvov	URS	1	2	0	1	1	3	4	-1	0	0.500	1.500

Pos'n	Club	Cnty	Pts	P	W	D	L	F	A	Diff	B	Pts/P	F/P
453	Angers	Fra	1	2	0	1	1	2	3	-1	0	0.500	1.000
454	Odra Opole	Pol	1	2	0	1	1	2	3	-1	0	0.500	1.000
455	Progresul Bucharest	Rom	1	2	0	1	1	1	2	-1	0	0.500	0.500
456	Lanerossi Vicenza	Ita	1	2	0	1	1	1	2	-1	0	0.500	0.500
457	Mersin Idmanyurdu	Tur	1	2	0	1	1	0	1	-1	0	0.500	0.000
458	UCD	Irl	1	2	0	1	1	0	1	-1	0	0.500	0.000
459	Tromsø IL	Nor	1	2	0	1	1	0	1	-1	0	0.500	0.000
460	Chemie Halle	GDR	1	2	0	1	1	3	5	-2	0	0.500	1.500
461	FH Hafnarfjördhur	Isl	1	2	0	1	1	3	5	-2	0	0.500	1.500
462	Salgótarján	Hun	1	2	0	1	1	2	4	-2	0	0.500	1.000
463	Chimia Râmnicu Vâlcea	Rom	1	2	0	1	1	2	4	-2	0	0.500	1.000
464	GKS Tychy	Pol	1	2	0	1	1	1	3	-2	0	0.500	0.500
465	Siófok	Hun	1	2	0	1	1	1	3	-2	0	0.500	0.500
466	Bray Wanderers	Irl	1	2	0	1	1	1	3	-2	0	0.500	0.500
467	Kastoria	Gre	1	2	0	1	1	0	2	-2	0	0.500	0.000
468	PSV Schwerin	GDR	1	2	0	1	1	0	2	-2	0	0.500	0.000
469	Baia Mare	Rom	1	2	0	1	1	2	5	-3	0	0.500	1.000
470	Etar Veliko Tarnovo	Bul	1	2	0	1	1	0	3	-3	0	0.500	0.000
471	Pogon Szczecin	Pol	1	4	0	1	3	3	7	-4	0	0.250	0.750
472	Rot-Weiss Essen	FRG	1	2	0	1	1	1	5	-4	0	0.500	0.500
473	Sigma Olomouc	Tch	1	2	0	1	1	1	5	-4	0	0.500	0.500
474	Willem II	Ned	1	2	0	1	1	2	7	-5	0	0.500	1.000
475	KTP Kotka	Fin	1	2	0	1	1	0	5	-5	0	0.500	0.000
476	Lugano	Sui	1	4	0	1	3	1	7	-6	0	0.250	0.250
477	Home Farm	Irl	1	2	0	1	1	1	7	-6	0	0.500	0.500
478	Cork Celtic	Irl	1	4	0	1	3	2	10	-8	0	0.250	0.500
479	Aarau	Sui	1	4	0	1	3	2	11	-9	0	0.250	0.500
480	Distillery	Nir	1	4	0	1	3	4	15	-11	0	0.250	1.000
481	Ankaragücü	Tur	1	6	0	1	5	1	13	-12	0	0.167	0.167
482	OB Odense	Den	1	8	0	1	7	7	21	-14	0	0.125	0.875
483	OPS Oulu	Fin	1	4	0	1	3	2	19	-17	0	0.250	0.500
484	St. Patrick's Athletic	Irl	1	8	0	1	7	6	26	-20	0	0.125	0.750
485	Finn Harps	Irl	1	8	0	1	7	5	37	-32	0	0.125	0.625
486	Anorthosis Famagusta	Cyp	1	8	0	1	7	2	35	-33	0	0.125	0.250
487	Progrès Niedercorn	Lux	1	10	0	1	9	1	37	-36	0	0.100	0.100
488	Olympiakos Nicosia	Cyp	1	10	0	1	9	5	57	-52	0	0.100	0.500
489	Tasmania Berlin	FRG	0	2	0	0	2	3	5	-2	0	0.000	1.500
490	Racing Club Paris	Fra	0	2	0	0	2	2	4	-2	0	0.000	1.000
491	Union Teplice	Tch	0	2	0	0	2	2	4	-2	0	0.000	1.000
492	Napredak Krusevac	Yug	0	2	0	0	2	0	2	-2	0	0.000	0.000
493	Zaglebie Lubin	Pol	0	2	0	0	2	0	2	-2	0	0.000	0.000
494	Tresnjevka Zagreb	Yug	0	2	0	0	2	1	4	-3	0	0.000	0.500
495	Gençlerbirligi	Tur	0	2	0	0	2	1	4	-3	0	0.000	0.500
496	Flacara Moreni	Rom	0	2	0	0	2	1	4	-3	0	0.000	0.500
497	Wiener Neustadt	Aut	0	2	0	0	2	0	3	-3	0	0.000	0.000
498	Celta Vigo	Esp	0	2	0	0	2	0	3	-3	0	0.000	0.000
499	Dukla Banská Bystrica	Tch	0	2	0	0	2	3	7	-4	0	0.000	1.500
500	SK Frigg	Nor	0	2	0	0	2	2	6	-4	0	0.000	1.000
501	Plastika Nitra	Tch	0	2	0	0	2	1	5	-4	0	0.000	0.500
502	Boluspor	Tur	0	2	0	0	2	0	4	-4	0	0.000	0.000
503	NEA Salamina Famagusta	Cyp	0	2	0	0	2	0	5	-5	0	0.000	0.000
504	Morton	Sco	0	2	0	0	2	3	9	-6	0	0.000	1.500
505	Botev Vratsa	Bul	0	2	0	0	2	2	8	-6	0	0.000	1.000
506	Skoda Plzen	Tch	0	2	0	0	2	1	7	-6	0	0.000	0.500
507	Køge BK	Den	0	2	0	0	2	1	7	-6	0	0.000	0.500
508	Pirin Blagoevgrad	Bul	0	2	0	0	2	1	7	-6	0	0.000	0.500
509	IF Sarpsborg	Nor	0	2	0	0	2	0	6	-6	0	0.000	0.000

Pos'n	Club	Cnty	Pts	P	W	D	L	F	A	Diff	B	Pts/P	F/P
510	Labinoti Elbasan	Alb	0	2	0	0	2	0	6	-6	0	0.000	0.000
511	Cork City	Irl	0	2	0	0	2	0	6	-6	0	0.000	0.000
512	Swift Hesperange	Lux	0	2	0	0	2	0	6	-6	0	0.000	0.000
513	Vanløse IF	Den	0	2	0	0	2	1	8	-7	0	0.000	0.500
514	Go Ahead Eagles	Ned	0	2	0	0	2	0	7	-7	0	0.000	0 000
515	Akritas Morphou	Cyp	0	2	0	0	2	0	7	-7	0	0 000	0.000
516	Galway United	Irl	0	4	0	0	4	4	12	-8	0	0.000	1.000
517	Lechia Gdańsk	Pol	0	2	0	0	2	2	10	-8	0	0.000	1.000
518	Cliftonville	Nir	0	2	0	0	2	0	8	-8	0	0.000	0.000
519	Apolonia Fier	Alb	0	2	0	0	2	0	8	-8	0	0.000	0.000
520	Gzira United	Mlt	0	2	0	0	2	0	9	-9	0	0.000	0.000
521	Moss FK	Nor	0	6	0	0	6	5	15	-10	0	0.000	0.833
522	Fola Esch	Lux	0	2	0	0	2	1	11	-10	0	0.000	0.500
523	Sligo Rovers	Irl	0	4	0	0	4	0	10	-10	0	0.000	0.000
524	B 1901 Nykobing	Den	0	4	0	0	4	6	11	-11	0	0.000	1.500
525	HIFK Helsinki	Fin	0	6	0	0	6	5	16	-11	0	0.000	0.833
526	Marsa	Mlt	0	2	0	0	2	0	11	-11	0	0.000	0.000
527	Alki Larnaca	Cyp	0	2	0	0	2	0	12	-12	0	0.000	0.000
528	Drogheda United	Irl	0	2	0	0	2	0	14	-14	0	0.000	0.000
529	Anorthosis Nicosia	Cyp	0	2	0	0	2	0	16	-16	0	0.000	0.000
530	HPS Helsinki	Fin	0	4	0	0	4	2	19	-11	0	0.000	0.500
531	KPV Kokkola	Fin	0	4	0	0	4	2	23	-21	0	0.000	0.500
532	Jeunesse Hautcharage	Lux	0	2	0	0	2	0	21	-21	0	0.000	0.000
533	EPA Larnaca	Cyp	0	6	0	0	6	0	22	-22	0	0.000	0.000
534	Vikingur Reykjavik	Isl	0	8	0	0	8	3	27	-24	0	0.000	0.315
535	Zurrieq	Mlt	0	6	0	0	6	1	27	-26	0	0.000	0.167
536	Stade Dudelange	Lux	0	4	0	0	4	1	32	-31	0	0 000	0.250
537	Rabat Ajax	Mlt	0	8	0	0	8	0	40	-40	0	0.000	0.000
538	KR Reykjavik	Isl	0	14	0	0	14	10	66	-56	0	0.000	0.714
	Total		**16325**	**14946**	**6041**	**2864**	**6041**	**22424**	**22424**	**0**	**1379**	**1.092**	**3.001**

Above: Dinamo Tbilisi's Georgi Tawadse is challenged by Carl Zeiss Jena defender Wolfgang Schilling during the 1980-81 European Cup Winners' Cup final in Düsseldorf. Tbilisi won 2-1.

Club Performance by Points

1981-82 to 1990-91

Pos'n	Club	Cnty	Pts	P	W	D	L	F	A	Diff	B	Pts/P	F/P
1	Juventus	Ita	125	13	49	11	13	155	56	99	16	1.712	2.123
2	Bayern Munich	FRG	120	76	43	17	16	154	72	82	17	1.579	2.026
3	Anderlecht	Bel	118	77	44	14	19	132	76	56	16	1.532	1.714
4	Real Madrid	Esp	112	77	40	15	22	146	88	58	17	1.455	1.896
5	Barcelona	Esp	105	70	31	15	18	119	63	56	16	1.500	1.700
6	Inter Milan	Ita	91	70	33	16	21	101	63	38	9	1.300	1.443
7	Dundee United	Sco	85	64	31	16	17	102	62	40	7	1.328	1.594
8	IFK Gothenburg	Swe	83	52	30	13	9	103	50	53	10	1.596	1.981
9	Benfica	Por	82	51	30	11	16	86	44	42	11	1.439	1.509
10	FC Porto	Por	77	54	31	7	16	97	55	42	8	1.426	1.796
11	Spartak Moscow	URS	75	56	30	12	14	91	60	31	3	1.339	1.625
12	Cologne	FRG	72	52	28	10	14	94	51	43	6	1.385	1.808
13	Sporting Lisbon	Por	68	54	24	15	15	96	51	45	5	1.259	1.778
14	Red Star Belgrade	Yug	67	49	25	11	13	102	59	43	6	1.367	2.082
15	Aberdeen	Sco	66	47	24	12	11	73	40	33	6	1.404	1.553
16	Roma	Ita	64	47	25	6	16	65	41	24	8	1.362	1.383
17	Dinamo Kiev	URS	63	43	21	13	9	75	37	38	8	1.465	1.744
18	Girondins Bordeaux	Fra	63	48	23	12	13	62	47	15	5	1.313	1.292
19	Rapid Vienna	Aut	60	49	24	7	18	95	70	25	5	1.224	1.939
20	Hamburg	FRG	59	43	24	4	15	75	45	30	7	1.372	1.744
21	Austria Vienna	Aut	56	48	19	14	15	85	67	18	4	1.167	1.771
22	Liverpool	Eng	54	30	21	4	5	61	20	41	8	1.800	2.033
23	Werder Bremen	FRG	53	42	19	10	13	71	46	25	5	1.262	1.690
24	Steaua Bucharest	Rom	52	38	18	8	12	61	41	20	8	1.368	1.605
25	Dinamo Bucharest	Rom	51	48	19	8	21	67	52	15	5	1.063	1.396
26	Lokomotive Leipzig	GDR	50	39	18	10	11	59	36	23	4	1.282	1.513
27	Tottenham Hotspur	Eng	48	32	17	8	7	67	24	43	6	1.500	2.094
28	Dynamo Dresden	GDR	48	38	18	7	13	69	54	15	5	1.263	1.816
29	Hajduk Split	Yug	48	40	20	5	15	67	52	15	3	1.200	1.615
30	Rangers	Sco	46	38	19	7	12	68	43	25	1	1.211	1.189
31	AC Milan	Ita	46	32	15	9	8	46	22	24	7	1.438	1.438
32	Olympique Marseille	Fra	45	25	16	6	3	47	17	30	7	1.800	1.880
33	PSV Eindhoven	Ned	44	41	14	11	16	56	36	20	5	1.073	1.366
34	Sampdoria	Ita	44	28	15	7	6	39	21	18	7	1.571	1.393
35	CSKA Sofia	Bul	44	42	16	7	19	57	62	-5	5	1.048	1.357
36	Amsterdam, Ajax	P-B	43	34	16	5	13	59	33	26	6	1.265	1.735
37	KV Mechelen	Bel	43	25	15	7	3	37	14	23	6	1.720	1.480
38	Manchester United	Eng	43	27	14	9	4	42	22	20	6	1.593	1.556
39	Universitatea Craiova	Rom	43	38	18	4	16	43	40	3	3	1.132	1.132
40	Neuchâtel Xamax	Sui	38	32	13	10	9	49	37	12	2	1.188	1.531
41	Napoli	Ita	38	32	11	13	8	35	31	4	3	1.188	1.094
42	Partizan Belgrade	Yug	36	34	16	3	15	60	51	9	1	1.059	1.765
43	Sparta Prague	Tch	36	32	14	6	12	51	47	4	2	1.125	1.594
44	Standard Liège	Bel	34	25	13	5	7	50	30	20	3	1.360	2.000
45	Aston Villa	Eng	34	23	13	4	6	39	20	19	4	1.478	1.696
46	Dinamo Minsk	URS	34	26	12	7	7	41	25	16	3	1.308	1.577
47	Bayer Leverkusen	FRG	34	24	11	9	4	31	16	15	3	1.417	1.292
48	Legia Warsaw	Pol	33	28	10	10	8	36	31	5	3	1.179	1.286
49	Dynamo Berlin	GDR	33	32	13	6	13	44	45	-1	1	1.031	1.375
50	Bor. Mönchengladbach	FRG	32	26	12	6	8	45	36	9	2	1.231	1.731
51	VFB Stuttgart	FRG	32	28	10	9	9	40	33	7	3	1.143	1.429
52	Real Sociedad	Esp	32	26	11	7	8	28	22	6	3	1.231	1.077
53	Dukla Prague	Tch	32	30	10	10	10	36	36	0	2	1.061	1.200

Pos'n	Club	Cnty	Pts	P	W	D	L	F	A	Diff	B	Pts/P	F/P
54	Club Bruges	Bel	32	34	12	6	16	53	56	-3	2	0.941	1.559
55	Torpedo Moscow	URS	31	22	12	5	5	39	25	14	2	1.409	1.773
56	Bohemians Prague	Tch	31	28	12	5	11	42	33	9	2	1.107	1.500
57	Atlético Madrid	Esp	31	25	13	2	10	29	30	-1	3	1.240	1.160
58	Panathinaikos	Gre	31	34	11	6	17	43	61	-18	3	0.912	1.265
59	Kaiserslautern	FRG	30	22	13	1	8	41	22	19	3	1.364	1.864
60	FC Liège	Bel	30	24	13	2	9	40	24	16	2	1.250	1.667
61	Brøndby IF	Den	30	24	10	7	7	33	24	9	3	1.250	1.375
62	Malmö FF	Swe	30	30	10	9	11	40	35	5	1	1.000	1.333
63	Celtic	Sco	29	30	12	5	13	41	36	5	0	0.967	1.367
64	Valencia	Esp	29	24	10	7	7	31	26	5	2	1.208	1.292
65	Monaco	Fra	29	28	8	10	10	34	32	2	3	1.036	1.214
66	Feyenoord	Ned	28	26	12	4	10	37	33	4	0	1.077	1.423
67	Olympiakos Pireus	Gre	28	30	10	8	12	32	35	-3	0	0.933	1.067
68	Widzew Lódź	Pol	27	26	10	5	11	34	36	-2	2	1.038	1.308
69	FC Tirol	Aut	27	26	11	3	12	42	53	-11	2	1.038	1.615
70	Fiorentina	Ita	26	20	8	7	5	16	17	-1	3	1.300	0.800
71	Honvéd	Hun	26	24	12	2	10	34	46	-12	0	1.083	1.417
72	Servette	Sui	25	22	10	5	7	37	20	17	0	1.136	1.682
73	Beveren	Bel	25	22	11	3	8	38	23	15	0	1.136	1.727
74	Dnepr Dnepropetrovsk	URS	25	24	8	7	9	27	28	-1	2	1.042	1.125
75	Verona	Ita	23	16	8	6	2	23	15	8	1	1.438	1.438
76	Athletic Bilbao	Esp	23	22	10	3	9	30	28	2	0	1.045	1.364
77	Galatasaray	Tur	23	22	8	5	9	25	31	-6	2	1.045	1.136
78	Velez Mostar	Yug	22	18	8	6	4	33	25	8	0	1.222	1.833
79	Paris Saint-Germain	Fra	22	20	8	5	7	30	24	6	1	1.100	1.500
80	Borussia Dortmund	FRG	22	18	10	2	6	23	17	6	0	1.222	1.278
81	Videoton	Hun	22	20	8	3	9	23	24	-1	3	1.100	1.150
82	Vitória Guimarães	Por	22	20	9	3	8	20	25	-5	1	1.100	1.000
83	Atalanta	Ita	21	18	6	6	6	18	15	3	3	1.167	1.000
84	Groningen	Ned	21	20	9	3	8	30	29	1	0	1.050	1.500
85	Dinamo Moscow	URS	20	14	7	4	3	22	11	11	2	1.429	1.571
86	Español	Esp	20	12	7	3	2	17	7	10	3	1.667	1.417
87	Dinamo Tbilisi	URS	20	16	7	4	5	20	15	5	2	1.250	1.250
88	Heart of Midlothian	Sco	20	16	8	3	5	22	19	3	1	1.250	1.375
89	Everton	Eng	19	9	7	2	0	16	2	14	3	2.111	1.778
90	Nottingham Forest	Eng	19	12	7	3	2	12	7	5	2	1.583	1.000
91	Waregem	Bel	19	14	7	3	4	24	20	4	2	1.357	1.714
92	Admira Wacker	Aut	19	16	8	2	6	17	17	0	1	1.188	1.063
93	Lech Poznań	Pol	19	18	8	3	7	22	28	-6	0	1.056	1.222
94	Bayer Uerdingen	FRG	18	14	7	2	5	33	14	19	2	1.286	2.357
95	Eintracht Frankfurt	FRG	18	14	7	2	5	17	14	3	2	1.286	1.214
96	Banik Ostrava	Tch	18	20	7	4	9	30	28	2	0	0.900	1.500
97	Radnicki Nis	Yug	18	16	7	2	7	23	21	2	2	1.125	1.438
98	Sion	Sui	18	18	7	3	8	24	33	-9	1	1.000	1.333
99	Levski Sofia	Bul	18	24	6	5	13	27	44	-17	1	0.750	1.125
100	Grasshoppers Zürich	Sui	17	24	6	4	14	25	38	-13	1	0.708	1.042
101	Omonia Nicosia	Cyp	17	26	7	3	16	31	47	-16	0	0.654	1.192
102	Auxerre	Fra	16	14	6	3	5	25	15	10	1	1.143	1.786
103	Torino	Ita	16	12	5	5	2	19	11	8	1	1.333	1.583
104	Victoria Bucharest	Rom	16	14	6	3	5	21	17	4	1	1.143	1.500
105	Antwerp	Bel	16	16	5	5	6	28	26	2	1	1.000	1.150
106	Real Zaragoza	Esp	15	12	5	3	4	15	13	2	2	1.250	1.250
107	AGF Aarhus	Den	15	16	6	2	8	21	20	1	1	0.938	1.313
108	TJ Vitkovice	Tch	15	12	5	4	3	12	12	0	1	1.250	1.000
109	PAOK Salonika	Gre	15	16	5	5	6	14	17	-3	0	0.938	0.875
110	Ujpesti Dózsa	Hun	15	18	6	2	10	20	28	-8	1	0.833	1.111

Pos'n	Club	Cnty	Pts	P	W	D	L	F	A	Diff	B	Pts/P	F/P
111	Waterschei Thor	Bel	14	8	6	0	2	19	9	10	2	1.750	2.375
112	Zeljeznicar Sarajevo	Yug	14	10	5	2	3	18	11	1	2	1.400	1.800
113	Trakia Plovdiv	Bul	14	16	5	4	1	29	26	3	0	0.875	1.813
114	Larissa	Gre	14	12	5	3	4	12	11	1	1	1.167	1.000
115	Nantes	Fra	14	14	4	5	5	21	24	-3	1	1.000	1.500
116	Sportul Studentesc Bucharest	Rom	14	16	5	4	7	16	24	-8	0	0.875	1.000
117	HJK Helsinki	Fin	14	18	7	0	11	17	45	-28	0	0.778	0.944
118	Inter Bratislava	Tch	13	14	6	1	7	30	23	1	0	0.929	2.143
119	Seville	Esp	13	12	5	3	4	17	15	2	0	1.083	1.417
120	Sturm Graz	Aut	13	14	3	6	5	13	14	-1	1	0.929	0.929
121	17 Nëntori Tirana	Alb	13	16	6	1	9	16	24	-8	0	0.813	1.000
122	Glentoran	Nir	13	22	3	7	12	18	36	-18	0	0.591	0.818
123	FC Kuusysi Lahti	Fin	13	20	4	4	12	16	37	-21	1	0.650	0.800
124	Hammarby IF	Swe	12	10	5	2	3	22	14	8	0	1.200	2.200
125	Real Valladolid	Esp	12	8	4	3	1	12	6	6	1	1.500	1.500
126	Lyngby BK	Den	12	14	4	4	6	18	19	-1	0	0.857	1.286
127	Carl Zeiss Jena	GDR	12	16	4	4	8	22	26	-4	0	0.750	1.375
128	Ferencváros	Hun	12	16	4	4	8	18	24	-6	0	0.750	1.125
129	Linzer ASK	Aut	12	12	5	2	5	9	15	-6	0	1.000	0.750
130	Dinamo Tirana	Alb	12	16	4	4	8	9	19	-10	0	0.750	0.563
131	Rába ETO	Hun	12	14	5	2	7	22	33	-11	0	0.857	1.571
132	Lokeren	Bel	11	12	3	5	4	14	14	0	0	0.917	1.167
133	Wrexham	Wal	11	12	4	3	5	14	14	0	0	0.917	1.167
134	Zenit Leningrad	URS	11	12	5	1	6	14	22	-8	0	0.917	1.167
135	RoPS Rovaniemi	Fin	11	12	3	4	5	5	15	-10	1	0.917	0.417
136	Besiktas	Tur	11	18	3	4	11	14	33	-19	1	0.611	0.778
137	Shakhtyor Donetsk	URS	10	6	4	1	1	15	8	7	1	1.667	2.500
138	First Vienna	Aut	10	8	4	2	2	14	8	6	0	1.250	1.750
139	AZ'67 Alkmaar	Ned	10	8	4	2	2	11	9	2	0	1.250	1.375
140	Bologna	Ita	10	8	4	1	3	10	9	1	1	1.250	1.250
141	Sparta Rotterdam	Ned	10	10	3	4	3	14	15	-1	0	1.000	1.400
142	Gent	Bel	10	12	3	4	5	14	19	-5	0	0.833	1.167
143	GKS Katowice	Pol	10	14	4	2	8	15	21	-6	0	0.714	1.071
144	TPS Turku	Fin	10	14	4	2	8	10	17	-7	0	0.714	0.714
145	Magdeburg	GDR	10	12	4	2	6	8	15	-7	0	0.833	0.667
146	Haka Valkeakoski	Fin	10	12	3	3	6	14	22	-8	1	0.833	1.167
147	Trabzonspor	Tur	10	12	4	2	6	9	21	-12	0	0.833	0.750
148	Linfield	Nir	10	20	1	8	11	18	37	-19	0	0.500	0.900
149	Toulouse	Fra	9	8	4	1	3	12	10	2	0	1.125	1.500
150	Montpellier	Fra	9	8	3	2	3	11	9	2	1	1.125	1.375
151	Lens	Fra	9	8	3	3	2	10	10	0	0	1.125	1.250
152	Lokomotiv Sofia	Bul	9	8	3	3	2	12	14	-2	0	1.125	1.500
153	Belenenses	Por	9	8	3	3	2	4	6	-2	0	1.125	0.500
154	Dinamo Zagreb	Yug	9	10	3	3	4	8	11	-3	0	0.900	0.800
155	Boavista	Por	9	12	4	1	7	15	19	-4	0	0.750	1.250
156	Górnik Zabrze	Pol	9	14	3	3	8	19	25	-6	0	0.643	1.357
157	FC Zürich	Sui	9	10	3	3	4	12	19	-7	0	0.900	1.200
158	Fenerbahçe	Tur	9	14	4	1	9	14	27	-13	0	0.643	1.000
159	AEK Athenes	Gre	9	14	4	1	9	11	27	-16	0	0.643	0.768
160	Fram Reykjavik	Isl	9	20	4	1	15	11	50	-38	0	0.450	0.600
161	Swansea City	Wal	8	12	3	2	7	27	15	12	0	0.667	2.250
162	Sochaux	Fra	8	6	3	2	1	15	3	12	0	1.333	2.500
163	AIK	Swe	8	8	3	2	3	17	9	8	0	1.000	2.125
164	DAC Dunajská Streda	Tch	8	8	4	0	4	16	11	5	0	1.000	2.000
165	Sarajevo	Yug	8	8	3	2	3	18	18	0	0	1.000	2.250
166	Roda JC	Ned	8	8	3	1	4	8	10	-2	1	1.000	1.000
167	Utrecht	Ned	8	10	3	2	5	11	17	-6	0	0.800	1.100

Pos'n	Club	Cnty	Pts	P	W	D	L	F	A	Diff	B	Pts/P	F/P
168	Flamurtari Vlorë	Alb	8	14	3	2	9	14	22	-8	0	0.571	1.000
169	Vitesse	Ned	7	6	3	1	2	7	4	3	0	1.167	1.167
170	Southampton	Eng	7	8	1	5	2	8	9	-1	0	0.875	1.000
171	St. Mirren	Sco	7	10	2	3	5	8	11	-3	0	0.700	0.800
172	IFK Norrköping	Swe	7	8	2	3	3	6	9	-3	0	0.875	0.750
173	Young Boys Berne	Sui	7	8	3	0	5	7	12	-5	1	0.875	0.875
174	Shamrock Rovers	Irl	7	12	2	3	7	9	15	-6	0	0.583	0.750
175	Kalmar FF	Swe	7	8	3	1	4	7	16	-9	0	0.875	0.875
176	Tatabánya	Hun	7	10	2	3	5	7	17	-10	0	0.700	0.700
177	Lillestrøm SK	Nor	7	14	2	3	9	11	30	-19	0	0.500	0.786
178	Hamrun Spartans	Mlt	7	14	3	1	10	5	30	-25	0	0.500	0.357
179	Queen's Park Rangers	Eng	6	4	3	0	1	13	6	7	0	1.500	3.250
180	SKA Rostov on Don	URS	6	4	3	0	1	6	2	4	0	1.500	1.500
181	Wisla Kraków	Pol	6	6	3	0	3	10	11	-1	0	1.000	1.667
182	Arsenal	Eng	6	6	3	0	3	9	10	-1	0	1.000	1.500
183	Chernomorets Odessa	URS	6	8	2	2	4	9	10	-1	0	0.750	1.125
184	Fortuna Sittard	Ned	6	6	2	1	3	6	1	-1	1	1.000	1.000
185	OFI Crete	Gre	6	6	3	0	3	5	8	-3	0	1.000	0.833
186	Politehnica Timisoara	Rom	6	6	3	0	3	6	13	-7	0	1.000	1.000
187	Rosenborg BK	Nor	6	8	2	2	4	6	17	-11	0	0.750	0.750
188	Valur Reykjavik	Isl	6	12	2	2	8	6	29	-23	0	0.500	0.500
189	Wettingen	Sui	5	4	2	1	1	6	2	4	0	1.250	1.500
190	Hibernian	Sco	5	4	2	1	1	4	1	3	0	1.250	1.000
191	Aris Salonika	Gre	5	4	2	1	1	9	1	2	0	1.250	2.250
192	Rijeka	Yug	5	6	2	1	3	8	8	0	0	0.833	1.333
193	Djurgården SIF	Swe	5	6	1	3	2	8	8	0	0	0.833	1.333
194	Lausanne-Sports	Sui	5	6	2	1	3	9	10	-1	0	0.833	1.500
195	Watford	Eng	5	6	2	1	3	10	12	-2	0	0.833	1.667
196	Karl-Marx-Stadt	GDR	5	8	2	1	5	9	12	-3	0	0.625	1.125
197	Saint-Etienne	Fra	5	6	1	3	2	5	8	-3	0	0.833	0.833
198	Winterslag	Bel	5	6	2	1	3	5	9	-4	0	0.833	0.833
199	KB Copenhagen	Den	5	6	1	3	2	5	10	-5	0	0.833	0.833
200	Bryne IL	Nor	5	6	2	1	3	5	11	-6	0	0.833	0.833
201	Lucerne	Sui	5	8	1	3	4	4	10	-6	0	0.625	0.500
202	Vålerengen SIF	Nor	5	10	1	3	6	9	20	-11	0	0.500	0.900
203	IL Viking	Nor	5	10	1	3	6	6	20	-14	0	0.500	0.600
204	Apollon Limassol	Cyp	5	8	1	3	4	7	28	-21	0	0.625	0.875
205	Vllaznia Shkodër	Alb	4	4	2	0	2	6	2	4	0	1.000	1.500
206	Bastia	Fra	4	4	1	2	1	7	4	3	0	1.000	1.750
207	Arges Pitesti	Rom	4	4	1	2	1	7	6	1	0	1.000	1.750
208	FC Den Haag	Ned	4	4	2	0	2	5	4	1	0	1.000	1.250
209	Békéscsaba	Hun	4	4	2	0	2	5	4	1	0	1.000	1.250
210	Osasuna	Esp	4	4	2	0	2	4	4	0	0	1.000	1.000
211	Corvinul Hunedoara	Rom	4	4	1	2	1	8	9	-1	0	1.000	2.000
212	Laval	Fra	4	4	1	2	1	4	5	-1	0	1.000	1.000
213	Stahl Brandenburg	GDR	4	4	1	2	1	3	4	-1	0	1.000	0.750
214	Estrela Amadora	Por	4	4	1	2	1	3	4	-1	0	1.000	0.750
215	Slovan Bratislava	Tch	4	4	2	0	2	5	7	-2	0	1.000	1.250
216	Zhalgiris Vilnius	URS	4	6	2	0	4	1	11	-4	0	0.667	1.167
217	Vorwärts Frankfurt/Oder	GDR	4	6	2	0	4	5	9	-4	0	0.667	0.833
218	Wismut Aue	GDR	4	6	1	2	3	4	8	-4	0	0.667	0.667
219	Bohemians	Irl	4	6	1	2	3	7	12	-5	0	0.667	1.167
220	Slask Wroclaw	Pol	4	6	1	2	3	4	11	-7	0	0.667	0.667
221	Metz	Fra	4	8	1	2	5	11	20	-9	0	0.500	1.375
222	Öster SIF	Swe	4	8	2	0	6	3	16	-13	0	0.500	0.375
223	Apoel Nicosia	Cyp	4	12	1	2	9	13	33	-20	0	0.333	1.083
224	IA Akranes	Isl	4	14	0	4	10	8	41	-33	0	0.286	0.571

Pos'n	Club	Cnty	Pts	P	W	D	L	F	A	Diff	B	Pts/P	F/P
225	Jeunesse Esch	Lux	4	14	1	2	11	8	48	-40	0	0.286	0.571
226	Vasas SC	Hun	3	6	1	1	4	13	10	3	0	0.500	2.167
227	Metallist Kharkov	URS	3	4	1	1	2	4	3	1	0	0.750	1.000
228	Cardiff City	Wal	3	4	1	1	2	5	6	-1	0	0.750	1.250
229	NEC Nijmegen	Ned	3	4	1	1	2	4	6	-2	0	0.750	1.000
230	Spartak Varna	Bul	3	4	1	1	2	2	4	-2	0	0.750	0.500
231	Haarlem	Ned	3	4	1	1	2	6	9	-3	0	0.750	1.500
232	Ipswich Town	Eng	3	4	1	1	2	5	8	-3	0	0.750	1.250
233	Sporting Gijón	Esp	3	4	1	1	2	2	5	-3	0	0.750	0.500
234	Iraklis	Gre	3	4	1	1	2	1	4	-3	0	0.750	0.250
235	B 1903 Copenhagen	Den	3	4	1	1	2	2	8	-6	0	0.750	0.500
236	IK Brage	Swe	3	6	1	1	4	8	15	-7	0	0.500	1.333
237	MTK-VM	Hun	3	6	1	1	4	5	13	-8	0	0.500	0.833
238	Naestved IF	Den	3	4	1	1	2	3	11	-8	0	0.750	0.750
239	Vardar Skoplje	Yug	3	6	1	1	4	3	11	-8	0	0.500	0.500
240	Vejle BK	Den	3	6	1	1	4	4	13	-9	0	0.500	0.667
241	AEL Limassol	Cyp	3	6	1	1	4	3	15	-12	0	0.500	0.500
242	Slavia Sofia	Bul	3	6	1	1	4	8	21	-13	0	0.500	1.333
243	Coleraine	Nir	3	10	0	3	7	4	24	-20	0	0.300	0.400
244	Dundalk	Irl	3	12	1	1	10	7	28	-21	0	0.250	0.583
245	Cercle Bruges	Bel	2	2	1	0	1	4	4	0	0	1.000	2.000
246	CSKA Moscow	URS	2	2	1	0	1	2	2	0	0	1.000	1.000
247	IF Elfsborg	Swe	2	2	0	2	0	2	2	0	0	1.000	1.000
248	Vojvodina Novi Sad	Yug	2	2	1	0	1	2	2	0	0	1.000	1.000
249	Stal Mielec	Pol	2	2	0	2	0	1	1	0	0	1.000	0.500
250	Fredrikstad FK	Nor	2	2	0	2	0	1	1	0	0	1.000	0.500
251	AaB Aalborg	Den	2	2	1	0	1	1	1	0	0	1.000	0.500
252	Nuremberg	FRG	2	2	1	0	1	3	4	-1	0	1.000	1.500
253	Merthyr Tydfil	Wal	2	2	1	0	1	2	3	-1	0	1.000	1.000
254	Rad Belgrade	Yug	2	2	1	0	1	2	3	-1	0	1.000	1.000
255	Chernomorets Bourgas	Bul	2	2	1	0	1	3	5	-2	0	1.000	1.500
256	Real Betis	Esp	2	4	1	0	3	3	5	-2	0	0.500	0.750
257	Ikast FS	Den	2	4	1	0	3	3	5	-2	0	0.500	0.750
258	Borac Banja Luka	Yug	2	2	1	0	1	2	4	-2	0	1.000	1.000
259	Slavia Prague	Tch	2	2	1	0	1	1	3	-2	0	1.000	0.500
260	IBA Akureyri	Isl	2	2	1	0	1	1	3	-2	0	1.000	0.500
261	Chaves	Por	2	4	1	0	3	6	9	-3	0	0.500	1.500
262	Portimonense	Por	2	2	1	0	1	1	4	-3	0	1.000	0.500
263	Bangor City	Wal	2	4	0	2	2	1	4	-3	0	0.500	0.250
264	Sakaryaspor	Tur	2	4	1	0	3	3	7	-4	0	0.500	0.750
265	Limerick	Irl	2	4	0	2	2	2	6	-4	0	0.500	0.500
266	Twente Enschede	Ned	2	4	0	2	2	2	6	-4	0	0.500	0.500
267	Mjøndalen IF	Nor	2	2	1	0	1	1	5	-4	0	1.000	0.500
268	CSU Galati	Rom	2	2	1	0	1	1	5	-4	0	1.000	0.500
269	Krems	Aut	2	2	1	0	1	1	5	-4	0	1.000	0.500
270	Pécsi MSC	Hun	2	4	1	0	3	1	5	-4	0	0.500	0.250
271	B 93 Copenhagen	Den	2	1	1	0	3	5	10	-5	0	0.500	1.250
272	Grazer AK	Aut	2	4	0	2	2	3	8	-5	0	0.500	0.750
273	Athlone Town	Irl	2	4	0	2	2	7	14	-7	0	0.500	1.750
274	Ilves Tampere	Fin	2	4	1	0	3	3	10	-7	0	0.500	0.750
275	Partizani Tirana	Alb	2	5	1	0	4	2	9	-7	0	0.400	0.400
276	Sliven	Bul	2	4	1	0	3	3	13	-10	0	0.500	0.750
277	Derry City	Irl	2	6	0	2	4	1	11	-10	0	0.333	0.167
278	Paralimni	Cyp	2	4	1	0	3	4	15	-11	0	0.500	1.000
279	Sporting Braga	Por	2	4	1	0	3	1	12	-11	0	0.500	0.250
280	Union Luxembourg	Lux	2	10	0	2	8	3	33	-30	0	0.200	0.300
281	Sliema Wanderers	Mlt	2	12	1	0	11	5	48	-43	0	0.167	0.417

Pos'n	Club	Cnty	Pts	P	W	D	L	F	A	Diff	B	Pts/P	F/P
282	Avenir Beggen	Lux	2	16	1	0	15	4	73	-69	0	0.125	0.250
283	Mersin Idmanyurdu	Tur	1	2	0	1	1	0	1	-1	0	0.500	0.000
284	UCD	Irl	1	2	0	1	1	0	1	-1	0	0.500	0.000
285	Spartak Trnava	Tch	1	2	0	1	1	0	1	-1	0	0.500	0.000
286	Tromsø IL	Nor	1	2	0	1	1	0	1	-1	0	0.500	0.000
287	FH Hafnarfjördhur	Isl	1	2	0	1	1	3	5	-2	0	0.500	1.500
288	Szombierki Bytom	Pol	1	2	0	1	1	1	3	-2	0	0.500	0.500
289	Siófok	Hun	1	2	0	1	1	1	3	-2	0	0.500	0.500
290	Beroe Stara Zagora	Bul	1	2	0	1	1	1	3	-2	0	0.500	0.500
291	Bray Wanderers	Irl	1	2	0	1	1	1	3	-2	0	0.500	0.500
292	PSV Schwerin	GDR	1	2	0	1	1	0	2	-2	0	0.500	0.000
293	Hvidovre IF	Den	1	2	0	1	1	4	7	-3	0	0.500	2.000
294	Baia Mare	Rom	1	2	0	1	1	2	5	-3	0	0.500	1.000
295	GAIS	Swe	1	2	0	1	1	2	5	-3	0	0.500	1.000
296	Pogon Szczecin	Pol	1	4	0	1	3	3	7	-4	0	0.250	0.750
297	Ruch Chorzów	Pol	1	2	0	1	1	2	6	-4	0	0.500	1.000
298	Sigma Olomouc	Tch	1	2	0	1	1	1	5	-4	0	0.500	0.500
299	Molde FK	Nor	1	2	0	1	1	1	5	-4	0	0.500	0.500
300	SK Brann	Nor	1	4	0	1	3	1	5	-4	0	0.250	0.250
301	KTP Kotka	Fin	1	2	0	1	1	0	5	-5	0	0.500	0.000
302	Pezoporikos Larnaca	Cyp	1	4	0	1	3	4	10	-6	0	0.250	1.000
303	Glenavon	Nir	1	4	0	1	3	2	9	-7	0	0.250	0.500
304	St-Gallen	Sui	1	4	0	1	3	2	10	-8	0	0.250	0.500
305	Progrès Niedercorn	Lux	1	4	0	1	3	1	9	-8	0	0.250	0.250
306	St. Patrick's Athletic	Irl	1	4	0	1	3	1	9	-8	0	0.250	0.250
307	KuPS Kuopio	Fin	1	4	0	1	3	3	12	-9	0	0.250	0.750
308	Aarau	Sui	1	4	0	1	3	2	11	-9	0	0.250	0.500
309	IBV Vestmannaeyjar	Isl	1	6	0	1	5	3	14	-11	0	0.167	0.500
310	Floriana	Mlt	1	4	0	1	3	1	13	-12	0	0.250	0.250
311	Red Boys Differdange	Lux	1	8	0	1	7	1	46	-45	0	0.125	0.125
312	Akademik Sofia	Bul	0	2	0	0	2	1	3	-2	0	0.000	0.500
313	Zaglebie Lubin	Pol	0	2	0	0	2	0	2	-2	0	0.000	0.000
314	Lokomotiv Plovdiv	Bul	0	2	0	0	2	2	5	-3	0	0.000	1.000
315	West Bromwich Albion	Eng	0	2	0	0	2	1	4	-3	0	0.000	0.500
316	IK Start	Nor	0	2	0	0	2	1	4	-3	0	0.000	0.500
317	Gençlerbirligi	Tur	0	2	0	0	2	1	4	-3	0	0.000	0.500
318	Flacara Moreni	Rom	0	2	0	0	2	1	4	-3	0	0.000	0.500
319	Dukla Banská Bystrica	Tch	0	2	0	0	2	3	7	-4	0	0.000	1.500
320	Plastika Nitra	Tch	0	2	0	0	2	1	5	-4	0	0.000	0.500
321	Sligo Rovers	Irl	0	2	0	0	2	0	4	-4	0	0.000	0.000
322	EPA Larnaca	Cyp	0	2	0	0	2	0	4	-4	0	0.000	0.000
323	Petrolul Ploiesti	Rom	0	2	0	0	2	0	4	-4	0	0.000	0.000
324	Adanaspor	Tur	0	2	0	0	2	2	7	-5	0	0.000	1.000
325	Hansa Rostock	GDR	0	2	0	0	2	2	7	-5	0	0.000	1.000
326	Waterford United	Irl	0	2	0	0	2	1	6	-5	0	0.000	0.500
327	Panionios	Gre	0	2	0	0	2	1	6	-5	0	0.000	0.500
328	Ankaragücü	Tur	0	2	0	0	2	0	5	-5	0	0.000	0.000
329	NEA Salamina Famagusta	Cyp	0	2	0	0	2	0	5	-5	0	0.000	0.000
330	B 1901 Nykobing	Den	0	2	0	0	2	3	9	-6	0	0.000	1.500
331	Pirin Blagoevgrad	Bul	0	2	0	0	2	1	7	-6	0	0.000	0.500
332	Labinoti Elbasan	Alb	0	2	0	0	2	0	6	-6	0	0.000	0 000
333	Cork City	Irl	0	2	0	0	2	0	6	-6	0	0.000	0.000
334	Swift Hesperange	Lux	0	2	0	0	2	0	6	-6	0	0.000	0.000
335	KR Reykjavik	Isl	0	2	0	0	2	0	7	-7	0	0.000	0.000
336	Bursaspor	Tur	0	2	0	0	2	0	7	-7	0	0.000	0 000
337	Galway United	Irl	0	4	0	0	4	4	12	-8	0	0.000	1.000
338	Lechia Gdańsk	Pol	0	2	0	0	2	2	10	-8	0	0.000	1.000

Pos'n	Club	Cnty	Pts	P	W	D	L	F	A	Diff	B	Pts/P	F/P
339	Moss FK	Nor	0	4	0	0	4	2	10	-8	0	0.000	0.500
340	OPS Oulu	Fin	0	2	0	0	2	0	8	-8	0	0.000	0.000
341	Apolonia Fier	Alb	0	2	0	0	2	0	8	-8	0	0.000	0.000
342	Örgryte IS	Swe	0	4	0	0	4	5	14	-9	0	0.000	1.250
343	B 1913 Odense	Den	0	2	0	0	2	1	10	-9	0	0.000	0.500
344	OB Odense	Den	0	4	0	0	4	2	13	-11	0	0.000	0.500
345	Anorthosis Famagusta	Cyp	0	2	0	0	2	0	11	-11	0	0.000	0.000
346	Portadown	Nir	0	2	0	0	2	1	13	-12	0	0.000	0.500
347	Vikingur Reykjavik	Isl	0	6	0	0	6	3	16	-13	0	0.000	0.500
348	Drogheda United	Irl	0	2	0	0	2	0	14	-14	0	0.000	0.000
349	Aris Bonnevoie	Lux	0	2	0	0	2	0	15	-15	0	0.000	0.000
350	Spora Luxembourg	Lux	0	4	0	0	4	2	19	-17	0	0.000	0.500
351	Ballymena United	Nir	0	6	0	0	6	1	19	-18	0	0.000	0.167
352	Zurrieq	Mlt	0	6	0	0	6	1	27	-26	0	0.000	0.167
353	Hibernians	Mlt	0	8	0	0	8	4	32	-28	0	0.000	0.500
354	Rabat Ajax	Mlt	0	8	0	0	8	0	40	-40	0	0.000	0.000
355	Valletta	Mlt	0	10	0	0	10	1	50	-49	0	0.000	0.100
	Total		**5386**	**4966**	**1966**	**1034**	**1966**	**6799**	**6799**	**0**	**420**	**1.085**	**2.738**

Above: Gerd Müller of Bayern Munich scores the second goal for his team during the 1974-75 final of the European Champions' Cup Final against Leeds at the Parc des Princes stadium. Bayern won 2-0. Leeds defender Paul Reaney (2) and goalkeeper David Stewart can only watch.

Club Performance by Points

1986-87 to 1990-91

Pos'n	Club	Cnty	Pts	P	W	D	L	F	A	Diff	B	Pts/P	F/P
1	Bayern Munich	FRG	67	41	25	7	9	84	38	46	10	1.634	2.049
2	Juventus	Ita	62	36	27	2	7	82	26	56	6	1.722	2.278
3	Barcelona	Esp	55	38	19	9	10	58	30	28	8	1.447	1.526
4	Real Madrid	Esp	52	34	19	7	8	68	36	32	7	1.529	2.000
5	Anderlecht	Bel	47	33	18	5	10	49	31	18	6	1.424	1.485
6	Red Star Belgrade	Yug	46	29	17	8	4	61	28	33	4	1.586	2.103
7	Inter Milan	Ita	46	34	16	10	8	41	23	18	4	1.353	1.206
8	Olympique Marseille	Fra	45	25	16	6	3	47	17	30	7	1.800	1.880
9	FC Porto	Por	43	29	18	3	8	63	27	36	4	1.483	2.172
10	KV Mechelen	Bel	43	25	15	7	3	37	14	23	6	1.720	1.480
11	Benfica	Por	41	27	15	5	7	43	14	29	6	1.519	1.593
12	AC Milan	Ita	41	26	13	8	5	37	13	24	7	1.577	1.423
13	Sampdoria	Ita	39	24	13	6	5	36	18	18	7	1.625	1.500
14	Werder Bremen	FRG	38	28	13	7	8	48	28	20	5	1.357	1.714
15	Girondins Bordeaux	Fra	38	26	14	7	5	27	17	10	3	1.462	1.038
16	Steaua Bucharest	Rom	37	27	14	4	9	48	35	13	5	1.370	1.778
17	IFK Gothenburg	Swe	36	22	13	6	3	36	16	20	4	1.636	1.636
18	Dundee United	Sco	36	28	13	7	8	34	26	8	3	1.286	1.214
19	Ajax	Ned	35	22	14	1	7	40	18	22	6	1.591	1.818
20	Sporting Lisbon	Por	34	26	12	7	7	53	23	30	3	1.308	2.038
21	Bayer Leverkusen	FRG	34	24	11	9	4	31	16	15	3	1.417	1.292
22	Napoli	Ita	34	26	10	11	5	30	23	7	3	1.308	1.154
23	Dinamo Kiev	URS	30	22	10	7	5	39	20	19	3	1.364	1.773
24	Brøndby IF	Den	30	24	10	7	7	33	24	9	3	1.250	1.375
25	Torpedo Moscow	URS	29	20	12	3	5	38	24	14	2	1.450	1.900
26	Cologne	FRG	29	22	10	7	5	32	18	14	2	1.318	1.455
27	Roma	Ita	29	20	12	2	6	31	20	11	3	1.450	1.550
28	Spartak Moscow	URS	29	26	10	7	9	33	29	4	2	1.115	1.269
29	VFB Stuttgart	FRG	28	22	10	5	7	33	23	10	3	1.273	1.500
30	Rangers	Sco	27	22	10	6	6	34	22	12	1	1.227	1.545
31	PSV Eindhoven	Ned	27	23	7	8	8	27	18	9	5	1.174	1.174
32	FC Liège	Bel	26	20	11	2	7	35	19	16	2	1.300	1.750
33	Dinamo Bucharest	Rom	26	22	9	5	8	29	18	11	3	1.182	1.318
34	Dynamo Dresden	GDR	26	20	9	5	6	31	22	9	3	1.300	1.550
35	Club Bruges	Bel	25	24	9	5	10	41	37	4	2	1.042	1.708
36	Monaco	Fra	23	20	6	8	6	25	17	8	3	1.150	1.250
37	FC Tirol	Aut	23	20	9	3	8	37	37	0	2	1.150	1.850
38	CSKA Sofia	Bul	23	22	9	2	11	34	35	-1	3	1.045	1.545
39	Borussia Dortmund	FRG	21	16	10	1	5	23	15	8	0	1.313	1.438
40	Malmö FF	Swe	21	20	6	8	6	27	22	5	1	1.050	1.350
41	Atalanta	Ita	21	18	6	6	6	18	15	3	3	1.167	1.000
42	Español	Esp	20	12	7	3	2	17	7	10	3	1.667	1.417
43	Lokomotive Leipzig	GDR	20	15	6	5	4	17	9	8	3	1.333	1.133
44	Partizan Belgrade	Yug	20	20	9	1	10	37	31	6	1	1.000	1.850
45	Real Sociedad	Esp	20	16	7	5	4	17	13	4	1	1.250	1.063
46	Rapid Vienna	Aut	20	18	9	2	7	32	29	3	0	1.111	1.778
47	Vitória Guimarães	Por	20	18	8	3	7	19	20	-1	1	1.111	1.056
48	Manchester United	Eng	19	9	7	2	0	17	4	13	3	2.111	1.889
49	Heart of Midlothian	Sco	19	14	8	2	4	20	13	7	1	1.357	1.429
50	Admira Wacker	Aut	19	14	8	2	4	16	10	6	1	1.357	1.143
51	Fiorentina	Ita	19	14	5	6	3	8	7	1	3	1.357	0.571
52	Legia Warsaw	Pol	19	16	6	5	5	21	21	0	2	1.188	1.313
53	Austria Vienna	Aut	18	18	7	4	7	21	26	-5	0	1.000	1.167

Pos'n	Club	Cnty	Pts	P	W	D	L	F	A	Diff	B	Pts/P	F/P
54	Velez Mostar	Yug	17	14	7	3	4	24	21	3	0	1.214	1.714
55	Groningen	Ned	17	16	7	3	6	23	22	1	0	1.063	1.438
56	Panathinaikos	Gre	17	20	7	2	11	29	40	-11	1	0.850	1.450
57	Neuchâtel Xamax	Sui	16	14	6	4	4	22	17	5	0	1.143	1.571
58	Bucarest Victoria	Pou	16	14	6	3	5	21	17	4	1	1.143	1.500
59	Olympiakos Pireus	Gre	16	16	5	6	5	22	19	3	0	1.000	1.375
60	Hamburg	FRG	15	12	7	0	5	21	11	10	1	1.250	1.750
61	Real Zaragoza	Esp	15	12	5	3	4	15	13	2	2	1.250	1.250
62	Dinamo Minsk	URS	15	12	5	4	3	13	11	2	1	1.250	1.083
63	Aberdeen	Sco	15	14	6	3	5	12	11	1	0	1.071	0.857
64	TJ Vitkovice	Tch	15	12	5	4	3	12	12	0	1	1.250	1.000
65	Galatasaray	Tur	15	14	5	3	6	16	20	-4	2	1.071	1.143
66	Bor. Mönchengladbach	FRG	14	12	4	4	4	16	14	2	2	1.167	1.333
67	Honvéd	Hun	14	14	6	2	6	18	30	-12	0	1.000	1.286
68	Auxerre	Fra	13	10	5	2	3	20	7	13	1	1.300	2.000
69	AGF Aarhus	Den	13	10	5	2	3	17	7	10	1	1.300	1.700
70	Feyenoord	Ned	13	12	6	1	5	21	16	5	0	1.083	1.750
71	Sion	Sui	13	12	5	2	5	17	17	0	1	1.083	1.417
72	Dynamo Berlin	GDR	13	12	5	3	4	17	18	-1	0	1.083	1.417
73	Torino	Ita	12	8	4	3	1	14	5	9	1	1.500	1.750
74	Verona	Ita	12	8	4	3	1	12	7	5	1	1.500	1.500
75	Celtic	Sco	12	12	5	2	5	17	15	2	0	1.000	1.417
76	Lech Poznań	Pol	12	8	5	2	1	15	13	2	0	1.500	1.875
77	Dukla Prague	Tch	12	12	4	4	4	14	13	1	0	1.000	1.167
78	Eintracht Frankfurt	FRG	11	8	4	2	2	11	8	3	1	1.375	1.375
79	Sparta Prague	Tch	11	14	4	3	7	23	24	-1	0	0.786	1.643
80	Antwerp	Bel	11	12	3	4	5	16	18	-2	1	0.917	1.333
81	Dnepr Dnepropetrovsk	URS	11	12	3	4	5	11	15	-4	1	0.917	0.917
82	RoPS Rovaniemi	Fin	11	12	3	4	5	5	15	-10	1	0 917	0.417
83	Real Valladolid	Esp	10	6	3	3	0	10	2	8	1	1.667	1.667
84	First Vienna	Aut	10	8	4	2	2	14	8	6	0	1.250	1.750
85	Bologna	Ita	10	8	4	1	3	10	9	1	1	1.250	1.250
86	Atlético Madrid	Esp	10	10	5	0	5	8	9	-1	0	1.000	0.800
87	Sportul Studentesc Bucharest	Rom	10	10	4	2	4	10	13	-3	0	1.000	1.000
-	Universitatea Craiova	Rom	10	10	5	0	5	10	13	-3	0	1.000	1.000
89	TPS Turku	Fin	10	12	4	2	6	9	13	-4	0	0.833	0.750
90	GKS Katowice	Pol	10	14	4	2	8	15	21	-6	0	0.714	1.071
91	Wrexham	Wal	9	8	3	3	2	10	7	3	0	1.125	1.250
92	Toulouse	Fra	9	8	4	1	3	12	10	2	0	1.125	1.500
93	Valencia	Esp	9	8	3	3	2	12	10	2	0	1.125	1.500
94	Montpellier	Fra	9	8	3	2	3	11	9	2	1	1.125	1.375
95	Beveren	Bel	9	10	4	1	5	9	8	1	0	0.900	0.900
96	Górnik Zabrze	Pol	9	12	3	3	6	17	19	-2	0	0.750	1.417
97	Belenenses	Por	9	8	3	3	2	4	6	-2	0	1.125	0.500
98	17 Nëntori Tirana	Alb	9	12	4	1	7	12	17	-5	0	0.750	1.000
99	Besiktas	Tur	9	12	3	2	7	10	20	-10	1	0.750	0.833
100	DAC Dunajská Streda	Tch	8	8	4	0	4	16	11	5	0	1.000	2.000
101	Athletic Bilbao	Esp	8	8	4	0	4	11	13	-2	0	1.000	1.375
102	Roda JC	Ned	8	8	3	1	4	8	10	-2	1	1.000	1.000
103	Hajduk Split	Yug	8	10	3	2	5	10	14	-4	0	0.800	1.000
104	Flamurtari Vlorë	Alb	8	12	3	2	7	11	17	-6	0	0.667	0.917
105	Grasshoppers Zürich	Sui	8	12	2	3	7	11	19	-8	1	0.667	0.917
106	Levski Sofia	Bul	8	12	3	1	8	14	23	-9	1	0.667	1.167
107	Bayer Uerdingen	FRG	7	6	3	1	2	9	4	5	0	1.167	1.500
108	Trakia Plovdiv	Bul	7	8	2	3	3	16	12	4	0	0.875	2.000
109	Vitesse	Ned	7	6	3	1	2	7	4	3	0	1.167	1.167
110	Young Boys Berne	Sui	7	8	3	0	5	7	12	-5	1	0.875	0.875

Pos'n	Club	Cnty	Pts	P	W	D	L	F	A	Diff	B	Pts/P	F/P
111	Omonia Nicosia	Cyp	7	14	2	3	9	11	27	-16	0	0.500	0.786
112	Sochaux	Fra	6	4	2	2	0	13	1	12	0	1.500	3.250
113	Aston Villa	Eng	6	4	3	0	1	7	5	2	0	1.500	1.750
114	Dinamo Tbilisi	URS	6	6	2	2	2	8	7	1	0	1.000	1.333
115	Ferencváros	Hun	6	8	2	2	4	9	9	0	0	0.750	1.125
116	Gent	Bel	6	6	2	2	2	7	8	-1	0	1.000	1.167
117	OFI Crete	Gre	6	6	3	0	3	5	8	-3	0	1.000	0.833
118	Rosenborg BK	Nor	6	8	2	2	4	6	17	-11	0	0.750	0.750
119	Wettingen	Sui	5	4	2	1	1	6	2	4	0	1.250	1.500
120	Dinamo Moscow	URS	5	4	2	1	1	5	2	3	0	1.250	1.250
121	Hibernian	Sco	5	4	2	1	1	4	1	3	0	1.250	1.000
122	Waregem	Bel	5	4	2	1	1	8	6	2	0	1.250	2.000
123	Standard Liège	Bel	5	4	2	1	1	6	5	1	0	1.250	1.500
124	Djurgården SIF	Swe	5	6	1	3	2	8	8	0	0	0.833	1.333
125	Banik Ostrava	Tch	5	6	2	1	3	10	11	-1	0	0.833	1.667
126	Dinamo Zagreb	Yug	5	6	1	3	2	5	6	-1	0	0.833	0.833
127	Trabzonspor	Tur	5	4	2	1	1	6	8	-2	0	1.250	1.500
128	Magdeburg	GDR	5	6	2	1	3	2	4	-2	0	0.833	0.333
129	Karl-Marx-Stadt	GDR	5	8	2	1	5	9	12	-3	0	0.625	1.125
130	AEK Athenes	Gre	5	8	2	1	5	7	12	-5	0	0.625	0.875
131	Dinamo Tirana	Alb	5	8	2	1	5	7	13	-6	0	0.625	0.875
132	Lucerne	Sui	5	8	1	3	4	4	10	-6	0	0.625	0.500
133	Zenit Leningrad	URS	5	6	2	1	3	5	12	-7	0	0.833	0.833
134	Ujpesti Dózsa	Hun	5	8	2	1	5	4	11	-7	0	0.625	0.500
135	Lillestrøm SK	Nor	5	10	1	3	6	8	16	-8	0	0.500	0.800
136	Kalmar FF	Swe	5	6	2	1	3	3	12	-9	0	0.833	0.500
137	Glentoran	Nir	5	10	0	5	5	5	18	-13	0	0.500	0.500
138	Vllaznia Shkodër	Alb	4	4	2	0	2	6	2	4	0	1.000	1.500
139	FC Den Haag	Ned	4	4	2	0	2	5	4	1	0	1.000	1.250
140	Békéscsaba	Hun	4	4	2	0	2	5	4	1	0	1.000	1.250
141	Utrecht	Ned	4	4	1	2	1	4	3	1	0	1.000	1.000
142	Stahl Brandenburg	GDR	4	4	1	2	1	3	4	-1	0	1.000	0.750
143	Seville	Esp	4	4	1	2	1	3	4	-1	0	1.000	0.750
144	Estrela Amadora	Por	4	4	1	2	1	3	4	-1	0	1.000	0.750
145	Widzew Lódź	Pol	4	4	1	2	1	2	3	-1	0	1.000	0.500
146	Wismut Aue	GDR	4	4	1	2	1	2	3	-1	0	1.000	0.500
147	Servette	Sui	4	4	1	2	1	2	3	-1	0	1.000	0.500
148	St. Mirren	Sco	4	4	1	2	1	1	2	-1	0	1.000	0.250
149	Paris Saint-Germain	Fra	4	6	1	2	3	6	8	-2	0	0.667	1.000
150	Inter Bratislava	Tch	4	6	2	0	4	9	12	-3	0	0.667	1.500
151	Fenerbahçe	Tur	4	6	2	0	4	9	12	-3	0	0.667	1.500
152	Zhalgiris Vilnius	URS	4	6	2	0	4	7	11	-4	0	0.667	1.167
153	Politehnica Timisoara	Rom	4	4	2	0	2	4	8	-4	0	1.000	1.000
154	Linfield	Nir	4	8	0	4	4	6	11	-5	0	0.500	0.750
155	HJK Helsinki	Fin	4	6	2	0	4	5	11	-6	0	0.667	0.833
156	Valur Reykjavik	Isl	4	8	1	2	5	4	18	-14	0	0.500	0.500
157	Metallist Kharkov	URS	3	4	1	1	2	4	3	1	0	0.750	1.000
158	Chernomorets Odessa	URS	3	4	1	1	2	4	4	0	0	0.750	1.000
159	Cardiff City	Wal	3	4	1	1	2	5	6	-1	0	0.750	1.250
160	PAOK Salonika	Gre	3	4	0	3	1	1	2	-1	0	0.750	0.250
161	Tatabánya	Hun	3	4	1	1	2	3	5	-2	0	0.750	0.750
162	Rába ETO	Hun	3	4	1	1	2	5	8	-3	0	0.750	1.250
163	Boavista	Por	3	6	1	1	4	4	7	-3	0	0.500	0.667
164	IFK Norrköping	Swe	3	4	1	1	2	3	6	-3	0	0.750	0.750
165	Iraklis	Gre	3	4	1	1	2	1	4	-3	0	0.750	0.250
166	Carl Zeiss Jena	GDR	3	6	1	1	4	7	12	-5	0	0.500	1.167
167	MTK-VM	Hun	3	6	1	1	4	5	13	-8	0	0.500	0.833

Pos'n	Club	Cnty	Pts	P	W	D	L	F	A	Diff	B	Pts/P	F/P
168	Apollon Limassol	Cyp	3	4	1	1	2	3	11	-8	0	0.750	0.750
169	FC Kuusysi Lahti	Fin	3	8	1	1	6	5	22	-17	0	0.375	0.625
170	Jeunesse Esch	Lux	3	8	1	1	6	5	26	-21	0	0.375	0.625
171	Fram Reykjavik	Isl	3	12	1	1	10	5	32	-27	0	0.250	0.417
172	Larissa	Gre	2	2	1	0	1	3	3	0	0	1.000	1.500
173	Lausanne-Sports	Sui	2	2	1	0	1	3	3	0	0	1.000	1.500
174	Vojvodina Novi Sad	Yug	2	2	1	0	1	2	2	0	0	1.000	1.000
175	AaB Aalborg	Den	2	2	1	0	1	1	1	0	0	1.000	0.500
176	Lokomotiv Sofia	Bul	2	2	1	0	1	3	4	-1	0	1.000	1.500
177	Nuremberg	FRG	2	2	1	0	1	3	4	-1	0	1.000	1.500
178	Slovan Bratislava	Tch	2	2	1	0	1	3	4	-1	0	1.000	1.500
179	Merthyr Tydfil	Wal	2	2	1	0	1	2	3	-1	0	1.000	1.000
180	Rad Belgrade	Yug	2	2	1	0	1	2	3	-1	0	1.000	1.000
181	Lens	Fra	2	2	1	0	1	1	2	-1	0	1.000	0.500
182	B 1903 Copenhagen	Den	2	2	1	0	1	1	2	-1	0	1.000	0.500
183	Bohemians Prague	Tch	2	2	1	0	1	1	2	-1	0	1.000	0.500
184	Kaiserslautern	FRG	2	2	1	0	1	1	2	-1	0	1.000	0.500
185	Chernomorets Bourgas	Bul	2	2	1	0	1	3	5	-2	0	1.000	1.500
186	Ikast FS	Den	2	4	1	0	3	3	5	-2	0	0.500	0.750
187	Ilves Tampere	Fin	2	2	1	0	1	2	4	-2	0	1.000	1.000
188	Borac Banja Luka	Yug	2	2	1	0	1	2	4	-2	0	1.000	1.000
189	Bryne IL	Nor	2	2	1	0	1	2	4	-2	0	1.000	1.000
190	Sporting Gijón	Esp	2	2	1	0	1	1	3	-2	0	1.000	0.500
191	IBA Akureyri	Isl	2	2	1	0	1	1	3	-2	0	1.000	0.500
192	Chaves	Por	2	4	1	0	3	6	9	-3	0	0.500	1.500
193	Linzer ASK	Aut	2	4	0	2	2	1	4	-3	0	0.500	0.250
194	Sakaryaspor	Tur	2	4	1	0	3	3	7	-4	0	0.500	0.750
195	Öster SIF	Swe	2	2	1	0	1	2	6	-4	0	1.000	1.000
196	Twente Enschede	Ned	2	4	0	2	2	2	6	-4	0	0.500	0.500
197	Mjøndalen IF	Nor	2	2	1	0	1	1	5	-4	0	1.000	0.500
198	CSU Galati	Rom	2	2	1	0	1	1	5	-4	0	1.000	0.500
199	Krems	Aut	2	2	1	0	1	1	5	-4	0	1.000	0.500
200	Pécsi MSC	Hun	2	4	1	0	3	1	5	-4	0	0.500	0.250
201	Haka Valkeakoski	Fin	2	4	0	2	2	5	11	-6	0	0.500	1.250
202	AEL Limassol	Cyp	2	4	1	0	3	1	9	-8	0	0.500	0.250
203	Apoel Nicosia	Cyp	2	6	1	0	5	7	16	-9	0	0.333	1.167
204	Derry City	Irl	2	6	0	2	4	1	11	-10	0	0.333	0.167
205	Slavia Sofia	Bul	2	4	1	0	3	4	15	-11	0	0.500	1.000
206	Hamrun Spartans	Mlt	2	6	1	0	5	2	16	-14	0	0.333	0.333
207	Sliema Wanderers	Mlt	2	8	1	0	7	3	23	-20	0	0.250	0.375
208	IA Akranes	Isl	2	8	0	2	6	2	24	-22	0	0.250	0.250
209	Avenir Beggen	Lux	2	8	1	0	7	3	28	-25	0	0.250	0.375
210	Swansea City	Wal	1	2	0	1	1	5	6	-1	0	0.500	2.500
211	Vasas SC	Hun	1	2	0	1	1	4	5	-1	0	0.500	2.000
212	Rijeka	Yug	1	2	0	1	1	1	2	-1	0	0.500	0.500
213	Spartak Trnava	Tch	1	2	0	1	1	0	1	-1	0	0.500	0.000
214	Vålerengen SIF	Nor	1	2	0	1	1	0	1	-1	0	0.500	0.000
215	Lokeren	Bel	1	2	0	1	1	0	1	-1	0	0.500	0.000
216	Tromsø IL	Nor	1	2	0	1	1	0	1	-1	0	0.500	0.000
217	Bohemians	Irl	1	2	0	1	1	0	1	-1	0	0.500	0.000
218	Sturm Graz	Aut	1	2	0	1	1	0	1	-1	0	0.500	0.000
219	Floriana	Mlt	1	2	0	1	1	0	1	-1	0	0.500	0.000
220	FH Hafnarfjördhur	Isl	1	2	0	1	1	3	5	-2	0	0.500	1.500
221	Pogon Szczecin	Pol	1	2	0	1	1	2	4	-2	0	0.500	1.000
222	Beroe Stara Zagora	Bul	1	2	0	1	1	1	3	-2	0	0.500	0.500
223	AIK	Swe	1	2	0	1	1	1	3	-2	0	0.500	0.500
224	Naestved IF	Den	1	2	0	1	1	1	3	-2	0	0.500	0.500

Pos'n	Club	Cnty	Pts	P	W	D	L	F	A	Diff	B	Pts/P	F/P
225	Bray Wanderers	Irl	1	2	0	1	1	1	3	-2	0	0.500	0.500
226	Slask Wroclaw	Pol	1	2	0	1	1	0	2	-2	0	0.500	0.000
227	PSV Schwerin	GDR	1	2	0	1	1	0	2	-2	0	0.500	0.000
228	GAIS	Swe	1	2	0	1	1	2	5	-3	0	0.500	1.000
229	Ruch Chorzów	Pol	1	2	0	1	1	2	6	-4	0	0.500	1.000
230	KuPS Kuopio	Fin	1	2	0	1	1	2	6	-4	0	0.500	1.000
231	Coleraine	Nir	1	4	0	1	3	2	6	-4	0	0.250	0.500
232	Sigma Olomouc	Tch	1	2	0	1	1	1	5	-4	0	0.500	0.500
233	Nantes	Fra	1	2	0	1	1	1	5	-4	0	0.500	0.500
234	Molde FK	Nor	1	2	0	1	1	1	5	-4	0	0.500	0.500
235	Shamrock Rovers	Irl	1	4	0	1	3	0	4	-4	0	0.250	0.000
236	Lyngby BK	Den	1	4	0	1	3	1	6	-5	0	0.250	0.250
237	Glenavon	Nir	1	4	0	1	3	2	9	-7	0	0.250	0.500
238	St. Patrick's Athletic	Irl	1	4	0	1	3	1	9	-8	0	0.250	0.250
239	Union Luxembourg	Lux	1	8	0	1	7	2	28	-26	0	0.125	0.250
240	IK Brage	Swe	0	2	0	0	2	2	4	-2	0	0.000	1.000
241	Zaglebie Lubin	Pol	0	2	0	0	2	0	2	-2	0	0.000	0.000
242	Gençlerbirligi	Tur	0	2	0	0	2	1	4	-3	0	0.000	0.500
243	Flacara Moreni	Rom	0	2	0	0	2	1	4	-3	0	0.000	0.500
244	SK Brann	Nor	0	2	0	0	2	0	3	-3	0	0.000	0.000
245	Metz	Fra	0	2	0	0	2	1	5	-4	0	0.000	0.500
246	Plastika Nitra	Tch	0	2	0	0	2	1	5	-4	0	0.000	0.500
247	EPA Larnaca	Cyp	0	2	0	0	2	0	4	-4	0	0.000	0.000
248	Moss FK	Nor	0	2	0	0	2	0	4	-4	0	0.000	0.000
249	Videoton	Hun	0	2	0	0	2	0	4	-4	0	0.000	0.000
250	Petrolul Ploiesti	Rom	0	2	0	0	2	0	4	-4	0	0.000	0.000
251	Vejle BK	Den	0	2	0	0	2	0	4	-4	0	0.000	0.000
252	Pezoporikos Larnaca	Cyp	0	2	0	0	2	2	7	-5	0	0.000	1.000
253	Hansa Rostock	GDR	0	2	0	0	2	2	7	-5	0	0.000	1.000
254	Waterford United	Irl	0	2	0	0	2	1	6	-5	0	0.000	0.500
255	Panionios	Gre	0	2	0	0	2	1	6	-5	0	0.000	0.500
256	IL Viking	Nor	0	2	0	0	2	0	5	-5	0	0.000	0.000
257	NEA Salamina Famagusta	Cyp	0	2	0	0	2	0	5	-5	0	0.000	0.000
258	Galway United	Irl	0	2	0	0	2	2	8	-6	0	0.000	1.000
259	Vardar Skoplje	Yug	0	2	0	0	2	0	6	-6	0	0.000	0.000
260	Cork City	Irl	0	2	0	0	2	0	6	-6	0	0.000	0.000
261	Swift Hesperange	Lux	0	2	0	0	2	0	6	-6	0	0.000	0.000
262	Partizani Tirana	Alb	0	3	0	0	3	0	6	-6	0	0.000	0.000
263	Sliven	Bul	0	2	0	0	2	1	8	-7	0	0.000	0.500
264	Bursaspor	Tur	0	2	0	0	2	0	7	-7	0	0.000	0.000
265	Zurrieq	Mlt	0	2	0	0	2	0	7	-7	0	0.000	0.000
266	Aarau	Sui	0	2	0	0	2	0	7	-7	0	0.000	0.000
267	Apolonia Fier	Alb	0	2	0	0	2	0	8	-8	0	0.000	0.000
268	Örgryte IS	Swe	0	4	0	0	4	5	14	-9	0	0.000	1.250
269	B 1913 Odense	Den	0	2	0	0	2	1	10	-9	0	0.000	0.500
270	Rabat Ajax	Mlt	0	2	0	0	2	0	10	-10	0	0.000	0.000
271	Ballymena United	Nir	0	2	0	0	2	0	10	-10	0	0.000	0.000
272	Portadown	Nir	0	2	0	0	2	1	13	-12	0	0.000	0.500
273	Hibernians	Mlt	0	4	0	0	4	0	15	-15	0	0.000	0.000
274	Spora Luxembourg	Lux	0	4	0	0	4	2	19	-17	0	0.000	0.500
275	Dundalk	Irl	0	6	0	0	6	0	19	-19	0	0.000	0.000
276	Valletta	Mlt	0	6	0	0	6	1	24	-23	0	0.000	0.167
	Total		**2688**	**2478**	**972**	**534**	**972**	**3163**	**3163**	**0**	**210**	**1.085**	**2.553**

Club Participation Details by Country 1955-56 to 1990-91

Albania

Club	Pts	P	W	D	L	F	A	Diff	B	Part	C1	C2	C3
Labinoti Elbasan	8	2	0	0	2	0	6	-6	–	1	0	–	–
Apolonia Fier	0	2	0	0	2	0	8	-8	–	1	–	–	0
Besa Kavajë	3	4	0	3	1	3	9	-6	–	1	–	3	–
Vllaznia Shkodër	6	6	3	0	3	9	6	3	–	2	2	4	–
Dinamo Tirana	13	20	4	5	11	10	24	-14	–	8	1	6	6
17 Nëntori Tirana	16	22	6	4	12	19	33	-14	–	8	9	7	–
Partizani Tirana	14	23	5	4	14	15	35	-20	–	11	8	6	0
Flamurtari Vlorë	8	14	3	2	9	14	22	-8	–	5	–	0	8
Total	**60**	**93**	**21**	**18**	**54**	**70**	**143**	**-73**	**–**	**37**	**20**	**26**	**14**

Austria

Club	Pts	P	W	D	L	F	A	Diff	B	Part	C1	C2	C3
Grazer AK	3	14	0	3	9	11	32	-21	–	6	–	2	1
Sturm Graz	25	28	8	7	13	29	35	-6	2	7	–	6	19
FC Tirol	53	58	21	8	29	79	106	-27	3	18	18	14	21
Krems	2	2	1	0	1	1	5	-4	–	1	–	2	–
Linzer ASK	18	23	7	4	12	20	43	-23	–	9	0	3	15
Vöest Linz	4	8	1	2	5	5	18	-13	–	4	1	–	3
SV Salzburg	6	8	3	0	5	11	17	-6	–	3	–	0	6
Admira Wacker	24	24	10	3	11	22	28	-6	1	7	1	8	15
Austria Vienna	107	104	35	28	41	147	156	-9	9	25	50	35	22
First Vienna	10	8	4	2	2	14	8	6	–	2	–	–	10
Rapid Vienna	138	128	51	26	51	201	186	15	10	31	57	48	33
Wiener Sport-Club	29	33	11	5	17	46	58	-12	2	10	14	–	15
Wiener Neustadt	0	2	0	0	2	0	3	-3	–	1	–	0	–
Total	**419**	**438**	**152**	**88**	**198**	**586**	**695**	**-109**	**27**	**124**	**141**	**118**	**160**

Belgium

Club	Pts	P	W	D	L	F	A	Diff	B	Part	C1	C2	C3
Anderlecht	246	176	95	25	56	335	224	111	31	31	82	73	91
Beerschot	6	10	2	2	6	13	15	-2	–	4	–	5	1
Antwerp	37	40	14	8	18	54	63	-9	1	11	0	–	37
Beveren	46	38	18	8	12	56	34	22	2	8	6	17	23
Cercle Bruges	2	2	1	0	1	4	4	0	–	1	–	2	–
Club Bruges	98	89	38	12	39	152	135	17	10	20	37	10	51
Charleroi	6	4	3	0	1	8	5	3	–	1	–	–	6
Gent	15	22	4	7	11	20	36	-16	–	8	–	3	12
FC Liège	60	48	25	6	17	68	48	20	4	9	–	7	53
Standard Liège	144	112	57	18	37	193	134	59	12	21	54	45	45
Lierse	15	18	6	2	10	27	30	-3	1	5	0	6	9
Lokeren	28	24	9	9	6	29	24	5	1	5	–	–	28
KV Mechelen	43	25	15	7	3	37	14	23	6	4	8	34	1
RWD Molenbeek	37	34	12	11	11	42	39	3	2	9	4	–	33
Union St-Gilloise	12	17	4	2	11	23	30	-7	2	5	–	–	12
Waregem	25	20	10	3	7	30	29	1	2	4	–	2	23
Waterschei Thor	19	12	8	1	3	26	11	15	2	2	–	19	–
Winterslag	5	6	2	1	3	5	9	-4	–	1	–	–	5
Total	**844**	**697**	**323**	**122**	**252**	**1122**	**884**	**238**	**76**	**149**	**191**	**223**	**430**

Bulgaria

Club	Pts	P	W	D	L	F	A	Diff	B	Part	C1	C2	C3
Pirin Blagoevgrad	0	2	0	0	2	1	7	-6	–	1	–	–	0

Chernomorets Bourgas	2	2	1	0	1	3	5	-2	–	1	–	2	–
Lokomotiv Plovdiv	26	30	10	6	14	40	50	-10	–	10	–	–	26
Trakia Plovdiv	31	36	11	8	17	53	56	-3	1	13	5	15	11
Dunav Ruse	2	2	1	0	1	1	2	-1	–	1	–	–	2
Sliven	2	4	1	0	3	3	13	-10	–	2	–	0	2
Akademik Sofia	4	6	2	0	4	8	10	-2	–	2	–	–	4
CSKA Sofia	124	116	48	18	50	173	169	4	10	30	93	22	9
Levski Sofia	68	74	25	14	35	126	131	-5	4	21	12	28	28
Lokomotiv Sofia	23	26	9	4	13	43	55	-12	1	7	7	2	14
Slavia Sofia	37	41	14	6	21	49	66	-17	3	13	–	24	13
Marek Stanke Dimitrov	6	6	3	0	3	8	10	-2	–	2	–	2	4
Beroe Stara Zagora	24	22	10	3	9	39	23	16	1	5	1	12	11
Spartak Varna	4	6	1	2	3	4	9	-5	–	2	–	4	–
Etar Veliko Tarnovo	1	2	0	1	1	0	3	-3	–	1	–	–	1
Botev Vratsa	0	2	0	0	2	2	8	-6	–	1	–	–	0
Total	**354**	**377**	**136**	**62**	**179**	**553**	**617**	**64**	**20**	**112**	**118**	**111**	**125**

Cyprus

Club	Pts	P	W	D	L	F	A	Diff	B	Part	C1	C2	C3
Anorthosis Famagusta	1	8	0	1	7	2	35	-33	–	4	0	1	0
Paralimni	2	8	1	0	7	8	36	-28	–	4	–	2	0
NEA Salamina Famagusta	0	2	0	0	2	0	5	-5	–	1	–	0	–
Alki Larnaca	0	2	0	0	2	0	12	-12	–	1	–	–	0
EPA Larnaca	0	6	0	0	6	0	22	-22	–	3	0	–	0
Pezoporikos Larnaca	4	14	0	4	10	10	52	-42	–	7	0	2	2
AEL Limassol	3	8	1	1	6	3	27	-24	–	4	0	3	–
Apollon Limassol	5	12	1	3	8	8	43	-35	–	6	–	3	2
Akritas Morphou	0	2	0	0	2	0	7	-7	–	1	–	–	0
Anorthosis Nicosia	0	2	0	0	2	0	16	-16	–	1	–	0	–
Apoel Nicosia	13	36	4	5	27	28	109	-81	–	16	4	6	3
Olympiakos Nicosia	1	10	0	1	9	5	57	-52	–	5	1	0	0
Omonia Nicosia	29	48	12	5	31	53	109	-56	–	19	24	1	4
Total	**58**	**158**	**19**	**20**	**119**	**117**	**530**	**-413**	**–**	**72**	**29**	**18**	**11**

Czechoslovakia

Club	Pts	P	W	D	L	F	A	Diff	B	Part	C1	C2	C3
Dukla Banská Bystrica	0	2	0	0	2	3	7	-4	–	1	–	–	0
Inter Bratislava	30	28	14	2	12	55	42	13	–	7	5	3	22
Slovan Bratislava	59	45	24	6	15	80	59	21	5	12	13	36	10
Zbrojovka Brno	47	41	18	8	15	65	52	13	3	10	5	4	38
DAC Dunajská Streda	8	8	4	0	4	16	11	5	–	2	–	6	2
TJ Gottwaldov	5	4	2	1	1	6	5	1	–	1	–	5	–
Spartak Hradec Králové	5	4	1	2	1	2	5	-3	1	1	5	–	–
Lokomotiv Kosice	12	10	4	4	2	9	8	1	–	3	–	10	2
VSS Kosice	4	4	2	0	2	5	8	-3	–	2	–	–	4
Plastika Nitra	0	2	0	0	2	1	5	-4	–	1	–	–	0
Sigma Olomouc	1	2	0	1	1	1	5	-4	–	1	–	–	1
Banik Ostrava	63	56	25	9	22	80	69	11	4	13	14	20	29
Skoda Plzen	0	2	0	0	2	1	7	-6	–	1	–	0	–
Bohemians Prague	37	36	14	7	15	52	46	6	2	9	6	–	31
Dukla Prague	112	93	40	24	29	138	119	19	8	22	59	29	24
Slavia Prague	13	14	6	1	7	18	20	-2	–	6	–	2	11
Sparta Prague	80	72	31	12	29	130	105	25	6	18	38	21	21
Tatran Presov	4	6	1	2	3	12	15	-3	–	2	–	1	3
Union Teplice	0	2	0	0	2	2	4	-2	–	1	–	–	0
Spartak Trnava	45	38	16	9	13	54	41	13	4	9	37	4	4
TJ Vitkovice	15	12	5	4	3	12	12	0	1	2	5	–	10
Dynamo Zilina	7	4	3	0	1	7	6	1	1	1	–	7	–

Total	**547**	**485**	**210**	**92**	**183**	**749**	**651**	**98**	**35**	**125**	**187**	**148**	**212**

Denmark

Club	Pts	P	W	D	L	F	A	Diff	B	Part	C1	C2	C3
AaB Aalborg	3	6	1	1	4	3	12	-9	–	3	–	3	–
BK Fremad Amager	2	2	0	2	0	1	1	0	–	1	–	2	–
AGF Aarhus	36	40	14	6	20	50	58	-8	2	12	17	14	5
AB Copenhagen	7	10	3	1	6	17	19	-2	–	3	3	–	4
B 1903 Copenhagen	17	26	6	5	15	31	50	-19	–	10	5	7	5
B 93 Copenhagen	2	4	1	0	3	5	10	-5	–	1	–	2	–
KB Copenhagen	21	35	7	6	22	58	94	-36	1	13	10	1	10
Brøndby IF	30	24	10	7	7	33	24	9	3	5	11	–	19
BK Frem	9	16	4	1	11	17	43	-26	–	7	–	4	5
Hvidovre IF	11	18	3	5	10	22	39	-17	–	7	6	4	1
Esbjerg FB	20	24	7	6	11	22	45	-23	–	8	9	1	10
Holbaek BIF	2	4	1	0	3	2	10	-8	–	2	–	–	2
Ikast FS	2	4	1	0	3	3	5	-2	–	2	–	0	2
Køge BK	0	2	0	0	2	1	7	-6	–	1	0	–	–
Lyngby BK	12	14	4	4	6	18	19	-1	–	5	5	6	1
Naestved IF	4	8	1	2	5	5	21	-16	–	4	–	–	4
B 1901 Nykobing	0	4	0	0	4	6	17	-11	–	2	–	0	0
OB Odense	1	8	0	1	7	7	21	-14	–	4	1	–	0
B 1909 Odense	10	16	3	3	10	27	44	-17	1	6	1	9	0
B 1913 Odense	6	14	3	0	11	24	46	-22	–	6	4	0	2
Randers Freja FC	12	12	4	3	5	17	16	1	1	4	–	10	2
Vanløse IF	0	2	0	0	2	1	8	-7	–	1	–	0	–
Vejle BK	19	24	7	4	13	29	43	-14	1	8	10	9	0
Total	**226**	**317**	**80**	**57**	**180**	**399**	**652**	**-253**	**9**	**115**	**82**	**72**	**72**

East Germany

Club	Pts	P	W	D	L	F	A	Diff	B	Part	C1	C2	C3
Wismut Aue	4	6	1	2	3	4	8	-4	–	2	–	–	4
Dynamo Berlin	68	60	23	18	19	87	80	7	4	15	40	19	9
Stahl Brandenburg	4	4	1	2	1	3	4	-1	–	1	–	–	4
Karl-Marx-Stadt	20	26	7	5	14	37	40	-3	1	6	15	–	5
Dynamo Dresden	118	98	42	25	31	156	121	35	9	20	33	17	68
Vorwärts Frankfurt/Oder	39	43	17	3	23	56	64	-8	2	13	22	9	8
Chemie Halle	1	2	0	1	1	3	5	-2	–	1	–	1	–
Carl Zeiss Jena	104	87	39	18	30	140	114	26	8	18	11	34	59
Chemie Leipzig	5	6	2	1	3	9	10	-1	–	2	0	5	–
Lokomotive Leipzig	100	94	38	17	39	135	125	10	7	23	–	32	68
Magdeburg	86	72	32	15	25	115	86	29	7	16	6	47	33
Hansa Rostock	8	10	4	0	6	15	19	-4	–	3	–	–	8
PSV Schwerin	1	2	0	1	1	0	2	-2	–	1	–	1	–
Sachsenning Zwickau	13	12	4	3	5	6	10	-4	2	3	–	13	–
Total	**571**	**522**	**210**	**111**	**201**	**766**	**688**	**78**	**40**	**124**	**127**	**178**	**26**

England

Club	Pts	P	W	D	L	F	A	Diff	B	Part	C1	C2	C3
Birmingham City	41	25	14	6	5	52	39	13	7	4	–	–	41
Aston Villa	46	33	17	7	9	55	31	24	5	6	25	–	21
Burnley	17	12	6	3	3	24	13	11	2	2	5	–	12
Coventry City	6	4	3	0	1	9	8	1	0	1	–	–	6
Derby County	28	22	11	4	7	50	29	21	2	4	16	–	12
Ipswich Town	72	50	29	9	12	100	51	49	5	10	6	9	57
Leeds United	144	91	50	24	17	165	67	98	20	11	30	16	98
Leicester City	5	4	2	1	1	8	5	3	–	1	–	5	–

Everton	57	41	21	11	9	65	31	34	4	10	10	24	23
Liverpool	224	140	84	26	30	278	106	172	30	21	128	23	73
Arsenal	73	51	27	11	13	92	42	50	8	8	9	16	48
Chelsea	64	42	23	10	9	86	44	42	8	6	–	25	39
Queen's Park Rangers	18	12	8	1	3	39	18	21	1	2	–	–	18
Tottenham Hotspur	141	87	53	16	18	208	84	124	19	11	11	40	90
West Ham United	45	30	15	6	9	58	42	16	9	4	–	45	–
Manchester City	45	34	15	9	10	54	34	20	6	7	1	29	15
Manchester United	149	95	53	23	19	198	100	98	20	14	70	43	36
Newcastle United	39	28	14	7	7	43	26	17	4	4	–	–	39
Nottingham Forrest	59	38	22	7	9	52	30	22	8	7	34	–	25
Sheffield Wednesday	11	10	5	0	5	25	18	7	1	2	–	–	11
Southampton	25	22	8	8	6	37	26	11	1	6	–	9	16
Stoke City	4	4	1	2	1	4	6	-2	–	2	–	–	4
Sunderland	6	4	3	0	1	5	3	2	–	1	–	6	–
Watford	5	6	2	1	3	10	12	-2	–	1	–	–	5
West Bromwich Albion	23	22	8	5	9	30	27	3	2	5	–	7	16
Wolverhampton Wanderers	43	32	16	6	10	59	44	15	5	7	7	4	32
Total	**1390**	**939**	**510**	**203**	**226**	**1806**	**936**	**870**	**167**	**157**	**352**	**301**	**737**

Finland

Club	Pts	P	W	D	L	F	A	Diff	B	Part	C1	C2	C3
HIFK Helsinki	0	6	0	0	6	5	16	-11	–	3	0	–	0
HJK Helsinki	16	30	8	0	22	28	90	-62	–	12	10	6	0
HPS Helsinki	0	4	0	0	4	2	19	-17	–	2	0	0	–
KPV Kokkola	0	4	0	0	4	2	23	-21	–	2	0	–	0
KTP Kotka	1	2	0	1	1	0	5	-5	–	1	–	1	–
KuPS Kuopio	8	22	2	4	16	18	67	-49	–	10	1	2	5
FC Kuusysi Lahti	13	20	4	4	12	16	37	-21	1	8	10	2	1
Reipas Lahti	11	24	3	5	16	23	93	-70	–	10	6	5	–
MP Mikkeli	3	6	1	1	4	4	18	-14	–	3	–	3	0
OPS Oulu	1	4	0	1	3	2	19	-17	–	2	1	–	–
RoPS Rovaniemi	11	12	3	4	5	5	15	-10	1	3	–	7	4
Ilves Tampere	4	8	2	0	6	10	22	-12	–	4	0	0	4
TPS Turku	13	26	5	3	18	15	48	-33	–	9	2	1	10
Haka Valkeakoski	15	28	5	4	19	27	73	-46	1	11	2	12	1
Total	**96**	**196**	**33**	**27**	**136**	**157**	**545**	**-388**	**3**	**80**	**32**	**39**	**25**

France

Club	Pts	P	W	D	L	F	A	Diff	B	Part	C1	C2	C3
Angers	1	2	0	1	1	2	3	-1	–	1	–	–	1
Angoulême	2	2	1	0	1	3	4	-1	–	1	–	–	2
Auxerre	16	14	6	3	5	25	15	10	1	4	–	–	16
Bastia	25	18	9	4	5	35	26	9	3	3	–	5	20
Girondins Bordeaux	76	64	29	13	22	83	81	2	5	15	23	15	38
Laval	4	4	1	2	1	4	5	-1	–	1	–	–	4
Lens	18	18	7	4	7	32	26	6	–	4	–	3	15
Olympique Lyon	37	38	14	6	18	59	69	-10	3	10	–	26	11
Olympique Marseille	67	49	26	8	15	79	56	23	7	12	35	20	12
Metz	5	12	1	3	8	16	30	-14	–	5	–	3	2
Monaco	41	46	12	14	20	62	65	-3	3	13	13	14	14
Montpellier	9	8	3	2	3	11	9	2	1	2	–	9	0
Nancy	3	4	1	1	2	7	6	1	–	1	–	3	–
Nantes	54	52	18	15	19	78	77	1	3	14	16	16	22
Nice	29	28	12	3	13	45	50	-5	2	7	18	–	11
Nîmes Olympique	2	4	1	0	3	4	6	-2	–	2	–	–	2
Paris Saint-Germain	22	20	8	5	7	30	24	6	1	5	1	15	6
Racing Club Paris	0	2	0	0	2	2	4	-2	–	1	–	–	0

Stade Français	5	6	1	3	2	3	3	0	–	2	–	–	5
Stade Reims	38	24	14	3	7	63	30	33	7	4	38	–	–
Stade Rennes	2	4	0	2	2	1	4	-3	–	2	–	2	–
Rouen	5	6	2	1	3	5	5	0	–	1	–	–	5
Saint-Etienne	81	69	29	15	25	103	80	23	8	16	51	5	25
Sedan	2	4	1	0	3	5	12	-7	–	2	–	0	2
Sochaux	22	20	7	6	7	32	22	10	2	5	–	–	22
Strasbourg	32	30	11	8	11	33	43	-10	2	6	8	5	19
Toulouse	11	10	5	1	4	16	16	1	–	3	–	–	11
Total	**609**	**558**	**219**	**123**	**216**	**838**	**770**	**68**	**48**	**142**	**203**	**141**	**265**

Greece

Club	Pts	P	W	D	L	F	A	Diff	B	Part	C1	C2	C3
AEK Athens	48	58	19	7	32	74	107	-33	3	18	17	4	27
Panathinaikos	69	81	23	17	41	96	131	-35	6	25	41	10	18
Panionios	8	11	4	0	7	11	22	-11	–	4	–	4	4
OFI Crete	6	6	3	0	3	5	8	-3	–	2	–	4	2
Kastoria	1	2	0	1	1	0	2	-2	–	1	–	1	–
Larissa	14	12	5	3	4	12	11	1	1	4	2	10	2
Panahaiki	5	4	2	1	1	4	9	-5	–	1	–	–	5
Olympiakos Pireus	71	77	28	15	34	86	116	-30	–	26	20	28	23
Aris Salonika	24	28	9	6	13	41	61	-20	–	10	–	1	23
Iraklis	6	10	2	2	6	5	25	-20	–	5	–	1	5
PAOK Salonika	44	44	16	11	17	46	68	-22	1	16	3	22	19
Total	**296**	**333**	**111**	**63**	**159**	**380**	**560**	**-180**	**11**	**112**	**83**	**85**	**128**

Hungary

Club	Pts	P	W	D	L	F	A	Diff	B	Part	C1	C2	C3
Békéscsaba	4	4	2	0	2	5	4	1	–	1	–	4	–
Csepel	1	2	0	1	1	3	4	-1	–	1	1	–	–
Ferencváros	133	108	50	19	39	188	142	45	14	22	21	29	83
Honvéd	78	70	34	8	28	126	111	15	2	17	22	12	44
MTK-VM	54	44	20	7	17	85	74	11	7	10	12	25	17
Vasas SC	49	51	19	8	24	94	70	24	3	14	33	3	13
Diósgyöri VTK	14	12	7	0	5	19	23	-4	–	3	–	6	8
Rába ETO	46	42	19	5	18	73	76	-3	3	11	17	15	14
Komló	2	2	1	0	1	4	8	-4	–	1	–	2	–
Pécs Dózsa	4	6	2	0	4	6	7	-1	–	1	–	–	4
Pécsi MSC	2	4	1	0	3	1	5	-4	–	2	–	0	2
Salgótarján	1	2	0	1	1	2	4	-2	–	1	–	–	1
Siófok	1	2	0	1	1	1	3	-2	–	1	–	1	–
Videoton	30	28	11	5	12	32	35	-3	3	6	–	–	30
Haladás	4	4	1	2	1	9	4	5	–	1	–	4	–
Tatabánya	7	10	2	3	5	7	17	-10	–	5	–	1	6
Ujpesti Dózsa	122	105	46	18	41	188	158	30	12	23	46	29	47
Total	**552**	**496**	**215**	**78**	**203**	**843**	**745**	**98**	**44**	**120**	**152**	**131**	**269**

Iceland

Club	Pts	P	W	D	L	F	A	Diff	B	Part	C1	C2	C3
IA Akranes	8	32	1	6	25	18	99	-81	–	15	5	2	1
IBA Akureyri	2	4	1	0	3	2	17	-15	–	2	2	0	–
FH Hafnarfjördhur	1	2	0	1	1	3	5	-2	–	1	–	–	1
IBK Keflavik	4	20	1	2	17	12	70	-58	–	9	0	1	3
Fram Reykjavik	11	32	5	1	26	16	91	-75	–	14	0	11	0
KR Reykjavik	0	14	0	0	14	10	66	-56	–	7	0	0	0
Valur Reykjavik	14	32	3	8	21	18	92	-74	–	15	7	2	5
Vikingur Reykjavik	0	8	0	0	8	3	27	-24	–	4	0	0	0

IBV Vestmannaeyjar	5	18	0	5	13	7	46	-39	–	8	1	0	4
Total	**45**	**162**	**11**	**23**	**128**	**89**	**513**	**-424**	**–**	**75**	**15**	**16**	**14**

Italy

Club	Pts	P	W	D	L	F	A	Diff	B	Part	C1	C2	C3
Atalanta	23	21	7	6	8	22	21	1	3	4	–	11	12
Bologna	53	39	18	13	8	55	36	19	4	8	3	4	46
Cagliari	7	10	3	1	6	10	12	-2	–	3	4	–	3
Cesena	2	2	1	0	1	3	4	-1	–	1	–	–	2
Fiorentina	112	81	42	16	23	112	81	31	12	18	22	34	56
Sampdoria	50	32	18	7	7	43	27	16	7	5	–	44	6
AC Milan	220	151	77	35	39	268	147	121	31	24	108	53	59
Inter Milan	247	178	87	41	50	283	161	122	32	29	84	16	147
Napoli	104	85	36	26	23	102	89	13	6	18	7	25	72
Penigia	4	4	1	2	1	2	4	-2	–	1	–	–	4
Roma	139	102	51	20	31	154	101	53	17	17	14	30	95
Lazio	11	14	5	1	8	20	28	-8	–	4	–	–	11
Torino	66	59	23	15	21	81	67	14	5	14	4	26	36
Juventus	319	208	122	36	50	368	176	192	39	31	112	46	161
Verona	23	16	8	6	2	23	15	8	1	3	5	–	18
Lanerossi Vicenza	1	2	0	1	1	1	2	-1	–	1	–	–	1
Total	**1381**	**1004**	**499**	**226**	**279**	**1547**	**971**	**576**	**157**	**181**	**363**	**289**	**729**

Luxembourg

Club	Pts	P	W	D	L	F	A	Diff	B	Part	C1	C2	C3
Avenir Beggen	2	22	1	0	21	6	102	-96	–	11	0	0	2
Aris Bonnevoie	9	22	3	3	16	16	72	-56	–	10	1	6	2
Red Boys Differdange	3	20	1	1	18	8	103	-95	–	10	2	0	1
Alliance Dudelange	2	4	0	2	2	4	18	-14	–	2	–	2	–
Stade Dudelange	0	4	0	0	4	1	32	-31	–	2	0	–	–
Fola Esch	0	2	0	0	2	1	11	-10	–	1	–	0	–
Jeunesse Esch	20	49	7	6	36	48	162	-114	–	22	15	1	4
Jeunesse Hautcharage	0	2	0	0	2	0	21	-21	–	1	–	0	–
Swift Hesperange	0	2	0	0	2	0	6	-6	–	1	–	0	–
Spora Luxembourg	4	19	2	0	17	12	87	-75	–	9	2	0	2
Union Luxembourg	6	30	2	2	26	12	114	-102	–	15	0	6	0
Progrès Niedercorn	1	10	0	1	9	1	37	-36	–	5	1	0	0
US Rumelange	2	8	1	0	7	3	48	-45	–	4	–	2	0
Total	**49**	**194**	**17**	**15**	**162**	**112**	**813**	**-701**	**–**	**93**	**21**	**17**	**11**

Malta

Club	Pts	P	W	D	L	F	A	Diff	B	Part	C1	C2	C3
Gzira United	0	2	0	0	2	0	9	-9	–	1	–	0	–
Hamrun Spartans	7	14	3	1	10	5	30	-25	–	6	2	4	1
Valletta	3	28	1	1	26	9	123	-114	–	14	2	1	0
Floriana	8	32	2	4	26	15	126	-111	–	16	2	4	2
Hibernians	12	34	4	4	26	15	103	-88	–	16	4	6	2
Marsa	0	2	0	0	2	0	11	-11	–	1	–	–	0
Rabat Ajax	0	8	0	0	8	0	40	-40	–	4	0	–	0
Sliema Wanderers	19	48	8	3	37	28	140	-112	–	22	9	9	1
Zurrieq	0	6	0	0	6	1	27	-26	–	3	–	0	0
Total	**49**	**174**	**18**	**13**	**143**	**73**	**609**	**-536**	**–**	**83**	**19**	**24**	**6**

Netherlands

Club	Pts	P	W	D	L	F	A	Diff	B	Part	C1	C2	C3
AZ'67 Alkmaar	37	26	13	8	5	62	26	36	3	5	5	6	26

Ajax	196	135	76	19	40	262	133	129	25	27	116	37	43
FC Amsterdam	29	24	11	5	8	43	32	11	2	5	10	–	19
Vitesse	7	6	3	1	2	7	4	3	–	1	–	–	7
NAC Breda	6	6	2	2	2	5	8	-3	–	2	–	6	–
Go Ahead Eagles	0	2	0	0	2	0	7	-7	–	1	–	0	–
PSV Eindhoven	142	109	53	21	35	197	108	89	15	22	58	33	51
Twente Enschede	72	58	26	12	20	103	69	34	8	11	–	15	57
Groningen	21	20	9	3	8	30	29	1	–	4	–	6	15
Haarlem	3	4	1	1	2	6	9	-3	–	1	–	–	3
Roda JC	8	12	3	1	8	14	21	-7	1	4	0	8	–
FC Den Haag	23	20	10	2	8	34	27	7	1	5	–	20	3
NEC Nijmegen	3	4	1	1	2	4	6	-2	–	1	–	3	–
Feyenoord	145	105	57	19	29	220	120	100	12	21	56	14	75
Sparta Rotterdam	36	32	14	7	11	64	44	20	1	7	7	11	18
Fortuna Sittard	7	8	2	2	4	9	12	-3	1	2	–	7	–
Willem II	1	2	0	1	1	2	7	-5	–	1	–	1	–
Utrecht	29	36	11	7	18	48	73	-25	–	13	0	2	27
Total	**765**	**609**	**292**	**112**	**205**	**1110**	**735**	**375**	**69**	**133**	**252**	**169**	**344**

Northern Ireland

Club	Pts	P	W	D	L	F	A	Diff	B	Part	C1	C2	C3
Ballymena United	2	10	1	0	9	3	29	-26	–	5	–	0	2
Cliftonville	0	2	0	0	2	0	8	-8	–	1	–	0	–
Crusaders	2	10	0	2	8	5	37	-32	–	5	0	2	–
Distillery	1	4	0	1	3	4	15	-11	–	2	1	0	–
Glentoran	34	58	8	17	33	50	123	-73	1	25	12	14	8
Linfield	29	51	7	14	30	52	109	-57	1	23	21	4	4
Carrick Rangers	2	4	1	0	3	7	12	-5	–	1	–	2	–
Coleraine	9	26	2	5	19	27	85	-58	–	11	0	1	8
Derry City*	2	5	1	0	4	8	20	-12	–	2	2	0	–
Glenavon	2	12	0	2	10	6	32	-26	–	6	1	0	1
Ards	3	8	1	1	6	9	35	-26	–	4	0	1	2
Portadown	6	8	2	2	4	8	27	-19	–	3	0	2	4
Total	**92**	**198**	**23**	**44**	**131**	**179**	**532**	**-353**	**2**	**88**	**37**	**26**	**29**

Norway

Club	Pts	P	W	D	L	F	A	Diff	B	Part	C1	C2	C3
SK Brann	10	14	4	2	8	18	24	-6	–	5	–	10	0
SFK Bodø/Glimt	2	6	1	0	5	5	12	-7	–	2	–	2	–
Bryne IL	5	6	2	1	3	5	11	-6	–	3	–	2	3
Strømgodset IF	3	8	1	1	6	6	33	-27	–	4	0	2	1
Fredrikstad FK	5	16	1	3	12	9	37	-28	–	7	3	2	0
Gjøvik/Lyn	2	2	1	0	1	1	6	-5	–	1	–	2	–
Haugar FC	4	4	1	2	1	3	7	-4	–	1	–	4	–
IK Start	7	14	3	1	10	13	29	-16	–	6	0	–	7
Lillestrøm SK	13	22	4	5	13	15	41	-26	–	9	11	0	2
Mjøndalen IF	2	6	1	0	5	3	29	-26	–	3	–	0	2
Molde FK	4	6	1	2	3	5	18	-13	–	3	–	–	4
Moss FK	0	6	0	0	6	5	15	-10	–	3	0	0	0
SK Frigg	0	2	0	0	2	2	6	-4	–	1	–	–	0
FK Skeid	10	16	3	4	9	14	35	-21	–	7	1	4	5
SFK Lyn	11	22	4	2	16	29	73	-44	1	8	4	6	1
Vålerengen SIF	7	18	1	5	12	18	42	-24	–	9	4	1	2
IF Sarpsborg	0	2	0	0	2	0	6	-6	–	1	–	–	0
IL Viking	13	26	4	5	17	20	56	-36	–	11	3	0	10
Tromsø IL	1	2	0	1	1	0	1	-1	–	1	–	1	–
Rosenborg BK	19	26	8	3	15	31	61	-30	–	10	5	4	10
Total	**118**	**224**	**40**	**37**	**147**	**202**	**542**	**-340**	**1**	**95**	**31**	**40**	**47**

Poland

Club	Pts	P	W	D	L	F	A	Diff	B	Part	C1	C2	C3
Polonia Bytom	4	6	2	0	4	7	13	-6	–	2	4	–	–
Szombierki Bytom	3	6	1	1	4	5	10	-5	–	2	2	–	1
Ruch Chorzów	28	32	10	6	16	49	60	-11	2	8	15	–	13
Wisla Kraków	22	20	8	5	7	34	32	2	1	5	7	10	5
Lechia Gdańsk	0	2	0	0	2	2	10	-8	–	1	–	0	–
Arka Gdynia	2	2	1	0	1	3	4	-1	–	1	–	2	–
GKS Katowice	10	16	4	2	10	17	25	-8	–	6	–	5	5
LKS Lódź	2	2	1	0	1	2	6	-4	–	1	2	–	–
Widzew Lódź	37	38	13	9	16	47	58	-11	2	9	11	2	24
Zaglebie Lubin	0	2	0	0	2	0	2	-2	–	1	–	–	0
Stal Mielec	13	16	4	4	8	11	14	-3	1	5	0	–	13
Odra Opole	1	2	0	1	1	2	3	-1	–	1	–	–	1
Lech Poznań	19	20	8	3	9	24	38	-14	–	7	8	10	1
Stal Rzeszów	5	4	2	1	1	9	4	5	–	1	–	5	–
Zaglebie Sosnowiec	7	13	2	3	8	11	28	-17	–	6	–	5	2
Pogon Szczecin	1	4	0	1	3	3	7	-4	–	2	–	–	1
GKS Tychy	1	2	0	1	1	1	3	-2	–	1	–	–	1
Gwardia Warsaw	15	17	6	3	8	18	28	-10	–	5	4	2	9
Legia Warsaw	92	75	33	19	23	110	81	29	7	18	27	40	25
Zaglebie Walbrzych	5	4	2	1	1	6	5	1	–	1	–	–	5
Slask Wroclaw	29	28	10	8	10	41	46	-5	1	7	1	11	17
Górnik Zabrze	80	68	31	13	24	118	100	18	5	17	49	26	5
Total	**376**	**379**	**138**	**81**	**160**	**520**	**577**	**57**	**19**	**107**	**130**	**118**	**128**

Portugal

Club	Pts	P	W	D	L	F	A	Diff	B	Part	C1	C2	C3
Estrela Amadora	4	4	1	2	1	3	4	-1	–	1	–	4	–
Barreirense	10	11	5	0	6	11	16	-5	–	4	–	–	10
Sporting Braga	10	12	5	0	7	14	23	-9	–	4	–	8	2
Chaves	2	4	1	0	3	6	9	-3	–	1	–	–	2
Academica Coimbra	9	10	3	2	5	5	10	-5	1	3	–	7	2
Vitória Guimarães	30	28	12	5	11	32	40	-8	1	7	–	2	28
Belenenses	19	24	5	9	10	24	33	-9	–	9	–	1	18
Benfica	253	179	88	42	49	324	179	145	35	32	179	38	36
Sporting Lisbon	156	135	57	32	46	243	169	74	10	31	24	46	86
Leixões	10	10	2	5	3	13	16	-3	1	3	–	7	3
Portimonense	2	2	1	0	1	1	4	-3	–	1	–	–	2
Boavista	28	30	11	6	13	42	39	3	–	9	–	14	14
FC Porto	142	118	57	19	42	182	140	42	9	29	47	41	54
Vitória Setúbal	63	56	26	7	23	90	72	18	4	11	–	6	57
Total	**738**	**623**	**274**	**129**	**220**	**990**	**754**	**236**	**61**	**145**	**250**	**174**	**314**

Republic of Ireland

Club	Pts	P	W	D	L	F	A	Diff	B	Part	C1	C2	C3
Athlone Town	6	8	1	4	3	11	19	-8	–	3	2	–	4
Finn Harps	1	8	0	1	7	5	37	-32	–	4	–	1	0
Bray Wanderers	1	2	0	1	1	1	3	-2	–	1	–	1	–
Cork Celtic	1	4	0	1	3	2	10	-8	–	2	0	1	–
Cork City	0	2	0	0	2	0	6	-6	–	1	–	0	–
Cork Hibernians	5	10	2	1	7	9	21	-12	–	4	0	5	0
Derry City*	2 2 } 4	6 5 } 11	0 1 } 1	2 0 } 2	4 4 } 8	1 8 } 9	11 20 } 31	-10 -12 } -22	– – } –	3 2 } 5	0 2 } 2	1 0 } 1	1 – } 1
Drogheda United	0	2	0	0	2	0	14	-14	–	1	–	–	0
Bohemians	15	26	4	7	15	18	49	-31	–	11	4	5	6
Drumcondra	6	13	3	0	10	12	46	-34	–	5	2	–	4

Home Farm	1	2	0	1	1	1	7	-6	–	1	–	1	–
St. Patrick's Athletic	1	8	0	1	7	6	26	-20	–	4	1	0	0
Shamrock Rovers	22	38	7	8	23	37	66	-29	–	16	4	12	6
Shelbourne	5	11	1	3	7	6	18	-12	–	4	0	0	5
UCD	1	2	0	1	1	0	1	-1	–	1	–	1	–
Dundalk	18	34	6	6	22	23	83	60	–	13	9	5	4
Galway United	0	4	0	0	4	4	12	-8	–	2	–	0	0
Limerick	2	12	0	2	10	7	32	-25	–	6	0	1	1
Sligo Rovers	0	4	0	0	4	0	10	-10	–	2	0	0	–
Waterford United	9	22	4	1	17	21	61	-40	–	9	6	3	–
Total	**96**	**218**	**28**	**40**	**150**	**164**	**532**	**-368**	**–**	**93**	**28**	**37**	**31**

Romania

Club	**Pts**	**P**	**W**	**D**	**L**	**F**	**A**	**Diff**	**B**	**Part**	**C1**	**C2**	**C3**
UT Arad	11	16	3	4	9	16	31	-15	1	4	2	–	9
Bacau	9	8	3	2	3	12	11	1	1	1	–	–	9
Baia Mare	1	2	0	1	1	2	5	-3	–	1	–	1	–
Red Flag Brasov	7	11	3	1	7	14	25	-11	–	3	–	–	7
Dinamo Bucharest	103	100	40	18	42	157	133	24	5	25	52	23	28
Progresul Bucharest	1	2	0	1	1	1	2	-1	–	1	–	1	–
Rapid Bucharest	17	22	7	2	13	24	38	-14	1	6	3	8	6
Sportul Studentesc Bucharest	16	20	6	4	10	20	31	-11	–	6	–	–	16
Steaua Bucharest	91	81	32	18	31	114	112	2	9	22	56	34	1
Victoria Bucharest	16	14	6	3	5	21	17	4	1	3	–	–	16
Universitatea Cluj	6	6	3	0	3	8	12	-4	–	2	–	4	2
Universitatea Craiova	69	62	28	10	24	75	69	6	3	16	9	10	50
CSU Galati	2	4	1	0	3	3	10	-7	–	2	–	0	2
Convinul Hunedoara	4	4	1	2	1	8	9	-1	–	1	–	–	4
Flacara Moreni	0	2	0	0	2	1	4	-3	–	1	–	–	0
Jiul Petrosani	2	2	1	0	1	2	3	-1	–	1	–	2	–
Arges Pitesti	26	26	10	6	10	38	42	-4	–	8	8	–	18
Petrolul Ploiesti	26	25	12	1	12	24	34	-10	1	8	5	2	19
Chimia Râmnicu Vâlcea	1	2	0	1	1	2	4	-2	–	1	–	1	–
Politehnica Timisoara	14	14	7	0	7	14	25	-11	–	4	–	6	8
ASA Tîrgu Mures	3	6	1	1	4	4	13	-9	–	3	–	–	3
Total	**425**	**429**	**164**	**75**	**190**	**560**	**630**	**-70**	**22**	**119**	**135**	**92**	**198**

Scotland

Club	**Pts**	**P**	**W**	**D**	**L**	**F**	**A**	**Diff**	**B**	**Part**	**C1**	**C2**	**C3**
Aberdeen	98	79	37	18	24	125	86	39	6	20	15	50	33
Dundee	21	20	9	1	10	40	39	1	2	5	12	1	8
Dundee United	127	102	46	26	30	149	98	51	9	20	13	7	107
Dunfermline Athletic	55	42	23	5	14	83	45	38	4	7	–	19	36
Heart of Midlothian	36	36	14	7	15	56	63	-7	1	10	2	2	32
Hibernian	86	70	34	13	23	125	99	26	5	15	9	8	69
Celtic	174	128	66	24	38	235	126	109	18	27	112	47	15
Rangers	185	147	70	27	50	245	193	52	18	30	64	74	47
Morton	0	2	0	0	2	3	9	-6	–	1	–	–	0
Kilmarnock	25	24	9	5	10	38	39	-1	2	5	4	–	21
St. Mirren	11	14	3	5	6	10	14	-4	–	4	–	4	7
St. Johnstone	6	6	3	0	3	8	-8	0	–	1	–	–	6
Partick Thistle	6	6	3	0	3	10	11	-1	–	2	–	–	6
Total	**830**	**676**	**317**	**131**	**228**	**1127**	**830**	**297**	**65**	**147**	**231**	**212**	**387**

Spain

Club	**Pts**	**P**	**W**	**D**	**L**	**F**	**A**	**Diff**	**B**	**Part**	**C1**	**C2**	**C3**
Español	44	34	18	3	13	49	41	8	5	5	–	–	44

Barcelona	342	233	123	49	61	463	260	203	47	35	56	122	164
Athletic Bilbao	103	86	40	16	30	121	111	10	7	18	14	6	83
Sporting Gijón	9	12	3	3	6	9	13	-4	–	5	–	–	9
Las Palmas	11	12	4	3	5	20	17	3	–	3	–	–	11
Atlético Madrid	179	130	68	22	40	210	144	66	21	26	57	79	43
Castilla Madrid	2	2	1	0	1	4	6	-2	–	1	–	2	–
Real Madrid	362	235	133	38	64	514	255	259	58	35	271	40	51
Osasuna	4	4	2	0	2	4	4	0	–	1	–	–	4
Sabadell	2	2	1	0	1	3	5	-2	–	1	–	–	2
Real Sociedad	43	40	14	12	14	42	49	-7	3	9	12	5	26
Real Zaragoza	92	70	35	11	24	129	98	31	11	11	–	30	62
Real Betis	10	12	3	3	6	10	15	-5	1	4	–	7	3
Seville	25	24	9	6	9	32	39	-7	1	7	7	2	16
Valencia	149	111	54	26	31	205	135	70	15	19	6	29	114
Real Valladolid	12	8	4	3	1	12	6	6	1	2	–	10	2
Celta Vigo	0	2	0	0	2	0	3	-3	–	1	–	–	0
Total	**1389**	**1017**	**512**	**195**	**310**	**1827**	**1201**	**626**	**170**	**183**	**423**	**332**	**634**

Sweden

Club	Pts	P	W	D	L	F	A	Diff	B	Part	C1	C2	C3
Åtvidaberg SFF	19	18	6	5	7	26	30	-4	2	5	9	8	2
IF Elfsborg	5	8	1	3	4	8	15	-7	–	4	–	–	5
IK Brage	3	6	1	1	4	8	15	-7	–	2	–	–	3
GAIS	3	4	1	1	2	6	10	-4	–	2	–	–	3
IFK Gothenburg	101	74	37	16	21	135	98	37	11	15	42	8	51
Örgryte IS	5	10	1	3	6	12	28	-16	–	4	0	–	5
Halmstad SBK	3	4	1	1	2	4	6	-2	–	2	3	–	–
Hammarby IF	12	10	5	2	3	22	14	8	–	2	–	3	9
Kalmar FF	10	12	4	2	6	11	22	-11	–	5	–	8	2
Landskrona BOIS	2	4	1	0	3	1	9	-8	–	2	–	2	0
Malmö FF	90	89	31	22	36	106	123	-17	6	27	45	27	18
IFK Norrköping	30	34	9	12	13	42	47	-5	–	11	9	10	11
AIK	21	22	7	7	8	37	32	5	–	8	–	6	15
Djurgården SIF	20	28	6	7	15	34	55	-21	1	11	6	6	8
Öster SIF	17	28	7	3	18	29	50	-21	–	11	3	2	12
Total	**341**	**351**	**118**	**85**	**148**	**481**	**554**	**-73**	**20**	**111**	**117**	**80**	**144**

Switzerland

Club	Pts	P	W	D	L	F	A	Diff	B	Part	C1	C2	C3
Aarau	1	4	0	1	3	2	11	-9		2	–	1	0
FC Basle	34	55	13	7	35	85	135	-50	1	21	23	1	10
Young Boys Berne	29	29	9	8	12	41	53	-12	3	9	21	7	1
Servette	66	67	25	14	28	97	103	-6	2	20	16	28	22
La Chaux-de-Fonds	6	6	2	2	2	11	16	-5	–	2	4	2	–
Lausanne-Sports	32	47	12	6	29	68	107	-39	2	16	1	15	16
Lucerne	5	10	1	3	6	6	19	-13	–	4	0	0	5
Lugano	1	4	0	1	3	1	7	-6	–	2	–	0	1
Neuchâtel Xamax	38	32	13	10	9	49	37	12	2	7	8	2	28
St-Gallen	4	8	1	2	5	4	16	-12	–	3	–	3	1
Sion	26	28	10	5	13	38	54	-16	1	9	–	13	13
Wettingen	5	4	2	1	1	6	2	4	–	1	–	–	5
FC Zürich	60	63	22	10	31	88	109	-21	6	16	28	13	19
Grasshoppers Zürich	79	82	30	13	39	135	128	7	6	21	19	7	53
Total	**386**	**439**	**140**	**83**	**216**	**631**	**797**	**-166**	**23**	**133**	**120**	**92**	**174**

Turkey

Club	Pts	P	W	D	L	F	A	Diff	B	Part	C1	C2	C3
Adanaspor	3	6	1	1	4	6	20	-14	–	3	–	–	3
Sakaryaspor	2	4	1	0	3	3	7	-4	–	1	–	2	–
Gençlerbirligi	0	2	0	0	2	1	4	-3	–	1	–	0	–
Ankaragücü	1	6	0	1	5	1	13	-12	–	3	–	1	–
Boluspor	0	2	0	0	2	0	4	-4	–	1	–	–	0
Bursaspor	7	8	2	2	4	5	12	-7	1	2	–	7	–
Eskisehirspor	8	14	3	2	9	13	26	-13	–	5	–	3	5
Besiktas	18	32	6	5	21	21	62	-41	1	15	10	3	5
Fenerbahçe	44	62	18	7	37	62	118	-56	1	22	22	8	14
Galatasaray	62	69	21	16	32	81	120	-39	4	20	38	18	6
Altay	7	12	2	3	7	14	32	-18	–	6	–	4	3
Göztepe	24	30	10	2	18	36	49	-13	2	7	–	10	14
Mersin Idmanyurdu	1	2	0	1	1	0	1	-1	–	1	–	1	–
Orduspor	2	2	1	0	1	2	6	-4	–	1	–	–	2
Trabzonspor	20	22	9	2	11	19	35	-16	–	9	13	5	2
Total	**199**	**273**	**74**	**42**	**157**	**264**	**509**	**-245**	**9**	**97**	**83**	**62**	**54**

USSR

Club	Pts	P	W	D	L	F	A	Diff	B	Part	C1	C2	C3
Dnepr Dnepropetrovsk	25	24	8	7	9	27	28	-1	2	6	15	–	10
Shakhtyor Donetsk	24	18	10	3	5	30	24	6	1	5	–	11	13
Ararat Erevan	25	16	11	2	3	37	15	22	1	3	11	4	10
Metallist Kharkov	3	4	1	1	2	4	3	1	–	1	–	3	–
Dinamo Kiev	159	106	59	25	22	173	84	89	16	20	75	54	30
Zenti Leningrad	11	21	5	1	6	14	22	-8	–	4	6	–	5
Karpaty Lvov	1	2	0	1	1	3	4	-1	–	1	–	1	–
Dinamo Minsk	34	26	12	7	7	41	25	16	3	5	9	8	17
CSKA Moscow	7	6	3	1	2	7	5	2	–	2	5	–	2
Dinamo Moscow	59	43	20	11	12	61	40	21	8	9	–	46	13
Spartak Moscow	111	86	44	18	24	134	92	42	5	17	24	12	75
Torpedo Moscow	61	47	22	14	11	72	46	26	3	12	3	30	28
Chernomorets Odessa	8	10	3	2	5	10	13	-3	–	3	–	–	8
SKA Rostov on Don	6	4	3	0	1	6	2	4	–	1	–	6	–
Dinamo Tbilisi	63	51	25	8	18	76	57	19	5	10	2	30	31
Zhalgiris Vilnius	4	6	2	0	4	7	11	-4	–	2	–	–	4
Zaria Voroshilovgrad	5	4	2	1	1	3	1	2	–	1	5	–	–
Total	**606**	**465**	**230**	**102**	**133**	**705**	**472**	**233**	**44**	**102**	**155**	**205**	**24**

Wales

Club	Pts	P	W	D	L	F	A	Diff	B	Part	C1	C2	C3
Bangor City	4	7	1	2	4	5	9	-4	–	2	–	4	–
Cardiff City	49	45	16	13	16	62	50	12	4	12	–	49	–
Borough United	3	4	1	1	2	2	4	-2	–	1	–	3	–
Merthyr Tydfil	2	2	1	0	1	2	3	-1	–	1	–	2	–
Newport County	8	6	2	3	1	12	3	9	1	1	–	8	–
Swansea Town	10	16	3	4	9	31	27	4	–	6	–	10	–
Wrexham	28	26	10	7	9	34	34	0	1	7	–	28	–
Total	**104**	**106**	**34**	**30**	**42**	**148**	**130**	**18**	**6**	**30**	**–**	**104**	**–**

West Germany

Club	Pts	P	W	D	L	F	A	Diff	B	Part	C1	C2	C3
Hertha Berlin	48	36	20	5	11	54	42	12	3	8	–	–	48
Tasmania Berlin	0	2	0	0	2	3	5	-2	–	1	–	–	0
Werder Bremen	65	50	24	11	15	89	55	34	6	10	13	6	46

Eintracht Braunschweig	21	21	8	4	9	34	25	9	1	4	5	–	16
Cologne	223	165	86	30	49	318	195	123	21	26	25	18	180
Viktoria Cologne	2	2	1	0	1	5	7	-2	–	1	–	–	2
Borussia Dortmund	65	51	26	7	18	100	71	29	6	10	22	24	19
MSV Duisburg	21	14	8	3	3	38	19	19	2	2	–	–	21
Fortuna Düsseldorf	34	29	11	8	10	45	36	9	4	5	–	22	12
Rot-Weiss Essen	1	2	0	1	1	1	5	-4	–	1	1	–	–
Eintracht Frankfurt	116	85	45	13	27	170	113	57	13	15	13	35	68
Schalke 04	44	31	17	6	8	53	41	12	4	5	9	23	12
Hamburg	182	125	70	20	35	252	147	105	22	19	43	54	85
Hannover 96	15	21	6	3	12	30	50	-20	–	7	–	–	15
Kaiserslautern	58	46	25	3	18	92	61	31	5	8	–	2	56
Bayer Leverkusen	34	24	11	9	4	31	16	15	3	4	–	–	34
Bor. Mönchengladbach	181	115	67	25	23	259	127	132	22	16	46	14	121
Bayern Munich	282	178	101	39	38	372	175	197	41	24	159	62	61
1860 Munich	40	30	15	6	9	70	42	28	4	6	6	17	17
Nuremberg	26	20	10	3	7	33	27	6	2	6	12	11	3
Kickers Offenbach	2	2	1	0	1	2	3	-1	–	1	–	2	–
Saarbrücken	2	2	1	0	1	5	7	-2	–	1	2	–	–
VFB Stuttgart	92	70	34	17	19	128	77	51	7	13	2	3	87
Bayer Uerdingen	18	14	7	2	5	33	14	19	2	2	–	11	7
Wuppertal	2	2	1	0	1	6	8	-2	–	1	–	–	2
Total	**1574**	**1137**	**595**	**215**	**327**	**2223**	**1368**	**855**	**169**	**196**	**358**	**304**	**912**

Yugoslavia

Club	Pts	P	W	D	L	F	A	Diff	B	Part	C1	C2	C3
Borac Banja Luka	8	6	4	0	2	17	8	9		2	–	8	–
Red Star Belgrade	216	167	82	30	55	323	222	101	22	32	103	30	83
OFK Belgrade	54	49	20	8	21	90	90	0	6	10	–	11	43
Partizan Belgrade	81	77	32	11	34	132	122	10	6	19	35	5	41
Rad Belgrade	2	2	1	0	1	2	3	-1	–	1	–	–	2
Borovo	2	2	1	0	1	2	3	-1	–	1	–	2	–
Napredak Krusevac	0	2	0	0	2	0	2	-2	–	1	–	–	0
Olimpija Ljubljana	2	6	0	2	4	6	20	-14	–	3	–	1	1
Velez Mostar	33	28	12	8	8	47	40	7	1	6	–	10	23
Radnicki Nis	27	22	11	3	8	34	31	3	2	3	–	–	27
Vojvodina Novi Sad	39	36	14	8	14	39	42	-3	3	10	12	–	27
Rijeka	15	16	5	4	7	16	17	-1	1	4	–	10	5
Sarajevo	13	14	4	5	5	29	30	-1	–	4	4	–	9
Zeljeznicar Sarajevo	23	22	8	4	10	41	35	6	3	4	0	–	23
Vardar Skoplje	5	8	2	1	5	5	16	-11	–	3	0	2	3
Hajduk Split	104	86	43	10	33	144	102	42	8	17	28	22	54
Sloboda Tuzla	2	2	1	0	1	4	8	-4	–	1	–	–	2
Dinamo Zagreb	105	100	35	25	40	133	126	7	10	24	3	29	73
NK Zagreb	9	12	3	3	6	20	18	2	–	4	–	–	9
Tresnjevka Zagreb	0	2	0	0	2	1	4	-3	–	1	–	–	0
Total	**740**	**659**	**278**	**122**	**259**	**1085**	**939**	**146**	**62**	**150**	**185**	**130**	**423**

Notes:

*** In 1988-89 Derry City left the Irish League (Northern Ireland) and joined the League of Ireland (Republic of Ireland)**

National Classification by Cumulative Year-by-Year Index

1955-56 to 1990-91

Pos	Cnty	Total	5556	5657	5758	5859	5960	6061	6162	6263	6364	6465	6566	6667	6768	6869	6970
1	Esp	293.155	13.000	13.000	11.000	15.000	15.000	7.666	15.800	7.166	11.800	8.428	13.666	4.000	6.666	6.666	3.000
2	Ita	275.896	9.000	12.000	10.500	2.000	4.000	9.750	7.400	12.000	9.600	8.142	4.666	11.000	10.200	6.000	8.571
3	FRG	275.771	1.500	5.000	5.000	9.000	5.000	4.000	4.200	4.200	8.500	6.333	8.166	6.833	6.714	5.833	5.666
4	Eng	265.315	–	12.000	11.333	1.000	9.000	8.000	5.000	7.666	4.000	14.500	12.333	8.200	11.200	8.285	12.500
5	Sco	200.499	9.000	2.000	2.000	2.000	13.000	6.000	6.250	6.000	5.500	5.200	7.400	11.600	6.400	8.166	6.000
6	Bel	189.115	0.000	0.000	0.000	9.000	3.500	0.500	6.000	5.500	5.666	3.000	4.000	5.000	3.800	2.500	8.200
7	Ned	189.981	2.000	0.000	6.000	0.000	7.000	1.000	3.500	6.666	3.666	5.000	1.000	4.500	2.500	5.600	9.500
8	Hun	184.146	6.000	1.000	12.000	4.000	1.500	2.666	8.666	6.333	8.666	12.000	7.666	6.333	11.666	18.000	2.750
9	Yug	180.831	6.000	9.000	4.500	1.000	4.666	3.500	5.600	8.000	3.500	3.600	3.750	6.200	4.800	2.166	3.200
10	Por	177.699	1.000	0.000	1.000	4.000	0.000	18.000	5.250	4.400	7.500	5.000	4.200	2.600	5.800	5.166	5.500
11	Fra	174.682	13.000	8.000	2.000	15.000	5.500	3.000	0.500	3.333	5.333	3.600	1.200	3.000	4.750	1.666	2.600
12	Tch	156.233	–	4.000	2.000	5.000	5.000	4.500	5.333	5.000	9.000	4.000	6.000	4.500	4.000	11.000	1.800
13	GDR	156.080	–	–	2.500	10.000	2.000	2.000	6.333	1.666	1.000	1.000	4.666	7.666	1.250	2.000	7.750
14	URS	149.765	–	–	–	–	–	–	–	–	–	–	10.000	3.000	7.000	–	3.500
15	Aut	126.698	4.000	2.000	2.000	6.000	8.000	7.500	3.500	2.666	3.333	2.500	1.333	3.666	2.000	2.500	1.250
16	Pol	124.600	1.000	2.000	3.000	0.000	2.000	2.000	2.000	2.500	4.000	6.500	6.000	3.500	7.000	7.000	8.500
17	Rom	117.348	–	4.000	2.000	2.000	1.000	–	1.000	4.666	2.000	4.666	5.000	3.000	3.250	2.250	2.500
18	Bul	109.280	–	5.000	2.000	2.000	1.000	3.000	1.000	6.500	3.000	5.666	3.666	8.333	1.333	1.500	4.250
19	Swe	108.915	4.000	1.000	1.000	5.000	4.000	8.000	0.000	4.000	3.000	1.333	2.333	1.333	0.000	4.000	1.333
20	Sui	108.865	0.000	4.000	2.666	12.000	0.333	2.000	2.250	1.666	3.250	3.500	1.750	2.250	2.750	0.800	1.500
21	Wal	104.000	–	–	–	–	–	–	1.000	2.000	3.000	8.000	0.000	1.000	13.000	1.000	6.000
22	Gre	19.581	–	–	–	–	1.000	1.000	1.000	0.000	2.333	2.333	2.750	0.666	0.333	5.000	1.250
23	Tur	72.078	–	2.000	–	1.000	5.000	2.000	0.000	4.000	6.000	1.666	1.666	0.000	2.000	4.000	5.666
24	Den	71.912	1.000	1.000	3.000	2.000	0.500	6.000	1.666	3.250	0.000	0.250	1.333	0.500	1.333	4.000	1.500
25	Nor	38.079	–	–	–	–	–	3.000	0.000	0.000	1.000	1.333	2.000	1.000	0.666	2.666	1.500
26	Fin	35.575	–	–	–	0.000	–	0.000	0.000	0.000	1.000	2.000	0.000	0.500	0.000	3.000	0.500
27	Alb	34.499	–	–	–	–	–	–	–	1.000	2.000	1.000	1.000	–	–	2.000	1.000
28	Nir	33.911	–	–	1.000	0.000	2.000	–	0.000	1.000	1.000	0.500	1.000	4.500	1.333	0.666	1.250
29	Irl	32.658	–	–	0.000	0.000	1.000	0.000	0.000	1.333	1.000	1.666	1.000	1.666	0.333	1.000	0.666
30	Lux	21.158	–	2.000	0.000	2.000	2.000	0.000	0.500	0.333	1.666	0.666	0.000	0.333	0.666	2.000	0.666
31	Cyp	20.162	–	–	–	–	–	–	–	–	1.000	0.000	0.500	0.000	0.500	0.000	0.000
32	Mlt	17.160	–	–	–	–	–	–	0.000	0.000	0.500	0.000	1.000	0.500	0.500	1.000	1.666
33	Isl	15.661	–	–	–	–	–	–	–	–	–	0.000	0.000	0.500	1.000	0.500	0.000

	Pts	P	W	D	L	F	A	Diff	B	F/P
Total	**16325**	**14946**	**6041**	**2864**	**6041**	**22424**	**22424**	**0**	**1379**	**3.001**

1955-56 to 1990-91

Pos	Cnty	Total	7071	7172	7273	7374	7475	7576	7677	7778	7879	7980	8081	8182	8283	8384	8485
1	Esp	293.155	6.333	3.500	5.200	5.200	6.400	5.800	10.000	7.600	6.400	6.666	6.333	7.600	8.000	3.600	3.833
2	Ita	275.896	5.666	9.166	8.333	4.000	5.600	4.500	7.833	4.333	3.666	3.833	6.500	3.750	6.800	10.750	11.000
3	FRG	275.771	7.666	6.333	9.833	10.500	12.333	10.285	9.285	6.714	14.000	13.714	8.571	9.000	8.833	3.500	7.166
4	Eng	265.315	12.375	9.571	11.000	9.333	6.000	7.666	8.000	7.333	9.142	6.285	8.000	7.142	3.857	12.666	9.428
5	Sco	200.499	4.333	9.600	3.500	5.600	2.000	4.750	2.250	3.250	4.250	4.750	4.000	5.500	10.500	7.200	3.200
6	Bel	189.115	6.200	4.800	2.500	3.800	3.750	10.500	9.400	10.250	4.400	2.750	5.166	8.500	8.400	6.800	4.400
7	Ned	189.981	9.600	8.200	8.500	7.500	11.200	8.000	4.250	12.500	3.250	7.250	8.666	3.800	2.000	3.833	3.750
8	Hun	184.146	2.250	7.000	4.500	5.000	6.000	4.000	5.400	2.750	4.500	3.500	3.250	1.750	2.500	3.750	5.500
9	Yug	180.831	3.833	5.600	6.000	3.250	8.750	5.500	3.250	4.250	6.500	6.500	3.800	7.750	5.000	5.400	5.600
10	Por	177.699	5.000	5.200	5.200	6.500	3.000	6.250	2.250	4.250	2.000	3.750	5.750	6.000	8.750	7.000	2.750
11	Fra	174.682	2.000	2.200	0.800	4.250	5.000	5.250	3.500	7.500	3.000	8.500	7.750	2.800	4.400	3.800	4.000
12	Tch	156.233	4.750	1.000	5.250	5.250	5.000	3.000	3.000	3.000	7.500	5.800	5.250	2.500	6.000	6.000	3.800
13	GDR	156.080	7.666	6.333	6.250	9.250	2.750	7.000	4.750	7.750	4.400	5.500	6.200	5.600	1.800	5.000	4.000
14	URS	149.765	1.500	7.333	6.750	5.750	9.000	6.800	6.750	6.500	4.000	4.000	5.800	5.666	4.200	8.250	10.000
15	Aut	126.698	3.000	2.500	1.000	2.000	2.200	2.750	3.000	5.750	4.000	0.500	0.250	3.250	4.000	7.500	7.500
16	Pol	124.600	5.250	3.000	3.750	3.750	3.500	5.750	4.000	1.600	4.000	1.500	2.750	2.000	5.000	2.000	3.000
17	Rom	117.348	2.500	6.250	3.500	2.750	2.750	1.500	0.800	2.500	3.250	5.000	1.750	4.250	5.750	4.666	3.500
18	Bul	109.280	2.000	2.000	3.750	5.750	0.750	4.250	4.000	2.000	2.200	3.000	5.750	3.750	2.000	2.250	3.500
19	Swe	108.915	0.333	2.500	2.750	2.000	5.000	2.400	2.000	1.500	4.500	3.750	2.250	7.500	2.500	2.000	3.000
20	Sui	108.865	2.250	1.500	2.250	4.250	2.000	1.500	5.000	4.400	4.750	2.750	4.750	5.500	4.000	1.250	3.000
21	Wal	104.000	10.000	2.000	5.000	1.000	0.000	8.000	4.000	1.000	2.000	2.000	8.000	0.000	6.000	1.000	2.000
22	Gre	19.581	4.000	2.000	2.750	3.750	2.750	2.250	4.500	4.000	1.500	3.500	1.250	2.250	2.000	3.750	7.666
23	Tur	72.078	2.000	1.666	1.000	1.750	1.250	1.000	3.250	1.500	1.000	1.000	1.000	0.333	2.000	1.000	1.000
24	Den	71.912	1.250	1.333	1.500	2.250	1.250	0.000	0.500	2.750	3.250	3.500	3.000	2.666	1.333	0.250	2.000
25	Nor	38.079	0.666	2.000	1.250	1.500	0.000	0.750	0.500	3.000	2.000	0.250	1.333	1.000	1.666	1.000	1.000
26	Fin	35.575	0.666	0.666	1.000	0.333	1.666	0.666	1.333	0.333	1.500	0.000	0.333	0.333	1.666	2.666	0.333
27	Alb	34.499	2.000	0.500	3.000	–	–	–	–	–	2.000	2.000	0.500	2.000	1.500	2.000	0.000
28	Nir	33.911	1.666	0.000	–	3.000	1.333	0.000	1.333	1.000	1.000	0.333	1.000	1.666	0.666	0.333	1.333
29	Irl	32.658	1.666	0.333	2.333	0.000	0.333	2.000	1.666	1.000	2.333	2.666	1.000	2.000	1.666	0.000	1.666
30	Lux	21.158	0.666	0.333	0.000	0.333	0.000	0.000	0.666	0.000	1.000	2.000	0.000	0.666	0.000	0.000	0.666
31	Cyp	20.162	0.500	0.000	0.666	0.333	–	1.000	1.666	0.333	1.000	1.333	0.666	1.000	1.333	0.666	1.000
32	Mlt	17.160	0.333	2.000	0.666	0.000	1.333	0.333	0.666	0.666	0.666	1.333	0.666	0.000	0.000	0.000	1.333
33	Isl	15.661	0.000	1.000	0.333	0.333	0.333	0.666	0.333	0.666	1.333	0.666	0.333	0.666	0.000	0.666	0.333

	Pts	P	W	D	L	F	A	Diff	B	F/P
Total	**16325**	**14946**	**6041**	**2864**	**6041**	**22424**	**22424**	**0**	**1379**	**3.001**

National Classification by Cumulative Year-by-Year Index

1955-56 to 1990-91

Pos	Cnty	Total	8586	8687	8788	8889	8990	9091
1	Esp	293.155	10.166	7.400	9.800	9.800	5.500	6.166
2	Ita	275.896	7.166	6.000	6.166	12.166	1.714	12.125
3	FRG	275.771	8.833	7.666	8.666	8.428	11.500	7.000
4	Eng	265.315	–	–	–	–	–	12.500
5	Sco	200.499	4.800	7.000	4.800	5.000	3.200	4.500
6	Bel	189.115	6.400	4.800	9.400	5.833	9.800	4.600
7	Ned	188.981	2.600	7.250	9.200	4.250	3.200	2.250
8	Hun	184.146	3.000	1.750	3.500	2.750	1.250	1.000
9	Yug	180.831	5.400	4.200	2.600	5.000	4.500	8.666
10	Por	177.699	4.600	8.400	5.833	4.400	5.800	5.600
11	Fra	174.682	3.200	4.200	8.000	3.500	8.800	9.750
12	Tch	156.233	3.400	2.600	5.500	1.250	3.000	2.250
13	GDR	156.080	3.000	5.000	1.750	6.250	3.250	2.750
14	URS	149.765	8.400	6.400	4.500	2.666	5.000	1.000
15	Aut	126.698	4.250	5.250	2.000	2.400	6.600	4.750
16	Pol	124.600	2.500	3.750	1.500	2.500	0.750	5.750
17	Rom	117.348	5.000	2.500	4.800	9.250	4.750	3.000
18	Bul	109.280	1.666	3.250	1.250	3.250	3.333	1.333
19	Swe	108.915	7.000	7.500	2.000	3.600	2.500	2.000
20	Sui	108.865	4.000	4.000	2.750	2.250	3.750	2.250
21	Wal	104.000	2.000	6.000	2.000	3.000	1.000	3.000
22	Gre	79.581	1.000	2.250	3.250	2.250	3.500	1.750
23	Tur	72.078	2.666	2.333	1.000	4.666	0.333	3.333
24	Den	71.912	2.000	3.333	3.333	4.666	0.666	3.750
25	Nor	38.079	1.000	1.333	2.333	1.000	0.333	1.000
26	Fin	35.575	4.666	1.666	4.333	2.666	1.250	0.500
27	Alb	34.499	2.000	2.333	3.333	1.000	2.000	0.333
28	Nir	33.911	1.333	1.000	1.000	1.000	0.000	0.666
29	Irl	32.658	0.333	0.000	0.666	0.333	0.000	1.000
30	Lux	21.158	0.000	0.333	0.666	0.000	0.333	0.666
31	Cyp	20.162	2.000	1.666	1.000	0.000	1.000	1.000
32	Mlt	17.160	0.333	0.000	0.000	1.000	0.666	0.000
33	Isl	15.661	2.000	0.000	1.000	1.000	0.000	2.000

	Pts	P	W	D	L	F	A	Diff	B	F/P
Total	**16325**	**14946**	**6041**	**2864**	**6041**	**22424**	**22424**	**0**	**1379**	**3.001**

National Classification by Cumulative Year-by-Year Index

1981-82 to 1990-91

Pos	Cnty	Total	8182	8283	8384	8485	8586	8687	8788	8889	8990	9091
1	Ita	87.637	3.750	6.800	10.750	11.000	7.166	6.000	6.166	12.166	11.714	12.125
2	FRG	80.592	9.000	8.833	3.500	7.166	8.833	7.666	8.666	8.428	11.500	7.000
3	Esp	71.865	7.600	8.000	3.600	3.833	10.166	7.400	9.800	9.800	5.500	6.166
4	Bel	68.933	8.500	8.400	6.800	4.400	6.400	4.800	9.400	5.833	9.800	4.600
5	URS	62.082	5.666	4.200	8.250	10.000	8.400	6.400	4.500	2.666	5.000	7.000
6	Por	59.133	6.000	8.750	7.000	2.750	4.600	8.400	5.833	4.400	5.800	5.600
7	Sco	55.700	5.500	10.500	7.200	3.200	4.800	7.000	4.800	5.000	3.200	4.500
8	Yug	54.116	7.750	5.000	5.400	5.600	5.400	4.200	2.600	5.000	4.500	8.666
9	Fra	52.450	2.800	4.400	3.800	4.000	3.200	4.200	8.000	3.500	8.800	9.750
10	Aut	47.500	3.250	4.000	7.500	7.500	4.250	5.250	2.000	2.400	6.600	4.750
11	Rom	47.466	4.250	5.750	4.666	3.500	5.000	2.500	4.800	9.250	4.750	3.000
12	Eng	45.593	7.142	3.857	12.666	9.428	–	–	–	–	–	12.500
13	Ned	42.133	3.800	2.000	3.833	3.750	2.600	7.250	9.200	4.250	3.200	2.250
14	Swe	39.600	7.500	2.500	2.000	3.000	7.000	7.500	2.000	3.600	2.500	2.000
15	GDR	38.400	5.600	1.800	5.000	4.000	3.000	5.000	1.750	6.250	3.250	2.750
16	Tch	36.300	2.500	6.000	6.000	3.800	3.400	2.600	5.500	1.250	3.000	2.250
17	Sui	32.750	5.500	4.000	1.250	3.000	4.000	4.000	2.750	2.250	3.750	2.250
18	Gre	29.666	2.250	2.000	3.750	7.666	1.000	2.250	3.250	2.250	3.500	1.750
19	Pol	28.750	2.000	5.000	2.000	3.000	2.500	3.750	1.500	2.500	0.750	5.750
20	Hun	26.750	1.750	2.500	3.750	5.500	3.000	1.750	3.500	2.750	1.250	1.000
21	Wal	26.000	0.000	6.000	1.000	2.000	2.000	6.000	2.000	3.000	1.000	3.000
22	Bul	25.582	3.750	2.000	2.250	3.500	1.666	3.250	1.250	3.250	3.333	1.333
23	Den	23.997	2.666	1.333	0.250	2.000	2.000	3.333	3.333	4.666	0.666	3.750
24	Fin	20.079	0.333	1.666	2.666	0.333	4.666	1.666	4.333	2.666	1.250	0.500
25	Tur	18.664	0.333	2.000	1.000	1.000	2.666	2.333	1.000	4.666	0.333	3.333
26	Alb	16.499	2.000	1.500	2.000	0.000	2.000	2.333	3.333	1.000	2.000	0.333
27	Nor	11.665	1.000	1.666	1.000	1.000	1.000	1.333	2.333	1.000	0.333	1.000
28	Cyp	10.665	1.000	1.333	0.666	1.000	2.000	1.666	1.000	0.000	1.000	1.000
29	Nir	8.997	1.666	0.666	0.333	1.333	1.333	1.000	1.000	1.000	0.000	0.666
30	Isl	7.665	0.666	0.000	0.666	0.333	2.000	0.000	1.000	1.000	0.000	2.000
31	Irl	7.664	2.000	1.666	0.000	1.666	0.333	0.000	0.666	0.333	0.000	1.000
32	Mlt	3.332	0.000	0.000	0.000	1.333	0.333	0.000	0.000	1.000	0.666	0.000
33	Lux	3.330	0.666	0.000	0.000	0.666	0.000	0.333	0.666	0.000	0.333	0.666

	Pts	P	W	D	L	F	A	Diff	B	F/P
Total	**5386**	**4966**	**1966**	**1034**	**1966**	**6799**	**6799**	**0**	**420**	**2.738**

National Classification by Cumulative Year–by–Year Index

1986–87 to 1990–91

Pos	Cnty	Total	8687	8788	8889	8990	9091
1	Ita	48.171	6.000	6.166	12.166	11.714	12.125
2	FRG	43.260	7.666	8.666	8.428	11.500	7.000
3	Esp	38.666	7.400	9.800	9.800	5.500	6.166
4	Bel	34.433	4.800	9.400	5.833	9.800	4.600
5	Fra	34.250	4.200	8.000	3.500	8.800	9.750
6	Por	30.033	8.400	5.833	4.400	5.800	5.600
7	Ned	26.150	7.250	9.200	4.250	3.200	2.250
8	URS	25.566	6.400	4.500	2.666	5.000	7.000
9	Yug	24.966	4.200	2.600	5.000	4.500	8.666
10	Sco	24.500	7.000	4.800	5.000	3.200	4.500
11	Rom	24.300	2.500	4.800	9.250	4.750	3.000
12	Aut	21.000	5.250	2.000	2.400	6.600	4.750
13	GDR	19.000	5.000	1.750	6.250	3.250	2.750
14	Swe	17.600	7.500	2.000	3.600	2.500	2.000
15	Den	15.748	3.333	3.333	4.666	0.666	3.750
16	Wal	15.000	6.000	2.000	3.000	1.000	3.000
–	Sui	15.000	4.000	2.750	2.250	3.750	2.250
18	Tch	14.600	2.600	5.500	1.250	3.000	2.250
19	Pol	14.250	3.750	1.500	2.500	0.750	5.750
20	Gre	13.000	2.250	3.250	2.250	3.500	1.750
21	Eng	12.500	–	–	–	–	12.500
22	Bul	12.416	3.250	1.250	3.250	3.333	1.333
23	Tur	11.665	2.333	1.000	4.666	0.333	3.333
24	Fin	10.415	1.666	4.333	2.666	1.250	0.500
25	Hun	10.250	1.750	3.500	2.750	1.250	1.000
26	Alb	8.999	2.333	3.333	1.000	2.000	0.333
27	Nor	5.999	1.333	2.333	1.000	0.333	1.000
28	Cyp	4.666	1.666	1.000	0.000	1.000	1.000
29	Isl	4.000	0.000	1.000	1.000	0.000	2.000
30	Nir	3.666	1.000	1.000	1.000	0.000	0.666
31	Irl	1.999	0.000	0.666	0.333	0.000	1.000
32	Lux	1.998	0.333	0.666	0.000	0.333	0.666
33	Mlt	1.666	0.000	0.000	1.000	0.666	0.000

	Pts	P	W	D	L	F	A	Diff	B	F/P
Total	2688	2478	972	534	972	3163	3163	0	210	2.553

Country Records – Points Gained 1955-56 to 1990-91

Albania

Pos'n	Cnty	Pts	P	W	D	L	F	A	Diff	B	Pts/P	Q	E
1	Malta	11	8	5	1	2	15	3	12	0	1.375	4	0
2	Sweden	8	12	2	4	6	6	17	-11	0	0.667	1	5
3	Romania	6	6	3	0	3	4	5	-1	0	1.000	1	2
4	Austria	5	8	2	1	5	9	14	-5	0	0.625	0	4
5	Scotland	5	8	1	3	4	4	14	-10	0	0.625	0	4
6	Spain	4	4	1	2	1	3	5	-2	0	1.000	0	2
–	East Germany	4	4	2	0	2	3	5	-2	0	1.000	1	1
8	Bulgaria	4	6	2	0	4	7	10	-3	0	0.667	1	2
9	Yugoslavia	2	2	1	0	1	3	2	1	0	1.000	1	0
10	Northern Ireland	2	2	1	0	1	2	2	0	0	1.000	1	0
11	Italy	2	2	1	0	1	2	3	-1	0	1.000	0	1
12	Denmark	2	4	0	2	2	1	7	-6	0	0.500	1	1
13	Belgium	1	2	0	1	1	1	4	-3	0	0.500	0	1
14	Netherlands	1	4	0	1	3	2	7	-5	0	0.250	0	2
15	Portugal	1	3	0	1	2	0	5	-5	0	0.333	0	2
16	West Germany	1	4	0	1	3	1	8	-7	0	0.250	0	2
17	France	1	4	0	1	3	1	13	-12	0	0.250	0	2
18	Poland	0	2	0	0	2	2	4	-2	0	0.000	0	1
19	Turkey	0	2	0	0	2	0	3	-3	0	0.000	0	1
20	Finland	0	4	0	0	4	3	7	-4	0	0.000	0	2
21	Greece	0	2	0	0	2	1	5	-4	0	0.000	0	1
	Total	**60**	**93**	**21**	**18**	**54**	**70**	**143**	**-73**	**0**	**0.645**	**11**	**36**

Austria

Pos'n	Cnty	Pts	P	W	D	L	F	A	Diff	B	Pts/P	Q	E
1	East Germany	33	23	12	4	7	33	27	6	5	1.435	8	3
2	Italy	25	33	8	7	18	41	69	-28	2	0.758	5	11
3	USSR	23	26	6	7	13	28	41	-13	4	0.885	7	6
4	Turkey	22	16	10	1	5	35	17	18	1	1.375	6	2
5	Hungary	22	19	8	4	7	25	27	-2	2	1.158	4	5
6	West Germany	22	34	8	6	20	29	78	-49	0	0.647	0	17
7	Spain	20	31	4	10	17	28	68	-40	2	0.645	2	13
8	Denmark	17	14	6	4	4	24	19	5	1	1.214	5	2
9	Czechoslovakia	17	18	6	2	10	14	28	-14	3	0.944	4	5
10	Belgium	16	19	7	2	10	28	38	-10	0	0.842	4	6
11	Yugoslavia	15	21	3	8	10	16	31	-15	1	0.714	2	8
12	Finland	14	10	7	0	3	22	12	10	0	1.400	3	2
13	Scotland	14	16	5	2	9	14	19	-5	2	0.875	3	5
14	Romania	14	18	4	6	8	15	25	-10	0	0.778	3	6
15	Luxembourg	12	6	6	0	0	34	0	34	0	2.000	3	0
16	Malta	12	6	6	0	0	22	1	21	0	2.000	3	0
17	Norway	11	6	4	2	0	17	6	11	1	1.833	3	0
18	Albania	11	8	5	1	2	14	9	5	0	1.375	4	0
19	France	11	8	5	1	2	16	15	1	0	1.375	3	1
20	Sweden	11	10	4	2	4	11	11	0	1	1.100	2	3
21	England	11	17	3	5	9	11	28	-17	0	1.647	0	9
22	Greece	10	12	3	4	5	19	14	5	0	0.833	4	2
23	Netherlands	10	14	4	1	9	17	22	-5	1	0.714	3	4
24	Poland	10	15	4	2	9	20	29	-9	0	0.667	1	6
25	Bulgaria	9	12	4	1	7	16	23	-7	0	0.750	4	2
26	Cyprus	6	4	3	0	1	12	3	9	0	1.500	2	0
27	Switzerland	6	6	2	2	2	5	4	1	0	1.000	2	1

28	Portugal	5	10	1	3	6	10	29	-19	0	0.500	0	5
29	Rep. of Ireland	4	2	2	0	0	5	0	5	0	2.000	1	0
30	Iceland	3	2	1	0	1	4	2	2	1	1.500	1	0
31	Wales	3	2	1	1	0	1	0	1	0	1.500	1	0
	Total	**419**	**438**	**152**	**88**	**198**	**586**	**695**	**-109**	**27**	**0.957**	**93**	**124**

Belgium

Pos'n	Cnty	Pts	P	W	D	L	F	A	Diff	B	Pts/P	Q	E
1	Spain	61	60	24	7	29	72	88	-16	6	1.017	14	16
2	Italy	60	59	17	16	26	55	70	-15	10	1.017	13	16
3	West Germany	52	53	16	12	25	57	83	-26	8	0.981	12	15
4	England	47	58	17	9	32	62	102	-40	4	0.810	10	20
5	Yugoslavia	42	33	17	3	13	53	46	7	5	1.273	9	7
6	Scotland	41	46	13	11	22	49	76	-27	4	0.891	11	12
7	Northern Ireland	38	21	17	3	1	73	16	57	1	1.810	11	0
8	Portugal	37	36	14	5	17	46	47	-1	4	1.028	8	10
9	Norway	35	22	15	5	2	45	12	33	0	1.591	11	0
10	Netherlands	33	25	13	4	8	36	24	12	3	1.320	7	6
11	Romania	32	20	13	4	3	28	11	17	2	1.600	9	1
12	France	29	24	11	5	8	39	34	5	2	1.208	7	5
13	Cyprus	28	14	3	1	0	47	8	39	1	2.000	7	0
14	East Germany	27	24	9	5	10	37	33	4	4	1.125	5	7
15	Czechoslovakia	27	25	11	2	12	37	38	-1	3	1.080	7	5
16	Luxembourg	26	14	12	2	0	40	6	34	0	1.857	7	0
17	Austria	24	19	10	2	7	38	28	10	2	1.263	6	4
18	Denmark	23	12	11	0	1	35	8	27	1	1.917	6	0
19	Greece	22	14	8	3	3	28	16	12	3	1.571	6	1
20	USSR	20	16	7	2	7	20	18	2	4	1.250	6	2
21	Poland	18	16	6	6	4	19	17	2	0	1.125	4	4
22	Finland	17	8	8	0	0	34	5	29	1	2.125	4	0
23	Iceland	14	8	6	2	0	30	5	25	0	1.750	4	0
24	Hungary	14	14	5	2	7	22	25	-3	2	1.000	3	4
25	Sweden	14	14	5	3	6	16	19	-3	1	1.000	3	4
26	Turkey	12	8	4	3	1	19	7	12	1	1.500	3	1
27	Switzerland	12	12	5	1	6	24	25	-1	1	1.000	2	4
28	Bulgaria	11	6	4	2	0	16	6	10	1	1.833	3	0
29	Malta	8	4	4	0	0	22	1	21	0	2.000	2	0
30	Wales	8	4	3	1	0	5	2	3	1	2.000	2	0
31	Belgium	5	4	2	0	2	3	3	0	1	1.250	1	1
32	Rep. of Ireland	4	2	2	0	0	11	4	7	0	2.000	1	0
33	Albania	3	2	1	1	0	4	1	3	0	1.500	1	0
	Total	**844**	**697**	**323**	**122**	**252**	**1122**	**884**	**238**	**76**	**1.211**	**205**	**145**

Bulgaria

Pos'n	Cnty	Pts	P	W	D	L	F	A	Diff	B	Pts/P	Q	E
1	Yugoslavia	24	31	8	7	16	39	71	-32	1	0.774	3	12
2	Spain	23	31	9	4	1	34	62	-28	1	0.742	3	12
3	Poland	20	14	8	2	4	31	16	15	2	1.429	6	1
4	West Germany	18	32	7	4	21	31	69	-38	0	0.563	3	13
5	Romania	17	14	8	0	6	34	23	11	1	1.214	5	2
6	Italy	17	30	5	7	18	25	58	-33	0	0.567	1	13
7	Czechoslovakia	16	12	6	2	4	25	16	9	2	1.333	4	2
8	Hungary	16	22	7	2	13	34	48	-14	0	0.727	3	8
9	Austria	15	12	7	1	4	23	16	7	0	1.250	2	4
10	Greece	15	12	7	0	5	18	14	4	1	1.250	4	2
11	France	14	14	5	3	6	16	18	-2	1	1.000	4	3

12	USSR	14	18	4	5	9	16	24	-8	1	0.778	2	7
13	Netherlands	14	18	4	3	11	16	33	-17	3	0.778	3	6
14	Malta	12	6	6	0	0	19	1	18	0	2.000	3	0
15	Rep. of Ireland	12	6	5	1	0	12	2	10	1	2.000	3	0
16	Switzerland	12	11	3	4	4	13	9	4	2	1.091	2	3
17	Turkey	11	6	5	1	0	11	2	9	0	1.833	3	0
18	Finland	8	4	4	0	0	30	4	26	0	2.000	2	0
19	Albania	8	6	4	0	2	10	7	3	0	1.333	2	1
20	Portugal	8	10	1	5	4	11	16	-5	1	0.800	1	4
21	England	8	14	3	1	10	9	23	-14	1	0.571	2	5
22	Luxembourg	7	4	3	1	0	16	2	14	0	1.750	2	0
23	Northern Ireland	7	4	2	1	1	6	4	2	2	1.750	2	0
24	Cyprus	7	6	3	1	2	14	13	1	0	1.167	2	1
25	Iceland	6	4	3	0	1	11	1	10	0	1.500	2	0
26	Denmark	5	4	2	1	1	6	4	2	0	1.250	2	0
27	Sweden	5	10	2	1	7	20	21	-1	0	0.500	2	3
28	East Germany	5	6	2	1	3	6	10	-4	0	0.833	0	3
29	Scotland	5	8	2	1	5	6	13	-7	0	0.625	0	4
30	Wales	3	2	1	1	0	5	1	4	0	1.500	1	0
31	Belgium	2	6	0	2	4	6	16	-10	0	0.333	0	3
	Total	**354**	**377**	**136**	**62**	**179**	**553**	**617**	**-64**	**20**	**0.939**	**74**	**112**

Cyprus

Pos'n	Cnty	Pts	P	W	D	L	F	A	Diff	B	Pts/P	Q	E
1	Rep. of Ireland	7	10	3	1	6	8	13	-5	0	0.700	2	3
2	Bulgaria	5	6	2	1	3	13	14	-1	0	0.833	1	2
3	Greece	5	8	1	3	4	4	8	-4	0	0.625	1	3
4	Malta	4	2	2	0	0	10	0	10	0	2.000	1	0
5	Finland	4	4	2	0	2	5	6	-1	0	1.000	1	1
6	Romania	4	14	1	2	11	7	41	-34	0	0.286	0	7
7	Sweden	3	6	1	1	4	4	25	-21	0	0.500	0	3
8	Norway	2	2	1	0	1	6	1	5	0	1.000	1	0
9	Luxembourg	2	2	1	0	1	7	3	4	0	1.000	1	0
10	East Germany	2	2	1	0	1	2	4	-2	0	1.000	0	1
11	Iceland	2	2	1	0	1	2	5	-3	0	1.000	0	1
12	Austria	2	4	1	0	3	3	12	-9	0	0.500	0	2
13	Hungary	2	4	1	0	3	1	17	-16	0	0.500	0	2
14	Italy	2	8	0	2	6	2	19	-17	0	0.250	0	4
15	Netherlands	2	4	1	0	3	4	27	-23	0	0.500	0	2
16	Czechoslovakia	2	8	0	2	6	5	36	-31	0	0.250	0	4
17	Spain	2	8	0	2	6	3	39	-36	0	0.250	0	4
18	Poland	1	2	0	1	1	3	7	-4	0	0.500	0	1
19	Switzerland	1	4	0	1	3	3	9	-6	0	0.250	0	2
20	Wales	1	2	0	1	1	0	8	-8	0	0.500	0	1
21	Yugoslavia	1	6	0	1	5	6	17	-11	0	0.167	0	3
22	USSR	1	6	0	1	5	1	15	-14	0	0.167	0	3
23	Belgium	1	14	0	1	13	8	47	-39	0	0.071	0	7
24	Denmark	0	2	0	0	2	0	7	-7	0	0.000	0	1
25	Scotland	0	4	0	0	4	1	17	-16	0	0.000	0	2
26	Portugal	0	4	0	0	4	1	22	-21	0	0.000	0	2
27	West Germany	0	20	0	0	20	8	111	-103	0	0.000	0	10
	Total	**58**	**158**	**19**	**20**	**119**	**117**	**530**	**-413**	**0**	**0.367**	**8**	**71**

Czechoslovakia

Pos'n	Cnty	Pts	P	W	D	L	F	A	Diff	B	Pts/P	Q	E
1	Spain	32	33	12	8	13	43	47	-4	0	0.970	6	11

2	Switzerland	30	22	12	3	7	38	33	5	3	1.364	6	5
3	Belgium	30	25	12	2	11	38	37	1	4	1.200	5	7
4	Yugoslavia	27	26	11	5	10	38	42	-4	0	1.038	1	9
5	West Germany	27	48	9	7	32	54	107	-53	2	0.563	4	20
6	Scotland	25	24	8	6	10	28	28	0	3	1.042	7	5
7	England	25	30	10	4	16	33	60	-27	1	0.833	2	13
8	Italy	24	24	9	4	11	22	27	-5	2	1.000	4	8
9	Hungary	23	24	8	6	10	36	36	0	1	0.958	5	7
10	Portugal	23	20	8	4	8	19	19	0	3	1.150	5	5
11	Austria	22	18	10	2	6	28	14	14	0	1.222	5	4
12	East Germany	22	16	8	3	5	26	19	7	3	1.375	5	3
13	Denmark	21	12	7	5	0	30	6	24	2	1.750	6	0
14	France	19	16	7	5	4	16	10	6	0	1.188	5	3
15	Poland	17	17	6	3	8	25	21	4	2	1.000	5	3
16	Greece	17	10	6	2	2	13	11	2	3	1.700	4	1
17	Sweden	16	12	5	5	2	20	13	7	1	1.333	5	1
18	Malta	15	8	7	1	0	34	3	31	0	1.875	4	0
19	Iceland	15	8	7	1	0	25	3	22	0	1.875	4	0
20	Cyprus	14	8	6	2	0	36	5	31	0	1.750	4	0
21	Finland	12	6	5	1	0	30	5	25	1	2.000	3	0
22	Turkey	12	8	6	0	2	17	5	12	2	1.500	3	1
23	Rep. of Ireland	12	6	5	1	0	13	5	8	1	2.000	3	0
24	Norway	12	8	5	2	1	13	7	6	0	1.500	4	0
25	Netherlands	12	10	5	1	4	11	14	-3	1	1.200	2	3
26	USSR	11	16	3	4	9	9	26	-17	1	0.688	1	7
27	Bulgaria	10	12	4	2	6	16	25	-9	0	0.833	2	4
28	Romania	7	10	2	3	5	12	20	-8	0	0.700	1	4
29	Luxembourg	6	4	3	0	1	18	2	16	0	1.500	2	0
30	Wales	5	2	2	0	0	4	0	4	1	2.500	1	0
31	Northern Ireland	4	2	2	0	0	4	1	3	0	2.000	1	0
	Total	**547**	**485**	**210**	**92**	**183**	**749**	**651**	**98**	**35**	**1.128**	**118**	**124**

Denmark

Pos'n	Cnty	Pts	P	W	D	L	F	A	Diff	B	Pts/P	Q	E
1	West Germany	14	37	5	3	29	41	97	-56	1	0.378	2	16
2	Luxembourg	13	8	6	1	1	38	6	32	0	1.625	4	0
3	Austria	13	14	4	4	6	19	24	-5	1	0.929	2	5
4	Rep. of Ireland	12	10	5	2	3	16	15	1	0	1.200	3	2
5	France	12	16	4	4	8	18	33	-15	0	0.750	2	6
6	Switzerland	11	14	4	2	8	27	34	-7	1	0.786	3	4
7	Northern Ireland	10	6	4	2	0	12	3	9	0	1.667	3	0
8	Sweden	10	8	3	4	1	11	9	2	0	1.250	3	1
9	Malta	9	4	4	0	0	18	2	16	1	2.250	2	0
10	Finland	9	6	4	1	1	16	7	9	0	1.500	2	0
11	Norway	8	4	3	1	0	5	0	5	1	2.000	2	0
12	East Germany	8	6	2	3	1	8	7	1	1	1.333	2	1
13	Poland	8	12	3	2	7	9	18	-9	0	0.667	2	4
14	Portugal	8	18	3	2	13	14	35	-21	0	0.444	1	8
15	Spain	8	22	2	4	16	18	71	-53	0	0.364	0	11
16	Hungary	7	4	3	1	0	10	3	7	0	1.750	2	0
17	Wales	7	6	2	2	2	6	3	3	1	1.667	1	2
18	Albania	6	4	2	2	0	7	1	6	0	1.500	1	1
19	Yugoslavia	6	8	2	2	4	10	19	-9	0	0.750	0	4
20	USSR	6	14	2	1	11	12	32	-20	1	0.429	1	6
21	Romania	5	8	2	1	5	9	19	-10	0	0.625	0	4
22	Scotland	5	16	2	1	13	12	35	-23	0	0.313	1	7
23	Czechoslovakia	5	12	0	5	7	6	30	-24	0	0.417	0	6

24	Cyprus	4	2	2	0	0	7	0	7	0	2.000	1	0
25	Iceland	4	2	2	0	0	3	0	3	0	2.000	1	0
26	Greece	4	4	1	1	2	4	4	0	1	1.000	1	1
27	Bulgaria	3	4	1	1	2	4	6	-2	0	0.750	0	2
28	Netherlands	3	18	1	1	16	12	51	-42	0	0.167	0	9
29	Turkey	2	2	1	0	1	2	1	1	0	1.000	1	0
30	Italy	2	6	0	2	4	7	15	-8	0	0.333	0	3
31	England	2	10	0	2	8	10	34	-24	0	0.200	0	5
32	Belgium	2	12	1	0	11	8	35	-27	0	0.167	0	6
	Total	**226**	**317**	**80**	**57**	**180**	**399**	**652**	**-253**	**9**	**0.713**	**43**	**115**

East Germany

Pos'n	Cnty	Pts	P	W	D	L	F	A	Diff	B	Pts/P	Q	E
1	Italy	40	39	17	4	18	47	51	-4	2	1.026	9	11
2	Portugal	37	22	12	6	4	29	18	11	7	1.682	9	2
3	Yugoslavia	34	33	12	7	14	52	51	1	3	1.030	9	7
4	France	33	28	12	6	10	39	34	5	3	1.179	8	6
5	Belgium	27	24	10	5	9	33	37	-4	2	1.125	7	5
6	Switzerland	26	19	9	5	5	47	30	17	3	1.368	6	3
7	Sweden	26	18	9	5	4	35	22	13	3	1.444	7	2
8	Hungary	25	21	9	3	9	28	23	5	4	1.190	6	4
9	West Germany	25	34	8	8	18	44	69	-25	1	0.735	3	14
10	England	25	40	9	6	25	30	63	-33	1	0.625	3	17
11	Poland	22	18	9	4	5	27	20	7	0	1.222	5	3
12	Austria	19	23	7	4	12	27	33	-6	1	0.826	3	8
13	Northern Ireland	18	13	7	4	2	29	10	19	0	1.385	7	0
14	Wales	18	12	6	5	1	24	14	10	1	1.500	6	0
15	Netherlands	18	23	6	6	11	20	32	-12	0	0.783	2	10
16	Finland	16	10	7	1	2	31	8	23	1	1.600	5	0
17	Luxembourg	16	8	7	1	0	24	4	20	1	2.000	4	0
18	USSR	16	19	5	5	9	19	26	-7	1	0.842	3	7
19	Romania	15	14	6	2	6	25	15	10	1	1.071	4	2
20	Czechoslovakia	14	16	5	3	8	19	26	-7	1	0.875	3	5
21	Scotland	14	16	5	3	8	16	24	-8	1	0.875	3	5
22	Spain	14	16	5	3	8	17	27	-10	1	0.875	2	6
23	Rep. of Ireland	12	7	5	1	1	23	3	20	1	1.714	3	0
24	Iceland	12	8	4	4	0	13	4	9	0	1.500	4	0
25	Turkey	12	9	4	4	1	15	8	7	0	1.333	3	1
26	Greece	10	8	4	2	2	12	8	4	0	1.250	3	1
27	Norway	8	6	4	0	2	15	9	6	0	1.333	2	1
28	Bulgaria	8	6	3	1	2	10	6	4	1	1.333	3	0
29	Denmark	5	6	1	3	2	7	8	-1	0	0.833	1	2
30	Albania	4	4	2	0	2	5	3	2	0	1.000	1	1
31	Cyprus	2	2	1	0	1	4	2	2	0	1.000	1	0
	Total	**571**	**522**	**210**	**111**	**201**	**766**	**688**	**78**	**40**	**1.094**	**135**	**123**

England

Pos'n	Cnty	Pts	P	W	D	L	F	A	Diff	B	Pts/P	Q	E
1	West Germany	114	85	37	22	26	138	101	37	18	1.341	30	15
2	Spain	103	89	33	25	31	129	138	-9	12	1.157	22	23
3	Netherlands	86	60	32	15	13	112	62	50	7	1.433	22	8
4	Portugal	83	53	33	8	12	108	59	49	9	1.566	19	8
5	Belgium	83	58	32	9	17	102	62	40	10	1.431	20	10
6	Italy	80	70	26	19	25	81	84	-3	9	1.143	19	17
7	Scotland	70	44	23	13	8	68	36	32	11	1.591	17	5
8	East Germany	68	40	25	6	9	63	30	33	12	1.700	17	3

9	Hungary	63	41	24	8	9	60	32	28	7	1.537	13	7
10	Yugoslavia	60	42	21	9	12	61	49	12	9	1.429	13	8
11	Romania	48	25	18	3	4	56	17	39	9	1.920	11	1
12	Switzerland	47	28	19	3	6	66	26	40	6	1.679	11	3
13	Czechoslovakia	44	30	16	4	10	60	33	27	8	1.467	13	2
14	Rep. of Ireland	41	22	18	4	0	89	8	81	1	1.864	11	0
15	England	38	32	10	12	10	28	28	0	6	1.188	8	8
16	Norway	37	20	18	1	1	92	12	80	0	1.850	10	0
17	Poland	37	24	13	6	5	47	22	25	5	1.542	9	3
18	France	35	24	12	5	7	45	26	19	6	1.458	10	2
19	Greece	33	22	13	4	5	49	21	28	3	1.500	8	3
20	Austria	29	17	9	5	3	28	11	17	6	1.706	9	0
21	Sweden	24	15	8	7	0	29	8	21	1	1.600	6	2
22	Bulgaria	24	14	10	1	3	23	9	14	3	1.714	5	2
23	Northern Ireland	21	12	10	0	2	35	8	27	1	1.750	6	0
24	Turkey	21	14	8	4	2	23	7	16	1	1.500	6	1
25	Iceland	20	10	10	0	0	49	4	45	0	2.000	5	0
26	Denmark	20	10	8	2	0	34	10	24	2	2.000	5	0
27	Finland	17	10	7	2	1	38	7	31	1	1.700	5	0
28	USSR	17	14	5	4	5	23	24	-1	3	1.214	3	4
29	Luxembourg	11	6	5	1	0	40	1	39	0	1.833	3	0
30	Malta	11	6	5	1	0	25	1	24	0	1.833	3	0
31	Wales	5	2	2	0	0	5	0	5	1	2.500	1	0
	Total	**1390**	**939**	**510**	**203**	**226**	**1806**	**936**	**870**	**167**	**1.480**	**340**	**135**

Finland

Pos'n	Cnty	Pts	P	W	D	L	F	A	Diff	B	Pts/P	Q	E
1	Malta	9	8	4	1	3	13	8	5	0	1.125	4	0
2	Albania	9	4	4	0	0	7	3	4	1	2.250	2	0
3	Sweden	7	14	2	2	10	12	29	-17	1	0.500	1	6
4	Austria	6	10	3	0	7	12	22	-10	0	0.600	2	3
5	Poland	5	10	1	3	6	8	25	-17	0	0.500	1	4
6	East Germany	5	10	2	1	7	8	31	-23	0	0.500	0	5
7	USSR	5	14	1	2	11	11	39	-28	1	0.357	1	6
8	Rep. of Ireland	4	2	2	0	0	4	0	4	0	2.000	1	0
9	Yugoslavia	4	2	2	0	0	4	2	2	0	2.000	1	0
10	Cyprus	4	4	2	0	2	6	5	1	0	1.000	1	1
11	Northern Ireland	4	4	0	4	0	2	2	0	0	1.000	2	0
12	Norway	4	6	2	0	4	4	9	-5	0	0.667	1	2
13	Switzerland	4	8	1	2	5	5	21	16	0	0.500	0	4
14	England	4	10	1	2	7	7	38	-31	0	0.400	0	5
15	Portugal	3	4	1	1	2	2	4	-2	0	0.750	0	2
16	Denmark	3	6	1	1	4	7	16	-9	0	0.500	1	2
17	Romania	3	8	1	1	6	3	14	-11	0	0.375	0	4
18	France	3	16	0	3	13	2	48	-46	0	0.188	0	8
19	Luxembourg	2	4	1	0	3	4	7	-3	0	0.500	0	2
20	Turkey	2	4	0	2	2	2	7	-5	0	0.500	0	2
21	Italy	2	10	1	0	9	2	21	-19	0	0.200	0	5
22	Scotland	2	6	1	0	5	3	27	-24	0	0.333	0	3
23	Hungary	1	4	0	1	3	4	22	-18	0	0.250	0	2
24	Czechoslovakia	1	6	0	1	5	5	30	-25	0	0.167	0	3
25	Netherlands	0	4	0	0	4	5	23	-18	0	0.000	0	2
26	West Germany	0	6	0	0	6	7	28	-21	0	0.000	0	3
27	Bulgaria	0	4	0	0	4	4	30	-26	0	0.000	0	2
28	Belgium	0	8	0	0	8	5	34	-29	0	0.000	0	4
	Total	**96**	**196**	**33**	**27**	**136**	**158**	**545**	**-387**	**3**	**0.490**	**18**	**80**

France

Pos'n	Cnty	Pts	P	W	D	L	F	A	Diff	B	Pts/P	Q	E
1	Portugal	40	43	14	11	18	42	60	-18	1	0.930	9	12
2	Italy	38	51	11	14	26	42	79	-37	2	0.745	5	20
3	USSR	35	26	11	7	8	35	31	4	6	1.346	10	3
4	Scotland	35	31	14	4	13	42	43	-1	3	1.129	6	9
5	West Germany	34	44	12	7	25	43	81	-38	3	0.773	4	18
6	Finland	31	16	13	3	0	48	2	46	2	1.938	8	0
7	East Germany	28	28	10	6	12	34	39	-5	2	1.000	6	8
8	Netherlands	27	28	8	9	11	29	35	-6	2	0.964	6	8
9	Greece	26	18	8	6	4	38	26	12	4	1.444	6	3
10	Spain	26	33	7	10	16	40	60	-20	2	0.788	6	11
11	Romania	25	16	10	2	4	27	17	10	3	1.563	5	3
12	Belgium	23	24	8	5	11	34	39	-5	2	0.958	5	7
13	Denmark	21	16	8	4	4	33	18	15	1	1.313	6	2
14	Luxembourg	20	10	10	0	0	51	4	47	0	2.000	5	0
15	England	20	24	7	5	12	26	45	-19	1	0.833	2	10
16	Northern Ireland	19	10	9	1	0	27	5	22	0	1.900	5	0
17	Switzerland	18	16	6	3	7	25	21	4	3	1.125	5	3
18	Yugoslavia	17	15	5	5	5	29	24	5	2	1.133	4	4
19	Bulgaria	16	14	6	3	5	18	16	2	1	1.143	3	4
20	Rep. of Ireland	14	8	6	2	0	26	9	17	0	1.750	4	0
21	Poland	14	12	5	2	5	23	16	7	2	1.167	5	1
22	Czechoslovakia	14	16	4	5	7	10	16	-6	1	0.875	3	5
23	Iceland	12	8	6	0	2	22	7	15	0	1.500	4	0
24	Turkey	11	11	4	2	5	17	13	4	1	1.000	2	3
25	Hungary	11	10	4	2	4	19	25	-6	1	1.100	3	2
26	Norway	10	6	4	1	1	14	4	10	1	1.667	3	0
27	Albania	7	4	3	1	0	13	1	12	0	1.750	2	0
28	Sweden	6	8	2	2	4	11	11	0	0	0.750	2	2
29	Austria	6	8	2	1	5	15	16	-1	1	0.750	1	3
30	Wales	5	4	2	0	2	5	7	-2	1	1.250	1	1
	Total	**609**	**558**	**219**	**123**	**216**	**838**	**770**	**68**	**48**	**1.091**	**136**	**142**

Greece

Pos'n	Cnty	Pts	P	W	D	L	F	A	Diff	B	Pts/P	Q	E
1	Italy	26	42	8	10	24	36	74	-38	0	0.619	3	18
2	Yugoslavia	25	22	11	1	10	28	41	-13	2	1.136	4	7
3	Switzerland	16	12	7	1	4	14	15	-1	1	1.333	2	4
4	England	16	22	5	4	13	21	49	-28	2	0.727	3	8
5	France	15	18	4	6	8	26	38	-12	1	0.833	3	6
6	Austria	14	12	5	4	3	14	19	-5	0	1.167	2	4
7	Hungary	14	15	5	3	7	22	36	-14	1	0.933	3	5
8	Spain	14	18	5	4	9	9	31	-22	0	0.778	1	8
9	Malta	13	8	6	1	1	24	5	19	0	1.625	4	0
10	Poland	13	15	5	3	7	17	24	-7	0	0.867	3	4
11	Cyprus	11	8	4	3	1	8	4	4	0	1.375	3	1
12	Luxembourg	10	6	5	0	1	18	4	14	0	1.667	3	0
13	Bulgaria	10	12	5	0	7	14	18	-4	0	0.833	2	4
14	Netherlands	10	13	3	4	6	11	23	-12	0	0.769	3	4
15	Romania	10	16	5	0	11	12	31	-19	0	0.625	1	7
16	Belgium	9	14	3	3	8	16	28	-12	0	0.643	1	6
17	Sweden	8	6	3	1	2	6	5	1	1	1.333	2	1
18	Northern Ireland	7	4	2	2	0	10	8	2	1	1.750	2	0
19	Czechoslovakia	7	10	2	2	6	11	13	-2	1	0.700	1	4
20	USSR	7	12	2	3	7	7	17	-10	0	0.583	1	5
21	West Germany	7	16	2	3	11	9	33	-24	0	0.438	0	8

22	Denmark	6	4	2	1	1	4	4	0	1	1.500	1	1
23	Portugal	6	10	3	0	7	14	17	-3	0	0.600	2	3
24	East Germany	6	8	2	2	4	8	12	-4	0	0.750	1	3
25	Scotland	5	4	2	1	1	6	5	1	0	1.250	1	1
26	Albania	4	2	2	0	0	5	1	4	0	2.000	1	0
27	Iceland	4	2	2	0	0	4	0	4	0	2.000	1	0
28	Wales	3	2	1	1	0	6	5	1	0	1.500	1	0
	Total	**296**	**333**	**111**	**63**	**159**	**380**	**560**	**-180**	**11**	**0.889**	**55**	**112**

Hungary

Pos'n	Cnty	Pts	P	W	D	L	F	A	Diff	B	Pts/P	Q	E
1	Yugoslavia	40	32	16	3	13	58	53	5	5	1.250	9	7
2	Spain	34	39	14	3	22	46	71	-25	3	0.872	5	14
3	Scotland	32	26	14	1	11	37	41	-4	3	1.231	6	7
4	England	31	41	9	8	24	32	60	-28	5	0.756	7	13
5	Bulgaria	30	22	13	2	7	48	34	14	2	1.364	8	3
6	Portugal	30	28	12	4	12	39	46	-7	2	1.071	6	8
7	Italy	30	34	8	11	15	35	51	-16	3	0.882	6	11
8	Czechoslovakia	28	24	10	6	8	36	36	0	2	1.167	7	5
9	Turkey	25	19	10	3	6	40	24	16	2	1.316	6	3
10	East Germany	23	21	9	3	9	23	28	-5	2	1.095	4	6
11	West Germany	23	24	8	4	12	40	52	-12	3	0.958	4	8
12	Netherlands	20	17	6	4	7	24	24	0	4	1.176	4	4
13	Greece	18	15	7	3	5	36	22	14	1	1.200	5	3
14	Austria	18	19	7	4	8	27	25	2	0	0.947	5	4
15	Switzerland	18	18	7	3	8	25	29	-4	1	1.000	4	5
16	Sweden	17	12	6	4	2	26	11	15	1	1.417	6	0
17	Belgium	17	14	7	2	5	25	22	3	1	1.214	4	3
18	Iceland	16	8	7	1	0	30	5	25	1	2.000	4	0
19	Rep. of Ireland	15	8	7	1	0	22	5	17	0	1.875	4	0
20	Romania	15	14	7	0	7	21	19	2	1	1.071	4	3
21	Poland	14	12	5	3	4	18	12	6	1	1.167	3	3
22	Malta	13	8	6	1	1	40	6	34	0	1.625	4	0
23	France	10	10	4	2	4	25	19	6	0	1.000	2	3
24	Finland	7	4	3	1	0	22	4	18	0	1.750	2	0
25	USSR	7	11	3	0	8	16	28	-12	1	0.636	2	4
26	Cyprus	6	4	3	0	1	17	1	16	0	1.500	2	0
27	Norway	6	4	3	0	1	15	3	12	0	1.500	2	0
28	Luxembourg	4	2	2	0	0	11	3	8	0	2.000	1	0
29	Wales	4	2	2	0	0	6	1	5	0	2.000	1	0
30	Denmark	1	4	0	1	3	3	10	-7	0	0.250	0	2
	Total	**552**	**496**	**215**	**78**	**203**	**843**	**745**	**98**	**44**	**1.113**	**127**	**119**

Iceland

Pos'n	Cnty	Pts	P	W	D	L	F	A	Diff	B	Pts/P	Q	E
1	Northern Ireland	7	8	2	3	3	6	7	-1	0	0.875	2	2
2	Sweden	6	6	2	2	2	6	4	2	0	1.000	2	1
3	East Germany	4	8	0	4	4	4	13	-9	0	0.500	0	4
4	France	4	8	2	0	6	7	22	-15	0	0.500	0	4
5	Malta	3	4	1	1	2	2	7	-5	0	0.750	0	2
6	Scotland	3	14	0	3	11	9	47	-38	0	0.214	0	7
7	Cyprus	2	2	1	0	1	5	2	3	0	1.000	1	0
8	Luxembourg	2	2	0	2	0	4	4	0	0	1.000	1	0
9	Austria	2	2	1	0	1	2	4	-2	0	1.000	0	1
10	Rep. of Ireland	2	4	1	0	3	2	12	-10	0	0.500	0	2
11	Bulgaria	2	4	1	0	3	1	11	-10	0	0.500	0	2

12	Belgium	2	8	0	2	6	5	30	-25	0	0.250	0	4
13	West Germany	2	10	0	2	8	5	40	-35	0	0.200	0	5
14	Norway	1	8	0	1	7	2	20	-18	0	0.125	0	4
15	Czechoslovakia	1	8	0	1	7	3	25	-22	0	0.125	0	4
16	Portugal	1	4	0	1	3	1	23	-22	0	0.250	0	2
17	Hungary	1	8	0	1	7	5	30	-25	0	0.125	0	4
18	Turkey	0	2	0	0	2	3	6	-3	0	0.000	0	1
19	Denmark	0	2	0	0	2	0	3	-3	0	0.000	0	1
20	Greece	0	2	0	0	2	0	4	-4	0	0.000	0	1
21	Romania	0	2	0	0	2	0	5	-5	0	0.000	0	1
–	USSR	0	2	0	0	2	0	5	-5	0	0.000	0	1
23	Yugoslavia	0	2	0	0	2	1	9	-8	0	0.000	0	1
24	Italy	0	2	0	0	2	0	11	-11	0	0.000	0	1
25	Switzerland	0	4	0	0	4	3	25	-22	0	0.000	0	2
26	Poland	0	10	0	0	10	4	30	-26	0	0.000	0	5
27	Netherlands	0	4	0	0	4	2	31	-29	0	0.000	0	2
28	Spain	0	12	0	0	12	3	34	-31	0	0.000	0	6
29	England	0	10	0	0	10	4	49	-45	0	0.000	0	5
	Total	**45**	**162**	**11**	**23**	**128**	**89**	**513**	**-424**	**0**	**0.278**	**6**	**75**

Italy

Pos'n	Cnty	Pts	P	W	D	L	F	A	Diff	B	Pts/P	Q	E
1	West Germany	132	102	42	24	36	152	121	31	24	1.294	33	17
2	Yugoslavia	95	64	30	22	12	93	55	38	13	1.484	24	7
3	Spain	91	90	36	12	42	107	137	-30	7	1.011	15	31
4	Belgium	80	59	26	16	17	70	55	15	12	1.356	16	13
5	England	77	70	25	19	26	84	81	3	8	1.100	17	19
6	France	76	51	26	14	11	79	42	37	10	1.490	20	5
7	Greece	62	42	24	10	8	74	36	38	1	1.476	18	3
8	Scotland	61	42	22	7	13	73	41	32	10	1.452	16	5
9	Poland	58	48	23	9	16	47	40	7	3	1.208	13	12
10	Austria	50	33	18	7	8	69	41	28	7	1.515	11	5
11	Hungary	48	34	15	11	8	51	35	16	7	1.412	11	6
12	Bulgaria	47	30	18	7	5	58	25	33	4	1.567	13	1
13	East Germany	45	39	18	4	17	51	47	4	5	1.154	11	9
14	Poland	44	29	15	10	4	50	28	22	4	1.517	10	4
15	Turkey	42	22	19	2	1	59	12	47	2	1.909	11	0
16	Romania	41	29	14	8	7	39	18	21	5	1.414	11	4
17	Switzerland	39	22	16	3	3	51	20	31	4	1.773	10	1
18	Sweden	39	28	14	8	6	41	24	17	3	1.393	12	2
19	USSR	31	26	8	10	8	21	19	2	5	1.192	8	5
20	Netherlands	31	27	10	6	11	32	32	0	5	1.148	9	6
21	Czechoslovakia	30	24	11	4	9	27	22	5	4	1.250	8	4
22	Luxembourg	24	12	12	0	0	52	1	51	0	2.000	6	0
23	Italy	23	20	7	6	7	16	16	0	3	1.150	5	5
24	Finland	20	10	9	0	1	21	2	19	2	2.000	5	0
25	Malta	16	8	8	0	0	33	2	31	0	2.000	4	0
26	Norway	16	8	7	1	0	15	1	14	1	2.000	4	0
27	Cyprus	15	8	6	2	0	19	2	17	1	1.875	4	0
28	Northern Ireland	12	6	5	1	0	15	1	14	1	2.000	3	0
29	Denmark	11	6	4	2	0	15	7	8	1	1.833	3	0
30	Wales	11	7	5	0	2	11	6	5	1	1.571	3	0
31	Rep. of Ireland	7	4	3	1	0	8	0	8	0	1.750	2	0
32	Iceland	4	2	2	0	0	11	0	11	0	2.000	1	0
33	Albania	3	2	1	0	1	3	2	1	1	1.500	1	0
	Total	**1381**	**1004**	**499**	**226**	**279**	**1547**	**971**	**576**	**157**	**1.375**	**338**	**164**

Luxembourg

Pos'n	Cnty	Pts	P	W	D	L	F	A	Diff	B	Pts/P	Q	E
1	Finland	6	4	3	0	1	7	4	3	0	1.500	2	0
2	Northern Ireland	6	8	2	2	4	11	24	-13	0	0.750	0	4
3	Sweden	3	10	1	1	8	2	23	-21	0	0.300	0	5
4	Denmark	3	8	1	1	6	6	38	-32	0	0.375	0	4
5	Sweden	3	9	1	1	7	3	42	-39	0	0.333	0	4
6	Yugoslavia	3	10	1	1	3	10	53	-43	0	0.300	0	5
7	Iceland	2	2	0	2	0	4	4	0	0	1.000	0	1
8	Malta	2	2	1	0	1	2	2	0	0	1.000	0	1
9	Norway	2	2	1	0	1	2	4	-2	0	1.000	0	1
10	Cyprus	2	2	1	0	1	3	7	-4	0	1.000	0	1
11	Poland	2	6	1	0	5	7	15	-8	0	0.333	1	2
12	Turkey	2	6	1	0	5	5	16	-11	0	0.333	0	3
13	Greece	2	6	1	0	5	4	18	-14	0	0.333	0	3
14	Czechoslovakia	2	4	1	0	3	2	18	-16	0	0.500	0	2
15	Belgium	2	14	0	2	12	6	40	-34	0	0.143	0	7
16	West Germany	2	13	1	0	12	8	62	-54	0	0.154	0	6
17	Netherlands	2	14	0	2	12	5	84	-79	0	0.143	0	7
18	Bulgaria	1	4	0	1	3	2	16	-14	0	0.250	0	2
19	East Germany	1	8	0	1	7	4	24	-20	0	0.125	0	4
20	England	1	6	0	1	5	1	40	-39	0	0.167	0	3
21	Rep. of Ireland	0	2	0	0	2	2	8	-6	0	0.000	0	1
22	Romania	0	2	0	0	2	0	6	-6	0	0.000	0	1
23	Hungary	0	2	0	0	2	3	11	-8	0	0.000	0	1
24	USSR	0	2	0	0	2	0	9	-9	0	0.000	0	1
25	Scotland	0	2	0	0	2	1	11	-10	0	0.000	0	1
26	Austria	0	6	0	0	6	0	34	-34	0	0.000	0	3
27	Spain	0	10	0	0	10	5	48	-43	0	0.000	0	5
28	France	0	10	0	0	10	4	51	-47	0	0.000	0	5
29	Portugal	0	8	0	0	8	2	49	-47	0	0.000	0	4
30	Italy	0	12	0	0	12	1	52	-51	0	0.000	0	6
	Total	**49**	**194**	**17**	**15**	**162**	**112**	**813**	**-701**	**0**	**0.253**	**3**	**93**

Malta

Pos'n	Cnty	Pts	P	W	D	L	F	A	Diff	B	Pts/P	Q	E
1	Finland	7	8	3	1	4	8	13	-5	0	0.875	0	4
2	Iceland	5	4	2	1	1	7	2	5	0	1.250	2	0
3	Albania	5	8	2	1	5	3	15	-12	0	0.625	0	4
4	Northern Ireland	4	2	2	0	0	3	1	2	0	2.000	1	0
5	Rep. of Ireland	4	4	2	0	2	2	6	-4	0	1.000	0	2
6	Portugal	4	10	2	0	8	7	40	-33	0	0.400	0	5
7	Greece	3	8	1	1	6	5	24	-19	0	0.375	0	4
8	Romania	3	8	1	1	6	2	22	-20	0	0.375	0	4
9	Hungary	3	8	1	1	6	6	40	-34	0	0.375	0	4
10	Luxembourg	2	2	1	0	1	2	2	0	0	1.000	1	0
11	Sweden	2	2	1	0	1	2	5	-3	0	1.000	0	1
12	Netherlands	1	6	0	1	5	2	22	-20	0	0.167	0	3
13	England	1	6	0	1	5	1	25	-24	0	0.167	0	3
14	Spain	1	10	0	1	9	1	27	-26	0	0.100	0	5
15	Wales	1	6	0	1	5	0	26	-26	0	0.167	0	3
16	West Germany	1	6	0	1	5	1	30	-29	0	0.167	0	3
17	Czechoslovakia	1	8	0	1	7	3	34	-31	0	0.125	0	4
18	Scotland	1	10	0	1	9	1	42	-41	0	0.100	0	5
19	Norway	0	2	0	0	2	0	9	-9	0	0.000	0	1
20	Cyprus	0	2	0	0	2	0	10	-10	0	0.000	0	1
21	USSR	0	4	0	0	4	0	13	-13	0	0.000	0	2

22	Denmark	0	4	0	0	4	2	18	-16	0	0.000	0	2
23	Bulgaria	0	6	0	0	6	1	19	-18	0	0.000	0	3
24	Poland	0	6	0	0	6	3	23	-20	0	0.000	0	3
25	Austria	0	6	0	0	6	1	22	-21	0	0.000	0	3
–	Belgium	0	4	0	0	4	1	22	-21	0	0.000	0	2
27	Switzerland	0	6	0	0	6	4	29	-25	0	0.000	0	3
28	Italy	0	8	0	0	8	2	33	-31	0	0.000	0	4
29	Yugoslavia	0	10	0	0	10	3	35	-32	0	0.000	0	5
	Total	**49**	**174**	**18**	**13**	**143**	**73**	**609**	**-536**	**0**	**0.282**	**4**	**83**

Netherlands

Pos'n	Cnty	Pts	P	W	D	L	F	A	Diff	B	Pts/P	Q	E
1	West Germany	56	58	21	9	28	81	98	-17	5	0.966	11	18
2	Spain	49	42	16	10	16	53	55	-2	7	1.167	12	9
3	England	43	60	13	15	32	62	112	-50	2	0.717	8	22
4	Switzerland	38	25	16	4	5	41	23	18	2	1.520	8	4
5	France	38	28	11	9	8	35	29	6	7	1.357	8	6
6	Denmark	35	18	16	1	1	54	12	42	2	1.944	9	0
7	Poland	34	18	13	3	2	45	13	32	5	1.889	9	0
8	East Germany	33	23	11	6	6	32	20	12	5	1.435	10	2
9	Italy	31	27	11	6	10	32	32	0	3	1.148	6	9
10	Bulgaria	29	18	11	3	4	33	16	17	4	1.611	6	3
11	Scotland	29	30	12	4	14	40	41	-1	1	0.967	7	8
12	Northern Ireland	27	14	13	1	0	69	8	61	0	1.929	7	0
13	Luxembourg	26	14	12	2	0	84	5	79	0	1.857	7	0
14	Portugal	25	30	8	5	17	31	45	-14	4	0.833	6	9
15	Yugoslavia	24	20	8	3	9	35	32	3	5	1.200	5	5
16	Turkey	23	14	11	0	3	37	11	26	1	1.643	7	0
17	Sweden	23	15	10	1	4	40	17	23	2	1.533	7	0
18	Belgium	22	25	8	4	13	24	36	-12	2	0.880	6	7
19	Norway	20	12	8	2	2	25	10	15	2	1.667	5	1
20	Austria	20	14	9	1	4	22	17	5	1	1.429	4	3
21	Hungary	19	17	7	4	6	24	24	0	1	1.118	4	4
22	Rep. of Ireland	18	12	7	4	1	26	7	19	0	1.500	5	1
23	Yugoslavia	18	10	6	3	1	20	3	17	3	1.800	4	1
24	Greece	17	13	6	4	3	23	11	12	1	1.308	4	3
25	USSR	15	18	5	4	9	16	27	-11	1	0.833	2	7
26	Malta	11	6	5	1	0	22	2	20	0	1.833	3	0
27	Czechoslovakia	11	10	4	1	5	14	11	3	2	1.100	3	2
28	Northern Ireland	8	4	4	0	0	31	2	29	0	2.000	2	0
29	Finland	8	4	4	0	0	23	5	18	0	2.000	2	0
30	Cyprus	7	4	3	0	1	27	4	23	1	1.750	2	0
31	Albania	7	4	3	1	0	7	2	5	0	1.750	2	0
32	Wales	1	2	0	1	1	2	5	-3	0	0.500	0	1
	Total	**765**	**609**	**292**	**112**	**205**	**1110**	**735**	**375**	**69**	**1.256**	**181**	**125**

Northern Ireland

Pos'n	Cnty	Pts	P	W	D	L	F	A	Diff	B	Pts/P	Q	E
1	Norway	13	12	3	5	4	21	18	3	2	1.083	3	3
2	Luxembourg	10	8	4	2	2	24	11	13	0	1.250	4	0
3	Iceland	9	8	3	3	2	7	6	1	0	1.125	2	2
4	East Germany	8	13	2	4	7	10	29	-19	0	0.615	0	7
5	Belgium	5	21	1	3	17	16	73	-57	0	0.238	0	11
6	Finland	4	4	0	4	0	2	2	0	0	1.000	0	2
7	Scotland	4	10	1	2	7	8	24	-16	0	0.400	1	4
8	Romania	4	8	1	2	5	5	25	-20	0	0.500	1	3

9	England	4	12	2	0	10	8	35	-27	0	0.333	0	6
10	Bulgaria	3	4	1	1	2	4	6	-2	0	0.750	0	2
11	Switzerland	3	4	1	1	2	6	9	-3	0	0.750	0	2
12	Rep. of Ireland	3	6	0	3	3	3	8	-5	0	0.500	1	2
13	Sweden	3	4	1	1	2	6	13	-7	0	0.750	0	2
14	Yugoslavia	3	6	1	1	4	7	25	-18	0	0.500	0	3
15	Portugal	3	10	0	3	7	8	34	-26	0	0.300	0	5
16	Albania	2	2	1	0	1	2	2	0	0	1.000	0	1
17	Turkey	2	2	1	0	1	3	4	-1	0	1.000	0	1
18	Greece	2	4	0	2	2	8	10	-2	0	0.500	0	2
19	Denmark	2	6	0	2	4	3	12	-9	0	0.333	0	3
20	Wales	1	2	0	1	1	0	4	-4	0	0.500	0	1
21	USSR	1	6	0	1	5	3	16	-13	0	0.167	0	3
22	Italy	1	6	0	1	5	1	15	-14	0	0.167	0	3
23	France	1	10	0	1	9	5	27	-22	0	0.100	0	5
24	Netherlands	1	14	0	1	13	8	69	-61	0	0.071	0	7
25	Malta	0	2	0	0	2	1	3	-2	0	0.000	0	1
26	Czechoslovakia	0	2	0	0	2	1	4	-3	0	0.000	0	1
27	Spain	0	6	0	0	6	5	23	-18	0	0.000	0	3
28	West Germany	0	6	0	0	6	4	25	-21	0	0.000	0	3
	Total	**92**	**198**	**23**	**44**	**131**	**179**	**532**	**353**	**2**	**0.465**	**12**	**88**

Norway

Pos'n	Cnty	Pts	P	W	D	L	F	A	Diff	B	Pts/P	Q	E
1	Iceland	15	8	7	1	0	20	2	18	0	1.875	4	0
2	Northern Ireland	13	12	4	5	3	18	21	-3	0	1.083	3	3
3	West Germany	10	18	4	2	12	14	54	-40	0	0.556	1	8
4	Belgium	9	22	2	5	15	12	15	-33	0	0.409	0	11
5	Finland	8	6	4	0	2	9	4	5	0	1.333	2	1
6	Sweden	6	8	2	1	5	8	19	-11	1	0.750	1	3
7	Netherlands	6	12	2	2	8	10	25	-15	0	0.500	1	5
8	Malta	4	2	2	0	0	9	0	9	0	2.000	1	0
9	East Germany	4	6	2	0	4	9	15	-6	0	0.667	1	2
10	Czechoslovakia	4	8	1	2	5	7	13	-6	0	0.500	0	4
11	Switzerland	3	2	1	1	0	3	1	2	0	1.500	1	0
12	Romania	3	4	1	1	2	3	6	-3	0	0.750	0	2
13	Spain	3	6	1	1	4	8	14	-6	0	0.500	0	3
14	France	3	6	1	1	4	4	14	-10	0	0.500	0	3
15	Wales	3	6	0	3	3	3	19	-16	0	0.500	0	3
16	USSR	3	12	1	1	10	9	32	-23	0	0.250	0	6
17	England	3	20	1	1	18	12	92	-80	0	0.150	0	10
18	Luxembourg	2	2	1	0	1	4	2	2	0	1.000	1	0
19	Turkey	2	2	1	0	1	5	4	1	0	1.000	1	0
20	Cyprus	2	2	1	0	1	1	6	-5	0	1.000	0	1
21	Austria	2	6	0	2	4	6	17	-11	0	0.333	0	3
22	Hungary	2	4	1	0	3	3	15	-12	0	0.500	0	2
23	Poland	2	6	0	2	4	5	18	-13	0	0.333	0	3
24	Scotland	2	14	0	2	12	9	34	-25	0	0.143	0	7
25	Rep. of Ireland	1	2	0	1	1	2	4	-2	0	0.500	0	1
26	Denmark	1	4	0	1	3	0	5	-5	0	0.250	0	2
27	Italy	1	8	0	1	7	1	15	-14	0	0.125	0	4
28	Yugoslavia	1	10	0	1	9	5	28	-23	0	0.100	0	5
29	Portugal	0	6	0	0	6	3	18	-15	0	0.000	0	3
	Total	**118**	**224**	**40**	**37**	**147**	**202**	**542**	**-340**	**1**	**0.527**	**17**	**95**

Poland

Pos'n	Cnty	Pts	P	W	D	L	F	A	Diff	B	Pts/P	Q	E
1	Turkey	25	17	10	1	6	24	14	10	4	1.471	6	2
2	Austria	21	15	9	2	4	29	20	9	1	1.400	6	1
3	Czechoslovakia	21	17	8	3	6	21	25	-4	2	1.235	3	5
4	Iceland	20	10	10	0	0	30	4	26	0	2.000	5	0
5	Italy	20	29	4	10	15	28	50	-22	2	0.690	4	10
6	Greece	17	15	7	3	5	24	17	7	0	1.133	4	3
7	England	17	24	5	6	13	22	47	-25	1	0.708	3	9
8	Denmark	16	12	7	2	3	18	9	9	0	1.333	4	2
9	Sweden	16	16	6	4	6	26	26	0	0	1.000	4	4
10	Finland	15	10	6	3	1	25	8	17	0	1.500	4	1
11	Belgium	15	16	4	6	6	17	19	-2	1	0.938	4	4
12	USSR	14	12	5	3	4	10	11	-1	1	1.167	3	3
13	East Germany	14	18	5	4	9	20	27	-7	0	0.778	3	5
14	Scotland	14	16	4	4	8	18	26	-8	2	0.875	3	5
15	West Germany	14	30	4	6	20	36	70	-34	0	0.467	3	12
16	France	13	12	5	2	5	16	23	-7	1	1.083	1	5
17	Malta	12	6	6	0	0	23	3	20	0	2.000	3	0
18	Hungary	12	12	4	3	5	12	18	-6	1	1.000	3	3
19	Bulgaria	11	14	4	2	8	16	31	-15	1	0.786	1	6
20	Norway	10	6	4	2	0	18	5	13	0	1.667	3	0
21	Luxembourg	10	6	5	0	1	15	7	8	0	1.667	2	1
22	Switzerland	8	8	2	3	3	9	15	-6	1	1.000	2	2
23	Spain	8	16	2	4	10	12	23	-11	0	0.500	0	8
24	Romania	7	8	3	1	4	15	11	4	0	0.875	1	3
25	Netherlands	7	18	2	3	13	13	45	-32	0	0.389	0	9
26	Rep. of Ireland	5	2	2	0	0	4	0	4	1	2.500	1	0
27	Albania	4	2	2	0	0	4	2	2	0	2.000	1	0
28	Yugoslavia	4	6	1	2	3	5	9	-4	0	0.667	1	2
29	Cyprus	3	2	1	1	0	7	3	4	0	1.500	1	0
30	Portugal	2	2	1	0	1	2	6	-4	0	1.000	0	1
31	Wales	1	2	0	1	1	1	3	-2	0	0.500	0	1
	Total	**376**	**379**	**138**	**81**	**160**	**520**	**577**	**-57**	**19**	**0.992**	**79**	**107**

Portugal

Pos'n	Cnty	Pts	P	W	D	L	F	A	Diff	B	Pts/P	Q	E
1	France	50	43	18	11	14	60	42	18	3	1.163	12	9
2	Spain	50	52	20	8	24	80	80	0	2	0.962	11	15
3	Italy	48	48	16	9	23	40	47	-7	7	1.000	12	13
4	Netherlands	43	30	17	5	8	45	31	14	4	1.433	9	6
5	Belgium	41	36	17	5	14	47	46	1	2	1.139	10	8
6	West Germany	38	43	11	14	18	45	73	-28	2	0.884	5	17
7	England	37	53	12	8	33	59	108	-49	5	0.698	8	19
8	Romania	35	22	12	7	3	38	17	21	4	1.591	9	2
9	Hungary	33	28	12	4	12	46	39	7	5	1.179	8	6
10	Denmark	32	18	13	2	3	35	14	21	4	1.778	8	1
11	Scotland	32	30	13	4	13	40	53	-13	2	1.067	4	11
12	Yugoslavia	31	30	12	7	11	45	38	7	0	1.033	8	7
13	Switzerland	25	18	8	6	4	31	19	12	3	1.389	6	3
14	USSR	23	14	7	6	1	19	8	11	3	1.643	5	2
15	Czechoslovakia	22	20	8	4	8	19	19	0	2	1.100	5	5
16	Northern Ireland	17	10	7	3	0	34	8	26	0	1.700	5	0
17	Austria	17	10	6	3	1	29	10	19	2	1.700	5	0
18	Luxembourg	16	8	8	0	0	49	2	47	0	2.000	4	0
19	Malta	16	10	8	0	2	40	7	33	0	1.600	5	0

20	Rep. of Ireland	16	11	6	4	1	18	5	13	0	1.455	4	1
21	Bulgaria	16	10	4	5	1	16	11	5	3	1.600	4	1
22	East Germany	16	22	4	6	12	18	29	-11	2	0.727	2	9
23	Greece	15	10	7	0	3	17	14	3	1	1.500	3	2
24	Norway	12	6	6	0	0	18	3	15	0	2.000	3	0
25	Sweden	12	8	4	1	3	17	6	11	3	1.500	4	0
26	Wales	11	10	4	3	3	12	12	0	0	1.100	2	3
27	Cyprus	9	4	4	0	0	22	1	21	1	2.250	2	0
28	Iceland	8	4	3	1	0	23	1	22	1	2.000	2	0
29	Turkey	5	6	2	1	3	13	7	6	0	0.833	2	1
30	Albania	5	3	2	1	0	5	0	5	0	1.667	2	0
31	Finland	5	4	2	1	1	4	2	2	0	1.250	2	0
32	Poland	2	2	1	0	1	6	2	4	0	1.000	1	0
	Total	**738**	**623**	**274**	**129**	**220**	**990**	**754**	**236**	**61**	**1.185**	**172**	**141**

Republic of Ireland

Pos'n	Cnty	Pts	P	W	D	L	F	A	Diff	B	Pts/P	Q	E
1	Cyprus	13	10	6	1	3	13	8	5	0	1.300	3	2
2	Northern Ireland	9	6	3	3	0	8	3	5	0	1.500	2	1
3	Denmark	8	10	3	2	5	15	16	-1	0	0.800	2	3
4	Iceland	6	4	3	0	1	12	2	10	0	1.500	2	0
5	Portugal	6	11	1	4	6	5	18	-13	0	0.545	1	4
6	Netherlands	6	12	1	4	7	7	26	-19	0	0.500	1	5
7	West Germany	6	18	2	2	14	10	50	-40	0	0.333	0	9
8	Scotland	6	22	1	4	17	17	61	-44	0	0.273	0	11
9	Luxembourg	4	2	2	0	0	8	2	6	0	2.000	1	0
10	Malta	4	4	2	0	2	6	2	4	0	1.000	2	0
11	England	4	22	0	4	18	8	89	-81	0	0.182	0	11
12	Norway	3	2	1	1	0	4	2	2	0	1.500	1	0
13	East Germany	3	7	1	1	5	3	23	-20	0	0.429	0	3
14	Wales	2	4	0	2	2	1	7	-6	0	0.500	0	2
15	Turkey	2	6	0	2	4	5	12	-7	0	0.333	0	3
16	Switzerland	2	6	1	0	5	4	19	-15	0	0.333	0	3
17	France	2	8	0	2	6	9	26	-17	0	0.250	0	4
18	Yugoslavia	2	6	1	0	5	1	18	-17	0	0.333	0	3
19	Spain	2	14	0	2	12	9	39	-30	0	0.143	0	7
20	Sweden	1	2	0	1	1	1	2	-1	0	0.500	0	1
21	Czechoslovakia	1	6	0	1	5	5	13	-8	0	0.167	0	3
22	Italy	1	4	0	1	3	0	8	-8	0	0.250	0	2
23	Romania	1	4	0	1	3	1	10	-9	0	0.250	0	2
24	Bulgaria	1	6	0	1	5	2	12	-10	0	0.167	0	3
25	Hungary	1	8	0	1	7	5	22	-17	0	0.125	0	4
26	Finland	0	2	0	0	2	0	4	-4	0	0.000	0	1
–	Poland	0	2	0	0	2	0	4	-4	0	0.000	0	1
28	Austria	0	2	0	0	2	0	5	-5	0	0.000	0	1
29	Belgium	0	2	0	0	2	4	11	-7	0	0.000	0	1
30	USSR	0	6	0	0	6	1	18	-17	0	0.000	0	3
	Total	**96**	**218**	**28**	**40**	**150**	**164**	**532**	**-368**	**0**	**0.440**	**15**	**93**

Romania

Pos'n	Cnty	Pts	P	W	D	L	F	A	Diff	B	Pts/P	Q	E
1	Spain	28	34	11	5	18	39	66	-27	1	0.824	5	12
2	Cyprus	25	14	11	2	1	41	7	34	1	1.786	7	0
3	Turkey	24	20	10	3	7	30	28	2	1	1.200	6	4
4	Greece	23	16	11	0	5	31	12	19	1	1.438	7	1
5	Austria	23	18	8	6	4	25	15	10	1	1.278	6	3

6	Italy	22	29	7	8	14	18	39	-21	0	0.759	4	11
7	Yugoslavia	21	26	8	4	14	26	50	-24	1	0.808	2	11
8	Scotland	19	16	6	4	6	15	19	-4	3	1.188	4	4
9	USSR	18	14	6	4	4	18	16	2	2	1.286	4	3
10	West Germany	17	25	5	5	15	27	51	-24	2	0.680	2	10
11	Finland	15	8	6	1	1	14	3	11	2	1.875	4	0
12	Hungary	15	14	7	0	7	19	21	-2	1	1.071	3	4
13	East Germany	15	14	6	2	6	15	25	-10	1	1.071	2	4
14	Portugal	14	22	3	7	12	17	38	-21	1	0.636	2	9
15	Malta	13	8	6	1	1	22	2	20	0	1.625	4	0
16	Czechoslovakia	13	10	5	3	2	20	12	8	0	1.300	4	1
17	Northern Ireland	12	8	5	2	1	25	5	20	0	1.500	3	1
18	Denmark	12	8	5	1	2	19	9	10	1	1.500	4	0
19	Bulgaria	12	14	6	0	8	23	34	-11	0	0.857	2	5
20	France	11	16	4	2	10	17	27	-10	1	0.688	3	5
21	Belgium	11	20	3	4	13	11	28	-17	1	0.550	1	9
22	England	11	25	4	3	18	17	56	-39	0	0.440	1	11
23	Poland	9	8	4	1	3	11	15	-4	0	1.125	3	1
24	Rep. of Ireland	7	4	3	1	0	10	1	9	0	1.750	2	0
25	Sweden	7	10	3	0	7	13	15	-2	1	0.700	2	3
26	Albania	6	6	3	0	3	5	4	1	0	1.000	2	1
27	Norway	5	4	2	1	1	6	3	3	0	1.250	2	0
28	Netherlands	5	10	1	3	6	3	20	-17	0	0.500	1	4
29	Luxembourg	4	2	2	0	0	6	0	6	0	2.000	1	0
30	Iceland	4	2	2	0	0	5	0	5	0	2.000	1	0
31	Switzerland	4	4	1	2	1	12	9	3	0	1.000	1	1
	Total	**425**	**429**	**164**	**75**	**190**	**560**	**630**	**-70**	**22**	**0.991**	**95**	**118**

Scotland

Pos'n	Cnty	Pts	P	W	D	L	F	A	Diff	B	Pts/P	Q	E
1	West Germany	73	67	24	17	26	99	98	1	8	1.090	16	18
2	Belgium	62	46	22	11	13	76	49	27	7	1.348	12	11
3	Spain	54	55	20	10	25	71	95	-24	4	0.982	8	18
4	Yugoslavia	44	35	17	4	14	60	50	10	6	1.257	10	7
5	Switzerland	42	29	16	7	6	62	34	28	3	1.448	10	4
6	Rep. of Ireland	40	22	17	4	1	61	17	44	2	1.818	11	0
7	Netherlands	36	30	14	4	12	41	40	1	4	1.200	8	7
8	Italy	35	42	13	7	22	41	73	-32	2	0.833	5	16
9	Portugal	34	30	13	4	13	53	40	13	4	1.133	11	4
10	England	32	44	8	13	23	36	68	-32	3	0.727	5	17
11	France	31	31	13	4	14	43	42	1	1	1.000	9	6
12	Czechoslovakia	30	24	10	6	8	28	28	0	4	1.250	5	7
13	Denmark	29	16	13	1	2	35	12	23	2	1.813	7	1
14	Norway	26	14	12	2	0	34	9	25	0	1.857	7	0
15	Sweden	26	20	9	7	4	35	22	13	1	1.300	6	4
16	Hungary	26	26	11	1	14	41	37	4	3	1.000	7	6
17	Iceland	25	14	11	3	0	47	9	38	0	1.786	7	0
18	Poland	22	16	8	4	4	26	18	8	2	1.375	5	3
19	Austria	22	16	9	2	5	19	14	5	2	1.375	5	3
20	East Germany	21	16	8	3	5	24	16	8	2	1.313	5	3
21	Malta	20	10	9	1	0	42	1	41	1	2.000	5	0
22	Northern Ireland	16	10	7	2	1	24	8	16	0	1.600	4	1
23	Romania	16	16	6	4	6	19	15	4	0	1.000	4	4
24	USSR	13	11	4	4	3	17	13	4	1	1.182	4	2
25	Albania	12	8	4	3	1	14	4	10	1	1.500	4	0
26	Bulgaria	12	8	5	1	2	13	6	7	1	1.500	4	0
27	Finland	10	6	5	0	1	27	3	24	0	1.667	3	0

28	Cyprus	8	4	4	0	0	17	1	16	0	2.000	2	0
29	Turkey	5	4	2	1	1	6	1	5	0	1.250	1	1
30	Luxembourg	4	2	2	0	0	11	1	10	0	2.000	1	0
31	Greece	4	4	1	1	2	5	6	-1	1	1.000	1	1
	Total	**830**	**676**	**317**	**131**	**228**	**1127**	**830**	**297**	**65**	**1.228**	**192**	**144**

Spain

Pos'n	Cnty	Pts	P	W	D	L	F	A	Diff	B	Pts/P	Q	E
1	Italy	115	90	42	12	36	137	107	30	19	1.278	31	15
2	West Germany	110	91	38	19	34	129	125	4	15	1.209	24	21
3	England	102	89	31	25	33	138	129	9	15	1.146	23	22
4	Yugoslavia	80	57	30	9	18	98	76	22	11	1.404	19	9
5	Belgium	75	60	29	7	24	88	72	16	10	1.250	16	14
6	Scotland	71	55	25	10	20	95	71	2	11	1.291	18	8
7	Switzerland	62	39	25	5	9	92	42	50	7	1.590	17	3
8	Portugal	60	52	24	8	20	80	80	0	4	1.154	15	11
9	Hungary	54	39	22	3	14	71	46	25	7	1.385	14	5
10	Austria	52	31	17	10	4	68	28	40	8	1.677	13	2
11	Romania	47	34	18	5	11	66	39	27	6	1.382	12	5
12	France	47	33	16	10	7	60	40	20	5	1.424	11	6
13	Spain	47	40	16	8	16	72	72	0	7	1.175	10	10
14	Bulgaria	46	31	18	4	9	62	34	28	6	1.484	12	3
15	Netherlands	46	42	16	10	16	55	53	2	4	1.095	9	12
16	Denmark	41	22	16	4	2	71	18	53	5	1.864	11	0
17	Czechoslovakia	39	33	13	8	12	47	43	4	5	1.182	11	6
18	USSR	36	27	10	12	5	31	24	7	4	1.333	8	6
19	Poland	27	16	10	4	2	23	12	11	3	1.688	8	0
20	Rep. of Ireland	26	14	12	2	0	39	9	30	0	1.857	7	0
21	Iceland	25	12	12	0	0	34	3	31	1	2.083	6	0
22	Luxembourg	22	10	10	0	0	48	5	43	2	2.200	5	0
23	Greece	22	18	9	4	5	31	9	22	0	1.222	8	1
24	Sweden	22	12	8	2	2	27	11	16	1	1.833	5	1
25	East Germany	22	16	8	3	5	27	17	10	3	1.375	6	2
26	Malta	20	10	9	1	0	27	1	26	1	2.000	5	0
27	Turkey	17	12	7	2	3	20	11	9	1	1.417	4	2
28	Wales	15	8	4	3	1	10	5	5	4	1.875	4	0
29	Cyprus	14	8	6	2	0	39	3	36	0	1.750	4	0
30	Northern Ireland	12	6	6	0	0	23	5	18	0	2.000	3	0
31	Norway	10	6	4	1	1	14	8	6	1	1.667	3	0
32	Albania	5	4	1	2	1	5	3	2	1	1.250	2	0
	Total	**1389**	**1017**	**512**	**195**	**310**	**1827**	**1201**	**626**	**170**	**1.366**	**344**	**164**

Sweden

Pos'n	Cnty	Pts	P	W	D	L	F	A	Diff	B	Pts/P	Q	E
1	Finland	24	14	10	2	2	29	12	17	2	1.714	6	1
2	Italy	21	28	6	8	14	24	41	-17	1	0.750	2	12
3	West Germany	20	32	7	5	20	32	72	-40	1	0.625	2	14
4	Albania	18	12	6	4	2	17	6	11	2	1.500	5	1
5	Poland	18	16	6	4	6	26	26	0	2	1.125	4	4
6	Belgium	17	14	6	3	5	19	16	3	2	1.214	4	3
7	Bulgaria	16	10	7	1	2	21	20	1	1	1.600	3	2
8	Scotland	16	20	4	7	9	22	35	-13	1	0.800	4	6
9	Luxembourg	15	9	7	1	1	42	3	39	0	1.667	4	0
10	Romania	15	10	7	0	3	15	13	2	1	1.500	3	2
11	East Germany	13	18	4	5	9	22	35	-13	0	0.722	2	7
12	Austria	12	10	4	2	4	11	11	0	2	1.200	3	2

13	USSR	12	12	4	3	5	13	15	-2	1	1.000	2	4
14	Norway	11	8	5	1	2	19	8	11	0	1.375	3	1
15	France	10	8	4	2	2	11	11	0	0	1.250	2	2
16	Cyprus	9	6	4	1	1	25	4	21	0	1.500	3	0
17	Czechoslovakia	9	12	2	5	5	13	20	-7	0	0.750	1	5
18	Netherlands	9	15	4	1	10	17	40	-23	0	0.600	0	7
19	Switzerland	8	10	3	2	5	9	13	-4	0	0.800	1	4
20	Hungary	8	12	2	4	6	11	26	-15	0	0.667	0	6
21	England	8	15	0	7	8	8	29	-21	1	0.533	2	6
22	Turkey	7	6	2	2	2	12	9	3	1	1.167	2	1
23	Portugal	7	8	3	1	4	6	17	-11	0	0.875	0	4
24	Spain	7	12	2	2	8	11	27	-16	1	0.583	1	5
25	Greece	6	6	2	1	3	5	6	-1	1	1.000	1	2
26	Denmark	6	8	1	4	3	9	11	-2	0	0.750	1	3
27	Iceland	6	6	2	2	2	4	6	-2	0	1.000	1	2
28	Northern Ireland	5	4	2	1	1	13	6	7	0	1.250	2	0
29	Rep. of Ireland	3	2	1	1	0	2	1	1	0	1.500	1	0
30	Malta	2	2	1	0	1	5	2	3	0	1.000	1	0
31	Yugoslavia	2	4	0	2	2	6	10	-4	0	0.500	0	2
32	Wales	1	2	0	1	1	2	3	-1	0	0.500	0	1
	Total	**341**	**351**	**118**	**85**	**148**	**481**	**554**	**-73**	**20**	**0.972**	**66**	**109**

Switzerland

Pos'n	Cnty	Pts	P	W	D	L	F	A	Diff	B	Pts/P	Q	E
1	Spain	24	39	9	5	25	42	92	-50	1	0.615	3	17
2	Hungary	20	18	8	3	7	29	25	4	1	1.111	5	4
3	Scotland	20	29	6	7	16	34	62	-28	1	0.690	4	10
4	Denmark	18	14	8	2	4	34	27	7	0	1.286	4	3
5	France	18	16	7	3	6	21	25	-4	1	1.125	3	5
6	Czechoslovakia	18	22	7	3	12	33	38	-5	1	0.818	5	6
7	East Germany	18	19	5	5	9	30	47	-17	3	0.947	3	6
8	Luxembourg	17	10	8	1	1	23	2	21	0	1.700	5	0
9	Netherlands	17	25	5	4	16	23	41	-18	3	0.680	4	8
10	Portugal	16	18	4	6	8	19	31	-12	2	0.889	3	6
11	West Germany	16	33	3	9	21	36	81	-45	1	0.485	2	15
12	England	15	28	6	3	19	26	66	-40	0	0.536	3	11
13	Belgium	14	12	6	1	5	25	24	1	1	1.167	4	2
14	Finland	13	8	5	2	1	21	5	16	1	1.625	4	0
15	Sweden	13	10	5	2	3	13	9	4	1	1.300	4	1
16	Bulgaria	13	11	4	4	3	9	13	-4	1	1.182	3	2
17	Malta	12	6	6	0	0	29	4	25	0	2.000	3	0
18	Yugoslavia	12	20	4	4	12	23	49	-26	0	0.600	0	10
19	USSR	11	18	3	3	12	18	29	-11	2	0.611	3	6
20	Rep. of Ireland	10	6	5	0	1	19	4	15	0	1.667	3	0
21	Poland	10	8	3	3	2	15	9	6	1	1.250	2	2
22	Italy	10	22	3	3	16	20	51	-31	1	0.455	1	10
23	Greece	9	12	4	1	7	15	14	1	0	0.750	4	2
24	Iceland	8	4	4	0	0	25	3	22	0	2.000	2	0
25	Turkey	8	7	3	1	3	13	12	1	1	1.143	2	1
26	Cyprus	7	4	3	1	0	9	3	6	0	1.750	2	0
27	Austria	6	6	2	2	2	4	5	-1	0	1.000	1	2
28	Northern Ireland	5	4	2	1	1	9	6	3	0	1.250	2	0
29	Romania	4	4	1	2	1	9	12	-3	0	1.000	1	1
30	Wales	3	4	1	1	2	4	5	-1	0	0.750	0	2
31	Norway	1	2	0	1	1	1	3	-2	0	0.500	0	1
	Total	**386**	**439**	**140**	**83**	**216**	**631**	**797**	**-166**	**23**	**0.879**	**85**	**133**

Turkey

Pos'n	Cnty	Pts	P	W	D	L	F	A	Diff	B	Pts/P	Q	E
1	Romania	17	20	7	3	10	28	30	-2	0	0.850	4	6
2	Hungary	15	19	6	3	10	24	40	-16	0	0.789	3	6
3	Poland	14	17	6	1	10	14	24	-10	1	0.824	2	6
4	France	13	11	5	2	4	13	17	-4	1	1.182	3	2
5	Austria	11	16	5	1	10	17	35	-18	0	0.688	2	6
6	Luxembourg	10	6	5	0	1	16	5	11	0	1.667	3	0
7	Rep. of Ireland	10	6	4	2	0	12	5	7	0	1.667	3	0
8	Switzerland	8	7	3	1	3	12	13	-1	1	1.143	1	2
9	Spain	8	12	3	2	7	11	20	-9	0	0.667	2	4
10	England	8	14	2	4	8	7	23	-16	0	0.571	1	6
11	Portugal	7	6	3	1	2	7	13	-6	0	1.167	1	2
12	Yugoslavia	7	12	2	2	8	6	15	-9	1	0.583	1	5
13	Finland	6	4	2	2	0	7	2	5	0	1.500	2	0
14	Sweden	6	6	2	2	2	9	12	-3	0	1.000	1	2
15	East Germany	6	9	1	4	4	8	15	-7	0	0.667	1	3
16	Netherlands	6	14	3	0	11	11	37	-26	0	0.429	0	7
17	Albania	5	2	2	0	0	3	0	3	1	2.500	1	0
18	Belgium	5	8	1	3	4	7	19	-12	0	0.625	1	3
19	Czechoslovakia	5	8	2	0	6	5	17	-12	1	0.625	1	3
20	West Germany	5	16	1	3	12	8	40	-32	0	0.313	0	8
21	Iceland	4	2	2	0	0	6	3	3	0	2.000	1	0
22	Scotland	4	4	1	1	2	1	6	-5	1	1.000	1	1
23	USSR	4	18	1	2	15	6	37	-31	0	0.222	0	9
24	Italy	4	22	1	2	19	12	59	-47	0	0.182	0	11
25	Wales	3	2	1	0	1	3	1	2	1	1.500	1	0
26	Northern Ireland	3	2	1	0	1	4	3	1	1	1.500	1	0
27	Norway	2	2	1	0	1	4	5	-1	0	1.000	0	1
28	Denmark	2	2	1	0	1	1	2	-1	0	1.000	0	1
29	Bulgaria	1	6	0	1	5	2	11	-9	0	0.167	0	3
	Total	**199**	**273**	**74**	**42**	**157**	**264**	**509**	**-245**	**9**	**0.729**	**37**	**97**

USSR

Pos'n	Cnty	Pts	P	W	D	L	F	A	Diff	B	Pts/P	Q	E
1	West Germany	49	46	20	6	20	51	68	-17	3	1.065	5	18
2	Austria	36	26	13	7	6	41	28	-13	3	1.385	6	7
3	Turkey	35	18	15	2	1	37	6	31	3	1.944	9	0
4	Switzerland	29	18	12	3	3	29	18	11	2	1.611	6	3
5	Italy	27	26	8	10	8	19	21	-2	1	1.038	5	8
6	Spain	26	27	5	12	10	24	31	-7	4	0.963	6	8
7	Czechoslovakia	25	16	9	4	3	26	9	17	3	1.563	7	1
8	Yugoslavia	25	20	11	2	7	37	22	15	1	1.250	6	4
9	Netherlands	25	18	9	4	5	27	16	11	3	1.389	7	2
10	France	25	26	8	7	11	31	35	-4	2	0.962	3	10
11	Finland	24	14	11	2	1	39	11	28	0	1.714	6	1
12	Denmark	24	14	11	1	2	32	12	20	1	1.714	6	1
13	Bulgaria	24	18	9	5	4	24	16	8	1	1.333	7	2
14	East Germany	24	19	9	5	5	26	19	7	1	1.263	7	3
15	Norway	22	12	10	1	1	32	9	23	1	1.833	6	0
16	Greece	19	12	7	3	2	17	7	10	2	1.583	5	1
17	Hungary	17	11	8	0	3	28	16	12	1	1.545	4	2
18	Belgium	16	16	7	2	7	18	20	-2	0	1.000	2	6
19	England	15	14	5	4	5	24	23	1	1	1.071	4	3
20	Rep. of Ireland	14	6	6	0	0	18	1	17	2	2.333	3	0
21	Poland	14	12	4	3	5	11	10	1	3	1.167	3	3
22	Romania	14	14	4	4	6	16	18	-2	2	2.000	3	4

23	Sweden	13	12	5	3	4	15	13	2	0	1.083	4	2
24	Cyprus	11	6	5	1	0	15	1	14	0	1.833	3	0
25	Northern Ireland	11	6	5	1	0	16	3	13	0	1.833	3	0
26	Scotland	11	11	3	4	4	13	17	-4	1	1.000	2	4
27	Malta	9	4	4	0	0	13	0	13	1	2.250	2	0
28	Portugal	9	14	1	6	7	8	19	-11	1	0.643	2	5
29	Iceland	5	2	2	0	0	5	0	5	1	2.500	1	0
30	Luxembourg	4	2	2	0	0	9	0	9	0	2.000	1	0
31	Wales	4	5	2	0	3	4	3	1	0	0.800	1	1
	Total	**606**	**465**	**230**	**102**	**133**	**705**	**472**	**233**	**44**	**1.303**	**135**	**99**

Wales

Pos'n	Cnty	Pts	P	W	D	L	F	A	Diff	B	Pts/P	Q	E
1	Malta	11	6	5	1	0	26	0	26	0	1.833	3	0
2	Norway	10	6	3	3	0	19	3	16	1	1.667	3	0
3	Portugal	10	10	3	3	4	12	12	0	1	1.000	3	2
4	USSR	7	5	3	0	2	3	4	-1	1	1.400	1	1
5	East Germany	7	12	1	5	6	14	24	-10	0	0.583	0	6
6	Rep. of Ireland	6	4	2	2	0	7	1	6	0	1.500	2	0
7	Denmark	6	6	2	2	2	3	6	-3	0	1.000	2	1
8	France	5	4	2	0	2	7	5	2	1	1.250	1	1
9	Switzerland	5	4	2	1	1	5	4	1	0	1.250	2	0
10	Spain	5	8	1	3	4	5	10	-5	0	0.625	0	4
11	Netherlands	4	2	1	1	0	5	2	3	1	2.000	1	0
12	Poland	4	2	1	1	0	3	1	2	1	2.000	1	0
13	Yugoslavia	4	4	2	0	2	5	6	-4	0	1.000	0	2
14	Italy	4	7	2	0	5	6	11	-5	0	0.571	0	3
15	Cyprus	3	2	1	1	0	8	0	8	0	1.500	1	0
16	Northern Ireland	3	2	1	1	0	4	0	4	0	1.500	1	0
17	Sweden	3	2	1	1	0	3	2	1	0	1.500	1	0
18	Turkey	2	2	1	0	1	1	3	-2	0	1.000	0	1
19	Greece	1	2	0	1	1	5	6	-1	0	0.500	0	1
20	West Germany	1	2	0	1	1	3	4	-1	0	0.500	0	1
21	Austria	1	2	0	1	1	0	1	-1	0	0.500	0	1
22	Belgium	1	4	0	1	3	2	5	-3	0	0.250	0	2
23	Bulgaria	1	2	0	1	1	1	5	-4	0	0.500	0	1
24	Czechoslovakia	0	2	0	0	2	0	4	-4	0	0.000	0	1
25	Hungary	0	2	0	0	2	1	6	-5	0	0.000	0	1
26	England	0	2	0	0	2	0	5	-5	0	0.000	0	1
	Total	**104**	**106**	**34**	**30**	**42**	**148**	**130**	**18**	**6**	**0.981**	**22**	**30**

West Germany

Pos'n	Cnty	Pts	P	W	D	L	F	A	Diff	B	Pts/P	Q	E
1	Italy	101	102	36	24	42	121	152	-31	8	1.020	17	33
2	Spain	101	91	34	19	38	125	129	-4	14	1.110	21	24
3	England	83	85	26	22	37	101	138	-37	9	0.976	15	30
4	Czechoslovakia	79	48	32	7	9	107	54	53	8	1.646	20	4
5	Scotland	78	67	26	17	24	98	99	-1	9	1.164	18	16
6	Netherlands	74	58	28	9	21	98	81	17	9	1.276	18	11
7	Belgium	71	53	25	12	16	83	57	26	9	1.340	15	12
8	Denmark	65	37	29	3	5	97	41	56	4	1.757	16	2
9	France	64	44	25	7	12	81	43	38	7	1.455	18	4
10	Portugal	62	43	18	14	11	73	45	28	12	1.442	17	5
11	Switzerland	58	33	21	9	3	81	36	45	7	1.758	15	2
12	USSR	55	46	20	6	20	68	51	17	9	1.196	18	5
13	Yugoslavia	54	40	20	7	13	72	53	19	7	1.350	13	7
14	West Germany	54	44	19	6	19	72	72	0	10	1.227	11	11

15	Austria	53	34	20	6	8	78	29	49	7	1.559	17	0
16	Bulgaria	53	32	21	4	7	69	31	38	7	1.656	13	3
17	Poland	50	30	20	6	4	70	36	34	4	1.667	12	3
18	East Germany	49	34	18	8	8	69	44	25	5	1.441	11	3
19	Sweden	48	32	20	5	7	72	32	40	3	1.500	11	2
20	Cyprus	41	20	20	0	0	111	8	103	1	2.050	10	0
21	Romania	39	25	15	5	5	51	27	24	4	1.560	10	2
22	Rep. of Ireland	33	18	14	2	2	50	10	40	3	1.833	9	0
23	Hungary	33	24	12	4	8	52	40	12	5	1.375	8	4
24	Turkey	30	16	12	3	1	40	8	32	3	1.875	8	0
25	Greece	27	16	11	3	2	33	9	24	2	1.688	8	0
26	Norway	26	18	12	2	4	54	14	40	0	1.444	8	1
27	Luxembourg	24	13	12	0	1	62	8	54	0	1.846	6	0
28	Iceland	18	10	8	2	0	40	5	35	0	1.800	5	0
29	Northern Ireland	13	6	6	0	0	25	4	21	1	2.167	3	0
30	Finland	12	6	6	0	0	28	7	21	0	2.000	3	0
31	Malta	11	6	5	1	0	30	1	29	0	1.833	3	0
32	Albania	8	4	3	1	0	8	1	7	1	2.000	2	0
33	Wales	4	2	1	1	0	4	3	1	1	2.000	1	0
	Total	**1574**	**1137**	**595**	**215**	**327**	**2223**	**1368**	**855**	**169**	**1.384**	**386**	**184**

Yugoslavia

Pos'n	Cnty	Pts	P	W	D	L	F	A	Diff	B	Pts/P	Q	E
1	Spain	49	57	18	9	30	76	98	-22	4	0.860	9	19
2	Italy	48	64	12	22	30	55	93	-38	2	0.750	7	24
3	Bulgaria	41	31	16	7	8	71	39	32	2	1.323	12	3
4	England	39	42	12	9	21	49	61	-12	6	0.929	8	13
5	East Germany	38	33	14	7	12	51	52	-1	3	1.152	7	9
6	West Germany	38	40	13	7	20	53	72	-19	5	0.950	7	13
7	Scotland	37	35	14	4	17	50	60	-10	5	1.057	7	10
8	Romania	36	26	14	4	8	50	26	24	4	1.385	11	2
9	Hungary	32	32	13	3	16	53	58	-5	3	1.000	7	9
10	Belgium	31	33	13	3	17	46	53	-7	2	0.939	7	9
11	Switzerland	30	20	12	4	4	49	23	26	2	1.500	10	0
12	Czechoslovakia	30	26	10	5	11	42	38	4	5	1.154	9	4
13	Portugal	30	30	11	7	12	38	45	-7	1	1.000	7	8
14	Austria	28	21	10	8	3	31	16	15	0	1.333	8	2
15	Netherlands	25	20	9	3	8	32	35	-3	4	1.250	5	5
16	Greece	22	22	10	1	11	41	28	13	1	1.000	7	4
17	Malta	20	10	10	0	0	35	3	32	0	2.000	5	0
18	Norway	20	10	9	1	0	28	5	23	1	2.000	5	0
19	Luxembourg	19	10	8	1	1	53	10	43	2	1.900	5	0
20	Turkey	19	12	8	2	2	15	6	9	1	1.583	5	1
21	USSR	18	20	7	2	11	22	37	-15	2	0.900	4	6
22	France	16	15	5	5	5	24	29	-5	1	1.067	4	4
23	Denmark	12	8	4	2	2	19	10	9	2	1.500	4	0
24	Cyprus	11	6	5	1	0	17	6	11	0	1.833	3	0
25	Northern Ireland	10	6	4	1	1	25	7	18	1	1.667	3	0
26	Rep. of Ireland	10	6	5	0	1	18	1	17	0	1.667	3	0
27	Poland	8	6	3	2	1	9	5	4	0	1.333	2	1
28	Sweden	7	4	2	2	0	10	6	4	1	1.750	2	0
29	Wales	5	4	2	0	2	6	5	1	1	1.250	2	0
30	Yugoslavia	5	4	2	0	2	4	4	0	1	1.250	1	1
31	Iceland	4	2	2	0	0	9	1	8	0	2.000	1	0
32	Albania	2	2	1	0	1	2	3	-1	0	1.000	0	1
33	Finland	0	2	0	0	2	2	4	-2	0	0.000	0	1
	Total	**740**	**659**	**278**	**122**	**259**	**1085**	**939**	**146**	**62**	**1.123**	**177**	**149**

Comparative Country v Country Performance Chart

1955-56 to 1990-91

	Total		%	No.	Albania		Austria		Belgium		Bulgaria		Cyprus		Czechoslovacia		Denmark		E. Germany	
	Q	E	Qual	Adv	Q	E	Q	E	Q	E	Q	E	Q	E	Q	E	Q	E	Q	E
Albania	11	36	23.4%	21	–	–	0	4	0	1	1	2	–	–	–	–	1	1	1	1
Austria	93	124	42.9%	31	4	0	–	–	4	6	4	2	2	0	4	5	5	2	8	3
Belgium	205	145	58.6%	33	1	0	6	4	1	1	3	0	7	0	7	5	6	0	5	7
Bulgaria	74	112	39.8%	31	2	1	2	4	0	3	–	–	2	1	4	2	2	0	0	3
Cyprus	8	71	10.1%	27	–	–	–	–	0	7	1	2	–	–	0	4	0	1	0	1
Czechoslovakia	118	124	48.8%	31	–	–	5	4	5	7	2	4	4	0	–	–	6	0	5	3
Denmark	43	115	27.2%	32	1	1	2	5	0	6	0	2	1	0	0	6	–	–	2	1
East Germany	135	123	52.3%	31	1	1	3	8	7	5	3	0	1	0	3	5	1	2	–	–
England	340	135	71.6%	31	–	–	9	0	20	10	5	2	–	–	13	2	5	0	17	3
Finland	18	80	18.4%	28	2	0	2	3	0	4	0	2	1	1	0	3	1	2	0	5
France	136	142	48.9%	30	2	0	1	3	5	7	3	4	–	–	3	5	6	2	6	8
Greece	55	112	32.9%	28	1	0	2	4	1	6	2	4	3	1	1	4	1	1	1	3
Hungy	127	119	51.6%	30	–	–	5	4	4	3	8	3	2	0	7	5	0	2	4	6
Iceland	6	75	7.4%	29	–	–	0	1	0	4	0	2	1	0	0	4	0	1	0	4
Italy	338	164	67.3%	33	1	0	11	5	16	13	13	1	4	0	8	4	3	0	11	9
Luxembourg	3	93	3.1%	30	–	–	0	3	0	7	0	2	0	1	0	2	0	4	0	4
Malta	4	83	4.6%	29	0	4	0	3	0	2	0	3	0	1	0	4	0	2	–	–
Netherlands	181	125	59.2%	32	2	0	4	3	6	7	6	3	2	0	3	2	9	0	10	2
N. Ireland	12	88	12.0%	28	0	1	–	–	0	11	0	2	–	–	0	1	0	3	0	7
Norway	17	95	15.2%	29	–	–	0	3	0	11	–	–	0	1	0	4	0	2	1	2
Poland	79	107	42.5%	31	1	0	6	1	4	4	1	6	1	0	3	5	4	2	3	5
Portugal	172	141	55.0%	32	2	0	5	0	10	8	4	1	2	0	5	5	8	1	2	9
Rep. of Ireland	15	93	13.9%	30	–	–	0	1	0	1	0	3	3	2	0	3	2	3	0	3
Romania	95	118	44.6%	31	2	1	6	3	1	9	2	5	7	0	4	1	4	0	2	4
Scotland	192	144	57.1%	31	4	0	5	3	12	11	4	0	2	0	5	7	7	1	5	3
Spain	344	164	67.7%	32	2	0	13	2	16	14	12	3	4	0	11	6	11	0	6	2
Sweden	66	109	37.7%	32	5	1	3	2	4	3	3	2	3	0	1	5	1	3	2	7
Switzerland	85	133	39.0%	31	–	–	1	2	4	2	3	2	2	0	5	6	4	3	3	6
Turkey	37	97	27.6%	29	–	–	2	6	1	3	0	3	–	–	1	3	0	1	1	3
USSR	135	99	57.7%	31	–	–	6	7	2	6	7	2	3	0	7	1	6	1	7	3
Wales	22	30	42.3%	26	–	–	0	1	0	2	0	1	1	0	0	1	2	1	0	6
West Germany	386	184	67.7%	33	2	0	17	0	15	12	13	3	10	0	20	4	16	2	14	3
Yugoslavia	177	149	54.3%	33	0	1	8	2	7	9	12	3	3	0	9	4	4	0	7	9
					Elim	**Qual**	**Elim**	**Qual**	**Elim**	**Qual**	**Elim**	**Qual**	**Elim**	**Qual**	**Elim**	**Qual**	**Elim**	**Qual**	**Elim**	**Qual**
Total	**3729**	**3729**	**50.0%**		**36**	**11**	**124**	**93**	**145**	**205**	**112**	**74**	**71**	**8**	**124**	**118**	**115**	**43**	**123**	**135**

	England		Finland		France		Greece		Hungary		Iceland		Italy		Luxembourg		Malta		Netherlands	
	Q	E	Q	E	Q	E	Q	E	Q	E	Q	E	Q	E	Q	E	Q	E	Q	E
Albania	–	–	0	2	0	2	0	1	–	–	–	–	0	1	–	–	4	0	0	2
Austria	0	9	3	2	3	1	4	2	4	5	1	0	5	11	3	0	3	0	3	4
Belgium	10	20	4	0	7	5	6	1	3	4	4	0	13	16	7	0	2	0	7	6
Bulgaria	2	5	2	0	4	3	4	2	3	8	2	0	1	13	2	0	3	0	3	6
Cyprus	–	–	1	1	–	–	1	3	0	2	0	1	0	4	1	0	1	0	0	2
Czechoslovakia	2	1	3	0	5	3	4	1	5	7	4	0	4	8	2	0	4	0	2	3
Denmark	0	5	2	1	2	6	1	1	2	0	1	0	0	3	4	0	2	0	0	9
East Germany	3	17	5	0	8	6	3	1	6	4	4	0	9	11	4	0	–	–	2	10
England	8	8	5	0	10	2	8	3	13	7	5	0	19	17	3	0	3	0	22	8
Finland	0	5	–	–	0	8	–	–	0	2	–	–	0	5	0	2	4	0	0	2
France	2	10	8	0	–	–	6	3	3	2	4	0	5	20	5	0	–	–	6	8
Greece	3	8	–	–	3	6	–	–	3	5	1	0	3	18	3	0	4	0	3	4
Hungary	7	13	2	0	2	3	5	3	–	–	4	0	6	11	1	0	4	0	4	4
Iceland	0	5	–	–	0	4	0	1	0	4	–	–	0	1	1	0	0	2	0	2
Italy	17	19	5	0	20	5	18	3	11	6	1	0	5	5	6	0	4	0	9	6
Luxembourg	0	3	2	0	0	5	0	3	0	1	–	1	0	6	–	–	0	1	0	7
Malta	0	3	0	4	–	–	0	4	0	4	2	0	0	4	1	0	–	–	0	3
Netherlands	8	22	2	0	8	6	4	3	4	4	2	0	6	9	7	0	3	0	–	–
N. Ireland	0	6	0	2	0	5	0	2	–	–	2	2	0	3	4	0	0	1	0	7
Norway	0	10	2	1	0	3	–	–	0	2	4	0	0	4	1	0	1	0	1	5
Poland	3	9	4	1	1	5	4	3	3	3	5	0	4	10	2	1	3	0	0	9
Portugal	8	19	2	0	12	9	3	2	8	6	2	0	12	13	4	0	5	0	9	6
Rep. of Ireland	0	11	0	1	0	4	–	–	0	4	2	0	0	2	1	0	2	0	1	5
Romania	1	11	4	0	3	5	7	1	3	4	1	0	4	11	1	0	4	0	1	4
Scotland	5	17	3	0	9	6	1	1	7	6	7	0	5	16	1	0	5	0	8	7
Spain	23	22	–	–	11	6	8	1	14	5	6	0	31	15	5	0	5	0	9	12
Sweden	2	6	6	1	2	2	1	2	0	6	1	2	2	12	4	0	1	0	0	7
Switzerland	3	11	4	0	3	5	4	2	5	4	2	0	1	10	5	0	3	0	4	8
Turkey	1	6	2	0	3	2	–	–	3	6	1	0	0	11	3	0	–	–	0	7
USSR	4	3	6	1	3	10	5	1	4	2	1	0	5	8	1	0	2	0	7	2
Wales	0	1	–	–	1	1	0	1	0	1	–	–	0	3	–	–	3	0	1	0
West Germany	15	30	3	0	18	4	8	0	8	4	5	0	17	33	6	0	3	0	18	11
Yugoslavia	8	13	0	1	4	4	7	4	7	9	1	0	7	24	5	0	5	0	5	5
	Elim	**Qual**	**Elim**	**Qual**	**Elim**	**Qual**	**Elim**	**Qual**	**Elim**	**Qual**	**Elim**	**Qual**	**Elim**	**Qual**	**Elim**	**Qual**	**Elim**	**Qual**	**Elim**	**Qual**
Total	**135**	**340**	**80**	**18**	**142**	**136**	**112**	**55**	**119**	**127**	**75**	**6**	**164**	**338**	**93**	**3**	**83**	**4**	**125**	**181**

1955-56 to 1990-91

	N. Ireland		Norway		Poland		Portugal		Rep. of Ire.		Romania		Scotland		Spain		Sweden		Switzerland	
	Q	E	Q	E	Q	E	Q	E	Q	E	Q	E	Q	E	Q	E	Q	E	Q	E
Albania	1	0	–	–	0	1	0	2	–	–	1	2	0	4	0	2	1	5	–	–
Austria	–	–	3	0	1	6	0	5	1	0	3	6	3	5	2	13	2	3	2	1
Belgium	11	0	11	0	4	4	8	10	1	0	9	1	11	12	14	16	3	4	2	4
Bulgaria	2	0	–	–	6	1	1	4	3	0	5	2	0	4	3	12	2	3	2	3
Cyprus	–	–	1	0	0	1	0	2	2	3	0	7	0	2	0	4	0	3	0	2
Czechoslovakia	1	0	4	0	5	3	5	5	3	0	1	4	7	5	6	11	5	1	6	5
Denmark	3	0	2	0	2	4	1	8	3	2	0	4	1	7	0	11	3	1	3	4
East Germany	7	0	2	1	5	3	9	2	3	0	4	2	3	5	2	6	7	2	6	3
England	6	0	10	0	9	3	19	8	11	0	11	1	17	5	22	23	6	2	11	3
Finland	2	0	1	2	1	4	0	2	1	0	0	4	0	3	–	–	1	6	0	4
France	5	0	3	0	5	1	9	12	4	0	5	3	6	9	6	11	2	2	5	3
Greece	2	0	–	–	3	4	2	3	–	–	1	7	1	1	1	8	2	1	2	4
Hungary	–	–	2	0	3	3	6	8	4	0	4	3	6	7	5	14	6	0	4	5
Iceland	2	2	0	4	0	5	0	2	0	2	0	1	0	7	0	6	2	1	0	2
Itally	3	0	4	0	10	4	13	12	2	0	11	4	16	5	15	31	12	2	10	1
Luxembourg	0	4	0	1	1	2	0	4	0	1	0	1	0	1	0	5	0	4	0	5
Malta	1	0	0	1	0	3	0	5	0	2	0	4	0	5	0	5	0	1	0	3
Netherlands	7	0	5	1	9	0	6	9	5	1	4	1	7	8	12	9	7	0	8	4
Northern Ireland	–	–	3	3	–	–	0	5	1	2	1	3	1	4	0	3	0	2	0	2
Norway	3	3	–	–	0	3	0	3	0	1	0	2	0	7	0	3	1	3	1	0
Poland	–	–	3	0	–	–	0	1	1	0	1	3	3	5	8	0	4	4	2	2
Portugal	5	0	3	0	1	0	–	–	4	1	9	2	4	11	11	15	4	0	6	3
Rep. of Ireland	2	1	1	0	0	1	1	4	–	–	0	2	0	11	0	7	0	1	0	3
Romania	3	1	2	0	3	1	2	9	2	0	–	–	4	4	5	12	2	3	1	1
Scotland	4	1	7	0	5	3	11	4	11	0	4	4	–	–	8	18	6	4	10	4
Spain	3	0	3	0	8	0	15	11	7	0	12	5	18	8	10	10	5	1	17	3
Sweden	2	0	3	1	4	4	0	4	1	0	3	2	4	6	1	5	–	–	1	4
Switzerland	2	0	0	1	2	2	3	6	3	0	1	1	4	10	3	17	4	1	–	–
Turkey	1	0	0	1	2	6	1	2	3	0	4	6	1	1	2	4	1	2	1	2
USSR	3	0	6	0	3	3	2	5	3	0	3	4	2	4	6	8	4	2	6	3
Wales	1	0	3	0	1	0	3	2	2	0	–	–	–	–	0	4	1	0	2	0
West Germany	3	0	8	1	12	3	17	5	9	0	10	2	18	16	21	24	14	2	15	2
Yugoslavia	3	0	5	0	2	1	7	8	3	0	11	2	7	10	9	19	2	0	10	0
	Elim	**Qual**	**Elim**	**Qual**	**Elim**	**Qual**	**Elim**	**Qual**	**Elim**	**Qual**	**Elim**	**Qual**	**Elim**	**Qual**	**Elim**	**Qual**	**Elim**	**Qual**	**Elim**	**Qual**
Total	**88**	**12**	**95**	**17**	**107**	**79**	**141**	**172**	**93**	**15**	**118**	**95**	**144**	**192**	**164**	**344**	**109**	**66**	**133**	**85**

1955-56 to 1990-91

	Turkey		USSR		Wales		W. Germany		Yugoslavia	
	Q	**E**	**Q**	**E**	**Q**	**E**	**Q**	**E**	**Q**	**E**
Albania	0	1	–	–	–	–	0	2	1	0
Austria	6	2	7	6	1	0	0	17	2	8
Belgium	3	1	6	2	2	0	12	15	9	7
Bulgaria	3	0	2	7	1	0	3	13	3	12
Cyprus	–	–	0	3	0	1	0	10	0	3
Czechoslovakia	3	1	1	7	1	0	4	20	4	9
Denmark	1	0	1	6	1	2	2	16	0	4
East Germany	3	1	3	7	6	0	3	14	9	7
England	6	1	3	4	1	0	30	15	13	8
Finland	0	2	1	6	–	–	0	3	1	0
France	2	3	10	3	1	1	4	18	4	4
Greece	–	–	1	5	1	0	0	8	4	7
Hungary	6	3	2	4	1	0	4	8	9	7
Iceland	0	1	0	1	–	–	0	5	0	1
Italy	11	0	8	5	3	0	33	17	24	7
Luxembourg	0	3	0	1	–	–	0	6	0	5
Malta	–	–	0	2	0	3	0	3	0	5
Netherlands	7	0	2	7	0	1	11	18	5	5
Northern Ireland	0	1	0	3	0	1	0	3	0	3
Norway	1	0	0	6	0	3	1	8	0	5
Poland	6	2	3	3	0	1	3	12	1	2
Portugal	2	1	5	2	2	3	5	17	8	7
Rep. of Ireland	0	3	0	3	0	2	0	9	0	3
Romania	6	4	4	3	–	–	2	10	2	11
Scotland	1	1	4	2	–	–	16	18	10	7
Spain	4	2	8	6	4	0	24	21	19	9
Sweden	2	1	2	4	0	1	2	14	0	2
Switzerland	2	1	3	6	0	2	2	15	0	10
Turkey	–	–	0	9	1	0	0	8	1	5
USSR	9	0	–	–	1	1	5	18	6	4
Wales	0	1	1	1	–	–	0	1	0	2
West Germany	8	0	18	5	1	0	11	11	13	7
Yugoslavia	5	1	4	6	2	0	7	13	1	1
	Elim	**Qual**	**Elim**	**Qual**	**Elim**	**Qual**	**Elim**	**Qual**	**Elim**	**Qual**
Total	**97**	**37**	**99**	**135**	**30**	**22**	**184**	**386**	**149**	**177**

Second-leg Outcomes 1955-56 to 1990-91

First-leg: 0-0

Second-leg	1-0	2-0	3-0	4-0	5-0	2-1	3-1	4-1	5-1	3-2	4-2	5-2	4-3
	21	8	1	0	0	8	4	1	1	1	0	1	0
Second-leg	5-3	5-4	0-0	1-1	2-2	3-3	4-4	5-5	0-1	0-2	0-3	0-4	0-5
	0	0	11	28	7	0	0	0	45	53	15	11	8
Second-leg	1-2	1-3	1-4	1-5	2-3	2-4	2-5	3-4	3-5	4-5	5>	<5	
	21	12	5	4	7	1	1	1	0	0	0	10	

First-leg 1-0

Second-leg	1-0	2-0	3-0	4-0	5-0	2-1	3-1	4-1	5-1	3-2	4-2	5-2	4-3
	29	9	6	4	0	16	11	2	0	7	2	3	0
Second-leg	5-3	5-4	0-0	1-1	2-2	3-3	4-4	5-5	0-1	0-2	0-3	0-4	0-5
	0	0	39	40	13	3	0	0	31	79	28	16	10
Second-leg	1-2	1-3	1-4	1-5	2-3	2-4	2-5	3-4	3-5	4-5	5>	<5	
	45	14	12	9	11	5	1	2	1	0	1	10	

First-leg 2-0

Second-leg	1-0	2-0	3-0	4-0	5-0	2-1	3-1	4-1	5-1	3-2	4-2	5-2	4-3
	19	14	4	1	2	17	6	1	1	7	2	0	0
Second-leg	5-3	5-4	0-0	1-1	2-2	3-3	4-4	5-5	0-1	0-2	0-3	0-4	0-5
	1	0	21	39	20	4	0	0	51	25	34	13	7
Second-leg	1-2	1-3	1-4	1-5	2-3	2-4	2-5	3-4	3-5	4-5	5>	<5	
	36	12	10	5	9	0	1	1	0	0	1	8	

First-leg 3-0

Second-leg	1-0	2-0	3-0	4-0	5-0	2-1	3-1	4-1	5-1	3-2	4-2	5-2	4-3
	17	11	9	1	1	8	9	4	1	7	0	0	0
Second-leg	5-3	5-4	0-0	1-1	2-2	3-3	4-4	5-5	0-1	0-2	0-3	0-4	0-5
	0	0	6	21	10	1	1	0	29	29	9	5	4
Second-leg	1-2	1-3	1-4	1-5	2-3	2-4	2-5	3-4	3-5	4-5	5>	<5	
	23	13	3	2	5	3	1	0	0	0	1	1	

First-leg 1-1

Second-leg	1-0	2-0	3-0	4-0	5-0	2-1	3-1	4-1	5-1	3-2	4-2	5-2	4-3
	11	8	2	0	0	10	4	3	0	4	2	0	0
Second-leg	5-3	5-4	0-0	1-1	2-2	3-3	4-4	5-5	0-1	0-2	0-3	0-4	0-5
	0	0	30	23	6	1	0	0	43	39	11	18	5
Second-leg	1-2	1-3	1-4	1-5	2-3	2-4	2-5	3-4	3-5	4-5	5>	<5	
	37	19	9	7	7	1	3	1	1	0	1	15	

First-leg 2-1

Second-leg	1-0	2-0	3-0	4-0	5-0	2-1	3-1	4-1	5-1	3-2	4-2	5-2	4-3
	19	7	2	0	1	12	6	3	0	3	0	0	1
Second-leg	5-3	5-4	0-0	1-1	2-2	3-3	4-4	5-5	0-1	0-2	0-3	0-4	0-5
	0	0	9	26	9	4	1	0	40	31	31	7	5
Second-leg	1-2	1-3	1-4	1-5	2-3	2-4	2-5	3-4	3-5	4-5	5>	<5	
	16	13	9	1	6	4	1	1	1	1	0	13	

First-leg 3-1

Second-leg	1-0	2-0	3-0	4-0	5-0	2-1	3-1	4-1	5-1	3-2	4-2	5-2	4-3
	15	5	3	0	0	6	3	3	0	1	1	1	0

Second-leg	5-3	5-4	0-0	1-1	2-2	3-3	4-4	5-5	0-1	0-2	0-3	0-4	0-5
	1	0	12	10	5	0	0	0	20	15	10	6	3

Second-leg	1-2	1-3	1-4	1-5	2-3	2-4	2-5	3-4	3-5	4-5	5>	<5
	18	7	5	5	1	3	0	0	0	0	2	3

First-leg 4-1

Second-leg	1-0	2-0	3-0	4-0	5-0	2-1	3-1	4-1	5-1	3-2	4-2	5-2	4-3
	7	3	0	1	0	5	2	1	0	0	0	0	0

Second-leg	5-3	5-4	0-0	1-1	2-2	3-3	4-4	5-5	0-1	0-2	0-3	0-4	0-5
	0	0	5	7	3	1	0	0	9	12	3	3	3

Second-leg	1-2	1-3	1-4	1-5	2-3	2-4	2-5	3-4	3-5	4-5	5>	<5
	6	5	0	3	2	1	1	0	0	1	0	1

First-leg 5-1

Second-leg	1-0	2-0	3-0	4-0	5-0	2-1	3-1	4-1	5-1	3-2	4-2	5-2	4-3
	3	1	0	0	0	4	3	1	1	1	0	0	0

Second-leg	5-3	5-4	0-0	1-1	2-2	3-3	4-4	5-5	0-1	0-2	0-3	0-4	0-5
	0	0	4	5	4	0	0	0	5	3	1	1	0

Second-leg	1-2	1-3	1-4	1-5	2-3	2-4	2-5	3-4	3-5	4-5	5>	<5
	5	2	2	0	3	0	0	0	0	0	2	1

First-leg 2-2

Second-leg	1-0	2-0	3-0	4-0	5-0	2-1	3-1	4-1	5-1	3-2	4-2	5-2	4-3
	7	4	0	0	0	2	0	0	0	2	0	0	0

Second-leg	5-3	5-4	0-0	1-1	2-2	3-3	4-4	5-5	0-1	0-2	0-3	0-4	0-5
	0	0	9	6	1	0	1	0	13	9	8	7	4

Second-leg	1-2	1-3	1-4	1-5	2-3	2-4	2-5	3-4	3-5	4-5	5>	<5
	17	6	8	3	7	2	0	0	0	0	1	3

First-leg 3-2

Second-leg	1-0	2-0	3-0	4-0	5-0	2-1	3-1	4-1	5-1	3-2	4-2	5-2	4-3
	3	1	0	0	0	9	2	0	1	1	0	1	0

Second-leg	5-3	5-4	0-0	1-1	2-2	3-3	4-4	5-5	0-1	0-2	0-3	0-4	0-5
	0	0	9	6	3	3	0	0	13	12	4	7	1

Second-leg	1-2	1-3	1-4	1-5	2-3	2-4	2-5	3-4	3-5	4-5	5>	<5
	9	4	0	1	0	1	1	1	0	0	2	4

First-leg 4-2

Second-leg	1-0	2-0	3-0	4-0	5-0	2-1	3-1	4-1	5-1	3-2	4-2	5-2	4-3
	1	2	1	0	0	2	2	1	0	0	1	1	0

Second-leg	5-3	5-4	0-0	1-1	2-2	3-3	4-4	5-5	0-1	0-2	0-3	0-4	0-5
	0	0	4	1	1	2	1	0	3	7	2	0	0

Second-leg	1-2	1-3	1-4	1-5	2-3	2-4	2-5	3-4	3-5	4-5	5>	<5
	4	4	1	0	0	0	2	0	0	0	0	1

First-leg 5-2

Second-leg	1-0	2-0	3-0	4-0	5-0	2-1	3-1	4-1	5-1	3-2	4-2	5-2	4-3
	2	1	0	0	0	1	0	0	0	1	0	0	0
Second-leg	5-3	5-4	0-0	1-1	2-2	3-3	4-4	5-5	0-1	0-2	0-3	0-4	0-5
	0	0	0	0	0	0	0	0	1	0	1	0	0
Second-leg	1-2	1-3	1-4	1-5	2-3	2-4	2-5	3-4	3-5	4-5	5>	<5	
	0	2	2	1	0	0	0	0	0	0	0	0	

First-leg 6-2

Second-leg	1-0	2-0	3-0	4-0	5-0	2-1	3-1	4-1	5-1	3-2	4-2	5-2	4-3
	0	0	1	0	0	0	0	0	0	0	0	0	0
Second-leg	5-3	5-4	0-0	1-1	2-2	3-3	4-4	5-5	0-1	0-2	0-3	0-4	0-5
	0	0	0	3	0	0	0	0	0	0	0	1	1
Second-leg	1-2	1-3	1-4	1-5	2-3	2-4	2-5	3-4	3-5	4-5	5>	<5	
	1	0	0	0	0	0	0	0	0	0	0	0	

First-leg 3-3

Second-leg	1-0	2-0	3-0	4-0	5-0	2-1	3-1	4-1	5-1	3-2	4-2	5-2	4-3
	1	0	0	0	0	1	0	0	0	0	0	0	0
Second-leg	5-3	5-4	0-0	1-1	2-2	3-3	4-4	5-5	0-1	0-2	0-3	0-4	0-5
	0	0	0	1	2	0	0	0	2	1	2	1	1
Second-leg	1-2	1-3	1-4	1-5	2-3	2-4	2-5	3-4	3-5	4-5	5>	<5	
	1	0	0	1	0	0	2	0	0	0	0	1	

First-leg 4-3

Second-leg	1-0	2-0	3-0	4-0	5-0	2-1	3-1	4-1	5-1	3-2	4-2	5-2	4-3
	1	0	0	0	0	0	0	0	0	0	0	0	0
Second-leg	5-3	5-4	0-0	1-1	2-2	3-3	4-4	5-5	0-1	0-2	0-3	0-4	0-5
	0	0	1	1	0	2	0	0	1	2	1	1	0
Second-leg	1-2	1-3	1-4	1-5	2-3	2-4	2-5	3-4	3-5	4-5	5>	<5	
	2	2	1	0	0	0	0	0	0	0	0	0	

First-leg 5-3

Second-leg	1-0	2-0	3-0	4-0	5-0	2-1	3-1	4-1	5-1	3-2	4-2	5-2	4-3
	0	2	0	0	0	0	0	0	0	0	0	0	0
Second-leg	5-3	5-4	0-0	1-1	2-2	3-3	4-4	5-5	0-1	0-2	0-3	0-4	0-5
	0	0	1	0	0	0	0	0	0	0	1	0	0
Second-leg	1-2	1-3	1-4	1-5	2-3	2-4	2-5	3-4	3-5	4-5	5>	<5	
	0	0	0	1	0	0	0	1	0	0	0	0	

First-leg 0-1

Second-leg	1-0	2-0	3-0	4-0	5-0	2-1	3-1	4-1	5-1	3-2	4-2	5-2	4-3
	2	5	1	1	0	0	1	0	0	0	1	0	0
Second-leg	5-3	5-4	0-0	1-1	2-2	3-3	4-4	5-5	0-1	0-2	0-3	0-4	0-5
	0	0	14	20	4	1	0	0	24	22	22	17	10
Second-leg	1-2	1-3	1-4	1-5	2-3	2-4	2-5	3-4	3-5	4-5	5>	<5	
	12	7	4	0	5	1	0	1	0	0	1	13	

First-leg 0-2

Second-leg	1-0	2-0	3-0	4-0	5-0	2-1	3-1	4-1	5-1	3-2	4-2	5-2	4-3
	3	0	0	1	0	3	1	0	0	1	0	0	0
Second-leg	5-3	5-4	0-0	1-1	2-2	3-3	4-4	5-5	0-1	0-2	0-3	0-4	0-5
	0	0	5	7	4	0	0	0	12	6	6	8	8
Second-leg	1-2	1-3	1-4	1-5	2-3	2-4	2-5	3-4	3-5	4-5	5>	<5	
	13	6	3	3	0	3	1	1	0	0	0	16	

First-leg 1-2

Second-leg	1-0	2-0	3-0	4-0	5-0	2-1	3-1	4-1	5-1	3-2	4-2	5-2	4-3
	4	0	0	0	0	1	1	0	0	0	0	0	0
Second-leg	5-3	5-4	0-0	1-1	2-2	3-3	4-4	5-5	0-1	0-2	0-3	0-4	0-5
	0	0	13	20	3	1	0	0	16	12	9	6	4
Second-leg	1-2	1-3	1-4	1-5	2-3	2-4	2-5	3-4	3-5	4-5	5>	<5	
	10	11	7	5	2	1	0	2	0	0	0	7	

First-leg 1-3

Second-leg	1-0	2-0	3-0	4-0	5-0	2-1	3-1	4-1	5-1	3-2	4-2	5-2	4-3
	2	1	0	0	0	1	2	0	0	0	0	0	0
Second-leg	5-3	5-4	0-0	1-1	2-2	3-3	4-4	5-5	0-1	0-2	0-3	0-4	0-5
	0	0	3	5	1	2	0	0	9	6	6	7	3
Second-leg	1-2	1-3	1-4	1-5	2-3	2-4	2-5	3-4	3-5	4-5	5>	<5	
	9	6	2	2	1	3	0	0	1	0	0	7	

First-leg 2-4

Second-leg	1-0	2-0	3-0	4-0	5-0	2-1	3-1	4-1	5-1	3-2	4-2	5-2	4-3
	2	0	0	0	0	0	0	1	0	0	0	0	0
Second-leg	5-3	5-4	0-0	1-1	2-2	3-3	4-4	5-5	0-1	0-2	0-3	0-4	0-5
	0	0	1	0	0	0	0	0	1	1	2	1	0
Second-leg	1-2	1-3	1-4	1-5	2-3	2-4	2-5	3-4	3-5	4-5	5>	<5	
	3	1	1	0	0	0	0	0	0	0	0	0	

First-leg 3-4

Second-leg	1-0	2-0	3-0	4-0	5-0	2-1	3-1	4-1	5-1	3-2	4-2	5-2	4-3
	0	0	0	0	0	1	0	1	0	0	0	0	0
Second-leg	5-3	5-4	0-0	1-1	2-2	3-3	4-4	5-5	0-1	0-2	0-3	0-4	0-5
	0	0	0	2	0	0	0	0	0	1	0	0	0
Second-leg	1-2	1-3	1-4	1-5	2-3	2-4	2-5	3-4	3-5	4-5	5>	<5	
	1	0	0	0	1	0	0	0	0	1	0	1	

Qualification/Eliminations after First-leg Score

First-leg Score	No. Matches	Qualifications No.	%	Eliminations No.	%
0-0	286	85	29.72%	201	70.28%
1-0	459	254	55.34%	205	44.66%
2-0	372	278	74.73%	94	25.27%
3-0	235	215	91.49%	20	8.51%
1-1	321	64	19.94%	257	80.06%
2-1	283	123	43.46%	160	56.54%
3-1	164	115	70.12%	49	29.88%
4-1	85	73	85.88%	12	14.12%
5-1	52	50	96.15%	2	3.85%
2-2	120	19	15.83%	101	84.17%
3-2	99	43	43.43%	56	56.57%
4-2	44	30	68.18%	14	31.82%
5-2	12	8	66.67%	4	33.33%
6-2	7	5	71.43%	2	28.57%
3-3	17	3	17.65%	14	82.35%
4-3	15	6	40.00%	9	60.00%
5-3	6	4	66.67%	2	33.33%
0-1	189	11	5.82%	178	94.18%
0-2	111	2	1.80%	109	98.20%
1-2	135	2	1.48%	133	98.52%
1-3	79	1	1.27%	78	98.73%
2-4	14	1	7.14%	13	92.86%
3-4	9	1	11.11%	8	88.89%

Home Match Statistics

	1-0	2-0	3-0	4-0	5-0	2 -1	3-1	4-1	5-1	3-2	4-2	5-2	4-3
Number	864	780	470	268	156	604	323	182	114	178	80	30	30
	5-3	5-4	0-0	1-1	2-2	3-3	4-4	5-5	0-1	0-2	0-3	0-4	0-5
Number	10	4	497	624	234	47	9	0	383	211	104	44	37
	1-2	1-3	1-4	1-5	2-3	2-4	2-5	3-4	3-5	4-5	5>	<5	
Number	271	142	74	19	86	30	18	11	7	0	301	71	
	1-0	2-0	3-0	4-0	5-0	2-1	3-1	4-1	5-1	3-2	4-2	5-2	4-3
Percent	12	11	6	4	2	8	4	2	2	2	1	0	0
	5-3	5-4	0-0	1-1	2-2	3-3	4-4	5-5	0-1	0-2	0-3	0-4	0-5
Percent	0	0	7	9	3	1	0	0	5	3	1	1	1
	1-2	1-3	1-4	1-5	2-3	2-4	2-5	3-4	3-5	4-5	5>	<5	
Percent	4	2	1	0	1	0	0	0	0	0	4	1	

Number of matches **7313**

Qualification Percentages after Particular First-leg Scores

All Three Cups

	Qualifications No.	Qualifications %	Eliminations No.	Eliminations %	Total
0-0	85	29.72%	201	70.28%	286
1-0	254	55.34%	205	44.66%	459
2-0	278	74.73%	94	25.27%	372
3-0	215	91.49%	20	8.51%	235
1-1	64	19.94%	257	80.06%	321
2-1	123	43.46%	160	56.54%	283
3-1	115	70.12%	49	29.88%	164
4-1	73	85.88%	12	14.12%	85
5-1	50	96.15%	2	3.85%	52
2-2	19	15.83%	101	84.17%	120
3-2	43	43.43%	56	56.57%	99
4-2	30	68.18%	14	31.82%	44
5-2	8	66.67%	4	33.33%	12
6-2	5	71.43%	2	28.57%	7
3-3	3	17.65%	14	82.35%	17
4-3	6	40.00%	9	60.00%	15
5-3	4	66.67%	2	33.33%	6
0-1	11	5.82%	178	94.18%	189
0-2	2	1.80%	109	98.20%	111
1-2	2	1.48%	133	98.52%	135
1-3	1	1.27%	78	98.73%	79
2-4	1	7.14%	13	92.86%	14
3-4	1	11.11%	8	88.89%	9

Champions Cup

	Qualifications No.	Qualifications %	Eliminations No.	Eliminations %	Total
0-0	25	33.33%	50	66.67%	75
1-0	51	45.95%	60	54.05%	111
2-0	74	81.32%	17	18.68%	91
3-0	65	94.20%	4	5.80%	69
1-1	16	21.92%	57	78.08%	73
2-1	39	44.83%	48	55.17%	87
3-1	35	76.09%	11	23.91%	46
4-1	21	80.77%	5	19.23%	26
5-1	13	100.00%	0	0.00%	13
2-2	5	14.29%	30	85.71%	35
3-2	13	52.00%	12	48.00%	25
4-2	8	72.73%	3	27.27%	11
5-2	2	100.00%	0	0.00%	2
6-2	2	100.00%	0	0.00%	2
3-3	1	14.29%	6	85.71%	7
4-3	4	66.67%	2	33.33%	6
5-3	2	50.00%	2	50.00%	4
0-1	1	2.38%	41	97.62%	42
0-2	0	0.00%	30	100.00%	30
1-2	0	0.00%	44	100.00%	44
1-3	1	4.00%	24	96.00%	25
2-4	0	0.00%	2	100.00%	2
3-4	1	25.00%	3	75.00%	4

Cup Winners' Cup

	Qualifications No.	Qualifications %	Eliminations No.	Eliminations %	Total
0-0	23	27.71%	60	72.29%	83
1-0	57	54.29%	48	45.71%	105
2-0	68	69.39%	30	30.61%	98
3-0	49	90.74%	5	9.26%	54
1-1	19	18.81%	82	81.19%	101
2-1	25	40.98%	36	59.02%	61
3-1	22	73.33%	8	26.67%	30
4-1	11	91.67%	1	8.33%	12
5-1	11	100.00%	0	0.00%	11
2-2	1	4.00%	24	96.00%	25
3-2	8	40.00%	12	60.00%	20
4-2	5	62.50%	3	37.50%	8
5-2	1	100.00%	0	0.00%	1
6-2	1	50.00%	1	50.00%	2
3-3	0	0.00%	2	100.00%	2
4-3	2	66.67%	1	33.33%	3
5-3	1	100.00%	0	0.00%	1
0-1	2	3.64%	53	96.36%	55
0-2	0	0.00%	33	100.00%	33
1-2	0	0.00%	26	100.00%	26
1-3	0	0.00%	16	100.00%	16
2-4	1	25.00%	3	75.00%	4
3-4	0	0.00%	3	100.00%	3

UEFA Cup

	Qualifications No.	Qualifications %	Eliminations No.	Eliminations %	Total
0-0	37	28.91%	91	71.09%	128
1-0	146	60.08%	97	39.92%	243
2-0	136	74.32%	47	25.68%	183
3-0	101	90.18%	11	9.82%	112
1-1	29	19.73%	118	80.27%	147
2-1	59	43.70%	76	56.30%	135
3-1	58	65.91%	30	34.09%	88
4-1	41	87.23%	6	12.77%	47
5-1	26	92.86%	2	7.14%	28
2-2	13	21.67%	47	78.33%	60
3-2	22	40.74%	32	59.26%	54
4-2	17	68.00%	8	32.00%	25
5-2	5	55.56%	4	44.44%	9
6-2	2	66.67%	1	33.33%	3
3-3	2	25.00%	6	75.00%	8
4-3	0	0.00%	6	100.00%	6
5-3	1	100.00%	0	0.00%	1
0-1	8	8.70%	84	91.30%	92
0-2	2	4.17%	46	95.83%	48
1-2	2	3.08%	63	96.92%	65
1-3	0	0.00%	38	100.00%	38
2-4	0	0.00%	8	100.00%	8
3-4	0	0.00%	2	100.00%	2

Above: PSV goalkeeper Hans Van Breukelen (with trophy) and captain Erik Gerets. Van Breukelen was PSV's hero in the penalty shoot out during his sides defeat of Benfica in the 1987-88 final in Stuttgart.

Roll of Honour – the Winners and the Runners-up

Champions' Cup Winners

1.	England	8
2.	Italy	7
3.	Spain	6
4.	Netherlands	5
5.	West Germany	4
6.	Portugal	3
7.	Scotland	1
8.	Romania	1
9.	Yugoslavia	1
	Total	**36**

Champions' Cup Runners-up

1.	Italy	7
2.	Spain	6
3.	West Germany	5
4.	Portugal	5
5.	France	4
6.	England	2
7.	Yugoslavia	1
8.	Netherlands	1
9.	Scotland	1
10.	Greece	1
11.	Belgium	1
12.	Sweden	1
13.	Romania	1
	Total	**36**

Cup Winners Cup Winners

1.	England	6
2.	Italy	5
3.	Spain	5
4.	West Germany	3
5.	USSR	3
6.	Belgium	3
7.	Scotland	2
8.	Portugal	1
9.	Czechoslovakia	1
10.	East Germany	1
11.	Netherlands	1
	Total	**31**

Cup Winners Cup Runners-up

1.	Spain	6
2.	England	4
3.	Italy	3
4.	West Germany	3
5.	Belgium	3
6.	Scotland	2
7.	Hungary	2
8.	Austria	2
9.	East Germany	2
10.	Poland	1
11.	USSR	1
12.	Portugal	1
13.	Netherlands	1
	Total	**31**

UEFA Cup Winners

1.	England	9
2.	Spain	8
3.	Italy	5
4.	West Germany	4
5.	Netherlands	2
6.	Sweden	2
7.	Hungary	1
8.	Yugoslavia	1
9.	Belgium	1
	Total	**33**

UEFA Cup Runners-up

1.	England	6
2.	Spain	5
3.	West Germany	5
4.	Italy	4
5.	Hungary	3
6.	Belgium	3
7.	Yugoslavia	2
8.	Netherlands	2
9.	France	1
10.	Portugal	1
11.	Scotland	1
	Total	**33**

All Three Cups' Winners

1.	England	23
2.	Spain	19
3.	Italy	17
4.	West Germany	11
5.	Netherlands	8
6.	Portugal	4
7.	Belgium	4
8.	Scotland	3
9.	USSR	3
10.	Yugoslavia	2
11.	Sweden	2
12.	Romania	1
13.	Czechoslovakia	1
14.	East Germany	1
15.	Hungary	1
	Total	**100**

All Three Cups' Runners-up

1.	Spain	17
2.	Italy	14
3.	West Germany	13
4.	England	12
5.	Portugal	7
6.	Belgium	7
7.	France	5
8.	Hungary	5
9.	Netherlands	4
10.	Scotland	4
11.	Yugoslavia	3
12.	Austria	2
13.	East Germany	2
14.	Greece	1
15.	Sweden	1
16.	Poland	1
17.	USSR	1
18.	Romania	1
	Total	**100**

Above: Barcelona's José Ramon Alesanco attempts to head the ball as Steaua Bucharest goalkeeper Helmut Ducadam punches clear in the 1985-86 European Champions' Cup Final.

The Winners – Classification by Country and Team

Country/Team	C1	C2	C3	C1	C2	C3	Total
Albania	–	–	–	–	–	–	–
Austria	–	–	–	–	–	–	–
Belgium							
Anderlecht	–	1976, 1978	1983	–	2	1	3
KV Mechelen	–	1988	–	–	1	–	1
Bulgaria	–	–	–	–	–	–	–
Cyprus	–	–	–	–	–	–	–
Czechoslovakia							
Slovan Bratislava	–	1969	–	–	1	–	1
Denmark	–	–	–	–	–	–	–
East Germany							
Magdeburg	–	1974	–	–	1	–	1
England							
Arsenal	–	–	1970	–	–	1	1
Aston Villa	1982	–	–	1	–	–	1
Chelsea	–	1971	–	–	1	–	1
Everton	–	1985	–	–	1	–	1
Ipswich Town	–	–	1981	–	–	1	1
Leeds United	–	–	1968, 1971	–	–	2	2
Liverpool	1977, 1978, 1981, 1984	–	1973, 1976	4	–	2	6
Manchester City	–	1970	–	–	1	–	1
Manchester United	1968	1991	–	1	1	–	2
Newcastle United	–	–	1969	–	–	1	1
Nottingham Forest	1979, 1980	–	–	2	–	–	2
Tottenham Hotspur	–	1963	1972, 1984	–	1	2	3
West Ham United	–	1965	–	–	1	–	1
Finland	–	–	–	–	–	–	–
France	–	–	–	–	–	–	–
Greece	–	–	–	–	–	–	–
Hungary							
Ferencváros	–	–	1965	–	–	1	1
Iceland	–	–	–	–	–	–	–
Italy							
Fiorentina	–	1961	–	–	1	–	1
AC Milan	1963, 1969, 1989 1990	1968, 1973	–	4	2	–	6
Inter Milan	1964, 1965	–	1991	2	–	1	3
Roma	–	–	1961	–	–	1	1
Juventus	1985	1984	1977, 1990	1	1	2	4
Napoli	–	–	1989	–	–	1	1
Sampdoria	–	1990	–	–	1	–	1
Luxembourg	–	–	–	–	–	–	–
Malta	–	–	–	–	–	–	–
Netherlands							
Ajax	1971, 1972, 1973	1987	–	3	1	–	4
PSV Eindhoven	1988	–	1978	1	–	1	2
Feyenoord	1970	–	1974	1	–	1	2
Northern Ireland	–	–	–	–	–	–	–
Norway	–	–	–	–	–	–	–
Poland	–	–	–	–	–	–	–

Country/Team	C1	C2	C3	C1	C2	C3	Total
Portugal							
Benfica	1961, 1962	–	–	2	–	–	2
Sporting Lisbon	–	1964	–	–	1	–	1
FC Porto	1987	–	–	1	–	–	1
Republic of Ireland	–	–	–	–	–	–	–
Romania							
Steaua Bucharest	1986	–	–	1	–	–	1
Scotland							
Aberdeen	–	1983	–	–	1	–	1
Celtic	1967	–	–	1	–	–	1
Rangers	–	1972	–	–	1	–	1
Spain							
Barcelona	–	1979, 1982, 1989	1958, 1960, 1966	–	3	3	6
Atlético Madrid	–	1962	–	–	1	–	1
Real Madrid	1956, 1957, 1958 1959, 1960, 1966	–	1985, 1986	6	–	2	8
Valencia	–	1980	1962, 1963	–	1	2	3
Real Zaragoza	–	–	1964	–	–	1	1
Sweden							
IFK Gothenburg	–	–	1982, 1987	–	–	2	2
Switzerland	–	–	–	–	–	–	–
Turkey	–	–	–	–	–	–	–
USSR							
Dinamo Kiev	–	1975, 1986	–	–	2	–	2
Dinamo Tbilisi	–	1981	–	–	1	–	1
Wales	–	–	–	–	–	–	–
West Germany							
Borussia Dortmund	–	1966	–	–	1	–	1
Eintracht Frankfurt	–	–	1980	–	–	1	1
Hamburg	1983	1977	–	1	1	–	2
B. Mönchengladbach	–	–	1975, 1979	–	–	2	2
Bayern Munich	1974, 1975, 1976	1967	–	3	1	–	4
Bayer Leverkusen	–	–	1988	–	–	1	1
Yugoslavia							
Dinamo Zagreb	–	–	1967	–	–	1	1
Red Star Belgrade	1991	–	–	1	–	–	1

The Runners-up – Classification by Country and Team

Country/Team	C1	C2	C3	C1	C2	C3	Total
Albania	–	–	–	–	–	–	–
Austria							
Austria Vienna	–	1978	–	–	1	–	1
Rapid Vienna	–	1985	–	–	1	–	1
Belgium							
Anderlecht	–	1977, 1990	1970, 1984	–	2	2	4
Club Bruges	1978	–	1976	1	–	1	2
Standard Liège	–	1982	–	–	1	–	1
Bulgaria	–	–	–	–	–	–	–
Cyprus	–	–	–	–	–	–	–
Czechoslovakia	–	–	–	–	–	–	–
Denmark	–	–	–	–	–	–	–
East Germany							

Country	C1	C2	C3	C1	C2	C3	Total
Carl Zeiss Jena	–	1981	–	–	1	–	1
Leipzig Lokomotiv	–	1987	–	–	1	–	1
England							
Arsenal	–	1980	–	–	1	–	1
Birmingham	–	–	1960, 1961	–	–	2	2
Chelsea	–	–	1958	–	–	1	1
Leeds United	1975	1973	1967	1	1	1	3
Liverpool	1985	1966	–	1	1	–	2
Tottenham Hotspur	–	–	1974	–	–	1	1
West Ham United	–	1976	–	–	1	–	1
Wolverhampton Wand	–	–	1972	–	–	1	1
Finland	–	–	–	–	–	–	–
France							
Bastia	–	–	1978	–	–	1	1
Stade Reims	1956, 1959	–	–	2	–	–	2
Saint-Etienne	1976	–	–	1	–	–	1
Olympique Marseille	1991	–	–	1	–	–	1
Greece							
Panathinaikos	1971	–	–	1	–	–	1
Hungary							
MTK-VM	–	1964	–	–	1	–	1
Ferencváros	–	1975	1968	–	1	1	2
Videoton	–	–	1985	–	–	1	1
Ujpesti Dózsa	–	–	1969	–	–	1	1
Iceland	–	–	–	–	–	–	–
Italy							
Fiorentina	1975	1962	1990	1	1	1	3
AC Milan	1958	1974	–	1	1	–	2
Inter Milan	1967, 1972	–	–	2	–	–	2
Roma	1984	–	1991	1	–	1	2
Juventus	1973, 1983	–	1965, 1971	2	–	2	4
Sampdoria	–	1989	–	–	1	–	1
Luxembourg	–	–	–	–	–	–	–
Malta	–	–	–	–	–	–	–
Netherlands							
AZ'67 Alkmaar	–	–	1981	–	–	1	1
Ajax	1969	1988	–	1	1	–	2
Twente Enchede	–	–	1975	–	–	1	1
Northern Ireland	–	–	–	–	–	–	–
Norway	–	–	–	–	–	–	–
Poland							
Górnik Zabrze	–	1970	–	–	1	–	1
Portugal							
Benfica	1963, 1965, 1968 1988, 1990	–	1983	5	–	1	6
FC Porto	–	1984	–	–	1	–	1
Republic of Ireland	–	–	–	–	–	–	–
Romania							
Steaua Bucharest	1989	–	–	1	–	–	1
Scotland							
Celtic	1970	–	–	1	–	–	1
Rangers	–	1961, 1967	–	–	2	–	2
Dundee United	–	–	1987	–	–	1	1
Spain							
Barcelona	1961, 1986	1969, 1991	1962	2	2	1	5

Country	C1	C2	C3	C1	C2	C3	Total
Athletic Bilbao	–	–	1977	–	–	1	1
Atlético Madrid	1974	1963, 1986	–	1	2	–	3
Real Madrid	1962, 1964, 1981	1971, 1983	–	3	2	–	5
Valencia	–	–	1964	–	–	1	1
Real Zaragoza	–	–	1966	–	–	1	1
Español	–	–	1988	–	–	1	1
Sweden							
Malmö FF	1979	–	–	1	–	–	1
Switzerland	–	–	–	–	–	–	–
Turkey	–	–	–	–	–	–	–
USSR							
Dinamo Moscow	–	1972	–	–	1	–	1
Wales	–	–	–	–	–	–	–
West Germany							
Fortuna Düsseldorf	–	1979	–	–	1	–	1
Eintracht Frankfurt	1960	–	–	1	–	–	1
Hamburg	1980	1968	1982	1	1	1	3
B. Mönchengladbach	1977	–	1973, 1980	1	–	2	3
Bayern Munich	1982, 1987	–	–	2	–	–	2
1860 Munich	–	1965	–	–	1	–	1
Cologne	–	–	1986	–	–	1	1
VFB Stuttgart	–	–	1989	–	–	1	1
Yugoslavia							
Red Star Belgrade	–	–	1979	–	–	1	1
Partizan Belgrade	1966	–	–	1	–	–	1
Dinamo Zagreb	–	–	1963	–	–	1	1

The Winners – Classification by Results

Pos'n	Club	Cnty	Wins	Competitions
1	Real Madrid	Esp	8	6xC1, 2xC3
2	AC Milan	Ita	6	4xC1, 2xC2
3	Liverpool	Eng	6	4xC1, 2xC3
4	Barcelona	Esp	6	3xC2, 3xC3
5	Ajax	Ned	4	3xC1, 1xC2
6	Bayern Munich	FRG	4	3xC1, 1xC2
7	Juventus	Ita	4	1xC1, 1xC2, 2xC3
8	Inter Milan	Ita	3	2xC1, 1xC3
9	Anderlecht	Bel	3	2xC2, 1xC3
10	Tottenham Hotspur	Eng	3	1xC2, 2xC3
11	Valencia	Esp	3	1xC2, 2xC3
12	Benfica	Por	2	2xC1
13	Nottingham Forest	Eng	2	2xC1
14	Manchester United	Eng	2	1xC1, 1xC2
15	Hamburg	FRG	2	1xC1, 1xC2
16	Feyenoord	Ned	2	1xC1, 1xC3
17	PSV Eindhoven	Ned	2	1xC1, 1xC3
18	Dinamo Kiev	URS	2	2xC2
19	Leeds United	Eng	2	2xC3
20	Borussia Mönchengladbach	FRG	2	2xC3
21	IFK Gothenburg	Swe	2	2xC3
21	Celtic	Sco	1	1xC1
23	Aston Villa	Eng	1	1xC1
24	Steaua Bucharest	Rom	1	1xC1
25	FC Porto	Por	1	1xC1

26	Red Star Belgrade	Yug	1	1xC1
27	Fiorentina	Ita	1	1xC2
28	Atlético Madrid	Esp	1	1xC2
29	Sporting Lisbon	Por	1	1xC2
30	West Ham United	Eng	1	1xC2
31	Borussia Dortmund	FRG	1	1xC2
32	Slovan Bratislava	Tch	1	1xC2
33	Manchester City	Eng	1	1xC2
34	Chelsea	Eng	1	1xC2
35	Rangers	Sco	1	1xC2
36	Magdeburg	GDR	1	1xC2
37	Dinamo Tbilisi	URS	1	1xC2
38	Aberdeen	Sco	1	1xC2
39	Everton	Eng	1	1xC2
40	KV Mechelen	Bel	1	1xC2
41	Roma	Ita	1	1xC3
42	Sampdoria	Ita	1	1xC2
43	Real Zaragoza	Esp	1	1xC3
44	Ferencváros	Hun	1	1xC3
45	Dinamo Zagreb	Yug	1	1xC3
46	Newcastle United	Eng	1	1xC3
47	Arsenal	Eng	1	1xC3
48	Eintracht Frankfurt	FRG	1	1xC3
49	Ipswich Town	Eng	1	1xC3
50	Bayer Leverkusen	FRG	1	1xC3
51	Napoli	Ita	1	1xC3
	Total		**100**	

Liverpool's Alan Kennedy moves away from Real Madrid's Juan Juanito during the 1980-81 European Champions' Cup Final in Paris. Liverpool won 1-0.

Number of Appearances in all Three Competitions
Classification by Results

Pos'n	Club	Cnty	App	Wins
1	Real Madrid	Esp	13	8
2	Barcelona	Esp	11	6
3	AC Milan	Ita	8	6
4	Liverpool	Eng	8	6
5	Juventus	Ita	8	4
6	Benfica	Ita	8	2
7	Anderlecht	Bel	7	3
8	Ajax	Ned	6	4
9	Bayern Munich	FRG	6	4
10	Inter Milan	Ita	5	3
11	Hamburg	FRG	5	2
12	Leeds United	Eng	5	2
13	Borussia Mönchengladbach	FRG	5	2
14	Tottenham Hotspur	Eng	4	3
15	Valencia	Esp	4	3
16	Fiorentina	Ita	4	1
17	Atlético Madrid	Esp	4	1
18	Roma	Ita	3	1
19	Rangers	Sco	3	1
20	Ferencváros	Hun	3	1
21	Manchester United	Eng	2	2
22	Feyenoord	Ned	2	2
23	PSV Eindhoven	Ned	2	2
24	Nottingham Forest	Eng	2	2
25	Dinamo Kiev	URS	2	2
26	IFK Gothenburg	Swe	2	2
27	Celtic	Sco	2	1
28	FC Porto	Por	2	1
29	Steaua Bucharest	Rom	2	1
30	West Ham United	Eng	2	1
31	Chelsea	Eng	2	1
32	Real Zaragoza	Esp	2	1
33	Dinamo Zagreb	Yug	2	1
34	Arsenal	Eng	2	1
35	Eintracht Frankfurt	FRG	2	1
36	Sampdoria	Ita	2	1
37	Stade Reims	Fra	2	0
38	Club Bruges	Bel	2	0
39	Birmingham City	Eng	2	0
40	Aston Villa	Eng	1	1
41	Sporting Lisbon	Por	1	1
42	Borrusia Dortmund	FRG	1	1
43	Slovan Bratislava	Tch	1	1
44	Manchester City	Eng	1	1
45	Magdeburg	GDR	1	1
46	Dinamo Tbilisi	URS	1	1
47	Aberdeen	Sco	1	1
48	Everton	Eng	1	1
49	Newcastle United	Eng	1	1
50	Ipswich Town	Eng	1	1
51	KV Mechelen	Bel	1	1
52	Bayer Leverkusen	FRG	1	1
53	Napoli	Ita	1	1
54	Red Star Belgrade	Yug	1	1
55	Partizan Belgrade	Yug	1	0
56	Panathinaikos	Gre	1	0
57	Saint-Etienne	Fra	1	0
58	Malmö FF	Swe	1	0
59	MTK-VM	Hun	1	0
60	1860 Munich	FRG	1	0
61	Górnik Zabrze	Pol	1	0
62	Dinamo Moscow	URS	1	0
63	Austria Vienna	Aut	1	0
64	Fortuna Düsseldorf	FRG	1	0
65	Carl Zeiss Jena	GDR	1	0
66	Standard Liège	Bel	1	0
67	Rapid Vienna	Aut	1	0
68	Lokomotive Leipzig	GDR	1	0
69	Ujpesti Dózsa	Hun	1	0
70	Wolverhampton Wanderers	Eng	1	0
71	Twente Enschede	Ned	1	0
72	Athletic Bilbao	Esp	1	0
73	Bastia	Fra	1	0
74	AZ'67 Alkmaar	Ned	1	0
75	Videoton	Hun	1	0
76	Cologne	FRG	1	0
77	Dundee United	Sco	1	0
78	Español	Esp	1	0
79	VFB Stuttgart	FRG	1	0
80	Olympique Marseille	Fra	1	0
	Total		**200**	**100**

The Most Number of Appearances in a Final

Champions' Cup

Pos'n	Cnty	App	Won
1	Italy	14	7
2	Spain	12	6
3	England	10	8
4	West Germany	9	4
5	Portugal	8	3
6	Netherlands	6	5
7	France	4	0
8	Scotland	2	1
9	Yugoslavia	2	1
10	Romania	2	1
11	Greece	1	0
12	Belgium	1	0
13	Sweden	1	0
	Total	**72**	**36**

Cup Winners' Cup

Pos'n	Cnty	App	Won
1	Spain	11	5
2	England	10	6
3	Itlay	8	5
4	West Germany	6	3
5	Belgium	6	3
6	USSR	4	3
7	Scotland	4	2
8	East Germany	3	1
9	Portugal	2	1
10	Netherlands	2	1
11	Hungary	2	0
12	Austria	2	0
13	Czechoslovakia	1	1
14	Poland	1	0
	Total	**62**	**31**

UEFA Cup

Pos'n	Cnty	App	Won
1	England	15	9
2	Spain	13	8
3	Italy	9	5
4	West Germany	9	4
5	Netherlands	4	2
6	Hungary	4	1
7	Belgium	4	1
8	Yugoslavia	3	1
9	Sweden	2	2
10	France	1	0
11	Portugal	1	0
12	Scotland	1	0
	Total	**66**	**33**

All Three Cups

Pos'n	Cnty	App	Won
1	Spain	36	19
2	England	35	23
3	Italy	31	17
4	West Germany	24	11
5	Netherlands	12	8
6	Belgium	11	4
7	Portugal	11	4
8	Scotland	7	3
9	Hungary	6	1
10	Yugoslavia	5	2
11	France	5	0
12	USSR	4	3
13	East Germany	3	1
14	Sweden	3	1
15	Romania	2	1
16	Austria	2	0
17	Czechoslovakia	1	1
18	Greece	1	0
19	Poland	1	0
	Total	**200**	**100**

Alphabetical List of Clubs by Country

Including Previous Names of Clubs

Albania
Apolonia Fier
Besa Kavajë
Dinamo Tirana
Flamurtari Vlorë
Labinoti Elbasan
17 Nëntori Tirana
Partizani Tirana
Vllaznia Shkodër

Austria
Admira Wacker
Austria Vienna
FC Tirol (ex Wacker Innsbruck)
First Vienna
Grazer AK
Krems
Linzer ASK
Rapid Vienna
SV Salzburg
Sturm Graz
Vöest Linz
Wiener Sport-Club
Wiener Neustadt

Belgium
Anderlecht
Antwerp
Beerschot
Beveren
Cercle Bruges
Charleroi
Club Bruges
FC Liège
Gent
KV Mechelen
Lierse
Lokeren
RWD Molenbeek
Standard Liège
Union St-Gilloise
Waregem
Waterschei Thor
Winterslag

Bulgaria
Akademik Sofia
Beroe Stara Zagora
Botev Vratsa
Chernomorets Bourgas
CSKA Sofia (ex CDNA Sofia and Sredets Sofia)
Dunav Ruse
Etar Veliko Tarnovo
Levski Sofia (ex Levski Spartak Sofia and Vitosha Sofia)
Lokomotiv Plovdiv
Lokomotiv Sofia
Marek Stanke Dimitrov
Pirin Blagoevgrad
Slavia Sofia
Sliven
Spartak Varna
Trakia Plovdiv

Cyprus
AEL Limassol
Akritas Morphou
Alki Larnaca
Anorthosis Famagusta
Anorthosis Nicosia
Apoel Nicosia
Apollon Limassol
EPA Larnaca
NEA Salamina Famagusta
Olympiakos Nicosia
Omonia Nicosia
Paralimni
Pezoporikos Larnaca

Czechoslovakia
Banik Ostrava
Bohemians Prague
DAC Dunajská Streda
Dukla Banská Bystrica
Dukla Prague
Dynamo Zilina
Inter Bratislava
Lokomotiv Kosice
Plastika Nitra
Sigma Olomouc
Skoda Plzen
Slavia Prague
Slovan Bratislava
Sparta Prague
Spartak Hradec Králové
Spartak Trnava
Tatran Presov
TJ Gottwaldov
TJ Vitkovice
Union Teplice
VSS Kosice
Zbrojovka Brno

Denmark
AaB Aalborg
AB Copenhagen
AGF Aarhus
B 1901 Nykobing
B 1903 Copenhagen
B 1909 Odense
B 1913 Odense
B 93 Copenhagen
BK Frem
BK Fremad Amager
Brøndby IF
Esbjerg FB
Holbaek BIF
Hvidovre IF
Ikast FS
KB Copenhagen
Køge BK
Lyngby BK
Naestved IF
OB Odense
Randers Freja FC
Vanløse IF
Vejle BK

East Germany
Carl Zeiss Jena
Chemie Halle
Chemie Leipzig
Dynamo Berlin
Dynamo Dresden
Hansa Rostock
Karl-Marx-Stadt
Lokomotive Leipzig
Magdeburg
PSV Schwerin
Sachsenning Zwickau
Stahl Brandenburg
Vorwärts Frankfurt/Oder
Wismut Aue

England
Arsenal
Aston Villa
Birmingham City
Burnley
Chelsea
Coventry City
Derby County
Everton
Ipswich Town
Leeds United
Leicester City
Liverpool
Manchester City
Manchester United
Newcastle United
Nottingham Forest
Queen's Park Rangers
Sheffield Wednesday
Southampton
Stoke City
Sunderland
Tottenham Hotspur
West Ham United
Watford
West Bromwich Albion
Wolverhampton Wanderers

Finland
FC Kuusysi Lahti
Haka Valkeakoski
HIFK Helsinki
HJK Helsinki
HPS Helsinki
Ilves Tampere
KPV Kokkola
KTP Kotka
KuPS Kuopio
MP Mikkeli
OPS Oulu
Reipas Lahti
RoPS Rovaniemi
TPS Turku

France
Angers
Angoulême
Auxerre
Bastia
Girondins Bordeaux
Laval
Lens
Metz
Monaco
Montpellier
Nancy
Nantes
Nice
Nîmes Olympique
Olympique Lyon
Olympique Marseille
Paris Saint-Germain
Racing Club Paris
Rouen
Saint-Etienne
Sedan
Sochaux
Stade Français
Stade Reims
Stade Rennes

Strasbourg
Toulouse

Greece

AEK Athenes
Aris Salonika
Iraklis
Kastoria
Larissa
OFI Crete
Olympiakos Pireus
Panathinaikos
Panahaiki
Panionios
PAOK Salonika

Hungary

Békéscsaba
Csepel
Diósgyöri VTK
Ferencváros
Haladás
Honvéd
Komló
MTK-VM
Pécs Dózsa †
Pécsi MSC
Rába ETO
Salgótarján
Siófok
Tatabánya
Ujpesti Dózsa
Vasas SC
Videoton

Iceland

FH Hafnarfjördhur
Fram Reykjavik
IA Akranes
IBA Akureyri
IBK Keflavik
IBV Vestmannaeyjar
KR Reykjavik
Valur Reykjavik
Vikingur Reykjavik

Italy

AC Milan
Atalanta
Bologna
Cagliari
Cesena
Fiorentina
Inter Milan
Juventus
Lanerossi Vicenza
Lazio
Napoli
Penigia
Roma
Sampdoria
Torino
Verona

Luxembourg

Alliance Dudelange
Aris Bonnevoie
Avenir Beggen
Fola Esch
Jeunesse Esch
Jeunesse Hautcharage
Progrès Niedercorn
Red Boys Differdange
Spora Luxembourg
Stade Dudelange
Swift Hesperange
Union Luxembourg
US Rumelange

Malta

Floriana
Gzira United
Hamrun Spartans
Hibernians
Marsa
Rabat Ajax
Sliema Wanderers
Valletta
Zurrieq

Netherlands

Ajax
AZ'67 Alkmaar
FC Amsterdam (ex DWS)
FC Den Haag
Feyenoord
Fortuna Sittard
Go Ahead Eagles
Groningen
Haarlem
NAC Breda
NEC Nijmegen
PSV Eindhoven
Roda JC
Sparta Rotterdam
Twente Enschede
Utrecht
Vitesse
Willem II

Northern Ireland
Ards
Ballymena United
Carrick Rangers
Cliftonville
Coleraine
Crusaders
Derry City*
Distillery
Glenavon
Glentoran
Linfield
Portadown

Norway
Bryne IL
FK Skeid
Fredrikstad FK
Gjøvik/Lyn
Haugar FC
IF Sarpsborg
IK Start
IL Viking
Lillestrøm SK
Mjøndalen IF
Molde FK
Moss FK
Rosenborg BK
SFK Bodø/Glimt
SFK Lyn
SK Brann
SK Frigg
Strømgodset IF
Tromsø IL
Vålerengen SIF

Poland
Arka Gdynia
GKS Katowice
GKS Tychy
Górnik Zabrze
Gwardia Warsaw
Lech Poznań
Lechia Gdańsk
Legia Warsaw
LKS Lódź
Odra Opole
Pogon Szczecin
Polonia Bytom
Ruch Chorzów
Slask Wroclaw
Stal Mielec
Stal Rzeszów
Szombierki Bytom
Widzew Lódź
Wisla Kraków
Zaglebie Lubin
Zaglebie Sosnowiec
Zaglebie Walbrzych

Portugal
Academica Coimbra
Barreirense
Belenenses
Benfica
Boavista
Chaves
Estrela Amadora
FC Porto
Leixões
Portimonense
Sporting Braga
Sporting Lisbon
Vitória Guimarães
Vitória Setúbal

Republic of Ireland
Athlone Town
Bohemians
Bray Wanderers
Cork Celtic
Cork City
Cork Hibernians
Derry City*
Drogheda United
Drumcondra
Dundalk
Finn Harps
Galway United
Home Farm
Limerick
Shamrock Rovers
Shelbourne
Sligo Rovers
St. Patrick's Athletic
UCD
Waterford United

Romania
Arges Pitesti
ASA Tîrgu Mures
Bacau
Baia Mare
Chimia Râmnicu Vâlcea
Corvinul Hunedoara
CSU Galati
Dinamo Bucharest
Flacara Moreni
Jiul Petrosani
Petrolul Ploiesti
Politehnica Timisoara
Progresul Bucharest

Rapid Bucharest
Red Flag Brasov
Sportul Studentesc Bucharest
Steaua Bucharest
Universitatea Cluj
Universitatea Craiova
UT Arad
Victoria Bucharest

Scotland
Aberdeen
Celtic
Dundee
Dundee United
Dunfermline Athletic
Heart of Midlothian
Hibernian
Kilmarnock
Morton
Partick Thistle
Rangers
St. Johnstone
St. Mirren

Spain
Athletic Bilbao
Atlético Madrid
Barcelona
Castilla Madrid
Celta Vigo
Español
Las Palmas
Osasuna
Real Betis
Real Madrid
Real Sociedad
Real Valladolid
Real Zaragoza
Sabadell
Seville
Sporting Gijón
Valencia

Sweden
AIK
Åtvidaberg SFF
Djurgården SIF
GAIS
Halmstad SBK
Hammarby IF
IF Elfsborg
IFK Gothenburg
IFK Norrköping
IK Brage
Kalmar FF
Landskrona BOIS
Malmö FF
Örgryte IS
Öster SIF

Switzerland
Aarau
FC Basle
FC Zürich
Grasshoppers Zürich
La Chaux-de-Fonds
Lausanne-Sports
Lucerne
Lugano
Neuchâtel Xamax
Servette
Sion
St-Gallen
Wettingen
Young Boys Berne

Turkey
Adanaspor
Altay
Ankaragücü
Besiktas
Boluspor
Bursaspor
Eskisehirspor
Fenerbahçe
Galatasaray
Gençlerbirligi
Göztepe
Mersin Idmanyurdu
Orduspor
Sakaryaspor
Trabzonspor

USSR
Ararat Erevan
Chernomorets Odessa
CSKA Moscow
Dinamo Kiev
Dinamo Minsk
Dinamo Moscow
Dinamo Tbilisi
Dnepr Dnepropetrovsk
Karpaty Lvov
Metallist Kharkov
Shakhtyor Donetsk
SKA Rostov on Don
Spartak Moscow
Torpedo Moscow
Zaria Voroshilovgrad
Zenit Leningrad
Zhalgiris Vilnius

Wales

Bangor City
Borough United
Cardiff City
Merthyr Tydfil
Newport County
Swansea City (ex Swansea Town)
Wrexham

West Germany

Bayer Leverkusen
Bayer Uerdingen
Bayern Munich
Borussia Dortmund
Borussia Mönchengladbach
Cologne
Eintracht Braunschweig
Eintracht Frankfurt
Fortuna Düsseldorf
Hamburg
Hannover 96
Hertha Berlin
Kaiserslautern
Kickers Offenbach
MSV Duisburg
Nuremberg
Rot-Weiss Essen
Saarbrücken
Schalke 04
Tasmania Berlin
VFB Stuttgart
Viktoria Cologne
Werder Bremen
Wuppertal
1860 Munich

Yugoslavia

Borac Banja Luka
Borovo
Dinamo Zagreb
Hajduk Split
Napredak Krusevac
NK Zagreb
OFK Belgrade
Olimpija Ljubljana
Partizan Belgrade
Rad Belgrade
Radnicki Nis
Red Star Belgrade
Rijeka
Sarajevo
Sloboda Tuzla
Tresnjevka Zagreb
Vardar Skoplje
Velez Mostar
Vojvodina Novi Sad
Zeljeznicar Sarajevo

Notes:
*** In 1988-89 Derry City left the Irish League (Northern Ireland) and joined the League of Ireland (Republic of Ireland)**

† In 1973 Pécs Dózsa merged with Pécsi MSC

Number of Participating Teams per Country per Cup

County		55-56	56-57	57-58	58-59	59-60	60-61	61-62	62-63	63-64	64-65	65-66	66-67
Albania	C1	–	–	–	–	–	–	–	1	1	1	1	–
	C2	–	–	–	–	–	–	–	–	–	–	–	–
	C3	–	–	–	–	–	–	–	–	–	–	–	–
	Tot	–	–	–	–	–	–	–	1	1	1	1	–
Austria	C1	1	1	1	1	1	1	1	1	1	1	1	1
	C2	–	–	–	–	–	1	1	1	1	1	1	1
	C3	–	–	–	–	–	–	–	1	1	2	1	1
	Tot	1	1	1	1	1	2	2	3	3	4	3	3
Belgium	C1	1	1	1	1	1	1	1	1	1	1	1	1
	C2	–	–	–	–	–	–	–	–	–	1	1	1
	C3	–	–	–	(1	)	1	1	1	2	3	3	3
	Tot	1	1	1	1.5	1.5	2	2	2	3	5	5	5
Bulgaria	C1	–	1	1	1	1	1	1	1	1	1	1	1
	C2	–	–	–	–	–	–	1	1	1	1	1	1
	C3	–	–	–	–	–	–	–	–	1	1	1	1
	Tot	–	1	1	1	1	1	2	2	3	3	3	3
Cyprus	C1	–	–	–	–	–	–	–	–	1	–	1	1
	C2	–	–	–	–	–	–	–	–	1	1	1	1
	C3	–	–	–	–	–	–	–	–	–	–	–	–
	Tot	–	–	–	–	–	–	–	–	2	1	2	2
Czechoslovakia	C1	–	1	1	1	1	1	1	1	1	1	1	1
	C2	–	–	–	–	–	1	1	1	1	1	1	1
	C3	–	–	–	–	–	–	1	1	1	1	1	2
	Tot	–	1	1	1	1	2	3	3	3	3	3	4
Denmark	C1	1	1	1	1	1	1	1	1	1	1	1	1
	C2	–	–	–	–	–	–	1	1	1	1	1	1
	C3	–	(1	)	(1	)	1	1	2	1	2	1	2
	Tot	1	1.5	1.5	1.5	1.5	2	3	4	3	4	3	4
East Germany	C1	–	–	1	1	1	1	1	1	1	1	1	1
	C2	–	–	–	–	–	1	1	1	1	1	1	1
	C3	–	(1	)	(1	)	1	1	1	1	1	1	1
	Tot	–	0.5	1.5	1.5	1.5	3	3	3	3	3	3	3

County		67-68	68-69	69-70	70-71	71-72	72-73	73-74	74-75	75-76	76-77	77-78	78-79
Albania	C1	–	–	1	1	1	–	–	–	–	–	–	1
	C2	–	1	–	1	1	1	–	–	–	–	–	–
	C3	–	–	–	–	–	–	–	–	–	–	–	–
	Tot	–	1	1	2	2	1	–	–	–	–	–	1
Austria	C1	1	1	1	1	1	1	1	1	1	1	1	1
	C2	1	1	1	1	1	1	1	1	1	1	1	1
	C3	1	2	2	2	2	2	2	3	2	2	2	2
	Tot	3	4	4	4	4	4	4	5	4	4	4	4
Belgium	C1	1	1	1	1	1	1	1	1	1	1	1	1
	C2	1	1	1	1	1	1	1	1	1	2	1	2
	C3	3	4	3	3	3	2	3	2	2	2	2	2
	Tot	5	6	5	5	5	4	5	4	4	5	4	5
Bulgaria	C1	1	–	1	1	1	1	1	1	1	1	1	1
	C2	1	–	1	1	1	1	1	1	1	1	1	1
	C3	1	2	2	2	2	2	2	2	2	2	2	3
	Tot	3	2	4	4	4	4	4	4	4	4	4	5
Cyprus	C1	1	1	1	1	1	1	1	–	1	1	1	1
	C2	1	1	1	1	1	1	1	–	1	1	1	1
	C3	–	–	–	–	1	1	1	–	1	1	1	1
	Tot2	2	2	2	2	3	3	3	–	3	3	3	3
Czechoslovakia	C1	1	1	1	1	1	1	1	1	1	1	1	1
	C2	1	1	2	1	1	1	1	1	1	1	1	1
	C3	1	1	2	2	2	2	2	2	2	2	2	2
	Tot	3	3	5	4	4	4	4	4	4	4	4	4
Denmark	C1	1	1	1	1	1	1	1	1	1	1	1	1
	C2	1	1	1	1	1	1	1	1	1	1	1	1
	C3	1	1	2	2	1	2	2	2	2	2	2	2
	Tot	3	3	4	4	3	4	4	4	4	4	4	4
East Germany	C1	1	–	1	1	1	1	1	1	1	1	1	1
	C2	1	–	1	1	1	1	1	1	1	1	1	1
	C3	2	2	2	1	1	2	2	2	2	2	2	3
	Tot	4	2	4	3	3	4	4	4	4	4	4	5

County		79-80	80-81	81-82	82-83	83-84	84-85	85-86	86-87	87-88	88-89	89-90	90-91
Albania	C1	1	1	1	1	–	1	–	1	1	1	1	1
	C2	–	1	–	1	1	–	1	1	1	1	1	1
	C3	–	–	1	–	–	–	1	1	1	–	1	1
	Tot	1	2	2	2	1	1	2	3	3	2	3	3
Austria	C1	1	1	1	1	1	1	1	1	1	1	1	1
	C2	1	1	1	1	1	1	1	1	1	1	1	1
	C3	2	2	2	2	2	2	2	2	3	3	3	2
	Tot	4	4	4	4	4	4	4	4	5	5	5	4
Belgium	C1	1	1	1	1	1	1	1	1	1	1	1	1
	C2	1	1	1	1	1	1	1	1	1	2	1	1
	C3	2	4	4	3	3	3	3	3	3	3	3	3
	Tot	4	6	6	5	5	5	5	5	5	6	5	5
Bulgaria	C1	1	1	1	1	1	1	1	1	1	1	1	1
	C2	1	1	1	1	1	1	–	1	1	1	1	1
	C3	2	2	2	2	2	2	2	2	2	2	1	1
	Tot	4	4	4	4	4	4	3	4	4	4	3	3
Cyprus	C1	1	1	1	1	1	1	1	1	1	1	1	1
	C2	1	1	1	1	1	1	1	1	1	1	1	1
	C3	1	1	1	1	1	1	1	1	1	1	1	1
	Tot	3	3	3	3	3	3	3	3	3	3	3	3
Czechoslovakia	C1	1	1	1	1	1	1	1	1	1	1	1	1
	C2	1	1	1	1	1	1	1	1	1	1	1	1
	C3	3	2	2	2	3	3	3	3	2	2	2	2
	Tot	5	4	4	4	5	5	5	5	4	4	4	4
Denmark	C1	1	1	1	1	1	1	1	1	1	1	1	1
	C2	1	1	1	1	1	1	1	1	1	1	1	1
	C3	2	1	1	1	2	2	1	1	1	1	1	2
	Tot	4	3	3	3	4	4	3	3	3	3	3	4
East Germany	C1	1	1	1	1	1	1	1	1	1	1	1	1
	C2	1	1	1	1	1	1	1	1	1	1	1	1
	C3	2	3	3	3	3	2	2	3	2	2	2	2
	Tot	4	5	5	5	5	4	4	5	4	4	4	4

Number of Participating Teams per Country per Cup

County		55-56	56-57	57-58	58-59	59-60	60-61	61-62	62-63	63-64	64-65	65-66	66-67
England	C1	–	1	1	1	1	1	1	1	1	1	1	1
	C2	–	–	–	–	–	1	1	1	2	1	2	1
	C3	–	(2	)	(2	)	1	3	1	2	2	3	3
	Tot	–	2	2	2	2	3	5	3	5	4	6	5
Finland	C1	–	–	–	1	–	1	1	1	1	1	1	1
	C2	–	–	–	–	–	–	–	–	1	1	1	1
	C3	–	–	–	–	–	–	–	–	–	–	–	–
	Tot	–	–	–	1	–	1	1	1	2	2	2	2
France	C1	1	1	1	1	1	1	1	1	1	1	1	1
	C2	–	–	–	–	–	–	1	1	1	1	1	1
	C3	–	–	–	(1	)	1	2	1	1	3	3	3
	Tot	1	1	1	1.5	1.5	2	4	3	3	5	5	5
Greece	C1	–	–	–	–	1	1	1	1	1	1	1	1
	C2	–	–	–	–	–	–	1	–	1	1	1	1
	C3	–	–	–	–	–	–	1	–	1	1	2	1
	Tot	–	–	–	–	1	1	3	1	3	3	4	3
Hungary	C1	1	1	1	1	1	1	1	1	1	1	1	1
	C2	–	–	–	–	–	1	1	1	1	1	1	1
	C3	–	–	–	(1	)	1	1	1	1	1	1	1
	Tot	1	1	1	1.5	1.5	3	3	3	3	3	3	3
Iceland	C1	–	–	–	–	–	–	–	–	–	1	1	1
	C2	–	–	–	–	–	–	–	–	–	–	1	1
	C3	–	–	–	–	–	–	–	–	–	–	–	–
	Tot	–	–	–	–	–	–	–	–	–	1	2	2
Italy	C1	1	1	1	1	1	1	1	1	2	2	1	1
	C2	–	–	–	–	–	1	1	1	1	1	1	1
	C3	–	(1	)	(2	)	2	3	2	2	4	4	3
	Tot	1	1.5	1.5	2	2	4	5	4	5	7	6	5
Luxembourg	C1	–	1	1	1	1	1	1	1	1	1	1	1
	C2	–	–	–	–	–	–	1	1	1	1	1	1
	C3	–	–	–	–	–	–	–	1	1	1	1	1
	Tot	–	1	1	1	1	1	2	3	3	3	3	3

County		67-68	68-69	69-70	70-71	71-72	72-73	73-74	74-75	75-76	76-77	77-78	78-79
England	C1	1	2	1	1	1	1	1	1	1	1	1	2
	C2	1	1	1	2	2	1	1	1	1	1	1	1
	C3	3	4	4	5	4	4	4	4	4	4	4	4
	Tot	5	7	6	8	7	6	6	6	6	6	6	7
Finland	C1	1	1	1	1	1	1	1	1	1	1	1	1
	C2	1	–	1	1	1	1	1	1	1	1	1	–
	C3	–	–	–	1	1	–	1	1	1	1	1	1
	Tot	2	1	2	3	3	2	3	3	3	3	3	2
France	C1	1	1	1	1	1	1	1	1	1	1	1	1
	C2	1	1	1	1	1	1	1	1	1	1	1	1
	C3	2	4	3	3	3	3	2	2	2	2	2	2
	Tot	4	6	5	5	5	5	4	4	4	4	4	4
Greece	C1	1	1	1	1	1	1	1	1	1	1	1	1
	C2	1	1	1	1	1	1	1	1	1	1	1	1
	C3	1	2	2	2	1	2	2	2	2	2	2	2
	Tot	3	4	4	4	3	4	4	4	4	4	4	4
Hungary	C1	1	–	1	1	1	1	1	1	1	1	1	1
	C2	1	–	1	1	1	1	1	1	1	1	1	1
	C3	1	1	2	2	2	2	2	2	2	3	2	2
	Tot	3	1	4	4	4	4	4	4	4	5	4	4
Iceland	C1	1	1	1	1	1	1	1	1	1	1	1	1
	C2	1	1	1	1	1	1	1	1	1	1	1	1
	C3	–	–	1	1	1	1	1	1	1	1	1	1
	Tot	2	2	3	3	3	3	3	3	3	3	3	3
Italy	C1	1	1	2	1	1	1	1	–	1	1	1	1
	C2	1	1	1	1	1	1	1	1	1	1	1	1
	C3	3	4	4	4	4	4	4	4	4	4	4	4
	Tot	5	6	7	6	6	6	6	5	6	6	6	6
Luxembourg	C1	1	1	1	1	1	1	1	1	1	1	1	1
	C2	1	1	1	1	1	1	1	1	1	1	1	1
	C3	1	–	1	1	1	1	1	1	1	1	1	1
	Tot	3	2	3	3	3	3	3	3	3	3	3	3

County		79-80	80-81	81-82	82-83	83-84	84-85	85-86	86-87	87-88	88-89	89-90	90-91
England	C1	2	2	2	2	1	1	–	–	–	–	–	–
	C2	1	1	1	1	1	1	–	–	–	–	–	1
	C3	4	3	4	4	4	5	–	–	–	–	–	1
	Tot	7	6	7	7	6	7	–	–	–	–	–	2
Finland	C1	1	1	1	1	1	1	1	1	1	1	1	1
	C2	1	1	1	1	1	1	1	1	1	1	1	1
	C3	1	1	1	1	1	1	1	1	1	1	2	2
	Tot	3	3	3	3	3	3	3	3	3	3	4	4
France	C1	1	1	1	1	1	1	1	1	1	1	1	1
	C2	1	1	1	1	1	1	1	1	1	1	1	1
	C3	2	2	3	3	3	3	3	3	2	2	3	2
	Tot	4	4	5	5	5	5	5	5	4	4	5	4
Greece	C1	1	1	1	1	1	1	1	1	1	1	1	1
	C2	1	1	1	1	1	1	1	1	1	1	1	1
	C3	2	2	2	2	2	1	2	2	2	2	2	2
	Tot	4	4	4	4	4	3	4	4	4	4	4	4
Hungary	C1	1	1	1	1	1	1	1	1	1	1	1	1
	C2	1	1	1	1	1	1	1	1	1	1	1	1
	C3	2	2	2	2	2	2	2	2	2	2	2	2
	Tot	4	4	4	4	4	4	4	4	4	4	4	4
Iceland	C1	1	1	1	1	1	1	1	1	1	1	1	1
	C2	1	1	1	1	1	1	1	1	1	1	1	1
	C3	1	1	1	1	1	1	1	1	1	1	1	1
	Tot	3	3	3	3	3	3	3	3	3	3	3	3
Italy	C1	1	1	1	1	1	1	2	1	1	1	2	2
	C2	1	1	1	1	1	1	1	1	1	1	1	2
	C3	4	2	2	3	2	2	3	4	4	4	4	4
	Tot	6	4	4	5	4	4	6	6	6	6	7	8
Luxembourg	C1	1	1	1	1	1	1	1	1	1	1	1	1
	C2	1	1	1	1	1	1	1	1	1	1	1	1
	C3	1	1	1	1	1	1	1	1	1	1	1	1
	Tot	3	3	3	3	3	3	3	3	3	3	3	3

County		55-56	56-57	57-58	58-59	59-60	60-61	61-62	62-63	63-64	64-65	65-66	66-67
Malta	C1	–	–	–	–	–	–	1	1	1	1	1	1
	C2	–	–	–	–	–	–	1	1	1	1	1	1
	C3	–	–	–	–	–	–	–	–	–	–	–	–
	Tot	–	–	–	–	–	–	2	2	2	2	2	2
Netherlands	C1	1	1	1	1	1	1	1	1	1	1	1	1
	C2	–	–	–	–	–	–	1	1	1	1	1	1
	C3	–	–	–	–	–	–	–	1	1	1	1	2
	Tot	1	1	1	1	1	1	2	3	3	3	3	4
Northern Ireland	C1	–	–	1	1	1	–	1	1	1	1	1	1
	C2	–	–	–	–	–	–	1	1	1	1	1	1
	C3	–	–	–	–	–	–	–	1	1	–	1	–
	Tot	–	–	1	1	1	–	2	3	3	2	3	2
Norway	C1	–	–	–	–	–	1	1	1	1	1	1	1
	C2	–	–	–	–	–	–	–	–	1	1	1	1
	C3		–	–	–	–	–	–	–	–	1	1	1
	Tot	–	–	–	–	–	1	1	1	2	3	3	3
Poland	C1	1	1	1	1	1	1	1	1	1	1	1	1
	C2	–	–	–	–	–	–	–	1	1	1	–	1
	C3	–	–	–	–	–	–	–	–	–	–	–	–
	Tot	1	1	1	1	1	1	1	2	2	2	1	2
Portugal	C1	1	1	1	1	1	1	2	2	1	1	1	1
	C2	–	–	–	–	–	–	1	1	1	2	1	1
	C3	–	–	–	–	–	–	1	2	2	2	3	3
	Tot	1	1	1	1	1	1	4	5	4	5	5	5
Rep. of Ireland	C1	–	–	1	1	1	1	1	1	1	1	1	1
	C2	–	–	–	–	–	–	1	1	1	1	1	1
	C3	–	–	–	–	–	–	–	1	1	1	1	1
	Tot	–	–	1	1	1	1	2	3	3	3	3	3
Romania	C1	–	1	1	1	1	–	1	1	1	1	1	1
	C2	–	–	–	–	–	–	1	1	1	1	1	1
	C3	–	–	–	–	–	–	–	1	1	1	1	1
	Tot	–	1	1	1	1	–	2	3	3	3	3	3

County		67-68	68-69	69-70	70-71	71-72	72-73	73-74	74-75	75-76	76-77	77-78	78-79
Malta	C1	1	1	1	1	1	1	1	1	1	1	1	1
	C2	1	1	1	1	1	1	1	1	1	1	1	1
	C3	–	1	1	1	1	1	1	1	1	1	1	1
	Tot	2	3	3	3	3	3	3	3	3	3	3	3
Netherlands	C1	1	1	1	2	2	1	1	1	1	1	1	1
	C2	1	1	1	1	1	1	1	1	1	1	1	1
	C3	2	3	2	2	2	2	2	3	2	2	2	2
	Tot	4	5	4	5	5	4	4	5	4	4	4	4
Northern Ireland	C1	1	1	1	1	1	–	1	1	1	1	1	1
	C2	1	1	1	1	1	–	1	1	1	1	1	1
	C3	1	1	2	1	1	–	1	1	1	1	1	1
	Tot	3	3	4	3	3	–	3	3	3	3	3	3
Norway	C1	1	1	1	1	1	1	1	1	1	1	1	1
	C2	1	1	1	1	1	1	1	1	1	1	1	1
	C3	1	1	2	1	1	2	2	2	2	2	2	2
	Tot	3	3	4	3	3	4	4	4	4	4	4	4
Poland	C1	1	–	1	1	1	1	1	1	1	1	1	1
	C2	1	–	1	1	1	1	1	1	1	1	1	1
	C3	–	1	2	2	2	2	2	2	2	2	3	2
	Tot	2	1	4	4	4	4	4	4	4	4	5	4
Portugal	C1	1	1	1	1	1	1	1	1	1	1	1	1
	C2	1	1	1	1	1	1	1	1	1	1	1	1
	C3	3	4	4	3	3	3	1	2	2	2	2	2
	Tot	5	6	6	5	5	5	3	4	4	4	4	4
Rep. of Ireland	C1	1	1	1	1	1	1	1	1	1	1	1	1
	C2	1	1	1	1	1	1	1	1	1	1	1	1
	C3	1	1	1	1	1	1	1	1	1	1	1	1
	Tot	3	3	3	3	3	3	3	3	3	3	3	3
Romania	C1	1	1	1	1	1	1	1	1	1	1	1	1
	C2	1	1	1	1	1	1	1	1	1	1	1	1
	C3	2	2	2	2	2	2	2	2	2	3	2	2
	Tot	4	4	4	4	4	4	4	4	4	5	4	4

County		79-80	80-81	81-82	82-83	83-84	84-85	85-86	86-87	87-88	88-89	89-90	90-91
Malta	C1	1	1	1	1	1	1	1	1	1	1	1	1
	C2	1	1	1	1	1	1	1	1	1	1	1	1
	C3	1	1	1	1	1	1	1	1	1	1	1	1
	Tot	3	3	3	3	3	3	3	3	3	3	3	3
Netherlands	C1	1	1	1	1	1	1	1	1	1	1	1	–
	C21	1	1	1	1	1	1	1	1	2	1	1	1
	C3	2	4	3	3	4	2	3	2	2	2	3	3
	Tot	4	6	5	5	6	4	5	4	5	4	5	4
Northern Ireland	C1	1	1	1	1	1	1	1	1	1	1	1	1
	C2	·1	1	1	1	1	1	1	1	1	1	1	1
	C3	1	1	1	1	1	1	1	1	1	1	1	2
	Tot	3	3	3	3	3	3	3	3	3	3	3	4
Norway	C1	1	1	1	1	1	1	1	1	1	1	1	1
	C2	1	1	1	1	1	1	1	1	1	1	1	1
	C3	2	1	1	1	1	1	1	1	1	1	1	1
	tot	4	3	3	3	3	3	3	3	3	3	3	3
Poland	C1	1	1	1	1	1	1	1	1	1	1	1	1
	C2	1	1	1	1	1	1	1	1	1	1	1	1
	C3	2	2	2	2	1	2	2	2	2	2	2	2
	Tot	4	4	4	4	3	4	4	4	4	4	4	4
Portugal	C1	1	1	1	1	1	1	1	1	2	1	1	1
	C2	1	1	1	1	1	1	1	1	1	1	1	1
	C3	2	2	2	2	2	2	3	3	3	3	3	3
	Tot	4	4	4	4	4	4	5	5	6	5	5	5
Rep. of Ireland	C1	1	1	1	1	1	1	1	1	1	1	1	1
	C2	1	1	1	1	1	1	1	1	1	1	1	1
	C3	1	1	1	1	1	1	1	1	1	1	1	1
	Tot	3	3	3	3	3	3	3	3	3	3	3	3
Romania	C1	1	1	1	1	1	1	1	1	1	1	1	1
	C2	1	1	1	1	–	1	1	1	1	1	1	1
	C3	2	2	2	2	2	2	2	2	3	2	2	3
	Tot	4	4	4	4	3	4	4	4	5	4	4	5

County		55-56	56-57	57-58	58-59	59-60	60-61	61-62	62-63	63-64	64-65	65-66	66-67
Scotland	C1	1	1	1	1	1	1	1	1	1	1	1	1
	C2	–	–	–	–	–	1	1	1	1	1	1	1
	C3	–	–	–	–	–	1	2	3	2	3	3	3
	Tot	1	1	1	1	1	3	4	5	4	5	5	5
Spain	C1	1	2	2	2	2	2	1	1	1	1	1	2
	C2	–	–	–	–	–	–	1	2	1	1	1	1
	C3	–	(1	)	(1	)	1	3	3	3	5	4	4
	Tot	1	2.5	2.5	2.5	2.5	3	5	6	5	7	6	7
Sweden	C1	1	1	1	1	1	1	1	1	1	1	1	1
	C2	–	–	–	–	–	–	–	–	–	–	–	–
	C3	–	–	–	–	–	–	–	–	–	2	2	2
	Tot	1	1	1	1	1	1	1	1	1	3	3	3
Switzerland	C1	1	1	1	1	1	1	1	1	1	1	1	1
	C2	–	–	–	–	–	1	1	1	1	1	1	1
	C3	–	(2	)	(2	)	1	2	1	2	2	2	2
	Tot	1	2	2	2	2	3	4	3	4	4	4	4
Turkey	C1	–	1	–	1	1	1	1	1	1	1	1	1
	C2	–	–	–	–	–	–	–	–	1	1	1	1
	C3	–	–	–	–	–	–	–	1	–	1	1	1
	Tot	–	1	–	1	1	1	1	2	2	3	3	3
USSR	C1	–	–	–	–	–	–	–	–	–	–	–	1
	C2	–	–	–	–	–	–	–	–	–	–	1	1
	C3	–	–	–	–	–	–	–	–	–	–	–	–
	Tot	–	–	–	–	–	–	–	–	–	–	1	2
Wales	C1	–	–	–	–	–	–	–	–	–	–	–	–
	C2	–	–	–	–	–	–	1	1	1	1	1	1
	C3	–	–	–	–	–	–	–	–	–	–	–	–
	Tot	–	–	–	–	–	–	1	1	1	1	1	1
West Germany	C1	2	1	1	1	1	1	1	1	1	1	1	1
	C2	–	–	–	–	–	1	1	1	1	1	1	2
	C3	–	(1	)	(2	)	2	3	3	2	4	4	3
	Tot	2	1.5	1.5	2	2	4	5	5	4	6	6	6

County		67-68	68-69	69-70	70-71	71-72	72-73	73-74	74-75	75-76	76-77	77-78	78-79
Scotland	C1	1	1	1	1	1	1	1	1	1	1	1	1
	C2	1	1	1	1	1	1	1	1	1	1	1	1
	C3	3	4	3	4	3	2	3	2	2	2	2	2
	Tot	5	6	5	6	5	4	5	4	4	4	4	4
Spain	C1	1	1	1	1	1	1	1	1	1	1	1	1
	C2	1	1	1	1	1	1	1	1	1	1	1	1
	C3	4	4	4	4	4	3	3	3	3	3	3	3
	Tot	6	6	6	6	6	5	5	5	5	5	5	5
Sweden	C1	1	1	1	1	1	1	1	1	1	1	1	1
	C2	–	1	1	1	1	1	1	1	1	1	1	1
	C3	1	1	1	1	2	2	2	2	3	2	2	2
	Tot	2	3	3	3	4	4	4	4	5	4	4	4
Switzerland	C1	1	1	1	1	1	1	1	1	1	1	1	1
	C2	1	1	1	1	1	1	1	1	1	1	1	1
	C3	2	3	2	2	2	2	2	2	2	2	3	2
	Tot	4	5	4	4	4	4	4	4	4	4	5	4
Turkey	C1	1	1	1	1	1	1	1	1	1	1	1	1
	C2	1	1	1	1	1	1	1	1	1	1	1	–
	C3	1	1	1	1	1	2	2	2	2	2	2	2
	Tot	3	3	3	3	3	4	4	4	4	4	4	3
USSR	C1	1	–	1	1	1	1	1	1	1	1	1	1
	C2	1	–	1	1	1	1	1	1	1	1	1	1
	C3	–	–	–	–	2	2	2	3	2	2	2	2
	Tot	2	–	2	2	4	4	4	5	4	4	4	4
Wales	C1	–	–	–	–	–	–	–	–	–	–	–	–
	C2	1	1	1	1	1	1	1	1	1	1	1	1
	C3	–	–	–	–	–	–	–	–	–	–	–	–
	Tot	1	1	1	1	1	1	1	1	1	1	1	1
West Germany	C1	1	1	1	1	1	1	1	1	2	2	1	1
	C2	2	1	1	1	1	1	1	1	1	1	2	1
	C3	4	4	4	4	4	4	4	4	4	4	4	4
	Tot	7	6	6	6	6	6	6	6	7	7	7	6

County		79-80	80-81	81-82	82-83	83-84	84-85	85-86	86-87	87-88	88-89	89-90	90-91
Scotland	C1	1	1	1	1	1	1	1	1	1	1	1	1
	C2	1	1	1	1	2	1	1	1	1	1	1	1
	C3	2	2	2	2	2	3	3	3	3	3	3	2
	Tot	4	4	4	4	4	5	5	5	5	5	5	4
Spain	C1	1	1	1	1	1	1	1	1	1	1	1	1
	C2	2	2	1	2	1	1	1	1	1	1	2	1
	C3	3	3	3	4	3	4	4	3	3	3	3	4
	Tot	6	6	5	7	5	6	6	5	5	5	6	6
Sweden	C1	1	1	1	1	1	1	1	1	1	1	1	1
	C2	1	1	1	1	1	1	1	1	1	1	1	1
	C3	2	2	2	2	2	2	2	2	2	3	2	2
	Tot	4	4	4	4	4	4	4	4	4	5	4	4
Switzerland	C1	1	1	1	1	1	1	1	1	1	1	1	1
	C2	1	1	1	1	1	1	1	1	1	1	1	1
	C3	2	2	2	2	2	2	2	2	2	2	2	2
	Tot	4	4	4	4	4	4	4	4	4	4	4	4
Turkey	C1	1	1	1	1	1	1	1	1	1	1	1	1
	C2	1	1	1	1	1	1	1	1	1	1	1	1
	C3	2	1	1	1	1	1	1	1	1	1	1	1
	Tot	4	3	3	3	3	3	3	3	3	3	3	3
USSR	C1	1	1	1	1	1	1	1	1	1	1	1	1
	C2	1	1	2	1	1	1	1	1	1	1	1	1
	C3	2	3	3	3	2	2	3	3	4	4	4	3
	Tot	4	5	6	5	4	4	5	5	6	6	6	5
Wales	C1	–	–	–	–	–	–	–	–	–	–	–	–
	C2	1	1	1	1	1	1	1	1	1	1	1	1
	C3	–	–	–	–	–	–	–	–	–	–	–	–
	Tot	1	1	1	1	1	1	1	1	1	1	1	1
West Germany	C1	1	1	1	1	1	1	1	1	1	1	1	1
	C2	1	1	1	1	1	1	1	1	1	1	1	1
	C3	5	5	4	4	4	4	4	4	4	5	4	4
	Tot	7	7	6	6	6	6	6	6	6	7	6	6

County		55-56	56-57	57-58	58-59	59-60	60-61	61-62	62-63	63-64	64-65	65-66	66-67
Yugoslavia	C1	1	1	1	1	1	1	1	1	1	1	1	1
	C2	–	–	–	–	–	1	1	1	1	1	1	1
	C3	–	(1	)	(2	)	2	3	3	2	3	2	3
	Tot	1	1.5	1.5	2	2	4	5	5	4	5	4	5

County		67-68	68-69	69-70	70-71	71-72	72-73	73-74	74-75	75-76	76-77	77-78	78-79
Yugoslavia	C1	1	1	1	1	1	1	1	1	1	1	1	1
	C2	1	1	1	1	1	1	1	1	1	1	1	1
	C3	3	4	3	4	3	3	2	2	2	2	2	2
	Tot	5	6	5	6	5	5	4	4	4	4	4	4

County		79-80	80-81	81-82	82-83	83-84	84-85	85-86	86-87	87-88	88-89	89-90	90-91
Yugoslavia	C1	1	1	1	1	1	1	1	1	1	1	1	1
	C2	1	1	1	1	1	1	1	1	1	1	1	–
	C3	2	3	2	2	3	3	3	3	3	3	2	2
	Tot	4	5	4	4	5	5	5	5	5	5	4	3

Bonus Points Gained

1955-56 to 1990-91

Cnty	5556	5657	5758	5859	5960	6061	6162	6263	6364	6465	6566	6667	6768	6869	6970
Albania	–	–	–	–	–	–	–	–	–	–	–	–	–	–	–
Austria	1	–	–	1	1	3	–	–	–	–	–	1	–	1	–
Belgium	–	–	–	1	2	–	2	1	2	–	1	2	1	–	4
Bulgaria	–	1	–	–	–	–	–	1	–	–	–	4	–	–	1
Cyprus	–	–	–	–	–	–	–	–	–	–	–	–	–	–	–
Czechoslovakia	–	–	–	–	–	2	2	2	3	–	1	2	1	5	–
Denmark	–	–	1	–	–	2	–	1	–	–	–	–	–	1	–
East Germany	–	–	1	1	–	–	2	–	–	–	1	1	–	–	2
England	–	2	7	–	5	6	3	3	1	7	11	4	6	7	9
Finland	–	–	–	–	–	–	–	–	–	–	–	–	–	–	–
France	3	1	–	3	1	–	–	1	2	1	–	–	1	–	–
Greece	–	–	–	–	–	–	–	–	–	–	–	–	–	1	–
Hungary	1	–	2	–	–	–	4	2	4	5	3	1	4	3	–
Iceland	–	–	–	–	–	–	–	–	–	–	–	–	–	–	–
Italy	2	3	3	–	2	8	5	6	6	8	2	5	7	4	5
Luxembourg	–	–	–	–	–	–	–	–	–	–	–	–	–	–	–
Malta	–	–	–	–	–	–	–	–	–	–	–	–	–	–	–
Netherlands	–	–	1	–	1	–	–	2	1	1	–	1	–	3	5
Northern Ireland	–	–	–	–	–	–	–	–	–	–	–	1	–	–	–
Norway	–	–	–	–	–	–	–	–	–	–	–	–	–	1	–
Poland	–	–	–	–	–	–	–	–	–	1	–	–	1	–	5
Portugal	–	–	–	–	–	3	4	3	3	3	1	–	3	2	1
Rep. of Ireland	–	–	–	–	–	–	–	–	–	–	–	–	–	–	–
Romania	–	–	–	–	–	–	–	1	–	–	–	–	–	–	1
Scotland	2	–	–	–	2	5	2	3	2	1	3	8	3	5	3
Spain	3	4	7	5	8	4	13	6	9	6	11	2	4	4	–
Sweden	1	–	–	–	–	1	–	–	–	–	–	–	–	–	–
Switzerland	–	1	2	2	–	1	–	–	2	1	–	1	1	–	–
Turkey	–	–	–	–	–	–	–	1	1	–	–	–	–	2	2
USSR	–	–	–	–	–	–	–	–	–	–	1	–	1	–	–
Wales	–	–	–	–	–	–	–	–	–	1	–	–	2	–	–
West Germany	–	–	1	1	3	4	2	3	5	4	4	5	6	2	3
Yugoslavia	1	2	1	–	3	3	3	6	1	1	3	4	1	–	1

1955-56 to 1990-91

Cnty	7071	7172	7273	7374	7475	7576	7677	7778	7879	7980	8081	8182	8283	8384	8485
Albania	–	–	–	–	–	–	–	–	–	–	–	–	–	–	–
Austria	–	–	–	–	–	1	–	4	2	–	–	–	2	3	4
Belgium	1	2	–	–	1	6	6	6	2	–	2	5	5	3	–
Bulgaria	–	–	–	2	–	1	1	–	–	1	2	2	–	–	–
Cyprus	–	–	–	–	–	–	–	–	–	–	–	–	–	–	–
Czechoslovakia	–	–	3	1	1	–	–	–	3	1	1	–	2	1	1
Denmark	–	–	–	–	–	–	–	1	–	–	–	–	–	–	–
East Germany	2	2	1	5	–	3	2	3	2	1	3	1	–	1	1
England	12	7	10	4	3	6	5	4	6	6	7	6	2	10	8
Finland	–	–	–	–	–	–	–	–	–	–	–	–	–	1	–
France	–	–	–	–	2	3	1	3	–	4	3	–	1	–	2
Greece	3	–	–	1	–	–	2	–	–	–	–	–	–	–	3
Hungary	–	3	1	2	3	–	1	–	1	–	–	–	–	1	3
Iceland	–	–	–	–	–	–	–	–	–	–	–	–	–	–	–
Italy	3	7	6	3	2	1	5	2	1	2	2	–	5	6	6
Luxembourg	–	–	–	–	–	–	–	–	–	–	–	–	–	–	–
Malta	–	–	–	–	–	–	–	–	–	–	–	–	–	–	–
Netherlands	6	4	5	3	6	3	1	6	–	2	5	–	–	–	1
Northern Ireland	–	–	–	1	–	–	–	–	–	–	–	–	–	–	–
Norway	–	–	–	–	–	–	–	–	–	–	–	–	–	–	–
Poland	2	–	–	1	1	1	1	–	1	–	–	1	2	–	–
Portugal	1	2	1	3	1	1	–	2	–	–	2	1	4	4	–
Rep. of Ireland	–	–	–	–	–	–	–	–	–	–	–	–	–	–	–
Romania	–	2	1	–	–	–	–	–	–	–	–	1	2	2	–
Scotland	1	5	1	2	–	1	–	–	1	1	–	1	4	4	–
Spain	5	–	2	3	3	4	6	4	3	6	3	5	7	1	3
Sweden	–	1	–	–	2	–	–	–	3	1	–	3	–	–	1
Switzerland	–	–	–	2	–	–	2	2	2	–	1	1	–	–	–
Turkey	–	–	–	–	1	–	–	–	–	–	–	–	–	–	–
USSR	–	3	2	–	4	1	2	2	–	1	4	3	1	3	4
Wales	1	–	–	–	–	1	–	–	–	–	1	–	–	–	–
West Germany	3	2	6	8	9	8	7	3	12	14	5	9	5	–	3
Yugoslavia	2	2	3	1	3	1	–	1	3	2	1	3	–	2	2

1955-56 to 1990-91

Cnty	8586	8687	8788	8889	8990	9091
Albania	–	5	6	7	7	–
Austria	1	2	–	–	1	–
Belgium	4	1	6	2	6	2
Bulgaria	–	1	–	2	1	–
Cyprus	–	–	–	–	–	–
Czechoslovakia	2	–	1	–	–	–
Denmark	–	1	–	1	–	2
East Germany	1	3	–	2	–	1
England	–	–	–	–	–	3
Finland	1	–	1	–	–	–
France	1	2	3	1	5	4
Greece	–	–	1	–	–	–
Hungary	–	–	–	–	–	–
Iceland	–	–	–	–	–	–
Italy	3	2	3	10	12	12
Luxembourg	–	–	–	–	–	–
Malta	–	–	–	–	–	–
Netherlands	–	3	6	2	1	–
Northern Ireland	–	–	–	–	–	–
Norway	–	–	–	–	–	–
Poland	–	–	–	–	–	2
Portugal	2	4	4	–	3	3
Rep. of Ireland	–	–	–	–	–	–
Romania	3	–	2	5	2	–
Scotland	1	3	1	1	–	–
Spain	9	5	6	6	1	4
Sweden	2	4	–	1	–	–
Switzerland	1	1	1	–	1	–
Turkey	–	1	–	2	–	–
USSR	3	3	1	–	1	4
Wales	–	–	–	–	–	–
West Germany	6	5	6	7	7	2
Yugoslavia	2	1	–	–	1	3

Number of Countries in the Quarter Final

Out of a maximum of 24

Season	5556	5657	5758	5859	5960	6061	6162
Number	8	7	10	7	10	12	11
Season	6263	6364	6465	6566	6667	6768	6869
Number	16	14	13	12	15	15	14
Season	6970	7071	7172	7273	7374	7475	7576
Number	13	13	13	13	15	15	16
Season	7677	7778	7879	7980	8081	8182	8283
Number	14	14	14	13	15	14	13
Season	8384	8485	8586	8687	8788	8889	8990
Number	14	14	16	17	14	13	13
Season	9091						
Number	12						

Above: Ajax celebrate with the 1970-71 European Champions' Cup after their 2-0 win over Panathinaikos at Wembley. Below: Everton's Graeme Sharp, Kevin Sheedy, Trevor Steven and Andy Gray with the European Cup Winners' Cup after their 3-1 win over Rapid Vienna in the 1984-85 final.

Club Rankings by Country and by Cup – 1955-56 to 1990-91

Albania

Rank	Club	C1.C2.C3 Place	C1 Rank	C1 Place	C2 Rank	C2 Place	C3 Rank	C3 Place
7	Labinoti Elbasan	510	5)	248		–		–
8	Apolonia Fier	519		–		–	4)	419
6	Besa Kavajë	390		–	5)	240		–
5	Vllaznia Shkodër	311	3)	189	4)	204		–
3	Dinamo Tirana	239	4)	221	2)	170	2)	229
1	17 Nëntori Tirana	220	1)	117	1)	158		–
2	Partizan Tirana	233	2)	126	3)	173	3)	388
4	Flamurtari Vlorë	290		–	6)	362	1)	206

Austria

Rank	Club	C1.C2.C3 Place	C1 Rank	C1 Place	C2 Rank	C2 Place	C3 Rank	C3 Place
11	Grazer AK	396		–	8)	286	11)	377
5	Sturm Graz	172		–	5)	168	4)	120
3	FC Tirol	95	3)	68	3)	95	3)	114
12	Krems	430		–	7)	277		–
7	Linzer ASK	210	7)	230	6)	233	7)	151
10	Vöest Linz	375	6)	219		–	10)	298
9	SV Salzburg	323		–	10)	365	9)	222
6	Admira Wacker	176	5)	211	4)	141	5)	147
2	Austria Vienna	39	2)	26	2)	29	2)	107
8	First Vienna	264		–		–	8)	185
1	Rapid Vienna	29	1)	19	1)	11	1)	72
4	Wiener Sport-Club	150	4)	81		–	6)	149
13	Wiener Neustadt	497		–	9)	340		–

Belgium

Rank	Club	C1.C2.C3 Place	C1 Rank	C1 Place	C2 Rank	C2 Place	C3 Rank	C3 Place
1	Anderlecht	7	1)	12	1)	4	1)	10
16	Beerschot	317		–	9)	186	16)	368
8	Antwerp	126	8)	252		–	5)	63
5	Beveren	103	5)	138	5)	78	8)	99
18	Cercle Bruges	402		–	11)	248		–
3	Club Bruges	49	3)	40	6)	125	3)	43
15	Charleroi	312		–		–	13)	221
13	Gent	226		–	10)	237	11)	173
4	FC Liège	83		–	7)	149	2)	38
2	Standard Liège	24	2)	23	2)	17	4)	51
12	Lierse	224	7)	240	8)	167	12)	198
9	Lokeren	156		–		–	7)	83
6	KV Mechelen	112	4)	121	3)	31	15)	353
7	Molenbeek	125	6)	165		–	6)	70
14	Union St-Gilloise	250		–		–	10)	171
10	Waregem	169		–	12)	263	9)	101
11	Waterschei Thor	200		–	4)	73		–
17	Winterslag	341		–		–	14)	244

Bulgaria

Rank	Club	C1.C2.C3 Place	C1 Rank	C1 Place	C2 Rank	C2 Place	C3 Rank	C3 Place
16	Pirin Blagoevgrad	508		–		–	14)	407
12	Chernomorets Bourgas	420		–	8)	266		–
5	Lokomotiv Plovdiv	163		–		–	2)	91
4	Trakia Plovdiv	141	4)	155	4)	87	6)	180
11	Dunav Ruse	412		–		–	10)	315
13	Sliven	439		–	10)	360	11)	325
9	Akademik Sofia	362		–		–	9)	268
1	CSKA Sofia	32	1)	10	3)	64	7)	205
2	Levski Sofia	71	2)	95	1)	47	1)	85
7	Lokomotiv Sofia	184	3)	130	9)	287	3)	153
3	Slavia Sofia	129		–	2)	60	4)	164
8	Marek Stanke Dimitrov	318		–	7)	264	8)	260
6	Beroe Stara Zagora	174	5)	212	5)	100	5)	174
10	Spartak Varna	371		–	6)	221		–
14	Etar Veliko Tarnovo	470		–		–	12)	364
15	Botev Vratsa	505		–		–	13)	405

Cyprus

Rank	Club	C1.C2.C3 Place	C1 Rank	C1 Place	C2 Rank	C2 Place	C3 Rank	C3 Place
7	Anorthosis Famagusta	486	5)	238	7)	333	7)	424
6	Paralimni	447		–	4)	288	10)	428
9	NEA Salamina Famagusta	503		–	8)	350		–
11	Alki Larnaca	527		–		–	8)	425
13	EPA Larnaca	533	7)	260		–	5)	409
4	Pezoporikos Larnaca	379	4)	237	5)	295	4)	344
5	AEL Limassol	397	6)	257	2)	245		–
3	Apollon Limassol	352		–	3)	247	3)	339
10	Akritas Morphou	515		–		–	6)	415
12	Anorthosis Nicosia	529		–	10)	375		–
2	Apoel Nicosia	244	2)	172	1)	184	2)	301
8	Olympiakos Nicosia	488	3)	227	9)	359	9)	426
1	Omonia Nicosia	153	1)	54	6)	330	1)	271

Czechoslovakia

Rank	Club	C1.C2.C3 Place	C1 Rank	C1 Place	C2 Rank	C2 Place	C3 Rank	C3 Place
20	Dukla Banská Bystrica	499		–		–	17)	392
8	Inter Bratislava	142	7)	146	11)	243	5)	105
4	Slovan Bratislava	86	5)	88	1)	27	8)	184
5	Zbrojovka Brno	101	8)	148	9)	213	1)	61
12	DAC Dunajská Streda	286		–	7)	162	13)	304
14	TJ Gottwaldov	334		–	8)	191		–
15	Spartak Hradec Králové	340	10)	156		–		–
11	Lokomotiv Kosice	248		–	5)	124	14)	308
17	VSS Kosice	366		–		–	11)	274
21	Plastika Nitra	501		–		–	18)	396
18	Sigma Olomouc	473		–		–	15)	366
3	Banik Ostrava	80	4)	83	4)	70	3)	79
22	Skoda Plzen	506		–	14)	352		–
7	Bohemians Prague	124	6)	136		–	2)	76
1	Dukla Prague	37	1)	16	2)	45	4)	96
10	Slavia Prague	236		–	12)	253	7)	178

2	Sparta Prague	59	2)	37	3)	68	6)	113
16	Tatran Presov	365		–	13)	297	12)	288
19	Union Teplice	491		–		–	16)	385
6	Spartak Trnava	107	3)	39	10)	223	10)	273
9	TJ Vitkovice	222	9)	154			9)	187
13	Dynamo Zilina	298		–	6)	150		–

Denmark

		C1.C2.C3	C1		C2		C3	
Rank	**Club**	**Place**	**Rank**	**Place**	**Rank**	**Place**	**Rank**	**Place**
15	AaB Aalborg	393		–	9)	244		–
16	BK Fremad Amager	403		–	10)	252		–
1	AGF Aarhus	132	1)	69	1)	93	4)	250
12	AB Copenhagen	299	10)	178		–	7)	262
6	B1903 Copenhagen	215	8)	157	5)	148	5)	256
18	B 93 Copenhagen	432		–	11)	279		–
3	KB Copenhagen	194	3)	105	13)	319	3)	194
2	Brøndby IF	143	2)	101		–	1)	116
11	BK Frem	280		–	8)	216	6)	258
9	Hvidovre IF	260	6)	141	7)	208	14)	376
4	Esbjerg FB	198	5)	118	12)	316	2)	189
19	Holbaek BIF	437		–		–	11)	340
17	Ikast FS	419		–	14)	337	9)	306
21	Køge BK	507	13)	246		–		–
8	Lyngby BK	249	7)	145	6)	171	13)	367
14	Naestved IF	377		–		–	8)	283
23	B 1901 Nykobing	524		–	16)	351	17)	400
20	OB Odense	482	11)	220		–	18)	412
10	B 1909 Odense	273	12)	222	3)	131	15)	393
13	B 1913 Odense	327	9)	169	15)	344	12)	342
7	Randers Freja FC	247		–	2)	123	10)	307
22	Vanløse IF	513		–	17)	358		–
5	Vejle BK	203	4)	106	4)	132	16)	399

East Germany

		C1.C2.C3	C1		C2		C3	
Rank	**Club**	**Place**	**Rank**	**Place**	**Rank**	**Place**	**Rank**	**Place**
12	Wismut Aue	369		–		–	10)	276
5	Dynamo Berlin	70	1)	35	4)	74	5)	203
11	Stahl Brandenburg	360		–		–	9)	267
7	Karl-Marx-Stadt	195	4)	77		–	8)	243
1	Dynamo Dresden	34	2)	45	5)	79	1)	25
6	Vorwärts Frankfurt/Oder	120	3)	58	7)	133	7)	212
13	Chemie Halle	460		–	9)	304		–
2	Carl Zeiss Jena	42	5)	100	2)	32	3)	30
10	Chemie Leipzig	338	7)	233	8)	188		–
3	Lokomotive Leipzig	47	3)	35	2)	26		–
4	Magdeburg	55	6)	137	1)	13	4)	69
9	Hansa Rostock	288		–		–	6)	210
14	PSV Schwerin	468		–	10)	313		–
8	Sachsenning Zwickau	238		–	6)	98		–

England

		C1.C2.C3	C1		C2		C3	
Rank	**Club**	**Place**	**Rank**	**Place**	**Rank**	**Place**	**Rank**	**Place**
10	Aston Villa	102	5)	50		–	13)	111

14	Birmingham City	115		–		–	6)	57
20	Burnley	213	12)	152		–	19)	166
23	Coventry City	314		–		–	21)	223
16	Derby County	155	6)	72		–	18)	165
6	Ipswich Town	65	11)	134	11)	130	4)	31
3	Leeds United	23	4)	46	8)	81	1)	8
24	Leicester City	332		–	14)	187		–
9	Everton	89	8)	104	6)	59	12)	98
1	Liverpool	8	1)	4	7)	61	3)	20
5	Arsenal	64	9)	110	9)	82	5)	45
7	Chelsea	77		–	5)	55	8)	60
19	Queen's Park Rangers	207		–		–	14)	124
4	Tottenham Hotspur	27	7)	98	3)	22	2)	11
12	West Ham United	106	1)	18		–		–
11	Manchester City	105	13)	209	4)	42	17)	145
2	Manchester United	20	2)	14	2)	20	9)	64
15	Newcastle United	118		–		–	7)	59
8	Nottingham Forest	85	3)	43		–	11)	95
21	Sheffield Wednesday	252		–		–	20)	175
17	Southampton	167		–	10)	128	15)	138
26	Stoke City	363		–		–	23)	269
22	Sunderland	313		–	13)	164		–
25	Watford	339		–		–	22)	240
18	West Bromwich Albion	182		–	12)	147	16)	139
13	Wolverhampton Wanderers	113	10)	131	15)	205	10)	73

Finland

Rank	Club	C1.C2.C3 Place	C1 Rank	C1 Place	C2 Rank	C2 Place	C3 Rank	C3 Place
12	HIFK Helsinki	525	9)	250		–	7)	397
1	HJK Helsinki	221	2)	109	3)	180	10)	430
13	HPS Helsinki	530	10)	253	11)	368		–
14	KPV Kokkola	531	11)	259		–	9)	413
10	KTP Kotka	475		–	9)	324		–
7	KuPS Kuopio	293	6)	224	6)	280	2)	259
3	FC Kuusysi Lahti	240	1)	107	7)	285	5)	352
6	Reipas Lahti	262	3)	143	4)	201		
9	MP Mikkeli	395		–	5)	242	8)	410
11	OPS Oulu	483	7)	225		–		–
5	RoPS Rovaniemi	258		–	2)	156	4)	279
8	Ilves Tampere	373	8)	239	10)	343	3)	272
4	TPS Turku	242	5)	202	8)	299	1)	192
2	Haka Valkeakoski	229	4)	200	1)	104	6)	370

France

Rank	Club	C1.C2.C3 Place	C1 Rank	C1 Place	C2 Rank	C2 Place	C3 Rank	C3 Place
26	Angers	453		–		–	22)	350
22	Angoulême	404		–		–	18)	311
14	Auxerre	217		–		–	7)	135
10	Bastia	168		–	8)	189	5)	115
2	Girondins Bordeaux	63	4)	55	5)	88	1)	62
20	Laval	359		–		–	17)	266
13	Lens	209		–	11)	227	8)	143
7	Olympique Lyon	127		–	1)	54	13)	183
3	Olympique Marseille	72	3)	41	2)	71	10)	168
19	Metz	349		–	13)	239	21)	341

5	Monaco	116	7)	87	6)	94	9)	152
16	Montpellier	276		–	7)	129	24)	402
21	Nancy	382		–	12)	230		–
4	Nantes	92	6)	74	3)	83	4)	108
9	Nice	148	5)	67		–	12)	182
23	Nîmes Olympique	416		–		–	19)	319
27	Racing Club Paris	490		–		–	23)	384
12	Paris Saint-Germain	186	9)	207	4)	86	14)	224
18	Stade Français	337		–		–	16)	238
6	Stade Reims	121	2)	36		–		–
24	Stade Rennes	422		–	14)	274		–
1 7	Rouen	336		–		–	15)	237
1	Saint-Etienne	57	1)	25	10)	197	2)	93
25	Sedan	434		–	15)	342	20)	324
11	Sochaux	185		–		–	3)	106
8	Strasbourg	139	8)	123	9)	193	6)	121
15	Toulouse	254		–		–	11)	177

Greece

		C1.C2.C3	C1		C2		C3	
Rank	**Club**	**Place**	**Rank**	**Place**	**Rank**	**Place**	**Rank**	**Place**
3	AEK Athenes	100	3)	71	7)	218	1)	88
2	Panathinaikos	69	1)	34	4)	127	5)	129
7	Panionios	291		–	5)	206	8)	281
8	OFI Crete	320		–	6)	210	10)	327
11	Kastoria	467		–	9)	312		–
6	Larissa	230	5)	187	3)	122	9)	313
10	Panahaiki	342		–		–	6)	245
1	Olympiakos Pireus	67	2)	65	1)	50	2)	103
5	Aris Salonika	178		–	10)	320	3)	104
9	Iraklis	326		–	8)	311	7)	257
4	PAOK Salonika	110	4)	182	2)	66	4)	123

Hungary

		C1.C2.C3	C1		C2		C3	
Rank	**Club**	**Place**	**Rank**	**Place**	**Rank**	**Place**	**Rank**	**Place**
11	Békéscsaba	355		–	8)	207		–
15	Csepel	451	7)	206		–		–
1	Ferencváros	30	4)	62	2)	44	1)	15
3	Honvéd	62	3)	60	5)	101	3)	52
4	MTK-VM	91	6)	91	3)	57	5)	133
5	Vasas SC	97	2)	44	9)	232	7)	162
8	Diósgyöri VTK	231		–	6)	172	8)	207
6	Rába ETO	104	5)	70	4)	84	6)	155
13	Komló	424		–	10)	275		–
12	Pécs Dózsa	358		–		–	10)	264
14	Pécsi MSC	429		–	13)	341	11)	316
16	Salgótarján	462		–		–	12)	358
17	Siófok	465		–	11)	309		–
7	Videoton	144		–		–	4)	78
10	Haladás	354		–	7)	203		–
9	Tatabánya	303		–	12)	323	9)	230
2	Ujpesti Dózsa	33	1)	30	1)	43	2)	47

Iceland

Rank	Club	C1.C2.C3 Place	C1 Rank	C1 Place	C2 Rank	C2 Place	C3 Rank	C3 Place
3	IA Akranes	294	2)	159	2)	291	5)	380
6	IBA Akureyri	442	3)	191	6)	373		–
7	FH Hafnarfjördhur	461		–		–	4)	357
5	IBK Keflavik	380	8)	266	4)	317	3)	303
2	Fram Reykjavik	263	6)	264	1)	112	8)	431
9	KR Reykjavik	538	7)	265	7)	377	6)	416
1	Valur Reykjavik	234	1)	133	3)	294	1)	253
8	Vikingur Reykjavik	534	5)	236	5)	372	7)	418
4	IBV Vestmannaeyjar	353	4)	210	8)	382	2)	278

Italy

Rank	Club	C1.C2.C3 Place	C1 Rank	C1 Place	C2 Rank	C2 Place	C3 Rank	C3 Place
11	Atalanta	183		–	9)	110	10)	169
8	Bologna	94	10)	177	10)	209	7)	50
13	Cagliari	300	8)	161		–	14)	289
15	Cesena	405		–		–	15)	312
5	Fiorentina	36	4)	59	4)	30	6)	35
9	Sampdoria	96		–	3)	19	12)	228
3	AC Milan	10	2)	8	1)	8	5)	29
2	Inter Milan	6	3)	11	8)	80	2)	4
6	Napoli	43	6)	127	7)	56	4)	22
14	Penigia	364		–		–	13)	270
4	Roma	28	5)	80	5)	40	3)	9
12	Lazio	256		–		–	11)	181
7	Torino	73	9)	162	6)	53	8)	67
1	Juventus	3	1)	7	2)	14	1)	3
10	Verona	179	7)	151		–	9)	126
16	Lanerossi Vicenza	456		–		–	16)	354

Luxembourg

Rank	Club	C1.C2.C3 Place	C1 Rank	C1 Place	C2 Rank	C2 Place	C3 Rank	C3 Place
8	Avenir Beggen	450	8)	268	12)	383	2)	346
2	Aris Bonnevoie	282	5)	226	11)	181	4)	348
5	Red Boys Differdange	400	2)	193	11)	381	5)	381
6	Alliance Dudelange	441		–	4)	292		–
13	Stade Dudelange	536	7)	267		–		–
11	Fola Esch	522		–	7)	370		–
1	Jeunesse Esch	199	1)	79	5)	322	1)	285
12	Jeunesse Hautcharage	532		–	10)	379		–
10	Swift Hesperange	512		–	6)	355		–
4	Spora Luxembourg	381	3)	203	9)	378	3)	347
3	Union Luxembourg	329	6)	263	2)	183	8)	435
9	Progrès Niedercorn	487	4)	223	8)	371	6)	421
7	US Rumelange	449		–	3)	290	7)	434

Malta

Rank	Club	C1.C2.C3 Place	C1 Rank	C1 Place	C2 Rank	C2 Place	C3 Rank	C3 Place
6	Gzira United	520		–	6)	366		–
4	Hamrun Spartans	309	3)	199	3)	225	3)	355
5	Valletta	401	5)	205	5)	335	8)	432

3	Floriana	295	4)	204	4)	226	1)	333
2	Hibernians	251	2)	175	2)	182	2)	349
7	Marsa	526		–		–	6)	422
9	Rabat Ajax	537	6)	262		–	7)	429
1	Sliema Wanderers	206	1)	120	1)	134	4)	379
8	Zurrieq	535		–	7)	376	5)	414

Netherlands

		C1.C2.C3	C1		C2		C3	
Rank	**Club**	**Place**	**Rank**	**Place**	**Rank**	**Place**	**Rank**	**Place**
5	AZ'67 Alkmaar	123	6)	147	10)	174	6)	90
1	Ajax	12	1)	5	1)	26	4)	54
7	FC Amsterdam	147	4)	103		–	7)	117
12	Vitesse	296		–		–	10)	217
14	NAC Breda	319		–	11)	176		–
18	Go Ahead Eagles	514		–	15)	361		–
3	PSV Eindhoven	25	2)	17	2)	34	3)	41
4	Twente Enschede	66		–	4)	85	2)	32
10	Groningen	193		–	9)	165	9)	146
16	Haarlem	387		–		–	12)	291
11	Roda JC	289	8)	229	7)	140	13)	395
9	FC Den Haag	180		–	3)	69	11)	287
15	NEC Nijmegen	385		–	12)	234		–
2	Feyenoord	22	3)	20	5)	92	1)	18
6	Sparta Rotterdam	130	5)	128	6)	107	8)	125
13	Fortuna Sittard	301		–	8)	157		–
17	Willem II	474		–	14)	321		–
8	Utrecht	152	7)	228	13)	265	5)	89

Northern Ireland

		C1.C2.C3	C1		C2		C3	
Rank	**Club**	**Place**	**Rank**	**Place**	**Rank**	**Place**	**Rank**	**Place**
8	Ballymena United	446		–	11)	380	5)	321
11	Cliftonville	518		–	9)	364		–
9	Crusaders	448	8)	261	5)	289		–
10	Distillery	480	4)	218	8)	353		–
1	Glentoran	137	2)	96	1)	96	2)	215
2	Linfield	154	1)	64	2	212	4)	284
6	Carrick Rangers	431		–	4)	278		–
3	Coleraine	283	6)	255	7)	334	1)	214
7	Glenavon	444	3)	214	10)	367	7)	378
5	Ards	398	5)	251	6)	332	6)	328
4	Portadown	325	7)	256	3)	272	3)	277

Norway

		C1.C2.C3	C1		C2		C3	
Rank	**Club**	**Place**	**Rank**	**Place**	**Rank**	**Place**	**Rank**	**Place**
5	SK Brann	269		–	1)	114	16)	423
15	SFK Bodø/Glimt	436		–	8)	282		–
9	Bryne IL	343		–	6)	269	6)	295
13	Strømgodset IF	399	9)	243	10)	293	10)	369
10	Fredrikstad FK	351	5)	184	9)	284	14)	403
14	Gjøvik/Lyn	433		–	7)	281		–
11	Haugar	370		–	4)	220		–
7	IK Start	305	10)	254		–	3)	219
2	Lillestrøm SK	241	1)	102	16)	374	7)	338
16	Mjøndalen IF	445		–	15)	369	9)	345

12	Molde FK	376		–		–	5)	282
20	Moss FK	521	8)	235	13)	345	12)	383
18	SK Frigg	500		–		–	13)	394
6	FK Skeid	274	7)	208	5)	224	4)	251
4	SFK Lyn	261	4)	174	2)	178	11)	375
8	Vålerengen SIF	308	3)	171	12)	314	8)	343
19	IF Sarpsborg	509		–		–	15)	408
3	IL Viking	243	6)	185	14)	349	2)	193
17	Tromsø IL	459		–	11)	303		–
1	Rosenborg BK	205	2)	160	3)	211	1)	191

Poland

		C1.C2.C3	C1		C2		C3	
Rank	**Club**	**Place**	**Rank**	**Place**	**Rank**	**Place**	**Rank**	**Place**
14	Polonia Bytom	372	8)	168		–		–
15	Szombierki Bytom	389	9)	192		–	14)	362
5	Ruch Chorzów	159	3)	78		–	5)	163
6	Wisla Kraków	187	6)	129	4)	116	8)	241
22	Lechia Gdańsk	517		–	12)	363		–
16	Arka Gdynia	406		–	10)	255		–
10	GKS Katowice	270		–	7)	192	10)	249
17	LKS Lódź	427	10)	194		–		–
3	Widzew Lódź	128	4)	99	9)	250	2)	97
21	Zaglebie Lubin	493		–		–	17)	387
9	Stal Mielec	237	12)	234		–	4)	159
18	Odra Opole	454		–		–	12)	351
7	Lech Poznań	204	5)	125	5)	121	16)	374
12	Stal Rzeszów	330		–	6)	185		–
11	Zaglebie Sosnowiec	306		–	8)	200	11)	330
20	Pogon Szczecin	471		–		–	15)	365
19	GKS Tychy	464		–		–	13)	361
8	Gwardia Warsaw	225	7)	164	11)	283	6)	201
1	Legia Warsaw	52	2)	49	1)	24	1)	94
13	Zaglebie Walbrzych	335	7)	235		–		–
4	Slask Wroclaw	149	11)	213	3)	108	3)	134
2	Górnik Zabrze	60	1)	27	2)	52	9)	246

Portugal

		C1.C2.C3	C1		C2		C3	
Rank	**Club**	**Place**	**Rank**	**Place**	**Rank**	**Place**	**Rank**	**Place**
12	Estrela Amadora	361		–	9)	214		–
9	Barreirense	267		–		–	8)	190
10	Sporting Braga	271		–	5)	142	13)	337
13	Chaves	421		–		–	10)	323
11	Academica Coimbra	279		–	6)	151	12)	335
5	Vitória Guimarães	146		–	10)	260	5)	84
7	Belenenses	202		–	11)	318	6)	127
1	Benfica	5	1)	2	3)	25	4)	66
2	Sporting Lisbon	19	3)	53	1)	15	1)	13
8	Leixões	266		–	7)	152	9)	292
14	Portimonense	423		–		–	11)	326
6	Boavista	157		–	4)	91	7)	154
3	FC Porto	26	2)	28	2)	21	3)	37
4	Vitória Setúbal	79		–	8)	177	2)	33

Republic of Ireland

Rank	Club	C1.C2.C3 Place	C1 Rank	C1 Place	C2 Rank	C2 Place	C3 Rank	C3 Place
5	Athlone Town	324	5)	195		–	4)	265
16	Finn Harps	485		–	7)	306	13)	433
12	Bray Wanderers	466		–	9)	310		–
14	Cork Celtic	478	11)	245	8)	308		–
17	Cork City	511		–	16)	354		–
7	Cork Hibernians	346	10)	244	2)	194	9)	401
9	Derry City	378	6)	197	12)	328	7)	356
20	Drogheda United	528		–		–	12)	427
3	Bohemians	228	3)	170	3)	198	2)	233
6	Drumcondra	328	7)	201		–	5)	280
13	Home Farm	477		–	10)	325		–
15	St. Patrick's Athletic	484	8)	216	17)	357	11)	420
1	Shamrock Rovers	188	4)	173	1)	103	1)	225
8	Shelbourne	347	9)	242	14)	346	3)	242
11	UCD	458		–	6)	302		–
2	Dundalk	212	1)	119	4)	199	6)	286
18	Galway United	516		–	13)	336	10)	406
10	Limerick	443	13)	258	11)	327	8)	363
19	Sligo Rovers	523	12)	247	15)	348		–
4	Waterford United	281	2)	144	5)	241		–

Romania

Rank	Club	C1.C2.C3 Place	C1 Rank	C1 Place	C2 Rank	C2 Place	C3 Rank	C3 Place
10	UT Arad	259	7)	198		–	8)	202
11	Bacau	277		–	7)	199		–
20	Baia Mare	469		–	11)	315		–
12	Red Flag Brasov	304		–		–	10)	220
1	Dinamo Bucharest	44	2)	24	2)	62	2)	80
18	Progresul Bucharest	455		–	9)	300		–
6	Rapid Bucharest	214	6)	176	4)	144	11)	231
8	Sportul Studentesc Bucharest	219		–		–	6)	141
2	Steaua Bucharest	53	11)	22	1)	33	16)	372
7	Victoria Bucharest	218		–		–	5)	137
13	Universitatea Cluj	321		–	6)	217	14)	309
3	Universitatea Craiova	68	3)	115	3)	118	1)	44
17	CSU Galati	436		–	12)	338	15)	332
14	Corvinul Hunedoara	357		–		–	12)	263
21	Flacara Moreni	496	17)	390		–		–
16	Jiul Petrosani	409		–	7)	258		–
4	Arges Pitesti	162	4)	122		–	4)	128
5	Petrolul Ploiesti	164	5)	158	8)	268	3)	118
19	Chimia Râmnicu Vâlcea	463		–	10)	305		–
9	Politehnica Timisoara	232		–	5)	179	9)	211
15	ASA Tîrgu Mures	392		–	13)	299		–

Scotland

Rank	Club	C1.C2.C3 Place	C1 Rank	C1 Place	C2 Rank	C2 Place	C3 Rank	C3 Place
4	Aberdeen	48	3)	76	2)	9	5)	71
9	Dundee	192	5)	90	9)	296	9)	209
3	Dundee United	31	4)	85	6)	154	1)	7
6	Dunfermline Athletic	90		–	4)	72	4)	65
7	Heart of Midlothian	131	8)	196	8)	271	6)	74

5	Hibernian	56	6)	112	5)	135	2)	23
2	Celtic	17	1)	6	3)	12	8)	144
1	Rangers	13	2)	15	1)	3	3)	48
13	Morton	504		–		–	13)	404
8	Kilmarnock	170	7)	166		–	7)	112
10	St. Mirren	255		–	7)	215	10)	218
11	St. Johnstone	315		–		–	11)	226
12	Partick Thistle	316		–		–	12)	227

Spain

		C1.C2.C3	C1		C2		C3	
Rank	**Club**	**Place**	**Rank**	**Place**	**Rank**	**Place**	**Rank**	**Place**
7	Español	109		–		–	6)	53
2	Barcelona	2	3)	21	1)	1	1)	2
5	Athletic Bilbao	45	4)	82	8)	175	3)	17
13	Sporting Gijón	278		–		–	11)	204
11	Las Palmas	253		–		–	10)	176
3	Atlético Madrid	16	2)	18	2)	2	7)	56
15	Castilla Madrid	417		–	10)	262		–
1	Real Madrid	1	1)	1	3)	23	5)	42
14	Osasuna	356		–		–	12)	261
16	Sabadell	418		–		–	14)	320
8	Real Sociedad	114	5)	93	9)	190	8)	92
6	Real Zaragoza	51		–	4)	39	4)	27
12	Real Betis	268		–	7)	155	13)	294
9	Seville	173	6)	132	11)	267	9)	140
4	Valencia	21	7)	140	5)	41	2)	6
10	Real Valladolid	246		–	6)	113	15)	322
17	Celta Vigo	498		–		–	16)	391

Sweden

		C1.C2.C3	C1		C2		C3	
Rank	**Club**	**Place**	**Rank**	**Place**	**Rank**	**Place**	**Rank**	**Place**
6	Åtvidaberg SFF	201	3)	114	3)	143	12)	310
10	IF Elfsborg	344		–		–	8)	247
14	IK Brage	391		–		–	11)	297
13	GAIS	388		–		–	10)	293
1	IFK Gothenburg	46	2)	33	4)	145	1)	40
11	Örgryte IS	350	8)	232		–	9)	254
12	Halmstad SBK	384	6)	180		–		–
8	Hammarby IF	245		–	8)	228	6)	196
9	Kalmar FF	272		–	5)	146	13)	334
15	Landskrona BOIS	438		–	10)	270	14)	411
2	Malmö FF	54	1)	3	1)	51	2)	130
3	IFK Norrköping	145	4)	116	2)	120	5)	179
4	AIK	191		–	6)	161	3)	148
5	Djurgården SIF	197	5)	142	7)	169	7)	213
7	Öster SIF	216	7)	183	9)	249	4)	172

Switzerland

		C1.C2.C3	C1		C2		C3	
Rank	**Club**	**Place**	**Rank**	**Place**	**Rank**	**Place**	**Rank**	**Place**
14	Aarau	479		–	10)	307	13)	417
5	FC Basle	136	2)	56	11)	329	7)	195
7	Young Boys Berne	151	3)	63	6)	160	10)	359
2	Servette	74	5)	73	1)	48	3)	109
9	La Chaux-de-Fonds	322	7)	167	9)	254		–

6	Lausanne–Sports	140	8)	217	2)	89	5)	142
11	Lucerne	348	9)	241	13)	356	9)	239
13	Lugano	476		–	12)	347	11)	360
4	Neuchâtel Xamax	122	6)	124	8)	251	2)	82
12	St–Gallen	374		–	7)	238	12)	373
8	Sion	165		–	4)	99	6)	161
10	Wettingen	331		–		–	8)	234
3	FC Zürich	84	1)	48	3)	97	4)	122
1	Grasshoppers Zürich	61	4)	66	5)	153	1)	39

Turkey

		C1.C2.C3	C1		C2		C3	
Rank	**Club**	**Place**	**Rank**	**Place**	**Rank**	**Place**	**Rank**	**Place**
9	Adanaspor	394		–		–	7)	302
10	Sakaryaspor	426		–	9)	276		–
14	Gençlerbirligi	495		–	12)	339		–
13	Ankaragücü	481		–	11)	331		–
15	Boluspor	502		–		–	10)	398
7	Bursaspor	302		–	4)	159		–
6	Eskisehirspor	292		–	7)	229	5)	255
5	Besiktas	211	4)	108	8)	246	4)	248
2	Fenerbahçe	111	2)	61	3)	139	1)	156
1	Galatasaray	81	1)	38	1)	76	3)	232
8	Altay	307		–	6)	222	6)	300
3	Göztepe	177		–	2)	119	2)	157
12	Mersin Idmanyurdu	457		–	10)	301		–
11	Orduspor	428		–		–	8)	331
4	Trabzonspor	196	3)	89	5)	196	9)	336

USSR

		C1.C2.C3	C1		C2		C3	
Rank	**Club**	**Place**	**Rank**	**Place**	**Rank**	**Place**	**Rank**	**Place**
8	Dnepr Dnepropetrovsk	171	3)	75		–	9)	188
9	Shakhtyor Donetsk	175		–	6)	109	6)	158
7	Ararat Erevan	166	4)	97	9)	202	8)	186
16	Metallist Kharkov	383		–	10)	231		–
1	Dinamo Kiev	18	1)	13	1)	6	3)	77
10	Zenit Leningrad	257	6)	139		–	11)	252
17	Karpaty Lvov	452		–	11)	298		–
6	Dinamo Minsk	133	5)	111	7)	138	5)	131
12	CSKA Moscow	297	7)	149		–	13)	305
5	Dinamo Moscow	87		–	2)	16	7)	160
2	Spartak Moscow	38	2)	52	5)	102	1)	19
4	Torpedo Moscow	82	9)	179	4)	38	4)	81
11	Chernomorets Odessa	287		–		–	10)	208
13	SKA Rostov on Don	310		–	8)	163		–
3	Dinamo Tbilisi	78	10)	188	3)	37	2)	75
15	Zhalgiris Vilnius	367		–		–	12)	275
14	Zaria Voroshilovgrad	333	8)	150		–		–

Wales

		C1.C2.C3	C1		C2		C3	
Rank	**Club**	**Place**	**Rank**	**Place**	**Rank**	**Place**	**Rank**	**Place**
5	Bangor City	368		–	5)	219		–
1	Cardiff City	98		–	1)	10		–
6	Borough United	386		–	6)	235		–

7	Merthyr Tydfil	410		–	7)	259		–
4	Newport County	285		–	4)	137		–
3	Swansea City	265		–	3)	117		–
2	Wrexham	158		–	2)	49		–

West Germany

		C1.C2.C3	C1		C2		C3	
Rank	**Club**	**Place**	**Rank**	**Place**	**Rank**	**Place**	**Rank**	**Place**
10	Hertha Berlin	99		–		–	8)	46
25	Tasmania Berlin	489		–		–	22)	382
7	Werder Bremen	75	6)	84	12)	166	9)	49
17	Eintracht Braunschweig	190	11)	153		–	14)	136
2	Cologne	9	4)	51	7)	75	1)	1
23	Viktoria Cologne	415		–		–	21)	318
8	Borussia Dortmund	76	5)	57	4)	58	12)	119
16	MSV Duisburg	189		–		–	11)	110
14	Fortuna Düsseldorf	135		–	6)	65	17)	170
24	Rot–Weiss Essen	472	14)	215		–		–
5	Eintracht Frankfurt	35	7)	86	3)	28	5)	24
11	Schalke 04	108	9)	113	5)	63	16)	167
3	Hamburg	14	3)	32	2)	7	4)	14
19	Hannover 96	227		–		–	15)	150
9	Kaiserslautern	88		–	15)	261	7)	34
13	Bayer Leverkusen	134		–		–	10)	68
4	Borussia Mönchengladbach	15	2)	29	9)	90	2)	5
1	Bayern Munich	4	1)	3	1)	5	6)	28
12	1860 Munich	117	10)	135	8)	77	13)	132
15	Nuremberg	161	8)	92	11)	106	19)	296
20	Kickers Offenbach	408		–	14)	257		–
22	Saarbrücken	414	13)	190		–		–
6	VFB Stuttgart	50	12)	186	13)	236	3)	12
18	Bayer Uerdingen	208		–	10)	105	18)	216
21	Wuppertal	413		–		–	20)	317

Yugoslavia

		C1.C2.C3	C1		C2		C3	
Rank	**Club**	**Place**	**Rank**	**Place**	**Rank**	**Place**	**Rank**	**Place**
13	Borac Banja Luka	284		–	7)	136		–
1	Red Star Belgrade	11	1)	9	1)	36	1)	16
5	OFK Belgrade	93		–	4)	111	4)	55
4	Partizan Belgrade	58	2)	42	8)	195	5)	58
16	Rad Belgrade	411		–		–	14)	314
15	Borovo	407		–	9)	256		–
19	Napredak Krusevac	492		–		–	17)	386
18	Olimpija Ljubljana	440		–	11)	326	16)	371
7	Velez Mostar	138		–	5)	115	9)	102
8	Radnicki Nis	160		–		–	6)	86
6	Vojvodina Novi Sad	119	4)	94		–	7)	87
10	Rijeka	223		–	6)	126	12)	236
11	Sarajevo	235	5)	163		–	11)	200
9	Zeljeznicar Sarajevo	181	7)	231		–	8)	100
14	Vardar Skoplje	345	8)	249	10)	273	13)	290
3	Hajduk Split	41	3)	47	3)	67	3)	36
17	Sloboda Tuzla	425		–		–	15)	329
2	Dinamo Zagreb	40	6)	181	2)	46	2)	21
12	NK Zagreb	275		–		–	10)	197
20	Tresnjevka Zagreb	494		–		–	18)	389

Club Rankings by Country and by Cup – 1981-82 to 1990-91

Albania

Rank	Club	C1.C2.C3 Place	C1 Rank	C1 Place	C2 Rank	C2 Place	C3 Rank	C3 Place
6	Labinoti Elbasan	332	4)	131		–		–
7	Apolonia Fier	341		–		–	4)	271
4	Vllaznia Shkodër	205		–	3)	94		–
2	Dinamo Tirana	130	3)	115	2)	85	2)	127
1	17 Nëntori Tirana	121	1)	63	1)	67		–
5	Partizani Tirana	275	2)	98		–	3)	239
3	Flamurtari Vlorë	168		–	4)	200	1)	108

Austria

Rank	Club	C1.C2.C3 Place	C1 Rank	C1 Place	C2 Rank	C2 Place	C3 Rank	C3 Place
9	Grazer AK	272		–	6)	161	8)	223
5	Sturm Graz	120		–		–	3)	73
3	FC Tirol	69	3)	39	4)	104	4)	74
8	Krems	270		–	5)	148		–
6	Linzer ASK	129		–		–	5)	79
4	Admira Wacker	92		–	3)	59	6)	82
2	Austria Vienna	21	1)	19	2)	36	1)	34
7	First Vienna	138		–		–	7)	84
1	Rapid Vienna	19	2)	22	1)	10	2)	55

Belgium

Rank	Club	C1.C2.C3 Place	C1 Rank	C1 Place	C2 Rank	C2 Place	C3 Rank	C3 Place
1	Anderlecht	3	1)	8	2)	15	1)	5
8	Antwerp	105		–		–	5)	54
6	Beveren	73	5)	64	6)	82	6)	56
13	Cercle Bruges	245		–	7)	123		–
4	Club Bruges	54	4	49	9)	154	3)	33
11	Gent	142		–	8)	143	9)	110
5	FC Liège	60		–	5)	62	2)	32
3	Standard Liège	44	3)	47	3)	18	8)	107
10	Lokeren	132		–		–	7)	80
2	KV Mechelen	37	2)	46	1)	6	11)	213
7	Waregem	91		–		–	4)	42
9	Waterschei Thor	111		–	4)	28		–
12	Winterslag	198		–		–	10)	142

Bulgaria

Rank	Club	C1.C2.C3 Place	C1 Rank	C1 Place	C2 Rank	C2 Place	C3 Rank	C3 Place
12	Pirin Blagoevgrad	331		–		–	9)	263
7	Chernomorets Bourgas	257		–	5)	137		–
11	Lokomotiv Plovdiv	314		–		–	8)	240
3	Trakia Plovdiv	113	4)	117	2)	61	1)	112
8	Sliven	276		–	7)	197	6)	197
10	Akademik Sofia	312		–		–	7)	237
1	CSKA Sofia	35	1)	15	1)	32	4)	143
2	Levski Sofia	99	2)	76	3)	65	3)	120
4	Lokomotiv Sofia	152		–	6)	145	2)	114

6	Slavia Sofia	242		–		–	5)	178
9	Beroe Stara Zagora	290	3)	108		–		–
5	Spartak Varna	230		–	4)	115		–

Cyprus

		C1.C2.C3	C1		C2		C3	
Rank	**Club**	**Place**	**Rank**	**Place**	**Rank**	**Place**	**Rank**	**Place**
9	Anorthosis Famagusta	345		–		–	6)	274
5	Paralimni	278		–	3)	151		–
8	NEA Salamina Famagusta	329		–	6)	193		–
7	EPA Larnaca	322		–		–	5)	249
6	Pezoporikos Larnaca	302	3)	124		–	4)	211
4	AEL Limassol	241		–	1)	121		–
2	Apollon Limassol	204		–	2)	122	2)	206
3	Apoel Nicosia	223	2)	97	5)	189	3)	209
1	Omonia Nicosia	101	1)	32	4)	184	1)	155

Czechoslovakia

		C1.C2.C3	C1		C2		C3	
Rank	**Club**	**Place**	**Rank**	**Place**	**Rank**	**Place**	**Rank**	**Place**
12	Dukla Banská Bystrica	319		–		–	10)	244
6	Inter Bratislava	118		–	4)	120	4)	83
8	Slovan Bratislava	215		–	3)	102		–
7	DAC Dunajská Streda	164		–	2)	69	7)	180
13	Plastika Nitra	320		–		–	11)	247
11	Sigma Olomouc	299		–		–	9)	227
4	Banik Ostrava	96	4)	72		–	3)	64
3	Bohemians Prague	56	2)	58		–	1)	28
2	Dukla Prague	53	5)	90	1)	13	6)	109
9	Slavia Prague	259		–		–	8)	195
1	Sparta Prague	43	1)	21		–	2)	57
10	Spartak Trnava	285		–	5)	158		–
5	TJ Vitkovice	108	3)	70		–	5)	87

Denmark

		C1.C2.C3	C1		C2		C3	
Rank	**Club**	**Place**	**Rank**	**Place**	**Rank**	**Place**	**Rank**	**Place**
8	AaB Aalborg	251		–	3)	129		–
2	AGF Aarhus	107	4)	79	1)	39	4)	208
5	B1903 Copenhagen	235		–	4)	133	6)	230
10	B 93 Copenhagen	271		–	6)	149		–
4	KB Copenhagen	199	3)	75	7)	171		–
1	Brøndby IF	61	1)	38		–	1)	40
11	Hvidovre IF	293	5)	109		–		–
9	Ikast FS	256		–	8)	182	3)	184
3	Lyngby BK	126	2)	65	2)	76	5)	229
6	Naestved IF	238		–		–	2)	177
12	B 1901 Nykobing	330		–	9)	194		–
14	OB Odense	344	7)	130		–	8)	255
13	B 1913 Odense	343	8)	134		–		–
7	Vejle BK	240	6)	110	5)	138	7)	252

East Germany

		C1.C2.C3	C1		C2		C3	
Rank	**Club**	**Place**	**Rank**	**Place**	**Rank**	**Place**	**Rank**	**Place**
9	Wismut Aue	218		–		–	8)	158

3	Dynamo Berlin	49	1)	14	3)	73		–
7	Stahl Brandenburg	213		–		–	6)	152
6	Karl–Marx–Stadt	196		–		–	5)	141
2	Dynamo Dresden	28	2)	44	2)	22	2)	35
8	Vorwärts Frankfurt/Oder	217		–		–	7)	157
4	Carl Zeiss Jena	127		–	4)	108	3)	101
1	Lokomotive Leipzig	26		–	1)	8	1)	29
5	Magdeburg	145		–	5)	119	4)	117
11	Hansa Rostock	325		–		–	9)	256
10	PSV Schwerin	292		–	6)	167		–

England

		C1.C2.C3	C1		C2		C3	
Rank	**Club**	**Place**	**Rank**	**Place**	**Rank**	**Place**	**Rank**	**Place**
4	Aston Villa	45	2)	17		–	4)	94
11	Ipswich Town	232		–		–	9)	168
5	Everton	89		–	2)	17		–
1	Liverpool	22	1)	2		–		–
9	Arsenal	182		–		–	7)	124
8	Queen's Park Rangers	179		–		–	6)	121
2	Tottenham Hotspur	27		–	3)	19	1)	17
3	Manchester United	38		–	1)	7	3)	69
6	Nottingham Forest	90		–		–	2)	41
7	Southampton	170		–		–	5)	116
10	Watford	195		–		–	8)	139
12	West Bromwich Albion	315		–		–	10)	242

Finland

		C1.C2.C3	C1		C2		C3	
Rank	**Club**	**Place**	**Rank**	**Place**	**Rank**	**Place**	**Rank**	**Place**
1	HJK Helsinki	117	2)	51	3)	78	7)	280
7	KTP Kotka	301		–	6)	178		–
8	KuPS Kuopio	307		–	5)	172	6)	258
2	FC Kuusysi Lahti	123	1)	42	4)	150	4)	212
9	OPS Oulu	340	4)	133		–		–
3	RoPS Rovaniemi	135		–	2)	64	2)	162
6	Ilves Tampere	274	3)	125		–	3)	194
4	TPS Turku	144		–		–	1)	91
5	Haka Valkeakoski	146		–	1)	48	5)	254

France

		C1.C2.C3	C1		C2		C3	
Rank	**Club**	**Place**	**Rank**	**Place**	**Rank**	**Place**	**Rank**	**Place**
5	Auxerre	102		–		–	2)	50
12	Bastia	206		–	6)	95		–
1	Girondins Bordeaux	18	2)	18	3)	30	1)	24
13	Laval	212		–		–	10)	151
9	Lens	151		–		–	6)	97
2	Olympique Marseille	32	1)	12	1)	25		–
14	Metz	221		–	7)	118	11)	226
3	Monaco	65	3)	54	4)	34	4)	88
8	Montpellier	150		–	5)	49	12)	260
6	Nantes	115	4)	89		–	3)	77
4	Paris Saint–Germain	79	5)	104	2)	26	8)	123
11	Saint–Etienne	197	6)	107		–	9)	150
10	Sochaux	162		–		–	7)	102
7	Toulouse	149		–		–	5)	96

Greece

Rank	Club	C1.C2.C3 Place	C1 Rank	C1 Place	C2 Rank	C2 Place	C3 Rank	C3 Place
5	AEK Athenes	159	3)	80	6)	130	5)	163
1	Panathinaikos	58	1)	31	3)	52	3)	99
9	Panionios	327		–		–	9)	259
6	OFI Crete	185		–	4)	98	8)	199
4	Larissa	114	4)	87	1)	46	7)	188
2	Olympiakos Pireus	67	2)	41	2)	50	2)	98
7	Aris Salonika	191		–		–	4)	134
8	Iraklis	234		–		–	6)	171
3	PAOK Salonika	109	5)	119	5)	24	1)	72

Hungary

Rank	Club	C1.C2.C3 Place	C1 Rank	C1 Place	C2 Rank	C2 Place	C3 Rank	C3 Place
7	Békéscsaba	209		–	2)	97		–
4	Ferencváros	128	3)	91	4)	109	3)	118
1	Honvéd	71	1)	33		–	2)	70
9	MTK–VM	237	4)	92		–	8)	231
8	Vasas SC	226		–	3)	106		–
5	Rába ETO	131	2)	62		–	5)	130
10	Pécsi MSC	267		–	7)	185	7)	190
11	Siófok	289		–	5)	164		–
2	Videoton	81		–		–	1)	36
6	Tatabánya	176		–	6)	177	4)	129
3	Ujpesti Dózsa	110	5)	129	1)	35	6)	164

Iceland

Rank	Club	C1.C2.C3 Place	C1 Rank	C1 Place	C2 Rank	C2 Place	C3 Rank	C3 Place
3	IA Akranes	224	3)	116	2)	139	4)	235
4	IBA Akureyri	260	1)	94		–		–
5	FH Hafnarfjördhur	287		–		–	2)	217
1	Fram Reykjavik	160	5)	139	1)	53	5)	266
7	KR Reykjavik	335		–		–	6)	267
2	Valur Reykjavik	188	2)	102	3)	181	1)	153
8	Vikingur Reykjavik	347	4)	123		–	7)	270
6	IBV Vestmannaeyjar	309		–	4)	201	3)	224

Italy

Rank	Club	C1.C2.C3 Place	C1 Rank	C1 Place	C2 Rank	C2 Place	C3 Rank	C3 Place
9	Atalanta	83		–	4)	51	8)	76
11	Bologna	140		–		–	9)	86
7	Fiorentina	70		–		–	5)	26
5	Sampdoria	34		–	1)	2		–
4	AC Milan,	31	2)	10		–	10)	106
2	Inter Milan	6	6)	106	5)	75	1)	1
6	Napoli	41	4)	53		–	4)	18
3	Roma	16	3)	27	3)	27	3)	13
10	Torino	103		–		–	7)	51
1	Juventus	1	1)	4	2)	5	2)	11
8	Verona	75	5)	68		–	6)	44

Luxembourg

Rank	Club	C1.C2.C3 Place	C1 Rank	C1 Place	C2 Rank	C2 Place	C3 Rank	C3 Place
3	Avenir Beggen	282	5)	142	5)	208	1)	210
7	Aris Bonnevoie	349		–		–	7)	278
5	Red Boys Differdange	311		–	4)	207	3)	236
1	Jeunesse Esch	225	1)	103	2)	176	2)	234
6	Swift Hesperange	334		–	3)	196		–
8	Spora Luxembourg	350	4)	135		–	5)	269
2	Union Luxembourg	280	3)	127	1)	153	6)	273
4	Progrès Niedercorn	305	2)	112		–	4)	248

Malta

Rank	Club	C1.C2.C3 Place	C1 Rank	C1 Place	C2 Rank	C2 Place	C3 Rank	C3 Place
1	Hamrun Spartans	178	2)	101	1)	105	1)	214
7	Valletta	355	4)	140	3)	205	4)	276
3	Floriana	310		–	2)	179		–
5	Hibernians	353	3)	138		–	5)	279
6	Rabat Ajax	354	5)	141		–	6)	281
2	Sliema Wanderers	281	1)	96	5)	209	3)	275
4	Zurrieq	352		–	4)	206	2)	265

Netherlands

Rank	Club	C1.C2.C3 Place	C1 Rank	C1 Place	C2 Rank	C2 Place	C3 Rank	C3 Place
5	AZ'67 Alkmaar	139	2)	67	5)	87		–
2	Ajax	36	3)	82	1)	4	7)	131
9	Vitesse	169		–		–	5)	113
1	PSV Eindhoven	33	1)	16	9)	160	2)	47
14	Twente Enschede	266		–		–	9)	200
4	Groningen	84		–	3)	74	3)	59
13	Haarlem	231		–		–	8)	167
7	Roda JC	166		–	2)	58	10)	245
11	FC Den Haag	208		–	6)	96		–
12	NEC Nijmegen	229		–	7)	114		–
3	Feyenoord	66	4)	105		–	1)	23
6	Sparta Rotterdam	141		–		–	4)	89
10	Fortuna Sittard	184		–	4)	77		–
8	Utrecht	167		–	8)	136	6)	128

Northern Ireland

Rank	Club	C1.C2.C3 Place	C1 Rank	C1 Place	C2 Rank	C2 Place	C3 Rank	C3 Place
6	Ballymena United	351		–	4)	204		–
1	Glentoran	122	2)	61	1)	79	4)	233
2	Linfield	148	1)	52		–	2)	207
3	Coleraine	243		–	3)	198	1)	179
4	Glenavon	303		–	2)	188	3)	220
5	Portadown	346	3)	137		–		–

Norway

Rank	Club	C1.C2.C3 Place	C1 Rank	C1 Place	C2 Rank	C2 Place	C3 Rank	C3 Place
9	SK Brann	298		–	5)	173		–

3	Bryne IL	200		–	2)	141	2)	172
6	Fredrikstad FK	250		–	1)	128		–
11	IK Start	316	5)	120		–		–
1	Lillestrøm SK	177	1)	69	8)	203	5)	205
7	Mjøndalen IF	268		–		–	4)	201
10	Molde FK	300		–		–	7)	228
12	Moss FK	339	6)	122	6)	186		–
4	Vålerengen SIF	202	3)	83	4)	168	6)	215
5	IL Viking	203	4)	113	7)	192	1)	161
8	Tromsø IL	286		–	3)	159		–
2	Rosenborg BK	187	2)	77		–	3)	187

Poland

		C1.C2.C3	C1		C2		C3	
Rank	**Club**	**Place**	**Rank**	**Place**	**Rank**	**Place**	**Rank**	**Place**
9	Szombierki Bytom	288		–		–	6)	218
11	Ruch Chorzów	297	4)	111		–		–
6	Wisla Kraków	181		–	3)	72	11)	246
13	Lechia Gdańsk	338		–	7)	202		–
4	GKS Katowice	143		–	4)	83	3)	144
2	Widzew Lódź	68	1)	37	5)	126	1)	65
12	Zaglebie Lubin	313		–		–	9)	238
8	Stal Mielec	249		–		–	5)	185
3	Lech Poznań	93	3)	50	2)	44	7)	219
10	Pogon Szczecin	296		–		–	8)	225
1	Legia Warsaw	48		–	1)	14	2)	78
7	Slask Wroclaw	220		–	6)	166	4)	174
5	Górnik Zabrze	156	2)	45		–	10)	241

Portugal

		C1.C2.C3	C1		C2		C3	
Rank	**Club**	**Place**	**Rank**	**Place**	**Rank**	**Place**	**Rank**	**Place**
7	Estrela Amadora	214		–	4)	100		–
10	Sporting Braga	279		–	6)	142	9)	272
8	Chaves	261		–		–	7)	196
4	Vitória Guimarães	82		–	5)	134	3)	39
5	Belenenses	153		–	7)	170	6)	105
1	Benfica	9	1)	6	2)	45	2)	27
3	Sporting Lisbon	13	3)	56	3)	70	1)	6
9	Portimonense	262		–		–	8)	198
6	Boavista	155		–		–	5)	100
2	FC Porto	10	2)	9	1)	11	4)	63

Republic of Ireland

		C1.C2.C3	C1		C2		C3	
Rank	**Club**	**Place**	**Rank**	**Place**	**Rank**	**Place**	**Rank**	**Place**
5	Athlone Town	273	2)	99		–		–
8	Bray Wanderers	291		–	4)	165		–
12	Cork City	333		–	9)	195		–
6	Derry City	277	4)	126	5)	174	3)	216
14	Drogheda United	348		–		–	8)	277
2	Bohemians	219		–		–	2)	160
9	St. Patrick's Athletic	306	3)	114		–	5)	250
1	Shamrock Rovers	174	1)	84		–	1)	146
7	UCD	284		–	3)	157		–
3	Dundalk	244	5)	136	1)	117	6)	261

13	Galway United	337		–	6)	180	7)	262
4	Limerick	265		–	2)	155	4)	222
10	Sligo Rovers	321		–	7)	187		–
11	Waterford United	326		–	8)	190		–

Romania

		C1.C2.C3	C1		C2		C3	
Rank	Club	Place	Rank	Place	Rank	Place	Rank	Place
10	Baia Mare	294		–	5)	169		–
2	Dinamo Bucharest	25	2)	20	1)	12	4)	115
5	Sportul Studentesc Bucharest	116		–		–	3)	67
1	Steaua Bucharest	24	1)	5	2)	103		–
4	Victoria Bucharest	104		–		–	2)	52
3	Universitatea Craiova	39	3)	60	3)	113	1)	15
9	CSU Galati	269		–		–	8)	202
8	Corvinul Hunedoara	211		–		–	6)	149
11	Flacara Moreni	318		–		–	9)	243
7	Arges Pitesti	207		–		–	5)	147
12	Petrolul Ploiesti	323		–		–	10)	251
6	Politehnica Timisoara	186		–	4)	144	7)	159

Scotland

		C1.C2.C3	C1		C2		C3	
Rank	Club	Place	Rank	Place	Rank	Place	Rank	Place
2	Aberdeen	15	4)	34	1)	3	4)	53
1	Dundee United	7	3)	29	4)	99	1)	3
5	Heart of Midlothian	88		–		–	3)	38
7	Hibernian	190		–		–	6)	133
4	Celtic	63	1)	24	3)	90	5)	95
3	Rangers	30	2)	26	2)	54	2)	30
6	St. Mirren	171		–	5)	101	7)	165

Spain

		C1.C2.C3	C1		C2		C3	
Rank	Club	Place	Rank	Place	Rank	Place	Rank	Place
7	Español	86		–		–	3)	37
2	Barcelona	5	2)	30	1)	1	5)	45
6	Athletic Bilbao	76	4)	73		–	4)	43
12	Sporting Gijón	233		–		–	11)	170
4	Atlético Madrid	57		–	2)	21	7)	66
1	Real Madrid	4	1)	3	3)	23	1)	10
11	Osasuna	210		–		–	10)	148
3	Real Sociedad	52	3)	35	6)	81	6)	58
8	Real Zaragoza	106		–	5)	47	9)	135
13	Real Betis	255		–		–	12)	192
9	Seville	119		–		–	8)	71
5	Valencia	64		–		–	2)	19
10	Real Valladolid	125		–	4)	40	13)	193

Sweden

		C1.C2.C3	C1		C2		C3	
Rank	Club	Place	Rank	Place	Rank	Place	Rank	Place
10	IF Elfsborg	247		–		–	7)	183
9	IK Brage	236		–		–	6)	175
11	GAIS	295		–		–	9)	221
1	IFK Gothenburg	8	1)	11	7)	162	1)	7

12	Örgryte IS	342	4)	121		–	10)	257
3	Hammarby IF	124		–	5)	107	3)	92
6	Kalmar FF	175		–	2)	66	11)	264
2	Malmö FF	62	2)	40	1)	42	2)	85
5	IFK Norrköping	172		–	6)	132	4)	140
4	AIK	163		–	3)	80	5)	173
7	Djurgården SIF	193		–	4)	84		–
8	Öster SIF	222	3)	100		–	8)	203

Switzerland

		C1.C2.C3	C1		C2		C3	
Rank	**Club**	**Place**	**Rank**	**Place**	**Rank**	**Place**	**Rank**	**Place**
11	Aarau	308		–	7)	163	10)	268
6	Young Boys Berne	173	5)	95	4)	88		–
2	Servette	72	2)	74	1)	56	2)	68
8	Lausanne-Sports	194		–	5)	111	8)	181
9	Lucerne	201	6)	128		–	7)	138
1	Neuchâtel Xamax	40	1)	48	6)	127	1)	21
10	St-Gallen	304		–		–	9)	232
3	Sion	98		–	3)	68	3)	81
7	Wettingen	189		–		–	6)	132
5	FC Zürich	157	4)	85		–	4)	119
4	Grasshoppers Zürich	100	3)	78	2)	63	5)	126

Turkey

		C1.C2.C3	C1		C2		C3	
Rank	**Club**	**Place**	**Rank**	**Place**	**Rank**	**Place**	**Rank**	**Place**
8	Adanaspor	324		–		–	5)	253
5	Sakaryaspor	264		–	3)	147		–
7	Gençlerbirligi	317		–	6)	183		–
9	Ankaragücü	328		–	7)	191		–
10	Bursaspor	336		–	8)	199		–
2	Besiktas	136	2)	57	5)	175	3)	176
4	Fenerbahçe	158	3)	71		–	1)	154
1	Galatasaray	77	1)	36	1)	60	2)	169
6	Mersin Idmanyurdu	283		–	4)	156		–
3	Trabzonspor	147	4)	81	2)	91	4)	204

USSR

		C1.C2.C3	C1		C2		C3	
Rank	**Club**	**Place**	**Rank**	**Place**	**Rank**	**Place**	**Rank**	**Place**
5	Dnepr Dnepropetrovsk	74	2)	25		–	4)	90
9	Shakhtyor Donetsk	137		–	5)	41		–
13	Metallist Kharkov	227		–	8)	100		–
2	Dinamo Kiev	17	1)	13	1)	9	5)	93
8	Zenit Leningrad	134	5)	59		–	9)	145
3	Dinamo Minsk	46	4)	43	6)	57	2)	48
14	CSKA Moscow	246		–		–	11)	182
6	Dinamo Moscow	85		–	3)	29	7)	122
1	Spartak Moscow	11	3)	28		–	1)	4
4	Torpedo Moscow	55		–	2)	20	3)	61
11	Chernomorets Odessa	183		–		–	8)	125
10	SKA Rostov on Don	180		–	7)	71		–
7	Dinamo Tbilisi	87		–	4)	33	6)	104
12	Zhalgiris Vilnius	216		–		–	10)	156

Wales

Rank	Club	C1.C2.C3 Place	C1 Rank	C1 Place	C2 Rank	C2 Place	C3 Rank	C3 Place
5	Bangor City	263		–	5)	146		–
3	Cardiff City	228		–	3)	112		–
4	Merthyr Tydfil	253		–	4)	131		–
2	Swansea City	161		–	2)	55		–
1	Wrexham	133		–	1)	38		–

West Germany

Rank	Club	C1.C2.C3 Place	C1 Rank	C1 Place	C2 Rank	C2 Place	C3 Rank	C3 Place
4	Werder Bremen	23	3)	55		–	2)	9
2	Cologne	12		–	5)	92	1)	2
9	Borussia Dortmund	80		–	4)	86	9)	49
11	Eintracht Frankfurt	95		–	2)	24	12)	191
3	Hamburg	20	2)	23	6)	93	3)	12
8	Kaiserslautern	59		–	8)	135	6)	20
5	Bayer Leverkusen	47		–		–	4)	14
6	Borussia Mönchengladbach	50		–		–	5)	16
1	Bayern Munich	2	1)	1	1)	16	8)	31
12	Nuremberg	252		–		–	11)	186
7	VFB Stuttgart	51	4)	86	7)	116	7)	22
10	Bayer Uerdingen	94		–	3)	37	10)	111

Yugoslavia

Rank	Club	C1.C2.C3 Place	C1 Rank	C1 Place	C2 Rank	C2 Place	C3 Rank	C3 Place
13	Borac Banja Luka	258		–	5)	140		–
1	Red Star Belgrade	14	1)	7	1)	31	5)	62
3	Partizan Belgrade	42	2)	66	3)	89	2)	25
12	Rad Belgrade	254		–			11)	189
4	Velez Mostar	78		–	2)	43	6)	75
5	Radnicki Nis	97		–		–	3)	46
11	Vojvodina Novi Sad	248	3)	88		–		–
9	Rijeka	192		–		–	8)	136
8	Sarajevo	165	5)	118		–	7)	103
6	Zeljeznicar Sarajevo	112		–		–	4)	60
10	Vardar Skoplje	239	6)	132		–	10)	166
2	Hajduk Split	29		–	6)	152	1)	8
7	Dinamo Zagreb	154	4)	93	4)	125	9)	137

Club Rankings by Country and by Cup – 1986-87 to 1990-91

Albania

Rank	Club	C1.C2.C3 Place	C1 Rank	C1 Place	C2 Rank	C2 Place	C3 Rank	C3 Place
6	Apolonia Fier	267		–		–	3)	201
4	Vllaznia Shkodër	138		–	2)	54		–
3	Dinamo Tirana	131	2)	70	3)	55		–
1	17 Nëntori Tirana	98	1)	42	1)	49		–
5	Partizani Tirana	260	3)	73		–	2)	174
2	Flamurtari Vlorë	104		–	4)	122	1)	61

Austria

Rank	Club	C1.C2.C3 Place	C1 Rank	C1 Place	C2 Rank	C2 Place	C3 Rank	C3 Place
8	Sturm Graz	218		–		–	7)	155
1	FC Tirol	37	1)	18	4)	83	2)	41
7	Krems	200		–	5)	88		–
6	Linzer ASK	193		–		–	6)	138
3	Admira Wacker	50		–	1)	28	1)	39
4	Austria Vienna	53	3)	37	3)	70	5)	49
5	First Vienna	84		–		–	3)	43
2	Rapid Vienna	46	2)	34	2)	58	4)	47

Belgium

Rank	Club	C1.C2.C3 Place	C1 Rank	C1 Place	C2 Rank	C2 Place	C3 Rank	C3 Place
1	Anderlecht	5	1)	10	2)	6	4)	44
5	Antwerp	80		–		–	3)	42
6	Beveren	95		–		–	5)	56
4	Club Bruges	35	3)	28	4)	93	2)	20
7	Gent	116		–		–	6)	76
3	FC Liège	32		–	3)	31	1)	13
9	Standard Liège	123		–		–	8)	85
10	Lokeren	215		–		–	10)	153
2	KV Mechelen	10	2)	24	1)	4	9)	150
8	Waregem	122		–		–	7)	82

Bulgaria

Rank	Club	C1.C2.C3 Place	C1 Rank	C1 Place	C2 Rank	C2 Place	C3 Rank	C3 Place
5	Chernomorets Bourgas	186		–	3)	84		–
3	Trakia Plovdiv	108		–		–	1)	65
8	Sliven	263		–	4)	129		–
1	CSKA Sofia	38	1)	23	1)	14	3)	128
2	Levski Sofia	106	3)	75	2)	34	5)	147
4	Lokomotiv Sofia	176		–		–	2)	125
6	Slavia Sofia	205		–		–	4)	146
7	Beroe Stara Zagora	222	2)	64		–		–

Cyprus

Rank	Club	C1.C2.C3 Place	C1 Rank	C1 Place	C2 Rank	C2 Place	C3 Rank	C3 Place
7	NEA Salamina Famagusta	257		–	4)	121		–
5	EPA Larnaca	247		–		–	4)	183

6	Pezoporikos Larnaca	252	3)	76		–		–
3	AEL Limassol	202		–	2)	92		–
2	Apollon Limassol	168		–	1)	89	2)	164
4	Apoel Nicosia	203	2)	55		–	3)	177
1	Omonia Nicosia	111	1)	47	3)	114	1)	102

Czechoslovakia

		C1.C2.C3	C1		C2		C3	
Rank	**Club**	**Place**	**Rank**	**Place**	**Rank**	**Place**	**Rank**	**Place**
6	Inter Bratislava	150		–	5)	123	4)	94
7	Slovan Bratislava	178	3)	76		–		–
4	DAC Dunajská Streda	100		–	1)	36	5)	120
11	Plastika Nitra	246		–		–	9)	180
10	Sigma Olomouc	232		–		–	8)	166
5	Banik Ostrava	125		–		–	3)	86
8	Bohemians Prague	183		–		–	6)	133
2	Dukla Prague	77		–	2)	41	2)	69
3	Sparta Prague	79	1)	19		–	7)	148
9	Spartak Trnava	213		–	4)	96		–
1	TJ Vitkovice	64	2)	39		–	1)	46

Denmark

		C1.C2.C3	C1		C2		C3	
Rank	**Club**	**Place**	**Rank**	**Place**	**Rank**	**Place**	**Rank**	**Place**
3	AaB Aalborg	175		–	2)	75		–
2	AGF Aarhus	69	2)	45	1)	15		–
4	B1903 Copenhagen	182		–	3)	80		–
1	Brøndby IF	24	1)	16		–	1)	14
5	Ikast FS	185		–	5)	111	2)	122
7	Lyngby BK	236	4)	101	4)	179		–
6	Naestved IF	224		–		–	3)	160
9	B 1913 Odense	269	3)	84		–		–
8	Vejle BK	251		–		–	5)	187

East Germany

		C1.C2.C3	C1		C2		C3	
Rank	**Club**	**Place**	**Rank**	**Place**	**Rank**	**Place**	**Rank**	**Place**
7	Wismut Aue	146		–		–	6)	100
3	Dynamo Berlin	72	2)	31	2)	39		–
6	Stahl Brandenburg	142		–		–	5)	97
5	Karl-Marx-Stadt	129		–		–	4)	90
1	Dynamo Dresden	34	1)	22		–	1)	19
8	Carl Zeiss Jena	166		–	3)	64	8)	198
2	Lokomotive Leipzig	43		–	1)	11	2)	78
4	Magdeburg	128		–		–	3)	89
10	Hansa Rostock	253		–		–	7)	188
9	PSV Schwerin	227		–	4)	104		–

England

		C1.C2.C3	C1		C2		C3	
Rank	**Club**	**Place**	**Rank**	**Place**	**Rank**	**Place**	**Rank**	**Place**
2	Aston Villa	113		–		–	1)	73
1	Manchester United	48		–	1)	7		–

Finland

Rank	Club	C1.C2.C3 Place	C1 Rank	C1 Place	C2 Rank	C2 Place	C3 Rank	C3 Place
3	HJK Helsinki	155	1)	43		–		–
7	KuPS Kuopio	231		–	3)	106		–
4	FC Kuusysi Lahti	169	2)	59	4)	125	4)	149
1	RoPS Rovaniemi	82		–	1)	33	2)	105
5	Ilves Tampere	187		–		–	3)	135
2	TPS Turku	89		–		–	1)	52
6	Haka Valkeakoski	201		–	2)	90		–

France

Rank	Club	C1.C2.C3 Place	C1 Rank	C1 Place	C2 Rank	C2 Place	C3 Rank	C3 Place
4	Auxerre	68		–		–	2)	31
2	Girondins Bordeaux	15	2)	17	2)	13	1)	27
9	Lens	181		–		–	7)	132
1	Olympique Marseille	8	1)	8	1)	9		–
11	Metz	245		–	5)	117		–
3	Monaco	36	3)	33	3)	17	4)	66
6	Montpellier	94		–	4)	19	9)	191
10	Nantes	233		–		–	8)	167
8	Paris Saint-Germain	149	4)	61		–	6)	109
7	Sochaux	112		–		–	5)	70
5	Toulouse	92		–		–	3)	54

Greece

Rank	Club	C1.C2.C3 Place	C1 Rank	C1 Place	C2 Rank	C2 Place	C3 Rank	C3 Place
4	AEK Athenes	130	1)	46		–	6)	143
1	Panathinaikos	56	3)	56	2)	35	1)	59
8	Panionios	255		–		–	7)	190
3	OFI Crete	117		–	3)	59	5)	139
7	Larissa	172	2)	48		–		–
2	Olympiakos Pireus	59	4)	62	1)	21	2)	75
6	Iraklis	165		–		–	4)	118
5	PAOK Salonika	160		–		–	3)	111

Hungary

Rank	Club	C1.C2.C3 Place	C1 Rank	C1 Place	C2 Rank	C2 Place	C3 Rank	C3 Place
4	Békéscsaba	140		–	1)	57		–
2	Ferencváros	115		–	2)	65	4)	113
1	Honvéd	67	1)	40		–	1)	53
7	MTK-VM	167	2)	50		–	7)	169
9	Vasas SC	211		–	4)	95		–
6	Rába ETO	162		–		–	5)	114
8	Pécsi MSC	197		–	5)	116	6)	131
10	Videoton	249		–		–	8)	185
5	Tatabánya	161		–		–	3)	112
3	Ujpesti Dózsa	134	3)	80	3)	77	2)	110

Iceland

Rank	Club	C1.C2.C3 Place	C1 Rank	C1 Place	C2 Rank	C2 Place	C3 Rank	C3 Place
4	IA Akranes	208		–	2)	98	3)	171
3	IBA Akureyri	191	11)	51		–		–
5	FH Hafnarfjördhur	220		–		–	2)	157
2	Fram Reykjavik	171	3)	89	11)	71		–
1	Valur Reykjavik	156	2)	60	3)	109	1)	123

Italy

Rank	Club	C1.C2.C3 Place	C1 Rank	C1 Place	C2 Rank	C2 Place	C3 Rank	C3 Place
7	Atalanta	41		–	3)	23	8)	37
11	Bologna	85		–	9)	45		–
8	Fiorentina	51		–	5)	16		–
4	Sampdoria	13		–	1)	1		–
3	AC Milan	12	1)	3		–	10)	108
2	Inter Milan	7	4)	63		–	1)	1
5	Napoli	22	2)	29		–	4)	9
6	Roma	27		–	4)	73	3)	8
9	Torino	73		–		–	6)	34
1	Juventus	2	3)	32	2)	8	2)	2
10	Verona	74		–		–	7)	35

Luxembourg

Rank	Club	C1.C2.C3 Place	C1 Rank	C1 Place	C2 Rank	C2 Place	C3 Rank	C3 Place
2	Avenir Beggen	209	3)	81	3)	134	1)	142
1	Jeunesse Esch	170	1)	57		–	2)	170
4	Swift Hesperange	262		–	2)	128		–
5	Spora Luxembourg	274	4)	85		–	3)	200
3	Union Luxembourg	239	2)	78	1)	108	4)	202

Malta

Rank	Club	C1.C2.C3 Place	C1 Rank	C1 Place	C2 Rank	C2 Place	C3 Rank	C3 Place
1	Hamrun Spartans	206	2)	58	2)	127		–
7	Valletta	276	4)	87		–	2)	203
3	Floriana	219		–	1)	99		
6	Hibernians	273		–		–	3)	204
5	Rabat Ajax	270	3)	86		–		–
2	Sliema Wanderers	207	1)	53	4)	132	1)	197
4	Zurrieq	265		–	3)	131		–

Netherlands

Rank	Club	C1.C2.C3 Place	C1 Rank	C1 Place	C2 Rank	C2 Place	C3 Rank	C3 Place
1	Ajax	19		–	1)	3	7)	196
6	Vitesse	109		–		–	3)	67
2	PSV Eindhoven	31	1)	9	5)	100		–
9	Twente Enschede	196		–		–	5)	141
3	Groningen	55		–	3)	40	2)	40
5	Roda JC	102		–	2)	27	6)	178
7	FC Den Haag	139		–	4)	56		–
4	Feyenoord	70		–		–	1)	32
8	Utrecht	141		–		–	4)	95

Northern Ireland

Rank	Club	C1.C2.C3 Place	C1 Rank	C1 Place	C2 Rank	C2 Place	C3 Rank	C3 Place
5	Ballymena United	271		–	3)	133		–
1	Glentoran	137	2)	65	1)	63	4)	182
2	Linfield	154	1)	54		–	1)	124
3	Coleraine	229		–		–	3)	165
4	Glenavon	237		–	2)	118	2)	162
6	Portadown	272	3)	88		–		–

Norway

Rank	Club	C1.C2.C3 Place	C1 Rank	C1 Place	C2 Rank	C2 Place	C3 Rank	C3 Place
8	SK Brann	244		–	4)	115		–
3	Bryne IL	189		–	1)	86		–
2	Lillestrøm SK	135	1)	38	3)	112	5)	181
4	Mjøndalen IF	198		–		–	2)	144
7	Molde FK	234		–		–	4)	168
9	Moss FK	248	3)	74		–		–
5	Vålerengen SIF	214		–		–	3)	152
10	IL Viking	256		–	5)	120		–
6	Tromsø IL	216		–	2)	97		–
1	Rosenborg BK	118	2)	44		–	1)	127

Poland

Rank	Club	C1.C2.C3 Place	C1 Rank	C1 Place	C2 Rank	C2 Place	C3 Rank	C3 Place
8	Ruch Chorzów	230	3)	67		–		–
3	GKS Katowice	90		–	3)	44	2)	92
5	Widzew Lódź	145		–		–	3)	99
9	Zaglebie Lubin	241		–		–	5)	173
2	Lech Poznań	76	2)	35	2)	38		–
6	Pogon Szczecin	221		–		–	4)	158
1	Legia Warsaw	57		–	1)	12	1)	91
7	Slask Wroclaw	226		–	4)	103		–
4	Górnik Zabrze	96	1)	21		–	6)	175

Portugal

Rank	Club	C1.C2.C3 Place	C1 Rank	C1 Place	C2 Rank	C2 Place	C3 Rank	C3 Place
6	Estrela Amadora	144		–	3)	61		–
8	Chaves	192		–		–	7)	137
4	Vitória Guimarães	47		–	4)	81	2)	18
5	Belenenses	97		–	5)	105	4)	60
2	Benfica	11	2)	7	2)	42	5)	83
3	Sporting Lisbon	20		–	1)	37	1)	7
7	Boavista	163		–		–	6)	115
1	FC Porto	9	1)	4		–	3)	58

Republic of Ireland

Rank	Club	C1.C2.C3 Place	C1 Rank	C1 Place	C2 Rank	C2 Place	C3 Rank	C3 Place
3	Bray Wanderers	225		–	1)	102		–
8	Cork City	261		–	5)	126		–
1	Derry City	204	3)	77	2)	107	2)	156

2	Bohemians	217		–		–	1)	154
5	St. Patrick's Athletic	238	1)	68		–	3)	184
4	Shamrock Rovers	235	2)	69		–		–
9	Dundalk	275	4)	83	4)	124	4)	193
7	Galway United	258		–		–	5)	194
6	Waterford United	254		–	3)	119		–

Romania

Rank	Club	C1.C2.C3 Place	C1 Rank	C1 Place	C2 Rank	C2 Place	C3 Rank	C3 Place
2	Dinamo Bucharest	33	2)	41	1)	5		–
4	Sportul Studentesc Bucharest	87					2)	50
1	Steaua Bucharest	16	1)	5	2)	68		–
3	Victoria Bucharest	58		–		–	1)	22
5	Universitatea Craiova	87		–		–	3)	50
7	CSU Galati	199		–		–	5)	145
8	Flacara Moreni	243		–		–	6)	176
9	Petrolul Ploiesti	250		–		–	7)	186
6	Politehnica Timisoara	153		–		–	4)	104

Scotland

Rank	Club	C1.C2.C3 Place	C1 Rank	C1 Place	C2 Rank	C2 Place	C3 Rank	C3 Place
4	Aberdeen	63		–	1)	30	4)	62
1	Dundee United	18		–	2)	60	1)	4
3	Heart of Midlothian	49		–		–	2)	15
6	Hibernian	121		–		–	5)	81
5	Celtic	75	2)	25	4)	72	6)	129
2	Rangers	30	1)	12		–	3)	33
7	St. Mirren	148		–	3)	62		–

Spain

Rank	Club	C1.C2.C3 Place	C1 Rank	C1 Place	C2 Rank	C2 Place	C3 Rank	C3 Place
3	Español	42		–		–	1)	12
1	Barcelona	3		–	1)	2	2)	17
9	Athletic Bilbao	101		–		–	6)	63
11	Sporting Gijón	190		–		–	9)	136
7	Atlético Madrid	86		–		–	4)	48
2	Real Madrid	4	1)	2		–		–
4	Real Sociedad	45		–	4)	43	3)	26
5	Real Zaragoza	61		–	3)	18	7)	84
10	Seville	143		–		–	8)	98
8	Valencia	93		–		–	5)	55
6	Real Valladolid	83		–	2)	16		–

Sweden

Rank	Club	C1.C2.C3 Place	C1 Rank	C1 Place	C2 Rank	C2 Place	C3 Rank	C3 Place
9	IK Brage	240		–		–	7)	172
8	GAIS	228		–		–	6)	163
1	IFK Gothenburg	17	1)	15		–	1)	10
10	Örgryte IS	268	3)	72		–	8)	189
4	Kalmar FF	136		–	3)	52	9)	195
2	Malmö FF	40	2)	20	1)	24	2)	106
5	IFK Norrköping	164		–	4)	79	5)	161

7	AIK	223		–		–	4)	159
3	Djurgården SIF	124		–	2)	46		–
6	Öster SIF	195		–		–	3)	140

Switzerland

Rank	Club	C1.C2.C3 Place	C1 Rank	C1 Place	C2 Rank	C2 Place	C3 Rank	C3 Place
9	Aarau	266		–		–	8)	199
4	Young Boys Berne	110	2)	52	3)	48		–
7	Servette	147		–		–	5)	101
8	Lausanne-Sports	173		–		–	6)	121
6	Lucerne	132	4)	79		–	4)	88
1	Neuchâtel Xamax	57	1)	26	4)	74	1)	71
2	Sion	71		–	1)	29	2)	77
5	Wettingen	119		–		–	3)	79
3	Grasshoppers Zürich	105	3)	66	2)	32	7)	192

Turkey

Rank	Club	C1.C2.C3 Place	C1 Rank	C1 Place	C2 Rank	C2 Place	C3 Rank	C3 Place
5	Sakaryaspor	194		–	2)	87		–
6	Gençlerbirligi	242		–	4)	113		–
7	Bursaspor	264		–	5)	130		–
2	Besiktas	99	2)	36	3)	110	3)	117
4	Fenerbahçe	151	3)	71		–	1)	96
1	Galatasaray	65	1)	14		–	2)	116
3	Trabzonspor	127		–	1)	151		–

USSR

Rank	Club	C1.C2.C3 Place	C1 Rank	C1 Place	C2 Rank	C2 Place	C3 Rank	C3 Place
5	Dnepr Dnepropetrovsk	81	3)	27		–	10)	119
10	Metallist Kharkov	157		–	4)	66		–
1	Dinamo Kiev	23	1)	11	2)	25	3)	57
8	Zenit Leningrad	133		–		–	7)	93
4	Dinamo Minsk	62		–	3)	26	4)	68
7	Dinamo Moscow	120		–		–	6)	80
3	Spartak Moscow	28	2)	13		–	1)	25
2	Torpedo Moscow	25		–	1)	10	2)	29
11	Chernomorets Odessa	158		–		–	9)	107
6	Dinamo Tbilisi	114		–		–	5)	74
9	Zhalgiris Vilnius	152		–		–	8)	103

Wales

Rank	Club	C1.C2.C3 Place	C1 Rank	C1 Place	C2 Rank	C2 Place	C3 Rank	C3 Place
2	Cardiff City	159		–	2)	67		–
3	Merthyr Tydfil	179		–	3)	78		–
4	Swansea City	210		–	4)	94		–
1	Wrexham	91		–	1)	22		–

West Germany

Rank	Club	C1.C2.C3 Place	C1 Rank	C1 Place	C2 Rank	C2 Place	C3 Rank	C3 Place
2	Werder Bremen	14	2)	30		–	2)	5
4	Cologne	26		–		–	3)	6
6	Borussia Dortmund	39		–	2)	47	5)	21
9	Eintracht Frankfurt	78		–	1)	20	11)	134
7	Hamburg	60		–	3)	53	8)	38
12	Kaiserslautern	184		–	5)	82		–
3	Bayer Leverkusen	21		–		–	1)	3
8	Borussia Mönchengladbach	66		–		–	7)	30
1	Bayern Munich	1	1)	1		–	6)	23
11	Nuremberg	177		–		–	10)	126
5	VFB Stuttgart	29		–	4)	69	4)	11
10	Bayer Uerdingen	107		–		–	9)	64

Yugoslavia

Rank	Club	C1.C2.C3 Place	C1 Rank	C1 Place	C2 Rank	C2 Place	C3 Rank	C3 Place
8	Borac Banja Luka	188		–	3)	85		–
1	Red Star Belgrade	6	1)	6		–	2)	28
2	Partizan Belgrade	44		–	2)	50	1)	24
7	Rad Belgrade	180		–		–	6)	130
3	Velez Mostar	54		–	1)	45	3)	36
6	Vojvodina Novi Sad	174	2)	49		–		–
9	Rijeka	212		–		–	7)	151
10	Vardar Skoplje	259	3)	82		–		–
4	Hajduk Split	103		–	4)	91	4)	72
5	Dinamo Zagreb	126		–		–	5)	87

Of Goals and Indexes

These final pages of 100 European Cups provide some of the statistical information in the Year by Year section of the book in a graphical form.

Pages 734 to 736 contain charts showing the evolution of national indexes from 1955-56 to 1990-91. There are five charts in all, one each for the countries whose clubs have dominated the first 100 European Cups, namely England, France, Italy, Spain and West Germany.

The charts show how consistent the sides from England, Italy and Spain have been in 35 years. After the early years France suffered a fierce decline but have shown a slow but gradual rise since 1973. The West Germans rise from the lower reaches is also clearly charted but will take several more seasons to attain the highest point reached in 1966.

Evolution of National Indexes by Country 1955-56 to 1990-91

England

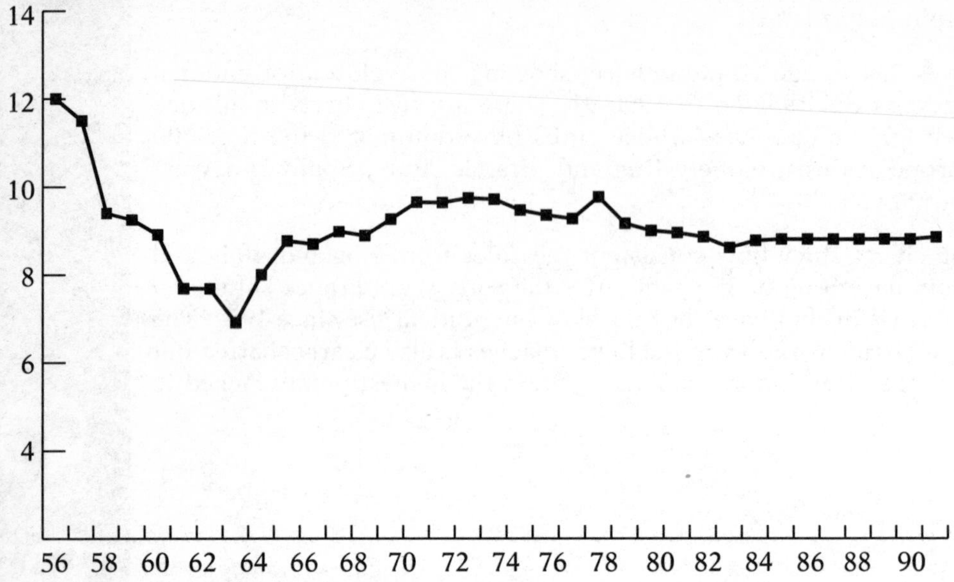

France

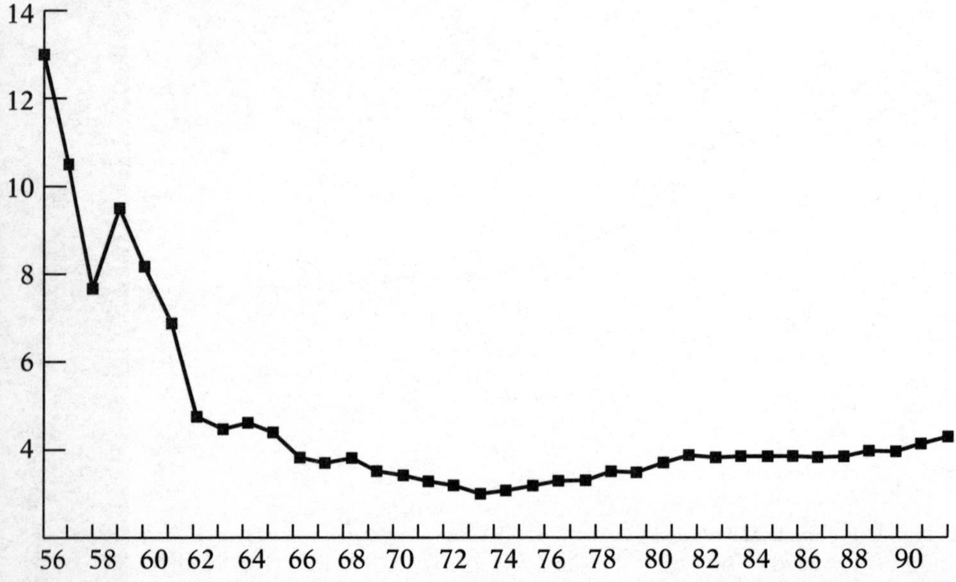

Italy

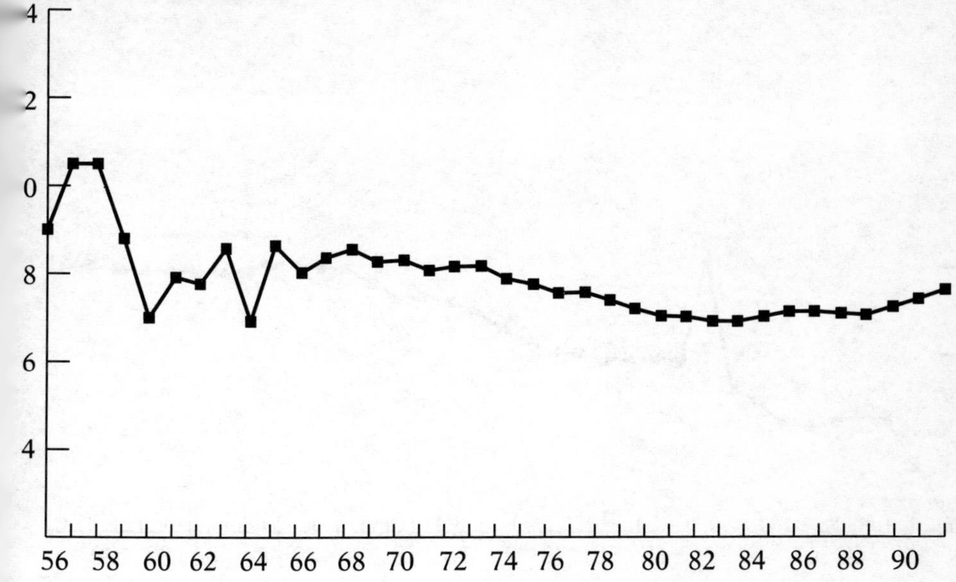
4
2
0
8
8
6
4
56 58 60 62 64 66 68 70 72 74 76 78 80 82 84 86 88 90

Spain

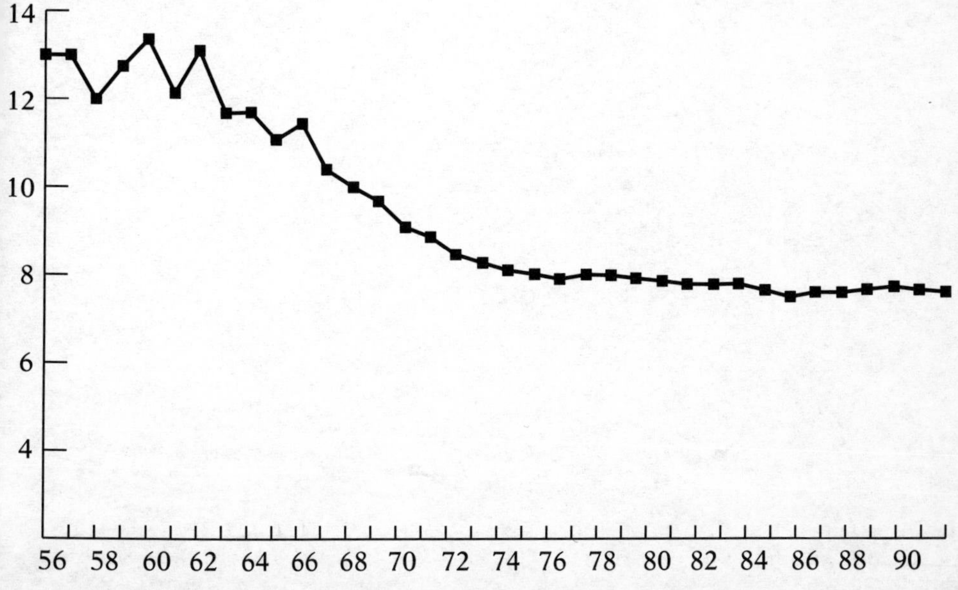
14
12
10
8
6
4
56 58 60 62 64 66 68 70 72 74 76 78 80 82 84 86 88 90

West Germany

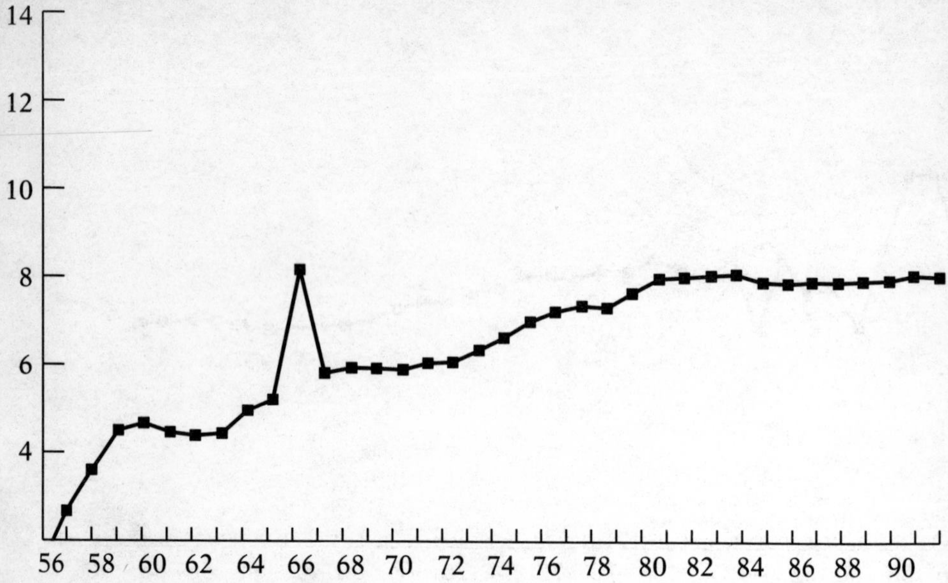